REAL ESTATE MANAGEMENT LAW

Real Estate Management Law

Seventh Edition

RICHARD CARD
Emeritus Professor of Law, De Montfort University, Leicester

JOHN MURDOCH
Emeritus Professor of Law, University of Reading

SANDI MURDOCH
Honorary Fellow, University of Reading

OXFORD
UNIVERSITY PRESS

OXFORD

UNIVERSITY PRESS

Great Clarendon Street, Oxford, OX2 6DP,
United Kingdom

Oxford University Press is a department of the University of Oxford.
It furthers the University's objective of excellence in research, scholarship,
and education by publishing worldwide. Oxford is a registered trade mark of
Oxford University Press in the UK and in certain other countries

Published in the United States of America by Oxford University Press
198 Madison Avenue, New York, NY 10016, United States of America

British Library Cataloguing in Publication Data
Data available

ISBN 978–0–19–957204–5

Preface

Like its previous editions, this book is intended to serve as a comprehensive textbook for real estate management students studying courses in basic legal topics, particularly ones that treat the subject matter in some depth.

We have had in mind the syllabuses for examinations in the core legal subjects for degrees and diplomas in real estate management, land management, surveying and allied fields. Despite its title, the book should also prove useful for those following similar courses in law for other types of qualifications.

This book is divided into six parts. Part I outlines the English legal system. The remaining Parts deal with the law of contract, the law of tort, land law, landlord and tenant and planning law respectively.

In addition to the usual flood of case law, this edition has had to incorporate quite a number of pieces of new legislation, in particular the Planning and Compulsory Purchase Act 2004; the Housing Act 2004; the Companies Act 2006; the Compensation Act 2006; the Commons Act 2006; the Tribunals, Courts and Enforcement Act 2007; the Housing and Urban Regeneration Act 2008; the Planning Act 2008, and the Mortgage Repossessions (Protection of Tenants etc) Act 2010.

Besides the inevitable updating and associated rewriting, this edition sees substantial changes to the structure of the book. In order to reflect changes in the needs of our readership, we have introduced chapter overviews at the start of each chapter, summaries of key points at appropriate stages, and questions at the end of chapters. We have also increased the coverage of land law and of landlord and tenant law.

We thank Ann Skippers, Principal of Ann Skippers Planning and Immediate Past President of the Royal Town Planning Institute, who contributed the chapters on planning law. Changes since the last edition have necessitated substantial re-writing of these chapters.

We have tried to summarise and explain the law as it had been reported on 1 January 2011.

Richard Card
John Murdoch
Sandi Murdoch
April 2011

New to this edition

- Increased coverage of both land law and landlord and tenant law.

- Reworked section on planning law.

- Introduction of a range of aids to learning, including chapter overviews, summaries of key points at appropriate stages, and self-test and scenario questions at the end of each chapter.

- Incorporation of pieces of new legislation, in particular the Planning and Compulsory Purchase Act 2004; the Housing Act 2004; the Companies Act 2006; the Compensation Act 2006; the Commons Act 2006; the Tribunals, Courts and Enforcement Act 2007; the Housing and Urban Regeneration Act 2008; the Planning Act 2008, and the Mortgage Repossessions (Protection of Tenants etc) Act 2010.

- Contents fully updated since last edition.

Contents

Table of abbreviations   xxxv

Table of statutes   xxxvii

Table of cases   xlix

Part I Outline of the English legal system

1 Introduction   3
Chapter Overview   3
Civil law and criminal law   3
Common law and legislation   3
Common law and equity   4
Questions   5

2 Administration of the Law   6
Chapter Overview   6
The civil courts   6
  County courts   7
    Jurisdiction   7
    Small claims track   7
    Fast track claims   8
    Multi-track claims   8
    Appeals   8
  The High Court of Justice   8
    Chancery Division   8
    Queen's Bench Division   9
    Family Division   10
    Appeals   10
  The Court of Appeal   10
    Jurisdiction   10
  The Supreme Court   11
    Jurisdiction   11
  The Court of Justice of the European Union (European Court)   11
    Jurisdiction   12
Specialist courts and tribunals   12
  The Technology and Construction Court   12
  Tribunals   13
  The Upper Tribunal (Lands Chamber)   14
Alternative Dispute Resolution   14
  Arbitration   14
  Early neutral evaluation   15
  Expert determination   15
  Mediation   15
  Conciliation   15
Questions   16

3 Sources of English Law — 17

Chapter Overview — 17

Legislation — 17

Acts of Parliament — 17

Commencement and repeal — 18

Subordinate legislation — 18

Delegated legislation — 18

Interpretation — 19

Literal construction — 19

Purposive construction — 20

Rules of interpretation — 21

Words must be understood in their context — 22

Ejusdem generis rule — 22

Presumptions — 22

Aids to interpretation — 23

Intrinsic aids — 23

Extrinsic aids — 23

Cases where a Convention right or EU law is involved — 25

Acts giving effect to international conventions — 25

European Convention on Human Rights and Human Rights Act 1998 — 25

Impact of the Act — 26

Statutory interpretation — 26

Declaration of incompatibility — 27

Unlawful actions — 27

The Convention rights — 28

Application of Convention rights — 28

Judicial precedent — 29

Ratio decidendi and *obiter dictum* — 29

The hierarchy of the courts and judicial precedent — 30

The Court of Justice of the European Union — 30

The Supreme Court and the House of Lords — 30

The Court of Appeal (Civil Division) — 31

Divisional courts — 32

High Court judges — 32

County courts — 32

Tribunals — 32

Effect of Human Rights Act 1998 — 32

Application of judicial precedents — 33

Custom — 34

European Union legislation — 35

Regulations, directives and decisions — 35

Direct applicability and direct effect — 35

Transposition — 36

Untransposed directives: any effect in English law? — 37

Supremacy of EU law — 37

Validity of EU legislation — 38

Interpretation of EU legislation — 38

Questions — 39

Part II **The law of contract**

4 **Introduction** 43
Chapter Overview 43
The essential elements of a contract 43
Form 44
   Contracts which must be made by deed 44
      Leases for three years or more 44
      Contracts in which there is no consideration 44
      What is a 'deed'? 44
   Contracts which must be in writing 45
   Contracts which must be evidenced in writing 45
   E-mail 45
Capacity 45
   Companies 46
      Legal status 46
      Contractual capacity 46
   Limited liability partnerships 47
   Partnerships 48
   Illegality 49
Questions 50

5 **Agreement** 51
Chapter Overview 51
Ascertaining an agreement 51
General requirement of offer and acceptance 51
Offer 52
   Invitation to treat 53
      Exposure for sale 53
      Advertisements 53
      Auctions 54
      Tenders 54
Acceptance 55
   Requirements 55
      Counter-offers distinguished 56
      Acceptance by conduct 57
      Acceptance of tenders 57
   Communication of acceptance 58
      Dispensation from need for communication of acceptance 58
      Postal acceptance 59
      Prescribed mode of acceptance 60
Termination of offers 61
   Revocation 61
      Communication of revocation 61
      Unilateral contracts 62
   Lapse of time 62
   Death 63
Uncertain, incomplete and conditional agreements 63
   Uncertainty 63

Incomplete agreements 65
'Subject to contract' and similar phrases 66
Conditional agreements 67
Condition precedent 67
Condition subsequent 68
Payment for work done in anticipation of concluding a contract 69
Questions 69

6 Binding Agreement 71
Chapter Overview 71
Introduction 71
Intention to be legally bound 71
Consideration 72
Executed and executory consideration 74
Past consideration 74
Adequacy of consideration 75
Sufficiency of consideration 75
Performance of, or promise to perform, an existing duty imposed by law 75
Performance of, or promise to perform, an existing contractual
duty owed to the other party 76
Performance of an existing contractual duty owed to a third party 77
Part payment of debts 77
Promissory estoppel 79
Agreements to discharge or vary a contract 82
Mutual discharge 82
Unilateral discharge 83
Variation 83
Questions 84

7 Contractual Terms 85
Chapter Overview 85
Express terms 85
Parol evidence rule and exceptions and qualifications 85
Implied terms 85
Conditions precedent 85
Invalidating factors 85
Written agreement not the whole contract 86
Collateral contracts 86
Effect of 'entire agreement clauses' 86
Determination of whether a written term is a term of contract 87
Notice must be given before or at the time of the contract 87
The notice must be contained in a contractual document 88
Reasonable notice of the term must be given 88
Contractual terms and mere representations 89
Execution of a written contract 89
The importance of the representation 89
Invitation to verify 90
Statements of fact, of opinion or as to the future 90
Ability of the parties to ascertain the accuracy of the representation 90
Implied terms 92

Terms implied by custom or usage   92

Terms implied by statute   92

Terms implied by the courts   95

Implication of a term which is a necessary incident of the type of contract in question   95

Implication to give effect to the parties' imputed intentions   96

Unfair contract terms   97

Questions   98

8 Performance and Breach   100

Chapter Overview   100

Performance   100

Payment   101

Tender of payment   101

Tender of acts   102

Breach   102

Repudiatory breach   103

Option to terminate or affirm   103

Termination   103

Affirmation   106

Types of repudiatory breach   106

Renunciation   106

Incapacitation   107

Defective performance   107

Anticipatory breach   110

Time of performance   112

Questions   114

9 Exemption Clauses and Unfair Terms in Consumer Contracts   115

Chapter Overview   115

Interpretation of exemption clauses   115

Liability can only be excluded or restricted by clear words   116

All ambiguities in the exemption clause are interpreted against the party relying on it   117

Exclusion or limitation of liability for negligence   117

General limitations on the application of an exemption clause   118

Misrepresentation   118

Inconsistent undertakings   118

Unfair Contract Terms Act 1977   119

Avoidance of liability for negligence   119

Avoidance of liability for breach of contract   120

Standard written terms   121

Dealing as consumer   121

Matters common to ss 2 and 3   122

Excepted agreements   122

The 'requirement of reasonableness'   122

Avoidance of liability arising from sale or supply of goods   123

Sale and hire purchase   123

Miscellaneous contracts under which the ownership or possession of goods passes   124

The 'requirement of reasonableness' in relation to ss 6 and 7   125
Varieties of exemption clauses   126
Unfair Terms in Consumer Contracts Regulations 1999   127
Terms to which the Regulations apply   127
Unfair terms   128
Test of fairness   129
Consequence of inclusion of unfair term   131
Interpretation of written terms in consumer contracts   131
Questions   132

10 Discharge by Frustration   133

Chapter Overview   133
Scope   133
Supervening destruction or unavailability   134
Fundamental change of circumstances   134
Death or other personal incapacity   135
Supervening illegality   135
Supervening destruction of a basic assumption on which the parties contracted   136
Limits   136
Express provision for frustrating event   137
Foreseen and foreseeable events   137
Fault of a party   138
Effect   139
Money paid or payable under the contract before the occurrence
of the frustrating event   139
Money payable under the contract after the occurrence of the frustrating event   140
Award for valuable benefit obtained   140
Scope of LR(FC)A 1943   142
Questions   143

11 Remedies for Breach of Contract   144

Chapter Overview   144
Damages   145
Purpose of damages   145
For what can compensation be awarded?   146
Loss of expectation   146
Consequential loss   150
Causal connection   151
Remoteness of loss   151
Reasonable contemplation of loss   151
Assumption of responsibility   154
Mitigation   157
Contributory negligence   158
Liquidated damages and penalties   159
Penalty   160
Parties' intention   160
Other remedies for breach of contract   162
Action for price or other agreed sum   162
Agreed sum not due at time of reputiatory breach   162

Account of profits from breach   164
Quantum meruit   165
Specific performance   166
Injunction   168
Limitation of actions   171
Limitation periods   171
Extending the limitation period   172
Equitable relief   172

Questions   173

12 Misrepresentation, Duress and Undue Influence   175

Chapter Overview   175
Misrepresentation   175
Active misrepresentation   176
Active misrepresentations which have remained mere representations   176
Misrepresentation by words or conduct   176
Misrepresentation of fact   177
The misrepresentation must have been addressed by the
misrepresentor to the person misled   179
The misrepresentation must have been intended by the misrepresentor to be acted
on by the misrepresentee or by a class of person including the misrepresentee   180
The misrepresentation must have induced the misrepresentee to
make the contract   180
Remedies for active misrepresentations which have remained
mere representations   181
Rescission   181
Damages   184
Indemnity   189
Active misrepresentations which have become contractual terms   190
Breach of contract   190
Misrepresentation Act 1967, s 1(a)   190
Avoidance of provision excluding or limiting liability for misrepresentation   191
Misrepresentation through non-disclosure   193
Insurance contracts   194
Contracts where one party is in a fiduciary relationship of
confidence with the other   194
Duress and undue influence   195
Duress   195
Undue influence   196
Actual undue influence   196
Presumed undue influence   197
Undue influence or misrepresentation by a third party   198
Unconscionable bargains   198
Bars to rescission   199

Questions   200

13 Third Party Rights or Obligations Under a Contract   201

Chapter Overview   201
Contractual rights and third parties   201

Contracts (Rights of Third Parties) Act 1999 202
Right of third party to enforce contractual term 202
Exemption clauses: protection of third party 202
Discharge and variation 203
Defences etc available to the promisor 204
Cases where s 1 does not apply 204
Other exceptions and qualifications 205
Collateral contracts 205
Action in tort by third party 205
Enforcement by a party to the contract 206
Contractual obligations and third parties 207
Third party generally not bound by an exemption clause 208

Questions 209

14 Agency 210

Chapter Overview 210
Principal and agent 210
Creation of agency 210
Capacity 211
Appointment by express agreement 211
Appointment by implied agreement 211
Ratification 211
Agency of necessity 214
Duties of an agent 214
Duty to act 214
Duty to obey instructions 214
Duty to exercise care and skill 215
Fiduciary duties 215
Other duties 216
Rights of agents 216
Remuneration 216
Indemnity 217
Sub-agents 218
Termination of agency 218
Act of parties 218
Death 219
Mental incapacity 219
Bankruptcy 220
Effects of termination 220
Principal and third parties 221
The authority of agents 221
Actual authority 221
Ostensible authority 221
The disclosed principal 223
The undisclosed principal 223
Limitations on the right of the undisclosed principal to sue 223
Election 224
Agents and third parties 225
Contracts made by deed 225
Trade usage 225

Where the agent is in reality the principal 225
Other cases 226
Rights of third parties against agents 226
On the contract 226
For breach of warranty of authority 226
In tort 227
Estate agents and auctioneers 227
Questions 228

Part III The law of tort

15 Introduction 231
Chapter Overview 231
Aims and functions of the law of tort 231
Definition of a tort 232
Tort and crime 232
Tort and contract 232
Tort and restitution 233
Tort and breach of trust 233
Scope of the law of tort 233
Interests protected 233
The relevance of damage 234
Mental element 234
Motive 235
Fault liability 236
Human rights 236
Questions 237

16 Negligence—Duty of Care 238
Chapter Overview 238
Duty of care 239
A general principle 239
Donoghue v Stevenson 239
The current position 240
Omissions 241
Duties of protection 242
Damage caused by third parties 243
Economic loss 245
'Pure' and 'consequential' economic loss 246
Transferred loss 246
Defective products 247
The interaction of contract and tort 248
Negligent statements 248
Physical damage 248
Hedley Byrne v Heller 249
Professional liability 252
Public authorities 254

Judicial process   256
   Judges and other decision-makers   256
   Advocates   257
   Other participants   258
Psychiatric injury   258

Questions   260

17 Negligence—Breach of Duty   261

Chapter Overview   261
The reasonable man   261
   The objective standard   262
   Physical defects   262
   Age   262
   Experience of others   263
   Professional status   264
      Valuers and surveyors   266
The principle of risk   267
   Likelihood of injury   267
   Seriousness of consequences   267
   Value of conduct   268
   Cost of precautions   268
The proof of negligence   269
   Res ipsa loquitur   270
      Control by the defendant   270
      Inference of negligence   270

Questions   271

18 Negligence—the Causing of Damage   272

Chapter Overview   272
Causation in fact   273
   The 'but for' test   273
   Proof of causation   274
   Loss of a chance   275
   Multiple causes   275
Intervening causes   277
   Conduct of a third party   277
      'Innocent' conduct   277
      'Guilty' conduct   278
   Conduct of the claimant   278
      Rescue cases   279
      Emergencies   279
      Legal rights   279
Remoteness of damage   280
   The 'foreseeability' test   280
      Kind of damage   281
      Manner of infliction of damage   281
      Extent of damage   282
      The 'egg-shell skull'   282
Policy considerations   283

Questions   284

19 Defences to Negligence 285

Chapter Overview 285
Consent and assumption of risk 285
  Consent to torts other than negligence 285
    Meaning of consent 286
  Assumption of risk in negligence cases 286
    Express consent 286
    Implied consent 287
Contributory negligence 287
  Standard of care 288
  Causation 289
  Apportionment 289

Questions 290

20 Breach of Statutory Duty 292

Chapter Overview 292
Existence of civil liability 292
Elements of liability 294
  Class protected 294
  Type of injury 295
  Breach by defendant 295
  Causation 296
  Defences 297

Questions 298

21 Liability for Dangerous Premises 299

Chapter Overview 299
Lawful visitors 299
  Scope of the duty 299
    Exclusion of liability by contract 299
    Exclusion of liability by notice 300
  Occupier 300
    Multiple occupation 301
  Premises 302
  Visitor 302
    Limited permission 303
    Entry as of right 303
    Rights of way 304
    Visitors under contract 304
  The common duty of care 305
    Children 306
    Specialists 307
    Warnings 308
    Independent contractors 308
    Assumption of risk 309
Trespassers and other 'non-visitors' 310
  Occupiers' Liability Act 1984 310
    Scope of the duty 310
    The statutory conditions 311
    The duty of care 311

Injury suffered on access land 312
Defences 312
Exclusion of liability 312

Purchasers 313
Caveat emptor 313
Common law developments 313
Defective Premises Act 1972 314

Landlords 315

Questions 316

22 Trespass to Land 317

Chapter Overview 317
Land 317
Intrusion 318
Possession 319
Defences 319
Access to neighbouring land 320

Remedies 321
Damages 321
Injunction 321
Action of ejectment 322
Self-redress 322

Questions 323

23 Nuisance 324

Chapter Overview 324
Private nuisance 324
Interference 325
Physical damage to land 325
Use and enjoyment 325
Unlawfulness 326
Degree of interference 326
Sensitivity 327
Locality 327
Continuity 328
Utility of the defendant's conduct 328
Order of events 329
The defendant's state of mind 329
Who is protected? 331
Who is liable? 331
Creator 331
Occupier 332
Landlord 333
Defences 335
Statutory authority 335
Other defences 336
Remedies 336
Damages 336
Injunction 337
Abatement 337

Public nuisance   338
   Highways   339
   Action for damages   340
Questions   341

24 Strict Liability   342

Chapter Overview   342
Rylands v Fletcher   342
  Elements of liability   343
    Land   343
    Accumulation   344
    Dangerous things   344
    Escape   345
    Non-natural use   345
    Damage   346
  Defences   347
    Consent of the claimant   347
    Default of the claimant and hypersensitivity 348
    Act of God   348
    Act of a stranger   349
    Statutory authority   349
    Fire   350
Statutory liability   351
Questions   352

25 Animals   353

Chapter Overview   353
Liability at common law   353
  Nuisance   353
  Negligence   354
Animals Act 1971   355
  Dangerous animals   355
    Classification of species   355
    Dangerous species   356
    Non-dangerous species   356
    Defences   358
  Straying livestock   359
    Defences   359
    Detention and sale   360
  Dogs worrying livestock   360
    Liability for dogs   360
    Protection of livestock   360
Questions   361

26 Vicarious Liability   363

Chapter Overview   363
Employer and employee   364
  Who is an employee?   364
    Control and other criteria   364

Function of employee 365
'Business' test 365
Borrowed employees 366
What is the course of employment? 367
Authorised acts 367
Implied authority 368
Ostensible authority 369
Prohibitions 369
Intentional wrongdoing 370
Liability of employee 372
Independent contractors 372
General principle 372
Non-delegable duties 373
Statutory duties 373
Withdrawal of support 373
Strict liability 374
Operations on the highway 374
Extra-hazardous acts 374
Other cases 374
Collateral negligence 375
Questions 375

27　Remedies 377

Chapter Overview 377
Damages 377
Kinds of damages 377
Personal injury 379
Loss of amenity 379
Pain and suffering 379
Loss of expectation of life 380
Medical and other expenses 380
Loss of earnings 380
Collateral benefits 381
Death 382
Fatal accidents 382
Damage to property 383
Measure of damages 383
Date of assessment 384
Multiple tortfeasors 385
Contribution between tortfeasors 385
Injunctions 386
Kinds of injunction 386
Damages in lieu of injunction 387
Other remedies 388
Limitation of actions 388
Commencement of limitation period 388
Personal injury 389
Latent damage 389
Extension of time 390

Injunctions 390

Questions 391

Part IV Land law

28 Land, its Ownership and Use 395

Chapter Overview 395

What is land? 396

General definition of land 397

Physical extent 397

Artificial things brought onto land 398

Things growing on the land 400

Limitations on the physical extent of a landowner's rights 400

Airspace 401

Minerals 401

Things found on or under the land 402

Wild animals 402

Water 402

Demarcating the physical extent of land: boundaries 403

The general law 403

Presumptions 404

Alteration of boundaries 405

Boundary structures 406

Legal nature of proprietary rights to land 407

Ownership interests: estates and tenure 407

Tenure 407

Estates 408

Third party rights: interests in land 410

Legal and equitable rights to land 410

What is an equitable interest? 410

Personal rights to use land: licences 412

Gratuitous licences 412

Contractual licences 413

Nature 413

Revocability 414

Enforceability against third parties 414

Questions 415

29 The Formal Acquisition of Rights to Land 416

Chapter Overview 416

Formal requirements governing contracts for the sale of land 417

The statutory requirements 417

Amplification by the courts 418

Signatures 418

More than one document 419

Additional terms 419

Options and rights of pre-emption 420

Compliance   420
Non-compliance   421
Reform: electronic documents   422
Formal requirements governing the creation of legal and equitable interests   422
Legal estates and interests: the general law   422
Short lease exception   423
Legal estates and interests: registration of title   424
The Land Register   424
Title not yet registered: first registration   425
Title already registered   427
Electronic conveyancing   429
Equitable interests   429
A typical sale of land   430
Initial negotiation   430
Inquiries and searches   432
Local land charges and supplementary inquiries   432
Draft contract   433
Contract   433
Exchange   433
Deposit   434
Terms   434
Vendor's liability for defects   434
Remedies   435
Sale by auction   436
Transfer stage   436
Registered land   436

Questions   438

30 The Informal Acquisition of Rights to Land   439

Chapter Overview   439
Informal transactions   439
An example: informal leases   440
The overall principle   442
Informal arrangements   442
Implied, resulting and constructive trusts   442
Resulting trusts   443
Constructive trusts   443
Proprietary estoppel   444
Expectation   445
Acts in reliance   445
Detriment   446
Effect of the doctrine   446
Conveyancing problems   447
Proprietary estoppel and constructive trusts   448
The doctrine of benefit and burden   449
Adverse possession   450
Introduction   450
Land Registration Act 2002: claims to registered land   452
Introduction   452

Adverse possession 452
The effect of completing the requisite period of adverse possession 456
Adverse possession and leases 457
Adverse possession against a tenant of an unregistered lease 457
The position of the landlord of an unregistered lease 458
Adverse possession against tenants of registered leases 458
Adverse possession by tenants 459

Questions 460

31 Concurrent Ownership 461

Chapter Overview 461
The forms of concurrent ownership 461
Introduction 461
Joint tenancy 462
The right of survivorship 462
The four unities 463
Tenancy in common 463
No right of survivorship 463
Four unities not essential 463
How concurrent ownership arises 464
Express creation 464
How to decide whether the beneficial interest is held on a joint tenancy
or a tenancy in common 464
Co-ownership by implication 466
Direct financial contributions 466
No direct financial contributions 466
Reform 467
Quantification of shares 468
The conversion of a joint tenancy into a tenancy in common: severance 469
Acquiring a greater interest in the land 470
By disposition of the equitable interest 470
By mutual agreement to sever 470
By notice in writing 470
Course of dealings 471
Ending co-ownership 471
The potential problems arising from concurrent ownership 472
Some of the problems 472
The old solutions 472
The modern mechanism for owning land concurrently: trusts of land 473
The imposition of a trust of land 474
Tenancy in common 474
Joint tenancy 475
Why a trust? 475
The position of the trustees 475
Powers and duties 475
Restrictions on powers 476
The position of the beneficiaries 476
The sale of trust land 477
The basic principles 477

Disputes over trusts of land	480
'Matrimonial' property	480
Other trust property	481
Questions	483
32 Easements	**485**
Chapter Overview	485
The nature of easement	485
The essential characteristics of an easement	486
There must be a dominant and servient piece of land	486
The easement must 'accommodate' the dominant land	486
The dominant and servient owners must be different persons	487
The right must be capable of forming the subject matter of a grant, ie be capable of being granted	487
Rights similar to easements	491
Natural rights	491
Restrictive covenants	491
Public rights	492
Licences	492
Non-derogation from grant	492
Profits à prendre	492
Customary rights	493
Acquisition of easements	494
Legal and equitable easements	494
Expressly created easements	495
Grants and reservations	495
Implied easements	495
Implied grants	495
Implied reservations	497
Creation of easements by the operation of the LPA 1925, s 62	498
The ambit of s 62	498
The operation of s 62	499
Exclusion of s 62 and the rule in *Wheeldon v Burrows*	500
Prescription	500
Continuous enjoyment	501
In fee simple	501
As of right	501
The three methods of prescription	502
Extinguishment of easements	505
Particular easements	506
Rights of way	506
Rights of light	507
Acquisition by prescription	507
Extent of right	508
Rights of support	509
Questions	510
33 Restrictive Covenants	**512**
Chapter Overview	512

Covenants where there is no relationship of landlord and tenant   512
The running of the burden   513
    Positive covenants   513
      Commonhold   514
      Devices to achieve the enforcement of positive covenants   515
    Restrictive covenants   516
      The covenant must be essentially negative   517
      The covenantee must retain land capable of being benefited   517
      The parties must intend that the covenant should run   518
      Registration and notice   518
The running of the benefit   519
    Positive covenants   519
      The covenant must touch and concern the land of the covenantee   519
      It was intended that the benefit should run   520
      The land to be benefited should be identifiable   520
      The successor must acquire a legal estate   520
    Restrictive covenants   520
      Annexation   520
      Assignment   522
      Scheme of development   522
Remedies   525
Discharge of restrictive covenants   526
    Development, planning law and restrictive covenants   526
Discharge at common law   527
    Change in character of neighbourhood   527
    Release of the covenant   527
    Unity of ownership   527
    Acquisition for planning or statutory purposes   527
Application to the Upper Tribunal (Lands Chamber)   528
    Obsolescence   529
    Agreement   529
    No injury   529
    Impedes reasonable use   529
Housing Act 1985, s 610   531
Proposals for reform   531
Questions   532

34 Mortgages   533
Chapter Overview   533
Creation of mortgages   533
    Historical background   533
    Modern mortgages   534
      Legal mortgages   534
      Informal mortgages   534
Mortgagor's right to redeem (repay)   535
    Commercial arrangements for repayment   535
    The differing approaches of the common law and
    equity to repayment   535
      Legal date of redemption   535
      The equity of redemption and the equitable right to redeem   535

Impediments to full redemption   536
  Provisions excluding redemption   537
  Oppressive or unconscionable terms   537
  Restraint of trade   540
  Statutory regulation   540
Mortgagee's remedies   542
  Possession of the mortgaged property   542
  Restrictions on the mortgagee's right to possession   542
    Express restriction   542
    Implied restriction   543
    Duty to account strictly   543
    The existence of a prior claim to possession   543
    Restrictions on claims to possession of dwellings   544
  Sale   546
    The power of sale   546
    Exercise of the power   547
    Court's power to order sale   548
  Action on the personal covenant   549
  Appointment of a receiver   550
  Foreclosure   551
  Leasing   552
  Insurance   553
  Priorities   554
  Priority   554
  Tacking of further advances   554
  Questions   555

35 Enforceability of Interests in Land   556
  Chapter Overview   556
  The background   556
    The pre-1926 rules   556
      Legal rights   557
      Equitable interests   557
      The bona fide purchaser of a legal estate for value   558
    The solutions adopted in 1925   558
      Two systems of registration   559
      Unregistered land   560
  Registered land   562
    Introduction   562
      The classification of rights to registered land   562
      The effect of registration of title   562
    Registered charges   563
    'Overriding' interests   564
      Introduction   564
      Short legal leases   565
      Rights of persons in actual occupation   565
      Easements and profits à prendre   569
      Miscellaneous overriding interests   570

Interests that require protection by an entry on the register 570
  Methods of protection 570
  The search procedure 572
  Failure to register 572
Alteration, rectification and indemnity 573
  Alteration 573
    Indemnity 574

Questions 575

Part V The law of landlord and tenant

36 Landlord and Tenant: the General Law 579
  Chapter Overview 579
  Characteristics of leasehold interests 580
    Certainty of term 580
      Fixed-term leases 580
      Periodic tenancies 581
      Leases for life 582
      Perpetually renewable leases 582
    Exclusive possession 582
      The distinction between a lease and a licence 583
  Particular types of tenancy 585
    Fixed-term leases 585
    Periodic tenancies 586
    Tenancy at will 587
    Tenancy at sufferance 587
    Tenancy by estoppel 587
    Concurrent leases 588
    Reversionary leases 588
  Rights and obligations under a lease: an introduction 589
  Lease negotiations 589
    Introduction 589
      New leases 589
      Existing leases 590
      Commercial premises 590
      Residential property 590
      Flexibility through form: absolute, qualified and fully qualified covenants 591
  The principal lease covenants 591
    Disposition 592
      Assignment, sub-letting, or parting with possession 592
  Use and enjoyment 595
    Landlord covenants 595
    Tenant covenants 598
    Other restrictions on use 599
    Enforcement of user covenants 599
    Physical state 600
      Implied repairing obligations: tenants 600

Implied repairing obligations: landlords   601
Express repairing obligations   603
Covenants against alterations   606
Outgoings   607
Rent   607
Rent reviews   608
Service charges   612
Insurance   613
Remedies for breach of covenant   613
For breach of covenants other than for payment of rent   613
Forfeiture   614
For breach of repairing covenants   616
For non-payment of rent   617
Distress   617
Forfeiture   618
Enforceability of covenants by and against assignees   619
Leases entered into before 1 January 1996   619
Touching and concerning   620
Assignment of the lease   620
Assignment of the reversion   622
Assignment of both the lease and the reversion   622
Leases entered into on or after 1 January 1996   623
The broad effect of the LT(C)A 1995   623
The transmission of covenants on assignment of the lease or the reversion   623
Release of tenant on assignment of the lease   624
Authorised guarantee agreements   624
Illustrations   625
Release of landlord on assignment of the reversion   625
Default notices and overriding leases   626
Sureties and sub-tenants   627
Sureties   627
Sub-tenants   628
Bringing leases to an end: the common law   629
Forfeiture   629
Surrender   629
Merger   629
Expiry   630
Notice   630
Enlargement   630
Frustration   631
Repudiation   631
Disclaimer   631

Questions   631

37 Landlord and Tenant: Statutory Protection   633

Chapter Overview   633
Residential tenancies   634
Introduction   634
Rent Act tenancies   635

Housing Act tenancies 636
Introduction 636
Assured shorthold tenancies 637
Assured tenancies 640
Long residential tenancies 642
Security of tenure 642
Enfranchisement 642
Right to manage 646
Public sector tenancies 646
Secure tenancies 647
Introductory, demoted and family intervention tenancies 648
Miscellaneous statutory provisions 651
Harassment and unlawful eviction 651
Information for tenants 652
Business tenancies 653
Introduction 653
Tenancies within the Act 653
Termination of tenancies governed by the LTA 1954 656
The renewal process 658
Opposing renewal 660
The new tenancy 664
Agricultural tenancies 667
Agricultural holdings 667
Farm business tenancies 669
Questions 670

Part VI Planning law

38 The Operation of the Planning System and its Legal Framework 675
Chapter Overview 675
Introduction 675
The origins of the planning system 675
The framework for planning control 676
Legislation 676
Principal Planning Acts 676
Human Rights legislation 677
Subordinate legislation 677
Government policy: Planning Policy Guidance Notes, Planning Policy Statements and Circulars 678
The planning institutions—a mixture of central and local government 679
Central government 679
The role of the Secretary of State 679
Local government: the local planning authority 680
The role of the LPA 680
Identifying the LPA 681
The operation of LPAs 682
Development plans 684
Introduction 684

Regional spatial strategies   684
Local Development Frameworks   685
   Process   686
   Legal challenges   687
Strategic environmental assessment   687
Sustainable development   687
The significance of the 'development plan'   688
The legal liabilities of LPAs   689
The power of planning officers to bind the authority   690
Legitimate expectation   690
Local Government Ombudsman   690

Questions   691

39 The Law of Development Management and Enforcement   692

Chapter Overview   692
Introduction   692
The definition of development   693
   Operational development   693
   Material change of use   694
   What constitutes a material change of use?   695
   What does not constitute a material change of use?   695
   Other uses excluded from development   696
   The Use Classes Order   696
The need for planning permission   699
   Permitted development   699
   Local Development Orders   700
   Article 4 directions   700
Applications for planning permission   701
   Outline and full planning applications   701
   Submitting an application   701
   What the LPA does on receipt of an application   702
   The decision   702
   Material considerations   703
   Making a decision   704
   Grant of permission   705
      Conditions   705
      Planning obligations   706
Appeals to the Secretary of State   708
   Written representations   709
   Informal hearing   709
   Public inquiry   709
   The inspector's decision   710
   Award of costs in appeals   710
   Challenging an inspector's decision   710
Environmental impact assessment   711
Listed buildings and conservation areas   712
   Listed buildings   712
   Conservation areas   713
Enforcement   714

Time limits	715
The four-year rule	715
The 10-year rule	716
Lawful use	716
Certificates of lawfulness	716
Enforcement powers	717
The Localism Bill	721
Questions	722
Index	725

Table of abbreviations

AA 1971	Animals Act 1971
AA 1996	Arbitration Act 1996
AHA 1986	Agricultural Holdings Act 1986
AJA 1982	Administration of Justice Act 1982
ANLA 1992	Access to Neighbouring Land Act 1992
ATA 1995	Agricultural Tenancies Act 1995
CA 1985	Companies Act 1985
CA 2006	Companies Act 2006
CCA 1974	Consumer Credit Act 1974
CL(C)A 1978	Civil Liability (Contribution) Act 1978
CLRA 2002	Commonhold and Leasehold Reform Act 2002
CRWA 2000	Countryside and Rights of Way Act 2000
DPA 1972	Defective Premises Act 1972
ECA 1972	European Communities Act 1972
FAA 1976	Fatal Accidents Act 1976
FSMA 2000	Financial Services and Markets Act 2000
GPDO 1995	Town and Country Planning General Permitted Development Order 1995
HA 1985	Housing Act 1985
HA 1988	Housing Act 1988
HA 1996	Housing Act 1996
HRA 1998	Human Rights Act 1998
IA 1986	Insolvency Act 1986
LA 1980	Limitation Act 1980
LCA 1972	Land Charges Act 1972
LDA 1986	Latent Damage Act 1986
LLPA 2000	Limited Liability Partnerships Act 2000
LPA 1907	Limited Partnerships Act 1907
LPA 1922	Law of Property Act 1922
LPA 1925	Law of Property Act 1925
LP(MP)A 1989	Law of Property (Miscellaneous Provisions) Act 1989
LP(R)A 1938	Leasehold Property (Repairs) Act 1938
LRA 1925	Land Registration Act 1925
LRA 1967	Leasehold Reform Act 1967
LRA 2002	Land Registration Act 2002
LRHUDA 1993	Leasehold Reform, Housing and Urban Development Act 1993

LR(FC)A 1943	Law Reform (Frustrated Contracts) Act 1943
LTA 1927	Landlord and Tenant Act 1927
LTA 1954	Landlord and Tenant Act 1954
LTA 1985	Landlord and Tenant Act 1985
LTA 1987	Landlord and Tenant Act 1987
LT(C)A 1995	Landlord and Tenant (Covenants) Act 1995
MA 1967	Misrepresentation Act 1967
MR(PT)A 2010	Mortgage Repossessions (Protection of Tenants) Act 2010
OLA 1957	Occupiers' Liability Act 1957
OLA 1984	Occupiers' Liability Act 1984
PA 1832	Prescription Act 1832
PA 1890	Partnership Act 1890
PAA 1971	Powers of Attorney Act 1971
PCPA 2004	Planning and Compulsory Purchase Act 2004
PEA 1977	Protection From Eviction Act 1977
RA 1977	Rent Act 1977
RcA 1977	Rentcharges Act 1977
RTA 1988	Road Traffic Act 1988
SCA 1981	Supreme Court Act 1981
SGA 1979	Sale of Goods Act 1979
SG(IT)A 1973	Supply of Goods (Implied Terms) Act 1973
SGSA 1982	Supply of Goods and Services Act 1982
SSAA 1992	Social Security Administration Act 1992
TA 1996	Treasure Act 1996
TCPA 1947	Town and Country Planning Act 1947
TCPA 1990	Town and Country Planning Act 1990
TLATA 1996	Trusts of Land and Appointment of Trustees Act 1996
UCTA 1977	Unfair Contract Terms Act 1977

Table of statutes

Paragraph references printed in bold type where the Act is set out in part or in full.

Abortion Act 1967 ... 3.10
Access to Neighbouring Land Act 1992 ... 22.6, 28.28
  s.1(1) ... 22.6
  s.1(2)(b) ... 22.6
  s.1(3) ... 22.6
  s.1(4) ... 22.6
  s.1(5) ... 22.6
  s.2(1) ... 22.6
  s.2(2) ... 22.6
  s.2(4) ... 22.6
  s.2(5) ... 22.6
  s.2(6) ... 22.6
  s.3(3) ... 22.6
Accidents Act 1976
  s.2(3) ... 3.27
Administration of Justice Act 1970 ... 34.25
  s.36 ... 34.25–34.26
Administration of Justice Act 1973 ... 34.26
  s.8 ... 34.26, 34.37
Administration of Justice Act 1982
  s.1(1) ... 27.6
  s.1(1)(b) ... 27.6
  s.1(2) ... 27.6, 27.8
  s.3 ... 27.11
  s.4 ... 27.10
  s.5 ... 27.9
Agricultural Holdings Act 1986 ... 37.46
  Pt V ... 37.47
  ss.1–5 ... 37.47
  s.1(4) ... 37.47
  s.10 ... 28.13
  s.12 ... 37.47
  s.13 ... 37.47
  ss.25–27 ... 37.47
  s.26(2) ... 37.47
  ss.36–48 ... 37.47
  ss.50–58 ... 37.47
  s.60 ... 37.47
  ss.64–69 ... 37.47
  s.66 ... 37.47
  s.71 ... 37.47
  s.72 ... 37.47
  s.84 ... 37.47
  Sch.2 ... 37.47
  Sch.3 ... 37.47
  Sch.9 para.2 ... 37.47
  Sch.14 para.12 ... 34.39
Agricultural Tenancies Act 1995 ... 37.46, 37.48
  Pt II ... 37.48

  Pt III ... 37.48
  s.1 ... 37.48
  s.1(3) ... 37.48
  s.1(4) ... 37.48
  s.4(1) ... 37.47
  s.5(1) ... 37.48
  s.6 ... 37.48
  s.8 ... 28.13
  s.9 ... 37.48
  s.9(c) ... 37.48
  s.20 ... 37.48
  s.20(4A) ... 37.48
  s.20(4B) ... 37.48
Animals Act 1971 ... 25.4
  s.2 ... 25.5, 25.7, 25.11
  s.2(1) ... 25.5
  s.2(2) ... 25.6
  s.3 ... 25.11
  s.4 ... 25.9–25.11
  s.4(1) ... 25.8
  s.5(1) ... 25.7, 25.9
  s.5(2) ... 25.7
  s.5(3) ... 25.7
  s.5(4) ... 25.11–25.12
  s.5(5) ... 25.8
  s.5(6) ... 25.9
  s.6(2) ... 25.4
  s.6(3) ... 25.5
  s.6(4) ... 25.5
  s.6(5) ... 25.7
  s.7 ... 25.8, 25.10
  s.8 ... 25.8
  s.8(1) ... 25.3
  s.8(2) ... 25.3
  s.9 ... 25.12
  s.11 ... 25.4, 25.8
Anti-Social Behaviour Act 2003 ... 37.18, 37.21
Arbitration Act 1996 ... 36.59, 37.47
  s.29 ... 16.25, 36.59
  s.33 ... 36.59
  s.34(1)(g) ... 36.59
  s.34(2)(d) ... 36.59
  s.34(2)(f) ... 36.59
  s.52(4) ... 36.59
  ss.59–65 ... 36.59
  s.68 ... 36.59
  s.69 ... 36.59
  s.90 ... 9.24
Civil Aviation Act 1982
  s.76 ... 22.2

s.76(1) ... 28.16
Civil Evidence Act 1968
    s.11 ... 17.15
Civil Liability (Contribution) Act 1978 ... 18.4
    s.1(1) ... 27.15
    s.3 ... 14.38
    s.4 ... 27.14
Civil Partnership Act 2004 ... 31.39
    s.72 ... 31.39
    s.81 ... 37.3–37.4
    Sch.5 ... 31.39
    Sch.8 para.13 ... 37.3
    Sch.8 para.41 ... 37.4
    Coal Industry Act 1994
    s.1(1) ... 28.17
    s.7(3) ... 28.17
Common Law Procedure Act 1852
    s.10 ... 36.70
Commonhold and Leasehold Reform Act
    2002 ... 28.7, 28.34, 33.5, 36.60, 37.13
    Pt II ... 37.16
    s.1 ... 28.34
    s.1(1) ... 28.34
    s.3 ... 37.13
    s.3(1) ... 28.34
    s.3(1)(b) ... 33.5
    s.11(2) ... 28.34
    s.14 ... 28.34
    s.25(1) ... 28.34
    s.26 ... 28.34
    s.34 ... 28.34
    s.74 ... 37.16
    s.79 ... 37.16
    s.96 ... 37.16
    s.97 ... 37.16
    s.117 ... 37.15
    s.120 ... 37.15
    ss.122–124 ... 37.15
    s.138 ... 37.14
    s.139 ... 37.14
    s.141 ... 37.14
    s.158 ... 36.60
    s.164 ... 36.61
    s.167 ... 36.70
    s.168 ... 36.65
    Sch.3 ... 28.34
    Sch.8 ... 37.15
    Sch.11 ... 36.60
Commons Act 2006 ... 32.21
Commons Registration Act 1965 ... 32.21
Companies Act 1985
    s.36C ... 14.8
Companies Act 2006 ... 4.11, 4.14
    s.31(1) ... 4.14
    s.39(1) ... 4.14
    s.40 ... 4.15
    s.42 ... 4.14
    s.44(1)(a) ... 29.11
    s.44(2)(a)–(b) ... 29.11
    s.44(5) ... 29.11

s.171(1)(a) ... 4.14
    s.739 ... 34.10
Compensation Act 2006
    s.1 ... 17.13
Compulsory Purchase Act 1965
    s.10 ... 33.37
Consumer Credit Act 1974 ... 4.7, 34.15,
    34.17–34.18
    s.16 ... 34.17
    s.58 ... 34.17
    s.60 ... 34.17
    s.65 ... 4.7
    s.93 ... 34.17
    s.126 ... 34.17, 34.25
    s.140A ... 34.17
    s.140B ... 34.17
Consumer Credit Act 2006 ... 34.15, 34.17
Consumer Protection Act 1987 ... 17.18
Consumer Safety Act 1978 ... 20.2
Contracts (Rights of Third Parties) Act
    1999 ... 13.1–13.2, 13.12, 28.2, 33.3
    s.1 ... 9.10, 13.4, 13.7–13.9, 13.12–13.13, 13.15,
        30.10, 36.39
    s.1(1)(a) ... 13.3
    s.1(1)(b) ... 13.3
    s.1(2) ... 13.3
    s.1(3) ... 13.3
    s.1(5) ... 13.3
    s.1(6) ... 13.5
    s.2(1) ... 13.6
    s.2(2) ... 13.6
    s.2(4) ... 13.6
    s.2(5) ... 13.6
    s.2(6) ... 13.6
    s.3(2) ... 13.7
    s.3(3) ... 13.7
    s.3(4) ... 13.7
    s.3(5) ... 13.7
    s.3(6) ... 13.4
    s.4 ... 13.12
    s.5 ... 13.13
    s.6(3) ... 13.8
    s.6(4) ... 13.8
    s.7(2) ... 9.10
Control of Pollution Act 1974 ... 23.1, 24.18
Countryside Act 1968
    s.15(4) ... 33.13
Countryside and Rights of Way Act 2000 ...
    21.9, 21.19, 32.16
    Pt I ... 32.16
    Pt II ... 32.16
    s.2 ... 21.23
    s.13 ... 21.23
    s.68 ... 32.43
County Courts Act 1984 ... 36.70
    s.138(2) ... 36.70
    s.138(3) ... 36.70
    s.138(7) ... 36.70
    s.138(9A) ... 36.70
    s.139(1) ... 36.70

Courts Act 2003
  s.100 . . . 27.8
Courts and Legal Services Act 1990
  s.62 . . . 16.26
  s.108 . . . 16.25
Criminal Law Act 1977 . . . 22.1, 22.10
  s.6 . . . 36.65
  s.6(1) . . . 34.18
Damages Act 1996
  s.2 . . . 27.8
Defective Premises Act 1972 . . . 27.20, 29.30
  s.1 . . . 21.29
  s.1(1) . . . 21.29
  s.1(2) . . . 21.29
  s.1(3) . . . 21.29
  s.1(4) . . . 21.29
  s.4 . . . 21.30, 23.17, 36.46
  s.6(3) . . . 21.29
Disability Discrimination Act 1995
  Pt III . . . 36.53
  s.22(3)(c) . . . 37.18
Distress for Rent Act 1689 . . . 36.69
Distress for Rent Act 1733 . . . 36.16, 36.69
Easter Act 1928 . . . 3.4
Electronic Communications Act 2000
  s.8 . . . 29.10
Enduring Powers of Attorney Act 1985 . . .
  14.22, 14.25, 14.27
Enterprise Act 2002
  s.261 . . . 31.41
Estate Agents Act 1979 . . . 2.23, 3.4
European Communities Act 1972 . . . 3.6
  s.2(1) . . . 3.49, 3.52
  s.2(2) . . . 3.50
  s.2(4) . . . 3.50
  s.3(1) . . . 3.36
Factories Act 1937 . . . 3.14
Family Law Act 1996
  s.31(10(b) . . . 35.24
Fatal Accidents Act 1976 . . . 15.7, 16.12, 27.11
  s.2(3) . . . 3.27
  s.3(3) . . . 27.11
  s.4 . . . 27.11
Finance Act 1976 . . . 3.21
  s.63(2) . . . 3.21
Financial Services Act 1986 . . . 29.1
Financial Services and Markets Act 2000 . . .
  34.16–34.17
  s.22 . . . 34.16
  s.23(1) . . . 34.16
  s.26(1) . . . 34.16
  s.26(2) . . . 34.16
  s.28(2) . . . 34.16
  s.150(1) . . . 34.16
Fires Prevention (Metropolis) Act 1774 . . .
  24.17
  s.83 . . . 34.40
  s.86 . . . 24.16
Greater London Authority Act 1999 . . . 38.12
Greater London Authority Act 2007 . . . 38.12

Government of Wales Act 2006
  Pt 4 . . . 3.1
Guard Dogs Act 1975 . . . 20.2, 25.7
Health and Social Care (Community Health
  and Standards) Act 2003
  s.150 . . . 27.9
Highways Act 1980 . . . 23.25, 28.25
  Pt IV . . . 21.10
  s.31(1) . . . 32.16
  s.41(1) . . . 20.3
Hotel Proprietors Act 1956
  s.2(3) . . . 21.2
Housing Act 1985 . . . 33.33, 37.2
  Pt IV . . . 37.17
  s.4ZA(3)–(7) . . . 37.22
  s.11 . . . 36.60
  s.12ZA . . . 37.10
  s.79 . . . 37.27
  s.79(1) . . . 37.18
  s.79(3) . . . 37.18
  s.80 . . . 37.18
  s.81 . . . 37.18
  s.82(1) . . . 37.18
  s.82(1A) . . . 37.18
  s.82A . . . 37.10, 37.18
  s.82A(3) . . . 37.21
  s.82A(4) . . . 37.21
  s.83 . . . 37.18
  s.86(1) . . . 37.18
  s.87(b) . . . 37.18
  s.89(1) . . . 37.18
  s.89(2)(a) . . . 37.18
  s.113(1)(a) . . . 37.18
  s.609 . . . 33.13
  Sch.1 . . . 37.18
  Sch.1 para.11 . . . 37.27
  Sch.2 . . . 37.18
Housing Act 1988 . . . 28.40, 34.23, 36.2, 36.9,
  37.2–37.4, 37.11, 37.12, 37.17, 37.23
  s.1 . . . 37.4, 37.27
  s.5 . . . 36.95, 37.4, 37.6
  s.5(1) . . . 37.6, 37.10
  s.5(2) . . . 37.6, 37.10
  s.7 . . . 37.4, 37.6, 37.10
  s.7(6) . . . 37.10
  s.8 . . . 37.10
  s.9(6) . . . 37.10
  s.13 . . . 37.4, 37.7, 37.11
  s.13(1) . . . 37.7
  s.14 . . . 37.4, 37.7, 37.11
  s.17 . . . 37.4
  s.19 . . . 36.69
  s.19A . . . 37.5, 37.9
  s.20A . . . 37.24
  s.21 . . . 37.6
  s.21(1)(a) . . . 37.6
  s.21(4)(a) . . . 37.6
  s.21(5) . . . 37.6
  s.22 . . . 37.4, 37.7
  s.27 . . . 15.8, 20.2, 36.34, 37.23

s.28 . . . 27.2, 37.23
Sch.1 . . . 37.4
Sch.1 para.4 . . . 37.27
Sch.2 . . . 37.10
Sch.2A . . . 37.5
Housing Act 1996 . . . 37.20
  s.1 . . . 36.65
  s.82 . . . 36.65
  s.96 . . . 37.5
  s.124 . . . 37.20
  s.124(2) . . . 37.20
  s.125(1) . . . 37.20
  s.125(2) . . . 37.20
  s.125A . . . 37.20
  s.127 . . . 37.20
  s.128(1) . . . 37.20
  s.130 . . . 37.20
  s.143E . . . 37.21
  s.143F . . . 37.21
  ss.159—174 . . . 37.17
  Sch.1 para.1A . . . 37.20
Housing Act 2004 . . . 36.44, 37.20
  s.4 . . . 36.44
  s.5(1) . . . 36.44
  s.7(1) . . . 36.44
  ss.212–215 . . . 37.8
  s.215(1) . . . 37.8
  s.215(2) . . . 37.8
  Sch.10 paras.3–8 . . . 37.8
  Sch.10 para.10 . . . 37.8
Housing and Town Planning Act 1909 . . . 38.2
Housing and Urban Regeneration Act
  2008 . . . 37.17–37.18, 37.22
  s.298 . . . 37.22
  Sch.11 Pt I . . . 37.18
Human Rights Act 1998 . . . 3.5, 3.22, 3.24–3.26,
  3.43, 15.12, 23.13, 38.4
  s.2(1) . . . 3.31
  s.3 . . . 3.27
  s.3(1) . . . 3.22, 3.27
  s.3(2) . . . 3.25
  s.4 . . . 3.28
  s.6 . . . 15.12
  ss.6(1)–(3) . . . 3.29
  s.6(1) . . . 36.46
  s.9(1) . . . 3.29
  s.10 . . . 3.28
  Sch.1 . . . 3.25, 3.30, 15.12
Insolvency Act 1986
  s.178 . . . 36.99
  s.283A . . . 31.41
  s.315 . . . 36.99
  s.335A . . . 31.41, 34.34
Interpretation Act 1978 . . . 3.21
  s.8 . . . 3.21
  s.15 . . . 3.4
  s.16 . . . 3.4
  Sch.1 . . . 3.21
Judicature Acts 1873–1875 . . . 1.5
Judicature Act 1873 . . . 8.31, 11.55

Land Charges Act 1972 . . . 35.9–35.13
  s.4(5) . . . 35.12, 35.23
  s.4(6) . . . 35.12, 35.23
Land Registration Act 1925 . . . 29.13,
  35.9–35.12, 35.14, 35.20, 35.38, 35.43
  s.4 . . . 36.19
  s.23(2) . . . 34.39
  s.27 . . . 34.4
  s.51 . . . 34.4
  s.62 . . . 35.31
  s.70(1)(g) . . . 35.23, 35.27
  s.70(1)(k) . . . 35.29
  s.71 . . . 35.21
  s.115 . . . 35.24
  s.116 . . . 35.24
  Sch.2 para.8 . . . 34.4
Land Registration Act 2002 . . . 29.1, 29.13,
  30.19, 30.28, 30.34–30.35, 35.9–35.12, 35.14,
  35.20
  s.3 . . . 29.16
  s.3(1)(d) . . . 32.20
  s.4 . . . 29.15–29.16, 35.22, 36.2
  s.6 . . . 29.15
  s.7(1) . . . 29.15
  s.7(2)(a) . . . 29.15
  s.7(2)(b) . . . 29.15
  s.8 . . . 29.15
  s.9 . . . 29.17
  s.10 . . . 29.17
  s.11(3) . . . 29.17
  s.11(4) . . . 29.17
  s.11(6) . . . 29.17
  s.12(3) . . . 29.17
  s.12(4) . . . 29.17
  s.12(5) . . . 29.17
  s.12(6) . . . 29.17, 33.15
  s.23 . . . 29.18
  s.23(1)(a) . . . 34.4
  s.23(2) . . . 34.30
  s.25 . . . 29.37
  s.26 . . . 29.18
  s.27 . . . 32.24, 35.19
  s.27(1) . . . 29.18, 35.30
  s.27(2)(a) . . . 29.18
  s.27(2)(b) . . . 29.18
  s.27(2)(d) . . . 32.24
  s.27(2)(e) . . . 33.9
  s.27(2)(f) . . . 34.4, 35.19
  s.27(7) . . . 35.30
  s.28 . . . 35.35
  s.29 . . . 29.19, 32.24, 35.37
  s.29(2) . . . 33.15, 34.5, 35.35
  s.29(2)(a) . . . 35.19
  s.29(2)(b) . . . 33.15
  s.30 . . . 32.24, 34.42
  s.32(1) . . . 35.35
  s.32(3) . . . 35.35
  s.33 . . . 30.5, 35.35
  s.33(c) . . . 33.15
  s.34(2) . . . 35.35

s.34(3) . . . 35.35
s.35 . . . 35.35
s.37 . . . 32.24
s.40 . . . 35.34
s.42 . . . 35.34
s.43(1) . . . 35.34
s.44 . . . 35.34
s.46 . . . 35.34
s.48 . . . 34.42
s.49(1) . . . 34.43
s.49(3) . . . 34.43
s.49(4) . . . 34.43
s.49(6) . . . 34.43
s.60 . . . 28.22
s.62 . . . 29.14
s.65 . . . 29.17, 35.38
s.66 . . . 29.14
s.67 . . . 29.37
s.70 . . . 35.36
s.71 . . . 32.24
s.77 . . . 35.35
s.91(3) . . . 29.11
s.91(4) . . . 29.11
s.91(5) . . . 29.11
s.93 . . . 29.10
s.96 . . . 30.20, 30.22
s.97 . . . 30.22
s.103 . . . 29.37
s.115 . . . 29.7
s.117(1) . . . 35.32
s.131(1) . . . 35.43
s.131(2) . . . 35.43
s.132 . . . 29.19
Sch.1 . . . 29.17, 35.16–35.17, 35.21, 35.32
Sch.1 para.2 . . . 35.29
Sch.1 para.3 . . . 35.31
Sch.1 paras.4–9 . . . 35.32
Sch.1 paras.10–14 . . . 35.32
Sch.2 para.2 . . . 29.18
Sch.2 para.3(2)(a) . . . 29.18
Sch.2 para.3(2)(b) . . . 29.18
Sch.2 para.7 . . . 32.24, 33.9
Sch.2 para.7(2) . . . 29.18, 35.30
Sch.2 para.8 . . . 35.19
Sch.3 . . . 35.17, 35.21, 35.22, 35.25–35.32,
   35.37
Sch.3 para.1 . . . 34.23
Sch.3 para.2 . . . 34.23, 35.23
Sch.3 para.2(a) . . . 35.24
Sch.3 para.2(b) . . . 35.26
Sch.3 para.2(c) . . . 30.22
Sch.3 para.2(d) . . . 35.24
Sch.3 para.3 . . . 32.24
Sch.3 para.3(1) . . . 35.30
Sch.3 para.3(2) . . . 35.30
Sch.3 paras.4–9 . . . 35.32
Sch.3 paras.10–14 . . . 35.32
Sch.4 . . . 29.17, 35.38
Sch.4 para.2 . . . 35.38
Sch.4 para.3(2) . . . 35.43

Sch.4 para.3(3) . . . 35.38
Sch.4 para.5 . . . 35.38
Sch.4 para.5(3) . . . 35.38
Sch.4 para.6(2) . . . 35.43
Sch.6 . . . 30.22, 30.31
Sch.6 para.1 . . . 30.22
Sch.6 para.1(1) . . . 30.28, 30.30
Sch.6 para.2 . . . 30.22, 30.30
Sch.6 para.3(1) . . . 30.22
Sch.6 para.4 . . . 30.22, 30.30, 30.35
Sch.6 para.5 . . . 30.22, 30.30
Sch.6 para.5(1) . . . 30.35
Sch.6 para.5(2) . . . 30.31
Sch.6 para.6 . . . 30.30, 30.32
Sch.6 para.7 . . . 30.32, 30.35
Sch.6 para.9(1) . . . 30.29, 30.35
Sch.6 para.9(2) . . . 30.30
Sch.6 para.11 . . . 30.28
Sch.6 para.11(1) . . . 30.23
Sch.8 . . . 35.44
Sch.8 para.1(1)(a) . . . 35.44
Sch.8 paras.1(1)(b)–(g) . . . 35.44
Sch.8 para.1(1)(c) . . . 29.37
Sch.8 para.5 . . . 35.44
Sch.12 para.10 . . . 35.30
Sch.12 para.18 . . . 30.22
Landlord and Tenant Act 1730 . . . 36.16
Landlord and Tenant Act 1927
   Pt I . . . 36.53
   s.1 . . . 36.53
   s.3 . . . 36.53
   s.19(1) . . . 36.28, 36.32
   s.19(1A) . . . 36.31, 36.81
   s.19(2) . . . 36.53
   s.19(3) . . . 36.37
   s.42 . . . 36.60
   s.42A . . . 36.60
   s.42B . . . 36.60
Landlord and Tenant Act 1954 . . . 28.40, 37.25,
   37.26, 37.27, 37.29, 37.30
   Pt I . . . 37.12
   Pt II . . . 34.39, 36.9, 37.25
   s.23 . . . 37.26
   s.23(2) . . . 37.27
   s.23(3) . . . 37.42
   s.23(4) . . . 37.27
   s.24(1) . . . 37.30, 37.33
   s.24(2) . . . 37.30
   ss.24A–D . . . 37.35
   s.24A . . . 37.35
   s.24A(1) . . . 37.35
   s.24C . . . 37.35
   s.24C(3) . . . 37.35
   s.24D(1)(b) . . . 37.35
   s.25 . . . 37.31–37.33, 37.35–37.36, 37.39–37.40
   s.25(1) . . . 37.31
   s.25(2) . . . 37.31
   s.25(3) . . . 37.31
   s.25(4) . . . 37.31
   s.25(6) . . . 37.31

s.25(7) . . . 37.31
s.25(8) . . . 37.31
s.26 . . . 37.31–37.36, 37.39
s.26(1) . . . 37.32
s.26(3) . . . 37.32
s.26(4) . . . 37.31
s.26(5) . . . 37.32
s.26(6) . . . 37.32
s.27(1) . . . 37.32
s.27(1A) 37.30, 37.32
s.29(1) . . . 37.41
s.29(2) . . . 37.33
s.29(3) . . . 37.33
s.29(5) . . . 37.33
s.29A(2) . . . 37.33
s.29B . . . 37.33, 37.34
ss.30(1)(a)–(g) . . . 37.36
s.30(1)(e) . . . 37.39
s.30(1)(f) . . . 37.37–37.40
s.30(1)(g) . . . 37.38–37.39, 37.43
s.30(2) . . . 37.38
s.30(3) . . . 37.38
s.31A . . . 37.37
ss.32–35 . . . 37.41
s.32(1) . . . 37.42
s.32(2) . . . 37.42
s.32(3) . . . 37.42
s.33 . . . 37.43
s.34(1) . . . 37.45
s.34(2) . . . 37.45
s.34(3) . . . 37.45
s.35 . . . 37.44
s.35(2) . . . 37.44
s.36(2) . . . 37.41
s.37(1) . . . 37.39
s.37(1A) . . . 37.39
s.37(1B) . . . 37.39
s.37(1C) . . . 37.39
s.37(3)(a) . . . 37.39
s.37(3)(b) . . . 37.39
s.37A(1) . . . 37.40
s.37A(2) . . . 37.40
s.38(2) . . . 37.39
s.38(4) . . . 37.29
s.38A . . . 37.29
s.41(1) . . . 37.26
s.42 . . . 37.26
s.43 . . . 37.28
s.44 . . . 37.31
s.55 . . . 37.40
s.64 . . . 37.33–37.34, 37.35
s.69 . . . 37.30
Landlord and Tenant Act 1985 . . . 7.28, 36.47,
  36.60
s.3 . . . 36.77
s.3(1) . . . 37.24
s.3(3A) . . . 37.24
s.3(3B) . . . 37.24
ss.11–14 . . . 23.17, 36.45, 36.54
s.11(1A) . . . 36.45

s.11(1B) . . . 36.45
s.17 . . . 36.67
s.18 . . . 36.60, 36.67
s.18(2) . . . 36.67
s.19 . . . 36.60
s.19(2A) . . . 36.60
s.19(2B) . . . 36.60
s.20 . . . 36.60
s.20ZA . . . 36.60
s.20B(1) . . . 36.60
s.21 . . . 36.60
s.21A . . . 36.60
Landlord and Tenant Act 1987
Pt II . . . 36.67
Pt III . . . 36.67
s.24 . . . 36.67
s.47(1) . . . 37.24
s.47(1)(b) . . . 37.24
s.48(1) . . . 37.24
s.48(2) . . . 37.24
Landlord and Tenant Act 1988 . . . 36.29, 36.32,
  36.37, 36.39
s.1(6) . . . 36.30
s.3(5) . . . 36.30
Landlord and Tenant (Covenants) Act 1995 . . .
  36.71, 36.74, 36.78, 36.83–36.86, 37.44
s.3 . . . 36.39
s.3(1) . . . 36.79
s.3(6)(a) . . . 36.79
s.4 . . . 36.79
s.5(2) . . . 36.80
s.6(2) . . . 36.83
s.7 . . . 36.83
s.8 . . . 36.83
s.11 . . . 36.80
s.12 . . . 36.79
s.16(1) . . . 36.81
s.16(2) . . . 36.81
s.16(3) . . . 36.81
s.16(4)(b) . . . 36.81
s.17(2) . . . 36.74, 36.85
s.17(3) . . . 36.88
s.17(6) . . . 36.85
s.18 . . . 36.74
s.19(1) . . . 36.74, 36.86, 36.88
s.20(6) . . . 35.24
s.22 . . . 36.31, 36.81
s.24(2) . . . 36.88
s.25(1) . . . 36.78
s.26(1)(a) . . . 36.83
s.28(1) . . . 36.79
Landlord and Tenant (Licensed Premises) Act
  1990 . . . 37.28
Latent Damage Act 1986 . . . 27.23
Law of Property Act 1922
s.145 . . . 36.7
Sch.15 . . . 36.7
Law of Property Act 1925 . . . 31.7, 31.25–31.26,
  31.29–31.30, 33.3, 34.3, 34.28, 36.3
s.1 . . . 28.33, 28.35, 28.37

s.1(2) . . . 28.37, 32.24, 33.9
s.1(3) . . . 28.37–28.38
s.1(6) . . . 31.17, 31.30
s.2(1) . . . 31.36
s.2(2) . . . 31.26
s.4(3) . . . 33.9
s.27(1) . . . 31.36
s.27(2) . . . 31.36
s.28 . . . 31.23
s.34 . . . 31.30, 31.34
s.35 . . . 31.30
s.36 . . . 31.31, 31.34
s.36(2) . . . 31.21
s.38 . . . 28.28
s.41 . . . 8.31
s.49(1) . . . 29.37
s.49(2) . . . 29.28, 29.35
s.52 . . . 32.24
s.52(1) . . . 29.11, 36.28, 36.92
s.53 . . . 29.21, 30.8, 31.16
s.53(2) . . . 29.21, 30.8
s.54(2) . . . 29.12, 30.3, 36.14, 36.28
s.56 . . . 33.3
s.62 . . . 28.5, 30.5, 32.24, 32.28, 32.32,
    32.34–32.39, 32.51, 35.30
s.77(1)(c) . . . 36.74
s.78 . . . 33.21, 33.26–33.27
s.79 . . . 33.7, 33.14, 33.26, 36.74
s.84 . . . 2.24, 33.38, 33.45
s.84(1) . . . 33.38, 33.42–33.43
s.84(1)(a) . . . 33.39
s.84(1)(aa) . . . 33.42
s.84(1)(b) . . . 33.40
s.84(1)(c) . . . 33.41
s.84(1A) . . . 33.42
s.84(1B) . . . 33.38
s.84(1C) . . . 33.38
s.84(2) . . . 33.32
s.84(3A) . . . 33.38
s.84(12) . . . 33.38
s.87(1) . . . 34.4
s.88 . . . 34.30
s.88(2) . . . 34.36
s.89 . . . 34.30
s.91(2) . . . 34.33, 34.38
s.99 . . . 34.39
s.101 . . . 34.29, 34.35, 34.40
s.101(3) . . . 34.29
s.103 . . . 34.29
s.104 . . . 34.30–34.31
s.105 . . . 34.32
s.108 . . . 34.40
s.109 . . . 34.35
s.111 . . . 31.11
s.141 . . . 36.76
s.142 . . . 36.76
s.146 . . . 36.65–36.67
s.146(4) . . . 36.70
s.147 . . . 36.67
s.149(3) . . . 36.19

s.149(6) . . . 36.6
s.152(1) . . . 34.39
s.153 . . . 36.96
s.193(4) . . . 32.43
s.198(1) . . . 35.12
s.199 . . . 35.12
s.205(1)(ix) . . . 28.6–28.7, 28.35
s.205(1)(xxi) . . . 31.36, 35.1
Sch.2 . . . 36.74
Law of Property Act 1969 . . . 37.25
Law of Property (Miscellaneous Provisions) Act
    1989 . . . 28.5, 29.2
s.1 . . . 29.11
s.1(2) . . . 4.6
s.1(3) . . . 4.6
s.1(5) . . . 29.11
s.2 . . . 4.4, 28.5, 29.3, 29.5–29.10, 29.23, 29.27,
    30.3, 30.6–30.7, 32.24, 34.5
s.2(1) . . . 29.2
s.2(5) . . . 29.2, 29.9, 29.36, 30.8
s.2A . . . 29.10
Law Reform (Contributory Negligence) Act
    1945 . . . 12.30
s.1(1) . . . 19.6, 19.9
s.4 . . . 19.6
Law Reform (Frustrated Contracts) Act 1943 . . .
    10.17–10.18, 10.20–10.23
s.1(2) . . . 10.17, 10.19–10.20, 10.22
s.1(3) . . . 10.19–10.22
s.1(4) . . . 10.17
s.2(3) . . . 10.22
s.2(4) . . . 10.21
s.2(5) . . . 10.23
s.36(1) . . . 11.55
Law Reform (Miscellaneous Provisions) Act
    1934 . . . 27.10
Law Reform (Personal Injuries) Act 1948
    s.2(4) . . . 27.7
Leasehold Property (Repairs) Act 1938 . . . 36.67
s.1(2) . . . 36.67
Leasehold Reform Act 1967 . . . 37.13–37.14
s.1(1ZC) . . . 37.14
s.2 . . . 37.14
s.2(1)(b) . . . 37.14
s.2(3) . . . 37.14
s.8 . . . 37.14
s.9(1) . . . 37.14
s.9(1A) . . . 37.14
s.9(1B) . . . 37.14
s.9(1C) . . . 37.14
s.9A . . . 37.14
Leasehhold Reform, Housing and Urban
    Development Act 1993 . . . 37.3
Pt I . . . 37.13
s.3(1) . . . 37.15
s.3(2) . . . 37.15
s.4(4) . . . 37.15
s.5(1) . . . 37.15
s.5(5) . . . 37.15
s.13 . . . 37.15

s.13(2)(b) ... 37.15
s.24(1) ... 37.15
s.32 ... 37.15
s.39(3) ... 37.15
s.42 ... 37.15
s.48(1) ... 37.15
s.56 ... 37.15
s.56(2) ... 37.15
s.57 ... 37.15
Sch.6 ... 37.15
Sch.13 ... 37.15
Limitation Act 1980 ... 11.52–11.53, 27.20,
    27.25, 29.17, 30.20–30.21
s.5 ... 11.53, 13.3
s.8 ... 11.53, 13.3
s.11 ... 27.22
s.11(4) ... 11.53
s.14A ... 27.23
s.14B ... 27.23
s.15 ... 30.23
s.15(1) ... 30.20–30.21
s.17 ... 30.20–30.21, 30.33
s.20 ... 34.34
s.28 ... 11.53, 27.24
ss.29–31 ... 11.54
s.32 ... 11.53
s.33 ... 11.53, 27.24
Sch.1 para.1 ... 30.21
Sch.1 para.4 ... 30.34
Sch.1 para.8 ... 30.21
Limited Partnerships Act 1907 ... 4.18
s.4 ... 4.18
s.6 ... 4.18
Limited Liability Partnerships Act 2000 ...
    4.16
s.1(3) ... 4.17
s.1(5) ... 4.18
Local Government Act 1972
s.100A ... 38.15
s.100E ... 38.15
s.101 ... 38.17
Local Government Act 1992 ... 38.12, 38.21
Local Government and Housing Act 1989
Sch.10 ... 37.12
Local Government (Miscellaneous Provisions)
    Act 1982
s.33 ... 33.4
Local Land Charges Act 1975 ... 29.25
s.10 ... 29.25
Married Women's Property Act 1882
s.11 ... 13.9
Matrimonial Causes Act 1973 ... 31.39
ss.23–25 ... 31.39
Matrimonial Proceedings and Property Act
    1970
s.37 ... 31.13
Merchant Shipping Act 1995 ... 24.18
Mines (Working Facilities and Support) Act
    1966
s.1 ... 28.17

Misrepresentation Act 1967 ... 12.21
s.1(a) ... 12.43
s.2(1) ... 12.22, 12.24–12.26, 12.28–12.34,
    12.38
s.2(2) ... 12.36–12.38
s.3 ... 9.9, 12.45–12.46, 12.48–12.50, 29.30
Mortgage Repossessions (Protection of Tenants
    etc) Act 2010 ... 34.39
s.1(2) ... 34.39
s.1(4) ... 34.39
s.2 ... 34.39
National Parks and Access to the Countryside
    Act 1949 ... 21.9, 21.19, 22.5
National Trust Act 1937
s.8 ... 33.13
Nuclear Installations Act 1965 ... 20.2, 24.18
Occupiers' Liability Act 1957 ... 9.10, 21.1, 21.4,
    21.7, 21.10–21.11, 21.18–21.19, 21.24, 25.1
s.1(3) ... 21.1, 21.4, 21.6, 21.21
s.1(3)(a) ... 21.6
s.1(4) ... 21.9
s.1(7) ... 21.10
s.2(1) ... 21.1–21.2
s.2(2) ... 21.12
s.2(3)(a) ... 21.13
s.2(3)(b) ... 21.14
s.2(4)(a) ... 21.3, 21.15
s.2(4)(b) ... 21.16
s.2(5) ... 21.3, 21.17
s.2(6) ... 21.9
s.3 ... 21.11
s.4 ... 21.30
s.5 ... 21.11
Occupiers' Liability Act 1984 ... 21.9–21.10,
    21.18–21.20, 21.23–21.25, 25.7
s.1(5) ... 21.24
s.2 ... 21.2
Offices, Shops and Railway Premises Act 1963
    ... 20.4
Partnership Act 1890 ... 4.18
s.1 ... 4.18
s.5 ... 4.19, 14.43
Party Wall etc Act 1996 ... 22.6, 28.28
Petroleum Act 1998
s.1(a) ... 28.17
s.2(1) ... 28.17
Planning Act 2008 ... 38.3, 39.33
s.14 ... 38.6
s.196 ... 39.35
s.205 ... 39.33
Planning (Consequential Provisions)
    Act 1990 ... 38.3
Planning (Hazardous Substances)
    Act 1990 ... 38.3
Planning (Listed Buildings and Conservation
    Areas) Act 1990, 39.45
s.72 ... 39.50
Planning and Compensation Act 1991 ... 38.3,
    38.28, 39.52
Pt I ... 39.52

s.26 . . . 38.28

Planning and Compulsory Purchase Act
2004 . . . 38.3, 38.9, 38.11–38.12, 38.21,
38.24–38.25, 38.27, 39.33, 39.52
Pt 2 . . . 38.23
s.15 . . . 38.23
s.17 . . . 38.23
s.18 . . . 38.23
s.35 . . . 38.23
s.38 . . . 38.28
s.38(6) . . . 38.22, 38.28, 39.27
s.39 . . . 38.27
s.40 . . . 39.19
s.42(1) . . . 39.23
ss.46–48 . . . 39.33
s.52 . . . 39.65
ss.56–59 . . . 39.40
s.113 . . . 38.25

Poor Law Amendment Act 1857
s.3 . . . 3.11

Powers of Attorney Act 1971 . . . 14.27
s.4 . . . 14.22
s.5 . . . 14.27
s.7 . . . 14.35

Powers of Criminal Courts Act 1973 . . . 15.3

Prescription Act 1832 . . . 32.40, 32.42,
32.48–32.49, 32.55
s.2 . . . 32.50–32.51
s.3 . . . 32.55
s.4 . . . 32.50, 32.55
s.7 . . . 32.50

Protection from Eviction Act 1977 . . . 37.23
s.1 . . . 22.3, 36.34
s.1(2) . . . 37.23
s.1(3) . . . 37.23
s.1(3A) . . . 37.23
s.1(3B) . . . 37.23
s.2 . . . 36.65
s.3(1) . . . 37.6
s.5(1)(a) . . . 36.95
s.5(1)(b) . . . 36.95

Rent Act 1977 . . . 34.23, 36.9, 36.69, 37.2,
37.3–37.4
s.2(1) . . . 37.3
s.24(3) . . . 37.27
s.70 . . . 37.3
s.70(2) . . . 37.3
s.98 . . . 37.3
s.147 . . . 36.69
Sch.1 . . . 37.3
Sch.1 para.2 . . . 37.3
Sch.15 . . . 37.3

Rentcharges Act 1977 . . . 33.9
s.1 . . . 33.9
s.2 . . . 33.9

Rights of Light Act 1959 . . . 2.24, 29.25, 32.55
s.2 . . . 32.55
s.3 . . . 32.55

Road Traffic Act 1988
s.34 . . . 32.43

s.148(7) . . . 13.9
s.149(3) . . . 19.4

Sale of Goods Act 1979 . . . 7.25
s.7 . . . 10.23
s.10 . . . 8.30
s.11(3) . . . 8.21
ss.12–15 . . . 8.22
s.12 . . . 7.25, 9.17
s.12(1) . . . 7.25
s.12(2) . . . 7.25
s.12(5A) . . . 7.25
ss.13–15 . . . 9.18
s.13 . . . 7.25, 9.4
s.13(1) . . . 7.25, 8.2
s.13(1A) . . . 7.25
s.14(2) . . . 7.25, 8.24, 9.13
s.14(2A) . . . 7.25
s.14(2B)–(2F) . . . 7.25
s.14(3) . . . 7.25
s.15(2) . . . 7.25
s.15(3) . . . 7.25
s.15A . . . 8.2, 8.23
s.29 . . . 8.5
s.29(3) . . . 8.28
s.49 . . . 11.36
s.52 . . . 11.44
s.55 . . . 7.26
s.61(5A) . . . 8.23

Social Security Administration Act 1992
Pt IV . . . 27.9

Social Security (Recovery of Benefits) Act 1997
. . . 27.9

Statute of Frauds 1677
s.4 . . . 4.8

Supply of Goods and Services Act 1982
ss.2–5 . . . 7.26–7.27, 8.22, 9.19
s.2 . . . 9.19
s.5A . . . 8.23
ss.7–10 . . . 7.26, 8.22, 9.19
s.10A . . . 8.23
s.11 . . . 7.26
s.12(2) . . . 7.27
s.12(3) . . . 7.27
ss.13–15 . . . 7.27
s.14 . . . 8.28
s.16 . . . 7.27
s.18 . . . 7.27

Supply of Goods (Implied Terms) Act 1973
ss.8–11 . . . 7.26, 8.22
s.8 . . . 9.17
ss.9–11 . . . 9.18
s.11A . . . 8.23

Supreme Court Act 1981
s.31 . . . 39.42
s.32A . . . 27.8
s.37 . . . 36.67
s.49(1) . . . 30.4
s.50 . . . 33.30

Supreme Court of Judicature Act 1873
s.25(11) . . . 30.4

Town and Country Planning Act 1947 . . .
    32.52, 38.2–38.3, 38.21
Town and Country Planning Act 1968 . . .
    38.21
Town and Country Planning Act 1990 . . . 38.3,
    38.10, 38.21, 38.28, 39.6, 39.9, 39.32, 39.34,
    39.52
    s.54A . . . 38.28
    s.55 . . . 39.2
    s.55(1) . . . 28.17, 38.2
    s.55(1A) . . . 39.4
    s.55(2) . . . 39.8
    s.55(3) . . . 39.7
    s.57 . . . 39.1
    s.57(1) . . . 39.1, 39.17
    s.57(2) . . . 39.1
    s.57(3) . . . 39.1
    s.62(5) . . . 39.23
    s.69 . . . 39.23
    s.70(1) . . . 39.25, 39.31
    s.78 . . . 38.10, 39.34, 39.35
    s.106(3) . . . 33.13
    s.171B . . . 39.53
    s.171C . . . 39.60
    s.171D . . . 39.60
    s.172(1) . . . 39.61
    s.174(2) . . . 39.62
    s.183 . . . 39.64
    s.187A . . . 39.63
    s.187B . . . 39.66
    s.191 . . . 39.57
    s.195 . . . 39.57
    s.196A . . . 39.67
    s.196B . . . 39.67
    s.196C . . . 39.67
    s.233 . . . 33.37
    s.284 . . . 39.39
    s.288 . . . 39.42
    s.289(4A) . . . 39.64
    s.303 . . . 39.23
    s.319A . . . 39.35
    Sch.6 para.3 . . . 38.10
Trade Union and Labour Relations
    (Consolidation) Act 1992
    s.179 . . . 6.4
    s.236 . . . 11.48
Tramways Act 1870
    s.25 . . . 20.6
Treasure Act 1996
    s.1 . . . 28.18
    s.4 . . . 28.18
    s.6 . . . 28.18
    s.10 . . . 28.18
    s.11 . . . 28.18
Tribunals, Courts and Enforcement Act 2007
    . . . 2.23
    Pt 3 . . . 36.69
    s.72 . . . 36.69
    Sch.12 . . . 36.69

Trustee Act 1925
    s.34(1) . . . 31.33
Trustee Act 2000 . . . 31.33
Trusts of Land and Appointment of Trustees
    Act 1996 . . . 31.28–31.29, 31.40
    s.1 . . . 31.28
    s.1(2)(a) . . . 31.28
    s.2 . . . 31.28
    s.4 . . . 31.28, 31.33
    s.5 . . . 31.28–31.29
    s.6 . . . 31.34
    s.6(1) . . . 31.33
    ss.6(2)–(6) . . . 31.33
    s.7 . . . 31.33–31.34
    s.8 . . . 31.34
    s.10 . . . 31.34
    s.11 . . . 31.33, 31.36
    s.12 . . . 31.35
    s.13 . . . 31.35, 31.40, 31.42
    s.14 . . . 31.23, 31.33, 31.35, 31.41–31.42
    s.14(1) . . . 31.40
    s.14(2) . . . 31.40
    s.15 . . . 31.40–31.42
    s.15(2) . . . 31.40
    s.15(4) . . . 31.41
    s.17(1) . . . 31.33
    s.34 . . . 31.29
    s.36 . . . 31.29
    Sch.2 . . . 31.28
    Sch.2 paras.3–4 . . . 31.29
Unfair Contract Terms Act 1977 . . . 7.26–7.27,
    7.30, 7.34, 8.15, 8.23, 9.1, 9.9, 9.13, 9.22, 9.28,
    13.4, 16.18, 21.2, 21.11, 26.7
    s.1(1) . . . 9.10
    s.1(3) . . . 9.9
    s.2 . . . 9.14, 9.20–9.21
    s.2(1) . . . 9.10
    s.2(2) . . . 9.10
    s.2(3) . . . 19.4
    s.3 . . . 9.12, 9.14, 9.20
    s.3(1) . . . 9.11
    s.3(2) . . . 9.11
    s.6 . . . 9.16, 9.21
    s.6(1) . . . 9.17–9.18
    s.6(2) . . . 9.18
    s.6(3) . . . 9.18
    s.6(4) . . . 9.18
    s.7 . . . 9.16, 9.19, 9.21
    s.7(2) . . . 9.19
    s.7(3) . . . 9.19
    s.7(3A) . . . 9.19
    s.7(4) . . . 9.19
    s.9 . . . 8.15
    s.11(1) . . . 9.15, 12.45
    s.11(2) . . . 9.20
    s.11(4) . . . 9.15
    s.11(5) . . . 9.15
    s.12(1) . . . 9.13, 9.18
    s.12(1A) . . . 9.13, 9.18

s.12(2) . . . 9.13, 9.18
s.12(3) . . . 9.13, 9.18
s.13(1) . . . 9.21
s.14 . . . 9.9
Sch.1 . . . 9.10, 9.14
Sch.2 . . . 9.15, 9.20
Water Act 1981 . . . 24.18
Water Act 1989 . . . 28.20
Water Industry Act 1991 . . . 23.16

Water Resources Act 1963 . . . 28.20
Water Resources Act 1991
s.24 . . . 28.20
s.27 . . . 28.20
s.48 . . . 28.20
Wildlife and Countryside Act 1981
s.9 . . . 28.19
Wills Act 1861
s.3 . . . 3.20

Table of Cases

139 High Street, Deptford, Re [1951] Ch
884 . . . 35.39

4 Eng Ltd v Harper [2008] EWHC 915
(Ch) . . . 12.28

A v Hoare [2008] UKHL 6, HL . . . 27.22

A & B v Essex County Council [2003] EWCA
Civ 1848, CA . . . 16.24

AB v South West Water Services Ltd [1993] 1 All
ER 609, CA . . . 23.23, 27.2

A-G for Ontario v Orange Productions Ltd
(1971) 21 DLR (3d) 257 . . . 23.23

A-G of Southern Nigeria v John Holt & Co
(Liverpool) Ltd [1915] AC 599, PC . . . 32.11

A-G v Blake (Jonathan Cape Ltd, third party)
[2000] 4 All ER 385, HL . . . 11.38, 11.39

A-G v Corke [1933] Ch 89 . . . 24.6

A-G v Cory Bros & Co Ltd [1921] 1 AC 521,
HL . . . 24.10

A-G v Morgan [1891] 1 Ch 432, CA . . . 28.17

A-G v PYA Quarries Ltd [1957] 1 All ER 894,
CA . . . 23.23

A-G v Sheffield Gas Consumers Co (1853) 3 De
GM & G 304 . . . 23.21, 27.16

A-G v Stone (1895) 12 TLR 76 . . . 24.6

A-G of Belize v Belize Telecom Ltd [2009]
UKPC 11, PC . . . 7.32

A-G's Reference (No 1 of 1988) [1989] 2 All ER
1, HL . . . 3.21

AG Securities v Vaughan and Antoniades v
Villiers [1988] 3 All ER 1058, HL . . . 36.10

A Prosser & Son Ltd v Levy [1955] 3 All ER 577,
CA . . . 24.10

Abbahall Ltd v Smee [2002] EWCA Civ 1831,
[2003] 1 All ER 465 . . . 23.16

Abbey National Building Society v Cann [1990]
1 All ER 1085 . . . 35.25

Abbey National Mortgages plc v Key Surveyors
Nationwide Ltd [1996] 2 EGLR 99, CA . . .
17.7

Abbott v Abbott [2007] UKPC 53 . . . 31.14

Abernethie v AH & J Kleiman Ltd [1969] 2 All
ER 790 . . . 37.27

Abrahams v Deakin [1891] 1 QB 516, CA . . .
26.14

Adami v Lincoln Grange Management Ltd
[1998] 17 EG 148, CA . . . 36.46

Adams v Lindsell (1818) 1 B & Ald 681 . . . 5.21

Adams v Ursell [1913] 1 Ch 269 . . . 23.10,
23.12

Addis v Gramophone Co Ltd [1909] AC 488,
HL . . . 11.1, 11.11

Addiscombe Garden Estate Ltd v Crabbe [1957]
3 All ER 563, CA . . . 37.27

Aerial Advertising Co v Batchelors Peas Ltd
(Manchester) [1938] 2 All ER 788 . . . 8.25

Ahmed v HM Treasury (No 2) [2010] UKSC
5 . . . 3.44

Ailsa Craig Fishing Co Ltd v Malvern Fishing
Co Ltd [1983] 1 All ER 101, HL . . . 9.4

Aircool Installations v British
Telecommunications [1995] CLY 821 . . .
28.11

Ajayi v R T Briscoe (Nigeria) Ltd [1964] 3 All ER
556, PC; BP Exploration (Libya) Ltd v Hunt
(No 2) [1982] 1 All ER 925 . . . 6.22, 6.23

Al-Kandari v JR Brown & Co [1988] 1 All ER
833, CA . . . 16.21, 16.27

Al-Nakib Investments (Jersey) Ltd v Longcroft
[1990] 3 All ER 321 . . . 16.18

Al Saudi Banque v Clark Pixley [1989] 3 All ER
361 . . . 16.21

Alan Wibberley Building Ltd v Insley [1999] 2
All ER 897, HL . . . 28.24

Albert Place Mansions (Freehold) Ltd v Craft
rule Ltd [2010] EWHC 1230 . . . 37.15

Alcock v Chief Constable of the South Yorkshire
Police [1991] 4 All ER 907, HL . . . 16.6,
16.28

Alcock v Wraith (1991) 59 BLR 20 . . . 26.17,
26.19, 26.22

Alderslade v Hendon Laundry Ltd [1945] 1 All
ER 244, CA . . . 9.6

Aldham v United Dairies (London) Ltd [1939] 4
All ER 522, CA . . . 25.3

Aldin v Latimer Clark, Muirhead & Co [1894] 2
Ch 437 . . . 32.18, 36.35

Aldred's Case (1610) 9 Co Rep 57b . . . 23.4,
25.2, 32.15

Aldwych Club Ltd v Copthall Property Co Ltd
(1962) 185 Estates Gazette 219 . . . 37.44

Alec Lobb (Garages) Ltd v Total Oil GB Ltd
[1985] 1 All ER 303, CA . . . 12.67

Alexandrou v Oxford [1993] 4 All ER 328,
CA . . . 16.10

Alfred F Beckett Ltd v Lyons [1967] 1 All ER
833, CA . . . 32.4

Ali v Furness Withy (Shipping) Ltd [1988] 2
Lloyd's Rep 379 . . . 16.9

Allen v Greenwood [1979] 1 All ER 819,
CA . . . 32.56

Allen v Gulf Oil Refining Ltd [1981] 1 All ER
353, HL . . . 23.8, 23.18

Alliance and Leicester Building Society v
Edgestop Ltd [1994] 2 All ER 38 . . . 19.6

Allied Dunbar Assurance plc v Homebase Ltd
[2002] 2 EGLR 23, CA . . . 36.32

Allied Maples Group Ltd v Simmons &
Simmons [1995] 4 All ER 907, CA . . . 11.10,
18.5

Allied Maritime Transport Ltd v Vale do Rio
Doce Navegaeao SA ("The Leonidas D")
[1985] 2 All ER 796, CA . . . 6.22

Almeroth v Chivers & Sons Ltd [1948] 1 All ER
53, CA . . . 23.25

Alpenstow Ltd v Regalian Properties plc [1985]
2 All ER 545 . . . 5.34, 5.36

Alvis v Harrison (1991) 62 P & CR 10, HL . . .
32.53

Amalgamated Estates v Joystretch
Manufacturing (1980) 257 Estates Gazette
489, CA . . . 36.57

Amalgamated Investment and Property Co Ltd
v John Walker & Sons Ltd [1976] 3 All ER
509, CA . . . 10.11

American Cyanamid Co v Ethicon Ltd [1975] 1
All ER 504, HL . . . 27.17

AMF International Ltd v Magnet Bowling Ltd
[1968] 2 All ER 789 . . . 21.1, 21.4, 21.16,
26.16

An Bord Bainne Co-operative v Milk
Marketing Board [1988] 1 FTLR 145,
CA . . . 20.3

Anangel Atlas Compania Naviera SA v
Ishikawajima-Harima Heavy Industries Co
[1990] 1 Lloyd's Rep 167 . . . 14.15

Ancell v McDermott [1993] 4 All ER 355,
CA . . . 16.7

Anchor Brewhouse Developments Ltd v Berkley
House (Docklands Developments) Ltd [1987]
2 EGLR 173 . . . 22.2, 22.8, 28.16

André & Cie v Ets Michel Blanc & Fils [1979] 2
Lloyd's Rep 427, CA . . . 12.10

Andreae v Selfridge & Co Ltd [1937] 3 All ER
255, CA . . . 23.12

Andrews Bros (Bournemouth) Ltd v Singer &
Co Ltd [1934] 1 KB 17, CA . . . 9.4

Andrews v Ramsay & Co [1903] 2 KB 635,
CA . . . 14.15

Andrews v Schooling [1991] 3 All ER 723,
CA . . . 21.29

Anglia Building Society v Secretary of State for
the Environment [1984] JPL 175 . . . 39.29

Anns v Merton London Borough Council [1977]
2 All ER 492, HL . . . 3.37, 16.6, 16.22, 21.27

Anstruther-Gough-Calthorpe v McOscar
[1924] 1 KB 716, CA . . . 36.49

Appleby v Myers (1867) LR 2 CP 651 . . . 10.19

Applegate v Moss [1971] 1 All ER 747,
CA . . . 27.24

Arab Bank plc v Mercantile Holdings Ltd [1994]
2 All ER 74 . . . 34.33

Archer v Brown [1985] QB 401 . . . 12.29, 27.2

Arcos Ltd v E A Ronaasen & Sons [1933] AC
470, HL . . . 8.2

Arenson v Casson, Beckman, Rutley & Co
[1975] 3 All ER 901, HL . . . 16.25

Argy Trading Development Co Ltd v Lapid
Developments Ltd [1977] 3 All ER 785 . . .
16.20

Aribisala v St James Homes (Grosvenor Docks)
Ltd (No 2) [2008] EWHC 456 . . . 29.28

Armagas v Mundogas SA [1986] AC 717,
HL . . . 14.34

Armstrong v Jackson [1917] 2 KB 822 . . .
12.19

Armstrong v Sheppard and Short Ltd [1959] 2
QB 384 . . . 22.5, 27.16

Arthur JS Hall & Co v Simons [2000] 3 All ER
673, HL . . . 16.26

Arthur v Anker [1996] 3 All ER 783, CA . . .
22.10

Ashburn Anstalt v Arnold [1989] Ch 1; [1988]
2 All ER 147, CA . . . 28.44, 30.10, 36.2, 36.4,
36.5, 36.9, 36.55

Ashdown v Samuel Williams & Sons Ltd [1957]
1 All ER 35, CA . . . 21.3

Asher v Whitlock (1865) LR 1 QB 1 . . . 22.9

Ashford Shire Council v Dependable Motors
Pty Ltd [1961] 1 All ER 96, PC . . . 14.4

Ashworth Frazer Ltd v Gloucester City Council
[2001] UKHL 59, [2002] 1 All ER 377 . . .
36.30

Aslan v Murphy (Nos 1 and 2) [1989] 3 All ER
130, CA . . . 36.9

Aspinall Finance Ltd v Viscount Chelsea [1989]
1 EGLR 103, CA . . . 37.26

Assam Railways and Trading Co Ltd v IRC
[1935] AC 445, HL . . . 3.21

Associated British Ports v CH Bailey plc [1990]
1 All ER 929, HL . . . 36.67

Associated Provincial Picture Houses v
Wednesbury Corpn [1948] 1 KB 223 . . . 39.31

Aswan Engineering Establishment Co v
Lupdine Ltd [1987] 1 All ER 135, CA . . . 16.15

Atkinson v Cotesworth (1825) 3 B & C
647 . . . 14.22

Atkinson v Newcastle and Gateshead
Waterworks Co (1877) 2 Ex D 441,
CA . . . 20.3

Att-Gen of the British Virgin Islands v Hartwell
[2004] UKPC 12, PC . . . 26.14

Attica Sea Carriers Corpn v Ferrostaal Poseidon
Bulk Reederei GmbH ("The Puerto Buitrago")
[1976] 1 Lloyd's Rep 250, CA . . . 11.37

Attwood v Small (1838) 6 Cl & Fin 232,
HL . . . 12.14

Austerberry v Oldham Corpn (1885) 29 Ch D
750, CA . . . 33.4

Australia Asset Management Corpn v York
Montague Ltd [1996] 3 All ER 365,
HL . . . 18.1

Australian Blue Metal Ltd v Hughes [1963] AC
74 . . . 28.43

Auty v National Coal Board [1985] 1 All ER 930,
CA . . . 27.8

Avery v Bowden (1855) 5 E & B 714 . . . 8.27

Avonridge Property Co Ltd v Mashru [2005]
UKHL 70 . . . 36.83
Avramides v Colwill [2006] EWCA Civ 1533,
CA . . . 13.3

B v Camden London Borough Council [2001]
PIQR P9 . . . 21.30
Bacchiocchi v Academic Agency Ltd [1998] 2
All ER 241 . . . 37.39
Baddeley v Earl of Granville (1887) 19 QBD 423,
DC . . . 20.8
Badger v Ministry of Defence [2005] EWHC
2491, QB . . . 19.8
Bailey v Armes [1999] EGCS 21, CA . . . 21.4
Bailey v Bullock [1950] 2 All ER 1167 . . . 11.5
Bailey v Stephens (1862) 12 CBNS 91 . . . 32.6
Bainbrigge v Browne (1881) 18 Ch D 188 . . . 12.63
Baird v Williamson (1863) 15 CBNS 376 . . . 24.5
Bairstow Eves London Central Ltd v Smith
[2004] EWHC 263 (QB) . . . 9.25
Baker v Baker (1993) 25 HLR 408, CA . . . 30.15
Baker v Willoughby [1969] 3 All ER 1528,
HL . . . 18.6
Bakewell Management Ltd v Brandwood [2004]
2 AC 519 . . . 32.43
Baldry v Marshall [1925] 1 KB 260, CA . . . 8.13
Balfour v Balfour [1919] 2 KB 571, CA . . . 6.2
Balfour v Barty-King [1957] 1 All ER 156,
CA . . . 24.15
Ballard's Conveyance, Re [1937] 2 All ER
691 . . . 33.12, 33.18
Balsamo v Medici [1984] 1 WLR 951 . . . 14.20
Bank of Cyprus (London) Ltd v Gill [1980] 2
Lloyds Rep 51 . . . 34.31
Bank of Nova Scotia v Hellenic Mutual War
Risks Association (Bermuda) Ltd [1989] 3 All
ER 628, CA . . . 16.10
Bank of Scotland v Grimes [1985] 2 All ER 254,
CA . . . 34.26
Bankway Properties Ltd v Pensfold-Dunsford
[2001] EWCA Civ 528 . . . 37.11
Bannister v Bannister [1948] 2 All ER 133 . . .
30.10
Banque Bruxelles Lambert SA v Eagle Star
[1995] 2 All ER 769 . . . 17.9, 19.7
Banque Financière de la Cité SA v Westgate
Insurance Co Ltd [1989] 2 All ER 952,
CA . . . 12.54, 12.56, 16.10, 16.19
Barclays Bank plc v Fairclough Building Ltd
[1995] 1 All ER 289, CA . . . 11.28
Barclays Bank plc v O'Brien [1993] 4 All ER 417,
HL . . . 12.60, 12.66
Barclays Bank plc v Savile Estates Ltd [2002] 24
EG 142, CA . . . 36.57
Barclays Bank plc v Schwartz [1995] CLY 2492,
CA . . . 7.8
Barclays Bank v Fairclough Building Ltd [1995]
QB 214, CA . . . 19.6
Barker v Corus (UK) Ltd [2006] UKHL 20,
HL . . . 18.4

Barnard Marcus & Co v Ashraf [1988] 1 EGLR
7, CA . . . 14.18
Barnes and Co v Malvern Hills District Council
[1985] 274 Estates Gazette 830 . . . 39.64
Barnes v Lucille Ltd (1907) 96 LT 680 . . . 25.6
Barnes v Nayer (1986) Times, 19 December,
CA . . . 19.6
Barnett v Chelsea and Kensington Hospital
Management Committee [1968] 1 All ER
1068 . . . 16.9, 18.3
Barrett v Enfield LBC [2001] 2 AC 550, HL . . .
16.22, 16.24
Barrett v Lounova (1982) Ltd [1989] 1 All ER
351, CA . . . 36.46
Barrett v Ministry of Defence [1995] 3 All ER 87,
CA . . . 16.9
Barrow & Bros v Dyster, Nalder & Co (1884) 13
Qbd 635, DC . . . 14.39
Barry v Heathcote-Ball & Co (Commercial
Auctions) Ltd [2001] 1 All ER 944,
CA . . . 5.7, 6.7
Barton v Armstrong [1975] 2 All ER 465, PC
. . . 12.59
Barvis Ltd v Secretary of State for the
Environment (1971) 22 P & CR 710 . . . 39.4
Basely v Clarkson (1681) 3 Lev 37. . . . 22.1
Basham, Re [1986] 1 WLR 1498 . . . 30.17
Basildon District Council v J E Lesser
(Properties) Ltd [1985] 1 All ER 20 . . . 11.28
Basma v Weekes [1950] 2 All ER 146, PC . . .
14.43
Bass Ltd's Application, Re (1973) 26 P & CR
156 . . . 33.42
Batchelor v Marlow [2001] EWCA Civ
1051 . . . 32.11
Bates v Donaldson [1896] 2 QB 241,
CA . . . 36.30
Batsford Estates (1983) Co Ltd v Taylor [2005]
EWCA Civ 489 . . . 30.27
Baxall Securities Ltd v Sheard Walshaw
Partnership [2002] EWCA Civ 09 . . . 18.9
Baxter v Four Oaks Properties Ltd [1965] 1 All
ER 906 . . . 33.29
Baxter v Mannion [2011] EWCA Civ 120 . . . 30.30
Bayliffe v Butterworth (1847) 1 Exch 425 . . .
14.29
Beard v London General Omnibus Co [1900] 2
QB 530, CA . . . 26.9
Beattie v Lord Ebury (1872) 7 Ch App 777,
CA . . . 12.10, 14.45
Beaulieu v Finglam (1401) YB 2 Hen 4 . . .
24.15
Beaumont v Humberts [1990] 2 EGLR 166,
CA . . . 17.7
Bedford Insurance Co Ltd v Instituto de
Resseguros do Brasil [1984] 3 All ER
766 . . . 14.9
Beer v Bowden [1981] l All ER 1070, CA . . . 5.33
Begbie v Phosphate Sewage Co (1875) LR 10 QB
491 . . . 12.14

Behn v Burness (1863) 3 B & S 751 . . . 8.22
Behnke v Bede Shipping Co Ltd [1927] 1 KB 649 . . . 11.44
Behrens v Bertram Mills Circus Ltd [1957] 1 All ER 583 . . . 25.4
Bell Hotels (1935) Ltd v Motion (1952) 159 Estates Gazette 496 . . . 17.9
Bendles Motors Ltd v Bristol Corpn [1963] 1 WLR 247 . . . 39.6
Beningfield v Baxter (1886) 12 App Cas 167, PC . . . 12.63
Benn v Hardinge (1992) 66 P & CR 246, CA . . . 32.52
Bentsen v Taylor, Sons & Co (No 2) [1893] 2 QB 274, CA . . . 8.17
Bernard v Att-Gen of Jamaica [2004] UKPC 47, PC . . . 26.14
Bernstein v Skyviews and General Ltd [1977] 2 All ER 902 . . . 22.2, 28.15, 28.16
Berrisford v Mexfield Housing Co-operative Ltd [2010] EWCA Civ 811 . . . 36.5
Berrycroft Management Co Ltd v Sinclair Gardens Investments (Kensington) Ltd [1997] 1 EGLR 47, CA . . . 36.60
Bertram, Armstrong & Co v Godfray (1830) 1 Knapp 381 . . . 14.13
Beswick v Beswick [1967] 2 All ER 1197, HL . . . 3.17, 11.44, 13.2, 12.12
BHP Petroleum Great Britain Ltd v Chesterfield Properties Ltd [2001] EWCA Civ 1797 . . . 36.83
Biff a Waste Services Ltd v Maschinenfabrik Ernst Hese GmbH [2008] EWCA Civ 1257, CA . . . 26.7, 26.22
Billson v Residential Apartments Ltd [1992] 1 AC 494, HL . . . 36.65
Birch v Paramount Estates Ltd (1956) 167 Estates Gazette 396, CA . . . 7.6
Bircham & Co Nominees (No 2) Ltd v Worrell Holdings Ltd [2001] EWCA Civ 775 . . . 29.7
Bird v Brown (1850) 4 Exch 786 . . . 14.7
Bird v Holbrook (1828) 4 Bing 628 . . . 21.18
Birmingham and District Land Co Ltd v London and North Western Rly Co (1888) 40 Ch D 268 . . . 6.23
Birmingham Citizens Permanent Building Society v Caunt [1962] 1 All ER 163 . . . 34.21
Birmingham Midshires Mortgage Services Ltd v Sabherwal (1999) 80 P & CR 256 . . . 30.17
Birmingham, Dudley and District Banking Co v Ross (1888) 38 Ch D 295 . . . 36.35
Birse Construction Ltd v Haiste Ltd [1996] 2 All ER 1, CA . . . 27.15
Bisset v Wilkinson [1927] AC 177, PC . . . 12.8
Bize v Dickason (1786) 1 Term Rep 285 . . . 11.52
Blackburn Bobbin Co v T W Allen & Sons [1918] 2 KB 467, CA . . . 10.4
Black-Clawson International Ltd v Papierwerke Waldhof-Aschaffenburg AG [1975] 1 All ER 810 . . . 3.10, 3.21

Blackpool and Fylde Aero Club Ltd v Blackpool Borough Council [1990] 3 All ER 25, CA . . . 5.8
Blades v Free (1829) 9 B & C 167 . . . 14.24
Blades v Higgs (1865) 11 HL Cas 621 . . . 28.19
Blake v Galloway [2004] EWCA Civ 814 . . . 17.5
Blaustein v Maltz, Mitchell & Co [1937] 1 All ER 497, CA . . . 14.16
Bliss v South East Thames Regional Health Authority [1987] ICR 700, CA . . . 8.16, 11.6
Blue Circle Industries plc v Ministry of Defence [1998] 3 All ER 385 . . . 20.5
Blyth v Birmingham Waterworks Co (1856) 11 Exch 781 . . . 17.2
Blythe Valley District Council v Persimmon Homes (North East) Ltd [2008] EWCA Civ 861 . . . 38.24
Boardman v Phipps [1966] 3 All ER 721, HL . . . 14.15
Bocardo SA v Star Energy UK Onshore Ltd [2009] EWCA Civ 579 . . . 22.2, 28.7, 28.17
Boden v French (1851) 10 CB 886 . . . 14.13
Bolam v Friern Hospital Management Committee [1957] 2 All ER 118 . . . 17.7
Bolitho v City and Hackney Health Authority [1997] 4 All ER 771, HL . . . 17.7
Bolton Partners v Lambert (1889) 41 Ch D 295 . . . 14.6, 14.7
Bolton v Stone [1951] 1 All ER 1078, HL . . . 17.11, 17.14
Bone v Seale [1975] 1 All ER 787, CA . . . 23.20
Bonita, The; Charlotte, The (1861) 1 Lush 252 . . . 14.10
Bonnington Castings Ltd v Wardlaw [1956] 1 All ER 615, HL . . . 18.4
Boosey v Davis (1987) 55 P & CR 83 . . . 30.25
Boots the Chemist v Pinkland Ltd [1992] 2 EGLR 98 . . . 37.44
Borman v Griffith [1930] 1 Ch 493 . . . 32.31, 32.38
Boss Holdings Ltd v Grosvenor West End Properties Ltd [2008] UKHL 5 . . . 37.14
Bostock v Bryant (1990) 22 HLR 449, CA . . . 36.9
Boston Deep Sea Fishing and Ice Co v Ansell (1888) 39 Ch D 339, CA . . . 14.15
Boston Deep Sea Fishing and Ice Co Ltd v Farnham (Inspector of Taxes) [1957] 1 WLR 1051 . . . 14.8
Boston Fruit Co v British and Foreign Marine Insurance Co [1906] AC 336, HL . . . 14.8
Boulcott Golf Club Inc v Engelbrecht [1945] NZLR 556 . . . 24.15
Bourgoin SA v Ministry of Agriculture, Fisheries and Food [1985] 3 All ER 585, CA . . . 20.3
Bourhill v Young [1942] 2 All ER 396, HL . . . 16.5
Bourne Leisure Ltd v Marsden [2009] EWCA Civ 671, CA . . . 21.13

Bower v Peate (1876) 1 QBD 322 . . . 26.19

Box v Jubb (1879) 4 Ex D 76 . . . 24.13

Boyd v Great Northern Rly Co [1895] 2 IR 555 . . . 23.26

Boyle v Kodak Ltd [1969] 1 WLR 661, HL . . . 20.7

Boyter v Thomson [1995] 3 All ER 135, HL . . . 7.25

BP Exploration Co (Libya) Ltd v Hunt (No 2) [1982] 1 All ER 925 . . . 10.19, 10.22

BP Properties Ltd v Buckler [1987] 2 EGLR 168, CA . . . 30.27

Brace v Calder [1895] 2 QB 253, CA . . . 11.25

Brace v South-East Regional Housing Association Ltd [1984] 1 EGLR 144, CA . . . 23.12, 32.57

Bracey v Read [1962] 3 All ER 472 . . . 37.26

Bradburn v Great Western Rly Co (1874) LR 10 Exch 1 . . . 27.9

Bradburn v Lindsay [1983] 2 All ER 408 . . . 32.12, 32.57

Bradbury v Morgan (1862) 1 H & C 249 . . . 5.29

Bradford Corpn v Pickles [1895] AC 587, HL . . . 15.8, 15.10, 23.12, 28.20

Bradford v Robinson Rentals Ltd [1967] 1 All ER 267 . . . 18.16

Branchett v Beaney, Coster and Swale Borough Council (1992) 24 HLR 348, CA . . . 11.6

Brasserie du Pêcheur SA v Germany (C-46/93); R v Secretary of State for Transport, ex p Factortame (No 4) (C-48/93) [1996] All ER (EC) 301, ECJ . . . 3.51

Braymist Ltd v Wise Finance Co Ltd [2002] EWCA Civ 127 . . . 14.8

Brennan v Bolt Burdon [2004] EWCA Civ 1017, CA . . . 12.10

Brent Kelly v Cooper Associates [1993] AC 205, PC . . . 14.15

Brew Bros Ltd v Snax (Ross) Ltd [1970] 1 All ER 587, CA . . . 23.3, 23.17

Brew Bros v Snax (Ross) Ltd [1970] 1 QB 612 . . . 36.49

Brian Cooper & Co v Fairview Estates (Investments) Ltd [1987] 1 EGLR 18, CA . . . 14.18

Bridges v Mees [1957] 2 All ER 577 . . . 35.24

Bridlington Relay Ltd v Yorkshire Electricity Board [1965] 1 All ER 264 . . . 23.4, 23.7

Brikom Investments Ltd v Carr [1979] 2 All ER 753, CA . . . 30.16

Brinkibon v Stahag Stahl GmbH [1982] 1 All ER 293, HL . . . 5.17

Bristol & West plc v Bartlett [2002] EWCA Civ 1181 . . . 34.34

Bristol and West Building Society v Henning [1985] 2 All ER 606, CA . . . 34.24, 35.24

Britannia Building Society v Earl [1990] 2 All ER 469, CA . . . 34.39

British Bakeries (Midlands) Ltd v Michael Testler & Co Ltd [1986] 1 EGLR 64 . . . 36.30

British Bank of the Middle East Ltd v Sun Life Assurance Co of Canada (UK) Ltd [1983] 2 Lloyd's Rep 9, HL . . . 14.34

British Celanese Ltd v A H Hunt (Capacitors) Ltd [1969] 2 All ER 1252 . . . 23.9, 24.8, 24.9

British Crane Hire Corpn Ltd v Ipswich Plant Hire Ltd [1974] 1 All ER 1059, CA . . . 7.11

British Fermentation Products Ltd v Compare Reavell Ltd [1999] 2 All ER (Comm) 389 . . . 9.12

British Railways Board v Glass [1964] 3 All ER 418, CA . . . 32.53

British Railways Board v Herrington [1972] AC 877, HL . . . 21.18

British Road Services Ltd v Arthur V Crutchley Ltd [1968] 1 All ER 811, CA . . . 5.13, 26.23

British Shipbuilders v VSEL Consortium plc [1997] 1 Lloyd's Rep 106 . . . 36.59

British Steel Corpn v Cleveland Bridge and Engineering Co Ltd [1984] 1 All ER 504 . . . 5.38

British Telecommunications plc v Sun Life Assurance Society plc [1995] 4 All ER 44, CA . . . 36.48

British Westinghouse Electric and Manufacturing Co Ltd v Underground Electric Rlys Co of London [1912] AC 673 . . . 11.26

Broadway Investments hackney Ltd v Grant [2006] EWCA Civ 1709 . . . 37.27

Brogden v Metropolitan Rly Co (1877) 2 App Cas 666, HL . . . 5.14

Bromley Park Garden Estates Ltd v Moss [1982] 2 All ER 890. CA. . . . 36.30

Brooks v Home Office [1999] FLR 33 . . . 17.8

Broomfield v Williams [1897] 1 Ch 602 . . . 32.35

Brown v Corus (UK) Ltd [2004] EWCA Civ 374, CA . . . 18.4

Brown v National Coal Board [1962] 1 All ER 81, HL . . . 20.6

Brown v Raphael [1958] 2 All ER 79 . . . 12.8

Brown v Robinson [2004] UKPC 56, PC . . . 26.14

Brown's Estate, Re; Brown v Brown [1893] 2 Ch 300 . . . 34.34

Browne v Flower [1911] 1 Ch 219 . . . 32.18, 36.34, 36.35

Browne v Lockhart (1840) 10 Sim 420 . . . 34.8

Brunner v Greenslade [1970] 3 All ER 833 . . . 33.28, 33.36

Bryant v Lefever (1879) 4 CPD 172 . . . 32.9

Buckinghamshire County Council v Moran [1989] 2 All ER 225 . . . 30.25, 30.26

Buckpitt v Oates [1968] 1 All ER 1145 . . . 19.4

Bulli Coal Mining Co v Osborne [1899] AC 351, PC . . . 28.17

Bulstrode v Lambert [1953] 1 WLR 2064 . . . 32.53

Bunge Corpn v Tradax SA [1981] 2 All ER 513, HL . . . 8.22, 8.29, 8.30

Bunker v Charles Brand & Son Ltd [1969] 2 All
ER 59 . . . 21.15, 21.17

Burgess v Rawnsley [1975] 3 All ER 142, CA . . .
31.20, 31.22

Burnett v British Waterways Board [1973] 2 All
ER 631, CA . . . 21.17

Burns v Burns [1984] 1 All ER 244, CA. . . .
31.14

Burroughs Bay v Bristol City Council [1996] 1
PLR 78 . . . 39.5

Burton v Winters [1993] 3 All ER 847, CA . . .
22.10

Bushwall Properties Ltd v Vortex Properties Ltd
[1976] 2 All ER 283, CA . . . 5.31

Business Computers International Ltd v
Registrar of Companies [1987] 3 All ER
465 . . . 16.27

Butler Machine Tool Co Ltd v Ex-Cell-O Corpn
(England) Ltd [1979] 1 All ER 965, CA . . .
5.13

Bybrook Barn Centre Ltd v Kent County
Council [2001] BLR 55, CA . . . 23.16

Byrne v Hall Pain & Foster [1999] 1 EGLR 73,
CA . . . 27.21

Byrne v Van Tienhoven (1880) 5 CPD 344 . . .
5.26

C A Taylor (Wholesale) Ltd v Hepworths Ltd
[1977] 2 All ER 784 . . . 27.12

C and P Haulage v Middleton [1983] 3 All ER
94, CA . . . 11.8

C v Imperial Design Ltd [2001] Env LR 33,
CA . . . 17.5

Cachia v Faluyi [2001] EWCA Civ 998,
CA . . . 3.27

Cadogan v 26 Cadogan Square Ltd and Howard
de Walden Estates Ltd v Aggio [2008] UKHL
44 . . . 37.15

Cadogan v Royal Brompton Hospital National
Health Trust [1996] 2 EGLR 115 . . . 33.37

Calico Printers' Association Ltd v Barclays Bank
(1931) 145 LT 51 . . . 14.20

Calveley v Chief Constable of Merseyside [1989]
1 All ER 1025, HL . . . 16.23

Calvert v William Hill Credit Ltd [2008] EWCA
Civ 1427, CA . . . 16.9

Cambridge Water Co Ltd v Eastern Counties
Leather plc [1994] 1 All ER 53, HL . . . 23.12,
24.8, 24.9

Caminer v Northern and London Investment
Trust Ltd [1950] 2 All ER 486, HL . . .
23.25

Campbell v Griffin [2001] EWCA Civ 990 . . .
30.13

Campden Hill Towers Ltd v Gardner [1977] 1
All ER 739, CA . . . 36.45

Candler v Crane, Christmas & Co [1951] All ER
426 . . . 16.18

Cann v Willson (1888) 39 Ch D 39 . . . 16.21

Cannon v Hartley [1949] 1 All ER 50 . . . 11.44

Cannon v Villars (1878) 8 Ch D 415 . . . 32.53

Caparo Industries plc v Dickman [1990] 1 All
ER 568, HL . . . 16.6, 16.11, 16.21

Capital and Counties plc v Hampshire County
Council [1997] 2 All ER 865, CA . . . 16.8, 16.23

Capp v Topham (1805) 6 East 392 . . . 14.19

Capps v Miller [1989] 2 All ER 333, CA . . .
19.8

Car and Universal Finance Co Ltd v Caldwell
[1964] 1 All ER 290, CA . . . 12.18, 12.19

Cardshops v Davies [1971] 2 All ER 721,
CA . . . 37.45

Carega Properties SA v Sharratt [1979] 2 All ER
1084, HL . . . 37.3

Carlgarth, The [1927] P 93 . . . 21.8

Carlill v Carbolic Smoke Ball Co [1893] 1 QB
256, CA . . . 5.3, 5.6, 5.19, 5.20

Carmel Southend v Strachan & Henshaw [2007]
3 EGLR 15 . . . 36.52

Carr-Glynn v Frearsons [1997] 2 All ER
614 . . . 16.21

Carr-Saunders v Dick McNeil Associates Ltd
[1986] 2 All ER 888 . . . 32.56

Casey's Patents, Re; Stewart v Casey [1892] 1 Ch
104, CA . . . 6.10

Cassell & Co Ltd v Broome [1972] 1 All ER 801,
HL . . . 27.2

Cassidy v Ministry of Health [1951] 1 All ER
574, CA . . . 3.34, 17.18, 26.5, 26.23

Castle v St Augustine's Links (1922) 38 TLR
615 . . . 23.25

Caswell v Powell Duffryn Associated Collieries
Ltd [1939] 3 All ER 722, HL . . . 20.8

Cattle v Stockton Waterworks Co (1875) LR 10
QB 453 . . . 16.12, 24.9

Caunce v Caunce [1969] 1 All ER 722 . . . 35.13

Cavalier v Pope [1906] AC 428 at 433 . . . 21.4,
21.26, 21.30

CCC Films (London) Ltd v Impact Quadrant
Films Ltd [1984] 3 All ER 298 . . . 11.8

Cehave NV v Bremer Handelsgesellschaft mbH
("The Hansa Nord") [1975] 3 All ER 739,
CA . . . 8.24, 8.25

Cellulose Acetate Silk Co Ltd v Widnes Foundry
(1925) Ltd [1933] AC 20, HL . . . 11.31, 11.34

Celsteel Ltd v Alton House Holdings Ltd (No 2)
[1987] 2 All ER 240, CA . . . 36.34

Cemp Properties (UK) Ltd v Dentsply Research
and Development Corpn [1991] 2 EGLR 197,
CA . . . 16.21

Centaploy Ltd v Matlodge Ltd [1973] 2 All ER
720 . . . 36.5

Central Estates (Belgravia) Ltd v Woolgar
(No 2) [1972] 3 All ER 610, CA . . . 36.64

Central Estates Ltd v Secretary of State for the
Environment [1997] 1 EGLR 239, CA . . .
36.57

Central London Property Trust Ltd v High
Trees House Ltd [1956] 1 All ER 256n . . .
3.34, 6.20, 6.22, 6.23

Central London Rly Co v City of London Land Tax Comrs [1911] 1 Ch 467 . . . 28.25

Century Insurance Co Ltd v Northern Ireland Road Transport Board [1942] 1 All ER 491, HL . . . 26.9

Chadburn v Moore (1892) 61 LJ Ch 674 . . . 14.47

Chadwick v Keith Marshall [1984] CLY 1037 . . . 23.20

Chambers v Randall [1923] 1 Ch 149 . . . 33.27

Chandler Bros Ltd v Boswell [1936] 3 All ER 179, CA . . . 10.13

Chandler v Kerley [1978] 2 All ER 942, CA . . . 28.42, 28.43, 30.15

Chandler v Webster [1904] 1 KB 493, CA . . . 10.15, 10.16

Chapelton v Barry UDC [1940] 1 All ER 356, CA . . . 7.12

Chaplin v Hicks [1911] 2 KB 786, CA . . . 11.10

Chapman v Honig [1963] 2 All ER 513, CA . . . 15.10

Chappell v Bray (1860) 6 H & N 145 . . . 14.27

Chaproniere v Mason (1905) 21 TLR 633 . . . 17.18

Charge Card Services Ltd, Re [1988] 3 All ER 702, CA . . . 8.3

Charing Cross West End and City Electric Supply Co v Hydraulic Power Co [1914] 3 KB 772, CA . . . 23.18, 24.4

Charing Cross West End and Electric Supply Co v Hydraulic Power Co [1914] 3 KB 772, CA . . . 24.14

Charles Clement(London) Ltd v Rank City Wall Ltd [1978] 1 EGLR 47 . . . 37.44

Charlton v Forrest Printing Ink Co Ltd [1980] IRLR 331, CA . . . 16.11

Chartered Trust plc v Davies [1997] 2 EGLR 83, CA . . . 36.34, 36.35, 36.98

Chatsworth Estates Co v Fewell [1931] 1 Ch 224 . . . 33.34, 33.35

Chaudhry v Prabhakar [1988] 3 All ER 718, CA . . . 14.14, 16.20

Checkpoint Ltd v Strathclyde Pension Fund [2003] EWCA Civ 84, [2003] 14 EG 124, CA . . . 36.59

Cheese v Thomas [1994] 1 All ER 35, CA . . . 12.19

Chelsea Yacht & Boat Co Ltd v Pope [2001] 2 All ER 409, CA . . . 28.5, 28.9

Cheltenham and Gloucester Building Society v Norgan [1996] 1 All ER 449, CA . . . 34.27, 34.33

Chemco Leasing SpA v Rediffusion [1987] 1 FTLR 201, CA . . . 5.28

Cheryl Investments Ltd v Saldanha [1979] 1 All ER 5, CA . . . 37.27

Cheshire County Council v Woodward [1962] 2 QB 126 . . . 39.4

Chester v Afshar [2004] UKHL 41, HL . . . 19.3

Chestertons v Barone [1987] 1 EGLR 15, CA . . . 14.38

Chhokar v Chhokar [1984] FLR 313 . . . 35.25

Chief Constable of Hertfordshire Police v Van Colle; Smith v Chief Constable of Sussex [2008] UKHL 50, [2008] 3 All ER 977, HL . . . 16.23

China & South Sea Bank Ltd v Tan [1989] 3 All ER 839, PC . . . 34.31

Chinnock v Sainsbury (1860) 30 LJ Ch 409 . . . 14.22

Chipchase v British Titan Products Co Ltd [1956] 1 All ER 613, CA . . . 20.6

Christie v Davey [1893] 1 Ch 316 . . . 23.12

CIBC Mortgages plc v Pitt [1993] 4 All ER 433, HL . . . 12.61, 12.66

City and Westminster Properties (1934) Ltd v Mudd [1958] 2 All ER 733 . . . 7.6

City of London Building Society v Flegg [1987] 3 All ER 435, HL . . . 31.36, 34.24, 35.27

Cityland and Property (Holdings) Ltd v Dabrah [1967] 2 All ER 635 . . . 34.11

Civil Service Co-operative Society Ltd v McGrigor's Trustee [1923] 2 Ch 347 . . . 36.65

Clapman v Edwards [1938] 2 All ER 507 . . . 32.5

Clark v MacLennan [1983] 1 All ER 416 . . . 17.7

Clarke v Bruce Lance & Co [1988] 1 All ER 364, CA . . . 16.21

Clarke v Dunraven [1897] AC 59, HL . . . 5.2

Clarke v Price (1819) 2 Wils Ch 157 . . . 11.44

Clarkson, Booker Ltd v Andjel [1964] 3 All ER 260, CA . . . 14.38

Clauss v Pir [1987] 2 All ER 752 . . . 14.1

Clayards v Dethick and Davis (1848) 12 Qb 439 . . . 18.13

Clear Channel UK Ltd v Manchester City Council [2006] 04 EG 168 . . . 36.8

Clegg v Dearden (1848) 12 QB 576 . . . 22.7

Clore v Theatrical Properties Ltd [1936] 3 All ER 483 . . . 28.44

Close v Steel Co of Wales Ltd [1961] 2 All ER 953, HL . . . 20.5

Clough v First Choice Holidays & Flights Ltd [2006] EWCA Civ 15, CA . . . 18.4

Clunis v Camden and Islington Health Authority [1998] 3 All ER 180, CA . . . 18.20

Co-operative Group (CWS) Ltd v Pritchard [2011] EWCA Civ 329, CA . . . 19.4

Co-operative Insurance Society Ltd v Argyll Stores (Holdings) Ltd [1997] 3 All ER 297, HL . . . 11.44, 36.39

Co-operative Wholesale Society Ltd v National Westminster Bank plc [1995] 1 EGLR 97, CA . . . 36.58

Cocktails Ltd v Secretary of State for Communities and Local Government [2008] EWCA Civ 1523 . . . 39.16

Cogent v Gibson (1864) 33 Beav 557 . . . 11.44

Coghurst Wood Leisure Park Ltd v Secretary of State for Transport, Local Government and the Regions [2002] EWHC 1091(Admin) . . . 38.30, 38.31

Cohen v Kittell (1889) 22 Qbd 680, DC . . . 14.12

Colchester Estates (Cardiff) v Carlton Industries plc [1984] 2 All ER 601 . . . 3.40

Colledge v Bass Mitchells & Butlers [1988] ICR 125, CA . . . 27.9

Collen v Gardner (1856) 21 Beav 540 . . . 14.29

Collen v Wright (1857) 8 E & B 647 . . . 14.45

Collier v P & M J Wright Holdings Ltd [2007] EWCA Civ 1329, CA . . . 6.18, 6.22, 6.23

Collingwood v Home and Colonial Stores Ltd [1936] 3 All ER 200, CA . . . 24.8, 24.16, 24.17

Collins v Associated Greyhound Racecourses Ltd [1930] 1 Ch 1 . . . 14.37

Collins v Flynn [1963] 2 All ER 1068 . . . 36.50

Collins v Godefroy (1831) 1 B & Ad 950 . . . 6.13, 6.14

Collins v Howell-Jones (1980) 259 Estates Gazette 331, CA . . . 12.49

Colls v Home and Colonial Stores Ltd [1904] AC 179, HL . . . 32.56

Colour Quest Ltd v Total Downstream UK plc [2010] EWCA Civ 180, CA. . . . 16.14, 24.6, 24.10

Colvilles Ltd v Devine [1969] 2 All ER 53, HL . . . 18.12

Combe v Combe [1951] 1 All ER 767, CA . . . 6.24

Commercial Union Life Assurance Co Ltd v Label Ink [2001] L & TR 29 . . . 36.51

Commission for the New Towns v Cooper (Great Britain) Ltd [1995] 2 All ER 929, CA . . . 29.4

Compagnie de Commerce et Commission SARL v Parkinson Stove Co [1953] 2 Lloyd's Rep 487, CA . . . 5.23

Computastaff Ltd v Ingledew, Brown, Bennison and Garrett [1983] 2 EGLR 150 . . . 16.21

Conlon v Simms [2006] EWCA Civ 1749, CA . . . 12.56

Connolly-Martin v Davis [1999] PNLR 826, CA . . . 16.27

Cooke v Eshelby (1887) 12 App Cas 271, HL . . . 14.37

Cooper v Phibbs (1867) LR 2 HL 149 . . . 28.20

Copeland v Greenhalf [1952] 1 All ER 809 . . . 32.11

Corby Group Litigation, Re [2008] EWCA Civ 463, CA . . . 23.26

Corisand Investments Ltd v Druce & Co [1978] 2 EGLR 86 . . . 17.9

Cornwal v Wilson (1750) 1 Ves Sen 509 . . . 14.7, 14.10

Corr v IBC Vehicles Ltd [2008] UKHL 13, HL . . . 18.17

Cory, Re (1912) 29 TLR 18 . . . 6.5

Costa v ENEL (C-6/64) [1964] ECR 585, ECJ . . . 3.52

Costain Property Developments Ltd v Finlay & Co Ltd [1989] 1 EGLR 237 . . . 36.39

Costello v Chief Constable of the Northumbria Police [1999] 1 All ER 550, CA . . . 16.11

Cottage Holiday Associates Ltd v Customs and Excise Comrs [1983] QB 735 . . . 36.4

Cotton v Derbyshire Dales District Council (1994) Times, 20 June, CA . . . 21.12

Couch v McCann (1977) 77 DLR (3d) 387 . . . 21.4

Coulthart v Clementson (1879) 5 QBD 42 . . . 5.29

County Ltd v Girozentrale Securities [1996] 3 All ER 834, CA . . . 11.13

Cowan v Chief Constable for Avon & Somerset Constabulary [2002] HLR 42, CA . . . 16.23

Coward v Motor Insurers' Bureau [1962] 1 All ER 531, CA . . . 6.3

Cox v Binfield [1989] 1 EGLR 97, CA . . . 37.38

Cox v First Secretary of State [2003] EWHC 1290 Admin . . . 38.31

Cox v Glue (1848) 5 CB 533 . . . 22.2

Crabb v Arun District Council [1975] 3 All ER 865, CA . . . 30.13–30.15

Crago v Julian [1992] 1 All ER 744, CA . . . 29.12, 36.28

Crédit Lyonnais Bank Nederland NV v Burch [1997] 1 All ER 144 . . . 12.67

Credit Suisse v Beegas Nominees [1994] 4 ALL ER 803 . . . 36.50

Cremdean Properties Ltd v Nash (1977) 244 EG 547, CA . . . 12.46, 12.49

Cresswell v Proctor [1968] 2 All ER 682, CA . . . 33.38

Cresswell v Sirl [1947] 2 All ER 730, CA . . . 25.12

Crest Nicholson Residential (South) Ltd v McAllister [2004] EWCA Civ 410 . . . 33.26

Cricket Ltd v Shaftesbury plc [1999] 2 EGLR 57 . . . 37.28

Cricklewood Property and Investment Trust Ltd v Leighton's Investment Trust Ltd [1945] 1 All ER 252, HL . . . 10.8

Cripps, Re [1946] Ch 265, CA . . . 34.35

Croke v Wiseman [1981] 3 All ER 852, CA . . . 27.8

Cromwell Property Investment Co Ltd v Western and Toovey [1934] Ch 322 . . . 34.8

Cross v David Martin and Mortimer [1989] 1 EGLR 154 . . . 17.9

Crow v Wood [1970] 3 All ER 425, CA . . . 32.12

Crowhurst v Amersham Burial Board (1878) 4 Ex D 5 . . . 24.5, 24.6, 24.8

Crown Estate Commissioners v Signet group plc [1996] 2 EGLR 200 . . . 36.30

Crown River Cruises Ltd v Kimbolton Fireworks Ltd [1996] 2 Lloyd's Rep 533 . . . 23.13, 24.4

Croydon London Borough Council v Gladden [1994] JPL 723 . . . 39.8

Crump v Lambert (1867) LR 3 Eq 409 . . . 23.4

CTN Cash and Carry Ltd v Gallaher Ltd [1994] 4 All ER 714, CA . . . 12.59

Cuckmere Brick Co Ltd v Mutual Finance Ltd [1971] 2 All ER 633, CA . . . 34.31

Cullen v Chief Constable of the Royal Ulster Constabulary [2003] UKHL 39 . . . 20.2

Cullinane v British Rema Manufacturing Co Ltd [1953] 2 All ER 1257, CA . . . 11.9

Cumming v Ince (1847) 11 QB 112 . . . 12.58

Cummings v Granger [1977] 1 All ER 104, CA . . . 19.2, 25.7

Cunard v Antifyre Ltd [1933] 1 KB 551 . . . 23.2

Cundy v Lindsay (1878) 3 App Cas 459, HL . . . 5.3, 12.17

Cunliffe-Owen v Teather and Greenwood [1967] 3 All ER 561 . . . 7.23

Cunningham v Reading Football Club [1992] PIQR P141 . . . 16.11, 21.12

Cunningham v Whelan (1917) 52 ILT 67 . . . 25.2

Curran v Northern Ireland Co-ownership Housing Association Ltd [1987] 2 All ER 13, HL . . . 16.23

Currie v Misa (1875) LR 10 Exch 153 . . . 6.7

Curtis v Betts [1990] 1 All ER 769, CA . . . 25.6

Curtis v Chemical Cleaning and Dyeing Co Ltd [1951] 1 All ER 631, CA . . . 7.8, 9.7

Curtis v London Rent Assessment Committee [1997] 4 All ER 842, CA . . . 37.3

Customs & Excise Commissioners v Barclays Bank [2006] UKHL 28, HL . . . 16.10

Cutler v United Dairies (London) Ltd [1933] 2 KB 297, CA . . . 18.11, 19.5

Cutler v Wandsworth Stadium Ltd [1949] 1 All ER 544, HL . . . 20.3

D & C Builders Ltd v Rees [1965] 3 All ER 837, CA . . . 6.18, 6.22

D & F Estates Ltd v Church Comrs for England [1988] 2 All ER 992, HL . . . 21.27, 26.16

D v East Berkshire Community Health NHS Trust [2005] UKHL 23, HL . . . 16.22, 16.23

D'Eyncourt v Gregory (1866) LR 3 Eq 382 . . . 28.11

D'Silva v Lister House Development Ltd [1970] 1 All ER 858 . . . 37.26

Da Costa en Schaake NV v Nederlandse Belastingadministratie (C–28–30/62) [1963] CMLR 224, ECJ . . . 3.36

Daborn v Bath Tramways Motor Co Ltd [1946] 2 All ER 333, CA . . . 17.13

Daiches v Bluelake Investments Ltd [1985] 2 EGLR 67 . . . 36.67

Daily Office Cleaning Contractors v Shefford [1977] RTR 361, DC . . . 27.12

Daley v Ramdath (1993) Times, 21 January, CA . . . 27.2

Dalton v Angus (1881) 6 App Cas 740 at 801, HL . . . 32.45, 32.48

Daly v General Steam Navigation Co Ltd [1980] 3 All ER 696, CA . . . 27.4

Daly v Liverpool Corpn [1939] 2 All ER 142 . . . 17.5

Daniells v Mendonca (1999) 78 P & CR 401, CA . . . 22.8

Daniels v Whetstone Entertainments Ltd [1962] 2 Lloyd's Rep 1, CA . . . 26.14

Dann v Hamilton [1939] 1 All ER 59 . . . 19.5

Darbishire v Warran [1963] 3 All ER 310, CA . . . 27.12

Darby v National Trust for Places of Historic Interest or Natural Beauty [2001] EWCA Civ 189, 3 LGLR 29 . . . 21.12

Dare's and Beck's Application, Re (1974) 28 P & CR 354 . . . 33.40

Darling v A-G [1950] 2 All ER 793 . . . 26.18

Darlington Borough Council v Wiltshier Northern Ltd [1995] 3 All ER 895, CA . . . 11.2

Das v Linden Mews Ltd [2002] EWCA Civ 590 . . . 32.4, 32.53

Daulia Ltd v Four Millbank Nominees Ltd [1978] 2 All ER 557 . . . 5.27

Davey v Harrow Corpn [1957] 2 All ER 305, CA . . . 28.27

David Blackstone Ltd v Burnetts (West End) Ltd [1973] 3 All ER 782 . . . 36.64

Davies v Davies [1975] Qb 172, CA . . . 25.3

Davies v Dennis [2009] EWCA Civ 1081 . . . 32.9

Davies v Jones [2009] EWCA Civ 1164 . . . 30.18, 33.10

Davies v Law Mutual Building Society (1971) 219 Estates Gazette 309, DC . . . 34.23

Davies v Yadegar [1990] 1 EGLR 71, CA . . . 22.2, 28.23

Davis Contractors Ltd v Fareham UDC [1956] 2 All ER 145, HL . . . 10.2

Davis v City and Hackney Health Authority [1989] 2 Med LR 366 . . . 27.22

Davis v Johnson [1978] 1 All ER 1132, HL . . . 3.21

De Bussche v Alt (1878) 8 Ch D 286, CA . . . 14.16

Dean v Allin & Watts [2001] EWCA Civ 758, [2001] Lloyd's Rep PN 605, CA . . . 16.21

Deane v Clayton (1817) 7 Taunt 489 . . . 21.18

Deepak Fertilizers & Petrochemical Corpn v Imperial Chemical Industries plc [1999] 1 Lloyd's Rep 387, CA . . . 7.7, 12.47

Delaney v T P Smith Ltd [1946] 2 All ER 23, CA . . . 22.4

Delaware Mansions Ltd v Westminster City Council [2001] UKHL 55 . . . 23.13

Dellneed Ltd v Chin [1987] 1 EGLR 75 . . . 36.11

Denmark Productions Ltd v Boscobel Productions Ltd [1968] 3 All ER 513, CA . . . 10.14, 11.37

Dennis v Ministry of Defence [2003] EWHC 793 . . . 23.10, 23.12

Department of Transport v North West Water Authority [1983] 3 All ER 273, HL . . . 23.18, 24.14

Dept. of the Environment v Thomas Bates & Son Ltd [1990] 2 All ER 943, HL . . . 21.27

Derry v Peek (1889) 14 App Cas 337, HL . . . 12.23, 16.17

Design Progression Ltd v Thurloe Properties Ltd [2004] EWHC 324 (Ch) . . . 36.29

Deyong v Shenburn [1946] 1 All ER 226 . . . 16.10

Di Luca v Juraise (Springs) Ltd [1998] 2 EGLR 125, CA . . . 8.30

Dick Bentley (Productions) Ltd v Harold Smith (Motors) Ltd [1965] 2 All ER 65, CA . . . 7.20

Dickinson v Abel [1969] 1 All ER 484 . . . 6.6

Dickinson v Dodds (1876) 2 Ch D 463, CA . . . 5.26

Dillwyn v Llewelyn (1862) 4 De GF & J 517 . . . 30.15

Diment v NH Foot Ltd [1974] 2 All ER 785 . . . 32.41

Dimmock v Hallett (1866) 2 Ch App 21 . . . 12.7, 12.11

Dinefwr Borough Council v Jones [1987] 2 EGLR 58 . . . 36.45

Director General of Fair Trading v First National Bank plc [2001] UKHL 52, HL . . . 9.25, 9.28

Dobson v Thames Water Utilities Ltd [2009] EWCA Civ 28, CA . . . 23.13

Dodd Properties (Kent) Ltd v Canterbury CC [1980] 1 All ER 928, CA . . . 18.19, 27.13

Dodsworth v Dodsworth (1973) 228 Estates Gazette 1115, CA . . . 30.15

Doherty v Birmingham City Council [2008] UKHL 57 . . . 37.20

Dolgellau Golf Club v Hett [1998] L & TR 217, CA . . . 37.38

Dolphin Quays Developments Ltd v Mills [2006] EWHC 931 . . . 29.6

Dolphin's Conveyance, Re; Birmingham Corpn v Boden [1970] 2 All ER 664 . . . 33.29

Domb v Isoz [1980] 1 All ER 942, CA . . . 29.27

Dominion Mosaics and Tile Co Ltd v Trafalgar Trucking Co Ltd [1990] 2 All ER 246, CA . . . 27.12

Donaghey v Boulton and Paul Ltd [1967] 2 All ER 1014, HL . . . 20.5

Dong Bang Minerva v Davina Ltd [1995] 1 EGLR 41 . . . 36.29

Donnelly v Joyce [1973] 3 All ER 475, CA . . . 27.7

Donoghue v Folkestone Properties Ltd [2003] EWCA Civ 231, CA . . . 21.21

Donoghue v Stevenson [1932] AC 562, HL . . . 3.45, 16.3, 16.4, 16.6, 16.15

Doughty v Turner Manufacturing Co Ltd [1964] 1 All ER 98, CA . . . 18.17

Douglas-Scott v Scorgie [1984] 1 All ER 1086, CA . . . 36.45

Downsview Nominees Ltd v First City Corporation Ltd [1993] AC 295 . . . 34.31

Doyle v Olby (Ironmongers) Ltd [1969] 2 All ER 119, CA . . . 12.25

DPP v Schildkamp [1969] 3 All ER 1640, HL . . . 3.20

Drane v Evangelou [1978] 2 All ER 437, CA . . . 27.2

Draper v Hodder [1972] 2 All ER 210, CA . . . 25.3, 25.6

Draper's Conveyance, Re; Nihan v Porter [1967] 3 All ER 853 . . . 31.21

Draycott v Hannells Lettings Ltd [2010] EWHC 217 (QB) . . . 37.8

Drew v Nunn (1879) 4 Qbd 661, CA . . . 14.25

Dubai Aluminium Co Ltd v Salaam [2002] UKHL 48, HL . . . 26.8

Duchess of Argyll v Beuselinck [1972] 2 Lloyd's Rep 172 . . . 17.7

Dudley and District Benefit Building Society v Emerson [1949] 2 All ER 252, CA . . . 34.39

Duffy v Lamb [1997] NPC 52, CA . . . 32.12

Duffen v FRA Bo SpA [2000] 1 Lloyd's Rep 180 . . . 8.15

Duke v GEC Reliance Ltd [1988] 1 All ER 626, HL . . . 3.51

Duncan Investments Ltd v Underwoods [1997] PNLR 521 . . . 16.21

Dunlop Pneumatic Tyre Co Ltd v New Garage and Motor Co Ltd [1915] AC 79 . . . 11.34

Dunlop Pneumatic Tyre Co Ltd v Selfridge & Co Ltd [1915] AC 847, HL . . . 6.7, 13.2, 13.2

Dunn v Birmingham Canal Navigation Co (1872) LR 7 Qb 244 . . . 24.11

Dunne v North Western Gas Board [1963] 3 All ER 916, CA . . . 24.5, 23.18

Dunton v Dover District Council (1977) 76 LGR 87 . . . 23.4, 23.10

Durley House Ltd v Cadogan [2001] 1 EGLR 60 . . . 37.45

Durrant v Child (1611) 1 Bulst 157 . . . 25.8

Dutton v Bognor Regis UDC [1972] 1 All ER 462, CA . . . 21.27

Dwyer v Mansfield [1946] 2 All ER 247 . . . 23.24

Dyason v Secretary of State for the Environment [1998] JPL 778 . . . 39.37

Dyer v Dyer (1788) 2 Cox Eq Cas 92 . . . 30.9

Dymond v Pearce [1972] 1 All ER 1142, CA . . . 18.3, 23.24

Dyster v Randall & Sons [1926] Ch 932 . . . 14.37

E Christopher & Co v Essig [1948] WN 461 . . . 14.47

E R Ives Investments Ltd v High [1967] 1 All ER 504, CA . . . 35.13

Eagles v Minister for the Environment Sustainability and Housing and Welsh Assembly Government and another [2009] EWHC 1028 (Admin) . . . 39.16

Easson v London North Eastern Rly Co [1944] 2 All ER 425, CA . . . 17.17

East Suffolk Rivers Catchment Board v Kent [1940] 4 All ER 527, HL . . . 16.8

East v Maurer [1991] 2 All ER 733, CA . . . 12.28

Eastern and South African Telegraph Co Ltd v Cape Town Tramways Companies Ltd [1902] AC 381, PC . . . 24.11

Eastman Photographic Materials Co Ltd v Comptroller-General of Patents, Designs and Trade Marks [1898] AC 571, HL . . . 3.13

Eastman v South West Thames Area Health Authority [1991] RTR 389, CA . . . 19.9

Ecay v Godfrey (1947) 80 Lloyd's LR 286 . . . 7.18

Eco-Energy (GB) Ltd v First Secretary of State [2004] EWCA Civ 1566 (CA) . . . 39.42

Edgington v Fitzmaurice (1885) 29 Ch D 459, CA . . . 12.9, 12.15

Edis's Application, Re (1972) 23 P & CR 421 . . . 33.38

Edward Wong Finance Co v Johnson, Stokes and Master [1984] AC 296, PC . . . 17.7

Edwards v Railway Executive [1952] 2 All ER 430 . . . 21.7

Edwards v Skyways Ltd [1964] 1 All ER 494 . . . 6.2

Ee v Kakar (1979) 40 P & CR 223 . . . 5.36

Egyptian International Foreign Trade Co v Soplex Wholesale Supplies and Refson (PS) & Co [1985] 2 Lloyd's Rep 36 . . . 14.31

Ehlmer v Hall [1993] 1 EGLR 137, CA . . . 22.4

Elguzouli-Daf v Metropolitan Police Comr [1995] 1 All ER 833, CA . . . 16.27

Elitestone Ltd v Morris [1997] 2 All ER 513, HL . . . 28.8–28.10

Ellen Street Estates Ltd v Minister of Health [1934] 1 KB 590, CA . . . 3.4

Ellenborough Park, Re; Davies, Powell v Maddison, Re [1955] 3 All ER 667, CA . . . 32.3, 32.5, 32.6, 32.9

Ellerman Lines Ltd v Murray [1931] AC 126, HL . . . 3.20

Elliott v Islington London Borough Council [1991] 1 EGLR 167, CA . . . 27.18

Elliott v Turquand (1881) 7 App Cas 79, HL . . . 14.26

Ellis v Goulton [1893] 1 QB 350, CA . . . 29.28

Ellison v Ministry of Defence (1996) 81 BLR 101 . . . 24.5, 24.8

Elliston v Reacher [1908] 2 Ch 374 . . . 33.29

Elm Avenue, Re [1984] 3 All ER 632 . . . 33.32

Elmcroft Developments Ltd v Tankersley-Sawyer (1984) 270 EG 140 . . . 36.52

Emile Elias & Co Ltd v Pine Groves Ltd [1993] 1 WLR 305, PC . . . 33.29

Entick v Carrington (1765) 19 State Tr 1029 . . . 22.1

Entores v Miles Far East Corpn [1955] 2 All ER 493, CA . . . 5.17

ER Ives Investments Ltd v High [1967] 1 All ER 504, CA . . . 30.13, 30.15, 30.16, 30.18

Eric v Stansfield v South East Nursing Home Services Ltd [1986] 1 EGLR 29 . . . 14.15

Erlanger v New Sombrero Phosphate Co (1878) 3 App Cas 1218 . . . 12.19

Errington v Errington and Woods [1952] 1 All ER 149, CA . . . 5.27, 28.44

Ertel Bieber & Co v Rio Tinto Co Ltd [1918] AC 260, HL . . . 10.12

Esselte AB v Pearl Assurance plc [1997] 2 All ER 41, CA . . . 37.26, 37.30

Essex Water Co v Secretary of State for the Environment [1989] JPL 914 . . . 39.15

Essexcrest Ltd v Evenlex Ltd [1988] 1 EGLR 69, CA . . . 37.29

Esso Petroleum Co Ltd v Alstonbridge Properties Ltd [1975] 3 All ER 358 . . . 34.21, 34.34

Esso Petroleum Co Ltd v Harper's Garage (Stourport) Ltd [1967] 1 All ER 699, HL . . . 34.14

Esso Petroleum Co Ltd v Mardon [1976] 2 All ER 5, CA . . . 7.19, 12.32

Etheridge v K [1999] Ed CR 550 . . . 17.5

Euston Centre Properties v H & J Wilson [1982] 1 EGLR 57 . . . 37.45

Evans v Llewellin (1787) 1 Cox Eq Cas 333 . . . 12.67

Everett v Comojo (UK) Ltd 2011] EWCA Civ 13, CA . . . 16.11, 21.12

Eves v Eves [1975] 3 All ER 768, CA . . . 31.14

EWP Ltd v Moore [1992] Qb 460, CA . . . 37.47

Ex p. Mather (1797) 3 Ves 373 . . . 14.19

Experience Hendrix LLC v PXX Enterprises Inc [2003] EWCA Civ 323,CA . . . 11.7, 11.39

Expert Clothing Service and Sales Ltd v Hillgate House Ltd [1985] 2 All ER 998, CA . . . 36.64, 36.65

F v Wirral Metropolitan Borough Council [1991] 2 All ER 648, CA . . . 20.3

Fabbri v Morris [1947] 1 All ER 315, DC . . . 23.24

Faccenda Chicken Ltd v Fowler [1986] 1 All ER 617, CA . . . 7.31

Fairchild v Glenhaven Funeral Services Ltd [2002] UKHL 22 . . . 18.4

Fairclough v Swan Brewery Co Ltd [1912] AC 565, PC . . . 34.10

Fairlie v Fenton (1870) LR 5 Exch 169 . . . 14.42

Fairweather v St Marylebone Property Co Ltd [1962] 2 All ER 288, HL . . . 30.21, 30.34

Family Management v Gray [1980] 1 EGLR 46, CA . . . 37.45

Fardon v Harcourt-Rivington (1932) 146 LT 391 . . . 17.11

Farley v Skinner [2001] UKHL 49, HL . . . 11.6

Farmer Giles Ltd v Wessex Water Authority [1990] 1 EGLR 177, CA . . . 27.12

Farrar v Farrars Ltd (1888) 40 Ch D 395 . . .
34.30
Farrell v Avon Health Authority [2001] Lloyd's
Rep Med 458 . . . 16.28
Farrer v Nelson (1885) 15 QBD 258 . . . 23.3,
25.2
Farrow v Wilson (1869) LR 4 CP 744 . . . 14.24,
14.27
Fawke v Viscount Chelsea [1979] 3 All ER 568,
CA . . . 36.58, 37.45
Fay v Prentice (1845) 1 CB 828 . . . 23.20
FC Shepherd & Co Ltd v Jerrom [1986] 3 All ER
589, CA . . . 10.14
Federated Homes Ltd v Mill Lodge Properties
Ltd [1980] 1 All ER 371, CA . . . 33.24,
33.26
Felthouse v Bindley (1862) 11 CBNS 869 . . .
5.20
Fenna v Clare & Co [1895] 1 QB 199, DC . . .
23.25
Fennelly v Connex Southeastern Ltd [2001]
IRLR 390, CA . . . 26.14
Fercometal SARL v Mediterranean Shipping Co
SA ("The Simona") [1988] 2 All ER 742,
HL . . . 8.27
Ferguson v John Dawson & Partners
(Contractors) Ltd [1976] 3 All ER 817,
CA . . . 26.3
Ferguson v Welsh [1987] 3 All ER 777,
HL . . . 21.16
Fibrosa Spolka Akcyjna v Fairbairn Lawson
Combe Barbour Ltd [1942] 2 All ER 122,
HL . . . 10.16
Field Common Ltd v Elmbridge DC [2008]
EWHC 2079 (Ch) . . . 22.7
Filliter v Phippard (1847) 11 Qb 347 . . . 24.16
Financings Ltd v Stimson [1962] 3 All ER 386,
CA . . . 5.23, 36.60
First Energy (UK) Ltd v Hungarian
International Bank Ltd [1993] 2 Lloyd's Rep
194, CA . . . 14.34
First National Bank plc v Syed [1991] 2 All ER
250 . . . 34.27
First National Securities Ltd v Hegerty [1985]
QB 850 . . . 31.19, 35.39
First Plus Financial Group v Hewett [2010]
EWCA Civ 312 . . . 12.55
First Secretary of State v Chelmsford BC [2003]
EWHC 2800 (Admin) . . . 39.54
First Sport Ltd v Barclays Bank plc [1993] 3 All
ER 789, CA . . . 14.30
Firstpost Homes Ltd v Johnson [1995] 4 All ER
355 . . . 29.4, 29.5
Firth v Bowling Iron Co (1878) 3 CPD
254 . . . 24.6
Fisher v Bell [1960] 3 All ER 731, DC . . . 5.5
Fisher v Brooker [2009] UKHL 41, HL . . . 11.55
Fisher v CRT Ltd (No 2) [1966] 1 All ER 88,
CA . . . 21.5
Fitzgerald v Lane [1987] Qb 781, CA . . . 18.4

Fitzgerald v Lane [1988] 2 All ER 961, HL . . . 19.9
Fitzkriston v Panayi [2008] EWCA Civ
283 . . . 29.12
Fitzleet Estates Ltd v Cherry [1977] 3 All ER
996, HL . . . 3.37
Fitzmaurice v Bayley (1856) 6 E & B 868 . . .
14.10
Flack v Hudson [2001] QB 698, CA . . . 25.6
Flairline Properties Ltd v Hassan [1999] 1 EGLR
137 . . . 37.26
Flight v Bolland (1828) 4 Russ 298 . . . 11.44
Floods of Queensferry Ltd v Shand
Construction Ltd (No 3) [2000] BLR 81 . . .
12.37
Fluor Daniels Properties v Shortlands
Investments [2001] 2 EGLR 103 . . . 36.52
Foakes v Beer (1884) 9 App Cas 605, HL . . .
6.18, 6.23
Foalquest Ltd v Roberts [1990] 1 EGLR 50 . . .
14.39
Fontana NV v Mautner (1979) 254 Estates
Gazette 199 . . . 6.22
Forman & Co Pty Ltd v The Liddesdale [1900]
AC 190, PC . . . 14.10
Forsikringsaktieselskapet Vesta v Butcher
[1988] 2 All ER 43, CA . . . 11.28, 19.6
Forster v Outred & Co [1982] 2 All ER 753,
CA . . . 27.21
Fosbroke-Hobbes v Airwork Ltd and British
American Air Services Ltd [1937] 1 All ER
108 . . . 17.18
Foskett v Mistry [1984] RTR 1, CA . . . 17.5
Foster v British Gas (C-188/89) [1990] ECR
3313 . . . 3.49
Fothergill v Monarch Airlines Ltd [1980] 2 All
ER 696, HL . . . 3.23
Foto-Frost v Hauptzollant Lubeck-Ost [1988] 3
CMLR 57, ECJ . . . 3.53
Four-Maids Ltd v Dudley Marshall (Properties)
Ltd [1957] 2 All ER 35 . . . 34.18
Fourbouys plc v Newport Borough Council
[1994] 1 EGLR 138 . . . 37.45
Fowler v Barron [2008] EWCA Civ 377 . . .
31.11
Fowley Marine (Emsworth) Ltd v Gafford [1968]
1 All ER 979, CA . . . 22.4
Fox & Widley v Guram [1998] 1 EGLR 91 . . .
36.57
Fox v PG Wellfair Ltd [1981] 2 Loyd's Rep 514,
CA . . . 36.59
Francis v Cockrell (1870) LR 5 Qb 501 . . . 21.6
Francovich v Italy (Cases C-6 & 9/90) [1993] 2
CMLR 66, ECJ . . . 3.51
Franklin v Jeffries (1985) Times,
11 March . . . 22.3
Franklin v South Eastern Rly Co (1858) 3 H & N
211 . . . 27.11
Frawley v Neill [2000] CP Rep 20, CA . . . 11.55
Frederick Lawrence Ltd v Freeman, Hardy &
Willis [1959] 3 All ER 77 . . . 37.38

Freeman and Lockyer v Buckhurst Park
　Properties (Mangal) Ltd [1964] 1 All ER 630,
　CA . . . 14.30, 14.31
Freeman v Higher Park Farm [2008] EWCA Civ
　1185, CA . . . 25.7
Freeman v Marshall & Co(1966) 200 Estates
　Gazette 777 . . . 17.8
Friend v Young [1897] 2 Ch 421 . . . 14.24
Friends' Provident Life Office v British Railways
　Board [1995] 48 EG 106 . . . 36.74
Fritz v Hobson (1880) 14 Ch D 542 . . . 23.26
Froom v Butcher [1975] 3 All ER 520, CA . . . 19.8
Fruin v Fruin [1983] CA . . . 30.26
Fulford v Secretary of State [1997] JPL
　163 . . . 38.6
FW Woolworth & Co v Lambert [1937] Ch
　37 . . . 36.53

G Percy Trentham Ltd v Archital Luxfer Ltd
　[1993] 1 Lloyd's Rep 25 . . . 5.31
Galoo Ltd v Bright Grahame Murray [1995] 1
　All ER 16, CA . . . 11.13
Garden Cottage Foods Ltd v Milk Marketing
　Board [1983] 2 All ER 770, HL . . . 20.3
Gardiner v Heading [1928] 2 KB 284, CA . . .
　14.42
Gardner v Hodgson's Kingston Brewery Co
　[1903] AC 229, HL . . . 32.51
Gasson v Cole (1910) 26 TLR 468 . . . 14.19
Gator Shipping Corpn v Trans-Asiatic Oil Ltd
　SA ("The Odenfeld") [1978] 2 Lloyd's Rep
　357 . . . 11.37
Gaussen v Morton (1830) 10 B & C 731 . . . 14.22
Gayler and Pope Ltd v B Davies & Son Ltd
　[1924] 2 KB 75 . . . 25.3
Gee v Metropolitan Rly Co (1873) LR 8 QB
　161 . . . 17.17
Geier v Kujawa, Weston and Warne Bros
　(Transport) Ltd [1970] 1 Lloyd's Rep
　364 . . . 7.13
General Billposting Co Ltd v Atkinson [1909]
　AC 118, HL . . . 8.11
General Engineering Services Ltd v Kingston
　and St Andrew Corpn [1988] 3 All ER 867,
　PC . . . 26.9
Ghaidan v Godin Mendoza [2004] UKHL 30,
　HL . . . 3.27
GHSP Inc v AB Electronic Ltd [2010] EWHC
　1828 (Comm) . . . 5.13
Giannoukakis Ltd v Saltfleet Ltd [1988] 1 EGLR
　73, CA . . . 37.45
Gibbs and Houlder Bros' Lease, Re [1925] Ch
　575, CA . . . 36.30
Gibson v Government of the USA [2007] UKPC
　520, PC . . . 3.45
Gibson v Manchester City Council [1978] 2 All
　ER 583 . . . 5.2, 5.4
Giedo Van Der Garde BV v Force India Formula
　One Team Ltd [2010] EWHC 2373
　(QB) . . . 8.13

Gilbert Ash (Northern) Ltd v Modern
　Engineering (Bristol) Ltd [1973] 3 All ER 195,
　HL . . . 8.21
Gilbert v Spoor [1982] 2 All ER 576, CA . . .
　32.15, 33.42
Giles v Walker (1890) 24 Qbd 656 . . . 24.5
Gill v Edouin (1895) 72 LT 579, CA . . . 24.10
Gillespie Bros & Co v Cheney, Eggar & Co
　[1896] 2 QB 59 . . . 7.2
Gillett v Holt [2000] 2 All ER 289 . . . 30.11
Gillett v Peppercorne (1840) 3 Beav 78 . . .
　14.15
Gillingham BC v Medway (Chatham) Dock Co
　Ltd [1993] QB 343 . . . 23.8
Ginty v Belmont Building Supplies Ltd [1959] 1
　All ER 414 . . . 20.7, 20.8
Gissing v Gissing [1971] AC 886 . . . 31.13, 31.14
GKN Distributors Ltd v Tyne Tees Fabrication
　Ltd (1985) 50 P & CR 403 . . . 29.35
Gladstone v Bower [1960] 2 Qb 384 . . . 37.47
Glaister v Appleby-in-Westmoreland Town
　Council [2009] EWCA Civ 1325, CA . . . 16.7
Glanville v Sutton & Co Ltd [1928] 1 KB
　571 . . . 25.6
Glasbrook Bros Ltd v Glamorgan County
　Council [1925] AC 270, HL . . . 6.14
Glasgow Corpn v Taylor [1922] 1 AC 44,
　HL . . . 21.13
Gloster v Chief Constable of Greater
　Manchester [2000] PIQR P114, CA . . . 25.6
Go West Ltd v Spigarolo [2003] EWCA
　Civ 17, . . . 36.29
Gold v Brighton Corpn [1956] 3 All ER 442,
　CA . . . 37.44
Goldberg v Edwards [1950] Ch 247, CA . . .
　32.37, 32.38
Golden Strait Corpn v Nippon Yusen Kubishika
　Kaisha [2007] UKHL 12, HL . . . 11.12
Goldman v Hargrave [1966] 2 All ER 989, PC . . .
　16.9, 17.14, 23.16, 24.16
Goldmile Properties Ltd v Lechouritis [2003]
　EWCA Civ 49 . . . 36.34
Gomberg v Smith [1962] 1 All ER 725,
　CA 25.3
Good Harvest Partnership LLP v Centaur
　Services Ltd [2010] EWHC 330 . . . 36.88
Good v Cheesman (1831) 2 B & Ad 328 . . .
　6.19
Gooden v Northamptonshire County Council
　[2002] 1 EGLR 137, CA . . . 16.24
Goodman v Gallant [1986] 1 All ER 311,
　CA . . . 31.10, 31.16
Goodwill v British Pregnancy Advisory Service
　[1996] 2 All ER 161, CA . . . 16.20
Gordon v Selico Co Ltd [1986] 1 EGLR 71,
　CA . . . 12.5
Gordon v Selico Ltd [1986] 1 EGLR 71,
　CA. . . . 14.47
Gorringe v Calderdale BC [2004] UKHL
　15 . . . 2.3

Gorringe v Calderdale MBC [2004] UKHL 15, HL . . . 16.22, 16.23, 20.3

Gorris v Scott (1874) LR 9 Exch 125 . . . 20.5

Gorse v Durham County Council [1971] 2 All ER 666 . . . 8.18

Gosling v Anderson (1972) 223 Estates Gazette 1743, CA . . . 12.24, 14.47

Gott v Measures [1947] 2 All ER 609, DC . . . 25.12

Gough v Thorne [1966] 3 All ER 398, CA . . . 17.5

Grad v Finanzamt Traustein (C-90/70) [1970] ECR 325, ECJ . . . 3.49

Grainger & Son v Gough [1896] AC 325, HL . . . 5.6

Gran Gelato Ltd v Richcliff (Group) Ltd [1992] 1 All ER 865 . . . 12.30, 16.21

Grant v Edwards [1986] 2 All ER 426, CA . . . 31.14

Grant v National Coal Board [1956] 1 All ER 682, HL . . . 20.5

Gratitudine, The (1801) 3 Ch Rob 240 . . . 14.11

Gray v Pullen (1864) 5 B & S 970 . . . 26.18

Graysim Holdings Ltd v P & O Property Holdings Ltd [1995] 4 All ER 831, HL . . . 37.26

Graystone Property Investments Ltd v Margulies (1983) 47 P & CR 472, CA . . . 28.23

Greasley v Cooke [1980] 3 All ER 710 . . . 30.13, 30.15, 30.17

Great Central Rly Co v Bates [1921] 3 KB 578 . . . 21.7

Great Northern Rly Co v Witham (1873) LR 9 CP 16 . . . 5.15

Greater Nottingham Co-operative Society Ltd v Cementation Piling & Foundations Ltd [1988] 2 All ER 971, CA . . . 16.16

Greatorex v Greatorex [2000] 4 All ER 769 . . . 16.28

Green v Ashco Horticulturist Ltd [1966] 1 WLR 889 . . . 32.35

Green v Chelsea Waterworks Co (1894) 70 LT 547, CA . . . 24.14

Greenhalgh v British Railways Board [1969] 2 All ER 114, CA . . . 21.10, 21.19

Greenock Corpn v Caledonian Rly Co [1917] AC 556, HL . . . 24.12

Greer v Downs Supply Co [1927] 2 KB 28, CA . . . 14.37

Gregg v Scott [2005] UKHL 2, HL . . . 18.5

Gregory v Ford [1951] 1 All ER 121 . . . 7.31

Gregory v Kelly [1978] RTR 426 . . . 19.7

Gregson v Cyril Lord Ltd [1962] 3 All ER 907, CA . . . 37.38

Grescot v Green (1700) 1 Salk 199 . . . 36.75

Grey v Pearson (1857) 6 HL Cas 61 . . . 3.12

Griffiths v Williams (1977) 248 Estates Gazette 947, CA . . . 30.15

Grigsby v Melville [1973] 3 All ER 455, CA . . . 28.7, 32.11

Groos, Re [1904] P 269 . . . 3.20

Gross v Lewis Hillman Ltd [1969] 3 All ER 1476, CA . . . 12.12

Groveside Properties Ltd v Westminster Medical School (1983) 47 P & CR 507, CA . . . 37.26, 37.27

GS Fashions Ltd v B & Q plc [1995] 4 All ER 899 . . . 36.63

Guardcliffe Properties Ltd v City and St James [2003] EWHC 215 (Ch) . . . 36.59

Guardian Assurance Co Ltd v Gants Hill Holdings Ltd [1983] 2 EGLR 36 . . . 36.37

Guppys (Bridport) Ltd v Brookling [1984] 1 EGLR 29, CA . . . 27.2

Gurton v Parrott [1991] 1 EGLR 98, CA . . . 37.27

Gwilliam v West Hertfordshire Hospital NHS Trust [2002] EWCA Civ 1041, CA . . . 21.16

H and N Emanuel Ltd v Greater London Council [1971] 2 All ER 835, CA . . . 24.15

H P Bulmer Ltd v J Bollinger SA [1974] 2 All ER 1226, CA . . . 2.20, 3.54

H Parsons (Livestock) Ltd v Uttley Ingham & Co Ltd [1978] 1 All ER 525, CA . . . 11.16

H West & Son Ltd v Shephard [1963] 2 All ER 625, HL . . . 27.4

Habib Bank Ltd v Habib Bank AG Zurich [1981] 2 All ER 650, CA . . . 30.11

Habib Bank Ltd v Tailor [1982] 3 All ER 561, CA . . . 34.26

Habton Farms v Nimmo [2004] QB 1 . . . 14.45

Haddon v Lynch [1911] VLR 230 . . . 23.6

Hadley v Baxendale (1854) 23 LJ Ex 179 . . . 11.15, 11.18, 11.22, 11.23

Hagee (London) Ltd v AB Erikson and Larson [1975] 3 All ER 234, CA . . . 37.29

Hair v Gillman (2000) 80 P & CR 108 . . . 32.11, 32.36

Halbot v Lens [1901] 1 Ch 344 . . . 14.45

Hale v Jennings Bros [1938] 1 All ER 579, CA . . . 24.6, 24.7, 24.9, 24.13

Haley v London Electricity Board [1964] 3 All ER 185, HL . . . 17.6

Halifax Building Society v Clark [1973] 2 All ER 33 . . . 34.26

Hall v Beckenham Corpn [1949] 1 All ER 423 . . . 23.14

Hall v Dorling (1997) 74 P & CR 400, CA . . . 28.24

Hall v Ewin (1887) 37 Ch D 74 . . . 33.13

Halsall v Brizell [1957] 1 All ER 371 . . . 33.10

Halsey v Esso Petroleum Co Ltd [1961] 2 All ER 145 . . . 23.3, 23.8, 23.26, 24.6, 24.9

Hamble Parish Council v Haggard [1992] 4 All ER 147 . . . 32.53

Hamlin v Edwin Evans [1996] 2 EGLR 106, CA . . . 27.23

Hammersmith and City Rly Co v Brand (1869) LR 4 HL 171, HL . . . 23.18

Hammersmith and Fulham London Borough
Council v Monk [1992] 1 AC 478, HL . . .
36.14, 36.95

Hammond v St Pancras Vestry (1874) LR 9 CP
316 . . . 23.18

Hamp v Bygrave [1983] 1 EGLR 174 . . . 28.11

Hancock v BW Brazier (Anerley) Ltd [1966] 2
All ER 901, CA . . . 7.31, 21.29

Hanning v Top Deck Travel Group Ltd (1993) 68
P & CR 14, CA . . . 32.43

Hanstown Properties Ltd v Green [1978] 1
EGLR 185, CA . . . 14.37

Harben Style Ltd v Rhodes trust [1995] 1 EGLR
118 . . . 36.57

Harborough District Council v Wheatcroft
[1996] JPL B128 . . . 39.66

Hardaker v Idle District Council [1896] 1 QB
335, CA . . . 26.21

Hardy v Central London Rly Co [1920] 3 KB
459, CA . . . 21.7

Harmer v Cornelius (1858) 5 CB (NS) 236 . . .
7.31

Harmsworth Pension Fund Trustees Ltd v
Charringtons Industrial Holdings Ltd [1985]
1 EGLR 97 . . . 36.58

Harold Wood Brick Co Ltd v Ferris [1935] 2 KB
198, CA . . . 8.31

Harper v GN Haden & Sons Ltd [1933] Ch 298,
CA . . . 23.24

Harris v Birkenhead Corpn [1976] 1 All ER 341,
CA . . . 21.4

Harris v Evans [1998] 3 All ER 522, CA . . .
16.23

Harris v Flower (1904) 74 LJ Ch 127, CA . . .
32.53

Harris v Goddard [1983] 1 WLR 1203 . . .
31.21

Harris v James (1876) 45 LJQB 545 . . . 23.17

Harris v Jones [1832] 1 Moo & R 173 . . . 36.51

Harris v Nickerson (1873) LR 8 QB 286 . . . 5.7

Harrison v British Railways Board [1981] 3 All
ER 679 . . . 18.11, 19.7, 26.10

Harrison v Vincent [1982] RTR 8, CA . . . 21.17

Harrods Ltd v Lemon [1931] 2 KB 157,
CA . . . 14.15

Hart v Emelkirk [1983] 1 WLR 1289 . . . 36.67

Hart v Windsor (1843) 12 M & W 68 . . . 7.31,
36.44

Hartas v Ribbons (1889) 22 Qbd 254, CA . . .
14.7

Hartley v Birmingham City District Council
[1992] 2 All ER 213, CA . . . 27.24

Hartley v Mayoh & Co [1954] 1 All ER 375,
CA . . . 20.4

Hartley v Ponsonby (1857) 7 E & B 872 . . . 6.15

Harvela Investments Ltd v Royal Trust Co of
Canada (CI) Ltd [1985] 2 All ER 966,
HL . . . 5.8

Harvey v Facey [1893] AC 552, PC . . . 5.3

Harvey v Pratt [1965] 1 WLR 1025 . . . 36.3

Harvey v RG O'Dell Ltd [1958] 2 QB 78 . . .
26.10

Harvey v Stagg (1977) 247 Estates Gazette 463,
CA . . . 36.14

Haseldine v C A Daw & Son Ltd [1941] 3 All ER
156, CA . . . 13.16, 17.8, 21.16

Havenridge Ltd v Boston Dyers Ltd [1994] 49
EG 111, CA . . . 36.60

Hawley v Luminar Leisure Ltd [2006] EWCA
Civ 18, CA . . . 26.7

Haycocks v Neville [2007] EWCA Civ 78 . . .
28.27

Hayes v James & Charles Dodd (a firm) [1990] 2
All ER 815, CA . . . 11.6

Haynes v Harwood [1935] 1 KB 146, CA . . .
18.8, 18.11, 19.3

Head v Tattersall (1871) LR 7 Exch 7 . . . 5.37

Heap v Ind Coope and Allsopp Ltd [1940] 3 All
ER 634, CA . . . 23.17

Heasmans v Clarity Cleaning Co [1987] ICR
949, CA . . . 26.14

Heath v Brighton Corpn (1908) 98 LT 718 . . .
23.6

Heath v Keys [1984] CLY 3568 . . . 27.12

Hector v Lyons (1988) 58 P & CR 156, CA . . .
14.42

Hedley Byrne & Co Ltd v Heller & Partners Ltd
[1963] 2 All ER 575, HL . . . 3.34, 12.32, 12.33,
12.34, 14.46, 16.18, 16.20, 16.21

Heil v Rankin [2000] 3 All ER 138, CA . . . 27.3

Heilbut, Symons & Co v Buckleton [1913] AC
30, HL . . . 7.6, 7.16, 7.21

Helby v Matthews [1895] AC 471, HL . . . 29.7

Hely-Hutchinson v Brayhead Ltd [1967] 2 All
ER 14 . . . 14.29

Hemmens v Wilson Browne [1993] 4 All ER
826 . . . 16.21

Hemmings v Stoke Poges Golf Club [1920] 1 KB
720, CA . . . 22.10

Henderson v Merrett Syndicates Ltd [1994] 3 All
ER 506, HL . . . 15.4, 16.16, 16.19

Hennessy v Craigmyle & Co Ltd [1986] ICR 461,
CA . . . 12.59

Henry Kendall & Sons v William Lillico & Sons
Ltd [1969] 2 AC 31, HL . . . 7.11

Henry Smith & Son v Muskett [1979] 1 EGLR
13 . . . 14.15

Henthorn v Fraser [1892] 2 Ch 27, CA . . . 5.21

Herbert v Doyle [2008] EWHC 1950 . . . 29.9

Herne Bay Steam Boat Co v Hutton [1903] 2 KB
683, CA . . . 10.10

Heslop v Burns [1974] 3 All ER 406 . . . 36.15

Hewett v Alf Brown's Transport [1992] ICR 530,
CA . . . 16.5

Hey v Moorhouse (1839) 6 Bing NC 52 . . .
22.4

Heyman v Darwins Ltd [1942] 1 All ER 337 . . .
8.9, 8.15, 10.15

Heywood v Wellers [1976] 1 All ER 300,
CA . . . 11.6

Heyworth v Hutchinson (1867) LR 2 QB 447 . . . 8.21

Hickman v Maisey [1900] 1 QB 752, CA . . . 22.3

Hicks v Chief Constable of the South Yorkshire Police [1992] 2 All ER 65, HL . . . 27.5

HIH Casualty and General Insurance Ltd v Chase Manhattan Bank [2003] UKHL 6, HL . . . 12.49

Hill v C A Parsons & Co Ltd [1971] 3 All ER 1345, CA . . . 11.49

Hill v Chief Constable of West Yorkshire [1988] 2 All ER 238, HL . . . 16.10, 16.23

Hill v Lovett 1992 SLT 994 . . . 25.1

Hill v Tupper (1863) 2 H & C 121 . . . 22.4, 32.5

Hillas & Co Ltd v Arcos Ltd (1932) 147 LT 503, HL . . . 5.31

Hillas-Drake, Re; National Provincial Bank v Liddell [1944] 1 All ER 375 . . . 3.40

Hillil Property and Investment Co Ltd v Naraine Pharmacy Ltd (1979) 39 P & CR 67, CA . . . 37.27

Hillingdon Estates Co v Stonefield Estates Ltd [1952] 1 All ER 853 . . . 10.11

Hillman v Rogers [1997] NPC 183, CA . . . 32.39

Hills (Patents) Ltd v University College Hospital Board of Governors [1955] 3 All ER 365 . . . 37.27

Hilton v James Smith & Sons (Norwood) Ltd [1979] 2 EGLR 44, CA . . . 36.34

Hindcastle Ltd v Barbara Attenborough Associates Ltd [1996] 1 All ER 737, HL . . . 36.99

Hippisley v Knee Bros [1905] 1 KB 1, DC . . . 14.15

Hirachand Punamchand v Temple [1911] 2 KB 330, CA . . . 6.19

Hirji Mulji v Cheong Yue Steamship Co Ltd [1926] AC 497, PC . . . 10.15

Hivac Ltd v Park Royal Scientific Instruments Ltd [1946] 1 All ER 350, CA . . . 7.31

HKRUK II (CHC) Ltd v Heaney [2010] EWHC 2245 (Ch) . . . 32.56

Hoare & Co v McAlpine [1923] 1 Ch 167 . . . 23.3, 24.6, 24.11

Hodgson v Marks [1971] Ch 892 . . . 35.26, 35.28

Hodgson v Trapp [1988] 3 All ER 870, HL . . . 27.8

Holbeck Hall Hotel Ltd v Scarborough Borough Council [2000] 2 All ER 705, CA . . . 23.16, 32.57

Holden v Chief Constable of Lancashire [1986] 3 All ER 836, CA . . . 27.2

Holden v White [1982] 2 All ER 328, CA . . . 21.10, 21.19

Holgate v Lancashire Mental Hospitals Board [1937] 4 All ER 19 . . . 16.11

Holland v Hodgson (1872) LR 7 CP 328 . . . 28.10

Hollebone v Midhurst and Fernhurst Builders [1968] 1 Lloyd's Rep 38 . . . 27.12

Holliday v National Telephone Co [1899] 2 QB 392, CA . . . 23.25, 26.24

Hollier v Rambler Motors (AMC) Ltd [1972] 1 All ER 399, CA . . . 7.11, 9.6

Holling v Yorkshire Traction Co [1948] 2 All ER 662 . . . 23.25

Hollywood Silver Fox Farm Ltd v Emmett [1936] 1 All ER 825 . . . 15.10, 23.12

Holman v Howes [2007] EWCA Civ 877 . . . 31.16

Holmes v Wilson (1839) 10 Ad & El 503 . . . 22.7

Holwell Securities Ltd v Hughes [1974] 1 All ER 161, CA . . . 5.21

Home Brewery Ltd v William Davis & Co (Leicester) Ltd [1987] 1 All ER 637 . . . 23.3

Home Office v Dorset Yacht Co Ltd [1970] 2 All ER 294, HL . . . 16.6, 16.11

Homepace Ltd v Sita South East Ltd [2008] EWCA Civ 1 . . . 36.59

Homes v Smith [2000] Lloyd's Rep Bank 139, CA . . . 8.3

Honeywill and Stein Ltd v Larkin Bros Ltd [1934] 1 KB 191, CA . . . 26.22

Hong Kong Fir Shipping Co Ltd v Kawasaki Kisen Kaisha Ltd [1962] 1 All ER 474, CA . . . 8.22, 8.24, 8.25

Hood v National Farmers Union [1994] 1 EGLR 1, CA . . . 16.19

Hooper v Treffry (1847) 1 Exch 17. . . . 14.19

Hopgood v Brown [1955] 1 All ER 550, CA . . . 28.27

Hopkin's Lease, Re; Caerphilly Concrete Products Ltd v Owen [1972] 1 All ER 248 CA . . . 36.7

Horrocks v Forray [1976] 1 All ER 737, CA . . . 28.42

Horsey Estate Ltd v Steiger [1899] 2 Qb 79, CA . . . 36.65

Horsham Properties Group Ltd v Clark [2008] EWHC 2327 . . . 34.18, 34.25, 34.28

Hosebay Ltd v Day [2010] EWCA Civ 748 . . . 37.14

Hotson v East Berkshire Health Authority [1987] 2 All ER 909, HL . . . 18.5

Houghton v Trafalgar Insurance Co [1953] 2 All ER 1409, CA . . . 9.5

Hounslow London Borough Council v Pilling (1993) 25 HLR 305, CA . . . 36.95

Hounslow London Borough Council v Twickenham Garden Developments Ltd [1970] 3 All ER 326 . . . 28.42, 28.43

Hounslow London Borough v Minchinton (1997) 74 P & CR 221, CA . . . 30.24, 30.25

House Property and Investment Co, Re [1953] 2 All ER 1525 . . . 3.45

Howard de Walden Estates Ltd v Aggio [2008] UKHL 44 . . . 37.15

Howard Houlder & Partners Ltd v Manx Isles Steamship Co Ltd [1923] 1 KB 110 . . . 14.17

Howard Marine and Dredging Co Ltd v A Ogden & Sons (Excavations) Ltd [1978] 2 All ER 1134 . . . 7.15

Howard Marine and Dredging Co Ltd v A Ogden & Sons (Excavations) Ltd. [1978] 2 All ER 1134, CA . . . 12.24

Howard v Patent Ivory Manufacturing Co (1888) 38 Ch D 156 . . . 14.8

Howes v Bishop [1909] 2 KB 390, CA . . . 12.63

Howitt v Alfred Bagnall & Sons Ltd [1967] 2 Lloyd's Rep 370 . . . 21.14

Hubbard v Pitt [1975] 3 All ER 1, CA . . . 23.4

Huddersfield Police Authority v Watson [1947] 2 All ER 193, DC . . . 3.39

Hudson v Cripps [1896] 1 Ch 265 . . . 36.34

Hughes v Hughes (1971) 221 Estates Gazette 145, CA . . . 14.10

Hughes v Lord Advocate [1963] 1 All ER 705, HL . . . 18.17, 20.5

Hughes v Metropolitan Rly Co (1877) 2 App Cas 439, HL . . . 6.22, 6.23

Hughes v National Union of Mineworkers [1991] 4 All ER 278 . . . 16.11

Humble v Hunter (1848) 12 Qb 310 . . . 14.37

Humphreys v Dreamland (Margate) Ltd (1930) 144 LT 529, HL . . . 21.4

Hunt v Luck [1901] 1 Ch 45 . . . 35.6, 35.23

Hunt v Severs [1994] 2 All ER 385, HL . . . 27.7

Hunt v Silk (1804) 5 East 449 . . . 8.13

Hunt v Wallis [1994] PIQR P128 . . . 25.6

Hunter v Babbage (1994) 69 P & CR 548 . . . 31.20

Hunter v Canary Wharf Ltd [1997] 2 All ER 426, HL . . . 23.3, 23.4, 23.13, 23.20, 32.10

Hunter v Chief Constable of West Midlands [1981] 3 All ER 727, HL . . . 16.26

Hunter v Parker (1840) 7 M & W 322 . . . 14.10

Hurst v Bryk [2000] 2 All ER 193, HL . . . 8.11

Hurst v Picture Theatres Ltd [1915] 1 KB 1, CA . . . 28.43

Hurstfell Ltd v Leicester Square Property Co Ltd [1988] 2 EGLR 105, CA . . . 37.36

Hussain v Lancaster City Council [1999] 4 All ER 125, CA . . . 23.17

Hussain v New Taplow Paper Mills Ltd [1988] 1 All ER 541, HL . . . 27.9

Hussein v Mehlman [1992] 2 EGLR 87 . . . 36.98

Hutton v Warren (1836) 1 M & W 466 . . . 7.23

Hyde v Wrench (1840) 3 Beav 334 . . . 5.9, 5.11

Hyett v Great Western Rly Co [1947] 2 All ER 264, CA . . . 18.11

Hypo-Mortgage Services Ltd v Robinson [1997] 2 FLR 71 . . . 35.25

Hyundai Heavy Industries Co Ltd v Papodopolous [1980] 2 All ER 29, HL . . . 8.14

I v DPP [2001] UKHL 10, HL . . . 3.21

IDC Group Ltd v Clark (1992) 65 P & CR 179, CA . . . 32.25

Ilkiw v Samuels [1963] 2 All ER 879, CA . . . 26.9

Ilott v Wilkes (1820) 3 B & Ald 304 . . . 21.18

Imageview Management Ltd v Jack [2009] EWCA Civ 63 . . . 14.15

Imperial Chemical Industries Ltd v Shatwell [1964] 2 All ER 999, HL . . . 20.8

Inche Noriah v Shaik Allie Bin Omar [1929] AC 127, PC . . . 12.63

Inclusive Technology Ltd v Williamson [2009] EWCA Civ 718 . . . 37.40

Inco Europe Ltd v First Choice Distribution [2000] 2 All ER 109, HL . . . 3.15

Industries and General Mortgage Co Ltd v Lewis [1949] 2 All ER 573 . . . 14.15

Infiniteland Ltd v Artisan Contracting Ltd [2005] EWCA Civ 758, CA . . . 5.31

Inglewood Investment Co Ltd v Baker [2003] 1 P & CR 23 . . . 30.26

Inntrepreneur Pub Co (Co Ltd) v East Crown Ltd [2000] 2 Lloyd's Rep 611 . . . 7.7

Interfoto Picture Library Ltd v Stiletto Ltd [1988] 1 All ER 348, CA . . . 7.13

International Drilling Fluids Ltd v Louisville Investments (Uxbridge) Ltd [1986] 1 All ER 321, CA . . . 36.30

International Tea Stores Co v Hobbs [1903] 2 Ch 165 . . . 32.36

Inverugie Investments Ltd v Hackett [1995] 3 All ER 841, PC . . . 22.7

Inwards v Baker [1965] 1 All ER 446, CA . . . 28.44, 30.13, 30.15, 30.16

Iqbal v Thakrar [[2004] 3 EGLR 21, CA . . . 36.53

IRC v Hoogstraten [1984] 3 All ER 25, CA . . . 16.27

Iron Trades Employers Insurance Association v Union of House and Land Investors Ltd [1937] 1 All ER 481 . . . 34.39

Irvine v Union Bank of Australia (1877) 2 App Cas 366, PC . . . 14.6

Irving v Post Office [1987] IRLR 289, CA . . . 26.14

J Evans & Son (Portsmouth) Ltd v Andrea Merzario Ltd [1976] 2 All ER 930, CA . . . 7.5, 7.16, 7.17

J F Perrott & Co Ltd v Cohen [1951] 1 KB 705 . . . 30.36

J Lauritzen AS v Wijsmuller BV ("The Super Servant Two") [1990] 1 Lloyd's Rep 1, CA . . . 10.14

J Lyons & Co Ltd v Knowles [1943] 1 All ER 477 . . . 36.75

J Pereira Fernandes SA v Mehta [2006] EWHC 813 (Ch) . . . 4.9

J Sainsbury plc v London Borough of Enfield [1989] 2 All ER 817 . . . 33.25, 33.27

J Spurling Ltd v Bradshaw [1956] 2 All ER 121, CA . . . 7.11

JA Pye (Oxford) Ltd v Graham [2002] UKHL 30 . . . 30.23–30.26

J.A. Pye (Oxford) Ltd v The United Kingdom (Application no. 44302/02), ECHR (Grand Chamber) . . . 30.20

Jackson v Horizon Holidays Ltd [1975] 3 All ER 92, CA . . . 13.12

Jackson v Royal Bank of Scotland Ltd [2003] UKHL 3, HL . . . 11.16

Jacobs v Batavia and General Plantations Trust Ltd [1924] 1 Ch 287 . . . 7.1

Jacobs v Morton and Partners (1994) 72 BLR 92 . . . 21.28, 21.29

Jaggard v Sawyer [1995] 2 All ER 189, CA . . . 27.18, 33.30

James McNaughton Papers Group Ltd v Hicks Anderson & Co [1991] 1 All ER 134 . . . 16.19, 16.21

James v Evans [2000] 3 EGLR 1, CA . . . 29.9, 30.12

Janmohamed v Hassam (1976) 241 Estates Gazette 609 . . . 5.34

Jarvis v Swans Tours Ltd [1973] 1 All ER 71, CA . . . 11.6

Jaundrill v Gillett (1996) Times, 30 January, CA . . . 25.6

Javad v Aqil [1990] EWCA Civ 1 . . . 37.26

Javad v Aqil [1991] 1 All ER 243, CA . . . 36.14, 36.15

Jayes v IMI (Kynoch) Ltd [1985] ICR 155, CA . . . 19.9

Jeancharm Ltd v Barnet Football Club Ltd [2003] EWCA Civ 58, CA . . . 11.34

JEB Fasteners Ltd v Marks, Bloom & Co Ltd [1983] 1 All ER 583 . . . 12.34

Jebson v Ministry of Defence [2000] 1 WLR 2055, CA . . . 16.9

Jelbert v Davis [1968] 1 All ER 1182, CA . . . 32.53

Jelson Ltd v Derby City Council [1999] 3 EGLR 91 . . . 29.2, 29.4

Jennings v Rice [2003] 1 P & CR 8 . . . 30.15

Jervis v Harris [1996] 1 ALL ER 303 . . . 36.67

Jeune v Queens Cross Properties Ltd [1974] Ch 97 . . . 33.30, 36.67

Jobling v Associated Dairies Ltd [1981] 2 All ER 752, HL . . . 18.6

Jobson v Johnson [1989] 1 All ER 621, CA . . . 11.30

Jobson v Record (1997) 75 P & CR 375, CA . . . 32.4

Joel v Law Union and Crown Insurance Co [1908] 2 KB 863, CA . . . 12.54

John McCann & Co v Pow [1975] 1 All ER 129, CA . . . 14.47

John Summers & Sons Ltd v Frost [1955] 1 All ER 870, HL . . . 20.6

John Young & Co v Bankier Distillery Co [1893] AC 691, HL . . . 28.20

Johnson v Agnew [1979] 1 All ER 883 . . . 11.12

Johnson v BJW Property Developments Ltd [2002] EWHC 1131 (TCC) . . . 24.8, 24.15, 24.16

Johnson v Unisys Ltd [2001] UKHL 13 . . . 11.1, 11.11

Joint London Holdings Ltd v Mount Cook Land Ltd [2005] EWCA Civ 1171 . . . 36.37

Jolley v Sutton London Borough Council [2000] 3 All ER 409, HL . . . 18.17

Jollybird Ltd v Fairzone Ltd [1990] 1 EGLR 253 . . . 36.60

Jones v Boyce (1816) 1 Stark 493 . . . 18.12

Jones v Chapman (1847) 2 Exch 803 . . . 22.4

Jones v Chappell (1875) LR 20 Eq 539 . . . 23.13

Jones v Department of Employment [1988] 1 All ER 725, CA . . . 16.23

Jones v Festinig Rly Co (1868) LR 3 Qb 733 . . . 24.17

Jones v Festiniog Rly Co (1868) LR 3 Qb 733 . . . 24.6

Jones v Gooday (1841) 8 M & W 146 . . . 27.12

Jones v Jenkins [1986] 1 EGLR 113, CA . . . 37.38

Jones v Kernott [2009] EWHC 1713 (Ch) . . . 31.16

Jones v Lavington [1903] 1 KB 253, CA . . . 36.34

Jones v Lee [1980] ICR 310, CA . . . 11.50

Jones v Lipman [1962] 1 WLR 832 . . . 35.37

Jones v Livox Quarries Ltd [1952] 2 Qb 608, CA . . . 19.8

Jones v Llanrwst UDC [1911] 1 Ch 393 . . . 22.4, 23.13

Jones v Morgan [2001] EWCA Civ 995 . . . 34.10, 34.11

Jones v Price [1965] 2 All ER 625, CA . . . 32.12

Jones v Price and Morgan (1992) 64 P & CR 404, CA . . . 32.51

Jones v Pritchard [1908] 1 Ch 30 . . . 23.19, 32.12, 32.30

Jones v Rhys-Jones (1974) 30 P & CR 451, CA . . . 33.38

Jones v Sherwood Computer Services plc [1992] 2 All ER 170, CA . . . 36.59

Jones v Stones [1999] 1 WLR 1739, CA . . . 22.5

Jones v Williams (1843) 11 M & W 176 . . . 23.22

Joseph Constantine Steamship Line Ltd v Imperial Smelting Corpn Ltd [1941] 2 All ER 165, HL . . . 10.14

Joseph Travers & Sons Ltd v Cooper [1915] 1 KB 73, CA . . . 9.6

Joyce v Rigolli [2004] EWCA Civ 79 . . . 28.27

K v Secretary of State for the Home Dept [2002] EWCA Civ 983, CA . . . 16.11

K, Re; F, Re [1988] 1 All ER 358 . . . 14.25

K/S Victoria Street v House of Fraser (Stores Management) Ltd [2010] EWHC 3006 (Ch) . . . 36.88

Kalsep Ltd v X-Flow BV [2001] All ER (D) 113 (Mar) . . . 12.67

Kane v New Forest DC [2001] 3 All ER 914, CA . . . 16.24

Keighley, Maxsted & Co v Durant [1901] AC 240, HL . . . 14.8

Kelner v Baxter (1866) LR 2 CP 174 . . . 14.8

Kelsen v Imperial Tobacco Co (of Great Britain and Ireland) Ltd [1957] 2 All ER 343 . . . 22.2

Kemble v Farren (1829) 6 Bing 141 . . . 11.34

Kennaway v Thompson [1980] 3 All 329,
CA . . . 23.10

Kennedy v Broun (1863) 13 CBNS 677 . . . 6.10

Kenney v Hall, Pain and Foster [1976] 2 EGLR
29 . . . 17.9

Kenny v Electricity Supply Board [1932] IR
73 . . . 21.6

Kent v Griffiths [2000] 2 All ER 474, CA . . .
16.23

Keown v Coventry Healthcare NHS Trust
[2006] EWCA Civ 39 . . . 21.20

Keppel Bus Co Ltd v Sa'ad bin Ahmad [1974] 2
All ER 700, PC . . . 26.14

Keppel v Wheeler [1927] 1 KB 577, CA . . . 14.15,
14.18

Kernott v Jones [2010] EWCA Civ 578 . . . 31.11

KH Enterprise (Cargo Owners) v Pioneer
Container (Owners) ("The Pioneer
Container") [1994] 2 All ER 250, PC . . . 13.14

Khan v Secretary of State for Environment
[1997] JPL B126 . . . 39.29

Kiddle v City Business Properties Ltd [1942] 2
All ER 216 . . . 24.10

Kilgour v Gaddes [1904] 1 KB 457,
CA . . . 32.42

King v David Allen & Sons Billposting Ltd
[1916] 2 AC 54 . . . 28.44

King v Liverpool City Council [1986] 3 All ER
544, CA . . . 16.10

King v South Northamptonshire District
Council [1992] 1 EGLR 53, CA . . . 7.31, 32.12,
36.46

King, Re; Robinson v Gray [1963] 1 All ER 781,
CA . . . 36.76

Kirby v Leather [1965] 2 All ER 441, CA . . . 27.24

Kirby v School Board of Harrogate [1896] 1 Ch
436 . . . 33.37

Kirkham v Boughey [1957] 3 All ER 153 . . .
16.12

Kirkham v Chief Constable of the Greater
Manchester Police [1990] 3 All ER 246,
CA . . . 16.9

Kleinwort Benson Ltd v Lincoln City Council
(1999) 2 AC 349 . . . 12.10

Kleinwort Benson Ltd v Malaysia Mining Corpn
Bhd [1989] 1 All ER 785, CA . . . 4.1

Knight v Home Office [1990] 3 All ER 237 . . . 16.9

Knightley v Johns [1982] 1 All ER 851, CA . . .
18.8, 18.9

Knightsbridge Estates Trust Ltd v Byrne [1938]
4 All ER 618, CA . . . 34.12

Knott v Secretary of State for the Environment
[1997] JPL 713 . . . 39.31

Knox v Gye (1872) LR 5 HL 656 . . . 11.55

Kofi Sunkersette Obu v Strauss & Co Ltd [1951]
AC 243, PC . . . 14.17

Kooragang Investment Pty Ltd v Richardson
and Wrench Ltd [1981] 3 All ER 65, PC . . .
26.12

Koufos v C Czarnikow Ltd ("The Heron II")
[1967] 3 All ER 686, HL . . . 11.15, 11.17, 11.20

Kreglinger v New Patagonia Meat and Cold
Storage Co Ltd [1914] AC 25, HL . . . 34.13

Krell v Henry [1903] 2 KB 740, CA . . . 10.9,
10.18

L v Reading Borough Council [2001] EWCA Civ
346 . . . 16.24

L'Estrange v F Graucob Ltd [1934] 2 KB 394,
DC . . . 7.8

L'Office Cherifien des Phosphates Unitramp SA
v Yamashita-Shinnihon Steamship Co Ltd
[1994] 1 All ER 20, HL . . . 3.19

Lace v Chantler [1944] 1 All ER 305, CA . . .
36.4

Ladies' Hosiery and Underwear Ltd v Parker
[1930] 1 Ch 304 . . . 36.14

Laemthong International Lines Co Ltd v Artis
("The Laemthong Glory") (No 2) [1005]
EWCA Civ 519, CA . . . 13.3

Lagan Navigation Co v Lambeg Bleaching Co
[1927] AC 226, HL . . . 23.22

Lagden v O'Connor [2003] UKHL 64, HL . . .
18.19

Lambert v Barratt Homes Ltd [2010] EWCA Civ
681, CA . . . 23.16

Lambert v Lewis [1980] 1 All ER 978, CA . . .
16.20

Lambeth LBC v Kay [2006] UKHL 10 . . . 3.31

Lambourn v McLellan [1903] 2 Ch 268,
CA . . . 28.13

Lambton v Mellish [1894] 3 Ch 163 . . . 23.19

Lampleigh v Brathwait (1615) Hob 105 . . . 6.10

Lancaster v Bird [1998] 73 Con LR 22,
CA . . . 7.23

Land Securities v Westminster City Council
(No 2) [1995] 1 EGLR 245 . . . 36.52

Lane v Holloway [1967] 3 All ER 129, CA . . .
19.2

Langbrook Properties Ltd v Surrey County
Council [1969] 3 All ER 1424 . . . 28.20

Larner v British Steel plc [1993] 4 All ER 102,
CA . . . 20.6

Laskar v Laskar [2008] EWCA Civ 347 . . . 31.11,
31.13

Lauritzencool AB v Lady Navigation Inc [2005]
EWCA Civ 579 . . . 11.48

Law v Redditch Local Board [1892] 1 QB
127 . . . 11.32

Lawntown Ltd v Camenzuli [2007] EWCA Civ
949 . . . 33.44

Laws v Florinplace Ltd [1981] 1 All ER
659 . . . 23.4

Lay v Drexler [2007] EWCA Civ 464 . . . 37.33

LCC v Agricultural Food Products Ltd [1955] 2
All ER 229, CA . . . 14.1

LCC v Allen [1914] 3 KB 642, CA . . . 33.13

LCC v Cattermoles (Garages) Ltd [1953] 2 All
ER 582, CA . . . 26.12

Le Foe v Le Foe [2001] 2 FLR 970 . . . 31.13

Leach v R [1912] AC 305, HL . . . 3.19

Leaf v International Galleries [1950] 1 All ER 693, CA . . . 12.19

League Against Cruel Sports Ltd v Scott [1985] 2 All ER 489 . . . 22.1, 25.1

Leakey v National Trust for Places of Historic Interest or Natural Beauty [1980] 1 All ER 17, CA . . . 23.16

Lease Management Services Ltd v Purnell Secretarial Services Ltd (1994) 13 Tr LR 337 . . . 9.15

Lee-Parker v Izzet (No 2) [1972] 2 All ER 800 . . . 5.36

Lee v Leeds City Council [2002] 1 WLR 1488, CA . . . 36.46, 36.49

Lee-Verhulst (Investments) Ltd v Harwood Trust [1972] 3 All ER 619, CA . . . 37.26

Leeds City Council v Hall; Birmingham City Council v Frisby [2011] UKSC 8 . . . 37.20, 37.21, 37.22

Leeman v Montagu [1936] 2 All ER 1677 . . . 25.2

Leigh & Sillivan Ltd v Aliakmon Shipping Co Ltd [1986] 2 All ER 145, HL . . . 16.14

Leigh and Sillivan Ltd v Aliakmon Shipping Co Ltd ("The Aliakmon") [1986] 2 All ER 145, HL . . . 13.16

Leigh v Jack (1879) 5 Ex D 264, CA . . . 30.24, 30.25

Leigh v Taylor [1902] AC 157, HL . . . 28.11

Lemmon v Webb [1894] 3 Ch 1, CA . . . 22.3, 23.3, 23.22

Lennon v Commissioner of Police of the Metropolis [2004] EWCA Civ 130, CA . . . 16.20

Les Affréteurs Réunis SA v Leopold Walford (London) Ltd [1919] AC 801, HL . . . 7.24

Level Properties Ltd v Ball Brothers Ltd [2007] EWHC 744 . . . 36.59

Levet v Gas Light and Coke Co Ltd [1919] 1 Ch 24 . . . 32.54

Lewis v Frank Love Ltd [1961] 1 All ER 446 . . . 34.10

Lewis v Weldcrest [1978] 3 All ER 1226, CA . . . 37.27

Lexgorge Ltd v Howard de Walden Estates Ltd [2010] EWCA Civ 748 . . . 37.14

Liesbosch Dredger v SS Edison [1933] AC 449, HL . . . 18.19, 27.12

Lilley v Doubleday (1881) 7 Qbd 510 . . . 14.13

Lim Poh Choo v Camden and Islington Area Health Authority [1979] 2 All ER 910, HL . . . 27.7

Lim Teng Huan v Ang Swee Chuan [1992] 1 WLR 113 . . . 30.11, 30.15, 30.16

Limpus v London General Omnibus Co (1862) 1 H & C 526 . . . 26.12

Linden Gardens Trust Ltd v Lenesta Sludge Disposals Ltd [1993] 3 All ER 417, HL . . . 11.2

Linden v Department of Health and Social Security [1986] 1 All ER 691 . . . 37.26

Link Lending Ltd v Bustard [2010] EWCA 424 . . . 35.25

Lippiatt v South Gloucestershire Council [1999] 4 All ER 149, CA . . . 23.16

Lips v Older [2004] EWHC 1686, QB . . . 21.12

Lister v Hesley Hall Ltd [2001] UKHL 22, HL . . . 26.8, 26.14

Lister v Romford Ice and Cold Storage Co Ltd [1957] AC 555, HL . . . 7.30, 26.15

Litster v Forth Dry Dock and Engineering Co Ltd [1989] 1 All ER 1134, HL . . . 3.54

Littledale v Liverpool College [1900] 1 Ch 19, CA . . . 30.26

Liverpool City Council v Irwin [1976] 2 All ER 39, HL . . . 7.29–7.32, 32.12, 36.46

Liverpool Corpn v H Coghill & Son [1918] 1 Ch 307 . . . 32.45

Lloyd v Butler [1990] 2 EGLR 155 . . . 17.9

Lloyd v Grace, Smith & Co [1912] AC 716, HL . . . 14.32, 26.11, 26.14

Lloyd v Stanbury [1971] 2 All ER 267 . . . 11.8

Lloyd's v Harper (1880) 16 Ch D 290, CA . . . 11.2

Lloyds Bank plc v Rosset [1991] 1 AC 107, HL . . . 30.10, 30.17, 31.13, 31.14, 35.25

Lock v Bell [1931] 1 Ch 35 . . . 8.31

Logicrose v Southend United Football Club [1988] 1 WLR 1256 . . . 14.15

London & Northern Bank, ex p Jones, Re [1900] 1 Ch 220 . . . 5.21

London & Suburban Land & Building Co (Holdings) Ltd v Carey (1991) 62 P & CR 480 . . . 32.53

London and Blenheim Estates Ltd v Ladbroke Retail Parks Ltd [1993] 4 All ER 157, CA . . . 32.4, 32.11

London and County (A & D) Ltd v Wilfred Sportsman Ltd [1970] 2 All ER 600, CA . . . 36.76

London and Leeds Estates Ltd v Paribas Ltd [1993] 2 EGLR 149, CA . . . 36.58

London and Manchester Assurance Co Ltd v O & H Construction Ltd [1989] 2 EGLR 185 . . . 22.8

London and South Western Rly Co v Gomm (1882) 20 Ch D 562 . . . 32.15

London Borough of Croydon v Gladden [1994] JPL 723 . . . 39.66

London Borough of Enfield v Secretary of State for Environment [1975] JPL 155 . . . 38.28

London Borough of Lewisham v Malcolm [2008] UKHL 43 . . . 37.18

London Borough of Tower Hamlets v Barrett [2005] EWCA Civ 923 . . . 30.36

London Corpn v Riggs (1880) 13 Ch D 798 . . . 32.29, 32.53

London Tara Hotel Ltd v Kensington Close Hotel Ltd [2010] EWHC 2749 . . . 32.46, 32.48

Long v Gowlett [1923] 2 Ch 177 . . . 32.35

Long v Lloyd [1958] 2 All ER 402, CA . . . 12.19

Long v London Borough of Tower Hamlets [1996] 2 All ER 683 . . . 29.12, 36.2, 36.19

Longrigg, Burrough and Trounson v Smith (1979) 251 Estates Gazette 847, CA . . . 36.14

Longstaff v Birtles [2001] EWCA Civ 1219, CA . . . 12.68

Lonrho Ltd v Shell Petroleum Co Ltd (No 2) [1981] 2 All ER 456 . . . 20.2

Looe Fuels Ltd v Looe Harbour [2008] EWCA Civ 414 . . . 29.2

Lord Advocate v Dumbarton District Council [1990] 1 All ER 1, HL . . . 3.19

Lord Waring v London and Manchester Assurance Co Ltd [1935] Ch 310 . . . 34.30

Lotus Ltd v British Soda Co Ltd [1971] 1 All ER 265 . . . 32.57

Love v Port of London Authority [1959] 2 Lloyd's Rep 541 . . . 18.19

Lovelock v Franklyn (1846) 8 QB 371 . . . 8.26

Lovely and Orchard Services Ltd v Daejan Investment (Grove Hall) Ltd [1978] 1 EGLR 44 . . . 37.45

Lowery v Walker [1911] AC 10, HL . . . 21.7

Lucas v Beale (1851) 10 CB 739 . . . 14.43

Lumley v Wagner (1852) 1 De GM & G 604 . . . 11.48

Lurcott v Wakely and Wheeler [1911] 1 KB 905, CA . . . 36.49

Lusty v Finsbury Securities Ltd (1991) 58 BLR 66, CA . . . 11.41, 11.42

Luxor (Eastbourne) Ltd v Cooper [1941] 1 All ER 33, HL . . . 4.2, 5.27, 14.18, 14.47

Lyell v Kennedy (1889) 14 App Cas 437, HL . . . 14.10

Lynch v Thorne [1956] 1 All ER 744, CA . . . 7.30, 7.31

Lyons, Sons & Co v Gulliver [1914] 1 Ch 631, CA . . . 23.24

Lysaght v Edwards (1876) 2 Ch D 499 . . . 29.8

Lyus v Prowsa Developments Ltd [1982] 1 WLR 1044. . . . 30.10, 35.37

McAdams Homes Ltd v Robinson [2004] EWCA 214 . . . 32.52

McAnarney v Hanrahan [1993] IR 492 . . . 16.21

McArdle, Re [1951] 1 All ER 905, CA . . . 6.9, 6.10

Macarthys Ltd v Smith (C-129/79) [1980] ECR 1275, ECJ . . . 3.49, 3.52

McAuley v Bristol City Council [1992] 1 All ER 749, CA . . . 21.30

McCall v Abelesz [1976] 1 All ER 727, CA . . . 20.2

McCall v Australian Meat Co Ltd (1870) 19 WR 188 . . . 14.26

McCamley v Cammell Laird Shipbuilders Ltd [1990] 1 All ER 854, CA . . . 27.9

McCarrick v Liverpool Corpn [1946] 2 All ER 646, HL . . . 36.48

McCausland v Duncan Lawrie Ltd [1996] 4 All ER 995, CA . . . 29.2

McCullagh v Lane Fox & Partners Ltd [1996] 1 EGLR 35, CA . . . 16.21

McCutcheon v David MacBrayne Ltd [1964] 1 All ER 430, HL . . . 7.11

McDermid v Nash Dredging and Reclamation Co Ltd [1987] 2 All ER 878, HL . . . 26.23

McDonald v Dennys Lascelles Ltd (1933) 48 CLR 457 . . . 8.14

McGeown v Northern Ireland Housing Executive [1994] 3 All ER 53, HL . . . 21.10

McGhee v National Coal Board [1972] 3 All ER 1008, HL . . . 18.4

McGivney v Golderslea Ltd (2001) 17 Const LJ 454, CA . . . 21.12

McGruther v Pitcher [1904] 2 Ch 306, CA . . . 13.14

Mackay v Dick (1881) 6 App Cas 251, HL . . . 5.36

McKenna v British Aluminium Ltd (2002) Times, 25 April . . . 23.13, 24.9

McKenny v Foster [2008] EWCA Civ 173, CA . . . 25.6

McKew v Holland and Hannen and Cubitts (Scotland) Ltd [1969] 3 All ER 1621, HL . . . 18.10, .17

McKinnon Industries Ltd v Walker [1951] 3 DLR 577 . . . 23.7

McLaughlin v Duffill [2008] EWCA Civ 1627 . . . 14.4

McLean v Brett (1919) 49 DLR 162 . . . 25.8

McLoughlin v Jones [2001] EWCA Civ 1743 . . . 16.28

McMath v Rimmer Bros (Liverpool) Ltd [1961] 3 All ER 1154, CA . . . 20.7

McMonagle v Westminster City Council [1990] 1 All ER 993, HL . . . 3.12

Macnab v Richardson [2008] EWCA Civ 1631, CA . . . 22.10

McNerny v Lambeth London Borough Council [1989] 1 EGLR 81, CA . . . 21.26

McPherson v Watt (1877) 3 App Cas 254, HL . . . 14.15

McWilliams v Sir William Arrol & Co Ltd [1962] 1 All ER 623, HL . . . 18.3

Maga v Birmingham Roman Catholic Archdiocese Trust [2010] EWCA Civ 256, CA . . . 26.14

Magor and St Mellons RDC v Newport Corporation [1951] 2 All ER 839 . . . 3.15

Maguire v Harland & Wolff plc [2005] EWCA Civ, CA . . . 16.5

Maguire v Sefton MBC [2006] EWCA Civ 316, CA . . . 21.11

Maharaj v Chand [1986] 3 All ER 107, PC . . . 30.16

Mahesan S/O Thambiah v Malaysia Government Officers' Co-operative Housing Society Ltd [1978] 2 All ER 405, PC . . . 14.15

Maitland v Raisbeck and AT and J Hewitt Ltd [1944] 2 All ER 272, CA . . . 23.24

Majrowski v Guy's and St Thomas's NHS Trust
[[2006] UKHL 34, HL . . . 26.14

Malayan Credit Ltd v Jack Chia-MPH Ltd
[1986] 1 All ER 711, PC . . . 31.11

Malcolm v Broadhurst [1970] 3 All ER
508 . . . 18.19

Malik v Bank of Credit and Commerce
International SA [1997] 3 All ER 1, HL . . .
7.31, 11.11

Maloney v Torfaen CBC [2005] EWCA Civ 1762,
CA . . . 21.21

Malpas v St Ermine's Property Ltd [1992] 1
EGLR 109 . . . 37.14

Mancetter Developments Ltd v Garmanson Ltd
[1986] 1 All ER 449, CA . . . 28.13, 36.43

Manchester City Council v Pinnock [2010]
UKSC 45 . . . 37.18, 37.21, 37.22

Manchester Corpn v Farnworth [1930] AC 171,
HL . . . 23.18, 24.14

Manchester Ship Canal Co v Manchester
Racecourse Co [1901] 2 Ch 37 . . . 11.47

Manfield & Sons Ltd v Botchin [1970] 3 All ER
143 . . . 36.14, 36.15

Manjang v Drammeh (1990) 61 P & CR 194,
PC . . . 32.29

Mansel v Webb (1918) 88 LJKB 323, CA . . .
24.15

Mansfield v Weetabix Ltd [1998] 1 WLR 1263,
CA . . . 17.4

Marc Rich & Co AG v Bishop Rock Marine Co
Ltd [1995] 3 All ER 307, HL . . . 16.6,
16.21

Marcan Shipping (London) v Polish Steamship
Co [1989] 2 Lloyd's Rep 138, CA . . . 14.18

Marchant v Charters [1977] 3 All ER 918,
CA . . . 36.8, 36.9

Marcic v Thames Water Utilities Ltd [2003]
UKHL 66, HL . . . 23.16

Maredelante Cia Naviera SA v Bergbau-Handel
GmbH ("The Mihalis Angelos") [1970] 3 All
ER 125, CA . . . 8.22, 11.42

Marintrans AB v Comet Shipping Co Ltd [1985]
3 All ER 442 . . . 11.29

Maritime National Fish Ltd v Ocean Trawlers
Ltd [1935] AC 524, PC . . . 10.14

Marjorie Burnett v Barclay (1980) 258 Estates
Gazette 642 . . . 36.7

Market Investigations Ltd v Minister of Social
Security [1968] 3 All ER 732 . . . 26.6

Marquess of Zetland v Driver [1938] 2 All ER
158, CA . . . 33.18, 33.24

Marriage v East Norfolk Rivers Catchment
Board [1949] 2 All ER 1021, CA . . . 23.18

Marsden v Edward Heyes Ltd [1927] 2 KB 1 . . .
36.42, 36.43

Marsden v Miller (1992) 64 P & CR 239,
CA . . . 22.4, 30.25

Marshall v Southampton and South West
Hampshire Area Health Authority (C-152/84)
[1986] 2 All ER 584, ECJ . . . 3.49

Marten v Flight Refuelling Ltd [1962] Ch 115 . . .
33.18, 33.25, 33.27

Marten v Whale [1917] 2 KB 480, CA . . . 5.36

Martin's Application, Re [1989] 1 EGLR 193,
CA . . . 33.31, 33.42

Martine v South East Kent Health Authority
(1993) 20 BMLR 51, CA . . . 16.23

Mason v Levy Auto Parts of England Ltd [1967]
2 All ER 62 . . . 24.6, 24.17

Massey v Boulden [2002] EWCA Civ 1634 . . .
32.4, 32.53

Masters v Brent London Borough Council
[1978] 2 All ER 664 . . . 27.21

Matania v National Provincial Bank Ltd [1936]
2 All ER 633, CA . . . 26.22

Mathew v Bobbins (1980) 41 P & CR 1,
CA . . . 12.63

Matthews v Kuwait Bechtel Corpn [1959] 2 All
ER 345, CA . . . 7.31

Matthews v Smallwood [1910] 1 Ch 777 . . .
36.64

Matthews v Wicks (1987) Times, 25 May,
CA . . . 25.8

Mattis v Pollock [2003] EWCA Civ 887, [2003] 1
WLR 2158, CA . . . 26.14

May and Butcher Ltd v R [1934] 2 KB 17n,
HL . . . 5.33

Mayer v Hurr (1983) 49 P & CR 56, CA . . .
28.22

Maynard v West Midlands Regional Health
Authority [1985] 1 All ER 635, HL . . . 17.7

Meah v McCreamer (No 2) [1986] 1 All ER
943 . . . 18.20

Medforth v Blake [1999] 3 ALL ER 97 . . . 34.35

Mediana, The [1900] AC 113, HL . . . 27.12

Mediterranean Salvage and Towage Ltd v
Seamar Trading and Commerce Inc [2009]
EWCA Civ 531, CA . . . 7.32

Mehmet v Perry [1977] 2 All ER 529, DC . . .
27.11

Melluish (Inspector of Taxes) v BMI (No 3) Ltd
[1995] 4 All ER 453, HL . . . 28.5, 28.10

Mendelssohn v Normand Ltd [1969] 2 All ER
1215, CA . . . 9.8

Mercer v Denne [1905] 2 Ch 538 . . . 3.46,
32.22

Mercury Communications Ltd v Director
General of Telecommunications [1996] 1 All
ER 575, HL . . . 36.59

Merlin v British Nuclear Fuels plc [1990] 3 All
ER 711 . . . 20.5

Merrett v Babb [2001] EWCA Civ 214 . . . 16.19,
26.15

Merritt v Merritt [1970] 2 All ER 760, CA . . .
6.2

Mersey Docks and Harbour Board v Coggins
and Griffith (Liverpool) Ltd [1946] 2 All ER
345, HL . . . 26.7

Mersey Steel and Iron Co v Naylor Benzon and
Co (1884) 9 App Cas 434, HL . . . 8.18

Metropolitan Asylum District Managers v Hill (1881) 6 App Cas 193, HL . . . 23.18

Metropolitan Asylums Board (Managers) v Kingham & Sons (1890) 6 TLR 217 . . . 14.10

Metropolitan Electric Supply Co Ltd v Ginder [1901] 2 Ch 799 . . . 11.47

Metropolitan Police District Receiver v Palacegate Properties Ltd [2000] EWCA Civ 33 . . . 37.29

Metropolitan Water Board v Dick Kerr & Co Ltd [1918] AC 119, HL . . . 10.5, 10.12

Midland Bank plc v Bardgrove Property Services Ltd [1992] 2 EGLR 168, CA . . . 23.20, 32.57

Midland Bank Ltd v Reckitt [1933] AC 1, HL . . . 14.6

Midland Rly Co's Agreement, Re [1971] 1 All ER 1007 . . . 36.5

Midtown Ltd v City of London Real Property Co Ltd [2005] EWHC 33 (Ch) . . . 32.56

Miles v Forest Rock Granite Co (Leicestershire) Ltd (1918) 34 TLR 500, CA . . . 24.5, 24.9

Miller v Duggan [1996] CLY 4444 . . . 25.3

Miller v Emcer Products Ltd [1956] 1 All ER 237, CA . . . 32.11, 36.34

Miller v Jackson [1977] 3 All ER 338, CA . . . 23.10

Millman v Ellis (1995) 71 P & CR 158, CA . . . 32.31

Mills v Brooker [1919] 1 KB 555 . . . 23.22

Mills v Silver [1991] 1 All ER 449, CA . . . 32.12, 32.46, 32.53

Mills v Winchester Diocesan Board of Finance [1989] 2 All ER 317 . . . 16.23

Milmo v Carreras [1946] 1 All ER 288, CA . . . 36.28

Miner v Gilmour (1859) 12 Moo PCC 131 . . . 28.20

Ministry of Housing and Local Government v Sharp [1970] 1 All ER 1009, CA . . . 20.6

Ministry of Sound (Ireland) Ltd v Online Ltd [2003] EWHC 2178 (Comm) . . . 11.37

Mint v Good [1950] 2 All ER 1159, CA . . . 21.30, 23.17

Mira v Aylmer Square Investments Ltd [1990] 1 EGLR 45, CA . . . 36.34

Miro Properties Ltd v J Trevor & Sons [1989] 1 EGLR 151 . . . 14.8

Mirvahedy v Henley [2003] UKHL 16 . . . 25.6

Mitchell v Glasgow CC [2009] UKHL 11, HL . . . 16.10

Mitchell v Mosley [1914] 1 Ch 438, CA . . . 28.6, 28.7

Mitchell v Mulholland (No 2) [1971] 2 All ER 1205, CA . . . 27.8

Mohammad Zadeh v Joseph [2006] EWHC 1040 . . . 33.26

Moloney v Lambeth London Borough Council (1966) 64 LGR 440 . . . 21.4, 21.13

Moncrieff v Jamieson [2007] UKHL 42 . . . 32.11, 32.53

Monsanto plc v Tilly [2000] Env LR 313, CA . . . 22.5

Montgomerie v United Kingdom Mutual Steamship Association [1891] 1 Qb 370 . . . 14.35

Montross Associated Investments SA v Moussaieff [1990] 2 EGLR 61, CA . . . 36.37

Moody v Steggles (1879) 12 Ch D 261 . . . 32.5

Moore v Metropolitan Rly Co (1872) LR 8 QB 36 . . . 26.14

Moorgate Mercantile Co Ltd v Twitchings [1976] 2 All ER 641, HL . . . 16.10

Morales v Eccleston [1991] RTR 151, CA. . . . 17.5

Morgan Crucible Co plc v Hill Samuel Bank Ltd [1991] 1 All ER 148, CA . . . 16.21

Morgan Sindall plc v Sawston Farms (Cambs) Ltd [1999] 1 EGLR 90 . . . 36.59

Morgan v Fear [1907] AC 425, HL . . . 32.55

Morgan v Manser [1947] 2 All ER 666 . . . 10.7

Morgan v Stainer [1993] 2 EGLR 73 . . . 36.60

Morley v Bird (1798) 3 Ves 628 . . . 31.11

Morris v Blaenau Gwent District Council (1982) 80 LGR 793, CA . . . 25.10

Morris v C W Martin & Sons Ltd [1965] 2 All ER 725, CA . . . 26.14

Morris v Murray [1991] 2 QB 6 . . . 19.5

Morrison Holdings Ltd v Manders Property (Wolverhampton) Ltd [1976] 2 All ER 205 . . . 37.26

Morros Marks v British Waterways Board [1963] 1 WLR 1008, CA . . . 37.36

Morse v Barratt (Leeds) Ltd (1992) 9 Const LJ 158 . . . 21.28

Mortimer v Bailey [2004] EWCA Civ 1514 . . . 33.30

Morton v William Dixon Ltd 1909 SC 807 . . . 17.7

Moschi v LEP Air Services Ltd [1972] 2 All ER 393, HL . . . 8.14

Moss Bros Group plc v CSC Properties Ltd [1999] EGCS 47 . . . 36.30

Motion v Michaud (1892) 8 TLR 253 . . . 14.22

Mount Banking Corpn Ltd v Brian Cooper & Co [1992] 2 EGLR 142 . . . 17.9

Mount Carmel Investments Ltd v Peter Thurlow Ltd [1988] 3 All ER 129, CA . . . 30.21, 30.25, 30.27

Mountford v Scott [1975] 1 All ER 198, CA . . . 6.11

Moy v Stoop (1909) 25 TLR 262 . . . 23.12

Muirhead v Industrial Tank Specialities Ltd [1985] 3 All ER 705, CA . . . 16.15

Mullaney v Chief Constable of West Midlands Police [2001] EWCA Civ 700, CA . . . 16.11

Mullaney v Maybourne Grange (Croydon) Management Co [1986] 1 EGLR 70 . . . 36.60

Mullard v Ben Line Steamers Ltd [1971] 2 All ER 424, CA . . . 20.8

Mullens v Miller (1882) 22 Ch D 194 . . . 14.47

Mullin v Richards [1998] 1 All ER 920, CA . . . 17.5

Multiservice Bookbinding Ltd v Marden [1978] 2 All ER 489 . . . 34.11

Murdoch v Glacier Metal Co Ltd [1998] Env LR 732, CA . . . 23.6

Murphy v Bradford Metropolitan Borough Council [1992] PIQR P68, CA . . . 21.12

Murphy v Brentwood District Council [1990] 2 All ER 908, HL . . . 3.37, 16.6, 16.15, 21.27, 21.28, 36.46

Murphy v Gooch [2007] EWCA Civ 608 . . . 31.42

Murray v Birmingham City Council [1987] 2 EGLR 53 . . . 36.52

Musgrove v Pandelis [1919] 2 KB 43, CA . . . 24.15–24.17

Mutual Life and Citizens Assurance Co Ltd v Evatt [1971] 1 All ER 150, PC . . . 16.20

N and J Vlassopulos Ltd v Ney Shipping Ltd [1977] 1 Lloyd's Rep 478, CA . . . 14.43

Nahhas v Pier House (Cheyne Walk) Management Ltd [1984] 1 EGLR 160 . . . 26.14

Nash v Finlay (1901) 85 LT 682, DC . . . 3.9

Nash v Paragon Finance plc [2001] EWCA Civ 1466 . . . 34.11

National Building Society v Cann [1990] 1 All ER 1085, HL . . . 34.24

National Car Parks Ltd v Colebrook Estates Ltd [1983] 1 EGLR 78 . . . 37.45

National Car Parks Ltd v Trinity Development Co [2001] 2 EGLR 43 . . . 36.11

National Carriers Ltd v Panalpina (Northern) Ltd [1981] 1 All ER 161, HL . . . 10.11

National Grid plc v M 25 Group Ltd [1999] 1 EGLR 65, CA . . . 36.59

National Provincial Bank Ltd v Ainsworth [1965] AC 1175 . . . 35.24

National Telephone Co v Baker [1893] 2 Ch 186 . . . 24.6

National Trust for Places of Historic Interest or National Beauty v White [1987] 1 WLR 907 . . . 32.53

Naylor v Payling [2004] EWCA Civ 560, CA . . . 21.16

NCR Ltd v Riverland Portfolio No 1 Ltd [2004] EWHC 921 . . . 36.32

Neaverson v Peterborough Rural District Council [1902] 1 Ch 557 . . . 32.48

Neil Martin Ltd v Revenue and Customs Commissioners [2007] EWCA Civ 1041, CA . . . 16.23

Nettleship v Weston [1971] 3 All ER 581, CA . . . 17.3, 17.8

Network Rail Infrastructures Ltd v CJ Morris [2004] EWCA Civ 172, CA . . . 23.4

New Windsor Corpn v Mellor [1975] 3 All ER 44, CA . . . 3.46

New Zealand and Australian Land Co v Watson (1881) 7 Qbd 374, CA . . . 14.20

New Zealand Shipping Co Ltd v A M Satterthwaite & Co Ltd, ("The Eurymedon") [1974] 1 All ER 1015, PC . . . 6.17

Newbigging v Adam (1886) 34 Ch D 582, CA . . . 12.39

Newbury District Council v Secretary of State for the Environment [1981] AC 578 . . . 39.31

Newman v Real Estate Debenture Corpn Ltd and Flower Decorations Ltd [1940] 1 All ER 131 . . . 36.35

News Group Newspapers Ltd v Society of Graphical and Allied Trades 1982 (No 2) [1987] ICR 181 . . . 23.25, 23.26

Newton Abbot Co-operative Society Ltd v Williamson and Treadgold Ltd [1952] 1 All ER 279 . . . 33.13

Niazi Services Ltd v van der Loo [2004] EWCA Civ 53 . . . 36.45

Nicholls v Ely Beet Sugar Factory [1931] 2 Ch 84, CA . . . 22.4, 23.20

Nicholls v Kinsey [1994] 1 EGLR 131 . . . 37.29

Nichols v Marsland (1876) 2 Ex D 1, CA . . . 24.12

Nickerson v Barraclough [1981] 2 All ER 369 . . . 32.35, 32.29

Nickoll and Knight v Ashton Edridge & Co [1901] 2 KB 126, CA . . . 10.3

Nicolene Ltd v Simmonds [1953] 1 All ER 822, CA . . . 5.32

Nisbet and Potts' Contract, Re [1906] 1 Ch 386 . . . 30.21

Nisshin Shipping Co Ltd v Cleaves & Co Ltd [2003] EWHC 2602 (Comm) . . . 13.3

Nixon v Nixon [1969] 1 WLR 1676 . . . 31.13

Noakes & Co Ltd v Rice [1902] AC 24, HL . . . 34.13

Noble v Harrison [1926] 2 KB 332 . . . 24.8

North Eastern Properties Ltd v Coleman [2010] EWCA Civ 277 . . . 29.6

North Ocean Shipping Co Ltd v Hyundai Construction Co, ("The Atlantic Baron") [1978] 3 All ER 1170 . . . 6.15

North, Re; North v Cusden [1952] 1 All ER 609 . . . 31.10

Northumberland and Durham District Banking Co, ex p Bigge, Re (1858) 28 LJ Ch 50 . . . 12.14

Northwestern Utilities Ltd v London Guarantee and Accident Co Ltd [1936] AC 108, PC . . . 24.4, 24.6, 24.10, 24.13

Norwest Holst Group Administration Ltd v Harrison [1985] ICR 668, CA . . . 8.26

Norwich and Peterborough Building Society v Steed [1993] 1 All ER 330, CA . . . 35.39

Norwich City Council v Harvey [1989] 1 All ER 1180, CA . . . 13.5, 16.16

Norwich Union Life Insurance Society v British Railways Board [1987] 2 EGLR 137 . . . 36.50, 36.58

Norwich Union Life Insurance Society v Shopmoor Ltd [1999] 1 WLR 531 . . . 36.29

Notcutt v Universal Equipment Co (London) Ltd [1986] 3 All ER 582, CA . . . 10.7

Nottingham County Council and Broxtowe Borough Council v Secretary of State for the Environment, Transport and the Regions [1999] EGCS 35. . . . 39.30

Nottingham v Aldridge [1971] 2 All ER 751 . . . 26.10

NV Algemen Transporten Expeditie Onderneming van Gend en Loos v Nederlandse Administratie der Belastingen (C-26/62) [1963] ECR 1, ECJ . . . 3.49

Nweze v Nwoko [2004] 2 P & CR 33, CA . . . 29.2, 29.4

Nye Saunders v Bristow (1987) 37 BLR 92, CA . . . 14.14

Nykredit Mortgage Bank plc v Edward Erdman Group Ltd (No 2) [1998] 1 All ER 305, HL . . . 27.21

Nynehead Developments Ltd v RH Fibreboard Containers Ltd [1999] 1 EGLR 7 . . . 36.34, 36.98

O'Brien v Robinson [1973] 1 All ER 583, HL . . . 36.45

O'Connell v Jackson [1971] 3 All ER 129, CA . . . 19.8

O'May v City of London Real Property Co Ltd [1982] 1 All ER 660, HL . . . 37.44

O'Rourke v Camden London Borough Council [1997] 3 All ER 23, HL . . . 20.2

Oates v Stimson [2006] EWCA Civ 548 . . . 29.9

Ocean Tramp Tankers Corpn v V/O Sovfracht ("The Eugenia") [1964] 1 All ER 161, CA . . . 10.13, 10.14

Oceanic Village Ltd v United Attractions Ltd [2000] 1 All ER 975 . . . 36.89

Office of Fair Trading v Abbey National plc [2009] UKSC 6, S . . . 9.25

Office of Fair Trading v Foxtons Ltd [2009] EWHC 1681 (Ch) . . . 9.24, 9.28

Official Solicitor to the Supreme Court v Thomas [1986] 2 EGLR 1, CA . . . 8.3

Ofulue v Bossert [2009] UKHL 16 . . . 30.23, 30.26

Ogwo v Taylor [1987] 3 All ER 961, HL . . . 21.14

Old Groveboury Manor Farm Ltd v W Seymour Plant Sales & Hire Ltd (No 2) [1979] 3 All ER 504 . . . 36.28

OLL Ltd v Secretary of State for Transport [1997] 3 All ER 897 . . . 16.23

Olley v Marlborough Court Ltd [1949] 1 All ER 127, CA . . . 7.10

Olotu v Home Office [1997] 1 All ER 385, CA . . . 20.2

Omak Maritime Ltd v Mamola Challenger Shipping Co [2010] EWHC 2026 (Comm) . . . 11.8

Omar v El Wakil [2001] EWCA Civ 1090 . . . 29.28

Omega Trust Co Ltd v Wright Son & Pepper [1997] 1 EGLR 120, CA . . . 16.21

Onslow v Corrie (1817) 2 Madd 330 . . . 36.75

Orange v Chief Constable of West Yorkshire Police [2001] EWCA Civ 611, CA . . . 16.9

Orchard v Lee [2009] EWCA Civ 295 . . . 17.5

Orlando Investments Ltd v Grosvenor Estate Belgravia [1989] 2 EGLR 74, CA . . . 36.30

Oropesa, The [1943] 1 All ER 211, CA . . . 18.8

Oscar Chess Ltd v Williams [1957] 1 All ER 325 . . . 7.15, 7.16, 7.19, 7.20, 8.21

Osman v UK (1998) 29 EHRR 245 . . . 16.23

Ostle v Stapleton [1996] CLY 4443 . . . 25.3

Ough v King [1967] 3 All ER 859, CA . . . 32.56

Outram v Academy Plastics Ltd [2001] ICR 367, CA . . . 16.7

Overbrooke Estates Ltd v Glencombe Properties Ltd [1974] 3 All ER 511 . . . 12.48, 14.33

Overend Gurney and Co v Gibb (1872) LR 5 HL 480, HL . . . 14.13

Overseas Tankship (UK) v Miller Steamship Co Pty ("The Wagon Mound") (No 2) [1966] 2 All ER 709 . . . 17.14, 18.15, 23.12, 23.20, 23.26

Overseas Tankship (UK) v Morts Dock and Engineering Co ("The Wagon Mound") [1961] 1 All ER 404, PC . . . 18.14, 18.15, 18.16, 18.19

Owen v Gadd [1956] 2 QB 99 . . . 36.34

Owens v Brimmell [1977] Qb 859 . . . 19.7

Oxley v Hiscock [2005] Fam 211 . . . 31.16

P & A Swift Investments v Combined English Stores Group plc [1988] 2 All ER 885, HL . . . 33.18, 36.73

P & S Platt Ltd v Crouch [2004] 1 P & CR 242 . . . 32.35

Pacific Associates Inc v Baxter [1989] 2 All ER 159, CA . . . 16.21

Padbury v Holliday and Greenwood Ltd (1912) 28 TLR 494, CA . . . 26.24

Paddington Building Society v Mendelsohn (1985) 50 P & CR 244 . . . 35.24

Page Motors Ltd v Epsom and Ewell Borough Council (1981) 80 LGR 337, CA . . . 23.16

Page One Records Ltd v Britton [1967] 3 All ER 822 . . . 11.48, 11.49, 14.22

Page v Smith [1995] 2 All ER 736, HL . . . 16.28

Pagnan SpA v Feed Products [1987] 2 Lloyd's Rep 601, CA . . . 5.33

Paine v Meller (1801) 6 Ves 349 . . . 10.11

Palacath v Flanagan (1985) 274 Estates Gazette 143 . . . 36.59

Palk v Mortgage Services Funding plc [1993] 2 All ER 481, CA . . . 34.27, 34.33

Pan Atlantic Insurance Co Ltd v Pine Top Insurance Co Ltd [1994] 3 All ER 581, HL . . . 12.15, 12.54

Pankhania v Hackney London Borough Council [2002] EWHC 2441 (Ch) . . . 12.10, 12.37

Panorama Developments Ltd v Fidelis Furnishing Fabrics Ltd [1971] 3 All ER 16, CA . . . 14.29

Pao On v Lau Yiu Long [1979] 3 All ER 65, PC . . . 6.10, 6.17, 12.58, 12.59

Parc Battersea Ltd v Hutchinson [1999] 2 EGLR 33 . . . 37.26

Paris v Stepney Borough Council [1951] 1 All ER 42, HL . . . 17.12

Parkash v Irani Finances Ltd [1969] 1 All ER 930 . . . 29.37

Parker v British Airways Board [1982] QB 1004, CA . . . 28.18

Parker v Ibbetson (1858) 4 CBNS 346 . . . 14.22

Parker v South Eastern Rly Co (1877) 2 CPD 416, CA . . . 7.13

Parkins v Westminster City Council [1998] 1 EGLR 22, CA . . . 37.18

Parry v Cleaver [1969] 1 All ER 555, HL . . . 27.9

Partridge v Crittenden [1968] 2 All ER 421, DC . . . 5.6

Pascoe v Turner [1979] 2 All ER 945, CA . . . 30.13, 30.15

Pasternack v Poulton [1973] 2 All ER 74 . . . 19.9

Patchett v Swimming Pool and Allied Trades Association Ltd [2009] EWCA Civ 717, CA . . . 16.20

Patel v Ali [1984] 1 All ER 978 . . . 11.45

Patel v Keles [2009] EWCA Civ 1187 . . . 37.38

Paterson v Gandasequi (1812) 15 East 62 . . . 14.38

Patience v Andrews [1983] RTR 447 . . . 19.8

Patrick v Colerick (1838) 3 M & W 483 . . . 22.5

Paul v Summerhayes (1878) 4 Qbd 9, DC . . . 25.1

Pavledes v Ryesbridge Properties (1989) 58 P & CR 459 . . . 30.27

Payne v Cardiff RDC [1932] 1 KB 241 . . . 34.29

Payne v Cave (1789) 3 Term Rep 148 . . . 5.7

Payne v Inwood (1996) 74 P & CR 42, CA . . . 32.35

Payzu Ltd v Saunders [1919] 2 KB 581, CA . . . 11.25

Peabody Donation Fund Governors v Sir Lindsay Parkinson & Co Ltd [1984] 3 All ER 529, HL . . . 16.6

Peacock v Custins [2001] 2 All ER 827, CA . . . 32.4, 32.53

Pearce v Scotcher (1882) 9 QBD 162, DC . . . 28.20

Pearson v Coleman Bros [1948] 2 All ER 274, CA . . . 21.8

Pearson v North Western Gas Board [1968] 2 All ER 669 . . . 24.14

Peckham v Ellison (1998) 31 HLR 1030, CA . . . 32.33

Peek v Gurney (1873) LR 6 HL 377, HL . . . 12.13

Peffer v Rigg [1978] 3 All ER 745 . . . 35.37

Pell Frischmann Engineering Ltd v Bow Valley Iran Ltd [2009] UKPC 45, PC . . . 11.7

Pembery v Lamdin [1940] 2 All ER 434 . . . 36.49

Penn v Bristol and West Building Society [1997] 3 All ER 470, CA . . . 14.45

Penn v Wilkins [1975] 2 EGLR 113 . . . 23.4

Penniall v Harborne (1848) 11 QB 368 . . . 36.61

Penny v Wimbledon UDC [1899] 2 QB 72, CA . . . 26.21

Pepper v Hart [1993] 1 All ER 42, HL . . . 3.21

Percy v Hall [1996] 4 All ER 523, CA . . . 3.9

Perera v Vandiyar [1953] 1 All ER 1109, CA . . . 15.8, 22.3, 36.34

Performance Cars Ltd v Abraham [1961] 3 All ER 413, CA . . . 18.6

Perl (P) (Exporters) Ltd v Camden London Borough Council [1983] 3 All ER 161, CA . . . 16.10

Perry v Butlins Holiday World [1998] Ed CR 39, CA . . . 21.13

Perry v Kendricks Transport Ltd [1956] 1 All ER 154, CA . . . 24.9, 24.13

Petra Investements Ltd v Jeffrey Rogers plc [2000] 3 EGLR 120 . . . 36.35

Petrol Filling Station, Vauxhall Bridge Road, London, Re; sub nom. Rosemex Service Station Ltd v Shell Mex and BP Ltd (1968) 20 P & CR 1 . . . 34.13

Peyman v Lanjani [1984] 3 All ER 703, CA . . . 8.16, 12.19

Pharmaceutical Society of Great Britain v Boots Cash Chemists (Southern) Ltd [1953] 1 All ER 482, CA . . . 5.5

Pharmaceutical Society of Great Britain v Dickson [1968] 2 All ER 686, HL . . . 4.13

Phelps v Hillingdon LBC [2001] 2 AC 619, HL . . . 16.24

Philco Radio Ltd v J Spurling Ltd [1949] 2 All ER 882, CA . . . 18.9

Philcox v Civil Aviation Authority [1995] 27 LS Gaz R 33, CA . . . 16.21

Philips v Ward [1956] 1 All ER 874, CA . . . 17.9

Philips v William Whiteley Ltd [1938] 1 All ER 566 . . . 17.8

Phillips Hong Kong Ltd v A-G of Hong Kong (1993) 61 BLR 41, PC . . . 11.34

Phillips Products Ltd v Hyland [1987] 2 All ER 620, CA . . . 9.15, 9.20, 9.21, 26.7

Phillips v Britannia Hygienic Laundry Co Ltd [1923] 1 KB 539, DC . . . 26.21

Phipps v Pears [1964] 2 All ER 35 . . . 32.3, 32.10, 32.35

Phipps v Rochester Corpn [1955] 1 All ER 129 . . . 21.13

Photo Production Ltd v Securicor Transport Ltd [1980] 1 All ER 556, HL . . . 8.15, 9.1, 26.14

Pickering v Busk (1812) 15 East 38 . . . 14.47

Pickering v Liverpool Daily Post and Echo Newspapers plc [1991] 1 All ER 622, HL . . . 20.3

Pickering v Rudd (1815) 4 Camp 219 . . . 28.16

Pidduck v Eastern Scottish Omnibuses Ltd [1990] 2 All ER 69, CA . . . 27.11

Pilcher v Rawlins (1872) 7 Ch App 259 . . . 35.4

Pilmore v Hood (1838) 5 Bing NC 97 . . . 12.12

Pinnel's Case (1602) 5 Co Rep 117a . . . 6.18

Pinner v Everett [1969] 3 All ER 257 . . . 3.17

Pirbakaran v Patel [2006] EWCA Civ 685 . . . 36.65, 37.23

Pitt v PHH Asset Management Ltd [1993] 4 All ER 961, CA . . . 29.2, 29.23, 5.35

Pitts v Hunt [1990] 3 All ER 344, CA . . . 19.9

PK Finans International (UK) Ltd v Andrew Downs & Co Ltd [1992] 1 EGLR 172 . . . 17.7

Planché v Colburn (1831) 8 Bing 14 . . . 11.41

Platform Home Loans Ltd v Oyston Shipways Ltd [1998] 13 EG 148, CA . . . 19.7

Platt v Liverpool CC [1997] CLY 4864, CA . . . 21.22

Platt v London Underground Ltd [2001] 2 EGLR 121 . . . 36.35

Plinth Property Investments Ltd v Mott, Hay and Anderson (1978) 38 P & CR 361, CA . . . 36.37, 36.58

Plumb v Cobden Flour Mills Co Ltd [1914] AC 62 . . . 26.12

Pointon York Group plc v Poulton [2006] EWCA Civ 1001 . . . 37.26

Poland v John Parr & Sons [1927] 1 KB 236, CA . . . 26.14

Polsue and Alfieri Ltd v Rushmer [1907] AC 121, HL . . . 23.8

Pontardawe RDC v Moore-Gwyn [1929] 1 Ch 656 . . . 24.5

Ponting v Noakes [1894] 2 Qb 281 . . . 24.7

Pool v Pool (1889) 58 LJP 67 . . . 14.24, 14.27

Pope v Fraser and Southern Rolling and Wire Mills Ltd (1938) 55 TLR 324 . . . 23.25

Poppleton v Trustees of the Portsmouth Youth Activities Committee [2008] EWCA Civ 646, CA . . . 21.12

Port v Griffith [1938] 1 All ER 295 . . . 36.35

Portman Building Society v Hamlyn [1998] 4 All ER 202 . . . 11.38

Portuguese Consolidated Copper Mines Ltd, Re (1890) 45 Ch D 16, CA . . . 14.10

Posner v Scott-Lewis [1987] Ch 25 . . . 11.44

Possfund Custodian Trustee Ltd v Diamond [1996] 2 All ER 774 . . . 16.18

Post Office v Aquarius Properties Ltd [1987] 1 All ER 1055, CA . . . 36.49

Post Office v Estuary Radio [1967] 3 All ER 663, CA . . . 3.23

Postlethwaite v Freeland (1880) 5 App Cas 599, HL . . . 8.28

Potton Developments Ltd v Thompson [1998] NPC 49 . . . 28.9

Potts and Densley [2011] EWHC 1144 QB . . . 37.8

Poussard v Spiers and Pond (1876) 1 QBD 410 . . . 8.7

Powell and Thomas v Evan Jones & Co [1905] 1 KB 11, CA . . . 14.20

Powell v Brent London Borough Council [1987] IRLR 466, CA . . . 11.49

Powell v Kempton Park Racecourse Co Ltd [1899] AC 143, HL . . . 3.18

Powell v May [1946] 1 All ER 444, DC . . . 3.9

Powell v McFarlane (1977) 38 P & CR 452 . . . 30.23, 30.24

Prager v Blatspiel; Stamp and Heacock Ltd [1924] 1 KB 566 . . . 14.11

Pratt v George J Hill Associates (1987) 38 BLR 25, CA . . . 26.16

Pratt v Richards [1951] 2 KB 208 . . . 21.6

Prebble & Co v West (1969) 211 Estates Gazette 831, CA . . . 14.47

Predeth v Castle Phillips Finance Co Ltd [1986] 2 EGLR 144, CA . . . 34.31

Prekookeanska Plovidba v Felstar Shipping Corpn ("The Carniva") [1994] 2 Lloyd's Rep 14, CA . . . 18.17

Prendergast v Sam and Dee [1989] 1 Med LR 36, CA . . . 18.9

Presentaciones Musicales SA v Secunda [1994] 2 All ER 737, CA . . . 14.10

Pretoria Warehousing Co Ltd v Shelton [1993] NPC 98, CA . . . 32.35

Pride of Derby and Derbyshire Angling Association Ltd v British Celanese Ltd [1953] 1 All ER 179 . . . 23.19

Pritchard v Briggs [1980] Ch 338, CA . . . 29.7

Property and Bloodstock Ltd v Emerton [1967] 3 All ER 321, CA . . . 34.30

Property Point Ltd v Kirri [2009] EWHC 2958 . . . 32.53

Prospect Estates Ltd v Grosvenor Estates Ltd [2008] EWCA 1281 . . . 37.14

Proudfoot v Hart (1890) 25 QBD 42, CA . . . 36.48, 36.52

Proudfoot v Montefiore (1867) LR 2 Qb 511 . . . 14.1

Prudential Assurance Co v London Residuary Body [1992] 3 All ER 504, HL . . . 36.4, 36.5

Pugh v Savage [1970] 2 All ER 353, CA . . . 32.6

Pulleyn v Hall Aggregates (Thames Valley) (1992) 65 P & CR 276, CA . . . 30.25

Punjab National Bank v de Boinville [1992] 3 All ER 104, CA . . . 14.43

Pwllbach Colliery Co Ltd v Woodman [1915] AC 634, HL . . . 32.30

Pyer v Carter (1857) 1 H & N 916 . . . 32.31

Pym v Campbell (1856) 6 E & B 370 . . . 5.36, 7.3

Quazi v Quazi [1979] 3 All ER 897, HL . . . 3.18

Quennell v Maltby [1979] 1 All ER 568,
CA . . . 34.39

Quick v Taff-Ely Borough Council [1986] QB
809, CA . . . 36.44, 36.49

Quinn v Scott [1965] 2 All ER 588 . . . 23.25

R & B Customs Brokers Co Ltd v United
Dominions Trust [1988] 1 All ER 847,
CA . . . 9.13

R (Beresford) v Sunderland City Council [2003]
UKHL 60 . . . 32.46

R (on the application of Cooperative Group Ltd)
v Northumberland County Council [2010]
EWHC 373 (Admin) . . . 39.44

R (on the application of Copeland) v Tower
Hamlets LBC [2010] EWHC 1845
(Admin) . . . 39.29

R (on the application of Hall Hunter) v First
Secretary of State [2006] EWHC 3482
(Admin) . . . 39.4

R (on the application of Purdy) v DPP [2009]
UKHL 45, HL . . . 3.37

R (on the application of Quintavelle) v Secretary
of State for Health [2003] UKHL 13 . . . 3.17

R (on the application of W) v Lambeth London
Borough Council [2002] EWCA Civ 613,
CA . . . 3.38

R (on the application of Westminster City
Council) v National Asylum Support Service
[2002] UKHL 38 . . . 3.20

R (Wilson) v Wychavon DC and anor [2007]
EWCA Civ 52 . . . 39.65

R Addie & Sons (Collieries) Ltd v Dumbreck
[1929] AC 358, HL . . . 21.7, 21.18

R v Allen [1985] 2 All ER 641, HL . . . 3.21

R v Ayres [1984] 1 All ER 619, HL . . . 3.21

R v Bristol City Council, ex p Anderson [2000]
PLCR 104 . . . 39.31

R v City of London Corpn, ex p Masters,
Governors and Commonlity of the Mystery
of the Barbers of London [1996] 2 EGLR
128 . . . 33.37

R v City of London Corpn, ex p Mystery of the
Barbers of London (1997) 73 P & CR 59 . . .
32.52

R v Clarke (1927) 40 CLR 227 . . . 5.10

R v Deputy Governor of Parkhurst Prison, ex p
Hague; Weldon v Home Office [1991] 3 All ER
733, HL . . . 20.2

R v East Sussex CC, ex p Reprotech (Pebsham)
Ltd [2002] JPL 821 . . . 38.30

R v Hazelton (1874) LR 2 CCR 134 . . . 12.18

R v Horncastle [2009] UKSC 14, SC . . . 3.31

R v House [2010] EWCA Crim 2270, CA . . . 3.15

R v J [2004] UKHL 42, HL . . . 3.11

R v Jones; R v Smith [1976] 3 All ER 54,
CA . . . 21.8

R v Kelt [1977] 3 All ER 1099, CA . . . 3.20

R v Kuxhaus [1988] 2 All ER 705 . . . 39.64

R v Lloyd (1802) 4 Esp 200 . . . 23.23

R v London Borough of Hillingdon, ex p Royco
Homes [1974] QB 720 . . . 39.31

R v Northumberland Compensation Appeal
Tribunal, ex p Shaw [1952] 1 All ER 122,
CA . . . 3.39

R v Secretary of State for Environment,
Transport and the Regions, ex p Alconbury
Developments [2001] UKHL 23 . . . 38.10

R v Secretary of State for Transport, ex p
Factortame (No 5) [1999] 4 All ER 906,
HL . . . 3.51

R v Secretary of State for Transport, ex p
Factortame (No 7) [2001] 1 WLR 942 . . . 3.51

R v Shorrock [1993] 3 All ER 917, CA . . . 23.24

R v Teignbridge District Council, ex p
Teignmouth Quay Co [1995] JPL 828 . . . 39.60

R v TJB [2009] UKHL 30, HL . . . 3.21

R v Townley (1871) LR 1 CCR 315 . . . 28.19

R v Vale of Glamorgan DC, ex p Adams [2001]
JPL 93 . . . 39.29

R v Wicks [1997] JPL 1049 . . . 39.61

Rae v Mars (UK) Ltd [1990] 1 EGLR 161 . . .
21.15, 21.17

Rahman v Arearose Ltd [2001] QB 351,
CA . . . 18.9

Railways Comr v Valuer-General [1974] AC 328,
PC . . . 28.15

Rainbow Estates Ltd v Tokenhold Ltd [1998] 2
All ER 860 . . . 36.67

Raineri v Miles [1980] 2 All ER 145,
HL . . . 8.31, 29.29

Rainham Chemical Works v Belvedere Fish
Guano Co [1921] 2 AC 465, HL . . . 24.4, 24.6

Raja v Austin Gray [2002] EWCA Civ 1965,
CA . . . 16.21, 34.31

Ramsden v Dyson (1866) LR 1 HL 129 . . . 30.11

Ramsgate Victoria Hotel v Montefiore (1866) LR
1 Ex Ch 109 . . . 5.28

Ramzan v Brookwide Ltd [2010] EWHC Ch
2453 . . . 27.2

Rance v Elvin (1985) 50 P & CR 9, CA . . . 32.12

Rann v Hughes (1778) 7 Term Rep 350n,
HL . . . 4.5

Rapier v London Tramways Co [1893] 2 Ch 588,
CA . . . 23.4, 23.12

Ratcliff v McConnell [1999] 1 WLR 670,
CA . . . 21.24

Ravenseft Properties Ltd v Davstone (Holdings)
Ltd [1979] 1 All ER 929 . . . 36.49

RCA Corpn v Pollard [1982] 3 All ER 771,
CA . . . 20.2

Read v J Lyons & Co Ltd [1946] 2 All ER 471,
HL . . . 24.7, 24.8

Ready- Mixed Concrete (South- East) Ltd v
Minister of Pension and National Insurance
[1968] 1 All ER 433 . . . 26.6

Reardon Smith Line Ltd v Hansen- Tangen
[1976] 3 All ER 570 . . . 8.24

Record v Bell [1991] 4 All ER 471 . . . 29.5, 29.6

Red House Farms (Thorndon) Ltd v Catchpole (1977) 244 Estates Gazette 295 . . . 30.25

Redgrave v Hurd (1881) 20 Ch D 1, CA . . . 12.14

Redland Bricks Ltd v Morris [1969] 2 All ER 576, HL . . . 27.17, 32.57

Reeman v Department of Transport [1997] 2 Lloyd's Rep 648, CA . . . 16.21

Rees v Skerrett [2001] EWCA Civ 760 . . . 32.10, 32.57

Reeve v Lisle [1902] AC 461, HL . . . 34.10

Reeve v Reeve (1858) 1 F & F 280 . . . 14.17

Reeves v Metropolitan Police Comr [1998] 2 All ER 381, HL . . . 16.9, 18.20, 19.3, 19.7

Regal (Hastings) Ltd v Gulliver [1942] 1 All ER 378, HL . . . 14.15

Regalian Properties plc v London Development Corpn [1995] 1 All ER 1005 . . . 5.38

Regent Oil Co Ltd v J A Gregory (Hatch End) Ltd [1965] 3 All ER 673, CA . . . 33.13

Regis Property Co Ltd v Redman [1956] 2 All ER 335, CA . . . 32.12, 32.35

Reid v Bickerstaff [1909] 2 Ch 305 . . . 33.24, 33.28

Reid v Rush & Tompkins Group plc [1989] 3 All ER 228, CA . . . 16.7, 16.19

Rely- a-Bell Burglar and Fire Alarm Co Ltd v Eisler [1926] Ch 609 . . . 11.48

Renals v Cowlishaw (1878) 9 Ch D 125 . . . 33.24

Resolute Maritime Inc v Nippon Kaiji Kyokai [1983] 2 All ER 1 . . . 12.24, 14.46

Revill v Newbery [1996] 1 All ER 291, CA . . . 21.18

Reynolds v Ashby & Son [1904] AC 466, HL . . . 28.11

Reynolds v Atherton (1921) 125 LT 690, CA . . . 5.29

Rhind v Astbury Water Park Ltd [2004] EWCA Civ 756, CA . . . 21.21

RHJ Ltd v FT Patten (Holdings) Ltd [2008] EWCA Civ 151 . . . 32.55

Rhodes v Forwood (1876) 1 App Cas 256, HL . . . 14.23

Rhone v Stephens [1994] 2 All ER 65, HL . . . 30.18, 33.4, 33.10, 33.12, 33.26

Rialas v Mitchell (1984) Times, 17 July, CA . . . 27.7

Ribee v Norrie [2001] PIQR P8, CA . . . 24.15

Richard Thomas and Baldwins Ltd v Cummings [1955] 1 All ER 285, HL . . . 3.14

Richardson v Pitt-Stanley [1995] ICR 303, CA . . . 20.2

Richardson v Williamson and Lawson (1871) LR 6 Qb 276 . . . 14.45

Riches v News Group Newspapers Ltd [1986] QB 256, CA . . . 27.2

Richley v Faull [1965] 3 All ER 109 . . . 17.18

Rickards v Lothian [1913] AC 263, PC . . . 24.8, 24.10, 24.13

Rickless v United Artists Corpn [1987] 1 All ER 679, CA . . . 20.2

Ridley v Taylor [1965] 2 All ER 51, CA . . . 33.38, 33.41

Rigby v Chief Constable of Northamptonshire [1985] 1 WLR 1242 . . . 22.5, 24.4–24.5

Rignall Developments Ltd v Halil [1987] 3 All ER 170 . . . 29.36

Rimmer v Liverpool City Council [1984] 1 All ER 930, CA . . . 21.26, 36.46

Rivers v Cutting [1982] 3 All ER 69, CA . . . 26.16

Roake v Chadha [1983] 3 All ER 503 . . . 33.26, 33.27

Roberts v J Hampson & Co [1989] 2 All ER 504 . . . 17.9

Roberts v Macord (1832) 1 Mood & R 230 . . . 32.9

Robertson v British Gas Corpn [1983] ICR 351, CA . . . 6.4

Robinson v Beaconsfield RDC [1911] 2 Ch 188, CA . . . 26.16

Robinson v Davison (1871) LR 6 Exch 269 . . . 10.7

Robinson v Harman (1848) 1 Exch 850 . . . 11.3

Robinson v Kilvert (1889) 41 Ch D 88, CA . . . 23.7

Robinson v Post Office [1974] 2 All ER 737, CA . . . 18.9, 18.17, 18.19

Robson v Hallett [1967] 2 All ER 407, DC . . . 21.7, 28.41

Rock Refrigeration Ltd v Jones [1997] 1 All ER 1, CA . . . 8.11

Roe v Minister of Health [1954] 2 All ER 131, CA. . . . 17.7

Roe v Sheffield CC [2003] EWCA Civ 1 . . . 20.6

Rogan v Woodfield Building Services Ltd [1995] 1 EGLR 72, CA . . . 37.24

Rogers v Hosegood [1900] 2 Ch 388 . . . 33.18, 33.24

Rogers v Night Riders [1983] RTR 324, CA . . . 26.23

Rom Securities Ltd v Rogers (Holdings) Ltd (1967) 205 Estates Gazette 427 . . . 10.11

Romer and Haslam, Re [1893] 2 QB 286, CA . . . 8.3

Romulus Trading v Comet Properties [1996] 2 EGLR 70 . . . 36.35

Rondel v Worsley [1967] 3 All ER 993, HL . . . 16.26

Rookes v Barnard [1964] 1 All ER 367, HL . . . 27.2

Ropaigealach v Barclays Bank plc [2000] QB 263, CA . . . 34.18, 34.25, 34.28

Rose and Frank Co v J R Crompton & Bros Ltd [1925] AC 445, HL . . . 6.4

Rose v Miles (1815) 4 M & S 101 . . . 23.26

Rose v Plenty [1976] 1 All ER 97, CA . . . 26.13

Roseberry Limited v Rocklee Limited [2011] All ER (D) 139 . . . 28.23

Rosling v Pinnegar (1986) 54 P & CR 124, CA . . . 32.53

Ross River Ltd v Cambridge City FC Ltd [2007] EWHC 2115 (Ch) . . . 12.14

Roth & Co v Taysen Townsend & Co (1895) 1 Com Cas 240 . . . 11.27

Rouse v Gravelworks Ltd [1940] 1 All ER 26, CA . . . 24.8

Rouse v Squires [1973] 2 All ER 903, CA . . . 18.3

Routledge v Grant (1828) 4 Bing 653 . . . 5.25

Rover International Ltd v Cannon Film Sales Ltd (No 3) [1989] 3 All ER 423, CA . . . 8.13

Rowe v Herman [1997] 1 WLR 1390, CA . . . 26.21

Rowling v Takaro Properties Ltd [1988] 1 All ER 163, PC . . . 16.23

Royal Bank of Scotland plc v Jennings [1997] 19 EG 152 . . . 36.57

Royal Bank of Scotland v Etridge (No 2) [2001] UKHL 44, HL . . . 12.63, 12.64, 12.65, 12.66

Royal Bank of Scotland v Victoria Street (No 3) Ltd [2008] EWHC 3052 . . . 36.30

Royal College of Nursing of the United Kingdom v Department of Health and Social Security [1981] 1 All ER 545, HL . . . 3.10

Royal Trust Co of Canada v Markham [1975] 3 All ER 433, CA . . . 34.27

Royal Victoria Pavilion, Ramsgate, Re [1961] 3 All ER 83 . . . 33.14

Royscot Trust Ltd v Rogerson [1991] 3 All ER 294, CA . . . 12.25, 12.26

RTS Flexible Systems Ltd v Molkerei Alois Muller Gmbh & Co KG (UK Production) [2010] UKSC 14, SC . . . 5.33, 5.34

Ruddiman & Co v Smith (1889) 60 LT 708, DC . . . 26.10, 26.12

Rugby Football Union v Secretary of State for the Environment, Transport and the Regions [2002] EWCA Civ 1169 . . . 39.13

Rugby School (Governors) v Tannahill [1935] 1 KB 87, CA . . . 36.65

Ruxley Electronics and Construction Ltd v Forsyth [1995] 3 All ER 268, HL . . . 11.4, 11.6

Ryan v Fildes [1938] 3 All ER 517 . . . 26.14

Ryan v Mutual Tontine Westminster Chambers Association [1893] 1 Ch 116 . . . 11.44

Rylands v Fletcher (1868) LR 3 HL 330, HL . . . 15.9, 24.2–24.9, 24.13–24.14, 24.17, 25.1, 26.17, 26.20

S Pearson & Son Ltd v Dublin Corpn [1907] AC 351, HL . . . 12.14

S v Walsall Metropolitan Borough Council [1985] 3 All ER 294, CA . . . 26.16

Safeway Food Stores Ltd v Banderway Ltd (1983) 267 EG 850 . . . 36.59

Sage v Secretary of State for the Environment, Transport and the Regions and Maidstone BC [2003] UKHL 22 . . . 39.54

Salmon v Seafarer Restaurants Ltd [1983] 3 All ER 729 . . . 21.14

Salomon v Salomon & Co Ltd [1897] AC 22, HL . . . 4.12

Salomons v Pender (1865) 3 H & C 639 . . . 14.18

Salsbury v Woodland [1969] 3 All ER 863, CA . . . 23.25, 26.21

Samuel Smith (Southern) Ltd v Howard de Walden Estates Ltd [2007] 1 EGLR 107 . . . 37.44, 37.45

Samuel v Jarrah Timber and Wood Paving Corpn Ltd [1904] AC 323, HL . . . 34.10

Sansom v Metcalfe Hambleton & Co [1998] 2 EGLR 103, CA . . . 17.7

Sarch v Blackburn (1830) 4 C & P 297 . . . 19.3

Sard v Rhodes (1836) 1 M & W 153 . . . 8.3

Sargeant v Macepark (Whittlebury) [2004] 4 All ER 662 . . . 36.53

Saunders v Leeds Western Health Authority [1993] 4 Med LR 355 . . . 17.18

Saunders v Vautier (1841) 10 LJ Ch 354 . . . 31.33

Savills v Scott [1988] 1 EGLR 20 . . . 14.43

Savva v Hussein [1996] 47 EG 138, CA . . . 36.65

Saxon v Blake (1861) 29 Beav 438 . . . 14.36, 14.39

Sayers v Harlow UDC [1958] 2 All ER 342, CA . . . 18.13

Scala House and District Property Co Ltd v Forbes [1973] 3 All ER 308, CA . . . 36.65

Scammell and Nephew Ltd v Ouston [1941] 1 All ER 14, HL . . . 5.31

Scancarriers A/S v Aotearoa International Ltd [1985] 2 Lloyd's Rep 419, PC . . . 5.3

Scandinavian Trading Tanker Co AB v Flota Petrolera Ecuatoriana ("The Scaptrade") [1983] 1 All ER 301, CA . . . 6.22

Scarfe v Adams [1981] 1 All ER 843, CA . . . 28.22

Schack v Anthony (1813) 1 M & S 573 . . . 14.39

Schimizu (UK) Ltd v Westminster City Council [1997] JPL 523 . . . 39.51

Schmaltz v Avery (1851) 16 Qb 655 . . . 14.42

Schuler AG v Wickman Machine Tool Sales Ltd [1973] 2 All ER 39, HL . . . 8.22

SCM (UK) Ltd v W J Whittall & Son Ltd [1970] 2 All ER 417, CA . . . 23.9

SCM (UK) Ltd v WJ Whittall & Son Ltd [1970] 3 All ER 245, CA . . . 16.13

Scotson v Pegg (1861) 6 H & N 295 . . . 6.17

Scott v London and St Katherine Docks Co (1865) 3 H & C 596 . . . 17.16, 17.18

Scott v Shepherd (1773) 2 Wm Bl 892 . . . 18.8

Scottish & Newcastle plc v Raguz [2008] UKHL 65 . . . 36.85

Scottish Mutual Assurance plc v Jardine Public Relations Ltd [1999] EGCS 43 . . . 36.60

Scrimshire v Alderton (1743) 2 Stra 1182 . . . 14.36

Scruttons Ltd v Midland Silicones Ltd [1962] 1 All ER 1, HL . . . 13.2

Seddon v Smith (1877) 36 LT 168 . . . 30.25

Sedleigh-Denfield v O'Callaghan [1940] 3 All ER 349, HL . . . 23.3, 23.5, 23.16

See also Nynehead Developments Ltd v RH Fibreboard Containers Ltd [1999] 1 EGLR 7 . . . 36.35

Sekhon v Alissa [1989] 2 FLR 94 . . . 30.9

Selectmove Ltd, Re [1995] 2 All ER 531, CA . . . 6.13, 6.16

Seligman v Docker [1948] 2 All ER 887 . . . 25.2

Shankie-Williams v Heavey [1986] 2 EGLR 139, CA . . . 16.21

Shanklin Pier Ltd v Detel Products Ltd [1951] 2 All ER 471 . . . 13.10

Sharif v Sadiq [2004] EWHC 1931 (Ch) . . . 29.2

Sharp v Avery [1938] 4 All ER 85, CA . . . 16.17

Sharpe (a bankrupt), Re [1980] 1 All ER 198 . . . 30.9, 30.16

Sharpe v Duke Street Securities (1987) 55 P & CR 331, CA . . . 37.14

Shaw v Doleman [2009] EWCA Civ 279 . . . 36.99

Sheldon v RHM Outhwaite (Underwriting Agencies) Ltd [1995] 2 All ER 558, HL . . . 27.24

Shelfer v City of London Electric Lighting Co [1895] 1 Ch 287, CA . . . 23.10, 27.18

Shelfer v City of London Electric Lighting Co. [1891–4] All ER Rep 838 . . . 33.30

Shell-Mex and BP Ltd v Manchester Garages Ltd [1971] 1 All ER 841 . . . 36.9, 36.11

Shell-Mex & BP Ltd v Manchester Garages Ltd [1971] 1 All ER 841, CA . . . 37.26

Shiffman v Hospital of the Order of St John of Jerusalem [1936] 1 All ER 557 . . . 24.6, 24.9

Shillito v Thompson (1875) 1 QBD 12 . . . 23.23

Shiloh Spinners Ltd v Harding [1973] 1 All ER 90, HL . . . 33.8

Shipton, Anderson & Co v Weil Bros & Co [1912] 1 KB 574 . . . 8.2

Shipway v Broadwood [1899] 1 Qb 36 . . . 14.15

Shirlcar v Heinitz (1983) 268 Estates Gazette 362 . . . 36.57

Short v J and W Henderson Ltd (1946) 62 TLR 427 . . . 26.3, 26.4

Shropshire County Council v Edwards (1982) 46 P & CR 270 . . . 33.25

Sidaway v Board of Governors of the Bethlem Royal Hospital and the Maudsley Hospital [1985] 1 All ER 643, HL . . . 19.3

Siddorn v Patel [2007] EWHC 1248, QB . . . 21.20

Sight and Sound Education Ltd v Books etc Ltd [2000] L & TR 146 . . . 37.39

Silven Properties Ltd v Royal Bank of Scotland plc [2004] EWCA 1409 . . . 34.31, 34.35

Simkiss v Rhondda Borough Council (1982) 81 LGR 460, CA . . . 21.13

Simmons v Dobson (1991) 62 P & CR 485, CA . . . 32.48

Simms v Leigh Rugby Football Club Ltd [1969] 2 All ER 923 . . . 21.17

Simpson v Edinburgh Corpn, 1961 SLT 17 . . . 38.28

Simpson v Savage (1856) 1 CBNS 347 . . . 23.13

Simpson v Thomson (1877) 3 App Cas 279, HL . . . 16.12

Singer and Friedlander Ltd v John D Wood & Co [1977] 2 EGLR 84 . . . 17.9

Singer Co (UK) Ltd v Tees and Hartlepool Port Authority [1988] 1 FTLR 442 . . . 13.16

Single Horse Properties Ltd v Surrey County Council [2002] EWCA Civ 367 . . . 37.32

Sirros v Moore [1974] 3 All ER 776, CA . . . 16.25

Skeet v Powell-Sheddon [1988] 2 EGLR 112, CA . . . 37.38

Skerritts of Nottingham Ltd v Secretary of State for Environment Transport and the Region (No 2) [2000] JPL 1025 . . . 39.4

Skinner v London, Brighton and South Coast Rly Co (1850) 5 Exch 787 . . . 17.18

Skipton Building Society v Clayton (1993) 25 HLR 596, CA . . . 36.6

Sledmore v Dalby (1996) 72 P & CR 196, CA . . . 30.15

Smallman v Smallman [1971] 3 All ER 717, CA . . . 5.36

Smally v Smally (1700) 1 Eq Cas Abr 6 . . . 14.3

Smeaton v Ilford Corpn [1954] 1 All ER 923 . . . 23.18, 24.5, 24.8

Smirk v Lyndale Developments Ltd [1975] Ch 317 . . . 30.36

Smith and Snipes Hall Farm Ltd v River Douglas Catchment Board [1949] 2 All ER 179, CA . . . 33.18–33.21

Smith New Court Securities Ltd v Scrimgeour Vickers (Asset Management) Ltd [1996] 4 All ER 769, HL . . . 12.21, 12.25, 12.26

Smith v Ainger (1990) Times, 5 June, CA . . . 25.6

Smith v Baker & Sons [1891] AC 325 HL . . . 19.3

Smith v Butler [1900] 1 Qb 694, CA . . . 5.36

Smith v Chadwick (1884) 9 App Cas 187 . . . 12.14

Smith v Cologan (1788) 2 Term Rep 188n . . . 14.7

Smith v Draper [1990] 2 EGLR 69, CA . . . 37.36

Smith v Eric S Bush; Harris v Wyre Forest District Council [1989] 2 All ER 514, HL . . . 9.15, 9.21, 16.18, 16.19, 16.21

Smith v Kenrick (1849) 7 CB 515 . . . 24.5

Smith v Land and House Property Corpn (1884) 28 Ch D 7, CA . . . 12.8, 14.47

Smith v Leech Brain & Co Ltd [1961] 3 All ER 1159 . . . 18.19

Smith v Littlewoods Organisation Ltd [1987] 1 All ER 710, HL . . . 16.10, 16.11

Smith v Scott [1972] 3 All ER 645 . . . 23.17

Smith v Stages [1989] 1 All ER 833, HL . . . 26.10

Smoker v London Fire and Civil Defence Authority; Wood v British Coal Corpn [1991] 2 All ER 449, HL . . . 27.9

Smoldon v Whitworth [1997] ELR 249, CA . . . 16.9

Sneesby v Goldings [1995] 2 EGLR 102, CA . . . 17.9

Snell & Prideaux Ltd v Dutton Mirrors Ltd [1995] 1 EGLR 259, CA . . . 32.52

Snook v Mannion [1982] RTR 321, DC . . . 21.7

Soames v Spencer (1822) 1 Dow & Ry KB 32 . . . 14.10

Sochacki v Sas [1947] 1 All ER 344 . . . 24.8, 24.16, 24.17

Société Commerciale de Réassurance v ERAS (International) [1992] 2 All ER 82n, CA . . . 27.23

Société Italo-Belge pour le Commerce et l'Industrie SA v Palm and Vegetable Oils (Malaysian) Sdn Bhd ("The Post Chaser") [1982] 1 All ER 19 . . . 6.22

Sorrell v Finch [1976] 2 All ER 371, HL . . . 14.47

Sotiros Shipping Inc v Sameiet Solholt ("The Solholt") [1983] 1 Lloyd's Rep 605 . . . 11.26

South Cambridgeshire DC v Persons Unknown, Times Law Reports, 11 November 2004 . . . 39.66

South Lakeland District Council v Secretary of State for the Environment [1992] 2 AC 141, HL . . . 39.50

South Western General Property Co Ltd v Marton (1982) 263 Estates Gazette 1090 . . . 12.46

Southern Water Authority v Carey [1985] 2 All ER 1077 . . . 14.8

Southwark London Borough Council v Mills [1999] 4 All ER 449, HL . . . 23.5, 36.34, 36.35

Southwark London Borough Council v Williams [1971] 2 All ER 175, CA . . . 22.5

Sovmots Investments Ltd v Secretary of State for the Environment [1976] 1 All ER 178 . . . 32.31, 32.35, 32.38

Spall v Owen (1981) 44 P & CR 36 . . . 28.22

Spartan Steel and Alloys Ltd v Martin & Co (Contractors) Ltd [1972] 3 All ER 557, CA . . . 16.13

Spath Holme Ltd v Chairman of Greater Manchester and Lancashire Rent Assessment Panel (1995) 28 HLR 107, CA . . . 37.3

Spectrum Plus Ltd, Re [2005] UKHL 41, HL . . . 3.44

Spence v Crawford [1939] 3 All ER 271 . . . 12.19

Spencer v Harding (1870) LR 5 CP 561 . . . 5.8

Spencer v Wincanton Holdings Ltd [2009] EWCA Civ 1404, CA . . . 18.10, 18.17

Spencer's Case (1583) 5 Co Rep 16a . . . 36.74

Spice Girls Ltd v Aprilia World Service BV [2002] EWCA Civ 15, CA . . . 12.5, 12.11

Spicer v Smee [1946] 1 All ER 489 . . . 23.9

Spiro v Glencrown Properties Ltd [1991] 1 All ER 600 . . . 29.7

Spiro v Lintern [1973] 3 All ER 319, CA . . . 14.8

Spring v Guardian Assurance plc [1994] 3 All ER 129, HL . . . 16.19, 16.20

Springer v Great Western Rly Co [1921] 1 KB 257, CA . . . 14.11

Squarey v Harris-Smith (1981) 42 P & CR 118, CA . . . 32.39

St Albans City and District Council v International Computers Ltd [1996] 4 All ER 481 . . . 9.12, 11.2

St Anne's Well Brewery Co v Roberts (1928) 140 LT 1, CA . . . 23.17, 24.4

St Edmundsbury and Ipswich Diocesan Board of Finance v Clark (No 2) [1975] 1 All ER 772, CA . . . 32.25

St Edmundsbury and Ipswich Diocesan Board of Finance v Clark (No 2) [1975] 1 All ER 772, CA . . . 32.53

St Helen's Smelting Co v Tipping (1865) 11 HL Cas 642 . . . 23.3, 23.8

St Marylebone Property Co Ltd v Tesco Stores Ltd [1988] 27 EG 72 . . . 36.37

Stack v Dowden [2007] 2 AC 432 . . . 31.11, 31.13, 31.14, 31.16, 31.42

Stafford v Lee (1992) 65 P & CR 172, CA . . . 32.30

Standard Chartered Bank Ltd v Walker [1982] 3 All ER 938, CA . . . 34.31

Standard Chartered Bank v Pakistan National Shipping Corpn (No 2) [2002] UKHL 43, HL . . . 12.30, 19.6

Stansbie v Troman [1948] 1 All ER 599, CA . . . 16.11, 18.9

Stanton v Callaghan [2000] QB 75, CA . . . 16.27

Staples v West Dorset District Council (1995) 93 LGR 536, CA . . . 21.12

Stapley v Gypsum Mines Ltd [1953] 2 All ER 478 . . . 19.9

Starmark Enterprises Ltd v CPL Distribution Ltd [2001] EWCA Civ 1252 . . . 36.57

Starmark Enterprises v CPL Distribution Ltd [2001] EWCA Civ 1252, CA . . . 3.38

Startup v Macdonald (1843) 6 Man & G 593 . . . 8.5

State Bank of India v Sood [1997] 1 All ER 169, CA . . . 31.36, 35.27

Staton v National Coal Board [1957] 2 All ER 667 . . . 26.10

Steele v Northern Ireland Office [1988] 12 NIJB 1 . . . 16.11

Steiglitz v Egginton (1815) Holt NP 141 . . . 14.4

Steinberg v Secretary of State for the Environment [1989] JPL 258 . . . 39.50

Stent v Monmouth District Council [1987] 1 EGLR 59, CA . . . 36.49

Stephens v Anglian Water Authority [1987] 3 All ER 379, CA . . . 28.20

Sterling Hydraulics Ltd v Dictomatik Ltd [2006] EWHC 2004 (QB) . . . 5.13

Stevens v Woodward (1881) 6 Qbd 318, DC . . . 24.13, 26.12

Stevenson v Rogers [1999] 1 All ER 613, CA . . . 7.25, 9.13

Stevenson, Jacques & Co v McLean (1880) 5 QBD 346 . . . 5.12

Stevenson, Jordan and Harrison Ltd v Macdonald and Evans [1952] 1 TLR 101 ... 26.3, 26.5

Stewart Gill Ltd v Horatio Myer & Co Ltd [1992] 2 All ER 257, CA ... 9.15, 9.21

Stickney v Keeble [1915] AC 386, HL ... 8.31, 11.45

Stilk v Myrick (1809) 2 Camp 317 ... 6.15

Stock v David Wilson Homes (Anglia) [1993] NPC 83, CA ... 28.22

Stock v Frank Jones (Tipton) Ltd [1978] 1 All ER 948, HL ... 3.15

Stocznia Gdanska SA v Latvian Shipping Co [1998] 1 All ER 883, HL ... 8.13, 10.16, 11.37

Stone and Saville's Contract, Re [1963] 1 All ER 353, CA ... 29.37

Stone v Cartwright (1795) 6 Term Rep 411 ... 26.1

Stone v Taffe [1974] 3 All ER 1016, CA ... 21.8

Storer v Manchester City Council [1974] 3 All ER 824 ... 5.1

Stovin v Wise [1996] 3 All ER 801, HL ... 16.22, 16.23

Strand Securities v Caswell [1965] 1 All ER 820 ... 35.25, 35.28

Street v Mountford [1985] 2 All ER 289, H ... 36.9

Stribling v Wickham (1989) 21 HLR 381, CA ... 36.10

Stringer v Minister of Housing and Local Government [1970] 1 WLR 1281 ... 39.28

Strover v Harrington [1988] 1 All ER 769 ... 12.14

Stuart v Joy [1904] 1 KB 362, CA ... 36.76

Stubbs v Holywell Rly Co Ltd (1867) LR 2 Exch 311 ... 10.7

Sturge v Hackett [1962] 1 WLR 1257, CA ... 28.23

Sturges v Bridgman (1879) 11 Ch D 852, CA ... 23.11, 23.19

Sudbrook Trading Estate Ltd v Eggleton [1982] 3 All ER 1, HL ... 5.31

Sugarman v Porter [2006] EWHC 331 (Ch) ... 33.26

Suleman v Shahsavari [1989] 2 All ER 460 ... 11.12, 14.45

Sumpter v Hedges [1898] 1 QB 673 ... 8.12

Sunnyfield, Re [1932] 1 Ch 79 ... 33.32

Supershield Limited v Siemens Building Technologies FE Limited [2010] EWCA Civ 7, CA ... 11.23, 11.24

Surrey CC v Bredero Homes Ltd [1993] 3 All ER 705, CA ... 11.1

Surrey County Council v Bredero Homes Ltd [1993] 3 All ER 705, CA ... 33.30

Sussex Peerage case (1844) 11 Cl & Fin 85 ... 3.13

Sutcliffe v Thackrah [1974] 1 All ER 859, HL ... 16.21, 16.25

Sutradhar v Natural Environment Research Council [2006] UKHL 33, HL ... 16.7

Sutton's Hospital Case (1612) 10 Co Rep 23a ... 4.13

Swain v Natui Ram Puri [1996] PIQR P442, CA ... 21.21

Swan v Great Northern Rly (1864) 4 De GJ & SM 211 ... 23.9

Swinney v Chief Constable of Northumbria Police [1996] 3 All ER 449, CA ... 16.24

Swiss Air Transport Co Ltd v Palmer [1976] 2 Lloyd's Rep 604 ... 14.31

Swordheath Properties Ltd v Tabet [1979] 1 All ER 240, CA ... 22.7

Sylvia Shipping Co Ltd v Progress Bulk Carriers Ltd [2010] EWHC 542 (Comm) ... 11.23

T (a minor) v Surrey County Council [1994] 4 All ER 577 ... 16.24

Tagro v Cafane [1991] 2 All ER 235, CA ... 36.34

Tai Hing Cotton Mill Ltd v Kamsing Knitting Factory [1978] 1 All ER 515, PC ... 11.12

Tai Hing Cotton Mill Ltd v Liu Chong Bank Ltd [1985] 2 All ER 947, PC ... 7.30

Tamlin v Hannaford [1950] 1 KB 18, CA ... 3.19

Tandon v Trustees of Spurgeon's Homes [1982] 1 All ER 1086, HL ... 37.14

Target Home Loans Ltd v Clothier [1994] 1 All ER 439, CA ... 34.27

Targett v Torfaen Borough Council [1992] 1 EGLR 275, CA ... 21.28, 36.46

Tarry v Ashton (1876) 1 QBD 314 ... 23.25, 26.21

Tate & Lyle Industries Ltd v Greater London Council [1983] 1 All ER 1159, HL ... 23.26, 28.20

Tate v Williamson (1866) 2 Ch App 55 ... 12.55

Taylor v Allon [1965] 1 All ER 557 ... 5.14, 5.20

Taylor v Caldwell (1863) 3 B & S 826 ... 10.3

Taylor's Fashions Ltd v Liverpool Victoria Trustees Co Ltd [1982] QB 133n ... 30.11

Tehidy Minerals Ltd v Norman [1971] 2 All ER 475, CA ... 32.48, 32.52

Tekdata Interconnections Ltd v Amphenol Ltd [2009] EWCA Civ 1209, CA ... 5.13

Tenax Steamship Co Ltd v Reinante Transoceania Navegacion SA ("The Brimnes") [1974] 3 All ER 88, CA ... 5.26

Tennant Radiant Heat Ltd v Warrington Development Corpn [1988] 1 EGLR 41, CA ... 11.29, 19.6

Tennent v Earl of Glasgow (1864) 2 M 22 ... 24.12

Tesco Stores Ltd v Wards Construction (Investment) Ltd (1995) 76 BLR 94 ... 21.28

Tetley v Chitty [1986] 1 All ER 663 ... 23.17

Texaco Antilles Ltd v Kernochan [1973] 2 All ER 118, PC ... 33.36

Thamesmead Town Ltd v Allotey [1998] 3 EGLR 97, CA ... 33.10

The Picture Warehouse Ltd v Cornhill Ltd [2008] EWHC 45 . . . 37.42

Theyer v Purnell [1918] 2 KB 333 . . . 25.8

Thomas v BPE Solicitors [2010] EWHC 306 (Ch) . . . 5.22

Thomas v British Railways Board [1976] 3 All ER 15, CA . . . 21.10

Thomas v National Union of Mineworkers [1985] 2 All ER 1 . . . 23.25

Thomas v Sorrell (1673) Vaugh 330 . . . 28.40

Thomas Witter Ltd v TBP Industries Ltd [1996] 2 All ER 573 . . . 12.23, 12.37, 12.38

Thompson-Schwab v Costaki [1956] 1 All ER 652, CA . . . 23.4

Thompson v Alexander (1992) 59 BLR 81 . . . 21.29

Thompson v Brown Construction (Ebbw Vale) Ltd [1981] 2 All ER 296, HL . . . 27.24

Thompson v Gibson (1841) 7 M & W 456 . . . 23.14

Thompson v London, Midland and Scottish Rly Co [1930] 1 KB 41, CA . . . 7.13

Thompson v Park [1944] 2 All ER 477 . . . 28.43

Thompson v T Lohan (Plant Hire) Ltd [1987] 2 All ER 631, CA . . . 9.10, 26.7

Thomson v Davenport (1829) 9 B & C 78 . . . 14.36, 14.38

Thorne v University of London [1966] 2 All ER 338, CA . . . 16.23

Thorner v Major [2009] UKHL 18 . . . 30.12

Thornton v Shoe Lane Parking Ltd [1971] 1 All ER 686, CA . . . 7.13

Tichborne v Weir (1892) 67 LT 735 . . . 30.21, 30.33

Tiedemann and Ledermann Frères, Re [1899] 2 Qb 66 . . . 14.9

Tillett v Ward (1882) 10 Qbd 17 . . . 25.3

Tiltwood, Sussex, Re; Barrett v Bond [1978] 2 All ER 1091 . . . 33.36

Tinn v Hoffmann & Co (1873) 29 LT 271 . . . 5.10

Tinsley v Milligan [1994] AC 330 . . . 30.9

Tito v Waddell (No 2) [1977] 3 All ER 129 . . . 30.18

Tollemache and Cobbold Breweries Ltd v Reynolds [1983] 2 EGLR 158, CA . . . 22.8

Tomlinson v Congleton BC [2003] UKHL 47, HL . . . 17.13, 21.20, 21.22

Tool Metal Manufacturing Co Ltd v Tungsten Electric Co Ltd [1955] 2 All ER 657, HL . . . 6.22, 6.23

Tootal Clothing Ltd v Guinea Properties Management Ltd (1992) 64 P & CR 452, CA . . . 29.2, 29.6

Tophams Ltd v Sefton [1967] 1 AC 50, HL . . . 33.26

Topp v London Country Bus (South West) Ltd [1993] 3 All ER 448, CA . . . 16.10

Torvald Klaveness A/S v Arni Maritime Corpn, The Gregos [1994] 4 All ER 998, HL . . . 8.19

Town and Country Building Society v Julien (1991) 24 HLR 312, CA . . . 34.27

TP and KM v UK [2001] FLR 549, EHCR . . . 16.23

Transco plc v Stockport MBC [2003] UKHL 61, HL . . . 24.3–24.4, 24.8, 24.9

Transfield Shipping Inc v Mercator Inc ("The Achilleas") [2008] UKHL 48, HL . . . 11.22, 11.23, 11.24

Transworld Land Co Ltd v J Sainsbury plc [1990] 2 EGLR 255 . . . 36.39

Tredegar Iron and Coal Co Ltd v Hawthorn Bros & Co (1902) 18 TLR 716, CA . . . 8.27

Treloar v Nute [1976] 1 WLR 1295 . . . 30.25

Trent Strategic Health Authority v Jain [2009] UKHL 4, HL . . . 16.23

Trevett v Lee [1955] 1 All ER 406, CA . . . 23.24

Trickett v Tomlinson (1863) 13 CBNS 663 . . . 14.32

Truman, Hanbury, Buxton & Co Ltd's Application, Re [1955] 3 All ER 559, CA . . . 33.39

Trustee in Bankruptcy of St John Poulton v Ministry of Justice [2010] EWCA Civ 392, CA . . . 20.2

Tsakiroglou & Co Ltd v Noblee Thorl GmbH [1961] 2 All ER 179, HL . . . 10.4, 10.5

TSB Bank plc v Botham [1996] EGCS 149, CA . . . 28.5, 28.11

Tse Kwong Lam v Wong Chit Sen [1983] 3 All ER 54, PC . . . 34.30, 34.31

Tudor v Hamid [1988] 1 EGLR 251, CA . . . 29.28

Tulk v Moxhay (1848) 18 LJ Ch 83 . . . 33.11, 33.12

Turberville v Stamp (1697) 1 Ld Raym 264 . . . 24.15

Turner v Goldsmith [1891] 1 Qb 544, CA . . . 14.23

Turner v Green [1895] 2 Ch 265 . . . 12.11, 12.52

Turpin v Bilton (1843) 5 Man & G 455 . . . 14.12

Tutin v Mary Chipperfield Promotions Ltd (1980) 130 NLJ 807 . . . 25.5

Tutton v AD Walter Ltd [1985] 3 All ER 757 . . . 21.7

Twentieth Century Banking Corpn Ltd v Wilkinson [1976] 3 All ER 361 . . . 34.36, 34.38

Twine v Bean's Express Ltd (1946) 175 LT 131, CA . . . 26.13

Tye v House [1997] 2 EGLR 171 . . . 5.35, 29.23

Tysoe v Davies [1984] RTR 88 . . . 23.25

UK Housing Alliance (North West) Ltd v Francis [2010] EWCA Civ 117, CA . . . 9.27

Union Eagle Ltd v Golden Achievement Ltd [1997] 2 All ER 215, PC . . . 8.29

Union Lighterage Co v London Graving Dock Co [1902] 2 Ch 557, CA . . . 32.45

Union of London and Smith's Bank Ltd's
Conveyance, Re; Miles v Easter [1933] Ch 611,
CA . . . 33.27
United Bank of Kuwait v Sahib [1997] Ch
107 . . . 29.9
United Dominions Trust Ltd v Shellpoint
Trustees Ltd [1993] 4 All ER 310, CA . . .
36.70
United Kingdom Mutual Steamship Assurance
Ltd v Nevill (1887) 19 Qbd 110, CA . . . 14.37
United Scientific Holdings v Burnley Borough
Council [1978] AC 904, HL . . . 36.57
Universal Cargo Carriers Corpn v Citati [1957]
2 All ER 70 . . . 8.19
Universal Corpn v Five Ways Properties Ltd
[1979] 1 All ER 552, CA . . . 29.28
Universe Tankships Inc of Monrovia v
International Transport Workers Federation
("The Universe Sentinel") [1982] 2 All ER 67,
HL . . . 12.59
Uratemp Ventures Ltd v Collins [2001] UKHL
43 . . . 37.4

Vacwell Engineering Co Ltd v BDH Chemicals
Ltd [1970] 3 All ER 553n, CA . . . 18.18
Vale of White Horse District Council v Parker
[1997] JPL 660 . . . 39.61
Van Duyn v Home Office (C-41/74) [1975] 3 All
ER 190, ECJ . . . 3.49, 3.54
Van Oppen v Clerk to the Bedford Charity
Trustees [1989] 3 All ER 389, CA . . . 16.7
Vanderpant v Mayfair Hotel Co Ltd [1930] 1 Ch
138 . . . 23.12
Vasey v Surrey Free Inns [1996] PIQR P373,
CA . . . 26.14
Vellino v Chief Constable of the Greater
Manchester Police [2001] EWCA Civ
1249 . . . 16.9
Verity and Spindler v Lloyds Bank [1996] Fam
Law 213 . . . 16.19
Verrall v Great Yarmouth Borough Council
[1980] 1 All ER 839, CA . . . 28.43
Viasystems (Tyneside) Ltd v Thermal Transfer
(Northern) Ltd [2005] EWCA Civ 1151,
CA . . . 26.7
Victoria Laundry (Windsor) Ltd v Newman
Industries Ltd [1949] 1 All ER 997, CA . . .
11.15, 11.16, 11.19, 11.22
Vincent v Premo Enterprises (Voucher Sales)
Ltd [1969] 2 All ER 941, CA . . . 4.6, 29.11
Vision Enterprises Ltd v Tiensia [2010] EWCA
Civ 1224 . . . 37.8
Vitol SA v Norelf Ltd [1996] 3 All ER 193,
HL . . . 8.10
Vodden v Gayton [2001] PIQR P52 . . . 21.10
Voice v Bell (1993) 68 P & CR 441, CA . . . 32.4
Vowles v Evans [2003] EWCA Civ 318 . . . 16.9
Vowles v Miller (1810) 3 Taunt 137 . . . 28.24
Voyce v Voyce (1991) 62 P & CR 290, CA . . .
30.15

W J Alan & Co Ltd v El Nasr Export and Import
Co [1972] 2 All ER 127 . . . 6.22, 6.28
W v Essex CC [2001] 2 AC 592, HL . . . 16.28
W v Essex County Council [2000] 2 All ER 237,
HL . . . 16.24
W v Home Office [1997] Imm AR 302,
CA . . . 16.23
W v Meah [1986] 1 All ER 935 . . . 18.20
Wadlow v Samuel [2007] EWCA Civ 155,
CA . . . 12.63
Wake v Renault (UK) Ltd (1996) 15 Tr LR 514,
CA . . . 7.6
Wakeham v Wood (1981) 43 P & CR 40, CA . . .
32.15, 33.30
Walford v Miles [1992] 1 All ER 453, HL . . .
5.31, 5.35
Walker v Arkay Caterers Ltd [1997] EGCS
107 . . . 36.36
Walker v Boyle [1982] 1 All ER 634 . . . 9.15,
12.46
Walker v Northumberland County Council
[1995] 1 All ER 737 . . . 16.28
Wall v Rederiaktiebolaget Luggude [1915] 3 KB
66 . . . 11.33
Wallace v Newton [1982] 2 All ER 106 . . . 25.6
Wallington v Secretary of State for Wales [1990]
JPL 112 . . . 39.8
Wallis Fashions Group plc v CGU Life
Assurance Ltd [2000] L & TR 520 . . . 37.44
Wallis, Son and Wells v Pratt and Haynes [1911]
AC 394, HL . . . 9.4
Walsh v Lonsdale (1882) 21 Ch D 9 . . . 11.45,
30.4, 30.5
Walter v Selfe (1851) 4 De G & Sm 315 . . . 23.6
Walton Harvey Ltd v Walker and Homfrays Ltd
[1931] 1 Ch 274, CA . . . 10.13
Wandsworth LBC v Secretary of State for
Transport, Local Government and the
Regions and BT Cellnet [2003] EWHC
622 . . . 38.30
Wandsworth London Borough Council v
Railtrack plc [2001] EWCA Civ 1236 . . .
23.23, 25.2
Ward v Kirkland [1966] 1 All ER 609 . . . 32.31
Ward v Ritz Hotel (London) [1992] PIQR P315,
CA . . . 21.12
Ward v Tesco Stores Ltd [1976] 1 All ER 219,
CA . . . 17.18
Ward v Warnke (1990) 22 HLR 496, CA . . . 6.3
Ware v Garston Haulage Co Ltd [1943] 2 All ER
558, CA . . . 23.24
Warehousing and Forwarding Co of East Africa
Ltd v Jafferali & Sons Ltd [1963] 3 All ER 571,
PC . . . 14.7
Warlow v Harrison (1859) 1 E & E 309 . . . 5.7
Warner Bros Pictures Inc v Nelson [1936] 3 All
ER 160 . . . 11.48
Warren v Henlys Ltd [1948] 2 All ER 935 . . .
26.14
Warren v Keen [1954] 1 QB 15 . . . 36.42

Warren v Mendy [1989] 3 All ER 103, CA . . .
11.48
Waterman v Boyle [2009] EWCA Civ 115 . . .
32.11, 32.53
Watford Electronics Ltd v Sanderson CFL Ltd
[2001] EWCA Civ 317, CA . . . 12.48
Watkins v Birmingham City Council (1975) 126
NLJ 442 . . . 17.5, 26.5
Watson v British Boxing Board of Control
[2001] QB 1134, CA . . . 16.9
Watson v Croft Promo-Sport Ltd [2009] EWCA
Civ 15, CA . . . 23.8, 23.10
Watson v Swann (1862) 11 CBNS 756 . . . 14.8
Watt v Hertfordshire County Council [1954] 2
All ER 368, CA . . . 17.13
Watts v Morrow [1991] 4 All ER 937, CA . . .
11.6, 27.12
Waverley Borough Council v Fletcher [1995] 4
All ER 756, CA . . . 28.18
Way v Latilla [1937] 3 All ER 759, HL . . . 14.17
Wayling v Jones (1983) 69 P & CR 170 . . . 30.13,
30.15
Webb v Barclays Bank plc and Portsmouth
Hospitals NHS Trust [2001] Lloyd's Rep Med
500, CA . . . 18.9
Webb v Bird (1861) 10 CBNS 268 . . . 32.9
Webb v Pollmount [1966] 1 All ER 481 . . . 35.24
Webb's Lease, Re [1951] Ch 808 . . . 28.23
Webb's Lease, Re; Sandom v Webb [1951] Ch
808, CA . . . 32.33
Webbv EMO Air Cargo (UK) Ltd [1992] 4 All
ER 929 . . . 3.51
Weedon v Hindwood, Clarke and Esplin [1975]
1 EGLR 82 . . . 17.9
Weigall & Co v Runciman & Co (1916) 85 LJKB
1187, CA . . . 14.13
Weir v Chief Constable of Merseyside Police
[2003] EWCA Civ 111 . . . 26.14
Weld- Blundell v Stephens [1920] AC 956,
HL . . . 11.13
Weller & Co v Foot and Mouth Disease
Research Institute [1965] 3 All ER 560 . . .
16.12, 24.9
Wells v Cooper [1958] 2 All ER 527, CA. . . . 17.8
Wells v Wells [1998] 3 All ER 481, HL . . . 27.8
Wells, Re; Swinburne-Hanham v Howard
[1933] Ch 29 . . . 34.10
Welsh v Stokes [2007] EWCA Civ 796,
CA . . . 25.6
Welton v North Cornwall District Council
[1997] 1 WLR 570, CA . . . 16.24
Wentworth v Wiltshire County Council [1993]
2 All ER 256, CA . . . 20.5
Wessex Dairies Ltd v Smith [1935] 2 KB 80,
CA . . . 7.31
West Bromwich Albion Football Club Ltd v El-
Safty [2006] EWCA Civ 1299, CA . . . 16.12
West Lancashire District Council v Secretary of
State for the Environment [1998] EGCS
33 . . . 39.38

West London Commercial Bank v Kitson (1884)
13 QBD 360 . . . 12.10
West Wiltshire District Council v Garland
[1995] 2 All ER 17, CA . . . 20.4
Western Bank Ltd v Schindler [1976] 2 All ER
39 . . . 34.21
Westminster City Council v British Waterways
Board [1985] AC 676 . . . 39.15
Westminster City Council v Clarke [1992] 1 All
ER 695, HL . . . 36.8, 36.9, 37.18
Westripp v Baldock [1939] 1 All ER 279,
CA . . . 22.3
Westwood v Post Office [1973] 3 All ER 184,
HL . . . 19.8, 20.4, 21.8
Wheat v E Lacon & Co Ltd [1966] 1 All ER 582,
HL . . . 21.4, 21.5
Wheaton v Maple & Co [1893] 3 Ch 48,
CA . . . 32.42
Wheeldon v Burrows (1879) 12 Ch D 31 . . .
32.29, 32.31, 32.32, 32.34, 32.37–32.39
Wheeler v Copas [1981] 3 All ER 405 . . . 21.6
Wheeler v JJ Saunders Ltd [1995] 2 All ER 697,
CA . . . 23.8, 32.31, 32.39, 37.26
Wheeler v Trustees of St Mary's Hall,
Chislehurst (1989) Times, 10 October . . .
21.12
Whincup v Hughes (1871) LR 6 CP 78 . . . 8.13
White (Contractors) Ltd v Tarmac Civil
Engineering Ltd [1967] 3 All ER 586,
HL . . . 26.7
White and Carter (Councils) Ltd v McGregor
[1962] AC 413, HL . . . 11.37
White and Carter Ltd v Carbis Bay Garage Ltd
[1941] 2 All ER 633, CA . . . 10.8
White v Bijou Mansions Ltd [1937] 3 All ER 269
. . . 33.3
White v Blackmore [1972] 3 All ER 158,
CA . . . 21.3
White v Chief Constable of the South Yorkshire
Police [1999] 1 All ER 1, HL . . . 16.28
White v City of London Brewery Co (1889) 42
Ch D 237, CA . . . 34.22
White v Garden (1851) 10 CB 919 . . . 12.17,
12.19
White v John Warrick & Co Ltd [1953] 2 All ER
1021, CA. . . . 9.6
White v Jones [1995] 1 All ER 691, HL . . .
16.21
White v St Albans City and District Council
(1990) Times, 12 March, CA . . . 21.21
Whitehouse v Jordan [1981] 1 All ER 267,
HL . . . 17.7
Whiteley v Chappell (1868) LR 4 QB 147 . . .
3.11
Whittington v Seale-Hayne (1900) 82 LT
49 . . . 12.39
Whitwham v Westminster Brymbo Coal Co
[1896] 2 Ch 538, CA . . . 22.7
Whyte v Redland Aggregates Ltd [1998] CLY
3989, CA . . . 21.12

Wieland v Cyril Lord Carpets Ltd [1969] 3 All ER 1006 . . . 18.17

Wilbeam v Ashton (1807) 1 Camp 78 . . . 11.33

Wilkes v Hungerford Market Co (1835) 2 Bing NC 281 . . . 23.26

Wilkinson v Coverdale (1793) 1 Esp 74, CA . . . 14.12

Wilkinson v Lloyd (1845) 7 QB 27 . . . 8.13

William Aldred's Case (1610) 9 Co Rep 57b . . . 32.9

William Ashton v Secretary of State for Communities and Local Government and Local Government and Coin Street Community Builders Ltd [2010] EWCA Civ 600 . . . 39.42

William Cory & Son Ltd v Wingate Investments (London Colney) Ltd (1978) 17 BLR 104, CA . . . 11.12

William Hill (Southern) Ltd v Cabras Ltd [1987] 1 EGLR 37, CA . . . 32.5

William Hill Organisation v Bernard Sunley & Sons (1982) 22 BLR 8, CA . . . 16.16, 27.24

William Sindall plc v Cambridgeshire County Council [1994] 3 All ER 932 . . . 12.38

Williams & Glyn's Bank Ltd v Boland [1980] 2 All ER 408, HL . . . 34.24, 35.23–35.26, 35.28

Williams Bros Direct Supply Ltd v Raftery [1957] 3 All ER 593, CA . . . 30.24, 30.25

Williams v Bayley (1866) LR 1 HL 200, HL . . . 12.61

Williams v Carwardine (1833) 5 C & P 566 . . . 5.10

Williams v Fawcett [1985] 1 All ER 787, CA . . . 3.38

Williams v Jones [2002] EWCA Civ 1097 . . . 30.36

Williams v Kiley [2002] EWCA Civ 1645 . . . 33.28, 36.39

Williams v Linnit [1951] 1 All ER 278, CA . . . 21.2

Williams v Natural Life Health Foods Ltd [1998] 2 All ER 577, HL. . . . 16.19

Williams v Roffey Bros & Nicholls (Contractors) Ltd [1990] 1 All ER 512, CA . . . 6.16

Williams v Wellingborough Borough Council [1975] 3 All ER 462, CA . . . 34.30

Willis v Association of Universities of the British Commonwealth [1965] 1 QB 140, CA . . . 37.38

Willis' Application, Re [1997] 28 EG 137 . . . 33.42

Wills v Wills [2004] 1 P & CR 37 . . . 30.25

Willson v Ministry of Defence [1991] 1 All ER 638 . . . 27.8

Wilmott v Barber (1880) 15 Ch D 96 . . . 30.11

Wilsher v Essex Area Health Authority [1986] 3 All ER 801, CA . . . 17.8, 18.4

Wilson Smithett & Cape (Sugar) Ltd v Bangladesh Sugar and Food Industries Corpn [1986] 1 Lloyd's Rep 378 . . . 5.14

Wilson v Finch Hatton (1877) 2 Ex D 336 . . . 36.44

Wilson v Tumman (1843) 6 Man & G 236 . . . 14.8

Wiltshire County Council v Frazer [1986] 1 All ER 65 . . . 22.9

Wimpey Construction UK Ltd v Poole (1984) 27 BLR 58 . . . 17.7

Windsor Life Assurance Co Ltd v Lloyds bank plc [2009] 47 EG 134 . . . 37.33

Winn v Bull (1877) 7 Ch D 29 . . . 5.34

Winter Garden Theatre (London) Ltd v Millennium Productions Ltd [1947] 2 All ER 331, HL . . . 28.43

Winter v Traditional & Contemporary Contracts Ltd [2007] EWCA Civ 1088 . . . 33.43

Winterbottom v Lord Derby (1867) LR 2 Exch 316 . . . 23.26

With v O'Flanagan [1936] 1 All ER 727, CA . . . 12.11

Withers v Perry Chain Co Ltd [1961] 3 All ER 676, CA . . . 17.14

Wolstanton Ltd v Newcastle-under-Lyme Borough Council [1940] 3 All ER 101, HL . . . 3.46

Wong v Beaumont Property Trust Ltd [1964] 2 All ER 119, CA . . . 32.20

Wood v Law Society [1993] NLJR 1475 . . . 16.23

Woodar Investment Development Ltd v Wimpey Construction UK Ltd [1980] 1 All ER 571, HL . . . 8.18, 13.12

Woodar Investment Ltd v Wimpey Construction Ltd [1980] 1 All ER 517, HL . . . 11.2

Woodhouse A C Israel Cocoa Ltd SA v Nigerian Produce Marketing Co Ltd [1972] 2 All ER 271, HL . . . 6.22

Woodman v Richardson [1937] 3 All ER 866, CA . . . 21.6

Woodward v Hastings Corpn [1944] 2 All ER 565, CA . . . 21.16

Wooldridge v Sumner [1962] 2 All ER 978 . . . 19.5

Woollerton and Wilson Ltd v Richard Costain Ltd [1970] 1 All ER 483 . . . 22.8

Woollins v British Celanese Ltd (1966) 1 KIR 438, CA . . . 21.14, 21.15

Woolwich Building Society v Dickman [1996] 3 All ER 204 . . . 34.23

Worboys v Carter [1987] 2 EGLR 1, CA . . . 14.8

Workers Trust and Merchant Bank Ltd v Dojap Investments Ltd [1993] 2 All ER 370, PC . . . 29.28

Worth v Gilling (1866) LR 2 CP 1 . . . 25.6

Wright v Carter [1903] 1 Ch 27, CA . . . 12.63

Wright v Lodge [1993] 4 All ER 299, CA . . . 18.7

Wright v Macadam [1949] 2 All ER 565, CA . . . 32.11, 32.36

Wright v Robert Leonard (Developments) Ltd
    [1994] NPC 49, CA . . . 29.6
Wringe v Cohen [1939] 4 All ER 241, CA . . .
    23.17, 23.25
Wroth v Tyler [1973] 1 All ER 897 . . . 11.16
Wrotham Park Estate Co Ltd v Parkside Homes
    Ltd [1974] 2 All ER 321 . . . 11.7, 11.38, 11.39,
    11.40, 33.13, 33.30
WWF World Wide Fund for Nature v World
    Wrestling Federation Entertainment Inc
    [2007] EWCA Civ 286, CA . . . 11.40
Wycombe Health Authority v Barnett (1982) 47
    P & CR 394 . . . 36.42
Wyld v Silver [1962] 3 All ER 309, CA . . . 32.22

X v Bedfordshire County Council [1995] 3 All
    ER 353, HL . . . 16.22, 16.23, 16.24, 20.2
Xenos v Danube and Black Sea Rly Co (1863) 13
    CBNS 825 . . . 8.26

Yasuda Fire and Marine Insurance Co of
    Europe Ltd v Orion Marine Insurance
    Underwriting Agency Ltd [1995] 3 All ER
    211 . . . 14.1, 14.16

Yates Building Co Ltd v RJ Pulleyn & Sons
    (York) Ltd (1975) 119 Sol Jo 370, CA . . . 5.23
Yaxley v Gotts [2000] 1 All ER 711, CA . . . 29.9
Yeoman's Row Management Ltd v Cobbe [2008]
    EWHL1139 . . . 29.9, 30.12
Yetton v Eastwood Froy Ltd [1966] 3 All ER 3
    53 . . . 11.26
Yewens v Noakes (1880) 6 QBD 530 . . . 26.4
Yonge v Toynbee [1910] 1 KB 215, CA . . . 14.25,
    14.27, 14.45
Young & Co Ltd v White (1911) 28 TLR
    87 . . . 14.38
Young v Bristol Aeroplane Co Ltd [1944] 2 All
    ER 293, CA . . . 3.38
Young v Dalgety plc [1987] 1 EGLR 116 . . .
    28.12
Yuen Kun- yeu v A-G of Hong Kong [1987] 2 All
    ER 705, PC . . . 16.23

Z v UK [2001] 2 FLR 612, EHCR . . . 16.23
Zanzibar v British Aerospace (Lancaster House)
    Ltd [2000] 1 WLR 2333 . . . 12.37
Zarvos v Pradhan [2003] EWCA Civ 208 . . .
    37.38

PART I

Outline of the English legal system

1

Introduction

CHAPTER OVERVIEW

This book is concerned with those aspects of the civil law of England and Wales which are of direct relevance to the property professional. In the rest of this book 'English law' and 'English legal system' are used to describe the law and legal system respectively of England and Wales. The laws and legal systems of Scotland and, to a lesser extent Northern Ireland, are distinct from those of England and Wales.

In this chapter we explain three distinctions which are fundamental to the understanding of English law:

- the distinction between civil law and criminal law;
- the distinction between common law and legislation as sources of English law; and
- the distinction between common law and equity as sources of English law.

Civil law and criminal law

1.1 Criminal cases, which are called prosecutions, are normally initiated by the state, but they may be brought by a private citizen, although this is rare. If a prosecution is successful the defendant is liable to punishment. This affords no direct benefit to the victim (V) since V does not receive fines payable or the fruits of a criminal's labours in prison. V cannot prevent a prosecution nor order its discontinuance.

1.2 In contrast, civil actions are brought by an individual (the claimant) who is seeking to obtain compensation for loss suffered or to establish legal rights. If damages are awarded, they are payable to the claimant and are generally assessed on the basis that they should compensate the claimant and not on the basis of punishing the defendant. A claimant can discontinue a civil action at any time before judgment.

1.3 Facts which disclose a criminal offence may also form the basis of a civil action. If A, a taxi driver, collides with C's car while driving B to the station, the civil law of contract, the civil law of tort and the criminal law may all be applicable. A has certainly broken his contract to drive B to the station, and if his driving was careless this may occasion not only criminal liability for an offence of careless driving but also tortious liability to C for the damage caused to C's car.

Common law and legislation[1]

1.4 Common law and legislation are sources of law.[1] Common law means judge-made law. It is contained in the decisions or judgments made by the English judiciary over many centuries. Legislation comprises Acts of Parliament and Acts of the Welsh Assembly, subordinate legislation (such as statutory instruments deriving their authority from Acts of Parliament) and the legislation of the European Union.

[1] Chapter 3.

Common law and equity

1.5 The common law can be further subdivided into common law and equity. The difference between these two species of judge-made law is that of their origins. Prior to the Judicature Acts of 1873–1875 there were two systems of courts in England, the common law courts and the Court of Chancery. Although the court system was fused in 1875, the law which they applied was not. Thus it is still possible to speak of common law and equity as distinct bodies of law.

1.6 The common law courts had evolved from the centralised system for the administration of justice developed between the eleventh and thirteenth centuries. Therefore, common law is that body of law developed by the common law courts prior to the fusion of the administration of justice in 1875, and modifications and extensions effected since 1875.

1.7 Equity is that body of law developed in the Court of Chancery prior to 1875 and its subsequent amendments and developments. The Court of Chancery developed because the common law courts entangled themselves in an extremely rigid procedure which made it difficult to initiate actions and severely limited the development of the common law, and the remedies available in the common law courts were inadequate. Thus, the habit arose in the fourteenth and fifteenth centuries of petitioning the King to remedy injustice. After a while, the King delegated the task of determining these petitions to his Chancellor. In due course, the Lord Chancellor began to hear cases in the Court of Chancery. The procedure in the Court of Chancery was originally less rigid than that of the common law courts; and the basis of decisions was supposed to be the merits of each action and what was just between the parties, with little reference to previous cases. Subsequently, both procedure and substantive law became more rigid; the notion of creating a remedy to fit the particular case before the court disappeared and the Court of Chancery became as much influenced by previous cases as the common law courts.

The rules of equity developed by the Court of Chancery were concerned either with entirely new rights totally unknown to the common law or with remedies (such as injunctions and specific performance)[1] designed to counter the inefficacy or injustice of the common law. Equity did not amend the common law but enabled a litigant who had failed to establish a claim at common law, or been disappointed by the remedies available there, to seek an equitable remedy which made good the defects of the common law in a particular case. For example, if the parties to a contract agree to vary their agreement the common law provides that the variation cannot take effect unless it is made by deed or supported by consideration, whereas equity may prevent the agreement being enforced in its unvaried form, for a time at least.[2]

[1] Paras 11.43–11.51.
[2] Paras 6.20–6.24.

1.8 If there is a conflict between the rules of the common law and those of equity, the rules of equity prevail. It cannot be emphasised too much that the remedies developed by equity cannot be demanded as of right (unlike common law remedies) but, reflecting the origins of equity in conscience, are discretionary.

Questions

1. What are the differences between criminal law and civil law?

2. What is meant by the term 'common law'?

2

Administration of the law

CHAPTER OVERVIEW

In this chapter we describe:

- the system of courts with a civil jurisdiction;
- specialist courts and tribunals;
- alternative methods of dispute resolution.

The civil courts

2.1 We describe below those courts with a civil jurisdiction which would be of relevance to a property professional in his or her capacity as such. We do not, therefore, describe magistrates' courts or the Crown Court which have jurisdiction over criminal matters; such jurisdiction as they have over civil matters (eg family proceedings in the case of a magistrates' court) is of no such relevance. The chart below shows the civil court structure in England and Wales.

THE CIVIL COURT STRUCTURE IN ENGLAND AND WALES

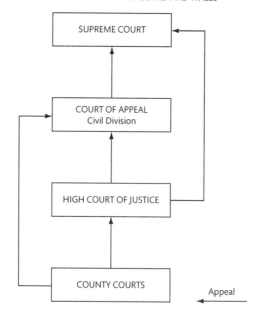

County courts

2.2 The jurisdiction of the county courts is exclusively civil. County courts are sited in many locations in England and Wales.

The full jurisdiction of the county courts is typically exercised by circuit judges, judges who are appointed to serve in the Crown Court and in county courts. It can also be exercised by deputy circuit judges (retired circuit judges appointed to serve on a part-time basis) and recorders (part-time judges otherwise normally engaged in professional legal practice as a lawyer).

There are also district judges and part-time deputy district judges. These judges deal with the work of the county courts at the interim stage of proceedings and also have jurisdiction to try claims not exceeding £25,000 in value and to try claims for the recovery of land. In addition, they have the full jurisdiction of a circuit judge in all undefended claims.

Jurisdiction

2.3 County courts have jurisdiction over a wide range of civil matters. This jurisdiction includes:

- *Jurisdiction over actions in contract or tort or for money recoverable by statute.* An action in contract or tort may be *commenced* in a county court or in the High Court, save that a claim must be commenced in a county court where the value of a claim does not exceed £25,000 (or £50,000 where the proceedings include a claim for personal injury).
- *Jurisdiction over actions for the recovery of land.*
- *An equity jurisdiction*, eg in cases of administration of estates, foreclosure of mortgages and specific performance of contracts for the sale of land, where the amount of the estate, the amount owing under the mortgage or purchase price, as the case may be, does not exceed £30,000.
- *Matters under the Rent, Landlord and Tenant and Housing Acts.*

Once started in a county court or the High Court, proceedings are allocated to one of three tracks, as explained below.

Small claims track

2.4 A defended action will normally be allocated to the 'small claims track' and tried in a county court if the amount involved is not in excess of £5,000. In the case of:

- a claim in respect of personal injuries, the amount claimed for personal injuries must not exceed £1,000;
- a claim by a residential tenant for an order requiring the landlord to repair the premises, the repair-cost must not exceed £1,000.

If an action is allocated to the small claims track, the court can adopt any method of proceeding which it considers fair, including an inquisitorial approach under which it questions witnesses before the parties can. Proceedings are normally heard by a district judge or deputy district judge.

If the amount in dispute exceeds the relevant limit a suitable claim can still be allocated to the 'small claims track' if the parties agree to this.

The advantage of the 'small claims track' is that it is eminently suitable for the litigant in person in small claims cases, which are mainly 'consumer disputes', since it is even more informal and inexpensive than trial in the county court. Legal representation is discouraged by the fact that, contrary to the usual rule, a successful party cannot normally recover the costs of legal representation from the other.

Fast track claims

2.5 The fast track is the normal track for any claim for which the small claims track is not the normal track where the claim has a value of not more than £25,000, but only if the trial is not expected to exceed one day and will not involve more than one expert witness per party in any expert field (with a maximum of two such fields). Fast-track cases should be completed within 30 weeks of allocation. The majority of fast track claims are heard in a county court; otherwise they are heard in the High Court.

Multi-track claims

2.6 The 'multi-track' is the normal track to which claims for which neither of the other two tracks is the normal track are allocated. Multi-track cases are heard in a county court or the High Court, depending on their complexity and/or value.

Appeals

2.7 Appeal from a district judge or deputy district judge lies to a circuit judge but the permission of the judge appealed from or the circuit judge is required. Appeal from any other judge of a county court lies, in some cases, to the Court of Appeal, and, in the rest, to the High Court, in either case with the permission of the judge appealed from or the court appealed to.

The High Court of Justice

2.8 The High Court is divided into three Divisions.

Most cases are heard by High Court judge, but a significant number, mainly in the Queen's Bench Division, are heard by deputy High Court judges who are appointed on a temporary basis.

The High Court has an extensive appellate jurisdiction. Except for isolated exceptions where an order affects the liberty of an individual, an appeal to the High Court requires the permission of the court from whom it is sought to appeal or of the High Court.

Unless there are special circumstances where the interests of justice so require, an appeal will not be a rehearing but a review of the lower court's decision. The comments in para 2.16 about appeals to the Court of Appeal apply equally here.

Sometimes an appeal is required to be by case stated. An appeal by case stated is never reheard; the court simply hears legal arguments relating to the facts set out in the stated case.

An appeal will only be allowed where the decision of the lower court was wrong, or where it was unjust because of a serious procedural or other irregularity in the lower court. The same rule also applies in a county court to an appeal to a circuit judge from the decision of a district judge.

Chancery Division

2.9 The jurisdiction of the Chancery Division, which is entirely civil, is exercised in London and a number of regional centres. It can be split into original and appellate jurisdictions.

Original jurisdiction Matters within this jurisdiction include:

- the administration of estates of deceased persons;
- the redemption and foreclosure of mortgages;
- the rectification or cancellation of deeds;
- the dissolution of partnerships;
- the sale, exchange or partition of land, or the raising of charges on land; and
- all causes and matters under enactments relating to companies.

Appellate jurisdiction This covers appeals in 'Chancery matters' from a county court. In addition, a few appeals of other types may be heard, eg income tax appeals from the Commissioners of Revenue and Customs.

Queen's Bench Division

2.10 This division is the largest of the three divisions and has the most varied jurisdiction which is exercised in certain regional centres, as well as in London.

2.11 The civil jurisdiction of the Queen's Bench Division can be divided into three heads, the first of which is the busiest:

- *Original civil jurisdiction* The principal aspects of this are actions in contract and tort. Commercial matters are dealt with by specialist judges in the Commercial Court which sits in London, and whose procedure is more flexible than the normal High Court procedure. Small and medium-sized commercial cases are also heard by specialist circuit judges sitting as High Court judges in the Mercantile Courts which sit in London and a number of regional centres.

- *Appellate civil jurisdiction* A single judge has jurisdiction to hear appeals from decisions in the county courts. In addition, a single judge (or, if the court so directs, a divisional court) hears appeals by way of case stated on a miscellaneous collection of civil matters from magistrates' courts (excluding family proceedings) and the Crown Court. A divisional court consists of two or more judges, increasingly two, of whom one will normally be a Lord (or Lady) Justice of Appeal (a member of the Court of Appeal). An appeal by case stated must be on the ground that the determination or decision is wrong in law or is in excess of jurisdiction.

- *Judicial review jurisdiction* This jurisdiction is exercised by the Administrative Court. Normally, the case is heard by a single judge, but it may be heard by a divisional court.

  Permission to claim judicial review must be obtained from a judge. Judicial review proceedings can be brought in respect of the decisions of magistrates' courts, county courts, the Crown Court (except in respect of trials on indictment) and other decision-making bodies of a public nature, such as local authorities. As in an appeal by case stated, the court simply hears legal argument and decides on that basis.

  On a claim for judicial review the court can make a mandatory order, a prohibitory order or a quashing order. A mandatory order is used to compel the body to whom it is directed to carry out a public duty imposed on it by law. It cannot be used to compel the body to exercise its discretion in a particular way, but it may be used to compel it to hear and determine a case. A prohibitory order or a quashing order will only be issued in relation to an order or decision of a body which is under a public duty to 'act judicially' or 'act fairly' in making that decision, as opposed to purely administratively. This does not mean that a prohibitory order and a quashing order will be issued only to courts or tribunals, for many other bodies, such as local authorities, may sometimes be required to act judicially, and in other cases are required to act fairly. A prohibitory order is issued to prevent such a body from reaching a decision or acting in a way which is in excess of jurisdiction or otherwise acting improperly. A quashing order covers much the same area but after such a body has decided or done something and it is desired to review it and, if necessary, quash it on the ground of excess of jurisdiction or otherwise acting improperly or unreasonably. It is not concerned with the correctness of the decision on its merits but with whether it was lawfully and reasonably made.

Family Division

2.12 The Family Division deals with all aspects of family law, including:

- proceedings for the determination of title to property in dispute between spouses; and
- proceedings concerning the occupation of the matrimonial home and/or the exclusion of a violent spouse.

Appeals

2.13 Appeals from the original or appellate civil jurisdiction of any division of the High Court lie to the Court of Appeal (Civil Division), as do appeals from decisions in judicial review cases.[1]

  [1] But note the 'leap-frogging' exception mentioned in para 2.18.

The Court of Appeal

2.14 The Court of Appeal is composed of the Lord Chief Justice (who is President of the Courts of England and Wales and Head of Criminal Justice), the Master of the Rolls (Head of Civil Justice), the Chancellor of the High Court (Head of the Chancery Division), the Presidents of the Queen's Bench and Family Divisions, and Lord (or Lady) Justices of Appeal. A High Court judge may be required to sit in the Court of Appeal if this is necessary. The Court of Appeal is divided into a civil and a criminal division. The number of judges who hear an appeal is normally three.

Jurisdiction

2.15 The Court of Appeal (Civil Division) hears appeals from:

- The decisions of the High Court in civil matters.
- The final decisions by a county court judge in a multi-track claim or in certain specialist proceedings and decisions by a county court judge when hearing an appeal.
- The decisions of the Upper Tribunal.[1]

Save for isolated exceptions where an order affects the liberty of an individual, an appeal to the Court of Appeal requires the permission of the court or the chamber of the Upper Tribunal from whom it is sought to appeal or of the Court of Appeal. There is no right of further appeal to the Court of Appeal from the determination of an appeal to a county court, the High Court or the Upper Tribunal unless the Court of Appeal considers that:

- the appeal would raise an important point of principle or practice; or
- there is some other compelling reason for the Court of Appeal to hear it.

  [1] Paras 2.23 and 2.24.

2.16 While most civil appeals to the Court of Appeal are on points of law, an appeal from a court may be against a finding of fact or the exercise of discretion by the trial judge or the damages awarded. An appeal will not be a re-hearing but a review of the decision of the lower court, unless in the circumstances it would be in the interests of justice to hold a re-hearing. The Court of Appeal cannot interfere with the lower court's findings of fact unless that court has misdirected itself in making its findings. The Court of Appeal will only allow an appeal if the lower court's decision was wrong or where it was unjust because of a serious procedural or other irregularity in the lower court's proceedings.

The Supreme Court

2.17 The Supreme Court replaced the House of Lords as the final appeal court in England and Wales in October 2009. It consists of a President, Vice-President and 10 other Justices of the Supreme Court; acting justices may be appointed. Cases before the Supreme Court are heard by a court consisting of an uneven number of judges, normally five, seven or nine. The Supreme Court has both a civil and a criminal jurisdiction under English law.

Jurisdiction

2.18 Under its appellate civil jurisdiction, the Supreme Court hears:

- Appeals from the Court of Appeal (Civil Division), provided that leave has been granted by that Court or by the Supreme Court.
- 'Leap-frog' appeals from the High Court. This procedure may only be used where:
  - the parties agree to it;
  - the High Court judge grants a certificate to sanction it (which may only be done if a point of law is involved which is of general public importance and which either relates to a matter of construction of legislation or else is one in respect of which the judge is 'bound' by a previous decision); and
  - the Supreme Court gives leave to appeal.

  The 'leap-frog' procedure is used in comparatively few cases.

The Supreme Court will not generally interfere with findings of fact on which the trial judge and appellate court are agreed, unless it can be shown that both courts were clearly wrong.

The Court of Justice of the European Union (European Court)

2.19 The European Court operates under the treaties, including amending treaties, establishing the European Union (EU) and its predecessor, the European Community.

The Court consists of 27 judges. The Court sits in plenary session, ie as a 'court' (generally consisting of 13 judges), unless the decision has been made to hear the case in a 'chamber' of three or five judges. A court or chamber is assisted by one of the eight Advocates-General, a type of official unknown to English law. The duty of an Advocate-General is, with complete impartiality and independence, to make reasoned submissions in open court on cases brought before the Court in order to assist in the performance of its functions.

Before 1973 the House of Lords was the final court of appeal in all cases in this country but the accession of the United Kingdom to membership of the European Community meant that the European Court became the ultimate court (ie its decisions are binding on the Supreme Court and other United Kingdom courts) in matters within its jurisdiction.

Nevertheless, in the great majority of cases arising within the United Kingdom the Supreme Court is the final court. The fundamental point that the treaties under which the European Court operates are concerned only with those matters which have a European element must be firmly grasped in order to understand the relationship of the European Court to the rest of our legal system.

Jurisdiction

2.20 The jurisdiction of the European Court can be divided into the following principal categories:

- Matters concerning the conduct of member states or of the institutions of the Community, which are outside the scope of this book.
- Matters of direct concern to litigation in a member state, which have been referred for a preliminary ruling on the interpretation or validity of EU law by the European Court by a court or tribunal in a member state.

The essence of a preliminary ruling is that it should precede the judgment of the referring court or tribunal. Where a question of EU law is raised before any court or tribunal of a member state, the court or tribunal *may*, if it considers that a decision on the question is necessary to enable it to give judgment, refer the matter to the European Court for a preliminary ruling. Where a court or tribunal of a member state has doubts about the validity of a EU law it *must* refer that question for a ruling. In addition, where any question of EU law is raised in a case pending before a court or tribunal of a member state, against whose decisions there is no judicial remedy under national law, that court or tribunal *must* generally refer the matter to the European Court for a ruling. This provision refers to the Supreme Court where an appeal lies to the Supreme Court. On the other hand, where there is no right of appeal at all from a lower court to a higher court in respect of the matter in issue, that court is the court of 'last resort'.

Where a matter is referred to the European Court for a preliminary ruling, only the request for interpretation or decision on validity is referred. The case itself is not transferred. Consequently, the court making the reference remains 'in charge' of it, although its procedure is suspended until the European Court has given its ruling on the reference.

In terms of the relationship between the European Court and English courts it is important to distinguish between the task of interpreting EU law – to see what it means – and the task of applying it to the case in hand.

The English judges have the final say in applying EU law: only they are empowered to find the facts and give judgment for one side or the other. However, before they can apply EU law they have to see what it means, and in this task of interpretation English judges are not the final authority: the European Court is.[1]

---

[1] See *H P Bulmer Ltd v J Bollinger SA* [1974] 2 All ER 1226, CA.

Specialist courts and tribunals

The Technology and Construction Court

2.21 Some cases in the High Court are heard by the Technology and Construction Court, which consists of a High Court judge (who is in charge) and circuit judges assigned to it. The Court's business includes any Chancery or Queen's Bench cause or matter:

- which involves a prolonged examination of documents or accounts, or technical, scientific or local investigation, such as could more conveniently be conducted by a specialist judge in that court; or
- for which trial by a specialist judge is desirable in the interests of one or more of the parties on grounds of expedition, economy or convenience or otherwise.

The majority of cases in the Technology and Construction Court come from the construction industry and concern architects, engineers, surveyors, contractors, house-builders, developers and others involved in that industry. However, the Court also decides cases about computer hardware or software, and other disputes of a technical or scientific nature or of an environmental nature (such as pollution or noise).

Another specialist court is the Judicial Committee of the Privy Council, referred to in para 3.45.

Tribunals

2.22 Tribunals have been created to deal with particular matters arising under modern legislation, especially social welfare legislation. The function of most administrative tribunals is to enable individual citizens to challenge the administrative decisions of a government department or agency. Some tribunals, however, adjudicate disputes between individuals; the Lands Chamber of the Upper Tribunal and Employment Tribunals are examples. Tribunals are usually composed of a legally qualified member and lay members. The hallmarks of tribunals have traditionally been said to be informality, cheapness and freedom from technicality. For these reasons they have been compared favourably with the civil courts. More cases are heard by tribunals than by civil courts.

2.23 The Tribunals, Courts and Enforcement Act 2007 established the First-tier Tribunal and the Upper Tribunal to take over the functions of a range of separate tribunals.

The First-tier Tribunal has jurisdiction over appeals against administrative decisions of a government department or agency. It is divided into six chambers representing broad areas of jurisdiction. One is the General Regulatory Chamber which has jurisdiction (among other things) over appeals under the Estate Agents Act 1979 relating to an order prohibiting a person from acting as an estate agent or to a warning that a person has not complied with duties under that Act. A tribunal hearing a case as a First-tier Tribunal consists of a judge of the First-tier Tribunal and other members of that Tribunal; the number and nature of those members who sit in a particular case varies.

The Upper Tribunal has jurisdiction:

- over appeals from, and enforcement of, First-tier Tribunal decisions;
- over certain cases that do not go through the First-tier Tribunal.

The Upper Tribunal has also taken over from the High Court the power to conduct judicial review proceedings in respect of specified decisions of the First-tier Tribunal, in particular those which cannot be appealed. So far, only two classes of case have been specified. Appeal from the Upper Tribunal on a point of law normally lies to the Court of Appeal (Civil Division) with the permission of that Tribunal or Court. The Upper Tribunal itself is subject to the judicial review by the High Court but only in the unlikely case of an outright excess of jurisdiction or denial of fundamental justice by the Upper Tribunal.

The Upper Tribunal is divided into four chambers, one of which is the Lands Chamber. A case heard by the Upper Tribunal is normally heard by an individual judge of the Upper Tribunal but it may be heard by more than one such judge in more difficult cases or by a judge (or judges) and an expert member (or members) in appropriate cases. An Upper Tribunal cannot consist of more than three persons.

The Upper Tribunal (Lands Chamber)

2.24 The Upper Tribunal (Lands Chamber) has permanent hearing rooms in London but it also sits elsewhere to determine cases. It consists of a President, who is its judicial head, and a number of other members. Members of the Upper Tribunal (Lands Chamber) must be lawyers or chartered surveyors,

The Upper Tribunal (Lands Chamber) has jurisdiction over a number of matters, including:

- assessment of compensation for the compulsory purchase of land, where this has not been agreed between the parties, or of compensation for certain other matters, such as compensation for planning restrictions restricting new development;

- applications for the modification or discharge of restrictive covenants under the Law of Property Act 1925, s 84;[1]

- applications for certificates as to notice under the Rights of Light Act 1959;[2]

- land taxation appeals;

- hearing appeals from a leasehold valuation tribunal, a residential property tribunal (rent and leasehold disputes), the Valuation Tribunal for England or a valuation tribunal in Wales (rateable values for non-domestic premises); and

- in the specified classes of case (see para 2.23) judicial review in respect of a decision of one of these tribunals.

[1] Paras 34.38–34.43.
[2] Para 32.55.

Alternative Dispute Resolution

2.25 Alternative dispute resolution (ADR) refers to any method of resolving civil matters without resorting to the courts. Examples of ADR are arbitration, early neutral evaluation, expert determination, mediation and conciliation. A court must encourage resort to ADR if it considers that appropriate. If the parties agree to refer a dispute, or a future dispute, to ADR, their agreement is binding.

ADR is a quicker and cheaper method than litigation in the courts. It is therefore of interest both to consumers and to businesses involved in commercial disputes. In addition to speeding up settlement, ADR has the advantage of making it possible to reach settlements reflecting commercial or personal interests, as well as strict rights.

Arbitration

2.26 Particularly in commercial and consumer matters, the parties to a dispute may prefer to go straight to arbitration rather than become involved in court proceedings. Hence, they may voluntarily agree before or after the dispute to refer it to arbitration. Many construction contracts provide for such a reference, as do various codes of practice initiated by trade associations which are incorporated in their standard form contracts used by members.

The parties are free to agree on the number of persons whom they wish to act as arbitrators. They may appoint the arbitrators themselves or provide a procedure for the appointments to be made. They may, for example, provide that the appointment shall be made by the President of a relevant professional society, such as the Royal Institution of Chartered Surveyors.

An arbitration decision is binding on the parties unless an arbitration agreement provides otherwise.

Early neutral evaluation

2.27 Under this process a neutral person, commonly a lawyer, hears a summary of each party's case and gives a non-binding assessment of the merits. This can then be used as a basis for settlement or further negotiation.

Expert determination

2.28 Here a neutral person who is an expert in the subject matter is appointed to decide a disputed matter, the decision being binding on the parties. Expert determination is sometimes used, for example, in boundary disputes where it involves the appointment of a chartered surveyor to decide the correct boundary line.

Mediation

2.29 In mediation a neutral mediator helps the parties to reach a common position. It can be 'facilitative' or 'evaluative'. It is 'facilitative' if the mediator does not advise the parties of his (or her) own opinion of the merits of the dispute. It is 'evaluative' if the mediator is expected to express his (or her) own opinion.

Mediation is particularly appropriate where the claim is small or not complex, or both. It is also appropriate where it is particularly important to reduce conflict and bitterness between the parties. Mediation may be conducted as 'virtual mediation' via a secure chat room provided by a specialist Internet organisation.

When mediation is successful and an agreement is reached, it is written down and forms a binding contract, unless the parties otherwise state.

Conciliation

2.30 This is similar to mediation but differs in that the conciliator moves from one party to the other, discussing the merits of each side's case and the risks in litigation. Sometimes, if the conciliation does not directly lead to a settlement, the conciliator's role may extend to advising the parties of his assessment of the likely result of a trial. Of course, this is not binding, but it often leads to a settlement.

ADMINISTRATION OF THE LAW: KEY POINTS

- Civil cases before the courts commence either in a county court or in the High Court.
- A claim will normally be allocated to:
  - the small claims track if it is not in excess of £5,000 (or £1,000 in the case of a personal injuries or property repair claim);
  - the fast track if it is not a small claims track claim and is not in excess of £25,000 (unless certain conditions apply);
  - the multi-track if neither of the other tracks is the normal track.

- Small track claims are always heard in a county court. Fast track claims and multi-track claims are heard in a county court or in the High Court, depending on their complexity and/or value. Fast track cases are normally heard in a county court.

- A district judge's decision can be appealed to a circuit judge. Otherwise a decision made by a judge in a county court can be appealed to the Court of Appeal or to the High Court, depending on the circumstances.

- There are three Divisions of the High Court: Chancery, Queen's Bench and Family. Appeal from their decisions lies to the Court of Appeal.

- The final court of appeal in England and Wales is the Supreme Court.

- Appeals in the above cases can only be made with the permission of the court (or judge) appealed from or the court appealed to.

- Matters relating to the interpretation or validity of EU law may (and sometimes must) be referred to the Court of Justice of the EU for a preliminary ruling.

- Tribunals exist to resolve disputes arising under various pieces of modern legislation. The First-tier Tribunal has taken over the functions of a range of tribunals. The Upper Tribunal hears appeals from the First-tier Tribunal and also certain cases which do not go through the First-tier Tribunal.

- Civil disputes can also be resolved outside the system of courts and tribunals by the adoption of one of the methods of alternative dispute resolution: arbitration; early neutral evaluation; expert determination; mediation; and conciliation.

Questions

1. Which judges sit in:
   - a county court;
   - the Court of Appeal?

2. Paula made a contract with Dan. Paula claims that Dan has broken the contract and that the breach has caused her £4,500 loss. Dan also made a contract with Hal. Hal claims that Dan has broken the contract and caused him a loss of over £1m. Hal's claim is a complex one. The case will probably involve a trial of two weeks. Advise Paula and Hal about the court in which their claims will be tried.

3. To which court or courts does an appeal lie from the decision of a circuit judge in a county court?

4. Over what matters does the Chancery Division have jurisdiction?

5. Over what civil matters does the Queen's Bench Division have jurisdiction?

6. What appeals does the Court of Appeal (Civil Division) hear? What pre-conditions, if any, are there for an appeal to that court?

7. What is the jurisdiction of the Upper Tribunal (Lands Chamber)?

8. What is alternative dispute resolution? What are its advantages?

3

Sources of English law

CHAPTER OVERVIEW

In this chapter we explain the direct means by which English law is made by:

- legislation;

- judicial precedent;

- custom (which is now of very little relevance).

Since it impacts on English law, we also explain the legislation of the European Union.

Legislation

3.1 There are two types of domestic legislation: Acts of the United Kingdom Parliament and Acts of the Welsh Assembly,[1] and subordinate legislation.

[1] The Government of Wales Act 2006, Pt 4 ('the Welsh Assembly Act provisions') enables the National Assembly for Wales to enact its own Acts of the Assembly, limited in their effect to Wales, on any matter within its legislative competence (ie in any of the 20 devolved areas). The devolved areas include town and country planning, housing and environmental matters. On 3 March 2011, the majority of the voters in a referendum were in favour of the Welsh Assembly Act provisions coming into force. The effect is to empower the Welsh ministers (who are appointed from among the Welsh Assembly members) to bring the provisions into force. It is anticipated that the Welsh Assembly Act provisions will come into force on 5 May 2011. An Act of the Welsh Assembly is not law if it is outside the Assembly's legislative competence, and can be questioned on this ground. Acts of the Welsh Assembly are not further discussed in this book, but what is said from paras 3.10 on about Acts of Parliament is generally equally applicable to them.

3.2 In terms of the law covered in this book, legislation plays a particularly important part in the areas of land law and planning law. In these areas, legislation lays down the foundations of the relevant law which then has to be interpreted by the courts and applied by them and others involved. In the case of contract law and tort law, on the other hand, the foundations of that law are laid down by judicial precedent and legislation has only served to amend or add to it to a limited extent.

Acts of Parliament

3.3 The validity of an Act of Parliament cannot be questioned in an English or Welsh court. Subject to an exception which discussed in para 3.52, an Act has to be applied by an English or Welsh court.

Commencement and repeal

3.4 An Act of Parliament comes into operation when it receives royal assent unless, as frequently occurs, some other date is specified in the Act or it is to be appointed by a commencement order made by a government minister. Sometimes a commencement order is not made for a considerable time. An extreme example concerns the Easter Act 1928; the Act provides a fixed date for Easter but a commencement order has not yet been made.

A commencement order may only relate to certain parts of an Act, so that the legislation is brought into force in a piecemeal fashion. For example, while most of the Estate Agents Act 1979 has been brought into force, a commencement order has not yet been made in relation to the requirement for insurance cover in respect of clients' money and the provisions on standards of competence.

An Act of Parliament may be repealed expressly by a subsequent Act, or impliedly by being inconsistent with it[1] (although there is a presumption against implied repeal).[2] Unless the contrary intention appears, repeal does not:

- revive a previously repealed rule of law; or
- affect existing rights and liabilities, or legal proceedings, civil or criminal.[3]

[1] *Ellen Street Estates Ltd v Minister of Health* [1934] 1 KB 590, CA.
[2] Para 3.19.
[3] Interpretation Act 1978, ss 15 and 16.

Subordinate legislation

3.5 Various extra-Parliamentary institutions have limited legislative powers. Legislation made by them is subordinate since it is made by bodies with limited powers and may be held invalid by the courts in the types of case described in para 3.9. Subordinate legislation can be disregarded in appropriate cases if it is incompatible with a 'Convention right' under the Human Rights Act 1998.[1]

There are two types of subordinate legislation: delegated legislation and autonomic legislation (which is made by the Queen by Order in Council under the royal prerogative in respect of the dependent territories, the armed forces and the civil service). A property professional will have to refer to delegated legislation in the course of his or her professional practice.

[1] Para 3.28.

Delegated legislation

3.6 Delegated legislation comprises the great bulk of subordinate legislation. Delegated legislation is legislation made by some executive body under powers delegated to it by an Act of Parliament. An Act of Parliament often gives powers to some bodies, such as the Queen in Council (in effect the Government), a minister, the ministers of the Welsh Assembly or a local authority, to make regulations and prescribe for their breach.

There is a vast amount of delegated legislation – the number of pieces made annually being numbered in thousands, whereas the number of Public and Private Acts of Parliament a year rarely exceeds 50 and often is considerably less. An example of an Act giving very wide powers of delegated legislation is the European Communities Act 1972.[1] Governmental delegated legislation made by the central executive may be required to be made by Order in Council made by the Queen in Council, otherwise it takes the form of regulations or rules made by a minister (or the Welsh Ministers). Generally, delegated legislation of these types must be made by statutory instrument.

[1] Para 3.50.

3.7 A statutory instrument comes into effect when made unless, as is usual, it specifies a later date.

3.8 Another type of delegated legislation is the byelaw. Byelaws are made by local authorities and certain other bodies authorised by an Act of Parliament. Although general in operation, they are restricted to the locality or undertaking to which they apply. They are not made by statutory instrument.

3.9 All forms of delegated legislation are invalid if they are proved to be ultra vires. Delegated legislation is ultra vires if it is in excess of the powers conferred by the enabling Act on the rule-making body; or if it is made in breach of a mandatory part of the procedure concerning its making prescribed by that Act; or, in the case of byelaws only, if it is patently unreasonable, or so uncertain as to have no ascertainable meaning, or so unclear in its effect as to be incapable of certain application in any given situation, or repugnant to the general law.[1]

The invalidity of delegated legislation is either challenged directly before the courts on an application for judicial review or raised as a defence to a court action which concerns the application of the delegated legislation.

[1] *Nash v Finlay* (1901) 85 LT 682, DC; *Powell v May* [1946] 1 All ER 444, DC; *Percy v Hall* [1996] 4 All ER 523, CA.

Interpretation

3.10 What follows is concerned with the interpretation of Acts of Parliament but, essentially, the same rules apply to the interpretation of subordinate legislation.

It is often said that, in interpreting Acts, the courts are trying to discover Parliament's intentions from the words of the Act.[1] However, as Lord Reid observed in *Black-Clawson International Ltd v Papierwerke Waldhof-Aschaffenburg AG*,[2] 'that is not quite accurate. We are seeking the meaning of the words which Parliament used. We are seeking not what Parliament meant but the true meaning of what they said'. In seeking that meaning of a provision, a court does not have to give it its historical meaning (ie interpret it as if it was doing so when it was enacted). Acts are almost always intended to operate for many years and, unless they are not, a court is free to apply the current meaning of the provision to the context and conditions of the present day. In *Royal College of Nursing of the United Kingdom v Department of Health and Social Security*,[3] for example, the House of Lords interpreted the Abortion Act 1967 as applying to a medical method of inducing an abortion whose first reported use was in 1971, so that Parliament could not have had it in mind when it enacted the legislation.

In interpreting a statutory provision the courts may give it a literal construction or give it a purposive one instead, as explained in the following paragraphs.

[1] But see para 3.22.
[2] [1975] 1 All ER 810 at 814.
[3] [1981] 1 All ER 545, HL.

Literal construction

3.11 This refers to the process whereby the meaning of an Act is found by interpreting the words used in their ordinary, literal and grammatical sense. If the words can be so interpreted a court must normally give effect to that interpretation, unless the Act or the legal context in which the words are used compels it to give the word a special meaning, irrespective of the desirability or justice of the result. In *Whiteley v*

Chappell,[1] for example, the defendant was acquitted of personating at an election 'any person entitled to vote', contrary to the Poor Law Amendment Act 1857, s 3, because he had personated a dead voter and such a person is not entitled to vote. In a more modern case it has been held that, if a provision is clear and unambiguous, the court cannot decline to give effect to it on the ground that its rationale is anachronistic, discredited or unconvincing.[2]

The process of literal construction is modified if the 'golden rule', described in the next paragraph, applies and will be abandoned for a purposive construction where to apply the literal meaning of the statutory provision would clearly defeat its purpose.

[1] (1868) LR 4 QB 147.
[2] *R v J* [2004] UKHL 42, HL.

3.12 It may happen that to interpret statutory words according to their ordinary, literal and grammatical sense in their context would give rise to manifest absurdity, repugnancy or inconsistency *with the rest of the Act*. In such a case, the so-called 'golden rule' permits a court to modify the literal interpretation so as to avoid such a result.[1]

A modern example is provided by the House of Lords' decision in *McMonagle v Westminster City Council*.[2] M was charged with the offence of using premises as a 'sex encounter establishment' without a licence, contrary to the Local Government (Miscellaneous Provisions) Act 1982. The definition of such an establishment was 'premises at which performances which are *not* unlawful are given, which…comprise the sexual stimulation of persons admitted to the premises…'. M's defence was that it had not been proved that the performances in question were *not* unlawful and that, if they were unlawful, a licence was not required under the plain words of the Act. The House of Lords rejected this interpretation as being absurd, and held that the words 'which are not unlawful' were mere surplusage which had been introduced by an incompetent draftsman solely to emphasise that a licence conferred no immunity from the ordinary criminal law. Thus, the prosecution did not have to prove that the performances were not unlawful and it was no defence that they were unlawful.

[1] *Grey v Pearson* (1857) 6 HL Cas 61 at 106.
[2] [1990] 1 All ER 993, HL.

Purposive construction

3.13 Literal construction breaks down, in particular, in the case of an ambiguity. In such a case, the court may apply the 'mischief rule'. This rule is best paraphrased by the statement by Lord Halsbury in *Eastman Photographic Materials Co Ltd v Comptroller-General of Patents, Designs and Trade Marks*: 'We are to see what was the law before the Act was passed, and what was the mischief or defect for which the law had not provided, what remedy Parliament appointed, and the reason for the remedy.'[1] The mischief rule only applies where the provision is ambiguous.[2]

The mischief rule is now of little importance because of the development of wider principles of purposive construction which are not limited to cases of ambiguous statutes designed to remedy a particular mischief, to which we now turn.

[1] [1898] AC 571 at 573.
[2] *Sussex Peerage* case (1844) 11 Cl & Fin 85 at 143.

3.14 If the court thinks that the interpretation of the words in their ordinary, literal and grammatical sense would clearly produce a result contrary to the purpose of the Act as it understands it to be, the court may construe them in any other way consistent with that purpose which the words are capable of bearing. In *Richard Thomas and Baldwins Ltd v Cummings*,[1] for example, a provision in the Factories Act 1937, which required the fencing of dangerous parts of a machine while it was in motion, was held not to apply where a fitter modifying a machine turned the machine by hand. The machine could not have been modified while it was fenced, and the purpose of the statute was to protect workers operating machines with dangerous parts.

[1] [1955] 1 All ER 285, HL.

3.15 As part of purposive construction, courts can correct obvious drafting errors in suitable cases by adding, omitting or substituting words. In *Inco Europe Ltd v First Choice Distribution*,[1] the House of Lords held that, before doing so, a court must be abundantly sure of three matters:

- the intended purpose of the Act;
- that, by inadvertence, the draftsman and Parliament had failed to give effect to that purpose in the provision in question; and
- the substance of the provision that Parliament would have made, although not necessarily the precise words that it would have used, had the error in the Bill been noticed.

The House added that sometimes, even when these conditions are met, the court may find itself inhibited from interpreting the statute in accordance with what it is satisfied was Parliament's intention. The alteration in language required may be too far-reaching: the insertion must not be too big, or too much at variance with the language used by Parliament. Moreover, the subject matter of the legislation may call for a strict interpretation, as in the case of penal legislation.

If a court is faced with a factual situation for which the Act has not provided, for reasons other than a drafting error, even the purposive approach does not permit the court to fill the gap. To do so would be to attribute to Parliament an intention which it never had. Like literal construction, purposive construction is limited to giving effect to the words of the Act It does not extend to reading words into it to rectify an anomaly or absurdity, *unless clear reason is found within the body* of the Act itself;[2] nor does purposive construction extend to giving a provision a strained meaning in order to give effect to what Parliament might have intended had it contemplated a different situation from that which existed at the time of the Act.[3] A court cannot attribute to Parliament an intention which Parliament never had. For a court to do so was condemned by Lord Simonds in *Magor and St Mellons RDC v Newport Corpn*,[4] as a 'naked usurpation of the legislative function under the thin disguise of interpretation'. His Lordship added that if a gap is disclosed the remedy lies in an amending Act.

[1] [2000] 2 All ER 109, HL.
[2] *Stock v Frank Jones (Tipton) Ltd* [1978] 1 All ER 948, HL.
[3] *R v House* [2010] EWCA Crim 2270, CA.
[4] [1951] 2 All ER 839 at 841.

Rules of interpretation

3.16 In interpreting a statutory provision, the court will be assisted by various rules of interpretation. Indeed, if the provision proves to be uncertain or ambiguous, one or more of these rules may be determinative of the court's interpretation.

Words must be understood in their context

3.17 A word in itself does not have an absolute meaning; its meaning is relative to its context.[1] Part of this rule is the principle that an Act must be read as a whole. Every section must be read in the light of every other section,[2] including the interpretation section normally found towards the end of an Act. This can assist in resolving ambiguities, inconsistencies or redundancies in a particular provision. In addition, the Act as a whole must be read in the context of the historical situation which led to its enactment.[3]

> [1] See *Pinner v Everett* [1969] 3 All ER 257 at 258.
> [2] *Beswick v Beswick* [1967] 2 All ER 1197, HL.
> [3] *R (on the application of Quintavelle) v Secretary of State for Health* [2003] UKHL 13 at [8].

Ejusdem generis rule

3.18 An important example of the rule that words must be understood in their context is the *ejusdem generis* (of the same class) rule. Enactments often list things which are so similar as to form a class to which a provision is to apply, following the list with some general words implying that some other similar things are intended to fall within the class. Whether something which is not specified in the list of things falls within the general words depends upon whether or not it is ejusdem generis as the specified things. In *Powell v Kempton Park Racecourse Co Ltd*,[1] an Act prohibited the keeping of a 'house, office, room or other place' for betting with persons resorting thereto. The House of Lords held that Tattersall's Ring (an uncovered enclosure) at a racecourse was not ejusdem generis as the specified things, and was not therefore an 'other place' within the meaning of the Act, since the specific words 'house, office, room' created a *genus* (class) of indoor places. There cannot be a *genus* for the purposes of the present rule unless the 'other' thing is preceded by a list of at least two or more specific things which share the same common characteristics.[2]

> [1] [1899] AC 143, HL.
> [2] *Quazi v Quazi* [1979] 3 All ER 897, HL.

Presumptions

3.19 There are a number of presumptions as to the intentions of Parliament, which may be rebutted by the express words of the Act or by necessary implication from the subject matter of the Act itself.

- *Against retrospective effect of legislation* This presumption is concerned with whether an Act affects factual situations which arose before it came into operation. Parliament is presumed not to have intended to alter the law applicable to pre-existing events, contracts or other transactions in a manner which is unfair to those concerned in them, unless a contrary intention appears. The greater the degree of unfairness, the stronger will have to be the evidence that Parliament intended the legislation to have retrospective effect.[1]

- *Against alteration of the common law* Parliament is presumed not to intend to change the common law, with the result that, unless the words of the Act unmistakably indicate that the common law is changed, they must be interpreted so as not to alter it.[2]

- *Against the Crown being bound* The Crown (ie the State) is not bound by an Act unless there can be gathered from it an intention that it should be bound.[3] The presumption also extends to employees of the Crown, in the course of their duties, and to Crown property. However, Acts frequently provide that they are to bind the Crown. Even if an Act does not expressly bind the Crown, a court may construe it as doing so by necessary implication.

Other presumptions made in construing an Act include those against implied repeal of earlier legislation by later, apparently inconsistent, legislation (the earlier only being impliedly repealed if reconciliation is logically impossible); and against inconsistency with European Union law or international law.

¹ *L'Office Cherifien des Phosphates Unitramp SA v Yamashita-Shinnihon Steamship Co Ltd* [1994] 1 All ER 20, HL.
² *Leach v R* [1912] AC 305, HL.
³ *Tamlin v Hannaford* [1950] 1 KB 18, CA; *Lord Advocate v Dumbarton District Council* [1990] 1 All ER 1, HL.

Aids to interpretation

Intrinsic aids

3.20 The rule that an Act must be read as a whole makes it of obvious importance to know what parts of an Act may be regarded as intrinsic aids to interpretation.

- *Long title and short title* These are part of the Act, but, in practice, the courts do not refer to the short title and only refer to the long title to resolve an ambiguity; in other words the long title is not allowed to restrict the clear meaning of a provision. In *Re Groos*,¹ it was held that the Wills Act 1861, s 3, applied to the will of an alien, even though the long title read: 'An Act to amend the law with respect to wills of personal estates made by British subjects.'

- *Punctuation, headings to a group of sections and side notes to individual sections* are inserted into a Bill by the parliamentary draftsmen and can be altered any time up to royal assent. They are not debated by Parliament and are therefore not part of the Act. Nevertheless, they are admissible aids to interpretation, although less weight will be attached to them than to the parts of the Act open for debate in Parliament.²

- *Schedules* which are used, for instance, to list repeals and set out transitional or more detailed provisions, are part of the Act, but they cannot affect the interpretation of a word in the body of the Act unless it is ambiguous or uncertain.³

- *Explanatory notes* which, since 1999, have accompanied a Bill on its introduction and are updated during the Parliamentary process, cast light on the contextual scene of the Act and the mischief at which it is aimed, and are admissible aids to interpretation.⁴

¹ [1904] P 269.
² *DPP v Schildkamp* [1969] 3 All ER 1640, HL; *R v Kelt* [1977] 3 All ER 1099, CA.
³ *Ellerman Lines Ltd v Murray* [1931] AC 126, HL.
⁴ *R (on the application of Westminster City Council) v National Asylum Support Service* [2002] UKHL 38 at [5].

Extrinsic aids

3.21 Unlike most continental courts, an English or Welsh court may not generally look at material outside the four walls of the Act to find Parliament's intention. However, the following extrinsic aids can be looked at for limited purposes:

- *Dictionaries* can be consulted to ascertain the range of meaning, for the purpose of the literal construction of words which have no particular legal meaning.¹

- *Parliamentary debates* A court cannot generally look at reports of the parliamentary debates on the Bill which became the Act.[2] This may appear to fly in the face of common sense but it must be admitted that it might be difficult in some cases to determine a legislative intent from a two, or more, sided parliamentary debate, especially where the Bill has been subject to amendment in Parliament.

  In 1992, the majority of the House of Lords in *Pepper v Hart*[3] held, by way of exception, that the courts can refer to reports of debates in Parliament relating to the provision in question as an aid to its interpretation if it is ambiguous or absurd or if its literal meaning would lead to absurdity. Even in such cases, the House held, reference to parliamentary reports is only possible if:

  - it discloses the mischief aimed at or the legislative intention behind the ambiguous or obscure words;

  - the statements relied on were by the minister(s) promoting the Bill; and

  - those statements are clear.[4]

  Pepper v Hart was concerned with a provision in the Finance Act 1976 whereby the cash equivalent of an in-house benefit was taxable. The Act provided that the cash equivalent of the benefit was 'an amount equal to the cost of the benefit' and by s 63(2) the cost of the benefit was 'the amount of any expense incurred in or in connection with its provision'. The in-house benefit in question was a reduced school fees scheme for members of staff at a school. The majority of the House of Lords held that s 63(2) was clearly ambiguous because the 'expense incurred in or in connection with' the provision of in-house benefits could be interpreted either as the marginal cost caused by the provision of the benefit or as a proportion of the total cost incurred in providing the service for all parents (the average cost). The majority of the House held that the requirements set out above were satisfied and that reference to a statement made by the government minister in Parliament made it clear that Parliament had intended to assess the expense incurred in the provision of in-house benefits, particularly concessionary fees, on the basis of the marginal cost to the employer, and not on the average cost of the benefit.

- *Reports of committees or of the Law Commission and Government White Papers* containing proposals for legislation which have been presented to Parliament and resulted in the enactment in question can be looked at to discover the state of the pre-existing law and the mischief which the enactment was passed to remedy. An example is provided by the House of Lords' decision in *Black-Clawson International Ltd v Papierwerke Waldhof-Aschaffenburg AG*,[5] where their Lordships referred to the report of a committee, which had resulted in the passing of an Act, to discover what the pre-existing law was understood to be and what its mischief was. Two of the five Lords of Appeal, Viscount Dilhorne and Lord Simon, went further and stated that it was permissible to look at such a report for a direct statement of what the resulting enactment meant. This minority statement went further than our courts have been prepared to go in the past. Lord Reid and Lord Wilberforce disagreed with it expressly in *Black-Clawson,* and subsequent House of Lords' decisions have indicated that it is not correct.[6] However, in a more recent case the House of Lords was helped in determining the meaning of a section by reference to a Law Commission report which had resulted in the legislation in question.[7] We think that this approach will now prevail.

- *Judicial precedent* The interpretation given by a court to a statutory provision or word may be binding in relation to *that* provision or word in *that* Act, in accordance with the principles of the doctrine of judicial precedent (paras 3.32 to 3.45).

• *Interpretation Act 1978* The Act lays down various definitions which apply unless there is a contrary intention, express or implied, in a particular Act. For example, 'unless the contrary intention appears, (a) words importing the masculine gender shall include the feminine; and (b) words in the singular shall include the plural and words in the plural shall include the singular'. Again, '"person" includes a body of persons corporate or unincorporate'.[8]

[1] See, for example *A-G's Reference (No 1 of 1988)* [1989] 2 All ER 1, HL.
[2] *Assam Railways and Trading Co Ltd v IRC* [1935] AC 445, HL; *Davis v Johnson* [1978] 1 All ER 1132, HL.
[3] [1993] 1 All ER 42, HL.
[4] It is immaterial that an individual ministerial statement appears at odds with a particular meaning if otherwise ministerial statements clearly indicate the meaning of the words: *R v TJB* [2009] UKHL 30, HL.
[5] [1975] 1 All ER 810, HL.
[6] *R v Ayres* [1984] 1 All ER 619, HL; *R v Allen* [1985] 2 All ER 641, HL.
[7] *I v DPP* [2001] UKHL 10, HL.
[8] Section 6 and Sch 1 respectively.

Cases where a Convention right or EU law is involved

3.22 The frequent but somewhat inaccurate statement that, in interpreting an Act, a court is trying to discover Parliament's intentions, is particularly hard to accept where a Convention right under the Human Rights Act 1998 is involved. The reason is that a court is required by s 3(1) of the Act to interpret legislation to comply with a Convention right so far as possible, which involves an approach to interpretation radically different from that described above, as we shall see in para 3.27.

As to interpretation of an Act so as to be consistent with EU law see para 3.19.

Acts giving effect to international conventions

3.23 Where the purpose of an Act of Parliament is to put into domestic effect an international convention recourse may be had to the terms of the convention if a provision of the Act is ambiguous or vague.[1]

Sometimes, an Act actually incorporates the convention. In such a case there are no limits on recourse to the terms of the convention because they have been made provisions of the Act. Conventions are apt to be more loosely worded than Acts of Parliament. A court must interpret the English text of an incorporated convention in a broad and sensible purposive manner unconstrained by the technical rules of English law. In the event of ambiguity or obscurity in the convention, the court can look at material in the public records of the international conference at which it was drafted provided that that material was intended to clear up the ambiguity or obscurity.[2]

[1] *Post Office v Estuary Radio* [1967] 3 All ER 663, CA.
[2] *Fothergill v Monarch Airlines Ltd* [1980] 2 All ER 696, HL.

European Convention on Human Rights and Human Rights Act 1998

3.24 The European Convention on Human Rights (ECHR), taken together with the Human Rights Act 1998, is of major importance. The provisions of the Act referred to below have great influence over the interpretation and development of the law by the courts and over new legislation.

Impact of the Act

3.25 The Human Rights Act 1998 'brings home' those Convention rights set out in Sch 1 to the Act. Essentially what this means is that remedies are available in courts and tribunals (hereafter simply 'courts') in England and Wales in respect of the Convention rights. This has not been achieved by the incorporation of the Convention rights into English law. Unlike directly applicable or directly effective EU legislation,[1] the Convention does not automatically take priority over English law. Our domestic courts have not been given a power to disregard an inconsistent Act of Parliament, but the effect of the main provisions in the Act comes close to permitting disregard without disturbing Parliamentary sovereignty. On the other hand, subordinate legislation[2] incompatible with a Convention right can be disregarded unless (leaving aside the possibility of revocation) primary legislation (essentially Acts of Parliament) prevents removal of the incompatibility.[3]

[1] Para 3.49.
[2] For the purposes of the Human Rights Act 1998, 'subordinate legislation' includes Acts of the Welsh Assembly.
[3] Human Rights Act 1998, s 3(2).

3.26 The HRA 1998 gives teeth to the Convention rights:

- by a special provision about statutory interpretation designed, so far as possible, to give effect to legislation in a way which is compatible with the Convention rights;

- by providing for a court, other than a trial court, to make a declaration of incompatibility if legislation cannot be interpreted so as to be compatible; and

- by making it unlawful for a public authority to act in a way incompatible with a Convention right.

Statutory interpretation

3.27 The HRA 1998, s 3(1) provides that primary legislation and subordinate legislation must, '*so far as it is possible to do so*, be read and given effect in a way which is compatible with the Convention rights'.[1] This is called 'reading down' the legislation. The courts, where necessary, will prefer a strained but possible interpretation which is consistent with Convention rights to one more consistent with the statutory words themselves by giving them a narrower meaning than their ordinary meaning. The approach under HRA 1998, s 3(1) is radically different from traditional techniques of statutory interpretation. There are, however, limits, as indicated by 'as far as possible'. A court cannot construe an Act in a way which Parliament could not conceivably have intended. Perverse interpretation or extensive redrafting is not permissible. In the rare case where the mismatch between Convention rights and the Act is this great, an appeal court may make a declaration of incompatibility.

An example of the operation of HRA 1998, s 3(1) is provided by *Cachia v Faluyi*.[2] This was concerned with the Fatal Accidents Act 1976, s 2(3), which provides that: 'Not more than one action [by a dependant in respect of a wrongful act causing death] shall lie for and in respect of the same subject matter of complaint'. The question for the Court of Appeal was whether this prevented three dependant children pursuing a claim by writ for damages for the death of their mother when a previous writ in the action had been issued but never served on the defendant. On a literal construction, the first writ could be regarded as constituting an action, in which case the children would have been prevented from pursuing their claim by the subsequent writ. The Court of Appeal, however, noting that ECHR, Art 6 (a Convention right) gave the children a right of access to a court to claim damages for their loss of dependency, and noting HRA 1998, s 3, held that 'action' in the Accidents Act 1976, s 2(3) should be interpreted so as to refer to 'served process' (ie service of the writ) so as to give effect to Art 6. Consequently, the first writ not having been served, s 2(3) did not bar the children's pursuit of their claim by the writ in question.

The operation of HRA 1998, s 3(1) does not depend on any ambiguity in the legislative provision; it can require a provision to bear a meaning which departs from the unambiguous meaning which it would otherwise bear. However, s 3(1) reaches its limits if a compatible interpretation would be inconsistent with a fundamental feature of the legislation; to give such an interpretation would be to cross the constitutional boundary between interpreting the legislation and amending the legislation (which is not permitted under s 3(1)). Provided that boundary is not crossed, s 3(1) authorises (and may require) the court to insert or remove words which may change the meaning of the provision or depart from Parliament's intention in order to make the provision compatible, but only if this does not conflict with a fundamental feature of the legislation.[3]

[1] Emphasis added.
[2] [2001] EWCA Civ 998, CA.
[3] *Ghaidan v Godin Mendoza* [2004] UKHL 30, HL.

Declaration of incompatibility

3.28 If a trial court is unable to interpret primary legislation compatibly with a Convention right, it will have to proceed as normal. The issue of incompatibility can then be raised on appeal or in judicial review proceedings. The High Court, Court of Appeal and Supreme Court, if satisfied that a provision of primary legislation is incompatible with a Convention right, may then make a declaration of incompatibility.[1] They may also make such a declaration in respect of a provision of subordinate legislation which is so incompatible if satisfied that (disregarding the possibility of revocation) the primary legislation prevents removal of that incompatibility.[1]

If a declaration of incompatibility is made, the validity of the provision is unaffected. The Government and Parliament are not required to take remedial action, although normally they will. A fast-track route for doing so via a ministerial order is provided by HRA 1998, s 10.

[1] HRA 1998, s 4.

Unlawful actions

3.29 It is unlawful for a public authority to act[1] in a way incompatible with a Convention right, unless:

- as the result of one or more provisions of primary legislation, the authority could not have acted differently; or
- in the case of one or more provisions of, or made under, primary legislation which cannot be read or given effect in a way which is compatible with the Convention rights, the authority was acting so as to give effect to or enforce those provisions.[2]

A 'public authority' includes a court or tribunal, and any person or body which always acts in a public capacity. Where a person or body sometimes acts in a public capacity and sometimes in a private capacity, eg a privatised utility company, it is a public authority when it acts in the former capacity.

The victim of an alleged infringement may bring legal proceedings against any public authority in respect of any act which the victim considers to be unlawful in terms of the Convention rights. A court may grant such relief or remedy (including damages if this is necessary to afford just satisfaction to the person in whose favour they are made) or make an order as it considers appropriate within the terms of HRA 1998.

By HRA 1998, s 9(1), unlawful action of this sort by a court is normally remediable only by way of appeal or judicial review or in such other order as may be prescribed by rules.

Because the prohibition on acting incompatibly with a Convention right only applies to a public authority, it does not in itself permit an individual citizen to enforce a Convention right in proceedings against another private citizen. It is, however, arguable that since the court is a 'public authority' subject to the prohibition it must apply such a right in a dispute between private individuals because it is prohibited from acting in contravention of such a right.

[1] 'Act' includes a failure to act: HRA 1998, s 6(6).
[2] HRA 1998, s 6(1)–(3).

The Convention rights

3.30 The Convention rights specified in HRA 1998, Sch 1 include:

- the right not to be deprived of liberty save in specified cases, eg after conviction or lawful arrest, and in accordance with a procedure prescribed by law;
- the right to a fair trial;
- the right to respect for private and family life;
- the freedom of expression; and
- the freedom of assembly and association.

The exercise of the last three rights or freedoms mentioned may be restricted by the law on specified grounds if this is necessary in a democratic society in (for example) the interests of national security, for the prevention of disorder or crime, for the protection of health or morals or for the protection of the rights and freedoms of others.

Application of Convention rights

3.31 The HRA 1998, s 2(1) provides that, in determining a question which has arisen in connection with a Convention right, a court must *take into account* the case law of the European Court of Human Rights. The terms of s 2(1) make it clear that these decisions are not binding;[1] they are to be taken into account along with other relevant decisions. The right of individual petition to the European Court of Human Rights remains, however, and a failure by an English court to apply a decision of that Court could lead to an application to it.

[1] Although the Supreme Court will normally apply principles clearly established by the European Court of Human Rights, there will be rare occasions where the Supreme Court has concerns as to whether a decision of the European Court of Human Rights sufficiently appreciated or accommodated particular aspects of our domestic process. In such a case it can decline to follow the European Court of Human Right's decision, giving its reasons: *R v Horncastle* [2009] UKSC 14, SC.

In *Lambeth LBC v Kay* [2006] UKHL 10, the House of Lords held that where a domestic court would normally be bound to follow the decision of a court higher in the domestic hierarchy of courts, but that decision appears to be inconsistent with a later decision of the European Court of Human Rights, the domestic court is bound to follow the binding domestic precedent.

LEGISLATION: KEY POINTS

- There are two types of domestic legislation:
  - Acts of Parliament and Acts of the Welsh Assembly; and
  - subordinate legislation.
- Subordinate legislation includes delegated legislation (ie legislation made by an executive body authorised by an Act).
- In *interpreting* a provision in an Act or subordinate legislation, the court may give it a literal construction whereby its meaning is found by interpreting the words used in their ordinary, literal and grammatical sense in their context. This process is modified by the golden rule, whereby a court can modify the literal construction of the words to avoid a manifest absurdity or repugnance or inconsistency with the rest of the Act. In addition, the literal construction of a provision will be abandoned for a purposive construction (whereby a provision may be construed any other way consistent with its purpose) where to apply the literal meaning of the provision would clearly defeat its purpose.
- So far as possible, an Act or subordinate legislation must be interpreted in a way compatible with the European Convention on Human Rights.

Judicial precedent

3.32 This is the other important source of English law and consists of the 'decisions' of courts made in decided cases. As will be seen, the 'decisions' of certain courts are more than just authoritative statements of the law since they can be binding (ie must be applied) in subsequent cases where the legally material facts are the same. Whether a particular statement of law made by a judge in one case is binding in a subsequent case depends partly on whether the statement formed the *ratio decidendi* (the reason of the decision) of the case or was merely an *obiter dictum* (something said by the way), and partly on the relative position of the two courts. Even if it is not binding, a judicial statement of the law has a persuasive effect in subsequent cases, the strength of its persuasiveness being a matter of degree.

Ratio decidendi and *obiter dictum*

3.33 Only the ratio decidendi of a case can have binding effect. A judgment usually contains the following elements:

a. A statement of the facts found with an indication, express or implied, of which of them are material facts.

b. Statements by the judge of the legal principles which apply to the legal issues raised by the material facts and are the reason for the judge's decision.

c. The actual judgment, decree or order delivered by the judge after application of b. to a., eg that the defendant is liable coupled with an award of damages.

Part c. is binding only on the parties to the case and is not a precedent for the future, nor is part a. in itself. It is part b. of this process which constitutes the ratio decidendi.

3.34 Sometimes the statements of the applicable principles made by the judge may be wider than the material facts necessitate. In such a case the ratio of the decision will be limited to that part of it which applies to the material facts and, to the extent that the statement is wider, it will be obiter dictum.[1] There are two other types of obiter dictum.

First, a statement of legal principle is obiter if it relates to facts which were not found to exist in the case or, if found, were not material. For example, in *Central London Property Trust Ltd v High Trees House Ltd*, which we discuss later in this book,[2] Denning J's principal statement about promissory estoppel was obiter since it applied to a set of facts which were not found to exist in the case.

Second, a statement of legal principle which relates to some or all of the material facts but is not the basis of the court's decision, eg because it is given in a dissenting judgment or because another material fact prevents the principle applying, is also obiter. A leading example is *Hedley Byrne & Co Ltd v Heller & Partners Ltd*.[3] The House of Lords expressed the opinion that the maker of a statement owes a duty of care, in certain circumstances, to persons who suffer loss in reliance on it. This opinion was obiter because, although it was based on material facts found to exist in the case, the actual decision—that there was no breach of such a duty—was based on another material fact, that the maker of the statement had made it subject to an effective disclaimer of responsibility.

[1] *Cassidy v Ministry of Health* [1951] 1 All ER 574, CA.
[2] Para 6.20.
[3] [1963] 2 All ER 575, HL; para 16.18.

The hierarchy of the courts and judicial precedent

3.35 As already indicated, the system of courts is a hierarchy. Essentially, one court is bound by the ratio decidendi of a case decided by another court if it is lower in the hierarchy than the latter and will not be bound by it if it is higher. Some courts are also normally bound by their own previous rationes decidendi. This basic statement will be expanded by taking courts described in Chapter 2 in turn, starting from the top of the hierarchy. For convenience, the word 'decision' will be used to indicate 'ratio decidendi'.

The Court of Justice of the European Union

3.36 As stated in para 2.19, the European Court of Justice is now the ultimate court in respect of matters within its jurisdiction. Consequently, in these limited areas of jurisdiction the decisions of the European Court bind all English courts. Indeed, the European Communities Act 1972, s 3(1) provides that any question as to the validity, meaning or effect of EU law, shall be treated as a question of law (and, if not referred to the European Court, be for determination in accordance with the principles laid down by, and any relevant decision of, the European Court or any court attached to it).

The European Court does not observe a doctrine of binding precedent and does not regard itself as bound by its previous decisions,[1] although it leans in favour of consistency with its previous decisions.

[1] Cases C–28–30/62 *Da Costa en Schaake NV v Nederlandse Belastingadministratie* [1963] CMLR 224, ECJ.

The Supreme Court and the House of Lords

3.37 A decision of the House of Lords (and now of the Supreme Court) binds all courts inferior to it. Until 1966, a decision of the House of Lords also bound that House. This principle meant that a legal rule might become unalterable by the House of Lords, in which case legislation was the only remedy if a change in the law was desired. In 1966, the House of Lords reversed this principle declaring that it would not be bound by its own decisions where it appeared right to depart from them.[1] The declaration added that in this connection the House would bear in mind the danger of disturbing retrospectively the basis on which contracts, settlements of property and fiscal arrangements have been entered into and also the special need for certainty as to the criminal law. This declaration now applies to the Supreme Court in respect of its decisions and those of the House of Lords.

The House of Lords did not make much use of its declared freedom. It held that it is not enough that it should consider its previous decision was wrong; there must be an additional factor, such as a change of circumstances on which the previous decision was based or that it is productive of manifest injustice[2] or that the previous decision is inconsistent with a subsequent decision of the European Court of Human Rights.[3] One of the relatively few cases in which the House of Lords overruled one of its previous decisions is *Murphy v Brentwood District Council*[4] where it overruled its decision in *Anns v London Borough Council of Merton*[5] that a local authority, exercising its statutory function of controlling building works, was under a common law duty to take reasonable care to ensure that the building complied with building regulations. It is anticipated that the Supreme Court will be equally reluctant to overrule one of its previous decisions or a decision of the House of Lords.

[1] [1966] 3 All ER 77.
[2] *Fitzleet Estates Ltd v Cherry* [1977] 3 All ER 996, HL.
[3] *R (on the application of Purdy) v DPP* [2009] UKHL 45, HL.
[4] [1990] 2 All ER 908, HL. See paras 21.27–21.28
[5] [1977] 2 All ER 492, HL.

The Court of Appeal (Civil Division)

3.38 The Civil Division of the Court of Appeal is bound by the previous decisions of the European Court of Justice, Supreme Court and House of Lords. It is also bound by the previous decisions of either division of the Court of Appeal. This was settled by the Court of Appeal in *Young v Bristol Aeroplane Co Ltd*.[1] The Court, however, recognised that there were exceptional situations where an earlier Court of Appeal decision is not binding on the Civil Division. The three principal exceptional situations, all stated in *Young v Bristol Aeroplane*, are:

- Where two of its previous decisions conflict. Normally, the Court of Appeal should follow the later of its two decisions, but it does not have to do so if it considers that that decision was wrongly decided.[2] The decision not followed will be deemed to be overruled.[2]

- The Court must refuse to follow a previous decision of its own which, though not expressly overruled, is inconsistent with a later Supreme Court or House of Lords decision.

- The Court is not bound to follow its previous decision if that decision was given per incuriam (ie through lack of care). A decision is regarded as having been given per incuriam where some relevant legislation or binding precedent, which would have affected the decision, was overlooked by the court making it.[3] Only in very rare instances can a case not strictly within this formulation be held to have been decided per incuriam, since such a case must normally involve a manifest slip or error and it must be likely to cause serious inconvenience in the administration of justice or serious injustice or some equally serious consequence.[4]

[1] [1944] 2 All ER 293, CA.
[2] *Starmark Enterprises v CPL Distribution Ltd* [2001] EWCA Civ 1252, CA.

[3] See, for example, *R (on the application of W) v Lambeth London Borough Council* [2002] EWCA Civ 613, CA.

[4] *Williams v Fawcett* [1985] 1 All ER 787, CA.

Divisional courts

3.39 Divisional courts are bound by decisions of the European Court of Justice, the Supreme Court, the House of Lords and the Court of Appeal, except, apparently, a Court of Appeal decision which is per incuriam, in that a relevant contrary decision of the House of Lords or Supreme Court was not cited and was therefore ignored.[1] A divisional court is bound by one of its own previous decisions unless the *Young v Bristol Aeroplane* principles apply.[2]

[1] *R v Northumberland Compensation Appeal Tribunal, ex p Shaw* [1952] 1 All ER 122, CA.
[2] *Huddersfield Police Authority v Watson* [1947] 2 All ER 193, DC.

High Court judges

3.40 A High Court judge is bound by the decisions of the European Court of Justice, the Supreme Court, the House of Lords, the Court of Appeal and a divisional court. On the other hand, a High Court judge is not bound by a decision of another High Court judge although he (or she) will treat such a decision as strong persuasive authority and will only refuse to follow it if convinced that it is wrong, and with a clear statement of the reason for doing so.[1] Where a High Court judge is faced with two conflicting decisions of other High Court judges, that judge should normally treat the legal point at issue as settled by the second decision, provided that the judge's decision in that case was reached after full consideration of the first decision. The only, rare, exception is where the third judge is convinced that the second judge was wrong in not following the first.[2]

[1] *Re Hillas-Drake, National Provincial Bank v Liddell* [1944] 1 All ER 375.
[2] *Colchester Estates (Cardiff) v Carlton Industries plc* [1984] 2 All ER 601.

County courts

3.41 County courts are bound by the decisions of the European Court of Justice, the Supreme Court, the House of Lords, the Court of Appeal and a divisional court, and by those of High Court judges sitting alone. The decision of a judge in a county court does not bind another county court judge.

Tribunals

3.42 The Upper Tribunal is bound by the decisions of the European Court of Justice, the Supreme Court, the House of Lords, the Court of Appeal and a divisional court. It is not bound by its own decisions, but its decisions are binding on the First-tier Tribunals. First-tier Tribunal decisions have no binding effect

Effect of Human Rights Act 1998

3.43 Where a Convention right under the HRA 1998 is involved, the strict rules of judicial precedent outlined above may have to be relaxed because, as stated above:

- a court must not act in a way incompatible with such a right; and
- a court must, so far as possible, interpret legislation in a way compatible with Convention rights.

   The effect of each of these provisions is that a court can validly refuse to follow an otherwise binding decision if it considers that that decision is incompatible with a Convention right.

Application of judicial precedents

3.44 The fact that a judicial precedent may be binding or merely persuasive in a subsequent case has already been touched on. It may also be noticed that a judicial precedent will become devoid of effect if it is overruled by a court competent to do so (normally, one higher in the hierarchy). As opposed to overruling by Act of Parliament,[1] judicial overruling operates retrospectively,[2] which may have the effect of disturbing financial interests or vested rights generally. For this reason the courts are reluctant to overrule a previous decision unless they consider it is clearly wrong.

Where a precedent is binding on a court, that court must follow it unless that court can distinguish it on the facts. Suppose that the Supreme Court has held that if facts A and B exist, principle X applies, and that a case is heard by a High Court judge at first instance where facts A and B exist as well as fact E, which did not exist in the Supreme Court's case. The judge may distinguish the Supreme Court's case on its material facts and consequently, since that decision will not be binding in relation to the case before the judge, decide to apply some other principle or to apply principle X by analogy. Since the facts are never identical in any two cases there is wide scope for 'distinguishing'. However, a court inferior to that which gave the previous decision will not normally distinguish it on strained grounds.

[1] Para 3.4.

[2] By way of exception in wholly exceptional cases where it is in the interests of justice to do so, the Supreme Court may declare that one of its decisions is not to operate retrospectively: *Re Spectrum Plus Ltd* [2005] UKHL 41, HL; *Ahmed v HM Treasury (No 2)* [2010] UKSC 5 at [17].

3.45 There are various types of persuasive precedents:

- those decisions of courts inferior in the hierarchy to a court which subsequently hears a similar case. Into this category one can also put decisions of the Judicial Committee of the Privy Council on appeals from British dependent territories and a few Commonwealth states, which do not bind English courts or the Privy Council itself if it considers its previous decision incorrect.[1] However, the decisions of the Privy Council are particularly persuasive because the Judicial Committee is composed of Justices of the Supreme Court (plus, sometimes, a judge of the Court of Appeal or a judge of equal standing from a Commonwealth country);

- where an otherwise binding precedent is distinguishable; it will nevertheless have persuasive authority;[2]

- obiter dicta, the persuasiveness of which depends on the seniority of the court or prestige of the judge by whom the words were uttered and the relative position of that court and a subsequent court. One of the most significant examples is the 'neighbour principle' expounded by Lord Atkin in 1932 in *Donoghue v Stevenson*,[3] which was much wider than the actual case required but has become the basis of the modern tort of negligence and has been applied in numerous cases since;

- decisions of the European Court of Human Rights;

- decisions of Irish, Scottish, Commonwealth and US courts, which are being referred to increasingly by our courts.

[1] *Gibson v Government of the USA* [2007] UKPC 520, PC.

[2] Especially if it is a House of Lords or Supreme Court decision: *Re House Property and Investment Co* [1953] 2 All ER 1525.

[3] [1932] AC 562, HL.

> PRECEDENT: KEY POINTS
>
> - The decisions of some courts can create a legal precedent. Whether a particular judicial statement by such a court is binding in a subsequent case depends partly on whether that statement formed part of the *ratio decidendi* (the reason for the decision: henceforward the 'decision') of the case or was merely an *obiter dictum* (something said by the way) and partly on the relative standing of the two courts. Only the *ratio decidendi* can have binding effect. Essentially, one court is bound by the *ratio decidendi* of a case decided by another if it is lower in the hierarchy of courts than the latter and will not be bound if it is higher. Some courts are normally bound by their own *rationes decidendi*.
>
> - If a binding precedent can be distinguished, it will not bind the distinguishing court. A precedent can only be distinguished if the facts of the case before it differ materially from the precedent.

Custom

3.46 Local customs, ie customs operative in a particular locality or among a particular group of people in a particular locality, are occasionally recognised by the courts as establishing a local 'law' for the locality in question at variance with the general law of the land, although they must not be contrary to an Act of Parliament or to a fundamental principle of the common law.

Local customs are largely to be found in rights of way and common. Recognition of a local custom depends on a number of conditions being satisfied, the most important of which are that the alleged custom must:

- have existed since 'time immemorial', which, theoretically, it will only do if it goes back to 1189 (for reasons of historical accident);
- have been continuous. The custom must have been in existence continuously. This means that the right to exercise it must not have been interrupted; but the fact that the right has not actually been exercised for a period of time, even 100 years in one case,[1] does not negative the existence of a local custom (although if the evidence of custom is dubious it will go far to negative any customary right);
- not be unreasonable;[2]
- be certain; in other words the right claimed must be certain in nature and scope and prove to adhere to a defined locality or group of people;
- be recognised as compulsory.[3]

The first condition is not as strict as may appear since the claimant can succeed in proving it if he can prove that the practice in question has existed in the locality for a substantial time: the oldest local inhabitant is often called as a witness in this context. If the claimant proves this, existence since 1189 will be presumed,[4] provided, of course, that such a practice was possible in 1189.

---

[1] *New Windsor Corpn v Mellor* [1975] 3 All ER 44, CA.

[2] *Wolstanton Ltd v Newcastle-under-Lyme Borough Council* [1940] 3 All ER 101, HL.

[3] Blackstone's *Commentaries*: 'a custom that all the inhabitants shall be rated towards the maintenance of a bridge will be good, but a custom that every man is to contribute thereto at his own pleasure is idle and absurd, and indeed not custom at all'.

[4] *Mercer v Denne* [1905] 2 Ch 538 at 577.

CUSTOM: KEY POINTS

A usage cannot be recognised as a local custom unless it:

- has existed since 1189 (or is presumed to have done so);
- has been continuous;
- is not unreasonable;
- is certain; and
- is recognised as compulsory.

European Union legislation

3.47 The source of European Union law is the legislation of the European Union (EU).

The fundamental legislation of the EU is to be found in the treaties establishing the EU, and its predecessor, the European Community, including amending treaties.

The overwhelming mass of the EU legislation is found not in the treaties referred to above but in regulations, directives and decisions of the EU's organs. EU legislation is largely concerned with economic matters, such as agriculture, free trade and fair competition, but it also deals with other matters, such as immigration, employment and other social matters.

Regulations, directives and decisions

3.48 These types of legislation can only be made on a proposal from the European Commission (a supranational body composed of the highest officials in the EU), which has the sole right of initiative in drafting legislation.

Regulations have general application and are made by the Council of the EU (a political body composed of a minister from each member) in conjunction with the European Parliament or by the European Commission.

Directives can be issued by the Council of the EU in conjunction with the European Parliament or by the European Commission. Directives are directed to member states, who are obliged to implement them although they have a choice as to the form and methods of implementation.

Decisions, which are made by the Council of the EU, by the Council in conjunction with the European Parliament or by the European Commission, are addressed either to a member state or to an individual or institution. They are a formal method of enunciating administrative decisions giving effect to the policy of the EU and are binding on the addressee.

Direct applicability and direct effect

3.49 In order to understand how EU legislation affects English law, it is necessary to understand the concepts of direct applicability and direct effect:

- *Direct applicability* Only regulations are directly applicable.[1] This means that they are automatically incorporated into the law of a member state as soon as they are made, without the need for action by that state. Regulations also have direct effect (see below) except in the rare case where they fail the conditions for direct effect (below).

- *Direct effect* Any type of EU legislation can be relied on (whether by way of claim or defence) in a court of a member state if it is of direct effect.[2] For it to have direct effect:

  - the right in question must be clear, precise and unconditional;
  - it must not require implementation by adoption measures in the member states or by a EU institution; and
  - it must not leave scope for the exercise of discretion by a member state or EU institution.[3]

- There are two types of direct effect:

  - *Vertical direct effect*, which means that the piece of legislation creates legal obligations in national law on the state or an emanation of the state (ie any body which the state has made responsible for providing a public service and which provides that service under the supervision of the state, eg a local authority or an authority providing public health services)[4] which are enforceable against it in domestic court by an individual;[5] and
  - *Horizontal direct effect*, which means that the piece of legislation creates legal obligations on individuals which can be enforced against them in a domestic court by another individual or the state. Only EU treaty provisions and regulations can have this effect, but only if their wording indicates that they do. Thus, for example, if it has a direct effect a directive can only confer rights on an individual, and not obligations.

    A directive cannot have immediate direct effect. The reason is that member states are expected to implement them by transposing them into their domestic law by their own legislation, and thereby are enabled to tailor their response in a way most appropriate to their own legal system. For this reason, they are given a period of time in which to transpose a directive, usually two years, and it is only after this period has elapsed without the directive being transposed in law of a member state that a directive satisfying the three conditions above can have direct effect in that member state.

Directly applicable and directly effective EU legislation is given effect in the United Kingdom by the European Communities Act 1972, s 2(1).

[1] Treaty on the Functioning of the EU, art 288.

[2] Case C-90/70 *Grad v Finanzant Traustein* [1970] ECR 325, ECJ; Case C-41/74 *Van Duyn v Home Office* [1975] 3 All ER 190, ECJ ; Case C-129 79 *Macarthys Ltd v Smith* [1980] ECR 1275, ECJ.

[3] Case C-26/62 *NV Algemen Transporten Expeditie Onderneming van Gend en Loos v Nederlandse Administratie der Belastingen* [1963] ECR 1, ECJ.

[4] Case C-152/84 *Marshall v Southampton and South West Hampshire Area Health Authority* [1986] 2 All ER 584, ECJ; Case C-188/89 *Foster v British Gas* [1990] ECR 3313 at 3348.

[5] Case C-152/84 *Marshall v Southampton and South West Hampshire Area Health Authority*.

Transposition

3.50 Directives are transposed into law in the United Kingdom by delegated legislation made under powers given by the European Communities Act 1972, s 2(2), which also governs the implementation in further detail of regulations. Delegated legislation made under these powers can include any provision which might be made in an Act of Parliament.[1] This power to make delegated legislation is the widest given to the United Kingdom government in modern times apart from times of war. The power must be exercised by way of statutory instrument and such an instrument will be ultra vires, and therefore invalid, if it is not related to the affairs of the EU. There are a number of limits in this power of delegated legislation; for instance, it cannot be used to impose taxation.

[1] European Communities Act 1972, s 2(4).

Untransposed directives: any effect in English law?

3.51 A directive which has not been transposed into the law of a member state and is not of direct effect in the circumstances is not devoid of all effect under that law. It may have effect in two ways, even during the period for transposition.

First, a national court must have regard to an untransposed directive in interpreting national legislation; national legislation, whenever passed, must be interpreted by a national court in such a way as to give effect to EU directives *so far as possible*.[1] A national court cannot, however, eliminate national provisions contrary to a provision of an untransposed directive and substitute the terms of the directive.[2] To do so would be to introduce direct effect between individuals under the guise of interpretation. Thus, it is for an English court to construe an Act of Parliament so as to accord with a directive, if this can be done without distorting the meaning of the Act, whether the Act came after or before the directive.[3]

Second, the failure of a member state to transpose a directive, or to transpose it properly, may give rise to a liability in damages. A person may be able to claim from a member state in the courts of that state damages for loss suffered as a result of its failure to transpose nationally a directive.[4] This principle also applies where a directive has been transposed inadequately or erroneously.[5] In English law, such damages are awarded on the basis of the commission of a tort analogous to that of breach of statutory duty.[6] For an action for this tort to succeed it must be proved that:

- the relevant rule of EU law is one which is intended to confer rights on individuals;
- the breach is sufficiently serious; and
- there is a direct causal link between the breach and the loss complained of.

[1] Case C-06/89 *Marleasing SA v La Comercial Internacional de Alimentacion SA* [1992] 1 CMLR 305, ECJ.
[2] *Webb v EMO Air Cargo (UK) Ltd* [1992] 4 All ER 929 at 929–930.
[3] *Duke v GEC Reliance Ltd* [1988] 1 All ER 626, HL.
[4] Cases C–6,9/90 *Francovich v Italy* [1993] 2 CMLR 66, ECJ.
[5] Two cases are relevant: Case C–46/93 *Brasserie du Pêcheur SA v Germany*; Case C–48/93 *R v Secretary of State for Transport, ex p Factortame (No 4)* [1996] All ER (EC) 301, ECJ.
[6] *R v Secretary of State for Transport, ex p Factortame (No 5)* [1998] 1 All ER 736n, DC, affd [1999] 4 All ER 906, HL; *R v Secretary of State for Transport, ex p Factortame (No 7)* [2001] 1 WLR 942. For breach of statutory duty, see ch 20.

Supremacy of EU law

3.52 According to EU law, directly applicable or directly effective EU law takes precedence over domestic law,[1] and this is given effect to in English law by the European Communities Act 1972, s 2(1). If a provision of English legislation is incompatible with such a law an English court should set it aside.[1] The only exception would be where an inconsistent post-1972 Act passed after the EU law is expressly and deliberately in conflict with it, in which case the Act must prevail.[2] It was mentioned in para 3.19 that there is a presumption in interpreting an Act of Parliament that it is not inconsistent with EU law so that an English court will so far as possible interpret the Act so as to avoid inconsistency.

[1] Case C-6/64 *Costa v ENEL* [1964] ECR 585, ECJ
[2] *Macarthys Ltd v Smith* [1979] ICR 785, CA.

Validity of EU legislation

3.53 Regulations, directives and decisions are subject to review by the European Court. They can be held invalid by it (but not by a court of a member state[1]) on the grounds of lack of competence, or infringement of any essential procedural requirement, or infringement of the treaties or of any rule of law concerning their application, or misuse of power.

[1] Case C-314/85 *Foto-Frost v Hauptzollant Lubeck-Ost* [1988] 3 CMLR 57, ECJ.

Interpretation of EU legislation

3.54 The drafting of the legislation of the EU is quite unlike that of English legislation but, like the legislation of other European countries, is drafted in terms of broad principle, leaving the courts to supply the detail by giving effect to the general intention of the legislature.

The result of this difference in drafting is that the interpretation of the legislation of the EU, whether by the European Court or by an English court,[1] is not based on a slavish interpretation of the words or the grammatical structure of the sentences but on the purpose or intent of the legislation;[2] in other words, a purposive approach involving a preparedness to look at the policy underlying the words of the legislation is taken to the interpretation of such legislation.

[1] *HP Bulmer Ltd v J Bollinger SA* [1974] 2 All ER 1226 at 1237–1238.
[2] Case C-41/74 *Van Duyn v Home Office* [1975] 3 All ER 190, ECJ; *Litster v Forth Dry Dock and Engineering Co Ltd* [1989] 1 All ER 1134, HL.

EU LAW: KEY POINTS

- The source of EU law is the legislation of the EU. The types of legislation of the EU and their effects are as follows:

Type of legislation	Direct applicability	Direct effect (provided conditions met)	
		Vertical	Horizontal
Treaties	✗	✓	✓
Regulations	✓	✓	✓
Directives	✗	✓ (once implementation period lapsed)	✗
Decisions	✗	✓ (on addressee only)	✗

- In interpreting EU law, the European Court of Justice or an English court will take a purposive approach.

Questions

1. What types of legislation are made in England and Wales?

2. What are the two approaches to the interpretation of a statutory provision, and what do they involve?

3. What is the significance in terms of its interpretation that a statutory provision involves a Convention right under the Human Rights Act 1998?

4. What is meant by the terms:
    *   *ratio decidendi*; and
    *   *obiter dictum*?

5. To what extent, if any, are the following courts or judges not bound by the decision of another court or judge of the same status (eg the Supreme Court by another of its decisions):
    *   the Supreme Court;
    *   the Court of Appeal (Civil Division);
    *   a divisional court;
    *   a judge of the High Court;
    *   a judge of a county court?

6. In *Pharmaceutical Society of Great Britain v Boots Cash Chemists (Southern) Ltd* [1953] 1 All ER 482, an Act required certain drugs to be sold only under the supervision of a qualified pharmacist. A pharmacist in a self-service chemists was at the cash desk but, if the contract for the sale of drugs had been made before a customer reached it, the statute would have been infringed. The Court of Appeal had no hesitation in holding that the display of goods was only an invitation to treat, that, in a self-service shop, the offer to buy was made by the customer at the cash desk, and that the contract was concluded when the offer was accepted there. Consequently, Boots were not in breach of the statute. It was not necessary to decide precisely when a customer's offer is accepted at the cash desk, but one member of the Court of Appeal (Birkett LJ) agreed with the view that acceptance occurs when the payment of the price is accepted.

Consider the following:

A) Would the Court of Appeal's statement that, in a self-service shop, the offer to buy is made by the customer at the cash desk, and that the contract of sale is concluded when the offer is accepted there, bind:
    *   the Supreme Court;
    *   the Court of Appeal;
    *   a judge of the High Court,
    in a later case involving the issue of how and when a contract of sale is made in a self-service shop?

B) Would your answer to A) be different if the later case concerned a self-service china shop, at the entrance of which there was a sign saying:
    'Because of breakages, customers will be deemed to have accepted an offer to sell an item on picking it up. Thus, if you drop an item you will have to pay the contract price like anyone else who picks up an item.'

C) Would Birkett LJ's statement bind:
    *   the Supreme Court;

- the Court of Appeal;
- a judge of the High Court?

7. What is meant by the concepts of 'direct applicability' and 'direct effect' in respect of the legislation of the EU?

8. What effect, if any, in English law can an untransposed directive have?

PART II

The law of contract

4

Introduction

CHAPTER OVERVIEW

Contracts dominate our ability to transact with each other. Whenever a person buys a cup of coffee, gets a job, or rents a flat or agrees to conduct a survey for a client, that person makes a contract. Knowledge of the fundamental principles of the law of contract is an essential part of a property professional's knowledge base.

In this chapter we outline:

● the essential elements of a contract (dealt with further in chapters 5 and 6);

● the rules about the form of a contract; and

● the contractual capacity of companies and other business organisations.

The essential elements of a contract

4.1 For there to be a contract (ie a legally binding agreement):

● there must be an agreement;

● the parties must have intended their agreement to be legally binding; and

● the contract must be supported by consideration or be made by deed.

Although it is usual to talk about enforcing a contract, it must not be forgotten that what is being enforced is a promise by one party to an agreement by the other party to it. A mere statement of present fact to which another person agrees cannot be enforced, even if it relates to the fact of the present intentions of the party making the statement. Thus, if a company says 'it is our policy to ensure that any of our subsidiaries is always in a position to meet its liabilities in respect of a loan made to it', there is not a breach of contract if one of the subsidiaries becomes unable to meet its liabilities in respect of a loan.[1]

---

[1] *Kleinwort Benson Ltd v Malaysia Mining Corpn Bhd* [1989] 1 All ER 785, CA.

4.2 A contract may be either bilateral or unilateral.

A bilateral contract is one in which a party (A) promises to do something if the other party (B) promises to do something in return and B makes that counter-promise. In such a case, the mere exchange of promises normally renders both promises binding immediately. A unilateral contract, on the other hand, arises where A promises to do something in return for an act by B, rather than a counter-promise, as where A promises to pay B a reward if he finds some lost property or where A promises to pay B £100,000 if he sails round the world in less than six months, and B responds by doing the requested act. In such a case B is not bound to do anything at all; only if he does the act will A's promise become binding (because only then will a unilateral contract between A and B come into being). A less obvious example of a unilateral contract, though one which is of great commercial importance, is the normal type of commission agreement entered into by estate agents, mortgage brokers and the like. According to the decision of the House of Lords in *Luxor (Eastbourne) Ltd v Cooper*,[1] an estate agent instructed by a client to market a property is under no obligation to take any action at all; only when the estate agent satisfies the client's instructions as expressed in the agency agreement (eg finding the eventual purchaser) does the client's promise of commission become binding (because only then will a unilateral contract between the client and the estate agent come into being).

[1] [1941] 1 All ER 33, HL.

Form

4.3 With the exceptions mentioned below, English law does not require an agreement to be in writing in order to be a valid and enforceable contract, but there are obvious advantages in reducing it into writing.

Contracts which must be made by deed

Leases for three years or more

4.4 Leases for more than three years are void at law, and cannot therefore pass a legal estate to the purported tenant, unless made by deed. However, provided it complies with the provisions of the Law of Property (Miscellaneous Provisions) Act 1989, s 2, such a lease not made by deed can take effect as a contract to grant a lease, which can be specifically enforced and will create the same rights between the parties for many purposes.[1]

[1] See further, paras 30.2–30.5.

Contracts in which there is no consideration

4.5 If there is no consideration for the promise made by one party to the other there is no legally binding agreement unless it is made by deed.[1]

[1] *Rann v Hughes* (1778) 7 Term Rep 350n, HL.

What is a 'deed'?

4.6 A contract is not made by deed unless the instrument in which it is written:

- makes it clear on its face that it is intended to be a deed by the person making it or, as the case may be, by the parties to it (eg because it describes itself as a deed or because it expresses itself to be executed or signed as a deed); and

- it is validly executed as a deed by that person (or a person authorised to execute it on that person's behalf) or, as the case may be, by one or more of those parties (or a person authorised to execute it on behalf of one or more of those parties).[1]

An instrument is validly executed as a deed by an individual (I) only if:

- it is signed–
  - by I in the presence of a witness who attests the signature, or

- at I's direction and in I's presence and the presence of two witnesses who attest the signature; and

- it is delivered as a deed by I or a person authorised to do so on I's behalf.[2]

A deed is regarded as delivered as soon as there are acts which show that the person making it intends unconditionally to be bound by it: physical delivery of it to the other party is no longer required and a deed may be delivered even though it remains in the custody of its maker.[3]

There are special statutory provisions governing the execution of a deed by a company or a limited liability partnership.

[1] Law of Property (Miscellaneous Provisions) Act 1989, s 1(2).
[2] LP(MP)A 1989, s 1(3).
[3] *Vincent v Premo Enterprises (Voucher Sales) Ltd* [1969] 2 All ER 941, CA.

Contracts which must be in writing

4.7 Some contracts are invalid or unenforceable unless they are in writing. For example, an agreement for the sale or other disposition of land or an interest in land is generally invalid unless it is made in writing, as we explain in para 29.2. By way of further example, consumer credit agreements and consumer hire agreements which are not executed in writing in the manner required by the Consumer Credit Act 1974 are enforceable against the debtor or hirer only on an order of the court.[1]

[1] Consumer Credit Act 1974, s 65.

Contracts which must be evidenced in writing

4.8 Contracts of guarantee do not have to be written but if they are not there must be written evidence of their parties and terms; otherwise they cannot be enforced in legal proceedings.[1]

[1] Statute of Frauds 1677, s 4.

E-mail

4.9 An e-mail can satisfy a requirement for 'writing'. In *J Pereira Fernandes SA v Mehta*[1] it was held that a contract of guarantee had been evidenced in writing where its terms were contained in an e-mail. It was also held that, by including his name in an e-mail text, the sender signs it provided that it is clear that the sender's name was intended to act as a signature.

[1] [2006] EWHC 813 (Ch).

Capacity

4.10 There are special rules about the capacity of the following to make contracts:

- minors (ie people under 18);
- mentally disordered and intoxicated persons;
- companies;

- limited liability partnerships; and
- partnerships.

Property professionals are most unlikely to make contracts with people in the first two categories. Consequently, the contractual capacity of such people is not dealt with in this book. On the other hand, the contractual capacity of companies and limited liability partnerships and of partnerships of the traditional type is of importance to property professionals.

Companies

Legal status

4.11 Under English law, a company (which is an artificial legal person) may be formed by incorporation in any one of three ways:

- by registration under the Companies Act 2006, which simply involves submitting prescribed documentation to the Registrar of Companies and paying a fee (registered companies); or
- by Act of Parliament (statutory companies); or
- by Royal Charter (chartered companies). Chartered companies are typically charitable or quasi-charitable associations or non-trading bodies, such as the Royal Institution of Chartered Surveyors.

It is extremely rare (as well as difficult and expensive) to form a company other than by registration under the Companies Act 2006 (CA 2006). The CA 2006 permits the formation of private companies and public companies. Only public companies can apply for listing on the Stock Exchange.

4.12 Other associations of people may pursue some common purpose, such as trade unions, clubs and partnerships of the traditional type, but companies can be distinguished from such unincorporated associations in that they are themselves a legal person totally distinct from their shareholders (often called members) and employees. Even if a company is totally dominated by one shareholder, the company and that shareholder are distinct legal persons.[1]

Two consequences of the separate legal identities of a company and its members are:

- a company can sue and be sued in its own name;
- a company can make contracts on its own behalf (and its members cannot claim the benefit nor be subject to the burden of such contracts[2]).

[1] *Salomon v Salomon & Co Ltd* [1897] AC 22, HL.
[2] This is merely the effect of the doctrine of privity: ch 13.

Contractual capacity

4.13 Although a company is a legal person, it does not—except in the case of a chartered company[1]—necessarily have the contractual capacity of a natural person. The contractual capacity of a statutory company depends on the wording of the creating statute. The contractual capacity of a registered company is described in the next paragraph.

[1] *Sutton's Hospital Case* (1612) 10 Co Rep 23a; *Pharmaceutical Society of Great Britain v Dickson* [1968] 2 All ER 686, HL.

4.14 When a registered company is created, the people forming the company are required to lodge articles of association with the Registrar of Companies at Companies House in Cardiff, unless model articles promulgated by the Secretary of State are to be used. Articles of association are available for public inspection. The constitution of a registered company is to be found in its articles of association. Until CA 2006, a registered company's constitution was to be found in its memorandum of association which had to contain an 'objects clause' setting out the objects of the company (ie the purposes for which the company was formed and the aims and business it intended to pursue). An objects clause is now not required. The upshot of this is that, while a pre-CA 2006 company will have an objects clause (unless its constitution is amended), a post-CA 2006 will have unlimited objects unless its articles specifically restrict its objects.[1]

In terms of the law of contract the importance of this is that a registered company can only make contracts which fall within its objects. If a company's objects are unrestricted its contractual capacity is also unrestricted, but otherwise its capacity will be restricted to making contracts within its objects. Traditionally, a contract outside a company's objects (known as an ultra vires—beyond its powers—contract) was void but this has been amended by statute.[2] The CA 2006, s 39(1) provides that the validity of an act may not be called into question on the ground of lack of capacity by reason of anything in the company's constitution. This means that, if a registered company enters into a contract which is ultra vires, the contract will be binding and enforceable in respect of both parties. However, as the directors of the company are obliged to act in accordance with the company's constitution,[3] a director will be liable to compensate the company for any loss suffered by the company as a result of that director causing an ultra vires contract to be made.

[1] CA 2006, s 31(1).
[2] There are special rules in respect of companies which are charities: CA 2006, s 42.
[3] CA 2006, s 171(1)(a).

4.15 Although it is a person in law, a company obviously cannot negotiate contracts personally; it must act through agents. An agent, such as a director of the company, is subject to the usual rules of agency described in Chapter 14. Hence, an agreement entered into by an agent of a company is only binding on the company if that person had actual, implied or ostensible authority to enter into it.

The authority which an agent of a company appears to possess may be restricted and that restriction may be capable of discovery. For example, the directors have actual, implied or ostensible authority to enter into almost any transaction on behalf of the company but the company's constitution may say, for example, that transactions in excess of £500,000 in value must be approved by the shareholders. Can the directors bind the company by a transaction which is in breach of such a restriction? The CA 2006, s 40 provides that, in favour of a person dealing with the company in good faith, the power of the directors to bind the company (or to authorise others to do so) is deemed to be free of any limitations under the company's constitution. Thus, a company cannot enforce a contract which was entered into by an unauthorised agent but the other party may be able to do so. A person does not manifest bad faith simply by knowing that there is a restriction on the powers of the directors or by failing to inquire whether their powers are limited. A person is presumed to have acted in good faith unless the contrary is proved.

Limited liability partnerships

4.16 In 2000 a new form of business entity, the limited liability partnership (LLP), was created by the Limited Liability Partnerships Act 2000 (LLPA 2000). Despite its name the LLP is a body corporate, an artificial legal person quite distinct from its members.

A LLP has more in common with a company than a partnership and is largely regulated by the provisions of company law rather than by partnership law. A LLP is formed by the submission of specified documentation to the Registrar of Companies and the payment of a fee. One distinction between a LLP and most companies is that a LLP does not have shares held by shareholders in the same way.

4.17 A LLP can sue and be sued in its own name and can make contracts on its own behalf. It has the same capacity to contract as a natural person.[1] As in the case of a company, a LLP will act through an agent and will be bound by an agent who has actual, implied or ostensible authority to make the contract.

[1] LLPA 2000, s 1(3).

Partnerships

4.18 A partnership will usually be governed by the rules laid down in the Partnership Act 1890 (PA 1890), but it is possible to create limited partnerships which are governed by the Limited Partnerships Act 1907 (LPA 1907). The limited partnership, which is a partnership with some of the characteristics of a limited liability company, is uncommon in England and Wales, although much used in continental Europe. Unlike a 'limited liability partnership', a 'partnership' or 'limited partnership' is not a body corporate (ie is not a separate legal entity). With a few exceptions, the law relating to partnerships does not apply to a limited liability partnership.[1]

The PA 1890, s 1 defines a partnership as 'the relation existing between two or more persons carrying on a business in common with a view to profit'. Because the partners and the partnership are not separate legal entities, unlike the shareholders and the company in which they hold shares, there are important differences between being a partner and being a shareholder. For example:

- a partner is liable for the debts and liabilities of the partnership: a shareholder is not liable for the debts and liabilities of the company;

- a partner has a legal interest in the assets of the partnership: a shareholder does not have any legally recognised interest in the assets of the company;

- shares in a partnership are not transferable: shares in a company are; and

- the death of a partner technically terminates the partnership, although the remaining partners may agree to carry on the partnership: the death of a shareholder leaves the company unaffected.

A limited partnership is a partnership where one or more partners has only a limited liability for the debts of the partnership. Every limited partnership must have at least one general partner[2] (ie with full liability for debts) and any limited partner who is active in the affairs of the partnership becomes a general partner.[3] The limited partnership is only suitable for those who wish to invest money in a partnership but take no part in its running; their lack of popularity seems hardly surprising.

It is unusual to find large businesses run as partnerships. While there are advantages over companies (and limited liability partnerships) in that there is less publicity for the affairs of the partnership, and perhaps less tax to be paid, these benefits will probably be outweighed by the advantages enjoyed by a company (or limited liability partnership) of limited liability and tax saving once profits reach a certain size.

[1] LLPA 2000, s 1(5).
[2] LPA 1907, s 4.
[3] LPA 1907, s 6.

4.19 Because a partnership is not a separate legal person, it does not have its own contractual capacity. However, a partnership can usually sue, or be sued, in the name of the partnership, and is generally bound by contracts entered into by one of its partners since each partner is an agent for the partnership and fellow partners for the purposes of the business of the partnership. In theory, a partnership can make any contract it wishes. Whether a contract entered into by a partner binds the partnership and fellow partners depends on the usual rules of agency,[1] with the additional rule that any contract entered into by a partner which would be within the usual way of business of the kind carried on by the partnership will bind the partnership and fellow partners, unless the partner so acting (P) has no authority to make the particular contract and the other party either knows this or does not know or believe P to be a partner.[2]

[1] Chapter 14.
[2] PA 1890, s 5.

Illegality

4.20 Sometimes a contract may be tainted with illegality (either because it is prohibited by statute, or because it is performed in a way prohibited by statute, or because it involves an unlawful or immoral element or is in unjustifiable restraint of trade). In such cases, one or both parties may be unable to enforce it or the impermissible part of it. The relevant rules are outside the scope of this book.

INTRODUCTION TO CONTRACT LAW: KEY POINTS

- For there to be a contract (ie a legally binding agreement):
  – there must be an agreement;
  – the parties must have intended their agreement to be legally binding; and
  – the agreement must be supported by consideration or made by deed.

- A bilateral contract is one in which a party (A) promises to do something if the other party (B) promises to do something in return and B makes that counter-promise. In such a case, the mere exchange of promises normally renders both promises binding immediately. A unilateral contract, on the other hand, arises where A promises to do something in return for an act by B, rather than a counter-promise. In such a case B is not bound to do anything at all; only if he does the act will A's promise become binding.

- Writing is not normally required for a valid and enforceable contract but:
  – leases for three years or more must be made by deed, and so must a contract for which there is no consideration if it is to be valid;
  – an agreement for the sale or other disposition of an interest in land must generally be made in writing.

- The contractual capacity of a company may be limited but, in the case of a registered company, this does not normally prevent a contract entered into by it being binding and enforceable. A limited liability partnership has the same capacity as a natural legal person. A company or limited liability partnership will act through an agent.

- A partnership does not have contractual capacity but the partnership may become bound by a contract made by one of its partners acting as its agent.

Questions

1. What are the differences between a bilateral contract and a unilateral contract?

2. Aileen, an estate agent, is instructed by Bill on a sole agency basis at a commission rate of 1.5% to find a purchaser for his house. After many weeks of hard work trying to do so, Aileen finally finds someone, Charlie, who is willing to purchase the house. Bill and Charlie are, however, eventually unable to agree a price. Soon afterwards, the sole agency ends, a purchaser not having been found. Bill refuses to pay Aileen a penny. Advise Aileen.

3. What is a deed? When does a contract have to be made by deed or in writing?

4. Explain how it is determined whether:

   - a registered company; or
   - a partnership,

   is bound by a contract.

5

Agreement

CHAPTER OVERVIEW

We stated at the beginning of the last chapter that a contract is a legally binding agreement. In this chapter we consider the element of 'agreement'. This involves the examination of the following points:

- how an agreement is ascertained;
- the general, but not invariable, rule that proof of an agreement requires proof that one person made an offer to another which the latter accepted;
- what constitutes an offer;
- what constitutes an effective acceptance of an offer;
- how offers may be terminated before acceptance;
- the legal position if an agreement is uncertain in its terms, or is inconclusive, or is subject to the operation of a condition.

Ascertaining an agreement

5.1 An 'agreement' is often said to require a meeting of the minds of the parties to it, but this is rather misleading. The reason is that the law tends to take an objective, rather than a subjective, approach to an agreement. It is concerned not so much with what is actually in the minds of the parties, but with what a reasonable person would infer, from their conduct and the circumstances, as being in their minds (ie did they agree and, if so, on what terms?). This approach is not surprising: when the question of whether or not there is agreement is raised it is not possible to look back into the actual minds of the parties.

The following quotation indicates the approach of the courts:

'In contracts you do not look into the actual intent in a man's mind. You look at what he said and did. A contract is formed when there is, to all outward appearances, a contract.'[1]

---

[1] *Storer v Manchester City Council* [1974] 3 All ER 824 at 828.

General requirement of offer and acceptance

5.2 The agreement involved in most contracts can be analysed into an offer by one party to the other which has been accepted by the other. However, not all agreements can be so analysed. This is the case, for example, where two parties agree to terms suggested by a third person. It may also be the case where several parties agree independently with X that they will be bound by terms stipulated by him. In such an event the parties may have entered into a contract not merely with X but with each other. In *Clarke v Dunraven*,[1] yachtsmen wrote to the secretary of a yacht club agreeing to be bound by certain rules during a yacht race. The House of Lords held that a contract containing those rules existed between the yachtsmen with the result that a yachtsman whose yacht was damaged was able to recover damages in accordance with the rules. While there was agreement between the yachtsmen to be bound by the rules, it cannot be analysed in terms of offer and acceptance between them.

Despite exceptional cases such as these, it is the law that generally, for there to be an agreement, what has occurred must be capable of analysis into an offer by one party accepted by the other. Some judges have taken a more liberal approach. For example, in *Gibson v Manchester City Council*,[2] Lord Denning MR said: 'To my mind it is a mistake to think that all contracts can be analysed into the form of offer and acceptance... You should look at the correspondence as a whole and at the conduct of the parties... and see therefore whether the parties have come to an agreement on everything that was material'. However, on appeal in that case, Lord Denning's approach was disapproved by the House of Lords. For example, Lord Diplock said: 'My Lords there may be certain types of contract, *though I think they are exceptional*, which do not fit easily into the normal analysis of a contract as constituted by offer and acceptance; but a contract alleged to have been made by an exchange of correspondence between the parties in which the successive communications other than the first are in reply to one another is not one of these'.[3] Lord Diplock's statement represents the weight of judicial opinion, although Lord Denning's approach is a more appropriate reflection of what happens in business than a strict 'offer and acceptance approach'.

[1] [1897] AC 59, HL.
[2] [1978] 2 All ER 583.
[3] [1979] 1 All ER 972 at 974.

Offer

5.3 An offer is made where a person (the offeror) unequivocally expresses to another (the offeree) his willingness to make a binding agreement on the terms specified by him if they are accepted by the offeree.

An offer may be made to a specific person, to a group of people, or to the world at large.[1] An offer to a specific person cannot be accepted by anyone else.[2]

An offer may be made in writing or in spoken words, or may be inferred from conduct.

The fact that an offer requires an expression of unequivocal willingness to contract means that quotations of rates or prices are not offers.[3] It also means that inquiries and replies to inquiries are not offers, although sometimes they may resemble them. In *Harvey v Facey*,[4] one party inquired as to the lowest acceptable price for certain land, and the other party telegraphed his lowest acceptable price. This was held not to be an offer but merely a reply to the inquiry.

[1] *Carlill v Carbolic Smoke Ball Co* [1893] 1 QB 256, CA.
[2] *Cundy v Lindsay* (1878) 3 App Cas 459, HL.
[3] *Scancarriers A/S v Aotearoa International Ltd* [1985] 2 Lloyd's Rep 419, PC.
[4] [1893] AC 552, PC.

Invitation to treat

5.4 An offer must be distinguished from an 'invitation to treat' (ie an invitation to another person to make an offer or to enter into negotiations which may lead to the making of an offer). In *Gibson v Manchester City Council*,[1] where a letter had been sent saying that the council 'may be prepared to sell the house to you', it was held by the House of Lords that the letter did not constitute an offer to sell but merely an invitation to treat. In certain situations, what may appear to be an offer by X to Y will be regarded by a court merely as an invitation to treat, unless there is clear evidence that X was willing to be bound as soon as Y indicated his assent or satisfied a particular condition. The following examples of these situations can be given.

[1] [1979] 1 All ER 972, HL.

Exposure for sale

5.5 An invitation to treat is a starting point for contractual negotiations and precedes the making of an offer. In *Fisher v Bell*,[1] a shopkeeper was charged with offering for sale a flick knife which was on display in his shop window. A divisional court held that the display of goods in a shop window was not an offer to sell but an invitation to treat; it was for customers to make the offer. The rationale behind this decision is that a shop is a place for negotiation over the terms of a contract, including the price, and that the shopkeeper invites customers to make him an offer which he can accept or reject as he pleases. This is an unrealistic view of how shops operate today.

Like the display of goods in shop windows, the display of goods in self-service shops is an invitation to treat. In *Pharmaceutical Society of Great Britain v Boots Cash Chemists (Southern) Ltd*,[2] the Court of Appeal had no hesitation in holding that the display of goods was only an invitation to treat, that the offer to buy was made by the customer at the cash desk, and that the contract was concluded when the offer was accepted. It was not necessary to decide precisely when a customer's offer is accepted at the cash desk, but one member of the Court of Appeal agreed with the view that acceptance occurs when payment of the price is accepted.[3]

[1] [1960] 3 All ER 731, DC.
[2] [1953] 1 All ER 482, CA.
[3] [1953] 1 All ER 482, at 484.

Advertisements

5.6 Whether an advertisement is an offer or an invitation to treat depends on the intention with which it is made. Advertisements of rewards and the like are normally offers since the advertiser does not intend any further negotiation to take place. An example is provided by *Carlill v Carbolic Smoke Ball Co*,[1] where the defendants advertised that they would pay £100 to anyone catching influenza after using their product in a specified manner. The Court of Appeal held that, since no further negotiations on the defendants' part were intended, the advertisement constituted an offer made to all the world which would ripen into a contract with anyone who fulfilled the conditions.

On the other hand, an advertisement of goods for sale is presumptively an invitation to treat, and not an offer,[2] because otherwise the advertiser might find himself contractually obliged to supply the advertised goods to a greater number of people (those who had responded positively to the advertisement) than the number of specified goods which had been advertised.[3]

Circulars sent to potential customers are also invitations to treat for the supply of goods, and not offers.[4]

[1] [1893] 1 QB 256, CA.

[2] *Partridge v Crittenden* [1968] 2 All ER 421, DC.

Although the rule that the advertisement of goods for sale is presumptively an invitation to treat was established before the time of websites, there is no reason why it should not apply to advertisements on websites.

It may be noted that, unless parties who are not consumers have agreed otherwise, and unless the contract is concluded by exchange of e-mails, the service provider:

- must explain to customers in plain terms the technical steps to follow to complete a binding agreement;
- must acknowledge receipt of the order without undue delay and by electronic means; and
- must make available technical means to correct input errors prior to placing the order:

Electronic Commerce (EC Directive) Regulations 2002, regs 9 and 11, giving effect to the Directive on Electronic Commerce. Such an acknowledgement is not, without more, an acceptance of the offer contained in the order. A service provider who fails to comply with either of the first two bullet points is liable in damages for the tort of breach of statutory duty: reg 13.

[3] This reason would not apply if the advertiser was the manufacturer of the goods advertised, because he could make more. In *Partridge v Crittenden* [1968] 2 All ER 421 at 424, Lord Parker CJ suggested that an advertisement or circular for the sale of goods by a manufacturer could be interpreted as an offer.

[4] *Grainger & Son v Gough* [1896] AC 325, HL.

Auctions

5.7 An auctioneer who calls for bids at an auction does not offer them for sale. Instead, those who bid make an offer which the auctioneer is free to accept or reject, and an offer can be withdrawn at any time before the auctioneer accepts.[1] Because the advertisement of an auction is merely a declaration of an intention to hold the auction, potential buyers have no claim against the auctioneer if the auctioneer fails to hold the auction.[2] These rules even apply where an auctioneer advertises an auction as 'without reserve' (ie that the bid of the highest bona fide bidder will be accepted and that the property will not be withdrawn if a reserve price is not reached), so that there is no contract *of sale* if the auctioneer refuses to accept the highest bid and withdraws the property. However, the auctioneer is liable in such circumstances for breach of a collateral contract *that the sale will be without reserve*.[3] This contract comes into existence as follows: by advertising the sale as without reserve the auctioneer makes an offer to this effect to whoever is the highest bona fide bidder, which is accepted by the person who makes the highest bona fide bid before the property is withdrawn.[4]

[1] *Payne v Cave* (1789) 3 Term Rep 148; Sale of Goods Act 1979, s 57(2).

[2] *Harris v Nickerson* (1873) LR 8 QB 286.

[3] *Warlow v Harrison* (1859) 1 E & E 309; *Barry v Heathcote-Ball & Co (Commercial Auctions) Ltd* [2001] 1 All ER 944, CA.

[4] If the auctioneer refuses to sell to the highest bidder, the damages will be assessed in the same way as if the vendor had wrongfully refused to deliver goods to the buyer: *Barry v Heathcote-Ball & Co (Commercial Auctions) Ltd*.

Tenders

5.8 An announcement that the provision of goods or services (or the purchase of goods or services) is open to tender is not an offer but only an invitation to treat. Consequently, a person who submits a tender makes an offer, which may be accepted or rejected by the person seeking tenders.[1] In *Spencer v Harding*,[2] for example, the defendant issued a circular offering by tender the stock in trade of X. This was held not to be an offer. Thus, the defendant was not required to sell the goods to the claimant who had submitted the highest tender.

A person (A) seeking tenders who indicates that he (or she) will accept the highest or lowest tender, as the case may be, will be contractually bound to do so. The reason is that, in accompanying the request for tenders with such an indication, A thereby accompanies his (or her) invitation to treat with an offer of a unilateral contract to accept the highest or lowest tender, as the case may be. The highest or lowest tender, as the case may be, will constitute an acceptance of that offer, and A will be contractually obliged to accept that tender.[3]

Where an invitation to tender is made only to a small, selected group of persons, it will be held to be accompanied by an offer to consider all conforming tenders submitted by the stipulated deadline, which offer is accepted by so submitting such a tender. Consequently, in such a case, it will be a breach of contract (a contract to consider a conforming tender submitted in time) to fail to consider such a tender.[4] It will not, of course, be a breach of contract to fail to accept a conforming tender after considering it.

[1] For acceptance of tenders see para 5.15.
[2] (1870) LR 5 CP 561.
[3] *Harvela Investments Ltd v Royal Trust Co of Canada (CI) Ltd* [1985] 2 All ER 966, HL.
[4] *Blackpool and Fylde Aero Club Ltd v Blackpool Borough Council* [1990] 3 All ER 25, CA.

OFFER: KEY POINTS

- An offer is an unequivocal expression of willingness to make a binding agreement on specified terms if they are accepted by someone to whom it is addressed.

- An offer can be made to a specific person, to a group of people or to the world at large.

- An invitation to treat is not an offer but simply an invitation to another person to make an offer or to enter into negotiations.

- Displays of goods for sale, advertisements, calls for bids at auctions and invitations to tender are all generally regarded by the courts as invitations to treat.

Acceptance

Requirements

5.9 To convert an offer into a contract the offeree must unequivocally and unconditionally accept the offer; if, for example, A offers to sell B a car for £5,000, payable in advance, B does not accept the offer when he replies purporting to accept the offer but saying that he will pay the £5,000 on delivery.[1] In addition, the offeree is normally required to communicate his acceptance to the offeror.

[1] *Hyde v Wrench* (1840) 3 Beav 334; para 5.11.

5.10 It should come as no surprise to anyone to learn that one cannot accept an offer of which one is ignorant. This is important in the case where B offers a reward for the performance of a particular action, eg finding his lost dog. If A, who is ignorant of the offer, finds the dog, A's action cannot constitute an acceptance of the offer and A cannot claim the reward successfully.[1] Moreover, if someone who knows of the offer performs the specified action for reasons entirely unconnected with that offer, there is no acceptance.[1] But, if that person's conduct is motivated partly by the offer and partly by other reasons there is a valid acceptance.[2]

A related point is that, if two offers which are identical in terms cross in the post, there can be no contract. The courts will not construe one offer as the offer and the other offer as the acceptance.[3]

[1] *R v Clarke* (1927) 40 CLR 227.
[2] *Williams v Carwardine* (1833) 5 C & P 566.
[3] *Tinn v Hoffmann & Co* (1873) 29 LT 271.

Counter-offers distinguished

5.11 If an offeree in purporting to accept the offer seeks to alter a term or to introduce an entirely new term , eg as to the amount of goods to be delivered or the time of payment, this is not an acceptance, because there is not an unequivocal and unconditional acceptance of the terms of the offer. Instead, it is a counter-offer which may or may not be accepted by the original offeror.

A counter-offer puts an end to the original offer, so that it cannot subsequently be accepted by the offeree. In *Hyde v Wrench*,[1] for instance, the defendant offered to sell property to the claimant for £1,000. The claimant 'agreed' to buy the property for £950. This was rejected and the claimant then purported to accept the original offer of the property for £1,000. It was held that the claimant's purported acceptance for £950 was a counter-offer which destroyed the original offer, so that it was no longer capable of acceptance when the claimant purported to accept it.

[1] (1840) 3 Beav 334.

5.12 A counter-offer must be distinguished from an inquiry or request for information by an offeree. Such an inquiry or request, even if answered negatively by the offeror, does not destroy the offer. An example is *Stevenson, Jacques & Co v McLean*.[1] The defendant offered to sell iron to the claimants at 40 shillings a ton with immediate delivery. The claimants asked the defendant by telegram if the defendant would sell at the same price if delivery was staggered over two months. On receiving no reply, the claimants accepted the original offer but the defendant failed to deliver and claimed the telegram was a counter-offer. The court rejected the defendant's claim and held that the telegram was a mere request for information, and not a counter-offer, so that the original offer could still be accepted by the claimants.

[1] (1880) 5 QBD 346.

5.13 A contract may arise in the course of long and complicated negotiations, during which one party offers to contract on certain terms (eg terms A, B and C contained in a document sent by him) and the other agrees to contract, but plainly does so[1] on different terms (eg terms A, B and D contained in a document sent by him), and so on. Even if it is expressed to be an acceptance, such a response will in law be a counter-offer and not an acceptance. If neither party expressly accepts the other's terms, what is the legal situation? The orthodox approach is that if, after the communication of the last set of terms, the recipient does something which indicates a relevant agreement with the sender, for example by delivering the goods which the sender has ordered, the recipient will be held to have accepted[2] the sender's counter-offer and thus contracted on the sender's terms.[3] This approach is liable to result in a situation where there is no contract at all if the last set of terms is not followed by anything on the recipient's part which can be described as an acceptance of them. However, where the negotiations have concerned the sale (or other supply) of goods, which are actually delivered, a court may find from the *conduct* of the parties that a contract, containing neither set of terms, but including terms implied by statute into a contract for the sale (or other supply) of goods,[4] has been created.[5]

An alternative approach, taken by Lord Denning MR in *Butler Machine Tool Co Ltd v Ex-Cell-O Corpn (England) Ltd*,[6] is that where there is a 'battle of the forms' a 'compromise' contract can be constructed by the court on reasonable terms.

The orthodox approach must be adopted unless the documents passing between the parties and their course of dealings shows that their common intention was that some other terms were intended to prevail.[7]

[1] *Sterling Hydraulics Ltd v Dictomatik Ltd* [2006] EWHC 2004 (QB).
[2] Acceptance can be by conduct; see para 5.14.
[3] *British Road Services Ltd v Arthur V Crutchley Ltd* [1968] 1 All ER 811, CA; *Butler Machine Tool Co Ltd v Ex-Cell-O Corpn (England) Ltd* [1979] 1 All ER 965, CA.
[4] Paras 7.25 and 7.26.
[5] *GHSP Inc v AB Electronic Ltd* [2010] EWHC 1828 (Comm).
[6] [1979] 1 All ER 965 at 968–969.
[7] *Tekdata Interconnections Ltd v Amphenol Ltd* [2009] EWCA Civ 1209, CA.

Acceptance by conduct

5.14 An acceptance may be express, as where the offeree accepts the offer by a written or oral statement intended to constitute an acceptance,[1] or it may be manifested by the offeree's conduct. For instance, a cover note issued by an insurance company is an offer to insure which would be accepted by using a car in reliance on it.[2] A more complicated case of acceptance by conduct is that of *Brogden v Metropolitan Rly Co*,[3] in which Brogden was sued for failing to deliver coal. Brogden regularly supplied the company with coal and they decided to draw up a contract for such supply. A draft contract was submitted to Brogden with a blank space for the name of a mutually agreeable arbitrator. This constituted an offer. Brogden filled in the name of an arbitrator, marked the draft 'approved', and returned it to the agent of the company (who put it in a drawer where it remained). Brogden's action was not an acceptance but a counter-offer. Nevertheless, the parties bought and sold coal in accordance with the terms of the draft contract. Subsequently, Brogden refused to supply more coal and claimed that there was no binding contract for its supply. The House of Lords inferred from the conduct of the parties, the buying and selling of coal on terms exactly the same as those in the draft contract, that a contract had been concluded on the terms of the final draft, which came into effect either with the first order of coal by the company on the terms of the draft (since this conduct could be said to have manifested the company's acceptance of Brogden's counter-offer) or, at least, when Brogden supplied the coal. The first explanation is the more acceptable. The House of Lords stressed that mere mental acquiescence by the parties that the contract should exist would not have sufficed.

[1] See, for example, *Wilson Smithett & Cape (Sugar) Ltd v Bangladesh Sugar and Food Industries Corpn* [1986] 1 Lloyd's Rep 378 (letter of intent to supply materials as per terms of offer held to constitute an acceptance, because it was found to have been intended to constitute an acceptance).
[2] *Taylor v Allon* [1965] 1 All ER 557 at 559.
[3] (1877) 2 App Cas 666, HL.

Acceptance of tenders

5.15 The acceptance of tenders illustrates another aspect of acceptance. Tenders can be in two forms:

- People may be invited to tender, for example by a local authority, for the supply of *specified* goods or services over a given period. In such a case, a contract for the supply of those goods or services is constituted when a person's tender (offer) is accepted.

- People may be invited to tender for the supply of *such* goods and services *as may be required* over a given period. In such a case, a contract is not immediately concluded with the successful tenderer. Instead, that person's offer is treated as a standing offer and each time an order is placed this constitutes acceptance of the standing offer and there is a contract for the goods or services ordered. Because the person making the successful tender has no definite contract, that person can revoke his offer before any particular order is placed, and the person who invited tenders need never place an order.[1]

[1] *Great Northern Rly Co v Witham* (1873) LR 9 CP 16.

Communication of acceptance

5.16 If an offer has been made and the offeree has decided to accept, there is normally no completed agreement until that acceptance has been communicated to the offeror (or his agent), by words or conduct.[1] The reason for this is practical: if the offeror is not told that his offer has been accepted the offeror does not know whether he has made a contract or can make offers to others.

[1] Para 5.14.

5.17 Communication of acceptance usually requires actual communication. Consequently, an oral acceptance which is drowned by a passing aeroplane or is inaudible because of interference on the telephone is not effectively communicated.[1] It seems that fax messages sent during office hours are regarded as instantaneous communications and are subject to the same principles as oral acceptances; they take effect when printed out on the offeror's fax machine.[2] This rule would not apply where the communication was not instantaneous, as where a fax message is sent out of office hours; the time of acceptance in such a case would depend on the parties' intentions and sound business practice, and in some cases on a judgment as to where the risk should lie.

If an oral acceptance or one by fax does not completely reach the offeror and the party accepting does not realise this, there may be a valid communication of acceptance. But this will only be the case where the offeror realises that he (or she) has missed some of what the offeree is seeking to communicate and does not attempt to discover what has been missed.[3]

[1] *Entores v Miles Far East Corpn* [1955] 2 All ER 493, CA.
[2] In *Brinkibon v Stahag Stahl GmbH* [1982] 1 All ER 293, HL, this view was taken about messages sent by telex, a system now replaced by fax.
[3] *Entores v Miles Far East Corpn* [1955] 2 All ER 493 at 495.

5.18 Internet sales involve instantaneous communications. Consequently, it seems that an acceptance by the supplier of an offer to buy something advertised on a website must be communicated to the offeror in order to be effective. This raises the question of when communication occurs.

Dispensation from need for communication of acceptance

5.19 The offeror may by the terms of the offer expressly or impliedly dispense with the need to communicate acceptance. In particular, dispensation with the need for communication will normally be implied where the alleged contract is of the unilateral variety. An example is provided by *Carlill v Carbolic Smoke Ball Co*,[1] where the vendors of a product argued that a user of it, who claimed a reward which they had offered to anyone catching influenza after using the product, should have told them of her acceptance of their offer of a reward. The vendors' claim was rejected, since it was clear they had not intended a user of the product to write to them formally accepting the offer of a reward if illness was not avoided; consequently, the vendors had impliedly dispensed with the need for communication of acceptance.

[1] [1893] 1 QB 256, CA.

5.20 If the offeror does expressly or impliedly dispense with the need for communication of acceptance, the offeree's non-communication of acceptance does not enable the offeror successfully to deny that there is a contract enforceable against him.[1]

In addition, there will be a contract enforceable against the offeree if he has unambiguously manifested his acceptance, as by driving a car in reliance on an offer of motor insurance.[2] On the other hand, an offeree is not bound simply because an offeror has framed his offer in such terms that a contract is presumed to exist unless non-acceptance is communicated. Contractual liability cannot be imposed on the offeree in this way; as against the offeree, silence is not assent. In *Felthouse v Bindley*,[3] the claimant offered to buy T's horse and said that he would presume his offer to be accepted unless he heard to the contrary. T did not reply. The horse was sold by the defendant, an auctioneer, to another. It was held that no contract binding on T had been formed: the claimant was not entitled to presume acceptance unless he heard to the contrary.

[1] This is certainly the case in a unilateral contract, as *Carlill v Carbolic Smoke Ball Co*, para 5.19, shows.
[2] *Taylor v Allon* [1965] 1 All ER 557 at 559.
[3] (1862) 11 CBNS 869.

Postal acceptance

5.21 There is another exception to the general rule that acceptance must be actually communicated to be effective. It is that, subject to the qualifications referred to below, a posted acceptance is effective when it is posted, and this is so even if that acceptance is delivered late or is never delivered. This so-called 'postal rule' was first established in *Adams v Lindsell*.[1] A letter is 'posted' when it is placed, correctly stamped, in an official box or into the hands of a Post Office employee or agent authorised to receive letters;[2] most postmen who deliver letters are not so authorised.

The offeror can exclude the special postal acceptance rule by specifying in his offer that acceptance must be actually communicated to him.[3] In addition, the postal acceptance rule will be disregarded, and the general rule requiring communication prevail, if it is not reasonable to accept by post[4] or if the special rule would give rise to 'manifest inconvenience or absurdity'.[5] For example, it would not be reasonable to accept by post an offer by e-mail to sell highly perishable goods.

The justification for the special rule for postal acceptances seems to be that the offeror, by expressly or impliedly (eg by making the offer by post) allowing an acceptance to be made by post, must stand the risk of failures of the postal system. However, if a postal acceptance is delayed in the post because of the negligence of the offeree, as where the offeree wrongly addresses the letter, there seems no reason why the court should not decide that the acceptance was effective at whatever time is least advantageous to the negligent offeree.

[1] (1818) 1 B & Ald 681.
[2] *Re London & Northern Bank, ex p Jones* [1900] 1 Ch 220.
[3] For an example see *Holwell Securities Ltd v Hughes* [1974] 1 All ER 161, CA.
[4] *Henthorn v Fraser* [1892] 2 Ch 27, CA.
[5] *Holwell Securities Ltd v Hughes*.

5.22 There is no binding decision about whether the postal rule also applies to acceptance by e-mail. Such an acceptance is like a postal acceptance in that there is an interval, albeit normally a very short one, before it reaches its addressee and once sent it is outside the control of the offeree. These factors suggest that the postal rule applies by analogy and that acceptance by e-mail occurs when the 'send' button is clicked. However, there is persuasive authority that the anomaly involved in the postal rule does not apply to e-mail acceptances. This is provided by *Thomas v BPE Solicitors*,[1] where a High Court judge held, obiter, that the requirement of communication applies to e-mail acceptances, and that the issue of when acceptance by e-mail occurs is governed by the principles set out in para 5.17.

[1] [2010] EWHC 306 (Ch).

Prescribed mode of acceptance

5.23 Some offers require a particular form of acceptance to be employed (as where the offer states: 'Please send acceptance in writing by first class post to our Liverpool branch'). If the offer states that the acceptance may only be made in the specified manner, an acceptance in any other way cannot be effective (unless the offeror waives the requirement).[1] On the other hand, if the offer does not state that only the specified method may be used, an acceptance made in some other way (eg by fax to the Liverpool branch in the above example) can be effective as long as it is no less disadvantageous to the offeror than the prescribed method;[2] but if it is not, it is ineffective[3] (unless the offeror waives the specified mode).

[1] *Compagnie de Commerce et Commission SARL v Parkinson Stove Co* [1953] 2 Lloyd's Rep 487, CA.
[2] *Yates Building Co Ltd v RJ Pulleyn & Sons (York) Ltd* (1975) 119 Sol Jo 370, CA.
[3] *Financings Ltd v Stimson* [1962] 3 All ER 386, CA.

ACCEPTANCE: KEY POINTS

- To convert an offer into a contract an offeree must unequivocally and unconditionally accept the offer.

- One cannot accept an offer of which one is ignorant.

- An offeree who purports to accept the offer but seeks to alter a term or to add an entirely new term, makes a counter-offer. A counter-offer does not constitute an acceptance. Instead, it rejects (and terminates) the original offer and constitutes a new offer capable of acceptance by the original offeror.

- An acceptance may be made by written or spoken words, or be inferred from the offeree's conduct.

- Generally, acceptance must be communicated to the offeror in order to be effective. By way of exceptions, the offeror may dispense in the offeree's favour with the need for communication of acceptance, and a posted acceptance is effective on posting (the postal rule) unless the offeror expressly requires actual communication of acceptance or the use of the post to accept is unreasonable or the postal rule would give rise to manifest inconvenience or absurdity.

- If the mode of acceptance is prescribed, an acceptance in some other way is effective if it is no less disadvantageous to the offeror, unless the acceptance can only be made in the prescribed way.

Termination of offers

5.24 An offer may be terminated in several ways: by rejection (including a counter-offer[1]), by revocation, by lapse of time and by death. An offer which has terminated cannot subsequently be accepted.

[1] Para 5.11.

Revocation

5.25 At any time until acceptance by the offeree is effective, the offeror can withdraw the offer. The fact that the offeror has given the offeree time to make up his (or her) mind does not mean that the offeror is required to keep the offer open for that length of time. In *Routledge v Grant*,[1] an offer to lease premises was expressed to be open for acceptance for six weeks; it was held that nevertheless the offer could be withdrawn within that period.

There is an exception to the rule that the offer need not be kept open for a specified period. This is where there is a separate contract whereby the offeror contracts to keep the offer open for a given time. If there is such a contract the offer can be accepted at any time within the specified period. An example of such a contract is the granting of an option.

[1] (1828) 4 Bing 653.

Communication of revocation

5.26 The revocation of an offer only becomes effective when communicated to the offeree. In *Byrne v Van Tienhoven*,[1] the defendants wrote on 1 October to the claimants, offering to sell them goods. The claimants received the offer on 11 October and accepted it by telegram on the same day. Meanwhile, on 8 October the defendants had sent a letter to the claimants revoking their offer; this letter reached the claimants on 20 October. It was held that the revocation was ineffective because the claimants' acceptance had taken effect on 11 October (acceptance by telegram being treated in the same way as acceptance by letter) and therefore the defendants' offer was no longer capable of being revoked when their letter of revocation reached the claimants. Consequently, there was a contract between the claimants and defendants for the sale of the goods. There is no parallel rule to that which treats a posted acceptance as a communicated acceptance; a revocation must always be actually communicated.

This raises a question which has yet to be authoritatively determined. Does communication by letter, fax or e-mail require that the revocation is actually read by the offeror (or the offeror's agent) or does it occur at an earlier point of time, eg when the letter is delivered, or the fax is printed out, at the offeror's premises, regardless of whether it comes to his attention at that time? In the case of a business, it would appear that communication via a letter or fax probably occurs at the time of the delivery or print-out if this is during normal business hours.[2] The answer in other circumstances (or in the case of an e-mail) is less certain.

Communication of revocation may be indirect, in that, if the offeree hears from a reliable source that the offer has been withdrawn (and thereby knows beyond all question of the withdrawal), the courts will regard this as an effective revocation.[3] The difficulty inherent in this is that it is difficult to know what constitutes a reliable source.

[1] (1880) 5 CPD 344.

² Suggested by the decision in another context in *Tenax Steamship Co Ltd v Reinante Transoceania Navegacion SA, The Brimnes* [1974] 3 All ER 88, CA.
³ *Dickinson v Dodds* (1876) 2 Ch D 463, CA.

Unilateral contracts

5.27 Special rules apply in the case of unilateral contracts, where A does something (eg returning lost property) in response to B's offer (promise) to do something (eg to pay a reward) if he does it. The general rule is that once the offeree has embarked on the performance of the stipulated act or acts necessary for acceptance, as where B has found lost property and is en route to return it in response to the offer of a reward for its return, the offer cannot be withdrawn.¹ The reason is that, when the offer is made which will mature into a unilateral contract when accepted, there is alongside that principal offer a collateral offer to keep the principal offer open once performance in relation to it has begun, which is accepted by the offeree starting to perform the stipulated act or acts.² In *Errington v Errington and Woods*,³ a father purchased a house, partially by means of a mortgage, and allowed his daughter and her husband to live in it. The daughter and her husband paid the mortgage instalments in response to the father's offer that, if they did so, he would give them the house when it was paid for. The Court of Appeal held that this offer could not be revoked once the daughter and her husband had begun performance of the conduct specified in the offer. Of course, in the present type of case the offeror is not bound unless and until the offeree has fully performed the act or acts specified in the offer. This is subject to the important qualification that, if the offeror prevents performance of the necessary act or acts being completed, he cannot rely on the offeree's failure fully to perform as a defence to a breach of contract action by the offeree, because there is an implied obligation on the part of the offeror (which arises as soon as the offeree starts to perform) not to prevent performance by the offeree.⁴

The above rule does not apply if the terms of the offer, or its surrounding circumstances, indicate that it was not intended to become irrevocable before the offeree had completely performed the envisaged act. A good example is the kind of commission agreement commonly used by estate agents. Although this is an agreement which will ripen into a unilateral contract if the estate agent satisfies the client's instructions (as explained in para 4.2), it is settled that the client may revoke the instructions at any time, notwithstanding that the agent may have expended time and money in attempting to find a purchaser.⁵ The courts take the view that a change of mind by a client is simply one of the business risks which an estate agent must bear, and that the estate agent's fees for successful negotiations should be at a level sufficient to cover other abortive work.

¹ *Errington v Errington and Woods* [1952] 1 All ER 149, CA.
² *Daulia Ltd v Four Millbank Nominees Ltd* [1978] 2 All ER 557 at 561.
³ [1952] 1 All ER 149, CA.
⁴ *Daulia Ltd v Four Millbank Nominees Ltd* [1978] 2 All ER 557 at 561.
⁵ *Luxor (Eastbourne) Ltd v Cooper* [1941] 1 All ER 33, HL.

Lapse of time

5.28 Obviously, an offer which the offeror states is to remain open for a set time lapses at the end of that time and cannot thereafter be accepted. If no time limit is expressly set for the offer, it will normally lapse after a reasonable period.¹ In *Ramsgate Victoria Hotel v Montefiore*,² for example, it was held that an offer to buy shares, which was made in June, could not be accepted in November since the offer had lapsed by then. What is a reasonable period varies, depending on the facts of the case.

[1] *Chemco Leasing SpA v Rediffusion* [1987] 1 FTLR 201, CA.
[2] (1866) LR 1 Ex Ch 109.

Death

5.29 Death after an offer has been accepted cannot affect the validity of a contract.[1] There are, however, cases where either the offeror or the offeree dies before the offer is accepted.

If the offeror dies the offer does not seem to terminate automatically (except where the offer is clearly of such a type that it must end on death, eg an offer to work for X). However, the offeree cannot accept the offer once the offeree knows of the offeror's death.[2]

The effects of the offeree's death have not been decided conclusively but uncontradicted dicta suggest that the offer lapses. In *Reynolds v Atherton*,[3] it was suggested that an offer, being made to a living person, cannot survive that person's death and be accepted by someone else. This may be an illustration of the basic rule that an offer made to A cannot be accepted by B. On the other hand, if an offer is made to A or B there seems no reason why the death of B should prevent A accepting it.

[1] But it may discharge the contract: see para 10.6.
[2] *Bradbury v Morgan* (1862) 1 H & C 249; *Coulthart v Clementson* (1879) 5 QBD 42.
[3] (1921) 125 LT 690, CA; affd by the House of Lords who did not comment on this point.

Termination of Offers: Key Points

- An offer can be terminated by:
  - rejection;
  - revocation;
  - lapse of time, ie the time (if any) specified by the offeror or (if no time is specified) a reasonable time; or
  - the death of the offeror.
- To be effective, a revocation must be communicated directly or indirectly to the offeree.
- Where the contract would be a bilateral one, revocation before acceptance is effective. On the other hand, where the contract would be a unilateral contract, the offer cannot generally be revoked once the offeree has begun to perform the stipulated act or acts necessary for acceptance.

Uncertain, incomplete and conditional agreements

5.30 Although there may be an agreement, there may not be a legally binding contract because the agreement is uncertain in its terms, or is merely an agreement to agree in the future, or is subject to the operation of a condition.

Uncertainty

5.31 Where particular terms in an agreement are unclear or vague, the courts will try to divine the intention of the parties and find a contract, but if such intention cannot be discovered the agreement is not a contract (ie not legally binding) and cannot be enforced.[1] In *Bushwall Properties Ltd v Vortex Properties Ltd*,[2] for instance, A agreed to buy from

B 51½ acres of land for £500,000. Under the terms of the agreement the price was to be paid in three instalments and on each payment a 'proportionate part' of the land was to be conveyed to A. The Court of Appeal held that the agreement was void for uncertainty because it did not provide the machinery for identifying the proportionate part to be conveyed in each phase.

Another agreement which has been held not to be binding because of lack of certainty is an agreement to continue to negotiate in good faith for an unspecified period, since a party would never know whether he (or she) was entitled to withdraw from the negotiations and the court could not be expected to decide whether a proper reason existed for him (or her) to do so.[3] For similar reasons an agreement of unspecified duration not to negotiate with anyone else is void for uncertainty. We return to this type of agreement in para 5.35.

A court can supply the details of an apparently vague or unclear term, so that the agreement is a valid contract, if the parties have provided the machinery to ascertain its precise nature, as where there is an agreement for the sale of land at 'market price' (in which case the court can fix that price after making an inquiry),[4] or if the details which the parties must have intended can be implied by reference to the practices of a particular trade to which they belong or by reference to their previous dealings. In *Hillas & Co Ltd v Arcos Ltd*,[5] the parties had entered into an agreement for the sale and purchase of timber in 1930. The agreement contained an option to buy 100,000 standards of timber in 1931 but the size and quality of the timber were not specified. The House of Lords refused to find the agreement unenforceable, clarifying any uncertainties by reference to the previous dealings of the parties and usual practice in the timber trade. The judgment of the House is permeated by the view that the courts ought to strive to give effect to business arrangements and not zealously demand absolute certainty of all terms.

What if the parties have provided the machinery to fix the precise nature of a term and that machinery breaks down? This was answered in *Sudbrook Trading Estate Ltd v Eggleton*,[6] where the House of Lords dealt with the situation where a lease contained an option to purchase the land at a price to be agreed by two valuers, one to be nominated by each party, and one party failed to nominate a valuer. The question was whether the option agreement was unenforceable. The House of Lords held that where the machinery by which the value of the property was to be ascertained was *subsidiary and non-essential* to the main part of an agreement for the sale of the property at a fair and reasonable price assessed by applying objective standards, the court could, if the machinery for ascertaining the value of the property *broke down*, substitute other machinery, eg by appointing its own valuers, to ascertain such a price in order to ensure that the agreement did not fail. The House concluded that, where (as in the case before it) the price was to be decided by two valuers, one to be appointed by each party, the task of the valuers, expressly or impliedly, was to fix a fair and reasonable price and that the appointment of valuers by the parties was not essential to fixing a reasonable price, and that therefore the court should substitute its own machinery to ascertain the price.

The scope of *Sudbrook* is limited. First, as the House of Lords itself held, if the price was to be fixed by a named valuer or valuers, it could not be implied that the price was to be a fair and reasonable one because the implication was that the price was to be fixed by a specified means, the use of the named valuer or valuers. In such a case, it held, a court could not substitute its own machinery if for some reason the named valuer or valuers failed to fix the price, and there would not be an enforceable contract for the sale of the property.[7] Second, it seems that, where the breakdown in the machinery is due to the fault solely of the party seeking a substituted machinery, *Sudbrook* does not apply.[8]

There can be a valid contract for the sale of goods or the supply of a service, even though the price is not fixed, or left to be fixed in an agreed manner, and cannot be determined by a course of dealings between the parties. Statute provides that, in such a case, a reasonable price must be paid.[9]

Where an apparently uncertain term can be determined in one of the above ways, the contract is complete on the agreement of the parties even though the precise nature of that term remains to be fixed.[10]

If a transaction has been performed on both sides, it will be difficult for a party to submit successfully that there is no agreement or that there is not a legally binding contract on grounds of uncertainty or vagueness.[11]

[1] *Scammell and Nephew Ltd v Ouston* [1941] 1 All ER 14, HL.
[2] [1976] 2 All ER 283, CA.
[3] *Walford v Miles* [1992] 1 All ER 453, HL.
[4] *Bushwall Properties Ltd v Vortex Properties Ltd* [1976] 2 All ER 283 at 289.
[5] (1932) 147 LT 503, HL.
[6] [1982] 3 All ER 1, HL.
[7] *Sudbrook* was distinguished on this ground in *Bruce v Carpenter* [2006] EWHC 3301 (Ch).
[8] *Infiniteland Ltd v Artisan Contracting Ltd* [2005] EWCA Civ 758, CA.
[9] Sale of Goods Act 1979, s 8; Supply of Goods and Services Act 1982, s 15 (see para 7.27).
[10] *Sudbrook Trading Estate Ltd v Eggleton* [1982] 3 All ER 1, HL.
[11] *G Percy Trentham Ltd v Archital Luxfer Ltd* [1993] 1 Lloyd's Rep 25 at 27.

5.32 Sometimes it may be possible to ignore uncertainty in an agreement. This can be done, for instance, where the uncertainty relates to what is a meaningless term. In *Nicolene Ltd v Simmonds*,[1] the agreement contained the phrase 'I assume the usual conditions of acceptance apply'. There were no usual conditions of acceptance, but the Court of Appeal held that the phrase was meaningless and, since it did not relate to an important term or part of the contract, could be ignored; the rest of the agreement was enforceable as a binding contract.

[1] [1953] 1 All ER 822, CA.

Incomplete agreements

5.33 If a reasonable person would conclude from what the parties have said or done that the parties have agreed the essential terms[1] of an agreement and agreed to be bound immediately, there is a concluded agreement despite the fact that further terms must be negotiated.[2]

On the other hand, if an essential term of an agreement is open to further negotiation, or if the parties have not agreed to be bound immediately because further negotiation is necessary before a binding agreement can be concluded, there is no concluded agreement, but merely an agreement to agree. An example is where an agreement for the sale of goods leaves the price to be fixed by agreement between the parties. In *May and Butcher Ltd v R*,[3] the price of surplus tentage which was being sold by a government department was such as 'shall be agreed upon from time to time between the government department and the purchasers'. The House of Lords found that, because an essential term was left open for future negotiation, there was no concluded agreement.

However, if the parties have begun to perform the agreement or the agreement expressly or impliedly provides a method for resolving the lack of agreement, there will be a concluded agreement. An example of both these points is provided by *Foley v Classique Coaches Ltd*[4] where the Court of Appeal distinguished *May and Butcher Ltd v R* on two grounds. First, on the basis that the parties had acted on the agreement for three years and their implied belief that they had been contractually bound during that period must be given effect, and, second, because the contract provided that in the absence of agreement on price it was to be determined by arbitration. *Beer v Bowden*[5] provides another example. Premises were let for 10 years (later extended to 14) at a fixed rent for the first five years, but at a rent 'to be agreed' thereafter. The Court of Appeal implied a term that in the absence of agreement a reasonable rent determined by the court should be paid.

[1] Ie the terms which the parties had regarded, or the law required, as essential.

[2] *Pagnan SpA v Feed Products* [1987] 2 Lloyd's Rep 601, CA; *RTS Flexible Systems Ltd v Molkerei Alois Muller Gmbh & Co KG (UK Production)* [2010] UKSC 14, SC.

[3] [1934] 2 KB 17n, HL.

[4] [1934] 2 KB 1, CA.

[5] [1981] 1 All ER 1070, CA.

'Subject to contract' and similar phrases

5.34 The phrase 'subject to contract' is usually inserted initially in an agreement to buy land which is for sale by private treaty. Unless there are very exceptional circumstances which oust the prima facie meaning of the phrase[1] or, judged objectively, the parties have agreed the essential terms and agreed to be bound immediately,[2] such agreements are simply 'agreements to agree' and are not binding, nor are the parties required to try to ensure that a contract is concluded.[3] Phrases similar to 'subject to contract' have the same effect, except that where an agreement for the sale of land is made 'subject to the purchaser obtaining a mortgage *on terms satisfactory to himself*' a further term is implied that such satisfaction must not be unreasonably withheld.[4]

Because an agreement to buy land 'subject to contract' is not binding, it is legally permissible for the vendor to agree to sell the property to someone else offering a higher price. This is particularly common when property prices are rising; it is called 'gazumping'.

[1] *Alpenstow Ltd v Regalian Properties plc* [1985] 2 All ER 545.

[2] *RTS Flexible Systems Ltd v Molkerei Alois Muller Gmbh & Co KG (UK Production)* [2010] UKSC 14, SC. An agreement subject to contract which is not initially binding will become binding if the parties subsequently agree to waive the condition and the essential terms have been agreed: *RTS Flexible Systems Ltd v Molkerei Alois Muller Gmbh & Co KG (UK Production)*.

[3] *Winn v Bull* (1877) 7 Ch D 29.

[4] *Janmohamed v Hassam* (1976) 241 Estates Gazette 609.

5.35 The precarious position of a party to an agreement to buy property 'subject to contract' has led such parties, and their legal advisers, to seek ways of protecting their legal position by the use of 'lock-out agreements', with varying success. A lock-out agreement is one where, in return for consideration by the other party, one party (A) agrees to give the other party an exclusive opportunity to conclude a contract with A, ie A agrees not to negotiate with anyone else. A lock-out agreement whose duration is unlimited in time is not binding, but one which is subject to a time limit is.

This was held by the House of Lords in *Walford v Miles*.[1] In this case the claimants agreed in March 1987 'subject to contract' to buy a business from the defendants. Later that month there was a further agreement between one of the claimants and one of the defendants that, if the claimants obtained a 'comfort letter' from their bank that it was prepared to provide the finance for the purchase, the defendants would terminate negotiations with any third party. The comfort letter was provided, but at the end of March the defendants notified the claimants that they had decided to sell the business to a third party.

The claimants claimed that, although there was no binding contract for the sale of the business, their lock-out agreement with the defendants was binding, since they had provided consideration for the defendants' lock-out promise by providing the comfort letter and by promising to continue negotiations with the defendants.

The House of Lords held that, although it was possible for a lock-out agreement to be binding, the agreement in question was not binding because it was indefinite in duration.[2]

Walford v Miles can be contrasted with *Pitt v PHH Asset Management Ltd*[3] where a lock-out agreement for a specified period was held to be binding. In this case the defendant company had put on the market a property which attracted the interest of the claimant and of another person, B. The claimant and B made a number of offers, in which in effect they bid each other up. The claimant then entered an agreement through the defendant company's estate agents that the defendant company would sell the property to the claimant for £200,000 and would not consider any other offer provided that the claimant exchanged contracts within two weeks of receipt of a draft contract.

The defendant company sent a draft contract to the claimant. Eight days later the claimant indicated that he was ready to exchange contracts. However, on the same day, the claimant was notified that it had been decided to go ahead with a sale to B at £210,000 unless the claimant was prepared to exchange contracts that day at £210,000. The claimant refused to do so and the property was sold to B.

The claimant's action for breach of its lock-out agreement with the defendant company succeeded since it was of a specified duration (two weeks) and the defendant company was in breach of it. Of course, the defendant company was not bound by the lock-out agreement to sell to the claimant; it was only bound not to negotiate with another during the specified period. If it had waited for the two weeks to elapse, and not exchanged during that period, it would have been perfectly entitled thereafter to sell to B.

The appropriate remedy for breach of a lock-out agreement is an award of damages, and not an injunction, since the purpose of such an agreement is to protect a potential purchaser from wasting expenses incurred in getting ready to complete when the vendor elects to sell to another. The potential purchaser can recover as damages his costs which have been wasted.[4]

[1] [1992] 1 All ER 453, HL.

[2] The claimants had argued that the lock-out agreement was subject to an implied term that the defendants would continue to negotiate in good faith with the claimants. The House of Lords held that, even if such a term could be implied, it would not assist the claimants because an agreement to such an effect was void for uncertainty, as stated in para 5.31.

[3] [1993] 4 All ER 961, CA.

[4] *Tye v House* [1997] 41 EG 160.

Conditional agreements

Condition precedent

5.36 An agreement which appears to be a contract may never come into effect because its coming into effect is subject to a condition precedent which is not satisfied. An example is afforded by *Pym v Campbell*.[1] In this case an agreement to purchase a share in an invention was subject to the condition precedent that the invention be approved by X. X failed to approve and thus no contract to buy came into existence.[2]

An agreement subject to a condition precedent is not necessarily devoid of all effect. It all depends on the interpretation which the court gives to it.

On its true construction, the effect of an agreement subject to a condition precedent may be that, although the agreement containing it is not binding before the condition is satisfied, neither party can withdraw until it is clear whether or not the condition will be satisfied.[3]

Alternatively, or in addition, the effect of such an agreement may be that one party must do his best to fulfil the condition[4] or, at least, not obstruct its fulfilment.[5] For example, the phrase 'subject to survey' in an agreement for the sale of land has been construed as meaning that the purchaser must proceed with due diligence to obtain a surveyor's report and, having received it, consider it, and must act in good faith. If, in good faith, the purchaser is not satisfied with the report the purchaser is not obliged to proceed with the purchase, but in the meantime neither party can withdraw.[6]

Lastly, a condition precedent may be construed as imposing no obligation on either party. This is the prima facie construction[7] given to 'subject to contract' and similar conditions dealt with in para 5.34.

A condition precedent may be void for uncertainty, in which case the agreement in which it is contained is also void. An example is an agreement for the sale of land 'subject to the purchaser obtaining a *satisfactory mortgage*', since such a condition is too vague for the courts to enforce.[8]

[1] (1856) 6 E & B 370.
[2] In fact, it was held that there was no agreement at all.
[3] *Smith v Butler* [1900] 1 QB 694, CA. In *Smallman v Smallman* [1971] 3 All ER 717, CA, a buyer, who withdrew from an agreement to purchase which was subject to a condition precedent before it was clear whether the condition was satisfied, was unable to recover the deposit he had paid.
[4] *Marten v Whale* [1917] 2 KB 480, CA.
[5] *Mackay v Dick* (1881) 6 App Cas 251, HL.
[6] *Ee v Kakar* (1979) 40 P & CR 223.
[7] *Alpenstow Ltd v Regalian Properties plc* [1985] 2 All ER 545.
[8] *Lee-Parker v Izzet (No 2)* [1972] 2 All ER 800.

Condition subsequent

5.37   An agreement may also be subject to the operation of a condition subsequent. In such cases an agreement will be a contract unless and until the condition occurs. If it does occur, either the contract will automatically cease to bind or one party will have the right to cancel it, depending on the construction of the condition. In *Head v Tattersall*,[1] a contract for the sale of a horse was subject to the condition subsequent that, if the purchaser found within a given time that the horse did not meet its contractual description, the horse could be returned and the contract terminated. During that period, the purchaser found that the horse did not correspond with its description. It was held that he could return it and recover the price, even though it had been injured in the meanwhile.

[1] (1871) LR 7 Exch 7.

UNCERTAIN, INCOMPLETE AND CONDITIONAL AGREEMENTS: KEY POINTS

- Unless the court can supply the details of an apparently unclear or vague term, an uncertain agreement is not a contract (ie not legally binding). There is one qualification. Even if it is impossible to supply such details, the court can ignore an unclear or vague term which is meaningless; in such a case the court can enforce the rest of the agreement as a binding contract.

- If an essential term remains to be agreed there is no concluded agreement, and therefore no contract, unless the parties have begun to perform the agreement or the agreement expressly or impliedly provides a method to resolve the lack of agreement. An agreement 'subject to contract' is normally an agreement to agree and not binding.

- An agreement whose coming into effect is subject to a condition precedent will not come into operation as a contract unless and until the condition is satisfied. However, until the agreement is satisfied the agreement is not necessarily devoid of all effect.

- An agreement subject to a condition subsequent is a contract unless and until the condition occurs, whereupon the contract will either automatically cease to bind or one party will be entitled to cancel it, depending on the wording of the condition.

Payment for work done in anticipation of concluding a contract

5.38 Where, in anticipation of concluding a contract with the defendant, the claimant has commenced *at the defendant's request* to perform the work which would be required under the contract, but no contract is entered into, the defendant may be held liable to pay a reasonable sum for the work done pursuant to his request,[1] This is of obvious importance, for example, in the type of case where the defendant has given the claimant a 'letter of intent' to contract, which was not intended to have any legal effect, and asked him to start work immediately but never finally concluded a contract.

[1] *British Steel Corpn v Cleveland Bridge and Engineering Co Ltd* [1984] 1 All ER 504; cf *Regalian Properties plc v London Development Corpn* [1995] 1 All ER 1005.

Questions

1. Distinguish between an offer and an invitation to treat.

2. Distinguish between an acceptance of an offer and a counter-offer.

3. Anna, an auctioneer, calls for bids for Arcadia Cottage at an auction sale but refuses to accept the highest bid. At the same auction Anna calls for bids for Elm House, whose sale has been advertised as 'without reserve', but refuses to accept the highest bid. Explain with your reasons the legal position in these situations.

4. Explain whether or not there is an effective acceptance in the following cases:
   - Bob is offered a theodolite at a bargain price by Colin. Bob leaves a message, accepting the offer, on Colin's telephone answering machine. Before Colin can access the message the machine is destroyed when Colin's young son smashes it to smithereens with a hammer.
   - Dinah is offered some PCs for her estate agency office by Ed at £2,000 for the lot. The offer is made by e-mail. Dinah replies by post, saying that she accepts the offer and enclosing a cheque. She asks in her letter whether the PCs can be delivered within five days. Two hours after posting the letter, Dinah receives a telephone call from Ed who tells her that he has sold the PCs to Tom.

5. Felix, an estate agent, is instructed by Gus to find an eventual purchaser of Gus's house. Felix spends time and money in seeking to find an eventual purchaser. He is close to

introducing a potential purchaser but before he can do so Gus tells him that he has withdrawn his instructions. Advise Felix.

6. Explain whether or not it is true that an uncertain or incomplete agreement is always incapable of constituting a contract.

7. What is a 'lock-out agreement', when is it binding and what is the appropriate remedy for its breach?

6

Binding agreement

CHAPTER OVERVIEW

In this chapter we explain the rules relating to intention to be legally bound and to consideration. We conclude the chapter by explaining how a contract may validly be discharged (ie ended) or varied by agreement.

Introduction

6.1 An agreement which satisfies the rules in Chapter 5 will constitute a contract (ie a legally binding agreement), provided that:

- the parties intend to enter into a legally binding agreement; and
- it is supported by consideration.

Alternatively, it will constitute a contract if it is made by deed.

Intention to be legally bound

6.2 The parties to an agreement rarely state expressly whether or not they intend to create legal relations (ie to be legally bound). In the absence of an express indication of intention, the courts rely on two presumptions in deciding whether there was an intention to create legal relations, both of which can be rebutted expressly or impliedly by the parties:

- parties to social, domestic and family arrangements and other non-business agreements do not intend to be legally bound;[1] and
- parties to business agreements intend their agreements to be legally binding.[2]

[1] *Balfour v Balfour* [1919] 2 KB 571, CA. This presumption does not apply where the parties are married to each other but are, or are about to be, separated. They are presumed to intend to create legal relations: *Merritt v Merritt* [1970] 2 All ER 760, CA.
[2] *Edwards v Skyways Ltd* [1964] 1 All ER 494.

6.3 An example of the first type of arrangement is an agreement to give lifts to work, even if it is on an organised basis and involves payment to the car owners for their petrol.[1] While arrangements made within the family or household are presumed not to be intended to be legally binding, the nature of the agreement may clearly indicate that the parties intended a particular arrangement to be legally binding. In *Ward v Warnke*,[2] X allowed her son-in-law and her daughter (J) to occupy her holiday home under an agreement with the son-in-law that he would pay a modest rent (£3.50, later £6.00, per week). X paid the money into a building society account which named J as the beneficiary. The Court of Appeal held that on the facts the agreement constituted a legally binding tenancy agreement between the parties; the fact that it was between members of a family did not prevent the creation of a legal relationship.

¹ *Coward v Motor Insurers' Bureau* [1962] 1 All ER 531, CA.
² (1990) 22 HLR 496, CA.

6.4 In the case of a business agreement it is extremely difficult to rebut the presumption that the arrangement is to be legally binding, other than by clear words. A case where clear words led to the presumption being rebutted is *Rose and Frank Co v J R Crompton & Bros Ltd*,¹ in which the defendants appointed the claimants their agents to sell their products in America under an agreement which contained an 'honour clause', ie a clause which said the agreement was merely recording the intention of the parties and was binding in honour only and not in law. The claimants sued for alleged breach of contract. The Court of Appeal and the House of Lords held that the honour clause constituted a clearly expressed intention that the agency agreement was not to be legally binding and that effect had to be given to this intention.

Even where the presumption is rebutted by clear words, this does not prevent the subsequent conduct of the parties to the agreement constituting a legally binding agreement. In *Rose and Frank Co v J R Crompton & Bros Ltd*, the parties to the agency agreement ordered and supplied goods for sale in America. It was held that these orders and acceptances gave rise to legally binding agreements, even though the agency agreement was not legally binding.

An important statutory exception to the presumption that business agreements are intended to be legally binding is contained in the Trade Union and Labour Relations (Consolidation) Act 1992, s 179, which provides that collective agreements between employers and trade unions are presumed not to be legally enforceable unless they are made in writing and expressly state that the agreement is to be legally enforceable. However, if terms in a collective agreement are incorporated in an individual employee's contract of employment, they are presumed to be intended to be binding.²

¹ [1925] AC 445, HL.
² *Robertson v British Gas Corpn* [1983] ICR 351, CA.

INTENTION TO BE LEGALLY BOUND: KEY POINTS

An agreement is not legally binding if the parties did not intend it to be enter into legal relations. It is rebuttably presumed that parties to a non-business agreement do not intend to enter into legal relations, and that parties to a business agreement do intend to enter into legal relations.

Consideration

6.5 A promise in an agreement not made by deed¹ must be supported by consideration on the part of the party to whom it is made (the promisee) if it is to be legally binding. It is in the requirement of consideration that English law recognises the idea that a contract is a bargain.

In order to provide consideration for a promise, the promisee must promise to do, or do, an act (or refrain from doing an act; hereafter 'act' includes this):

- in return for *that* promise; and
- at the express or implied request of the promisor (the person making *that* promise).

It follows from the requirement that the promisee's act or promise must have been requested by the promisor that a 'gratuitous' act or promise by a promisee is not consideration. This is shown by *Re Cory*.[2] The YMCA wished to build a hall. It needed £150,000 to do so. £85,000 had been promised or was available. However, the YMCA decided not to commit itself to going on with the project until it saw that its efforts to raise the whole sum were likely to succeed. Cory then promised a donation of 1,000 guineas (£1,050) for the purpose of building the hall. The YMCA subsequently entered into a building contract for the hall, which they alleged they were largely induced to do by Cory's promise. Cory then died and the question arose whether his promise to pay was legally binding, in which case his estate would be bound by it. It was held that Cory's promise was not binding; the YMCA had not provided any consideration for Cory's promise because Cory had not expressly or impliedly requested the YMCA to do (or promise to do) anything in return.

[1] Para 4.6.
[2] (1912) 29 TLR 18.

6.6 It also follows from the definition of consideration that a promise (not made by deed) to give property on condition that something occurs is not legally binding if the promisee is not expressly or impliedly requested by the promisor to do or promise anything in return. In *Dickinson v Abel*,[1] A told B that he was willing to pay £100,000 for a farm which was vested in a bank as trustees. B had no proprietary interest in the farm but had previously passed on to the bank offers for the farm. B asked A: 'What's in it for me?' and was told that he would be paid £10,000 if A bought the farm for £100,000 or less. A did not ask B to perform any specific services, but B telephoned the bank and told them that an offer of £100,000 was on its way and that he personally would accept it. The farm was sold to A for less than £100,000 and B was paid the £10,000. The question later arose as to whether the £10,000 was taxable, which it would be if paid under a contract. It was somewhat surprisingly found as a fact that A had not expressly or impliedly requested B to do anything. Consequently, it was held, what B had done was not consideration for A's promise and there was therefore no legally binding agreement between A and B but merely a conditional gift. While the finding on the facts is hard to accept, the important legal point is the judge's application of the law to those facts.

[1] [1969] 1 All ER 484.

6.7 In a number of cases,[1] consideration has been defined as follows: that X provides consideration for Y's promise if X confers a benefit on Y, in return for which Y's promise is given, or if X incurs a detriment, in compensation for which Y's promise is given. Certainly if there is either a benefit or a detriment to the appropriate party that is good consideration, but this definition has been criticised and some cases cannot be explained in terms of benefit and detriment.

A better definition of consideration is that if one party's action or forbearance, promised or actual, is the price for which the other's promise is bought, and without that price there would be no bargain, the former party has provided consideration for the latter's promise.[2]

Executed and executory consideration

6.8 In the case of a unilateral contract, ie where a person does something at the request of another in return for a promise, such as finding a lost dog in return for the promise of a reward, the person doing the requested act thereby provides consideration for the other's promise. In a unilateral contract, consideration is only given by one party and only the other party is bound (hence the description 'unilateral contract'). The consideration provided in a unilateral contract is said to be 'executed' because it consists of the actual doing of something in response to a promise by the other party and at the other party's request.

In the case of a bilateral contract, ie where a party to an agreement promises to do something in response to a promise by the other party and at the other party's request, as where X promises to pay for goods to be supplied by Y, a party provides consideration by giving his (or her) promise. Thus, in the above example, X provides consideration for Y's promise to supply the goods and Y provides consideration for X's promise to pay for them. In a bilateral contract, consideration is given by both parties and both parties are bound (hence the description 'bilateral contract'). The consideration here is said to be 'executory' because it consists of a promise by each party which need not be executed (ie the promise need not be carried out) in order for the promise of the other party, for which it is exchanged, to be binding. The concept of executory consideration illustrates the difficulty of the benefit or detriment theory of consideration. When no one has done anything and there are merely promises there is no benefit or detriment to anyone, but it is possible to say that the price of one party's promise was the promise made by the other party.

Both executed and executory consideration are good consideration in law, unlike 'past consideration'.

Past consideration

6.9 'Past consideration' is said to have been given by a person (X) when, only after X has done something, a promise (eg to reward X) is made in return by another person. 'Past consideration' is an inaccurate expression, since it is not consideration at all and a person who has given it cannot enforce another's promise made in return for it.

The fact that past consideration is not good consideration illustrates the idea that consideration is the price of a promise. In *Re McArdle*,[1] work was done by X on a house which had been left to her and other members of her family. The other members then promised to reimburse the cost to her of the work but failed to keep their promise. X sued on the promise to pay but failed because she had provided no consideration for it, since her acts (doing the work on the house), which she alleged constituted consideration, pre-dated the promise by the relatives.

6.10 It would be wrong to think that all actions which are not preceded by an express promise constitute past consideration. If an act is done by X at the request of Y in circumstances where X and Y must have understood that the act was to be remunerated (so that a prior promise of remuneration by Y can be *implied*), the act by X is good consideration for the implied promise to pay, and a subsequent promise to pay, merely fixes the amount to be paid.[1]

What transforms apparently past consideration into good consideration is the fact that the action is in response to a request which raises an implied promise of payment.

The requested action is the price of the implied promise to pay. In *Re McArdle* there was no prior request or expectation of payment. In contrast, in *Re Casey's Patents, Stewart v Casey*,[2] where Y and Z wrote to Casey saying that 'in consideration of your [past] services as practical manager' (which Casey had provided at their request) they would give him a one-third share in certain patents, the Court of Appeal held that Casey's services as manager clearly raised an implication that they would be remunerated and thus Casey had provided consideration, the subsequent express promise merely fixing the amount of that remuneration.

[1] *Lampleigh v Brathwait* (1615) Hob 105; *Kennedy v Broun* (1863) 13 CBNS 677; *Re Casey's Patents, Stewart v Casey* [1892] 1 Ch 104, CA; *Pao On v Lau Yiu Long* [1979] 3 All ER 65, PC.
[2] [1892] 1 Ch 104, CA.

Adequacy of consideration

6.11 Provided that the alleged consideration has some economic value, the courts will not question its adequacy, even though one party made a very good bargain and the other did not. In *Mountford v Scott*,[1] £1, paid for an option to purchase a house, was found to be good consideration. Money is always considered to have an economic value and the fact that the amount was small was irrelevant.

Although the courts will not question the adequacy of consideration, the fact that the consideration is clearly inadequate may indicate that the contract has been procured by fraudulent misrepresentation, undue influence or duress on the part of the party benefiting from the inadequacy, in which case the contract may be set aside if the rules described in Chapter 12 are satisfied.

[1] [1975] 1 All ER 198, CA.

Sufficiency of consideration

6.12 The law refuses to recognise certain types of action or promise as capable of constituting consideration, with the result that a person making such an action or promise cannot enforce another's promise given in return for it. Such an action or promise is said not to be sufficient consideration, which is rather confusing since in law it is not consideration at all.

Performance of, or promise to perform, an existing duty imposed by law

6.13 The basic position is that performing or promising to perform an obligation imposed by law is not good consideration for the promise of another. This was stated in *Collins v Godefroy*,[1] in which the claimant gave evidence at the defendant's trial in response to a promise of payment. When he sued for the payment, it was held that he could not succeed because he had provided no consideration for the promise since he was obliged by law to give evidence. It is now clear that the principle in *Collins v Godefroy* has been refined by the principle in *Williams v Roffey Bros & Nicholls (Contractors) Ltd*, referred to in para 6.16. The result is that, unless the existing duty is to pay money,[2] where A makes a promise to B in return for B's performance of, or promise to perform, B's existing duty imposed by law to do something, B provides consideration for A's promise if, as a result of B's performance or promise, A obtains a practical benefit (or avoids a 'disbenefit').

[1] (1831) 1 B & Ad 950.
[2] *Re Selectmove Ltd* [1995] 2 All ER 531, CA.

6.14 The principle in *Collins v Godefroy* does not apply if the party (B) seeking to show that he (or she) provided consideration promised to do, or did, more than was required by law, as where B promises to pay (or pays) more than B is legally obliged, because that is good consideration. In *Glasbrook Bros Ltd v Glamorgan County Council*,[1] the company requested greater protection for its mine during a strike than the police thought necessary and offered to pay for the increased police presence. The company later refused to pay, claiming that, since the police were under a legal duty to protect property, they had provided no consideration for the company's promise of payment. The House of Lords held that the company was obliged to pay because the duty of the police was to take such steps as they reasonably thought necessary and, by providing protection beyond that level, they had done more than they were legally obliged to do and thus had provided consideration for the company's promise.

[1] [1925] AC 270, HL.

Performance of, or promise to perform, an existing contractual duty owed to the other party

6.15 If a person is under a contractual duty to do something, the basic position is that mere performance of that duty (or mere promise to perform it) cannot be good consideration for another promise by the person to whom the contractual duty is already owed. In *Stilk v Myrick*,[1] the crew of a ship were paid a lump sum for a voyage, including all normal emergencies. During the voyage two of the crew deserted and the captain promised to pay the wages of the deserters to the rest of the crew if they would continue the voyage short-handed. Once returned to England, the extra wages were not paid and the seamen sued. Their claim failed. The court held that they had provided no consideration for the captain's promise of extra wages since they were required to cope with normal emergencies by their existing contracts. Desertion by fellow crew members was a normal emergency so they had done no more than they had contracted to do. The court stressed that, if the seamen had promised to do more than they were obliged to do by their existing contracts, they would have provided good consideration. For example, if they had promised to face exceptional hazards that would have been consideration for the captain's promise.[2]

[1] (1809) 2 Camp 317.
[2] *Hartley v Ponsonby* (1857) 7 E & B 872; *North Ocean Shipping Co Ltd v Hyundai Construction Co, The Atlantic Baron* [1978] 3 All ER 1170.

6.16 In *Williams v Roffey Bros & Nicholls (Contractors) Ltd*[1] the Court of Appeal propounded a major limitation on the principle in *Stilk v Myrick*. It held that, where A makes a further promise to B in return for B's promise to perform (or performance of) B's contractual obligations already owed to A, and as a result of B's promise (or performance) A obtains a practical benefit (or avoids a 'disbenefit'), B provides good consideration for A's further promise. The facts of this case were that the claimant had been engaged by the defendants, who were the main contractors in refurbishing a block of flats, to carry out carpentry work for £20,000 which turned out to be unprofitable for him. The main contract contained a 'time penalty' clause and, fearful that the claimant would not complete the work on time, the defendants promised him an extra £10,300, payable at the rate of £575 per flat, if he carried out the work on time. The claimant promised to do so and completed the work in a number of flats, but was not paid the amount promised. The Court of Appeal held that the claimant could recover the unpaid amount; the defendants' promise was binding, consideration having been given for it by the claimant, since his promise benefited the defendants (apparently by avoiding the penalty for delay and avoiding the trouble and expense of engaging other people to complete the carpentry work). The Court of Appeal added that, if the defendant's promise had been obtained by duress or fraud, the contract could have been set aside on that ground.[2]

Since it is unlikely that A will make a further promise to B if A is not going to obtain some benefit from B's promise to perform (or performance of) B's contractual obligations owed to A, the decision appeared to refine the principle in *Stilk v Myrick* almost out of existence. However, in the subsequent case of *Re Selectmove Ltd*[3] the Court of Appeal took a restrictive approach to *Williams v Roffey Bros*, holding that it did not apply where the existing obligation was one to pay money. It held that a promise to pay (or the payment of) money already due could never be consideration for the promise of another. The Court emphasised that the existing obligation in *Williams v Roffey Bros* was to do work and supply materials and distinguished that case on that ground.

[1] [1990] 1 All ER 512, CA.
[2] Chapter 12.
[3] [1995] 2 All ER 531, CA.

Performance of an existing contractual duty owed to a third party

6.17 If a party (B) to a contract with T (the 'third party') is obliged by it to perform some action, a subsequent promise by B to perform that action (or his performance of it) can be good consideration for a promise by another person (A), whether or not there is any benefit to A. In *Scotson v Pegg*,[1] for example, B had contracted to deliver coal to T, or wherever T ordered it to be delivered. T sold the coal to A and told B to deliver it to A. A then promised B that if B delivered the coal A would unload it at a given rate. A failed to unload at this rate and, when sued, argued that B had not provided consideration for A's promise by delivering the coal, because B were obliged to do so under their contract with T. The court held that B had provided consideration.

In two modern cases,[2] the Privy Council has affirmed that a promise to discharge, or the discharge of, a pre-existing contractual obligation to a third party can be valid consideration for another's promise. In the former case, consideration for the promise consisted of unloading a ship which the promisee was already bound to unload under a contract with a third party.

[1] (1861) 6 H & N 295.
[2] *New Zealand Shipping Co Ltd v A M Satterthwaite & Co Ltd, The Eurymedon* [1974] 1 All ER 1015, PC and *Pao On v Lau Yiu Long* [1979] 3 All ER 65, PC.

Part payment of debts

6.18 *Position at common law* It is not surprising that, if B is under a contractual (or other) obligation to pay A and A promises to forego part of the debt, B's payment of the rest of the debt (ie B's performance of B's existing obligation to A) is not consideration for A's promise and, according to the common law, A can subsequently recover the remainder of the debt. In *Foakes v Beer*,[1] A was owed money under a judgment debt by B. A agreed to accept payment by instalments but the agreement did not refer to the question of interest, which is payable on a judgment debt. B paid the debt. A then sued for the interest. In reply, B pleaded the agreement between them, in which A had agreed to bring no further action on the judgment if B paid the debt by instalments. The House of Lords held that B had not provided consideration for A's promise and that, therefore, even if A's promise had included a promise to waive the interest element, it was not binding. B's payment by instalments of the judgment debts could not be consideration for a promise by A to take no further action. B was merely paying less than what he was obliged to do. The House of Lords regretted that this decision had to be reached, but considered itself bound by previous cases.

There are exceptions to the rule that part payment of a debt is no consideration for a promise to remit the rest of the debt. In *Pinnel's Case*,[2] it was said that, provided it was done at the creditor's request, early payment of part of a debt, or part payment at another place than that specified for payment, or payment in kind, even if the value of the goods is less than the debt, is good consideration for a promise by the creditor to forego the remainder of the debt. Thus, if B owes A £100 payable on 1 January at Reading and, at A's request, B pays £1 on 31 December (or pays £1 at Leicester on the correct day, or gives A a rose or a scarf on the correct day), the debt is validly discharged. It used to be thought that a part payment by cheque was good consideration for a promise to remit a debt payable in cash. This has been rejected by the Court of Appeal who decided that nowadays there is no effective difference between cash and a cheque which is honoured.[3]

[1] (1884) 9 App Cas 605, HL. For a recent example of the application of the principle in *Foakes v Beer*, see *Collier v P & M J Wright Holdings Ltd* [2007] EWCA Civ 1329, CA.
[2] (1602) 5 Co Rep 117a.
[3] *D & C Builders Ltd v Rees* [1965] 3 All ER 837, CA.

6.19 There are two somewhat anomalous areas where partial payment of a debt discharges it. First, where a debtor makes an arrangement with all his (or her) creditors that they will all be paid a given percentage of what they are owed, no creditor who has been paid it can recover more than that given percentage.[1] Second, when a third party pays part of a debt in full settlement, that is a valid discharge of the whole debt, and the creditor cannot recover the balance from the debtor.[2] The reason which has been given is that it would be a fraud on the third party if the creditor could do so.[3]

Neither of these areas can satisfactorily be explained in terms of principle (ie consideration by the debtor for the creditor's promise) and are best explained as based on grounds of public policy.

[1] *Good v Cheesman* (1831) 2 B & Ad 328.
[2] *Hirachand Punamchand v Temple* [1911] 2 KB 330, CA.
[3] *Hirachand Punamchand v Temple*.

6.20 *Position in equity* Apart from these exceptions it appeared that a debtor who paid part of a debt, believing that the creditor had agreed to remit the remainder of the debt, had no defence if the creditor sought to recover the amount foregone. However, in 1947 Denning J (as he was then) called upon equity to aid the debtor. In *Central London Property Trust Ltd v High Trees House Ltd*,[1] the claimants (C) let a block of flats to the defendants (D) in 1937 for 99 years at a rent of £2,500 per year. D intended to sub-let the flats but, because of World War 2, found they had many vacant flats and could not pay the rent out of profits. C agreed to accept a reduced rent of £1,250, which was paid quarterly from 1941 until September 1945, by which time all the flats were let. C demanded full rent in respect of the period from September 1945.

D had provided no consideration for the promise by C to remit the rent, but Denning J found that, while the common law could provide no defence in respect of an instalment to which the promise applied, equity could. Drawing on two little-known cases decided in the 19th century, Denning J held that where one party gave a promise which he intended to be binding, which he knew would be acted on, and which was acted on, that promise could be raised as a defence by the promisee if the promisor sought to enforce his strict legal rights. In this case C had promised to reduce the rent; they intended their promise to be binding, they knew D would act on it and D did so act; therefore the rent underpaid in the past could not have been recovered by C. However, Denning J found that the promise was understood by the parties only to apply under the conditions prevailing at the time it was made, namely when the flats were only partially let, and that when the flats became fully let, early in 1945, the promise to remit part of the rent ceased to bind C. As explained in para 6.23, even where a promise to accept part payment in settlement of a debt satisfies the above tests, the promise can be terminated by reasonable notice.

The *High Trees* case illustrates the equitable doctrine known as promissory estoppel, which applies to promises to remit debts (in whole or part) and also to promises not to enforce other contractual rights.

[1] [1956] 1 All ER 256n.

Promissory estoppel

6.21 Under the doctrine of promissory estoppel a promise not to enforce a contractual right (or other legal right) is given some effect, despite the absence of consideration for it, where it would be inequitable for the promisor simply to go back on his (or her) promise and enforce that right.

6.22 The requirements of promissory estoppel are as follows:

- *Unequivocal promise* There must be an unequivocal promise[1] by one party that he (or she) will not, at least for the time being, enforce his (or her) strict rights against the other. The promise may be either express or implied from conduct.[2] Silence and inaction cannot by themselves give rise to a promissory estoppel because they are by their nature equivocal, since there can be more than one reason why the party concerned is silent and inactive.[3]

- *Reliance* The promisee must have acted on the promise by doing something he (or she) would not otherwise have done or not doing what he (or she) would otherwise have done.[4] This requirement was satisfied in *Hughes v Metropolitan Rly Co*,[5] where a tenant, who had been given six months' notice to repair the premises in accordance with a repairing covenant but who had been induced by the landlord's conduct soon afterwards to believe that the lease would not be forfeited for failure to repair, failed to repair in reliance on this belief. In the *High Trees* case the requirement was satisfied by the fact that the lessees paid a lower rent as a result of the promise.[6]

  The present requirement means that promissory estoppel cannot arise if the promisee does nothing, by action or inaction, in reliance on the promise but simply does what the promisee was going to do anyway regardless of whether or not the promise was made.[7] This is illustrated by *Fontana NV v Mautner*.[8] M, the tenant of a flat, refused to leave when his tenancy expired. M was assured by the landlord's representative that he could stay on in the flat as long as he wished, but he subsequently received a notice to quit. In proceedings for possession, Balcombe J rejected M's claim that the assurance gave rise to a promissory estoppel, and made an order for possession. The judge held that this was not a case of promissory estoppel because M had done nothing, by action or inaction, in reliance on the assurance but had simply done what he was going to do anyway (and that was to sit tight for as long as he possibly could).

  There is no need for the promisee to have suffered 'detriment' by relying on the promise, eg by doing something the promisee was not previously obliged to do and suffering loss as a result,[9] but if the promisee has not suffered any detriment by relying on the promise it may not be inequitable for the promisor to go back on his (or her) promise (the next requirement).

- *Inequitable for promisor to resile* It must be inequitable for the promisor to go back on his (or her) promise, having regard to the course of dealings which has taken place between the parties.[10] This requirement will normally be satisfied if the promisee has simply relied on the promise by doing something the promisee would not otherwise have done or by not doing something the promisee would otherwise have done. However, this will not always be the case, as is shown by *The Post Chaser,*[11] where the promisors resiled from their promise not to enforce their strict rights only two days after making it. It was held that this was not inequitable because, in this short period, the promisees had not suffered any prejudice, despite having relied on the promise.

  The present requirement has another aspect; it is not inequitable for the promisor to go back on his (or her) promise, and the promisee is therefore not protected by promissory estoppel, if the promise has been procured by improper pressure or fraud on the part of the promisee or an associate (or by other similar conduct which would render it unfair to the promisor to hold the promise to his (or her) promise). In *D & C Builders Ltd v Rees,*[12] the claimants were owed £482 by the defendant who knew that they were in desperate need of money to stave off bankruptcy. The defendant's wife offered the claimants £300 in settlement of the debt, saying in effect that if they refused they would get nothing. The claimants accepted the £300 reluctantly in settlement of the debt but later sued successfully for the balance. Lord Denning MR refused to allow the defendant to rely on promissory estoppel; his wife's conduct had been improper and therefore it was not inequitable for the claimants to go back on their promise and insist on their strict contractual right to payment of the balance.

[1] *Woodhouse A C Israel Cocoa Ltd SA v Nigerian Produce Marketing Co Ltd* [1972] 2 All ER 271, HL.

[2] *Hughes v Metropolitan Rly Co* (1877) 2 App Cas 439, HL.

[3] *Allied Maritime Transport Ltd v Vale do Rio Doce Navegaeao SA, The Leonidas D* [1985] 2 All ER 796, CA.

[4] *Hughes v Metropolitan Rly Co; Central London Property Trust Ltd v High Trees House Ltd* [1956] 1 All ER 256n; *Tool Metal Manufacturing Co Ltd v Tungsten Electric Co Ltd* [1955] 2 All ER 657, HL; *Ajayi v R T Briscoe (Nigeria) Ltd* [1964] 3 All ER 556, PC; *BP Exploration (Libya) Ltd v Hunt (No 2)* [1982] 1 All ER 925, Goff J (affd by the House of Lords without reference to this point [1982] 1 All ER 925).

[5] (1877) 2 App Cas 439, HL.

[6] *D & C Builders Ltd v Rees* [1965] 3 All ER 837, CA; *Collier v P & MJ Wright* [2007] EWCA Civ 1329, CA.

[7] *Scandinavian Trading Tanker Co AB v Flota Petrolera Ecuatoriana, The Scaptrade* [1983] 1 All ER 301, CA (affd [1983] 2 All ER 763, HL).

[8] (1979) 254 Estates Gazette 199.

[9] *W J Alan & Co Ltd v El Nasr Export and Import Co* [1972] 2 All ER 127 at 140.

[10] *Hughes v Metropolitan Rly Co; Tool Metal Manufacturing Co Ltd v Tungsten Electric Co Ltd.*

[11] *Société Italo-Belge pour le Commerce et l'Industrie SA v Palm and Vegetable Oils (Malaysian) Sdn Bhd, The Post Chaser* [1982] 1 All ER 19.

[12] [1965] 3 All ER 837, CA.

6.23 *Effect of promissory estoppel* Generally, promissory estoppel only suspends, and does not discharge (ie does not wholly extinguish), an obligation. Where promissory estoppel operates to suspend an obligation, the promisor may, by giving reasonable notice to the promisee, revert to his strict contractual rights thereafter.[1] If a promise not to enforce a strict contractual right was clearly intended to be operative only for a certain period, as in the *High Trees* case, the promisor automatically reverts to that right on the expiry of the period, if he has not previously terminated his promise by giving reasonable notice.[2]

Where an obligation has been suspended, the effect of the promisor's reversion to the strict contractual position varies. If the obligation is to pay a lump sum or to perform some other act, such as to repair under a repairing covenant in a lease, the effect of a reversion is that after the period of reasonable notice the promisee must then perform his strict obligation. An example is provided by *Hughes v Metropolitan Rly Co*,[3] discussed above, where the House of Lords held that the six months' notice to repair which had been suspended ran from the time of the landlord's reversion to his strict contractual rights. On the other hand, where the obligation in question is to make periodic payments (such as the payment of rent) or to make some other performance by instalments, the effect of a reversion to the strict contractual position is as follows. The promisee is liable to make future payments (or other performance) in full in respect of instalments due after the period of reasonable notice, but (unless the promise otherwise provides) the promisee is not liable to pay (or perform) what was due, and unpaid (or unperformed), during the currency of the estoppel.[4]

Exceptionally, the effect of promissory estoppel may be to make a promise irrevocable, and thereby to discharge, and not just suspend, the promisee's obligations. A promise subject to promissory estoppel becomes irrevocable if the promisee cannot revert to his strict contractual position,[5] ie if it has become impossible for the promisee to perform his original obligation. An example would be where a building lease obliged the tenant to build by a specified date, but the landlord agreed to suspend the obligation and the land was subsequently compulsorily purchased by the local authority. Clearly, the landlord could not later revoke the promise to suspend the obligation to build; it would be impossible for the tenant to comply with that obligation.

In 2007, *one* member of the Court of Appeal[6] thought that part-payment of a debt in reliance on the creditor's promise not to sue for the remainder if the part-payment was made would in itself render the promise irrevocable (and thereby extinguish the debt) if the effect of the creditor going back on his promise was sufficiently inequitable. This would significantly extend the doctrine of promissory estoppel and would result in a conflict between it and the rule in *Foakes v Beer*. It does not represent the current state of the law.

[1] *Tool Metal Manufacturing Co Ltd v Tungsten Electric Co Ltd* [1955] 2 All ER 657, HL; *Ajayi v R T Briscoe (Nigeria) Ltd* [1964] 3 All ER 556, PC.

[2] *Birmingham and District Land Co Ltd v London and North Western Rly Co* (1888) 40 Ch D 268 at 288.

[3] (1877) 2 App Cas 439, HL.

[4] *Central London Property Trust Ltd v High Trees House Ltd* [1956] 1 All ER 256n; *Tungsten Electric Co Ltd v Tool Metal Manufacturing Co Ltd* (1950) 69 RPC 108, CA; *Tool Metal Manufacturing Co Ltd v Tungsten Electric Co Ltd* [1955] 2 All ER 657, HL.

[5] *Ajayi v R T Briscoe (Nigeria) Ltd* [1964] 3 All ER 556, PC.

[6] *Collier v P & M J Wright* [2007] EWCA Civ 1329 at [37].

6.24 *A shield, not a sword* Promissory estoppel only prevents the promisor from enforcing his (or her) strict rights (at least, without reasonable notice) despite the absence of consideration from the promisee for the promise; it cannot be used to found a cause of action. In *Combe v Combe*,[1] a husband promised to pay his wife maintenance shortly before they were divorced. In reliance on his promise she did not bring court proceedings for financial provision. He failed to pay and she sued him. She had provided no consideration for his promise because he had not requested her not to bring proceedings for financial provision. Consequently, she alleged that he was estopped from going back on his promise (so that it was binding on him) because she had relied on his promise. The Court of Appeal rejected her claim, on the ground that promissory estoppel was a shield and not a sword.

[1] [1951] 1 All ER 767, CA.

CONSIDERATION: KEY POINTS

- To be binding, a promise not made by deed must be supported by consideration on the part of the promisee.

- In order to provide consideration for a promise, the promisee must make a promise or do an act (or refrain from doing an act; hereafter 'act' includes this) in return for that promise and at the express or implied request of the promisor.

- Consideration consisting of a promise to do an act is described as 'executory consideration'; consideration consisting of actually doing an act is described as 'executed consideration'.

- An act done before a promise is 'past consideration', and therefore not consideration at all, unless it was done at the express or implied request of the promisor in circumstances where it must have been understood by both parties that the act would be remunerated.

- What is promised or done must have some economic value but, if it has, a court will not question its adequacy as consideration for the other party's promise.

- The performance, or a promise to perform, an existing duty imposed by law or a contractual duty owed to the other party is generally not sufficient consideration (ie is not consideration) for a promise by the other party, but it is where the other party obtains a practical benefit or avoids a disbenefit (unless the existing duty is to pay money).

- Part-payment of a debt is not generally sufficient consideration for a promise to forego the balance.

- Under the rules of promissory estoppel, a person owed a debt (or other obligation) who promises to accept part-payment (or part performance) cannot go back on that promise if his promise is unequivocal, is relied on by the promisee, and it would be inequitable for the promisor to go back on his (or her) promise. Generally, promissory estoppel merely suspends the promisor's right to full payment (or performance).

Agreements to discharge or vary a contract

6.25 The discharge of a contract by agreement may be either mutual or unilateral. It will be mutual, subject to the rules discussed later, where both parties still have contractual obligations to perform; it will be unilateral, subject to what we say in para 6.27, where one party still has contractual obligations to perform but the other party has completed his (or her) performance of the contract.

An agreement to vary or discharge made by deed is always effective. Otherwise, the situation is as follows.

Mutual discharge

6.26 If both parties still have contractual obligations to perform, any agreement to discharge the contract relieves both parties from further performance of it. In such a case, both parties have provided consideration, for each party promises not to require further performance of contractual obligations by the other party in return for being absolved from further performance of his (or her) own contractual obligations.

Unilateral discharge

6.27 An agreement for a unilateral discharge is only effective if the party to be absolved (B) has provided separate consideration for the other's promise to absolve. In other words, where one party (A) has performed all his (or her) contractual obligations prior to the agreement, A's promise to release the other party (B) from further performance does not bind A unless B provides separate consideration for A's promise to release. Unilateral discharge by agreement is also known as accord (agreement to discharge) and satisfaction (consideration for that agreement). In relation to whether simply performing (or promising to perform) the existing contractual obligation (in whole or part) in response to a promise of release can constitute consideration, the reader is referred to paras 6.15 and 6.18, in particular.

Accord without satisfaction is ineffective to discharge a contract. Satisfaction usually consists of doing something in return for the promise to discharge, but the satisfaction which is offered may be a promise to do something. Where there is a promise, the original contract is discharged from the moment of the accord (rather than later when the promise, which is the alleged satisfaction, has been translated into action) unless the accord expressly states that discharge of the original contract depends on *performance* of the promise to do something.

Promissory estoppel[1] may be available as a defence to a person who has been promised a release from further performance in circumstances where his (or her) obligations have not been discharged by accord and satisfaction because he (or she) has not provided consideration for the promise.

[1] Paras 6.21–6.24 above.

Variation

6.28 If a promised variation of a contract benefits both parties (or could benefit one or other of them[1] depending on the outcome of a contingency) it will have contractual effect because each party will provide consideration for the other's variation promise.

On the other hand, unless it is supported by some separate consideration, it will have no effect (because of lack of consideration) if it can only be of benefit to one party.

Suppose that a contract between A and B requires B to deliver 100 tons of copper to A in Leicester on 1 June. If B and A agree that B should, instead, deliver 95 tons on 1 May (or 100 tons on 1 July in Reading) the variation has contractual effect because it benefits both parties; in contrast, a variation whereby A agreed to accept the delivery of 95 tons in Leicester on 1 June would have no contractual effect, because it could only be of benefit to B, except that it might have a limited effect by virtue of the doctrine of promissory estoppel.

[1] As where the variation consists of the alteration of the currency of payment, whose exchange rate against the original currency of payment may go up or down by the time payment is due: *W J Alan & Co Ltd v El Nasr Export and Import Co* [1972] 2 All ER 127, CA.

AGREEMENTS TO DISCHARGE OR VARY A CONTRACT: KEY POINTS

- Unless such an agreement is made by deed the following rules apply. If both parties still have contractual obligations to perform, the promise of each party to discharge the other will be binding because each will have provided consideration for the other's promise.

- If one party has fully performed his (or her) side of the contract, a promise by that party to discharge the other party from his (or her) contractual obligations must be supported by consideration from the other in order for that promise to be binding.
- Unless it is supported by consideration from the other party, a party's promise to vary the contract for the benefit of the other is of no effect.

Questions

1. Consider the truth of the following statement: 'A business agreement is always legally binding'.

2. Locks reads in the *Estates Gazette* that Zimmer is raising funds to establish a care home for retired estate agents. Locks sends Zimmer an e-mail promising £10,000 towards the project. Later, Locks runs into financial difficulties and tells Zimmer that he can no longer pay the £10,000 (or, indeed, anything). Advise Zimmer as to whether Locks' promise is legally binding.

3. What do you understand by the terms 'executed consideration' and 'executory consideration'?

4. Ron was on holiday when his neighbour Sol telephoned to say that the roof of Ron's house had lost a number of tiles in a storm. Ron asked Sol to 'patch things up'. Sol agreed, and did so. On his return, Ron was so pleased with Sol's efforts that he promised to pay him £250 in respect of them. The day afterwards, Ron and Sol had a row. Ron now refuses to pay Sol anything. Advise Sol.

5. On 1 April, Zebedee Construction Ltd contracted with Estelle, a property developer, to erect an office block for Estelle within a year. On the following 21 September, Zebedee became seriously concerned about the ability of Bluechip Brick Ltd to deliver a specified quantity of bricks which it had contracted with Zebedee to deliver by 1 October. When Zebedee told Estelle of its concerns, Estelle contacted Bluechip and promised to pay it £10,000 if it delivered the specified quantity of bricks by 1 October. Estelle also promised Zebedee a bonus of £10,000 if Zebedee completed the office block on time. The bricks were delivered by 1 October and the office block was completed on time. Estelle has refused to honour either of the above promises. Explain whether or not she is legally obliged to do so.

6. Connor, a landlord, was told by Dinah, the tenant under a part-expired 21-year lease, that she was no longer able to pay the full rent. Connor said to Dinah that if she paid 75% of the instalments of rent due until the end of the lease he would not seek to forfeit the lease for non-payment of the full rent or to recover the unpaid rent. Thenceforth, Dinah has paid 75% of the rent. Now, a year later, Connor wishes to go back on his promise and claim the full rent, both in respect of the last year and in respect of the future. Advise Dinah.

7. What is required for an effective discharge of a contract where the parties agree to its discharge?

7

Contractual terms

CHAPTER OVERVIEW

In the last two chapters we dealt with what is required to create a contract (ie a legally binding agreement). In this chapter we are concerned with the terms (ie the contents) of a contract, which set out the rights and obligations of the parties. The terms of a contract may be:

- express; or

- implied.

Express terms

Parol evidence rule and exceptions and qualifications

7.1 Clearly, the ascertainment of its express terms is facilitated when the contract has been reduced into writing, particularly because under the 'parol evidence' rule oral or other evidence extrinsic to the document is not admissible generally to add to, vary, or contradict, the terms of the written agreement.[1] However, this rule is not as harsh as might be supposed, since in a number of cases extrinsic evidence is admissible, either as an exception to the parol evidence rule or because the circumstances fall outside its bounds. The following can be mentioned as examples.

[1] *Jacobs v Batavia and General Plantations Trust Ltd* [1924] 1 Ch 287 at 295.

Implied terms

7.2 The fact that a contract has been reduced into writing does not prevent extrinsic evidence being given to support or rebut the implication of a term into it.[1]

[1] *Gillespie Bros & Co v Cheney, Eggar & Co* [1896] 2 QB 59.

Conditions precedent

7.3 Extrinsic evidence is admissible to show that, although a written contract appears absolute on its face, it was not intended that a binding contract should be created (or that, although there was an immediate binding contract, a party's obligation to perform would not arise) until the occurrence of a particular event, such as a surveyor's report or the availability of finance.[1]

[1] *Pym v Campbell* (1856) 6 E & B 370; para 5.36.

Invalidating factors

7.4 Extrinsic evidence of a factor, such as misrepresentation, which invalidates the written contract is, of course, admissible.

Written agreement not the whole contract

7.5 While a document which looks like a contract is presumed to include all the terms of the contract, this presumption may be rebutted by evidence that the parties did not intend all the terms of their contract to be contained in the document. If the presumption is rebutted, extrinsic evidence is admissible to prove the other terms of the contract. An example is provided by the case of *J Evans & Son (Portsmouth) Ltd v Andrea Merzario Ltd*, which is discussed in para 7.17.

Collateral contracts

7.6 The parol evidence rule will also be circumvented if the court finds that the parties have made two contracts, the main written one and a contract collateral to it. An example is provided by *Birch v Paramount Estates Ltd*[1] where the D, who were developing a housing estate, offered C one of the house then under construction, stating orally that it would be as good as the show house. C agreed to buy the house but the written contract of sale made no reference to this statement. The completed house was not as good as the show house. The Court of Appeal held that there was an oral contract, to the effect that the house would be as good as the show house, collateral to the contract of sale and upheld the award of damages for its breach.

In essence, a collateral contract exists where A promises B something certain[2] in return for B making the main contract. A's promise must have been intended by the parties to be legally binding and to take effect as a collateral contract, and not merely as a term of the main contract, and it must be supported by separate consideration, although this may simply be B's making of the main contract.[3] Provided these requirements are satisfied, a collateral contract will be valid and enforceable by B, even though it conflicts with a term in the main contract. This is shown by *City and Westminster Properties (1934) Ltd v Mudd*.[4] In 1941, D became the tenant of a lock-up shop for three years. He was allowed by the landlords, C, to sleep in the shop. In 1944, a second lease for three years was granted to D. In 1947, during negotiations for a new lease, C inserted in the draft lease a clause restricting the use of the premises to trade purposes only. D objected and was told by C's agent that, if he accepted the new lease as it stood, C would not object to him residing on the premises. In consequence, D signed the lease. Later, C sought to forfeit the lease for breach of the covenant only to use the premises for trade purposes. It was held that D could plead the collateral contract as a defence to a charge of breach of the main contract, the lease.

[1] (1956) 167 Estates Gazette 396, CA.
[2] *Wake v Renault (UK) Ltd* (1996) 15 Tr LR 514, CA.
[3] *Heilbut, Symons & Co v Buckleton* [1913] AC 30, HL.
[4] [1958] 2 All ER 733.

Effect of 'entire agreement clauses'

7.7 A written agreement which has been formally drafted may well contain an 'entire agreement clause'. The precise wording of such a clause varies but it will normally state that the written agreement contains the entire and only contract between the parties in relation to the subject matter in question, each party acknowledging that in entering into the agreement it has not relied on any representation or undertaking which is not expressly incorporated in the written agreement.

The incorporation of an entire agreement clause is normally intended to prevent a party being liable for breach of contract in respect of statements not included in the written agreement. The effect of such a clause depends on its wording. However, one drafted in the explicit way described above will prevent parol evidence being given to prove that the written contract is not the whole contract (and that a statement not included in it is nevertheless a term of the contract) or that such a statement takes effect as a term of a contract collateral to the main contract; it will deprive that statement of any effect which it would otherwise have had as a contractual term.[1] We consider the effect of an entire agreement clause on liability for misrepresentation in paras 12.47 and 12.48.

[1] *Deepak Fertilizers & Petrochemical Corpn v Imperial Chemical Industries plc* [1999] 1 Lloyd's Rep 387, CA; *Inntrepreneur Pub Co (Co Ltd) v East Crown Ltd* [2000] 2 Lloyd's Rep 611.

Determination of whether a written term is a term of contract

7.8 The determination of whether what purports to be a term of the contract is indeed a term of the contract can sometimes give rise to nice questions. It depends very much on whether or not the term is contained in a signed contractual document. If it is, the general rule is that it is a contractual term binding on a party who signed the document, even though he was unaware of it because he had not read the document.[1] This is so even though that party is, to the other's knowledge, illiterate or unfamiliar with the English language.[2] An exception is where the party seeking to rely on a term has misrepresented to the other its contents or effect. In such a case, the term is rendered ineffective to the extent that it differs from the misrepresentation.[3]

[1] *L'Estrange v F Graucob Ltd* [1934] 2 KB 394, DC.
[2] *Barclays Bank plc v Schwartz* [1995] CLY 2492, CA.
[3] *Curtis v Chemical Cleaning and Dyeing Co Ltd* [1951] 1 All ER 631, CA.

7.9 In other cases, eg where the purported term is printed on a ticket or an order form or a notice, the purported term will only be a contractual term if reasonable notice of it is given. If reasonable notice of it is given, it is irrelevant that the party affected by the term is unaware of it. The following rules apply in this connection.

Notice must be given before or at the time of the contract

7.10 The term is ineffective unless it was brought to the party's notice before or at the time the contract was made. This is shown by *Olley v Marlborough Court Ltd.*[1] C and her husband were accepted as guests at a hotel. They paid for a week in advance and went to their room, on the wall of which was a notice exempting the hotel proprietors from liability for the loss or theft of property. Due to the negligence of the hotel staff, property was stolen from C's room. The Court of Appeal held that the hotel was not protected by the exemption clause because the contract had been made before the exemption clause was communicated so that it formed no part of the contract.

[1] [1949] 1 All ER 127, CA.

7.11 *Exceptions* There are two exceptions to the present rule.

The first is that, if there has been a course of dealings between the parties on the basis of documents incorporating similar terms, then, provided those dealings have been of a consistent nature[1] and each party would reasonably conclude that the term was a term of the contract,[2] the court will incorporate the term into a particular contract where express notice of it is given too late. In *J Spurling Ltd v Bradshaw*,[3] D had dealt with C, warehousemen, for many years. He delivered barrels of orange juice to them for storage. Later, he received a document from them which acknowledged receipt and referred to clauses on its back, one of which excluded C from any liability for loss or damage occasioned by their negligence. Subsequently, D refused to pay the storage charges because the barrels were empty on collection. He was sued for these charges and counterclaimed for negligence. The Court of Appeal held that the exemption clause was incorporated into the contract, and D was therefore bound by it, because in previous dealings he had received a document containing the clause, although he had never read it. Since incorporation of an exemption clause in this way depends on a previous consistent course of dealings between the parties it is less likely to occur in the case of contracts to which a private individual is a party, because normally such a party will have had insufficient dealings with the other party to constitute a course of dealings; three or four dealings over a five-year period, for instance, have been held insufficient to constitute a course of dealing.[4]

The second exception is that where a term is frequently used in a particular trade (as in the case of the standard terms of a trade association) a court will incorporate the term into a particular contract if the parties belong to the particular trade and can be presumed to have had a shared understanding that the term would apply.[5]

[1] *McCutcheon v David MacBrayne Ltd* [1964] 1 All ER 430, HL.
[2] *Henry Kendall & Sons v William Lillico & Sons Ltd* [1969] 2 AC 31, HL.
[3] [1956] 2 All ER 121, CA.
[4] *Hollier v Rambler Motors (AMC) Ltd* [1972] 1 All ER 399, CA.
[5] *British Crane Hire Corpn Ltd v Ipswich Plant Hire Ltd* [1974] 1 All ER 1059, CA.

The notice must be contained in a contractual document

7.12 A term is ineffective if it, or notice of it, is contained in a document which a reasonable person would not assume to contain contractual terms. Thus, in *Chapelton v Barry UDC*,[1] it was held that an exemption clause contained in a ticket for a deck chair on a beach was ineffective because no reasonable person would expect the ticket to be more than a receipt whose object was to enable a hirer to show that he had paid; he would not assume it contained contractual terms.

[1] [1940] 1 All ER 356, CA.

Reasonable notice of the term must be given

7.13 A leading authority is *Parker v South Eastern Rly Co*.[1] C left his bag at a station cloakroom. He received a ticket which said on its face: 'See back'. On the back were a number of terms, one of which limited the railway company's liability to £10 per package. C's bag was lost and he claimed its value of £24 10s (£24.50). It was held that C would be bound by the exemption clause, even though he had not read it, if the railway company had given reasonable notice of its terms. Notice can be reasonable even though it involves reference to other documents or to a notice.[2] The test laid down in *Parker v South Eastern Rly Co* is objective, and if reasonable notice has been given it is irrelevant that the party affected by the term was illiterate or otherwise unable to comprehend its meaning.[3] The only exception would be where the party relying on the term was aware of the other party's inability to comprehend; in such a case the clause would not be a term of the contract.[4]

What amounts to reasonable notice depends in part on the nature of the term. If it is particularly onerous or unusual and would not generally be known to the other party, more will be required (eg printing the term in a different type or colour from the other terms) in order that the notice be held to be reasonable[5] than would be required in a term of a less onerous or unusual type.

[1] (1877) 2 CPD 416, CA.
[2] *Thompson v London, Midland and Scottish Rly Co* [1930] 1 KB 41, CA.
[3] *Thompson v London, Midland and Scottish Rly Co*
[4] *Geier v Kujawa, Weston and Warne Bros (Transport) Ltd* [1970] 1 Lloyd's Rep 364.

[5] *Thornton v Shoe Lane Parking Ltd* [1971] 1 All ER 686, CA; *Interfoto Picture Library Ltd v Stiletto Ltd* [1988] 1 All ER 348, CA.

Contractual terms and mere representations

7.14 Problems can sometimes arise concerning whether a written or oral statement, which is made in contractual negotiations and not explicitly referred to at the time the contract is made, is nevertheless a term of the contract instead of being a mere representation. The present issue can be exemplified as follows. At the time the contract was made A may simply have said to B: 'I offer you £3,000 for the car' to which B replied 'I accept'. These two sentences will probably be the culmination of previous, and perhaps lengthy, negotiations between the parties during which B will have given A a number of assurances as to the condition of the car, its mileage and so on. Whether a pre-contractual statement is a contractual term, or simply a mere representation, is of importance. The reason is that, if the statement turns out to be false, the person to whom it was made can either seek a remedy for breach of contract or a remedy for misrepresentation if the statement is a contractual term, but can only seek a remedy for misrepresentation if the statement is a mere representation. Generally speaking, the remedies for misrepresentation are inferior to those for breach of contract. We discuss the subjects of breach of contract, remedies for breach and misrepresentation in Chapters 8, 11 and 12. For the present, we are concerned with the question of how it is ascertained whether a pre-contractual statement has become a contractual term.

7.15 A representation will be a contractual term if the parties intended that the representor was making a binding promise as to it.[1] Whether the parties did so intend can only be deduced from all the evidence. Of course, it is always possible for the parties actually to state that a particular representation is or is not a term of their contract. If they do not, then, if an intelligent bystander would infer from the words and behaviour of the parties that a binding promise was intended, that will suffice; ie the test is objective.[2] In approaching the question of the parties' objective intentions, the courts take into account factors such as the following.

[1] *Oscar Chess Ltd v Williams* [1957] 1 All ER 325 at 327–328.
[2] *Oscar Chess Ltd v Williams* [1957] 1 All ER 325 at 327–328. See also *Howard Marine and Dredging Co Ltd v A Ogden & Sons (Excavations) Ltd* [1978] 2 All ER 1134 at 1140.

Execution of a written contract

7.16 If the representation was followed by a written contract in which it does not appear, it will probably (but not necessarily) be regarded as a mere representation[1] since, because of the parol evidence rule, it can only take effect as a contractual term if the court finds that the parties intended that the contract should not be contained wholly in the written document or that the representation should form part of a collateral contract. An example of a case where a pre-contractual representation was found to be a contractual term despite the subsequent execution of a written contract is *J Evans & Son (Portsmouth) Ltd v Andrea Merzario Ltd*, which is discussed in the next paragraph.

[1] *Heilbut, Symons & Co v Buckleton* [1913] AC 30 at 50; *Oscar Chess Ltd v Williams* [1957] 1 All ER 325 at 329.

The importance of the representation

7.17 The more important the subject matter of the representation the more likely it is that the parties intended a binding promise concerning it. In particular, if the representation was so important that without it the representee would not have made the contract, the court is very likely to hold that it is a contractual term. In *J Evans & Son (Portsmouth) Ltd v Andrea Merzario Ltd*,[1] C bought some machines from an Italian company. They had previously employed D to arrange transport, and the machinery had always been packed in crates or trailers and carried below deck. On this occasion D's representative told C's that it was proposed that the machinery should be packed in containers. C's representative replied that if containers were used they must be stowed below, and not on deck, in case the machinery rusted. He was assured by D's representative that this would be done but this oral assurance was not included in the written agreement subsequently made between C and D. In fact, the containers were carried on deck and two fell into the sea. In the Court of Appeal, Roskill and Geoffrey Lane LJJ held that the oral assurance had become a term of the contract between the parties, which was not wholly written, and that C could recover damages for its breach. Roskill LJ stated that in the light of the totality of the evidence it was clear that C had only agreed to contract with D on the basis that the containers were stowed below deck, and therefore D's assurance concerning this had become a contractual term.

[1] [1976] 2 All ER 930, CA.

Invitation to verify

7.18 If a seller invites the buyer to check his representation it is very unlikely to be regarded as a contractual term. In *Ecay v Godfrey*,[1] for instance, the seller of a boat said that it was sound but advised a survey. It was held that this advice negatived any intention that the representation should be a contractual term. Conversely, if the seller assures the buyer that it is not necessary to verify the representation since he can take the seller's word for it, the representation is likely to be found to be intended to be a term of the resulting contract if the buyer contracts in reliance on it. In *Schawel v Reade*,[2] C, who required a stallion for stud purposes, went to D's stables to inspect a horse. While he was inspecting it, D said: 'You need not look for anything: the horse is perfectly sound. If there was anything the matter with the horse I would tell you.' C thereupon ended his inspection and a price was agreed three weeks later, C relying on D's statement. The House of Lords held that the jury's finding that D's statement was a contractual term was correct.

[1] (1947) 80 Lloyd's LR 286.
[2] [1913] 2 IR 64, HL.

Statements of fact, of opinion or as to the future

7.19 A statement of fact is more likely to be construed as intended to have contractual effect than a statement of opinion or as to future facts (eg a forecast).[1] A statement about something which is, or should be, within the promisor's control is very likely to be construed as a contractual term.[2]

[1] *Esso Petroleum Co Ltd v Mardon* [1976] 2 All ER 5 at 20.
[2] *Oscar Chess Ltd v Williams* [1957] 1 All ER 325 at 329.

Ability of the parties to ascertain the accuracy of the representation

7.20 If the representor had a special skill or knowledge, or was otherwise in a better position than the representee to ascertain the truth of the representation, this strongly suggests that the representation was intended to be a contractual term, and vice versa. An example is provided by *Dick Bentley (Productions) Ltd v Harold Smith (Motors) Ltd*.[1] C purchased a Bentley car from D in reliance on D's statement that the car had been fitted with a new engine and gear box and had done only 20,000 miles since then. The representation as to mileage, although honestly made, was untrue. The Court of Appeal held that the representation had become one of the terms of the contract because it had been made by a dealer who was in a position to know or find out the car's history, and it could therefore be inferred that the representation was intended to have contractual effect. The Court distinguished its previous decision in *Oscar Chess Ltd v Williams*.[2] There, Williams, a private person, represented in negotiations for the part-exchange of his Morris car that it was a 1948 model. This representation was based on the logbook which had been falsified by a person unknown. The representation was held not to have become a contractual term on the ground that Williams had no special knowledge as to the car's age, while the other party, who were car dealers, were in at least as good a position to ascertain whether the representation was true.

[1] [1965] 2 All ER 65, CA.
[2] [1957] 1 All ER 325, CA.

7.21 It must be emphasised that the factors mentioned above are only guides, not decisive tests or the only factors, to determining the parties' intentions.[1] Sometimes, they can point in different directions.

On many occasions, judges, having found that the parties intended a pre-contractual representation to have contractual effect, have found that it has taken effect under a collateral contract rather than as a term of the main contract.

[1] *Heilbut, Symons & Co v Buckleton* [1913] AC 30, HL.

EXPRESS TERMS: KEY POINTS

- The parol evidence rule states that extrinsic evidence is not admissible to add to, vary or contradict the terms of a written agreement. However, there are a number of exceptions or qualifications; extrinsic evidence is admissible to:
  - support or rebut the implication of a term;
  - show that the written agreement is subject to a condition precedent;
  - show the existence of an invalidating factor;
  - show that the written agreement is not the whole agreement;
  - establish a contract collateral to the main agreement.
- The last two qualifications cannot apply if the agreement contains an appropriately drafted 'entire agreement clause'.
- If what purports to be a term is contained in a signed contractual document it is generally a term of the contract. A purported term in an unsigned document is only a contractual term if:
  - notice was given before or at the time of the contract, unless it can be implied through a previous, consistent course of dealings between the parties or through trade usage;
  - the document was a contractual document (ie a document that a reasonable person would assume contained contractual terms); and
  - reasonable notice was given, the test of which is generally objective.
- It is important to distinguish between pre-contractual representations which are terms of the contract and those which are mere representations, because if the former are false a remedy for breach of contract or a remedy for misrepresentation may be sought, whereas in the latter case only a remedy for misrepresentation may be sought.
- Whether or not a pre-contractual representation has become a term of the contract depends on the parties' intentions. If the parties did not actually state them, their

intentions are judged by what an intelligent bystander would infer from their words and behaviour. Factors relevant to this objective test are:

- whether a written contract not containing the representation was subsequently made;
- the importance of the representation;
- whether the representor invited the respresentee to verify the representation;
- whether the representation was a statement of fact, of opinion or as to the future;
- the ability of the parties to ascertain the accuracy of the representation.

Implied terms

7.22 Although most of the terms of a contract will be express terms, it may also contain implied terms. Terms may be implied by custom or usage or by statute or by the courts.

Terms implied by custom or usage

7.23 Terms may be implied by the custom of a particular locality, as in *Hutton v Warren*,[1] or by the usage of a particular trade, as recognised in *Lancaster v Bird*.[2] Although the terms are often used interchangeably, 'usage' differs from 'custom' in that it need not be ancient or recognised as compulsory, but like custom it must be reasonable and certain in the sense that it is clearly established.[3] In *Hutton v Warren*, where a local custom was proved that a tenant was obliged to farm according to a certain course of husbandry for the whole of his tenancy and, on quitting, was entitled to a fair allowance for seeds and labour on the arable land, it was held that a term to this effect was implied in the lease. In *Lancaster v Bird*, the Court of Appeal recognised that in the case of a contract between those engaged in the building trade there was a term implied by usage that a price quoted was exclusive of value added tax, although it held that that usage did not apply to a contract between a builder and a consumer.

[1] (1836) 1 M & W 466. For the requirements of a valid local custom, see para 3.46.
[2] [1998] 73 Con LR 22, CA.
[3] *Cunliffe-Owen v Teather and Greenwood* [1967] 3 All ER 561 at 572.

7.24 A term cannot be implied by custom or usage if the express wording of the contract shows that the parties had a contrary intention. This is shown by *Les Affréteurs Réunis SA v Leopold Walford (London) Ltd*.[1] Walford acted as a broker in effecting the time charterparty of a ship. The charterparty provided that commission should be payable to Walford 'on signing this charter (ship lost or not lost)'. Before the charterparty could be operated, and therefore before any hire could be earned, the French government requisitioned the ship. The House of Lords held that Walford could recover his commission, despite a commercial usage in the case of a time charterparty that commission was payable only in respect of hire earned, because the usage was inconsistent with the express terms of the charterparty.

[1] [1919] AC 801, HL.

Terms implied by statute

7.25 The best-known examples of such terms are those implied into contracts for the sale of goods by the Sale of Goods Act 1979 (SGA 1979).

Section 12(1) provides that there is an implied condition[1] on the part of a seller of goods that he has a right to sell them. Section 12(2) provides, inter alia, that there is an implied warranty that the goods are free, and will remain free until the property passes, from any charge or encumbrance not known or disclosed to the buyer before the contract is made.

Section 13(1) provides that, where there is a contract for the sale of goods by description, there is an implied condition[2] that the goods will correspond with the description.

Section 14(2) provides that, where the seller sells goods in the course of a business, there is generally an implied condition[3] that the goods supplied under the contract are of satisfactory quality (ie of the standard that any reasonable person would regard as satisfactory, taking account of any description of the goods, the price (if relevant) and all the other relevant circumstances)[4]. Section 14(3) provides that, where the seller sells goods in the course of a business and the buyer expressly or impliedly makes known to him any particular purpose for which the goods are being bought, there is an implied condition that the goods supplied are reasonably fit for that purpose, whether or not that is a purpose for which such goods are commonly supplied.

Unlike ss 12 and 13, s 14(2) and (3) only apply where goods are sold *in the course of a business*. 'Business' is not limited to commercial activities in the ordinary sense because it is defined by s 61 to include 'a profession and the activities of any governmental department, or local or public authority'. A sale is 'in the course of a business' in the present context whenever the seller is a business, unless it is a purely private sale of goods outside the confines of the business carried on by the seller.[5] The seller's business need not be directed to sales of goods at all; a firm of surveyors which sells an obsolete PC sells it in the course of its business, for example. On the other hand, a sale of an obsolete PC bought for his children's use at home by a surveyor in sole practice would not be a sale 'in the course of business' because it would be a purely private sale outside the confines of his business.

If a private individual sells goods through an agent, such as an auctioneer, acting in the course of a business, s 14(2) and s 14(3) apply to the sale, unless the buyer knows that the seller is a private individual or reasonable steps have been taken to bring that fact to the buyer's attention before the contract is made.[6] This rule applies whether the private individual is a disclosed or undisclosed principal.[7] It follows that it is extremely important that an auctioneer acting on behalf of a private client should notify prospective bidders for the goods of this fact, so as to avoid exposing the client to the risk of liability under s 14(2) or s 14(3).

Finally, s 15(2) provides that where goods are sold by sample there is an implied condition[8] that the bulk will correspond with the sample in quality, and an implied condition that the goods will be free from any defect, rendering them unsatisfactory, which would not be apparent on reasonable examination of the sample.

---

[1] The classification of the implied terms under the SGA 1979, s 12(1) and (2) is made by s 12(5A).
[2] By the SGA 1979, s 13(1A) the term is classified as a condition.
[3] The classification of the implied terms under the SGA 1979, s 14 as conditions is made by s 14(6).
[4] SGA 1979, s 14(2A); see also ss 14(2B)–(2F).
[5] *Stevenson v Rogers* [1999] 1 All ER 613, CA.
[6] SGA 1979, s 14(5).
[7] *Boyter v Thomson* [1995] 3 All ER 135, HL. As to 'disclosed' and 'undisclosed', see paras 14.35 and 14.36.
[8] The classification of the implied term under the SGA 1979, s 15 is made by s 15(3).

7.26 Terms modelled on those implied into sale of goods contracts are implied:

- into contracts of hire purchase, by the Supply of Goods (Implied Terms) Act 1973, ss 8 to 11;

- into contracts of hire, by the Supply of Goods and Services Act 1982, ss 7 to 10; and

- into contracts analogous to sale under which a person transfers or agrees to transfer to another the property (ie ownership) in goods, by the Supply of Goods and Services Act 1982, ss 2 to 5. One example of a contract analogous to sale is a contract for work and materials, such as a building contract or a contract for double glazing; another is a contract of exchange.

Although the exclusion or restriction by the contract of one of the implied terms referred to in para 7.25 and this paragraph, or of liability for its breach, is permissible,[1] there are strict limitations on this under the Unfair Contract Terms Act 1977 (paras 9.17 to 9.20).

[1] Sale of Goods Act 1979, s 55; Supply of Goods and Services Act 1982, s 11.

7.27 By way of a further example, it may be noted that in a 'contract for the supply of a service' certain terms are implied by the Supply of Goods and Services Act 1982 (SGSA 1982), ss 13 to 15. Such a contract includes, for example, a contract between a surveyor and client (but does not include a contract of employment or apprenticeship[1]). The fact that goods are transferred or hired under the contract does not prevent it being a contract for the supply of a service.[2] Consequently, for example, while a contract for work and materials will be subject to the implied terms under the SGSA 1982, ss 2 to 5 in relation to the materials element, the work element will be subject to the terms implied into a contract for the supply of a service by ss 13 to 15.

The following terms are implied by the SGSA 1982 into a contract for the supply of a service:

- by s 13, where the supplier of the service is acting *in the course of a business*,[3] there is an implied term that he will carry out the service with reasonable care and skill;[4]
- by ss 14 and 15, where the time for the service to be carried out (s 14), or the consideration for the service (s 15):
  - is not stated by the contract, or
  - is not left to be determined in a manner agreed by the contract, or
  - is not determined by the course of dealings between the parties,

  there is an implied term that the service will be carried out within a reasonable time or, as the case may be, that a reasonable charge will be paid. The implied term as to the time of performance only applies where the contract is for the supply of a service by a supplier acting *in the course of a business*.

The SGSA 1982, s 16 permits the rights, duties and liabilities which may arise by virtue of ss 13 to 15 to be negatived or varied, subject to the relevant provisions of the Unfair Contract Terms Act 1977 (paras 9.9 to 9.15) and to any other legislation relating to the particular contract which defines or restricts rights, duties or liabilities.

[1] SGSA 1982, s 12(2).
[2] SGSA 1982, s 12(3).
[3] 'Business' includes a profession and the activities of any government department or local or public authority: SGSA 1982, s 18.
[4] There are very limited exceptions under the Supply of Services (Exclusion of Implied Terms) Orders 1982, 1983 and 1985, the most notable being that the implied term under s 13 does not apply to most services rendered by an advocate, nor to the services rendered by an arbitrator, nor to the services rendered by a company director to his company.

7.28 Under the Landlord and Tenant Act 1985 terms as to fitness for habitation and as to repairs are implied into certain types of leases. We discuss this in paras 36.44 and 36.45.

Terms implied by the courts

7.29 In *Liverpool City Council v Irwin*,[1] the House of Lords recognised that terms could be implied by the courts in two distinct situations:

- where the term was a necessary incident of the kind of contract in question (terms implied in law), and

- where it was necessary to give effect to the parties' imputed intentions (terms implied in fact).

  [1] [1976] 2 All ER 39, HL.

Implication of a term which is a necessary incident of the type of contract in question

7.30 When a court implies this type of term for the first time it lays down a general rule for contracts of the same type, eg employment contracts or leases, or a distinct species of that type of contract. The term will, therefore, be implied in subsequent cases concerning that type of contract,[1] subject to the rules of precedent, unless it is inconsistent with the express terms of the contract[2] or the contract validly excludes it.[3] In implying a term of the present type, the court is not trying to put the parties' intentions, actual or presumed, into effect but is implying it as a necessary incident of the type of contractual relationship in question.[4] Such an implication can only be made if the subject matter of the contract of necessity requires it; it is not enough that it would simply be reasonable to make it.[5]

  [1] *Lister v Romford Ice and Cold Storage Co Ltd* [1957] AC 555 at 576; *Liverpool City Council v Irwin* [1976] 2 All ER 39 at 46.
  [2] The Unfair Contract Terms Act 1977 (paras 9.9–9.21) may have the effect of automatically invalidating an inconsistent express term, in which case the implication can be made: *Johnstone v Bloomsbury Health Authority* [1991] 2 All ER 293, CA.
  [3] *Lynch v Thorne* [1956] 1 All ER 744, CA.
  [4] *Liverpool City Council v Irwin* [1976] 2 All ER 39, HL; *Tai Hing Cotton Mill Ltd v Liu Chong Bank Ltd* [1985] 2 All ER 947, PC.
  [5] *Liverpool City Council v Irwin* [1976] 2 All ER 39, HL.

7.31 It is only possible here to refer to a few of the terms implied into contracts under the present heading.

In contracts of employment a number of obligations on the employee are implied. The fundamental implied duty is that the employee will faithfully serve his (or her) employer (the implied duty of fidelity).[1] A number of more specific implied duties to which an employee is subject are merely instances of the duty of fidelity, for example:

- not to act against his (or her) employer's interests;[2]

- to use reasonable care and skill in performing his (or her) duties;[3]

- not to use or disclose a trade secret or confidential information relating to the employer's business contrary to the employer's interests.[4]

There is a separate implied duty whereby an ex-employee must not use or disclose a trade secret or information relating to the former employer's business which is so confidential that it requires the same protection as a trade secret.[5]

Reciprocal terms are implied in the employee's favour, the employer being obliged, for instance:

- not to require the employee to do any unlawful act;[6]

- to use reasonable care to ensure the health and safety of the employee;[7] and

- not, without reasonable and proper cause, to conduct his (or her) business in a manner likely to destroy or damage seriously the relationship of mutual trust and confidence between employer and employee.[8]

Another example of an implied term of the present type is provided by *Liverpool City Council v Irwin*.[9] That case concerned the situation where parts of a building have been let to different tenants (the case concerned a high-rise block of flats) and essential rights of access over parts of the building, such as stairs, retained by the landlord have been granted to the individual tenants. The House of Lords held that in such a situation a term could be implied into the tenancy agreements that the landlord would take reasonable care to keep the essential means of access reasonably safe and reasonably fit for use by tenants, their families and their visitors. Likewise, it has been held that, where a tenant has a right of way over a path which is an essential means of access to the tenant's premises, the landlord having retained control of the path, there is implied in the tenancy agreement a term that the landlord will take reasonable steps to keep the path in good repair.[10]

In a lease of furnished premises there is an implied term that they are fit for human habitation when let,[11] but for some obscure reason such a term is not implied by the courts in a contract for the sale of land with a house on it or for the letting of land with unfurnished premises on it[12] (although if the vendor or lessor is the builder he may be liable in tort to the purchaser, lessee, or even a visitor, who is injured as a result of negligent building[13]). Lastly, where a builder contracts to construct a dwelling there is a term implied by the courts that the dwelling, when completed, will be reasonably fit for human habitation.[14] However, this implication may be rebutted where the contract expressly specifies the way in which the work is to be done and the work is completed according to that specification.[15] This is an example of the rule that a term of the present type cannot be implied if it is inconsistent with the express terms of the contract.

[1] *Hivac Ltd v Park Royal Scientific Instruments Ltd* [1946] 1 All ER 350, CA.
[2] *Wessex Dairies Ltd v Smith* [1935] 2 KB 80, CA.
[3] *Harmer v Cornelius* (1858) 5 CB (NS) 236.
[4] *Faccenda Chicken Ltd v Fowler* [1986] 1 All ER 617, CA.
[5] *Faccenda Chicken Ltd v Fowler*.
[6] *Gregory v Ford* [1951] 1 All ER 121.
[7] *Matthews v Kuwait Bechtel Corpn* [1959] 2 All ER 345, CA.
[8] *Malik v Bank of Credit and Commerce International SA* [1997] 3 All ER 1, HL.
[9] [1976] 2 All ER 39, HL.
[10] *King v South Northamptonshire District Council* [1992] 1 EGLR 53, CA.
[11] Para 36.44. For other examples of terms implied into leases as a necessary incident, see paras 36.34, 36.35, 36.42 and 36.43.
[12] *Hart v Windsor* (1843) 12 M & W 68. For possible liability for breach of statutory duty see para 21.29.
[13] Para 21.28.
[14] *Hancock v BW Brazier (Anerley) Ltd* [1966] 2 All ER 901, CA.
[15] *Lynch v Thorne* [1956] 1 All ER 744, CA.

Implication to give effect to the parties' imputed intentions

7.32 The question of an implication of a term under this heading arises when the contract does not expressly provide for what is to happen when some event occurs. In *A-G of Belize v Belize Telecom Ltd*,[1] where the relevant law was clarified, the Privy Council held that, whenever it is said that some term ought to be implied in the contract to fill a gap, the question for the court is whether such a term would spell out in express terms what the contract, read as a whole against the relevant background, would reasonably be understood to mean. The Privy Council emphasised that a court's power to imply a term of the present type is limited to construing (interpreting) the contract to find out what it means, and that the court has no power to alter or improve the contract; it cannot introduce terms to make it fairer or more reasonable. The Privy Council recognised that the meaning of the contract is not necessarily what the parties would have intended. Instead, it held, it is the meaning which the contract would convey to a reasonable person having all the background knowledge which would reasonably be available to the parties.

In the *Belize* case, the Privy Council stated that, where the contract does not expressly provide for what is to happen when some event occurs, the most usual inference is that nothing is to happen; if the parties had intended something to happen the contract would have said so. It went on to point out that in some cases, however, a reasonable person would understand the contract to mean something else. He would consider that the only meaning consistent with the terms of the contract, read against the relevant background, is that something is to happen; the contract may not have expressly said so, but this is what it must mean.

In a case where the *Belize* case was applied, the Court of Appeal made clear that the necessity for the implication of the term remains a requirement of the present type of implication.[2] It is not enough, it held, that it is reasonable to imply the term;[3] its implication must be necessary to make the contract work.[4]

[1] [2009] UKPC 11, PC.

[2] *Mediterranean Salvage and Towage Ltd v Seamar Trading and Commerce Inc* [2009] EWCA Civ 531, CA.

[3] *Liverpool City Council v Irwin* [1976] 2 All ER 39, HL.

[4] *Mediterranean Salvage and Towage Ltd v Seamar Trading and Commerce Inc* [2009] EWCA Civ 531, CA.

7.33 Since the implication of a term under the above principles is always dependent on the particular circumstances of the case, the implication of a term under it does not lay down a general rule for the future.

Implied Terms: Key Points

A term may be implied into a contract:

- by a custom of a particular locality or the usage of a particular trade. Like a local custom, such a usage must be reasonable and certain. A term cannot be implied by custom or usage if the express words of the contract show that the parties had a contrary intention;

- by statute. Examples are provided by the implied terms as to the title of the seller, compliance with description, satisfactory quality and fitness for a particular purpose in contracts for the sale of goods. There are strict limits on the exclusion of these implied terms (and corresponding ones in similar contracts);

- by the courts where:
  - the term is a necessary incident of the kind of contract in question; or
  - the term is one which spells out in express words what the contract, read as a whole against the relevant background, would reasonably be understood to mean, and is one which is necessary to make the contract work.

Unfair contract terms

7.34 Under the Unfair Contract Terms Act 1977 and the Unfair Terms in Consumer Contracts Regulations 1999 there are special provisions relating to contract terms which are unfair. In some cases, these provisions render an unfair term of no effect. We deal with these provisions in Chapter 9.

Questions

1. What is the parol evidence rule? What exceptions or qualifications to it are there?

2. What is the importance of the distinction between a term and a mere representation?

3. Len, a quantity surveyor, drove to his local Computerglobe plc, a retail chain specialising in the sale of computers, to buy a new PC for his office. He parked in a nearby pay-on-exit car park operated by ABC Car Parks plc. Near the entrance barrier there was a sign referring to conditions under which vehicles were permitted to park and stating that they were displayed in the car park attendant's office. Len should not have driven to the car park because he was not wearing his spectacles. Because he was not wearing them he could not read what was on the sign.

    Len bought a PC in Computerglobe, signing a document 'Contract of Sale' without trying to read it. When he returned to his car he was injured, and his watch was smashed beyond repair, when a piece of masonry on the car park staircase fell on him due to negligently inadequate maintenance by ABC Car Parks.

    When Len first used his new PC he discovered that, through no fault of Computerglobe, it was not of satisfactory quality.

    When Len takes up these matters with ABC Car Parks plc and Computerglobe plc, ABC Car Parks plc tell him that one of their conditions displayed in the car park attendant's office was that 'ABC Car Parks plc will not be liable for any injury caused to persons using their car parks or for any loss or damage to such a person's belongings', and Computerglobe plc tell him that one of the clauses in the 'Contract of Sale' document which he signed stated that 'Computerglobe plc shall not be liable for breach of any term of this contract, express or implied, unless such breach is attributable to fault on their part'.

    Advise Len as to whether the condition displayed in the attendant's office and the clause in the Contract of Sale document are terms of his contracts with ABC Car Parks plc and Computerglobe plc. Note: other points arising in this question will be dealt with in one of the questions in Chapter 9.

4. Sunita wanted to employ an additional negotiator in her estate agent's office, so she placed an advertisement in the local newspaper. Anna was one of the applicants for the job. Sunita asked whether Anna could guarantee that she would work overtime when necessary if appointed. Anna replied: 'yes', at which Sunita said: 'Good. There'd have been no point in carrying on with this interview if you'd said "no". You do promise me that you will if you get the job, don't you?'. Anna replied: 'I promise'. The next day Sunita sent Anna a letter offering her the job as negotiator and enclosing a document headed 'Contract of Employment'. The document included a statement: 'The employee's working hours are 37 hours a week, based on a five-day working week', but it made no reference to overtime work. Anna signed the document, indicating that she accepted the offer of employment, and returned it to Sunita. The day after Anna took up her employment with Sunita, she was asked to work overtime which she refused to do.

    Is Anna contractually obliged to work overtime?

5. Eric was given a painting, 'The Blue Lagoon', in lieu of fees by Fiona, a wealthy client of his who was also his friend. Fiona told Eric that the painting was by John Constable but was not generally known about because it had always been in her family. After Fiona's death, Eric sold the painting for £1m to George, an art dealer specialising in British artists, repeating what he had been told by Fiona. It has now transpired that 'The Blue Lagoon' was painted years after Constable's death. The question has arisen whether Eric's statement to George that its artist was John Constable is an express term of the contract between Eric and George.

Is it? Give the reasons for your answer.

6. Give three examples of terms implied into a contract for the sale or hire of goods, and two examples of terms implied by statute into a contract for the supply of a service.

7. Explain with your reasons whether the following statement is correct: 'An unexpressed term can be implied into a contract by a court only if the court finds that the parties must actually have intended that term to form part of their contract'.

8

Performance and breach

CHAPTER OVERVIEW

In this chapter we examine:

- how a party to a contract can be discharged from his (or her) obligations under it by performing them (discharge by performance), and the legal effect of an unsuccessful tender of performance by a party;

- the legal effect of a breach of contract by a party, including the situations where the party not in breach is entitled to terminate the contract and thereby to be discharged from any obligations under it due thereafter (discharge by breach);

- the time for performance, and the legal consequences of failure to perform in time.

Performance

8.1 A contract may be discharged by agreement between the parties, by being broken by one of them, or by being frustrated, if the rules described elsewhere in this book[1] are satisfied. However, a contract is most frequently discharged by both parties performing their obligations under it, both parties being released from further liability thereby. If only one party (X) performs his (or her) contractual obligations X alone is discharged and X acquires a right of action against the other for breach of contract.

[1] Paras 6.25–6.27; 8.6–8.27; and 10.2–10.14.

8.2 For a party (X) to be discharged from his (or her) contractual obligations by performance X must have precisely performed all his (or her) obligations under the contract. Thus, to decide whether a party (X) is discharged by performance, one must first ascertain and construe the terms of the contract, express and implied, to see what X's contractual obligations were, and then look at what has happened to see whether what X has done precisely corresponds with those obligations. The requirement of precise performance is a strict one and, if it is not met, it is irrelevant that the performance effected is commercially no less valuable than that which was promised. In *Arcos Ltd v E A Ronaasen & Sons*,[1] C contracted to supply D with a certain quantity of timber which, as they knew, was to be used for constructing cement barrels. The contract specified that the timber should be half an inch thick but when it was delivered D discovered that 95% of it was over half an inch thick, although none of it exceeded three-quarters of an inch in thickness. It was still perfectly possible for D to use all the wood, as it had been delivered, for the construction of cement barrels but the House of Lords held that they were entitled to reject the whole consignment[2] since C had not performed a contractual obligation which was a condition of the contract.[3] Lord Atkin stated, obiter, that only if a deviation from the terms of the contract was 'microscopic' could the contract be taken to have been correctly performed. An example of this is provided by *Shipton, Anderson & Co v Weil Bros & Co*,[4] where a contract requiring the delivery of 4,950 tons of wheat was held to have been performed by the seller although he had delivered 4,950 tons 55 lbs.

[1] [1933] AC 470, HL.

[2] The decision that D were entitled to reject might now be different because of the Sale of Goods Act 1979, s 15A: para 8.23.

[3] The contractual obligation broken was the condition implied by the Sale of Goods Act 1979, s 13(1), viz, that in a sale of goods by description the goods must correspond with the description. See paras 7.25 and 8.21–8.22.

[4] [1912] 1 KB 574.

Payment

8.3 Where the obligation of one party (the debtor) to the other (the creditor) consists of the payment of a sum of money, that obligation is discharged by the payment of that sum. Payment should, primarily, be made in legal tender. Unless the creditor has expressly or impliedly agreed to do so, the creditor is not obliged to accept payment by cheque or other means.

Where a cheque is given, and accepted,[1] in payment, its effect may be absolutely to discharge the debtor or only conditionally to discharge the debtor.

The discharge will be *absolute* if the creditor promises expressly or impliedly, in accepting the cheque, to discharge the debtor from the debtor's existing obligations. If this occurs the creditor loses his (or her) right of action on the original contract but can sue on his (or her) rights under the cheque if it is dishonoured.[2]

The presumption is that the creditor only accepts a cheque as a *conditional* discharge, in which case the debtor is not discharged unless, and until, the cheque is honoured; if it is honoured, payment is deemed to have been made at the time the cheque is received.[3] If it is dishonoured, the debtor may be sued on the original contract or on the dishonoured cheque.[4]

Where payment is made by a credit card, the presumption is that it is accepted as an absolute discharge unless the contract states that it is only accepted as a conditional discharge.[5]

[1] *Official Solicitor to the Supreme Court v Thomas* [1986] 2 EGLR 1, CA.

[2] *Sard v Rhodes* (1836) 1 M & W 153.

[3] *Homes v Smith* [2000] Lloyd's Rep Bank 139, CA.

[4] *Re Romer and Haslam* [1893] 2 QB 286, CA.

[5] *Re Charge Card Services Ltd* [1988] 3 All ER 702, CA.

Tender of payment

8.4 If a party (X) makes a valid tender of payment of a debt by producing the amount owed in legal tender (or transferring it in a manner to which the creditor has expressly or impliedly agreed) but the creditor refuses to accept it, this does not discharge X's debt. If an action is brought for non-payment, all X has to do is to pay the money into court,[1] whereupon X is not liable in damages for non-performance, will not be liable for interest and must be paid his (or her) costs by the creditor.

[1] Civil Procedure Rules, r 37.3.

Tender of acts

8.5 Where a party (X) is obliged to perform some act, other than the payment of money, X will make a valid tender of performance if X attempts to perform the act in precise accordance with the terms of the contract. In the case of a contract for the sale of goods, the tender of them must be made at a reasonable hour.[1] A valid tender of an act other than payment discharges the tenderer from the obligation to perform that act and the tenderer can sue the other party for damages for breach of contract for refusing to accept the tendered performance. If the other party's refusal amounts to a renunciation of the contract the tenderer can elect to terminate the contract and recover damages.[2] If the other party sues the tenderer for non-performance, the tenderer can raise the refusal of the tender as a defence.[3]

[1] Sale of Goods Act 1979, s 29.
[2] *Startup v Macdonald* (1843) 6 Man & G 593.
[3] *Startup v Macdonald* (1843) 6 Man & G 593.

PERFORMANCE: KEY POINTS

- Precise performance of all of a party's contractual obligations discharges that party from further liability under the contract.

- Unless the creditor has expressly or impliedly agreed to payment by cheque or other means, payment of an amount due must be in legal tender in order to discharge the obligation to pay.

- Where an attempted performance of a contractual obligation is rejected, the effect of the tender depends on whether the tender was the tender of payment or the tender of some other act.

Breach

8.6 Breach of contract occurs where a party does not perform one or more of his contractual obligations precisely, in the sense discussed in para 8.2, and this failure is without lawful excuse. Thus, a breach occurs where a party without lawful excuse refuses to perform one or more contractual obligations, or simply fails to perform them, or incapacitates himself (or herself) from performing them, or performs them defectively.

8.7 A person (X) has a lawful excuse for failing to perform contractual obligations precisely in the following cases:

- if the contract has been discharged by frustration, as explained in Chapter 10;
- if there is impossibility of performance less than frustration; for instance, a temporary illness preventing an employee working provides a lawful excuse for the failure to work during the period of the illness;[1]
- if X has validly tendered performance of X's obligations but this has been rejected by the other party;
- if the other party has made it impossible for X to perform X's obligations.

[1] *Poussard v Spiers and Pond* (1876) 1 QBD 410.

8.8 Subject to a valid exemption clause to the contrary, whenever a party to the contract is in breach of contract, that party is legally liable to pay compensation (ie damages) to the other party (the 'injured party') for the loss sustained by the injured party in consequence of that breach but, unless the breach can be classified as a repudiatory breach and the injured party elects to terminate the contract, the contractual obligations of the parties so far as they have not been fully performed remain unchanged. The injured party may claim damages for breach either by bringing an action or by way of a counter-claim in an action brought against the injured party by the defaulting party, and even where no actual loss or damage to the injured party can be proved nominal damages (usually in the region of £2 to £20) will be awarded. Quite apart from damages, the injured party may be entitled, additionally or alternatively, to claim some other remedy, eg an order of specific performance of the contract or the recovery of an agreed sum. We consider the question of remedies in Chapter 11.

In the case of certain serious breaches of contract, commonly described as 'repudiatory breaches', the injured party can elect to treat the contract as repudiated by the other, accept the repudiation, and recover damages for breach, both parties being discharged from performance of their contractual obligations which would have been due thereafter. If the injured party does this, that party is said to terminate the contract for repudiatory breach.[1]

[1] Termination for repudiatory breach should not be confused with rescission for misrepresentation (discussed in ch 12), the effect of which (and the rules concerning which) are different.

Repudiatory breach

Option to terminate or affirm

8.9 A repudiatory breach does not automatically discharge the contract. Instead, the injured party has an option to terminate the contract or to affirm it.[1]

[1] *Heyman v Darwins Ltd* [1942] 1 All ER 337 at 340.

Termination

8.10 The injured party (X) will terminate the contract if X indicates to the defaulting party that X regards himself (or herself) as discharged by the repudiatory breach. No particular form of indication is required. It is sufficient that by words or conduct it is clearly and unequivocally conveyed to the repudiating party that X is treating the contract as at an end.[1] Thus, the contract will be terminated if X refuses to accept defective performance, or refuses to accept further performance, or simply refuses to perform X's own contractual obligations. Moreover, termination can be inferred if X simply does something incompatible with X's own continued performance of the contract, or simply fails to perform X's side of the contract, provided that this unequivocally points to the fact that X is treating the contract as at an end.[2] Suppose, for example, that an employer (Y) at the end of a day tells a contractor that Y is renouncing the contract and that the contractor need not return the next day. This would constitute a repudiatory breach of contract by Y.[3] The contractor does not return the next day or at all. The contractor's failure to return may, in the absence of any other explanation, convey a decision to terminate the contract.[4] X need not personally, or by an agent, notify the defaulting party of the election to terminate. It is sufficient that the election comes to the defaulting party's attention. For example, notification by an unauthorised intermediary can suffice.[5]

[1] *Vitol SA v Norelf Ltd* [1996] 3 All ER 193, HL.
[2] *Vitol SA v Norelf Ltd* [1996] 3 All ER 193, HL.
[3] Para 8.18.
[4] *Vitol SA v Norelf Ltd* [1996] 3 All ER 193, HL at 200.
[5] *Vitol SA v Norelf Ltd* [1996] 3 All ER 193, HL.

8.11 If the injured party elects to terminate the contract, the injured party is discharged for the future from obligations under the contract which would otherwise have been due or continuing thereafter. One result is that the injured party is not obliged to accept or pay for further performance. Another result is that an injured party who has terminated a contract for breach can resist successfully any action for failing thereafter to observe or perform a continuing obligation or an obligation due thereafter, even if the contract purports to make the obligation applicable after a repudiatory breach by the defaulting party.[1] Consequently, for example, if Fred, a wrongfully dismissed employee, has indicated that he regards himself as discharged by the repudiatory breach from his employment contract, Fred is no longer bound by terms in that contract restraining his future employment, even if his employment contract purports to make those terms applicable after a repudiatory breach by the employer.[2]

On the other hand, an injured party who has terminated is not generally discharged from obligations which are already due at the time of termination, since rights and obligations which arise from the partial execution of the contract—as well as causes of action which have accrued from its breach—continue unaffected.[3]

[1] *General Billposting Co Ltd v Atkinson* [1909] AC 118, HL.
[2] *Rock Refrigeration Ltd v Jones* [1997] 1 All ER 1, CA.
[3] *Hurst v Bryk* [2000] 2 All ER 193, HL.

8.12 An injured party who has terminated may be entitled to refuse to pay for partial or defective performance already received if complete and precise performance of the obligation broken by the defaulting party is a precondition of the right to be paid. However, if the injured party is in a position to return the partial or defective performance (eg faulty goods), and does not do so, the injured party must pay a reasonable sum or pro rata for the work done or goods supplied. It was held in *Sumpter v Hedges*[1] that, on the other hand, there is no such obligation where the injured party's acceptance of the partial or defective performance was not voluntary, ie the injured party had no choice. In that case C agreed to build two houses and a stable on D's land for a lump sum payable on completion. C did part of the work to the value of about three-fifths of the contract price but then abandoned the contract (a repudiatory breach) because of lack of money. It was held that C could not recover a reasonable sum for his work because D had no option but to accept the partial performance, viz the partly erected buildings.

[1] [1898] 1 QB 673.

8.13 In addition, an injured party who has terminated can recover back any money which the injured party has deposited or paid to the defaulting party under the contract if there has been a total failure of consideration on the part of the latter.[1]

There will be a total failure of consideration by the defaulting party if that party has not performed any part of that party's contractual duties in respect of which payment is due under the contract,[2] or if the injured party has not received any part of the benefit bargained for under the contract.[3] It has been held that these two definitions are not inconsistent with each other.[4]

Thus, if X pays Y £500 as a deposit on a car but Y fails to supply the car, X can terminate the contract and recover back the £500 which he paid.

If the failure of consideration is not total but only partial, money paid is not recoverable, so that, whether the contract is terminated or not, the appropriate remedy is an action for damages for breach of contract. Thus, if X employs Y to build a house and pays in advance, and Y starts the work but abandons it before it is finished, X cannot recover any part of that payment and must claim damages for breach of contract.[5] However, if:

- the partial performance is such as to entitle X to terminate the contract, and X elects to do so; and

- X is able to restore what he has received under the contract, and does so before he has received any benefit from it,[6]

X is said to bring about a total failure of consideration and is entitled to recover back any money paid.[7] A common example of this is where the buyer of defective goods rejects them immediately and claims back what he has paid for them.

If a contract consists of divisible parts and part of the consideration can be attributed to such a part, the injured party can recover the portion of money paid in respect of it, if there has been a total failure in respect of that part, albeit that there has not been a total failure of consideration in respect of other parts.[8]

[1] *Wilkinson v Lloyd* (1845) 7 QB 27.
[2] *Stocznia Gdanska SA v Latvian Shipping Co* [1998] 1 All ER 883, HL.
[3] *Rover International Ltd v Cannon Film Sales Ltd (No 3)* [1989] 3 All ER 423, CA.
[4] *Giedo Van Der Garde BV v Force India Formula One Team Ltd* [2010] EWHC 2373 (QB).
[5] *Whincup v Hughes* (1871) LR 6 CP 78.
[6] *Hunt v Silk* (1804) 5 East 449.
[7] *Baldry v Marshall* [1925] 1 KB 260, CA.
[8] *Giedo Van Der Garde BV v Force India Formula One Team Ltd* [2010] EWHC 2373 (QB).

8.14 After termination by the injured party, the position of the defaulting party (Y) is as follows:

- Y is not discharged from contractual obligations which are due at the time of the termination and have not been performed (so that, for instance, Y is still obliged to pay a sum of money then due[1]), and Y is also liable to pay damages to the injured party (X) for loss sustained by X in consequence of the breach of any such obligations;[2]

- Y's contractual obligations, so far as they are due or continuing after the termination, are discharged and there is substituted for them an obligation to pay damages to X for the loss sustained by X in consequence of their non-performance in the future.[2]

[1] *McDonald v Dennys Lascelles Ltd* (1933) 48 CLR 457 at 476–477; *Hyundai Heavy Industries Co Ltd v Papodopolous* [1980] 2 All ER 29, HL.
[2] *Moschi v LEP Air Services Ltd* [1972] 2 All ER 393, HL.

8.15 Termination for repudiatory breach does not necessarily extinguish the contract completely in relation to obligations whose performance is due thereafter, since an obligation will survive termination if on the proper interpretation of the contract the parties intended that it should.[1] Thus, for example, obligations relating to matters such as arbitration or jurisdiction may continue in existence if it was the intention of the parties, when they made the contract, that this should be so.[2] In addition, terms which validly 'liquidate' damages or which validly exclude or restrict liability remain in force.[3]

[1] *Duffen v FRA Bo SpA* [2000] 1 Lloyd's Rep 180 at 194–195.
[2] *Heyman v Darwins Ltd* [1942] 1 All ER 337, HL.

³ *Photo Production Ltd v Securicor Transport Ltd* [1980] 1 All ER 556, HL. For liquidated damages provisions, see para 11.30, and for exemption clauses: see ch 9. The proposition in the text has been given statutory force in relation to exemption clauses which must satisfy the requirement of reasonableness under the Unfair Contract Terms Act 1977 (see paras 9.9–9.20) by s 9 of that Act.

Affirmation

8.16 The injured party (X) will affirm the contract if, with full knowledge of the facts and of the right to terminate the contract,[1] X decides to treat it as still in existence, as where X decides to keep the defective goods delivered or, if the defaulting party has not completed performance, where X calls on the defaulting party to perform. X does not affirm a contract simply because X does not immediately terminate the contract but delays while considering whether or not to terminate it.[2]

[1] *Peyman v Lanjani* [1984] 3 All ER 703, CA.
[2] *Bliss v South East Thames Regional Health Authority* [1987] ICR 700, CA.

8.17 If the injured party elects to affirm, the contract remains in force, so that both parties are bound to continue performing any outstanding contractual obligations. Each party retains the right to sue for past or future breaches. Thus, if a seller of goods affirms the contract after a repudiatory breach by the buyer, the seller remains liable to deliver possession of the goods to the buyer and the buyer remains liable to accept delivery of the goods and pay the contract price. Another example is provided by *Bentsen v Taylor, Sons & Co (No 2)*,[1] where a charterparty described the ship as 'now sailed or about to sail' from a port to the United Kingdom. In fact, she did not sail for another month. This constituted a repudiatory breach of contract by the shipowner[2] but, instead of electing to terminate the contract, the charterers intimated to the shipowner that he was still bound to send the ship to the port of loading and that they, the charterers, would load her there, thereby affirming the contract. When the ship arrived, the charterers refused to load her. The Court of Appeal held that, since the contract had been affirmed, the shipowner was entitled to his contractual payment, subject to a set-off for the charterers for damages for the shipowner's breach of contract referred to above.

[1] [1893] 2 QB 274, CA.
[2] Because the term broken was a condition: see paras 8.21 and 8.22.

Types of repudiatory breach

Renunciation

8.18 Where one party renounces contractual obligations the other party is entitled to terminate the contract. A party is said to renounce contractual obligations if he (or she) has indicated an unconditional intention not to perform them or otherwise no longer to be bound by the contract or one of its essential terms.[1] Such an intention is easily established where there has been an express and unequivocal refusal to perform. Thus, if Fred, an employee, unqualifiedly refuses to carry out his contractual duties (or to carry out a duty which is an essential contractual term), his employer is entitled to dismiss him (ie terminate the contract of employment).[2] However, express refusal is not necessary; an intent no longer to be bound by the contract (or one of its essential terms) can also be implied by the words or conduct of a party. The actual intention of the party is not the crucial issue in such a case; the test is whether the party's words and conduct were such as to lead a reasonable person to believe that the party did not intend to be bound by the contract.[3]

[1] *Mersey Steel and Iron Co v Naylor Benzon and Co* (1884) 9 App Cas 434, HL.
[2] *Gorse v Durham County Council* [1971] 2 All ER 666.
[3] *Woodar Investment Development Ltd v Wimpey Construction UK Ltd* [1980] 1 All ER 571, HL.

Incapacitation

8.19 Even though a party has not demonstrated an intention not to be bound by the contract, a party who, *by that party's own act or default*, incapacitates himself (or herself) from performing contractual obligations is treated as if he (or she) had refused to perform them.[1] As Devlin J said in *Universal Cargo Carriers Corpn v Citati*,[2] 'To say "I would like to but cannot" negatives intent to perform as much as "I will not"'. An example of incapacitation is where Y has contracted to sell a specific thing to X but then sells it to T.

[1] *Torvald Klaveness A/S v Arni Maritime Corpn, The Gregos* [1994] 4 All ER 998, HL.
[2] [1957] 2 All ER 70.

Defective performance

8.20 Leaving aside termination for renunciation or incapacitation, an injured party can only terminate for failure to perform an obligation in two cases:

- where it involves breach of a term of the contract which is a condition;
- where it involves breach of an 'intermediate term' and the effect of the breach deprives the injured party of substantially the whole of the injured party's intended benefit under the contract.

8.21 *Breach of condition* Some contractual terms can be classified as conditions, others as intermediate terms, and others as warranties.

A condition is an essential term of the contract,[1] or, as it is sometimes put, one which goes to the root of the contract. If it is broken, the injured party may terminate the contract for breach of condition, as well as claiming damages, whether the effect of the breach is serious or trivial. In this context the word 'condition' does not bear its orthodox meaning, discussed in paras 5.36 and 5.37, of an event by which an obligation is suspended or cancelled but is used to describe a particular type of contractual term. It is certainly an odd word to use for this purpose.

An intermediate term is one whose breach may entitle the injured party to terminate the contract, depending on how serious the effect of the breach is. We explain this further in para 8.24.

A warranty is a contractual term concerning a less important or subsidiary statement of fact or promise.[2] If a warranty is broken this does not entitle the other party to terminate the contract. It simply entitles the other party to sue for damages or make a set-off and the party in breach is entitled to the contractual price less the damages or set-off.[3]

[1] *Heyworth v Hutchinson* (1867) LR 2 QB 447 at 451.
[2] *Oscar Chess Ltd v Williams* [1957] 1 All ER 325 at 328; Sale of Goods Act 1979, s 11(3).
[3] *Gilbert Ash (Northern) Ltd v Modern Engineering (Bristol) Ltd* [1973] 3 All ER 195, HL.

8.22 The classification of a term as a condition depends on the following considerations:

- Sometimes statute provides that particular terms are conditions, eg the implied conditions in sale of goods contracts, hire purchase contracts, contracts analogous to contracts for the sale of goods and hire contracts under the Sale of Goods Act 1979, ss 12 to 15, the Supply of Goods (Implied Terms) Act 1973, ss 8 to 11 and the Supply of Goods and Services Act 1982, ss 2 to 5 and 7 to 10 respectively.[1]

- In other cases, a term which has been classified as a condition in judicial decisions will be so classified thereafter, subject to the rules of judicial precedent.[2] An example is a stipulation as to time (other than the time for payment) in a commercial contract.[3]

- In the absence of classification by statute or case authority, a court has to decide whether the broken term is a condition by ascertaining the intention of the parties as at the time the contract was made.[3] The parties' intentions are particularly important and it is open to them to agree that what is a condition according to a previous judicial decision shall not be so treated in their contract, and vice versa. Because of the drastic consequences, the courts lean against construing a term as a condition: in fact, they are increasingly reluctant so to construe a term unless compelled by clear evidence of the parties' intentions.[4]

The approach of the courts is as follows:

- First, the court must seek to ascertain the intention of the parties as expressed in the contract. If, on its proper interpretation, the wording clearly reveals that the parties intended that any breach of the term should give rise to a right to terminate, that term will be regarded as a condition. But if the parties clearly did not so intend, the term will not be regarded as a condition even though it is described as a 'condition' in the contract. This is shown by *Schuler AG v Wickman Machine Tool Sales Ltd*.[5] A four-year distributorship agreement provided that the distributor should visit six named customers every week. The agreement described this provision as a 'condition'. The House of Lords held that the contract could not be terminated simply because of breach of this 'condition'. Its reasoning was that the parties could not have intended a mere failure to make one visit to result in a right to terminate. It thought that more probably 'condition' had been used simply to mean 'term'.

- If the wording of the contract, as interpreted by the court, does not conclude the matter, the court must ascertain the parties' intentions by inference from the nature, purpose and circumstances of the contract. If, in the context of the whole contract, it is clear that the term was so important that an injured party would always want to be entitled to terminate if it was broken it will be regarded as a condition. An example is *Behn v Burness*,[6] where one term of a charterparty was that the ship was 'now in the port of Amsterdam': the ship was not then there. The statement was held to be a condition because of the commercial importance attached to such a statement. On the other hand, a term in a charterparty that a ship is seaworthy has not been construed as a condition because it can be broken in a number of ways, in some of which the parties would clearly not intend that the charterer should be entitled to terminate.[7] As this decision indicates, if a term can be broken in a variety of ways it is unlikely that it will be inferred that the parties intended that the injured party should always be entitled to terminate the contract for breach of that term, since where a variety of breaches occur it is likely that some of them may not be serious. This can be compared with the situation where the term can only be broken in one way and that breach will always be serious.

---

[1] Paras 7.25 and 7.26.
[2] *Maredelante Cia Naviera SA v Bergbau-Handel GmbH, The Mihalis Angelos* [1970] 3 All ER 125, CA.
[3] *Bunge Corpn v Tradax SA* [1981] 2 All ER 513, HL.
[4] *Bunge Corpn v Tradax SA* [1981] 2 All ER 513 at 542, 551.
[5] [1973] 2 All ER 39, HL.
[6] (1863) 3 B & S 751.
[7] *Hong Kong Fir Shipping Co Ltd v Kawasaki Kisen Kaisha Ltd* [1962] 1 All ER 474, CA.

8.23 In the case of a contract for the sale or supply of goods, the right to terminate for breach of condition is subject to the Sale of Goods Act 1979, s 15A, which provides that, where in the case of a contract of sale:

- the buyer would otherwise have the right to reject goods (ie terminate the contract) by reason of a breach by the seller of one of the terms implied by ss 12 to 15 of the Act; but

- the seller proves that the breach is so slight that it would be unreasonable for him to do so,

then, if the buyer does not deal as consumer,[1] the breach is not to be treated as a breach of condition but only as a breach of warranty (with the result that there is no right to reject the goods).

Similar provision is made by the Supply of Goods (Implied Terms) Act 1973, s 11A, and the Supply of Goods and Services Act 1982, ss 5A and 10A, in relation to hire purchase contracts, contracts analogous to contracts for the sale of goods and contracts of hire, respectively.

[1] 'Dealing as consumer' has the same meaning as in the Unfair Contract Terms Act 1977 (see para 9.18): Sale of Goods Act 1979, s 61(5A).

8.24 *Breach of an intermediate term* If the term broken is not a condition, it must not be assumed that it is a warranty for which the only remedy is damages, unless statute or a judicial decision compels such a classification.[1] Instead, the contract must be construed and, unless the contract makes it clear (either by express provision or by necessary implication from its nature, purpose and circumstances) that the parties intended that no breach of the term should entitle the injured party to terminate the contract, the term will be classified as an intermediate (or innominate) term and not as a warranty.

If the term is so classified one must then ask whether the nature and effect of its breach is such as to deprive the injured party of substantially the whole benefit which it was intended that the injured party should obtain under the contract.[2] If it is, the injured party is entitled to terminate the contract, as well as claiming damages. In applying this test, account must be taken not only of the actual consequences of the breach but also of those whose occurrence is reasonably foreseeable.[3] There is high judicial authority in a number of cases that the present doctrine, whereby termination for breach of a term depends on the effects of the breach, is preferable to making termination dependent on whether the term itself is classified as a condition or a warranty, since it is far more likely to ensure that termination is possible when it is appropriate.[4]

A leading authority for the present doctrine is *Hong Kong Fir Shipping Co Ltd v Kawasaki Kisen Kaisha Ltd*.[5] C chartered a ship to D for 24 months. The ship was old and needed to be maintained by an adequate and competent engine room crew but C did not provide such a crew and thereby were in breach of a term of the charterparty to provide a ship 'in every way fitted for ordinary cargo service' (otherwise called a 'seaworthiness clause'). Because of the incompetence and inadequacy of the engine room crew and the age of the engines, the ship was held up for repairs for five weeks on her first voyage, and when she reached her destination it was found that further repairs, which would take 15 weeks, were necessary to make her seaworthy. D purported to terminate the charterparty and C sued for breach of contract on the ground that termination was wrongful. D pleaded that the seaworthiness clause was a condition of the contract, and that therefore D could terminate the contract for breach of it. Having held that the clause was not a condition for the reason set out towards the end of para 8.22, the Court of Appeal held that the effect of C's breach of the clause was not sufficiently serious to justify D in terminating the charterparty. One reason which it particularly relied on was the fact that after the repairs the ship was still available for 17 of the original 24 months. D's termination had therefore been wrongful.

The same decision was reached in *The Hansa Nord*.[6] A contract for the sale of citrus pulp pellets included a term that shipment was to be made in good condition. On delivery at Rotterdam, the buyers (B) rejected the whole consignment (ie terminated the contract) and the goods were sold by the order of a Dutch court to a third person. Subsequently, they were re-sold at one-third the original contract price to B who then used the whole consignment for a purpose (cattle food) similar to that for which they had originally bought it (animal feed)—though at a lower rate of inclusion in the case of the damaged pellets. The Court of Appeal held that the 'shipment in good condition' term was not a condition of the contract because it could not have been intended that any breach of it should entitle B to terminate the contract.[7] The Court then turned to the present doctrine and held that B were not entitled to terminate under it because, particularly in the light of the subsequent events, the effect of the breach was not sufficiently serious to justify termination. Thus, B were only entitled to damages and could not treat themselves as discharged from their obligation to accept the pellets and pay the contract price.

[1] *Hong Kong Fir Shipping Co Ltd v Kawasaki Kisen Kaisha Ltd* [1962] 2 QB 26 at 63–64; *Reardon Smith Line Ltd v Hansen-Tangen* [1976] 3 All ER 570 at 573–573.
[2] *Hong Kong Fir Shipping Co Ltd v Kawasaki Kisen Kaisha Ltd* [1962] 2 QB 26 at 70.
[3] *Hong Kong Fir Shipping Co Ltd v Kawasaki Kisen Kaisha Ltd* [1962] 2 QB 26 at 64.
[4] Eg *Reardon Smith Line Ltd v Hansen-Tangen* [1976] 3 All ER 570 at 577.
[5] [1962] 1 All ER 474, CA.
[6] *Cehave NV v Bremer Handelsgesellschaft mbH, The Hansa Nord* [1975] 3 All ER 739, CA.
[7] The Court also held that there was no breach of the implied condition as to quality under the Sale of Goods Act 1979, s 14(2); see para 7.25.

8.25 *Hong Kong Fir Shipping* and *The Hansa Nord* can be contrasted with *Aerial Advertising Co v Batchelors Peas Ltd (Manchester)*.[1] C agreed to conduct an aerial advertising campaign for D. One term of the contract was that the pilot of the aeroplane should telephone D each day and obtain their approval for what he proposed to do. On Armistice Day 1937, the pilot, in breach of this term, failed to contact D and flew over Salford during the two minutes' silence. The aeroplane was towing a banner saying 'Eat Batchelors Peas'. Of course, the term broken was not a condition since breach of it might well only have had trivial consequences, so that the parties could not have intended that its breach should always entitle D to terminate the contract. However, the effect of the particular breach was disastrous since it aroused public hostility towards D and their products. It was held that D were entitled to terminate the contract.

[1] [1938] 2 All ER 788.

Anticipatory breach

8.26 So far we have been concerned with actual breaches of contract, ie breaches of contractual obligations whose performance is due at the time of the breach. An anticipatory breach of contract occurs where a party renounces[1] his (or her) contractual obligations, or incapacitates himself (or herself)[2] from performing them, *before the time fixed for their performance*. If a party commits such an anticipatory breach, the injured party can accept the breach as discharging the contract (ie terminate it) and immediately bring an action for damages for breach of contract; the injured party does not have to wait for the time of performance to become due. An example is provided by *Lovelock v Franklyn*,[3] where D agreed to assign his interest in a lease to C for £140. Before the agreed date of performance arrived, D assigned his interest to another person. It was held that C could bring an action for damages immediately: he did not have to wait for the time of performance to arrive.

If the injured party validly terminates the contract for anticipatory breach, the other party is not permitted to change his (or her) mind and seek to perform his (or her) contractual obligations,[4] but the other party may do so at any time *before* there is a valid termination by the injured party.[5]

[1] Para 8.18.
[2] Para 8.19.
[3] (1846) 8 QB 371.
[4] *Xenos v Danube and Black Sea Rly Co* (1863) 13 CBNS 825.
[5] *Norwest Holst Group Administration Ltd v Harrison* [1985] ICR 668, CA.

8.27 As in the other situations where a party can terminate a contract for the other's failure to perform, a contract is never automatically discharged by anticipatory breach; instead, the injured party has an election to terminate or affirm the contract. If the injured party refuses to accept the anticipatory breach as discharging the contract and continues to insist on performance, the injured party will affirm it. When a contract is affirmed after anticipatory breach the effects are as follows:

- the injured party loses the right to bring an action for damages for anticipatory breach;

- the contract remains in force. Each party remains liable to perform his (or her) obligations when they become due and will be liable for failure to perform them then. Thus, the party who committed the anticipatory breach is given an opportunity to perform his (or her) obligations, and will be liable only if there is a failure to do so. The contract remains in existence at the risk of both parties; consequently, if the party who has affirmed after anticipatory breach subsequently commits a breach of contract that party will be liable,[1] and either party can take advantage of any supervening circumstance which would justify non-performance;[2]

- as opposed to the case where the injured party immediately sues for damages for anticipatory breach, a party who affirms is under no duty to mitigate his (or her) loss before performance is due.[3] This may result in the recovery of larger damages in the event of ultimate non-performance by the other.

[1] *Fercometal SARL v Mediterranean Shipping Co SA, The Simona* [1988] 2 All ER 742, HL.
[2] *Avery v Bowden* (1855) 5 E & B 714.
[3] *Tredegar Iron and Coal Co Ltd v Hawthorn Bros & Co* (1902) 18 TLR 716, CA

B*REACH*: K*EY* P*OINTS*

- A breach of contract occurs where a party without lawful excuse:
  - refuses to perform one or more contractual obligations or simply fails to perform them;
  - incapacitates himself (or herself) from performing them; or
  - performs them defectively.

- Subject to a valid exemption clause to the contrary, a party in breach of contract is liable to pay damages to the other party.

- If a breach of contract is a repudiatory breach, the injured party, in addition to claiming damages, can elect to terminate or affirm the contract. If the injured party elects to

> terminate, both parties are discharged from performance of their obligations under the contract which would have been due thereafter; in addition, the injured party may have other rights additional to the recovery of damages depending on the facts.
>
> - There are the following types of repudiatory breach:
>   - renunciation;
>   - incapacitation;
>   - breach of condition; and
>   - breach of an intermediate term, if the effect of the breach is to deprive the injured party of substantially the whole benefit which it was intended that the injured party should obtain under the contract.
> - Renunciation or incapacitation may relate to a contractual obligation not yet due for performance. This type of repudiatory breach is known as an anticipatory breach.

Time of performance

8.28 When a contract does not stipulate a time within which a party's contractual obligations must be performed, they must be performed within a reasonable time.[1]

[1] *Postlethwaite v Freeland* (1880) 5 App Cas 599, HL. The Sale of Goods Act 1979, s 29(3) gives this rule statutory effect in relation to a seller's obligation to send goods to a buyer. The Supply of Goods and Services Act 1982, s 14, has the like effect in relation to the provision of services by a supplier acting in the course of a business: see para 7.27.

8.29 Whether a time is stipulated for performance of a party's obligations by the contract or whether it is implied that they must be performed within a reasonable time, the question arises whether time is 'of the essence of the contract'. If it is, the stipulation or implied obligation as to time will be classified as a condition[1] and a party's failure to perform in that time will not only constitute a breach of contract entitling the other party to maintain an action for damages but also a repudiatory breach of the contract, which the other party can accept as discharging the other party from that party's contractual obligations (termination of the contract).[2] The rule is a strict one; it applies even though the party in default tenders performance shortly after a stipulated time for performance. This was re-affirmed by the Privy Council in *Union Eagle Ltd v Golden Achievement Ltd*,[3] where a purchaser of a flat was required to complete by 5 pm on a specified day, time being of the essence. The purchaser failed to complete by that time. The purchaser's vendor declared that the contract was terminated and the purchaser's deposit forfeited. Ten minutes after the time for completion, the purchaser tendered the purchase price. The Privy Council refused to intervene by ordering the specific performance of the contract of sale on the ground that it had no power to do so.

[1] This point was made by the majority of the Court of Appeal in *Bunge Corpn v Tradax SA* [1981] 2 All ER 513 and is implicit in the leading speeches in the House of Lords in that case: [1981] 2 All ER 513. With regard to conditions, see para 8.21.
[2] See, in particular, *Bunge Corpn v Tradax SA* [1981] 2 All ER 513, HL. See also paras 8.9–8.15.
[3] [1997] 2 All ER 215, PC.

8.30 Whether time is of the essence of a contract, other than a contract which is specifically enforceable (see para 8.31), depends on the parties' intentions when the contract is made. If they are not expressed in the contract, they must be inferred from the nature of the subject matter of the contract and of the obligation which has not been performed in time. In this context certain presumptions have been established. For instance, a stipulation as to time in a contract granting an *option* to purchase land is presumptively of the essence.[1] Likewise, a stipulation as to time in a commercial contract is presumptively of the essence of the contract.[2] However, the Sale of Goods Act 1979, s 10 provides that a term *as to the time of payment for goods* is deemed not to be of the essence of the contract, unless the contrary intention appears from the contract.

[1] *Di Luca v Juraise (Springs) Ltd* [1998] 2 EGLR 125, CA.
[2] *Bunge Corpn v Tradax SA* [1981] 2 All ER 513, HL.

8.31 Before the Judicature Act 1873, common law and equity had different rules about when the time for performance was of the essence in a contract which was specifically enforceable,[1] such as a contract for the sale[2] of an interest in land or for the sale of a unique chattel, but since that Act the equitable rules prevail.[3] The result is that time is not of the essence in such a contract unless it falls within one of the following three categories where equity treated it as of the essence:

- where the contract expressly states that obligations as to time must be strictly complied with. In *Harold Wood Brick Co Ltd v Ferris*[4] for instance, a stipulation that the purchase of a brickfield should be completed by 31 August which added that 'the purchase shall in any event be completed not later than 15 September' was held to make time (15 September) of the essence of the contract;

- where the contract does not expressly make time of the essence of the contract, but the stipulated or impliedly required time has passed by, the party who has been subjected to delay can make time of the essence by invoking a period of notice for performance (eg completion in the case of a contract for the sale of land) if one is specified in the contract or, if one is not specified, by giving a notice fixing a reasonable time for performance;[5]

- where the subject matter of the contract, or the circumstances surrounding it, makes punctual compliance with an obligation as to time imperative, time must be taken to be of the essence of the contract. For example, under this heading time has been held to be of the essence of a contract for the sale of business premises as a going concern.[6]

Even if time is not of the essence of a contract for the sale of an interest in land or of some other specifically enforceable contract, a party who fails to complete within the required time is, of course, in breach of that term and liable in damages, provided that the failure was not due to some conveyancing difficulty or some difficulty with regard to title.[7] Inability to raise the necessary finance is no defence.[8]

[1] Paras 11.43–11.45.
[2] As opposed to a contract granting an option to purchase: para 8.30.
[3] Law of Property Act 1925, s 41.
[4] [1935] 2 KB 198, CA.
[5] *Stickney v Keeble* [1915] AC 386, HL.
[6] *Lock v Bell* [1931] 1 Ch 35.
[7] *Raineri v Miles* [1980] 2 All ER 145, HL.
[8] *Raineri v Miles* [1980] 2 All ER 145, HL.

TIME OF PERFORMANCE: KEY POINTS

- If a party fails to perform his (or her) contractual obligations within the time stipulated in the contract or (if no time is stipulated) within a reasonable time, the other party is entitled not only to recover damages for breach of contract but also to terminate the contract for breach of condition if time is of the essence of the contract.
- Whether, in the case of a contract which is not specifically enforceable, time is of the essence depends on the parties' intentions. In a contract which is specifically enforceable, time is not of the essence unless the contract falls within one of three categories.

Questions

1. What is required for a party's contractual obligations to be discharged by performance?

2. What is meant by tender of performance, and what are its effects?

3. What is required for there to be:
   - a 'mere' breach of contract;
   - a repudiatory breach of contract?

4. What are the consequences of a repudiatory breach?

5. Describe the types of repudiatory breach.

6. Two years ago, Arnold made a five-year contract with Kleenkleen Ltd for that company to clean the five offices in Arnold's chain of estate agents. The contract contains 30 terms, all of which appear under the heading 'Conditions' in the contractual document. One of these terms is that 'Kleenkleen shall use cleaning products manufactured by Megasuds plc unless an alternative product has been approved by Arnold'. Two weeks ago Kleenkleen used a floor cleaning agent manufactured by Strongsuds Ltd without seeking Arnold's approval. The product was a more expensive and effective one than the equivalent produced by Megasuds but, because of its special nature, the floor in one room in one of Arnold's offices was unexpectedly ruined and will have to be replaced. Advise Arnold, who has lost faith in Kleenkleen and does not want to continue with Kleenkleen's services.

7. When is time of the essence in a contract for the sale of land? What are the consequences if time is of the essence?

9

Exemption clauses and unfair terms in consumer contracts

CHAPTER OVERVIEW

A contract may contain an exemption clause. An exemption clause may:

- purport to exclude or restrict one of the parties' liability for breach of contract, or some other liability, such as for misrepresentation or for the tort of negligence, or both; or

- purport to exclude or modify the obligations of a party which would normally be implied by law from the legal nature of the contract.

Uncontrolled, exemption clauses could operate very unfairly in the case of standard form contracts, where one party has no real option but to accept the terms offered by the other.

Standard form contracts may also contain other types of term which, uncontrolled, could operate to the prejudice of a consumer.

In this chapter we consider:

- the requirement that a person who wishes to rely on an exemption clause must prove that, as a matter of interpretation, it covers the liability in question;

- two limitations on the operation of exemption clauses, which have been introduced by the courts;

- various limitations under the Unfair Contract Terms Act 1977 on the validity of exemption clauses; and

- the limitations which apply to exemption clauses and other standard terms in consumer contracts in general under the Unfair Terms in Consumer Contracts Regulations 1999.

Interpretation of exemption clauses

9.1 If an exemption clause is a term[1] of the contract it must be determined whether it applies to the liability in question.

There is no rule of law that an exemption clause is eliminated, or deprived of effect, regardless of its terms by a breach of contract, however fundamental that breach may be. The question whether, and to what extent, an exemption clause applies to the liability in question is answered by interpreting the contract to see whether the parties intended that the clause should apply to the loss or damage which has occurred in the circumstances in which it has occurred. This was stated by the House of Lords in *Photo Production Ltd v Securicor Transport Ltd*.[2]

In the *Photo Production* case, the claimant company (C) employed the defendant company (D) to check against burglaries and fires at their factory at night. One night, D's patrolman deliberately started a fire in the factory. It got out of control and a large part of the premises was burnt down. The loss and damage suffered amounted to £615,000. By way of defence to C's action to recover this amount as damages, D relied principally on an exemption clause in their contract with C which purported to exempt D from liability for any injurious act by an employee unless it could have been foreseen and avoided by due diligence on D's part. The clause added that D was not to be liable for any loss suffered by C through fire, except in so far as such loss was solely attributable to the negligence of D's employees acting within the scope of their employment. The House of Lords held that, although D would otherwise have been liable to C, on its true interpretation the exemption clause clearly and unambiguously applied to what had occurred, and protected D from liability.[3]

[1] See paras 7.8–7.13.

[2] [1980] 1 All ER 556, HL.

[3] The contract in this case was a standard form contract, but, since it was entered into before the Unfair Contract Terms Act 1977, the House of Lords was not concerned with the validity of the exemption clause under that Act.

9.2 In case it should be thought that the rule that the application of an exemption clause depends on the interpretation of the contract is liable to cause injustice in consumer contracts and other contracts based on standard terms, we would point out that exemption clauses in such a contract made nowadays are rendered either totally invalid or invalid unless fair and reasonable by legislation, as we explain later in this chapter, even though on their true interpretation they were intended to apply to what has occurred. It follows that the interpretation of an exemption clause is now generally of crucial importance only where the contract has been negotiated between businesses capable of looking after their own interests and of deciding how the risks inherent in the performance of the contract can most economically be borne, which is usually by one or other party insuring against such risks.

9.3 We set out below certain rules of interpretation which are applied to exemption clauses by the courts and which tend to favour the party affected by such a clause.

Liability can only be excluded or restricted by clear words

9.4 The liability in question must be precisely covered by the exemption clause relied on. In *Andrews Bros (Bournemouth) Ltd v Singer & Co Ltd*,[1] C entered into a contract to buy 'new Singer cars' from D. One of the cars delivered by D was not a new car, having run a considerable mileage. A clause in the contract exempted D from liability for breach of all 'conditions, warranties and liabilities *implied* by common law, statute or otherwise' but the Court of Appeal held that this did not protect D against liability for breach of an express term. A similar decision was reached in *Wallis, Son and Wells v Pratt and Haynes*.[2] D sold by sample to C seed described as 'common English sainfoin'. The contract stated that D gave 'no *warranty* express or implied' as to any matter concerning the seed. The seed turned out to be the inferior and cheaper 'giant sainfoin'. The House of Lords held that the exemption clause did not apply because there had been a breach of the *condition* implied by the Sale of Goods Act 1979, s 13 (that goods sold by description correspond with it) and the clause did not purport to exclude liability for breach of condition.

This rule of interpretation is applied more rigorously in the case of clauses purporting to exclude liability than in the case of those purporting to restrict it.[3]

¹ [1934] 1 KB 17, CA.

² [1911] AC 394, HL.

³ *Ailsa Craig Fishing Co Ltd v Malvern Fishing Co Ltd* [1983] 1 All ER 101, HL.

All ambiguities in the exemption clause are interpreted against the party relying on it

9.5 This is in accordance with the rule normally applied by the courts in the interpretation of contracts.¹ In relation to consumer contracts, the Unfair Terms in Consumer Contracts Regulations 1999, reg 7(2) gives this rule legislative force.²

¹ *Houghton v Trafalgar Insurance Co* [1953] 2 All ER 1409, CA.

² See para 9.30.

Exclusion or limitation of liability for negligence

9.6 The nature of liability for a breach of contract depends on the term broken. In the case of most terms, liability for their breach is strict (ie a party who does not comply with the term is liable despite the absence of any negligence); in the case of others, liability for their breach only arises if the party in question has been negligent (ie has failed to show reasonable care). This distinction depends upon whether the term broken simply imposes an obligation that something be done or that something be of a certain standard, or whether it imposes an obligation *to take reasonable care* (or the like) in relation to something. It should also be borne in mind that, where contractual liability for the breach in question is strict, the guilty party may also be liable in tort if proved to have been negligent.

If an exemption clause clearly purports to exclude or restrict *all* liability, effect must be given to it¹ (subject to the general rules as to the validity of exemption clauses), but if the clause is not so clearly drafted the law is as follows.

Where the liability for breach of contract in question to which the clause is sought to be applied is strict, the clause is normally interpreted as being confined to that contractual liability, and not as extending to any tortious liability for negligence, with the result that the guilty party is not protected by it if proved to have been negligent.² A leading example is *White v John Warrick & Co Ltd*.³ C hired a tricycle from D. While he was riding it the saddle tilted forward and he was injured. The contract of hire stated: 'nothing in this agreement shall render the owners liable for any personal injury'. The Court of Appeal held that the exemption clause would not protect D from liability in tort if they were found to have been negligent. Its reason was that, in the absence of the exemption clause, D could have been liable for breach of contract in supplying a defective tricycle⁴ irrespective of negligence and the operation of the clause had to be restricted to that strict liability.

Where liability can be based on negligence and nothing else, the exemption clause will normally be interpreted as extending to that head of damage, because if it were not so interpreted it would lack subject matter.⁵ This is shown by *Alderslade v Hendon Laundry Ltd*.⁶ D contracted to launder C's handkerchiefs, the contract limiting D's liability 'for lost or damaged articles' to 20 times the laundering charge. The handkerchiefs were lost through D's negligence. The Court of Appeal held that the only way in which D could be made liable for the loss of the handkerchiefs would be if D could be shown to have been guilty of negligence. It held that the exemption clause applied to limit D's liability for negligence because otherwise the clause would be left without any content at all.

Both these rules are only rules of interpretation and, although they will normally be adopted, the court is free to interpret the clause in another way if, on its wording or other evidence, the court considers that the parties had some other intention.⁷

[1] *Joseph Travers & Sons Ltd v Cooper* [1915] 1 KB 73, CA.
[2] *Alderslade v Hendon Laundry Ltd* [1945] KB 189, CA.
[3] [1953] 2 All ER 1021, CA.
[4] The term broken would have been an implied term that the tricycle was reasonably fit for the purpose
for which it was hired: paras 7.25 and 7.26.
[5] *Alderslade v Hendon Laundry Ltd* [1945] KB 189 at 192; *Hollier v Rambler Motors (AMC) Ltd* [1972] 1
All ER 399, CA.
[6] [1945] 1 All ER 244, CA.
[7] *Hollier v Rambler Motors (AMC) Ltd* [1972] 1 All ER 399, CA.

INTERPRETATION OF EXEMPTION CLAUSES: KEY POINTS

Whether, and to what extent, an exemption clause applies to the liability in question is always answered by interpreting the contract to see whether the parties intended that it should apply to the loss or damage which has occurred in the circumstances in which it has occurred. The following rules of interpretation apply:

- liability can only be excluded or restricted by clear words;

- ambiguities are interpreted against the party relying on the clause;

- unless the clause clearly purports to exclude or limit all liability, it will be interpreted as applying to liability for negligence if the only liability is for negligence, but if there are two bases for liability—one strict and the other based on negligence—the clause will normally be interpreted as limited to the strict liability.

General limitations on the application of an exemption clause

Misrepresentation

9.7 If the party favoured by an exemption clause induced the other party to accept it by misrepresenting its contents or effect, the clause is rendered ineffective to the extent that it is wider than the misrepresentation, even though the contract was signed by the other party and even though the misrepresentation was innocent. In *Curtis v Chemical Cleaning and Dyeing Co Ltd*,[1] C took a dress to D's shop for cleaning. The dress was trimmed with beads and sequins. C was asked to sign a receipt exempting D from all liability for any damage to articles cleaned. C asked why her signature was required and was told that the receipt exempted D from liability for damage to the sequins and beads. When the dress was returned it was badly stained. It was held that D were not protected by the clause because through their employee D had innocently induced C to believe that the clause only referred to damage to the beads and sequins and therefore the clause only protected D against liability for such damage.

[1] [1951] 1 All ER 631, CA.

Inconsistent undertakings

9.8 If, at or before the time the contract was made, the party favoured by an exemption clause gives an undertaking which is inconsistent with it, the exemption clause is rendered ineffective to the extent that it is inconsistent with the undertaking, even though the undertaking does not form part of the contract or of a contract collateral to it. In *Mendelssohn v Normand Ltd*,[1] C left his car in D's garage on terms contained in a ticket, one of which was that D would not accept any responsibility for any loss sustained by the vehicle or its contents, however caused. The car contained valuables and C wanted to lock it, but the attendant told C that this was not permissible. C told the attendant about the valuables and the attendant promised to lock the car after he had moved it. On his return, C discovered that the valuables had been stolen. The Court of Appeal held that D were not protected by the exemption clause because D's attendant had in effect promised to see that the valuables were safe, and this oral undertaking took priority over the exemption clause.

[1] [1969] 2 All ER 1215, CA.

GENERAL LIMITATIONS ON THE APPLICATION OF AN EXEMPTION CLAUSE: KEY POINTS

Where the party favoured by an exemption clause:

- induced the other to accept it by misrepresenting its contents or effect;

- gave an undertaking inconsistent with the clause,

the clause is rendered ineffective to the extent of the misrepresentation or inconsistency.

Unfair Contract Terms Act 1977

9.9 The Unfair Contract Terms Act 1977 (UCTA 1977) contains a number of provisions greatly limiting the extent to which it is possible to 'exclude or restrict liability' for negligence or breach of contract.[1] Generally these provisions only apply to clauses seeking to exclude or restrict 'business liability', which is defined as liability (whether in tort or for breach of contract) which arises *from things done or to be done in the course of a business or from the occupation of premises used for business purposes of the occupier.*[2] In UCTA 1977, '*business*' includes a profession and the activities of any government department or public or local authority.[3] The meaning of the phrase 'in the course of a business' in UCTA 1977 is discussed in para 9.13. The main impact of the 'business liability limitation' on the effect of the Act is that its provisions do not generally apply to exemption clauses in contracts made between private individuals. The exceptions are indicated at the appropriate point below.

It must be noted that UCTA 1977 is inappropriately named; it is not concerned with unfair contract terms in general but only with terms which are exemption clauses.

[1] The Misrepresentation Act 1967, s 3 contains provisions limiting the extent to which it is possible to exclude or restrict liability for misrepresentation: see ch 12.

[2] UCTA 1977, s 1(3). The liability of an occupier of premises for breach of an obligation or duty towards a person obtaining access to them for recreational or educational purposes, being liability based on the dangerous state of the premises, is not a business liability of the occupier unless granting that person such access for the purposes concerned falls within the business purposes of the occupier: ibid. Thus, the potential liability of Fred, a farmer in the Pennines, who grants free access to potholers is not a 'business liability', in so far as it relates to the dangerous state of the potholes and the rest of his premises.

[3] UCTA 1977, s 14.

Avoidance of liability for negligence

9.10 UCTA 1977, s 2(1) provides that a person cannot, by reference to an exemption clause or notice, exclude or restrict his liability for death or personal injury (including any disease or impairment of physical or mental condition) resulting from negligence.

In the case of other loss or damage, s 2(2) provides that a person cannot, by reference to an exemption clause or notice, exclude or restrict his liability for negligence, *except in so far as the clause or notice satisfies the 'requirement of reasonableness'.* Unlike s 2(1), s 2(2) does not apply where the negligence consists of breach of an obligation arising from a contract term and the person seeking to enforce that term is a third party to the contract acting in reliance on the Contracts (Rights of Third Parties) Act 1999, s 1.[1] In such a case, the exemption clause will be effective in the same way as any other exemption clause to which UCTA 1977 does not apply.

UCTA 1977, s 2(1) and (2) do not extend to a contract of employment, except in favour of the employee.[2]

'Negligence' in s 2 means the breach:

- of any obligation, arising from the express or implied terms of a contract, to take reasonable care or exercise reasonable skill in the performance of the contract; or
- of any common law duty to take reasonable care or exercise reasonable skill; or
- of the common duty of care imposed by the Occupiers' Liability Act 1957.[3]

Section 2 does not prevent the parties to a contract (eg for the hire of industrial plant) agreeing between themselves which of them should bear liability in negligence for any injury to a third party (eg injury arising from the negligent use of the plant) since this merely *allocates* liability (as opposed to excluding or restricting it).[4]

The fact that s 2 applies to non-contractual notices (see para 21.3) as well as exemption clauses is another reason why UCTA 1977 is inappropriately named.

[1] Contracts (Rights of Third Parties) Act 1999, s 7(2); for s 1 of that Act, see para 13.3.
[2] UCTA 1977, Sch 1.
[3] UCTA 1977, s 1(1). The duty at common law to take reasonable care or exercise reasonable skill, and the duty under the 1957 Act, are discussed in chs 16 and 21.
[4] *Thompson v T Lohan (Plant Hire) Ltd* [1987] 2 All ER 631, CA.

Avoidance of liability for breach of contract

9.11 UCTA 1977, s 3(2) lays down a special rule which applies *as between the contracting parties where one of them deals as consumer or on the other's written standard terms of business.*[1]

Section 3(2) provides that, *as against the party dealing as consumer or on the other's written standard terms of business*, the other party cannot by reference to any contract term:

- exclude or restrict his liability for breach of contract; or
- claim to be entitled:
  - to render a contractual performance substantially different from that which was reasonably expected of him, or
  - in respect of the whole or any part of his contractual obligation, to render no performance at all,

except in so far as the contract term satisfies the 'requirement of reasonableness'. This provision is widely drawn; for example, a term permitting a holiday company to provide accommodation in a different hotel from that specified in the contract may be held invalid, and so may a term entitling a theatre company to cancel a performance without a refund.

[1] UCTA 1977, s 3(1).

Standard written terms

9.12 A person 'deals on the other's written standard terms' if the contract which that person makes is on those terms. 'Deals' in this context means 'make a deal'.[1] It has been common for a party to contract on the basis of a standard form contract produced by that party's professional or trade association. In *British Fermentation Products Ltd v Compair Reavell Ltd*,[2] the judge held that s 3 does not apply to such 'standard terms', because they are not 'the other's' (ie the other party's) standard terms of business, although he suggested that it might be possible to prove that the other party has expressly or impliedly from practice adopted the association's standard terms as his (or her) standard terms and that this might make s 3 applicable. Clearly, the narrow interpretation in this case limits the extent of s 3, which is unfortunate.

[1] *St Albans City and District Council v International Computers Ltd* [1996] 4 All ER 481 at 491.
[2] [1999] 2 All ER (Comm) 389.

Dealing as consumer

9.13 In the present context, a party to a contract 'deals as consumer' in relation to another party if he neither makes the contract in the course of a business nor holds himself out as doing so, and the other party does make the contract in the course of a business.[1] A dictum by Dillon LJ in *R & B Customs Brokers Co Ltd v United Dominions Trust*[2] provides an explanation of the meaning of the phrase 'in the course of a business':

> 'There are some transactions which are clearly integral parts of the business concerned, and these should be held to have been carried out in the course of those businesses; this would cover, apart from much else, the instance of a one-off adventure in the nature of trade where the transaction itself would constitute a trade or business. There are other transactions, however,…which are at the highest only incidental to the carrying on of the relevant business; here a degree of regularity is required before it can be said that they are an integral part of the business carried on and so entered into in the course of that business.'

In *R & B Customs Brokers* the Court of Appeal held that a company operating as a freight forwarding agent, which had bought a car for the business and personal use of its two directors and sole shareholders, a husband and wife, had not made the purchase in the course of a business. The purchase was *not clearly* an *integral* part of the freight forwarding agency business. It was *only incidental* to it and there was *no regularity* of purchases of the type in question.

The meaning given to 'in the course of a business' in *R & B Customs Brokers* is narrower than that given to the same phrase in the Sale of Goods Act 1979, s 14(2) by the Court of Appeal in *Stevenson v Rogers*,[3] a later case referred to in para 7.25.

In the case of contracts for the sale, hire purchase or other supply[4] of goods there is an additional requirement in order for a party who is not an individual to be 'dealing as consumer', viz that the goods are of a type ordinarily supplied for private use or consumption[5] (see further para 9.18).

The definition of dealing as consumer' is subject to the following qualification. A buyer is not regarded as dealing as consumer:

- if the buyer is an individual and the goods are second-hand goods sold at public auction at which individuals have the opportunity of attending the sale in person; or
- if the buyer is not an individual and the goods are sold by auction or competitive tender.[6]

It is for those claiming that a party does not deal as consumer to show this.[7]

[1] UCTA 1977 s 12(1)(a) and (b).
[2] [1988] 1 All ER 847, CA.
[3] [1999] 1 All ER 613, CA.
[4] Ie those described in para 9.18.
[5] UCTA 1977, s 12(1)(c) and (1A).
[6] UCTA 1977, s 12(2).
[7] UCTA 1977, s 12(3).

Matters common to ss 2 and 3

Excepted agreements[1]

9.14 UCTA 1977, ss 2 and 3 do not extend to:

- any contract of insurance;
- any contract *so far* as it relates to the creation, transfer or termination of an interest in land[2] or of any right or interest in any patent, trade mark, copyright or the like;
- any contract *so far* as it relates:
  - to the formation or dissolution of a company or other corporation or of a partnership or other unincorporated association, or
  - to its constitution or the rights or obligations of its corporators or members;
- any contract *so far* as it relates to the creation or transfer of securities or of any right or interest in securities.

Contracts of insurance are totally excepted, but the other contracts are only excepted *so far* as they relate to the specified matters. Presumably, only those parts of such a contract which relate to the specified matters (such as the transfer of an interest in land) are excepted from ss 2 and 3 and the rest of the contract is subject to those sections.

Other exceptions relate to charterparties and the like, and are outside the scope of this book.

[1] UCTA 1977, Sch 1.
[2] A mere contractual licence does not create or transfer an interest in land (see para 28.44) and therefore an exemption clause contained in it is subject to ss 2 and 3.

The 'requirement of reasonableness'

9.15 The requirement of reasonableness is that the exemption clause must have been a fair and reasonable one to be included having regard to the circumstances which were, or ought reasonably to have been, known or in the contemplation of the parties when the contract was made.[1]

Where a party seeks to restrict liability to a specified sum in reliance on an exemption clause, then, in determining whether the clause satisfies the requirement of reasonableness, regard must be had in particular to:

- the resources which that party could expect to be available for the purpose of meeting the liability should it arise; and
- how far it was open to that party to cover the liability by insurance.[2]

It is for the party claiming that an exemption clause satisfies the requirement of reasonableness to show on the balance of probabilities that it does.[3]

In *Smith v Eric S Bush; Harris v Wyre Forest District Council*,[4] Lord Griffiths was of the opinion that the following matters should always be considered in relation to the requirement of reasonableness:

- Were the parties of equal bargaining power? If they were the requirement of reasonableness is more easily discharged than if they were not.

- How difficult is the task being undertaken to which the exemption clause applies? If the task is very difficult or dangerous there may be a high risk of failure, which would be a pointer to the requirement of reasonableness being satisfied.

- What are the practical consequences of the decision on the requirement of reasonableness? This involves the amount of money potentially at stake and the ability of the parties to bear the loss involved, which in turn raises the question of insurance.

The courts also apply by analogy the factors in Sch 2, set out in para 9.20.

It cannot be over-emphasised that it is the clause which must be reasonable in relation to the particular contract; the question is not whether its particular application in the particular case is reasonable. If a clause is drawn so widely as to be capable of applying in unreasonable circumstances it will not be held to be reasonable, even though in the actual situation which has arisen its application would not be unreasonable.[5] A clause may well have various parts to it but, because the whole clause must be subjected to the test of reasonableness, it is not permissible to look only at that part of it which is relied on.[6] A court will be particularly unwilling to find a clause reasonable if it purports to exclude all potential liability.[7]

[1] Unfair Contract Terms Act 1977, s 11(1).
[2] UCTA 1977, s 11(4).
[3] UCTA 1977, s 11(5); *Phillips Products Ltd v Hyland* [1987] 2 All ER 620, CA.
[4] [1989] 2 All ER 514, HL.
[5] *Walker v Boyle* [1982] 1 All ER 634; *Phillips Products Ltd v Hyland Ltd* [1987] 2 All ER 620 at 628.
[6] *Stewart Gill Ltd v Horatio Myer & Co Ltd* [1992] 2 All ER 257, CA.
[7] *Lease Management Services Ltd v Purnell Secretarial Services Ltd* (1994) 13 Tr LR 337.

Avoidance of liability arising from sale or supply of goods

9.16 UCTA 1977, ss 6 and 7 contain additional provisions dealing with attempts to avoid liability where the ownership or possession of goods has passed.

Sale and hire purchase

9.17 By s 6(1), liability for breach of the obligations arising from:

- the Sale of Goods Act 1979 (SGA 1979), s 12 (seller's implied undertakings as to title etc);[1]

- the Supply of Goods (Implied Terms) Act 1973 (SG(IT)A 1973), s 8 (the corresponding things in relation to hire purchase),

cannot be excluded or restricted by reference to an exemption clause.

[1] These terms are described in para 7.25.

9.18 Section 6(2) provides that, *as against a person dealing as consumer*, liability for breach of the obligations arising from:

- SGA 1979, ss 13, 14 or 15 (seller's implied undertakings as to conformity of goods with description or sample, or as to their quality or fitness for a particular purpose);[1]

- SG(IT)A 1973, ss 9, 10 or 11 (the corresponding things in relation to hire purchase), cannot be excluded or restricted by reference to an exemption clause. It must be emphasised that this provision is limited to the implied terms specified. The validity of a clause excluding or restricting liability for breach of any express term will depend on the application of the principles which we have mentioned in para 9.11.

Unlike s 6(1), s 6(2) only vitiates the exemption clause as against a person dealing as consumer. In the present context, a party to a contract (A) 'deals as consumer' in relation to another party if:

- he (A) neither makes the contract in the course of a business nor holds himself out as doing so; and

- the other party does make the contract in the course of a business.[2]

Where A is not an individual, it is also necessary, in order for A to deal as consumer, that the goods passing under or in pursuance of the contract are of a type ordinarily supplied for private use or consumption.[3]

We dealt with the meaning of 'in the course of a business' in para 9.13. The upshot of the above provision is that, if a company buys from a dealer a Rolls Royce or a yacht for its chairman, it will 'deal as consumer' and liability for breach of the implied terms just mentioned cannot be excluded or restricted.

The definition of 'dealing as consumer' is subject to the following qualification. A buyer is not regarded as dealing as consumer:

- if the buyer is an individual and the goods are second-hand goods sold at public auction at which individuals have the opportunity of attending the sale in person; or

- if the buyer is not an individual and the goods are sold by auction or competitive tender.[4]

It is for those claiming that a party does not deal as consumer to show this.[5]

Where a party does not deal as consumer, s 6(3) is the operative provision. Section 6(3) provides that, *as against a person dealing otherwise than as consumer*, liability for breach of the obligations arising from SGA 1979, ss 13–15, or SG(IT)A 1973, ss 9–11, can be excluded or restricted by an exemption clause, but *only in so far as the clause satisfies the 'requirement of reasonableness'*.

The provisions of s 6(1) and (3) are exceptional in that they are not limited to liabilities arising in the course of business.[6]

---

[1] These terms are described in para 7.25.
[2] UCTA 1977, s 12(1)(a) and (b).
[3] UCTA 1977, s 12(1)(c) and (1A).
[4] UCTA 1977, s 12(2)
[5] UCTA 1977, s 12(3).
[6] UCTA 1977, s 6(4).

Miscellaneous contracts under which the ownership or possession of goods passes

9.19 The Unfair Contract Terms Act 1977, s 7 deals with exemption clauses purporting to exclude or restrict liability for breach of obligations implied by law[1] into other contracts under which the ownership or possession of goods passes, eg contracts of hire or exchange or for work and materials. Section 7 applies to these contracts a regime which is broadly similar to that just mentioned in relation to sale of goods and hire purchase.

Section 7(2) provides that, *as against a person dealing as consumer* (in the same sense as in sale of goods and hire purchase), liability in respect of the goods' correspondence with description or sample, or their quality or fitness for any particular purpose, cannot be excluded or restricted by reference to an exemption clause.

On the other hand, as against a person dealing otherwise than as consumer, s 7(3) provides that such liability can be excluded or restricted by reference to such a clause, but *only in so far as the clause satisfies the 'requirement of reasonableness'*.

In relation to an exemption clause purporting to exclude or restrict liability for breach of the various terms as to title which are implied into contracts for work and materials and analogous contracts by the Supply of Goods and Services Act 1982, s 2, s 7(3A) provides that liability for breach of these terms cannot be excluded or restricted by reference to an exemption clause.

On the other hand, by s 7(4), liability in respect of breach of the various terms as to title etc which are implied otherwise than under s 2 of the 1982 Act into contracts for the transfer or supply of goods can be excluded or restricted by such a clause, but *only in so far as the clause satisfies the 'requirement of reasonableness'*. Thus, a different rule applies where such a clause appears in a contract of hire or of pledge from that which applies where it appears in a contract for, say, work and materials.

[1] Supply of Goods and Services Act 1982, ss 2–5 and 7–10; see para 7.26.

The 'requirement of reasonableness' in relation to ss 6 and 7

9.20 The provisions mentioned in para 9.15 concerning the requirement of reasonableness also apply where that requirement is relevant under ss 6 and 7. However, in addition, in determining for the purposes of these two sections whether a contract term satisfies the requirement of reasonableness, regard must be had in particular to the guidelines specified in UCTA 1977, Sch 2,[1] viz:

- the strength of the bargaining positions of the parties relative to each other;
- whether the customer received an inducement to agree to the term, or in accepting it had an opportunity of entering into a similar contract with other persons, but without having to accept a similar term;
- where the term excludes or restricts any relevant liability if some condition is not complied with, whether it was reasonable at the time of the contract to expect that compliance with that condition would be practicable;
- whether the goods were manufactured, processed or adapted to the special order of the customer;
- whether the customer knew or ought reasonably to have known of the existence and extent of the term (eg because it was in small print or was unlikely to be read in full by the customer). We saw in paras 7.8 to 7.13 that an exemption clause may be a term of the contract even though the customer was unaware of it, especially if the customer has signed a contractual document containing it. This provision of Sch 2 enables the court to hold an exemption clause which is undoubtedly a term of the contract unreasonable, and therefore invalid, because, for instance, the customer could not reasonably have known of its existence.

Although Sch 2 does not extend to the requirement of reasonableness as it relates to ss 2 or 3, the courts apply the factors in Sch 2 by analogy when considering the requirement of reasonableness in relation to those sections.[2]

[1] UCTA 1977, s 11(2).
[2] *Phillips Products Ltd v Hyland* [1987] 2 All ER 620, CA.

Varieties of exemption clauses

9.21 As we have shown, UCTA 1977 repeatedly refers to the 'exclusion or restriction of liability'. These words are given a wide interpretation by s 13(1) which provides that, to the extent that the provisions mentioned above prevent the exclusion or restriction of any liability, they also prevent:

- making the liability or its enforcement subject to restrictive or onerous conditions (eg a term requiring 14 days' notice of loss);

- excluding or restricting rules of evidence or procedure (eg a term that failure to complain within 14 days is deemed to be conclusive evidence of proper performance of the contract); or

- excluding or restricting any right or remedy in respect of the liability,[1] or subjecting a person to any prejudice in consequence of his pursuing any such right or remedy.

Section 13(1) also provides that, to the extent that ss 2, 6 and 7 prevent the exclusion or restriction of liability, they also prevent excluding or restricting liability by reference to terms which exclude or restrict the relevant obligation or duty. It follows that a clause purporting to disclaim any potential liability is caught by this provision, even though it purports to prevent a duty arising in the first place (as opposed simply to disclaiming liability for breach of an acknowledged duty).[2]

Whether or not a contract term has the effect of excluding or restricting liability within the above formulation is determined by looking at its effect and substance, and not at its form.[3]

---

[1] Eg a term which allows recovery of damages but which purports to remove any right to terminate the contract for repudiatory breach, or a term which excludes a right to set-off a claim by a buyer for damages for breach against a claim for the price by a seller: *Stewart Gill Ltd v Horatio Myer & Co Ltd* [1992] 2 All ER 257, CA.

[2] *Smith v Eric S Bush; Harris v Wyre Forest District Council* [1989] 2 All ER 514, HL.

[3] *Phillips Products Ltd v Hyland* [1987] 2 All ER 620, CA.

UNFAIR CONTRACT TERMS ACT 1977: KEY POINTS

- UCTA 1977 limits the extent to which it is possible to exclude or restrict liability. Generally, it is limited to attempts to exclude or restrict business liability.

- UCTA 1977 absolutely prohibits the exclusion or restriction by an exemption clause or notice of liability for death or personal injury caused by negligence. For other loss or damage an exemption clause or notice is only effective in respect of negligence liability if it satisfies the requirement of reasonableness.

- Where a clause excludes or restricts liability for breach of contract, the clause is of no effect against a party dealing as consumer or on the other party's standard written terms unless it satisfies the requirement of reasonableness.

- Liability for breach of the implied terms as to title implied in a contract of sale of goods or hire-purchase can never be excluded or restricted by a clause. Likewise, liability for breach of the other terms (as to quality etc) implied into such a contract by statute can never be excluded or restricted as against a consumer; on the other hand it may be excluded or restricted as against a non-consumer if the clause satisfies the requirement of reasonableness. Generally corresponding rules apply in respect of the equivalent implied term in respect of other contracts under which the ownership or possession of property passes.

Unfair Terms in Consumer Contracts Regulations 1999

9.22 These Regulations give effect to the EC Directive on Unfair Terms in Consumer Contracts.

The Regulations cover matters already covered by UCTA 1977. However, as will be seen, in some respects UCTA 1977 is wider than the Regulations since:

- the Regulations are limited to contracts made by a 'consumer', whereas UCTA 1977 is not;

- to the extent that UCTA 1977 has special provisions relating to 'consumers', 'consumer' has a wider meaning under the Act, because under the Regulations a 'consumer' means 'any natural person[1] who…is acting for purposes outside his trade, business or profession' (so that, for example, a company entering into a one-off contract which was not integral to its business would not be a 'consumer' under the Regulations, although it would be under the Act)[2];

- in the case of consumer contracts for the sale or supply of goods, liability for breach of statutorily implied terms as to description or quality cannot be excluded under UCTA 1977 regardless of whether they are reasonable or not, nor generally can liability for breach of the implied term as to title in any sale or supply contract, whereas under the Regulations an exemption clause of such a type in a consumer contract will only be invalid if it is unfair;

- the Regulations only apply to contracts which have not been individually negotiated, whereas UCTA 1977 generally applies to individually negotiated contracts as well.

On the other hand, in some respects the Regulations are wider than UCTA 1977, since they are not limited to exemption clauses, but extend to any 'unfair term' (as defined by the Regulations).

Despite these differences, there is a substantial area of overlap between UCTA 1977 and the Regulations. It follows that, in many cases involving exemption clauses, the application of the Act and of the Regulations must be considered.

[1] As opposed to an artificial legal person such as a company.
[2] Para 9.13.

9.23 The Regulations deal with two separate issues:

- unfair terms in consumer contracts; and
- interpretation of written terms in consumer contracts,

provided in each case that the term is one to which the Regulations apply.

Terms to which the Regulations apply

9.24 Regulation 4(1) provides that the Regulations apply to unfair terms in contracts, whether written or oral, between 'a *seller or a supplier*' and 'a *consumer*'. 'Seller or supplier' means any natural or legal person who, in contracts covered by the Regulations, is acting for purposes relating *to his trade, business or profession, whether publicly owned or privately owned*. 'Consumer' means any natural person who, in contracts covered by the Regulations, is acting for purposes which *are outside his trade, business or profession*.[1] Thus, if a property developer makes a contract with a surveyor for a survey of a house which the developer is buying as his (or her) private residence the developer is a 'consumer' for the purposes of the Regulations, but not if the survey related to property to be developed for commercial purposes. In both instances, of course, the surveyor is a 'supplier' under the Regulations. While a 'professional' or 'commercial' landlord who makes a letting agency contract in respect of his (or her) properties is not a 'consumer' in relation to that contract, a person who has become a landlord of a small number of premises as an alternative to pensions and savings is a 'consumer' in relation to such a contract.[2] A company or other legal person cannot be a 'consumer' for the purpose of the Regulations.[3]

[1] Reg 3(1).

[2] This was assumed in *Office of Fair Trading v Foxtons Ltd* [2009] EWHC 1681 (Ch).

[3] The Arbitration Act 1996, s 90 provides one exception: where a term is one to submit disputes to arbitration a 'consumer' includes a company or other legal person who satisfies the requirements in the text.

Unfair terms

9.25 The Regulations subject any term to which they apply to a test of fairness, save for an exception set out in reg 6(2). This provides that, *in so far as it is in plain, intelligible language*, the assessment of the fairness of a term must not relate to:

- the definition of the main subject matter of the contract, or
- the adequacy[1] of the price or remuneration as against the goods or services supplied in exchange.

In other words, terms of these types are excluded from the requirement of fairness. The meaning of these exceptions, especially the first, is obscure. In *Director General of Fair Trading v First National Bank plc*,[2] the House of Lords held that they should not be given a liberal interpretation; the object of the Regulations would be frustrated if reg 6(2) was interpreted so as to exclude from the assessment of fairness a term which did not fall plainly within it. The House held that a term in a credit agreement providing for the payment by the borrower of interest 'after as well as before' any judgment against him in the event of default plainly did not concern the adequacy of the interest earned by the bank as its remuneration but was designed to ensure that the bank's entitlement to interest did not come to an end on the entry of judgment, as otherwise it would have. It was therefore not excluded by reg 6(2) from the requirement of reasonableness. The House of Lords concluded, however, that the term was not an unfair term on the facts.

The restrictive approach of the House of Lords in *First National Bank* was applied in *Bairstow Eves London Central Ltd v Smith*[3] to clauses in an estate agent's standard terms under which the 'standard commission' payable was 3% of the sale price, but 'early payment' (ie within 10 days) attracted a 'discount rate' of 1.5%. Gross J held on appeal that the applicability of reg 6(2) depended on the interpretation of the contract to find what both parties contemplated when they made it: did the clauses provide for a 3% commission rate with the client having the option to pay 1.5% (in which case reg 6(2) would apply), or did they provide for a rate of 1.5% with a '10 day default' provision (in which cases reg 6(2) would not apply)? Basing his answer on the prevailing market, the pre-contractual negotiations between the parties and their expectation that the 1.5% commission would be paid within 10 days, Gross J concluded that the latter option was the answer, despite the use of 'standard commission' and 'discount rate'. The issue of unfairness was not appealed.

By way of contrast to the above two cases, the Supreme Court in *Office of Fair Trading v Abbey National plc*[4] held that charges levied by banks on personal account holders in respect of unauthorised overdrafts were part of the price or remuneration paid by the customer in exchange for the package of banking services which made up a current account and therefore, in so far as the terms were in plain and intelligible language, were excluded from the requirement of fairness in respect of their adequacy as against the services supplied.

[1] 'Adequacy' is to be read in the sense of 'appropriateness': *Director General of Fair Trading v First National Bank plc* [2001] UKHL 52 at [64].
[2] [2001] UKHL 52, HL.
[3] [2004] EWHC 263 (QB).
[4] [2009] UKSC 6, SC.

Test of fairness

9.26 By reg 5(1), a contractual term which has not been individually negotiated is to be regarded as unfair if, contrary to the requirement of good faith, it causes a significant imbalance in the parties' rights and obligations arising under the contract, to the detriment of the consumer.

9.27 Regulation 5(2) provides that a term is always to be regarded as not having been individually negotiated where it has been *drafted in advance and the consumer has not been able to influence the substance of the term*. Regulation 5(3) adds that, notwithstanding that a specific term or certain aspects of it in a contract has been individually negotiated, the Regulations apply to the rest of a contract if an overall assessment of the contract indicates that it is a pre-formulated standard contract. The fact that a consumer has had the opportunity of considering the terms of an agreement does not mean that a term has been individually negotiated.[1]

If a *seller or supplier* claims that a term was *individually negotiated*, that person has the burden of proving this.[2]

[1] *UK Housing Alliance (North West) Ltd v Francis* [2010] EWCA Civ 117, CA.
[2] Reg 5(4).

9.28 Two elements can be derived from reg 5(1):

- the term must cause significant imbalance to the parties' rights and obligations to the detriment of the consumer; and
- this 'significant imbalance' must be 'contrary to the requirement of good faith'.

Regulation 5(1) lays down a composite test covering both the making and the substance of the contract; in applying it regard must be had to the object of the Regulations.[1]

In *Director General of Fair Trading v First National Bank plc*,[2] the House of Lords held that the requirement of significant imbalance was met if, looking at the contract as a whole, a term was so weighted in favour of the seller or supplier as to tilt the parties' rights and obligations under the contract significantly in the seller or supplier's favour.

Turning to the requirement of good faith, it held that it was one of 'fair and open dealing'. 'Openness', it held, required that the terms should be expressed fully, clearly and legibly, containing no traps. Appropriate prominence should be given to terms potentially disadvantageous to the consumer. 'Fair dealing', it continued, required that a seller or supplier should not take advantage, even unconsciously, of the consumer's necessity, lack of money, lack of experience, unfamiliarity with the subject matter, weak bargaining position or any other factor listed in or analogous to those listed in Sch 2 to the Regulations referred to below.

Schedule 2 to the Regulations contains an indicative, non-exhaustive and lengthy list of terms which *may* be regarded as unfair. These are terms which have the object or effect of, for example:

- excluding or limiting the legal liability of a seller or supplier in the event of the death of a consumer or personal injury to the latter resulting from an act or omission of that seller or supplier;

- inappropriately excluding or limiting the legal rights of the consumer vis-à-vis the seller or supplier or another party in the event of total or partial non-performance or inadequate performance by the seller or supplier of any of the contractual obligations, including the option of offsetting a debt owed to the seller or supplier against any claim which the consumer may have against the seller or supplier;

- making an agreement binding on the consumer whereas provision of services by the seller or supplier is subject to a condition whose realisation depends on the seller or supplier's own will alone;

- permitting the seller or supplier to retain sums paid by the consumer where the latter decides not to conclude or perform the contract, without providing for the consumer to receive compensation of an equivalent amount from the seller or supplier where the latter is the party cancelling the contract;

- requiring any consumer who fails to fulfil his obligation to pay a disproportionately high sum in compensation;

- irrevocably binding the consumer to terms with which the consumer had no real opportunity of becoming acquainted before the conclusion of the contract;

- enabling the seller or supplier to alter unilaterally without a valid reason any characteristics of the product or service to be provided;

- giving the seller or supplier the right to determine whether the goods or services supplied are in conformity with the contract, or giving the seller or supplier the exclusive right to interpret any term of the contract;

- obliging the consumer to fulfil all his obligations where the seller or supplier does not perform his;

- giving the seller or supplier the possibility of transferring his rights and obligations under the contract, where this may serve to reduce the guarantees for the consumer, without the latter's agreement.

By way of example of a potentially unfair term outside the above list, it was held by Mann J in *Office of Fair Trading v Foxtons Ltd*[3] that terms under which an estate agent charged commission on the renewal of the lease by the tenant and on the sale of the property to the tenant were unfair in the circumstances. Mann J emphasised that his decision did not mean that all such terms were unfair; the terms in question were unfair because they could operate onerously and insufficient had been done to draw them to the attention of the consumer,

As with the test of reasonableness under UCTA 1977,[4] the test of fairness is assessed as at the time of the conclusion of the contract. Regulation 6(1) provides that the unfairness of a contractual term must be assessed, taking into account the nature of the goods or services for which the contract was concluded and by referring, as at the time of the conclusion of the contract, to all circumstances attending the conclusion of the contract and to all the other terms of the contract or of another contract on which it is dependent.

Unlike the provisions relating to the requirement of reasonableness in UCTA 1977, no provision is made concerning the burden of proof. Thus, it is for the consumer to prove that the test of fairness is not satisfied.

¹ *Director General of Fair Trading v First National Bank plc* [2001] UKHL 52, [at [17].
² [2001] UKHL 52.
³ [2009] EWHC 1681 (Ch).
⁴ Para 9.15.

Consequence of inclusion of unfair term

9.29 An unfair term under the provisions of the Regulations is not binding on the consumer.¹ However, the rest of the contract continues to bind the parties if it is capable of continuing in existence without the unfair term.²

¹ Reg 8(1).
² Reg 8(2).

Interpretation of written terms in consumer contracts

9.30 By reg 7(1), a seller or supplier must ensure that any written contractual term to which the Regulations apply is expressed in plain, intelligible language. Regulation 7(2) provides that, where there is doubt about the meaning of a written term, the interpretation most favourable to the consumer prevails; the term is not rendered ineffective.

UNFAIR TERMS IN CONSUMER CONTRACTS REGULATIONS 1999: KEY POINTS

- The Regulations apply to unfair terms in contracts between a 'seller' or 'supplier' and a 'consumer'.
- The regulations subject any term to which they apply to a test of fairness, except that, *in so far as it is in plain, intelligible language*, the assessment of the fairness of a term must not relate to:
  - the definition of the main subject matter of the contract, or
  - the adequacy of the price or remuneration as against the goods or services supplied in exchange.
- With regard to the test of fairness, a contractual term which has not been individually negotiated is to be regarded as unfair if it causes a significant imbalance in the parties' rights and obligations arising under the contract, to the detriment of the consumer, and this imbalance is contrary to the requirement of good faith.
- A term has not been individually negotiated where it has been drafted in advance and the consumer has not been able to influence the substance of the term. Notwithstanding that a specific term or certain aspects of it in a contract has been individually negotiated, the Regulations apply to the rest of a contract if an overall assessment of it indicates that it is a pre-formulated standard contract.
- Schedule 2 to the Regulations contains an indicative, non-exhaustive list of terms which may be regarded as unfair.
- If a term is unfair under the Regulations that term does not bind the consumer.

Questions

1. What rules apply to the interpretation of exemption clauses?

2. What types of liability:
    *   can never be excluded;
    *   can only be excluded if they satisfy the requirement of reasonableness, under the Unfair Contract Terms Act 1977?

3. What is the requirement of reasonableness under the Unfair Contract Terms Act 1977, and who has the burden of proof in relation to it?

4. To what terms do the Unfair Terms in Consumer Contracts Regulations 1999 apply?

5. What is the test of fairness under the 1999 Regulations, and what is the effect of a term which is unfair under them?

6. Compare and contrast the different approaches taken under the Unfair Contract Terms Act 1977 and the Unfair Terms in Consumer Contracts Regulations 1999.

7. Len, a quantity surveyor, drove to his local Computerglobe plc, a retail chain specialising in the sale of computers, to buy a new PC for his office. He parked in a nearby pay-on-exit car park operated by ABC Car Parks plc. Near the entrance barrier there was a sign referring to conditions under which vehicles were permitted to park and stating that they were displayed in the car park attendant's office. Len should not have driven to the car park because he was not wearing his spectacles. Because he was not wearing them he could not read what was on the sign.

    Len bought a PC in Computerglobe, signing a document 'Contract of Sale' without trying to read it. When he returned to his car he was injured, and his watch was smashed beyond repair, when a piece of masonry on the car park staircase fell on him due to negligently inadequate maintenance by ABC Car Parks.

    When Len first uses his new PC he discovers that, through no fault of Computerglobe, it is not of satisfactory quality.

    When Len takes up these matters with ABC Car Parks plc and Computerglobe plc, ABC Car Parks plc tell him that one of their conditions displayed in the car park attendant's office was that 'ABC Car Parks plc will not be liable for any injury caused to persons using their car parks or for any loss or damage to such a person's belongings', and Computerglobe plc tell him that one of the clauses in the 'Contract of Sale' document which he signed stated that 'Computerglobe plc shall not be liable for breach of any term of this contract, express or implied, unless such breach is attributable to fault on their part'.

    Advise Len as to his rights against ABC Car Parks plc and Computerglobe plc. Would your answer be affected, in relation to ABC Car Parks plc, if Len had read the sign and had gone to the car park attendant's office before entering the car park and inquired about the conditions referred to on the sign, and been told that the conditions simply excluded the liability of ABC Car Parks plc for the loss of a vehicle? If so, give your reasons.

    In answering this question note your answer to question 3 in Chapter 7.

10

Discharge by frustration

CHAPTER OVERVIEW

Under the doctrine of frustration a contract is automatically discharged in certain circumstances. We consider in turn:

- the scope of the doctrine of frustration;
- certain limits on its application;
- the legal effect of the frustration of a contract.

Scope

10.1 A contract may be automatically discharged by frustration if, because of a change of circumstances subsequent to its formation, a contractual obligation has become impossible of being performed. Examples are where, for example, *subsequent to the formation of the contract*:

- a thing essential to its performance is destroyed or becomes unavailable; or
- a fundamental change of circumstances occurs; or
- a party to a contract of a personal nature dies or is otherwise incapacitated from performing it; or
- performance of it is rendered illegal; or
- a basic assumption on which the parties contracted is destroyed.

10.2 A contract is not discharged by frustration simply because a subsequent event makes its performance more costly or difficult than envisaged when the contract was made. This is shown by *Davis Contractors Ltd v Fareham UDC*.[1] In 1946, the contractors entered into a contract with the council to build 78 houses for the fixed sum of £94,000. Owing to an unexpected shortage of skilled labour and of certain materials, the contract took 22 months to complete instead of the anticipated eight months and cost £115,000. The contractors contended that the contract had been frustrated by the long delay and that they were entitled to a sum in excess of the contract price on a restitutionary basis (ie reasonable recompense for the benefit which they had conferred). The House of Lords disagreed, holding that the mere fact that unforeseen circumstances had delayed the performance of the contract and made it more costly to perform did not discharge the contract.

[1] [1956] 2 All ER 145, HL.

Supervening destruction or unavailability

10.3 A contract is discharged by frustration if performance of it is rendered impossible by the subsequent destruction or unavailability of a specific thing expressly or impliedly required by the contract for its performance. A leading authority is *Taylor v Caldwell*.[1] D agreed to hire a music hall and gardens to C on specified days for the purpose of concerts. Before the first of the specified days, the music hall was destroyed by fire without the fault of either party. D were held not liable for breach of contract because performance of the contract had become impossible through the destruction of the hall and D were not at fault. The contract was therefore frustrated and both parties discharged from their contractual obligations.

The subsequent unavailability of a thing will frustrate a contract if it renders performance of the contract in accordance with its terms impossible. This is shown by *Nickoll and Knight v Ashton Edridge & Co*.[2] D sold C a cargo of cotton seed to be shipped 'per steamship *Orlando* during the month of January'. Before the time for shipping arrived, the ship was so damaged by stranding as to be unable to load in January. It was held that the contract was discharged by frustration.

[1] (1863) 3 B & S 826.
[2] [1901] 2 KB 126, CA.

10.4 The point that, for a contract to be frustrated under the present heading, the thing which has been destroyed or is otherwise unavailable must have been expressly or impliedly required by the contract for its performance is well illustrated by *Tsakiroglou & Co Ltd v Noblee Thorl GmbH*.[1] That case concerned a contract for the sale of groundnuts which were to be shipped from the Sudan to Hamburg during November or December 1956. Both parties contemplated that the ship would proceed via the Suez Canal but this was not stated in the contract. On 2 November 1956, the Canal was closed (and remained so for five months). The House of Lords held that the unavailability of the Canal did not frustrate the contract. One of its reasons was that there was no express provision in the contract for shipping via the Canal, nor could a provision be implied to that effect, because the route was immaterial to the buyers.

Even more conclusively, unavailability of a thing does not frustrate the contract if it merely affects the method of performance contemplated by one of the parties.[2] In *Nickoll and Knight v Ashton Edridge & Co*, for instance, the contract would not have been frustrated if, instead of the name of the ship on which the cargo was to be loaded being stated in the contract, the sellers had merely intended to load on that ship.

[1] [1961] 2 All ER 179, HL.
[2] *Blackburn Bobbin Co v T W Allen & Sons* [1918] 2 KB 467, CA.

Fundamental change of circumstances

10.5 A contract is frustrated if an event occurs of such gravity that, although technically the contract could still be performed, it would be the performance of a radically different contract from that contemplated.

In *Metropolitan Water Board v Dick Kerr & Co Ltd*,[1] the company contracted with the Board to construct a reservoir within six years, subject to a proviso that time could be extended if delay was caused by difficulties, impediments or obstructions. After two years had elapsed the Minister of Munitions, acting under statutory powers, required the company to stop work on the contract and remove and sell their plant. The House of Lords held that the interruption created by the prohibition was of such a nature and duration that the contract, if resumed, would in effect be radically different from that originally made. Therefore it was frustrated.

This case can be contrasted with *Tsakiroglou & Co Ltd v Noblee Thorl GmbH*.[2] In that case, the House of Lords held that the contract was not frustrated by the closure of the Suez Canal because a voyage round the Cape of Good Hope would not be commercially or fundamentally different from shipping via the Canal, albeit it was more expensive for the sellers.

[1] [1918] AC 119, HL.
[2] Para 10.4.

Death or other personal incapacity

10.6 A contract for personal services (ie a contract of employment, or any other contract which can only be performed by a party personally, eg a contract to paint a portrait) is discharged by frustration if that party dies[1] or is otherwise rendered *permanently* incapable of performing it.[2]

[1] *Stubbs v Holywell Rly Co Ltd* (1867) LR 2 Exch 311.
[2] *Notcutt v Universal Equipment Co (London) Ltd* [1986] 3 All ER 582, CA.

10.7 If a person becomes *temporarily* incapable of performing a contract for personal services, it may be discharged. Whether or not the temporary incapacity frustrates such a contract depends on whether, in the light of the probable duration of the incapacity at its inception, performance after it has ceased would be radically different from what was envisaged by the contract and in effect be the substitution of a new contract. In *Morgan v Manser*,[1] D, a comedian, entered into a contract with C in 1938 whereby he engaged C's services as manager for 10 years. In 1940, D was called up and was not demobilised until 1946. It was held that the contract was discharged by frustration in 1940 since it was then likely that D would have to remain in the forces for a very long time. Similarly, if the duration of an employee's illness is likely to be so lengthy as to make performance of a contract of employment radically different from that envisaged, the contract will be discharged by frustration, and so will a contract to perform at a concert on a specified day by an illness of short duration.[2] Conversely, a contract of a personal nature is not frustrated by the illness of a party where this is likely to last for only a small part of the period of the contract: further performance after the party becomes available again will not be the performance of a radically different contract.

[1] [1947] 2 All ER 666.
[2] *Robinson v Davison* (1871) LR 6 Exch 269.

Supervening illegality

10.8 If a change in the law or in the circumstances makes it impossible to perform a contract legally, the contract is discharged by frustration. In *White and Carter Ltd v Carbis Bay Garage Ltd*,[1] for instance, it was held that a contract made in 1939 to display advertisements for three years was frustrated by wartime Defence Regulations prohibiting advertisements of the type in question. On the other hand, in *Cricklewood Property and Investment Trust Ltd v Leighton's Investment Trust Ltd*,[2] the House of Lords held that a 99-year building lease was not frustrated by Defence Regulations prohibiting building for only a small part of that term: performance had merely been suspended, not made impossible.

[1] [1941] 2 All ER 633, CA.
[2] [1945] 1 All ER 252, HL.

Supervening destruction of a basic assumption on which the parties contracted

10.9 A contract is discharged by frustration if, although it is physically and legally possible for each party to perform his (or her) obligations under the contract, a change of circumstances has destroyed a basic assumption on which both parties contracted. In *Krell v Henry*,[1] D agreed to hire a flat in Pall Mall from C for 26 and 27 June 1902, on one of which days Edward VII was to be crowned. To C's knowledge, D hired the flat in order to view the Coronation processions, but this was not mentioned in their written contract. The processions were postponed because of the King's illness.

The Court of Appeal held that a view of the processions was not simply D's purpose in hiring the flat but the basis of the contract for both parties, and that since the postponement of the processions prevented this being achieved the contract was frustrated.

[1] [1903] 2 KB 740, CA.

10.10 It is not enough that the purpose of one party in making the contract cannot be fulfilled; the basis on which both parties contracted must have been destroyed. This is shown by *Herne Bay Steam Boat Co v Hutton*,[1] which also reveals the difficulty in drawing the distinction. D chartered a ship from C for 28 and 29 June 1902, for the express purpose of taking fare-paying passengers to see the Coronation naval review at Spithead and to cruise round the fleet. The review was cancelled, but the fleet remained.

The Court of Appeal held that the charterparty was not frustrated because the holding of the review was not the basis on which both parties had contracted and it was irrelevant that D's purpose was defeated.

[1] [1903] 2 KB 683, CA.

SCOPE OF THE DOCTRINE OF FRUSTRATION: KEY POINTS

A contract may be frustrated if it becomes impossible of performance because of a change of circumstances. Frustrating events include:

- the destruction or unavailability of something essential to contractual performance;
- a fundamental change of circumstances;
- death or other personal incapacity in a personal services contract;
- performance becoming illegal;
- the destruction of a basic assumption on which the parties contracted.

Limits

10.11 There are no limits on the type of contract to which, as a matter of law, the doctrine of frustration can apply. In relation to most types of contract, the applicability of the doctrine is long-established; but it was only in 1980 in *National Carriers Ltd v Panalpina (Northern) Ltd*[1] that the House of Lords finally decided, with one dissentient, that the doctrine of frustration is applicable to a lease, although on the facts the particular lease was not frustrated. Their Lordships stated that cases where a lease would be frustrated would be extremely rare. In the case of a long lease, and it must be remembered that a lease may often be for 99 years or 999 years, a prime reason is that, if the lessee is only deprived temporarily of the use of the premises, the interruption of use will almost never be for long enough to frustrate the contract. Moreover, in the case of the destruction, or the like, of the premises, the lease will normally expressly provide for that event by covenants as to insurance and rebuilding, and thereby exclude the doctrine of frustration.

A contract for a lease and a contract for the sale of land can, of course, be discharged by frustration.[2] However, it is clear that such a contract will only be frustrated in the most extreme cases, since it has been held, for example, that a contract for the sale of premises is not frustrated simply because, before completion of the contract by conveyance, they are destroyed[3] or made subject to a compulsory purchase order.[4] In these cases, at least, the purchaser will be compensated by the payment of insurance moneys or compulsory purchase compensation. Much greater hardship will be suffered by the person who has contracted to lease or buy land for redevelopment but before completion the buildings on it are listed as being of special architectural interest, so that redevelopment becomes difficult or impossible and the land loses most of its value. It has been held that the contract is not frustrated in such a case,[5] and consequently the person who has contracted to lease or buy remains bound to go ahead with a venture which is financially disastrous.

[1] [1981] 1 All ER 161, HL.
[2] Contract for a lease: *Rom Securities Ltd v Rogers (Holdings) Ltd* (1967) 205 Estates Gazette 427; contract for sale of land: assumed in *Amalgamated Investment and Property Co Ltd v John Walker & Sons Ltd* [1976] 3 All ER 509, CA.
[3] *Paine v Meller* (1801) 6 Ves 349.
[4] *Hillingdon Estates Co v Stonefield Estates Ltd* [1952] 1 All ER 853.
[5] *Amalgamated Investment and Property Co Ltd v John Walker & Sons Ltd* [1976] 3 All ER 509, CA.

Express provision for frustrating event

10.12 The doctrine of frustration does not apply if the parties have made provision to deal with the frustrating event which has occurred. There is one exception: a contract is frustrated by supervening illegality despite an express provision to the contrary.[1]

A provision concerned with the effect of a possible future event is narrowly construed and, unless on its true construction it covers the frustrating event in question, the doctrine of frustration is not ousted. This is shown by *Metropolitan Water Board v Dick Kerr & Co Ltd*,[2] discussed above, where the contract for the reservoir provided that in the event of delays 'however caused' the contractors were to be given an extension of time. The House of Lords held that this provision did not prevent the doctrine of frustration applying because it did not cover the particular event which had occurred. Although the event was literally within the provision, the provision could be construed as limited to temporary difficulties, such as shortage of supplies, and not as extending to events which fundamentally altered the nature of the contract and which could not have been in the parties' contemplation when they made the contract.

[1] *Ertel Bieber & Co v Rio Tinto Co Ltd* [1918] AC 260, HL.
[2] [1918] AC 119, HL; para 10.5.

Foreseen and foreseeable events

10.13 If, by reason of special knowledge, the risk of the particular frustrating event was foreseen or foreseeable by only *one* party the doctrine of frustration cannot apply. It is up to that party to provide against the risk of that event and, if that party fails to do so and cannot perform the contract, that party is liable for breach.[1]

On the other hand, where the risk of the frustrating event was foreseen or foreseeable by both parties, but they did not make provision to deal with it, the doctrine of frustration can apply.[2] In each case, however, it is a question of construction whether the failure to make provision for the event means that each party took the risk of it rendering contractual performance impossible or whether, in the absence of any such intention, the doctrine of frustration should apply to discharge the contract.[3]

[1] *Walton Harvey Ltd v Walker and Homfrays Ltd* [1931] 1 Ch 274, CA.
[2] *Ocean Tramp Tankers Corpn v V/O Sovfracht, The Eugenia* [1964] 1 All ER 161, CA.
[3] *Chandler Bros Ltd v Boswell* [1936] 3 All ER 179, CA.

Fault of a party

10.14 A party cannot rely on the doctrine of frustration if it is proved that the frustrating event was brought about by that party's fault, but (assuming that the other party has not also contributed to the event by his (or her) fault) the other party can.[1]

A deliberate election to pursue a course of conduct which renders performance of the contract impossible or illegal is clearly established as fault in this context; that conduct may in itself be a breach of contract,[2] but it is not necessary that it should be.[3] In *Maritime National Fish Ltd v Ocean Trawlers Ltd*,[4] C chartered to D a trawler fitted with an otter trawl. Both parties knew that the use of an otter trawl without a licence from a minister was illegal. Later, D applied for licences for five trawlers which they were operating, including C's. They were only granted three licences and were asked to specify the three trawlers which they wished to have licensed. D named three trawlers other than C's. They then claimed that they were no longer bound by the charterparty because it had been frustrated. The Privy Council held that the frustration was due to D's deliberate act in not specifying Cs' trawler for a licence and that therefore they could not rely on the doctrine of frustration. Consequently, C could recover the hire under the charterparty.

Any deliberate choice of conduct which renders performance of the contract impossible or illegal suffices for present purposes, however reasonable it is to make that choice.[5]

It would seem that a negligent act by a party, as opposed to a deliberate choice of conduct, which renders performance of the contract impossible or illegal prevents that party relying on the doctrine of frustration.[5]

The onus of proof where fault is alleged is on the party alleging it.[6]

[1] *FC Shepherd & Co Ltd v Jerrom* [1986] 3 All ER 589, CA.
[2] As in *Ocean Tramp Tankers Corpn v V/O Sovfracht, The Eugenia* [1964] 1 All ER 161, CA.
[3] *Denmark Productions Ltd v Boscobel Productions Ltd* [1968] 3 All ER 513, CA.
[4] [1935] AC 524, PC.
[5] *J Lauritzen AS v Wijsmuller BV, The Super Servant Two* [1990] 1 Lloyd's Rep 1, CA.
[6] *Joseph Constantine Steamship Line Ltd v Imperial Smelting Corpn Ltd* [1941] 2 All ER 165, HL.

LIMITS: KEY POINTS

- The doctrine of frustration cannot apply where the contract expressly makes provision to deal with the frustrating event, or where it is foreseen or foreseeable by only one of the parties.

- A party cannot rely on frustration as discharging the contract if the frustrating event was brought about by that party's own fault.

Effect

10.15 Frustration does not merely make the contract terminable at the election of a party: the frustrating event *automatically* discharges the contract at the time that it is frustrated[1] (except that provisions intended by the parties to apply in the event of frustration, such as one dealing with its consequences, remain in force).[2] As noted in Chapter 8 a party whose obligations have been discharged by frustration has a lawful excuse for not performing them and is therefore not in breach of contract.

As explained in para 10.14, where the frustrating event is brought about by the fault of one party, the other party may rely on it as discharging the contract but the party at fault cannot.

Leaving aside the complicated question of the effect of frustration on money paid or payable under the contract, the effect of frustration on other obligations under the contract is governed by the common law and is as follows: the discharge of a contract by frustration releases a party from further performance of any such obligations due after the frustrating event[3] but not from any such obligations due before that time, which remain enforceable.[4]

Turning to the effect of frustration on money paid or payable under the contract, the position is as follows.

[1] *Hirji Mulji v Cheong Yue Steamship Co Ltd* [1926] AC 497, PC.
[2] *Heyman v Darwins Ltd* [1942] 1 All ER 337, HL.
[3] *Chandler v Webster* [1904] 1 KB 493, CA.
[4] *Chandler v Webster* [1904] 1 KB 493, CA.

Money paid or payable under the contract before the occurrence of the frustrating event

10.16 At common law, the original position was that an obligation to pay money due before the frustrating event remained enforceable and money paid under the contract before that event was irrecoverable.[1] However, in 1942, in *Fibrosa Spolka Akcyjna v Fairbairn Lawson Combe Barbour Ltd*,[2] a case where money payable in advance for machinery had been paid but the contract had been frustrated before any of the machinery had been delivered, the House of Lords held that the money could be recovered back on the ground of a total failure of consideration.

The decision in the *Fibrosa* case left the law unjust in two ways:

- The decision only permitted recovery if there had been a total failure of consideration. This could be unjust to the payer of the money because, if the payee had performed any part of the payee's contractual duties, however small, in respect of which the money was due, the payer could not recover a penny of what had been paid.

- The decision could also be unjust to a payee who was ordered to return a pre-payment because the payee might have incurred expenses in preparing to perform the contractual duties in respect of which the money was due.

[1] *Chandler v Webster* [1904] 1 KB 493, CA.
[2] [1942] 2 All ER 122, HL.

10.17 These injustices were removed by the Law Reform (Frustrated Contracts) Act 1943 (LR(FC)A 1943). Section 1(2) of the Act provides:

- all sums *payable* under the contract *before* the frustrating event *cease to be payable* whether or not there has been a total failure of consideration;

- all sums *paid* under the contract *before* the frustrating event are *recoverable* whether or not there has been a total failure of consideration;

- the court has a discretionary *power* to allow the payee to set off against the sums so paid or payable a sum not exceeding the value of the expenses he (or she) has incurred before the frustrating event in, or for the purpose of, the performance of the contract.

    If the court exercises this power, it allows the payee to retain the amount stipulated by it (if the payee has been paid) or to recover the stipulated amount (if money was payable but not paid). The stipulated amount, which may include an element in respect of overhead expenses and of any work or services performed personally by the payee,[1] cannot exceed the sums paid or payable to the payee. The following illustrates the operation of these provisions. X contracts with Y to manufacture and deliver certain machinery by 1 March for £5,000, £1,000 to be paid on 1 January and the balance of £4,000 on delivery. The contract is discharged by frustration on 1 February before the machinery is delivered but after X has incurred expenses of £500 in making the machinery. Pursuant to s 1(2), Y need not pay the £1,000 if Y has not paid it before 1 February or, if Y has, Y can recover the £1,000, but the court may order Y to pay X up to £500 for X's expenses or may allow X to retain up to £500, as the case may be.

[1] LR(FC)A 1943, s 1(4).

Money payable under the contract after the occurrence of the frustrating event

10.18 Such money is not recoverable by the party to whom it was due, in accordance with the rule that frustration releases both parties from performing any contractual obligation due after the frustrating event. Thus, in *Krell v Henry*,[1] it was held that the owner of the flat could not recover a sum payable for the hire of the flat because it was not due until a time after the processions had been postponed (the frustrating event). Likewise, the balance of £4,000 referred to in the example in the previous paragraph is not recoverable by X because it was not due until after the frustrating event. In further contrast to the rules outlined in para 10.17, the courts do not have power to allow a claim in respect of expenses by a party to whom money was payable only after the frustrating event, because LR(FC)A 1943 does not apply in such a case.

[1] [1903] 2 KB 740, CA; para 10.9.

Award for valuable benefit obtained

10.19 At common law, a party who had benefited another by partly performing the contract before it was frustrated could not recover any sum of money for this.[1] This rule was particularly harsh where payment was not due to the party conferring the benefit until after the occurrence of the frustrating event because where money was paid or payable before that time that party could retain or recover it, as the case might be.

The LR(FC)A 1943, s 1(3), now makes a monetary award available to either party for a valuable benefit conferred on the other. It provides that, where a party to a frustrated contract has, by reason of anything done by any other party in, or for the purpose of, the performance of the contract, obtained a valuable benefit before the frustrating event (other than the payment of money to which s 1(2) applies), that other party may recover from the benefited party such sum, if any, as the court considers just, having regard to all the circumstances of the case.

In assessing the amount of an award under s 1(3), the court must first identify and value the benefit obtained by the benefited party (Y). Where services rendered by the other party (X) have an end-product, Y's benefit is the end-product of those services.[2] It follows, for example, that, in the case of a building contract which is frustrated when the building is partially completed, the benefit to be valued is the uncompleted building, not the work put in by the builder. This is important because occasionally a relatively small service performed under a contract may confer a substantial benefit, and vice versa. Sometimes services will have no end-product, as where they consist of transporting goods. In such a case the benefit is the value of the services.[3] Generally speaking, valuation of the benefit must be made as at the date of the frustration and not at an earlier time when the benefit was received.[4] In particular, the court must take into account the effect in relation to the benefit of the circumstances giving rise to the frustration,[5] so that if a builder (X) contracts to do building work on Y's house and, when he has nearly finished, the house (including X's work) is seriously damaged by fire, and the building contract is thereby frustrated, the valuation of the benefit relates to the value of what remains of X's work as at the date of frustration. From the benefit valued in the above way there must be deducted any expenses incurred by the benefited party (Y) before the contract was frustrated, including any sums paid or payable by Y to X under the contract and retained or recoverable by X under s 1(2).[6]

The value of the benefit assessed by the court under the above principles forms the upper limit of an award under s 1(3) but not the award itself. This is because the court, having identified and valued the benefit, must then decide on a 'just sum' within that upper limit to award to X in respect of X's performance. Here, the court should take into particular account the contract consideration, since in many cases it will be unjust to award more than that consideration or a rateable part of it. The fact that X has broken the contract in some way before the frustration has no bearing on the just sum to be awarded to X, although Y's claim to damages for the breach may be the subject of a counterclaim or set-off if not statute-barred.[7]

[1] *Appleby v Myers* (1867) LR 2 CP 651.
[2] *BP Exploration Co (Libya) Ltd v Hunt (No 2)* [1982] 1 All ER 925; affd at 986, HL.
[3] *BP Exploration Co (Libya) Ltd v Hunt (No 2)* [1982] 1 All ER 925; affd at 986, HL.
[4] *BP Exploration Co (Libya) Ltd v Hunt (No 2)* [1982] 1 All ER 925; affd at 986, HL.
[5] LR(FC)A 1943, s 1(3).
[6] LR(FC)A 1943, s 1(3).
[7] *BP Exploration Co (Libya) Ltd v Hunt (No 2)* [1982] 1 All ER 925; affd at 986, HL.

10.20 The operation of LR(FC)A 1943 can be illustrated as follows: X, a jobbing decorator, contracts with Y to paint the outside of Y's house for £2,000, £500 to be paid on 1 September and the rest on completion. Y pays X the £500 on 1 September. After X has painted most of the house the contract is frustrated, X having been seriously incapacitated in a car crash. Under s 1(2), X must return the £500 to Y, unless and to the extent that the court exercises its discretion to allow X to retain some or all of it. Suppose that X's expenses were £350 and the court allows X to retain this, only £150 will be recoverable by Y. The obligation as to the further £1,500 is, of course, discharged by frustration and X cannot claim this from Y. However, as X has conferred a valuable benefit on Y before the frustrating event, s 1(3) comes into play. Suppose that the value of the paintwork completed by X is £1,200 as at the date of the frustration, the court must then deduct what it has allowed X to retain under s 1(2) and the resulting sum (ie £850) will be the upper limit of the 'just sum' awarded by the court under s 1(3).

Scope of LR(FC)A 1943

10.21 Where a contract to which LR(FC)A 1943 applies is severable,[1] eg a contract to work for a year at £2,400 a month, and a severable part of it is wholly performed before the frustrating event, or wholly performed except in respect of payment of sums which are or can be ascertained under the contract, that part is to be treated as if it were a separate contract and had not been frustrated, and the Act is only applicable to the remainder of the contract.[2] The result is that, if the employee under the above contract works for two months and two weeks and then dies before any salary has been paid, the employee's executors can recover the two months' salary owing to the employee (each month being treated as a separate contract) plus an award under s 1(3) for any valuable benefit conferred by the deceased on the employer during the remaining two weeks.

[1] Ie complete performance by one party is not a condition of the other party's obligations becoming due.
[2] Section 2(4).

10.22 Where a contract contains a provision (such as one precluding any recovery of any award under LR(FC)A 1943 or one limiting such an award) which is intended to have effect in the event of circumstances arising which operate, or would but for the provision operate, to frustrate the contract, or is intended to have effect whether such circumstances arise or not, the court must give effect to that provision and only give effect to LR(FC)A 1943, s 1(2) and (3) to such extent, if any, as is consistent with that provision.[1]

[1] Section 2(3). See, further, *BP Exploration Co (Libya) Ltd v Hunt (No 2)* [1982] 1 All ER 925; affd at 986, HL.

10.23 The LR(FC)A 1943 does not apply to the following types of contract:

- a contract of insurance.[1] Generally, a premium is not returnable once the risk has attached;
- a contract to which the Sale of Goods Act 1979, s 7 applies.[1] Section 7 provides that where there is an agreement to sell specific goods, and subsequently, without any fault on the part of the seller or buyer, the goods *perish before the risk passes to the buyer*, the agreement is thereby avoided. Where a contract is avoided under s 7, the principles laid down by the House of Lords in the *Fibrosa* case[2] apply. Under these a buyer who has paid for the goods before they perished can recover that payment only if there has been a total failure of consideration, in which case the seller has no right of set-off for any expenses incurred in seeking to perform the contract before the goods perished.

[1] Section 2(5).
[2] Para 10.16.

EFFECT OF FRUSTRATION: KEY POINTS

The effect of the automatic discharge of a contract for frustration is that a party is released from further performance of any non-monetary obligation due after the frustrating event. With specified exceptions:

- a sum of money payable or paid before the frustrating event ceases to be payable or is recoverable, respectively, but the court may allow the payee to set off against such sums an amount in respect of the expenses which the payee incurred in performing the contract;
- money payable after the frustrating event ceases to be payable;
- the court can award a monetary award to a party for any valuable benefit obtained by the other party before the frustrating event.

Questions

1. When may a contract be discharged by frustration?

2. What are the effects of a frustrating event?

3. Brix plc contracted to build a factory for £20m for PC Ltd. The agreed completion date was two years from the date of the contract. £5m was to be paid six months after that date and the balance on completion. The contract contained a 'Force Majeure' clause providing for the extension of time for the works (without additional payment) 'in the event of fire, flood, explosion or similar occurrence delaying completion of the works'.

   Ten months later, after the £5m instalment had been paid, there was major subsidence on the site caused by the collapse of a network of medieval tunnels below it, of which both parties had been unaware. The subsidence destroyed the foundations of the factory, which Brix had half completed. As a result, it will take four years to complete the factory and completion will involve a total expenditure of £30m.

   Discuss the legal position.

4. In January, Paul, a keen yachtsman, agreed to rent Jane's house overlooking Weymouth Bay for £6,000 for a week in June when an international yacht regatta was to take place in the Bay. Paul paid a deposit of £2,000. The balance was payable on 1 June.

   A term of the agreement was that Jane would make some minor alterations to a room overlooking the Bay so as to improve the view of the regatta. The cost of these alterations was £1,000.

   A few days before the scheduled start of the regatta, a large, laden tanker sank in the Bay and the resulting pollution necessitated cancellation of the regatta. Paul informed Jane that he no longer wanted to use the house, that he wanted his £2,000 deposit back and that he would not be paying the balance of the £6,000.

   Advise Jane.

   Would your answer be different if the reason for the cancellation was not oil pollution (because a tanker had sunk in the Bay) but the withdrawal of sponsorship of the regatta by Paul, the sole sponsor?

5. Explain:
   - how a 'valuable benefit' is identified and valued for the purposes of the Law Reform (Frustrated Contracts) Act 1943, s 1(3), and
   - the effect under s 1(3) of the conferment of such a benefit before the frustration of a contract.

11

Remedies for breach of contract

CHAPTER OVERVIEW

In the event of a breach of contract, the injured party may have one or more of the following remedies:

- The injured party may, subject to any applicable and effective exemption clause,[1] and to the rules discussed in paras 11.1–11.34, recover damages for any loss suffered as a result of the breach by bringing an action for damages for breach of contract.

- If a breach consists of the other party's failure to pay the agreed price or other remuneration due under the contract, the appropriate course for the injured party is to bring an action for the agreed sum to recover that amount, rather than an action for damages. See paras 11.35–11.37. A person who recovers an agreed sum may also recover damages for any further loss which he (or she) has suffered.

- In the case of a repudiatory breach, the injured party (X) may terminate the contract for breach, ie accept the breach as discharging the contract, thereby discharging X from any obligation to perform the contract further. If X elects to terminate for repudiatory breach, X may also bring an action for damages for any loss suffered. Termination for repudiatory breach was dealt with in paras 8.9–8.15.

- The injured party may sue for an account of profits accruing to the other party through the breach of contract. See paras 11.38–11.40.

- Where the injured party (X) has performed part of his (or her) own obligations, but is unjustifiably prevented from completing them by the other party, X may recover the value of what X has done *if X terminates the contract for breach*. See paras 11.41–11.42.

- Where the injured party (X) has paid the contractual price, but the other party has not performed any part of his (or her) contractual duties in respect of which the payment is due under the contract or X has not received any part of the benefit bargained for under the contract, X may recover the amount paid *if X terminates the contract for breach*. If the failure of consideration is not total but only partial, an action for the return of money paid is not available. These matters were dealt with in slightly more detail in para 8.13.

- Lastly, in appropriate cases, the injured party may seek a decree of specific performance or an injunction in addition to, or instead of, damages. See paras 11.43–11.51.

The chapter concludes by explaining how delay can result in an action for a remedy being barred.

---

[1] Chapter 9.

Damages

Purpose of damages

11.1 Damages for breach of contract are not awarded to punish the defaulting party (hereafter 'the defendant'),[1] with the result that the amount awarded is not affected by the deliberateness of the breach, manner of the breach or the motive behind it[2]. Instead, damages for breach of contract are awarded to compensate the injured party (hereafter 'the claimant') for the loss or damage which the claimant has suffered as a result of the breach of contract.[3]

This rule means that, where the claimant has not suffered any loss or damage as a result of the breach, the damages recoverable by the claimant will as a general rule be purely nominal (usually in the region of £2 to £20).

[1] In *Johnson v Unisys Ltd* [2001] UKHL 13, the House of Lords confirmed that exemplary damages (see para 27.2) are not available in a claim of breach of contract.
[2] *Addis v Gramophone Co Ltd* [1909] AC 488, HL.
[3] For a modern authority see *Surrey CC v Bredero Homes Lt*d [1993] 3 All ER 705, CA.

11.2 As part of the rule that damages for breach of contract are awarded to compensate the claimant, a claimant cannot, as a general principle, recover damages on behalf of a third party. This was established by the House of Lords in *Woodar Investment Ltd v Wimpey Construction Ltd*.[1] However, in a few exceptional cases, a claimant can recover substantial damages for a loss which the claimant has not suffered.

One exception is where the claimant made the contract as agent or trustee for another. If the contract is broken in such a case and the claimant sues for damages on the other's behalf the claimant can recover substantial damages for the loss suffered by the other as a result of the breach.[2]

Another exception was established by the decision in *St Albans City and District Council v International Computers Ltd*,[3] where the Court of Appeal held that a claimant could recover substantial damages in respect of loss suffered by a third party if the claimant was under a duty to act in the best interests of the third party, although not strictly a trustee. In this case, C purchased from D a computer program for its collection of community charge payments. The program was defective. As a result of this breach of contract the number of chargepayers was overstated when the program was used to extract the number of chargepayers. One result was that C had to pay £685,000 to the county council by way of increased precept payments. It could not recover that sum from the county council, and was obliged to recover it from chargepayers by setting a higher community charge for the following year. When sued for the £685,000, D argued that C had not itself suffered any loss as a result of its breach of contract because C had recouped its loss, and the only loss remaining was that of the chargepayers. The Court of Appeal upheld an award of £685,000 on the ground that, although not strictly a trustee, C had no less a capacity than a trustee to recover damages for breach of contract for the chargepayers' benefit. Otherwise the chargepayers would be out of pocket.[4]

[1] [1980] 1 All ER 517, HL.
[2] *Lloyd's v Harper* (1880) 16 Ch D 290, CA.
[3] [1996] 4 All ER 481, CA.
[4] For other exceptions to *Woodar v Wimpey* see *Linden Gardens Trust Ltd v Lenesta Sludge Disposals Ltd* [1993] 3 All ER 417, HL; *Darlington Borough Council v Wiltshier Northern Ltd* [1995] 3 All ER 895, CA.

For what can compensation be awarded?

Loss of expectation

11.3 The principal function of damages for breach of contract is to put the claimant into the same position, so far as money can, *as if the contract had been performed* as agreed.[1] In achieving this, damages are awarded to compensate the claimant for the loss of the claimant's expectations under the contract.

> [1] *Robinson v Harman* (1848) 1 Exch 850 at 855.

11.4 Lost expectations may consist of a loss of profit which the claimant expected to make if the contract had been properly performed but which has been lost as a result of the breach. Suppose, for example, that D agrees to sell some machinery to C, a manufacturer, who intends to use it to make goods for sale at a profit, and that D does not deliver the machinery on time. C's loss as a result of D's breach is the profit which C would have made from selling the goods if the machinery had been delivered on time.

Where the claimant did not contract with any expectation of making a profit, the claimant's loss of expectation in a case where the subject matter of the contract involved property will be quantified either by reference to the diminished value of what the claimant has received (ie the difference between what the thing would have been worth if the contract had been properly performed and its actual value) or by the cost of cure/repair/reinstatement of the thing so as to make it as it would have been if the contract had been properly performed.

In the case of many contracts there is no significant (if any) difference in the amount quantified by the 'diminution in value' measure and the 'cost of cure' measure. However, in some contracts, the two measures may produce significantly different sums. This is particularly likely to happen in the case of building contracts. Normally, the claimant's loss of expectations in respect of defective or incomplete workmanship is assessed by the cost of cure, but the choice between the two measures is essentially based on whether or not it is reasonable to use the cost of a cure measure. This was affirmed by the House of Lords in *Ruxley Electronics and Construction Ltd v Forsyth*.[1] D contracted with C for the construction by D of a swimming pool at C's house. A term of the contract specifically required the pool to be 7'6" deep at its deepest point. However, D constructed a pool which was, at most, 6' deep. More importantly, at a point where the diving board was situated, the pool was less than 6' deep. As indicated above, the House of Lords was faced with a choice of two options as to the quantification of damages in respect of the defect:

- capital value of pool in a non-defective state minus its value in its defective state ('diminution in value' measure). This was favoured by the trial judge, who found that there had been no diminution in value because, despite its defects, the pool still enhanced the value of C's property;
- cost of repair/reinstatement ('cost of cure' measure). This was favoured by the Court of Appeal and involved an award of damages in line with the expensive cost of digging up and extensively reconstructing the pool (£21,650).

The House of Lords took the same view as the trial judge and simply awarded C £2,500 for loss of amenity[2] and nothing in respect of the defect to the pool itself. It held that the cost of cure could only be recovered if it was reasonable to allow this. In assessing this, it was appropriate to consider the personal preferences of C and whether or not he intended to cure the defect (since if C did not intend to rebuild he would have lost nothing except the diminution in value). Moreover, the House held that, where the cost of cure was *less* than the diminution in value, the measure should be the cost of cure. On the other hand, where the cost of cure was *out of all proportion* to the good to be obtained, the appropriate measure was the diminution in value measure, and if there was no diminution in value substantial damages could not be awarded in respect of the defect in the pool itself.

[1] [1995] 3 All ER 268, HL.
[2] Para 11.6.

11.5 *Inconvenience or discomfort* As part of expectation loss, damages can be awarded for inconvenience or discomfort, resulting from the breach. *Bailey v Bullock*[1] provides an example of damages being awarded for physical inconvenience or discomfort. There, C and his wife and child were forced to live in discomfort with his in-laws for two years because of his solicitor's failure, in breach of contract, to take effective steps to obtain possession of a house.

[1] [1950] 2 All ER 1167.

11.6 *Disappointment or distress* Consistently with the rule that damages for breach of contract are awarded for loss of expectation, damages for disappointment or distress brought about by breach of contract may also be awarded, but only:

- where it is a consequence of injury or of physical inconvenience or discomfort caused by the breach;[1] or
- where a major or important object of the contract was the giving of pleasure or enjoyment or the prevention of disturbed peace of mind or of distress.[2]

In *Jarvis v Swans Tours Ltd*,[3] for instance, C booked a 15-day winter sports holiday with D. He did so on the faith of D's brochure, which described the holiday as a house party and promised a number of entertainments, including excellent skiing, a yodeller evening, a bar, and afternoon tea and cakes. In the first week there were 13 guests; in the second C was entirely alone. The entertainments fell far short of the promised standard. The Court of Appeal held that C was entitled to damages for mental distress and disappointment due to loss of enjoyment caused by the breach of contract. A similar decision was reached in *Heywood v Wellers*,[4] where a solicitor's client suffered distress as a result of the solicitor's incompetent handling of an injunction designed to prevent molestation of the client. In *Ruxley Electronics and Construction Ltd v Forsyth*, referred to in para 11.4, the award of damages for loss of amenity was held by the House of Lords to be justified on the basis that the object of the contract was the provision of a pleasurable amenity and that C's pleasure was not as great as it would have been if the pool had been 7'6" deep. The one Law Lord who considered the matter further justified the award for loss of amenity on the basis that it was a logical application of the existing exceptions to the rule that generally damages for distress or disappointment cannot be awarded.

In contrast, damages for disappointment or distress cannot be awarded where the breach is of an employment contract (eg wrongful dismissal) or of a covenant for quiet enjoyment[5] in a lease, since the giving of pleasure or peace of mind or the like is not an object of such a contract or covenant.[6] For example, in *Hayes v James & Charles Dodd (a firm)*,[7] a married couple, who suffered anxiety and distress when their car repair business failed because their solicitors had incorrectly advised them (in breach of contract) that there was a right of access to the rear of the workshop they were purchasing, were held by the Court of Appeal not to be entitled to damages for that distress (although they recovered damages for the financial loss which they had suffered). This case makes an interesting contrast to *Heywood v Wellers* where the object of the contract was to prevent the client suffering distress.

It can be seen from the above that normally damages for disappointment or distress are not recoverable for breach of a contract of survey, because the giving of pleasure or peace of mind or the like is not an object of such a contract.[8] *Farley v Skinner,*[9] however, shows that if a contract of survey has one of these things as its major or important object damages for distress can be awarded for its breach. In *Farley v Skinner*, a contract between D, a chartered surveyor, and C, a prospective purchaser, to inspect and report on the condition of a property included a requirement to advise about whether the property might be affected by aircraft noise; C did not want a property on a flight path. D negligently failed to discover that the property was from time to time badly so affected. The House of Lords held that C could recover damages for distress and disappointment suffered after he had bought the property in reliance on D's report, because a major or important object of the contract was to give pleasure, relaxation and peace of mind.

[1] *Watts v Morrow* [1991] 4 All ER 937, CA.
[2] *Farley v Skinner* [2001] UKHL 49, HL.
[3] [1973] 1 All ER 71, CA.
[4] [1976] 1 All ER 300, CA.
[5] Para 36.34.
[6] *Bliss v South East Thames Regional Health Authority* [1987] ICR 700, CA (breach of employment contract); *Branchett v Beaney, Coster and Swale Borough Council* (1992) 24 HLR 348, CA (breach of covenant for quiet enjoyment in a lease; for a description of this type of covenant, see para 36.34).
[7] [1990] 2 All ER 815, CA.
[8] *Watts v Morrow* [1991] 4 All ER 937, CA.
[9] [2001] UKHL 49, HL.

11.7 *Negative terms* Where the term broken is a negative one, ie not to do something (as in the case of a restrictive covenant relating to land), the expectation lost is that the conduct restrained will not take place (eg that building will not take place in breach of the restrictive covenant) unless a release from the negative term is negotiated at a price. If the breach prevents the negotiation of such a release damages can be awarded to compensate for loss of this expectation on the basis of what could reasonably have been demanded by the claimant as a quid pro quo for releasing the defendant from the negative term.

Damages were assessed on this basis by a High Court judge in *Wrotham Park Estate Co Ltd v Parkside Homes Ltd,*[1] where damages were awarded to compensate C for breach of a restrictive covenant against building on land. The judge assessed the damages at 5% of D's anticipated profits, this being the amount which C could reasonably have demanded for relaxation of the covenant. *Wrotham Park* was applied by the Court of Appeal in *Experience Hendrix LLC v PXX Enterprises Inc,*[2] where damages were awarded on the same basis in respect of breach of a term that D would not licence certain recordings in which Jimi Hendrix merely featured as a sideman. The Court of Appeal held that C was entitled to damages representing the sum which might reasonably have been demanded as a quid pro quo for agreeing to release D from the term not to licence the recordings as it had.

The sum which C might reasonably have demanded to release D from the negative term is assessed by reference to a notional agreement negotiated by C and D to release D from the negative term, and in the hypothetical negotiations the parties must be assumed to have acted willingly and reasonably.[3]

[1] [1974] 2 All ER 321.
[2] [2003] EWCA Civ 323, CA.
[3] *Pell Frischmann Engineering Ltd v Bow Valley Iran Ltd* [2009] UKPC 45, PC.

11.8 *Reliance loss* In some cases, damages are awarded to compensate the claimant for expenditure which the claimant has incurred in reliance on the contract being performed (ie in expectation of the contract being performed).[1] Damages of this type are called damages for reliance loss. By way of an extension, damages can even be recovered for expenses incurred prior to, and in anticipation of, the contract and wasted as a result of the breach. In *Lloyd v Stanbury*,[2] for instance, C, who had made a contract to buy a farm, which was broken by D's failure to complete, was awarded damages for (inter alia) the following losses incurred before there was a binding contract of sale: legal expenses incurred in carrying out pre-contract searches and drafting the contract, and the cost of moving a caravan to the farm, as a temporary home for D, prior to and in anticipation of the contract.

Because they compensate for expenditure which has been *incurred in reliance on the contract and wasted as a result of its breach*, damages for reliance loss cannot be awarded if this would make the claimant better off than if the contract had been performed, as where the claimant has made a bad bargain by agreeing to pay more for something than it was worth or where the claimant's expected profit from the contract was less than the claimant's expenditure. *C and P Haulage v Middleton*[3] provides an example of the operation of this limitation. C was granted by D a contractual licence (on a six-month renewable basis) to occupy premises as a workshop. C spent money in making the premises suitable, although the contract provided that fixtures installed by him were not to be removed. Ten weeks before the end of a six-month term, C was ejected in breach of the contractual licence. As a temporary measure, C was permitted by his local authority to use his own home as a workshop, which he did until well after the six-month term had expired. The Court of Appeal held that C could only recover nominal damages. C's ability to use his home as a workshop meant that he suffered no loss as a result of D's breach since, in the circumstances, he was no worse off than if the contract had been fully performed. C could not recover, as reliance loss, his expenditure in equipping the premises, because, it was held, if the contract had been wholly performed as agreed and lawfully terminated at the end of the six-month term, there would have been no question of him recovering that expenditure and, therefore, to award him such damages would leave him better off than if the contract had been wholly performed.

In order to defeat a claimant's claim for wasted expenditure, the onus is on the defendant to prove that the expenditure would not have been recovered if the contract had been performed.[4]

[1] *Omak Maritime Ltd v Mamola Challenger Shipping Co* [2010] EWHC 2026 (Comm).
[2] [1971] 2 All ER 267.
[3] [1983] 3 All ER 94, CA.
[4] *CCC Films (London) Ltd v Impact Quadrant Films Ltd* [1984] 3 All ER 298.

11.9 Damages for reliance loss and damages for loss of another expectation are not mutually exclusive, but damages cannot be awarded for both if this has the effect of compensating the claimant twice over for the same loss. For example, in *Cullinane v British Rema Manufacturing Co Ltd*,[1] D sold a machine to C. A term of the contract related to the machine's output rate. C claimed damages for breach of this term under two headings:

- loss of profits, and
- the capital cost of the machine and its installation (reliance loss).

It was held that C could not recover damages for both types of loss, as a claim for loss of profits could only be based on the fact that money had been spent on acquiring and installing the machine.

[1] [1953] 2 All ER 1257, CA.

11.10 *Difficulty of precise assessment* The fact that the precise assessment of the value of a lost expectation is difficult does not prevent an award being made, as is shown by *Chaplin* *v Hicks.*[1] D advertised that he would employ, as actresses, 12 women to be selected by him out of 50 chosen as the most beautiful by the readers of various newspapers, in which the candidates' photographs appeared. C was one of the 50 chosen by the readers but D made an unreasonable appointment for an interview with her, and selected 12 out of the 49 who were able to keep the appointment. In an action for breach of contract, D contended that only nominal damages were payable, since C would only have had a one in four chance of being selected. Nevertheless, the Court of Appeal refused to disturb an award of £100 damages for the loss of her chance of being selected. Where damages are claimed for a lost chance, C must prove that the chance was a real or substantial, and not merely speculative, one. The value of the lost chance will depend on where the chance lay on a range between a real or substantial one and a virtually certain one.[2]

[1] [1911] 2 KB 786, CA.
[2] *Allied Maples Group Ltd v Simmons & Simmons* [1995] 4 All ER 907, CA.

11.11 *Time of assessment* Where damages are awarded to compensate the claimant for loss of expectations, they are normally assessed as at the date of the breach. However, this is not an absolute rule since, if its observance would give rise to injustice, the court has power to fix such other date as may be appropriate in the circumstances.[1] For example, where the claimant could only reasonably have been expected to mitigate his (or her) loss at a point of time after the breach, damages should be assessed as at that point of time, or, if that point of time is not earlier, at the date of the judgment.[2] By way of further example, if, as has happened with house prices in the recent past, there has been a rapid and dramatic rise in the value of the subject matter of the contract, it may be more appropriate for damages to be assessed at the date of the judgment rather than the date of the breach.[3]

Damages may be reduced where subsequent events before the court hearing are known to have reduced the actual loss suffered.[4]

In the case of an anticipatory breach of contract, damages for loss of expectation are assessed by reference to the time when performance ought to have been made, and not by reference to the time of the anticipatory breach.[5]

[1] *Johnson v Agnew* [1979] 1 All ER 883 at 896.
[2] *William Cory & Son Ltd v Wingate Investments (London Colney) Ltd* (1978) 17 BLR 104, CA. For mitigation of loss, see paras 11.25–11.27.
[3] *Suleman v Shahsavari* [1989] 2 All ER 460.
[4] *Golden Strait Corpn v Nippon Yusen Kubishika Kaisha* [2007] UKHL 12, HL.
[5] *Tai Hing Cotton Mill Ltd v Kamsing Knitting Factory* [1978] 1 All ER 515, PC.

Consequential loss

11.12 Subject to the rules of remoteness, a claimant can recover not merely for loss of expectation resulting from the breach of contract, but also for expenses, personal injury (including pain and suffering) and injury to property which are an inevitable consequence of the breach.

Damages for injury to reputation are not as a general rule recoverable in a breach of contract action[1] but, where the loss of reputation results from breach of a term (as opposed to the manner of the breach) and leads to financial loss, damages (known as 'stigma damages') are recoverable for that loss. This was held by the House of Lords in *Malik v Bank of Credit and Commerce International SA,*[2] where C had been employees of D bank which, unknown to them, had been engaged in a massive fraud. D bank collapsed and went into liquidation. C were made redundant by the liquidator. Their association with the bank made it difficult to obtain employment in the banking field, and they suffered financial loss in consequence. The House of Lords held that D bank was in breach of its implied obligation not, without reasonable cause, to conduct its business in a manner likely to destroy or seriously damage the relationship of confidence between employer and employee,[3] and that, if C could prove that the injury to their reputation caused by this breach had handicapped them in the labour market and thereby caused them financial loss, C would be entitled to recover damages for that loss.

Malik was a case where the breach of the implied term of trust and confidence in the employment contract had occurred *during* that contract and was not related to any dismissal. In *Johnson v Unisys Ltd*,[4] the House of Lords held that an employee had no right of action at common law to recover financial losses resulting from his inability to work because of a nervous breakdown arising from the unfair manner of his *dismissal*, and that a conclusion to the contrary would be inconsistent with the statutory scheme for dealing with unfair dismissal.

[1] *Addis v Gramophone Co Ltd* [1909] AC 488, HL.
[2] [1997] 3 All ER 1, HL.
[3] Para 7.31.
[4] [2001] UKHL 13.

Causal connection

11.13 In order to succeed in an action for damages, the claimant must, of course, prove that the loss or damage (hereafter simply referred to as 'loss') which the claimant has suffered resulted from the defendant's breach of contract.[1] This requires that the claimant's loss would not have occurred but for the defendant's breach. The defendant's breach need not be the only cause of the loss, since the conduct of others or the occurrence of extraneous events may also contribute to it, but it must be the effective or dominant cause of the loss.[2]

[1] *Weld-Blundell v Stephens* [1920] AC 956, HL.
[2] See, eg *Galoo Ltd v Bright Grahame Murray* [1995] 1 All ER 16, CA; *County Ltd v Girozentrale Securities* [1996] 3 All ER 834, CA.

Remoteness of loss

11.14 Proof of a causal link between breach and loss is not in itself enough to entitle the claimant to damages for that loss, because a defendant will only be liable for it if it was not too 'remote'. A loss will not normally be too remote if it was reasonably contemplatable by the parties, and will normally be too remote if it was not so contemplatable, under the rule explained below. In exceptional circumstances the 'reasonable contemplation test' will be ousted and the question of remoteness will be answered by applying the test of whether the defendant can reasonably be said to have assumed responsibility for loss of the particular type suffered.

Reasonable contemplation of loss

11.15 Whether or not loss suffered is too remote is normally determined by applying the rule in *Hadley v Baxendale*[1] (as explained in *Victoria Laundry (Windsor) Ltd v Newman Industries Ltd*[2] and *Koufos v C Czarnikow Ltd, The Heron II*[3]).

The rule, as explained, provides that damage is not too remote if one of the two following sub-rules is satisfied:

- if the loss arises naturally, ie according to the usual course of things, from the breach of contract as a not unlikely result of it; or

- if the loss could reasonably be supposed to have been in the contemplation of the parties, when they made the contract, as a not unlikely result of the breach of it.

As we shall see, the first sub-rule deals with 'normal' damage which arises in the ordinary course of events, while the second sub-rule deals with 'abnormal' damage which arises from special circumstances.

[1]   (1854) 23 LJ Ex 179.
[2]   [1949] 1 All ER 997, CA.
[3]   [1967] 3 All ER 686, HL.

11.16 In the light of subsequent cases, a number of things can be said about both sub-rules.

First, the claimant can only recover for such loss as would, *at the time of the making of the contract*,[1] have been within the reasonable contemplation of the parties as a not unlikely result of its breach, *had they had their attention drawn to the possibility of the breach which has in fact occurred*.[2] It must be emphasised that the particular breach itself need not have been contemplated. Suppose that the loss has been caused by some defect in the subject matter of the contract which was unknown, or even unknowable, when the contract was made. The court has to assume, even though it is contrary to the facts, that the parties had in mind the breach which has occurred when it considers whether the claimant's loss was within their reasonable contemplation.[3]

Second, what was within the parties' reasonable contemplation depends on the knowledge 'possessed' by them at that time. For this purpose, knowledge 'possessed' is of two kinds: one imputed, the other actual. Under the first sub-rule, everyone is taken to know (ie knowledge is imputed) the 'ordinary course of things' and, consequently, what loss is a not unlikely result of a breach of contract in that ordinary course. In addition, 'knowledge possessed' may, in a particular case, include knowledge which the defaulting party (and the other party) actually possess of special circumstances, outside the ordinary course of things, of such a kind that in these special circumstances a further loss would not be unlikely to result. Such a case attracts the second sub-rule so as to make the additional loss recoverable.[4]

Third, provided the *type* of loss caused by a breach of contract was within the reasonable contemplation of the parties as not unlikely when the contract was made, the loss is not too remote, and damages can therefore be recovered for it, even though its extent was much greater than could have been reasonably contemplated[5] and even though it occurred in a way which could not have been reasonably contemplated.[6] An example is provided by *H Parsons (Livestock) Ltd v Uttley Ingham & Co Ltd*.[7] D supplied C with a hopper in which to store pig nuts. The hopper was not properly ventilated, and this constituted a breach of contract by D; as a result, the pig nuts became mouldy and many of Cs' pigs suffered a rare intestinal disease (E coli) from which 254 of them died. C were awarded damages by the Court of Appeal for the loss sustained by the death and sickness of the pigs. The reasoning of the majority of the Court of Appeal was that, if the breach had been brought to the parties' attention and they had asked themselves what was likely to happen as a result, they would have contemplated that it was not unlikely that the pigs would become ill, and that, since the type of loss caused (physical harm) was within the parties' reasonable contemplation, it was irrelevant that its extent and the way in which it occurred were not. This principle raises the issue of what constitutes a type of loss, as is shown by reference to *Victoria Laundry (Windsor) Ltd v Newman Industries Ltd*, referred to in para 11.19, and the speeches of Lord Rodger and Baroness

Hale in *Transfield Shipping Inc v Mercator Shipping Inc, The Achilleas*, referred to in para 11.22.

¹ This was confirmed in *Jackson v Royal Bank of Scotland Ltd* [2003] UKHL 3, HL.
² *H Parsons (Livestock) Ltd v Uttley Ingham & Co Ltd* [1978] 1 All ER 525, CA.
³ *H Parsons (Livestock) Ltd v Uttley Ingham & Co Ltd* [1978] 1 All ER 525, CA.
⁴ *Victoria Laundry (Windsor) Ltd v Newman Industries Ltd* [1949] 1 All ER 997, CA.
⁵ *Wroth v Tyler* [1973] 1 All ER 897; *H Parsons (Livestock) Ltd v Uttley Ingham & Co Ltd.*
⁶ *H Parsons (Livestock) Ltd v Uttley Ingham & Co Ltd* [1978] 1 All ER 525, CA.
⁷ [1978] 1 All ER 525, CA.

11.17 *Degree of risk* The degree of risk which is required to have been within the parties' reasonable contemplation in order to satisfy the test of remoteness has been variously described in the cases. In *Koufos v C Czarnikow Ltd, The Heron II*,[1] which can be taken as settling the point, the House of Lords made it clear that the degree of risk is more than mere possibility or a risk that is 'on the cards'. However, they were not unanimous in their terminology as to the degree of risk required. Lords Pearce and Upjohn favoured 'serious possibility' or 'real danger'; Lord Reid favoured 'not unlikely' (ie 'considerably less than even chance, but nevertheless not very unusual and easily foreseeable'). There is no difference of substance between these terms. With the exception of Lord Reid, the House was prepared to accept the phrase 'liable to result', a rather colourless and vague term which two of them thought was a convenient term to describe 'serious possibility' or 'real danger'. We have used 'not unlikely' in this book on the basis that it is the term which has tended to be used in subsequent decisions.

¹ [1967] 3 All ER 686, HL.

11.18 *Examples* The application of the contractual rule of remoteness can best be illustrated by reference to past decisions. In *Hadley v Baxendale*,[1] C's mill at Gloucester was brought to a halt when a crankshaft broke. The shaft had to be sent to its makers in Greenwich as a pattern for a new one. D undertook to deliver it at Greenwich the following day, but in breach of contract delayed its delivery so that the duration of the stoppage at the mill was extended. C's claim to recover damages for loss of profits caused by D's delay was unsuccessful since this loss was held to be too remote. The basis of the court's decision was that D only knew that they were transporting a broken shaft owned by C. The court applied the two sub-rules in turn, and held:

- C might have had a spare shaft or been able to borrow one, and therefore the loss of profits did not arise in the usual course of events from D's breach; and
- on the facts known to D (they were unaware of the lack of a substitute shaft), the loss of profits could not be supposed to have been within the reasonable contemplation of the parties at the time they made the contract as the probable result of the breach.

¹ (1854) 23 LJ Ex 179.

11.19 In *Victoria Laundry (Windsor) Ltd v Newman Industries Ltd*,[1] D agreed to sell to C, who were launderers and dyers, a boiler to be delivered on a certain date. The boiler was damaged in a fall and was not delivered until five months after the agreed delivery date. C claimed damages for loss of profits that would have been earned during the five-month period through the extension of their business, and also for loss of several highly lucrative dyeing contracts which they would have obtained with the Ministry of Supply. The Court of Appeal held that C could recover for the loss of 'normal' profits (ie those which would have been earned through an extension of the business) but not for the loss of 'exceptional' profits (ie loss of the highly lucrative contracts), which it treated as a different type of loss. This decision was based on the following application of the two sub-rules:

- D knew at the time of the contract that C were laundrymen and dyers and required the boiler for immediate use in their business and, with their technical experience and knowledge of the facts, it could be presumed that loss of 'normal' profits was foreseeable by them, and therefore within both parties' reasonable contemplation, as liable to result from the breach; but

- in the absence of special knowledge, D could not reasonably foresee the loss of the 'exceptional' profits under the highly lucrative contracts as liable to result from the breach.

[1] [1949] 1 All ER 997, CA.

11.20 In *Koufos v C Czarnikow Ltd, The Heron II*,[1] C sugar merchants chartered a ship from D to carry a cargo of sugar from Constanza to Basrah. The ship deviated in breach of contract and arrived in Basrah nine days later than expected. Because of a fall in the market price of sugar, C obtained £3,800 less for the cargo than would have been obtained if it had arrived on time. D did not know of C's intention to sell the sugar in Basrah, but D did know that there was a market for sugar at Basrah and that C were sugar merchants. The House of Lords held that C's loss of profits (£3,800) was not too remote under the first sub-rule, since knowledge could be imputed to D that the goods might be sold at market price on their arrival in Basrah and that market prices were apt to fluctuate daily, and therefore the loss of profits was within the reasonable contemplation of the parties at the time of the contract as not unlikely in the event of the breach in question.

[1] [1967] 3 All ER 686, HL.

Assumption of responsibility

11.21 The principle of assumption of responsibility has emerged in recent years. In the exceptional type of case where it applies, it operates to override the solution given by the reasonable contemplation test of remoteness, either by excluding from recovery a loss satisfying that test or by including a loss which does not.

11.22 *Exclusionary effect* Under the assumption of responsibility principle, in the exceptional cases where it applies, a defendant is not liable for a loss caused by his breach of contract which satisfies the reasonable contemplation test *if he cannot reasonably be regarded as having assumed responsibility for losses of the particular type suffered.*

The leading case for this is the decision of the House of Lords in *Transfield Shipping Inc v Mercator Shipping Inc, The Achilleas*.[1] In that case, D, charterers under a time charterparty of a ship, were obliged to re-deliver her by 2 May 2004 and had given notice that they would do so. The shipowners, C, then contracted to let the ship to new charterers for a four- to six-month period following on from the then existing charterparty, at a daily rate of $39,500 a day. The latest day for delivery to the new charterers was 8 May 2004, after which they were entitled to cancel. In breach of contract, D failed to re-deliver the ship until 11 May. By that time charterparty rates had fallen. The new charterer agreed to accept the ship late but only at a greatly reduced rate ($31,500 a day). C claimed damages from D for the loss of the difference between the original rate and the reduced rate over the period of the charterparty with the new charterers. It having been held that C could recover damages for this loss because the loss fell within the first sub-rule in *Hadley v Baxendale* as arising naturally, ie according to the usual course of things from the breach, D appealed to the House of Lords who allowed the appeal.

Lord Rodger decided the case solely by reference to the reasonable contemplation test, concluding that neither party could reasonably have contemplated that an overrun of nine days would 'in the ordinary course of things' cause C the *type* of loss for which they claimed damages. In other words, as in *Victoria Laundry v Newman Industries*, he regarded the loss as a different type of loss from that reasonably contemplatable by the parties. Baroness Hale, who was doubtful whether the appeal should be allowed, stated that if it was it would be for Lord Rodger's reason. Lord Walker may have allowed the appeal on similar grounds but caused confusion by expressly agreeing with the very different reasoning of Lords Hoffman and Hope. Those two law lords applied the assumption of responsibility principle, to which we now turn.

Lords Hoffman and Hope allowed the appeal on the ground that it was insufficient that a particular kind of loss was not unlikely if it was not reasonable to assume that D had undertaken responsibility for it, and that in the circumstances it was not reasonable to assume that D had undertaken responsibility for the loss of the follow-on charterparty, and so the damages were limited to the difference between the market rate and the charter rate for the period of the delay in re-delivery. It remains to be seen what factors will negate the assumption of responsibility. The two law lords both emphasised that the amount of the loss was outside D's control and was unpredictable at the time when the contract was made. Further guidance was given in *Sylvia Shipping*, below.

¹ [2008] UKHL 48, HL.

11.23 It is clear from subsequent cases in which *Transfield* has been referred to that the approach taken by Lords Hoffman and Hope (with Lord Walker's agreement) will only be applied in exceptional cases to exclude from recovery a loss which is not too remote under the reasonable contemplation test. In *Sylvia Shipping Co Ltd v Progress Bulk Carriers Ltd*,¹ Hamblen J, affirming that the assumption of responsibility principle had the support of the majority in *Transfield*, said that the reasonable contemplation test, remains the general test of remoteness applicable in the great majority of cases. However, he said, there may be 'unusual' cases in which the context, surrounding circumstances or general understanding in the relevant market make it necessary specifically to consider whether there has been an assumption of responsibility. This was most likely to be in those relatively rare cases where the application of the general test (ie that of reasonable contemplation) led or might lead to an unquantifiable, unpredictable or disproportionate liability or where there is clear evidence that such a liability would be contrary to market understanding and expectations.

In *Sylvia Shipping*, shipowners had broken their maintenance obligations under a time charterparty with the result that a sub-charter made by the charterers was cancelled. It was held that the arbitrators had not been wrong in law in holding that the charterers were entitled to the loss of profit on the cancelled sub-charter. Hamblen J held that the loss in question arose naturally within the first sub-rule in *Hadley v Baxendale*, and that the case was not one of those 'unusual' ones where the issue of whether or not there had been an assumption of responsibility had to be considered because it could not be said that the liability in question was likely to be unquantifiable, unpredictable, uncontrollable or disproportionate (loss of a sub-charter during a time charterparty could never be for longer than the time charterparty), and nor did the case involve volatile market conditions.

In *Supershield Limited v Siemens Building Technologies FE Limited*,[2] Toulson LJ, with whom the other two members of the Court of Appeal agreed, said that, while the reasonable contemplation test remains a standard rule on the basis that it reflects the expectation to be imputed to the parties in the ordinary case, ie that a contract-breaker should ordinarily be liable for loss resulting from the breach only if, at the time of the contract, it was reasonably contemplatable as not unlikely, *Transfield* is authority that there may be cases where the court, on examining the contract and the commercial background, decides that the reasonable contemplation approach would not reflect the expectation or intention reasonably to be imputed to the parties.

  [1] [2010] EWHC 542 (Comm).
  [2] [2010] EWCA Civ 7, CA.

11.24 *Inclusionary effect* In *Supershield*, Toulson LJ stated that logically the assumption of responsibility principle may have an inclusionary effect; if, on the proper analysis of the contract against its commercial background, the loss was within the scope of the duty (responsibility assumed), it could not be regarded as too remote, even though it would not have occurred in ordinary circumstances (ie an unlikely event would not be too remote if it fell within the scope of assumption of a responsibility to prevent it).

In *Supershield*, C entered into a sub-contract to supply and install the sprinkler system in a new office building. C had then sub-contracted the installation of the system to D. A float valve in the tank supplying the system, which D was obliged to install and had installed, failed, and water from the tank overflowed into a bunded area. The bunded area had a retaining wall and drains in its floor, but they were blocked by various material. The water overflowed the bund and caused extensive damage to electrical equipment. C was joined in proceedings against the main contractor for the loss caused by the flood and had settled the claims of the other parties. C in turn sued D for the amount of the settlement. D stated in reply that the escape of water was too remote for C to have been liable for the resulting loss on a proper application of the reasonable contemplation test of remoteness and this had not been reasonably reflected in C's settlement. The trial judge gave judgment for C.

Dismissing D's appeal, Toulson LJ (with whom the other two judges agreed) held as follows. On the facts, the valve and the drains were both designed to control the flow of water involved in the operation of the sprinkler system. They were part of a system of multiple protection devices fitted in the reasonable expectation that the risk of simultaneous failure of both or all the protection devices would have been minimal. The fulfilment of that expectation would, however, depend on those responsible for the protection devices doing as they ought. If they failed to do so and the unlikely happened, it should be no answer for one of them to say that that the occurrence was unlikely, when it was that party's responsibility to see that it did not occur.

It must be remembered that Toulson LJ prefaced his remarks by saying the reasonable contemplation test remains a standard rule on the basis that it reflects the expectation to be imputed to the parties in the ordinary case, ie that a contract-breaker should ordinarily be liable for loss resulting from the breach only if, at the time of the contract, it was reasonably contemplatable as not unlikely, but that *Transfield* was authority that there may be cases where the court, on examining the contract and the commercial background, decides that the reasonable contemplation approach would not reflect the expectation or intention reasonably to be imputed to the parties. The assumption of responsibility principle will only be operative on an inclusionary basis in exceptional cases, in the same way as it is limited on an exclusionary basis.

Mitigation

11.25 The claimant cannot recover for loss which the claimant could reasonably have avoided. Thus, the seller of goods which have been wrongly rejected by the buyer must not unreasonably refuse another's offer to buy them. Similarly, an employee who has been wrongfully dismissed must not unreasonably refuse an offer of employment from another.[1] If such refusals occur, the claimant is said to be in breach of' the duty to mitigate his (or her) loss and cannot recover the unmitigated loss but only the loss which the claimant would have suffered if the damage had been mitigated. If the claimant would have suffered no loss at all, only nominal damages are recoverable.[2]

A leading case on the duty to mitigate is *Payzu Ltd v Saunders*.[3] A contract for the sale of goods by D to C provided that delivery should be as required over a nine-month period and that payment should be made within one month of delivery. C failed to make prompt payment for the first instalment and D, in breach of contract, refused to deliver any more instalments under the contract. D did, however, offer to deliver goods at the contract price if C would pay cash with each order. C refused to do so and brought an action for breach of contract, claiming the difference between the contract price and the market price (which had risen). The Court of Appeal held that C should have mitigated their loss by accepting D's offer; consequently, the damages which C could recover were to be measured by the loss which they would have suffered if the offer had been accepted, and not by the difference between the contract and market prices.

[1] *Brace v Calder* [1895] 2 QB 253, CA.
[2] *Brace v Calder* [1895] 2 QB 253, CA.
[3] [1919] 2 KB 581, CA.

11.26 The following points may be noted about the duty to mitigate:

- The phrase 'duty to mitigate' is somewhat misleading because the claimant is not legally obliged to do so. The defendant is free to act as he (or she) judges to be best, but if the defendant does so the defendant cannot recover for loss which he (or she) could reasonably have avoided.[1]

- The duty to mitigate may require the claimant to do something positive. In the examples given in para 11.25, the seller and the employee would equally have been in breach of their duty to mitigate if they had not made reasonable efforts to seek other offers to buy the goods or alternative equivalent employment: it would not necessarily excuse them that no one had spontaneously made them an offer. Damages cannot be recovered for any loss which would have been avoided if such reasonable steps had been taken.[2]

- The duty to mitigate only requires the claimant to take reasonable steps to minimise his (or her) loss. The claimant is not required to act with lightning speed, nor to accept the first or, indeed, any offer that is made (unless it is a reasonable one). For example, Rita, a wrongfully dismissed managing director, is not expected to mitigate her loss by taking a job sweeping floors. Indeed, in one case it was held that it was reasonable for a person who had wrongfully been dismissed as managing director in an arbitrary and high-handed fashion to refuse the company's offer of a slightly lower post at the same salary.[3]

[1] *Sotiros Shipping Inc v Sameiet Solholt, The Solholt* [1983] 1 Lloyd's Rep 605 at 608.
[2] *British Westinghouse Electric and Manufacturing Co Ltd v Underground Electric Rlys Co of London* [1912] AC 673 at 689.
[3] *Yetton v Eastwood Froy Ltd* [1966] 3 All ER 353.

11.27 Where there is an anticipatory breach of contract,[1] the claimant (C) has an option either to terminate the contract and sue immediately for damages or to affirm the contract and await the time fixed for performance, in which case he (or she) can then bring an action for damages if the other party is still in breach. If C elects to terminate C is under a duty to mitigate his (or her) loss.[2] On the other hand, C is under no duty to mitigate his (or her) loss before performance is due if C affirms the contract.[3]

> [1] Para 8.26.
> [2] *Roth & Co v Taysen Townsend & Co* (1895) 1 Com Cas 240.
> [3] Para 8.27.

Contributory negligence

11.28 Where a claimant has by his (or her) own fault contributed to the loss or the event causing it, the damages for breach of contract are not generally reduced in proportion to the claimant's degree of responsibility for that loss or event.[1] The doctrine of contributory negligence, under which the damages awarded to a claimant in a tort action may be reduced on the ground that the claimant was partly at fault,[2] does not generally apply to an action for breach of contract.[3]

There is one exception. If the defendant is liable in tort for negligence independently of the contract and also for breach of a contractual obligation to take reasonable care which was the same as the common law duty in the tort of negligence,[4] a court may apportion the blame and reduce the damages awarded to the claimant for breach of contract by reason of the claimant's contributory negligence.[5] Suppose that C, a surveyor's client, is negligently given incorrect information by the surveyor, and relies on it when C should know better (ie is negligent in doing so), and suppose that, as a result of C and the surveyor's negligence, C suffers economic loss. The doctrine of contributory negligence would apply to an action by C for breach of contract because the surveyor's liability to C in the tort of negligence and for breach of contract would be based on the same obligation to take reasonable care.

> [1] *Basildon District Council v J E Lesser (Properties) Ltd* [1985] 1 All ER 20.
> [2] Law Reform (Contributory Negligence) Act 1945. See para 19.6.
> [3] *Barclays Bank plc v Fairclough Building Ltd* [1995] 1 All ER 289, CA.
> [4] As to when there may be concurrent liability in tort and in contract, see para 16.16.
> [5] *Forsikringsaktieselskapet Vesta v Butcher* [1988] 2 All ER 43, CA; affd on other grounds [1989] 1 All ER 402, HL.

11.29 Of course, in any breach of contract case, if the claimant's contribution to the loss is so great as to prevent the defendant's breach of contract being an effective cause of the claimant's loss, the claimant will not be able to recover any damages at all for it.[1] Moreover, if the defendant successfully brings a counter-claim to a successful claim by the claimant, the effect on the damages awarded to each party may be the same as if there was an apportionment of liability on grounds of contributory negligence. In *Tennant Radiant Heat Ltd v Warrington Development Corpn*,[2] for instance, C leased a unit in a warehouse owned by D. Goods stored there by C were damaged when the roof collapsed under an accumulation of rainwater. The roof would not have collapsed but for the facts that C in breach of covenant had failed to repair the roof over their unit and that D had failed to keep clear the water outlets on the roof as a whole (and were therefore liable in tort for negligence and nuisance).[3] The Court of Appeal held that the damages recoverable on the claim and the counterclaim should be assessed on the basis of the extent to which the damage to the goods (C's claim) and to the roof (D's counter-claim) were caused, respectively, by D's tortious behaviour and by C's breach of covenant.

¹ Para 11.13; *Marintrans AB v Comet Shipping Co Ltd* [1985] 3 All ER 442.
² [1988] 1 EGLR 41, CA.
³ See chs 16 and 23.

Liquidated damages and penalties

11.30 So far we have been concerned with unliquidated damages, ie damages which are assessed by the court and not by the agreement of the parties. It is, however, possible for the parties to agree in their contract, by way of a genuine pre-estimate of the loss, that in the event of a breach the damages shall be a fixed sum or be calculated in a specific way. Such damages are called liquidated damages. Liquidated damages have the obvious advantage that the amount recoverable as damages is always certain, whereas in the case of unliquidated damages it is uncertain until the court has decided the matter. Provision for liquidated damages is often found in contracts which have to be completed within a certain time. Thus, contracts for building or civil engineering work normally provide for a specified sum to be paid for every day or week of delay.

It is customary to refer to liquidated damages clauses and penalty clauses (below) as involving the payment of a sum of money, and for convenience we shall discuss them in that context. However, it should not be forgotten that such clauses may involve the transfer of property, and not the payment of money.¹

¹ *Jobson v Johnson* [1989] 1 All ER 621, CA.

11.31 If a contract containing a liquidated damages clause is broken, the claimant can recover the specified sum, whether this is greater or less than the actual loss suffered. This rule may benefit a claimant who has suffered little or no loss but can be to the claimant's disadvantage if the loss suffered greatly exceeds the specified sum. In *Cellulose Acetate Silk Co Ltd v Widnes Foundry (1925) Ltd*,¹ D agreed to build machinery for C in 18 weeks and, in the event of taking longer, to pay 'by way of penalty £20 per working week'. The machinery was completed 30 weeks late and C lost £5,850 in consequence. The House of Lords held that the provision for payment was one for liquidated damages and that C could only recover 30 weeks at £20, ie £600.

¹ [1933] AC 20, HL.

11.32 Liquidated damages provisions must be distinguished from two other provisions:

Exemption clauses restricting liability A liquidated damages clause is not an exemption clause limiting liability because it fixes the sum payable for breach whether the actual loss is greater or less, whereas (assuming it is valid) such an exemption clause merely fixes the maximum sum recoverable and, if the actual loss is less than that sum, only the actual loss can be recovered.

Penalty clauses Where the sum fixed by the contract is a genuine pre-estimate of the loss which will be caused by its breach, the provision is one for liquidated damages, but if instead the sum is intended to operate as a threat to hold a potential defaulter to his (or her) bargain it is a penalty.¹ The distinction between a penalty and liquidated damages is crucial because their effects are different.

¹ *Law v Redditch Local Board* [1892] 1 QB 127 at 132.

Penalty

11.33 If the actual loss suffered by a claimant is less than the sum specified in a penalty clause, the claimant can only recover that actual loss.[1]

Suppose that a broken contract contains a penalty clause providing for a £1,000 penalty but the claimant's actual loss is only £100, the claimant can only recover £100 (whereas if the clause had been one for liquidated damages the claimant could have recovered £1,000).

On the other hand, if the penalty is less than the actual loss suffered by the claimant, eg because of inflation since the contract was made, the claimant can recover the whole of the loss.[2]

Where a consumer is subject to a penalty clause and the Unfair Terms in Consumer Contracts Regulations 1999 apply to the clause, it is highly likely to be regarded as an unfair term, and therefore not binding on the consumer.[3]

[1] *Wilbeam v Ashton* (1807) 1 Camp 78.
[2] *Wall v Rederiaktiebolaget Luggude* [1915] 3 KB 66.
[3] See paras 9.24–9.29. Note, in particular, the fifth entry in the indicative list of unfair terms in Sch 2 to the Regulations set out in para 9.28.

Parties' intention

11.34 Whether an agreed sum is liquidated damages or a penalty depends on the parties' intention and, as is shown by the *Cellulose Acetate* case,[1] the use of the words 'penalty' or 'liquidated damages' in the contract is not conclusive. The crucial question is whether the parties intended the specified sum to be a genuine pre-estimate of the damage likely to be caused by the breach or to operate as a fine or penalty for breach. This intention is to be gathered from the terms and inherent circumstances of the contract at the time it was made, and not at the time of its breach.[2] This does not mean that what has happened subsequently is irrelevant, since it can provide valuable evidence as to what could reasonably have been expected to be the loss when the contract was made.[3]

Where the parties are of equal bargaining power, the courts must be cautious before finding that a clause is a penalty clause. This is because of the need for certainty, especially in commercial contracts. However, if the clause was clearly not intended to be a genuine pre-estimate of the damage likely to result from breach, other justifications of it as 'reasonable' between the parties and in the light of the other terms of the contract will be irrelevant.[4]

The determination of the parties' intention is aided by a number of rebuttable presumptions of intention summarised by Lord Dunedin in *Dunlop Pneumatic Tyre Co Ltd v New Garage and Motor Co Ltd*,[5] in terms which were endorsed by the Privy Council in *Phillips Hong Kong Ltd v A-G of Hong Kong*:[6]

- 'It will be held to be a penalty if the sum stipulated for is extravagant and unconscionable in amount in comparison with the greatest loss that could conceivably be proved to have followed from the breach.' In applying this presumption, comparisons must be made in respect of reasonably likely happenings, and not completely unlikely hypothetical situations.[7]

- 'It will be held to be a penalty if the breach consists only in not paying a sum of money, and the sum stipulated is a sum greater than the sum which ought to have been paid.'[8]

- 'There is a presumption (but no more) that it is a penalty when a single lump sum is made payable by way of compensation, on the occurrence of one or more or all of several events, some of which may occasion serious and others but trifling damage.' In *Kemble v Farren*,[9] for example, D agreed with C to appear at Covent Garden for four seasons at £3.6s.8d (£3.33) a night. The contract provided that if either party refused to fulfil the agreement, or any part of it, he should pay the other £1,000 as 'liquidated damages'. D refused to act during the second season. It was held that the stipulation was a penalty. The obligation to pay £1,000 might have arisen simply on C's failure to pay £3.6s.8d and was therefore quite obviously a penalty.

- 'It is no obstacle to the sum stipulated being a genuine pre-estimate of damage, that the consequences of the breach are such as to make precise pre-estimation almost an impossibility.' This is illustrated by the *Dunlop* case itself. C supplied tyres to D subject to an agreement that D would not sell below the list price and would pay £5 by way of liquidated damages for every tyre sold in breach of the agreement. The House of Lords held that the stipulated sum was one for liquidated damages. Clearly, the figure of £5 was, at most, only a rough and ready estimate of the possible loss which C might suffer if their price list was undercut.

[1] Para 11.31.
[2] *Dunlop Pneumatic Tyre Co Ltd v New Garage and Motor Co Ltd* [1915] AC 79 at 868–7.
[3] *Philips Hong Kong Ltd v A-G of Hong Kong* (1993) 61 BLR 41, PC.
[4] *Philips Hong Kong Ltd v A-G of Hong Kong* (1993) 61 BLR 41, PC.
[5] [1915] AC 79 at 86.
[6] (1993) 61 BLR 41, PC.
[7] *Philips Hong Kong Ltd v A-G of Hong Kong* (1993) 61 BLR 41, PC.
[8] This does not apply to a provision for the payment of interest in the event of late payment where the stipulated rate of interest represents a genuine pre-estimate of the likely loss suffered by the payee: *Jeancharm Ltd v Barnet Football Club Ltd* [2003] EWCA Civ 58, CA.
[9] (1829) 6 Bing 141.

DAMAGES: KEY POINTS

- Damages for breach of contract are awarded to compensate the claimant for his (or her) loss.
- The principal function of damages for breach of contract is to put the claimant into the same position as if the contract had been performed as agreed (compensation for expectation loss).
- As part of compensation for expectation loss, damages for breach of contract can be awarded to compensate the claimant for any expenditure incurred in reliance on the contract and wasted as a result of its breach.
- Damages for breach of contract cannot be recovered for distress or disappointment unless:
  - it is a consequence of physical injury or of physical inconvenience or discomfort caused by the breach; or
  - a major or important object of the contract was the giving of pleasure, enjoyment or the prevention of disturbed peace of mind or of distress.
- Damages for reliance loss and some other loss of expectation cannot both be recovered if this has the effect of compensating the claimant twice over for the same loss.
- Damages can also be awarded for loss other than loss of expectation which is an inevitable consequence of the breach (consequential loss).

- Damages for breach of contract can only be recovered for a loss where the breach was the effective or dominant cause of the loss and the loss is not too remote.

- Normally, loss is not too remote if the type of loss was reasonably contemplatable by both parties when they made the contract as not unlikely to result from the breach of contract in the ordinary course of things or in the light of special circumstances known to them and, normally, loss is too remote if it is not so contemplatable.

- However, in exceptional circumstances the 'reasonable contemplation test' will be ousted and the question of remoteness will be answered by applying the test of whether the defendant can reasonably be said to have assumed responsibility for loss of the particular type suffered.

- A claimant cannot recover damages for loss that could have been avoided by taking reasonable steps (mitigation of loss).

- If the defendant is liable in tort for negligence independently of the contract and also for breach of a contractual obligation to take reasonable care which was the same as the common law duty in tort, the claimant's damages may be reduced if he negligently contributed to the loss.

- Where a contract provides for a sum to be paid in the event of a breach, that sum may be liquidated damages or a penalty. If it is liquidated damages the claimant can recover the specified sum, whether greater or less than the actual loss. If it is a penalty, the claimant can only recover the actual loss; if this is greater than the penalty he may recover the whole loss.

Other remedies for breach of contract

Action for price or other agreed sum

11.35 If a breach consists of a party's failure to pay the contractually agreed price or other remuneration which is due under the contract, the appropriate course for the injured party (hereafter 'the claimant') is to bring an action for the agreed sum to recover that amount.

11.36 There is an important limitation on an action for the agreed sum in the case of a contract for the sale of goods. The Sale of Goods Act 1979, s 49 provides that, unless the agreed price is payable on a specified date irrespective of delivery, an action for it only lies if the property (ie ownership) in the goods has passed to the defendant buyer.

Agreed sum not due at time of repudiatory breach

11.37 Where a repudiatory breach is committed, the claimant may, of course, recover an agreed sum already due at the time of the breach, whether the claimant terminates or affirms the contract.

The position is more complicated where the agreed sum is not due at the time of the repudiatory breach but may become due subsequently. The position is as follows:

- *If the claimant elects to terminate the contract,* the claimant cannot claim an agreed sum which might have become due to the claimant subsequently.[1]

- *If the claimant elects to affirm the contract,* then, as already said,[2] the contract remains in force, so that both parties are bound to perform any outstanding contractual obligations. Consequently, if the claimant affirms the contract, the claimant party may be able to recover the agreed sum when it becomes due in the future. Whether or not the claimant will be able to recover that sum depends on the rules discussed in the rest of this paragraph.

It was recognised by the majority of the House of Lords in *White and Carter (Councils) Ltd v McGregor*[3] that, if further performance on the part of the claimant is required in order for the sum to become due, the claimant will be unable to recover the agreed sum if his (or her) further performance depends on the co-operation of the other party and it is withheld.[4] It is for this reason that a wrongfully dismissed employee cannot sue for his wages payable thereafter, even though he has subsequently indicated his willingness to go on working under the employment contract.[5] Instead that person must *either* sue for damages for breach of contract (the amount awarded being what would have been earned had the employment continued according to the contract, ie if contractual notice had been given, subject to the requirement to take reasonable steps to mitigate the loss by obtaining other employment), *or* seek payment under the law of restitution on a quantum meruit basis (see below) for the value of work already done.

It will not be often that the claimant can perform his (or her) side of the contract without the co-operation of the other party, although it was possible in *White and Carter (Councils) Ltd v McGregor*. C were advertising contractors. They carried on a business of supplying free litter bins to local authorities, the bins being paid for by businesses which hired advertising space on them. C agreed with D to display advertisements for his garage on bins for three years. On the same day, D renounced the contract and asked C to cancel it. C refused, thereby affirming the contract, and proceeded to prepare advertisement plates which they attached to bins and displayed. When D failed to pay at the appropriate time, C sued for the full contract price. The House of Lords held that C could recover the full contract price despite the fact that they had made no effort to mitigate their loss by getting other advertisers in substitution for D and had increased their loss after the renunciation by performing their side of the contract.

Even if the claimant can perform his (or her) side of the contract without the co-operation of the other party, and does so, the claimant cannot recover an agreed sum when it becomes due in the future (as opposed to such damages as would be available) if it is shown that the claimant had no legitimate interest, financial or otherwise, in performing the contract rather than claiming damages. This was stated by one of the Law Lords in *White and Carter*,[6] where a lack of a legitimate interest was not shown, and has subsequently been adopted in other cases.[7] 'Legitimate interest' in this context means that the claimant 'must have reasonable grounds for keeping the contract open, bearing in mind also the interests of the [other party]'.[8] By way of example, a commitment to a third party has been held to be a legitimate interest.[9]

---

[1] Para 8.14.

[2] Paras 8.16 and 8.27.

[3] [1961] 3 All ER 1178, HL.

[4] There is an exception. Where money becomes due under the contract independently of the claimant's performance, the claimant can recover the agreed sum without performing his obligations: *Ministry of Sound (Ireland) Ltd v Online Ltd* [2003] EWHC 2178 (Comm).

[5] *Denmark Productions Ltd v Boscobel Productions Ltd* [1968] 3 All ER 513, CA.

[6] [1962] AC 413 at 431.

[7] Eg *Attica Sea Carriers Corpn v Ferrostaal Poseidon Bulk Reederei GmbH, The Puerto Buitrago* [1976] 1 Lloyd's Rep 250, CA.

[8] *Stoczma Gdanska SA v Latvian Shipping Co* [1996] 2 Lloyd's Rep 132, CA (revsd on another ground [1998] 1 All ER 883, HL).

[9] *Gator Shipping Corpn v Trans-Asiatic Oil Ltd SA, The Odenfeld* [1978] 2 Lloyd's Rep 357.

Account of profits from breach

11.38   As seen in para 11.7, damages (*Wrotham Park* damages) can be awarded to compensate for loss of expectation where there has been a breach of a negative term even though there is no identifiable financial loss. An account of profits from breach is another remedy in a case where there is no identifiable loss to the claimant. If an account of profits is ordered it will order the recovery by the claimant of all the profits resulting to the defendant from the breach.

In *A-G v Blake (Jonathan Cape Ltd, third party)*,[1] the House of Lords recognised the availability of an account of profits from breach. It held that it is possible for the claimant to get an account of the profits accruing to the party in breach from that breach. Such an award is different from an award of damages, in that it requires the party in breach to disgorge an identifiable gain resulting from the breach of contract whereas damages require the defendant to compensate the claimant for the loss resulting from the breach.[2]

In *A-G v Blake*, Blake had for many years been employed by the British secret intelligence service. Unknown to them he had also worked for the KGB. In 1961 he was convicted of official secrets offences and imprisoned. He escaped from prison in 1965. He went to Russia where he remained. Some 20 years later he contracted with Cape to write his autobiography. The contract provided for an advance of royalties of £150,000 to be paid; of this £60,000 had actually been paid.

Blake had committed a breach of contract in writing the book because, when he had entered the British secret intelligence service, he had made a life-long contract with the Crown to keep everything he learnt confidential. The majority (4–1) of the House of Lords held that the Crown was entitled, by way of an account of profits, to the amount due and owing to Blake from Cape under the publishing contract on the ground that that money was the gain accruing to Blake through breach of his contract with it.

The decision in *A-G v Blake* is of limited effect. Lord Nicholls, with whom the rest of the majority agreed, made it clear that an account of profits was only available in exceptional circumstances as a remedy for breach of contract where the availability of damages, specific performance and injunction would provide an inadequate remedy. Moreover, as an equitable remedy the option of an account of profits is discretionary in the same way as specific performance or an injunction; it must be just and equitable to award it. Lord Nicholls stated that, in deciding whether to order an account of profits where damages, specific performance and injunction are inadequate, the court will have regard to all the circumstances, including the subject-matter of the contract, the purpose of the contractual provision broken, the circumstances in which the breach occurred, the consequences of the breach and the circumstances in which relief is sought. He said that a useful, but not exhaustive, guide is whether the claimant has a legitimate interest in preventing the defendant's profit-making activity and, hence, in depriving the defendant of his profit.

---

[1]   [2000] 4 All ER 385, HL.
[2]   *Portman Building Society v Hamlyn* [1998] 4 All ER 202 at 205.

11.39   The rule that an account of profits is only available for breach of contract in exceptional circumstances resulted in the Court of Appeal declining to order an account of profits in *Experience Hendrix LLC v PPX Enterprises Inc*.[1] In that case, under an agreement between C and D, D was entitled to license various recordings but not others. In breach of the agreement, all the recordings were licensed. D clearly made a profit from this but no identifiable financial loss appeared to have been suffered by C. The Court of Appeal refused to order an account of profits against D, although (as noted in para 11.7) it did award C damages on a *Wrotham Park* basis. Noting that in *A-G v Blake* the House of Lords had stated that an account of profits should only be ordered in exceptional circumstances, it drew 'obvious distinctions' between the case before it and *A-G v Blake*:

- there was nothing in *Hendrix* to parallel the state's special interest in preventing a spy benefiting by breaches of his contractual duty of secrecy and removing at least part of the financial attraction of such breaches;

- there was nothing in *Hendrix* to parallel the notoriety which accounted for the magnitude of Blake's royalty-earning capacity derived from his prior breaches of secrecy;

- there was no direct analogy between PPX's position and that of a fiduciary (Blake's position).

The court concluded that there were no exceptional circumstances and that an order to account for profits should not be made.

¹ [2003] EWCA Civ 323, CA.

11.40 In *WWF World Wide Fund for Nature v World Wrestling Federation Entertainment Inc*,¹ the Court of Appeal held that *Wrotham Park* damages and an account for profits from breach were compensatory in nature. It stated that both are granted by way of a just response to circumstances where the compensation which is the claimant's due cannot be measured by reference to identifiable financial loss. It recognised that the circumstances in which *Wrotham Park* damages may be an appropriate response differ in degree from those where an account for profits from breach is appropriate, but it held that the underlying feature in both cases is compensating the claimant where an identifiable financial loss cannot be established.

¹ [2007] EWCA Civ 286, CA.

Quantum meruit

11.41 In a particular situation, set out below, a claim on what is called a quantum meruit basis is available to a claimant as an *alternative* to a claim for damages for breach of contract.

If a party to a contract (D) unjustifiably prevents the other party (C) performing C's contractual obligations, as where D refuses to accept performance, or renders performance impossible, D's conduct will normally constitute a repudiatory breach of contract and C can recover damages for breach of contract, whether C elects to terminate or to affirm the contract. Alternatively, if C has partly performed his (or her) obligations under the contract C can claim under the law of restitution the reasonable value of the work done, provided that C has elected to terminate the contract.¹ *Lusty v Finsbury Securities Ltd*² provides an example of the rules. D contracted with C for C to act as its architect for an office block development. After C had done some work under the contract, D decided to use the land for residential development instead and cancelled future performance by C of the contract. This was clearly a repudiatory breach of contract. It was held that C could recover reasonable remuneration for his work on a quantum meruit basis.

¹ *Planché v Colburn* (1831) 8 Bing 14.
² (1991) 58 BLR 66, CA.

11.42 It must be emphasised that an award of damages and a quantum meruit award are distinct remedies. As we have already stated, damages are compensatory, their object generally being to put the claimant into the same position, so far as money can do it, as if the contract had been performed. Thus, if the claimant in a case like *Lusty v Finsbury Securities* decides to sue for damages, the damages awarded will be equivalent to the sum payable to the claimant on completion of the work, less any savings (eg on labour and materials) made through not completing performance. However, if it is shown that the claimant would in any event have been unable to perform the entire obligation, the claimant will at most be entitled to nominal damages.[1] The aim of a quantum meruit award is to prevent unjust enrichment to the defendant by awarding the claimant an amount equivalent to the value of the work which the claimant has done.

Generally, an award of damages will be more generous than a quantum meruit award, but the converse may be true if the claimant originally made a bad bargain or if only nominal damages would be awarded.

[1]   *Maredelanto Cia Naviera SA v Bergbau-Handel GmbH, The Mihalis Angelos* [1970] 3 All ER 125, CA.

Specific performance

11.43 The court may grant a decree of specific performance to the claimant instead of, or in addition to, awarding the claimant damages. Such a decree orders the defendant to carry out that party's contractual obligations.

11.44 Specific performance will not be granted in the following cases:

Where damages are an adequate remedy It is for this reason that specific performance of a contract to sell goods is not normally ordered; the payment of damages enables the claimant to go out into the market and buy the equivalent goods.[1] However, in exceptional cases, eg where the contract is for the sale of specific goods of a unique character or of special value or interest, the contract is specifically enforceable.[2] By way of contrast, every plot of land is unique, with the result that contracts for the sale or lease of land are always specifically enforceable. This has produced the rule that, since the contract is specifically enforceable in favour of the purchaser or lessee, a vendor or lessor of land can obtain an order of specific performance for the purchase price even though, in the particular case, damages would be an adequate remedy.[3]

It is because damages are normally adequate that a contractual obligation to pay money is not normally specifically enforceable. However, in addition to the exception just mentioned, there are other exceptions. For instance, as the House of Lords held in *Beswick v Beswick:*[4]

- a contract to pay money to a third party can be specifically enforced in favour of a party where, as is normally the case, any damages awarded to the party would be nominal; and

- where the contract is for an annuity or other periodical payment it can be specifically enforced (thereby avoiding the need to sue for damages every time a payment is not made).

Where consideration has not been provided The remedy of specific performance is an equitable one and, since equity does not recognise the making of a contract by deed as an effective substitute for consideration, specific performance cannot be awarded in favour of a person who has not provided consideration ('equity will not assist a volunteer') and that person is left to the common law remedy of damages.[5]

Where the court's constant supervision would be necessary to secure compliance with the order An example is provided by *Ryan v Mutual Tontine Westminster Chambers Association*.[6] In the lease of a flat in a block of flats the lessors agreed to keep a resident porter, who should be in constant attendance and perform specified duties. The person appointed got his duties done by deputies and was absent for hours at a time at another job. The court refused to order against the lessors specific performance of the agreement relating to the performance of the specified duties by the porter because such an order would have required its constant supervision. On the other hand, in *Posner v Scott-Lewis*,[7] specific performance was ordered against a lessor of a covenant to appoint a porter because what had to be done to comply with the order (appointing a porter) could be defined with sufficient certainty and enforcement of the order would not require the constant supervision of the court.

In *Co-operative Insurance Society Ltd v Argyll Stores (Holdings) Ltd*,[8] where the House of Lords allowed an appeal against the Court of Appeal's order for specific performance of a covenant in a lease of a supermarket which required it to be kept open for trade, the House of Lords held that specific performance should not be ordered if it would require a defendant to run a business (save in exceptional circumstances). One of the House's reasons was that to order someone to carry on a business would require the court's constant supervision.

Where the contract is for services of a personal nature The obvious example of such a contract is one of employment. The Trade Union and Labour Relations (Consolidation) Act 1992, s 236 prohibits an order of specific performance against an employee to compel the employee to do any work or to attend at any place for the doing of any work. It is well established by the cases that contracts for personal services not covered by the Act (for example an agency contract)[9] cannot be specifically enforced either, nor can an order of specific performance be made against an employer (except, possibly, in very exceptional circumstances). Reasons given are that such contracts would require constant supervision and that it is contrary to public policy to force one person to submit to the orders of another.

Lack of mutuality There is a rule that a claimant who has not performed his (or her) contractual obligations cannot obtain specific performance against the defendant if, in the circumstances, it would not be available to the defendant against the claimant. In *Flight v Bolland*,[10] for instance, it was held that a minor could not be awarded specific performance of the contract in question because such an order could not be made against the minor in the circumstances. While there is no doubting the present rule, its extent is uncertain.

[1] Apart from its inherent jurisdiction to order specific recovery of goods, the court has power under the Sale of Goods Act 1979, s 52 to order the specific performance of contracts for the sale of specific or ascertained goods. This power has not been used more liberally than the inherent power.

[2] *Behnke v Bede Shipping Co Ltd* [1927] 1 KB 649.

[3] *Cogent v Gibson* (1864) 33 Beav 557.

[4] [1967] 2 All ER 1197, HL; para 13.12.

[5] *Cannon v Hartley* [1949] 1 All ER 50.

[6] [1893] 1 Ch 116.

[7] [1987] Ch 25.

[8] [1997] 3 All ER 297, HL.

[9] *Clarke v Price* (1819) 2 Wils Ch 157.

[10] (1828) 4 Russ 298.

11.45 If the case does not fall within one of the above cases, specific performance may be ordered, but it must not be forgotten that, since specific performance is an equitable remedy, its award does not lie as of right (unlike the common law remedy of damages) but lies in the court's discretion.

Factors which make it unlikely that the court will exercise its discretion in favour of specific performance include:

- a mistake on the part of the defendant such that it would be unjust specifically to enforce the contract against the defendant;

- the severity of the hardship to the defendant if the contract is specifically enforced against the defendant;[1]

- breach of the contract by the claimant in circumstances where the grant of specific performance would be unjust to the defendant.[2]

Lastly, it is clearly established that the court will refuse specific performance of a contract for the sale of land in favour of a claimant who is in breach of a contractual stipulation concerning the time of completion where time is of 'the essence of the contract',[3] although it will normally grant it to such a claimant (subject to a condition that the claimant pays damages for the delay) where time is not 'of the essence' since this will not cause injustice to the defendant.

[1] *Patel v Ali* [1984] 1 All ER 978.
[2] *Walsh v Lonsdale* (1882) 21 Ch D 9.
[3] *Stickney v Keeble* [1915] AC 386 at 415–416.

Injunction

11.46 An injunction is a court order prohibiting the defendant from doing a specified thing. The remedy is not limited to breaches of contract, but in that context an injunction may be ordered to prevent breach of a negative stipulation contained in a contract. By way of comparison, specific performance is concerned with the enforcement of positive contractual stipulations.

Two types of injunction may be granted in contract cases:

- a mandatory injunction, which can be granted to compel the defendant to remedy an injury caused by a breach which has already occurred (eg to demolish a wall erected in breach of a restrictive covenant not to build). Mandatory injunctions are rarely granted.

- a prohibitory injunction, which can be granted to prevent a threatened or actual breach of contract.

11.47 While it is correct to say that injunctions are concerned with restraining breaches of negative contractual stipulations, it would be erroneous to assume that only an express negative stipulation can be remedied by an injunction. Generally, a breach of a positive stipulation can be enjoined if the stipulation can properly be construed as impliedly being a negative stipulation. Thus, in *Manchester Ship Canal Co v Manchester Racecourse Co*,[1] a stipulation for the grant of a 'first refusal' was construed as a stipulation, enforceable by injunction, not to sell to anyone else in breach of the stipulation. Similarly, in *Metropolitan Electric Supply Co Ltd v Ginder*,[2] where D had undertaken to take all the electricity required for his premises from C, it was held that this was impliedly an undertaking not to take electricity from any other person, which could be enforced by an injunction.

[1] [1901] 2 Ch 37.
[2] [1901] 2 Ch 799.

11.48 Although the courts are prepared to enforce negative stipulations in a contract for personal services, consistency with the rule that such a contract cannot normally be the subject of a decree of specific performance means that an injunction will not be issued to restrain an employee or the like from breaking a promise not to work for any other person, if this would indirectly amount to compelling the employee to perform the contract with the employer.[1] This is given statutory force in relation to contracts of employment by the Trade Union and Labour Relations (Consolidation) Act 1992, s 236, referred to in para 11.44, which applies to an injunction as it applies to an order of specific performance.

On the other hand, a negative promise by an employee or the like will be enforced against that person by injunction if it does not indirectly force that person to work for the employer. For example, in *Lumley v Wagner*,[2] D, an opera star, agreed to sing at C's theatre for three months and in no other theatre during that time. An injunction was granted restraining her from singing for another theatre owner during the three-month period. The approach taken in *Lumley v Wagner* was followed in *Warner Bros Pictures Inc v Nelson*.[3] D, whose stage name was Bette Davis, agreed with C not to work in a film or stage production for any other company for a year nor to be engaged in any other occupation. During the year she contracted to work for another film company. The judge stated that, while an injunction enforcing all the negative stipulations in the contract could not be granted (because it would force D either to be idle or to perform her contract with C), the injunction requested would be granted because it was limited to prohibiting her from working in a film or stage production for anyone other than C; she would still be free to earn her living in some other less remunerative way. The judge was unimpressed by the argument that the difference between what D could earn acting and what she could earn in any other capacity would be so substantial that the injunction would drive her to work for C. An argument of this type did, however, persuade the judge in *Page One Records Ltd v Britton*,[4] an employee against employer case referred to in para 11.49. In *Warren v Mendy*,[5] the Court of Appeal was also persuaded by such an argument on grounds of realism and practicality. Consequently, it is now the law that, contrary to the view of the judge in *Warner Bros v Nelson*, the question of whether an injunction against the defendant would compel the defendant to work for the claimant is not answered in the negative simply because the defendant is not debarred from doing other work. If the nature of, or remuneration for, that work is so different that effectively the defendant would be driven to work for the claimant, it will be held that an injunction would so compel the defendant and an injunction will not be ordered. Thus, if the facts of *Warner Bros v Nelson* arose today the decision on them would no doubt be against an injunction being ordered.

---

[1] *Rely-a-Bell Burglar and Fire Alarm Co Ltd v Eisler* [1926] Ch 609. There is no such rule where a contract concerns services of a non-personal nature, as in the case of a contract for services made between business concerns: *Lauritzencool AB v Lady Navigation Inc* {2005] EWCA Civ 579, CA.

[2] (1852) 1 De GM & G 604.

[3] [1936] 3 All ER 160.

[4] [1967] 3 All ER 822.

[5] [1989] 3 All ER 103, CA.

11.49 The law is similar where an employee seeks to enforce a negative stipulation against an employer. Thus, generally, an injunction will not be issued if its effect is to compel the employer to continue employment. But an injunction may be granted in exceptional cases where employer and employee retain their mutual confidence.

In *Page One Records Ltd v Britton*,[1] The Troggs, a pop group, appointed C as their manager for five years, agreeing not to let anyone else act as their manager during that time. After a year, The Troggs dismissed C, who sought an injunction restraining them from appointing anyone else as their manager. It was held that an injunction would indirectly compel The Troggs to continue to employ C because pop groups could not operate successfully without a manager, and it would be bad to pressure The Troggs into continuing to employ a person in whom they had lost confidence. Therefore the injunction sought was not granted.

In comparison, one may note the exceptional case of *Hill v C A Parsons & Co Ltd*.[2] D employers were forced by union pressure to dismiss C in breach of contract. An injunction was granted to restrain this breach, even though its effect was to compel the reinstatement of C. As the Court of Appeal pointed out, the circumstances were special, in particular because the parties retained their mutual confidence. Mutual confidence has been stressed as a pre-condition in other cases; it can be shown either by evidence that the employer and employee have expressed confidence in each other or by inference from evidence of an established and satisfactory employment relationship.[3]

  [1] [1967] 3 All ER 822.
  [2] [1971] 3 All ER 1345, CA.
  [3] *Powell v Brent London Borough Council* [1987] IRLR 466, CA.

11.50 Despite the general reluctance of the courts to grant an injunction in respect of a contract of employment, if the employee's contract requires a specified procedure to be followed before dismissal can take place, the courts will grant an injunction to restrain a proposed dismissal, or to restrain an employer giving effect to a dismissal notice, in breach of that procedure.[1]

  [1] *Jones v Lee* [1980] ICR 310, CA.

11.51 An injunction is like specific performance in that:

- it may be granted with or without an order for damages;

- where it is applicable, the grant of an injunction is discretionary (since it is an equitable remedy). In particular, an injunction will normally be refused if damages would be an adequate remedy.

REMEDIES OTHER THAN DAMAGES: KEY POINTS

- If a breach consists in the defendant's failure to pay a debt due under the contract, the appropriate course is for the claimant to bring an action for that sum (the agreed sum) to recover that amount. In the case of a contract for the sale of goods ownership must have passed to the defendant buyer.

- In exceptional circumstances a claimant may be able to recover an account of profits made by the defendant as a result of the breach, even though the claimant has not suffered an identifiable financial loss.

- A claimant may recover a reasonable sum based on work already done (quantum meruit) if the claimant has unjustifiably been prevented by the defendant from completing his (or her) obligations and has terminated the contract for repudiatory breach.

- In appropriate cases, a claimant may obtain an order of specific performance, an order requiring the defendant to fulfil his (or her) contractual obligations, instead of, or in addition to, damages.

- Specific performance is a discretionary remedy. It will not be granted where:
  - damages would be an adequate remedy;
  - consideration has not been provided;
  - the court's constant supervision to secure compliance would be necessary;
  - the contract is for services of a personal nature; or
  - there is lack of mutuality.
- In appropriate contractual cases, a mandatory injunction (order to remedy injury caused by breach of a negative stipulation) or a prohibitory injunction (order to restrain threatened or actual breach of a negative stipulation) may be granted. Mandatory injunctions are rarely granted.
- An injunction will not be granted to restrain breach of a negative stipulation in a contract for personal services if this would compel the defendant to continue working for or employing, as the case may be, the claimant. There is an exception where the defendant is an employer. It applies where parties retain their mutual confidence.
- An injunction may be granted with or without damages. It is a discretionary remedy.

Limitation of actions

11.52 An action for damages or other financial remedy will be barred if it is not brought within the relevant limitation period. The rules relating to these periods are statutory, the relevant Act being the Limitation Act 1980 (LA 1980). If an action is statute-barred this does not extinguish the claimant's substantive right but simply bars the procedural remedies available to the claimant. One consequence of this is that if a debtor pays a statute-barred debt, the creditor cannot recover the money as money not due.[1]

[1] *Bize v Dickason* (1786) 1 Term Rep 285 at 287.

Limitation periods

11.53 Under LA 1980:

- Actions founded on a simple contract (ie one not made by deed) cannot be brought after the expiry of six years from the date on which the cause of action arose[1], which is normally when the breach of contract occurs and never when the damage is suffered. However, if the damages claimed consist of or include damages for personal injuries caused by a breach of contract, the time limit is reduced to three years[2], although this period may be extended if it is equitable to so do.[3]
- Actions founded on a contract made by deed cannot be brought after the expiry of 12 years from the date on which the cause of action arose[4]. The special rules mentioned above concerning personal injuries claims also apply here.

There are special rules, described in para 27.24, about when the limitation period begins to run where the claimant was a minor or mentally ill when the cause of action accrued or where fraud, concealment or mistake is involved. In the former case time does not begin to run until the removal of the disability.[5] In the latter, time does not begin to run until the fraud, concealment or mistake has been, or ought to have been, discovered by the claimant.[6]

₁ LA 1980, s 5. For a special rule in relation to actions on certain contracts of loan, see LA 1980, s 6. If the claimant can establish a cause of action in tort for negligence, a cause of action arises (and time runs from) when the damage is suffered, although there are numerous exceptions, eg in personal injury cases and claims based on the negligent construction of buildings; see further paras 27.22 and 27.23.

[2] LA 1980, s 11(4).
[3] LA 1980, s 33; para 27.24.
[4] LA 1980, s 8.
[5] LA 1980, s 28.
[6] LA 1980, s 32.

Extending the limitation period

11.54 A written acknowledgement of liability to pay, or part payment of, a debt or other liquidated (ie agreed) pecuniary claim may start time running again, provided that the right of action has not previously become statute-barred (ie the acknowledgement or part payment must be made during the currency of the relevant limitation period).[1] A cause of action for unliquidated damages cannot be extended by an acknowledgement or part payment.[2]

[1] LA 1980, ss 29-31.
[2] LA 1980, ss 29-31.

Equitable relief

11.55 The provisions of LA 1980 do not apply to claims for equitable relief.[1] However, with one exception, the limitation periods under LA 1980 are applied to equitable claims by analogy.[2] The exception is where there is no corresponding remedy at common law, so that a claim for the type of relief in question could only have been entertained by the Court of Chancery before the Judicature Act 1873, eg a claim for specific performance or an injunction. Here, however, a claim may fail under the equitable doctrine of laches (delay). The test of whether a claimant is barred by laches is whether, broadly considered, the claimant's actions were such as to render it unconscionable for the claimant to be permitted to assert his (or her) rights.[3] Some sort of detrimental reliance by the defendant on the delay is usually required.[4] The avoidance of fixed limitation periods in this area is obviously more appropriate to the discretionary nature of equitable remedies.

[1] LA 1980, s 36(1).
[2] LA 1980, s 36(1); *Knox v Gye* (1872) LR 5 HL 656 at 674.
[3] *Frawley v Neill* [2000] CP Rep 20, CA.
[4] *Fisher v Brooker* [2009] UKHL 41, HL.

LIMITATION OF ACTIONS: KEY POINTS

- An action for damages or other financial remedy will be barred after a certain period of time.

- Actions concerning simple contracts (ie contracts not made by deed) must be brought within six years from the date on which the cause of action arose. Actions concerning

---

contracts made by deed must be brought within 12 years from that date. A personal injury claim must normally be brought within three years from that date.

- Written acknowledgement or part-payment during the limitation period may cause that period to start running again in respect of a debt or other agreed sum.
- The Limitation Act 1980 does not apply to claims for equitable relief but, with one exception, the limitation periods under the Act are applied to such claims by analogy. The exception is where there is no corresponding remedy at common law, as in the case of a claim for specific performance or for an injunction. Here the claim may fail under the equitable doctrine of laches (delay).

Questions

1. What is the law which applies to measure the damages payable where there is a significant difference between the amount quantified by the 'diminution in value' measure and the 'cost of cure' measure?

2. What are the rules relating to damages for distress caused by a breach of contract?

3. When is a loss not too remote for the purposes of an award of damages for breach of contract?

4. What is meant by the term 'liquidated damages'? What is the difference in effect between a provision for liquidated damages and a penalty?

5. On 1 October, Barry contracted with Daisy to build an extension to Daisy's hotel. Under the terms of the contract, the extension was to be completed by 1 April. The contract price was £200,000. The contract also provided that, in the event of delay in completing the extension by 1 April, Barry was to pay Daisy £1,000 for every week (or part) by which completion was delayed. Although completion was delayed by five weeks, Daisy's loss of profits as a result only amounted to £500.

    On 1 October Daisy sold Henry a strip of land at the bottom of the hotel's garden subject to a covenant that Henry would only build a bungalow on it. Henry has just obtained planning permission to build a block of flats on the site.

    Advise Daisy on her remedies in respect of the late completion and the proposed breach of the covenant.

6. Jock, the managing agent of a small block of flats, contracts with Simon, a decorator, whereby Simon agrees to paint and decorate the exterior of the flats for £8,000, the work to be done by 1 July. Simon hires scaffolding and a special stepladder from Ted, a one-man business supplier of decorators' equipment, to enable him to perform the contract with Jock. Simon takes immediate delivery as the stepladder but the scaffolding is to be delivered at the block of flats on 1 June.

    When Simon starts the work on 2 June he discovers that the scaffolding has not been delivered and that Ted has just gone on a three-week holiday. Simon hires scaffolding from DIY Ltd to enable him to carry out the contract despite Ted's breach. DIY Ltd has two tariffs for scaffolding: £600 (delivery when DIY's truck is next in the area, which is three days later) or £750 (express delivery). Simon chooses the latter option and the scaffolding is delivered an hour later.

    Two weeks later Simon uses the stepladder. It has a latent defect but Simon increases the risk of danger by carelessly assembling it. When Simon mounts the stepladder it collapses and Simon suffers a broken right arm as a result. This prevents him working as a decorator (he is right-handed) for two months and also prevents him earning a large fee when he is unable to appear on a reality television programme on which he is booked to appear.

Advise Simon as to his remedies.

7. What are the rules relating to the recovery of the price or other agreed sum?

8. What are the rules relating to the grant of a decree of specific performance?

12

Misrepresentation, duress and undue influence

CHAPTER OVERVIEW

It is not uncommon for a contract to be made after one party has made a misrepresentation (ie a false statement) to the other, has brought improper pressure to bear on the other, or has failed during negotiations to reveal an important fact relevant to the contract.
In this chapter we consider:

- the circumstances in which damages can be recovered, or a contract set aside, on grounds of active misrepresentation;

- the legal situation where an active misrepresentation has become a contractual term;

- the avoidance of a provision excluding or restricting liability for misrepresentation;

- the circumstances in which a contract can be set aside for non-disclosure of a material fact;

- the circumstances in which a contract can be set aside for duress or undue influence or on the ground of being an unconscionable bargain.

Misrepresentation

12.1 In certain very rare cases a contract is void if it is made in circumstances where one or both parties are mistaken as to the facts existing at the time of their agreement. In these cases, the mistake may have been induced by a misrepresentation by one of the parties, but this is not essential.

If a contract is void for mistake it has no legal effect; consequently, it is unenforceable by either party, money paid under it is recoverable back and title to property cannot pass under it. A party who has received goods under a void contract will be liable to the transferor in tort if he (or she) wrongfully interferes with them, and so will a third party who has bought them from that party.

A contract may be void for mistake:

- if:
  - it relates to a matter as to which the law or contract does not allocate the risk or provide some other solution;
  - both parties share the same mistake; and

- the mistake relates to the existence of the subject-matter, as to the possibility of performing the contract or as to a fundamental assumption underlying the contract; or

- if, because of a mistake which the parties do not share, they are fundamentally at cross-purposes because the mistake relates to:
    - the identity (as opposed to an attribute) of the other party;
    - the essence of the subject-matter of the contract; or
    - whether a particular matter is a term of the contract,

provided that the mistake is an operative one, in that a party knows of the other's mistake, or that the circumstances are so ambiguous that a reasonable party could not say whether the contract meant what one party thought it meant or what the other party thought it meant.

We are not concerned further in this chapter with the case where a mistake induced by misrepresentation is such as to render the contract void. We repeat that cases where a mistake has this effect are very rare.

12.2 Unless a mistake induced by a misrepresentation is such as to render the contract void, it is the rules which follow which govern the situation. These rules differ depending on whether there has been an active misrepresentation or a misrepresentation through non-disclosure.

Active misrepresentation

12.3 In a situation involving an 'active misrepresentation' the first question is whether the representation has become a term of the contract or not, applying the rules set out in paras 7.14 to 7.21. The division between active misrepresentations which have remained pre-contractual representations (mere representations) and those which have become terms of a resulting contract is fundamental since the remedies are different.

Active misrepresentations which have remained mere representations

12.4 The requirements for an actionable active misrepresentation are that:

- there must have been a misrepresentation by words or conduct;

- the misrepresentation must be one of fact, except that a misrepresentation of law may suffice in some cases;

- it must have been addressed to the person misled;

- it must have been intended to be acted on by that person; and

- it must have induced the contract.

Misrepresentation by words or conduct

12.5 Although a misrepresentation is normally made by words, it can be made by conduct. An example of a misrepresentation by conduct would be where the vendor of a house covered up dry rot in it.[1] Another example is provided by *Spice Girls Ltd v Aprilia World Service BV*.[2] Aprilia contracted to sponsor the Spice Girls after it had been induced to do so by a film and photographs showing all five members of the group. At the time that they participated in these activities the Spice Girls knew that Geri Halliwell would be leaving the group before the end of the sponsorship contract, but Aprilia was not told. When Geri Halliwell left the group, Aprilia successfully claimed damages for misrepresentation by Spice Girls Ltd. It was held that the conduct of the five Spice Girls, in appearing in the film and photo shoots, constituted a representation that they did not know or have reasonable grounds to believe that any of them intended to leave the group before the minimum term of the sponsorship contract. As they already knew that Geri Halliwell would leave before the end of the contract, their representation was false and therefore a misrepresentation.

[1] See *Gordon v Selico Co Ltd* [1986] 1 EGLR 71, CA.
[2] [2002] EWCA Civ 15, CA. See also para 12.11.

Misrepresentation of fact

12.6 With the possible exception of a misrepresentation of law, there must be a misrepresentation by words or conduct of a past or existing fact. The following must be distinguished from misrepresentation of fact.

12.7 *Mere puffs* A representation which is mere vague sales talk is not regarded as a representation of fact, as is shown by *Dimmock v Hallett*.[1] At a sale of land by auction, it was said to be 'fertile and improvable'; in fact it was partly abandoned and useless. The representation was held to be a 'mere flourishing description by an auctioneer' affording no ground for relief. It is a question of fact whether a particular statement is merely vague sales talk or the assertion of some verifiable fact.

[1] (1866) 2 Ch App 21.

12.8 *Statements of opinion* A statement which merely expresses an opinion or belief does not give grounds for relief if the opinion or belief turns out to be wrong. In *Bisset v Wilkinson*,[1] the vendor of a farm, which (as he knew) had never been used as a sheep farm, told a prospective purchaser that in his judgement the land would support 2,000 sheep. It was held that this statement was one of opinion, given that the farm had never been used for sheep, and that, since it was an honest statement, no relief was available.

In two cases, however, statements of opinion can involve an implied misrepresentation of fact and so give rise to relief:

- Where a person represents an opinion which that person does not honestly hold that person will at the same time make a misrepresentation of fact, viz that he (or she) holds the opinion.[2]

- Where a person represents an opinion for which that person does not have reasonable grounds, that person will at the same time make a misrepresentation of fact if he (or she) impliedly represents that there are reasonable grounds for the opinion. A classic example is *Smith v Land and House Property Corpn*.[3] The vendor of a hotel described it as let to 'Mr Frederick Fleck (a most desirable tenant)... for an unexpired term of 27 plus years, thus offering a first-class investment'. Fleck had not paid the last quarter's rent and had paid the previous one by instalments and under pressure. The Court of Appeal held that the above statement was not merely of opinion but also involved a misrepresentation of fact because the vendor impliedly stated that he had reasonable grounds for his opinion. Too much should not be read into this decision because the court will only find such an implied representation where the facts on which the opinion is based are particularly within the knowledge of the person stating the opinion, and not when the facts are equally known to both parties.[4]

[1] [1927] AC 177, PC.
[2] *Brown v Raphael* [1958] 2 All ER 79 at 81.

[3] (1884) 28 Ch D 7, CA.

[4] *Smith v Land and House Property Corpn* (1884) 28 Ch D 7 at 15.

12.9 *Statements as to the future* Such statements, the best example of which is a statement of intention, are obviously not statements of fact in themselves and no remedy is available if the future event does not occur. However, a statement as to the future will involve a misrepresentation of fact if its maker does not honestly believe in its truth. In the case of a misrepresentation of intention this rule is well summarised by the statement of Bowen LJ in *Edgington v Fitzmaurice*[1] that the state of a man's mind is as much a fact as the state of his digestion. In this case the claimant was induced to lend money to a company by representations made in a prospectus by the directors that the money would be used to improve the company's buildings and to expand its business. The directors' true intention was to use the money to pay off the company's debts. They were held liable in deceit (fraudulent misrepresentation) on the basis that their misrepresentation of present intentions was a misrepresentation of fact.

[1] (1885) 29 Ch D 459, CA.

12.10 *Statements of law* A statement of the *effect* of the law in a particular situation (eg that a particular alteration to a building will not require planning permission) is a statement of fact.

A statement of a rule of law made without reference to its effect in a particular situation is a statement of law (eg that under planning law planning permission is never required for advertising signs[1]).

It has customarily been stated that a person who is induced to contract by a misrepresentation of law has no remedy for misrepresentation.[2] To this proposition two qualifications have been recognised:

- where, as in the case of a statement of opinion or intention,[3] the representor does not honestly believe in the truth of the statement of law, the representor misrepresents the fact that he (or she) believes in it;[4] and

- where the misrepresentation relates to the existence or meaning of a foreign law; such a misrepresentation is regarded by our courts as one of fact. [5]

It may be that any misrepresentation of law can now suffice, even though it does not involve a misrepresentation of fact. In modern times, the House of Lords and the Court of Appeal have abolished the distinction between law and fact in relation to the law relating to restitution for mistake and contractual voidness for mistake[6]. There is much to be said for the argument that the law relating to misrepresentation should also reject such a distinction. This argument was accepted by a judge in the High Court in *Pankhania v Hackney London Borough Council*.[7] The judge thought that the common law rules should, so far as possible, be congruent with one another, and based on coherent principle, and that there was a stronger case for granting relief in favour of a party whose mistake has been induced by the other party's misrepresentation than where both parties have made the same mistake.

[1] Such a statement would be incorrect.

[2] *Beattie v Lord Ebury* (1872) 7 Ch App 777, CA in Chancery.

[3] See paras 12.8 and 12.9.

[4] See also *West London Commercial Bank v Kitson* (1884) 13 QBD 360 at 362–363.

[5] *André & Cie v Ets Michel Blanc & Fils* [1979] 2 Lloyd's Rep 427, CA.

[6] *Kleinwort Benson Ltd v Lincoln City Council* (1999) 2 AC 349 HL; *Brennan v Bolt Burdon* [2004] EWCA Civ 1017, CA.

[2002] EWHC 2441 (Ch).

12.11 *Silence* Not surprisingly, silence cannot generally constitute an active misrepresentation.[1] However, there are two exceptions:

- Where the representor's silence distorts an assertion of fact made by the representor there will be an active misrepresentation of fact if the representor knows or has reasonable grounds to believe that there has been the distortion. Thus, in *Dimmock v Hallett*,[2] it was said that if a vendor of land states that farms on it are let, but omits to say that the tenants have given notice to quit, his statement will be a misrepresentation of fact. The *Spice Girls* case referred to in para 12.5 provides a modern example of this principle.

- Where a representation of fact is falsified by later events, before the conclusion of the contract, there will be an active misrepresentation if the representor fails to notify the other of the change. This is shown by *With v O'Flanagan*.[3] Negotiations for the sale of a medical practice were begun in January 1934. D, the vendor, represented to C that the practice was producing £2,000 per annum, which was then true. Between January and May, D was seriously ill and the practice was looked after by a number of substitutes with the result that the receipts had fallen to £5 per week by 1 May 1934. On 1 May 1934, C, who had not been informed of the change of circumstances, signed a contract to purchase the practice. The Court of Appeal rescinded the contract on the ground that D ought to have communicated the change of circumstances to C. It said that the representation made to induce the contract must be treated as continuing until the contract was signed and what was initially a true representation had turned into a misrepresentation.

[1] *Turner v Green* [1895] 2 Ch 265 (para 12.52). See further paras 12.51–12.56.
[2] (1866) 2 Ch App 21.
[3] [1936] 1 All ER 727, CA.

The misrepresentation must have been addressed by the misrepresentor to the person misled

12.12 The present requirement is not as stringent as may appear at first sight because:

- It is possible for a representation to be made to the public in general, as in the case of an advertisement.

- A representation need not be made directly to the person misled, or that person's agent, in order to satisfy the present requirement. It suffices that the representor knew that the person to whom the misrepresentation was made would pass it on to the claimant.[1] An important limit on this rule is that, if the person (A) to whom the misrepresentation is originally made by D contracts with D as a result, the misrepresentation is deemed to be exhausted. Thus, if A then contracts to sell the property to C, repeating D's misrepresentation, as D knew A would, C has no redress against D because D's misrepresentation, being exhausted, is not regarded as addressed to C.[2] Of course, in such a case C is not remediless because C can pursue the normal remedies for misrepresentation against A who passed on the misrepresentation.

[1] *Pilmore v Hood* (1838) 5 Bing NC 97.
[2] *Gross v Lewis Hillman Ltd* [1969] 3 All ER 1476, CA.

The misrepresentation must have been intended by the misrepresentor to be acted on by the misrepresentee or by a class of person including the misrepresentee

12.13 *Peek v Gurney*[1] is the leading case on this point. The promoters of a company issued a prospectus which contained misrepresentations. The promoters' intention was to induce people to apply for shares on the formation of the company. C purchased shares on the market (ie not on formation of the company). C sued to recover their losses, claiming that they had been induced to buy the shares by the misrepresentations in the prospectus. Their claim was unsuccessful because the promoters had not intended that the prospectus should be relied on by people dealing in shares after the original allotment.

[1] (1873) LR 6 HL 377, HL.

The misrepresentation must have induced the misrepresentee to make the contract

12.14 The question of inducement is one of fact but, if the misrepresentor made a statement of a nature likely to induce a reasonable person to contract and with the intention of inducing this, it will normally be inferred that it did induce the misrepresentee to contract;[1] the inference is particularly strong where the misrepresentation was fraudulent.[2] However, this inference is rebuttable and will, for example, be rebutted in the following three cases:

- If the misrepresentee actually knew the truth,[3] or if an agent acting for the misrepresentee in the transaction knew the truth as a result of information received while acting in the scope of the agent's authority (since such knowledge is imputed to the misrepresentee). *Strover v Harrington*[4] provides an example. In the course of pre-contractual inquiries the solicitors of purchasers of land learned that, contrary to the representations of the vendors, the property was not connected to main drainage; the solicitors' knowledge was imputed to the purchasers.

- If the misrepresentee was ignorant of the misrepresentation when the contract was made. In *Re Northumberland and Durham District Banking Co, ex p Bigge*,[5] C, who had bought some shares in a company, sought to have the purchase rescinded on the ground that the company had published false reports of its financial state. C failed; one of the reasons was because he was unable to prove that he had read any of the reports or that anyone had told him of their contents.

- If the misrepresentee did not allow the representation to affect his (or her) judgement. Thus, if the misrepresentee investigates the truth of the representation (as where a prospective purchaser has a house surveyed) and relies on that investigation, rather than the representation, in making the contract, the inference of inducement is rebutted, except in the case of a fraudulent misrepresentation.[6] In *Attwood v Small*,[7] D offered to sell a mine, making exaggerated representations as to its earning capacity. C agreed to buy if they could verify D's representations and appointed agents to investigate the matter. The agents, who were experienced, visited the mine and were given every facility. They reported that the representations were true and the contract was made. The House of Lords held that the contract could not be rescinded for misrepresentation because C had not relied on the misrepresentations but on their own independent investigations. By way of contrast, the inference of inducement is not rebutted where the misrepresentee could have investigated and discovered the falsity of the representation but chose not to do so.[8]

[1] *Smith v Chadwick* (1884) 9 App Cas 187 at 196.

[2] *Ross River Ltd v Cambridge City FC Ltd* [2007] EWHC 2115 (Ch).
[3] *Begbie v Phosphate Sewage Co* (1875) LR 10 QB 491.
[4] [1988] 1 All ER 769.
[5] (1858) 28 LJ Ch 50.
[6] *S Pearson & Son Ltd v Dublin Corpn* [1907] AC 351, HL.
[7] (1838) 6 Cl & Fin 232, HL.
[8] *Redgrave v Hurd* (1881) 20 Ch D 1, CA.

12.15 Two general points about the requirement of inducement must be noted. First, provided that it was one of the inducements, the misrepresentation need not be the sole inducement. This is shown by *Edgington v Fitzmaurice*,[1] where C was induced to take debentures in a company partly by a misrepresentation in the prospectus and partly by his own mistaken belief that debenture holders would have a charge on the company's property. C was held entitled to rescission.

Second, the misrepresentation must not only have induced the misrepresentee to contract but it must also have been material, in that it related to a matter which would have influenced the judgment of a reasonable person.[2]

[1] (1885) 29 Ch D 459, CA.
[2] *Pan Atlantic Insurance Co Ltd v Pine Top Insurance Co Ltd* [1994] 3 All ER 581, HL (see especially at 600–610).

Remedies for active misrepresentations which have remained mere representations

12.16 Provided that the above requirements are satisfied, one or more of the following remedies:

- rescission,
- damages; and
- indemnity,

dealt with below may be available to the misrepresentee. Alternatively, the misrepresentee can refuse to carry out the contract and, provided (generally) that the misrepresentee returns what the misrepresentee obtained under it, successfully resist any claim for damages or specific performance.

Rescission

12.17 The effect of a misrepresentation is to make the contract voidable so that it remains valid unless and until the misrepresentee elects to rescind it on discovering the misrepresentation. Rescission entails setting the contract aside as if it had never been made, the misrepresentee recovering what he (or she) transferred under the contract but having to restore what was obtained under it. The effect of misrepresentation is important in relation to the rights of third parties. If A sells a car to B under a contract which is voidable for B's misrepresentation, a voidable title passes to B and, if P (an innocent purchaser) buys the car from B before A has rescinded, A loses the right to rescind and P obtains a valid title.[1] This must be distinguished from the situation where the contract is void for mistake.[2] There, title to the goods never passes and they can always be recovered, or damages obtained in lieu, from the other party or a third person to whom they have been transferred.[3]

[1] *White v Garden* (1851) 10 CB 919.
[2] Para 12.1.
[3] *Cundy v Lindsay* (1878) 3 App Cas 459, HL.

12.18 *How to rescind* Rescission can be effected in two ways. First, by bringing legal proceedings for an order for rescission. This may be necessary where a formal document or transaction, such as a lease, has to be set aside by a court order. In other cases a court order is not essential but may be advantageous if the misrepresentor is likely to prove unwilling to return what was obtained under the contract.

Second, rescission can be effected by the misrepresentee making it clear that he (or she) refuses to be bound by the contract. Normally, communication of this decision to the misrepresentor is required, but there is an exception. If a fraudulent misrepresentor absconds, it suffices that the misrepresentee records the intention to rescind the contract by some overt act that is reasonable in the circumstances. This was decided by the Court of Appeal in *Car and Universal Finance Co Ltd v Caldwell*.[1] D sold his car to N in return for a cheque which was dishonoured when he presented it the next day.[2] D immediately informed the police and the Automobile Association of the fraudulent transaction. Subsequently, N sold the car to X who knew of N's fraud. X sold the car to Y who did not know of the fraud. Y sold it sold it to C who bought it in good faith. It was held that in the circumstances D had done enough to rescind the contract before Y bought the car; title had therefore re-vested in him and C had not got title.

[1] [1964] 1 All ER 290, CA.
[2] By his conduct in drawing the cheque, N had fraudulently misrepresented that the existing state of facts was such that in the ordinary course of events the cheque would be honoured: *R v Hazelton* (1874) LR 2 CCR 134 at 140.

12.19 *Bars to rescission* There are four bars to the right to rescind:

a.   *Affirmation of contract by misrepresentee* This occurs if, after discovering that the misrepresentation is untrue and knowing of his (or her) right to rescind,[1] the misrepresentee declares the intention to waive the right to rescission or behaves in a way that such an intention can be inferred. An inference of such an intention was drawn in *Long v Lloyd*.[2] C bought a lorry as the result of D's misrepresentation that it was in excellent condition. On C's first business journey the dynamo broke and he noticed several other serious defects. On the next business journey the lorry broke down and C, realising that it was in a very bad condition, sought to rescind the contract. The Court of Appeal held that the second journey constituted an affirmation because C knew by then that the representation was untrue.

b.   *Lapse of time* This can provide evidence of affirmation where the misrepresentee fails to rescind for a considerable time after discovering the falsity. In addition, lapse of time can operate as a separate bar to rescission in cases where the misrepresentee has not delayed after discovering the falsity. This is shown by *Leaf v International Galleries*,[3] where C bought from D a picture of Salisbury Cathedral which D had innocently represented to be by Constable. Five years later, C discovered that this was a misrepresentation and immediately sought to rescind the contract. The Court of Appeal held that his right to rescind had been lost through lapse of a reasonable time to discover the falsity. This bar probably does not apply in the case of a fraudulent misrepresentation.

c.   *Inability to restore parties to their original position* The main objects of rescission are to restore the parties to their former position and to prevent unjust enrichment.[4] If it is not possible to restore the parties to their original position rescission is barred. Thus, if either party was never able to return what was received (as in the case of services) or has so changed or otherwise dealt with what was obtained under the contract that it cannot be restored, rescission is barred.[5] So, for example, the purchaser of a cake cannot rescind the contract if he has eaten the cake.

There are three qualifications on the present bar:

- A fraudulent misrepresentor cannot rely on his (or her) own dealings with what he (or she) has obtained as a bar to rescission by the misrepresentee.[6]

- The fact that a seller has spent the money received from the buyer does not make restitution impossible since one bank note is as good as another and the seller can restore what was obtained under the contract by handing over other notes.

- Precise restitution is not required for rescission. Provided the property in question can substantially be restored, rescission can be enforced even though the property has deteriorated, declined in value or otherwise changed. For example, in *Armstrong v Jackson*,[7] D fraudulently sold shares to C. Later, when the shares had fallen to one-twelfth of their value at the time of sale, C claimed rescission. It was held that, since C could return the actual shares, rescission would be ordered subject to D's repayment of the purchase price being credited with the dividends received by C.

  In ordering rescission, the court may do so on terms, eg to account for profits, to allow for deterioration or to pay equitable compensation, in order to achieve what is practically just.[8] Reference can also be made to *Cheese v Thomas*.[9] Here a contract between C and D for their joint purchase of a house had involved C contributing £43,000 to the purchase of a house at a price of £83,000 but, because of a fall in property values, the house had subsequently been sold for only £55,400. Rescission of the contract was ordered on the basis that C and D should share the loss brought about by the fall in value in the same proportions (43:40) as they had contributed to the price, and not on the basis of C's contribution of £43,000 being repaid.

  The Court of Appeal in *Cheese v Thomas* emphasised that the basic object of rescission is to restore each party as near as possible to his original position. Where a deterioration or loss of value results from the voluntary dealings with it by the person who obtained it under the contract, that person must not only account for any profits derived from it but also pay compensation for such deterioration or loss of value.[10]

d. *Bona fide purchaser for value* As has been indicated in para 12.17, if, before the misrepresentee elects to rescind, a third party has innocently purchased the property, or an interest in it, for value from the misrepresentor, the third party's rights are valid against the misrepresentee, who loses the chance to rescind. This is illustrated by *White v Garden*,[11] where a rogue induced D to sell him 50 tons of iron by a fraudulent misrepresentation. The rogue then sold the iron for value to C who acted in good faith (ie was unaware of the rogue's fraudulent misrepresentation) and D delivered the iron to C. When D realised the fraud, he seized and removed some of the iron. D was held liable for what is now the tort of conversion; he had purported to rescind the contract with the rogue too late, the rogue's voidable title having been made unavoidable when C innocently bought the iron from him. In *Car and Universal Finance Co Ltd v Caldwell*,[12] on the other hand, rescission was not barred because it occurred before the intervention of a bona fide purchaser for value.

---

[1] *Peyman v Lanjani* [1984] 3 All ER 703, CA.
[2] [1958] 2 All ER 402, CA.
[3] [1950] 1 All ER 693, CA.

[4] *Spence v Crawford* [1939] 3 All ER 271 at 288–289.
[5] *Clarke v Dickson* (1858) EB & E 148.
[6] *Spence v Crawford* [1939] 3 All ER 271 at 280–282.
[7] [1917] 2 KB 822.
[8] *Erlanger v New Sombrero Phosphate Co* (1878) 3 App Cas 1218 at 1278–1279.
[9] [1994] 1 All ER 35, CA.
[10] *Erlanger v New Sombrero Phosphate Co* (1878) 3 App Cas 1218 at 1278–1279.
[11] (1851) 10 CB 919.
[12] Para 12.18.

12.20 Quite apart from the above bars to rescission, the courts have power, in the case of non-fraudulent misrepresentations, to refuse rescission, or to refuse to recognise a purported rescission, and to award damages in lieu. This power is discussed in paras 12.36 and 12.37.

Damages

12.21 We are concerned here with damages for misrepresentation and not with damages for breach of contract, discussed in Chapter 11, which are a different species. Sometimes damages for misrepresentation can be recovered under the common law rules of tort: sometimes under the Misrepresentation Act 1967. Rescission and damages are alternative remedies in many cases, but if the victim of a fraudulent or negligent misrepresentation has suffered consequential loss the victim may rescind *and* sue for damages.

The duty to mitigate loss referred to in para 11.25, in respect of the assessment of damages for breach of contract, also applies to damages for misrepresentation; the duty arises when the misrepresentee discovers the truth.[1]

[1] *Smith New Court Securities Ltd v Scrimgeour Vickers (Asset Management) Ltd* [1996] 4 All ER 769, HL.

12.22 The discussion of the rules of assessment of damages for misrepresentation requires the division of the relevant law into five classes:

- fraudulent misrepresentation;
- negligent misrepresentation under the Misrepresentation Act 1967, s 2(1);
- negligent misrepresentation at common law;
- innocent misrepresentation;
- damages in lieu of rescission.

12.23 *Fraudulent misrepresentation* Fraudulent misrepresentation gives rise to an action for damages for the tort of deceit. The classic definition of fraud in this context was given by Lord Herschell in *Derry v Peek*.[1] Lord Herschell stated that fraud is proved where it is shown that a misrepresentation has been made:

- with knowledge of its falsity; or
- without belief in its truth; or
- recklessly, careless whether it be true or false.

A misrepresentation is not fraudulent if there is an honest belief in its truth when it is made, even though there are no reasonable grounds for that belief.[2] Motive is irrelevant:; an intention to cheat or injure is not required.

[1] (1889) 14 App Cas 337, HL.
[2] *Derry v Peek* (1889) 14 App Cas 337, HL; *Thomas Witter Ltd v TBP Industries Ltd* [1996] 2 All ER 573.

12.24 *Negligent misrepresentation under the Misrepresentation Act 1967 (MA 1967), s 2(1)* Section 2(1) provides that where a person has entered into a contract after a misrepresentation has been made to him by another party thereto and as a result of it has suffered loss, then, if the misrepresentor would be liable to damages for misrepresentation if it had been made fraudulently, he is to be so liable notwithstanding that the misrepresentation was not made fraudulently, unless he proves that he had reasonable grounds to believe and did believe up to the time the contract was made that the facts represented were true. In other words, the misrepresentor is deemed negligent, and liable to pay damages, unless he proves in the stated way that he was not negligent.

Whether the misrepresentor can prove this will depend, for instance, on whether the misrepresentor was an expert or not, the length of the negotiations and whether the misrepresentor had been misled by another. The misrepresentor's burden of proof is a difficult one to discharge. This is shown by *Howard Marine and Dredging Co Ltd v A Ogden & Sons (Excavations) Ltd.*[1] During negotiations for the hire of two barges, Howard's agent misrepresented their capacity in reliance on an error in Lloyd's Register. The Court of Appeal held that the burden of proof had not been discharged, since a file in Howard's possession disclosed the real capacity.

Section 2(1) applies where the misrepresentation was made on behalf of a party to the subsequent contract by an agent,[2] but in such a case the misrepresentee only has an action under s 2(1) against that party and not against the agent.[3]

  [1] [1978] 2 All ER 1134, CA.
  [2] *Gosling v Anderson* (1972) 223 Estates Gazette 1743, CA.
  [3] *Resolute Maritime Inc v Nippon Kaiji Kyokai* [1983] 2 All ER 1; an agent may be liable for a fraudulent misrepresentation or for negligent misrepresentation at common law.

12.25 *Damages for deceit or under MA 1967, s 2(1): remoteness and assessment of damages.* In the tort of deceit and under MA 1967 s 2(1), the rule of remoteness of damage is that the defendant is liable for all actual damage or loss directly flowing from the misrepresentation.[1] This is a more liberal rule than that of reasonable foreseeability of the possibility of the damage which applies in other torts, and also more liberal than the normal rule of remoteness which applies in the case of damages for breach of contract, where damages are limited to compensation for loss which was within the parties' reasonable contemplation, when the contract was made, as a not unlikely result of its breach.[2]

  [1] *Doyle v Olby (Ironmongers) Ltd* [1969] 2 All ER 119, CA; *Smith New Court Securities Ltd v Scrimgeour Vickers (Asset Management) Ltd* [1996] 4 All ER 769, HL (action for deceit); *Royscot Trust Ltd v Rogerson* [1991] 3 All ER 294, CA (action under MA 1967, s 2(1)).
  [2] See paras 18.14–18.19 (other torts) and paras 11.14–11.20 (breach of contract).

12.26 Damages for deceit or under MA 1967, s 2(1) are assessed according to the 'out of pocket rule',[1] ie an amount is awarded (in respect of direct loss) which puts the misrepresentee into the position in which the misrepresentee would have been had the misrepresentation never been made and the contract had not been made.

Where the claimant has been induced to buy something by a misrepresentation, the claimant is entitled to recover as damages the full price paid, but must give credit for any benefits received as a direct result of the transaction.[2] As a general rule, the benefits received by the claimant include the market value of the property acquired as at the date of acquisition, with the result that the damages awarded will be the difference between the price paid and the real value of the property at the date of the acquisition by the claimant.[2] However, this general rule is not inflexibly applied; it will not be applied where to do so would prevent the misrepresentee obtaining full compensation for the wrong suffered.[2] Examples of cases where the general rule will not apply are where:

- the misrepresentation has continued to operate after the date of the acquisition of the asset so as to cause the misrepresentee to retain the asset; or

- the circumstances are such that the claimant is, by reason of the fraud, locked into the property.[2]

One case where the general rule did not apply is *Smith New Court Securities Ltd v Scrimgeour Vickers (Asset Management) Ltd*,[3] where C were induced to buy some shares in company X for £23m by Ds' fraudulent misrepresentation. Because a fraud had been practised on company X before C acquired the shares, the shares were doomed to tumble in value and were therefore a flawed asset. There was a slump in their value and C were only able to sell them by degrees and only received £11m for them in total. C were awarded as damages the difference between what they had paid for the shares and what they had obtained by their sale of the shares (since the latter amount was to be regarded as the benefit received by them as a result of the transaction) because they could not have sold the shares at the value they had when they acquired them.

[1] *Smith New Court Securities Ltd v Scrimgeour Vickers (Asset Management) Ltd* [1996] 4 All ER 769, HL (action for deceit); *Royscot Trust Ltd v Rogerson* [1991] 3 All ER 294, CA (action under MA 1967, s 2(1)).
[2] *Smith New Court Securities Ltd v Scrimgeour Vickers (Asset Management) Ltd* [1996] 4 All ER 769, HL.
[3] [1996] 4 All ER 769, HL.

12.27 The 'out of pocket rule' should be contrasted with the measure of damages for breach of contract. Here the 'loss of expectation rule' applies, as has been explained in para 11.3, and the injured party recovers an amount which puts the injured party into the position in which (or she) would have been if the representation had been true. Where the breach relates to the thing's quality, this amount is the difference between the 'represented value' and the actual value.

12.28 The application of the 'out of pocket rule' does not mean that recovery as damages for deceit or under MA 1967, s 2(1) can never be made in respect of loss of profits. This is shown by *East v Maurer*,[1] where the seller of a hairdressing salon fraudulently represented that he would no longer be working at another salon in the area, in order to induce C to contract to buy the salon. C was induced by the representation to buy the salon. As a result of the untruth of the representation, C was unable to run a successful business at the salon. He was unable to sell it for three years. The Court of Appeal held that the damages for deceit were to be assessed on the basis that C should be compensated for all losses which he had suffered, including his loss on the resale *and his loss of profits*. The profits lost were assessed not on the basis of the profits which would have been earned if the representation had been true (which would have been the amount under the 'loss of expectation' rule) but on the basis of the profits which the misrepresentee would have made if he had not been induced into buying the salon but had bought a different one in the area (because this was the amount by which he was out of pocket as a result of the defendant's deceit).

Damages for loss of a chance are also recoverable as damages for deceit or under s 2(1) if the loss of the chance is directly caused by the defendant's deceit or negligent misrepresentation.[2]

[1] [1991] 2 All ER 733, CA.
[2] *4 Eng Ltd v Harper* [2008] EWHC 915 (Ch) (action for deceit).

12.29 A person who has been induced into a contract by a misrepresentation which is fraudulent or which is negligent under MA 1967, s 2(1) may also recover damages for any consequential loss or damage, such as expenses, personal injury, damage to property,[1] which may have been suffered, provided it is not too remote.

[1] Damages for distress or disappointment are also recoverable in an action in deceit: *Archer v Brown* [1985] QB 401.

12.30 The contributory negligence of the misrepresentee is not a ground for reducing damages awarded for deceit,[1] but it is such a ground if damages are awarded under MA 1967, s 2(1), provided that the defendant is also liable in tort for negligence, since the Law Reform (Contributory Negligence) Act 1945[2] applies in such a case.[3]

[1] *Standard Chartered Bank v Pakistan National Shipping Corpn (No 2)* [2002] UKHL 43, HL.
[2] Para 19.6.
[3] *Gran Gelato Ltd v Richcliff (Group) Ltd* [1992] 1 All ER 865.

12.31 Given that, where a fraudulent misrepresentation has been made, an action may normally be brought for the same amount of damages under MA 1967, s 2(1) without the need to prove fraud, or indeed negligence, it makes sense in many cases of suspected fraudulent misrepresentation for an action to be brought under s 2(1) rather than for deceit.

12.32 *Negligent misrepresentation at common law* The victim of a negligent misrepresentation may be able to sue the misrepresentor under the principles of the tort of negligence, particularly those enunciated in *Hedley Byrne v Heller & Partners*[1] which we discuss in paras 16.18 to 16.20. If the misrepresentee sues under the *Hedley Byrne* principles, the misrepresentee must prove:

- that the misrepresentor owed the misrepresentee a duty to take reasonable care in making the representation, which duty only arises if there is a 'special relationship' arising out of a voluntary assumption of responsibility by the misrepresentor;
- that the misrepresentor was in breach of that duty; and
- that damage resulted from that breach.

The circumstances in which a court may find a 'special relationship' are not entirely clear, as we explain in paras 16.18–16.20.

The *Hedley Byrne* principles were applied to a representation made in pre-contractual negotiations by the Court of Appeal in *Esso Petroleum Co Ltd v Mardon*.[2] In negotiations in 1963 for the tenancy of a filling station, Esso negligently told Mr Mardon that the station had an estimated annual throughput of 200,000 gallons. Mr Mardon was induced to take the tenancy but the actual annual throughput never exceeded 86,000 gallons and Mr Mardon was awarded damages against Esso. One reason for its decision given by the Court of Appeal was that Esso, having special knowledge and skill in estimating petrol throughput, were under the duty of care imposed by *Hedley Byrne*—which applied to pre-contractual statements—and were in breach of that duty. In this case, Mr Mardon could not have relied on the Misrepresentation Act 1967, s 2(1) because the misrepresentation had occurred before the Act came into force.

[1] [1963] 2 All ER 575, HL.
[2] [1976] 2 All ER 5, CA.

12.33 In practice, it is normally better to rely on MA 1967, s 2(1) in the case of a negligent misrepresentation because the claimant does not have the onus of proving negligence under s 2(1), unlike the position at common law. In addition, no special relationship is required under s 2(1). However, the *Hedley Byrne* principles are still important in cases of pre-contractual misrepresentation in four situations where there is a special relationship arising out of a voluntary assumption of responsibility by the defendant:[1]

- where the defendant is by a third party to the contract;
- where the contractual negotiations do not result in a contract between the defendant and the claimant but the claimant nevertheless suffers loss in reliance on the misrepresentation;
- where the limitation period for an action under s 2(1) has expired but that for negligence at common law (which runs from the suffering of loss, and not the misrepresentation) has not; and
- where there has been a misrepresentation by silence on the part of a defendant who is in the special relationship to the claimant.

In these cases, assuming their requirements are satisfied, there can be tortious liability under the principles in *Hedley Byrne*, although there can be no rescission for misrepresentation nor damages under MA 1967.

[1] Reliance on the defendant's voluntary assumption of responsibility may be difficult to prove if the parties are in arm's length commercial negotiations.

12.34 The measure of damages under *Hedley Byrne* is governed by the 'out of pocket' rule[1] and questions of remoteness of damage by the test of reasonable foreseeability at the time of the breach of duty (ie recovery can be had for such loss as is the reasonably foreseeable consequence of the statement being wrong, as opposed to the reasonably foreseeable loss caused by entering into the contract).[2] This is a narrower test of remoteness than that under the MA 1967, s 2(1), which is another reason for an action under s 2(1) being preferable to a claim based on negligent misrepresentation at common law when both actions are available.

[1] See, for example, *JEB Fasteners Ltd v Marks, Bloom & Co Ltd* [1983] 1 All ER 583 at 587.
[2] Paras 18.14–18.19.

12.35 *Innocent misrepresentation* Subject to what is said in paras 12.36 and 12.37, damages cannot be awarded for a misrepresentation which is not fraudulent or negligent, as defined above. However, an indemnity—which is different from damages—may be awarded.

12.36 *Damages in lieu of rescission* The MA 1967, s 2(2) provides that, where a person has entered into a contract after a non-fraudulent misrepresentation has been made to him which would entitle him to rescind the contract, then, if it is claimed in proceedings arising out of the contract that the contract ought to be or has been rescinded, the court or arbitrator may declare the contract subsisting and award damages in lieu of rescission, if of the opinion that it would be equitable to do so.

The rationale for this power is that rescission may be too drastic in some cases, eg where the misrepresentation was trifling. An award of damages under s 2(2) is discretionary. In exercising this discretion, a judge or arbitrator is required by s 2(2) to have regard to the nature of the misrepresentation and the loss that would be caused by it if the contract was upheld, as well as the loss that rescission would cause to the other party.

12.37 It is uncertain whether the power to award damages in lieu of rescission can only be exercised if rescission has not been barred, eg by affirmation of the contract. A literal interpretation, adopted by judges in three High Court cases, indicates that the power can only be exercised if rescission has not been barred.[1] However, in an earlier High Court case, to which these judges referred (but did not follow), it was held by the judge that this is not so and that the power to award damages under MA 1967, s 2(2) does not depend on an extant right to rescind, but only on a right having existed at some time after the contract was made.[2] The former interpretation is consistent with the purpose of s 2(2), to provide compensation where a court has refused to order rescission (or to recognise a rescission) which it would otherwise have done; the latter interpretation is not.

[1] *Zanzibar v British Aerospace (Lancaster House) Ltd* [2000] 1 WLR 2333; *Floods of Queensferry Ltd v Shand Construction Ltd (No 3)* [2000] BLR 81; *Pankhania v Hackney London Borough Council* [2002] EWHC 2441 (Ch).

[2] *Thomas Witter Ltd v TBP Industries Ltd* [1996] 2 All ER 573.

12.38 Important distinctions between MA 1967, s 2(1) and s 2(2) are:

- that damages cannot be awarded under s 2(1) if lack of negligence is proved, whereas they can be awarded in such a case under s 2(2);
- that damages under s 2(1) can be awarded in addition to rescission;
- that an award of damages under s 2(1) is not discretionary; and
- that s 2(3), described below, contemplates that the measure of damages under s 2(1) is different from, and more generous than, an award under s 2(2).[1]

In the light of this last point, obiter dicta in the Court of Appeal that, unlike damages under s 2(1), damages under s 2(2) cannot include damages for consequential loss, is not surprising. It seems that damages are assessed so as to compensate for the loss caused by refusing rescission (ie upholding the contract).[2]

Where a person has been held liable to pay damages under s 2(1), the judge or arbitrator, in assessing damages thereunder, is required by s 2(3) to take into account any damages in lieu of rescission under s 2(2).

[1] *William Sindall plc v Cambridgeshire County Council* [1994] 3 All ER 932 at 954; *Thomas Witter Ltd v TBP Industries Ltd* [1996] 2 All ER 573 at 591.

[2] *William Sindall plc v Cambridgeshire County Council* [1994] 3 All ER 932 at 954 and 961.

Indemnity

12.39 It has already been noted that the object of rescission is to restore the contracting parties to their former position as if the contract had never been made. As part of this restoration the misrepresentee can claim an indemnity against any *obligations necessarily created by the contract*.[1] The italicised words must be emphasised since they indicate that an indemnity is far less extensive than damages, as was recognised by the Court of Appeal in *Newbigging v Adam*.[2] A classic example of this distinction is provided by *Whittington v Seale-Hayne*.[3] C, breeders of prize poultry, were induced to take a lease of D's premises by D's innocent misrepresentation that the premises were in a thoroughly sanitary condition. Under the lease, C covenanted to execute all works required by any local or public authority. Owing to the insanitary condition of the premises the water supply was poisoned, C's manager and his family became very ill, and the poultry became valueless for breeding purposes or died. In addition, the local authority required the drains to be renewed. C sought an indemnity for the following losses: the value of the stock lost; loss of profit on sales; loss of breeding season; rent, and medical expenses on behalf of the manager. The trial judge rescinded the lease and held that C could recover an indemnity for what they had spent on rent, rates and repairs under the covenants in the lease, because these expenses arose necessarily out of the occupation of the premises or were incurred under the covenants in the lease and were thus obligations necessarily created by the contract. However, the judge refused to award an indemnity for the loss of stock, loss of profits, loss of breeding season or the medical expenses, since to do so would be to award damages, not an indemnity, there being no obligation created by the contract to carry on a poultry farm on the premises or to employ a manager, etc.

[1] *Whittington v Seale-Hayne* (1900) 82 LT 49, adopting the view of Bowen LJ in *Newbigging v Adam* (1886) 34 Ch D 582, CA.
[2] (1886) 34 Ch D 582, CA.
[3] (1900) 82 LT 49.

12.40 Two further points may be made concerning the award of an indemnity:

- Being ancillary to rescission, an indemnity cannot be awarded if rescission is barred.
- The remedy of an indemnity is redundant where the court can, and does, award damages for misrepresentation. However, where there has merely been an innocent misrepresentation and the court decides not to award damages in lieu of rescission, the availability of an award of an indemnity is very important.

Active misrepresentations which have become contractual terms

12.41 Whether a misrepresentation made during pre-contractual negotiations has become a term of the resulting contract, or of a contract collateral to it, is determined in accordance with the rules set out in paras 7.14 to 7.21.

If the misrepresentation has become a contractual term the misrepresentee has a choice between two courses of action.

Breach of contract

12.42 As in the case of the breach of any other contractual term, the misrepresentee can sue for damages for breach of contract (as opposed to damages for misrepresentation). The relevant law has already been discussed in detail in Chapter 11. In addition, if the misrepresentation has become a condition of the contract, or an 'intermediate term' and there has been a sufficiently serious breach of it, the misrepresentee can also terminate the contract for *breach*, as explained in Chapter 8.

Misrepresentation Act 1967, s 1(a)

12.43 The misrepresentee's alternative course of action is to make use of MA 1967, s 1(a). Under this provision a person who is induced to enter into a contract by an actionable misrepresentation, which has become a term of the contract, can elect to rescind the contract for misrepresentation subject to the bars to rescission.

However, if the misrepresentee does so rescind damages cannot be recovered for breach of contract since rescission for misrepresentation sets the contract aside for all purposes, including the right to claim damages for its breach, although the misrepresentee may be able to recover damages for *misrepresentation*, depending on the circumstances, in accordance with the rules set out in paras 12.21 to 12.38.

12.44 The choice of a particular course of action will depend very much on whether greater damages will be obtained for breach of contract or for misrepresentation and on whether the claimant wishes, and is able, to rescind for misrepresentation.

Avoidance of provision excluding or limiting liability for misrepresentation

12.45 The MA 1967, s 3 provides that if a contract contains a term (an exemption clause) which would exclude or restrict:

- any liability to which a party to a contract may be subject by reason of any misrepresentation made by him before the contract was made; or
- any remedy available to another party to the contract by reason of such a misrepresentation,

that clause is of no effect, except in so far as it satisfies the requirement of reasonableness. It is for the person claiming that it satisfies that requirement to show that it does. The requirement of reasonableness is that the clause must have been a fair and reasonable one to be included having regard to the circumstances which were, or ought reasonably to have been, known to or in the contemplation of the parties when the contract was made.[1]

Section 3 not only applies where the relevant misrepresentation has remained a mere representation but also where it has become a contractual term—at least as far as rescission for misrepresentation and damages for misrepresentation are concerned—although it is uncertain whether it applies if the misrepresentee elects to treat it as a breach of contract.

[1] Unfair Contract Terms Act 1977, s 11(1). See, further, para 9.15.

12.46 Section 3 is of great importance in relation to the purported exclusion or restriction of liability for misrepresentations made by estate agents.

Where an estate agent makes a misrepresentation about a property which he (or she) has been instructed to sell and thereby induces another to enter into a contract to purchase it, it is the client who is liable to the purchaser for misrepresentation,[1] although the client may seek to recover an indemnity from the agent[2] and the agent may be held liable to the other party in tort if deceit or negligence can be proved.

Not surprisingly, in an attempt to exclude or restrict a client's liability for a misrepresentation made by his (or her) estate agent, auction conditions, conditions of sale by tender and the like may contain a contract term (exemption clause) purporting to exclude or restrict it. Such a term is caught by MA 1967, s 3 and is of no effect except in so far as it satisfies the requirement of reasonableness. In this context, a 'contract term' is not limited to one which expressly excludes or restricts liability or a remedy, since it has been held that it also includes a term of the contract purporting to nullify any representation altogether so as to bring about a situation in law as if there was no representation, such as a term that 'although the particulars are believed to be correct their accuracy is not guaranteed and any intending purchaser must satisfy himself by inspection or otherwise as to their correctness'.[3]

[1] Para 14.28.
[2] Para 14.14.
[3] *Cremdean Properties Ltd v Nash* (1977) 244 Estates Gazette 547, CA; *Walker v Boyle* [1982] 1 All ER 634; *South Western General Property Co Ltd v Marton* (1982) 263 Estates Gazette 1090.

12.47 An entire agreement clause[1] which states that the written agreement containing it contains the entire and only contract between the parties in relation to the subject matter in question is not effective to exclude liability for misrepresentation.[2]

[1] Para 7.7 above.
[2] *Deepak Fertilizers & Petrochemical Corpn v Imperial Chemical Industries Ltd* [1998] 1 Lloyd's Rep 387, CA.

12.48 On the other hand, the wording of an entire agreement clause which states that the parties have not relied on any representation not set out in the written contract is sufficient to preclude the parties from asserting that they relied on any representation not contained in the written contract, and therefore to prevent any liability arising for any such misrepresentation actually made. In such a case, MA 1967, s 3 does not apply. The reason is that it would be bizarre to attribute to the parties an intention to exclude a liability which they must have thought could never arise.[1] In addition, a contract term which denies that an estate agent has any authority at all to make representations is not caught by s 3 and may therefore prevent the client from incurring liability for a misrepresentation by the estate agent.[2]

[1] *Watford Electronics Ltd v Sanderson CFL Ltd* [2001] EWCA Civ 317, CA. Such a statement would not prevent liability for deceit if there has been a fraudulent misrepresentation.
[2] *Overbrooke Estates Ltd v Glencombe Properties Ltd* [1974] 3 All ER 511.

12.49 It must be emphasised that MA 1967, s 3 is solely concerned with 'contract terms' (ie exemption clauses contained in a contract), and has no application to non-contractual clauses of the type commonly found in estate agents' particulars. Although it has been held that such a non-contractual clause denying that an estate agent has any authority to make representations is effective to prevent the client incurring liability for a misrepresentation by the estate agent,[1] it has been suggested that other non-contractual clauses purporting to exclude or restrict the client's liability for misrepresentation are ineffective to do so.[2]

[1] *Collins v Howell-Jones* (1980) 259 Estates Gazette 331, CA.
[2] *Cremdean Properties Ltd v Nash* (1977) 244 Estates Gazette 547 at 551.

12.50 Independently of MA 1967, s 3, the liability of a contracting party for that party's own fraudulent misrepresentation cannot validly be excluded or restricted by a contract term, but a suitably drafted clause can exclude or restrict the liability of a contracting party for a fraudulent misrepresentation by an agent.[1]

[1] *HIH Casualty and General Insurance Ltd v Chase Manhattan Bank* [2003] UKHL 6, HL.

ACTIVE MISREPRESENTATION: KEY POINTS

- For an active misrepresentation, there must be a misrepresentation of fact, except that a misrepresentation of law may suffice.

- A misrepresentation of fact must be distinguished from:
  - a mere puff;
  - a statement of opinion which turns out to be wrong, although a statement of opinion can involve an implied misrepresentation of fact;
  - a statement as to the future, although such a statement can involve a misrepresentation of fact if its maker does not honestly believe in its truth.

- A misrepresentation of law may involve a misrepresentation of fact in certain cases. In addition, it may be the law that a misrepresentation of law which does not involve a misrepresentation of fact suffices for an actionable misrepresentation.

- Silence cannot constitute an active misrepresentation, although there are two exceptions to this rule.

- The misrepresentation must have been addressed by the misrepresentor to the person misled.
- The misrepresentation must have been intended by the misrepresentor to be acted on by the misrepresentee or by a class of person including the misrepresentee.
- The misrepresentation must have induced the misrepresentee to make the contract; it will normally be rebuttably inferred that it did so if it was of a nature likely to induce a reasonable person to contract and was intended to do so.
- The remedy of rescission for misrepresentation is barred:
  - by affirmation of the contract by the misrepresentee after the misrepresentee has learnt that the misrepresentation is untrue and knows of the right to rescind;
  - by lapse of a reasonable time to discover the falsity;
  - if restitution of the property obtained under the contract is impossible. Provided that the property can substantially be restored, rescission can be enforced even though there has been a change in its physical nature, value or in some other way;
  - if a third party has innocently purchased the property or an interest in it for value from the misrepresentor.
- Damages for misrepresentation are available:
  - where the claimant proves that the misrepresentation was fraudulent;
  - where within the terms of the Misrepresentation Act 1967, s 2(1), the defendant does not prove that he (or she) was not negligent in making the misrepresentation;
  - where within the terms of the rule originated in *Hedley Byrne v Heller*, the claimant proves that the misrepresentation was made negligently;
  - under the Misrepresentation Act 1967, s 2(2), in lieu of rescission.
- The rules as to remoteness of damage and measure of damages vary as between these different heads of damages.
- Ancillary to rescission, an indemnity can be awarded in respect of any obligations necessarily created by the contract.
- If the misrepresentation has become a contractual term the misrepresentee has a choice between two courses of action:
  - to seek the appropriate remedy or remedies for breach of contract; or
  - to seek the appropriate remedy or remedies for misrepresentation.
- A contract term excluding or restricting liability for misrepresentation, or any remedy for it, is of no effect, except in so far as it satisfies the requirement of reasonableness. It is for the person claiming that it satisfies that requirement to prove that it does.

Misrepresentation through non-disclosure

12.51 Subject to certain exceptions, mere silence as to a material fact does not constitute a misrepresentation.

12.52 An example of the general rule that mere silence as to a material fact does not constitute a misrepresentation is *Turner v Green*.[1] There two solicitors arranged a compromise of certain legal proceedings. The failure of C's solicitor to inform D's of a material fact was held not to be a ground for relief, even though D would not have made the compromise if D had known of that fact.

[1] [1895] 2 Ch 205.

12.53 However, in certain situations there is a duty to disclose material facts, breach of which gives rise to relief.

Two of these situations have been referred to already: where silence distorts a positive assertion and where a positive assertion is falsified by later events (see para 12.11 above). In these cases silence is deemed to be an active misrepresentation.

In addition, in the case of contracts of the utmost good faith a duty to disclose fully all material facts is imposed, breach of which is regarded as a misrepresentation through non-disclosure for which relief is available.

Contracts of the utmost good faith can be divided into two main types:

- insurance contracts; and
- contracts where one party is in a fiduciary relationship with the other.

Insurance contracts

12.54 A person seeking to make an insurance contract (an intending insured or insurer) is under a duty to disclose to the other party all material facts[1] actually known by him (or her).[2] In the case of the duty imposed on an intending insured, a material fact is one which would have an effect, not necessarily a decisive influence, on the mind of a prudent insurer in deciding whether to accept the risk or as to the premium to be charged.[3] In the case of the duty imposed on an intending insurer, a material fact is one relating to the nature of the risk to be covered or the recoverability of a claim, which a prudent insured would take into account in deciding whether or not to place the risk in question with that insurer.[4] If a material fact is not disclosed as required, the other party cannot rely on it as a ground to avoid the contract if the non-disclosure did not induce that party to make the contract.[5]

[1] *Banque Financière de la Cité SA v Westgate Insurance Co Ltd* [1989] 2 All ER 952, CA; affd [1990] 2 All ER 947, HL.
[2] *Joel v Law Union and Crown Insurance Co* [1908] 2 KB 863, CA.
[3] *Pan Atlantic Insurance Co Ltd v Pine Top Insurance Co Ltd* [1994] 3 All ER 581, HL.
[4] *Banque Financière de la Cité SA v Westgate Insurance Co Ltd* [1989] 2 All ER 952, CA; affd [1990] 2 All ER 947, HL.
[5] See, for example *Pan Atlantic Insurance Co Ltd v Pine Top Insurance Co Ltd* [1994] 3 All ER 581, HL.

Contracts where one party is in a fiduciary relationship of confidence with the other

12.55 Where one prospective contracting party (Y) stands in a relationship with the other which is presumed to be confidential (such as parent and child; solicitor or account-ant and client; trustee and beneficiary; partner and partner; and principal and agent)[1] Y is under a duty to disclose to the other any material fact known to Y.

The same duty of disclosure applies where it is proved that a confidential relation-ship actually existed, ie proved that one party placed a sufficient degree of trust and confidence in the other party that the latter owed a duty of candour and fairness.[2] Thus, although the relationship of a husband and wife or banker and customer are not pre-sumed to be confidential, if it is proved that a particular relationship of such a type actu-ally was confidential, there will have been a duty to disclose a material fact. The duty in this type of case is not confined to cases where the 'trusting party' meekly follows the other's instructions.[3]

A material fact calling for disclosure is one which a reasonable person with appropriate legal knowledge would have thought relevant to the decision about whether or not to contract.[4]

[1] See Ch 14 in respect of agency.
[2] *Tate v Williamson* (1866) 2 Ch App 55; *First Plus Financial Group v Hewett* [2010] EWCA Civ 312.
[3] *First Plus Financial Group v Hewett* [2010] EWCA Civ 312.
[4] *First Plus Financial Group v Hewett* [2010] EWCA Civ 312.

12.56 The effect of a breach of the duty of disclosure in contracts of the utmost good faith is that the person to whom the duty was owed can have the contract rescinded, in which case an indemnity can be awarded where appropriate. The same bars to rescission apply as described above. Alternatively, the person to whom the duty was owed can refuse to carry out the contract and, provided (generally) that that person returns what he (or she) obtained under it, successfully resist any claim for damages for breach of duty.[1] Where there is a duty of disclosure, and there is a fraudulent failure to disclose, damages for deceit may be recovered.[2]

[1] *Banque Financière de la Cité SA v Westgate Insurance Co Ltd* [1989] 2 All ER 952, CA; affd [1990] 2 All ER 947, HL.
[2] *Conlon v Simms* [2006] EWCA Civ 1749, CA.

MISREPRESENTATION THROUGH NON-DISCLOSURE: KEY POINTS

- Generally, non-disclosure of a material fact is not a misrepresentation, but it will be if there is a duty of disclosure.
- There is a duty of disclosure in the case of contracts of the utmost good faith, ie insurance contracts and contracts where one party is in a fiduciary relationship with another.
- If there is a breach of this duty of disclosure, the resulting contract may be rescinded, subject to the bars on rescission, and an indemnity awarded. Only if a breach of the duty of disclosure is fraudulent can damages be awarded.

Duress and undue influence

12.57 In some situations a contract can be rescinded on the ground that it has been procured by illegitimate pressure or that unfair influence over a contracting party has been proved or may be presumed. The first case is governed by the common law of duress, and the second by principles of equity relating to undue influence and to what may be called 'unconscionable bargains'.

Duress

12.58 At one time only duress to the person, ie actual or threatened personal violence or imprisonment, sufficed for duress at common law.[1] In recent times, however, it has been held that economic duress, eg a threat to goods or to a person's business or a threat to break a contract, can also constitute duress at common law.[2]

[1] Co Litt 353b; *Cumming v Ince* (1847) 11 QB 112 at 120.
[2] *Pao On v Lau Yiu Long* [1979] 3 All ER 65, PC.

12.59 To constitute duress at common law, the pressure must be 'illegitimate'. Legitimate commercial pressure cannot constitute duress.[1] Pressure will be illegitimate if what is threatened is unlawful (ie a breach of contract, tort or crime).[2] Pressure can also be illegitimate, even though the threat is of lawful action, because of the nature of the pressure and of the demand to which it relates. Consequently, a threat to assault someone can amount to duress (because what is threatened is unlawful) and so can a threat to report a crime to the police unless a demand is complied with (because the pressure is illegitimate on the second ground).[3] Cases where a threat of lawful action amounts to illegitimate pressure will be rare in commercial dealings. The Court of Appeal has held that where parties are traders dealing at arm's length and one (Y) threatens lawful action (eg not to grant credit) thinking in good faith that the demand is valid, it will be particularly difficult to establish illegitimate pressure, and relatively rare if Y did not consider the demand valid.[4]

Even if there is illegitimate pressure, it will not constitute duress unless the victim has been coerced by that pressure into doing something because he (or she) had no practical alternative to submission to the pressure (and therefore cannot be regarded as having given a true consent).[5]

If duress is proved, it is irrelevant that that was not the sole or predominant cause inducing the contract, provided that it was a cause.[6]

It appears that duress renders a contract voidable, so that it is valid unless and until rescinded by the coerced party,[7] not void.

[1] *Pao On v Lau Yiu Long* [1979] 3 All ER 65, PC; *Hennessy v Craigmyle & Co Ltd* [1986] ICR 461, CA.
[2] *Universe Tankships Inc of Monrovia v International Transport Workers Federation, The Universe Sentinel* [1982] 2 All ER 67, HL.
[3] *Universe Tankships Inc of Monrovia v International Transport Workers Federation, The Universe Sentinel.*
[4] *CTN Cash and Carry Ltd v Gallaher Ltd* [1994] 4 All ER 714, CA.
[5] *Pao On v Lau Yiu Long* [1979] 3 All ER 65 PC; *Hennessy v Craigmyle & Co Ltd.*
[6] *Barton v Armstrong* [1975] 2 All ER 465, PC.
[7] *Universe Tankships Inc of Monrovia v International Transport Workers Federation, The Universe Sentinel.*

Undue influence

12.60 A contract which falls within the equitable doctrine of undue influence is voidable at the instance of the party influenced. There are two types of undue influence, actual and presumed. These were identified as types 1 and 2 by the House of Lords in *Barclays Bank plc v O'Brien,*[1] where the House also recognised a sub-division of presumed undue influence into types 2A and 2B.

[1] [1993] 4 All ER 417, HL.

Actual undue influence

12.61 The party alleging undue influence (C) must prove that the other party actually exerted unfair or improper influence over C and thereby procured a contract that would not otherwise have been made, as where a bank procured a mortgage from a father by a threat to prosecute his son for forgery otherwise.[1] There is no need for C to prove that the contract is manifestly disadvantageous to C.[2]

Developments in the common law rules of duress mean that there is now little difference in coverage between those rules and the equitable rules on actual undue influence.

[1] *Williams v Bayley* (1866) LR 1 HL 200, HL.
[2] *CIBC Mortgages plc v Pitt* [1993] 4 All ER 433, HL.

Presumed undue influence

12.62 There are two distinct types of presumed undue influence. The distinction between them is that the first—type 2A—involves two presumptions, while the second type—type 2B—only involves one presumption.

12.63 *Type 2A* In some types of relationship it is presumed that there exists a confidential relationship between the two parties, as a result of which the dominant party owes a duty to deal fairly with the other. Examples are the relationships of: parent and child;[1] solicitor or accountant and client;[2] and trustee and beneficiary,[3] in each of which the first-named party is presumed to be in a position to influence the other. While the list of relationships which can be presumed to be confidential is not closed, it has been held that the relationships between husband and wife[4] and between employer and employee[5] are not presumed to be confidential.

The above presumption does not suffice in itself to lead to a presumption of undue influence. That presumption will only operate if it is proved by the non-dominant party that the transaction is one which calls for an explanation; if it is this will raise a second rebuttable presumption that the dominant party exercised undue influence, and that party will be found to have exercised undue influence unless he (or she) proves the contrary.[6] For example, if a solicitor has bought land from a client at an under-value, a rebuttable presumption of undue influence will arise because the transaction calls for an explanation, but not if the solicitor has made a reasonable charge for professional services to a client because it does not call for an explanation.[7]

The presumption of undue influence is rebuttable by proof that the dominant party did deal fairly with the non-dominant party and that the latter's consent was given with knowledge of the true facts and was given freely, independent of any sort of influence. One, but not the only,[8] way of rebutting the presumption is by showing that the non-dominant party entered into the transaction only after its nature and effect were explained by an independent qualified person properly informed of the facts.[9]

[1] *Bainbrigge v Browne* (1881) 18 Ch D 188.
[2] *Wright v Carter* [1903] 1 Ch 27, CA.
[3] *Beningfield v Baxter* (1886) 12 App Cas 167, PC.
[4] *Howes v Bishop* [1909] 2 KB 390, CA.
[5] *Mathew v Bobbins* (1980) 41 P & CR 1, CA.
[6] *Royal Bank of Scotland v Etridge (No 2)* [2001] UKHL 44, HL.
[7] *Royal Bank of Scotland v Etridge (No 2)* [2001] UKHL 44 at [104].
[8] *Inche Noriah v Shaik Allie Bin Omar* [1929] AC 127, PC.
[9] See, for example, *Wadlow v Samuel* [2007] EWCA Civ 155, CA.

12.64 *Type 2B* Outside the relationships mentioned in para 12.63, it is open to a party (C) to prove that his (or her) relationship with the other was actually confidential (ie that the other has influence or ascendancy over C, so that C placed trust and confidence in the other) and that the transaction is one calling for an explanation. If both these things are proved a presumption of undue influence arises, and the dominant party will be found to have exercised undue influence unless the dominant party proves the contrary.[1]

[1] *Royal Bank of Scotland v Etridge (No 2)* [2001] UKHL 44, HL.

12.65 *Transaction must call for an explanation* As seen, in both type 2A and type 2B cases it is for the non-dominant party to prove that the transaction calls for an explanation. At one time there was a requirement that the transaction had to have caused that party 'manifest disadvantage', but this is no longer required,[1] although proof of manifest disadvantage is useful as evidence that the transaction calls for an explanation.

[1] *Royal Bank of Scotland v Etridge (No 2)* [2001] UKHL 44, HL.

Undue influence or misrepresentation by a third party

12.66 It can happen that a person makes a contract under the undue influence of a third party. A typical example is where someone under a third party's influence contracts with a bank to guarantee a loan by the bank to the third party. The unduly influenced person can have a contract which is not to his (or her) financial advantage rescinded if:

- the third party was an agent of the other party to the contract, which is normally unlikely; or

- when making the contract, the other contracting party had actual notice (ie actually knew) or constructive notice that there had been undue influence.[1]

The same rules apply where a dominant person in a confidential relationship has by misrepresentation induced the weaker one to contract with another.[2]

Whether or not there was constructive notice of any undue influence or misrepresentation depends on whether the other contracting party (X) knew of facts which should have put him (or her) on inquiry. If X did he (or she) will have constructive notice unless X proves that he (or she) took reasonable steps to satisfy himself (or herself) that the agreement of the party in question had been properly obtained. The law has been developed in relation to the situation where a wife offers to guarantee her husband's debts to a bank, and will be explained in that context. The following principles, however, are equally applicable where a husband guarantees his wife's debts or one sexual partner guarantees the other partner's debts. They were laid down by the House of Lords in *Royal Bank of Scotland plc v Etridge (No 2).*[3]

A bank is put on inquiry whenever a wife offers to stand surety for her husband's debts because on its face such a transaction is not to the wife's financial advantage and there is a substantial risk in such transactions of undue influence or misrepresentation by the husband.

Once a bank is put on inquiry it must bring home to the wife the risks of the transaction which she is offering to guarantee either personally or by ensuring that the wife is advised by a solicitor (which is the usual course of action).

Before the wife goes to a solicitor for advice, the bank must communicate directly with her, informing her that it will require written confirmation from the solicitor that the solicitor has fully explained to her the nature of the transaction and its practical consequences and telling her that the purpose of this requirement is the bank's own protection (ie that after receiving the independent legal advice she will not be able to dispute that she is legally bound by the guarantee). The bank must not proceed until it has received an appropriate response from the wife.

On receipt of a written confirmation from the solicitor the bank will be regarded as being discharged from its obligation to take reasonable steps to ensure that the wife's agreement has been properly obtained and it will be difficult, if not impossible, for the wife later to assert against it a defence based on the undue influence of the husband or misrepresentation by him.

[1] *Barclays Bank plc v O'Brien* [1993] 4 All ER 417, HL; *CIBC Mortgages plc v Pitt* [1993] 4 All ER 433, HL.
[2] *Barclays Bank plc v Boulter* [1999] 4 All ER 513, HL.
[3] [2001] UKHL 44, HL.

Unconscionable bargains

12.67 Acting under equitable principles, a court may rescind a contract on the basis that unfair advantage has been taken by one party (or that party's agent) of the other party who was poor, ignorant, weak-minded, illiterate, unfamiliar with the English language, or otherwise in need of special protection.[1] It is insufficient to prove that the terms of the contract were harsh or oppressive; it must also be shown that the 'dominant party' has imposed the terms in a morally reprehensible manner, ie in a way which affects the dominant party's conscience.[2] In other words, the other party must show impropriety in both the terms of the agreement and the manner in which it was arrived at.[3]

The law on unconscionable bargains has the same basis as the other areas of equitable intervention which have just been mentioned: inequality of bargaining power. Although there are dicta in some cases that this 'common thread' permits the courts to intervene in contractual situations other than those involving pressure or influence, or the taking of an unfair advantage of a poor, ignorant or weak-minded party or one otherwise in need of special protection, fairly recent decisions have rejected the argument that inequality of bargaining power is in itself a ground for rescinding a contract.[4]

[1] *Evans v Llewellin* (1787) 1 Cox Eq Cas 333.
[2] *Crédit Lyonnais Bank Nederland NV v Burch* [1997] 1 All ER 144 at 152–153.
[3] *Kalsep Ltd v X-Flow BV* [2001] All ER (D) 113 (Mar).
[4] Eg *Alec Lobb (Garages) Ltd v Total Oil GB Ltd* [1985] 1 All ER 303, CA.

Bars to rescission

12.68 Where a contract is voidable for duress or undue influence, or because it is an unconscionable bargain, it is valid unless and until it is rescinded. Rescission will be barred[1] by the same bars (besides lapse of time) as apply to rescission for misrepresentation.[2]

[1] Where a rescission is barred in a case involving a confidential relationship, equitable compensation for resulting loss is available because of the breach of the fiduciary duty: *Longstaff v Birtles* [2001] EWCA Civ 1219, CA.
[2] Para 12.19.

Duress and Undue Influence: Key Points

Subject to the bar to rescission, a contract may be rescinded on the ground that:

- it has been procured by duress (ie illegitimate pressure which coerced the victim into doing something because the victim had no practical alternative);

- there has been undue influence, either actual or presumed. Presumed undue influence occurs where there is a confidential relationship as a result of which the dominant party owes a duty to deal fairly with the other. In some types of relationship this is presumed to exist, and in these cases if it is proved that the transaction calls for an explanation there will be a rebuttable presumption of undue influence by the dominant party, which that party must disprove. In other relationships, if it is proved that the relationship was confidential and that the transaction calls for an explanation, undue influence will be presumed unless the dominant party disproves that conclusion. There are special rules to deal with the case where a person contracts with another under the undue influence of a third party;

- the contract is an unconscionable bargain, ie unfair advantage has been taken by one party (or that party's agent) of the other who is a person in need of special protection.

Questions

1. What are the requirements for an actionable active misrepresentation?

2. For the purposes of the law relating to an active misrepresentation, from what must a misrepresentation of fact be distinguished?

3. When can a statement of opinion, as to the future or of law, which turns out to be wrong, suffice for an actionable misrepresentation?

4. What are the bars to the remedy of rescission?

5. When are damages available for misrepresentation, and what are the essential differences between the various heads of damages for misrepresentation?

6. When can a contract term purporting to exclude or restrict liability for misrepresentation or a remedy for it be effective?

7. What exceptions are there to the general rule that mere silence cannot constitute a misrepresentation?

8. Colin was interested in buying some freehold premises and the wine bar in them from Delia. Delia told Colin that the average takings over the previous three years had been £3,000 per week but she omitted to tell Colin that the weekly takings had been declining over the last year; in the previous two years the average weekly takings had been £4,000. Delia also told Colin that in her opinion the average weekly takings would rise substantially because a number of halls of residence for students of the local university were under construction close to the wine bar. Delia made this statement despite the fact that she knew that each of the halls of residence would have its own bar and that the prices of bars in the halls of residence in the town were very low.

   Colin bought the premises and wine bar business from Delia. Immediately after the transfer of the premises and business to him Colin effected some structural alteration of the premises, involving the destruction of an outbuilding. He then discovered that the halls of residence were to have their own bars with low prices. Three months later Colin discovered that the weekly takings had been declining for the last year that Delia had been running the wine bar and were continuing to decline.

   Advise Colin as to his remedies, if any.

9. When can a contract be rescinded on the ground that it has been procured by illegitimate pressure or unfair influence over a contracting party?

10. How do presumptions operate under the law relating to undue influence?

13

Third party rights or obligations under a contract

CHAPTER OVERVIEW

This chapter explains the general rule that a third party to a contract cannot have rights or duties under it, and the exceptions and qualifications to that rule.

13.1 A long-established doctrine of contract law is the doctrine of privity of contract. This doctrine consists of two rules:

- only a party[1] to a contract can have rights under it, so that a third party (ie someone who is not a party to a contract) cannot enforce a contract; and

- a contract cannot impose obligations on a third party, so that a contractual obligation cannot bind a third party or be enforced against a third party.

Both rules are subject to exceptions or qualifications. In particular, the first rule has been made subject to a particularly significant exception by the Contracts (Rights of Third Parties) Act 1999 (C(RTP)A 1999).

[1] Although 'party to a contract' normally refers to a person who actually made the contract, a person on whose behalf an agent made an authorised contract is a party to it. In some cases the agent can also sue or be sued on the contract as well. See paras 14.39–14.44.

Contractual rights and third parties

13.2 Until C(RTP)A 1999, a third party could not generally enforce a contract, even if it was intended to benefit the third party. This was affirmed by the House of Lords in a number of cases in the 20th century.[1] It resulted from two rules:

- As stated in Chapter 6, unless a contract is made by deed, a person can only enforce a contractual promise if that person has provided consideration for that promise. It is not enough that there is consideration in the abstract; it is also necessary for a person seeking to enforce a promise to show that he (or she) has provided consideration for it.

- Even if a person can be said to have provided consideration for the promise in question, that person cannot enforce that promise unless he (or she) is a party to it (the doctrine of privity).[2]

These are the traditional rules which have to be satisfied (subject to (C(RTP)A 1999 and other exceptions or qualifications) before someone can enforce a promise (ie have a right under a contract). Suggested reasons for these rules have been that mere donees should not be able to enforce a contract (relevant only to the first rule) and that the parties to a contract should not have their freedom to vary it restricted by the existence of third party rights. Nevertheless, until C(RTP)A 1999, the law was open to criticism because—apart from the exceptions and qualifications mentioned in para 13.9—it prevented effect being given to the intention of the contracting parties where they had intended to benefit a third party, and it was unfair on a third party who had relied on a contract but could not enforce it; it caused difficulties in commercial life.

[1] Eg *Dunlop Pneumatic Tyre Co Ltd v Selfridge & Co Ltd* [1915] AC 847, HL; *Scruttons Ltd v Midland Silicones Ltd* [1962] 1 All ER 1, HL; *Beswick v Beswick* [1967] 2 All ER 1197, HL.
[2] *Dunlop Pneumatic Tyre Co Ltd v Selfridge & Co Ltd* [1915] AC 847, HL.

Contracts (Rights of Third Parties) Act 1999

Right of third party to enforce contractual term

13.3 The C(RTP)A 1999, s 1(1) provides that, subject to the provisions of the Act (described below), a third party to a contract may in his own right enforce a term of the contract if:

- the contract expressly provides that he may (s 1(1)(a)); or
- (unless on a proper construction of the contract the parties did not intend the term to be enforceable by the third party)[1] the term purports to confer a benefit on the third party (s 1(1)(b)).

In both cases, the third party must be expressly identified in the contract by name, as a member of a class (eg a reference to 'the employees' of a party) or as answering a particular description (eg a reference to a purchaser from a party in a sale of goods contract). This is provided by s 1(3).[2] The third party need not be in existence when the contract is entered into.[3] Thus, s 1 can apply to someone who was unborn when the contract was made if he (or she) is identifiable in one of the three ways referred to.

Section 1(5) provides that, for the purpose of exercising his right to enforce a term of the contract, a third party has any remedy (eg damages, an injunction or specific performance) which the third party would have had if the third party had been a party to the contract and was bringing an action for breach of contract, subject to the same rules as would have applied to that remedy in such a case.[4]

[1] C(RTP)A 1999, s 1(2). If the contract purports to confer a benefit on the third party and it is neutral as to the parties' intention as to its enforcement by the third party, s 1(2) does not prevent enforcement by the third party; s 1(2) does not require that for s 1(1)(b) to apply it must be shown that the parties positively intended that the benefit should be enforceable by the third party: *Nisshin Shipping Co Ltd v Cleaves & Co Ltd* [2003] EWHC 2602 (Comm); *Laemthong International Lines Co Ltd v Artis, The Laemthong Glory (No 2)* [2005] EWCA Civ 519, CA.
[2] Section 1(3) by the use of the word 'expressly' does not allow a person to be identified by a process of interpretation or implication: *Avramides v Colwill* [2006] EWCA Civ 1533, CA..
[3] C(RTP)A 1999, s 1(3).
[4] The same limitation periods apply as apply to a party to the contract: Limitation Act 1980, ss 5 and 8.

Exemption clauses: protection of third party

13.4 Where its terms are satisfied, C(RTP)A 1999, s 1 does not simply permit a third party to assert a positive right to sue for damages or some other remedy. It also enables a third party (T) to rely on an exemption clause in the contract as a defence to an action brought against T if:

- the contract expressly provides that T may rely on it;
- or purports to confer the benefit of the term on T,

and (in either case) T is identifiable from the contract. This is made clear by s 1(6), which provides that references in the Act to a third party enforcing a term of the contract include references to his availing himself of an exemption clause.

Thus, for example, if a contract between A and B for the carriage of machinery by B provides that B's liability for damage to the machinery is limited to £x and the machinery is damaged by the negligent driving of T, one of B's lorry drivers, T is not protected by the clause if T is sued in negligence by A. On the other hand, if the clause had expressly provided that the liability of B or any of B's employees for loss or damage was restricted to £x, T would be protected by the clause.

The C(RTP)A 1999, s 3(6) provides that where a third party (T) seeks the protection of an exemption clause in reliance on s 1, T may not do so unless T could have done so (whether by reason of any particular circumstances relating to T or otherwise) had T been a party to the contract. Thus, for example, if an exemption clause is of no effect between the parties because of the provisions of the Unfair Contract Terms Act 1977 it likewise cannot be effective in favour of the third party.

13.5 Although a third party (T) cannot directly take the benefit of an exemption clause if T falls outside the terms of C(RTPA) 1999, s 1(6), T may indirectly benefit from it in some cases. The reason is that an exemption clause in such a case may limit T's duty of care to one of the contracting parties, and hence T's liability in tort for negligence. For example, where an exemption clause in a building contract placed the risk of damage by fire on the employer (rather than the building contractor), it was held that it would not be just and reasonable to impose on a sub-contractor hired by the building contractor a duty of care to avoid causing damage by fire.[1]

[1] *Norwich City Council v Harvey* [1989] 1 All ER 1180, CA.

Discharge and variation

13.6 By C(RTP)A 1999, s 2(1), where a third party (T) has a right under s 1 to enforce a term of the contract, the parties to the contract may not, by agreement, discharge the contract, or vary it in such a way as to extinguish or alter T's entitlement under that right, without T's consent if:

- T has communicated his assent[1] to the term to the promisor party (ie the party against whom the term is enforceable by T) (s 2(1)(a));
- the promisor party is aware that T has relied on the term (s 2(1)(b)); or
- the promisor party can reasonably be expected to have foreseen that T would rely on the term and T has in fact relied on it (s 2(1)(c)).

However, by s 2(3), this is subject to any express term of the contract under which:

- the parties may by agreement discharge or vary the contract without the third party's consent; or
- the consent of the third party is required in circumstances specified in the contract instead of those set out in s 2(1)(a)–(c), above.

Where the third party's consent to a discharge or variation is required that consent can be dispensed with by a court or arbitral tribunal under s 2(4) or (5) in certain cases.

Section 2(4) provides that a court or arbitral tribunal may dispense with the third party's consent if satisfied that:

- his consent cannot be obtained because his whereabouts cannot reasonably be ascertained; or
- he is mentally incapable of giving consent.

In addition, by s 2(5), a court or arbitral tribunal may dispense with a consent required under s 2(1)(c) if it is satisfied that it cannot reasonably be ascertained whether or not the third party has in fact relied on the term.

If the court or arbitral tribunal dispenses with a third party's consent, it may impose such conditions as it thinks fit, including a condition requiring the payment of compensation to the third party.[2]

[1] This assent may be by words or conduct. If it is sent to the promisor party by post or other means, it is not regarded as communicated to the promisor until received by him: C(RTP)A 1999, s 2(2).
[2] C(RTP)A 1999, s 2(6).

Defences etc available to the promisor

13.7 Where proceedings are brought by a third party under C(RTP)A 1999, s 1 to enforce a term of a contract, the promisor party (ie the party against whom enforcement is sought) has available by way of defence or set-off any matter that:

- arises from or in connection with the contract and is relevant to the term, and
- would have been available to the promisor party by way of defence or set-off if the proceedings had been brought by the promisee party (ie the party by whom the term is enforceable against the promisor).

This is provided by s 3(2).

In addition, by s 3(4) the promisor party also has available to him:

- by way of defence or set-off, any matter; and
- by way of counter-claim, any matter not arising from the contract,

that would have been available to him by way of defence or set-off or, as the case may be, by way of counter-claim *against the third party* if the third party had been a party to the contract.

Section s 3(2) and (4) is subject to any express term of the contract as to the matters that are not to be available to the promisor party by way of defence, set-off or counter-claim.[1]

Lastly, s 3(3) provides that the promisor party also has available to him by way of defence or set-off against the third party any matter if:

- an express term of the contract provides for it to be available to him in proceedings brought by the third party, and
- it would have been available to him by way of defence or set-off if the proceedings had been brought by the promisee party.

It will be noted that s 3 does not permit a *counter-claim against the promisee party* to be raised against the third party.

[1] C(RTP)A 1999, s 3(5).

Cases where s 1 does not apply

13.8 The C(RTP)A 1999, s 1 does not apply in a handful of cases, two of which may be of interest to the property professional.

The first case is that any provision in the constitution of a company or limited liability partnership (such a constitution operates as a contract between the company or LLP and its members), which might benefit someone other than the company or LLP, or a member, does not confer rights on that third party and is not enforceable by him.

Secondly, s 1 does not confer any right on a third party to enforce any term of a contract of employment against an employee or other worker.[1] Thus, if an employment contract requires an employee not to divulge a trade secret supplied by a third party, that term cannot be enforced by the third party, although it could be enforced by the employer.

[1] C(RTP) A 1999, s 6(3) and (4).

Other exceptions and qualifications

13.9 The C(RTP)A 1999, s 1 does not affect any pre-existing exceptions or qualifications to the doctrine of privity of contract.

It is possible for a party to a contract to assign contractual rights to a third party.

Statutes have given a third party the right to enforce an insurance contract of certain types. For instance, a third party who has been injured in a road traffic accident can enforce the driver's insurance policy against the insurance company.[1] Likewise, where a man has insured his life for the express benefit of his wife and/or children, they can enforce payment under the policy on his death.[2]

The requirements of land law have also necessitated some modifications of the strict rules of privity. For example, the benefits of covenants in leases are transferred to successors in title of the landlord and tenant, despite the absence of privity, but in the case of leases created before 1 January 1996 only if the covenants affect the land.[3]

[1] Road Traffic Act 1988, s 148(7).
[2] Married Women's Property Act 1882, s 11.
[3] Paras 36.71–36.79.

Collateral contracts

13.10 The above situations are exceptions or qualifications to the doctrine of privity. It may also be possible to outflank the rule. For example, if a collateral contract can be found, a person not a party to the principal contract can sue on the collateral contract instead. In *Shanklin Pier Ltd v Detel Products Ltd*,[1] C employed contractors to paint their pier. They instructed the contractors to buy and use D's paint. They did so, having been promised by D, in consideration of C specifying the paint, that the paint would last for seven to ten years. The paint lasted for only three months. It was held that, while C could not sue on the contract of sale of the paint made between D and the contractors (the principal contract), to which they were not parties, they could sue on a collateral contract between them and D which contained a promise by D that the paint would last seven to ten years, for which promise C had provided consideration by requiring their contractors to use D's paint.

[1] [1951] 2 All ER 471.

Action in tort by third party

13.11 Where the doctrine of privity applies to prevent a third party to a contract being entitled by virtue of the contract itself to enforce a benefit arising under it, this does not mean that a contract can never indirectly benefit the third party. For example, if it is foreseeable that negligent performance of a contract by a party to it (Y) will cause physical injury to a third party (T), Y may owe a duty of care to T and be liable to T in the tort of negligence if Y is in breach of that duty. By way of another example, surveyors and other property professionals may be held liable in tort to people who are not their clients if they cause them foreseeable economic loss in negligently carrying out a contract made with a client. However, it is exceptional for a person to be held liable in tort for negligently causing foreseeable economic loss. We discuss liability in tort in Part III; Chapter 16 is particularly relevant in the present context. An action in tort may be a useful alternative where a third party could enforce the contract.

Enforcement by a party to the contract

13.12 Whether or not a third party could enforce a contract, the promisee party (the party who was promised that the benefit would be conferred on the third party) can enforce the contract if the promisor party does not carry out his (or her) contractual obligations.[1] Damages, the usual remedy for failure to perform contractual obligations, are available, but a promisee party cannot normally recover any damages on behalf of the third party in respect of the third party's loss. The reason is that, generally, as already said,[2] a claimant can only recover damages for the loss which the claimant has suffered.[3] If the contract was intended solely to benefit the third party, so that the contracting party has suffered no loss, only nominal damages (usually in the region of £2 to £20) will normally be recoverable by the contracting party.[4]

This being so, it is preferable for the contracting party to seek the enforcement of the contract by means of the equitable remedy of specific performance. The advantages of this remedy are illustrated by *Beswick v Beswick*.[5] In this case, in consideration of Peter Beswick transferring his business to his nephew, the nephew agreed to pay his uncle a pension and, after his death, a weekly annuity to his widow. The nephew paid his uncle the pension but only one payment of the annuity was made. The widow, in her capacity as the administratrix of her husband's estate, successfully sued her nephew for specific performance of the contract to pay the annuity. (Because the case was decided before C(RTP)A 1999, the widow would not have succeeded if she had sued merely as the intended recipient.) Thus, if specific performance of a contract can be ordered, a party to a contract or that party's personal representative can ensure enforcement of the contract for the benefit of a third party. However, it would be wrong to think that specific performance will always be ordered in the present type of case. It is a discretionary remedy and is subject to a number of other limitations described in para 11.44.

[1] The C(RTP)A 1999, s 4 expressly preserves the right of the promisee to enforce any term of the contract where a third party has a right of enforcement under s 1.

[2] For the general rule, and some exceptions to it, see para 11.2.

[3] If the contract is one to provide a contracting party with a benefit which others will also enjoy, such as a contract for a family holiday or a group coach trip, that contracting party is entitled to substantial damages for *his* (or *her*) loss (the family holiday or group coach trip) if the other party breaks the contract by failing to provide the benefit: *Jackson v Horizon Holidays Ltd* [1975] 3 All ER 92, CA, as explained in *Woodar Investment Development Ltd v Wimpey Construction (UK) Ltd* [1980] 1 All ER 571, HL.

[4] *Beswick v Beswick* [1967] 2 All ER 1197, HL.

[5] [1967] 2 All ER 1197, HL.

13.13 The C(RTP)A 1999, s 5 protects a promisor party from double liability where under s 1 a term of a contract is enforceable by a third party, and the promisee party has received from the promisor a sum in respect of:

- the third party's loss in respect of the term, or
- the expense to the promisee of making good to the third party the default of the promisor.

Section 5 provides that in such a case, where proceedings are then brought by the third party in reliance on s 1, the court or arbitral tribunal must reduce any award to the third party to such extent as it thinks appropriate to take account of the sum recovered by the promisee.

CONTRACTUAL RIGHTS AND THIRD PARTIES: KEY POINTS

- Privity of contract consists of two rules:
  - only a party to a contract can have rights under it, so that a third party (ie someone who is not a party to a contract) cannot enforce a contract, and
  - a contract cannot impose obligations on a third party, so that a contractual obligation cannot bind a third party or be enforced against a third party.

  Both rules are subject to exceptions or qualifications. In particular, the first rule has been made subject to a particularly significant exception by the Contracts (Rights of Third Parties) Act 1999.

- Under C(RTP)A 1999, a third party (T) may enforce a term of a contract if:
  - the term expressly states that T may enforce the contract or purports to confer a benefit on T; and
  - T is identified in the contract.

- In addition to enforcing a contract and obtaining a remedy, a third party may be protected under C(RTP)A 1999 by an exemption clause in the contract.

- Where a third party has a right under C(RTP)A 1999 to enforce a term of the contract, the Act sets out detailed provisions about the right of the parties to discharge the contract, or extinguish or alter the third party's entitlement. Generally, the third party's consent is required.

- Where a third party brings proceedings under C(RTP)A 1999 against a party to the contract, that party may rely on a defence or set-off which that party would have had against the other party or the third party. A counter-claim against a third party may also be relied on. These rules are subject to the express terms of the contract.

- Exceptions and qualifications existing before the C(RTP)A 1999 still apply. Thus, a third party can enforce rights under a contract if they have been assigned to him (or her) by a party or if some other statute expressly provides for third-party enforcement.

- A third party to a contract can enforce a contract collateral to it or may have an action in tort for negligence.

- If a party to a contract seeks to enforce a contractual obligation due in respect of a third party, the party can normally only recover nominal damages but that party may be able to obtain an order for specific performance of the contract.

Contractual obligations and third parties

13.14 As we have already indicated, the general rule is that only a person who is a party to a contract can be subject to any obligations contained in it. Consequently, a third party cannot generally be sued for contravening a provision in a contract made between others.[1]

Although there is good reason for generally refusing to allow a contract to impose obligations on third parties, there are some cases where this is possible. The principal exceptions or qualifications to the general rule can be summarised as follows:

- the burdens of covenants in leases are transferred to the successors in title of the landlord and tenant, despite the absence of privity of contract, but in the case of leases created before 1 January 1996 only if the covenants affect the land; we discuss this further in paras 36.71–36.79;

- the burdens of negative covenants affecting the use of land (ie restrictive covenants *not* to do specified things on the land), inserted in a contract of sale of land, bind subsequent purchasers of the land, provided certain conditions are satisfied; we discuss this further in paras 33.11–33.15;

- where someone hands over goods to another for repair, cleaning, carriage, loading or the like, the transaction gives rise to what is called a 'bailment', the transferor being the 'bailor' and the recipient the 'bailee'. If the bailee sub-contracts the work to someone else, the terms of the contract between the bailee and that person will bind the bailor (a third party to the contract, which involves a 'sub-bailment') if the bailee had the bailor's authority to make the sub-bailment and the bailor had expressly or impliedly consented to the bailee making the sub-bailment on the terms in question;[2]

- in certain cases, the rights of a person, by virtue of a contract to which he (or she) is party, to make use of a chattel are enforceable against a third party.

[1] *McGruther v Pitcher* [1904] 2 Ch 306, CA.
[2] *K H Enterprise (Cargo Owners) v Pioneer Container (Owners), The Pioneer Container* [1994] 2 All ER 250, PC; see, further, in respect of exemption clauses, para 13.16 .

Third party generally not bound by an exemption clause

13.15 Because a third party who can enforce a term of the contract by virtue of C(RTP) A 1999, s 1 may only do so subject to the other terms of the contract, the third party's enforcement of that term will be subject to any applicable, valid exemption clause.

13.16 On the other hand, a third party cannot be deprived of a right to sue in tort by an exemption clause contained in a contract between others, even though it purports to have that effect. An authority is *Haseldine v C A Daw & Son Ltd.*[1] The owners of a block of flats employed D to repair a lift in the block. D repaired the lift negligently and C was injured when the lift fell to the bottom of the lift shaft. D were held liable to C, it being irrelevant that the contract between D and the owners of the block purported to exempt D from liability for personal injury.

There is one exceptional type of case where an exemption clause can bind a third party who brings a tort action. This arises through the operation of the rule relating to sub-bailments referred to in para 13.14. If the sub-bailment contract contains an exemption clause it will bind the third party bailor if the requirements of the rule are satisfied.[2]

[1] [1941] 3 All ER 156, CA. See also *Leigh and Sillivan Ltd v Aliakmon Shipping Co Ltd, The Aliakmon* [1986] 2 All ER 145, HL.
[2] *Singer Co (UK) Ltd v Tees and Hartlepool Port Authority* [1988] 1 FTLR 442.

Questions

1. What is meant by 'privity of contract'?

2. What are the exceptions or qualifications to the doctrine of privity of contract?

3. Ann wants to make a gift of £15,000 to Ben and decides to sell her classic sailing boat to raise the money. Ben arranges for his brother, Don, to buy the boat from Ann for £25,000. The contract of sale made between Ann and Don provides that Don will pay £15,000 to Ben and the balance of £10,000 to Ann. After delivery of the boat, Don falls out with Ben. He pays Ann £10,000 but refuses to pay Ben £15,000.

   Advise Ben.

   Would your answer be different if the sale to Don had been on the understanding that Don would pay Ben £15,000 but the written contract of sale had simply said that the £15,000 would be paid by Don 'to the person who deserves it'?

4. Theo Dolite & Co Ltd, manufacturers of surveying equipment, wishes to amend its standard terms of business so as to enable its suppliers to rely, as against customers of Theo Dolite & Co Ltd, on the exemption clauses contained in those terms. The company also wishes to know whether an exemption clause can protect it against actions by third parties to any contract which it makes.

   Advise Theo Dolite & Co Ltd.

14

Agency

CHAPTER OVERVIEW

Agency concerns the activities of three parties: an agent, the principal for whom he (or she) acts and a third party with whom he (or she) deals.

The issues with which we are concerned in this chapter are:

- the relationship of principal and agent (ie the creation of agency, the duties and rights of agents and the termination of agency);

- the changes in the legal relationship of the principal and third parties which may be effected by an agent; and

- the legal relationship, if any, between the agent and third parties.

14.1 Agency is the relationship between two legal persons, whereby one person, the principal or client, appoints another, the agent, to act on his (or her) behalf. The relationship is usually, though not necessarily, contractual.[1] The major importance of agency lies in the fact that an authorised agent[2] may affect the legal position of the principal vis-à-vis third parties. In most cases, the agent does this by making a contract on the principal's behalf, or by disposing of property which the principal owns. However, the agent may also bind the principal in other ways, for example by signing a document,[3] receiving notice,[4] or committing a tort. With certain exceptions,[5] mostly statutory, a principal may do anything through the medium of an agent which he (or she) could lawfully do in person.

[1] *Yasuda Fire and Marine Insurance Co of Europe Ltd v Orion Marine Insurance Underwriting Agency Ltd* [1995] 3 All ER 211.
[2] Including one who, though not actually appointed, is given the appearance of authority by the principal: paras 14.30–14.34.
[3] *LCC v Agricultural Food Products Ltd* [1955] 2 All ER 229, CA.
[4] *Proudfoot v Montefiore* (1867) LR 2 Qb 511.
[5] See *Clauss v Pir* [1987] 2 All ER 752.

Principal and agent

Creation of agency

14.2 Agency may be created by agreement, express or implied, by ratification or by virtue of necessity. In determining whether a principal (P) has appointed another person to act as his agent (A), it is necessary to decide whether P had the capacity to appoint an agent and whether A had the capacity to act as an agent, before considering how an agent is appointed.

Capacity

14.3 An agent can be appointed to effect any transaction for which the principal has capacity.[1] However, an agent who lacks full contractual capacity cannot be personally liable on contracts which could not have been made on his (or her) own behalf.[2] Further, the agent may well not be liable on the contract of agency itself.

[1] For the law relating to capacity to contract, see paras 4.10–4.19.
[2] *Smally v Smally* (1700) 1 Eq Cas Abr 6; for when an agent is personally liable on contracts see paras 14.39–14.44.

Appointment by express agreement

14.4 An agent may be appointed by express agreement between principal and agent. This agreement is frequently, but not necessarily, a contract. If the appointment is by contract, the usual rules for the formation of contracts must be complied with. Normally, the appointment can be made informally, even if the agent is to transact contracts which must be made or evidenced in writing.[1] All that is necessary is a desire to appoint A as agent and A's consent to act as such. However, in some cases certain formalities are necessary to create agency. For instance, an agent who is to execute a deed must be appointed by a deed; this is known as a power of attorney.[2]

[1] *McLaughlin v Duffill* [2008] EWCA Civ 1627; [2009] 34 EG 80.
[2] *Steiglitz v Egginton* (1815) Holt NP 141, and see also the Powers of Attorney Act 1971, ss 1 and 7.

Appointment by implied agreement

14.5 If the parties have not expressly agreed to become principal and agent, it may be possible to find an implied agreement based on their conduct or relationship.[1] Factors which have been found relevant in determining whether agency has been created by implied agreement are whether one party acts for the other at the other's request and whether commission is payable.

[1] *Ashford Shire Council v Dependable Motors Pty Ltd* [1961] 1 All ER 96, PC.

Ratification

14.6 In certain circumstances, the relationship of principal and agent can be created or extended retrospectively under the doctrine of ratification. What this means is that, if A purports to act as agent for B in a particular transaction (although not authorised to do so), B may subsequently 'ratify' or adopt what A has done. In such a case, A is deemed to have been acting as an authorised agent when effecting the transaction.[1] However, ratification only validates past acts of the 'agent' and gives no authority for the future,[2] although frequent acts of ratification by an alleged principal may create agency by implied agreement or confer ostensible authority on the agent.[3]

[1] *Bolton Partners v Lambert* (1889) 41 Ch D 295.
[2] *Irvine v Union Bank of Australia* (1877) 2 App Cas 366, PC.
[3] *Midland Bank Ltd v Reckitt* [1933] AC 1, HL.

14.7 *Effects of ratification* A person who ratifies a transaction will be taken to have ratified the whole transaction, and not merely those parts which are to that person's advantage.[1] The effect of ratification is to make the transaction (which is usually a contract) binding on the principal from the moment it was made by the agent.[2] Since the acts of the agent are retrospectively validated, the agent cannot be liable to a third party for breach of warranty of authority, nor to the principal for acting outside the scope of authority,[3] and can claim commission and an indemnity.[4] Once a contract is ratified, the agent generally ceases to be liable on the contract, but ratification cannot vary rights in property which had vested before ratification.[5]

Perhaps the most controversial effect of ratification is that it allows the alleged principal to decide whether to accept a contract or reject it. The third party may wish to repudiate an agreement with the agent because of the agent's lack of authority, but find that the contract is binding if the alleged principal subsequently ratifies.[6] However, if a contract is explicitly made 'subject to ratification' the third party can withdraw prior to ratification and, if this is done, the contract cannot be ratified.[7]

[1] *Cornwal v Wilson* (1750) 1 Ves Sen 509.
[2] *Bolton Partners v Lambert* (1889) 41 Ch D 295.
[3] *Smith v Cologan* (1788) 2 Term Rep 188n. For breach of warranty of authority see para 14.45.
[4] *Hartas v Ribbons* (1889) 22 Qbd 254, CA. For indemnities see para 14.19.
[5] *Bird v Brown* (1850) 4 Exch 786.
[6] *Bolton Partners v Lambert* (1889) 41 Ch D 295.
[7] *Warehousing and Forwarding Co of East Africa Ltd v Jafferali & Sons Ltd* [1963] 3 All ER 571, PC.

14.8 *Who can ratify* Only the alleged principal can ratify the actions of an alleged agent and then only if the latter purported to act on the principal's behalf.[1] Thus an undisclosed principal cannot ratify.[2] A leading illustration of this is the case of *Keighley, Maxsted & Co v Durant*.[3] In this case an agent purchased wheat at a price which was higher than he had been authorised to pay. The agent had not revealed that he was acting as an agent when he bought the grain. The House of Lords held the defendant principal not liable for breach of contract when he refused to accept delivery of the grain, even though he had purported to ratify the contract of sale.

Provided that an agent reveals that he (or she) is acting as agent, the principal, even though unnamed, can ratify the agent's unauthorised actions.[4] However, an unnamed principal should be identifiable,[4] unless, perhaps, the third party has shown that the identity of the principal does not matter. Further, there is a strange rule by which unnamed, and possibly unidentifiable, principals can ratify contracts of marine insurance.[5]

A company which is a disclosed principal can only ratify if it is in existence at the time the agent enters into any contract.[6] Even if a company takes the benefit of a pre-incorporation contract it is not liable on it, although it will be liable if it makes a new contract post-incorporation on the same subject matter.[7] An agent who makes a pre-incorporation contract on behalf of a non-existent company is personally liable on it unless personal liability has been excluded 'by contract or otherwise'.[8]

To be able to ratify, the disclosed principal must have had capacity to make the contract at the date when the 'agent' contracted.[9]

[1] *Wilson v Tumman* (1843) 6 Man & G 236.
[2] However, an alleged principal who acts towards the third party as if the agent's act was authorised may become liable for it on the basis of estoppel: *Spiro v Lintern* [1973] 3 All ER 319, CA; *Worboys v Carter* [1987] 2 EGLR 1, CA.
[3] [1901] AC 240, HL.
[4] *Watson v Swann* (1862) 11 CBNS 756; *Southern Water Authority v Carey* [1985] 2 All ER 1077.
[5] *Boston Fruit Co v British and Foreign Marine Insurance Co* [1906] AC 336, HL.
[6] *Kelner v Baxter* (1866) LR 2 CP 174. However, a company may claim damages in tort for a negligent act committed before its incorporation: *Miro Properties Ltd v J Trevor & Sons* [1989] 1 EGLR 151.
[7] *Howard v Patent Ivory Manufacturing Co* (1888) 38 Ch D 156.

⁸ Companies Act 1985, s 36C. The agent is also entitled to enforce the contract personally: *Braymist Ltd v Wise Finance Co Ltd* [2002] EWCA Civ 127, [2002] 2 All ER 333, CA.

⁹ *Boston Deep Sea Fishing and Ice Co Ltd v Farnham (Inspector of Taxes)* [1957] 1 WLR 1051.

14.9 *What can be ratified* Apparently any action can be ratified (even where the purported agent was seeking personal benefit[1]) except those which are illegal[2] or otherwise void.

¹ *Re Tiedemann and Ledermann Frères* [1899] 2 Qb 66.

² *Bedford Insurance Co Ltd v Instituto de Resseguros do Brasil* [1984] 3 All ER 766.

14.10 *How to ratify* Ratification may be made by express affirmation of the unauthorised actions of the agent by the principal.[1] It need not, as a rule, take any special form, except that, where the agent has without authority executed a deed, ratification too must be by deed.[2] Ratification must take place within a reasonable time.[3] What is reasonable is a question of fact in every case but, if the time for performance of a contract has passed, ratification is impossible.[4] However, where an agent without authority commences legal proceedings, the client may ratify the agent's act even after the expiry of the limitation period within which proceedings must be commenced.[5]

Ratification may also be effected by conduct,[6] although mere passive acceptance of the benefit of a contract may be insufficient.[7] Examples of ratification are provided by the following cases. In *Lyell v Kennedy*,[8] A received rent from property for many years, although not authorised to do so. When the owner sued him for an account of the rents, it was held that the owner's action constituted ratification of A's receipt of the rents. Similarly, in *Cornwal v Wilson*,[9] A bought some goods in excess of the price authorised by P. P objected to the purchase but sold some of the goods; it was held that he had ratified the unauthorised act by selling the goods.

An action by the alleged principal will only be implied ratification if there was a choice whether or not to act. If the alleged principal had no real choice other than to accept the benefit of the unauthorised actions of the agent, accepting such benefit is not ratification. For example, if an agent has had unauthorised repairs done on a ship, merely retaking the ship with these repairs is not ratification by the alleged principal.[10]

Ratification will, generally, only be implied from conduct if the alleged principal has acted with full knowledge of the facts.[11] However an alleged principal who is prepared to take the risk of what the agent has done can choose to ratify without full knowledge. For instance, in *Fitzmaurice v Bayley*[12] an agent entered into an unauthorised contract for the purchase of property. The alleged principal wrote a letter saying he did not know what his agent had done but would stand by all that he had done. This was an express ratification by the principal, who had agreed to bear the risk of being bound by the unauthorised acts of the agent, whatever they were.

¹ *Soames v Spencer* (1822) 1 Dow & Ry KB 32.

² *Hunter v Parker* (1840) 7 M & W 322.

³ *Re Portuguese Consolidated Copper Mines Ltd* (1890) 45 Ch D 16, CA.

⁴ *Metropolitan Asylums Board (Managers) v Kingham & Sons* (1890) 6 TLR 217.

⁵ *Presentaciones Musicales SA v Secunda* [1994] 2 All ER 737, CA.

⁶ *Lyell v Kennedy* (1889) 14 App Cas 437, HL; *Cornwal v Wilson* (1750) 1 Ves Sen 50.

⁷ *Hughes v Hughes* (1971) 221 Estates Gazette 145, CA.

⁸ (1889) 14 App Cas 437, HL.

⁹ (1750) 1 Ves Sen 509.

¹⁰ *Forman & Co Pty Ltd v The Liddesdale* [1900] AC 190, PC.

¹¹ *The Bonita, The Charlotte* (1861) 1 Lush 252.

¹² (1856) 6 E & B 868.

Agency of necessity

14.11 Agency of necessity is a limited exception to the concept that agency is based on a consensual relationship between the parties. When certain emergencies occur, immediate action may be necessary and the courts may be prepared to find that the person taking such action was thereby acting as an agent of necessity. A common example of agency of necessity is that masters of ships faced with an emergency are agents of the shipowner, and have authority to enter into contracts with third parties on the shipowner's behalf.[1]

Frequently, agency of necessity will merely extend the authority of existing agents but in other cases it may create agency where none existed previously—for example, between masters of ships and cargo owners. In other cases, if a person claims to be an agent of necessity, such agency will only affect the relationship of the alleged principal and agent, and will confer no power on the 'agent' to deal with third parties on behalf of the 'principal'. This type of agency of necessity is more likely than the former if the parties were not already principal and agent; for example, someone who salvages a ship cannot make contracts on behalf of the shipowner.

Agency of necessity will only arise if the 'agent' has no practical way of communicating with the 'principal',[2] if the action of the 'agent' is reasonably necessary to benefit the principal[3] and if the agent has acted bona fide.

[1] *The Gratitudine* (1801) 3 Ch Rob 240.
[2] *Springer v Great Western Rly Co* [1921] 1 KB 257, CA.
[3] *Prager v Blatspiel, Stamp and Heacock Ltd* [1924] 1 KB 566.

CREATION OF AGENCY: KEY POINTS

- The relationship of principal and agent is usually, though not necessarily, a contractual one.
- Agency may be created by agreement (express or implied) in advance or by ratification after the event.
- In certain limited circumstances agency may arise out of necessity.

Duties of an agent

Duty to act

14.12 A paid agent is under a duty to act and will be liable to the principal for any loss suffered because of failure to act.[1] An agent who does not intend to act should inform the principal, but the agent cannot be made liable for failure to perform acts which are illegal or void.[2] A gratuitous agent does not appear to be under any positive duty to act, although one who chooses to act and does so negligently is liable.[3]

[1] *Turpin v Bilton* (1843) 5 Man & G 455.
[2] *Cohen v Kittell* (1889) 22 Qbd 680, DC.
[3] *Wilkinson v Coverdale* (1793) 1 Esp 74, CA.

Duty to obey instructions

14.13 An agent must act strictly in accordance with the instructions of the principal in so far as they are lawful and reasonable. An agent has no discretion to disobey instructions, even in what is honestly and reasonably regarded as being the principal's best interests.[1] An agent who carries out instructions cannot be liable for loss suffered by the principal because the instructions were at fault.[2] Conversely, an agent who does not will be responsible to the principal for any loss thereby suffered, even if the loss is not occasioned by any fault on the agent's part.[3] If an agent's instructions are ambiguous, the agent is not in breach of duty for making a reasonable but incorrect interpretation of them.[4] Similarly, if instructions confer a discretion on the agent, there is no liability if the agent exercises the discretion reasonably.[5]

[1] *Bertram, Armstrong & Co v Godfray* (1830) 1 Knapp 381.
[2] *Overend Gurney and Co v Gibb* (1872) LR 5 HL 480, HL.
[3] *Lilley v Doubleday* (1881) 7 Qbd 510.
[4] *Weigall & Co v Runciman & Co* (1916) 85 LJKB 1187, CA.
[5] *Boden v French* (1851) 10 CB 886.

Duty to exercise care and skill

14.14 An agent, whether paid or gratuitous,[1] is required to display reasonable care in carrying out the principal's instructions and also, where appropriate, such skill as may reasonably be expected from a member of the relevant profession.[2] An agent who fails to do so will be liable for any loss which the principal suffers. A negligent agent may also forfeit the right to remuneration where that negligence renders the agent's services to the principal worthless.[3]

[1] *Chaudhry v Prabhakar* [1988] 3 All ER 718, CA; see para 17.27.
[2] Supply of Goods and Services Act 1982, s 13. For examples, see paras 17.8 and 17.9.
[3] *Nye Saunders v Bristow* (1987) 37 BLR 92, CA.

Fiduciary duties

14.15 Every agent owes fiduciary duties, ie duties of good faith, to the principal. While these duties are based on the confidential nature of the agency relationship, it is important to appreciate that an agent who acts innocently may still be in breach of these duties.[1] There are two main fiduciary duties—a duty to disclose any conflict of interest and a duty not to take secret profits or bribes.

a. *Conflict of interest* Wherever an agent's own interests, or the interests of a third party, come into conflict with those of the principal, the agent must make a full disclosure to the principal of all relevant facts, so that the latter may decide whether to continue with the transaction. It is this rule which prevents an agent, in the absence of disclosure, from selling the agent's own property to the principal,[2] purchasing the principal's property personally[3] or acting as agent for both vendor and purchaser[4] or for two competing would-be purchasers.[5] Similarly, an estate agent instructed to sell property must not favour one potential purchaser at the expense of others, in the hope of reward from that purchaser.[6] If the agent is in breach of this duty, the principal may have any resulting transaction set aside, claim any profit accruing to the agent and refuse to pay commission.[7]

b. *Secret profits and bribes* An agent who, without the principal's knowledge and consent, makes a profit for himself out of his or her position, or out of property or information with which he or she is entrusted, must account for this profit to the principal.[8] Thus, an agent may not accept commission from both parties to a transaction,[9] nor keep the benefit of a trade discount while charging the principal the full price.[10] It makes no difference that the agent has acted honestly throughout, nor even that the agent's actions have conferred substantial benefits upon the principal.[11] However, an agent who has the principal's informed consent may keep whatever profit the agent makes.[12]

Where the secret profit takes the form of a payment from a third party who is aware that he (or she) is dealing with an agent, it is called a bribe, even if the payment is not made with any evil motive and even if the principal suffers no loss thereby.[13] The taking of a bribe entitles the principal to dismiss the agent,[14] recover either the amount of the bribe or the actual loss (if greater) from the agent or third party,[15] repudiate any transaction in respect of which the bribe was given[16] and refuse to pay commission.[17]

[1] *Keppel v Wheeler* [1927] 1 KB 577, CA.
[2] *Gillett v Peppercorne* (1840) 3 Beav 78.
[3] *McPherson v Watt* (1877) 3 App Cas 254, HL.
[4] *Harrods Ltd v Lemon* [1931] 2 KB 157, CA.
[5] *Eric V Stansfield v South East Nursing Home Services Ltd* [1986] 1 EGLR 29. An estate agent can of course act for more than one vendor, but must not disclose to one of them information which is confidential to another: *Brent Kelly v Cooper Associates* [1993] AC 205, PC.
[6] *Henry Smith & Son v Muskett* [1979] 1 EGLR 13.
[7] Para 14.18.
[8] *Regal (Hastings) Ltd v Gulliver* [1942] 1 All ER 378, HL. For an example concerning a football agent, see *Imageview Management Ltd v Jack* [2009] EWCA Civ 63; [2009] 2 All ER 666, CA.
[9] *Andrews v Ramsay & Co* [1903] 2 KB 635, CA.
[10] *Hippisley v Knee Bros* [1905] 1 KB 1, DC.
[11] *Boardman v Phipps* [1966] 3 All ER 721, HL.
[12] See *Anangel Atlas Compania Naviera SA v Ishikawajima-Harima Heavy Industries Co* [1990] 1 Lloyd's Rep 167.
[13] *Industries and General Mortgage Co Ltd v Lewis* [1949] 2 All ER 573.
[14] *Boston Deep Sea Fishing and Ice Co v Ansell* (1888) 39 Ch D 339, CA.
[15] *Mahesan S/O Thambiah v Malaysia Government Officers' Co-operative Housing Society Ltd* [1978] 2 All ER 405, PC.
[16] *Shipway v Broadwood* [1899] 1 Qb 369; *Logicrose v Southend United Football Club* [1988] 1 WLR 1256.
[17] Para 14.18.

Other duties

14.16 An agent has a duty not to delegate responsibilities to a sub-agent without the authority of the principal.[1] An agent must pay over to the principal any money received for the use of the principal in the course of the agency, even if it is claimed by third parties,[2] and must keep proper accounts. An agent must allow the principal to inspect all accounts, documents and records relating to acts done by the agent on the principal's behalf.[3]

[1] *De Bussche v Alt* (1878) 8 Ch D 286, CA.
[2] *Blaustein v Maltz, Mitchell & Co* [1937] 1 All ER 497, CA.
[3] *Yasuda Fire and Marine Insurance Co of Europe Ltd v Orion Marine Insurance Underwriting Agency Ltd* [1995] 3 All ER 211.

Rights of agents

Remuneration

14.17 A contract of agency may entitle the agent to be paid for services. The right to be paid may be an express term of the contract of agency or, in the absence of such a term, may be implied if it was clearly the intention of the parties that the agent was to be paid.[1] To be entitled to remuneration, the agent must have performed, precisely and completely, the obligations in the agency agreement. An agent who does less than is contractually required' can recover nothing unless the contract provides for payment for partial services.

If the contract of agency expressly provides the amount of remuneration for a given task, this is the amount payable. If the contract merely provides that the agent is to be paid without specifying an amount, the agent is entitled to recover a reasonable amount.[2] If the contract mentions remuneration, but on its true construction does not entitle the agent to payment, the agent can recover nothing. For instance, in *Kofi Sunkersette Obu v Strauss & Co Ltd*,[3] the Privy Council refused to allow an agent to recover any commission in a case where the contract of agency provided that the amount of commission, if any, was to be fixed by the principal. If there is an implied term providing for payment, the amount of such payment must be determined by the courts. Usually it will be on the basis of what is reasonable, but it may be possible to imply the fixed scale costs of professional men.[4]

In the absence of a contract of agency, an agent may be entitled to be paid on a *quantum meruit* ('reasonable sum') basis. However, where an agent is to be paid on the occurrence of a certain event, such as a commission on sale, there can be no claim for a quantum meruit if the event does not occur.[5]

[1] *Reeve v Reeve* (1858) 1 F & F 280. Also see the Supply of Goods and Services Act 1982, s 15.
[2] *Way v Latilla* [1937] 3 All ER 759, HL.
[3] [1951] AC 243, PC.
[4] For when the courts will imply terms into contracts see paras 7.29–7.33.
[5] *Howard Houlder & Partners Ltd v Manx Isles Steamship Co Ltd* [1923] 1 KB 110.

14.18 The mere occurrence of the transaction which the agent is commissioned to effect does not entitle the agent to remuneration; the occurrence must be brought about by the agent[1] unless the contract provides for payment however the desired result occurs.[2]

If the principal hinders the earning of commission by the agent, the agent cannot recover any commission thereby lost from the principal, unless the latter's action amounts to a breach of contract. The contract of agency may contain a term that the principal will not hinder the agent's efforts to earn commission,[3] but if it is not an express term the courts are reluctant to imply such a term into the contract of agency.[4]

An agent who complies with all instructions can nevertheless recover no commission in respect of a transaction rendered void or illegal by statute. An agent who is in breach of duties towards the principal normally forfeits all rights to commission,[5] unless the breach is a technical one and the agent has acted honestly.[6]

[1] *Millar, Son & Co v Radford* (1903) 19 TLR 575, CA.
[2] See *Brian Cooper & Co v Fairview Estates (Investments) Ltd* [1987] 1 EGLR 18, CA; *Barnard Marcus & Co v Ashraf* [1988] 1 EGLR 7, CA.
[3] A 'sole agency' is a good example of this.
[4] *Luxor (Eastbourne) Ltd v Cooper* [1941] 1 All ER 33, HL; *Marcan Shipping (London) v Polish Steamship Co* [1989] 2 Lloyd's Rep 138, CA. See also para 16.24.
[5] *Salomons v Pender* (1865) 3 H & C 639.
[6] *Keppel v Wheeler* [1927] 1 KB 577, CA.

Indemnity

14.19 An agent who has suffered loss or incurred liabilities in the course of carrying out authorised actions for his principal is entitled to be reimbursed or indemnified by the principal.[1] However, the agent has no right to reimbursement or an indemnity for losses or liabilities arising because of breaches of duty (eg failing to comply with instructions) or in carrying out an illegal transaction or a transaction rendered void by statute.[2] In *ex p Mather*,[3] a principal employed an agent to purchase smuggled goods. The agent was not entitled to recover the cost of these goods from the principal, even though the principal had obtained possession of them.

[1] *Hooper v Treffry* (1847) 1 Exch 17.
[2] *Capp v Topham* (1805) 6 East 392; *Gasson v Cole* (1910) 26 TLR 468.
[3] (1797) 3 Ves 373.

AGENTS' RIGHTS AND DUTIES: KEY POINTS

- Every agent owes the principal duties to obey instructions and to exercise care and skill; a paid agent also owes a positive duty to act on the principal's behalf.

- Every agent owes the principal a duty to avoid conflicts of interest and must not make any secret profit out of the agency.

- Unless otherwise agreed, an agent is entitled to be remunerated for services rendered to the principal.

- An agent is entitled to be indemnified by the principal against any expenses or legal liabilities incurred in the course of acting on the principal's behalf.

Sub-agents

14.20 Even where an agent is authorised to appoint a sub-agent to carry out the principal's instructions, it is presumed that the person appointed is merely an agent of the agent and does not, in the absence of clear evidence, become an agent of the principal.[1] As a result, the sub-agent has no claim against the principal for remuneration or indemnity, nor does he (or she) owe the principal any duty to act or to obey instructions. It has further been held, somewhat controversially, that the sub-agent owes the principal no duty of care in tort, unless the sub-agent is also a bailee of the principal's goods.[2] Whether the sub-agent owes fiduciary duties to the principal is unclear, for there are conflicting decisions of the Court of Appeal.[3]

[1] *Calico Printers' Association Ltd v Barclays Bank* (1931) 145 LT 51.
[2] *Balsamo v Medici* [1984] 1 WLR 951.
[3] *Powell and Thomas v Evan Jones & Co* [1905] 1 KB 11, CA; cf *New Zealand and Australian Land Co v Watson* (1881) 7 Qbd 374, CA.

Termination of agency

14.21 A contract of agency may be terminated, like any other contract, by agreement,[1] by performance,[2] by breach[3] or by frustration,[4] although it is important to remember that termination of agency between principal and agent need not terminate the agent's ostensible authority (which we discuss in paras 14.30 to 14.34). In addition, there are certain special rules applicable to agency, which we now discuss.

[1] Paras 6.25–6.28.
[2] Paras 8.2–8.5.
[3] Paras 8.9–8.27.
[4] Chapter 10.

Act of parties

14.22 A contract of agency will not be specifically enforced, because it is a contract for personal services.[1] As a corollary, either party may terminate the relationship at will. This may amount to a breach of contract, as where the agency was for a fixed period which has not expired, or where a required period of notice has not been given. If so, the innocent party is entitled to damages, but the agency itself is nonetheless determined.[2]

As to whether termination of an agency relationship without notice amounts to a breach of contract, we have already seen that, if an agent accepts a bribe, the contract of agency can be terminated without notice.[3] There are other contracts which on their true construction allow either principal or agent to terminate the agreement without any notice.[4] These include contracts, such as those of estate agents, under which an agent is employed on a commission basis.[5] Agency contracts which resemble contracts of employment, in that the agent is paid merely for being an agent, rather than for facilitating a particular transaction, require notice.[6]

There are some cases where the authority of an agent is irrevocable.[7] Under the Powers of Attorney Act 1971, s 4, a power of attorney expressed to be irrevocable, and given to secure a proprietary interest of the donee of the power, can be revoked neither by the donor of that power without the consent of the donee nor by the death, mental incapacity or bankruptcy of the donor. This is essentially a restatement of the common law rule that, if the agent is given authority by deed, or for valuable consideration, to effect a security or to protect an interest of the agent, that authority is irrevocable while the security or interest subsists.[8] Again, an authority coupled with an interest is not revoked by the death, mental incapacity or bankruptcy of the donor.

[1] *Chinnock v Sainsbury* (1860) 30 LJ Ch 409; para 11.44.
[2] *Page One Records Ltd v Britton* [1967] 3 All ER 822.
[3] Para 14.15.
[4] *Atkinson v Cotesworth* (1825) 3 B & C 647.
[5] *Motion v Michaud* (1892) 8 TLR 253, affd by the Court of Appeal (1892) 8 TLR 447, CA.
[6] *Parker v Ibbetson* (1858) 4 CBNS 346.
[7] See the Enduring Powers of Attorney Act 1985 (para 14.25).
[8] *Gaussen v Morton* (1830) 10 B & C 731.

14.23 A problem may arise where a principal, without actually revoking an agent's authority, effectively brings the agency to an end, for example by closing down the business to which it relates. In order to recover damages for loss of earnings, the agent must be able to prove that the principal's action amounts to a breach either of an express term of the contract of agency, or of one necessarily implied to give business efficacy.[1] The courts are slow to imply such terms. In *Rhodes v Forwood*,[2] a colliery owner appointed brokers as sole agents for the sale of his coal in Liverpool for seven years or as long as he did business there. After four years the colliery was sold. It was held that the owner had not contracted, either expressly or impliedly, to keep the brokers supplied with coal for sale, and he was therefore not liable for breach of contract. On the other hand, in *Turner v Goldsmith*,[3] a shirt manufacturer expressly agreed to employ a travelling salesman for five years, but his factory was destroyed by fire after only two years. It was held that the manufacturer was not released from his obligation, so that the agent was entitled to damages.

[1] Paras 7.31, 7.32.
[2] (1876) 1 App Cas 256, HL.
[3] [1891] 1 Qb 544, CA.

Death

14.24 The death of a principal or of an agent determines the agency.[1] An agent's rights to remuneration and indemnity cease with the death of the principal.[2] Most importantly, the actual authority (and, probably, his ostensible authority) of an agent ceases on the death of the principal and any transactions entered into thereafter bind the agent, but not the principal's estate, even if the agent does not know of the death.[3]

[1] *Blades v Free* (1829) 9 B & C 167; *Friend v Young* [1897] 2 Ch 421.
[2] *Farrow v Wilson* (1869) LR 4 CP 744; *Pool v Pool* (1889) 58 LJP 67.
[3] *Blades v Free* (1829) 9 B & C 167.

Mental incapacity

14.25 If a principal becomes mentally incapable the agency is terminated, and the agent can presumably claim no commission in relation to transactions entered into after the actual authority is determined. Where the agent has ostensible authority, this survives the principal's mental incapacity, and any contract entered into by him is binding upon the principal, unless the third party knew of the principal's incapacity.[1] Somewhat inconsistently, however, it has also been held that, provided that the third party did not know of the incapacity, the agent can be liable for breach of warranty of authority even if the agent was unaware of the principal's mental incapacity.[2]

Under the Mental Capacity Act 2005, it is now possible for a principal to execute a power of attorney, known as a 'lasting power of attorney', the authority of which will survive the principal's subsequent mental incapacity. To achieve this effect, various prescribed formalities must be complied with and the document must be registered with the Public Guardian.

[1] *Drew v Nunn* (1879) 4 Qbd 661, CA.
[2] *Yonge v Toynbee* [1910] 1 KB 215, CA.

Bankruptcy

14.26 The bankruptcy of a principal terminates a contract of agency.[1] On the other hand, the bankruptcy of an agent does not automatically determine the agency, unless it effectively prevents the agent from doing what the agent was appointed to do.[2]

[1] *Elliott v Turquand* (1881) 7 App Cas 79, HL.
[2] *McCall v Australian Meat Co Ltd* (1870) 19 WR 188.

Effects of termination

14.27 While the termination of agency cannot deprive the agent of any rights to commission or indemnity which have already accrued,[1] it prevents the future acquisition of such rights.[2] Furthermore, an agent who continues to act may become liable to a third party for breach of warranty of authority, even if the agent is unaware that the actual authority has been determined.[3]

In the absence of ostensible authority, a principal is not usually bound by anything which the agent does after termination of the agency. However, where the agency is created by deed, both an agent and a third party are given statutory protection in respect of transactions effected after termination, provided that they were unaware of this.[4]

[1] *Chappell v Bray* (1860) 6 H & N 145.
[2] *Farrow v Wilson* (1869) LR 4 CP 744; *Pool v Pool* (1889) 58 LJP 67.
[3] *Yonge v Toynbee* [1910] 1 KB 215, CA.
[4] Powers of Attorney Act 1971, s 5.

TERMINATION OF AGENCY: KEY POINTS

- Where an agency relationship is contractual, it may be brought to an end by act of the parties.

- Agency may be automatically terminated by the death, mental incapacity or bankruptcy of either party.

Principal and third parties

14.28 If an agent makes an authorised contract on behalf of the principal, it is as if the contract was made by the principal. The principal may sue and be sued on authorised contracts and for pre-contractual misrepresentations made by the agent. If a principal is undisclosed then both principal and agent can sue or be sued on the authorised contract. If a contract or other transaction, such as a disposition of property, is not authorised then it does not bind the principal, but the agent may incur personal liability in respect thereof. An agent's authority may take various forms.

The authority of agents

Actual authority

14.29 An agent who has been expressly appointed may have both express and implied actual authority. An agent appointed by implied agreement has implied actual authority.

Express authority is the authority conferred by the agreement (which is usually a contract) creating agency. Implied authority consists of those terms which will be implied into the contract of agency by applying the usual rules for the implication of terms into contracts.[1] Certain types of implied actual authority are well recognised, for instance incidental and customary authority.

Incidental authority is implied authority to do all subordinate acts incidental to and necessary for the execution of the agent's express authority.[2] It thus supplements the express authority of the agent. It is a question of fact in every case whether a particular action is incidental to the authorised purpose of the agent.

Customary authority means that an agent operating in a particular market or business has the authority which an agent operating in that market or business usually has.[3] This may arise where an agent has a particular position in his principal's business, such as company secretary or foreman, or where the agent engages in a recognised profession or trade, such as that of stockbroker or auctioneer.[4] In *Panorama Developments Ltd v Fidelis Furnishing Fabrics Ltd*,[5] a company appointed X their company secretary. As such he was an agent of the company, and the company was liable to pay for cars hired by X, even though he used them for his own and not the company's purposes, because hiring cars was within the customary or usual authority of an agent holding the position of company secretary.

It should be noted that, as between principal and agent, express authority is paramount. An agent who disobeys an express instruction cannot avoid liability on the ground that what was done was within the usual authority of such an agent. However, as far as third parties are concerned, they are entitled to assume, until they have notice to the contrary, that the agent has whatever authority would usually be implied in the circumstances.

[1] Paras 7.29–7.33.
[2] *Collen v Gardner* (1856) 21 Beav 540.
[3] *Bayliffe v Butterworth* (1847) 1 Exch 425.
[4] *Hely-Hutchinson v Brayhead Ltd* [1967] 2 All ER 14; affd on other grounds [1967] 3 All ER 98, CA.
[5] [1971] 3 All ER 16, CA.

Ostensible authority

14.30 Ostensible authority may result (for the benefit of a third party) in:

- a person who is not really an agent being regarded as one in a particular transaction; or
- the extension of the authority of an agent.[1]

It does not create a real agency relationship, nor does it extend the actual authority of the agent in relation to the principal, but merely allows the third party to deal with someone as if that person were an authorised agent. Thus, if a bank promises unequivocally and without qualification to honour cheques backed by a cheque guarantee card, a person (even a thief) in possession of both a cheque and a guarantee card has ostensible authority to bind the bank by forging a signature on the cheque, provided that a third party had no reason to believe that the signatory was not the genuine card-holder.[2]

[1] The important case of *Freeman and Lockyer v Buckhurst Park Properties (Mangal) Ltd* [1964] 1 All ER 630, CA, reaffirmed that ostensible authority operates in these two ways.
[2] *First Sport Ltd v Barclays Bank plc* [1993] 3 All ER 789, CA.

14.31 Ostensible authority can arise when the alleged principal represents to a third party that another person is authorised to act as agent and the third party relies on that representation.[1] If the third party can show that such was the case, the principal cannot deny the authority of the other.

Ostensible authority can operate in a single transaction. For instance, if P stands by and watches A acting on P's behalf, P conveys the impression to a third party that A is authorised so to act.[1] However, ostensible authority can also operate in a series of transactions; if P has frequently allowed A to act on P's behalf, P may be unable to deny A's authority to act in future transactions of a similar type. For example, if a company allows X to act as managing director, even though not appointed as such, third parties are entitled to assume that X is managing director.

If there is a single transaction, the ostensible authority of the agent is to effect that transaction and no more. That is all the 'principal' has represented to the world that the agent has authority to undertake. If the 'principal' has allowed a person to act on his behalf more than once, that person has ostensible authority to effect such transactions and similar transactions in the future, and may also have ostensible usual authority. Ostensible usual authority means that a person who is held out as occupying a particular position, for example managing director, will have all the usual authority that a person would have if properly appointed to that position.[2] If a person has invested an agent with ostensible authority, it is not necessarily limited to exactly the same transactions as those from which the ostensible authority arose. In *Swiss Air Transport Co Ltd v Palmer*,[3] an agent who was held out as having authority to ship wigs was held to have ostensible authority to arrange the shipment of wigs and other items over the same route, but not to buy himself an air ticket.

[1] See *Egyptian International Foreign Trade Co v Soplex Wholesale Supplies and Refson (PS) & Co* [1985] 2 Lloyd's Rep 36.
[2] *Freeman and Lockyer v Buckhurst Park Properties (Mangal) Ltd* [1964] 1 All ER 630, CA.
[3] [1976] 2 Lloyd's Rep 604.

14.32 Ostensible authority is of great importance where a principal has restricted or terminated the actual authority of a validly appointed agent. As between principal and agent, the restriction or termination is binding, and the agent will be liable to the principal for acting without actual authority. However, third parties are not bound by any restriction, provided that they are unaware of the restriction or termination.[1]

Acts within the ostensible authority of an agent bind the principal even if they are entered into for the agent's own purposes or are fraudulent, provided the fraud occurs while the agent is purporting to carry out what he or she is ostensibly authorised to do.[2]

[1] *Trickett v Tomlinson* (1863) 13 CBNS 663.
[2] *Lloyd v Grace, Smith & Co* [1912] AC 716, HL.

14.33 Ostensible authority is based on the belief raised in the mind of the third party by the representation of the alleged principal that a particular person is an agent or that a properly appointed agent has authority in excess of what really exists. It follows that a third party, who knows, or ought to know, the true position cannot rely on the doctrine of ostensible authority.[1]

[1] See, for example, *Overbrooke Estates Ltd v Glencombe Properties Ltd* [1974] 3 All ER 511; para 12.48.

14.34 It must be emphasised that ostensible authority depends upon a representation of fact made by the alleged principal. A statement by the 'agent' that he (or she) is authorised to carry out a particular transaction does not in itself confer ostensible authority to do so.[1] However, in exceptional circumstances an agent may have ostensible authority to describe his or her own authority (eg by assuring the third party that his or her actions have been approved by head office).[2]

[1] *British Bank of the Middle East Ltd v Sun Life Assurance Co of Canada (UK) Ltd* [1983] 2 Lloyd's Rep 9, HL; *Armagas v Mundogas SA* [1986] AC 717, HL.
[2] See *First Energy (UK) Ltd v Hungarian International Bank Ltd* [1993] 2 Lloyd's Rep 194, CA.

The disclosed principal

14.35 A disclosed principal is one whose existence, though not necessarily identity, is known to the third party at the time of contracting. To put it another way, a principal is disclosed wherever the third party is aware that he (or she) is dealing with an agent.

If the agent of a disclosed principal makes an authorised contract, the principal can almost invariably sue and be sued upon it.[1] Whether the agent also can sue or be sued on the contract is a question which we discuss in paras 14.39 to 14.44.

[1] *Montgomerie v United Kingdom Mutual Steamship Association* [1891] 1 Qb 370.

The undisclosed principal

14.36 If the third party is unaware that he (or she) is dealing with an agent, the principal is called an undisclosed principal. An undisclosed principal can sue and be sued on contracts made by an authorised agent.[1] The agent can also sue and be sued on such contracts.[2] It may seem odd that the third party can be sued by someone of whose existence he (or she) was unaware and with whom he or she may not have wished to contract. To protect the third party certain limitations have been placed on the right of the undisclosed principal to sue.

[1] *Scrimshire v Alderton* (1743) 2 Stra 1182; *Thomson v Davenport* (1829) 9 B & C 78.
[2] *Saxon v Blake* (1861) 29 Beav 438.

Limitations on the right of the undisclosed principal to sue

14.37 An undisclosed principal cannot sue in the following circumstances:

- where the undisclosed principal did not exist or lacked capacity at the time the agent contracted;[1]
- where the contract expressly prohibits the intervention of an undisclosed principal;[2]
- where the contract impliedly excludes the intervention of an undisclosed principal. For example, if the contract 'shows' the agent to be contracting as principal. In

the controversial case of *Humble v Hunter*,[3] the agent of an undisclosed principal signed a charterparty as 'owner' of the ship. This contract was found impliedly to regard the agent as owner, and the true owner (the principal) could not sue on the contract;

- where the third party can establish that there was a good reason for wishing to deal with the agent personally. For example, if the agent was a man of fine reputation and acknowledged skill, and the contract involved reliance on such integrity and skill;[4]

- where the third party would have a defence to an action by the agent. This most commonly arises where the third party has paid the agent what is due under the contract (for example, by setting-off money which the agent owes the third party). However, this only prevents the undisclosed principal from suing where it is his conduct which has enabled the agent to appear to be dealing personally;[5]

- where the third party's legal position would be materially worse as a result of the principal's intervention.[6] For example, where two persons became protected tenants of a flat, it was held that evidence could not be brought to show that they had taken the lease as agents for an undisclosed principal (consisting of themselves and a third person), since this would increase the number of people who would be entitled to security of tenure under the Rent Act.[7]

Apart from these cases, an undisclosed principal can intervene on the contract, even where it is clear that the third party would have refused for personal reasons to deal with the undisclosed principal, provided that there has been no positive misrepresentation.[8]

[1] Para 14.3.
[2] *United Kingdom Mutual Steamship Assurance Ltd v Nevill* (1887) 19 Qbd 110, CA.
[3] (1848) 12 Qb 310.
[4] *Greer v Downs Supply Co* [1927] 2 KB 28, CA.
[5] *Cooke v Eshelby* (1887) 12 App Cas 271, HL.
[6] *Collins v Associated Greyhound Racecourses Ltd* [1930] 1 Ch 1.
[7] *Hanstown Properties Ltd v Green* [1978] 1 EGLR 185, CA.
[8] *Dyster v Randall & Sons* [1926] Ch 932.

Election

14.38 Where the third party is in a position to sue either the agent or the principal (eg where the agent has acted on behalf of an undisclosed principal), the third party may, by taking action against one party, be deemed to have elected to pursue that party exclusively. In such a case, even if the third party fails to obtain satisfaction, there can be no recourse against the other party.[1] 'Election' in this sense may be express or implied. An implied election will only occur if a third party with full knowledge of all the relevant facts indicates clearly which party is to be held liable on the contract.[2] What constitutes implied election is a question of fact—beginning legal proceedings,[3] demanding payment, and debiting an account[4] are all relevant but not conclusive factors. Where principal and agent are jointly liable, the third party may even obtain judgment against one of them without forfeiting the right to sue the other.[5]

[1] *Paterson v Gandasequi* (1812) 15 East 62.
[2] *Thomson v Davenport* (1829) 9 B & C 78; *Chestertons v Barone* [1987] 1 EGLR 15, CA.
[3] *Clarkson, Booker Ltd v Andjel* [1964] 3 All ER 260, CA.
[4] *Young & Co Ltd v White* (1911) 28 TLR 87.
[5] Civil Liability (Contribution) Act 1978, s 3: para 27.15.

> PRINCIPAL AND THIRD PARTIES: KEY POINTS
>
> - A principal is legally bound by acts of the agent falling within the agent's express or implied authority.
> - A principal who leads a third party to believe that X has authority to do some act will be legally bound to the third party if the 'agent' does that act.
> - An undisclosed principal (ie one of whose existence the third party is unaware) may usually sue and be sued on any authorised contract made by an agent; however, there are limits to this principle.
> - A third party who has the right to sue both principal and agent may possibly, by choosing to pursue one of them, lose the right to pursue the other.

Agents and third parties

14.39 As we have seen, where an agent makes an authorised contract on behalf of an undisclosed principal, the agent can sue and be sued upon the contract.[1] Where an agent makes an authorised contract on behalf of a disclosed principal, the general rule is that the agent cannot sue or be sued on the contract.[2] However, in certain cases the agent is liable and entitled on the contract, either alone or jointly with the principal.

[1] *Saxon v Blake* (1861) 29 Beav 438.
[2] See, for example, *Foalquest Ltd v Roberts* [1990] 1 EGLR 50.

Contracts made by deed
14.40 An agent who enters into a contract made by deed is liable on it, even if it is known that the agent is contracting as an agent.[1]

[1] *Schack v Anthony* (1813) 1 M & S 573.

Trade usage
14.41 If a trade custom, not inconsistent with the contract, makes an agent liable on a contract the courts will give effect to that custom.[1]

[1] *Barrow & Bros v Dyster, Nalder & Co* (1884) 13 Qbd 635, DC.

Where the agent is in reality the principal
14.42 The result of some unsatisfactory case law is as follows. If an agent contracts on behalf of a non-existent principal then the agent must be contracting personally.[1] A person who purports to contract as agent, but who is in fact the principal, can sue and be sued on the contract.[2] However, if X, who is in fact a principal, appears to contract as agent for a named principal, X cannot sue or be sued on the contract[3] (though he or she can be sued for breach of warranty of authority[4]). The agent can sue if he or she contracts personally and the contract indicates, but does not name, a principal and shows that the identity of the principal is not relevant.[5]

[1] See in relation to unformed companies, the Companies Act 2006. s 51.
[2] *Gardiner v Heading* [1928] 2 KB 284, CA.
[3] *Fairlie v Fenton* (1870) LR 5 Exch 169; *Hector v Lyons* (1988) 58 P & CR 156, CA.
[4] Para 14.45.
[5] *Schmaltz v Avery* (1851) 16 Qb 655.

Other cases

14.43 Apart from these special cases, an agent may be jointly or solely liable on the contract entered into on behalf of an disclosed principal, if the contract expressly or impliedly reveals this to be the intention of the parties.[1] Under the Partnership Act 1890, s 5, a partner who contracts on behalf of the partnership is jointly liable with the rest of the partners on that contract. In other cases, whether there is an implied intention that an agent shall be jointly or solely liable on the contract is a question of construction.

Particular note is taken of the description of the agent in a written contract and of how the agent signed a written contract. An agent is not usually liable on a contract where either the description of the agent in the document, or the form of the agent's signature, makes it clear that he (or she) is acting merely as an agent.[2] If neither the document nor the signature has this effect, the agent is liable on the contract,[3] even if he (or she) is known to be acting as an agent. If the contract is oral and the agent is known to be an agent, the above rules for written contracts do not apply and every case is determined by reference to its particular facts.[4] An agent who is liable on a contract will probably also be entitled to sue on that contract, unless, as a matter of construction, the contract reveals that the agent is to be liable without having the benefit of the contract.

[1] See, for example, *Savills v Scott* [1988] 1 EGLR 20.
[2] *Lucas v Beale* (1851) 10 CB 739. Cf *Punjab National Bank v de Boinville* [1992] 3 All ER 104, CA.
[3] *Basma v Weekes* [1950] 2 All ER 146, PC.
[4] *N and J Vlassopulos Ltd v Ney Shipping Ltd* [1977] 1 Lloyd's Rep 478, CA.

Rights of third parties against agents

On the contract

14.44 If the agent is jointly or solely liable on the contract, the third party can, subject to the doctrine of election,[1] sue the agent.

[1] Para 14.38.

For breach of warranty of authority

14.45 A person who without authority purports to act as an agent is liable to the third party for breach of warranty of authority.[1] Purporting to act as agent constitutes a representation of authority, unless the third party knew or ought to have known of the lack of authority.[2]

Liability for breach of warranty of authority may arise where the agent is aware of the lack of authority. However, liability does not depend on such knowledge.[3] In *Yonge v Toynbee*,[4] an agent acting on behalf of his principal was held liable for breach of warranty of authority when, entirely unknown to him, his authority had been terminated by the mental incapacity of his principal. The third party can sue in such a case even where no contract has resulted, provided the third party's position has been altered in reliance on the representation.

If the untrue representation of authority made by the agent is one of law, not fact, there is no liability.[5] An action for breach of warranty cannot lie if the principal ratifies the unauthorised act.

The amount of damages which may be awarded under this head is the amount which would put the third party in the same position as if the representation (of authority) had been true.[6] Therefore, if the third party could have recovered nothing from the principal, even if the agent had had authority (for example because the principal is insolvent), only nominal damages can be recovered for breach of warranty of authority.

[1] *Collen v Wright* (1857) 8 E & B 647.
[2] *Halbot v Lens* [1901] 1 Ch 344.

[3] *Penn v Bristol and West Building Society* [1997] 3 All ER 470, CA.

[4] *Yonge v Toynbee* [1910] 1 KB 215, CA.

[5] *Beattie v Ebury* (1872) 7 Ch App 777, HL.

[6] *Richardson v Williamson and Lawson* (1871) LR 6 Qb 276; *Suleman v Shahsavari* [1988] 1 WLR 1181; *Habton Farms v Nimmo* [2004] QB 1.

In tort

14.46 An agent may be liable in tort even if the principal is also vicariously liable. Therefore, an agent may be liable in deceit, or under the rules in *Hedley Byrne & Co Ltd v Heller & Partners Ltd*[1] or, of course, for such actions as knocking down a third party by negligent driving. However, an agent may not be personally liable under the Misrepresentation Act 1967 unless the agent is a party to the contract which he (or she) makes on behalf of his principal.[2]

[1] [1963] 2 All ER 575, HL; para 17.18.

[2] *Resolute Maritime Inc v Nippon Kaiji Kyokai* [1983] 2 All ER 1; para 12.24.

AGENTS AND THIRD PARTIES: KEY POINTS

- An agent who makes an authorised contract on behalf of the principal is not usually either liable or entitled to sue on that contract; however, there are exceptions to this principle.

- A person who purports to act as an agent when lacking authority to do so is liable to the third party concerned for breach of warranty of authority.

Estate agents and auctioneers

14.47 The primary function of an estate agent is to effect an introduction between persons who wish to buy and sell land. The agent's implied or ostensible authority is very restricted. Unless expressly authorised, an estate agent cannot make a binding contract for the sale of the principal's property,[1] accept a pre-contract deposit,[2] or appoint a sub-agent.[3] In fact, the agent's implied authority is limited to the making of statements about the property. If a purchaser relies on a misrepresentation made by an estate agent, the principal cannot enforce the contract[4] and may be liable in damages.[5] It was on this basis that a landlord of a flat was held liable to an incoming tenant for the fraud of a managing agent in permitting evidence of dry rot to be covered up before the start of the tenancy.[6]

Unlike an estate agent, an auctioneer has implied authority to effect an actual sale of the principal's land or goods,[7] as well as to make statements about the property.[8]

The relationship between an estate agent and the client is a unilateral contract.[9] The agent is under no positive duty to act (except, perhaps, a 'sole agent'[10]) but, when acting, must display reasonable care and skill.[11] In order to be entitled to commission, the estate agent must fulfil precisely the terms of the client's instructions, which may vary from the mere introduction of a person who is willing to purchase the principal's property to the completion of a sale. The law on this matter is complex, but it may be said that the courts seldom award an estate agent commission unless there is an actual sale.[12]

[1] *Chadburn v Moore* (1892) 61 LJ Ch 674.

[2] *Sorrell v Finch* [1976] 2 All ER 371, HL.

[3] *John McCann & Co v Pow* [1975] 1 All ER 129, CA.

[4] *Mullens v Miller* (1882) 22 Ch D 194.

[5] *Gosling v Anderson* (1972) 223 Estates Gazette 1743, CA.

[6] *Gordon v Selico Ltd* [1986] 1 EGLR 71, CA.

[7] *Pickering v Busk* (1812) 15 East 38 at 43.

[8] *Smith v Land and House Property Corpn* (1884) 28 Ch D 7, CA.

[9] *Luxor (Eastbourne) Ltd v Cooper* [1941] 1 All ER 33, HL; para 4.2.

[10] *E Christopher & Co v Essig* [1948] WN 461.

[11] *Prebble & Co v West* (1969) 211 Estates Gazette 831, CA.

[12] For further discussion, see Murdoch *The Law of Estate Agency* (5th edn, 2009), ch 3.

Questions

1. In what ways may agency be created?

2. In what circumstances may agency be created retrospectively by ratification?

3. What are the requirements for, and the effects of, agency of necessity?

4. What duties does an agent owe to the principal?

5. What rights does an agent have against the principal?

6. What is the legal position of a sub-agent?

7. How may an agency relationship be brought to an end?

8. What are the requirements for, and the effects of, ostensible authority?

9. What is an 'undisclosed principal'; what is the legal position of such a principal?

10. In what circumstances can an agent sue on a contract which he or she has made as agent?

11. How may an agent incur liability under the doctrine of breach of warranty of authority?

12. Patrick has for several years employed Arthur to purchase used cars for Patrick at various car auctions; the auctioneers have always sent the invoices to Patrick, who has always paid the sums demanded. On one occasion Patrick instructs Arthur to purchase a boat for him, authorising Arthur to spend up to £30,000 on this acquisition. Arthur agrees to purchase a boat from Tessa at a price of £40,000, telling her that he is acting on behalf of Patrick. However, when Patrick receives the invoice from Tessa, he refuses to pay, arguing that Arthur has exceeded his authority.

    What is the legal position of all three parties?

PART III

The law of tort

15

Introduction

CHAPTER OVERVIEW

This chapter serves to introduce the main elements of the law of tort, which are dealt with in detail in the remainder of Part III. Here we discuss in particular:

- the nature of liability in tort;
- the distinction between tort and other areas of legal liability;
- the scope and limits of the law of tort;
- the relationship between 'fault' (intention or negligence) and liability;
- the impact of the Human Rights Act 1998 on English tort law.

Aims and functions of the law of tort

15.1 Wherever people live together, the acts, activities or omissions of one may cause losses of various kinds to another. Compensation for such losses may take a variety of forms; unemployment benefit from the state, sick pay from one's employer, the proceeds of a private insurance policy and so on. Apart from these sources, it is the law of tort which decides whether the primary loss should remain where it has fallen (on the claimant) or be transferred to the person who caused it (the defendant). It is important to appreciate that this is all that the law of tort can do; the loss which has occurred cannot be repaired but only allocated. In reaching a decision on this question, the law takes into account both the kind and the severity of the claimant's loss, and the defendant's reason for causing it: in short, it is for the law of tort to implement social policy by laying down the circumstances in which the loss ought to be transferred from one party to the other.

If a single main function can be ascribed to the law of tort, therefore, it is the provision of compensation for loss suffered, within the general confines of attempting to strike a fair balance between claimant and defendant. This is not to say, however, that there are no other aims to be fulfilled. The very fact that a defendant is not usually liable unless he or she is 'at fault' (in the sense of having deliberately or carelessly caused harm to the claimant) indicates an element of punishment for misconduct. The same principle, by enabling a careful defendant to avoid liability, also has a deterrent effect which plays a part in helping to prevent accidents.

Definition of a tort

15.2 A tort may be defined as the breach of a legal duty owed, independent of contract, by one person to another, for which a common law action for unliquidated damages may be brought. As we shall see in the next few paragraphs, this definition enables us to identify areas of legal liability which do not fall within the law of tort.

Perhaps the most important element of the definition is that of the 'common law action for unliquidated damages': unless this particular remedy is available, the defendant's liability (if any) does not lie within the law of tort. However, this is not to say that an action for damages is the only remedy available to a claimant in tort, nor even that it is necessarily always the most important. Some torts, such as nuisance, lend themselves readily to control by the grant of an injunction. A person who has been wrongfully dispossessed of land or goods may obtain an order for their return, and a limited amount of self-help (eg ejecting a trespasser) is tolerated by the courts in the interest of avoiding unnecessary litigation. Nonetheless, the possibility of damages on a common law basis must always be there and, further, these must be unliquidated, in the sense of being subject to assessment by the court rather than by prior agreement between the parties.[1]

[1] As to liquidated damages, see paras 11.30–11.34.

Tort and crime

15.3 A tort is the breach of a legal duty which is owed by one person to another; a crime, on the other hand, is the breach of a legal duty which is owed to, and enforceable by, society as a whole. Thus, the true distinction between these two fields of law lies, not in their subject matter (for such things as assault, theft and careless driving may be both crimes and torts), but in the purpose of the legal proceedings to which each gives rise. The main object of a criminal prosecution (which is usually instigated by the state) is to vindicate the rights of society against the offender through punishment. Such compensation as the offender may be ordered to pay to the victim[1] is an afterthought; the court's attention is focused primarily upon the question of what should be done with the defendant. The usual aim of a tort action, on the other hand, is to secure compensation for harm suffered by an individual claimant. It is true that, in very limited circumstances, a court is empowered to punish a defendant by awarding an extra sum as 'exemplary damages', over and above what is needed to compensate the claimant,[2] but this is subsidiary to the main object of the proceedings.

[1] Under the Powers of Criminal Courts (Sentencing) Act 2000.
[2] See para 27.2.

Tort and contract

15.4 It is sometimes said that duties in tort are automatically imposed upon a person by law, while contractual duties require voluntary acceptance. Both sides of this distinction, however, require some qualification. In the first place, there are many tortious duties which come into effect only as a result of some voluntary act by the defendant (eg permitting another person to enter land, or offering another person some advice). Second, while the existence of a contract depends upon the parties' agreement (although even this may be a question of interpreting their conduct rather than their secret thoughts), much of its content may be decided on by the general law, as in contracts for the sale of goods, which we discuss in Chapter 7.[1]

A better distinction, perhaps, lies in the purpose of each field of law. Tort, as we have seen, aims to compensate the claimant for harm done; it does this by awarding as damages a sum which will, as far as possible, restore the claimant's original position. In actions for breach of contract, by contrast, the claimant's basic complaint is of not having received some promised benefit, and damages are generally designed to fulfil the claimant's expectations, by putting the claimant into a financial position as if the contract had been performed.[2]

Theory apart, there are some significant practical distinctions between a breach of contract and a tort, with regard to such matters as the liability of minors, the awarding of exemplary damages (available in tort alone) and claims against bankrupt defendants. Most important, the rules as to limitation of actions are different. The time within which a claimant must serve his writ (or automatically lose the case) generally runs, in contract, from the date of the breach, while in tort the relevant date is usually that on which damage is suffered.[3]

It sometimes happens that a defendant's conduct is capable of constituting both a tort and a breach of contract. For instance, a surveyor who, on inspecting a property for a prospective purchaser, negligently fails to discover defects in it, is guilty of both a breach of contract (an implied term that the inspection will be carried out with due skill and care) and the tort of negligence. In such circumstances, the law allows the client to frame the case in either way (usually in tort, so as to gain the advantage of more generous limitation rules).[4]

[1] Para 7.25.
[2] Para 11.3.
[3] Paras 11.52–11.55, and 28.20–28.24.
[4] *Henderson v Merrett Syndicates Ltd* [1994] 3 All ER 506, HL; see para 16.16.

Tort and restitution

15.5 In some circumstances, a person who has been unjustly enriched at the expense of another may be compelled by law to make restitution. For instance, if A pays money to B under certain mistakes of fact, B may be ordered to return it. This area of law falls outside the definition of a tort because A is not claiming unliquidated damages; nor, indeed, can it meaningfully be said that B has broken any legal duty in merely receiving the money.

Tort and breach of trust

15.6 The obligations which a trustee owes to a beneficiary arise out of the trust relationship and may, if broken, lead to an award of damages. The whole matter, however (including the principles on which these damages are assessed) is governed by equity, rather than by common law, and the administration of trusts is today a function of the Chancery Division of the High Court; tort, by contrast, is normally regarded as within the province of the Queen's Bench Division.[1]

[1] Paras 2.0–2.11.

Scope of the law of tort

Interests protected

15.7 The most important interest to be recognised by any legal system is that of personal security which, broadly speaking, involves freedom from both physical injury[1] and wrongful deprivation of liberty. This particular interest also finds expression in other less obvious ways, such as the protection of a person's reputation and of certain status-based rights, eg the right to vote. Of rather less importance, though still well protected, are interests in the ownership and possession of land and goods.

As a general rule, since no person can own or possess another person, A is not allowed to sue in respect of an injury to B. However, an important statutory exception to this principle permits the dependants of a deceased person to sue the person responsible for the death for the loss of their breadwinner.[2]

It takes a fairly sophisticated legal system to recognise the possibility of compensating a claimant for those effects of the defendant's conduct which are purely financial. Even where protection is given to such economic interests (eg by the torts of conspiracy, intimidation and interference with contract) it is usually limited to cases where the defendant's conduct is deliberate. By and large, as we shall see, the causing of financial loss through mere carelessness is not actionable.[3]

[1] Including psychiatric damage; para 16.28.
[2] Fatal Accidents Act 1976; see para 27.11.
[3] Paras 16.12–16.15.

The relevance of damage

15.8 Even though a claimant may have suffered injury, damage or loss, there can be no compensation under the law of tort unless some recognised interest has been infringed. There is, for example, no right of privacy as such; consequently, a person who seeks legal protection against unwanted intrusions must, in order to succeed, show that the defendant has committed some recognised tort such as trespass or nuisance. Similarly, while injury to the claimant's feelings may aggravate the damages awarded in respect of a known tort, as where the defendant trespasses on the claimant's land in order to hurl abuse, it is not of itself an interest which the law will protect.

Examples of loss falling outside the scope of the law of tort are not difficult to find. In *Bradford Corpn v Pickles*,[1] the defendant, irritated by the claimant's refusal to buy his land, excavated in such a way that water which would otherwise have percolated into the claimant's reservoir instead collected on the defendant's property. The House of Lords held that, since the defendant was absolutely entitled to this water (unlike water flowing in a defined channel), the claimants could not complain when he intercepted it. Finally, in *Perera v Vandiyar*,[2] a landlord harassed his tenant by cutting off the supply of gas and electricity to the flat. This was undoubtedly a breach of contract, but it was held by the Court of Appeal that, since the landlord did not actually enter the premises, he was not guilty of any tort.[3]

The other side of the coin consists of circumstances in which the defendant's conduct may be actionable as a tort, notwithstanding that it has caused no actual damage to the claimant. The torts which come within this principle are said to be actionable per se; they are trespass in all its forms and libel (but not usually slander). The reasons for treating these torts differently and imposing liability are purely historical.

[1] [1895] AC 587, HL.
[2] [1953] 1 All ER 1109, [1953] 1 WLR 672, CA.
[3] A tort claim may now arise in such circumstances, under the Housing Act 1988, s 27.

Mental element

15.9 Some academic writers have attempted to identify a general principle of liability underlying the whole law of tort. However, this has proved very difficult (some would say impossible) to achieve, not least because different torts depend upon different mental elements on the part of the defendant. Three levels are involved. In the first place, some torts (such as assault, false imprisonment and deceit) depend upon proof of *intention*, that is to say that the defendant was aware of the likely consequences of an act and in fact desired those consequences. For this purpose, 'recklessness' is equivalent to intention. This covers cases where the defendant is well aware of the risks inherent in what is being done and those where, while not actually wanting to injure the claimant, the defendant is totally indifferent to the possibility that this will happen.

The second mental element which may be relevant to the law of tort is *negligence*, which normally signifies a blameworthy failure to appreciate and guard against the likely consequences of one's acts or omissions.[1] This concept, which today governs liability in the great majority of cases, involves testing the defendant's conduct against the objective yardstick of the hypothetical reasonable man; if it falls short of that standard, the defendant is liable, whatever his (or her) subjective state of mind.

Third, certain torts are based upon what is termed *strict liability*. This means that a defendant is liable for the consequences of his (or her) actions, even though they were neither desired nor could reasonably have been foreseen and avoided. This kind of liability includes the rule in *Rylands v Fletcher*,[2] liability for animals[3] and breach of statutory duty;[4] the vicarious liability of an employer for torts committed by employees is also strict.[5]

[1] Chapter 17.
[2] Paras 24.2–24.14.
[3] Chapter 25.
[4] Chapter 20.
[5] Paras 26.2–26.15.

Motive

15.10 'Intention' signifies a person's desire for certain consequences; 'motive', on the other hand, tells us why that person wants them to occur. Broadly speaking, the law of torts is not concerned with motive; it asks only what the defendant has done, not why. Thus, if A is exercising a legal right, the law does not inquire why. This principle, which helps to explain the case of *Bradford Corpn v Pickles*,[1] was also applied by a majority of the Court of Appeal in *Chapman v Honig*.[2] The defendant in that case was a landlord who, incensed that the claimant, his tenant, had given evidence against him on behalf of another tenant, served the claimant with a valid notice to quit. This, it was held, could not be regarded as wrongful, even though the defendant had clearly acted out of spite.

It is important to appreciate that bad motives are ignored only where the defendant is exercising an absolute legal right. In other cases, where the defendant's rights are qualified or limited, a bad motive may be the factor which tips some conduct over the line into what is unlawful. The tort of nuisance, for instance, permits a landowner to make some noise on his (or her) own land, provided that the interference which is thereby caused to his neighbours is not unreasonable. In deciding what noise level is acceptable, it is legitimate to ask why the noise is being made. In *Hollywood Silver Fox Farm Ltd v Emmett*,[3] the defendant fired guns near where his land adjoined that of the claimants, frightening the claimant's silver foxes and ruining their breeding season. A landowner is of course usually entitled to shoot over his own land; here, however, the defendant's actions were motivated by malice, and he was therefore held liable in nuisance.

[1] [1895] AC 587, HL; para 15.8.
[2] [1963] 2 All ER 513, CA.
[3] [1936] 1 All ER 825.

Fault liability

15.11 Although, as we have noted, it does not seem possible to reduce the law of tort to a single principle, one particular idea has, over the last century, come to occupy a dominant position. This is the notion that a person's liability should be related to 'fault', in the sense of intentional or negligent causing of harm. This principle, and its important corollary, that a person should not be liable *unless* he or she is at fault, became prominent at the time of the Industrial Revolution, when its moral appeal coincided with important vested interests. The vast increase in both traffic and industrial activity which occurred at this time were bound to lead to more accidents and, if liability for these were strict, development would thereby be retarded. Accordingly, 'no liability without fault' became the popular cry, and casualties were regarded merely as an unfortunate but inevitable price of progress. Today, 'fault' is established as the major, though not the only, criterion of liability in the law of tort.

Human rights

15.12 We describe, in Chapter 3, the role of the Human Rights Act 1998 in giving effect to certain rights enshrined in the European Convention on Human Rights.[1] Since October 2000, when the Act came into force, it has become clear that it will have a significant impact on the law of tort. As to the precise ways in which that impact will be felt, the most obvious is in relation to claims brought against local authorities and other public bodies, for harm caused by the manner in which they carry out (or fail to carry out) their statutory powers and duties. Since s 6 of the HRA 1998 makes it unlawful for a public authority to act in a way which is incompatible with a Convention right, it seems inevitable that torts such as negligence and nuisance should be redefined so as to ensure that they give adequate protection to those rights.

What is less obvious is the potential impact of the Human Rights Act upon tort claims between individuals or companies, since these are not specifically made subject to its operation. However, there is an argument to the effect that, since a court falls within the definition of 'public authority', the courts are therefore under a duty to interpret the law of tort in such a way that Convention rights are protected, even in cases where neither of the parties is a public authority. Whatever the merits of this argument, there are already silgns that the UK courts are prepared to adapt the law of tort in this way.

[1] Paras 3.24-3.31. The rights in question are those set out in Sch 1 to the HRA 1998.

Introduction to Tort: Key Points

- The main function of tort is to force wrongdoers to pay compensation to their victims.
- Tort is distinct from other areas of legal liability, though there are some overlaps.
- Tort protects a range of interests and normally requires proof of some kind of damage.
- The 'mental element' required for a tort ranges from intention to strict liability.
- The Human Rights Act 1998 has forced the English courts to revise certain principles of tort law.

Questions

1. How does tort differ from criminal law and contract law?

2. To what extent can a person maintain an action in tort despite having suffered no actual damage?

3. To what extent is liability in tort linked to 'fault' on the part of the defendant?

4. How has English tort law been affected by legislation on human rights?

16

Negligence–duty of care

CHAPTER OVERVIEW

The mere fact that a person acts 'negligently' or 'carelessly' is not in itself sufficient to render him (or her) liable in the tort of negligence. Liability can only arise if that person owes a legal duty to the claimant to take care.

In this chapter we examine the following issues:

- the principles used by the courts in deciding whether a particular situation gives rise to a duty of care;

- the extent to which the law imposes liability on one person for failing to protect another, for example against harm deliberately caused by a third party;

- the reluctance of the courts to permit a claim in respect of losses which are purely financial, and the treatment of defective products and buildings as 'pure financial loss';

- the way in which liability in the tort of negligence may be shaped by the existence of a contract;

- the extent to which liability for negligent words is different from liability for negligent acts;

- the problems involved in claims against a public authority for negligence in the exercise of its statutory powers;

- the extent to which judges, arbitrators, advocates and others are immune from liability in negligence;

- the extent to which damages may be claimed for injuries which are purely psychological.

16.1 Negligence today is by far the most important ground of liability in tort. Surprisingly, however, the emergence of negligence as a tort in its own right is a comparatively recent development; attempts to deduce general principles in this area are largely confined to the last 80 years or so.

As an independent tort, negligence may be defined as the breach of a legal duty to take care, owed by the defendant to the claimant, which results in damage to the claimant. There are thus three elements of liability, each of which must be proved by the claimant:

- a duty of care owed by the defendant to the claimant;
- breach by the defendant of that duty;
- damage to the claimant caused by the defendant's breach.

At first sight, this definition appears enormously wide, since it is not limited to any particular factual situation, nor to any particular interest of the claimant. However, the law does not suggest that a person should be liable for all the consequences of carelessness; such a burden would be an intolerably heavy one. The problem, therefore, is one of exclusion, and two of the elements of liability mentioned above are used by the courts to keep the tort of negligence within reasonable bounds. In the first place, however careless a defendant may have been, there is no liability to the claimant unless the defendant owed a legal duty to be careful. Second, even where the defendant is in breach of a duty of care, certain consequences of the breach are regarded by the courts as too remote to be actionable in law.[1]

[1] See paras 18.14–18.19.

Duty of care

16.2 A defendant is liable, not for all careless conduct, but only for that which occurs when the defendant is under a duty to take care. The emphasis on the idea of duty arose because, when the law first began to create positive obligations to take care, it did so in the context of certain easily recognisable relationships, whose common feature was that one party reasonably relied on the other to exercise the care and skill appropriate to a trade or profession. In this way liability for negligence was imposed upon the 'common callings' such as innkeepers, surgeons and attorneys.

At about the time of the Industrial Revolution, negligence as a basis of legal liability spread to more tenuous relationships, such as those between one highway user and another. In thus expanding the tort, judges continued to speak in terms of 'duty'. A claimant who wished to sue in negligence was required either to show that the case fell within an existing category of duty or to persuade the court that a new duty should be recognised to cover it.

A general principle

Donoghue **v** Stevenson

16.3 As the tort of negligence developed, the requirement of a duty of care served a useful practical purpose. If a court wished to exclude certain types of claimant who were regarded as lacking merit, such as trespassers, or certain types of injury which were not thought important enough to deserve protection, such as losses which were purely financial, it could simply declare that there was no duty of care to such a person or in respect of such harm. Conceptually, however, this was unsatisfactory, since there appeared to be no general principle underlying a judge's decision as to whether or not a duty of care existed.

An attempt to deduce such a general principle was eventually made in 1932 in the leading case of *Donoghue v Stevenson*.[1] The facts of that case were that the appellant was treated by a friend, in a café, to a bottle of ginger beer manufactured by the respondents. Having poured out and drunk part of the contents, the appellant discovered that the bottle contained a partially decomposed snail; this discovery, she claimed, caused her severe nervous shock and, later, an attack of gastro-enteritis. Since the appellant had no contract with the proprietor of the café, she sued the manufacturers of the ginger beer, who argued that their duty in respect of products was owed only to those to whom they sold them. In rejecting this argument, a majority of the House of Lords laid down that, in normal circumstances, a manufacturer owes a duty of care to the ultimate consumer of his products, notwithstanding the absence of any contractual relationship between them. In short, whatever else it may have done, *Donoghue v Stevenson* undoubtedly added a new duty to the existing list.

> [1] [1932] AC 562, HL.

16.4 The main importance of *Donoghue v Stevenson* for present purposes, however, lies in the speech of Lord Atkin, in which an attempt was made to formulate a general test for ascertaining whether or not a relationship is sufficient to found a duty of care. Having pointed out that 'the rule that you are to love your neighbour becomes, in law, you must not injure your neighbour', Lord Atkin went on to consider the question of duty in these terms: 'Who, then, in law is my neighbour? The answer seems to be—persons who are so closely and directly affected by my act that I ought reasonably to have them in contemplation as being so affected when I am directing my mind to the acts or omissions which are called in question.'

16.5 If taken at face value, this approach would impose a duty of care upon a defendant whenever he or she ought reasonably to have foreseen injury, loss or damage to the claimant. This is manifestly not the real position for, as we shall see, there are a number of areas in which the question whether or not there is a duty depends, not upon some purely mechanical test, but upon wider considerations of public policy. Nevertheless, foreseeability is always relevant in an exclusionary sense for, if it is not foreseeable to the defendant that the claimant may suffer damage, then no considerations of policy can justify a court in imposing a duty of care. Thus in *Bourhill v Young*,[1] where a motorcyclist carelessly collided with a car and was killed, an action by a woman who suffered psychiatric injury as a result of hearing the crash failed, since it was not foreseeable that she would suffer injury of any kind, either by impact or through shock alone. Lack of foreseeability has similarly ruled out claims by the wives of industrial workers who, after washing their husbands' contaminated clothes, have contracted lead poisoning[2] or mesothelioma.[3]

> [1] [1942] 2 All ER 396, HL.
> [2] *Hewett v Alf Brown's Transport* [1992] ICR 530, CA.
> [3] *Maguire v Harland & Wolff plc* [2005] EWCA Civ , CA.

The current position

16.6 In the years since *Donoghue v Stevenson*, the courts have come to recognise that 'foreseeability' alone is not sufficient to justify the imposition of a duty of care. However, what more might be required is an issue which has been debated in a large number of cases in the House of Lords.[1] Not surprisingly, the judges in these cases have expressed a wide range of opinions as to the true legal position. The most extreme view is that the situations in which a duty of care exists cannot be explained by reference to any general principle at all, and that the question which a judge should ask, when faced with a novel type of claim, is simply whether it is sufficiently similar to a situation in which a duty of care has previously been held to exist. In this way, it is said, the law can expand 'incrementally and by analogy with established categories of liability'.

If correct, this view would effectively return the law to its position prior to *Donoghue v Stevenson*.[2] However, we believe that it is not correct, and that in truth there remains a general principle, albeit one which is vague and flexible. This principle[3] is that a duty of care in tort will be recognised where:

- it is foreseeable to the defendant that negligence will cause injury, damage or loss to the claimant; and

- there is a relationship of sufficient 'proximity' between the parties; and

- it would be 'just and reasonable' to impose liability.

This three-fold test is not a mechanical one; the elements are recognised as convenient labels used to describe the features of a particular situation which call for the imposition of a duty of care.[4] None the less, despite its shortcomings it has been adopted and applied by the courts in a wide range of cases, including those in which a claimant suffers physical injury.[5]

[1] The most important of these cases are *Home Office v Dorset Yacht Co Ltd* [1970] 2 All ER 294, HL; *Anns v Merton London Borough Council* [1977] 2 All ER 492, HL, *Peabody Donation Fund Governors v Sir Lindsay Parkinson & Co Ltd* [1984] 3 All ER 529, HL; *Caparo Industries plc v Dickman* [1990] 1 All ER 568, HL; *Murphy v Brentwood District Council* [1990] 2 All ER 908, HL and *Alcock v Chief Constable of the South Yorkshire Police* [1991] 4 All ER 907, HL.

[2] [1932] AC 562, HL.

[3] Which was adopted by the House of Lords in *Caparo Industries plc v Dickman* [1990] 1 All ER 568, HL.

[4] See, for example, *Caparo Industries plc v Dickman* [1990] 1 All ER 568 at 574, 582, 585.

[5] *Marc Rich & Co AG v Bishop Rock Marine Co Ltd* [1995] 3 All ER 307, HL.

Omissions

16.7 The law is extremely reluctant to impose liability for pure omissions, in the sense of creating a positive duty to act for the benefit or protection of others, except where those others have given something in return. It has, for example, often been said that, in the absence of a prior legal relationship, there will be no liability involved in watching a blind man walk over a cliff edge, or a child drown in shallow water. Thus in *Sutradhar v Natural Environment Research Council*,[1] where the claimant became ill after drinking from an arsenic-contaminated well in Bangladesh, it was held that the defendants, who had tested the well as part of a geological survey but had never thought to test it for arsenic, owed no duty of care to the claimant. Likewise, in *Ancell v McDermott*,[2] where police officers discovered an oil spillage on a main road which was an obvious danger to traffic, it was held that they owed no duty of care to road users to remain at the scene and warn them of the danger. Again, in *Glaister v Appleby-in-Westmoreland Town Council*,[3] it was held that a local authority which permitted the holding of an annual horse fair owed no duty of care to see that the organisers took proper precautions in respect of tethered horses, nor to insist that the organisers took out public liability insurance to cover any possible injury to members of the public.

Judicial reluctance to impose obligations in this area is at its strongest in cases where the claimant is effectively demanding to be protected from harm which is purely financial. Thus it has been held that an employer owes no general duty to an employee to advise him to join the company pension scheme.[4] Nor is an employer, who sends an employee to work in a country where there is no compulsory insurance in respect of road accidents, under a duty to advise him to take out his own personal insurance policy.[5] Similarly, a school is under no legal obligation to warn its pupils or their parents of the desirability of taking out personal accident insurance to cover the risk of being injured during sporting activities at the school.[6]

[1] [2006] UKHL 33, HL.

[2] [1993] 4 All ER 355, CA.

[3] [2009] EWCA Civ 1325, CA.

[4] *Outram v Academy Plastics Ltd* [2001] ICR 367, CA.

[5] *Reid v Rush & Tompkins Group plc* [1989] 3 All ER 228, CA.

[6] *Van Oppen v Clerk to the Bedford Charity Trustees* [1989] 3 All ER 389, CA.

16.8 The 'no liability for pure omissions' principle has led the courts to conclude, further, that a person who would not be liable for failing to act at all is equally not liable for acting negligently, provided that this does not make the claimant's position worse. In *East Suffolk Rivers Catchment Board v Kent*,[1] the claimant's farm was flooded by the bursting of a sea wall. The defendants, who had a statutory power but no statutory duty to repair the wall, adopted such inefficient methods of doing so that the land remained under water for an unnecessarily long time. A majority of the House of Lords held that the defendants were not liable in negligence, for they had not created any new source of loss to the claimant, but had simply failed to reduce a loss which had already occurred and for which they were not themselves responsible.

The principle laid down in the *East Suffolk* case was strongly endorsed in *Capital and Counties plc v Hampshire County Council*,[2] which concerned the legal position of the fire brigade. The Court of Appeal there held that a fire brigade would be liable if, in the course of fighting a fire at the claimant's premises, it negligently increased the risk of damage (eg by turning off a sprinkler system). However, the fire brigade owed no positive duty either to turn up at the scene of the fire or, once there, to exercise care and skill in fighting the fire.

[1] [1940] 4 All ER 527, HL.
[2] [1997] 2 All ER 865, CA.

Duties of protection

16.9 Notwithstanding what was said in the previous two paragraphs, a duty positively to act for the protection of another is sometimes found to exist. This is especially so where there is a pre-existing relationship between the parties. It has accordingly been held that, where a patient is known to have suicidal tendencies,[1] a duty of care to prevent him from harming himself may be imposed upon those who have care of him, whether it be the police[2] or a hospital.[3] On the other hand, where a prisoner sustained serious injuries in attempting to escape from police custody, it was held that the police owed him no duty of care to prevent this.[4]

The pre-existing relationship which has featured most frequently in cases of this kind is that of employer and employee. It has been held that an employer may owe a duty to prevent a mentally disturbed seaman from throwing himself overboard,[5] or to protect an employee (a soldier) from injuries sustained while returning, in a drunken rowdy group, from a party organised by their commanding officer.[6] In *Barrett v Ministry of Defence*,[7] where a naval airman died in a drunken stupor following a heavy drinking session on a naval base, it was held by the Court of Appeal that the defendants owed no duty of care to prevent him from consuming large quantities of cheap alcohol. However, they were held liable for their failure to take care of him once he had collapsed, on the basis that they had assumed responsibility for him but had not called a doctor.

A positive duty to protect others has occasionally found to arise from less obvious relationships. In *Goldman v Hargrave*,[8] for example, a tall redgum tree on the defendant's land caught fire after being struck by lightning. The defendant could hardly be blamed for this, but he was held liable in negligence for leaving the fire to burn itself out, with the result that it spread to the claimant's land. Similarly, in *Barnett v Chelsea and Kensington Hospital Management Committee*,[9] the claimant's husband went to the casualty department of a hospital, complaining of vomiting and violent stomach pains, but the doctor on duty, who was himself feeling unwell, refused to examine him. In an action against the hospital authority for negligence,[10] it was held that on the facts a duty of care was owed, although the court left open the question of what the position would have been if the hospital had closed its doors altogether. Again, in *Smoldon v Whitworth*,[11] it was held that a referee in charge of an under-19 rugby match owed a duty of care to ensure the players' safety, and was accordingly liable to a player who suffered serious injuries when a scrum collapsed. And in *Watson v British Boxing Board of Control*,[12] the defendants were held liable in negligence to a professional boxer who suffered brain damage after being knocked out, for failing to ensure that immediate medical attention was available. On the other hand, it was held in *Calvert v William Hill Credit Ltd*[13] that a bookmaker which failed to fulfil its promise to a compulsive gambler not to accept any more telephone bets from him was not liable for the vast sums of money that he lost; it had not assumed any general duty to help control his addiction and, if prevented from telephone gambling, would have gambled and lost the same money in other ways.

[1] But not otherwise: *Orange v Chief Constable of West Yorkshire Police* [2001] EWCA Civ 611, [2002] QB 347, CA.

[2] *Kirkham v Chief Constable of the Greater Manchester Police* [1990] 3 All ER 246, CA; *Reeves v Metropolitan Police Comr* [1998] 2 All ER 381, HL.

[3] *Knight v Home Office* [1990] 3 All ER 237.

[4] *Vellino v Chief Constable of the Greater Manchester Police* [2001] EWCA Civ 1249, [2002] 3 All ER 78.

[5] *Ali v Furness Withy (Shipping) Ltd* [1988] 2 Lloyd's Rep 379.

[6] *Jebson v Ministry of Defence* [2000] 1 WLR 2055, CA.

[7] [1995] 3 All ER 87, CA.

[8] [1966] 2 All ER 989, PC.

[9] [1968] 1 All ER 1068.

[10] Which failed on the ground of causation; see para 18.3.

[11] [1997] ELR 249, CA; followed in *Vowles v Evans* [2003] EWCA Civ 318, [2003] 1 WLR 1607, which concerned an amateur rugby match between teams of adults.

[12] [2001] QB 1134, CA.

[13] [[2008] EWCA Civ 1427, CA.

Damage caused by third parties

16.10 One specific aspect of the principle of non-liability for omissions is that, in the absence of special circumstances, the defendant is not responsible for harm to the claimant which results from the unlawful (usually criminal) conduct of an independent third party, even where such harm is foreseeable. Thus a bus company is not liable if one of its vehicles, left unattended with its keys in the ignition, is stolen and then negligently driven so as to cause a fatal accident;[1] the management of a theatre owes no duty to actors to safeguard their belongings against theft from the dressing-room;[2] a social landlord who is aware of a tenant's violent tendencies is under no duty to warn other tenants;[3] and the owner of an empty and dilapidated building cannot be held responsible if neighbours suffer when it is used as a means of access by thieves[4] or as a playground by vandals[5] or fire-raising children.[6] Moreover, this approach has served to exclude actions by the victims of crime which allege negligence on the part of the police in failing to arrest a suspected murderer[7] or failing properly to investigate a burglary.[8]

Given the absence of any duty to prevent physical injury or damage to property, it is hardly surprising that there is no duty to prevent financial loss resulting from fraud. Thus, where tax authorities had obtained 'freezing injunctions' over the bank accounts of two companies, prohibiting them from withdrawing money, it was held that the bank (which was aware of the injunctions) owed no duty of care to the tax authorities to see that no money was withdrawn.[9] Similarly, where a finance company carelessly failed to register a hire purchase agreement concerning a car, it was held by a majority of the House of Lords that the company owed no duty of care to future purchasers; they were accordingly not liable when the hire purchaser, fraudulently concealing the existence of the agreement, 'sold' the vehicle to a dealer.[10] Even more extreme, it has been held that an insurance company is under no duty to inform a client that a broker is deliberately deceiving him or her as to the extent of the insurance cover,[11] nor to tell the assignee of a policy that the insured person is dishonestly jeopardising the cover.[12]

[1] *Topp v London Country Bus (South West) Ltd* [1993] 3 All ER 448, CA.
[2] *Deyong v Shenburn* [1946] 1 All ER 226.
[3] *Mitchell v Glasgow CC* [2009] UKHL 11, HL.
[4] *Perl (P) (Exporters) Ltd v Camden London Borough Council* [1983] 3 All ER 161, CA.
[5] *King v Liverpool City Council* [1986] 3 All ER 544, CA.
[6] *Smith v Littlewoods Organisation Ltd* [1987] 1 All ER 710, HL.
[7] *Hill v Chief Constable of West Yorkshire* [1988] 2 All ER 238, HL.
[8] *Alexandrou v Oxford* [1993] 4 All ER 328, CA.
[9] *Customs & Excise Commissioners v Barclays Bank* [2006] UKHL 28, HL.
[10] *Moorgate Mercantile Co Ltd v Twitchings* [1976] 2 All ER 641, HL.
[11] *Banque Financière de la Cité, SA v Westgate Insurance Co Ltd* [1989] 2 All ER 952, CA.
[12] *Bank of Nova Scotia v Hellenic Mutual War Risks Association (Bermuda) Ltd* [1989] 3 All ER 628, CA.

16.11 The problem of damage caused by third parties was examined by the House of Lords in *Smith v Littlewoods Organisation Ltd*.[1] The defendants there owned a disused cinema which they intended to demolish in order to redevelop the site. While the building was empty and unguarded, children broke in and caused damage in various ways, including the attempted lighting of fires. However, neither the defendants nor the police were told of these attempts, and eventually a serious fire was started which got out of control and damaged neighbouring property.

In holding the defendants not liable for this fire, a majority of the House of Lords took the view that a landowner's responsibility for the deliberate actions of a third party could be determined on the basis of 'foreseeability', albeit by using that term in a special sense. It would not, it was suggested, be enough that the third party's intervention was foreseeable as a mere possibility or even on the balance of probabilities; it must have been 'highly likely' to occur.

A minority view expressed by Lord Goff in *Smith v Littlewoods* was that, in practice, the courts had imposed liability in cases of this kind only in special circumstances, notably where the defendant had an existing relationship with either the claimant or the third party.[2] As to the relationships with the claimant which may be sufficient to create a duty of protection, it seems that an employer owes a duty not to expose his employee to a foreseeable wages snatch;[3] a police officer owes a duty to go to the aid of a fellow-officer who is under attack in a police station cell[4] or during an operation;[5] a decorator working alone in a client's house may be answerable for a theft which occurs when he leaves it empty and unlocked;[6] and the prison authorities may be liable for negligently revealing a sex offender's record to other prisoners, resulting in a foreseeable attack upon him.[7] As to relationships which are sufficient to create a duty to control the third party, it seems that an institution which assumes control of a potentially dangerous person such as a violent lunatic[8] or a borstal inmate[9] may be liable for negligently permitting its charge to escape and cause damage, provided that the escape creates an especially high risk to the claimant.[10]

The case of *Everett v Comojo (UK) Ltd*,[11] which concerned a knife attack by one night-club guest on another, may perhaps signal a more expansive approach to 'protective' duties of care in the future. In holding that the nightclub owners and occupiers owed a duty to prevent such an attack, the Court of Appeal stated that the existence or otherwise of a duty of care should be determined by reference to the threefold test of foreseeability, proximity and just and reasonableness laid down in *Caparo Industries plc v Dickman*.[12]

In the present case, all three elements were satisfied, so that a duty of care was owed although, on the facts, it had not been breached.

  1 [1987] 1 All ER 710, HL.
  2 Others mentioned are the negligent creation of a source of danger which might foreseeably be sparked off by other persons, and failure by a landowner to take reasonable steps to avert a known danger created on the land by other persons.
  3 *Charlton v Forrest Printing Ink Co Ltd* [1980] IRLR 331, CA (on the facts, employers not negligent). However, the police authorities owe no duty to individual officers in deciding on the policing of a potential riot: *Hughes v National Union of Mineworkers* [1991] 4 All ER 278.
  4 *Costello v Chief Constable of the Northumbria Police* [1999] 1 All ER 550, CA.
  5 *Mullaney v Chief Constable of West Midlands Police* [2001] EWCA Civ 700, CA.
  6 *Stansbie v Troman* [1948] 1 All ER 599, CA. As to possible liability under the Occupiers' Liability Act 1957, see *Cunningham v Reading Football Club* [1992] PIQR P141: para 21.12.
  7 *Steele v Northern Ireland Office* [1988] 12 NIJB 1.
  8 *Holgate v Lancashire Mental Hospitals Board* [1937] 4 All ER 19.
  9 *Home Office v Dorset Yacht Co Ltd* [1970] 2 All ER 294, HL.
  10 *K v Secretary of State for the Home Dept* [2002] EWCA Civ 983, CA.
  11 [2011] EWCA Civ 13, CA.
  12 [1990] 1 All ER 568, HL; see para 16.6.

DUTY OF CARE—GENERAL: KEY POINTS

- *Donoghue v Stevenson* suggested that a universal principle, that of 'foreseeability', underpins all legally recognised duties of care.

- The courts now recognise a threefold test: foreseeability, proximity and 'just and reasonableness'.

- The law does not normally impose any liability for a mere failure to act, nor for a positive act which does not worsen the claimant's position.

- A duty to act may, however, arise out of a pre-existing relationship.

- A person is not generally under any duty to prevent A from deliberately harming B, except where that person already has a certain kind of relationship with either A or B.

Economic loss

16.12 A person who is physically injured, or whose property is physically damaged, through the negligence of another, is entitled to recover damages in the tort of negligence for the financial consequences (eg loss of earnings or the cost of repairing damaged goods). As a general rule, however, no damages may be recovered for 'pure' economic or financial loss which results from the defendant's negligence, even where this is foreseeable. The leading case is *Cattle v Stockton Waterworks Co*,[1] where the claimant was employed under a fixed-price contract to build a tunnel through an embankment. His costs were greatly increased when the partly built tunnel was flooded by water escaping from the defendants' negligently laid main, and he sued in negligence to recover this loss. It was held that the claim must fail, since the claimant had not been injured; nor had any of his property been damaged.

The main reason for the 'economic loss' rule is the court's fear of 'opening the floodgates' to large numbers of legal claims arising out of a single act of negligence. This could occur because, while the physical effects of an act of negligence are normally felt by a restricted number of victims, the financial consequences may be felt by a great number of people. To allow them all to recover damages might, it is felt, produce a total liability out of all proportion to the defendant's wrong.

The principle laid down in *Cattle* has been consistently applied by the English courts in subsequent cases. For example, in *Weller & Co v Foot and Mouth Disease Research Institute*,[2] it was held that a person whose negligence caused an outbreak of foot and mouth disease among cattle could not be made liable to auctioneers who lost business when the Government ordered local markets to close; their liability, if any, would be restricted to farmers whose cattle were physically affected by the disease. Moreover, it has been extended to cases where the 'primary injury' is to a person, rather than to property. If an injury to A causes financial loss to B, who is dependent upon him, then that loss will not be recoverable in the tort of negligence.[3] This is demonstrated by the case of *Kirkham v Boughey*,[4] where the claimant and his wife were both injured in an accident caused by the negligence of the defendant. After the claimant had recovered from his injuries, he gave up his highly-paid job in order to be near his wife, who was still in hospital. It was held that, since this part of the claimant's loss of earnings resulted from his wife's injuries and not from his own, it was a purely financial loss; hence, even though it could be regarded as foreseeable, he could not claim for it.

[1] (1875) LR 10 QB 453. Approved by the House of Lords in *Simpson v Thomson* (1877) 3 App Cas 279, HL.
[2] [1965] 3 All ER 560.
[3] The position is different if B's loss results from A's death, but only by virtue of a statutory right to claim: see the Fatal Accidents Act 1976, para 27.11.
[4] [1957] 3 All ER 153. See also *West Bromwich Albion Football Club Ltd v El-Safty* [2006] EWCA Civ 1299, CA.

'Pure' and 'consequential' economic loss

16.13 As mentioned earlier, it is only 'pure' economic loss that lies outside the tort of negligence; there is no bar to recovering damages for economic loss which is the result of physical injury or damage. This principle can sometimes lead to fine distinctions, as in the case of *Spartan Steel and Alloys Ltd v Martin & Co (Contractors) Ltd*.[1] The defendants there negligently severed an electricity cable laid under the highway, thus cutting off power to the claimants' foundry. Molten metal being processed in a furnace threatened to solidify, which would have damaged both the metal and the furnace, and so the claimants had to incur expense (and damage the metal) in removing it. Furthermore, the loss of power meant that four more 'melts' which were planned could not be carried out, so that the claimants lost their expected profits on these. The Court of Appeal by a majority held that, while the defendants were liable for the physical damage and consequential loss of profit on the melt which had already been in progress, the inability to go ahead with the other four melts was pure economic loss and was therefore irrecoverable. It should be noted however that, if the metal had solidified in the furnace and production had been held up while it was cleaned out, the loss of profits would then have been classed as consequential economic loss and would thus have been recoverable.[2]

[1] [1972] 3 All ER 557, CA.
[2] *SCM (UK) Ltd v WJ Whittall & Son Ltd* [1970] 3 All ER 245, CA.

Transferred loss

16.14 The 'floodgates' reasoning which underpins the pure economic loss rule is easy to appreciate in cases where one person's property is negligently damaged, and the claimant is just one of the many persons who is in some way financially depend-ent upon that property. However, the courts have extended the rule of non-recovery to cases where, because of some contractual arrangement between the owner of the damaged property and the claimant, the financial effects of the damage are felt by the claimant instead of by the owner. In *Leigh & Sillivan Ltd v Aliakmon Shipping Co Ltd*,[1] the House of Lords held that, where a ship's cargo is damaged through the negligence of the carrier, only a person with ownership[2] of or a possessory title to the goods can recover damages from the carrier in negligence. Hence, if the cargo is in the process of being sold, under a contract which leaves ownership with the seller but places the risk of damage on the buyer (in the sense that he must still pay the full price), the buyer cannot recover damages.

[1] [1986] 2 All ER 145, HL.

[2] This may include beneficial, as well as legal, ownership: *Colour Quest Ltd v Total Downstream UK plc* [2010] EWCA Civ 180, CA.

Defective products

16.15 In *Donoghue v Stevenson*,[1] it was clearly laid down that a manufacturer of defec-tive goods, who was guilty of a breach of contract vis-à-vis the person to whom the goods were supplied, could at the same time be liable in the tort of negligence to a third party (the consumer) who suffered injury or whose property was damaged. What the House of Lords did not consider, far less decide, was whether a consumer could recover damages from the manufacturer where the goods in question did no actual harm to persons or property but were simply defective, in the sense of not being of the quality one would normally expect. In such a case, what the consumer had suffered would be perceived by the courts as pure economic loss, since he or she would not have received value for money.

It has now been clearly established that a manufacturer[2] owes no duty of care to a con-sumer to avoid causing pure economic loss of this kind.[3] Moreover, it makes no differ-ence that the defect has caused physical damage to the product itself, nor even that it has rendered the product dangerous.[4] The manufacturer can, however, be made liable where a defective product causes damage to other property, although there may be some difficulty in deciding what constitutes 'other property' for this purpose.[5]

[1] [1932] AC 562, HL; para 16.3.

[2] Most of the cases have in fact concerned defective buildings, but the relevant legal principles are identi-cal: see para 21.28.

[3] *Muirhead v Industrial Tank Specialities Ltd* [1985] 3 All ER 705, CA.

[4] *Murphy v Brentwood District Council* [1990] 2 All ER 908, HL.

[5] Eg where defective packaging results in damage to what is inside it: see *Aswan Engineering Establishment Co v Lupdine Ltd* [1987] 1 All ER 135, CA.

DUTY OF CARE—ECONOMIC LOSS: KEY POINTS

- In general there is no duty of care to avoid causing 'pure' (as opposed to 'consequential') economic loss to the claimant.

- This principle applies to cases of 'transferred loss'.

- It also applies so as to prevent claims in negligence against manufacturers or builders, where the negligence in question results in a defective product or building.

The interaction of contract and tort

16.16 The context in which an act of negligence occurs may involve a contractual relationship, either between the claimant and the defendant or between one of them and a
third party. Where this occurs, a court may well be called upon to decide whether it would
be just and reasonable to impose a duty of care upon the defendant, in circumstances
where a purely contractual analysis of the situation would suggest that none exists.

As far as contracts between claimant and defendant are concerned, it was decided by
the House of Lords in *Henderson v Merrett Syndicates Ltd*[1] that there is no objection in
principle to 'concurrent liability'. This means that, so long as the relationship between the
contracting parties is of sufficient proximity to found a duty of care in tort, the claimant is
entitled to frame an action in the most advantageous way.[2] However, this is subject to the
important qualification that where the contract places a clear limitation on the defendant's liability, it will not be just and reasonable to imply a duty of care in tort which is of
wider scope.[3]

As for contracts involving a third party, the courts have accepted in a number of cases
that these may have an effect upon tort claims between claimant and defendant. For
example, where a construction contract made between a client and a main contractor
makes clear that the contract works are to be at the client's sole risk, this may operate to
prevent the client from recovering damages from a sub-contractor who negligently causes
damage to the works.[4]

[1] [1994] 3 All ER 506, HL.
[2] In most cases, the only advantage to be gained by claiming in tort is that of the longer limitation period
which applies: see para 27.21.
[3] *William Hill Organisation v Bernard Sunley & Sons* (1982) 22 BLR 8, CA. Also see *Greater Nottingham
Co-operative Society Ltd v Cementation Piling & Foundations Ltd* [1988] 2 All ER 971, CA.
[4] *Norwich City Council v Harvey* [1989] 1 All ER 1180, CA.

Negligent statements

Physical damage

16.17 Where physical or psychiatric damage is concerned, there seems no good reason why the law should distinguish between negligent acts and negligent words. A doctor's liability to a patient who is treated with the wrong drug should surely be the same,
whether the doctor administers an injection or merely tells the patient which tablets
to take. Indeed, the law has found little difficulty in imposing liability where a person
is injured as a result of relying on negligent advice. In *Sharp v Avery*,[1] for example, the
defendant motorcyclist offered to lead a second motorcycle, on which the claimant was a
passenger, along a road which the defendant claimed to know. When the defendant went
off the road at a bend, the second motorcycle followed and the claimant fell off. The Court
of Appeal held that the defendant had assumed a duty of care towards the claimant and
was therefore liable for his injuries.

Where negligent words lead to purely financial loss, the position is more complicated.
The court's realisation that words may be used over and over again, reaching unsuspected
audiences without losing their power, has led to concerns that a single careless remark might
expose a defendant to wholly disproportionate liability. As a result, the law in this area has
been slower to develop and is based on the idea of a restricted duty of care. Indeed, for some
three-quarters of a century, the possibility of any legal remedy in this area was blocked by

the decision of the House of Lords in *Derry v Peek*,[2] in which it was held that company directors could not be liable for false statements made in a prospectus unless there was fraud.

[1] [1938] 4 All ER 85, CA.
[2] (1889) 14 App Cas 337, HL.

Hedley Byrne v Heller

16.18 The breakthrough, in the sense of judicial recognition that the tort of negligence might extend to statements leading to financial loss, came with the decision of the House of Lords in the leading case of *Hedley Byrne & Co Ltd v Heller & Partners Ltd*.[1] The claimants, a firm of advertising agents, were asked to arrange advertising space on behalf of a client. Since, in accordance with trade practice, the claimants would incur personal responsibility for paying for this space, they asked their bankers to check on the client's credit-worthiness. An inquiry was made of the defendants, the clients' bankers and financial backers, and they replied 'without responsibility' that the client was 'a respectably constituted company, considered good for its ordinary business engagements'. Relying on this reference, the claimants went ahead with the contracts; when, shortly afterwards the client became insolvent, the claimants lost some £17,000. It was held, at first instance and in the Court of Appeal, that the defendants were not liable because, although they had been careless, they did not owe the claimants any duty of care.

On appeal, the House of Lords held that the disclaimer ('without responsibility') prevented a duty from arising in the present case.[2] However, after an exhaustive review of the authorities, it was laid down that in an appropriate case a duty could arise. As to what would be an appropriate case, the test could not, it was said, be simply that of foreseeability, for this would impose an unacceptably heavy burden upon professional advisers. What was required was evidence of a special relationship between the parties, arising out of a voluntary assumption of responsibility by the defendant.

The circumstances in which a court might expect to find a special relationship and, with it, a duty of care were the subject of a considerable range of opinions in the House of Lords. The widest view expressed was that a duty of care will arise whenever the defendant realises or ought to realise that his or her skill and care are being relied upon, provided both that there is such reliance and that the reliance is reasonable in the circumstances. However, even under this wider approach, it is highly unlikely that a person would be held liable in respect of words casually uttered on a social occasion. It may also be necessary to show that the defendant gave the advice with a particular transaction in mind.[3] Thus a person who issues a prospectus inviting shareholders to take up a special 'rights issue' of shares is not liable if they decide, on the basis of misleading information in the prospectus, to purchase more shares on the open market,[4] unless the prospectus was clearly intended to encourage such further purchases.[5]

[1] [1963] 2 All ER 575, HL.
[2] Such a disclaimer would now, at least in business circumstances, be subject to a test of 'reasonableness' under the Unfair Contract Terms Act 1977 (paras 9.9–9.21): *Smith v Eric S Bush; Harris v Wyre Forest District Council* [1989] 2 All ER 514, HL.
[3] *Candler v Crane, Christmas & Co* [1951] All ER 426 at 435.
[4] *Al-Nakib Investments (Jersey) Ltd v Longcroft* [1990] 3 All ER 321.
[5] *Possfund Custodian Trustee Ltd v Diamond* [1996] 2 All ER 774.

16.19 The idea that liability in this area is dependent upon a voluntary assumption of responsibility by the defendant has been adopted in many subsequent cases, including some important decisions of the House of Lords.[1] In *Hood v National Farmers Union*,[2] for example, the defendants were sued by one of their members for failing to warn him of the strict time limits within which he must act if he wished to challenge the decision of a Milk Quota Tribunal. The reason they were held liable was specifically that they had taken upon themselves the role of adviser to their member in respect of such a challenge. Again, in *Verity and Spindler v Lloyds Bank*,[3] where the claimant sought a loan from the defendants in respect of a business venture, her bank manager took it upon himself to advise her as to the prudence of the venture. The advice was negligent and the bank was held liable for it.

The concept of a voluntary assumption of responsibility has been regarded as especially important in cases where a claim for negligence is brought, not against an organisation, but against the individual within that organisation who actually gave the offending advice. In *Williams v Natural Life Health Foods Ltd*,[4] where the managing director and major shareholder of a franchising company gave advice to a prospective franchisee, it was held that only the company, and not the individual, was liable, since the latter had not assumed personal responsibility for the advice which he gave. In *Merrett v Babb*,[5] by contrast, it was held that an employed valuer who signed a mortgage valuation report in his own name had assumed responsibility for it and therefore owed a duty of care to a house purchaser who relied on it.

Despite this emphasis on assumption of responsibility, it has been suggested in several cases that the idea is really a fiction. The important question, it is said, is not: 'did the defendant undertake, expressly or impliedly, to be responsible for advice?' but rather 'in what circumstances will the law impose a duty of care upon the defendant?'. In *Smith v Eric S Bush; Harris v Wyre Forest District Council*,[6] Lord Griffiths, having described the voluntary assumption of responsibility test as neither helpful nor realistic, suggested that the courts should approach this question as it would any other duty of care inquiry, by using a composite test involving foreseeability, proximity and 'justice and reasonableness'.[7] Nevertheless, it is only in rare cases that a duty of care in respect of financial loss will exist in the absence of a voluntary assumption of responsibility and/or reliance by the claimant on such an assumption.[8] All in all, the concept of assumption of responsibility remains a significant one.

In *James McNaughton Papers Group Ltd v Hicks Anderson & Co*,[9] an attempt was made in the Court of Appeal to identify those matters likely to be of importance when considering whether a duty of care arises in respect of an allegedly negligent statement. These are the purpose for which the statement was made; the purpose for which it was communicated; the relationship between the adviser, the advisee and any relevant third party; the size of any class to which the advisee belongs; the state of knowledge of the adviser; and reliance by the advisee.

---

[1] See, for example, *Spring v Guardian Assurance plc* [1994] 3 All ER 129, HL; *Henderson v Merrett Syndicates Ltd* [1994] 3 All ER 506, HL.

[2] [1994] 1 EGLR 1, CA.

[3] [1996] Fam Law 213.

[4] [1998] 2 All ER 577, HL.

[5] [2001] EWCA Civ 214, [2001] QB 1174, CA.

[6] [1989] 2 All ER 514 at 536.

[7] See para 16.6.

[8] *Banque Financière de la Cité SA v Westgate Insurance Co Ltd* [1989] 2 All ER 952 at 1009, CA; *Reid v Rush & Tompkins Group plc* [1989] 3 All ER 228 at 239, CA.

[9] [1991] 1 All ER 134 at 144.

16.20 The limits of the *Hedley Byrne* doctrine have been explored in a number of subsequent cases, and the courts have for the most part adopted a fairly liberal approach. A striking exception is the decision (by a bare majority) of the Privy Council in *Mutual Life and Citizens Assurance Co Ltd v Evatt*,[1] that a duty of care can only arise where the advice given was of a type which the defendant was in business to give. It is not easy to see why this should be so, and it is worth noting that, notwithstanding this decision, the Court of Appeal has imposed liability in negligence on an amateur car enthusiast who advised a friend on the purchase of a second-hand vehicle.[2]

One area in which the courts have so far been somewhat cautious is in their refusal to use *Hedley Byrne* as a basis for a positive duty to advise or warn of some danger[3] at least where there is no suggestion that the defendant has effectively said: 'Leave it all to me'.[4] Indeed, the case of *Argy Trading Development Co Ltd v Lapid Developments Ltd*[5] suggests that, even for those who choose to speak, the duty of care is subject to strict limits. In that case a lease of part of a warehouse placed the obligation to insure against fire upon the tenants. In fact, however, the landlords had a block policy which covered the whole building and so the tenants, at the landlords' suggestion, simply paid the landlords a proportionate part of the premiums. Some time later the landlords allowed the policy to lapse without telling the tenants, who consequently found themselves uninsured when fire gutted the building. In an action for negligence it was held that, although the relationship between the parties was such that the landlords owed the tenants a duty of care, this merely meant that they must not give inaccurate information as to the insurance position at the time; they were under no positive duty to notify the tenants if circumstances changed.

Another controversial issue is how far liability extends beyond cases where information or advice is specifically requested by and given to the claimant. It appears that a direct inquiry from the claimant is not a prerequisite for the imposition of a duty of care, so that an employer who gives a reference for an ex-employee may owe that person a duty of care, notwithstanding that the reference is requested by and given to a third party.[6] Indeed, a duty may occasionally arise without any request at all, so that a bank manager who takes it upon himself to explain to a customer the legal significance of a mortgage which she is about to execute in the bank's favour must do so with care and skill.[7] However, success in such cases is rare; the Court of Appeal has held that, where information had not been requested at all (it was contained in advertisements published by a manufacturer), the mere fact that a person might be expected to rely on it was not sufficient to establish a 'special relationship'.[8] A similar decision was reached in respect of misleading statements made on a trade association's website as to the insurance backing provided for customers of its members. It was held that, although the trade association might reasonably expect members of the public to rely on those statements, they would be expected first to obtain an 'information pack' as the website suggested; had they done so, they would not have been misled.[9]

Similarly, where a medical charity advised a man that, following a vasectomy operation, he need no longer use contraception, the charity was held to owe no duty of care to a future sexual partner who became pregnant when, most unexpectedly, the vasectomy spontaneously reversed itself.[10]

[1] [1971] 1 All ER 150, PC.
[2] *Chaudhry v Prabhakar* [1988] 3 All ER 718, CA.
[3] Para 16.10.
[4] As occurred in *Lennon v Commissioner of Police of the Metropolis* [2004] EWCA Civ 130, CA.
[5] [1977] 3 All ER 785.
[6] *Spring v Guardian Assurance plc* [1994] 3 All ER 129, HL.
[7] *Cornish v Midland Bank plc* [1985] 3 All ER 513, CA.
[8] *Lambert v Lewis* [1980] 1 All ER 978, CA.
[9] *Patchett v Swimming Pool and Allied Trades Association Ltd* [2009] EWCA Civ 717, CA.
[10] *Goodwill v British Pregnancy Advisory Service* [1996] 2 All ER 161, CA.

Professional liability

16.21 The greatest impact of *Hedley Byrne v Heller* has undoubtedly been in the sphere of professional work, where one person's reliance on advice from another is most likely to be regarded as reasonable. In fact, the principle has been extended to situations in which there is no discernible 'advice' at all, but where the professional adviser can be said to have assumed responsibility for services provided.

Of the various professionals who have been held liable in the tort of negligence to persons other than their clients, a number of examples may help to show what the courts regard as a 'special relationship' for this purpose. In *Shankie-Williams v Heavey*[1] the defendant timber specialist, who was instructed by the vendor of three flats in a converted house to investigate the ground floor flat, reported that it was free from dry rot. It was held by the Court of Appeal that the defendant, although instructed and paid by the vendor, owed a duty of care to a purchaser of that flat; however, no duty was owed to the purchaser of one of the other flats, who saw the report and jumped to the conclusion that the whole property must be rot-free.

A valuer who carries out a valuation of commercial property for a potential borrower, knowing that it will be shown to and relied upon by a lender, will owe a duty of care to the lender.[2] However, if the valuer in such circumstances makes it clear that the valuation is for the use only of a named lender, no duty of care will be owed to any other lender to whom it is passed on without the valuer's consent.[3] In residential cases, a valuer who is instructed by a building society or other lender to value a house for mortgage purposes will owe a duty of care to the purchaser; moreover, any attempt to disclaim liability is likely to be held unreasonable and thus invalid under the Unfair Contract Terms Act 1977.[4] However, a valuer or surveyor who advises a mortgage lender on the sale of a repossessed property owes no duty of care to the borrower to see that the property is sold at a reasonable price.[5]

The position of an estate agent who, while acting on behalf of a vendor, passes on false or misleading information about the property to a prospective purchaser, is not entirely clear. It has been held on two occasions[6] that, where the agent was responding to a specific inquiry form the purchaser, he had voluntarily assumed responsibility for the information and thus owed a duty of care. However, in *McCullagh v Lane Fox & Partners Ltd*[7] it was suggested by a majority of the Court of Appeal that, in normal circumstances, an agent would not be liable in negligence for false statements in sale particulars, since the purchaser would be expected to rely, not on this information, but on the investigations carried out by the purchaser's own solicitor and surveyor.

Turning to the legal profession, it appears that a vendor's solicitor owes no duty to the purchaser in answering preliminary inquiries before the conclusion of a contract for the sale of land.[8] However, a solicitor acting for a small firm in a loan transaction was held to have assumed responsibility to the lender, a private individual, and was liable in negligence for failing to warn the lender that the security might well prove ineffective.[9] Moreover, a solicitor who, on behalf of a client, gives an express or implied undertaking to take certain measures for the protection of a known third party, will owe a duty of care to that third party to fulfil the undertaking.[10] Of more far-reaching effect, it has been held that a solicitor instructed to draft a client's will owes a duty of care to those who are intended to benefit under it.[11] This ruling is especially interesting in that liability may be imposed upon the solicitor, even though it cannot be said that the beneficiaries have 'relied' upon any 'advice'. However, the duty imposed upon a solicitor in such circumstances appears limited to ensuring that the will achieves the testator's purpose;

he or she owes no duty towards a beneficiary to warn the testator that subsequent dealings with his property are likely to affect that beneficiary's interest,[12] nor to advise the testator of further steps which may be required if the gift to the beneficiary is to be effective.[13] Nor can this duty of care be extended beyond wills to a badly drafted and thus ineffective deed of gift, where the donor (the client's solicitor) refuses to execute a replacement deed.[14]

As for other professions, it has been held that accountants instructed by a company to audit its accounts owe a duty of care to its existing shareholders as a group, but not to an individual existing or potential investor[15] or a creditor,[16] unless they make a specific representation to an identified individual which is intended to be relied upon.[17] An architect or engineer undoubtedly owes a duty of care to a client in issuing certificates under a construction contract,[18] but it appears that no comparable duty is owed to the contractor.[19] Finally, it has been held that a surveyor who certifies a ship as seaworthy[20] or an aircraft as airworthy[21] owes no duty of care to a prospective purchaser, nor to the owner of cargo lost when the ship subsequently sinks.[22]

[1] [1986] 2 EGLR 139, CA.
[2] *Cann v Willson* (1888) 39 Ch D 39.
[3] *Omega Trust Co Ltd v Wright Son & Pepper* [1997] 1 EGLR 120, CA.
[4] *Smith v Eric S Bush; Harris v Wyre Forest District Council* [1989] 2 All ER 514, HL.
[5] *Raja v Austin Gray* [2002] EWCA Civ 1965, [2003] 13 EG 117, CA.
[6] *Computastaff Ltd v Ingledew, Brown, Bennison and Garrett* [1983] 2 EGLR 150; *Duncan Investments Ltd v Underwoods* [1997] PNLR 521. A similar principle applies to an auctioneer: *McAnarney v Hanrahan* [1993] IR 492.
[7] [1996] 1 EGLR 35, CA. The agents were in any event protected by an effective disclaimer in their sales particulars.
[8] *Cemp Properties (UK) Ltd v Dentsply Research and Development Corpn* [1991] 2 EGLR 197, CA; *Gran Gelato Ltd v Richcliff (Group) Ltd* [1992] 1 All ER 865.
[9] *Dean v Allin & Watts* [2001] EWCA Civ 758, [2001] Lloyd's Rep PN 605, CA.
[10] *Al-Kandari v JR Brown & Co* [1988] 1 All ER 833, CA.
[11] *White v Jones* [1995] 1 All ER 691, HL.
[12] *Clarke v Bruce Lance & Co* [1988] 1 All ER 364, CA.
[13] *Carr-Glynn v Frearsons* [1997] 2 All ER 614.
[14] *Hemmens v Wilson Browne* [1993] 4 All ER 826.
[15] *Caparo Industries plc v Dickman* [1990] 1 All ER 568, HL; *James McNaughton Papers Group Ltd v Hicks Anderson & Co* [1991] 1 All ER 134, CA.
[16] *Al Saudi Banque v Clark Pixley* [1989] 3 All ER 361.
[17] *Morgan Crucible Co plc v Hill Samuel Bank Ltd* [1991] 1 All ER 148, CA.
[18] *Sutcliffe v Thackrah* [1974] 1 All ER 859, HL: para 16.25.
[19] *Pacific Associates Inc v Baxter* [1989] 2 All ER 159, CA.
[20] *Reeman v Department of Transport* [1997] 2 Lloyd's Rep 648, CA.
[21] *Philcox v Civil Aviation Authority* [1995] 27 LS Gaz R 33, CA.
[22] *Marc Rich & Co AG v Bishop Rock Marine Co Ltd* [1995] 3 All ER 307, HL.

DUTY OF CARE—STATEMENTS: KEY POINTS

- Where the claimant's reliance on a negligent statement leads to financial loss, the defendant can only be liable if there has been a 'voluntary assumption of responsibility'.

- This is most likely to arise where specific advice is given directly by the defendant to the claimant.

- A duty of care in respect of statements means that professional advisers may, in appropriate circumstances, be liable to persons who are not their clients.

Public authorities

16.22 Public bodies such as local authorities operate against the background of detailed and complex statutory provisions. Parts of these statutory codes impose positive duties on the bodies in question, others confer discretionary powers. Where, in the exercise of its statutory functions, a public body causes injury, damage or loss to an individual, a question which arises is whether an action by the victim may lead to the recovery of damages.

The general principles of law governing such actions were subjected to detailed examination by the House of Lords in five important cases,[1] from which the following principles emerge:

- In certain limited circumstances, an action may lie for the breach by a public authority of a statutory duty, independent of any question of negligence. However, this requires the claimant to convince the court that Parliament intended the statute in question to create a civil right of action for damages.[2]

- The mere fact of carelessness by a public authority in the exercise of a statutory power or duty does not lead to liability. In order to succeed in an action for negligence, the claimant must establish a common law duty of care in accordance with the general principles described earlier.[3]

- Although a public authority may in principle owe a common law duty of care as to the manner in which it performs its statutory functions, it owes no such duty of care as to the way in which it exercises a statutory discretion; anything within the ambit of its discretion is a matter for the authority, not for the courts. Furthermore, if the factors relevant to the exercise of the discretion include matters of policy, the courts will not even consider whether or not the decision was within the ambit of the statutory discretion.[4]

- Where the claimant's complaint is that the public authority negligently failed to exercise a statutory power, the claimant can only succeed by showing that:
  - any rational public authority would have exercised the power in question (so that there was in effect a public law duty to act); and
  - the policy of the statute requires compensation to be paid to persons who suffer loss because the power was not exercised.

[1] *X v Bedfordshire County Council* [1995] 3 All ER 353, HL; *Stovin v Wise* [1996] 3 All ER 801, HL; *Barrett v Enfield London Borough Council* [1999] 3 All ER 193, HL; *Gorringe v Calderdale MBC* [2004] UKHL 15, HL; *D v East Berkshire Community Health NHS Trust* [2005] UKHL 23, HL.
[2] See ch 20.
[3] Para 16.6.
[4] The distinction between 'policy' and 'operational' decisions was given detailed consideration in *Anns v Merton London Borough Council* [1977] 2 All ER 492, HL.

16.23 The way in which the courts have applied these principles has made it difficult for a claimant to succeed in an action for negligence against a public authority. The courts for a long time showed enormous reluctance to recognise the kind of claims put forward in *X v Bedfordshire County Council*[1] (inadequate handling of potential child abuse cases, and failure to cater sufficiently for children with special educational needs). This reluctance has to some extent been overcome by decisions of the European Court of Human Rights[2] to the effect that the human rights of the child claimants in *X v Bedfordshire CC* had been infringed; in such circumstances there would be little point in the English courts continuing to deny the existence of a duty of care, at least to the child.[3]

The court's hesitancy in this area is perhaps not surprising, in view of the delicate decision-making processes involved, but a similar judicial attitude may be found in other less delicate areas. *Stovin v Wise*,[4] for example, concerned a claim by a motor-cyclist who was seriously injured when struck by a car emerging from a road junction. The junction was known to be dangerous, and the claimant claimed that the highway authority should have exercised its statutory power to remove a bank of earth which obstructed visibility. However, this claim was rejected by the House of Lords (albeit by a bare 3–2 majority).

In adopting such a restrictive approach to claims against public authorities, the courts clearly recognise that such actions raise a number of difficult issues which are not present in other cases of negligence. For example, it is always necessary to examine the particular statute under which the public body was acting at the time of its alleged negligence, to see whether its purpose was to protect the claimant from the type of harm suffered.[5] This approach has operated to deny a number of claims in which alleged negligence by a public authority has had a disastrous effect on the claimant's business.[6]

The courts have also shown an increasing awareness of the fact that, in many cases, the defendant has not positively caused harm to the claimant, but has merely failed to offer protection against harm arising naturally or from the acts of some third party. The law is slow to impose affirmative duties of protection,[7] and actions of this kind have failed against financial regulators,[8] a local authority responsible for vetting nursing homes,[9] the Law Society in its function of controlling solicitors,[10] the fire brigade[11] and the coast-guard.[12] By contrast, it has been held that, once an ambulance service 'accepts' a call for assistance, it assumes a duty of care towards the person concerned.[13] Moreover, while the common law of negligence continues to deny that the police may be liable to individuals for negligence in investigating or suppressing crime,[14] their failure to take action in the face of a 'real and immediate risk' to an identified individual may constitute a breach of that person's human rights.[15]

In a number of cases, claimants have sought to use the tort of negligence as a means in effect of challenging decisions reached by various officials or public bodies. In rejecting these claims, the policy grounds relied upon by the courts have included the availability of alternative remedies such as statutory appeal procedures, the need to avoid putting undue pressure on public decision makers and the undesirability of attempts by the courts to 'second-guess' the valid exercise of a discretion specifically conferred upon some other person or body. A combination of these factors has proved fatal to actions brought against an adjudicating officer deciding on a social security claim,[16] an immigration officer deal-ing with an asylum seeker,[17] a government minister exercising a discretionary power over foreign investment,[18] a police authority conducting disciplinary proceedings against a constable,[19] the charity commissioners[20] and university examiners.[21]

---

[1] [1995] 3 All ER 353, HL.

[2] *Z v UK* [2001] 2 FLR 612, EHCR; *TP and KM v UK* [2001] FLR 549, EHCR.

[3] *D v East Berkshire Community Health NHS Trust* [2005] UKHL 23, HL, where, however, it was held that no duty of care was owed to parents.

[4] [1996] 3 All ER 801, HL; followed in *Gorringe v Calderdale MBC* [2004] UKHL 15, HL.

[5] *Curran v Northern Ireland Co-ownership Housing Association Ltd* [1987] 2 All ER 13, HL.

[6] *Harris v Evans* [1998] 3 All ER 522, CA; *Neil Martin Ltd v Revenue and Customs Commissioners* [2007] EWCA Civ 1041, CA; *Trent Strategic Health Authority v Jain* [2009] UKHL 4, HL.

[7] See paras 16.7–16.11.

[8] *Yuen Kun-yeu v A-G of Hong Kong* [1987] 2 All ER 705, PC.

[9] *Martine v South East Kent Health Authority* (1993) 20 BMLR 51, CA.

[10] *Wood v Law Society* [1993] NLJR 1475.

[11] *Capital and Counties plc v Hampshire County Council* [1997] 2 All ER 865, CA.

[12] *OLL Ltd v Secretary of State for Transport* [1997] 3 All ER 897.

[13] *Kent v Griffiths* [2000] 2 All ER 474, CA.

[14] *Hill v Chief Constable of West Yorkshire* [1988] 2 All ER 238, HL; *Cowan v Chief Constable for Avon & Somerset Constabulary* [2002] HLR 42, CA.

[15] *Chief Constable of Hertfordshire Police v Van Colle; Smith v Chief Constable of Sussex* [2008] UKHL 50, [2008] 3 All ER 977, HL, applying the decision of the European Court of Human Rights in *Osman v UK* (1998) 29 EHRR 245.

[16] *Jones v Department of Employment* [1988] 1 All ER 725, CA.

[17] *W v Home Office* [1997] Imm AR 302, CA.

[18] *Rowling v Takaro Properties Ltd* [1988] 1 All ER 163, PC.

[19] *Calveley v Chief Constable of Merseyside* [1989] 1 All ER 1025, HL.

[20] *Mills v Winchester Diocesan Board of Finance* [1989] 2 All ER 317.

[21] *Thorne v University of London* [1966] 2 All ER 338, CA.

16.24 In contrast to the generally restrictive approach described above, the courts have shown greater willingness to impose a duty of care on a public authority where the authority can be said to have assumed responsibility towards the claimant, either individually[1] or, less commonly, as a member of a defined group. An example of the latter type of case is *Kane v New Forest DC*,[2] where a planning authority was held to owe a duty of care to pedestrians in permitting a footpath to be sited in such a way as to create a dangerous road crossing. As for the former type, it seems that, even in circumstances where there may be no positive duty to intervene for the benefit of a vulnerable child,[3] a public authority will owe a duty once it actually takes a child into care[4] or begins to teach a child with special educational needs.[5]

'Assumption of responsibility' is of particular importance in cases where a public authority offers specific advice to someone; the question is whether the circumstances are such as to indicate that it assumes responsibility for the accuracy of that advice.[6] The courts have thus accepted that a duty of care might be owed by a local planning authority which advised a property developer about the status of a highway;[7] an environmental health officer who advised the owners of a guest house that expensive building work was necessary to meet statutory requirements,[8] and by local authorities which recommended a child minder who then mistreated children in her care;[9] assured prospective foster parents that they would not be sent any child suspected of committing sexual abuse;[10] and failed to inform prospective adopters that the child placed with them for adoption had very serious behavioural problems.[11]

[1] *Swinney v Chief Constable of Northumbria Police* [1996] 3 All ER 449, CA; *L v Reading Borough Council* [2001] EWCA Civ 346, [2001] 1 WLR 1575.

[2] [2001] 3 All ER 914, CA.

[3] As in *X v Bedfordshire County Council* [1995] 3 All ER 353, HL: para 16.23.

[4] *Barrett v Enfield LBC* [2001] 2 AC 550, HL.

[5] *Phelps v Hillingdon LBC* [2001] 2 AC 619, HL.

[6] Para 16.19.

[7] *Gooden v Northamptonshire County Council* [2002] 1 EGLR 137, CA.

[8] *Welton v North Cornwall District Council* [1997] 1 WLR 570, [1997] PNLR 108, CA.

[9] *T (a minor) v Surrey County Council* [1994] 4 All ER 577.

[10] *W v Essex County Council* [2000] 2 All ER 237, HL.

[11] *A& B v Essex County Council* [2003] EWCA Civ 1848, CA.

Judicial process

Judges and other decision-makers

16.25 Until quite recently it could confidently be asserted that judges, barristers, solicitors, jurors and witnesses enjoy an absolute immunity from any form of civil action being brought against them in respect of anything they say or do in court during the course of a trial. Thus, for example, a judge (at least one who sits in a superior court of record)[1] has total immunity from any form of civil action in respect of anything said or done within his (or her) jurisdiction.[2] Even if that jurisdiction is exceeded, it seems that the judge is still immune from civil action, provided that he or she acts in good faith.[2] Statute has now in effect brought the legal position of magistrates into line with that of judges.[3]

The immunity of judges has been extended to certain other persons who exercise a judicial or quasi-judicial function. In particular, an arbitrator is not liable for anything which he does or fails to do unless the act or omission is shown to have been in bad faith.[4] However, merely because a third party is to make a decision by which two or more others have agreed to be bound does not in itself mean that the decision maker is immune from liability; such immunity arises only where the decision maker is appointed to settle an existing or future dispute in a judicial manner. This means that an architect who certifies whether or not a builder's work is up to the contractual standard, or a valuer by whose rental valuation a landlord and tenant have agreed to abide, will owe a duty of care in carrying out the work in question.[5]

[1] The Crown Court, High Court and higher courts.
[2] *Sirros v Moore* [1974] 3 All ER 776, CA.
[3] Courts and Legal Services Act 1990, s 108.
[4] Arbitration Act 1996, s 29.
[5] *Sutcliffe v Thackrah* [1974] 1 All ER 859, HL; *Arenson v Casson, Beckman, Rutley & Co* [1975] 3 All ER 901, HL.

Advocates

16.26 It was at one time the law that a barrister could not be held liable in negligence by a client, for the way in which he (or she) prepared and conducted a case in court.[1] Two main reasons were given for this immunity: first, that an advocate's primary duty lies, not to the client, but to the court to secure the true administration of justice, which may compel the barrister on occasion to disclose matters unfavourable to the client's case; and second, that there must at some point be an end to litigation (whereas an action against one's advocate would always in effect amount to a retrial of the original case, with the possibility of ending up with two conflicting decisions).

In *Arthur JS Hall & Co v Simons*,[2] the House of Lords decided that neither of these reasons was sufficient to justify giving advocates, alone among professional persons, immunity from liability for incompetence. Their lordships felt that the problem of conflicting duties was not a serious one, for the advocate's duty to the court would be taken into account in deciding whether or not he (or she) had acted with reasonable care and skill towards the client. As for the problem of conflicting decisions, the House of Lords felt that this could be avoided by a separate legal principle,[3] namely that no negligence action would be permitted if it would amount to a collateral attack upon a previous decision of a court of competent jurisdiction. An action by a disappointed litigant against a lawyer would normally fall foul of this principle, since the essence of the claimant's claim is that he (or she) should have won the previous case. However, there would be no bar to a negligence claim by a litigant who had, for example, successfully appealed against the original decision, but who claimed to have suffered loss in the time taken to appeal.

The exact scope of the 'no collateral attack' principle is far from clear, but it seems likely that it will in practice substantially reduce the effect of the removal of the advocate's immunity.

[1] *Rondel v Worsley* [1967] 3 All ER 993, HL: the principle was extended to other advocates, such as solicitors, by s 62 of the Courts and Legal Services Act 1990.
[2] [2000] 3 All ER 673, HL.
[3] Laid down in *Hunter v Chief Constable of West Midlands* [1981] 3 All ER 727, HL.

Other participants

16.27 The immunity described above has been extended to other persons who are involved in judicial proceedings. Indeed, it has been held that a litigant is owed no duty of care, as to the way in which legal proceedings are conducted by the opposing party,[1] nor by the opposing party's solicitor[2] or barrister.[3] This means that, for example, there is no liability for causing loss to another party by negligently serving a notice upon him or her at the wrong address. However, the immunity formerly given to expert witnesses was removed by the Supreme Court in the case of *Jones v Kaney*,[4] on grounds very similar to those used to justify removing the immunity of advocates.[5] Nor does the immunity extend to persons less closely connected with legal proceedings. A sequestrator, for example, owes a duty of care to the owner of property which is being administered, notwithstanding that he or she is acting as an officer of the court.[6]

[1] *Business Computers International Ltd v Registrar of Companies* [1987] 3 All ER 465. This includes the Crown Prosecution Service: *Elguzouli-Daf v Metropolitan Police Comr* [1995] 1 All ER 833, CA.
[2] *Al-Kandari v JR Brown & Co* [1988] 1 All ER 833 at 835, CA.
[3] *Connolly-Martin v Davis* [1999] PNLR 826, CA.
[4] [2011] UKSC 3, SC.
[5] Para 16.26.
[6] *IRC v Hoogstraten* [1984] 3 All ER 25, CA.

Psychiatric injury

16.28 Where a person recovers damages for physical injury, some compensation in respect of any accompanying psychological trauma is normally recoverable under the heading of pain and suffering.[1] Where, however, there is no 'impact injury', the courts have proved much less sympathetic to a claim in respect of purely mental harm. This may be due in part to an instinctive feeling that psychiatric damage is in some way less important that physical damage, or from a sense that claims for purely psychiatric harm are easier to counterfeit. There is also, no doubt, a fear of opening the floodgates, in the sense that a negligent driver, say, might be found liable, not only to someone who has been physically injured, but to a large number of the victim's relative and friends who may claim to have suffered psychiatric harm on seeing or hearing about the accident.

Whatever the reasons, there is no doubt that the law has sought to restrict claims by persons who have suffered psychiatric damage but not physical harm. The relevant legal rules, deriving mainly from three decisions of the House of Lords,[2] are extremely complex and somewhat uncertain: only a brief summary can be given here.

First, it must be emphasised that a claimant is only entitled to damages in respect of a recognised psychiatric illness, not for other mental responses such as distress or grief. Moreover, with one exception (noted below) it must have been foreseeable to the defendant that negligence might cause psychiatric harm to a person of reasonable fortitude. Thus, if the claimant is only affected because he (or she) is especially susceptible to psychiatric harm, the defendant is not liable for this.

A claimant who is a 'primary victim' (ie someone directly involved in the event caused by the defendant's negligence) is entitled to claim damages where for psychiatric injury where it was foreseeable that he (or she) would suffer either physical or psychiatric injury. This is the exceptional case mentioned above in that someone who has been put in physical danger (whether or not any physical injury actually results) can recover for psychiatric injury, even if that injury is unforeseeable. The courts have extended the category of 'primary victim' to include such claimants as an employee negligently exposed to stress at work,[3] a client sent to prison through the alleged negligence of a solicitor,[4] or the father of a new-born baby who was negligently told incorrectly that the child had died.[5] However, it is now clear that an accident witness is not to be regarded as a primary victim merely by virtue of being an employee of the defendant, nor of being a rescuer.

A claimant who is a 'secondary victim' (ie someone who suffers psychiatric injury merely from seeing or hearing injury to another[6]) must satisfy much more stringent requirements in order to recover damages. In *Alcock v Chief Constable of the South Yorkshire Police*[7] (a case arising out of the Hillsborough disaster, in which 95 Liverpool football supporters were crushed to death through the negligence of the police in controlling the crowd), the House of Lords stressed the importance of three criteria by which such cases were to be judged: the class of persons whose claims should be recognised; the proximity of such persons to the accident; and the means by which the shock is caused. On the facts of *Alcock*, the House of Lords held:

- there is no arbitrary list of relationships which are close enough to render it foreseeable that injury to or death of one partner may result in shock to the other. However, the only relationships close enough to raise a presumption that shock may be suffered are those of husband-wife and parent-child. In order for other relatives or friends to recover damages, they must positively prove an equivalent emotional tie.

- as a general rule, proximity requires a claimant to be physically close to the accident in time and space.

- as a general rule, proximity also requires the claimant to witness the accident or its immediate aftermath personally. It is not enough to be told of the accident by a third party, to see a televised recording of it or to read about it in a newspaper.

Applying these criteria, the House of Lords held that a local authority could be liable to the claimant foster parents for placing with them a 15-year-old boy with a history of sexual abuse; the boy sexually abused the claimants' four children, and the claimants themselves both suffered psychiatric illness as a result of this.[8]

---

[1] Para 27.5.

[2] *Alcock v Chief Constable of the South Yorkshire Police* [1991] 4 All ER 907, HL; *Page v Smith* [1995] 2 All ER 736, HL; *White v Chief Constable of the South Yorkshire Police* [1999] 1 All ER 1, HL.

[3] *Walker v Northumberland County Council* [1995] 1 All ER 737.

[4] *McLoughlin v Jones* [2001] EWCA Civ 1743, [2002] QB 1312.

[5] *Farrell v Avon Health Authority* [2001] Lloyd's Rep Med 458.

[6] There is no liability for a defendant who, by injuring himself (or herself), causes psychiatric injury to a witness: *Greatorex v Greatorex* [2000] 4 All ER 769.

[7] [1991] 4 All ER 907, HL.

[8] *W v Essex CC* [2001] 2 AC 592, HL.

Duty of Care—Miscellaneous: Key Points

- Actions for negligence against public authorities raise special problems, additional to those which apply to negligence actions in general.

- A public authority cannot be liable in negligence for the way in which it exercises a statutory discretion.

- However, a public authority may be liable if it has assumed responsibility towards the claimant.

- Judges are immune from civil liability for anything they do in the course of a trial.
- A similar immunity applies to arbitrators and to other participants in the judicial process, such as jurors and witnesses.
- A barrister or other advocate owes a duty of care to the client, although a negligence action will not be permitted if it would amount to a collateral attack upon a previous court decision.
- Where a person suffers psychiatric injury as a result of negligence, the right to recover damages will depend upon whether that person is a 'primary' or a 'secondary' victim.
- A primary victim (one who is directly involved in the traumatic event) may recover damages if psychiatric or other injury was foreseeable.
- A secondary victim (such as a person traumatised by the injury or death of a loved one) must satisfy more stringent criteria in order to recover damages.

Questions

1. To what extent is the duty of care in negligence based upon foreseeability?

2. In what circumstances does A owe a duty of care towards B to protect B against either accidental harm or harm deliberately caused by another?

3. Why can a claimant not normally recover damages in the tort of negligence for pure economic loss?

4. How may the existence or scope of a duty of care be affected by the terms of a contract?

5. What is meant by a 'voluntary assumption of responsibility' in the context of liability for negligent statements?

6. In what circumstances will a person be deemed to have assumed responsibility for a statement?

7. What problems are there in bringing a successful action for negligence against a public authority?

8. To what extent may a losing litigant sue his or her barrister for the way in which the barrister fought the case?

9. What is the difference between a primary victim and a secondary victim, in the context of a claim for psychiatric injury?

10. Barry recently purchased, with the aid of a mortgage from a bank, a converted barn from its second owner. Soon after moving in, he discovered that part of the conversion work had left the roof of the property in a dangerous condition which would cost £100,000 to rectify. Advise Barry whether he can recover damages in negligence from the following parties:

    - the builder who carried out the relevant work;
    - the vendor's estate agent, whose sales particulars described the property as 'renovated to an exceptionally high standard';
    - the vendor's solicitor, who had erroneously informed Barry's solicitor that the work had been done in accordance with the Building Regulations;
    - the surveyor instructed by the bank to inspect and value the property for mortgage purposes.

17

Negligence—breach of duty

CHAPTER OVERVIEW

Assuming that a defendant owed a duty of care to the claimant, the next question is whether or not he (or she) has breached that duty. In this chapter we consider:

- the concept of the 'reasonable man', and the extent to which this allows for disabilities or age;
- the standards of skill and care which the law demands from members of established professions;
- the modern 'risk/benefit' approach which is often used to determine negligence;
- the way in which a breach of duty is proved, and the circumstances in which it may be presumed.

17.1 In deciding whether a defendant has breached a duty of care owed to the claimant, the test to be applied is whether the defendant acted reasonably in all the circumstances of the case. In legal theory, this standard of 'reasonableness' is a uniform one. However, in practice it is capable of great flexibility, so that subtle differences of fact between one case and another may lead the court to apparently conflicting conclusions. Moreover, since decisions on the issue of breach of duty are based on the facts, they are not of binding authority for the future. Thus, even though a car driver in one case is held to have been negligent in turning right without giving a signal, this does not mean that such conduct will automatically amount to negligence in another case.

As we shall see, the tort of negligence imposes an objective standard of conduct. What is required, in order to avoid liability, is not to do one's best but to do what is reasonable. At first glance, this may appear rather harsh, in that a defendant is sometimes held liable in circumstances where no moral blame attaches. However, it may be pointed out that a court which sympathised with such a defendant, to the extent of denying that there had been negligence, would in effect be condemning an equally innocent claimant to shoulder his (or her) own loss.

The reasonable man

17.2 A long-established approach to the question of whether a duty of care has been breached is to measure the conduct of the defendant against such hypothetical creatures as 'the reasonable man', 'the man in the street', 'the man of ordinary prudence' or, most famously, 'the man on the Clapham omnibus'. As Alderson B put it in *Blyth v Birmingham Waterworks Co:*[1] 'Negligence is the omission to do something which a reasonable man guided upon those considerations which ordinarily regulate the conduct of human affairs, would do, or doing something which a prudent and reasonable man would not do.'

In considering whether the defendant's conduct has reached the requisite standard, various attributes of the defendant will be taken into account, and these we consider below. Further, modern courts frequently evaluate a person's conduct by reference to the risk which it creates, and this we discuss under the heading of 'The principle of risk'.

> [1] (1856) 11 Exch 781 at 784.

The objective standard

17.3 As a general rule, no allowance is made in law for any lack of intelligence or emotional restraint on the part of a particular defendant. Indeed, both judges and academic writers have expressed the view that, in an appropriate case, liability in negligence may be imposed upon a person who is mentally incapable, notwithstanding the obvious personal inability of such a person to reach the standard of reasonableness. This is on the ground that to excuse such a defendant would be unfair to innocent victims of conduct which is 'unreasonable'. Similar reasoning has been used to justify liability where the defendant is merely inexperienced, rather than mentally incapable; it was held by the Court of Appeal in *Nettleship v Weston*[1] that a learner-driver is negligent if he or she does not achieve the standard of an ordinarily competent and experienced driver.

> [1] [1971] 3 All ER 581, CA.

Physical defects

17.4 Although a person's psychological make-up is irrelevant to liability in negligence, the courts are more prepared to make allowances in the case of a defendant who suffers from some recognisable physical impediment. For example, a person who is blind or who has only one leg will be judged by what may reasonably be expected from someone in that condition. However, a problem arises where a person has a disability but is unaware of it. In *Mansfield v Weetabix Ltd*[1] a lorry belonging to the defendants crashed into the claimant's shop and caused extensive damage. It appeared that the driver was suffering from a medical condition, of which he was unaware, which rendered him incapable of driving safely. The Court of Appeal, having found that the driver would not have continued to drive had he known the truth, held that he could not be regarded as negligent. However, if the driver had ignored clear symptoms of possible danger, the decision might well have been different.

> [1] [1998] 1 WLR 1263, CA.

Age

17.5 Children are very seldom sued in negligence, for the practical reason that in most cases they would be unable to pay any damages awarded against them. Nevertheless, the courts are not infrequently called upon to consider the reasonableness or otherwise of a child's conduct, when an injured child's claim is met with a defence of contributory negligence.[1] In *Morales v Eccleston*,[2] for example, where an 11-year-old boy ran into the road without looking and was struck by a negligently driven car, the boy was held 75% responsible for his own injuries. It is clear that, in making this assessment, a court must take the child's age into account. Thus in *Foskett v Mistry*,[3] a 16-year-old who ran into the road without looking was held 75% responsible, but the Court of Appeal made it clear that an adult would have been held entirely to blame. On the other hand, in *Gough v Thorne*,[4] a 13-year-old girl was held not negligent in relying entirely upon a signal from the driver of a stationary lorry and stepping out into the road past the lorry, without looking for vehicles overtaking it. An extreme example is *C v Imperial Design Ltd*,[5] where a child deliberately lit a fire with a container of flammable liquid, which the defendants had negligently left outside their factory. The Court of Appeal reduced the claimant's contribution from 75% to 50%, on the ground that, though well aware of the dangers of fire, he had not realised that the chemical might cause an explosion.

In the few cases in which negligence actions have been brought against children, it has been made clear that allowance should again be made for the age of the child concerned. In *Mullin v Richards*,[6] two 15-year-old schoolgirls were fencing with plastic rulers when one of the rulers snapped, causing a serious eye injury to one of the girls. The Court of Appeal held that, when age was properly taken into account, it could not be said that a reasonable 15-year-old ought to have foreseen the likelihood of injury from what was nothing more than a children's game. A similar decision was reached in *Blake v Galloway*[7] where, in the course of some high-spirited and good-natured horseplay, a piece of bark chipping thrown by a 15-year-old boy struck his friend in the eye. Other children have escaped liability when their games have caused injury to outsiders.[8]

Of course, even a child is expected to achieve certain standards. In *Watkins v Birmingham City Council*,[9] a 10-year-old boy, while distributing school milk to various classrooms, left his tricycle in a position where a teacher fell over it. This was held to constitute negligence, a finding which was not challenged in the Court of Appeal, where the decision was reversed on another ground.[10]

Although there is less authority than in respect of children, it seems that elderly people too are to be judged in the light of their age. In *Daly v Liverpool Corpn*,[11] where a collision occurred between the claimant, a 69-year-old pedestrian, and the defendants' bus, it was held that a charge of contributory negligence against the claimant must take her age into account.

[1] Paras 19.6–19.9.
[2] [1991] RTR 151, CA.
[3] [1984] RTR 1, CA.
[4] [1966] 3 All ER 398, CA.
[5] [2001] Env LR 33, CA.
[6] [1998] 1 All ER 920, CA.
[7] [2004] EWCA Civ 814, [2004] 3 All ER 315, CA.
[8] See *Etheridge v K* [1999] Ed CR 550 (13-year-old not negligent in throwing a basketball down school stairs during an informal game, resulting in injury to a teacher) and *Orchard v Lee* [2009] EWCA Civ 295, CA (13-year-old colliding with playground supervisor when playing tag).
[9] (1975) 126 NLJ 442.
[10] See para 26.5.
[11] [1939] 2 All ER 142.

Experience of others

17.6 In order to attain the standard which the law demands of the reasonable man, the defendant must make due allowance for those shortcomings of others which can be reasonably foreseen. Thus, for example, if it is foreseeable that blind persons will use a city pavement, anyone who excavates there must erect a barrier sufficient to protect them, and not merely one which is sufficient to safeguard those who can see it.[1] Similarly, the reasonable man may have to recognise that others do not always act reasonably, and must thus take such precautions against their negligence as experience shows to be necessary. There may even be extreme cases in which a defendant ought to foresee and guard against even the criminal misconduct of others, although, as we have seen,[2] the law is reluctant to impose a duty of care in such circumstances.

[1] *Haley v London Electricity Board* [1964] 3 All ER 185, HL.
[2] Paras 16.10–16.11.

Professional status

17.7 A person's status within a trade or profession may demand a higher standard of conduct than normal, in the sense of requiring that person to exhibit skill as well as care. As to the degree of skill which must be shown, this is whatever may be expected of a reasonably competent practitioner, rather than a leading specialist (although a defendant who claims to be a specialist will probably be judged accordingly[1]). In *Roe v Minister of Health*,[2] the claimant underwent minor surgery in 1947, during which he became partially paralysed as a result of being injected with a contaminated anaesthetic. The danger of such contamination was appreciated by very few doctors until about 1951, after which the profession in general took action to prevent it from happening again. In acquitting the hospital staff of negligence, Denning LJ pointed out that: 'We must not look at the 1947 accident with 1954 spectacles.'

A person who acts in accordance with the generally accepted practice of a profession is unlikely to be found negligent,[3] although there have been occasions on which a court has declared such common practice to be unreasonable.[4] Conversely, a practitioner who ignores the usual procedures runs an increased risk of being judged negligent,[5] although failure to adhere to a professional institution's guidance notes is not conclusive evidence of negligence.[6] What, then, of the case in which professional opinion is split? In *Bolam v Friern Hospital Management Committee*,[7] McNair J made it clear that it was not for the court to select one body of opinion as correct and to discount all others; the question was simply whether it could be said that no reasonably competent practitioner could possibly hold the view which the defendant preferred. This statement of principle was approved by the House of Lords in *Maynard v West Midlands Regional Health Authority*.[8] However, the House of Lords has since made it clear that evidence from expert witnesses as to what is sound professional practice should not be followed blindly; a judge must be satisfied that it has a logical basis.[9]

It should always be remembered that a professional person's duty is to be skilful and careful, not necessarily to be correct. Nevertheless, it is not true to say that an error of judgment cannot amount to negligence; the vital question is whether the error is one which a reasonably competent practitioner would not have made.[10]

In deciding whether or not a charge of professional negligence has been established, the courts rely heavily upon evidence from expert witnesses as to what might reasonably be expected of a competent member of the profession. Such expert witnesses should be drawn from the same profession as the defendant; thus a structural engineer is not qualified to give evidence as to what a building surveyor should have seen or done.[11] Expert witnesses are almost always called by the parties, although a court has a power to appoint its own expert.[12]

1 *Duchess of Argyll v Beuselinck* [1972] 2 Lloyd's Rep 172; cf *Wimpey Construction UK Ltd v Poole* (1984) 27 BLR 58.

2 [1954] 2 All ER 131, CA.

3 *Morton v William Dixon Ltd* 1909 SC 807 at 809; *Beaumont v Humberts* [1990] 2 EGLR 166, CA.

4 See, for example, *Edward Wong Finance Co v Johnson, Stokes and Master* [1984] AC 296, PC.

5 See, for example, *Clark v MacLennan* [1983] 1 All ER 416.

6 See *PK Finans International (UK) Ltd v Andrew Downs & Co Ltd* [1992] 1 EGLR 172.

7 [1957] 2 All ER 118.

8 [1985] 1 All ER 635, HL.

9 *Bolitho v City and Hackney Health Authority* [1997] 4 All ER 771, HL.

10 *Whitehouse v Jordan* [1981] 1 All ER 267, HL. See also para 17.9.

11 *Sansom v Metcalfe Hambleton & Co* [1998] 2 EGLR 103, CA.

12 Under what is now Part 35 of the Civil Procedure Rules: see *Abbey National Mortgages plc v Key Surveyors Nationwide Ltd* [1996] 2 EGLR 99, CA.

17.8 An obligation to display professional skill as well as reasonable care is imposed, not only upon those who are actually members of that profession, but also on those who attempt to take on work which requires professional skill.[1] Indeed, some jobs so obviously require an expert that a defendant who attempts to carry them out personally is almost bound to be regarded as negligent.[2] In *Freeman v Marshall & Co*,[3] the claimant complained of a survey carried out for him by the defendant, which failed to diagnose rising damp. The defendant argued that, since he was unqualified and had little knowledge of structures, he had done all that could be reasonably expected of him. It was held, however, that, by advertising himself as an estate agent, valuer and surveyor, and by undertaking a structural survey, he had laid claim to the necessary expertise and must be judged accordingly. Similarly, a prison authority which elects to treat a pregnant inmate in prison, rather than sending her to hospital, must achieve the standard of skill and care of a hospital.[4]

Many jobs may as reasonably be undertaken by semi-skilled or unskilled persons as by professionals. Where this is so, the courts will not necessarily judge the defendant by the standard of the most skilled person who might be expected to do the work. In *Philips v William Whiteley Ltd*,[5] for example, a jeweller pierced a woman's ears. The instruments used were disinfected, although not to the standard which a surgeon would be expected to achieve, and she developed an abscess. It was held that, since this operation was frequently performed by jewellers, the defendants fell to be judged by the standards of a reasonable jeweller, and not those of a reasonable surgeon. A similar decision was reached in the case of *Wells v Cooper*,[6] where a door handle fitted by the defendant householder, who was an amateur carpenter of some experience, came off, with the result that the claimant was injured. The Court of Appeal held that, since this was the sort of job which the reasonable householder might be expected to do personally, the defendant was to be judged by amateur, and not professional, standards.

Some doubt is thrown on the latitude given to defendants in these two cases by the later decision in *Nettleship v Weston*.[7] There the Court of Appeal, no doubt influenced by their awareness of compulsory third party insurance for motorists, held that the standard which a learner-driver must achieve is not that of a reasonable learner, but that of a reasonable experienced driver.

1 However, there is no concept of 'team negligence' under which all members of, say, a medical unit would be judged by the standard of the unit as a whole: *Wilsher v Essex Area Health Authority* [1986] 3 All ER 801, CA.

2 Eg lift maintenance: *Haseldine v C A Daw & Son Ltd* [1941] 3 All ER 156, CA.

3 (1966) 200 Estates Gazette 777.

4 *Brooks v Home Office* [1999] FLR 33.

[5] [1938] 1 All ER 566.
[6] [1958] 2 All ER 527, CA.
[7] [1971] 3 All ER 581, CA.

Valuers and surveyors

17.9 In dealing with allegations of negligence against valuers and surveyors, it must be emphasised that valuation is not an exact science, and that to be wrong is not necessarily to be negligent. Nevertheless, a sizeable error in a valuation will normally require some explanation and justification from the valuer who made it. Indeed, it was said in one case that a valuation which departs from the 'correct' figure (as found by the judge with the help of expert witnesses) by more than 10% or 15% brings into question the competence of the valuer and the sort of care given to the task of valuation.[1] However, it has subsequently been doubted whether a single 'correct' value really exists, and it has been suggested that a better approach is to ask whether the defendant's figure lies within the 'bracket' of values which competent practitioners might reasonably have arrived at for the property in question.[2]

Even assuming that a valuer has reached a wrong conclusion, in the sense described above, damages for negligence can only be recovered if it is established that the error was due to a lack of reasonable care and skill. This has been found in such matters as failure to keep up to date with the principles of law which affect the type of valuation in question,[3] and, where the complaint was of an under-valuation, the overlooking of a potential market.[4] As far as the actual valuation process is concerned, the courts are careful not to lay down restrictive rules, since it is appreciated that an experienced valuer may often operate intuitively. Hence, the absence of comparables or detailed calculations does not of itself indicate negligence.[5] On the other hand, a valuer who does not trouble to visit the site which is to be valued,[6] who clearly ignores the price at which the property has recently changed hands[7] or who (after only three months' experience, all of it limited to properties worth less than £33,000) nonchalantly values a house at £100,000 without seeking confirmation from a more experienced colleague,[8] is unlikely to attract the sympathy of a judge when it is alleged that there was a lack of reasonable care and skill.

In relation to surveys and other inspections of property, the crucial question is normally whether the survey was too superficial to reveal obvious defects in the property.[9] This naturally depends, to some extent at least, on the type of survey carried out, although it has been held that the standard of skill and care required in carrying out a House Buyers Report and Valuation is identical to that for a structural survey.[10] In the case of a mortgage valuation ('a walking inspection by someone with a knowledgeable eye, experienced in practice, who knows where to look'[11]), a surveyor is not expected to move furniture or to lift floor coverings; however, if a limited inspection reveals clear evidence of a defect, it is then the surveyor's duty to 'follow the trail'.[12]

[1] *Singer and Friedlander Ltd v John D Wood & Co* [1977] 2 EGLR 84.
[2] See *Mount Banking Corpn Ltd v Brian Cooper & Co* [1992] 2 EGLR 142.
[3] *Weedon v Hindwood, Clarke and Esplin* [1975] 1 EGLR 82.
[4] *Bell Hotels (1935) Ltd v Motion* (1952) 159 Estates Gazette 496.
[5] *Corisand Investments Ltd v Druce & Co* [1978] 2 EGLR 86.
[6] *Singer and Friedlander Ltd v John D Wood & Co* [1977] 2 EGLR 84.
[7] *Banque Bruxelles Lambert SA v Eagle Star* [1995] 2 All ER 769.
[8] *Kenney v Hall, Pain and Foster* [1976] 2 EGLR 29.
[9] As it was in *Philips v Ward* [1956] 1 All ER 874, CA.
[10] *Cross v David Martin and Mortimer* [1989] 1 EGLR 154.
[11] *Lloyd v Butler* [1990] 2 EGLR 155.
[12] *Roberts v J Hampson & Co* [1989] 2 All ER 504; *Sneesby v Goldings* [1995] 2 EGLR 102, CA.

The Reasonable Man: Key Points

- The 'reasonable man' principle is objective and ignores the personal characteristics of an individual.
- However, broad characteristics such as age or physical disabilities are taken into account.
- A member of a recognised trade or profession must exercise appropriate skill as well as reasonable care.
- A similar responsibility attaches to anyone holding themselves out as competent to perform professional work.

The principle of risk

17.10 As an alternative to considering what the hypothetical reasonable man would have done in a particular situation, a court may choose to assess the defendant's conduct by asking whether the risks which it creates are such as to outweigh any value it may have, and the cost or difficulty of rendering it safe. In conducting this balancing operation a court will take into account one or both of the following matters:

- the likelihood that the activity in question will cause injury or damage; and
- the seriousness of the injury that may result if the risk materialises.

Against these factors may be set:

- the value, social utility or other desirability of the activity; and
- the cost and practicability of taking steps to reduce or eliminate the danger.

Likelihood of injury

17.11 As Lord Dunedin remarked in *Fardon v Harcourt-Rivington*:[1] 'People must guard against reasonable probabilities, but they are not bound to guard against fantastic possibilities'. This means that a risk may be so remote that the reasonable man is quite justified in ignoring it altogether. Perhaps the most famous example of this is the case of *Bolton v Stone*,[2] where the claimant was injured by a cricket ball which a visiting batsman had struck more than 100 yards, clearing a high fence on the way. The evidence indicated that shots of this kind had occurred on the ground no more than six times in 28 years. The House of Lords held that, while the risk was clearly foreseeable, from the very fact that there had been such shots in the past, it was sufficiently remote that the defendants might reasonably ignore it.

[1] (1932) 146 LT 391 at 392.
[2] [1951] 1 All ER 1078, HL.

Seriousness of consequences

17.12 Quite apart from the probability or improbability that a particular type of accident will occur, a court assessing a defendant's conduct may justifiably consider the gravity of the potential consequences. This principle was laid down by the House of Lords in *Paris v*

Stepney Borough Council,[1] where a one-eyed garage hand was struck in his remaining eye by a metal chip and became completely blind. It was not the practice of the employers to supply their workmen with safety spectacles, since they regarded the risk of eye injury as extremely remote. The House of Lords held that, although this approach was justifiable in relation to the other employees, special precautions should have been taken in the claimant's case, since he had so much more to lose.

[1] [1951] 1 All ER 42, HL.

Value of conduct

17.13 The number of accidents which occur every day could be drastically reduced if certain steps were taken. To take a simple example, it is obvious that road accidents would be far less likely to happen if everyone drove at no more than 10 mph. However, this does not mean that exceeding that speed is automatically negligent; most people would regard the increased risk as justified, in view of the enormous inconvenience which would be caused to the general public if all traffic were to move at a snail's pace.

The principle that important ends may be held to justify risky means was invoked in *Daborn v Bath Tramways Motor Co Ltd*,[1] where it was held that the use of a left-hand drive vehicle as an ambulance in wartime was reasonable in view of the shortage of suitable transport, notwithstanding the dangers which it created to other road users when turning right without giving any signal. In *Watt v Hertfordshire County Council*,[2] a heavy jack, which was needed to rescue a woman trapped under a bus, was carried on a lorry not suited to the purpose. During the journey the jack shifted, injuring the claimant, a fireman. The Court of Appeal held that the fire brigade's decision to use this unsuitable vehicle was a reasonable one, having regard to the emergency.

In *Tomlinson v Congleton BC*,[3] the House of Lords was emphatic in its view that local authorities should not be forced to close valuable public amenities from a fear of being held liable in negligence to persons using those amenities in a reckless and risky way. A wider version of this view has now been given statutory form: a court considering a claim in negligence may have regard to whether the imposition of liability might prevent a desirable activity from taking place or discourage persons (such as volunteers) from being involved in a desirable activity.[4]

[1] [1946] 2 All ER 333, CA.
[2] [1954] 2 All ER 368, CA.
[3] [2003] UKHL 47, HL: see para 21.22.
[4] Compensation Act 2006, s 1.

Cost of precautions

17.14 In deciding whether a defendant has dealt adequately with a particular risk, the courts will have regard to the ease with which that risk could have been reduced or eliminated. This is not simply a matter of money, although financial considerations are undoubtedly of importance; it also covers questions of convenience and practicability. In extreme cases, where the risk is a very serious one, it may be that the only course of action open to the reasonable man is to cease altogether the dangerous activity, although the courts are reluctant to impose such a heavy burden.[1] In *Withers v Perry Chain Co Ltd*,[2] for example, a woman who was susceptible to dermatitis (a skin complaint caused by contact with grease) was given the driest work which her employers had available; nevertheless, she again contracted the disease. Her argument that the defendants should have dismissed her for her own protection was rejected by the Court of Appeal, who held that such a drastic step could not possibly be justified by the relatively minor risk to which she was exposed.

At the other end of the scale, a person may be held liable for failing to eliminate even a small risk, if this could easily have been done. As Lord Reid put it:[3] 'It does not follow that, no matter what the circumstances may be, it is justifiable to neglect a risk of such a small magnitude. A reasonable man ... would not neglect such a risk if action to eliminate it presented no difficulty, involved no disadvantage, and required no expense.'

By and large, the objective standard of reasonable care applies to questions of cost and inconvenience as it does to other factors in the assessment of negligence. Thus, once a court decides that a reasonable man would have taken certain precautions (ie that they were not too costly in relation to the risk) a defendant who did not do so is liable, even if he or she personally could not afford them. However, a degree of subjectivity has been introduced for the benefit of an occupier upon whose land a danger arises through natural causes (and for which he naturally cannot be blamed). Where this happens, it has been held that the occupier may avoid liability to a neighbour by establishing that the actions necessary to eliminate the danger would have been beyond his or her personal means.[4]

[1] See *Bolton v Stone* [1951] 1 All ER 1078, HL; para 17.11.
[2] [1961] 3 All ER 676, CA.
[3] *The Wagon Mound (No 2)* [1966] 2 All ER 709 at 718.
[4] *Goldman v Hargrave* [1966] 2 All ER 989: para 24.16.

RISK AND BENEFIT: KEY POINTS

- A defendant's conduct may be judged by balancing the risks which it creates against any benefit which it produces, and against the cost of averting the risk.

- The 'size' of a risk depends on both the likelihood of its occurrence and the seriousness of the potential consequences.

- The creation of a risk may be justified by the social benefit provided by the activity concerned.

- The 'cost' of averting a risk is not merely a matter of finance.

The proof of negligence

17.15 The burden of proof in negligence actions, as in civil cases generally, lies on the claimant. This means that it is for the claimant to bring evidence which establishes on the balance of probabilities that the defendant has been careless. If the claimant cannot do this, the case will fail.

In seeking to establish negligence, a claimant may be able to rely on the Civil Evidence Act 1968, s 11 which provides that a criminal conviction for an offence which involves negligence (eg driving without due care and attention) is to be regarded in subsequent civil proceedings as sufficient evidence of negligence. This means that, in subsequent civil proceedings, the defendant's negligence will be presumed, although it is still open to the defendant to rebut this presumption.

Res ipsa loquitur

17.16 In many negligence actions, the claimant will have to rely on circumstantial evidence, since the full details of the accident will be known only to the defendant. In such circumstances, the claimant may gain assistance from the maxim *res ipsa loquitur*, meaning 'the thing speaks for itself'. The operation of this maxim is illustrated by the leading case of *Scott v London and St Katherine Docks Co*,[1] in which the claimant, who was walking past the defendant's warehouse, was injured when six bags of sugar fell on him. Neither party could offer any explanation of this occurrence, and the trial judge held that there was not enough evidence to allow the case to go to the jury. However, on appeal, this decision was held to be incorrect, and the following principle was laid down by Erle CJ:

> 'There must be reasonable evidence of negligence. But where the thing is shown to be under the management of the defendant or his servants, and the accident is such as in the ordinary course of things does not happen if those who have the management use proper care, it affords reasonable evidence, in the absence of explanation by the defendants, that the accident arose from want of care.'

It is clear, then, that for *res ipsa loquitur* to apply, it must be shown that:

- the thing which did the damage was under the management and control of the defendant or someone for whom the defendant was responsible; and
- the occurrence was such as would ordinarily indicate negligence.

[1] (1865) 3 H & C 596.

Control by the defendant

17.17 The mere fact that an unauthorised person *could* have tampered with the thing which causes injury to the claimant will not preclude reliance on *res ipsa loquitur*, provided that such intervention is improbable. Thus, where a railway passenger fell from a moving train immediately after leaving the station, it was held that the carriage doors could be regarded as under the control of the railway company.[1] However, the opposite conclusion was reached in the case of a child falling from the corridor of a train which had travelled a considerable distance since its last stop.[2]

[1] *Gee v Metropolitan Rly Co* (1873) LR 8 QB 161.
[2] *Easson v London North Eastern Rly Co* [1944] 2 All ER 425, CA.

Inference of negligence

17.18 The facts from which an inference of negligence may be drawn are extremely varied. Apart from the obvious case of objects falling from the upper floors of buildings,[1] the doctrine has been invoked in cases of railway collisions,[2] an aircraft which crashed on taking off,[3] the sudden and violent skid of a motor vehicle[4] and a stone in a bun.[5] In *Ward v Tesco Stores Ltd*,[6] where a supermarket customer slipped on some yoghurt which had been spilled on the floor, a majority of the Court of Appeal reached the somewhat doubtful conclusion that, in the absence of further evidence as to how the yoghurt came to be on the floor, its presence there could be attributed to negligence on the part of the defendants.

In practical terms, *res ipsa loquitur* is of most benefit to a claimant who is injured by a process the details of which he (or she) does not understand, or who cannot show which of the defendant's employees has been guilty of negligence. Common cases include consumers injured by defective products[7] and patients whose condition is rendered worse rather than better by the medical treatment which they receive, as in *Cassidy v Ministry of Health,*[8] where hospital treatment of the claimant's two stiff fingers left him with four stiff fingers.

[1] *Scott v London and St Katherine Docks Co* (1865) 3 H & C 596; para 17.16.

[2] *Skinner v London, Brighton and South Coast Rly Co* (1850) 5 Exch 787.

[3] *Fosbroke-Hobbes v Airwork Ltd and British American Air Services Ltd* [1937] 1 All ER 108.

[4] *Richley v Faull* [1965] 3 All ER 109.

[5] *Chaproniere v Mason* (1905) 21 TLR 633.

[6] [1976] 1 All ER 219, CA.

[7] Such victims may now hold the manufacturer strictly liable under the Consumer Protection Act 1987.

[8] [1951] 1 All ER 574, CA. Also see *Saunders v Leeds Western Health Authority* [1993] 4 Med LR 355 (*res ipsa loquitur* where heart of fit child stopped under anaesthetic).

PROOF OF NEGLIGENCE: KEY POINTS

- Where the precise cause of an accident is unknown, the facts may speak for themselves.

- For this to apply the situation must be under the defendant's control and the accident must be such as would not normally occur without negligence.

Questions

1. To what extent does the concept of the 'reasonable man' create an objective standard of care?

2. In what circumstances can a child be held guilty of negligence?

3. How is 'professional negligence' different from other negligence?

4. How can negligence be proved in an action against a valuer?

5. To what extent is negligence based upon the idea of 'risk-benefit analysis'?

6. In what circumstances may a claimant successfully assert that 'the facts speak for themselves'?

7. Following a head injury suffered while playing football, Duncan from time to time experiences severe headaches; moreover, he has on several occasions fainted in moments of extreme stress. One day, while driving his car past a school, Duncan sees Kylie, a 6-year-old girl, run into the road in front of him. Duncan swerves to avoid her, but blacks out momentarily and runs over Jason, who is standing on the pavement at the far side of the road. Kylie had just been collected from school by her mother, Debbie who, seeing another child in danger from a reversing car, had left Kylie unattended to run to the rescue.

   Advise Jason as to his rights, if any, against any other party.

18

Negligence—the causing of damage

CHAPTER OVERVIEW

A defendant who has committed a breach of a legal duty of care will be liable to the claimant, but only for those losses which have been caused by the breach and which are not too remote as consequences.

In this chapter we consider:

- the way in which the law seeks to decide whether or not a defendant's breach of duty has 'caused' the claimant's loss;

- the situations in which the 'chain of causation' is broken, either by the claimant himself or by a third party;

- the legal rules which govern 'remoteness of damage', that is, the range of consequences for which a defendant can be held responsible.

18.1 The mere fact that a defendant acts carelessly towards a claimant is not enough to render the defendant liable in tort. If a claim is to succeed, the claimant must be shown to have suffered damage of a kind which is actionable in the tort in question. In negligence, for example, a claim can only be based on personal injury, damage to property or (in certain circumstances) pure financial loss.

It was held by the House of Lords in *South Australia Asset Management Corpn v York Montague Ltd*[1] that, in order to recover damages, a claimant must show that the loss falls within the scope of the defendant's duty. Thus, where a valuer is commissioned to provide a valuation of property, on the basis of which the claimant will decide how much to lend, the valuer's duty is merely to take reasonable care to provide accurate information. If the valuer is negligent and thus inaccurate, there will be liability for the consequences of the information being wrong, but not for losses which the lender would have suffered in any event, even if the property had been worth as much as the valuer said (for example because there has been a sharp fall in property values generally).

In addition to proving that damage has been suffered, the claimant must show that the damage was caused by the defendant's breach of duty. In this connection it must be appreciated that 'causation' in legal terms has a rather more restricted meaning than that given to it in a purely factual sense. A court's concern is not to identify all the causes of an accident, but merely to consider whether any or all of a small number of identified conditions (normally the acts or omissions of the parties to a lawsuit) may be regarded as sufficiently important to rank as *legal* causes and thus to attract responsibility. This task, clearly, is one of selection in which the judge, aided by common sense and human experience, arrives at what in the end is a value judgement.

[1] [1996] 3 All ER 365, HL.

18.2 Causation in the legal sense is really two problems in one. In the first place, there must be an inquiry into whether the conduct of the defendant can be regarded as a cause of loss; if it cannot be so regarded, there can surely be no justification for holding the defendant liable for the claimant's misfortune. Second, assuming that the first question receives an affirmative answer, the law must decide whether the defendant's conduct and the claimant's damage are sufficiently closely connected that liability *ought* to be imposed.

Where a court concludes that a particular consequence of the defendant's breach of duty is not sufficiently connected to it to found liability, it may express this by stating that the conduct is not a legal cause or, more commonly, that the item of damage is too remote.

Causation in fact

The 'but for' test

18.3 In order to establish whether or not the defendant's act was a factual cause of the claimant's injury, a court will normally apply the 'but for' test. According to this test (which, as we show later, is subject to some important exceptions), the question to be asked is whether the damage would have happened but for the defendant's breach of duty. If the answer is that it would not, then that breach may be said, at least in a factual sense, to have been a cause of it.[1] If, however, it would have happened anyway, then the defendant's breach is not a cause.

The operation of the 'but for' test is strikingly shown by the case of *McWilliams v Sir William Arrol & Co Ltd*,[2] in which a steel erector fell to his death from a tower on which he was working. His employers had failed in their statutory obligation to provide him with a safety belt. Nevertheless, they defeated an action by the steel erector's widow by producing overwhelming evidence that, even if a belt had been provided, the deceased would not have worn it and would therefore in any event have fallen. Similarly, in *Barnett v Chelsea and Kensington Hospital Management Committee*,[3] a casualty doctor's negligent refusal to examine a poisoned night-watchman was held not to be a cause of his death, since the evidence established that accurate diagnosis would have been too late to save him.

It must be emphasised that the 'but for' test is essentially exclusive in nature. A cause which does not satisfy this requirement cannot be a legal cause; one which does satisfy it may be treated as legally operative, but only if a court regards it as sufficiently important. In *Rouse v Squires*,[4] for example, a negligently driven lorry jack-knifed and blocked two lanes of a motorway. In trying to avoid it, a second lorry, also negligently driven, skidded and killed a bystander. The accident would obviously not have happened but for the presence of both lorries, and the Court of Appeal held that both drivers were liable.[5] In *Dymond v Pearce*,[6] by contrast, where a motorcyclist injured his pillion passenger by negligently driving into a parked lorry, it was held that the lorry's presence, although again a necessary condition for the accident, was not a legal cause of it; responsibility here was attributed solely to the motorcyclist.

[1] Note that the defendant is in no way excused merely because other factors were also necessary.

Proof of causation

18.4 In matters of causation, as in all other elements of liability, it is for the claimant to prove the case on the balance of probabilities. In certain circumstances it may be enough to show that the defendant's breach of duty materially contributed to the claimant's damage, without proving that it was the only or even the main cause of it. This was accepted by the House of Lords in *Bonnington Castings Ltd v Wardlaw*,[1] where the claimant contracted pneumoconiosis from inhaling silica dust at work. This dust came from two sources, only one of which was due to a breach of duty by the employers, and there was no evidence as to the relative proportions. The claimant could not therefore prove that, but for the employers' breach, he would not have contracted the disease at all. Despite this, it was held that the employers, having made a material contribution to the disease, were liable.

The principle adopted in *Bonnington Castings v Wardlaw* was extended by the House of Lords in *McGhee v National Coal Board*,[2] where the claimant's job exposed him to abrasive brick dust. The claimant contracted dermatitis and claimed that this was due to the defendants' failure to provide washing facilities on site, as a result of which he had to cycle home each day still caked with dust and sweat. It was held that, although a positive connection could not be established between the defendants' failure and the claimant's injury (since his exposure to the brick dust might have been enough to cause dermatitis even if washing facilities had been provided), it was sufficient to impose liability upon the defendants that they had materially increased the risk.

The reasoning adopted in *McGhee* has been used to uphold a claim by an employee who suffered from vibration white finger, following negligent exposure by his employers to excessive levels of vibration from power tools.[3] However, where a case arises out of a single accident, as where a claimant is injured in slipping on the surround of a swimming pool, the defendant cannot be made liable merely by showing that the risk of slipping was increased by failure to use non-slip paint.[4]

The *McGhee* principle was severely criticised in *Wilsher v Essex Area Health Authority*,[5] where the House of Lords refused to apply it to a case where the defendants' medical negligence was only one of six possible causes of a premature baby's blindness. However, it was restored to favour by the House of Lords in *Fairchild v Glenhaven Funeral Services Ltd*,[6] where an employee had contracted mesothelioma (a form of cancer) through negligent exposure to asbestos fibres at work. The employee had worked for, and been exposed to, asbestos fibres by more than one employer, and it was impossible to say which exposure had caused the onset of the disease. The House of Lords, applying *McGhee*, ruled that any of the employers who had materially increased the risk could be made liable; to hold otherwise would be deeply offensive to notions of justice, since a claimant who could show that one employer was guilty, but not which one, would lose against all of them.

In both *Bonnington* and *Fairchild*, it was assumed that any defendant found guilty could be made liable for the claimant's entire loss, leaving it to the defendants to arrange contribution among themselves.[7] However, in *Barker v Corus (UK) Ltd*,[8] the House of Lords held that, wherever possible, defendants should only be held responsible for their fair share of the overall loss. Thus, where a claimant contracted mesothelioma (a form of cancer) following negligent exposure to asbestos fibres by more than one employer, the House of Lords suggested that liability should be apportioned on the basis of the length of time for which each employer was responsible. This ruling, though perfectly logical, provoked such an outcry that it was swiftly reversed by s 3 of the Compensation Act 2006. However, it is important to note that this statutory provision applies only in cases mesothelioma; the principle laid down by the House of Lords remains applicable in all other cases.

1 [1956] 1 All ER 615, HL.
2 [1972] 3 All ER 1008, HL. See also *Fitzgerald v Lane* [1987] Qb 781, CA.
3 *Brown v Corus (UK) Ltd* [2004] EWCA Civ 374, CA.
4 *Clough v First Choice Holidays & Flights Ltd* [2006] EWCA Civ 15, CA.
5 [1988] 1 All ER 871, HL.
6 [2002] UKHL 22, [2002] 3 All ER 305.
7 Under the Civil Liability (Contribution) Act 1978; para 27.15.
8 [2006] UKHL 20, HL.

Loss of a chance

18.5 In *Hotson v East Berkshire Health Authority*,[1] the claimant, who had been injured in a fall, claimed that the defendants' negligent failure to make a correct diagnosis of his injuries had allowed a more serious medical condition to develop. The evidence established that, when the claimant was first examined by the defendants, there was already a 75% likelihood that this condition would develop. The trial judge and the Court of Appeal awarded the claimant 25% of the damages claimed, on the basis that the defendants' negligence had turned a 75% risk into an inevitability. However, this approach was rejected by the House of Lords, which ruled that the claimant in these circumstances could only recover by showing that the defendants were responsible for his medical condition, something which, on the balance of probabilities, he was clearly unable to do. Similar reasoning was adopted, but this time only by a bare majority of the House of Lords, in *Gregg v Scott*,[2] where a doctor's negligence meant that the claimant's chance that his cancer could be successfully treated was reduced from 42% to 25%.

It should not be thought, on the basis of this decision, that damages can never be awarded for loss of a chance. In particular, such an award appears possible in cases where the claimant's loss depends on the hypothetical action of some third party. This was accepted by the Court of Appeal in *Allied Maples Group Ltd v Simmons & Simmons*.[3] The claimant company entered into a contract to purchase certain business property on the basis of advice from its solicitors, the defendants. The advice was negligent and, as a result, the claimants incurred liabilities. The claimants alleged that, had they been given the correct advice, they would have taken steps to protect themselves against these liabilities, but the defendants pointed out that the success of those steps would have depended upon negotiations with a third party. The Court of Appeal held that, once the claimants had proved that they would have taken the necessary steps, it was not necessary for them also to prove on the balance of probabilities that the negotiations with the third party would have succeeded; they were entitled to damages based on the chance that this would have been so.

1 [1987] 2 All ER 909, HL.
2 [2005] UKHL 2, HL.
3 [1995] 4 All ER 907, CA.

Multiple causes

18.6 Where damage is the result of more than one cause, the 'but for' test becomes an inadequate tool. Suppose, for example, that two independent fires, negligently lit by A and B, together destroy C's house. To allow each defendant to evade liability, by arguing that the house would in any event have been destroyed by the other fire, would be intolerable, and the law does not allow it: both A and B would be liable in full. However, this does not mean that the claimant can recover double damages. He may take his compensation as he chooses (all from one defendant, or some from each) and, once he has done so, the defendants may seek contribution from each other in proportions assessed by the court.[1]

A slightly different problem arises where the same injuries, or injuries which overlap each other, are 'caused' on separate occasions. The rule here is that the first cause in time is treated as the legally operative one, to the exclusion of all others. This may be illustrated by *Performance Cars Ltd v Abraham*,[2] where the defendant damaged the claimants' car in such a way that it required a repaint. In fact, however, as the result of a previous accident, the car already required a repaint, and it was accordingly held that the defendant could not be said to have caused this item of damage.

The principle of this case is that the second tortfeasor takes his victim as he finds him (ie in a damaged state). The effect which this has upon the liability of the first tortfeasor was considered in the important case of *Baker v Willoughby*,[3] in which the defendant was responsible for negligently injuring the claimant's leg and thereby reducing his earning capacity. Some time later, but before the case came to trial, the claimant was shot by robbers and his injured leg had to be amputated. The question was whether the defendant's liability for loss of earnings ceased at the time of the amputation. The Court of Appeal held that it did, on the ground that the second injury effectively 'swallowed up' the first. The House of Lords, however, pointed out that since the robbers, if sued, would be liable only for depriving the claimant of an already damaged leg, this solution would leave him out of pocket. It was accordingly held that, in assessing the defendant's liability, the second injury was to be ignored.

It should be noted that the approach adopted in *Baker v Willoughby* does not apply where the other cause of injury is natural, rather than tortious. In *Jobling v Associated Dairies Ltd*,[4] it was held that a claimant's damages for loss of earnings should only compensate him up to the date on which an earlier injury would in any case have rendered him totally disabled. The House of Lords there pointed out that any other result would over-compensate the claimant, and suggested that the *Baker v Willoughby* approach can only be justified by the need to prevent the claimant from falling between two tortfeasors, in the sense of being unable to obtain compensation from either of them.

[1] Paras 27.14–27.15.
[2] [1961] 3 All ER 413, CA.
[3] [1969] 3 All ER 1528, HL.
[4] [1981] 2 All ER 752, HL.

CAUSATION IN FACT: KEY POINTS

- In normal circumstances, proof of causation requires satisfaction of the 'but for' test.

- However, in exceptional circumstances it may be enough to show that the defendant's negligence made a material contribution to the risk.

- Where causation of actual loss cannot be established on the balance of probabilities, a defendant may nevertheless be liable for depriving the claimant of the chance of avoiding that loss.

- Special problems arise where there are multiple causes of the same loss.

Intervening causes

18.7 Where the injury or damage to the claimant is separated from the defendant's wrongful act by the act of another person (either the claimant or a third party), a court must decide whether the intervening act, whether by a third party or by the claimant himself, is sufficient to 'break the chain of causation' and thus to free the defendant from liability. This decision in truth requires a value judgement as to whether, in spite of the intervening conduct, total or partial responsibility should still attach to the defendant. A good example of this evaluation process is the case of *Wright v Lodge*,[1] in which a lorry, travelling at an excessive speed on a foggy night, crashed into a car which had broken down and was stationary on a dual carriageway road. The lorry then veered out of control on to the opposite carriageway and caused a fatal accident. The Court of Appeal held that, although the negligence of the car driver in failing to push her car off the road was a partial (10%) cause of the original collision, it was not a cause of the subsequent accident, for which the lorry driver was wholly responsible.

We now examine a number of examples of intervening acts.

[1] [1993] 4 All ER 299, CA.

Conduct of a third party

'Innocent' conduct

18.8 The chain of causation will seldom, if ever, be held to have been broken by the act of a third party who, for one reason or another, cannot be regarded as fully responsible for his or her actions. Where, for example, the defendant's negligence consists of leaving a horse untethered in the street, it is no defence to show that it was stampeded by mischievous children.[1] Similarly, the unthinking action of a person in an emergency will not be regarded as the conscious act of another volition. In *Scott v Shepherd*,[2] the defendant threw a lighted squib in a crowded market. Two people in turn, seeking to protect themselves and their goods, picked up the squib and threw it away; it finally exploded in the claimant's eye. The defendant was held liable.

The emergency principle can on occasion be extended beyond the instinctive reactions of an endangered person to cover also reasonable, albeit mistaken, decisions. In *The Oropesa*,[3] one of the many maritime collision cases to have raised this point, the master of a badly damaged ship launched a boat in heavy seas towards the *Oropesa*, which had been responsible for the collision, in order to discuss salvage. The boat overturned and a seaman was drowned. It was held that the seaman's death could be attributed to the negligence of the *Oropesa*; the decision of the other ship's master, made when under severe pressure, could not be said to break the chain of causation.

It should not be thought from what has been said above that a decision taken in an emergency can never be challenged on the ground of negligence. In *Knightley v Johns*,[4] a police inspector, who was in control following an accident in a one-way road tunnel, ordered a police motorcyclist to ride through the tunnel against the traffic flow, in order to stop cars from entering the tunnel. When the motorcyclist was struck by a car and injured, it was held by the Court of Appeal that the inspector's order was negligent; moreover, this broke the chain of causation between the injury to the claimant and the negligence of the motorist who had caused the original accident.

[1] *Haynes v Harwood* [1935] 1 KB 146, CA.
[2] (1773) 2 Wm Bl 892.
[3] [1943] 1 All ER 211, CA.
[4] [1982] 1 All ER 851, CA.

'Guilty' conduct

18.9 As shown by *Knightley v Johns*,[1] the negligent act of a third party may be sufficient to exempt the defendant from liability. This was also the case in *Baxall Securities Ltd v Sheard Walshaw Partnership*,[2] where the negligent failure of surveyors to discover an obvious defect in roof guttering broke the chain of causation from the negligence of the architects who designed it. However, it must be emphasised that such decisions represent judicial value judgements, and it cannot be assumed that this will always be the case. In *Prendergast v Sam and Dee*,[3] for example, where a doctor's bad handwriting led a pharmacist negligently to dispense the wrong drug, both the doctor and the pharmacist were held liable in negligence to the claimant. Generally speaking, where A's negligence causes B to require medical treatment, A will be liable, not only for the initial injury, but also for any further injury which results from that treatment.[4] This applies even where the medical treatment is itself negligent, so long as it is not wholly inappropriate.[5]

A negligent intervention by a third party may or may not break the chain of causation, but it might be thought that any deliberate, conscious act by a person of full capacity, in circumstances where there is no emergency, would always do so. However, even here the courts have occasionally been prepared to trace liability back to the defendant. In *Philco Radio Ltd v J Spurling Ltd*,[6] the defendants negligently misdelivered cases of highly inflammable material to the claimants' premises. A typist employed by the claimants (intending to do minor damage, although unaware of the true contents) touched a case with a lighted cigarette and a serious explosion and fire resulted. The defendants were held liable, notwithstanding the typist's act. Indeed, in extreme cases it has been held that even a deliberate criminal act may not break the chain of causation. This is shown by *Stansbie v Troman*,[7] where a decorator, who was working alone in the claimant's house, left it unlocked and unoccupied for two hours. He was held liable for a theft of jewellery which occurred during his absence.

[1] [1982] 1 All ER 851, CA; para 18.8.
[2] [2002] EWCA Civ 09, [2002] BLR 100.
[3] [1989] 1 Med LR 36, CA.
[4] *Robinson v Post Office* [1974] 2 All ER 737, CA.
[5] *Rahman v Arearose Ltd* [2001] QB 351, CA; *Webb v Barclays Bank plc and Portsmouth Hospitals NHS Trust* [2001] Lloyd's Rep Med 500, CA.
[6] [1949] 2 All ER 882, CA.
[7] [1948] 1 All ER 599, CA.

Conduct of the claimant

18.10 Principles similar to those which govern the conduct of a third party may also apply to an intervening act of the claimant, which may be held by the court to be so unreasonable that the effect of the defendant's original wrongdoing is entirely wiped out. In *McKew v Holland and Hannen and Cubitts (Scotland) Ltd*,[1] for example, an accident for which the defendants were responsible left the claimant's leg with a tendency to collapse suddenly and without warning. When, a few days later, knowing of this tendency, the claimant attempted to descend a steep staircase without assistance, it was held that he was entirely to blame for his resulting fall.

Decisions on the effect of a claimant's conduct in such cases are frequently made on the basis of contributory negligence,[2] so as to give more flexibility. Using this approach, a court can hold that the claimant's conduct, while not so outrageous as to exonerate the defendant entirely, is nevertheless a sufficiently significant cause of injury that the claimant should, by suffering a reduction in the damages awarded, be made to bear a proportion of the loss.[3]

In a number of situations, it can safely be said that the claimant's conduct will not affect causation, nor indeed amount to contributory negligence; these are considered below.

1 [1969] 3 All ER 1621, HL.
2 Paras 19.6–19.9.
3 See, for example, *Spencer v Wincanton Holdings Ltd* [2009] EWCA Civ 1404, CA.

Rescue cases

18.11 The act of a person who knowingly courts danger in attempting to rescue persons or even property[1] will not normally break the chain of causation. In *Haynes v Harwood*,[2] for example, the owner of a runaway horse was held liable to a policeman, who was injured in attempting to stop it in a crowded street. However, where the rescue attempt is unreasonable, for example because the danger outweighs the value of what is threatened, the chain of causation may be broken. In *Cutler v United Dairies (London) Ltd*,[3] the claimant was injured in helping the driver of a milk float whose runaway horse had come to rest safely in a field. The Court of Appeal held that, since the danger was over at the time of the claimant's intervention, he must be regarded as having caused his own injury. In one case a rescuer was held to be a partial cause of his own injury and thus to be guilty of contributory negligence,[4] although this related to the manner in which he went about the rescue rather than his initial decision to attempt it.[5]

1 *Hyett v Great Western Rly Co* [1947] 2 All ER 264, CA.
2 [1935] 1 KB 146, CA.
3 [1933] 2 KB 297, CA.
4 Paras 19.6–19.9.
5 *Harrison v British Railways Board* [1981] 3 All ER 679.

Emergencies

18.12 Like third parties, whom we discussed in para 18.8, claimants who are faced with an emergency are given considerable latitude by the courts, in the sense that an instinctive decision, albeit one which turns out to be wrong, will not break the chain of causation unless it is totally unreasonable. In *Jones v Boyce*,[1] the defendant's negligence led the claimant to believe that his stagecoach, in which the claimant was a passenger, was about to overturn. The coach did not in fact overturn but the claimant, in jumping to safety, broke his leg. The defendant was held liable.

1 (1816) 1 Stark 493. See also *Colvilles Ltd v Devine* [1969] 2 All ER 53, HL.

Legal rights

18.13 The generous treatment which is given by the courts to claimants in an emergency is also reflected in their attitude towards those who act in defence of their legal rights, where these are infringed by the defendant. In *Clayards v Dethick and Davis*,[1] for example, the defendant unlawfully dug a trench in such a way that the sole access to the claimant's stables became dangerous. When a horse which the claimant attempted to lead out was injured, the defendant was held liable; it could not be said that the claimant had caused his own loss, since this was a risk which he was perfectly entitled to take in exercising his right of way.

In the celebrated case of *Sayers v Harlow UDC*,[2] the Court of Appeal reached a compromise solution. The claimant there was trapped in a public toilet by the negligence of the defendant local authority, who were responsible for the fact that there was no handle on the inside of the toilet door. In trying to climb out in order to catch a bus, the claimant fell and was injured. It was held that, since the claimant's predicament was one of inconvenience rather than danger, her attempt to escape was unreasonable; she should, it was held, have endured her loss of liberty rather than run this risk. Nonetheless, her negligence could not be said to have wiped out altogether the effects of the defendants' negligence, and so the claimant was held to be 25% responsible for her injuries.

¹ (1848) 12 Qb 439.
² [1958] 2 All ER 342, CA.

INTERVENING CAUSES: KEY POINTS

- The 'chain of causation' between the defendant's act and the claimant's damage may on occasion be broken by the deliberate or negligent intervention of a third party.

- The chain of causation may also be broken by an act of the claimant, but this in unlikely where the claimant is attempting a rescue, acting in an emergency or seeking to exercise a legal right.

Remoteness of damage

18.14 Even where it can be shown that the defendant's breach of duty is a factual cause of the claimant's injury, and that the chain of causation has not been broken by an intervening cause, it is still not certain that the defendant will be held responsible for a particular consequence. In attempting to keep liability for a single act of negligence within bounds, the law regards certain consequences as too 'remote' from the original tort to found an action.¹ It was laid down by the Privy Council in *Overseas Tankship (UK) v Morts Dock and Engineering Co (The Wagon Mound)*² that a defendant will only be liable for those consequences of negligence which were reasonably foreseeable.

¹ The same principle applies to actions for breach of contract, although the detailed rules are different; paras 11.14–11.20.
² [1961] 1 All ER 404, PC.

The 'foreseeability' test

18.15 The facts of *The Wagon Mound*¹ were that the defendants negligently spilled large quantities of fuel oil into Sydney Harbour while their ship was being bunkered. Wind and tide carried this oil to the claimants' wharf, where two ships were being repaired by means of oxy-acetylene welding. The claimants ceased welding because of the fire risk but, on being assured by experts that fuel oil spread thus thinly on cool water would not ignite, recommended; as a result a catastrophic fire badly damaged both the wharf and the ships. The Australian courts held that, since some damage to the claimants' wharf (fouling of the slipways) was foreseeable, the defendants were also liable for the damage done by fire, notwithstanding that this was unforeseeable. However, on appeal, the Privy Council held that foreseeability must embrace, not only the fact of injury, but also its kind; therefore, in this case, the defendants were not liable for the damage done by fire, since it was unforeseeable.

In *Overseas Tankship (UK) v Miller Steamship Co Pty*,² (commonly known as *The Wagon Mound (No 2)*), a second action arose out of the same incident, this time brought by the owners of the damaged ships. The evidence which was put before the trial judge on this occasion indicated that a reasonable ship's officer would have regarded fire as a possibility, albeit a slight one. The Privy Council held that, so long as the risk was not so remote that a reasonable man would brush it aside as far-fetched, it was foreseeable enough; accordingly, the defendants were held liable.

The practical effects of the foreseeability test can be measured by considering separately three identifying characteristics of any particular consequence in respect of which damages may be claimed. These are the kind of damage, the manner of its infliction and its extent.

[1] [1961] 1 All ER 404, PC.
[2] [1966] 2 All ER 709, PC.

Kind of damage

18.16 Since *The Wagon Mound,* it is clear that a defendant is liable only for the kinds of damage which might reasonably have been foreseen. Thus, for example, the fact that damage by fouling is foreseeable will not render the defendant liable for damage by fire, if this what actually occurs. However, the general trend of decisions since 1961 has undoubtedly been against the drawing of fine distinctions. In *Bradford v Robinson Rentals Ltd,*[1] for example, a van driver, sent by his employers on a long journey in exceptionally cold weather in an unheated vehicle, suffered frostbite. It was held that, even if frostbite itself was unforeseeable, it was insufficiently akin to other foreseeable injuries from cold and fatigue to permit recovery.

[1] [1967] 1 All ER 267.

Manner of infliction of damage

18.17 The approach of judges to the question of how damage is caused is, by and large, to require foreseeability of the general outline, rather than precise details. For example, where the defendant negligently causes a ship to collide with a quay, the true test of remoteness is whether it is foreseeable that the ship will suffer damage to its hull, not whether it is foreseeable that its hull will be holed by a badly designed fender on the side of the quay.[1] Furthermore, there has been a readiness to impose liability upon the defendant where an injury caused to the claimant leads to a second accident,[2] at least where the claimant's own carelessness in respect of that accident is not enough to break the chain of causation altogether[3] or lead to a finding of contributory negligence.[4]

A defendant who is responsible for an initial injury to the claimant may also be held liable for the adverse effects of the resultant medical treatment,[5] or for even more unlikely consequences.[6] Thus, for example, a defendant who can foresee that the victim of a tort may suffer severe depression may be held legally liable for that victim's subsequent suicide.[7]

The general attitude of the courts is well illustrated by two cases decided by the House of Lords. In the first, *Hughes v Lord Advocate,*[8] employees of the Post Office had left an open manhole covered by a canvas shelter and surrounded by paraffin warning lamps. An eight-year-old boy took one of these lamps into the shelter, where he accidentally knocked it down the hole; there was a violent explosion and the boy was severely burned. The Scottish courts held that the defendants were not liable, on the ground that, while injury by burning was foreseeable, the explosion was not. The House of Lords, however, held that such a distinction was too fine to be accepted, and that the accident fell within the area of risk which the defendants had created.

The second case, *Jolley v Sutton London Borough Council*,[9] concerned a rotten wooden boat which had been abandoned on the defendants' land, near blocks of flats. The 14-year-old claimant and his friend, in attempting to repair the boat, jacked it up with a car jack, and the claimant was injured when the boat fell while he was working underneath it. The Court of Appeal held the defendants not liable, on the ground that the only foreseeable risk resulting from their failure to remove the boat was that children might climb on it and fall through the rotten deck. However, the House of Lords reversed this decision, ruling that the foreseeable risk was a more general one, of children meddling with the boat and being injured in the process.

Occasionally, a decision stands out as taking a much narrower line, although it may for that very reason be regarded with some doubt. One such is *Doughty v Turner Manufacturing Co Ltd*,[10] where the defendants' employee negligently dropped an asbestos cement cover into a cauldron of molten liquid. There was no splash, but two minutes later, due to an unforeseeable chemical reaction, the liquid erupted and the claimant was burned. The Court of Appeal held that, even if injury by splashing were foreseeable, the eruption was not; nor could it be treated as a mere variant of the foreseeable risk. The defendants were accordingly not liable.

[1] *Prekookeanska Plovidba v Felstar Shipping Corpn, The Carnival* [1994] 2 Lloyd's Rep 14, CA.
[2] *Wieland v Cyril Lord Carpets Ltd* [1969] 3 All ER 1006.
[3] As in *McKew v Holland and Hannen and Cubitts (Scotland) Ltd* [1969] 3 All ER 1621, HL; see para 18.10.
[4] As in *Spencer v Wincanton Holdings Ltd* [2009] EWCA Civ 1404, CA.
[5] *Robinson v Post Office* [1974] 2 All ER 737, CA.
[6] See the cases discussed in para 18.20.
[7] *Corr v IBC Vehicles Ltd* [2008] UKHL 13, HL.
[8] [1963] 1 All ER 705, HL.
[9] [2000] 3 All ER 409, HL.
[10] [1964] 1 All ER 98, CA.

Extent of damage

18.18 While the kind of damage, and the manner in which it is caused, must both be reasonably foreseeable, albeit in only a general sense, it appears that the extent of the damage need not be foreseeable at all. In *Vacwell Engineering Co Ltd v BDH Chemicals Ltd*,[1] for example, the defendants negligently failed to warn the claimants that a chemical which they had supplied was liable to explode on contact with water. An employee of the claimants placed a large quantity of this substance in a sink. This resulted in a violent explosion, which extensively damaged the claimants' premises. It was found that, while a minor explosion was foreseeable, one of this magnitude was not; nevertheless, the defendants were held liable for all the damage.

[1] [1970] 3 All ER 553n, CA.

The 'egg-shell skull'

18.19 It is well established that a defendant will be liable in full to a claimant whose injuries are aggravated by some inherent defect such as a thin skull or haemophilia, notwithstanding that the defendant could not possibly have foreseen this. Where the aggravated injury is of the same type, the defendant could equally be held liable on the basis that the extent of damage need not be foreseeable.[1] However, the 'egg-shell skull' principle extends also to cases where the secondary injury is of a different kind, based on the principle that 'a tortfeasor takes his victim as he finds him', a rule which was held, in *Smith v*

Leech Brain & Co Ltd,[2] to have survived *The Wagon Mound*. The defendants in that case negligently caused an employee's lip to be burned by molten metal. This burn activated an unsuspected pre-malignant cancerous condition which, three years later, led to the employee's death. The defendants were held liable, not only for the initial burn, but also for the death.

The egg-shell skull principle has been applied to claimants with a weak heart,[3] an allergy to certain vaccine[4] and even an 'egg-shell personality'.[5] Moreover, the House of Lords' 1933 ruling that it could not be extended to a claimant's lack of finance[6] has now been recognised as wrong and not to be followed.[7] A claimant may thus recover in circumstances where his (or her) impecuniosity means that financial losses caused by the defendant are increased.[8]

[1] See para 18.18.
[2] [1961] 3 All ER 1159.
[3] *Love v Port of London Authority* [1959] 2 Lloyd's Rep 541.
[4] *Robinson v Post Office* [1974] 2 All ER 737, CA.
[5] *Malcolm v Broadhurst* [1970] 3 All ER 508.
[6] *Liesbosch Dredger v SS Edison* [1933] AC 449, HL.
[7] *Lagden v O'Connor* [2003] UKHL 64, HL.
[8] See, eg, *Dodd Properties (Kent) Ltd v Canterbury CC* [1980] 1 All ER 928, CA; para 27.13.

Policy considerations

18.20 Decisions on both legal causation and remoteness of damage are, in truth, value judgments in which a judge's personal experience, common sense and notions of public policy all play their part. Notwithstanding the lip service which is habitually paid to the test of reasonable foreseeability, it must be all too obvious that many problems arise which no legal system can possibly answer by the mechanical application of such a principle. For example, only policy, and not foreseeability, can justify the ruling by the House of Lords that the police may be held liable in negligence for failing to prevent a person in custody from attempting or committing suicide.[1]

In *Clunis v Camden and Islington Health Authority*,[2] the claimant, a mentally disordered person, was in the care of the defendants when he killed a stranger in an unprovoked attack, for which he was convicted of manslaughter. He sued the defendants for negligently failing to control him, but this claim was rejected by the Court of Appeal, which ruled that a person could not recover damages on the basis of his own criminal act, unless he either did not know the nature and quality of that act or did not know that it was wrong.

The court in *Clunis* was not faced in that case by a claim on behalf of the victim, but such a claim was rejected in the earlier case of *Meah v McCreamer (No 2)*.[3] The claimant in that case, who had suffered serious head injuries in a road accident for which the defendant was responsible, subsequently carried out a series of sexual assaults for which he was sentenced to life imprisonment. When the claimant was successfully sued by two of his rape victims,[4] it was held that public policy would not allow him to reclaim from the driver the damages which he had to pay, nor would it permit those victims to sue the driver directly.

[1] *Reeves v Metropolitan Police Comr* [1999] 3 All ER 897, HL.
[2] [1998] 3 All ER 180, CA.
[3] [1986] 1 All ER 943.
[4] *W v Meah* [1986] 1 All ER 935.

REMOTENESS OF DAMAGE: KEY POINTS

- In general, a defendant is only liable for loss which could reasonably have been foreseen.
- The requirement of 'reasonable foreseeability' applies to the type of damage and the way in which it comes about, but not to its extent.
- The rule that a tortfeasor 'takes his victim as he finds him' forms an exception to the normal requirement of foreseeability.
- In addition to reasonable foreseeability, decisions as to the limits of a defendant's liability may be based on policy.

Questions

1. What is the 'but for' test of causation?

2. In what circumstances may a defendant be held liable for a claimant's loss merely for having increased the risk of it happening?

3. To what extent can a claimant recover damages for loss of a chance?

4. How do the courts deal with cases where there is more than one cause of the damage suffered by the claimant?

5. In what circumstances will an action by a third party or the claimant be held to have broken the 'chain of causation'?

6. What test is used by the courts to determine whether an item of damage is too remote from the defendant's negligence and is therefore not legally recoverable?

7. What is meant by the assertion that 'a tortfeasor takes his victim as he finds him'?

8. Bill, who has been employed as a pneumatic drill operator by three different companies during the past 20 years, develops repetitive strain injury (RSI). In consequence of this condition (of which Bill is well aware), when a bus which Bill has just boarded starts to move, Bill is unable to hold on tight to a safety bar. In consequence Bill falls and suffers a deep cut on his head; this, because of his pathological horror of blood, leads to serious depression.

   Advise Bill as to his rights, if any, against any or all of his employers.

19

Defences to negligence

CHAPTER OVERVIEW

Where a claimant has satisfied the court as to the three basic elements of a negligence claim (ie duty of care, breach of duty and resulting damage), the defendant may still be able to avoid liability by raising one of two long-established defences.

In this chapter we consider:

- consent as a defence in tort;

- assumption of risk (express and implied) in negligence cases;

- the scope of the Law Reform (Contributory Negligence) Act 1945;

- the meaning of contributory negligence;

- apportionment of responsibility under the 1945 Act.

19.1 In addition to arguing that the claimant has failed to establish the necessary elements of a case in negligence (or whatever tort is alleged), a defendant may seek to rely on two specific defences to liability. The first of these, called either 'consent' or 'assumption of risk' (depending on which tort is under consideration), operates to bar a claim altogether where a claimant has consented to the defendant's act or has voluntarily assumed the legal risk of injury from the defendant's conduct. The second defence, that of contributory negligence, leads to a reduction in the damages payable when the claimant's own fault is a partial cause of whatever injury or damage has been suffered.

Consent and assumption of risk

Consent to torts other than negligence

19.2 The idea of consent as a defence is easy to understand in relation to intentional torts such as assault and battery; a boxer cannot complain of a fair punch, for example, nor a patient of the bodily invasion inherent in a surgical operation.[1] Consent, however, has its limits; even a participant in a fist fight may not be precluded from claiming damages if an opponent inflicts serious injury with a savage blow which is quite out of proportion to the occasion.[2]

Consent is also relatively straightforward in relation to torts of strict liability, although the terminology here is different; the claimant will lose wherever it can fairly be said that he or she has assumed the legal risk of being injured. Thus, a person who knowingly keeps a vicious dog takes the initial legal risk that it will bite someone; but that legal risk will be transferred to the shoulders of anyone who ignores a clear 'Beware of the Dog' notice.[3]

[1] See para 19.3.
[2] *Lane v Holloway* [1967] 3 All ER 129, CA.
[3] *Cummings v Granger* [1977] 1 All ER 104, CA.

Meaning of consent

19.3 Although knowledge of a risk does not in itself indicate consent to run it, there can be no consent by someone who lacks full awareness of the nature and extent of the risk involved. Actual knowledge is required; thus in *Sarch v Blackburn*,[1] where the claimant was bitten by the defendant's dog, his right to recover damages was held to be unaffected by a large 'Beware of the Dog' notice, since he could not read.

Some legal systems adopt a principle of 'informed consent', whereby a patient who is not given full information about the risks involved in a proposed operation is not treated as having consented to it. This means that the operation is then actionable as a battery, even if it is carried out with all due care and skill. In *Sidaway v Board of Governors of the Bethlem Royal Hospital and the Maudsley Hospital*,[2] the House of Lords held that this doctrine has no place in English law and that a doctor's duty to warn of risks is merely part of the general duty of care which is owed to the patient. As a result, a patient who seeks legal redress for a failure to warn must show that any reasonably competent doctor would have given a warning. However, the House of Lords has held (controversially and by a bare majority) that, where a negligent failure to warn about operation risks is established, and those risks materialise, the patient can recover damages without proof that, had a warning been given, he or she would not have had the operation at all.[3]

To be of legal effect, a person's consent to assume a risk must be fully and freely given, neither induced by fraud nor resulting from some pressure sufficient to override his free will. For example, in cases of employer and employee, it is usually said that economic pressure on the employee not to lose a job prevents the implication that he or she assumes the risks inherent in it.[4] Similarly, in rescue cases, the defence of assumption of risk is ruled out by the moral obligation on the claimant to go to the aid of someone in danger.[5] At one time the courts held that, where a person of sound mind committed or attempted suicide, any action against police or hospital authorities for failing to prevent this would fail on the ground that the person had voluntarily assumed the risk. However, in *Reeves v Metropolitan Police Comr*,[6] the House of Lords held that the defence could not be raised in a case where the claimant's act was the very thing that the defendant was under a duty to prevent.

[1] (1830) 4 C & P 297.
[2] [1985] 1 All ER 643, HL.
[3] *Chester v Afshar* [2004] UKHL 41, HL.
[4] *Smith v Baker & Sons* [1891] AC 325 HL.
[5] *Haynes v Harwood* [1935] 1 KB 146, CA.
[6] [2000] AC 360, HL.

Assumption of risk in negligence cases

Express consent

19.4 Where the claimant is alleged to have expressly agreed to assume the risk of negligence by the defendant, the case is usually concerned with an exemption clause, although a non-contractual waiver is in principle also effective.[1] However, statute has now deprived the latter of one of its most important practical applications, namely, 'Ride at your own risk' as regards passengers in motor vehicles.[2] Further, the extent to which liability for negligence may be excluded by a contract term or notice is heavily restricted,[3] and the Unfair Contract Terms Act 1977, s 2(3) makes it clear that a person's agreement to or awareness of a purported exemption clause does not in itself lead to the conclusion that he or she assumes any risk.

[1] *Buckpitt v Oates* [1968] 1 All ER 1145.
[2] Road Traffic Act 1988, s 149(3).
[3] Paras 9.10 and 9.15.

Implied consent

19.5 Attempts to persuade a court to infer, from the claimant's conduct, that he or she assumed the risk of negligence by the defendant are seldom successful. Those which do succeed are usually cases in which the defendant's negligence takes place first, so that its full effects are visible to the claimant before going into danger. In *Cutler v United Dairies (London) Ltd*,[1] due to negligence for which the defendants were responsible, a horse ran away into a field. There was no danger, but the driver called for assistance in pacifying the animal, and the claimant was injured in helping him. The Court of Appeal held that the claimant had obviously assumed the risk and that he could not, therefore, recover damages.

The courts have shown little liking for the idea that a claimant may impliedly agree to exempt the defendant from liability for future acts of negligence; it has even been suggested that the defence can never apply in a normal case of negligence.[2] Nevertheless, it was applied by the Court of Appeal, albeit in extreme circumstances, in the case of *Morris v Murray*,[3] where the claimant accepted a flight in the defendant's light aircraft in bad weather when both parties were drunk. The claimant sought damages for injuries received in the ensuing crash, arguing that his own stupidity should lead only to a reduction of damages for contributory negligence. However, the Court of Appeal ruled that the claim should fail altogether on the ground of assumption of risk, stating that 'the wild irresponsibility of the venture is such that the law should not intervene to award damages and should leave the loss where it falls'.

[1] [1933] 2 KB 297, CA; para 18.11.
[2] *Dann v Hamilton* [1939] 1 All ER 59 at 60; *Wooldridge v Sumner* [1962] 2 All ER 978 at 990.
[3] [1991] 2 QB 6.

Consent and Assumption of Risk: Key Points

- A claimant who consents to what would otherwise be a tort may not then sue in respect of it.
- Consent for this purpose must be full and free and based upon knowledge of the risk.
- Assumption of risk is seldom a defence in an action for negligence.

Contributory negligence

19.6 The ability of a court to deal with cases where both parties are at fault by reducing the claimant's damages is entirely statute-based, dating from the enactment of the Law Reform (Contributory Negligence) Act 1945. Section 1(1) of that Act provides that where a person suffers damage as the result partly of his own fault and partly of the fault of another person, the damages recoverable by him shall be reduced to such extent as the court thinks just and equitable having regard to the claimant's share in the responsibility for the damage.

Interestingly, the Act speaks not of negligence but of *fault*. According to s 4, this means 'negligence, breach of statutory duty or other act or omission which gives rise to a liability in tort or would, apart from this Act, give rise to the defence of contributory negligence'. Clearly, then, this defence is available not only in cases of negligence, but also in a number of other torts. However, it appears to have no application to intentional torts such as assault and battery[1] or deceit.[2]

The 1945 Act is inapplicable to actions based purely on a breach of contract,[3] so that, if the claimant in such a case is also at fault, the court must either hold the claimant entirely responsible and thus deny compensation altogether, or ignore the claimant's share of the blame and award damages in full.[4] Where, however, a defendant's liability in contract is identical to what it would be in the tort of negligence, the claimant will not be able to avoid the operation of the 1945 Act by framing an action in contract; the court has the power to reduce the claimant's damages, whatever the action is called.[5]

[1] *Co-operative Group (CWS) Ltd v Pritchard* [2011] EWCA Civ 329, CA.
[2] *Alliance and Leicester Building Society v Edgestop Ltd* [1994] 2 All ER 38; *Standard Chartered Bank v Pakistan National Shipping Corporation (Nos 2 and 4)* [2002] UKHL 43, HL.
[3] *Barclays Bank v Fairclough Building Ltd* [1995] QB 214, CA; see para 11.28.
[4] In *Tennant Radiant Heat Ltd v Warrington Development Corpn* [1988] 1 EGLR 41, CA, the Court of Appeal managed to award partial compensation in such a case by ruling that the defendant had only caused part of the claimant's loss, but this seems wrong.
[5] *Forsikringsaktieselskapet Vesta v Butcher* [1988] 2 All ER 43, CA; para 11.28.

Standard of care

19.7 An allegation of contributory negligence does not require proof that the claimant owed anyone a legal duty of care; contributory negligence consists simply of failing to take such care of oneself as is reasonable in all the circumstances of the case. Thus, a mortgage lender who claims damages from a negligent valuer may suffer a reduction in those damages if either it was unreasonable for the lender to rely on the valuation[1] or the decision to lend was negligent for other reasons.[2]

As to the standard which the claimant is required to reach, this is evaluated in much the same way as is a defendant's for the purpose of establishing a breach of a duty of care.[3] Indeed, many of the factors which we considered in that context, such as the standard of care demanded of children, and the extent to which the reasonable man must foresee negligence in others, are of special relevance here. So too, those cases where the claimant's conduct tends not be regarded as an intervening cause,[4] such as rescue attempts, or the claimant's instinctive reactions to an emergency, may well today give rise to a finding of contributory negligence.[5] It has been held by the House of Lords that suicide, at least by a person of sound mind, may amount to contributory negligence in a claim against a defendant who owes a duty of care to prevent it.[6]

In considering the defence of assumption of risk, we noted that knowledge of a risk does not necessarily imply acceptance of it.[7] Such knowledge may, however, lead a court to the conclusion that the claimant was contributorily negligent in failing to take avoiding action. In *Owens v Brimmell*,[8] for example, a passenger in a car who knew that the driver had been drinking heavily lost 20% of his damages when the driver negligently crashed the car and the passenger was injured. So too, in *Gregory v Kelly*,[9] the claimant was held to be contributorily negligent in travelling in a car when he knew that the footbrake did not work.

[1] *Banque Bruxelles Lambert SA v Eagle Star* [1995] 2 All ER 769.
[2] *Platform Home Loans Ltd v Oyston Shipways Ltd* [1998] 13 EG 148, CA.
[3] Chapter 17.
[4] Paras 18.11–18.13.

⁵ See *Harrison v British Railways Board* [1981] 3 All ER 679; para 19.11.
⁶ *Reeves v Metropolitan Police Comr* [1999] 3 All ER 897, HL.
⁷ Para 19.3.
⁸ [1977] Qb 859, [1976] 3 All ER 765.
⁹ [1978] RTR 426.

Causation

19.8 It is not enough for a defendant to show that the claimant failed to take reasonable care; the lack of care must also be shown to have contributed, at least in part, to the claimant's damage. This, however, does not mean that it must have contributed to the accident which caused the damage. For example, a moped rider who is in no way responsible for a collision may nevertheless lose part of the damages payable if the injuries suffered are increased by the fact that the rider was not wearing a helmet[1] or that the helmet's chin strap was not fastened.[2] In the same way, failure by a driver of or a front-seat passenger in a motor vehicle to wear a seat belt normally leads to a reduction in damages of between 15% and 25%, depending on whether the injuries would have been substantially or even totally avoided,[3] but ignoring the question of what other injuries the seat belt itself might have caused.[4] In *Badger v Ministry of Defence*,[5] a similar principle was applied to a man who, having been exposed in the course of his employment to asbestos dust and fibres, contracted asbestosis which led to death from lung cancer. The damages payable by his employers were reduced by 20% on the ground of his contributory negligence in continuing to smoke cigarettes despite repeated medical advice to give up.

Since the attribution of legal cause is really, as we have seen,[6] a matter in which the judge exercises a choice, no hard and fast rules can be laid down. An important factor, however, is that of risk; if the claimant's damage does not fall within the scope of the risk which he or she unreasonably took on, then the negligence is not contributory. In *Jones v Livox Quarries Ltd*,[7] an employee who stood, contrary to instructions, on the back of a moving traxcavator was injured when another vehicle collided with it. The claimant argued that his negligence did not contribute to his injuries, since the only risk he had undertaken was that of falling off. The Court of Appeal, while accepting that he would not have been in any way to blame if, during his unauthorised ride, he had been shot by a negligent sportsman, nevertheless felt that the actual accident was within the risk. Accordingly damages were reduced by 20%. A similar problem arose in *Westwood v Post Office*,[8] where an employee was killed when he ignored a notice which read: 'Authorised personnel only', entered a lift motor room and fell through a defective trapdoor. A bare (3–2) majority of the House of Lords held that, since the notice gave no indication of danger, let alone of the specific danger, the trespasser's only fault was disobedience, and not contributory negligence.

¹ *O'Connell v Jackson* [1971] 3 All ER 129, CA.
² *Capps v Miller* [1989] 2 All ER 333, CA.
³ *Froom v Butcher* [1975] 3 All ER 520, CA.
⁴ *Patience v Andrews* [1983] RTR 447.
⁵ [2005] EWHC 2491, QB.
⁶ Paras 18.7–18.14.
⁷ [1952] 2 Qb 608, CA.
⁸ [1973] 3 All ER 184, HL.

Apportionment

19.9 Section 1(1) of the 1945 Act instructs the court to reduce the claimant's damages to such an extent as is just and equitable in view of the claimant's share in the responsibility for the damage. No statutory guidance is given for this process, but two factors are clearly regarded by the courts as relevant. The first of these, naturally, is the degree of fault which may be attributed to each party. This, however, cannot be the sole criterion for, in a case where the defendant is strictly liable, such as for a breach of statutory duty, it would lead to the absurd conclusion that a slightly negligent claimant receives nothing at all. Thus a second factor, that of 'causative importance', must also be considered.[1]

It should not be thought that equal carelessness compels equal division. For example, it is perfectly reasonable to place a greater burden upon a negligent motorist than upon an equally negligent passenger who is not wearing a seat belt, since the conduct of the former entails grave risks to others. All that can be said is that the courts make full use of the discretion which they are given; reductions have ranged from a mere 5% in the case of a passenger injured by negligent driving, whose failure to wear a seat belt was itself partly the driver's fault,[2] to 80% where safety regulations were deliberately flouted by a workman and his colleague.[3] In one case the Court of Appeal even held an injured workman 100% contributorily negligent,[4] although a differently constituted Court of Appeal described such a conclusion as 'logically unsupportable'.[5] It would be preferable in such a case to regard the claimant as the sole cause of his or her injuries.

Where an action is brought against more than one defendant, any contributory negligence by the claimant must be measured against the totality of the defendants' conduct, rather than against each of them separately. Thus, for example, if the claimant, defendant A and defendant B are all equally to blame, the claimant should be awarded two-thirds of his damages against each defendant rather than one-half.[6]

[1] *Stapley v Gypsum Mines Ltd* [1953] 2 All ER 478 at 486.
[2] *Pasternack v Poulton* [1973] 2 All ER 74. However, a passenger failed in her claim against a *non-negligent* driver for merely failing to advise her to wear a seat belt: *Eastman v South West Thames Area Health Authority* [1991] RTR 389, CA.
[3] *Stapley v Gypsum Mines Ltd* [1953] 2 All ER 478, HL.
[4] *Jayes v IMI (Kynoch) Ltd* [1985] ICR 155, CA.
[5] *Pitts v Hunt* [1990] 3 All ER 344, CA.
[6] *Fitzgerald v Lane* [1988] 2 All ER 961, HL.

CONTRIBUTORY NEGLIGENCE: KEY POINTS

- The Law Reform (Contributory Negligence) Act 1945 provides a partial defence where the claimant, as well as the defendant, is at fault.

- The standard of care demanded of a claimant is the same as that required of a defendant.

- Contributory negligence only applies where the claimant's fault is a partial cause of the damage suffered.

- Where contributory negligence is established it leads to a reduction of the damages payable.

Questions

1. To what extent does a claimant's 'consent' provide a defence to intentional torts or torts of strict liability?

2. To what extent does a claimant's 'consent' provide a defence to an action for negligence?

3. To what kinds of legal action does the claimant's contributory negligence provide a defence?

4. What is meant by 'contributory' and 'negligence' for this purpose?

5. Farmer Giles invites Alice, a guest at his farm, to accompany him on his supercharged tractor for an after-dinner tour of the property. Alice accepts the invitation, although she is aware that both of them have drunk a lot of wine during the evening. In the event, Giles (who drives as fast as the vehicle will permit), overturns the tractor and Alice is seriously injured.

   Advise Alice.

20

Breach of statutory duty

CHAPTER OVERVIEW

In this chapter we consider the following issues:

- the factors which influence the court's decision as to whether or not a particular statutory provision creates a civil right of action;
- the elements of liability in an action for breach of statutory duty.

20.1 It frequently happens that an act done by one person which causes injury or damage to another also constitutes a breach of some statutory obligation. This naturally renders the person concerned liable to whatever penalty is prescribed by the statute; but our present concern is with the effect, if any, which the statutory breach has upon that person's liability to pay damages to the claimant.

Many legal systems treat the fact that a defendant has or has not contravened a statutory rule as relevant only to the question whether or not there has been negligence. By contrast, English law takes the view that a breach of statutory duty may be a tort in itself, quite independent of negligence on the part of the defendant, and with its own elements of liability and defences. However, it is not suggested that every statutory obligation gives rise to a civil action, for such is the bulk of modern legislation that the universal imposition of liability would, it is thought, be an unacceptably heavy burden. Thus, a preliminary task for a claimant who wishes to frame an action in this way (in order to recover damages without the need to prove negligence) is to satisfy the court that the rule or regulation in question is one for breach of which damages may be awarded.

Existence of civil liability

20.2 In some cases, a particular statute or regulation states clearly that it either does[1] or does not[2] give rise to civil liability. Usually, however, the point is not specifically mentioned, and the question is therefore left for the courts to determine by interpreting the relevant provision. In carrying out this task, the courts claim to be giving effect to the intention of Parliament, but it is probably sensible to recognise this as a fiction: in reality, the lack of express provision in the statute indicates that there is no Parliamentary intention, so that what the courts are doing is based on their view of policy.

In their search for the intention of Parliament, the courts sometimes claim to gain assistance from a consideration of what sanction, if any, has been laid down for a breach of the provision in question. In particular, if there is a heavy criminal penalty attached, this may point to the absence of a civil action for damages.[3] However, the lack of any sanction at all does not necessarily mean that the statutory provision must be intended to provide a civil remedy.[4]

It has sometimes been said that statutes passed for the benefit of a particular class of persons give rise to a civil action, whereas those which benefit the public in general do not.[5] However, the House of Lords has emphasised[6] that the crucial question is not whether the claimant is in a 'protected class' but whether the legislature intended to create a civil right of action. Nor do the decided cases lend strong support to the 'class' theory. It has been held, for example, that no civil right of action arises under the Protection from Eviction Act 1977, s 1, which makes it a criminal offence to evict or harass a residential tenant;[7] nor for breach of the Prison Rules, which govern the conditions under which convicted prisoners are held;[8] nor for breach of the Prosecution of Offences (Custody Time Limits) Regulations 1987, which require the Crown Prosecution Service to bring an arrested person to court within a certain time;[9] nor for breach of a Northern Ireland statute giving a terrorist suspect detained by police a right to see a solicitor (at least where the denial of access has caused no actual loss);[10] nor for breach of a local authority's obligation to house a homeless person;[11] nor for breach by a local authority of generally worded statutory duties to protect the welfare and educational interests of children within its area.[12] Furthermore, while a person who commits a criminal offence by making an unauthorised recording of a live performance may be liable in damages to the performer,[13] there is no liability to a recording company which has an exclusive right to record that performance.[14]

---

[1] Eg the Nuclear Installations Act 1965 and the Consumer Safety Act 1978.

[2] Eg the Guard Dogs Act 1975.

[3] See *Richardson v Pitt-Stanley* [1995] ICR 303, CA.

[4] See *Trustee in Bankruptcy of St John Poulton v Ministry of Justice* [2010] EWCA Civ 392, CA (no claim where county court staff, in breach of insolvency legislation, failed to notify the Chief Land Registrar of a pending bankruptcy action, with the result that the bankrupt was able to sell property to the detriment of her creditors).

[5] See, for example, *Lonrho Ltd v Shell Petroleum Co Ltd (No 2)* [1981] 2 All ER 456 at 461.

[6] *R v Deputy Governor of Parkhurst Prison, ex p Hague; Weldon v Home Office* [1991] 3 All ER 733, HL.

[7] *McCall v Abelesz* [1976] 1 All ER 727, CA. An express right to damages in such cases has now been conferred by the Housing Act 1988, s 27.

[8] *R v Deputy Governor of Parkhurst Prison, ex p Hague; Weldon v Home Office* [1991] 3 All ER 733, HL.

[9] *Olotu v Home Office* [1997] 1 All ER 385, CA.

[10] *Cullen v Chief Constable of the Royal Ulster Constabulary* [2003] UKHL 39.

[11] *O'Rourke v Camden London Borough Council* [1997] 3 All ER 23, HL.

[12] *X v Bedfordshire County Council* [1995] 3 All ER 353, HL.

[13] *Rickless v United Artists Corpn* [1987] 1 All ER 679, CA.

[14] *RCA Corpn v Pollard* [1982] 3 All ER 771, CA.

20.3 It seems that the courts are very reluctant to use this tort to create new types of civil right, by allowing an action where there is no common law duty of care.[1] In *Atkinson v Newcastle and Gateshead Waterworks Co*,[2] for instance, the defendants, in breach of a statutory rule for which they could be fined £10, failed to maintain the prescribed pressure of water in their mains. As a result, a fire in the claimant's property could not be extinguished. It was held by the Court of Appeal that Parliament could not have intended to make the defendants virtual insurers of every property in the city and that consequently no civil action lay for breach of this duty. A similar decision was reached by the House of Lords in *Cutler v Wandsworth Stadium Ltd*,[3] where an individual bookmaker unsuccessfully claimed damages from the defendants for breach of their statutory duty to make space available for bookmakers at their greyhound racing track. Again, the Court of Appeal in *F v Wirral Metropolitan Borough Council*[4] held that a local authority in breach of a statutory code governing children in care could not be held liable in damages for 'interference with parental rights'.

It has been acknowledged by the House of Lords that 'directly applicable' legislation of the European Community[5] may confer upon individuals a right of action similar to that for breach of statutory duty.[6] In deciding whether or not this is the case, the courts do not, of course, refer to the intention of Parliament, but they nonetheless give attention to the criteria mentioned above. However, an important restriction upon this new form of civil liability lies in the fact that, even where a right of this kind is held to exist, it does not necessarily entitle a person aggrieved to recover damages; some other remedy may be appropriate.[7]

It must be acknowledged that it is very difficult to find any coherent principle by which to explain the 'intention of Parliament' in this context, although the actual decisions reached by the courts on this issue tend to fall clearly into two groups. Industrial safety regulations are almost invariably interpreted as conferring a civil right of action for damages; outside the field of industrial safety, the attitude of the courts towards claims for breach of statutory duty has been one of considerable and increasing reluctance. However, an injured road user is entitled to bring an action against a highway authority for breach of its duty under s 41(1) of the Highways Act 1980 to maintain the highway (although this duty does not extend to the erection of traffic signs in dangerous areas).[8]

[1] This is especially so where the claimant's 'injury' is not of a kind for which damages will normally be awarded: see *Pickering v Liverpool Daily Post and Echo Newspapers plc* [1991] 1 All ER 622, HL.

[2] (1877) 2 Ex D 441, CA.

[3] [1949] 1 All ER 544, HL.

[4] [1991] 2 All ER 648, CA.

[5] See paras 3.49–3.51.

[6] *Garden Cottage Foods Ltd v Milk Marketing Board* [1983] 2 All ER 770, HL.

[7] *Bourgoin SA v Ministry of Agriculture, Fisheries and Food* [1985] 3 All ER 585, CA; *An Bord Bainne Co-operative v Milk Marketing Board* [1988] 1 FTLR 145, CA.

[8] *Gorringe v Calderdale BC* [2004] UKHL 15.

Elements of liability

Class protected

20.4 Where a statutory provision is seen as having been passed for the protection of a defined class of persons, only members of that class can recover damages for a breach. A good illustration of this point is the case of *Hartley v Mayoh & Co*,[1] in which a fireman was killed by electrocution while fighting a fire at the defendants' factory. In an action by the fireman's widow it was held that the breach by the defendants of wiring regulations was irrelevant, since these were expressed to be for the benefit of persons employed at a factory, and this did not include the fireman.[2]

Even where a statute does not expressly define a 'protected class', a court may decide that Parliament intended to limit its protection. For example, it has been held that district auditors may be liable for breach of statutory duty to a local authority whose accounts they audit, but not to individual officers of that authority.[3] However, the courts are generally slow to impose limitations on the ambit of a statute in cases where Parliament has not done so. In *Westwood v Post Office*,[4] for example, a defective trapdoor, the condition of which constituted a breach of the Offices, Shops and Railway Premises Act 1963, led to the death of an employee at a telephone exchange. The trapdoor was in fact in a part of the premises which the deceased was not permitted to enter and it was argued by the defendants that, while the statute protected most employees, it did not cover trespassers. It was held by the House of Lords, however, that the employee's trespass did not deprive him of statutory protection.

[1] [1954] 1 All ER 375, CA.
[2] The claimant nevertheless succeeded in recovering damages on the ground of negligence.
[3] *West Wiltshire District Council v Garland* [1995] 2 All ER 17, CA.
[4] [1973] 3 All ER 184, HL; para 19.8.

Type of injury

20.5 The claimant in an action for breach of statutory duty must show that the injury or damage suffered is of a type which the statute is designed to prevent. The classic example of this principle is *Gorris v Scott*,[1] in which the absence of pens on the deck of the defendant's ship allowed the claimant's sheep to be swept overboard in a storm. Although pens were required by statute, this was held to be of no assistance to the claimant, for their purpose was merely to reduce the spread of disease among the animals. This principle also led to the rather harsh decision in *Close v Steel Co of Wales Ltd*,[2] where it was held that, since the purpose of a duty to fence dangerous machinery is to keep the operator out, it is of no relevance where the absence of a guard allows part of the machine to fly out and cause injury to the operator.

It is obvious that, the more precisely the purpose of a statute is interpreted by judges, the fewer cases will fall within it. The modern tendency, however, is to define the protected risk in fairly broad terms, an approach rather similar to that adopted towards the questions of how damage is caused in the tort of negligence.[3] Thus, in *Grant v National Coal Board*,[4] where a statutory breach allowed rock to fall from a mine roof, it was held that a miner could sue for injuries received when the bogie in which he was travelling was derailed by the fallen rock. So too, in *Donaghey v Boulton and Paul Ltd*,[5] the defendants failed in their statutory duty to supply an employee with crawling boards when he was working on a fragile asbestos roof. The employee fell, not through the asbestos, but through a hole in the roof adjacent to it. It was argued that this was outside the object of the statute, which was limited to fragile roofs, but the House of Lords rejected so narrow an interpretation and held that damages should be awarded.

It is noticeable that, in identifying the purpose of a statutory provision, the courts are usually reluctant to hold that it is intended to protect the claimant against pure economic loss.[6] This has even led to the rejection of a claim by a person whose house suffered radioactive contamination from the discharge of nuclear waste, on the ground that the damage suffered was not physical damage, but rather the devaluation of the property.[7]

[1] (1874) LR 9 Exch 125.
[2] [1961] 2 All ER 953, HL.
[3] See *Hughes v Lord Advocate* [1963] 1 All ER 705, HL; para 18.17.
[4] [1956] 1 All ER 682, HL.
[5] [1967] 2 All ER 1014, HL.
[6] See *Wentworth v Wiltshire County Council* [1993] 2 All ER 256, CA.
[7] *Merlin v British Nuclear Fuels plc* [1990] 3 All ER 711. Contrast *Blue Circle Industries plc v Ministry of Defence* [1998] 3 All ER 385.

Breach by defendant

20.6 Where a statutory rule is clear and exact, there is no liability for almost breaching it. In *Chipchase v British Titan Products Co Ltd*,[1] for example, the claimant fell from a working platform only 9 inches wide; had the platform been only slightly higher, statute would have required a width of 34 inches. On these facts the defendants were held not liable for either negligence or breach of statutory duty.

In deciding whether or not a particular obligation has been broken, it is important to realise that the standard of conduct required may vary, because of either the words used or their interpretation by the courts. For example, in *Ministry of Housing and Local Government v Sharp*,[2] the Court of Appeal held by a majority that the duty of a local land Registrar in issuing certificates of search was not absolute but merely one of reasonable care. Again, in *Roe v Sheffield CC*,[3] a majority of the Court of Appeal held that the duty imposed by section 25 of the Tramways Act 1870 (to lay tramlines on a level with the surrounding road surface was limited to what was technically feasible. A duty qualified by such words as 'so far as is reasonably practicable' is, it appears, equivalent to one of reasonable care;[4] at the other extreme, an unqualified duty may be held to impose an absolute obligation. In *John Summers & Sons Ltd v Frost*,[5] for instance, it was held by the House of Lords that a grinding wheel could not be described as 'securely fenced', as required by statute, if any part of the wheel remained exposed, even though to cover it completely would render it unusable.

Between these two levels lies an obligation 'to take such steps as may be necessary'. In deciding what steps are necessary, the courts consider only such dangers as the defendant ought reasonably to have foreseen. If this test establishes that steps are necessary, however, the defendant's obligation to take those steps is an absolute one.[6]

[1] [1956] 1 All ER 613, CA.
[2] [1970] 1 All ER 1009, CA.
[3] [2003] EWCA Civ 1.
[4] The onus of proof may well rest on the defendant: *Larner v British Steel plc* [1993] 4 All ER 102, CA.
[5] [1955] 1 All ER 870, HL.
[6] *Brown v National Coal Board* [1962] 1 All ER 81, HL.

Causation

20.7 As with any action in tort, the claimant must establish that the defendant's breach of duty was a legal cause of the injury, loss or damage suffered. With one exception the law on this matter, although complex, is no different from that which governs cases of negligence and which we have already considered.[1] The exception is where a statute is so drafted as to place identical duties on two parties (usually employer and employee) in such terms that an act or omission by one party constitutes a breach by both of them. In such a case, where a statute states simply that something 'shall be done', failure to do it puts both parties in breach, even though the moral blame may rest on only one of them. In *Ginty v Belmont Building Supplies Ltd*,[2] for example, it was provided by statute that, when work was being done on fragile roofs, crawling boards 'shall be used'. The defendants supplied such boards, together with full instructions as to their use, to the claimant, an experienced workman whom they employed, but he decided not to use the boards and consequently fell through the roof. This breach of statutory duty was undoubtedly one for which both claimant and defendants could have been criminally liable. However, it was held that the claimant was not entitled to claim damages from defendants, for their breach of statutory duty consisted entirely of his own breach.

It is important to note that the decision in *Ginty* does not apply where the defendant is guilty of some independent or extra fault, although the claimant in such a case may still lose a substantial proportion of the damages payable on the ground of contributory negligence. In *Boyle v Kodak Ltd*,[3] for instance, the House of Lords held the defendant employers two-thirds to blame for an accident at work, since they had failed to provide the claimant with adequate supervision or instruction in the relevant regulations. And, in *McMath v Rimmer Bros (Liverpool) Ltd*,[4] where the claimant fell from a ladder which no-one was 'footing', his employers were held liable for 50% of his damages, since the absence of anyone to foot the ladder was attributable to their fault.

[1] Chapter 18.
[2] [1959] 1 All ER 414.
[3] [1969] 1 WLR 661, HL.
[4] [1961] 3 All ER 1154, CA.

Defences

20.8 In principle, the defence of *assumption of risk*[1] is available in actions for breach of statutory duty. However, for reasons of public policy it has long been settled that an employer may not use it against an employee when the employer is personally in breach of a statutory obligation.[2] In cases where the employer is not personally in breach, but is made vicariously liable for breach by employees of statutory duties which are laid upon them, the defence is available.[3]

There is no doubt that the defence of contributory negligence[4] is available (and it should be noted that the claimant's 'fault' for this purpose may itself consist of some breach of statutory duty). However, if too liberally used, this defence would deprive many employees of the benefit of regulations specifically designed for their protection. Consequently, in dealing with industrial accident cases, the courts are careful to make full allowance for problems of fatigue, repetition, boredom and the like.[5]

Where the defendant is personally under a statutory duty, it is no defence to show that performance of the duty was delegated to the claimant. However, if the claimant's conduct is the sole cause of injury, the defendant may avoid liability on the basis of the rule in *Ginty v Belmont Building Supplies Ltd*.[6]

[1] Paras 19.2–19.5.
[2] *Baddeley v Earl of Granville* (1887) 19 QBD 423, DC.
[3] *Imperial Chemical Industries Ltd v Shatwell* [1964] 2 All ER 999, HL.
[4] Paras 19.6–19.9.
[5] See *Caswell v Powell Duffryn Associated Collieries Ltd* [1939] 3 All ER 722, HL; *Mullard v Ben Line Steamers Ltd* [1971] 2 All ER 424, CA.
[6] [1959] 1 All ER 414; para 20.7.

BREACH OF STATUTORY DUTY: KEY POINTS

- Where a statute is silent as to civil liability, the courts claim to be seeking to ascertain the intention of Parliament.

- It appears that, outside the field of industrial safety regulations, the courts are reluctant to interpret a statute as conferring a civil right of action.

- Where a claim is in principle acceptable, the claimant must show that he (or she) is within the protected class and that the injury suffered is of the type envisaged by the statute.

- Liability for breach of statutory duty may be strict, negligence-based or at an intermediate level.

Questions

1. What are the main factors considered by a court in deciding whether or not a particular statutory provision creates a civil right of action?

2. Assuming that a particular statute creates a civil right of action, what must a claimant prove in order to succeed in a claim?

3. To what extent does the claimant's own fault provide a defence to liability under this tort?

4. The town where Baskerville lives is subject to a local byelaw which imposes criminal liability on dog owners for any fouling of public places. Baskerville's dog fouls the pavement in the town's main shopping street and Dodder, an elderly person, slips and breaks his ankle.

    Advise Dodder as to his rights, if any, against Baskerville, on the assumption that he is unable to prove that Baskerville has been guilty of negligence in relation to this incident.

21

Liability for dangerous premises

CHAPTER OVERVIEW

Premises which are dangerous may result in injury or damage to persons on those premises. In this chapter we consider the following issues:

- the statutory duty which is owed by the occupier of premises to his (or her) lawful visitors;
- the lesser statutory duty which the occupier owes to those who are not lawful visitors (mainly trespassers);
- the liability which the law of tort imposes upon those who are negligent in the design or construction of buildings;
- the extent to which a person who sells or lets dangerous property can be held responsible for the consequences.

Lawful visitors

Scope of the duty

21.1 Section 2(1) of the Occupiers' Liability Act 1957 provides: 'An occupier of premises owes the same duty, the "common duty of care", to all his visitors, except in so far as he is free to and does extend, restrict, modify or exclude his duty to any visitor or visitors by agreement or otherwise.'

Most of the litigation in this area concerns personal injury or death, but s 1(3) of the Act provides that the statutory rules also apply to the obligations of a person occupying or having control over any premises or structure in respect of damage to property, including the property of persons who are not themselves visitors. Further, where damage to property is proved, the occupier's liability extends also to consequential financial loss, such as the expense of salvaging damaged goods.[1]

> [1] *AMF International Ltd v Magnet Bowling Ltd* [1968] 2 All ER 789.

Exclusion of liability by contract

21.2 Section 2(1) suggests that an occupier may exclude or restrict the duty which would otherwise be owed to a visitor. However, the qualification 'in so far as he is free to' indicates that there are circumstances in which the occupier is denied this freedom. It seems, for instance, that an innkeeper is not permitted to exclude liability for damage to the property of guests.[1] Any attempt by an occupier to exclude or restrict the statutory duty by means of a contractual term is subject to the rules which govern exemption clauses.[2] Of fundamental importance is the Unfair Contract Terms Act 1977. This, when it applies, prohibits the exclusion or restriction of liability for personal injury or death altogether, and makes the exclusion or restriction of liability for other kinds of damage subject to a test of reasonableness. The provisions of this Act are considered in detail elsewhere;[3] for present purposes it is sufficient to state that its operation is limited to duties which arise 'from the occupation of premises used for business purposes of the occupier'. However, a relaxation of the rules, which was introduced by the Occupiers' Liability Act 1984, s 2, permits a business occupier to exclude or restrict liability to those permitted to enter the occupier's land for recreational or educational purposes which do not themselves form part of the business. A private occupier is not affected by the Unfair Contract Terms Act, but any attempt to exclude or restrict liability by means of a contract term must still satisfy the stringent requirements of common law.

[1] *Williams v Linnit* [1951] 1 All ER 278, CA; see now the Hotel Proprietors Act 1956, s 2(3).
[2] Chapter 9.
[3] Paras 9.9–9.21.

Exclusion of liability by notice

21.3 Occupiers not infrequently seek to exclude or restrict their liability by displaying prominently on their premises notices which state, for example: 'No Liability is Accepted for any Injury or Damage'. It appears that, as a general principle, such notices can be effective. It has twice been held by the Court of Appeal, in *Ashdown v Samuel Williams & Sons Ltd*[1] and *White v Blackmore*,[2] that an occupier who is entitled to say: 'Keep Out' is equally entitled to impose conditions upon which persons may enter.[3] However, the principle has been substantially altered by the Unfair Contract Terms Act, at least where business premises are concerned.[4]

[1] [1957] 1 All ER 35, CA.
[2] [1972] 3 All ER 158, CA.
[3] For this reason it seems that a notice excluding liability will be of no effect against a person who enters the premises by some legal right.
[4] Para 9.10.

Occupier

21.4 The Occupiers' Liability Act 1957 contains no definition of 'occupier', indeed, the common law position is expressly preserved by s 1(3). Traditionally, this question has been approached by the courts on a commonsense basis, looking to the practicalities of the situation rather than to the technicalities of land law. Thus, for example, on a large-scale building project, the main contractor may well be held to be the occupier of the site (either alone or jointly with the owner).[1] Similarly, in a Canadian case where an auction was conducted on a farm, both the farmer and the auctioneer were held to be occupiers of the barn in which it took place.[2]

The most important single factor used in deciding who is an occupier is that of *control*. This need be neither entire nor exclusive but, unless a person is sufficiently in control of premises to realise that carelessness may lead to a visitor being injured, that person cannot be regarded as an occupier.[3] Thus a married couple were not occupiers of the flat roof of a supermarket, even though the window of their flat gave access to this roof and they allowed their own children to play on it. They therefore owed no duty to another child, who climbed from the garden on to the roof and then fell from it.[4]

It is on the basis of control that liability has been imposed upon a fairground concessionaire (who had no interest in the property)[5] and upon a local authority which, having acquired a house by compulsory purchase, ordered the resident to leave by serving a notice of intention to enter, even though the authority did not then take possession of the property.[6] Similarly, an owner of premises who licenses another to use them may well retain sufficient control to be treated as an occupier,[7] and it is then a question of fact whether the licensee is an occupier as well. On the other hand, where property is leased,[8] it is the tenant, and not the landlord, who is the occupier, although a landlord who is in breach of a repairing obligation may incur liability under a separate provision.[9] The landlord will also be regarded as the occupier of the common parts of premises, such as lifts and staircases in a block of flats, notwithstanding that the landlord cannot deny access to these areas to tenants' families or guests.[10]

  [1] *AMF International Ltd v Magnet Bowling Ltd* [1968] 2 All ER 789.
  [2] *Couch v McCann* (1977) 77 DLR (3d) 387.
  [3] See *Cavalier v Pope* [1906] AC 428 at 433.
  [4] *Bailey v Armes* [1999] EGCS 21, CA.
  [5] *Humphreys v Dreamland (Margate) Ltd* (1930) 144 LT 529, HL.
  [6] *Harris v Birkenhead Corpn* [1976] 1 All ER 341, CA.
  [7] *Wheat v E Lacon & Co Ltd* [1966] 1 All ER 582, HL.
  [8] For the distinction between a lease and a licence, see para 36.9.
  [9] Para 21.30.
  [10] *Moloney v Lambeth London Borough Council* (1966) 64 LGR 440.

Multiple occupation

21.5 The courts have repeatedly held that neither occupation, nor the control on which it is based, need be exclusive, and that consequently there may be more than one occupier of the same premises. In *Fisher v CRT Ltd (No 2)*,[1] for example, X owned a gaming club; a restaurant on the premises was held under licence by Y, who ran it as a separate business. Although detailed control over the restaurant was in the hands of Y, its sole entrance was through X's premises, and X had a right of entry. When a workman was injured in the restaurant, both X and Y were held liable as occupiers.

The leading case on the subject of multiple occupation, *Wheat v E Lacon & Co Ltd*,[2] concerned a public house with a resident manager. The brewery company which owned the public house permitted the manager and his wife (who occupied part of the premises as licensees) to take in paying guests, and one of these guests was killed when he fell down the unlighted back stairs. In an action by the guest's widow (which failed because she was unable to prove negligence), the House of Lords made some important comments on the question of occupation. The brewery, it was said, should be regarded as occupying the residential part of the premises, either vicariously (through its employee, the manager) or because it retained sufficient control. The manager, too, was an occupier of the relevant part. Both occupiers therefore owed visitors a duty of care; the content of their duties, however, might well differ. For example, the structure of the property would probably be the responsibility of the brewery, while liability for such matters as defective carpeting in the manager's flat would more appropriately be imposed upon the manager.

  [1] [1966] 1 All ER 88, CA.
  [2] [1966] 1 All ER 582, HL.

Premises

21.6 The Occupiers' Liability Act 1957 does not define what is meant by 'premises', although these clearly include land and buildings. In addition, it is provided by s 1(3)(a) that the statutory rules shall regulate 'the obligations of a person occupying or having control over any fixed or moveable structure, including any vessel, vehicle or aircraft', a list which seems apt to include both such permanent structures as grandstands[1] or pylons,[2] and more temporary erections such as scaffolding[3] or ladders.[4] However, in *Wheeler v Copas*,[5] it was held that the Act did not apply to a farmer who lent an unsuitable ladder to a bricklayer; the farmer could not be said to remain in occupation of the ladder once it was lent. As far as 'vessels, vehicles or aircraft' are concerned, it appears that the Act covers only damage caused by defective structure and not that which results from, say, negligent driving.

[1] *Francis v Cockrell* (1870) LR 5 Qb 501.
[2] *Kenny v Electricity Supply Board* [1932] IR 73.
[3] *Pratt v Richards* [1951] 2 KB 208, [1951] 1 All ER 90n.
[4] *Woodman v Richardson* [1937] 3 All ER 866, CA.
[5] [1981] 3 All ER 405.

Visitor

21.7 The simplification of occupiers' liability by the Act of 1957 leaves untouched one vital distinction, namely that between a lawful visitor and a trespasser; the statutory duty of care is owed only to the former. The most frequently cited definition of a trespasser is 'he who goes on the land without invitation of any sort and whose presence is either unknown to the proprietor or, if known, is practically objected to'.[1] This category embraces a wide variety of entrants, from the burglar or poacher to the lost rambler or wandering child. However, where bee-keepers complained that their bees had been killed by the chemical spray used by a neighbouring farmer on his crops, the judge refused to categorise the bees as either visitors or trespassers; he held nonetheless that a duty of care was owed.[2]

Whether or not a person is *expressly* permitted to enter premises is simply a question of fact. However, more difficulties arise where it is alleged that the occupier has *impliedly* given permission. As a general rule, the courts are reluctant to reach such a conclusion, as is illustrated by the case of *Great Central Rly Co v Bates*,[3] in which a policeman, seeing a warehouse door open at night and going in to investigate, was held to be a trespasser. On the other hand, the mere existence of a path across one's front garden is regarded as a tacit invitation to members of the public wishing to conduct lawful business with the occupier, although this licence extends no further than the front door.[4] Further, even this implication can be excluded, for example by a clearly displayed notice stating: 'No salesmen'. In the entertaining case of *Snook v Mannion*,[5] however, a householder's instruction to two police officers to 'F__ off' was held to constitute mere vulgar abuse, rather than a valid revocation of their implied permission to be on the premises.

Particular problems are caused by cases of repeated trespass, for instance where the occupier's land is frequently used by members of the public as a short cut, or for picnicking. No permission can be inferred if the occupier takes reasonable steps to keep such people out.[6] Even without such steps, however, it seems that acquiescence, rather than mere knowledge, is what must be proved; as Lord Goddard put it: 'How is it to be said that he had licensed what he cannot prevent?'[7] Nonetheless, in extreme cases, failure to take action may amount to permission, as it did in *Lowery v Walker*,[8] where a farmer's field had been used as a short cut to the local railway station for some 35 years. The farmer occasionally turned people back but otherwise took no action until, without warning, he put a savage horse in the field. The claimant, who was attacked and injured by this horse, was held by the House of Lords to be a lawful visitor and therefore entitled to sue the farmer for damages.

[1] *R Addie & Sons (Collieries) Ltd v Dumbreck* [1929] AC 358 at 371.
[2] *Tutton v AD Walter Ltd* [1985] 3 All ER 757.
[3] [1921] 3 KB 578.
[4] *Robson v Hallett* [1967] 2 All ER 407, DC.
[5] [1982] RTR 321, DC.
[6] *Hardy v Central London Rly Co* [1920] 3 KB 459, CA.
[7] *Edwards v Railway Executive* [1952] 2 All ER 430.
[8] [1911] AC 10, HL.

Limited permission

21.8 The permission, whether express or implied, by which a person enters premises may be limited in scope. If this is so, and the permission is exceeded, that person ceases to be a lawful visitor and becomes a trespasser.

The limitations which may be placed upon a licence to enter take various forms, of which the most common relates to area. A hotel guest, for example, becomes a trespasser by going through a door marked 'Private'. In *Westwood v Post Office*,[1] an employee who disregarded a notice on a door which stated: 'Authorised personnel only' was held to be a trespasser when he fell through a defective trapdoor in the room and was killed. On the other hand, where a limitation is not clearly shown, a visitor is given a certain amount of leeway. Thus, in *Pearson v Coleman Bros*,[2] a little girl was held to be a licensee when, in searching for a lavatory at a circus, she strayed into the zoo area and was mauled by a lion.

Permission may also be limited as to time, in which case it seems that, to be effective, the limitation must be brought to the entrant's notice. In *Stone v Taffe*,[3] where the manager of a public house gave an unauthorised after-hours party, it was held that the brewers were not entitled to treat a guest as a trespasser, as he did not know that they objected to this practice. This seems surprising since, as a general rule, a person may be a trespasser without being aware of it.[4]

The third limitation which may be placed upon permission to enter premises relates to the purpose of entry. This principle, which Scrutton LJ summarised by saying: 'When you invite a person into your house to use the staircase, you do not invite him to slide down the banisters',[5] was applied by the Court of Appeal in *R v Jones and R v Smith*.[6] The two defendants in that case, who were accused of stealing two television sets from the house of Smith's father, could only be convicted of burglary under the Theft Act 1968 if they had entered the house 'as trespassers'. Smith's father gave evidence that his son had unrestricted permission to enter it; it was held, however, that the father's general permission had been exceeded in this case, so that both defendants were trespassers.

[1] [1973] 1 All ER 283, CA; revsd on other grounds [1973] 3 All ER 184, HL.
[2] [1948] 2 All ER 274, CA.
[3] [1974] 3 All ER 1016, CA.
[4] Para 22.1.
[5] *The Carlgarth* [1927] P 93 at 110.
[6] [1976] 3 All ER 54, CA.

Entry as of right

21.9 It is provided by the Occupiers' Liability Act 1957, s 2(6) that 'persons who enter premises for any purpose in the exercise of a right conferred by law are to be treated as permitted by the occupier to be there for that purpose, whether they in fact have his permission or not'. As a result, the occupier owes the common duty of care to those officials, such as policemen, who have statutory powers of entry. Similarly, where a local authority provides such facilities as parks, playgrounds, lavatories or libraries, it seems that persons using these are lawful visitors.

An exception to the above rule is contained in s 1(4) of the 1957 Act, as amended. Persons who enter property under rights conferred by the Countryside and Rights of Way Act 2000, or by an access agreement or order made under the National Parks and Access to the Countryside Act 1949, are not trespassing; however, if injured, they are not to be treated as visitors.[1]

[1] They will now come within the Occupiers' Liability Act 1984: see para 21.19.

Rights of way

21.10 A person who uses a public right of way across land is of course not guilty of the tort of trespass. However, the common law did not regard such a person as a visitor to the land, with the result that the occupier was under no positive duty to make the way safe. In *Greenhalgh v British Railways Board*,[1] it was held by the Court of Appeal that this rule had not been altered by the Occupiers' Liability Act 1957, so that a woman who was injured when she tripped in a pothole on a railway bridge could not recover damages from the owners of the bridge, notwithstanding that it was crossed by a public footpath. Furthermore, the user of a public right of way cannot even take advantage of the statutory duty which an occupier of land owes to trespassers and other uninvited entrants,[2] for the Occupiers' Liability Act 1984, s 1(7) specifically provides that that duty is not owed to persons using the highway.

The occupier's immunity in such cases is subject to two qualifications. In the first place there may be liability where the danger arises, not from the condition of the way itself, but from activities which are carried on by the occupier on the same or adjoining land. In *Thomas v British Railways Board*,[3] for example, the defendants were held liable when their failure to repair a stile allowed a two-year-old girl to stray on to a railway line, where she was struck by a train. Second, where a right of way is maintainable at the public expense, the relevant highway authority is now under a positive statutory duty to repair and maintain the way, and can be liable for damages to anyone injured by its failure to do so.[4]

A person using a private right of way across land is likewise not treated, either by the common law or under the Occupiers' Liability Act 1957, as a visitor to the land.[5] However, such a person is now entitled to the more limited protection which is afforded to trespassers and other uninvited entrants by the Occupiers' Liability Act 1984.[6]

[1] [1969] 2 All ER 114, CA; affd in *McGeown v Northern Ireland Housing Executive* [1994] 3 All ER 53, HL.
[2] See para 21.19.
[3] [1976] 3 All ER 15, CA.
[4] Highways Act 1980, Part IV.
[5] *Holden v White* [1982] 2 All ER 328, CA.
[6] *Vodden v Gayton* [2001] PIQR P52, where the claim failed on the facts.

Visitors under contract

21.11 Persons who enter premises by virtue of a contract are subject to two specific provisions of the 1957 Act. First, where the contract is made between the occupier and the visitor (eg where entry is by ticket), s 5 provides in effect that the visitor's rights depend upon the terms of that contract; if the contract contains no relevant express terms, the common duty of care (and no stricter obligation) will be implied.[1] If the contract contains express terms which seek to exclude or limit the occupier's duty, these will now be subject to the Unfair Contract Terms Act 1977, which contains severe restrictions on the use of exemption clauses where the premises concerned are 'business premises'.[2]

Section 3 of the Act of 1957 deals with persons who enter premises under some contract to which they are not party. For instance, where an occupier employs a firm of builders to work on his house, the actual workmen are not normally parties to the contract under which the work is done. So too, a lease may grant access to 'common parts' of the landlord's building, such as staircases and lifts, not only to tenants, but also their families and guests. In all such cases, it is provided that, while the visitor may take the benefit of any additional obligations which the contract imposes upon the occupier, his rights may not be reduced below the level which is imposed by the common duty of care.

[1] *Maguire v Sefton MBC* [2006] EWCA Civ 316, CA.
[2] Paras 9.10 and 21.2.

OCCUPIERS AND LAWFUL VISITORS: KEY POINTS

- The Occupiers' Liability Act 1957 provides that an occupier of premises owes a 'common duty of care' to all lawful visitors.

- Such a duty can in principle be excluded or restricted by a contract term or by a notice on the premises. However, the extent to which this is possible is severely limited by the Unfair Contract Terms Act 1977.

- The question of who is an occupier for this purpose is determined by courts on a pragmatic basis, and there may be more than one 'occupier' of premises at the same time.

- 'Premises' normally consist of land and/or buildings, although other structures may be included.

- A lawful visitor is normally someone who is invited or at least permitted to be on the premises, and may lose that status (and become a trespasser) by abusing the terms on which he or she is permitted to be there.

- The occupier's duty of care extends to anyone who exercises a legal right to enter premises, even where the occupier personally objects to their entry.

- However, the duty does not extend to persons who cross the occupier's land in the exercise of a right of way.

The common duty of care

21.12 The duty which an occupier owes to lawful visitors is defined by the Occupiers' Liability Act 1957, s 2(2) as 'a duty to take such care as in all the circumstances of the case is reasonable to see that the visitor will be reasonably safe in using the premises for the purpose for which he is invited or permitted by the occupier to be there'. This definition is a straightforward application of the rules of negligence and, in deciding whether or not an occupier's duty has been breached, a court will consider all the circumstances of the case. To take a few examples, liability was imposed upon a local authority for allowing a school path which was swept free of snow to remain in a dangerously slippery condition,[1] a professional landlord (who was aware that a particular tenant was frequently very drunk) for failing to fence off a deep concrete stairwell next to the front door of the tenant's house;[2] and a hotel whose balcony balustrades were several inches lower than the height recommended by the British Standards Institution.[3] On the other hand, an occupier was held not liable for failing to replace a glass door panel which, though not conforming to current building regulations, had complied with those in force at the time of building.[4]

Moreover, there was held to be no duty on a local authority to put up warning notices in respect of obvious dangers such as a cliff path[5] or seaweed-covered rocks;[6] nor on the owners of a disused gravel pit[7] or a stately home with a lake[8] to erect 'no swimming' signs, where the dangers of swimming were obvious.

A crucial issue in many cases is the extent to which an occupier should predict what people will do on the premises. In *Wheeler v Trustees of St Mary's Hall, Chislehurst*,[9] it was held that the trustees of a church hall, who hired it out for a martial arts training session, could not be expected to ensure that the experienced hirer had supplied mats to cover the concrete floor. The trustees were accordingly not liable to a participant who suffered serious head injuries when he fell on the floor. Likewise, in *Poppleton v Trustees of the Portsmouth Youth Activities Committee*,[10] it was held that the defendants were under no duty either to train or supervise an adult in respect of the obvious risks inherent in 'bouldering', that is indoor simulated low-level rock-climbing. By contrast, in *Bell v Department of Health and Social Security*,[11] employers who knew that their employees frequently carried tea and coffee from the kitchen back to their offices in a four-storey building were held liable for a danger created by the spillage of drinks on pseudo-marble floors. It has even been held that a football club can be liable to visitors if, knowing of the risk, it fails to prevent visiting hooligans from tearing pieces of concrete from the terracing to use as missiles.[12]

The 1957 Act might well have left the courts to work out the details of the common duty of care; however, certain areas which had caused problems before 1957 are specifically dealt with, and these we consider in the next five paragraphs.

[1] *Murphy v Bradford Metropolitan Borough Council* [1992] PIQR P68, CA.
[2] *Lips v Older* [2004] EWHC 1686, QB.
[3] *Ward v Ritz Hotel (London)* [1992] PIQR P315, CA.
[4] *McGivney v Goldeslea Ltd* (2001) 17 Const LJ 454, CA.
[5] *Cotton v Derbyshire Dales District Council* (1994) Times, 20 June, CA.
[6] *Staples v West Dorset District Council* (1995) 93 LGR 536, CA.
[7] *Whyte v Redland Aggregates Ltd* [1998] CLY 3989, CA.
[8] *Darby v National Trust for Places of Historic Interest or Natural Beauty* [2001] EWCA Civ 189, 3 LGLR 29.
[9] (1989) Times, 10 October.
[10] [2008] EWCA Civ 646, CA.1.
[12] *Cunningham v Reading Football Club* [1992] PIQR P141. See also *Everett v Comojo (UK) Ltd* [2011] EWCA Civ 13, CA; para 16.11.

Children

21.13 In pointing out that the carefulness or otherwise which may be expected of a visitor is relevant to the occupier's duty, s 2(3)(a) provides that 'an occupier must be prepared for children to be less careful than adults'. That children are especially at risk is obvious. For example, in *Moloney v Lambeth London Borough Council*,[1] the defendants were held liable to a four-year-old who fell through a gap in a staircase balustrade which was too small to have endangered an adult.

A particular problem with children is that, even when on premises lawfully, they may be tempted by some dangerous and attractive object to exceed the scope of their permission. If this leads to injury, it is well established that the occupier may not use the child's technical trespass as a ground for avoiding liability. Thus in *Glasgow Corpn v Taylor*,[2] where a seven-year-old boy stole some attractive berries from an unfenced bush in a public park, it was held that his death by poisoning disclosed a good cause of action.

In relation to very young children, to whom almost anything is dangerous but who cannot understand warnings, the law seeks to balance the duty of the occupier with that of the parent. The courts take the view that an occupier, in taking precautions for the safety of small children, is entitled to assume that their parents will also take care. This approach was adopted by Devlin J in *Phipps v Rochester Corpn*,[3] where a five-year-old boy went blackberrying with his sister, aged seven, on a large grassy space forming part of the defendants' building site. The defendants were well aware that children frequently played in this place, so that they were to be regarded as lawful visitors.[4] When the boy fell into a trench and broke his leg, it was held that the defendants were not liable, since this was the kind of danger from which the occupier might expect a reasonable parent to protect his child. On the other hand, the owners of a holiday camp were held liable to a three-year-old who fell on to a low wall with sharp-edged bricks, because they could expect children to be in the area without close parental supervision.[5]

It should not be thought, on the basis of cases such as these, that an accident involving a small child must always be the fault of either the occupier or the parents. In *Bourne Leisure Ltd v Marsden*,[6] where a two-year-old wandered off from his parent's caravan on the defendants' site, climbed over the fence surrounding a pond and drowned, the Court of Appeal emphasised that this was a pure accident for which neither party could be blamed.

[1] (1966) 64 LGR 440.
[2] [1922] 1 AC 44, HL.
[3] [1955] 1 All ER 129. See also *Simkiss v Rhondda Borough Council* (1982) 81 LGR 460, CA.
[4] See para 21.8.
[5] *Perry v Butlins Holiday World* [1998] Ed CR 39, CA.
[6] [2009] EWCA Civ 671, CA.

Specialists

21.14 It is provided by s 2(3)(b) that 'an occupier may expect that a person, in the exercise of his calling, will appreciate and guard against any special risks ordinarily incident to it, so far as the occupier leaves him free to do so'. One important effect of this is that an occupier whose property becomes dangerous will not normally be liable to persons who come for the very purpose of repairing it. It might be thought that this would apply to the case of a fireman who is injured in fighting a fire which is caused by the occupier's negligence, but it has twice been held that such a person may recover damages from the occupier, provided that his presence at the fire was foreseeable and that he would be at risk despite exercising all the skill of his calling. Unfortunately, the first ruling to this effect[1] did not mention s 2(3)(b) of the Occupiers' Liability Act; the second[2] did not mention the Act at all but dealt with the case on the basis of common law negligence.

Whether or not a risk is 'incident to a person's calling' is a question of fact, but some guidance may be obtained from a comparison of two decisions. In *Howitt v Alfred Bagnall & Sons Ltd*,[3] a clerk of works fell from scaffolding on which he was standing to inspect roof repairs. The occupiers were held not liable, for the scaffolding was not defective; the only risk lay in using it at all, and this was inherent in the man's job. In *Woollins v British Celanese Ltd*,[4] on the other hand, a post office engineer fell through some hardboard roofing at the defendants' factory. It was held by the Court of Appeal that, while he could be expected to guard against live wires, the structure of the building was not connected with his job; he was therefore able to recover damages.

[1] *Salmon v Seafarer Restaurants Ltd* [1983] 3 All ER 729.
[2] *Ogwo v Taylor* [1987] 3 All ER 961, HL.
[3] [1967] 2 Lloyd's Rep 370.
[4] (1966) 1 KIR 438, CA.

Warnings

21.15 A reminder that an occupier's duty is to render the *visitor* safe, rather than the *premises,* is given by s 2(4)(a), which provides: 'Where damage is caused to a visitor by a danger of which he had been warned by the occupier, the warning is not to be treated without more as absolving the occupier from liability, unless in all the circumstances it was enough to enable the visitor to be reasonably safe'. The legal effect of compliance with this provision is that the common duty of care is fulfilled, which has two important consequences in deciding whether or not a warning is valid. First, the warning must come from the occupier personally,[1] although a warning from another source may lead to the conclusion that a visitor either assumes the risk of injury or is contributorily negligent. Second, it must be adequate, in the sense of both specifying the particular danger sufficiently clearly that the visitor can avoid it and being visible. In *Woollins v British Celanese Ltd,*[2] a warning hidden behind a door was held to be inadequate.[3]

---

[1] *Bunker v Charles Brand & Son Ltd* [1969] 2 All ER 59.
[2] (1966) 1 KIR 438, CA.
[3] In *Rae v Mars (UK) Ltd* [1990] 1 EGLR 161, it was held that no sufficient warning of danger had been given to a surveyor who, in inspecting an unlighted storehouse in a factory, fell on to the sunken floor and was injured.

Independent contractors

21.16 Section 2(4)(b) provides:

'Where damage is caused to a visitor by a danger due to the faulty execution of any work of construction, maintenance or repair by an independent contractor employed by the occupier, the occupier is not to be treated without more as answerable for the danger if in all the circumstances he had acted reasonably in entrusting the work to an independent contractor and had taken such steps (if any) as he reasonably ought in order to satisfy himself that the contractor was competent and that the work had been properly done.'

This, in effect, gives statutory approval to two earlier decisions of the Court of Appeal. In *Haseldine v CA Daw & Son Ltd,*[1] the claimant was injured when a lift in the defendants' block of flats fell to the bottom of the shaft. The accident resulted from negligent work by the firm of specialist engineers employed by the defendants to service the lift and it was held that, since the defendants had no reason to doubt the competence of their contractors, they had in no way failed in their duty towards the claimant.

The wording of s 2(4)(b) also endorses the principle laid down in *Woodward v Hastings Corpn,*[2] that an occupier who chooses to leave to an independent contractor jobs which could and should be done personally remains responsible for their proper execution. In that case a school cleaner (who was assumed to be an independent contractor) swept the snow from a step and carelessly left it in a dangerously icy condition. It was held that the local authority were liable in negligence to a person who slipped on the step, since this was not a specialist task.

Even where it is reasonable to entrust the work to an independent contractor, the occupier must take reasonable steps to see both that the contractor is competent and that the work is properly done. It has been held that on a large-scale construction job, for instance, the occupier may be obliged to appoint a qualified architect or surveyor (who would himself be an independent contractor of the occupier) to supervise the work.[3] However, the courts do not demand very much from an occupier who cannot be expected to understand the intricacies of the job, so that where a demolition contractor adopted an unsafe method of working and one of his employees was injured as a result, it was held that the occupier, who was unaware of what was happening, could not be liable.[4]

It may be noted in this connection that an occupier is not usually under any duty to check whether or not an independent contractor has public liability insurance.[5] However, such a duty may arise in special circumstances, for example where the contractor is to be involved in especially dangerous activities.[6]

[1] [1941] 3 All ER 156, CA.
[2] [1944] 2 All ER 565, CA.
[3] *AMF International Ltd v Magnet Bowling Ltd* [1968] 2 All ER 789.
[4] *Ferguson v Welsh* [1987] 3 All ER 777, HL.
[5] *Naylor v Payling* [2004] EWCA Civ 560, CA.
[6] *Gwilliam v West Hertfordshire Hospital NHS Trust* [2002] EWCA Civ 1041, CA.

Assumption of risk

21.17 Section 2(5) makes it clear that an occupier is not liable to a visitor in respect of risks which the latter willingly assumes. Thus, in *Simms v Leigh Rugby Football Club Ltd*,[1] where a professional Rugby League player was thrown against a concrete wall which surrounded the defendants' pitch, it was held that he could not recover damages for the injuries received; since the ground satisfied the League rules, it had to be assumed that players had accepted the risks inherent in playing on it.

Since s 2(5), in effect, applies the common law defence of assumption of risk, the rules which govern that defence are applicable.[2] In particular, it will not protect an occupier if the visitor has no real choice in the matter; for example, where his employer orders the visitor to enter the premises[3] or to incur the risk.[4]

It should also be noted that, although the Act is silent on the point, it has frequently been held that the defence of contributory negligence is available to an occupier.[5]

[1] [1969] 2 All ER 923. Cf *Harrison v Vincent* [1982] RTR 8, CA.
[2] Paras 19.2–19.5.
[3] *Burnett v British Waterways Board* [1973] 2 All ER 631, CA.
[4] *Bunker v Charles Brand & Son Ltd* [1969] 2 All ER 59.
[5] See, for example, *Rae v Mars (UK) Ltd* [1990] 1 EGLR 161.

THE COMMON DUTY OF CARE: KEY POINTS

- The occupier's duty is to take reasonable care to see that the lawful visitor will be reasonably safe. This may require the taking of extra steps where a visitor may be at greater risk (for example where a child may not understand a particular source of danger).

- On the other hand, an occupier is entitled to assume that a visitor who is a specialist will take care of himself (or herself) in respect of risks incidental to that specialism.

- An occupier who reasonably delegates work to an independent contractor, in circumstances where it is reasonable to do so, will not normally be liable if that contractor negligently creates a danger to visitors.

- An occupier's duty may be fulfilled by giving a visitor adequate warning of a danger; the occupier may also avoid liability where it is clear that the visitor has willingly assumed the risk of injury.

Trespassers and other 'non-visitors'

21.18 The Occupiers' Liability Act 1957 applies only to lawful visitors; injuries to trespassers were governed by the common law, which had to deal with two separate problems. First, there is the trespasser who is injured by the very steps which the occupier has taken to keep the trespasser out. The position here seems to be that static deterrents, such as broken glass or spikes on top of a wall, are permissible;[1] concealed instruments of retribution (such as man-traps or spring-guns), on the other hand, are not allowed,[2] although a trespasser who enters with full knowledge of their presence may be held to have assumed the risk of injury.[3] In *Revill v Newbery*,[4] the Court of Appeal imposed liability upon an allotment owner who fired a shotgun through a hole in the door of his shed and injured a trespasser who was attempting to break in.[5]

As for a trespasser injured by the condition of premises or by an activity taking place upon them, English law for many years took the view that the occupier could not be held responsible, even where the trespasser was only four years old and the occupier was well aware that small children often played on the haulage machinery which killed him.[6] That draconian view was eventually modified in the trespasser's favour by the House of Lords,[7] but this is now of purely historical interest, since the position of injured trespassers is today governed by the Occupiers' Liability Act 1984.

[1] *Deane v Clayton* (1817) 7 Taunt 489.
[2] *Bird v Holbrook* (1828) 4 Bing 628.
[3] *Ilott v Wilkes* (1820) 3 B & Ald 304.
[4] [1996] 1 All ER 291, CA.
[5] The claimant's damages were reduced by two-thirds on the ground of contributory negligence.
[6] *R Addie & Sons (Collieries) Ltd v Dumbreck* [1929] AC 358, HL.
[7] *British Railways Board v Herrington* [1972] AC 877, HL.

Occupiers' Liability Act 1984

21.19 The first point to note about the 1984 Act is that it applies, not only to trespassers, but to all persons other than those who are 'visitors' for the purposes of the Occupiers' Liability Act 1957. It thus embraces persons entering under the National Parks and Access to the Countryside Act 1949[1] and the Countryside and Rights of Way Act 2000,[2] and also those using a private right of way, although persons using the public highway are specifically excluded. The result appears to be that, while *Greenhalgh v British Railways Board*[3] remains good law, the effect of *Holden v White*[4] is reversed.

[1] See para 21.9.
[2] See para 21.23.
[3] [1969] 2 All ER 114, CA: para 21.10.
[4] [1982] 2 All ER 328, CA: para 21.10.

Scope of the duty

21.20 Where certain conditions are met, the 1984 Act imposes a duty on an occupier towards trespassers and other non-visitors. However, it should be noted that such a duty can only apply to a danger which is due to the state of the premises or to things done on them. This restriction has served to rule out a number of claims by trespassers whose injuries resulted from their own risky activities on premises which were not inherently dangerous, such as diving into shallow water,[1] an 11-year-old climbing on the underside of an external fire escape to impress his friends[2] or dancing on the roof a garage and falling through a plastic skylight.[3]

[1] *Tomlinson v Congleton BC* [2003] UKHL 47, [2004] 1 AC 46, HL.
[2] *Keown v Coventry Healthcare NHS Trust* [2006] EWCA Civ 39.
[3] *Siddorn v Patel* [2007] EWHC 1248, QB.

The statutory conditions

21.21 In attempting to strike the right balance between the interests of an occupier[1] of premises[2] and those of uninvited entrants, s 1(3) of the Act provides that the occupier shall only owe a duty to such a person if three conditions are satisfied. The first of these is that the occupier must be aware of the danger or have reasonable grounds to believe that it exists. In *Rhind v Astbury Water Park Ltd*,[3] the defendants were held to owe no duty to a 19-year-old who was injured when diving into a disused gravel pit, since they were unaware of the fibre glass container lying on the bottom on which the claimant struck his head.

The second condition is that the occupier must be aware or have reasonable grounds to believe that the uninvited entrant either is, or is likely to come into, the vicinity of the danger. This has served to defeat claims by a trespasser who dived into Folkestone Harbour in the middle of winter and struck a submerged grid pile;[4] one who took a dangerous short cut to his council flat across a steep grassy bank;[5] and one (aged nine) who surmounted a high fence before climbing on to a factory roof.[6] It should be noted that an occupier's 'knowledge' for this purpose cannot be assumed merely because the occupier has attempted to fence a dangerous area.[7] The third condition is that the risk in question is one against which the occupier may reasonably be expected to offer the other person some protection. To date this does not appear to have attracted much judicial attention, and it is difficult to see what it adds to the way in which a court would normally assess whether or not a duty of care has been fulfilled.

[1] 'Occupier' bears the same meaning as it does for the purpose of the Occupiers' Liability Act 1957; see paras 21.4–21.5.
[2] 'Premises' bears the same meaning as it does for the purposes of the Occupiers' Liability Act 1957; see para 21.7.
[3] [2004] EWCA Civ 756, CA.
[4] *Donoghue v Folkestone Properties Ltd* [2003] EWCA Civ 231, CA.
[5] *Maloney v Torfaen CBC* [2005] EWCA Civ 1762, CA.
[6] *Swain v Natui Ram Puri* [1996] PIQR P442, CA.
[7] *White v St Albans City and District Council* (1990) Times, 12 March, CA.

The duty of care

21.22 Where the statutory conditions are satisfied, the occupier is under a duty of reasonable care to see that the trespasser or other uninvited entrant is not killed or injured by the danger in question.[1] What is reasonable is of course a question of fact; thus a local authority was held not liable when it fenced off a vandalised house in dangerous condition, despite the fact that 14-year-old boys were still able to gain entry.[2]

In *Tomlinson v Congleton BC*,[3] the claimant was seriously injured when making a shallow dive into a lake at a country park run by the defendant local authority. Both swimming and diving were expressly forbidden, so that the claimant was trespassing at the time of his injury. In an extremely important ruling, and one which is likely to rule out many claims by trespassers, the House of Lords held that the defendants were under no duty to deny all public access to the lake (the only practical way in which to prevent trespassers like the claimant from taking such risks). Indeed it would be wholly unreasonable and against the public interest to sacrifice the pleasure of the vast majority of visitors in order to protect a few people from the consequences of their own recklessness.

[1] The Act specifically excludes liability for any loss of damage to property: s 1(8).
[2] *Platt v Liverpool CC* [1997] CLY 4864, CA.
[3] [2003] UKHL 47, HL.

Injury suffered on access land

21.23 The Countryside and Rights of Way Act 2000, s 2[1] creates a public right to enter, for the purposes of open-air recreation, any open country which has been officially designated 'access land'. A person who is injured while exercising this right comes within the Occupiers' Liability Act 1984, but the occupier's duty under that Act is a very restricted one. Section 13 of the CRWA 2000 excludes any claim for injuries caused by natural features (which include all plants, shrubs and trees, whether natural or planted), and also those suffered when passing over, under or through any wall, fence or gate, other than by proper use of a gate or stile, except where the occupier has intentionally or recklessly created the risk. Moreover, in considering other OLA 1984 claims by persons injured while exercising their right to enter access land, a court must have regard to the fact that the occupier should not be subjected to an undue financial or other burden, and also to the importance of maintaining the character of the countryside, including features of historic, traditional or archaeological interest.

[1] As extended by the Marine and Coastal Access Act 2009, Part 9.

Defences

21.24 The OLA 1984 provides an occupier with two defences against liability, similar to those which are available under the OLA 1957. First, s 1(5) provides that the occupier's duty may be discharged by taking such steps as are reasonable 'to give warning of the danger concerned or to discourage persons from incurring the risk'.[1] Second, s 1(6) makes it clear that the defence of assumption of risk is applicable,[2] and this defence was actually applied in the case of *Ratcliff v McConnell*[3] so as to rule out a claim by a student who climbed into his college's outdoor swimming pool at night and dived into the shallow end. Although it is not specifically mentioned, it seems likely that the defence of contributory negligence would also apply.[4]

[1] See para 21.15.
[2] See paras 19.2–19.5 and para 21.17. A trespasser failed on this ground in *Ratcliff v McConnell* [1999] 1 WLR 670, CA.
[3] [1999] 1 WLR 670, CA.
[4] See paras 19.6–19.9.

Exclusion of liability

21.25 We have already considered the extent to which an occupier may, by putting up a notice, exclude or restrict his liability to lawful visitors.[1] The OLA 1984 gives no guidance whatever as to whether the rights of non-visitors may be similarly affected, and the point has not yet arisen in any reported case. Should it do so, it could lead to the odd situation of a lawful visitor, who is perhaps more likely than a trespasser to see a notice excluding liability, being in a worse position than the trespasser if injuries occur. A possible solution to this problem might be for the courts to hold that, while the rights of a lawful visitor may be excluded by an appropriate notice, the visitor would then be left with rights equivalent to those enjoyed by a trespasser under the 1984 Act, and that neither lawful visitor nor trespasser may suffer any further reduction of their rights.

[1] Para 21.3.

THE DUTY TO TRESPASSERS AND OTHER 'NON-VISITORS': KEY POINTS

- The Occupiers' Liability Act 1984 provides that, in limited circumstances, an occupier of premises owes a duty to trespassers and other persons who are not lawful visitors.

- That duty arises only where the occupier is aware of both the danger and the trespasser's proximity to it, and where it is reasonable to expect the occupier to offer protection against that danger.

- Persons using a private right of way across land are owed the same duty. So too are persons using 'access land', although their rights are further limited by statute.

- An occupier may avoid liability by giving an adequate warning, or where it is clear that the trespasser has willingly assumed the risk of injury. However, it is unclear whether liability can be avoided by means of a notice excluding liability.

Purchasers

Caveat emptor

21.26   At one time, by virtue of a legal doctrine known as *caveat emptor* or 'let the buyer beware', a vendor or landlord of real property owed no duty of care to the purchaser or tenant (or to anyone else) in respect of injury or damage resulting from defects in the property. In relation to defects which the vendor/landlord has not positively created, this is still the case.[1] However, the legal position regarding defects created by the vendor or landlord has been the subject of both common law and legislative developments.

---

[1] *Rimmer v Liverpool City Council* [1984] 1 All ER 930, CA, where the Court of Appeal reluctantly followed the ruling by the House of Lords in *Cavalier v Pope* [1906] AC 428, HL. Also see *McNerny v Lambeth London Borough Council* [1989] 1 EGLR 81, CA.

Common law developments

21.27   In *Dutton v Bognor Regis UDC*,[1] the claimant was the second owner of a house which, a mere two years after being completed, was discovered to have inadequate foundations for its location (the site of an old rubbish tip). She sued the local authority, alleging that their building inspector had been guilty of negligence in passing the house's foundations as satisfactory. In upholding this claim, a majority of the Court of Appeal stated obiter that the builder would, if sued, also have been liable. This apparent reversal of the previous position was heavily criticised on the ground that the claim was in truth one for pure economic loss.[2] However, it was unanimously approved by the House of Lords in the similar case of *Anns v Merton London Borough Council*.[3]

For the next 10 years or so, the decision in *Anns v Merton* was used to justify the imposition of liability for negligence upon builders, sub-contractors, architects and other design consultants and, perhaps most importantly,[4] local authorities approving plans and inspecting buildings in the course of construction. However, a remarkable about-turn in the 1980s resulted in a series of decisions indicating that the House of Lords was extremely uneasy about this area of liability,[5] so far as it covered damage to the building itself. Eventually, in *Murphy v Brentwood District Council*,[6] the House of Lords declared that *Dutton v Bognor Regis*, *Anns v Merton* and all the cases which had followed them must be regarded as having been wrongly decided.

[1] [1972] 1 All ER 462, CA.

[2] See para 16.15.

[3] [1977] 2 All ER 492, HL.

[4] Since all the other potential defendants might well be insolvent and thus unable to pay any damages awarded.

[5] The most important of these decisions was that in *D & F Estates Ltd v Church Comrs for England* [1988] 2 All ER 992, HL.

[6] [1990] 2 All ER 908, HL. The House of Lords immediately applied this ruling in *Department of the Environment v Thomas Bates & Son Ltd* [1990] 2 All ER 943, HL.

21.28 As a result of *Murphy v Brentwood District Council*, the ability of a purchaser or tenant of a defective building to recover damages in the tort of negligence from whoever is responsible has been drastically restricted. The present legal position is as follows:

- A negligent designer, contractor or sub-contractor will be liable for a dangerous defect which causes death, personal injury or physical damage to property other than the building itself (eg where a defective garage roof falls on a car). However, once such a defect is discovered, a decision by the occupier to continue using the building might break the chain of causation from the defendant's negligence,[1] or might be held to constitute contributory negligence by the occupier.[2]

- A local authority which is guilty of negligence in approving plans, or inspecting a building in the course of construction, is probably liable to the same extent as a designer or builder as regards personal injury or death. However, the local authority will not be liable for physical damage to other property, since its statutory responsibilities in this area are limited to ensuring the health and safety of persons.[3]

- With two possible qualifications, there is no liability in negligence to a future owner in respect of damage to the building itself. This is perceived as pure economic loss and is therefore not recoverable. It makes no difference whether the building is merely defective or positively dangerous.

- The House of Lords in *Murphy v Brentwood District Council* suggested that, in two exceptional situations, a future owner might be able to recover damages in respect of damage to the building itself. Both of these have been recognised and applied in subsequent cases. The first is where the negligent work of one contractor or sub-contractor causes damage to other parts of the building which were not constructed by them (eg where a defective central heating boiler causes a fire); it appears that this may be treated as 'damage to other property', for which the negligent party would be liable.[4] Second, where a defective building constitutes a threat to adjoining property with the result that the owner is forced to incur the cost of repairing it, this cost may be recovered as damages from the person whose negligence caused the defect.[5]

[1] See paras 18.10.

[2] See *Targett v Torfaen Borough Council* [1992] 3 All ER 27, CA.

[3] *Tesco Stores Ltd v Wards Construction (Investment) Ltd* (1995) 76 BLR 94.

[4] *Jacobs v Morton and Partners* (1994) 72 BLR 92.

[5] *Morse v Barratt (Leeds) Ltd* (1992) 9 Const LJ 158.

Defective Premises Act 1972

21.29 Section 1 of this Act creates a legal remedy in respect of defects in dwellings (ie houses and flats, but not commercial property) which will run with the property for the benefit of purchasers or tenants. It provides that a person taking on work for or in connection with the provision of a dwelling (whether the dwelling is provided by the erection or by the conversion or enlargement of a building[1]) owes a duty:

- if the dwelling is provided to the order of any person, to that person; and
- without prejudice to paragraph a. above, to every person who acquires an interest (whether legal or equitable) in the dwelling,

to see that the work taken on is done in a workman-like or, as the case may be, professional manner, with proper materials and so that as regards that work the dwelling will be fit for habitation when completed.

This provision applies, not only to builders, but also to architects and other design consultants, sub-contractors, and the developer who arranges for someone else to do the work;[2] in short, to anyone whose work contributes to the completed dwelling. However, it does not extend to a manufacturer or supplier of standard components, nor to a builder who works entirely to a client's specification.[3]

The duty imposed by s 1(1) is not a duty of care, but rather a statutory version of the warranty which the common law implies into contracts to build and sell a dwelling.[4] It applies to omissions as well as to positive acts[5] and cannot be contracted out of.[6] However, it has been held to apply only to defects which are sufficiently serious to render the dwelling unfit for habitation,[7] an interpretation which considerably limits the usefulness of this statutory provision. It may also be noted that claims under the Act are subject to a limitation period of six years from the date on which the dwelling is completed.

[1] This does not include works of mere rectification or refurbishment; there must be a new dwelling: *Jacobs v Morton and Partners* (1994) 72 BLR 92.
[2] Section 1(4).
[3] Section 1(2) and (3).
[4] See *Hancock v B W Brazier (Anerley) Ltd* [1966] 2 All ER 901, CA; para 7.31.
[5] *Andrews v Schooling* [1991] 3 All ER 723, CA.
[6] Section 6(3).
[7] *Thompson v Alexander* (1992) 59 BLR 81.

Landlords

21.30 The law governing premises which are defective when disposed of applies to landlords just as it does to vendors. In respect of defects which arise after disposal, however, the position of the landlord requires separate treatment, since there may be a continuing obligation to repair. At common law, the breach of a landlord's repairing obligation was actionable by the tenant alone;[1] a visitor who was injured could neither recover damages for breach of the landlord's contractual obligation to repair the demised premises, nor treat the landlord as 'occupier' of these premises.[2] This unsatisfactory state of affairs was remedied by the Defective Premises Act 1972, s 4[3], which provides: 'Where premises are let under a tenancy which puts on the landlord an obligation to the tenant for the maintenance or repair of the premises, the landlord owes to all persons who might reasonably be expected to be affected by defects in the state of the premises a duty to take such care as is reasonable in all the circumstances to see that they are reasonably safe from personal injury or from damage to their property caused by a [defect within the repairing obligation].'

The effect of s 4 is that an injured person (who may be a visitor, trespasser or even someone off the premises) may sue the landlord for injury or damage caused by a defect which the landlord is under an obligation (express or implied) to repair. Further, while the landlord might be able to answer a claim by the tenant on the ground that the latter had failed to give notice of the defect,[4] this will be no defence against a third party,[5] provided that the landlord knew or ought to have known of the defect. It is important to note that s 4 also applies to the many cases where a landlord, although under no duty to repair the premises, nonetheless has an express or implied right to do so.[6]

¹ *Cavalier v Pope* [1906] AC 428, HL.
² Para 21.4.
³ Replacing the more limited provisions of the Occupiers' Liability Act 1957, s 4.
⁴ Paras 36.45 and 36.48.
⁵ Including a member of the tenant's family: see *B v Camden London Borough Council* [2001] PIQR P9.
⁶ See, for example, *Mint v Good* [1950] 2 All ER 1159. CA; *McAuley v Bristol City Council* [1992] 1 All ER 749, CA.

DEFECTIVE BUILDINGS: KEY POINTS

- The doctrine of '*caveat emptor*' means that a vendor or landlord is not liable for injuries arising out of defects in premises, where these are not themselves caused by the vendor or landlord.

- A person whose negligence in the design or construction of a building leads to defects will be liable to anyone injured as a result; however, there is no liability (for example to a subsequent owner of the property) in respect of the defects themselves.

- The Defective Premises Act 1972 imposes liability on designers and constructors for defects in residential (not commercial) premises; however, this liability lasts only for a limited period.

- A landlord of residential premises who is under an obligation to repair will be liable for injuries resulting from a defect in the premises falling within the repairing obligation.

Questions

1. Who is regarded as an 'occupier' for the purposes of the Occupiers' Liability Act 1957?

2. To what extent can an occupier exclude or restrict the duty which is owed to lawful visitors?

3. What duty is owed by an occupier to persons who exercise a right of way across the occupier's property?

4. What is the 'common duty of care'?

5. What is the legal effect of a warning of danger given by an occupier to visitors?

6. In what circumstances does an occupier owe a duty of care to trespassers?

7. To what extent can a designer or constructor of a building be held liable for negligence which results in defects in that building?

8. Porno, a former rock star, purchases a country estate and retires to its mansion. The entire estate is fenced, and notices all around the perimeter state: 'No access for vehicles'. One night Zoom, a freelance photographer seeking to take and sell unauthorised pictures of one of Porno's wild parties, rides his motorcycle across a footbridge which gives access to the estate. The footbridge collapses, zoom is seriously injured and his motorcycle is destroyed.
   Advise Zoom as to his rights, if any, against Porno.

22

Trespass to land

CHAPTER OVERVIEW

Trespass to land is one of the oldest of all torts. In this chapter we consider:

- the meaning of trespass and the extent to which it can be committed accidentally;
- the extent to which trespass can be committed above and below the surface of land;
- the range of acts and activities which may amount in law to a trespass;
- the question of who is entitled to bring an action for trespass;
- the circumstances in which the law permits one person to enter land belonging to another;
- the remedies, both legal and non-legal, available to a person whose land is trespassed upon.

22.1 This tort may be defined as a direct intrusion upon land in the possession of the claimant. It is actionable per se, which means that a claimant may succeed without having to prove that any damage has been done.[1] However, despite notices proclaiming that 'Trespassers will be prosecuted', trespass is not in itself normally a criminal offence.[2]

A defendant may commit trespass without meaning to, as in *Basely v Clarkson*,[3] where a man cutting his grass crossed an ill-defined boundary and cut some of the claimant's grass as well. However, where the actual intrusion on to the claimant's land is accidental, in the sense that the defendant did not intend it and took reasonable steps to prevent it, there will be a defence of inevitable accident. Thus in *League Against Cruel Sports Ltd v Scott*,[4] it was held that the master of a hunt would only be liable for trespass by the hounds if he either intended them to enter the claimant's land or negligently failed to prevent them from so doing.

[1] *Entick v Carrington* (1765) 19 State Tr 1029.
[2] Except where statute so provides, eg where the trespasser has an offensive weapon (Criminal Law Act 1977).
[3] (1681) 3 Lev 37.
[4] [1985] 2 All ER 489.

Land

22.2 In normal circumstances, possession of land carries with it possession of all underlying strata and of the airspace above, in which case the possessor may sue in trespass for intrusion at any level. Thus, for example, an oil company whose drilling pipelines intruded under the claimant's land at depths between 800 and 2,800 feet was held to have committed trespass.[1] Where, however, land is divided horizontally, such as in a block of flats[2] or on a sale of mineral rights, the possessor of the affected area is alone able to sue. Thus, for example, Y has rights of pasture over X's land, X may sue anyone who drives tent-pegs into the soil;[3] but only Y may take action against a person who merely rides across the grass.[4]

As far as the airspace above the land is concerned, it is clear that an unauthorised invasion of this is trespass, at least where it is not above the maximum height necessary for the occupier's ordinary use and enjoyment of the property. This may include, for example, a projecting advertisement[5] or the swinging jib of a crane.[6] In *Bernstein v Skyviews and General Ltd*,[7] however, the defendants were held not liable when they flew several hundred feet above the claimant's house to take unauthorised photographs of it, with a view to selling these to the claimant.

Over-flight is also subject to s 76 of the Civil Aviation Act 1982 which, broadly speaking, prevents the landowner from establishing a claim in either trespass or nuisance for the mere fact of the flight, provided that it takes place at a height which is reasonable, having regard to wind and weather. In *Bernstein*'s case, notwithstanding the purpose of their flight, the defendants were allowed to rely on this provision. However, the Act imposes strict liability in respect of any physical damage to the property below which results from an over-flight.

[1] *Bocardo SA v Star Energy UK Onshore Ltd* [2009] EWCA Civ 579.
[2] The tenant of a top floor flat is entitled to the air space above unless the lease defines an upper boundary: *Davies v Yadegar* [1990] 1 EGLR 71, CA.
[3] *Cox v Glue* (1848) 5 CB 533.
[4] *Cox v Mousley* (1848) 5 CB 533.
[5] *Kelsen v Imperial Tobacco Co (of Great Britain and Ireland) Ltd* [1957] 2 All ER 343.
[6] *Anchor Brewhouse Developments Ltd v Berkley House (Docklands Developments) Ltd* [1987] 2 EGLR 173.
[7] [1977] 2 All ER 902.

Intrusion

22.3 The most obvious form of trespass to land is entry by the defendant in person. The slightest crossing of the boundary, such as a hand across the threshold,[1] is sufficient but, in the absence of such a crossing (or at least some contact with the fabric of the property), there is no trespass. Thus a landlord who cuts off mains services to a tenant's flat from a point outside the flat may be guilty of both a breach of contract and a criminal offence,[2] but such conduct does not constitute the tort of trespass.[3]

A common form of trespass consists of causing objects to enter the claimant's land, for example by erecting a building which straddles the boundary. The most trivial invasion will suffice, such as leaning a ladder against the claimant's wall.[4] However, the invasion must be direct. Thus, someone who chops down a tree so that it falls into a neighbouring garden commits trespass; someone who merely allows roots or branches to grow across the boundary is guilty of nuisance.[5]

A person who is permitted or legally entitled to enter land may become a trespasser by exceeding or abusing the right of entry.[6] This rule is important in relation to rights of way, which permit only reasonable passage; thus, in *Hickman v Maisey*,[7] the defendant, who had patrolled a 15-yard stretch of highway across the claimant's land in order to spy on racehorse trials there, was held to be a trespasser. In such cases, action may be taken by the owner of the subsoil, which will in practice often be a highway authority.

[1] *Franklin v Jeffries* (1985) Times, 11 March.
[2] Protection from Eviction Act 1977, s 1.
[3] *Perera v Vandiyar* [1953] 1 All ER 1109, CA.

⁴ *Westripp v Baldock* [1939] 1 All ER 279, CA.
⁵ *Lemmon v Webb* [1894] 3 Ch 1, CA.
⁶ Para 21.8.
⁷ [1900] 1 QB 752, CA.

Possession

22.4 Trespass to land is a wrong to possession rather than to ownership. As a result, where land is let, it is only the tenant who can take action against a trespasser, unless permanent damage is done to the property, in which case the landlord may sue.[1] For the same reason, a tenant who fails to quit the premises when the lease expires is not thereby guilty of trespass, since the landlord is not in possession.[2] Conversely, where land is occupied under licence, the licensee normally[3] lacks the exclusive possession of the property which is necessary to found an action in trespass;[4] this remains in the hands of the licensor.

The common law's emphasis upon the protection of possession (based on its historical concern with preserving the peace) is such that even someone whose possession is wrongful may sue in trespass any other wrongdoer who disturbs that possession,[5] and it is no defence for the latter to show that the true right to possession lies with a third party. The only person who may override such wrongful possession is the true owner, or someone acting on the true owner's behalf.[6]

The question of what constitutes possession in law receives different answers in respect of different types of property. It is the occupation of a house which counts, but the possession of open land may depend upon evidence of actual use, so that the mere erection of a fence round an area of disputed land may not be enough.[7] If, as frequently happens in trespass actions, possession is disputed,[8] the law presumes in favour of the person with title[9] even if, on investigation, that title proves to be defective.[10]

A person who is not actually in possession of land cannot sue for trespass, even if he or she has an immediate right to possession. However, when such a person eventually enters upon the land, he or she is deemed to have been in possession from the moment the right accrued and is therefore entitled to claim damages in respect of trespass committed in the interim.

¹ *Jones v Llanrwst UDC* [1911] 1 Ch 393. If damage which is merely temporary causes financial loss to the landlord, there may be a claim in negligence: *Ehlmer v Hall* [1993] 1 EGLR 137, CA.
² *Hey v Moorhouse* (1839) 6 Bing NC 52.
³ But see para 36.9.
⁴ *Hill v Tupper* (1863) 2 H & C 121.
⁵ *Nicholls v Ely Beet Sugar Factory* [1931] 2 Ch 84, CA.
⁶ *Delaney v T P Smith Ltd* [1946] 2 All ER 23, CA.
⁷ See *Marsden v Miller* (1992) 64 P & CR 239, CA.
⁸ Especially where one party claims to have acquired title against the other by adverse possession: paras 30.19–30.36.
⁹ *Jones v Chapman* (1847) 2 Exch 803.
¹⁰ *Fowley Marine (Emsworth) Ltd v Gafford* [1968] 1 All ER 979, CA.

Defences

22.5 An entry cannot be a trespass if it is legally justified, and justification in this context may arise in various ways. Statutory powers of entry are conferred not only on the police, but also on a myriad of officials. More generally, an access agreement or order made under the National Parks and Access to the Countryside Act 1949 entitles any person to enter the land concerned, provided that the specified conditions are complied with.

A person who has a public or private right of way over land is not guilty of trespass unless the right in question is abused or exceeded.[1] Moreover, the exercise of certain other rights over land (such as easements, profits à prendre and local customary rights[2]) may entitle a person to do what would otherwise be a trespass. Indeed, even a bare permission or licence will also have this effect. Once such a licence is validly revoked,[3] any further intrusion is a trespass, although the licensee cannot be compelled to undo what has been done. Thus, in *Armstrong v Sheppard and Short Ltd*,[4] where the claimant withdrew the permission which he had given the defendants to lay and use a sewer under his land, it was held that further use of the sewer was a trespass, although the defendants could not be compelled to remove the sewer itself.

A person who discovers that goods belonging to him or her are on someone else's land is entitled to enter that land to retake them, at least if the other person is wrongfully responsible for their presence there.[5] Further, apparent acts of trespass may be justified by necessity (defence of the realm or the preservation of life or property) provided that they are in reasonable proportion to the threatened harm and that the need to trespass is not brought about by the defendant's own negligence.[6] However, the defence of necessity is kept within strict limits; it does not entitle homeless persons to 'squat' in vacant premises,[7] nor protesters against genetically modified crops to enter land on which such crops are growing.[8]

Finally, a person who acquiesces in a trespass cannot sue for it if it would be unconscionable to do so, for example where the defendant has been allowed or encouraged to incur expense. However, mere delay in complaining about a trespass does not itself amount to acquiescence.[9]

[1] Paras 21.8 and 22.3.
[2] Chapter 32.
[3] For revocation of licences, see paras 28.43–28.44.
[4] [1959] 2 QB 384, [1959] 2 All ER 651, CA.
[5] *Patrick v Colerick* (1838) 3 M & W 483.
[6] *Rigby v Chief Constable of Northamptonshire* [1985] 1 WLR 1242.
[7] *Southwark London Borough Council v Williams* [1971] 2 All ER 175, CA.
[8] *Monsanto plc v Tilly* [2000] Env LR 313, CA.
[9] *Jones v Stones* [1999] 1 WLR 1739, CA.

Access to neighbouring land

22.6 At common law, a landowner's need to carry out repairs to property did not justify a trespass upon adjoining land. However, there has been statutory intervention in this area. Under the Access to Neighbouring Land Act 1992,[1] any person wishing to carry out works of preservation to his land for which access to adjoining land is necessary,[2] but who cannot obtain the necessary permission for entry to that land, may apply to the county court for an access order.[3] It is for the court to decide whether any proposed works are works of preservation for this purpose, but certain works are presumed to be so.[4] The Act does *not* permit entry for the carrying out of improvements, alterations, or demolition work, except where these are incidental to works of preservation.[5]

An order under the Act must specify the works to be carried out, the land which can be entered and the period during which entry is authorised.[6] The court can impose such terms and conditions as are reasonably necessary for limiting or avoiding loss, damage, inconvenience or loss of privacy to the respondent or any other person,[7] and may require the applicant to insure against specified risks.[8] An order will not be granted where the entry would cause either interference to the use or enjoyment of the servient land, or hardship to any person in occupation of that land, to a degree which would make it unreasonable to make the order.[9] Once the work has been completed all waste must be removed and the servient land must be made good; the applicant is not authorised to leave anything on the servient land such as cables, pipes or drains.[10]

An order under the Act may require the applicant to pay *compensation* for any loss, damage or injury, or any substantial loss of privacy or other substantial inconvenience which might be caused.[11] In addition, except in the case of works to residential land, the court may order the payment of *consideration* for the entry; this sum is to be based on the likely financial advantage of the order to the applicant and the degree of inconvenience to the respondent or any other person.[12]

  [1] See also the Party Wall etc Act 1996.
  [2] Or which would be substantially more difficult to carry out without such access: s 1(2)(b).
  [3] Section 1(1). It may well be that the mere existence of the court's power will in future mean that parties are more prepared to negotiate access agreements.
  [4] These works, defined as 'basic preservation works', include such matters as the maintenance, repair or renewal of any part of a building, and the felling of trees or shrubs which are damaged or dangerous: s 1(4).
  [5] Section 1(5). The Act does not therefore solve the problem of tower cranes: see para 22.8.
  [6] Section 2(1).
  [7] Section 2(2).
  [8] Section 2(4)(b).
  [9] Section 1(3).
  [10] Section 3(3).
  [11] Section 2(4)(a).
  [12] Section 2(5). 'Likely financial advantage' is defined in s 2(6).

Remedies

Damages

22.7 Where actual damage is caused to land, the claimant is entitled to damages, and these will normally be assessed by reference to the amount by which the value of the property is diminished or, more commonly, the cost of reinstating it to its former condition.[1] Even where the land itself is not damaged, the claimant is entitled to claim for loss of use of the property. Here the appropriate measure is based either on the property's normal letting value[2] (whether or not it appears likely that the claimant could have let it)[3] or on the amount that the parties would hypothetically have negotiated as a fee for permitting the trespass.[4]

A defendant who is guilty of a continuing trespass, for example by remaining in occupation of or leaving goods on the claimant's land, is liable to successive actions until the offence ceases. Damages in each action will therefore be awarded for the effects of the trespass up to the date of judgment.[5] Where, however, the trespass consists of a single act, such as the digging of a hole in the claimant's land, that fact that its effects continue does not lead to the same result; here damages are awarded only once, and will therefore take into account both past and future effects of the trespass.[6]

  [1] Para 27.12.
  [2] *Whitwham v Westminster Brymbo Coal Co* [1896] 2 Ch 538, CA.
  [3] *Swordheath Properties Ltd v Tabet* [1979] 1 All ER 240, CA; *Inverugie Investments Ltd v Hackett* [1995] 3 All ER 841, PC.
  [4] *Field Common Ltd v Elmbridge DC* [2008] EWHC 2079 (Ch).
  [5] *Holmes v Wilson* (1839) 10 Ad & El 503.
  [6] *Clegg v Dearden* (1848) 12 QB 576.

Injunction

22.8 Where a trespass is continuous or repetitive, the claimant may seek an injunction to compel the defendant to cease the offending activity. Such an injunction will normally be granted as a matter of course, even though this may cause serious inconvenience or expense to the defendant. Thus, for example, the claimant can obtain an injunction order-ing the demolition of an encroaching building[1] or the immediate cessation of oversailing by a tower crane.[2]

Although an injunction will normally be granted, it must be borne in mind that it is a discretionary remedy.[3] It may accordingly be refused in special circumstances, such as where the court disapproves of the claimant's conduct.[4] Moreover, the court has a statu-tory discretion to award damages in lieu of an injunction in any case where it is felt to be appropriate.[5]

[1] *Daniells v Mendonca* (1999) 78 P & CR 401, CA.
[2] *Anchor Brewhouse Developments Ltd v Berkley House (Docklands Developments) Ltd* [1987] 2 EGLR 173; *London and Manchester Assurance Co Ltd v O & H Construction Ltd* [1989] 2 EGLR 185.
[3] *Woollerton and Wilson Ltd v Richard Costain Ltd* [1970] 1 All ER 483.
[4] *Tollemache and Cobbold Breweries Ltd v Reynolds* [1983] 2 EGLR 158, CA.
[5] See para 27.18.

Action of ejectment

22.9 This ancient action, more commonly known as the action for the recovery of land, enables the claimant to regain actual possession of his land.[1] It has often been said that, whereas a claimant seeking damages need only show that he was in possession of the land, one who seeks to recover the actual land must prove his title. However, in prac-tice it seems that proof of prior possession by the claimant raises a presumption of title which the defendant who is not entitled to the land will find almost impossible to rebut.[2] Whether proof that true title rests with a third party will suffice to defeat the claim-ant's claim is a matter of great controversy; even if it does, however, it is of no avail to a defendant whose possession is either wrongful as against the claimant or derives from the claimant.

[1] Under RSC Ord 113, a special summary procedure is available against persons who are unidentified, such as 'squatters' or 'sitters-in': see *Wiltshire County Council v Frazer* [1986] 1 All ER 65.
[2] *Asher v Whitlock* (1865) LR 1 QB 1.

Self-redress

22.10 As an alternative to taking legal action, a person in possession of land is entitled to use a reasonable degree of force either to eject or to deny entry to a trespasser.[1] Similarly, a person in possession of land may simply remove (or demolish) an encroaching object, but only in simple cases which do not justify the expense of legal proceedings or urgent cases which require an immediate remedy.[2] It has also been held that, so long as adequate notice is given, a person in possession of land may lawfully wheel clamp motor vehicles parked on that land without permission and charge the motorist a reasonable fee for releasing the vehicle.[3]

Where a person is wrongfully dispossessed of land, the use of reasonable force to recover that land will not amount to a tort. However, great care must be taken to avoid a breach of the criminal law. A residential tenant who refuses to quit, for example, cannot be evicted without a court order. Further, the Criminal Law Act 1977 makes it an offence for anyone except a 'displaced residential occupier' to use or threaten violence in order to secure entry to property.

[1] *Hemmings v Stoke Poges Golf Club* [1920] 1 KB 720, CA.
[2] *Burton v Winters* [1993] 3 All ER 847, CA; *Macnab v Richardson* [2008] EWCA Civ 1631, CA.
[3] *Arthur v Anker* [1996] 3 All ER 783, CA.

Trespass to Land: Key Points

- Trespass consists of an unauthorised entry onto the land of another.
- 'Land' for this purpose includes what lies below and, to an extent, the airspace above.
- A person who enters by mistake is still trespassing, but one who enters by accident may not be.
- Trespass is usually actionable by the possessor of land, rather than by the owner.
- A person who has some legal right to enter land does not commit trespass by exercising that right.
- Trespass may be justified in case of necessity, but the right to enter neighbouring land in order to maintain one's own property is strictly limited.
- A person whose land is trespassed upon may be entitled to damages for loss of use, or to an injunction to prevent further intrusions.
- In limited circumstances, the person in possession of land may use reasonable force to remove a trespasser or trespassing object.

Questions

1. To what extent does an intrusion into the airspace above land constitute an actionable trespass?

2. What is meant by the assertion that trespass must be 'direct'?

3. How accurate is it to say that trespass protects possession rather than ownership?

4. What are the rights of a landowner under the Access to Neighbouring Land Act 1992?

5. On what principles are damages assessed in cases of trespass?

6. Is it legally justifiable to remove something which has been placed on land without permission?

7. Silas owns a derelict building on the edge of town, which he has no plans either to use or to sell. Fastbuck Property Co begins construction of a 10-storey office block on an adjoining site, a project which can only be carried out by allowing a tower crane to swing over Silas's land. Fastbuck asks Silas for permission to do this, but Silas replies that the price for such permission is 50% of the profits from the development. Fastbuck refuses to agree and continues with the project, including the use of the tower crane.

    Advise Silas.

23

Nuisance

CHAPTER OVERVIEW

In terms of disputes between neighbours, one of the most important areas of the law of tort is that of nuisance. In this chapter we examine the following issues:

- the range of activities which may amount to a private nuisance;
- the factors which will determine whether or not an interference is a nuisance in the legal sense;
- the persons who are protected against, and those who may be held liable for, the commission of a nuisance;
- the special defences which apply to the tort of private nuisance, and the range of remedies available to the claimant;
- the legal definition of a public nuisance, and the extent to which such a nuisance may found liability in tort.

23.1 The term 'nuisance' is used to describe three separate areas of legal liability. First, a *private nuisance* consists of any unlawful interference which damages a person's land or adversely affects the use and enjoyment of it. Within this category there also falls any interference with a person's rights over land, such as easements or profits.[1] Second, a *public nuisance* is a criminal offence, consisting of an activity which endangers or inconveniences the public in general or which obstructs people in the exercise of public rights. The relevance of this class of nuisance to the law of tort is that damages may be awarded to any individual who suffers loss or damage over and above that which is incurred by the general public. Third, and not within the law of tort at all, is a *statutory nuisance* under various Acts of Parliament, such as the Control of Pollution Act 1974, the aim of which is to protect the environment. Enforcement in respect of this type of nuisance is in the hands of public bodies such as local authorities, although some of the statutes also make provision for an aggrieved individual to recover damages.

[1] Discussion of these rights belongs to land law; see chapter 32.

Private nuisance

23.2 It has been said that 'private nuisances, at least in the vast majority of cases, are interferences for a substantial length of time by owners or occupiers of property with the use of enjoyment of neighbouring land'.[1] The main function of the law is to balance the conflicting interests of neighbours, and to decide at what point an interference becomes intolerable and therefore actionable.

¹ *Cunard v Antifyre Ltd* [1933] 1 KB 551 at 557.

Interference

Physical damage to land

23.3 A person who *directly* causes something to enter the claimant's land is guilty of the tort of trespass.[1] Where the element of directness is lacking, however, the appropriate tort is private nuisance. Thus, for example, while it would be trespass to plant a tree in the claimant's garden, it is nuisance when the roots or branches of trees which the defendant has planted on his (or her) own land grow across the boundary.[2] Similarly, to build a wall on the claimant's land is a trespass, but to allow one's own wall to become so dilapidated that it falls onto the claimant's land is a nuisance.[3]

The simplest case of this type arises where something tangible is allowed to enter the claimant's property. A defendant has been held liable, for example, for causing water to overflow onto neighbouring land, both by carrying out filling operations on his (or her) own land[4] and by merely allowing a drain to become blocked.[5] However, damage may also be caused intangibly, as when vibrations shake the foundations of the claimant's building,[6] or fumes from a factory kill the claimant's shrubs.[7] It is clear from these cases that nuisance protects crops and buildings as well as the land itself; in *Farrer v Nelson*,[8] for instance, a person who overstocked land with pheasants was held liable for the effect which these had upon a neighbour's crops.

In *Hunter v Canary Wharf Ltd*,[9] the House of Lords emphasised that private nuisance is a tort to land, rather than to those who own or occupy it. This means that no one, not even the occupier, can recover damages in private nuisance for personal injury (for example where a person is made ill by fumes which render his (or her) house an unhealthy place in which to live). However, it seems that damage to an occupier's goods is regarded as consequential on the damage to the land, so that damages can be recovered for this.[10]

¹ Chapter 22.
² *Lemmon v Webb* [1894] 3 Ch 1, CA.
³ *Brew Bros Ltd v Snax (Ross) Ltd* [1970] 1 All ER 587, CA.
⁴ *Home Brewery Ltd v William Davis & Co (Leicester) Ltd* [1987] 1 All ER 637.
⁵ *Sedleigh-Denfield v O'Callaghan* [1940] 3 All ER 349, HL.
⁶ *Hoare & Co v McAlpine* [1923] 1 Ch 167.
⁷ *St Helen's Smelting Co v Tipping* (1865) 11 HL Cas 642.
⁸ (1885) 15 QBD 258.
⁹ [1997] 2 All ER 426, HL.
¹⁰ *Halsey v Esso Petroleum Co Ltd* [1961] 2 All ER 145.

Use and enjoyment

23.4 The feature of private nuisance which sets it apart from other torts is that it protects the amenity value of land, in the sense of the occupier's use and enjoyment of the property. Even where no physical damage is done, an occupier is entitled to complain if the intended use of the property (be it residential, agricultural or commercial) is unreasonably curtailed by the defendant's activities. It is on this basis that action in nuisance may be taken in respect of smoke from a factory chimney,[1] offensive smells from stables[2] or the periodic emptying of a neighbour's cess-pit,[3] the noise from a children's playground[4] or electromagnetic interference.[5] Examples of more subtle attacks on the enjoyment of land or upon its amenity include the picketing of a person's premises from the highway[6] and the use of neighbouring high-class residential premises for prostitution.[7]

In *Bridlington Relay Ltd v Yorkshire Electricity Board*,[8] it was suggested that an action in private nuisance could not be brought in respect of interference with television reception, since this would be a purely recreational use of land. However, the House of Lords in *Hunter v Canary Wharf Ltd*[9] took the view that television reception would in principle attract protection under this tort. Even so, the action there failed because the actual cause of the interference (the erection of a very large building on the defendants' land which blocked signals from the television transmitter) was held to be analogous to building so as to block a view from the claimant's property, something which is not in itself wrongful.[10]

[1] *Crump v Lambert* (1867) LR 3 Eq 409.
[2] *Rapier v London Tramways Co* [1893] 2 Ch 588, CA.
[3] *Penn v Wilkins* [1975] 2 EGLR 113.
[4] *Dunton v Dover District Council* (1977) 76 LGR 87.
[5] See *Network Rail Infrastructures Ltd v CJ Morris* [2004] EWCA Civ 172, CA.
[6] *Hubbard v Pitt* [1975] 3 All ER 1, CA.
[7] *Thompson-Schwab v Costaki* [1956] 1 All ER 652, CA. See also *Laws v Florinplace Ltd* [1981] 1 All ER 659 (sex shop in predominantly residential area).
[8] [1965] 1 All ER 264.
[9] [1997] 2 All ER 426, HL.
[10] *Aldred's Case* (1610) 9 Co Rep 57b.

Unlawfulness

23.5 Although private nuisance consists of an interference, not every interference constitutes a nuisance. The law does not demand absolute silence or absence of smell from neighbours; they must be allowed the occasional party or garden bonfire. Indeed, it has been held by the House of Lords that the tenant of a flat who uses the premises in the normal way cannot be guilty of nuisance by noise, even if the lack of sound proofing in the block means that other tenants are badly affected.[1] The law seeks to apply the broad principle of 'give and take', or 'live and let live'; as Lord Wright put it in *Sedleigh-Denfield v O'Callaghan*:[2] 'A balance has to be maintained between the right of the occupier to do what he likes with his own, and the right of his neighbour not to be interfered with'.

In striking this balance, the courts frequently refer to 'reasonableness'. However, the word is used in a different sense from that in which it features in negligence cases. There, the focus is on whether or not the defendant has acted 'reasonably'. In nuisance, by contrast, the court is concentrating on the interference itself, and asking whether this is so 'unreasonable' that the law should not require the claimant to put up with it.

In deciding whether a particular interference is 'unreasonable' in this sense, the courts have regard to a number of factors, which we now consider.

[1] *Southwark London Borough Council v Mills* [1999] 4 All ER 449, HL.
[2] [1940] 3 All ER 349 at 364.

Degree of interference

23.6 A matter of obvious importance is the seriousness of the interference in question. Where actual physical damage is caused, a fairly minor interference is sufficient to constitute nuisance but, where the claimant complains of interference with use and enjoyment, rather more is required. It has been said that there must be 'an inconvenience materially interfering with the ordinary comfort physically of human existence, not merely according to elegant or dainty modes and habits of living, but according to plain and sober and simple notions among the English people'.[1] In accordance with this approach, the Court of Appeal held that fluctuating night time noise from the defendants' factory was not sufficient to constitute a nuisance, even though it exceeded the maximum level recommended by the World Health Organisation.[2]

The matter here is purely one of degree. Thus in *Heath v Brighton Corpn*,[3] a buzzing noise from a power station, which disturbed a church congregation in a poor area, was held insufficient to be a nuisance. In *Haddon v Lynch*,[4] on the other hand, the persistent and early ringing of church bells on Sunday mornings was held to be actionable.

[1] *Walter v Selfe* (1851) 4 De G & Sm 315 at 322.
[2] *Murdoch v Glacier Metal Co Ltd* [1998] Env LR 732, CA.
[3] (1908) 98 LT 718.
[4] [1911] VLR 230.

Sensitivity

23.7 A person who is abnormally sensitive, or who puts property to an abnormally sensitive use, is not thereby entitled to a greater freedom from interference than anyone else. This rule, which is really no more than an application of the general principle outlined in the previous paragraph, is illustrated by *Robinson v Kilvert*,[1] in which heat from the defendant's premises damaged the claimant's stocks of brown paper. The amount of heat was not unreasonable; the damage was only caused because the paper was unduly sensitive, and the defendant was accordingly not liable. So too, in *Bridlington Relay Ltd v Yorkshire Electricity Board*,[2] it was held that a company which relayed television signals from its receiver to members of the public was not entitled to any greater freedom from interference than the average domestic user, on the basis that, unless it could offer a superior signal, it would have no customers.

Although the law gives no extra protection to those who are particularly sensitive, it does not abandon them altogether. If an interference is sufficiently substantial to constitute nuisance by ordinary standards, the claimant may recover damages for the full effect upon the extra-sensitive use to which the claimant's property is put, such as the growing of delicate orchids.[3]

[1] (1889) 41 Ch D 88, CA.
[2] [1965] 1 All ER 264.
[3] *McKinnon Industries Ltd v Walker* [1951] 3 DLR 577 at 581.

Locality

23.8 In assessing the standard of comfort to which the claimant is legally entitled, the character of the neighbourhood is an important factor. In *Halsey v Esso Petroleum Co Ltd*,[1] for instance, where the claimant complained of the nightly noise of tankers driving in and out of the defendants' oil depot, the judge regarded it as crucial that the depot was situated in a quiet residential part of Fulham. However, this does not mean that a person in a noisy area is left without protection altogether. For example, in *Polsue and Alfieri Ltd v Rushmer*,[2] the claimant, who lived in Fleet Street, was held entitled to complain of the nightly noise from a new printing press which the defendants had installed.

In *Allen v Gulf Oil Refining Ltd*,[3] claims in nuisance were made where a massive oil refinery, constructed under the authority of an Act of Parliament, caused severe dislocation of the environment. It was pointed out by Lord Wilberforce that, even if these claims were not completely defeated by the defence of statutory authority,[4] the appropriate standard of comfort for this locality was to be based on what Parliament had clearly authorised it to become, rather than on what it had been before the refinery was built. A similar 'change of character of the locality' argument may also be based upon a grant of planning permission.[5] However, the mere fact that planning permission has been granted for an activity does not automatically provide a defence to an action in private nuisance; it will only do so where there has been a strategic planning decision affected by considerations of public interest.[6]

It should be noted that, where physical damage is caused to the claimants property, the locality is irrelevant. Thus, in *St Helens Smelting Co v Tipping*,[7] where the claimant's shrubs were killed by fumes from the defendants' smelting works, the House of Lords regarded it as no defence that the area was devoted to such industrial activity.

[1]   [1961] 2 All ER 145.
[2]   [1907] AC 121, HL.
[3]   [1981] 1 All ER 353, HL.
[4]   Para 23.18.
[5]   *Gillingham BC v Medway (Chatham) Dock Co Ltd* [1993] QB 343.
[6]   *Wheeler v JJ Saunders Ltd* [1995] 2 All ER 697, CA. Also see *Watson v Croft Promo-Sport Ltd* [2009] EWCA Civ 15, CA.
[7]   (1865) 11 HL Cas 642.

Continuity

23.9 In most cases of private nuisance, especially those in which the claimant's use and enjoyment of land are affected, there is an element of continuity or repetition in the interference of which complaint is made. This does not mean that an isolated incident can never be a basis for liability (though a court is less likely to grant an injunction in such cases);[1] where actual damage results, as where a dilapidated building falls on to the claimant's land, there is no need for a repetition before action can be taken.

Cases in which there is a single occurrence of damage are sometimes explained as resulting from a continuing state of affairs for which the defendant is responsible. Thus in *Spicer v Smee*,[2] where defective wiring in the defendant's bungalow caused a fire which spread to the claimant's property, the defendant was held liable in nuisance. In *British Celanese Ltd v A H Hunt (Capacitors) Ltd*,[3] where light strips of metal foil, which were stored over a period of time on the defendants' land, blew on to adjoining property and caused damage, liability in nuisance was again imposed. In *SCM (UK) Ltd v W J Whittall & Son Ltd*,[4] on the other hand, where a workman negligently severed a cable and thus cut off the electricity supply to the claimant's factory, it was held that the defendants could not be liable in nuisance. Here there was nothing which could be described as a state of affairs, but merely an isolated act of negligence.

[1]   *Swan v Great Northern Rly* (1864) 4 De GJ & SM 211.
[2]   [1946] 1 All ER 489.
[3]   [1969] 2 All ER 1252.
[4]   [1970] 2 All ER 417, CA.

Utility of the defendant's conduct

23.10 A frequent plea of defendants in nuisance actions is that the offending activity is being carried on for the benefit of the public. This can undoubtedly have some bearing on the degree of interference which the claimant can be expected to put up with (the noise and dust which usually accompanies demolition and rebuilding, for example, would certainly be actionable if caused for no good reason). However, it cannot be a complete defence, for the courts will not allow the public interest to ride roughshod over private rights. In *Adams v Ursell*,[1] for instance, the smell from a fried-fish shop was held to be a nuisance, notwithstanding its value in supplying good food in a poor neighbourhood. Even more striking is the case of *Shelfer v City of London Electric Lighting Co*,[2] in which vibrations from the building of a power station damaged the claimant's house. The Court of Appeal held that the claimant was entitled to an injunction to stop the work, even though the laudable purpose of the building was to bring electric light to the City of London.

It may be that modern courts are more willing than their predecessors to give weight to the public interest, at least to the extent of refusing to stop a beneficial activity altogether.[3] In *Miller v Jackson*,[4] for example, the claimant bought a new house next to the ground on which the village team had played cricket for some 70 years. The Court of Appeal held, by a majority, that the danger from cricket balls constituted a nuisance; nevertheless, in view of the social value of the ground to the community, the claimant was denied an injunction and left to his remedy in damages. Likewise, in *Dunton v Dover District Council*,[5] where the claimant complained of the noise from a children's playground next to his hotel, the judge refused to order its closure, but restricted its opening times and the age-group of children permitted to use it. By contrast, the Court of Appeal in *Kennaway v Thompson*[6] granted an injunction which drastically curtailed the activities of a motor boat racing club, preferring to protect the interest of a neighbouring resident who complained about the noise.

[1] [1913] 1 Ch 269.
[2] [1895] 1 Ch 287, CA.
[3] In *Dennis v Ministry of Defence* [2003] EWHC 793, the claimants were limited to a claim for damages in respect of the 'fearsome' noise from Harrier jump-jets from a nearby RAF base used for training pilots.
[4] [1977] 3 All ER 338, CA.
[5] (1977) 76 LGR 87.
[6] [1980] 3 All 329, CA. In *Watson v Croft Promo-Sport Ltd* [2009] EWCA Civ 15, CA, the Court of Appeal similarly restricted the activities of a long-established motor racing circuit.

Order of events

23.11 Surprisingly, perhaps, it seems settled that a claimant is not precluded from complaining of a nuisance merely because by virtue of coming to it with his (or her) eyes wide open. In *Sturges v Bridgman*,[1] a doctor was held entitled to complain of the noise from machinery used by the defendant on adjoining premises, even though this caused him no inconvenience until he chose to build a consulting room at the end of his garden.

[1] (1879) 11 Ch D 852, CA.

The defendant's state of mind

23.12 The question whether liability in nuisance depends upon proof of any particular mental element on the part of the defendant is one of the most difficult and complex aspects of this tort. All that may safely be said is that the more unreasonable the defendant's conduct, the less likely it is that the claimant will be required to tolerate the interference in question. Thus, in *Christie v Davey*,[1] where the defendant banged a tray on the party wall in order to disrupt the claimant's music lessons, his malice was held to render this noise actionable as a nuisance, even though the volume itself might not have done so. Even clearer is *Hollywood Silver Fox Farm Ltd v Emmett*,[2] where the defendant fired guns near the boundary of his land for the specific purpose of disturbing the breeding season of the claimants' silver foxes. This was held to be actionable, although it could hardly be said that the sound of gunfire would normally amount to a nuisance, unless unduly prolonged. However, it should be noted that malice cannot make unlawful something which the defendant has an absolute right to do, such as the abstraction of percolating water from beneath his (or her) own land.[3]

Of less weight than malice, although still relevant to this question, is the possibility that the defendant has been negligent in failing to keep the interference to a minimum. If building operations cause more dust and noise than necessary,[4] or children in a day nursery are permitted to make excessive noise,[5] the defendant's lack of care may lead a court to the conclusion that the claimant should not be expected to put up with the consequences.

Although malice and negligence may thus both be highly relevant to liability in nuisance, it seems that neither is essential. The courts have repeatedly stressed that, if the interference caused by an activity is substantial enough to be a nuisance, the defendant cannot evade liability merely by showing that all reasonable steps have been taken to reduce it. Defendants who have taken all reasonable care have nevertheless been held liable in respect of the smell from stables[6] or from a fried-fish shop[7] and the noise from a hotel kitchen[8] or low-flying RAF jet aircraft.[9] The same principle applies where actual damage is caused; for example, where building works infringe a neighbour's right of support, it is no defence to show that the works were carried out without negligence.[10] In all these cases, however, the defendant was held liable as creator of the nuisance. As we shall see, where the defendant is sued as occupier of the land from which the nuisance emanates, proof that reasonable care has not been taken is normally essential to liability.[11]

The Privy Council in *The Wagon Mound (No 2)*[12] added to the confusion surrounding this issue by declaring that, while 'negligence in the narrow sense' might not always be needed for an action in nuisance, 'fault of some kind' is almost invariably necessary. What is meant by 'fault' in this context is far from clear. However, an important consequence of the decision is that, since fault involves foreseeability, the rules as to remoteness of damage in nuisance are identical to those in negligence.[13]

[1]   [1893] 1 Ch 316.
[2]   [1936] 1 All ER 825.
[3]   *Bradford Corpn v Pickles* [1895] AC 587, HL.
[4]   *Andreae v Selfridge & Co Ltd* [1937] 3 All ER 255, CA.
[5]   *Moy v Stoop* (1909) 25 TLR 262.
[6]   *Rapier v London Tramways Co* [1893] 2 Ch 588, CA.
[7]   *Adams v Ursell* [1913] 1 Ch 269.
[8]   *Vanderpant v Mayfair Hotel Co Ltd* [1930] 1 Ch 138.
[9]   *Dennis v Ministry of Defence* [2003] EWHC 793.
[10]   *Brace v South-East Regional Housing Association Ltd* [1984] 1 EGLR 144, CA.
[11]   Paras 23.15–23.16.
[12]   [1966] 2 All ER 709, PC.
[13]   *Cambridge Water Co Ltd v Eastern Counties Leather plc* [1994] 1 All ER 53 at 71–72, HL. We describe the relevant rules at paras 18.14–18.19.

THE ELEMENTS OF PRIVATE NUISANCE: KEY POINTS

- Private nuisance consists either of the indirect causing of physical damage to land or buildings, or of an unreasonable interference with the use and enjoyment (amenity value) of land.

- The 'unreasonableness' of an interference is a question of balance or 'give and take' between neighbours; it is dependent on a number of factors, including the level and duration of interference.

- A claimant whose use of land is hypersensitive is entitled to no greater degree of protection than anyone else.

- The grant of planning permission for an activity does not mean that it cannot constitute a nuisance; however, planning permission may alter the nature (and thus the standards) of the locality in question.

- An activity may be a nuisance even where it is in the public interest; however, a claimant in such circumstances may be refused an injunction and instead be limited to the recovery of damages.

- Interference which is deliberately or negligently caused is more likely to be an actionable nuisance, but neither malice nor negligence is an essential element of this tort.

Who is protected?

23.13 The tort of private nuisance is a means of protection for persons with a proprietary or possessory interest in affected land.[1] This does not mean that only the freehold owner can sue; a limited interest, such as a weekly tenancy,[2] will suffice, although someone with such an interest is unlikely to be awarded an injunction except in very serious cases. In exceptional circumstances, a person who is in exclusive possession of land but who is unable to prove title to it may be entitled to sue in private nuisance,[3] just as in trespass.[4]

The House of Lords has ruled that a person, such as a member of the occupier's family, who has neither an interest in the land nor exclusive possession of it is not entitled to maintain an action for private nuisance.[5] However, it has been suggested that this restriction might be in contravention of the Human Rights Act 1998.[6]

The requirement that a claimant has possession of land serves to exclude actions by the landlord of property, at least in respect of temporary interference with its use and enjoyment, even if the effect of these is to reduce its letting value.[6] The landlord can, however, sue to protect a reversionary interest against either physical damage or such nuisances as may, by the doctrine of prescription,[7] operate to deprive the landlord of rights or burden the land with obligations.[8]

Where a nuisance is continuous, its effects may be felt by successive owners or occupiers of the same property. In *Delaware Mansions Ltd v Westminster City Council*,[9] for example, the roots of trees for which the defendants were responsible encroached and damaged the foundations of property owned, at the time of the case, by the claimants. It was held by the House of Lords that, where there is a continuing nuisance of which the defendant knew or ought to have known, reasonable remedial expenditure may be recovered by the owner who has had to incur it.

[1] *Hunter v Canary Wharf* Ltd [1997] 2 All ER 426, HL. This includes a permanently moored barge to which the claimant has a right of exclusive use and occupation: *Crown River Cruises Ltd v Kimbolton Fireworks Ltd* [1996] 2 Lloyd's Rep 533.

[2] *Jones v Chappell* (1875) LR 20 Eq 539.

[3] *Hunter v Canary Wharf Ltd* [1997] 2 All ER 426, HL.

[4] Para 22.4.

[5] *Hunter v Canary Wharf Ltd* [1997] 2 All ER 426, HL.

[6] *McKenna v British Aluminium Ltd* (2002) Times, 25 April. As to what this would mean in terms of a legal remedy, see *Dobson v Thames Water Utilities Ltd* [2009] EWCA Civ 28, CA.

[6] *Simpson v Savage* (1856) 1 CBNS 347.

[7] Paras 32.40–32.51.

[8] *Jones v Llanrwst UDC* [1911] 1 Ch 393.

[9] [2001] UKHL 55, [2001] 4 All ER 737.

Who is liable?

Creator

23.14 In practice, most nuisance actions are brought against the occupier of the offending land. However, it seems that the person who actually creates a nuisance is always liable for it, whether the offending activity takes place on the creator's own land, someone else's land, or the public highway. This was assumed to be the case in *Hall v Beckenham Corpn*,[1] where the claimant complained of noise from model aeroplanes in a public park, although the individual enthusiasts were not in fact sued in that case. Further, a person who creates a nuisance on his or her own land remains liable for it, even where he (or she) subsequently parts with possession of the property and so becomes unable to prevent its continuance.[2]

[1] [1949] 1 All ER 423.

[2] *Thompson v Gibson* (1841) 7 M & W 456.

Occupier

23.15 An occupier may be held responsible for a nuisance which exists on the land, even where the occupier is not the creator of that nuisance. An extreme example of this is *Russell v London Borough Council of Barnet*,[1] in which a highway authority was held liable to a neighbouring householder for damage caused by the spreading roots of trees which were growing in the street, notwithstanding that the trees actually belonged to the house-holder! It may be noted in this connection that a highway authority is generally responsi-ble for all trees, whether self-sown or planted before or after adoption of the highway.[2] The simplest case of liability based on occupation is where the nuisance is created by someone for whom the occupier is responsible, such as a visitor. Here it seems that the occupier will be liable, provided that the nuisance is a foreseeable consequence of what the visitor has been permitted to do. Thus in *A-G v Stone*,[3] the defendant, who had allowed Gypsies to camp on his land, was held liable when the noise and insanitary conditions of their camp constituted a nuisance. A similar principle applies where work carried out on the occupier's behalf by an independent contractor causes a nuisance; if this consequence is foreseeable from the nature of the work, as where support is withdrawn from neighbour-ing property,[4] the defendant will be liable. In *Matania v National Provincial Bank Ltd*,[5] for instance, building operations carried on by a contractor on behalf of the occupier of a building's first floor involved a clear risk of nuisance by noise and dust to the occupiers of higher floors. When this happened, the occupier was held liable for it.

The general rule is that an occupier who is not also the creator of a nuisance can only be held responsible where he (or she) 'adopts' or 'continues' that nuisance. In effect, these terms mean having knowledge or the means of knowledge of the existence of a nuisance and then failing to take reasonable steps to abate it. In *Sedleigh-Denfield v O'Callaghan*,[6] for example, a drainage pipe, which had been negligently laid in the defendants' ditch by trespassers, became blocked, with the result that water overflowed onto the claimant's land. The defendants were held liable, for they had known of the pipe for three years and should have appreciated the danger. In *St Anne's Well Brewery Co v Roberts*,[7] on the other hand, part of the city wall of Exeter which was owned by the defendant collapsed and demolished the claimants' inn. The cause of this collapse was excavations which had been carried out by the defendant's predecessor. Since the defendant did not and could not know of these, he was held not liable.

There is one anomalous exception to the general rule that an occupier's liability is based on the foreseeability of the nuisance in question. It was laid down by the Court of Appeal, in the much-criticised case of *Wringe v Cohen*,[8] that, where premises abut upon a highway, the occupier (and landlord, if under a duty to repair) is strictly liable for dam-age resulting from disrepair, whether this is caused to neighbouring property or to the highway.[9] The extent of this liability is uncertain, since the court excluded cases in which the damage resulted from either the act of a trespasser or the 'secret and unobservable processes of nature'.

[1] [1984] 2 EGLR 44.

[2] *Hurst v Hampshire County Council* [1997] 2 EGLR 164, CA. It has (controversially) been held that liabil-ity can be imposed upon a non-occupier who has agreed with the occupier to take responsibility for the maintenance of trees: *Jones (LE) (Insurance Brokers) Ltd v Portsmouth CC* [2002] EWCA Civ 1723, CA.

[3] (1895) 12 TLR 76.

[4] *Bower v Peate* (1876) 1 QBD 321.

[5] [1936] 2 All ER 633, CA.

[6] [1940] 3 All ER 349, HL.

[7] (1928) 140 LT 1, CA.

[8] [1939] 4 All ER 241, CA.

[9] In the latter case the occupier would be liable for public nuisance; para 23.25.

23.16 At one time, an occupier could not be held responsible for a nuisance arising naturally on the land. However, since the decision of the Privy Council in *Goldman v Hargrave*,[1] it has been accepted that the occupier may be liable for failing to take reasonable steps to see that the condition of the property does not damage that of a neighbour. At the same time, the courts have sought to avoid the imposition of an unreasonable burden on an 'innocent' occupier. They have thus held that, in deciding whether the occupier has acted reasonably, regard should be had to the occupier's individual circumstances, including financial resources.[2] In this way, more may be demanded of a company or local authority than an individual, and more of a healthy and wealthy individual than of an infirm and impoverished one.

The concept of a subjective or 'measured' duty of care has been applied to cases of fire caused by lightning striking a tall tree,[3] earth falling from a natural geological mound;[4] a landslip of cliff land occupied by the defendants which withdraws support from the claimant's property;[5] and the deteriorating roof of a 'flying freehold' flat which permitted water to leak into the ground floor shop below.[6] A good illustration of the principle in operation is provided by the case of *Lambert v Barratt Homes Ltd*,[7] where the effect of a housing development on land sold to the developers by a local authority was that rainwater collecting on land retained by the local authority could no longer flow away naturally and instead caused flooding to neighbouring properties. It was held that the local authority's 'measured' duty of care required only that it should permit the neighbouring property owners to have access to its land in order to carry out remedial works at their own expense.

The idea of a reduced duty of care does not mean that the defendant always avoids liability. The courts have adopted it in relation to structures on the defendant's land which, though adequate when built, become a nuisance through increased usage, so that liability was imposed by the Court of Appeal on a highway authority in respect of a culvert taking a stream under a road, when an increase in the flow of water made the culvert insufficient.[8] However, a similar Court of Appeal ruling, which would have forced a water authority to upgrade a sewerage system or pay damages to occupiers whose properties were repeatedly flooded, was reversed by the House of Lords on the ground that this would conflict with the statutory scheme laid down by the Water Industry Act 1991, under which decisions as to the extent of sewerage authorities' responsibilities are made by the Director General of Water Services.[9]

We saw above that an occupier can be held liable for a nuisance created by a trespasser on his land, provided that the occupier has 'adopted' or 'continued' it.[10] In cases involving nuisance caused by Gypsies who were camping without permission on local authority land, it has been held that here, too, the local authority's duty of care is a 'measured' one.[11]

---

[1] [1966] 2 All ER 989, PC.

[2] This is unlike the normal standard of care in negligence, which is objective.

[3] *Goldman v Hargrave* [1966] 2 All ER 989, PC.

[4] *Leakey v National Trust for Places of Historic Interest or Natural Beauty* [1980] 1 All ER 17, CA.

[5] *Holbeck Hall Hotel Ltd v Scarborough Borough Council* [2000] 2 All ER 705, CA.

[6] *Abbahall Ltd v Smee* [2002] EWCA Civ 1831, [2003] 1 All ER 465.

[7] [2010] EWCA Civ 681, CA.

[8] *Bybrook Barn Centre Ltd v Kent County Council* [2001] BLR 55, CA.

[9] *Marcic v Thames Water Utilities Ltd* [2003] UKHL 66, HL.

[10] *Sedleigh-Denfield v O'Callaghan* [1940] 3 All ER 349, HL.

[11] *Page Motors Ltd v Epsom and Ewell Borough Council* (1981) 80 LGR 337, CA. See also *Lippiatt v South Gloucestershire Council* [1999] 4 All ER 149, CA (travellers).

Landlord

23.17 Where a nuisance arises from premises which are let, a claimant will normally take action against the tenant, who is the occupier. Whether or not the tenant is liable for the nuisance depends upon the rules discussed in the previous paragraph. In certain circumstances, however, the landlord may also be liable, although it is important to real-ise that this will not exonerate the tenant; it will simply provide the claimant with an additional person to sue.

In the first place, the landlord is legally responsible whenever it can be said that the landlord has 'authorised' the tenant to commit nuisance. This will be so where the nui-sance arises from the normal use of the land by the tenant for the very purpose for which it is let, as in *Harris v James*[1] (blasting and smoke from a lime quarry) or *Tetley v Chitty*[2] (disturbance from a go-kart club which operated as tenants of the local authority). It should be emphasised, however, that it is authority, and not merely foreseeability, which must be established. Thus, in *Smith v Scott*,[3] where a local authority placed a problem family in the next house to that of the claimants, it was held that the local authority were not liable for the foreseeable nuisances which ensued; having made their tenants covenant expressly not to commit nuisance, it could hardly be said that they had authorised them to do so. Similarly, in *Hussain v Lancaster City Council*,[4] the defendant local authority were held not liable for a campaign of racial harassment and abuse carried out by some of their tenants, where the offending conduct took place outside the tenants' property.

Where nuisance arises not from the use to which the property is put, but from the state of repair in which it is let, the landlord is liable if he (or she) knows or ought to know of its state at the commencement of the tenancy.[5] Further, the landlord remains liable in this situ-ation even though the tenant has covenanted to put the premises into repair; this is because a covenant between landlord and tenant cannot restrict the rights of third parties.[6]

In cases where the property falls into disrepair, and thus becomes a nuisance, dur-ing the currency of the lease, the landlord is only responsible if he (or she) has a duty to repair[7] or a right to enter and do repairs.[8] The common law on these points is somewhat uncertain, but s 4 of the Defective Premises Act 1972 contains similar principles which are rather more clearly expressed.[9]

The general rule is that a landlord, like an occupier, is only liable for nuisance by dis-repair where he or she knows or ought to know of it. Once again, however, the case of *Wringe v Cohen*[10] lays down that, if the premises adjoin a highway, liability is strict.

---

[1] (1876) 45 LJQB 545.
[2] [1986] 1 All ER 663.
[3] [1972] 3 All ER 645.
[4] [1999] 4 All ER 125, CA.
[5] *St Anne's Well Brewery Co v Roberts* (1928) 140 LT 1, CA.
[6] *Brew Bros Ltd v Snax (Ross) Ltd* [1970] 1 All ER 587, CA.
[7] This may be express or implied, eg under the Landlord and Tenant Act 1985, ss 11–14; para 36.45.
[8] *Heap v Ind Coope and Allsopp Ltd* [1940] 3 All ER 634, CA. This may be implied, eg in a weekly tenancy: *Mint v Good* [1950] 2 All ER 1159, CA.
[9] Para 21.30.
[10] [1939] 4 All ER 241, CA.

THE PARTIES IN PRIVATE NUISANCE: KEY POINTS

- An action in private nuisance can only be brought by someone who has a proprietary or possessory interest in land; this will almost always mean a freeholder or tenant.

- The creator of a nuisance is strictly liable for it.

- The occupier of land from which a nuisance comes may be under a 'measured duty of care' to prevent or stop it.

- The landlord of property from which a nuisance comes can only be held liable if he or she has 'authorised' the nuisance.

Defences

Statutory authority

23.18 Many actions in private nuisance arise out of the activities of local authorities and other public or quasi-public bodies, which are carried on under the auspices of a statute. Such bodies may have a defence against liability where they can prove that the nuisance they have created is an inevitable consequence of what the statute ordered or empowered them to do, in the sense that it would occur despite the use of all reasonable care and skill, according to the state of scientific knowledge at the time.[1] However, the position may be further affected if, as frequently occurs, the statute in question contains a specific statement to the effect that liability for nuisance is, or is not, excluded.

The case law on statutory authority as a defence is complex, but an attempt was made to rationalise it in the case of *Department of Transport v North West Water Authority*,[2] where the following propositions, formulated by the trial judge, were endorsed by the House of Lords:

- In the absence of negligence, a body is not liable for a nuisance caused by its performance of a statutory *duty*.[3]
- This is so, even if the statute in question expressly imposes liability for nuisance.[4]
- In the absence of negligence, a body is not liable for a nuisance caused by its exercise of a statutory *power*, where the statute does not expressly impose liability upon it.[5]
- Even without negligence, a body is liable for a nuisance caused by its exercise of a statutory power, if the statute expressly imposes liability upon it.[6]
- In all cases, immunity depends upon proof that the work has been carried out, or the operation conducted, with all reasonable regard and care for the interests of other persons.[7]

Whether or not a particular nuisance has been expressly or impliedly authorised in this sense is a matter of statutory interpretation. In the leading case of *Hammersmith and City Rly Co v Brand*,[8] for instance, where a railway company was expressly authorised to use railway engines, it was held by the House of Lords that no action in nuisance would lie against it in respect of damage caused by vibrations from passing trains. In *Allen v Gulf Oil Refining Ltd*,[9] the express authority of the defendants was limited to acquiring land and there *constructing* an oil refinery. A majority of the House of Lords, reversing the decision of the Court of Appeal, held that there was also implied authority to *operate* a refinery, so that no action in nuisance would lie in respect of the inevitable consequences (smell, noise, vibrations, etc) of its operation.

In the last two cases, the defendants were empowered to carry on the activity in question in a specific place. Frequently, however, this is not so, the defendants in question having a wide discretion under the statute as to the place and method of exercising their power. In such a case, a court is less likely to take the view that any nuisance arising from the exercise of the discretion is inevitable. Thus, in *Metropolitan Asylum District Managers v Hill*,[10] it was held that a general authority to build hospitals did not protect the defendants from liability when they chose to site a smallpox hospital in a residential area.

Where the statutory authority is to carry out not a specific undertaking, but such works of a particular kind as may from time to time be necessary, the courts have been somewhat reluctant to use private nuisance for the protection of private rights. This reflects the view that, if parliament has seen fit to confer an administrative discretion upon a public body, the bona fide exercise of that discretion should be challenged only through administrative channels and not through the ordinary courts of law.[11]

[1] *Manchester Corpn v Farnworth* [1930] AC 171, HL.
[2] [1983] 3 All ER 273, HL.
[3] *Hammond v St Pancras Vestry* (1874) LR 9 CP 316.
[4] *Smeaton v Ilford Corpn* [1954] 1 All ER 923.
[5] *Dunne v North Western Gas Board* [1963] 3 All ER 916, CA.
[6] *Charing Cross West End and City Electric Supply Co v Hydraulic Power Co* [1914] 3 KB 772, CA.
[7] *Allen v Gulf Oil Refining Ltd* [1981] 1 All ER 353, HL.
[8] (1869) LR 4 HL 171, HL.
[9] [1981] 1 All ER 353, HL.
[10] (1881) 6 App Cas 193, HL.
[11] *Marriage v East Norfolk Rivers Catchment Board* [1949] 2 All ER 1021, CA.

Other defences

23.19 The defences of assumption of risk and contributory negligence, which we have already considered in relation to negligence,[1] are clearly capable of applying to nuisance, at least where the claimant sues in respect of a single incident which causes physical damage. Where, however, the gist of the claimant's complaint is the general effect of the defendant's unreasonable use of land, these defences seem of little relevance. In particular, it is certainly no defence to prove that the claimant came to an existing nuisance,[2] nor that the claimant could have reduced its effects, eg by shutting windows against noise.

It seems in principle that the right to commit certain private nuisances may be acquired by 20 years' use, under the doctrine of prescription. For this to be so, however, the right in question must be capable of forming the subject matter of an easement,[3] such as the right to send smoke through flues in a party wall.[4] It is generally thought that this requirement would exclude the possibility of prescription in respect of such variable nuisances as noise and smells, although cases on long-standing nuisances of this kind have all been decided on other grounds.[5]

It is no defence to show that the defendant's interference only amounts to a nuisance when combined with interference by others.[6]

[1] Chapter 19.
[2] Para 23.11.
[3] Paras 32.4–32.12.
[4] *Jones v Pritchard* [1908] 1 Ch 630.
[5] See, for example, *Sturges v Bridgman* (1879) 11 Ch D 852, CA.
[6] *Lambton v Mellish* [1894] 3 Ch 163; *Pride of Derby and Derbyshire Angling Association Ltd v British Celanese Ltd* [1953] 1 All ER 179.

Remedies

Damages

23.20 Although private nuisance is in theory actionable only on proof that the claimant has suffered damage, the necessary damage will sometimes be presumed to exist. For example, the mere fact that the cornice of the defendant's house projects over the claimant's land is sufficient to found an action, without the need to prove that water falls from it.[1] So too, any interference with a proprietary right of the claimant is automatically actionable; this is important, since continued interference by the defendant might otherwise lead to the loss of the claimant's right altogether.[2]

Once it is established that the defendant is guilty of nuisance, the claimant is entitled to claim damages for consequential losses, provided that these are of a foreseeable kind.[3] As we have seen,[4] relevant losses include damage to goods and land,[5] together with the intangible 'use and enjoyment' of the claimant's property. The last category is obviously difficult to express in monetary terms; the courts have sometimes used the analogy of personal injury cases, so that damages for noise reflect those for deafness[6] and damages for smell reflect those awarded for loss of that sense.[7] However, the correctness of this approach was doubted in *Hunter v Canary Wharf Ltd*,[8] where it was stated that damages should be measured by the effect which the nuisance had on the value of the affected land.

[1] *Fay v Prentice* (1845) 1 CB 828.
[2] *Nicholls v Ely Beet Sugar Factory Ltd* [1936] Ch 343, CA.
[3] *The Wagon Mound (No 2)* [1966] 2 All ER 709, PC.
[4] Paras 23.3 and 23.4.
[5] For what is included in damage to land, see *Midland Bank plc v Bardgrove Property Services Ltd* [1992] 2 EGLR 168, CA; para 32.57.
[6] *Chadwick v Keith Marshall* [1984] CLY 1037.
[7] *Bone v Seale* [1975] 1 All ER 787, CA.
[8] [1997] 2 All ER 426 at 451, HL.

Injunction[1]

23.21 A commonly sought remedy in nuisance actions is that of injunction, whereby the claimant asks the court to order the termination of the offending activity. The award of this remedy lies in the discretion of the court, and it will seldom be granted in respect of injury which is trivial or temporary.[2] In more serious cases, however, the courts have displayed a notable tendency to grant an injunction even when the defendant's activity has public value,[3] which seems rather surprising in view of their statutory power to award damages in lieu of the injunction sought.[4]

[1] Paras 27.16–27.18.
[2] *A-G v Sheffield Gas Consumers Co* (1853) 3 De GM & G 304.
[3] Para 23.10.
[4] Para 27.18.

Abatement

23.22 The law has for centuries recognised the right of a person affected by a nuisance to take matters into his or her own hands and abate (ie remove) it. In a more sophisticated age, however, such self-help remedies are treated by the courts with suspicion and dislike, if for no other reason than that they may lead to a breach of the peace, and anyone claiming to exercise this right must therefore take great care not to exceed what the law permits. Where, for example, the defendant's tree overhangs the claimant's land, the claimant may lop off its branches[1] but must not, however, keep the fruit.[2] Further, where abatement involves entry on to the defendant's land, notice must first be given, except in an emergency.[3] And the overall requirement that damage be kept to a minimum means that, where there are alternative methods of abating a nuisance, the less mischievous must be chosen.[4]

[1] *Lemmon v Webb* [1895] AC 1, HL.
[2] *Mills v Brooker* [1919] 1 KB 555.
[3] *Jones v Williams* (1843) 11 M & W 176.
[4] *Lagan Navigation Co v Lambeg Bleaching Co* [1927] AC 226, HL.

Defences and Remedies: Key Points

- Where an activity is conducted under statutory provisions, the question of liability for nuisance is primarily dependent upon the wording of the statute.

- Liability in such cases will frequently depend on whether or not the activity in question was conducted with or without negligence.

- Damages for interference with the use and enjoyment of land are assessed by reference to the effect which the interference had on the value of the land.

Public nuisance

23.23 Public nuisance covers an even wider area than private nuisance, partly because it is not limited to interference with land. Public nuisance falls into two broad categories. First, the kind of interference, such as noise or smoke, which is commonly a private nuisance, will also become a public nuisance if it affects a sufficiently substantial neighbourhood or section of the public. Whether or not this is so is a question of fact;[1] thus, in *R v Lloyd*,[2] where only three people complained of noise, the defendant was held not guilty of public nuisance. Second, public nuisance may consist of interference with the exercise of public rights, for instance by obstructing a highway or navigable river. Within these two classes, liability has been imposed on such diverse activities as blasting operations causing widespread vibrations, dust, splinters and noise,[3] organising a pop festival which causes noise, traffic congestion and general inconvenience,[4] selling impure food[5] or water,[6] and failing to prevent pigeons roosting under a railway bridge from fouling the footpath.[7]

It must be remembered that public nuisance is essentially a matter of criminal law.[8] However, as noted below,[9] a private individual may in some circumstances seek damages for the effect of a public nuisance. Further, where the relevant criminal penalties are felt to be inadequate, the Attorney-General is empowered to obtain an injunction and thus to have the offending activity terminated.

[1] *A-G v PYA Quarries Ltd* [1957] 1 All ER 894, CA.
[2] (1802) 4 Esp 200.
[3] *A-G v PYA Quarries Ltd* [1957] 1 All ER 894, CA.
[4] *A-G for Ontario v Orange Productions Ltd* (1971) 21 DLR (3d) 257.
[5] *Shillito v Thompson* (1875) 1 QBD 12.
[6] *AB v South West Water Services Ltd* [1993] 1 All ER 609, CA.
[7] *Wandsworth London Borough Council v Railtrack plc* [2001] EWCA Civ 1236, [2002] QB 756.
[8] A very important consequence of this is that a public nuisance can never be legalised by prescription.
[9] Para 23.26.

23.24 Public nuisance, like private nuisance, involves the court in the task of balancing conflicting interests in accordance with the general idea of reasonableness. Therefore, a shopkeeper is not automatically liable when queues form outside the shop and obstruct the highway, since these may be due to circumstances beyond the shopkeeper's control, such as wartime shortages.[1] Liability will be imposed, however, on a theatre proprietor who takes no steps at all to reduce large nightly queues,[2] or on a shopkeeper who, by selling ice cream from a window, instead of inside the shop, positively increases the likelihood of obstruction.[3] The test is whether the defendant knows or ought to know that there is a real risk that nuisance of the kind which in fact occurs will be caused.[4]

Again, as with private nuisance, the court must apply the principle of 'give and take'. A builder may erect hoardings or scaffolding in the street,[5] vans may load and unload outside business premises[6] and vehicles may break down,[7] without liability arising in public nuisance. Indeed, where personal injury results from such an obstruction, as where the claimant collides at night with a parked vehicle, the modern tendency is to impose liability upon the defendant only where there has been negligence,[8] although it is not clear whether it is for the claimant to establish negligence or for the defendant to disprove it. Where, however, the obstruction is unreasonable in size or extent, as where a vehicle which has broken down is left for a long period in an unlighted or otherwise dangerous condition, the defendant will be liable in public nuisance.[9]

[1] *Dwyer v Mansfield* [1946] 2 All ER 247.
[2] *Lyons, Sons & Co v Gulliver* [1914] 1 Ch 631, CA.

3   *Fabbri v Morris* [1947] 1 All ER 315, DC.
4   *R v Shorrock* [1993] 3 All ER 917, CA.
5   *Harper v GN Haden & Sons Ltd* [1933] Ch 298, CA.
6   *Trevett v Lee* [1955] 1 All ER 406, CA.
7   *Maitland v Raisbeck and AT and J Hewitt Ltd* [1944] 2 All ER 272, CA.
8   *Dymond v Pearce* [1972] 1 All ER 1142, CA.
9   *Ware v Garston Haulage Co Ltd* [1943] 2 All ER 558, CA.

Highways

23.25 It is obvious from the previous paragraph that public nuisance frequently concerns the highway. In the first place, any obstruction, whether total or partial, of the highway is actionable, except where it can be justified on the broad ground of reasonableness. It has even been suggested[1] that it would be a public nuisance for pickets to harass workers in their use of the highway without actually obstructing it, but this has been doubted.[2]

Second, it is a public nuisance to carry on any activity, or to allow property to fall into a state, whereby users of the highway are endangered. This includes the creation of such obvious hazards as a pool of acid[3] or a pile of rubbish,[4] and the emission of large clouds of smoke from neighbouring premises[5] or defective vehicles[6] which obscure the vision of drivers. In *Castle v St Augustine's Links*,[7] liability was imposed upon a golf club which so sited one of its tees that golfers often sliced balls on to an adjoining public road. A person may even be liable for public nuisance for creating a danger which is not technically on the highway at all, provided that a passer-by may be endangered without making a substantial detour from the highway. Thus, for example, an unfenced excavation at the very edge of the road, or sharp outward-pointing spikes on a boundary fence,[8] can constitute a public nuisance.

Where danger arises from work which is being done on or in the highway itself, such as excavations, it is important to note that the defendant is liable even without negligence and, further, is responsible for any default of an independent contractor.[9]

The mere fact that a person's building or tree projects over the highway does not amount to a public nuisance, unless it is such as to interfere with reasonable passage. Where, however, it falls and does damage, there may undoubtedly be liability, although the basis of this is disputed. It seems that, where trees are concerned, the occupier is not liable unless there was reason to suspect the danger;[10] nor is the occupier responsible for the negligence of an independent contractor, eg in felling operations.[11] Where buildings collapse, liability appears to be strict, whether these project over[12] or merely adjoin[13] the highway.

As regards dangers arising from the condition of the highway itself, such as potholes or uneven flagstones, common law imposed no liability upon anyone for a mere failure to repair. In relation to highway authorities, this immunity was anomalous, and it was removed by statute in 1961. Under this provision (which is now contained in the Highways Act 1980), a highway authority may be liable in negligence, nuisance or breach of statutory duty for damage caused by its failure to maintain or repair a highway, subject to a statutory defence of proving that all reasonable care had been taken, by independent contractors or employees of the highway authority, to make the particular highway safe for the type and volume of traffic which might reasonably be expected to use it.

1   *Thomas v National Union of Mineworkers* [1985] 2 All ER 1.
2   *News Group Newspapers Ltd v Society of Graphical and Allied Trades 1982 (No 2)* [1987] ICR 181.
3   *Pope v Fraser and Southern Rolling and Wire Mills Ltd* (1938) 55 TLR 324.

[4] *Almeroth v Chivers & Sons Ltd* [1948] 1 All ER 53, CA.

[5] *Holling v Yorkshire Traction Co* [1948] 2 All ER 662.

[6] *Tysoe v Davies* [1984] RTR 88.

[7] (1922) 38 TLR 615.

[8] *Fenna v Clare & Co* [1895] 1 QB 199, DC.

[9] *Holliday v National Telephone Co* [1899] 2 QB 392, CA; see paras 26.21 and 26.24.

[10] *Caminer v Northern and London Investment Trust Ltd* [1950] 2 All ER 486, HL. See also *Quinn v Scott* [1965] 2 All ER 588.

[11] *Salsbury v Woodland* [1969] 3 All ER 863, CA.

[12] *Tarry v Ashton* (1876) 1 QBD 314.

[13] *Wringe v Cohen* [1939] 4 All ER 241, CA.

Action for damages

23.26 The fact that a person is inconvenienced by a public nuisance does not in itself justify a claim for damages in respect of it.[1] In order to recover damages, the claimant must be proved to have suffered some 'special' or 'particular' damage, over and above that which is sustained by the public in general. This requirement is obviously satisfied by personal injuries,[2] and, in *Halsey v Esso Petroleum Co Ltd*,[3] it was held that the claimant was entitled to complain of smuts from the defendants' oil depot, since these had caused actual damage to the paintwork of his car, which was parked in the street outside his house. Similarly, where unlawful industrial picketing obstructs the highway, the costs incurred by an employer in 'bussing' in workers and providing extra security for them was held recoverable as damages for public nuisance.[4]

In these cases, the damage to the claimant was of a different kind from that+ suffered by other persons, but it seems that a substantial difference in extent is also sufficient to found an action. In the Irish case of *Boyd v Great Northern Rly Co*,[5] for instance, a doctor with a busy practice recovered damages when he was delayed for 20 minutes at a level crossing, while in *Rose v Miles*,[6] where the defendant obstructed a creek and thus trapped the claimant's barges, the claimant was able to recover the considerable cost of unloading the cargo and transporting it by land. Again, in *Tate & Lyle Industries Ltd v Greater London Council*,[7] where the defendants caused serious siltation in navigable reaches of the River Thames, the claimants recovered for losses caused by the inability of large vessels to load and unload at their sugar refinery.

The obstruction of streets not infrequently leads to complaints by neighbouring tradesmen of loss of custom. Where access to the claimant's premises is blocked, this certainly gives rise to an action for damages.[8] Where the obstruction is further away, the legal position is less clear, although the better view is that an affected tradesman can sue,[9] provided that the effect of the obstruction upon business is foreseeable and therefore not too remote.[10]

[1] *Winterbottom v Lord Derby* (1867) LR 2 Exch 316.

[2] An argument that public nuisance, like private nuisance, no longer compensates for personal injuries was rejected by the Court of Appeal in *Re Corby Group Litigation* [2008] EWCA Civ 463, CA.

[3] [1961] 2 All ER 145.

[4] *News Group Newspapers Ltd v Society of Graphical and Allied Trades 1982 (No 2)* [1987] ICR 181.

[5] [1895] 2 IR 555.

[6] (1815) 4 M & S 101.

[7] [1983] 1 All ER 1159, HL.

[8] *Fritz v Hobson* (1880) 14 Ch D 542.

[9] *Wilkes v Hungerford Market Co* (1835) 2 Bing NC 281.

[10] *The Wagon Mound (No 2)* [1966] 2 All ER 709, PC; paras 18.14–18.19.

> PUBLIC NUISANCE: KEY POINTS
>
> - A public nuisance is one which affects a substantial section of the public, or which interferes with the exercise (or safe exercise) of public rights.
> - It is a public nuisance to obstruct the highway or unreasonably to endanger highway users.
> - Public nuisance is primarily a matter for the criminal law; however an action for damages may be brought by anyone who suffers 'special' damage, over and above that which everyone suffers.

Questions

1. What kinds of 'damage' may form the basis of a claim in private nuisance?

2. How do the courts seek to balance the competing interests of neighbours?

3. What factors are used in deciding whether or not an interference is 'unreasonable' and therefore an actionable nuisance?

4. To what extent is private nuisance a tort of strict (ie independent of negligence) liability?

5. Who is entitled to bring an action in private nuisance?

6. Who may be held liable for private nuisance, and on what basis?

7. To what extent is statutory authority a defence to an action in private nuisance?

8. In what circumstances does a nuisance become a 'public nuisance'?

9. In what circumstances does a public nuisance give rise to a civil action for damages?

10. Toby, the tenant of a house leased from Lionel, allows a local pop group to practise in his garage, to the great annoyance of Ned, his next-door neighbour. Fans of the group besiege the property, dropping large quantities of litter; this attracts rats, which soon infest Ned's property. On one occasion an especially loud session causes slates to fall off Toby's roof and into Ned's garden, breaking windows in his greenhouse.

    Advise Ned as to his rights, if any, against any other party.

24

Strict liability

CHAPTER OVERVIEW

In certain circumstances, the law of tort imposes liability upon someone without proof of negligence. In this chapter we consider the following issues:

- the rule of strict liability laid down in the leading case of *Rylands v Fletcher*;
- the requirements for liability under this rule, especially the need for an escape and a 'non-natural use' of land;
- the defences which are available in an action under *Rylands v Fletcher*;
- the special common law and statutory rules governing liability for damage caused by fire.

24.1 In this and the next chapter we consider several situations in which, unusually, liability may be imposed upon a defendant who is not guilty of any 'fault'. In these situations, the law in effect says that, while it is quite permissible to carry on high-risk activities, any losses which they cause must be borne by those who carry on the activities, and not by innocent members of society on whom those losses happen to fall.

Rylands v Fletcher

24.2 The defendants employed reputable independent contractors to construct a reservoir on their land, for the purpose of supplying water to their mill. In the course of construction, the contractors discovered some disused mine shafts on the reservoir site but negligently failed to seal these properly, with the result that water flowed down the shafts and flooded the claimant's mine, which connected with the disused workings. No negligence was found against the defendants themselves and, at first instance, they were held not liable for the damage caused. On appeal, however, the claimant was successful, upon grounds stated by Blackburn J:[1]

> 'We think that the true rule of law is, that the person who for his own purposes brings on his lands and collects and keeps there anything likely to do mischief if it escapes, must keep it in at his peril, and, if he does not do so, is prima facie answerable for all the damage which is the natural consequence of its escape. He can excuse himself by showing that the escape was owing to the claimant's default; or perhaps that the escape was the consequence of *vis major*, or the act of God; but as nothing of this sort exists here, it is unnecessary to inquire what excuse would be sufficient.'

This decision, together with the reasoning on which it was based, was expressly approved and upheld by the House of Lords,[2] although Lord Cairns LC rather complicated matters by stressing the importance of the fact that the defendants were at the relevant time putting their land to a 'non-natural use'.

[1] (1866) LR 1 Exch 265 at 279.
[2] (1868) LR 3 HL 330, HL.

24.3 The ruling in *Rylands v Fletcher* could undoubtedly have been used by the courts as the basis of a general principle of strict liability for ultra hazardous activities. However, this has not happened, due to the restrictive way in which it has been interpreted. In particular, the requirements of an escape from land[1] and a 'non-natural use' of land by the defendant[2] have served to keep the rule within strict limits, as has the House of Lords' insistence that the rule is a sub-species of private nuisance and therefore subject to the limitations of that tort in terms of who can sue and for what type of loss.[3] The specific defences available[4] also restrict the use of the rule, mainly by exonerating a non-negligent defendant.

The overall consequence of these restrictions is that it is virtually impossible to find a reported case in the last hundred years in which a claimant has succeeded in an action under *Rylands v Fletcher* where he (or she) would not have been equally successful in negligence. In these circumstances, it is perhaps surprising that the House of Lords has specifically resisted calls to abolish the rule altogether.[5]

[1] Para 24.7.
[2] Para 24.8.
[3] Para 24.9.
[4] Paras 24.10–24.14.
[5] *Transco plc v Stockport MBC* [2003] UKHL 61, HL.

Elements of liability

Land

24.4 The object that escapes and causes damage must be something which the defendant has brought on to his or her land. This does not mean, however, that liability is imposed only upon the freehold owner, or even the occupier, of the land in question. A licensee, for example, who introduces a dangerous substance on to land which he is permitted to use may be liable under *Rylands v Fletcher* for its subsequent escape, provided that it is then still under the licensee's (ineffective) control.[1] In such a case, it seems that an owner who is not in occupation is only liable if he (or she) has expressly or impliedly authorised the accumulation.[2]

The requirement of occupation of 'land' has been slightly relaxed, so as to include those who have a right to lay pipes, cables etc under the land of others or under the public highway. Indeed, an escape in such circumstances may render the defendant liable, not only to neighbouring landowners,[3] but also to other public bodies with similar rights.[4]

Whether the rule is capable of any further expansion must be regarded as doubtful. However, it may possibly apply where a dangerous thing escapes from the highway on to which the defendant has brought it.[5] It has also been suggested that it might apply to accumulations of dangerous objects in a vessel moored on a river.[6]

[1] *Rainham Chemical Works v Belvedere Fish Guano Co* [1921] 2 AC 465, HL.
[2] *St Anne's Well Brewery Co v Roberts* (1928) 140 LT 1, CA.
[3] *Northwestern Utilities Ltd v London Guarantee and Accident Co Ltd* [1936] AC 108, PC.

[4] *Charing Cross West End and City Electric Supply Co v Hydraulic Power Co* [1914] 3 KB 772, CA. However, this was specifically denied by Lord Scott in *Transco plc v Stockport MBC* [2003] UKHL 61, HL.

[5] *Rigby v Chief Constable of Northamptonshire* [1985] 2 All ER 985.

[6] *Crown River Cruises Ltd v Kimbolton Fireworks Ltd* [1996] 2 Lloyd's Rep 533.

Accumulation

24.5 Blackburn J spoke of the person who 'for his own purposes brings on his lands and collects and keeps there' something which, if it escapes, will be dangerous. Subsequent cases support this idea that the defendant is strictly liable only for artificial accumulations, and not for either natural material, such as earth, or material which accumulates naturally, such as rainwater.[1] For instance, in *Giles v Walker*,[2] an occupier who ploughed up forest land was held not liable for the subsequent spontaneous crop of thistles which spread to the claimant's land.[3] So too, in *Pontardawe RDC v Moore-Gwyn*,[4] it was held that *Rylands v Fletcher* had no application to a fall of rock from an outcrop due to the natural process of erosion. Again, where water is naturally on the defendant's land, the claimant cannot complain that the defendant's normal working of mines[5] or building works[6] causes it to flow on to the claimant's land.

Not surprisingly, an occupier who actively causes natural material to escape will be liable under *Rylands v Fletcher*.[7] For example, in *Miles v Forest Rock Granite Co (Leicestershire) Ltd*,[8] liability was imposed upon the defendants for damage done by the escape of rock caused by their blasting operations. A similar decision was reached in *Baird v Williamson*,[9] where the defendant pumped water which was naturally in his mine to a level from which it flowed into the claimant's mine.

The requirement that the accumulation be for the defendant's own purposes should not be taken too literally, as restricting *Rylands v Fletcher* to cases where the defendant acquires some personal benefit. It has been held to apply, for example, to a local authority compelled by statute to receive sewage into its sewers,[10] although the liability of statutory undertakers was doubted by the Court of Appeal on precisely this ground in *Dunne v North Western Gas Board*.[11]

[1] For the 'measured duty of care' which arises in respect of natural dangers, see para 23.16.

[2] (1890) 24 Qbd 656.

[3] Contrast *Crowhurst v Amersham Burial Board* (1878) 4 Ex D 5, where the defendants actually planted a poisonous tree.

[4] [1929] 1 Ch 656.

[5] *Smith v Kenrick* (1849) 7 CB 515, approved in *Rylands v Fletcher*.

[6] *Ellison v Ministry of Defence* (1996) 81 BLR 101.

[7] If the act is deliberate, the appropriate tort is trespass: *Rigby v Chief Constable of Northamptonshire* [1985] 2 All ER 985.

[8] (1918) 34 TLR 500, CA.

[9] (1863) 15 CBNS 376, again approved in *Rylands v Fletcher*.

[10] *Smeaton v Ilford Corpn* [1954] 1 All ER 923.

[11] [1963] 3 All ER 916, CA.

Dangerous things

24.6 As originally stated, the rule in *Rylands v Fletcher* applies to anything 'likely to do mischief if it escapes'. Such things have been held to include water in bulk,[1] gas,[2] electricity,[3] sparks,[4] acid smuts[5] and poisonous vegetation.[6] *Rylands v Fletcher* has also been held to apply to fire[7] and explosions,[8] notwithstanding that the thing which escapes in such cases is not necessarily the same as that which the defendant has accumulated.

All these seem to fall fairly within the rule as originally laid down, but some other candidates for inclusion are more questionable. In *Firth v Bowling Iron Co*,[9] for example, the defendants were held liable for a rusty wire fence which flaked on to the claimant's land and poisoned his cattle, while, in *Hale v Jennings Bros*,[10] the principle was invoked where a chair from a fairground 'chair-o-plane' became detached from the roundabout and, complete with its occupant, flew off and injured the occupier of a nearby booth. Even a falling flagpole[11] has been held to come within *Rylands v Fletcher*, although its application to vibrations,[12] where the invasion is intangible, has been criticised. Most extreme of all is the case of *A-G v Corke*,[13] where the doctrine was applied to human beings so as to justify the grant of an injunction against a man who allowed caravan dwellers to use his field, when these committed various acts of nuisance in the neighbourhood. The dubious nature of this decision is emphasised by the fact that liability could in any case have been imposed on the simple ground of nuisance.[14]

[1] *Rylands v Fletcher* itself.
[2] *Northwestern Utilities Ltd v London Guarantee and Accident Co Ltd* [1936] AC 108, PC.
[3] *National Telephone Co v Baker* [1893] 2 Ch 186.
[4] *Jones v Festiniog Rly Co* (1868) LR 3 Qb 733.
[5] *Halsey v Esso Petroleum Co Ltd* [1961] 2 All ER 145.
[6] *Crowhurst v Amersham Burial Board* (1878) 4 Ex D 5.
[7] *Mason v Levy Auto Parts of England Ltd* [1967] 2 All ER 62.
[8] *Rainham Chemical Works v Belvedere Fish Guano Co* [1921] 2 AC 465, HL; *Colour Quest Ltd v Total Downstream plc* [2009] EWHC 540, Comm.
[9] (1878) 3 CPD 254.
[10] [1938] 1 All ER 579, CA.
[11] *Shiffman v Hospital of the Order of St John of Jerusalem* [1936] 1 All ER 557.
[12] *Hoare & Co v McAlpine* [1923] 1 Ch 167.
[13] [1933] Ch 89.
[14] *A-G v Stone* (1895) 12 TLR 76; para 23.16.

Escape

24.7 *Rylands v Fletcher* requires an escape, in the sense that the damage complained of is suffered outside the land on which the defendant accumulates the dangerous thing. In *Ponting v Noakes*,[1] for instance, the claimant was unable to recover damages when his horse reached over the boundary of the defendant's land, ate some poisonous vegetation which grew there, and died. This principle was unanimously endorsed by the House of Lords in *Read v J Lyons & Co Ltd*,[2] where a munitions inspector was injured by the explosion of a shell at the defendants' weapons factory. It was admitted that such shells were 'dangerous things'; nevertheless it was held that, in the absence of either negligence or an escape, the defendants were not liable.

In deciding whether there has been a sufficient 'escape' for this purpose, the courts are concerned, not with the niceties of land law, but with the simple question of fact whether something has travelled from a place where the defendant has control to a place where beyond such control. As a result, a landlord may be liable to a tenant (or, possibly, to a licensee) when something escapes from a part of the property which the landlord has retained to another part which is in the occupation of the claimant.[3]

[1] [1894] 2 Qb 281.
[2] [1946] 2 All ER 471, HL.
[3] *Hale v Jennings Bros* [1938] 1 All ER 579, CA.

Non-natural use

24.8 In laying down the rule in *Rylands v Fletcher*, Blackburn J stressed the importance of the fact that the defendants had brought on to their land something which was not naturally there. This element of liability, like all the others, was expressly approved by Lord

Cairns LC, in the House of Lords, but the additional point was made that the defendant must be engaged in a 'non-natural' use of the land.

The effect of this requirement has been to introduce a great deal of flexibility into this area of law, because the courts are free not to impose strict liability upon a person whose use of land, although artificial, is an ordinary and usual one. The result of this discretion has been to tie *Rylands v Fletcher* more closely to the idea of exceptional risk, and it has been suggested that a non-natural use is one which brings with it increased danger to others and is not merely the ordinary use of the land or such a use as is proper for the general benefit of the community.[1]

It is difficult to predict how the courts will make what is in effect a value judgment, although decided cases offer some insight into judicial attitudes. Thus, while a domestic water supply,[1] or a house's electric wiring,[2] or a fire in a grate,[3] have all been held to be natural, similar utilities carried in bulk have not.[4] So too, trees, whether planted or self-sown, have been regarded as natural,[5] except where they are poisonous.[6] Such decisions do not necessarily mean that the dividing line lies between domestic or agricultural uses, on the one hand, and industrial uses, on the other. A number of cases have used the idea of natural use to avoid imposing strict liability on industrial activities which are regarded as for the public benefit,[7] even to the extent of suggesting that an armaments factory is a natural use of land in wartime.[8] However, in the recent case of *Cambridge Water Co Ltd v Eastern Counties Leather plc*,[9] the House of Lords regarded the storage of substantial quantities of chemicals on industrial premises as 'an almost classic case of non-natural use', even though the premises were in an industrial village and the defendants' activity created much-needed employment in the locality.

---

[1] *Rickards v Lothian* [1913] AC 263 at 279, PC.

[2] *Collingwood v Home and Colonial Stores Ltd* [1936] 3 All ER 200, CA.

[3] *Sochacki v Sas* [1947] 1 All ER 344; *Johnson v BJW Property Developments Ltd* [2002] EWHC 1131 (TCC), [2002] 3 All ER 574.

[4] *Smeaton v Ilford Corpn* [1954] 1 All ER 923 (sewage). However, the House of Lords in *Transco plc v Stockport MBC* [2003] UKHL 61, HL held that a pipe carrying water from a main to a block of 66 flats was a 'natural' use and therefore outside *Rylands v Fletcher*.

[5] *Noble v Harrison* [1926] 2 KB 332.

[6] *Crowhurst v Amersham Burial Board* (1878) 4 Ex D 5.

[7] Eg *Rouse v Gravelworks Ltd* [1940] 1 All ER 26, CA (working of mines and minerals); *British Celanese Ltd v A H Hunt (Capacitors) Ltd* [1969] 2 All ER 1252 (light engineering factory on an industrial estate); *Ellison v Ministry of Defence* (1996) 81 BLR 101 (construction of bulk fuel installations at airfield).

[8] *Read v J Lyons & Co Ltd* [1946] 2 All ER 471 at 475, 478, 484.

[9] [1994] 1 All ER 53 at 79.

Damage

24.9 It was said in *Rylands v Fletcher* that a defendant would be liable for 'all the damage which is the natural consequence' of the escape. This formulation does not indicate the appropriate test for remoteness of damage, but it is now established that the defendant can only be liable for damage of a type which could have been reasonably foreseen, even though foreseeability is irrelevant to liability itself.[1]

As to the *kinds* of damage which are actionable, the major question is whether *Rylands v Fletcher* is like private nuisance in protecting only those persons with an interest in or exclusive possession of land.[2] Until fairly recently, the balance of authority suggested that *Rylands v Fletcher* was not so limited; thus in *Halsey v Esso Petroleum Co Ltd*,[3] the claimant was able to claim for damage caused to the paintwork of his car, which was parked in the street, by acid smuts from the defendants' oil depot. So too, in *British Celanese Ltd v A H Hunt (Capacitors) Ltd*,[4] where strips of metal foil blew from the defendants' land on to an electricity sub-station, and the resulting power cut caused damage in the claimants' factory, it was held to be no defence that nothing had 'escaped' on to the claimants' land. However, these decisions appear irreconcilable with the views expressed by the House of Lords in *Cambridge Water Co Ltd v Eastern Counties Leather plc*[5] and *Transco plc v Stockport MBC*,[6] where *Rylands v Fletcher* was said to be a sub-species of private nuisance.[7] These views would also appear to exclude a claim in respect of personal injuries, contrary to earlier cases concerning claims by both occupiers[8] and non-occupiers.[9]

Whether or not it may accurately be described as a natural consequence, it is settled that no damages may be claimed under *Rylands v Fletcher* for pure economic loss.[10]

[1] *Cambridge Water Co Ltd v Eastern Counties Leather plc* [1994] 1 All ER 53.
[2] Para 23.13.
[3] [1961] 2 All ER 145.
[4] [1969] 2 All ER 1252.
[5] [1994] 1 All ER 53 at 69–71.
[6] [2003] UKHL 61, HL.
[7] In *McKenna v British Aluminium Ltd* (2002) Times, 25 April, it was accepted by the judge that restricting claimants in this way might be challenged under the Human Rights Act 1998.
[8] *Hale v Jennings Bros* [1938] 1 All ER 579, CA.
[9] *Miles v Forest Rock Granite Co (Leicestershire) Ltd* (1918) 34 TLR 500, CA; *Shiffman v Hospital of the Order of St John of Jerusalem* [1936] 1 All ER 557; *Perry v Kendricks Transport Ltd* [1956] 1 All ER 154, CA.
[10] *Cattle v Stockton Waterworks Co* (1875) LR 10 Qb 453; *Weller & Co v Foot and Mouth Disease Research Institute* [1965] 3 All ER 560. See paras 16.12–16.15.

ELEMENTS OF *RYLANDS V FLETCHER*: KEY POINTS

- Liability requires an escape of dangerous things which have been accumulated on land occupied by the defendant.
- The defendant must be shown to have been engaged in a 'non-natural use' of the land.
- The defendant is liable only for such damage to neighbouring land as is foreseeable.

Defences

Consent of the claimant

24.10 Where the claimant consents to the presence of the source of danger, the defendant is not liable in the absence of negligence.[1] This consent may be express;[2] however, it is more commonly implied from the circumstances. As to when consent will be implied, the legal position is confused; many of the cases have concerned an escape of water from an upper floor to a lower floor, and these could have been decided on an alternative ground, namely, that the installation in question was a natural use of land.[3] Apart from this, two main threads emerge from the cases as reasons for holding that the claimant has consented. First, and despite its apparent conflict with the principle that 'coming to a nuisance' is no defence,[4] the claimant (at least one who is the defendant's tenant) cannot complain of the condition of the demised property (or the landlord's property) at the commencement of the lease.[5] Second, consent to a dangerous installation will more easily be implied where it is maintained for the benefit of the claimant as well as the defendant.[6] This latter factor, however, is not conclusive, so that a consumer of gas is not precluded from suing the gas company by virtue of benefitting from the supply.[7]

It should be emphasised that the consent which is implied in these cases does not exonerate a defendant who is negligent,[8] unless the circumstances are so extreme that the claimant can be said to have assumed the risk of such negligence.

[1] Paras 19.2–19.5.
[2] As in *A-G v Cory Bros & Co Ltd* [1921] 1 AC 521, HL.
[3] *Rickards v Lothian* [1913] AC 263, PC; para 24.8.
[4] Para 23.11.
[5] *Kiddle v City Business Properties Ltd* [1942] 2 All ER 216.
[6] *Gill v Edouin* (1895) 72 LT 579, CA.
[7] *Northwestern Utilities Ltd v London Guarantee and Accident Co Ltd* [1936] AC 108, PC.
[8] *A Prosser & Son Ltd v Levy* [1955] 3 All ER 577, CA; *Colour Quest Ltd v Total Downstream plc* [2009] EWHC 540, Comm.

Default of the claimant and hypersensitivity

24.11 If the true legal cause of damage is some act or default of the claimant, no action will lie. In *Dunn v Birmingham Canal Navigation Co*,[1] for example, where a mine-owner, fully aware of the danger, worked his mine directly under the defendants' canal, he was held unable to sue in respect of the resulting flood. It also appears that the damages payable to a claimant who is partly responsible for the damage may be reduced on the ground of contributory negligence.[2]

Where injury or damage results from the hypersensitivity of the claimant or the claimant's property, it seems, by analogy with nuisance,[3] that the defendant should not be liable. In *Eastern and South African Telegraph Co Ltd v Cape Town Tramways Companies Ltd*,[4] where the escape of minute electric currents from the defendants' tramway system interfered with the claimants' submarine telegraph cable, the claimants failed to recover damages. Where, however, the claimant is not actively responsible for the sensitivity, the position is less clear. For example, in *Hoare & Co v McAlpine*,[5] it was said to be no defence to an action for causing damage by vibrations that the claimants' building was old and unstable.

[1] (1872) LR 7 Qb 244.
[2] Paras 19.6–19.9.
[3] Para 23.7.
[4] [1902] AC 381, PC.
[5] [1923] 1 Ch 167.

Act of God

24.12 The law recognises that there may be a natural catastrophe so overwhelming that even a system of strict liability should not hold the defendant responsible. Thus, where the escape is due to an operation of natural forces 'which no human foresight can provide against, and of which human prudence is not bound to recognise the possibility',[1] there is no liability. In *Nichols v Marsland*,[2] the defendant created artificial lakes on his land by damming a natural stream. A rainstorm of unprecedented violence broke down the banks which he had built, and the resulting flood swept away the claimant's bridges. The defendant was held not liable, on the basis that the storm constituted an act of God.

Nichols v Marsland appears to be the only reported English case in which the defence has succeeded, and even that decision has been heavily criticised. In *Greenock Corpn v Caledonian Rly Co*,[3] it was held by the House of Lords that, whatever the English position might be, an extraordinary rainfall in Scotland was no act of God!

[1] *Tennent v Earl of Glasgow* (1864) 2 M 22 at 26.
[2] (1876) 2 Ex D 1, CA.
[3] [1917] AC 556, HL.

Act of a stranger

24.13 Although difficult to reconcile with the theory of strict liability, it is well established that a defendant is not liable under *Rylands v Fletcher* where the escape is due to the deliberate and unforeseeable intervention of a 'stranger', that is, someone over whom the defendant has no control. This may be some unknown person who blocks up the waste-pipe of a washbasin and leaves the taps running,[1] a trespassing child who drops a lighted match into the petrol tank of a motor vehicle,[2] or even a neighbour who, by emptying a reservoir into the stream which feeds the defendant's reservoir, causes the latter to flood the claimant's land.[3] The defendant is responsible, however, for the acts of employees, unless they go where they are expressly forbidden[4] and, of course, for independent contractors.[5] Further, it appears that the defendant may be liable for the actions of anyone who is lawfully on the land. For example, in *Hale v Jennings Bros*,[6] where a chair flew off a fairground 'chair-o-plane' and injured a stallholder, it was held to be no defence that this was due to tampering by the person who was riding in it.

A defendant is responsible, even for the intervention of a 'stranger', if the defendant ought reasonably to have anticipated the danger and taken steps to prevent the accident. In *Northwestern Utilities Ltd v London Guarantee and Accident Co Ltd*,[7] for example, the claimants' hotel was destroyed by fire after gas escaped from the defendants' mains and exploded. The mains had fractured when support was withdrawn from it during the construction of a sewer. The Privy Council held the defendants liable, for they were aware of the construction work and should have appreciated the very grave danger which this involved.

[1] *Rickards v Lothian* [1913] AC 263, PC.
[2] *Perry v Kendricks Transport Ltd* [1956] 1 All ER 154, CA.
[3] *Box v Jubb* (1879) 4 Ex D 76.
[4] *Stevens v Woodward* (1881) 6 Qbd 318, DC (employee caused a flood by leaving the taps running in a lavatory which he was not permitted to use).
[5] *Rylands v Fletcher* itself.
[6] [1938] 1 All ER 579, CA.
[7] [1936] AC 108, PC.

Statutory authority

24.14 A person whose activity is authorised by statute is not liable under *Rylands v Fletcher* for any damage which it causes unless there has been negligence.[1] Thus in *Pearson v North Western Gas Board*,[2] where an explosion of gas which had escaped from the defendants' mains seriously injured the claimant, killed her husband and destroyed her home, the defendants were not liable, since they had not been negligent.

Whether or not an activity is authorised depends upon the statute in question, and the principles of interpretation used by the courts are similar to those which apply in cases of nuisance.[3] In *Green v Chelsea Waterworks Co*,[4] for example, the defendants were under a statutory duty to maintain a certain pressure of water in their mains, and the statute, unlike many of its kind, did not expressly state that they would be liable for any nuisance caused.[5] When a mains burst, it was held that they were not liable in the absence of negligence. By contrast, in *Charing Cross West End and Electric Supply Co v Hydraulic Power Co*,[6] the defendants merely had a statutory power to carry water in mains, and they were specifically made liable for nuisance. It was held that the statute did not exempt them from strict liability under *Rylands v Fletcher* in respect of a burst main.

[1] *Manchester Corpn v Farnworth* [1930] AC 171, HL.
[2] [1968] 2 All ER 669.
[3] Para 23.18.
[4] (1894) 70 LT 547, CA.

⁵ Even if there had been such a provision, the defendants would probably not have been liable: *Department of Transport v North West Water Authority* [1983] 3 All ER 273, HL.
⁶ [1914] 3 KB 772, CA.

DEFENCES TO *RYLANDS V FLETCHER*: KEY POINTS

- There is no liability where damage is due to the fault of the claimant.

- A claimant who has consented to the accumulation in question cannot succeed in the absence of negligence.

- A defendant is not liable where an escape is caused by an 'act of God' nor, in the absence of negligence, where it is caused by a third party over whom the defendant has no control.

Fire

24.15 Common law has for centuries imposed a form of strict liability upon anyone from whose property fire is allowed to spread and cause damage,[1] except where this is due to an act of God[2] or the intervention of a 'stranger'. The latter defence covers only those over whom the occupier has no control, so that liability has been imposed upon an occupier for the negligence of an employee who allowed a fire to spread,[3] an independent contractor who used a blowlamp to thaw frozen pipes and set fire to their lagging;[4] another contractor who negligently installed a fireplace in a party wall;[5] an individual tenant of a bedsit in a hostel who dropped a cigarette;[6] and even a golf club guest who dropped a lighted match.[7] In *H and N Emanuel Ltd v Greater London Council*,[8] a demolition contractor, on the defendants' land with their permission, lit a bonfire to burn rubbish; this was known to be his normal practice, although the contract specifically prohibited the lighting of fires on site. When sparks carried to the claimants' property and caused damage, the defendants were held liable.

Actions for the spread of fire are today usually governed by statute. Where this is not so, however, the common law rule still applies. Thus, for example, in *Mansel v Webb*,[9] the defendant was held strictly liable for the escape of sparks from his steam engine on the highway.

¹ *Beaulieu v Finglam* (1401) YB 2 Hen 4, fo 18, pl 6.
² *Turberville v Stamp* (1697) 1 Ld Raym 264.
³ *Musgrove v Pandelis* [1919] 2 KB 43, CA.
⁴ *Balfour v Barty-King* [1957] 1 All ER 156, CA.
⁵ *Johnson v BJW Property Developments Ltd* [2002] EWHC 1131 (TCC), [2002] 3 All ER 574.
⁶ *Ribee v Norrie* [2001] PIQR P8, CA.
⁷ *Boulcott Golf Club Inc v Engelbrecht* [1945] NZLR 556.
⁸ [1971] 2 All ER 835, CA.
⁹ (1918) 88 LJKB 323, CA.

24.16 The Fires Prevention (Metropolis) Act 1774, s 86 provides that no action shall be brought against any person in whose premises, or on whose estate, any fire shall accidentally begin. In view of the way in which this provision (which, in spite of its title, applies throughout the country) has subsequently been interpreted, the extent to which it modifies the common law rule is somewhat uncertain. In *Filliter v Phippard*,[1] 'accidentally' was said to refer only to a fire produced by mere chance or incapable of being traced to any cause. This rules out protection where a fire either begins or spreads through the negligence of the defendant[2] or someone for whom the defendant is responsible, such as an independent contractor;[3] but it seems that a person may avoid liability, even for a fire which he (or she) has deliberately lit, provided that there is no negligence. Thus in *Sochacki v Sas*,[4] a lodger who left his room for two or three hours with a fire burning was held not liable when a coal jumped out and set the house alight, since there was no evidence that the fire was too large for the grate. The operation of the statute is also shown by *Collingwood v Home and Colonial Stores Ltd*,[5] in which fire broke out at the defendants' shop as a result of defective electric wiring. In the absence of any negligence on the part of the defendants, they were held not liable.

It should be noted that, even where a fire is caused by an act of God or of a 'stranger', the defendant may still incur liability if, with knowledge of the danger on his land, he (or she) fails to take reasonable steps to abate it.[6]

[1] (1847) 11 Qb 347.
[2] *Musgrove v Pandelis* [1919] 2 KB 43, CA.
[3] *Johnson v BJW Property Developments Ltd* [2002] EWHC 1131 (TCC), [2002] 3 All ER 574.
[4] [1947] 1 All ER 344.
[5] [1936] 3 All ER 200, CA.
[6] *Goldman v Hargrave* [1966] 2 All ER 989, PC.

24.17 Apart from the special rules outlined above, it is established that either fire itself,[1] or the combustible material on which it feeds,[2] may be treated as a dangerous thing for the purposes of the rule in *Rylands v Fletcher*. This might appear to be of great significance in view of the much-criticised decision of the Court of Appeal, in *Musgrove v Pandelis*,[3] that the Fires Prevention (Metropolis) Act 1774 provides no defence to such an action. In practice, however, the benefits to the claimant may be more apparent than real. In the first place, either fire[4] or its cause[5] may be held to be a natural use of land, in which case *Rylands v Fletcher* does not apply.[6] Second, where the defendant accumulates materials, it has been held that liability under *Rylands v Fletcher* requires proof both that they were likely to ignite and that the resulting fire was likely to spread.[7] If this is correct, liability in such cases appears no different from ordinary negligence.

[1] *Jones v Festiniog Rly Co* (1868) LR 3 Qb 733.
[2] *Mason v Levy Auto Parts of England Ltd* [1967] 2 All ER 62.
[3] [1919] 2 KB 43, CA.
[4] *Sochacki v Sas* [1947] 1 All ER 344.
[5] *Collingwood v Home and Colonial Stores Ltd* [1936] 3 All ER 200, CA (electric wiring).
[6] Para 24.8.
[7] *Mason v Levy Auto Parts of England Ltd* [1967] 2 All ER 62.

LIABILITY FOR FIRE: KEY POINTS

- At common law, the occupier of property from which fire spreads is strictly liable, unless this is due to an 'act of God' or the action of someone over whom the occupier has no control.
- The Fires Prevention (Metropolis) Act 1774 provides a defence where a fire begins 'accidentally' (ie without negligence).

Statutory liability

24.18 One of the features of an industrialised urban society is that a single accident may disastrously affect an enormous number of people. A collapsing slag-heap, an explosion at a chemical plant or a crippled oil tanker, all may cause severe injury and damage over a wide area. In recent years, governments have sought by various statutes to provide for the possibility of certain of these incidents, and the provisions have often included the imposition of some form of strict liability for the consequences. Of special importance in this connection are the Nuclear Installations Act 1965 (injury or damage resulting from the radioactive, toxic, explosive or otherwise hazardous properties of nuclear matter, or from radiations emitted from waste); the Control of Pollution Act 1974 (injury or damage caused by the deposit of poisonous, noxious or polluting waste on land); the Water Act 1981 (escape of water from mains); and the Merchant Shipping Act 1995 (damage caused by the escape or discharge of persistent oil from a ship). The forms of liability, and the defences available, vary from one statute to another, but they may all be regarded as strict, in the sense that the absence of negligence provides no defence.

Questions

1. To what extent can the principle laid down in *Rylands v Fletcher* be described as one of strict liability?

2. What is meant by a 'non-natural use' of land?

3. What are the consequences of treating *Rylands v Fletcher* as a part of private nuisance?

4. What are the main defences to a claim under *Rylands v Fletcher*?

5. To what extent is an occupier strictly liable for a fire which starts on his or her land?

6. Sheila's house has a field attached in which, every year, she allows a local charity to hold a bonfire and firework display on November 5. On one occasion, in late October, a huge pile of combustible material had been collected for the bonfire when Toby, a nasty child, climbed over the fence and set fire to it. The fire spread rapidly to a neighbouring garden and to a shed in which Pyro stored a large quantity of fireworks for the display. These all exploded, causing damage to Justin's house and injuring Justin.
   What legal rights and liabilities arise in this situation?

25

Animals

CHAPTER OVERVIEW

The law has for centuries adopted special rules to govern liability for harm caused by animals. In this chapter we consider:

- the application of the general law of tort (especially nuisance and negligence) to damage caused by animals;
- the statutory rules governing damage caused by animals belonging to a dangerous species, or other animals which are known to be dangerous;
- the statutory rules governing straying livestock and dogs worrying livestock.

Liability at common law

25.1 Most torts are capable of arising out of the acts of an animal. It is, for example, an undoubted assault and battery to set one's dog on somebody, there seems no reason why teaching a parrot to repeat slanderous material should not lead to liability in defamation. Of more practical importance, an attack by an animal on a visitor to premises might also found a claim under the Occupier's Liability Act 1957,[1] the action of fox hunters in riding across a protesting farmer's land has been held to constitute trespass[2] and, while direct authority is lacking, the application of *Rylands v Fletcher*[3] to both vegetation and human beings suggests that it could also be used in cases of escaping animals, subject to the question of non-natural user.[4]

[1] *Hill v Lovett* 1992 SLT 994.
[2] *Paul v Summerhayes* (1878) 4 Qbd 9, DC. See also *League Against Cruel Sports Ltd v Scott* [1985] 2 All ER 489; para 23.1.
[3] Paras 24.2 to 24.14.
[4] Para 24.8.

Nuisance

25.2 The tort of nuisance is one in which animals frequently play a part. The smell of pigs[1] or the crowing of cockerels[2] may be actionable, while the obstruction of a highway by 24 cows has been held to be a public nuisance.[3] Where there is an invasion of the claimant's land by numbers of wild animals, such as rats or rabbits, escaping from the defendant's property, liability has traditionally turned upon whether the defendant is in any way responsible for their accumulation.[4] However, it is now clear that a defendant who is aware of a danger may become liable for a nuisance where by failing to take reasonable steps to avert it,[5] and this principle has been applied so as to render the owners of a rail-way bridge liable in public nuisance, for the fouling of the pavement under it by the large numbers of pigeons roosting there.[6]

[1] *Aldred's Case* (1610) 9 Co Rep 57b.
[2] *Leeman v Montagu* [1936] 2 All ER 1677.
[3] *Cunningham v Whelan* (1917) 52 ILT 67.
[4] *Farrer v Nelson* (1885) 15 Qbd 258; cf *Seligman v Docker* [1948] 2 All ER 887.
[5] See paras 23.15–23.16.
[6] *Wandsworth London Borough Council v Railtrack plc* [2001] EWCA Civ 1236, [2002] QB 756.

Negligence

25.3 A person in charge of an animal is under a general duty of care to keep it from caus-ing harm, and this can be of great assistance to a claimant who is unable to establish the necessary elements of strict liability under the Animals Act.[1] In *Gomberg v Smith*,[2] for example, a defendant who took his St Bernard for a walk in the street without a lead was held liable when it collided with and damaged the claimant's van. The dog in that case was merely clumsy, but the same principle may apply to a deliberate attack. For example, in *Aldham v United Dairies (London) Ltd*,[3] the defendants were held liable in negligence for leaving their pony unattended in the street for so long that it became restive and bit a passer-by. So too, in *Draper v Hodder*,[4] where a three-year-old child was attacked and seriously injured by a pack of Jack Russell terrier puppies, the defendant, a neighbouring breeder, was held negligent for allowing the dogs (which are known to be dangerous when in a pack) to wander both on his own property and on that of the claimant's family.

In a case of this nature, the claimant must show that there was a foreseeable risk of the type of injury suffered. This requirement proved fatal to two claims by persons injured when using public footpaths across fields. It has been held unforeseeable that a Limousin-cross cow with its calf would charge and butt a walker,[5] or that several horses would sur-round and push to the ground a person walking with his dog.[6]

There is no strict liability for livestock which stray from the highway,[7] but anyone who brings an animal on to the highway owes a duty of care to adjoining landowners. Thus in *Gayler and Pope Ltd v B Davies & Son Ltd*,[8] where the defendants left their pony and milk van unattended in the street they were held liable when it bolted and crashed through a draper's shop window. In *Tillett v Ward*,[9] by contrast, where an ox which was being driven along a street strayed into an ironmonger's shop, the defendant was found to have taken all reasonable care and was therefore not liable.

The old common law rule, that an occupier of land could not be held liable in negligence for failing to prevent domestic animals from straying on to the highway, was abolished by the s 8(1) of the Animals Act 1971. However, it is provided by s 8(2) that a person is not to be regarded as negligent by reason *only* of placing animals on unfenced land if:

- the land is common land; or
- it is situated in an area where fencing is not customary; or
- it is a town or village green;

and that person has a right (which includes permission from someone else who has a right[10]) to place the animals on that land.

This is not a return to the old immunity since, even in these areas, road and traffic con-ditions may be such that it is negligent to allow one's animals to stray.

[1] Para 25.6.
[2] [1962] 1 All ER 725, CA.

3 [1939] 4 All ER 522, CA.
4 [1972] 2 All ER 210, CA.
5 *Ostle v Stapleton* [1996] CLY 4443.
6 *Miller v Duggan* [1996] CLY 4444.
7 Para 25.8.
8 [1924] 2 KB 75.
9 (1882) 10 Qbd 17.
10 *Davies v Davies* [1975] Qb 172, [1974] 3 All ER 817, CA.

ANIMALS AT COMMON LAW: KEY POINTS

- Damage caused by an animal may give rise to a claim in tort, notably for nuisance.

- Any person in charge of an animal is under a duty of care to prevent it from causing damage.

Animals Act 1971

Dangerous animals

Classification of species

25.4 The Animals Act 1971, like the rules of common law which it replaced, makes the keeper of a dangerous animal strictly liable for all the damage it causes. The Act also follows the common law in treating two different kinds of animal as 'dangerous' for this purpose. First, certain species (lions, tigers etc) are regarded as so obviously dangerous that all their members automatically attract strict liability. Second, members of other less dangerous species may attract strict liability as individuals by exhibiting dangerous tendencies, but only when their keepers are aware of these tendencies.

The classification of species is thus clearly of prime importance, and this is dealt with by s 6(2), which provides that a dangerous species is a species:[1]

- which is not commonly domesticated in the British Islands; and

- whose fully grown animals normally have such characteristics that they are likely, unless restrained, to cause severe damage or that any damage they may cause is likely to be severe.

The wording of this definition seems apt to include both animals which are normally fierce, such as bears, tigers and gorillas, and animals which, though normally docile, are likely to cause severe damage if they cause damage at all. An elephant, for instance, is unlikely to cause damage, but its sheer bulk makes it dangerous on the occasions when it does get out of control. It also appears that a species may be classified as dangerous on account of the threat which it poses to property; this could even include, for example, rabbits, squirrels and Colorado beetles, provided that the damage which they are likely to cause can be described as severe.

It is important to appreciate that, once a species is classified as dangerous, no allowance is made for the amiable nature of a particular individual. A circus elephant may be as tame as a cow and, because of its training, much easier to control; nevertheless, since the species satisfies s 6(2), the individual is dangerous in law.[2]

A species which does not satisfy the statutory definition contained in s 6(2) is automatically a non-dangerous species.

¹ This includes sub-species and variety: s 11.
² *Behrens v Bertram Mills Circus Ltd* [1957] 1 All ER 583.

Dangerous species

25.5 Section 2(1) provides that where any damage is caused by an animal which belongs to a dangerous species, any person who is a keeper of the animal is liable for the damage, except as otherwise provided by the Act. This wide form of strict liability is not limited to damage which results from the animal's dangerous characteristics, since it also includes, for example, injuries caused by the blunderings of a frightened elephant, or a disease transmitted by an infected rat. So too, a person who suffers nervous shock on being faced by an escaped tiger, or who falls and breaks his leg in running away from it, can recover damages under this provision. It has even been held applicable to someone falling from a swaying camel, although the claimant's claim under s 2(1) failed on the ground that she had voluntarily assumed the risk.[1]

Liability under s 2 is imposed upon the animal's keeper, defined in s 6(3) as someone who 'owns the animal or has it in his possession; or is the head of a household of which a member under the age of 16 owns the animal or has it in his possession'. That subsection further provides that a person who loses the ownership or possession of an animal continues to be its 'keeper' unless and until someone else fulfils the definition. Thus, a person whose pet fox escapes and reverts to the wild remains responsible for its activities. However, a person who takes possession of an animal merely to prevent it from causing damage or to return it to its owner does not thereby become its 'keeper'.[2]

¹ *Tutin v Mary Chipperfield Promotions Ltd* (1980) 130 NLJ 807. The claimant recovered damages on the ground of negligence.
² Section 6(4).

Non-dangerous species

25.6 The strict liability which attaches to dangerous species also encompasses other individual animals with known dangerous characteristics, although in such a case the keeper is liable, not for all the damage done, but only for that which results from those dangerous characteristics. This is laid down by s 2(2), which provides that where damage is caused by an animal which does not belong to a dangerous species, a keeper of the animal is liable for the damage, except as otherwise provided by the Act, if:

- the damage is of a kind which the animal, unless restrained, was likely to cause or which, if caused by the animal, was likely to be severe; and

- the likelihood of the damage or of its being severe was due to characteristics of the animal which are not normally found in animals of the same species (ie the particular breed of dog, rather than dogs generally[1]) or are not normally so found except at particular times or in particular circumstances; and

- those characteristics were known to the keeper or were at any time known to a person who at that time had charge of the animal as the keeper's servant or, where the keeper was the head of a household, were known to another keeper of the animal who was a member of that household and under the age of 16.

The essence of this provision is that strict liability is imposed on the keeper of an animal where the keeper, or someone for whom the keeper is responsible, knows of some characteristic which renders the particular animal dangerous. The characteristic in question must be one which is either not common to the species in general, or common only in particular circumstances.

Section 2(2) is most easily understood and applied in cases where a particular animal is positively aggressive and the keeper is aware of this. If the vicious streak is permanent, it will be regarded as not common to the species in general; if it is dependent on circumstances, a claim against the keeper will not fail on the ground that it is shared by other members of the species in similar circumstances, such as the tendency of certain breeds of dog to show unusual aggression when defending their territory[2] or of a bitch to be aggressive towards humans when she has pups.[3]

Much more difficult are cases where an animal causes damage, not through aggression, but because it is nervous and unpredictable[4] or prone to panic when frightened. In *Mirvahedy v Henley*,[5] a bare majority of the House of Lords held the keeper of a horse liable when, in reacting to severe fright, it bolted out of a field through an electric fence and collided with the claimant's car. The majority regarded the horse's behaviour as unusual, since horses generally do not bolt, even though it might be usual in the particular circumstances of severe fright. The Court of Appeal has similarly imposed liability on the keeper of a horse which reared up and threw its rider, since the keeper was aware of its tendency to rear when ridden by an inexperienced rider.[6]

It should be noted that the damage for which a keeper is liable may extend beyond the direct results of an attack; thus a person injured in a fall when his or her dog is attacked by the defendant's dog may recover damages under s 2(2), provided of course that the requirements of that provision are satisfied.[7] However, the damage must be shown to have resulted from the dangerous characteristic. Thus, where horses were maliciously released from their field by an unidentified trespasser, their owner was held not liable for a traffic accident, since this was caused by the mere presence of the horses in the road rather than by any 'abnormal characteristic' which they possessed.[8] Moreover, it has been held than an Alsatian trained by the police to attack in certain circumstances does not then have an abnormal characteristic; its characteristic is its ability to respond to training, and this is common to the breed in general.[9]

A keeper is only liable under s 2(2) where the keeper, or certain of the keeper's family or employees, knows that the animal in question is dangerous.[10] Such knowledge is usually gained as the result of a previous attack, but this is not the only possibility. For example, in *Worth v Gilling*[11] it was sufficient that the defendant's dog habitually ran at passers-by to the limit of its chain, barking and trying to bite them. A horse's tendency to bite other horses, however, is not necessarily evidence that it is dangerous to people.[12]

Where the conditions of s 2(2) are satisfied, reasonable care is no defence; the animal is kept at the defendant's peril. The question of negligence may, however, be highly relevant in cases where, for some reason, s 2(2) does not apply.[13]

---

[1] *Hunt v Wallis* [1994] PIQR P128.

[2] *Curtis v Betts* [1990] 1 All ER 769, CA.

[3] See *Barnes v Lucille Ltd* (1907) 96 LT 680.

[4] *Wallace v Newton* [1982] 2 All ER 106.

[5] [2003] UKHL 16, [2003] 2 AC 491.

[6] *Welsh v Stokes* [2007] EWCA Civ 796, CA.

[7] *Smith v Ainger* (1990) Times, 5 June, CA.

[8] *Jaundrill v Gillett* (1996) Times, 30 January, CA. Also see *McKenny v Foster* [2008] EWCA Civ 173, CA, where a similar decision was reached in respect of an escaping cow.

[9] *Gloster v Chief Constable of Greater Manchester* [2000] PIQR P114, CA.

[10] Where an animal has more than one 'keeper', there is no reason why one should not be liable to the other: *Flack v Hudson* [2001] QB 698, CA.

[11] (1866) LR 2 CP 1.

[12] *Glanville v Sutton & Co Ltd* [1928] 1 KB 571.

[13] See *Draper v Hodder* [1972] 2 All ER 210, CA; para 25.3.

Defences

25.7 Liability under s 2 in respect of both dangerous and non-dangerous species is strict (ie independent of negligence). However, the liability is not absolute, since the Act expressly recognises four possible defences:

- Section 5(1) provides that a claimant cannot claim in respect of any damage which is due wholly to the claimant's own fault, as where he (or she) provokes a fierce dog or reaches into a leopard's cage.

- A claimant who is partly responsible for his (or her) own injuries may suffer a reduction of damages on the ground of contributory negligence.[1]

- The defence of assumption of risk[2] is made applicable to actions under s 2 by s 5(2), and operated to defeat a claim by an experienced rider who was bucked off by a horse which she knew to have this tendency.[3] The scope of this defence is, however, restricted by s 6(5), which provides that a keeper's employee is not to be treated as voluntarily accepting any risk which is incidental to employment.

- Section 5(3) lays down special rules for injured trespassers by providing that, where damage is caused by 'an animal kept on any premises or structure to a person trespassing there', the keeper is not liable under s 2 provided either that the animal was not kept there for the protection of persons or property or that, if it was so kept, it was reasonable to keep it there. Thus, a trespasser injured by an animal in a zoo or a safari park would probably not succeed in a claim under s 2,[4] for the animal would not be kept for protection. As to animals which it is reasonable to keep for protection, this is in practice most likely to apply to dogs. The Guard Dogs Act 1975, which makes it a criminal offence to have a guard dog on premises unless it is either secured or under the control of a handler, does not give rise to civil liability. However, it is thought that a court would regard someone as unreasonable for the purpose of the Animals Act 1971, s 5(3) for keeping a dog in circumstances which contravened the Guard Dogs Act.

All the defences mentioned above were considered in the case of *Cummings v Granger*[5] where an untrained alsatian, kept by the defendant to guard his scrapyard, attacked the claimant who, despite seeing a large 'Beware of the Dog' notice and knowing that the dog was there, entered the yard as a trespasser. The trial judge held that keeping the dog in these circumstances was unreasonable and that the defendant was accordingly liable, although he reduced the claimant's damages on the ground of contributory negligence. The Court of Appeal, however, held that keeping the dog was reasonable[6] and that the claimant had in any case voluntarily accepted the risk of injury.

[1] Section 10; paras 19.6–19.9.
[2] Paras 19.2–19.5.
[3] *Freeman v Higher Park Farm* [2008] EWCA Civ 1185, CA.
[4] An action might nevertheless lie under the Occupiers' Liability Act 1984; paras 21.19–21.25.
[5] [1977] 1 All ER 104, CA.
[6] These events preceded the coming into force of the Guard Dogs Act 1975.

THE ANIMALS ACT 1971 AND DANGEROUS ANIMALS: KEY POINTS

- The keeper of an animal which belongs to a dangerous species is strictly liable for any damage caused by the animal.

- The keeper of an animal which belongs to a non-dangerous species is strictly liable for any damage caused by the animal, where the keeper is aware that the particular animal has dangerous characteristics which are not common to the species as a whole.
- There are exceptions to this form of liability, notably where the claimant is at fault, has assumed the risk of injury or is a trespasser.

Straying livestock

25.8 Section 4(1) of the Act provides that where livestock belonging to any person strays on to land in the ownership or occupation of another and:

- damage is done by the livestock to the land or to any property on it which is in the ownership or possession of the other person; or
- any expenses are reasonably incurred by that other person in keeping the livestock while it cannot be restored to the person to whom it belongs or while it is detained in pursuance of s 7 of the Act, or in ascertaining to whom it belongs;

the person to whom the livestock belongs is liable for the damage or expenses, except as otherwise provided by the Act.

For the purpose of this provision, s 11 defines 'livestock' as 'cattle, horses, asses, mules, hinnies, sheep, pigs, goats and poultry [which means the domestic varieties of fowls, turkeys, geese, ducks, guinea-fowls, pigeons, peacocks and quails], and also deer not in the wild state'.

The right of action under s 4, which protects both owners and occupiers of land, but which imposes liability only upon a possessor of livestock, covers not only damage to the claimant's land and crops, but also damage to goods, including other animals. As a result, the claimant is entitled to damages, not only where animals are attacked, but also for other consequences such as infection[1] or the serving of a thoroughbred heifer by a bull of low birth.[2]

Where livestock stray on to the highway, it seems that the owner or occupier of the land across which the highway passes may claim under s 4(3).[3] A mere user of the highway, however, has no such right and must, in order to recover damages (eg where straying livestock cause a road accident), establish negligence.[4] Further, where livestock which are lawfully on the highway[5] stray from it, liability again depends on negligence; s 4 is expressly excluded.[6]

[1] *Theyer v Purnell* [1918] 2 KB 333.
[2] *McLean v Brett* (1919) 49 DLR 162.
[3] *Durrant v Child* (1611) 1 Bulst 157.
[4] See Animals Act 1971, s 8; para 25.3.
[5] But not those which have strayed on to it: *Matthews v Wicks* (1987) Times, 25 May, CA.
[6] Section 5(5).

Defences

25.9 Liability under s 4 is strict, but certain defences are recognised by the Act. A claim will fail altogether if the damage suffered is wholly due to the claimant's own fault;[1] if it is partly due to the claimant's fault, damages may be reduced on the ground of contributory negligence.[2]

The question of duties to fence is dealt with by s 5(6), which provides that a mere failure on the claimant's part to fence out the defendant's livestock does not amount to 'fault'.

However, the section goes on to provide that a defendant is nonetheless not liable where it is proved that the straying of the livestock on to the land would not have occurred but for a breach by any other person, being a person having an interest in the land, of a duty to fence. This, it should be noted, is not limited to the obvious case of the claimant who owes a fencing obligation to the defendant, since it also provides a defence where the claimant owes a legal duty to a third party, or where the duty is owed by a third party with an interest in the claimant's land, such as the landlord.

The defences of act of God, intervention by a 'stranger' and assumption of risk, all of which previously applied at common law, are not available in an action under s 4.

[1] Section 5(1).
[2] Section 10; paras 19.6–19.9.

Detention and sale

25.10 Section 7 of the Act provides that an occupier may detain any livestock which strays on to the occupier's land and which is not under anyone's control, provided the occupier gives notice within 48 hours to the police and to the possessor of the livestock, if known. The occupier must also treat the livestock with reasonable care, which includes feeding and watering it. The person entitled to possession of the livestock may demand its return but, if the detainor has a claim under s 4 for damage done by straying cattle, or for expenses incurred, this must first be met. It has been held that a local authority on to whose land animals frequently strayed was justified in making standard charges to cover its costs, rather than working out the exact expense caused by each stray.[1]

Once livestock has been lawfully detained for 14 days, then, provided neither party has commenced legal proceedings, the detainor may sell it at a market or by public auction and keep the amount of his claim under s 4 out of the net proceeds of sale.

[1] *Morris v Blaenau Gwent District Council* (1982) 80 LGR 793, CA.

Dogs worrying livestock

Liability for dogs

25.11 The worrying of livestock by dogs has long been a special problem and the Animals Act 1971, s 3, which deals with this, merely repeats with some modifications the rules laid down by earlier statutes. Section 3 provides that, where a dog causes damage by killing or injuring livestock, any person who is a keeper of the dog is liable for the damage, except as otherwise provided by the Act. For this purpose, 'livestock' includes the same animals as for the purpose of s 4,[1] but also includes pheasants, partridges and grouse in captivity; the meaning of 'keeper' is the same as it is under s 2.[2]

As with the other forms of strict liability under the Act, a claim may fail wholly under s 5(1),[3] or where loss results entirely from the claimant's own fault, or partly under the doctrine of contributory negligence. Section 5(4) also provides a defence where the attack takes place on land to which the livestock have strayed, so long as the presence of the dog there is authorised.

[1] Para 25.8.
[2] Para 25.6.
[3] Para 25.7.

Protection of livestock

25.12 At common law, a person whose animals were under attack from another animal could in certain circumstances act immediately in the defence of property, even if this involved killing or injuring the attacker. The common law rules on this matter, which were laid down in the case of *Cresswell v Sirl*,[1] apply to all kinds of animal, provided only that the latter belong to the person acting in their defence; there is therefore no right to shoot a dog which is attacking wild animals on the defendant's land.[2]

The common law rules remain in force but, in relation to a somewhat narrower area, namely the worrying[3] of livestock by dogs, the Animals Act 1971, s 9 confers even greater protection upon a person who takes matters into his (or her) own hands. According to this provision, it is a defence to an action for killing or injuring a dog that the defendant was entitled to and did act for the protection of livestock and that, within 48 hours of the incident, he (or she) notified the police.

Persons are entitled to act for the protection of livestock if and only if either the livestock or the land on which it is belongs to them, or if they are acting with the authority of such a person. However, if the circumstances in which a dog attacks livestock are such that the dog's keeper would have a defence under s 5(4),[4] then s 9 does not permit anyone to act for the protection of the livestock by killing or injuring the dog. The conditions under which the defendant may otherwise act are clearly stated by s 9, with the proviso that the defendant is protected if he (or she) reasonably believes them to be satisfied. These conditions are that either:

- the dog is worrying or is about to worry the livestock and there are no other reasonable means of ending or preventing the worrying; or

- the dog has been worrying livestock, has not left the vicinity and is not under the control of any person and there are no practicable means of ascertaining to whom it belongs.

[1] [1947] 2 All ER 730, CA.
[2] *Gott v Measures* [1947] 2 All ER 609, DC.
[3] This probably includes not only an actual attack, but also chasing in such a way as is likely to cause injury.
[4] Para 25.11.

THE ANIMALS ACT 1971 AND LIVESTOCK: KEY POINTS

- A person whose livestock stray on to the land of another is strictly liable for any damage done and for any expenses incurred by the other person in looking after the livestock pending their return.

- A person on to whose land livestock stray may detain the livestock until their keeper pays for any damage done or for any expenses incurred in detaining them.

- The keeper of a dog is strictly liable if it kills or injures livestock.

- The owner of livestock which are attacked by a dog is not liable if he or she kills or injures the dog in attempting to protect the livestock.

Questions

1. To what extent may the actions of an animal give rise to liability in nuisance or negligence?

2. What is the distinction, under the Animals Act 1971, between a 'dangerous' and a 'non-dangerous' species'? What is the legal effect of this distinction?

3. Where an animal belongs to a 'non-dangerous' species, in what circumstances is its keeper strictly liable for damage which it causes?

4. What defences are there to this form of strict liability?

5. Where A's livestock stray on to B's land, what are the respective rights and liabilities of A and B?

6. Where X's dog attacks Y's livestock and is shot by Y, what are the respective rights and liabilities of X and Y?

7. Farmer Brown's cows stray through a dilapidated fence onto Farmer Jones' land, where they are attacked by Farmer Green's dog. Farmer Jones shoots the dog, but not before it has attacked and bitten Farmer Brown, who is searching for the straying cows.

   How does the Animals Act 1971 apply to this situation?

26

Vicarious liability

CHAPTER OVERVIEW

In certain circumstances the law makes one person liable for a tort committed by another person. In this chapter we consider:

- how the law defines the relationship of employer and employee for the purposes of vicarious liability;
- the scope of an employer's liability for the torts of his employee;
- the extent to which the employer may be held liable for prohibited acts or deliberate misconduct;
- the extent to which damage caused by an independent contractor may result in liability for the client.

26.1 Vicarious liability arises when X is made answerable for a tort committed by Y, on the grounds that:

- there is a particular relationship between X and Y; and
- the tort is in some way connected to that relationship.

The only relationship which routinely gives rise to vicarious liability is that of employer and employee. Relationships of principal and agent[1] and between partners[2] may also create vicarious liability in limited circumstances. However, a superior employee is not vicariously liable for the torts of a subordinate,[3] nor a parent for those of a child. Most importantly, the relationship of independent contractor and client does not lead to vicarious liability as such. However, in certain circumstances the negligence of an independent contractor may put the client in breach of a personal non-delegable duty.[4]

It is important to appreciate that, where it exists, vicarious liability is a form of strict liability. It does not require proof that X specifically authorised Y to commit a tort, nor that X was negligent in the selection or instruction of Y. Of course, if such facts could be established, X would be liable for the consequences, but this would not be an example of vicarious liability.

[1] See, eg, para 14.46.
[2] For torts committed 'in the ordinary course of the business of the firm': Partnership Act 1890, s 10.
[3] *Stone v Cartwright* (1795) 6 Term Rep 411.
[4] Paras 26.16–26.24.

Employer and employee

26.2 As we have already seen, the relationship of employer and employee is the only one to which the law attaches a general principle of vicarious liability. It may be said that an employer is responsible for any tort which is committed by an employee in the course of employment. This raises two questions, which we consider below:

- who is an employee? and
- what is the course of employment?

Who is an employee?

26.3 Since an employer is not usually responsible for the torts of an independent contractor to whom work is entrusted, it is obvious that the distinction between an employee and an independent contractor is of paramount importance. The wording of the contract under which someone is working is relevant, but it is not decisive; if the court decides that the relationship as a whole falls into one category, it will be treated as such, notwithstanding that the parties have called it by another name. Thus, for example, in *Ferguson v John Dawson & Partners (Contractors) Ltd*,[1] where a building worker was expressly described as a 'labour only sub-contractor', a majority of the Court of Appeal held that the relationship between the parties was in reality that of employer and employee.

It is worth stating that, while the formulation of a precise yet simple test for distinguishing employees from independent contractors has caused serious problems, it is not usually difficult to see on which side of the line a particular case falls. As Lord Denning has said,[2] it is often easy to recognise a contract of service when you see it, but difficult to say wherein the distinction lies. A ship's master, a chauffeur and a reporter on the staff of a newspaper are all employed under a contract of service; but a ship's pilot, a taxi driver, and a newspaper contributor are employed under a contract for services.

Of the many attempts made by judges and writers to lay down some criteria by which a contract of service may be recognised, one of the best known is that of Lord Thankerton to *Short v J and W Henderson Ltd*:[3]

- the employer's power of selection of his employee;
- the payment of wages or other remuneration;
- the employer's right to control the method of doing the work; and
- the employer's right of suspension and dismissal.

It should always be borne in mind, however, not only that this list is far from exhaustive (one writer has identified no fewer than 15 relevant factors), but also that the feature which is in one case decisive may in the next be overwhelmed by other features which point to the opposite conclusion.

---

[1] [1976] 3 All ER 817, CA.
[2] *Stevenson, Jordan and Harrison Ltd v Macdonald and Evans* [1952] 1 TLR 101 at 111.
[3] (1946) 62 TLR 427 at 429.

Control and other criteria

26.4 There is no simple test by which employees and independent contractors may be distinguished. It used at one time to be thought that the crucial factor was the degree of control which the employer was entitled to exercise over each category. An independent contractor, it was said, could be told only what was to be done, whereas an employee was also subject to the command of the employer as to the *manner* in which it should be done.[1] However, modern conditions, especially the widespread employment by corporations of highly skilled and qualified personnel, have shown up the inadequacy of this test. For example, it cannot be doubted that a ship's captain works under a contract of service, but it would be ludicrous to suggest that the shipowners are in a position to dictate exactly how to do the job.

If control alone cannot be regarded as decisive, the same applies even more strongly to the other criteria mentioned above. The employer's rights of appointment and dismissal, which were regarded as characteristic of a contract of service in *Short v Henderson*, seem equally applicable to independent contractors, while the type of remuneration paid, although helpful, is far from conclusive.

[1] *Yewens v Noakes* (1880) 6 QBD 530 at 532.

Function of employee

26.5 It has been suggested that, instead of looking at the individual rights and duties which make up a contract of service or one for services, the courts should consider the *function* of the particular worker.[1] It is argued that, under a contract of service, a person is employed as part of a business, and his or her work is done as an integral part of the business; whereas, under a contract for services, the work, although done for the business, is not integrated into it but is only accessory to it. This 'organisation' test certainly serves to explain a number of cases in which a contract of service has been held to exist despite the lack of any real control by the employer, especially those in which, contrary to earlier authority, hospitals were held liable for the negligence of highly qualified staff.[2] However, in marginal cases, it seems merely to replace one difficult question: 'Is the person an employee?' with another: 'Is the person part of the employer's organisation?'

Concentration upon the actual work which is done by a particular individual should not be allowed to obscure the fact that vicarious liability depends upon the existence of a contract of service. In *Watkins v Birmingham City Council*,[3] where a schoolteacher was injured due to the negligence of a 10-year-old milk monitor, the trial judge held the local authority vicariously liable on the ground that the boy was doing a job which would otherwise have been done by a paid employee. However, the Court of Appeal reversed this decision, holding that the boy was delivering the milk as a pupil and not as an employee.

[1] *Stevenson, Jordan and Harrison Ltd v Macdonald and Evans* [1952] 1 TLR 101 at 111.
[2] *Cassidy v Ministry of Health* [1951] 1 All ER 574, CA.
[3] (1975) 126 NLJ 442, CA; para 17.5.

'Business' test

26.6 In a number of cases, the courts have adopted a slightly different approach to this problem, by considering whether it may fairly be said that the worker is in business on his (or her) own account.[1] Although this has links with the function test described above, it seems that the courts are concerned, not so much with the nature of the work done, but more with such questions as whether the work is done on the worker's own premises or with the worker's own equipment, whether the worker hires helpers and can delegate the task to them, whether the worker has a number of employers, what degree of financial risk the worker takes, what degree of responsibility the worker has for investment and management, and to what extent, if at all, the worker has an opportunity to profit from sound management.

Many of these factors were considered in *Ready-Mixed Concrete (South-East) Ltd v Minister of Pension and National Insurance*[2] a case concerning the drivers of lorries designed for the delivery of concrete. The drivers bought their own vehicles, although they could not alter or sell them without the company's consent, and they were obliged to maintain them and to use them exclusively for the company. The company was responsible for obtaining orders and supplying concrete, and it paid the drivers a rate based on mileage. After a thorough review of the authorities, MacKenna J held that the drivers were not employees of the company, but independent contractors, so that the company was not responsible for the payment of their national insurance contributions.

[1] *Market Investigations Ltd v Minister of Social Security* [1968] 3 All ER 732.
[2] [1968] 1 All ER 433.

Borrowed employees

26.7 A particular problem may arise in cases where an individual employee is lent (or, more commonly, hired) by a general employer to a third party. If the employee commits a tort while working for the third party, the question is where the burden of vicarious liability is to fall. The law usually insists that responsibility will lie on one or the other party but, where both parties have sufficient control over the employee's actions to bring with it the power and the responsibility to prevent a tort, it is possible to make both vicariously liable.[1]

In *Mersey Docks and Harbour Board v Coggins and Griffith (Liverpool) Ltd*,[2] a mobile crane, complete with its driver, was hired by the harbour board to a firm of stevedores. The driver was paid by the board but, for the period of hire, was subject to the detailed control of the stevedores. When the driver negligently injured a third party, the House of Lords held that vicarious responsibility must rest with the harbour board; this primary liability could, it was said, be transferred in an appropriate case, but the burden of proof upon a general employer would be a heavy one.[3] This heavy burden is perhaps most likely to be satisfied in cases where the employee in question is an unskilled labourer, since it is then more realistic to treat control as having been passed on. It was satisfied in *Hawley v Luminar Leisure Ltd*,[4] where a nightclub bouncer, who had been supplied to a nightclub by a general employer, punched the claimant in the face in the course of a fracas outside the club. The evidence showed that the nightclub owner exercised great and detailed control over how the bouncer did his job, and the Court of Appeal held that the nightclub owner and not the general employer was vicariously liable for this assault.

Where the contract of hire provides that any vicarious liability shall attach to the special employer, this cannot operate so as to deprive an injured third party of his rights against the general employer; its effect is merely to govern the position of the two employers.[5] Even to this extent, the provision may be subject to the test of reasonableness under the Unfair Contract Terms Act 1977.[6]

[1] *Viasystems (Tyneside) Ltd v Thermal Transfer (Northern) Ltd* [2005] EWCA Civ 1151, CA.
[2] [1946] 2 All ER 345, HL.
[3] See *Biffa Waste Services Ltd v Maschinenfabrik Ernst Hese GmbH* [2008] EWCA Civ 1257, CA.
[4] [2006] EWCA Civ 18, CA.
[5] *White (Contractors) Ltd v Tarmac Civil Engineering Ltd* [1967] 3 All ER 586, HL.
[6] See *Phillips Products Ltd v Hyland* [1987] 2 All ER 620, CA; *Thompson v T Lohan (Plant Hire) Ltd* [1987] 2 All ER 631, CA; paras 9.15, 9.20 and 9.21.

CONTRACTS OF EMPLOYMENT: KEY POINTS

- In deciding whether or not a contract of employment exists, an important factor is the degree of control exercised by the 'employer' over the 'employee's' actions.

- Some courts approach this question by asking whether the 'employee' is in reality part of the 'employer's' organisation, or whether he (or she) is in business on his (or her) own account.
- Where an employee is temporarily seconded to another employer, the question of vicarious liability for the employee's torts is usually dependent upon the degree of control exercised by each employer.

What is the course of employment?

26.8 An employer is not liable for every tort committed by an employee. However, the employer's liability is not restricted to torts which the employee has been specifically authorised to commit. The rule is that, for an employer to be liable, the employee must be shown to have committed the tort in the course of employment. As to what is meant by this expression, the principle which was traditionally used by the courts explained that an employer, as opposed to the client of an independent contractor, would be liable even for acts which had not been authorised, provided they were so connected with authorised acts that they might rightly be regarded as modes—although improper modes—of doing them. In other words, an employer was responsible not merely for what an employee was authorised to do, but also for the way in which the employee chose to do it. On the other hand, if the unauthorised and wrongful act of the employee was not so connected with the authorised act as to be a mode of doing it, but was an independent act, the employer would not be responsible: for in such a case the employee would not be acting in the course of his employment but would have gone outside it.

The 'authorised act: unauthorised manner' test served the courts well for almost a century. However, in *Lister v Hesley Hall Ltd*[1] it was replaced by the House of Lords with a wider and more vague test, namely that an employee's tort would be within the course of employment if it was so closely and directly connected with the employment that it would be fair and just to hold the employer vicariously liable for it. The House of Lords applied this new test (which it endorsed in *Dubai Aluminium Co Ltd v Salaam*)[2] in holding that, where the warden of a residential home for children attending a nearby school used his position to sexually abuse some of the children, the warden's employers were vicariously liable for his acts.

The extent to which the decision in *Lister* has changed the law is extremely unclear. However, two suggestions may be put forward. First, it seems unlikely that any case which resulted in vicarious liability under the old test would be decided differently under the new one. Secondly, it seems likely that the effects of *Lister* will be felt, not in cases of negligence, but in those where the employee (as in *Lister* itself) is guilty of intentional wrongdoing.[3] For this reason it is felt that the following discussion of the law, which is based mainly on cases decided prior to *Lister*, remains valid.

[1] [2001] UKHL 22, HL.
[2] [2002] UKHL 48, HL.
[3] Para 26.14.

Authorised acts

26.9 The principle adopted in *Lister*, like that which had been previously used, requires the court, when seeking to determine the course of employment, first to discover what acts are authorised and then to consider what, if any, connection exists between an authorised act and the tort in question. The decision of the House of Lords in *Century Insurance Co Ltd v*

Northern Ireland Road Transport Board[1] provides a good illustration of this approach in operation. The employee in that case was the driver of a petrol tanker who, while delivering petrol to a garage, lit a cigarette and dropped a match. The driver's employers sought to avoid liability for the resulting fire by claiming that they did not employ men to smoke. Not surprisingly, this argument was rejected for, given that the driver was specifically authorised to deliver petrol, it would be difficult to think of a more negligent manner of doing so. By contrast, in *General Engineering Services Ltd v Kingston and St Andrew Corpn*,[2] where firemen operating a 'go slow' policy in support of a pay claim took 17 minutes to reach a fire instead of the normal 3 or 4 minutes, it was held that their conduct was outside the course of their employment. Their employers, the local authority responsible for the fire brigade, were thus not liable to the owners of property destroyed by the fire.

The need to find an authorised act, with which the unauthorised tort can be linked, may be illustrated by cases in which a vehicle owned by the employer is driven by an employee who has no specific authority to do so. In *Beard v London General Omnibus Co*,[3] where a bus conductor took it upon himself to turn a bus round for its return journey, it was held that his negligent driving which caused an accident was outside the scope of his employment, since he was not permitted to drive. His employers were therefore not vicariously liable. In *Ilkiw v Samuels*,[4] on the other hand, where a lorry driver allowed an incompetent person to drive it, it was held that the *lorry driver's* negligence fell within the course of employment, for the driver's job included taking care of the vehicle. As a result, the lorry driver's employers were liable to a person injured in the ensuing accident.

[1] [1942] 1 All ER 491, HL.
[2] [1988] 3 All ER 867, PC.
[3] [1900] 2 QB 530, CA.
[4] [1963] 2 All ER 879, CA.

Implied authority

26.10 In considering exactly what acts of an employee may be regarded as authorised, it is important to realise that an employer's permission may be implied rather than express. To take a simple example, a person at work has implied authority to use lavatories, washbasins and so on. If that person negligently leaves a tap running and thereby floods adjoining premises, the employer will be vicariously liable and cannot argue that the employee was not in the course of his employment because he (or she) was not actually working at the time.[1] Thus in *Harvey v RG O'Dell Ltd*,[2] an employee sent out on an all-day job was held to be within the course of employment when riding his motorcycle into a neighbouring town to have lunch.

As far as travel to and from one's place of work is concerned, the course of employment will normally include those parts of the journey which take place on the employer's premises[3] and also journeys off the premises which are undertaken on the employer's business and in the employer's time.[4] However, ordinary commuting journeys are excluded, so that in *Nottingham v Aldridge*,[5] for example, an apprentice was held to be outside the scope of his employment while driving to a GPO training establishment after a weekend at home, even though, by giving a lift to a fellow-apprentice, he qualified for a mileage allowance from his employers. Occasionally, this distinction is not maintained. In *Harrison v British Railways Board*,[6] for example, a station foreman who attempted to board a moving train in order to leave work before his shift officially ended was held not be acting within the course of his employment.

[1] *Ruddiman & Co v Smith* (1889) 60 LT 708, DC.
[2] [1958] 2 QB 78, [1958] 1 All ER 657.

³ *Staton v National Coal Board* [1957] 2 All ER 667.
⁴ *Smith v Stages* [1989] 1 All ER 833, HL.
⁵ [1971] 2 All ER 751.
⁶ [1981] 3 All ER 679.

Ostensible authority

26.11 In one particular situation an employer may incur vicarious liability where the employee has not been expressly or even impliedly authorised to commit a particular act. This is where the employer has given third parties the impression that the employee is authorised, and a third party relies upon this appearance of authority. In such circumstances the employer will in effect be estopped (prevented) from denying that authority exists. As a result, liability for a tort of the employee may be attributed to the employer, notwithstanding that it was committed purely for the employee's own benefit, or that it had been specifically prohibited by the employer.

The leading case on the subject of ostensible authority is *Lloyd v Grace, Smith & Co*,¹ in which the claimant, a widow, sought advice from a firm of solicitors about certain property which she had inherited. She dealt entirely with the solicitors' managing clerk, who fraudulently induced her to sign documents which transferred the property to him. The clerk then misappropriated it. It was held by the House of Lords that the solicitors were responsible for this fraud; having permitted their employee to deal unsupervised with clients, they were liable for any tort which he might commit in what appeared to be the course of his employment.

¹ [1912] AC 716, HL.

Prohibitions

26.12 Where an employee commits a tort by doing something which the employer has forbidden, one might instinctively feel that the employer should never be held vicariously liable. However, the true legal position is more complex, turning on the question whether the employer has prohibited the act itself (in which case the employee cannot be within the course of employment when performing it) or has merely prohibited a particular mode of carrying it out. As was stated by Lord Dunedin, in *Plumb v Cobden Flour Mills Co Ltd*,¹ 'There are prohibitions which limit the sphere of employment, and prohibitions which only deal with conduct within the sphere of employment.'

Recognition that an employer may be legally responsible, even for an act of an employee which has been specifically prohibited, came as long ago as 1862, in the leading case of *Limpus v London General Omnibus Co*.² There, a bus driver, in attempting to obstruct a bus belonging to a rival company (a practice which his employers had expressly forbidden), caused an accident. Notwithstanding the prohibition, the employers were held vicariously liable, since the driver's negligence was undeniably committed in the course of performing an authorised act, namely, driving the bus. By contrast, where the prohibition is such as to remove all authority, the employee cannot then be said to act within the course of employment. In *Kooragang Investment Pty Ltd v Richardson and Wrench Ltd*,³ for example, a staff valuer was held to have gone outside the course of employment in carrying out valuations for a particular client whom the employers had blacklisted. Likewise, in *Stevens v Woodward*,⁴ an employee entered a washroom on the employer's premises, which he was not permitted to use, and, by leaving a tap running, caused a flood. The employer was held not liable because, if the employee's very presence in the washroom was forbidden, there was no authorised act in the course of which a tort could be committed. The effect of the prohibition in this case was to prevent any implication of authority.⁵ However, it should be noted that ostensible authority cannot be removed by a prohibition unless the third party is aware of it.

The difference between prohibiting a class of acts, and prohibiting a mode of carrying out permitted acts, depends upon how precisely a court defines the scope of the employee's employment in the first place, and the modern tendency is to adopt a fairly liberal approach. In *LCC v Cattermoles (Garages) Ltd*,[6] for example, a garage hand was expressly forbidden to drive customers' vehicles, although he was allowed, and indeed expected, to push them around the premises. When he drove a customer's car and caused an accident, his employers argued that he was acting outside the course of his employment. The Court of Appeal, however, held the employers vicariously liable, on the grounds that their employee was authorised to move cars; the prohibition applied only to the method used.

[1] [1914] AC 62 at 67.
[2] (1862) 1 H & C 526.
[3] [1981] 3 All ER 65, PC.
[4] (1881) 6 QBD 318, DC.
[5] Cf *Ruddiman & Co v Smith* (1889) 60 LT 708, DC, para 26.10.
[6] [1953] 2 All ER 582, CA.

26.13 Particular problems have been raised by cases in which a driver has negligently injured someone to whom the driver has given a lift contrary to the employer's instructions. Clearly the invitation is unauthorised, but the injury is actually caused by negligent driving, which is precisely what the driver is employed to do. In *Twine v Bean's Express Ltd*,[1] the Court of Appeal held the employer not liable since, while the employee could be regarded as within the course of employment vis-à-vis other road users, he must be treated as outside it vis-à-vis the unauthorised passenger. Once again, however, the modern approach seems to be a rather broader one. In *Rose v Plenty*,[2] a milk roundsman took a young boy on the float to help with deliveries, strictly against the instructions of his employers. When, due to the milkman's negligent driving, the boy was injured, a majority of the Court of Appeal held the employers liable on the ground that, in taking him on, the employee was doing in an unauthorised way what he was authorised to do, namely, deliver the milk.

[1] (1946) 175 LT 131, CA.
[2] [1976] 1 All ER 97, CA.

Intentional wrongdoing

26.14 An intentional wrong[1] may be held to fall within the course of employment, provided that there is a sufficiently close connection between the wrong and what the employee is employed to do lawfully that it would be fair and just to hold the employer responsible for it. This test is most likely to be satisfied where the employee is acting in what he or she, however mistakenly, believes to be the best interests of the employer. Thus, in *Moore v Metropolitan Rly Co*,[2] where a railway official arrested the claimant in the mistaken belief that he had not paid his fare, the railway company were held liable. In *Abrahams v Deakin*,[3] on the other hand, it was held that a barman had no implied authority to give someone into custody on a mistaken charge of attempting to pass bad money. In taking this step, the barman was not protecting the interests of his employer, for the attempt to defraud him had failed; he was rather furthering the course of justice.

A similar approach can be found in cases of assaults committed by employees. There may well be vicarious liability in respect of excessive corporal punishment administered by a schoolteacher;[4] a blow given by a driver to a boy suspected of stealing sugar from a cart;[5] an over-zealous ejection of a troublemaker by a dance-hall doorman;[6] or an assault by a railway ticket inspector suspicious that a passenger was travelling without a ticket.[7] In extreme circumstances, employers have even been held liable for the shooting of claimants by a police officer[8] or a security guard,[9] provided that the shooting has some connection with an attempt by the employee to assert authority.[10]

On the other hand, the short-tempered petrol pump attendant[11] or bus conductor[12] who strikes a customer in the course of an argument (or as an act of revenge following an argument) will not normally render the employer responsible, even where the original cause of the dispute is connected with the employer's business. However, it seems that the more liberal approach adopted in *Lister v Hesley Hall Ltd*[13] may have a significant effect in this area; thus vicarious liability has been imposed in respect of an assault by an off-duty policeman in a borrowed police van[14] and a stabbing by a nightclub bouncer in revenge after an earlier altercation.[15]

The most difficult cases are those in which an employee has quite clearly acted (usually dishonestly) for his or her personal benefit. While such conduct will normally be held to fall outside the scope of employment,[16] we have already seen from the case of *Lloyd v Grace, Smith & Co*,[17] that it will not always do so. Indeed, the *Lloyd* principle has been applied to torts other than deceit. In *Morris v C W Martin & Sons Ltd*,[18] the defendants, a firm of specialist cleaners, entrusted the claimant's mink coat to one of their employees. Instead of cleaning the garment, the employee stole it, and the defendants were held liable for this act of conversion. However, it should be noted that, had a third party or even another employee been guilty of the theft, the defendants would probably not have been liable; only in relation to the employee to whom the coat had actually been entrusted would it be fair and just to impose vicarious liability on the employer. Similar reasoning led to the imposition of vicarious liability in *Photo Production Ltd v Securicor Transport Ltd*,[19] where a patrolman employed by the defendants deliberately started a fire in one of the factories which it was his duty to visit.

Recent years have seen a number of cases in which employees have committed acts of abuse (usually of a sexual nature) against children. Provided the employee in question is in a position vis-a-vis the child of control (such as the warden of a children's home) or of trust (such as a priest), the courts have shown themselves ready to impose vicarious liability on the abuser's employer.[20]

---

[1] Which may include even the breach of a statutory duty imposed upon the employee personally: *Majrowski v Guy's and St Thomas's NHS Trust* [[2006] UKHL 34, HL (harassment).

[2] (1872) LR 8 QB 36.

[3] [1891] 1 QB 516, CA.

[4] *Ryan v Fildes* [1938] 3 All ER 517.

[5] *Poland v John Parr & Sons* [1927] 1 KB 236, CA.

[6] *Daniels v Whetstone Entertainments Ltd* [1962] 2 Lloyd's Rep 1, CA; *Vasey v Surrey Free Inns* [1996] PIQR P373, CA.

[7] *Fennelly v Connex Southeastern Ltd* [2001] IRLR 390, CA.

[8] *Bernard v A-G of Jamaica* [2004] UKPC 47, PC.

[9] *Brown v Robinson* [2004] UKPC 56, PC.

[10] *A-G of the British Virgin Islands v Hartwell* [2004] UKPC 12, PC.

[11] *Warren v Henlys Ltd* [1948] 2 All ER 935.

[12] *Keppel Bus Co Ltd v Sa'ad bin Ahmad* [1974] 2 All ER 700, PC.

[13] Para 26.8.

[14] *Weir v Chief Constable of Merseyside Police* [2003] EWCA Civ 111.

[15] *Mattis v Pollock* [2003] EWCA Civ 887, [2003] 1 WLR 2158, CA.

[16] *Heasmans v Clarity Cleaning Co* [1987] ICR 949, CA (office cleaning contractors not liable for their employee's unauthorised use of client's telephone); *Irving v Post Office* [1987] IRLR 289, CA (Post Office not liable for racist remarks written on mail by a sorter).

[17] [1912] AC 716, HL; para 26.11.

[18] [1965] 2 All ER 725, CA. See also *Nahhas v Pier House (Cheyne Walk) Management Ltd* [1984] 1 EGLR 160.

[19] [1980] 1 All ER 556, HL. On the facts, a term in the contract between the parties was effective to exclude the defendants' liability; see para 9.1.

[20] *Lister v Hesley Hall Ltd* [2001] UKHL 22, HL; *Maga v Birmingham Roman Catholic Archdiocese Trust* [2010] EWCA Civ 256, CA.

Liability of employee

26.15 It is important to emphasise that, although a claimant will normally choose to make an employer vicariously liable, the employee who actually commits a tort may always be held personally responsible for it. Thus in *Merrett v Babb*,[1] where a valuer's employer became insolvent, the house purchaser successfully sued the individual valuer for his negligence in carrying out a mortgage valuation. Moreover, an employer who has been forced to pay damages on the basis of vicarious liability is legally entitled to recover those damages from the guilty employee.[2] However, employers hardly ever exercise this right of indemnity, except in cases of collusion or wilful misconduct by the employee.

[1] [2001] EWCA Civ 214, [2001] QB 1174.
[2] *Lister v Romford Ice and Cold Storage Co Ltd* [1957] 1 All ER 125, HL.

THE COURSE OF EMPLOYMENT: KEY POINTS

- Vicarious liability can only arise where a tort is closely and directly connected to what the employee is employed to do and that it would be fair and just to hold the employer responsible for it.

- The course of employment covers both acts which are specifically authorised and acts which are impliedly authorised.

- An employer who clothes an employee with the appearance of certain authority will be treated as if the employee actually has that authority.

- In certain circumstances, even an act which the employer has specifically prohibited may fall within the course of employment.

- In certain circumstances, an employer may be vicariously liable for a tort committed by an employee intentionally and for the employee's own benefit.

Independent contractors

General principle

26.16 As a general rule, a person (hereafter referred to as the client) who entrusts work to an independent contractor is not legally responsible for any torts committed by the contractor or the contractor's employees in the course of carrying out that work. Where, for example, the police arrange for an abandoned car to be towed away, and the car is damaged due to the negligence of the garage to whom the job is entrusted, the police cannot be held responsible; it is the garage alone which is liable.[1] Likewise a local authority is not vicariously liable for injuries to a child caused by negligence on the part of foster-parents which it has selected.[2] The client will, of course, be liable for any tort which he (or she) authorises or ratifies, and may also be liable for any negligence in selecting an incompetent contractor[3] or in giving the contractor inadequate instructions.[4] Whether the client may be liable for failing to exercise reasonable supervision over the independent contractor depends on whether any duty of care is owed in this respect. Such a duty has been imposed upon an occupier of land in respect of work carried out there by a building contractor;[5] however, the House of Lords has held that a building contractor owes no duty of care in tort to a subsequent owner of the building to supervise the work of a sub-contractor.[6]

[1] *Rivers v Cutting* [1982] 3 All ER 69, CA.
[2] *S v Walsall Metropolitan Borough Council* [1985] 3 All ER 294, CA.
[3] *Pratt v George J Hill Associates* (1987) 38 BLR 25, CA.
[4] *Robinson v Beaconsfield RDC* [1911] 2 Ch 188, CA.
[5] *AMF International Ltd v Magnet Bowling Ltd* [1968] 2 All ER 789; see para 21.16.
[6] *D & F Estates Ltd v Church Comrs for England* [1988] 2 All ER 992, HL.

Non-delegable duties

26.17 Apart from these possibilities, there are a number of cases in which the law is prepared to say that the client owes a personal, non-delegable duty to third parties. In such cases the client, while entitled to delegate the performance of the duty to another, remains responsible for its due fulfilment. These exceptions to the general rule of non-liability for an independent contractor's torts do not appear to be based upon any coherent principle, but rather to have evolved to meet particular situations. Nevertheless, the main categories (which we describe in paras 28.23 to 28.28) are well established.[1]

It should be emphasised that the standard of liability which is imposed by these non-delegable duties is not entirely uniform. In some instances, such as the rule in *Rylands v Fletcher* and under many statutes, the client's duty is a strict one, in the sense that it can be broken even when there is no negligence on anyone's part. Other cases, such as the duty of a bailee of goods, depend upon proof that someone is negligent; the client here may be said to owe a duty that reasonable care be taken. The choice as to which standard is imposed by any particular duty does not appear to be based on any clear principle.

[1] See *Alcock v Wraith* (1991) 59 BLR 20 at 23.

Statutory duties

26.18 Many, if not most, of the statutory duties which give rise to civil liability[1] are non-delegable. In *Gray v Pullen*,[2] for example, where the defendants were obliged by statute to reinstate the highway after laying a drain in it, they were held liable when their independent contractor failed to do so.

Furthermore, it seems that a person with a statutory power to do something which would otherwise be unlawful delegates the exercise of this at his (or her) peril. Thus, in *Darling v A-G*,[3] where the Ministry of Works employed a contractor to drill trial bore holes on the claimant's land, the Ministry was held liable for the contractor's negligence in leaving a pile of timber there which injured the claimant's horse.

[1] Paras 20.2–20.3.
[2] (1864) 5 B & S 970.
[3] [1950] 2 All ER 793.

Withdrawal of support

26.19 A landowner who has a right to have land or buildings supported by those of a neighbour[1] may sue if that support is withdrawn, either by the neighbour personally or by the neighbour's independent contractor. This principle, which was established in *Bower v Peate*,[2] was perhaps the first non-delegable duty to be recognised by common law.

It extends to cases in which work on an adjoining property damages a party wall and, by analogy, to work negligently done on a roof above a party wall which permitted damp to penetrate the claimant's property.[3]

   [1] Para 32.57.
   [2] (1876) 1 QBD 321.
   [3] *Alcock v Wraith* (1991) 59 BLR 20, CA.

Strict liability

26.20 In Chapters 24 and 25 we considered a number of areas in which the common law imposes strict liability, notably the rule in *Rylands v Fletcher*, the escape of fire and damage of various kinds caused by animals. In all these cases a client may be held responsible for the default of an independent contractor.

Operations on the highway

26.21 Where work is done by an independent contractor on or under the highway, the client is liable if the contractor negligently causes damage to a highway user, for example by leaving an unlighted heap of soil in the road,[1] or to the occupier of adjoining premises, for example by fracturing a gas main and thus causing an explosion.[2] This principle extends to the negligent repair by a contractor of an overhanging lamp which consequently falls on a passer-by;[3] it does not, however, cover the negligent felling of trees near a highway,[4] nor the obstruction of the highway by a contractor working on the client's property,[5] nor the negligent repair by a contractor of a motor vehicle which the employer then drives along the road.[6]

   [1] *Penny v Wimbledon UDC* [1899] 2 QB 72, CA.
   [2] *Hardaker v Idle District Council* [1896] 1 QB 335, CA.
   [3] *Tarry v Ashton* (1876) 1 QBD 314.
   [4] *Salsbury v Woodland* [1969] 3 All ER 863, CA.
   [5] *Rowe v Herman* [1997] 1 WLR 1390, CA.
   [6] *Phillips v Britannia Hygienic Laundry Co Ltd* [1923] 1 KB 539, DC.

Extra-hazardous acts

26.22 In *Honeywill and Stein Ltd v Larkin Bros Ltd*,[1] the defendants, a firm of photographers, were employed by the claimants to take pictures inside a cinema owned by third parties. Due to the negligence of the defendants in the use of magnesium flares (which were then necessary for indoor photography), the premises were damaged by fire. It was held by the Court of Appeal that, since this was a 'dangerous operation', the claimants' duty in respect of it was a non-delegable one, and they were accordingly liable. A similar line of thinking can be found in *Matania v National Provincial Bank Ltd*,[2] where noise and dust from building works caused a nuisance; the builders' clients were held liable, since this was no mere ordinary building operation, but an extensive job involving a high risk of nuisance.

Perhaps because it is so difficult to say precisely when an operation becomes 'dangerous' or an act 'extra-hazardous', the courts have shown no great enthusiasm for this particular category.[3]

   [1] [1934] 1 KB 191, CA.
   [2] [1936] 2 All ER 633, CA.
   [3] See, for example, *Alcock v Wraith* (1991) 59 BLR 20, CA; *Biffa Waste Services Ltd v Maschinenfabrik Ernst Hese GmbH* [2008] EWCA Civ 1257, CA.

Other cases

26.23 Of the other situations in which courts have declared a person's duty to be non-delegable, so as to fix that person with responsibility for the default of an independent contractor, three worthy of note are the duty of a contractual bailee to safeguard the bailor's goods;[1] the duty of an employer to take care for the safety of all employees;[2] and (probably) the duty of a hospital to look after its patients.[3] The emphasis in all these cases is on the relationship between the *client* and the victim, and it may well be that courts will be increasingly ready to find that a client has 'undertaken' a non-delegable duty, at least where the client and the victim are parties to a contract.[4]

[1] *British Road Services Ltd v Arthur V Crutchley & Co Ltd* [1968] 1 All ER 811, CA.
[2] *McDermid v Nash Dredging and Reclamation Co Ltd* [1987] 2 All ER 878, HL.
[3] *Cassidy v Ministry of Health* [1951] 1 All ER 574, CA.
[4] See *Rogers v Night Riders* [1983] RTR 324, CA.

Collateral negligence

26.24 Even in circumstances where the law recognises a non-delegable duty, it is usually said that the client is not responsible for *casual* or *collateral* negligence of the independent contractor, but only for negligence in the very act which the contractor is employed to carry out. Thus in *Padbury v Holliday and Greenwood Ltd*,[1] where a workman employed by sub-contractors negligently left an iron tool on a window-sill and it fell on to a passer-by, the clients of the sub-contractors were held not liable.

The difficulty of deciding when negligence is collateral in this sense is well illustrated by *Holliday v National Telephone Co*,[2] where the defendants, who were laying telephone wires under a street, employed a plumber to make certain connections. The plumber negligently dipped his blow-lamp into molten solder, and a passer-by was injured by the resulting explosion. The Divisional Court thought that this was about as typical a case of casual negligence as it was possible to imagine, but the Court of Appeal held that this was negligence in the very act which the contractor was engaged to perform.

[1] (1912) 28 TLR 494, CA.
[2] [1899] 2 QB 392, CA.

INDEPENDENT CONTRACTORS: KEY POINTS

- The principle of vicarious liability does not apply to the relationship between independent contractor and client.
- However, in a number of cases where the client owes a personal duty to a third party, the actions of an independent contractor may constitute a breach of that duty.

Questions

1. How does a court decide whether the relationship between A and B is one of employer and employee or client and independent contractor?

2. Where a person who is generally employed by X commits a tort while temporarily seconded to work for Y, who will be held vicariously responsible for that tort?

3. When will a tort be held to have been committed within the course of employment?

4. What is meant by 'implied' and 'ostensible' authority in the context of vicarious liability?

5. On what basis can an employer be held responsible where an employee disobeys an explicit instruction?

6. On what basis can an employer be held responsible for an employee's deliberate tort?

7. In what circumstances is a client responsible for torts committed by an independent contractor?

8. Pat sets up a parcel delivery business in central London, using a team of motorcycle couriers who supply their own motorcycles and are paid on the basis of mileage they cover. Pat insists that the couriers do not carry passengers when engaged on deliveries. While carrying a parcel on behalf of Charles, Fred, one of the couriers, diverts to see his girlfriend Gemma and gives her a lift on the pillion seat of his motorcycle. When Fred negligently crashes, Gemma is injured and the parcel is destroyed.

   Advise Pat as to his liability, if any, to Charles and Gemma.

27

Remedies

CHAPTER OVERVIEW

A claimant who successfully brings an action in tort will, if successful, be entitled to one or more legal remedies. In this chapter we examine the following issues:

- the extent to which an award of damages in tort may depart from its main aim, that of compensating the claimant for loss suffered;
- the way in which damages are assessed in cases of personal injury, death and damage to property;
- the statutory mechanism for allocating liability where responsibility for the claimant's loss is shared by more than one person;
- the availability of remedies other than an award of damages, especially that of injunction;
- the time limits within which actions in tort must be commenced if they are not to be statute-barred.

Damages

27.1 The availability of an action for damages is the hallmark of a tort; the absence of such a remedy is what serves to distinguish other civil wrongs, such as breach of trust. Moreover, it should be emphasised that damages are available even in respect of those torts which are actionable without the need to prove that the claimant has suffered any actual loss. In such a case, the sum awarded may, but need not, be nominal. Where other torts are concerned, the claimant is called upon to establish a loss and, having done so, is entitled to be compensated for it.

Kinds of damages

27.2 As a general rule, the sole object of awarding damages to a claimant is to compensate for loss suffered as a result of the defendant's tort. With a few minor exceptions, matters such as the punishment of the defendant, or the restoration of benefits wrongfully obtained, have no place in the law of tort. It should also be noted that, whereas damages for breach of contract generally endeavour to put the claimant, in monetary terms, into the position in which he or she would have been had the contract been performed,[1] and thus take into account any profit which would have resulted from the bargain, damages for tort attempt to restore the claimant's original position, as if the tort had not been committed at all.

In a number of instances, the courts may depart, or appear to depart, from the principle of compensation in assessing the amount of damages to be awarded to a successful claimant. For example, where the claimant has a bare legal claim, but the court feels that it is morally wrong to pursue it, there may be an award of *contemptuous* damages, usually the smallest coin of the realm. In such a case the defendant may well not be ordered to pay the claimant's costs, in which case the claimant will end up out of pocket to a considerable extent.

Not to be confused with contemptuous damages are *nominal* damages, which are awarded in respect of torts actionable per se to mark the infringement of the claimant's legal rights, in cases where no actual loss has been incurred. An award of, say, £2 for trespass in no way signifies that the court is critical of the claimant for bringing the case; on the contrary, such an award is frequently accompanied by an injunction restraining the defendant from committing further acts of trespass.

In torts such as trespass or assault, where damages are incapable of precise assessment in money terms, the manner in which the defendant commits the tort may be taken into account by the court; if this is such as to injure the claimant's dignity or pride, *aggravated* damages may be awarded. Indeed, even where the claimant has suffered a quantifiable financial loss, as where he or she has been defrauded by the defendant, an additional sum may be awarded as compensation for injury to feelings.[2] However, a claimant cannot recover damages for indignation at the high-handed attitude displayed by the defendant following the commission of a tort.[3]

Quite apart from any question of aggravation, there remains the possibility that, where the defendant's conduct is particularly outrageous, the court may order the payment of *exemplary* or *punitive* damages, over and above what is necessary to compensate the claimant, for the explicit purpose of punishing the defendant and of emphasising that tort does not pay. Such awards are open to criticism on the grounds that the defendant is being punished for something which is not a crime, and without the protection of a criminal trial. It might also be argued that what is in effect a fine should be paid to the state rather than to the claimant, since the latter has, after all, already received sufficient to compensate for whatever loss has been suffered. Nevertheless, the power to award exemplary damages is well established, although in *Rookes v Barnard*[4] the House of Lords laid down that it should only be exercised in three classes of case:

- where statute authorises such an award;

- in cases of oppressive, arbitrary or unconstitutional acts by the servants of the Government, such as assault or wrongful arrest by police officers, who are regarded for this purpose as the servants of the Government;[5] or

- where the defendant has quite cold-bloodedly decided to infringe the claimant's rights after calculating that the profit in doing so will outweigh any compensation which may be awarded. This has been held to include such cases as the publication of a book[6] or a newspaper[7] containing sensational libels in order to boost sales, the eviction of a protected tenant by a landlord[8] anxious to turn a flat to more profitable use,[9] and the deliberate usurpation by a property company of a 'flying freehold' which protruded from adjoining premises over its property.[10]

---

[1] Para 11.3.

[2] *Archer v Brown* [1984] 2 All ER 267.

[3] *AB v South West Water Services Ltd* [1993] 1 All ER 609, CA.

[4] [1964] 1 All ER 367, HL.

[5] Exemplary damages may be awarded for wrongful arrest, even where the behaviour is not 'oppressive': *Holden v Chief Constable of Lancashire* [1986] 3 All ER 836, CA.

⁶ *Cassell & Co Ltd v Broome* [1972] 1 All ER 801, HL, in which it was held to be irrelevant that no profit was in fact made.

⁷ As to the assessment of exemplary damages where a newspaper article libels a group of claimants, see *Riches v News Group Newspapers Ltd* [1986] QB 256, CA.

⁸ But not the landlord's agent, unless he (or she) stands to benefit personally from the eviction: *Daley v Ramdath* (1993) Times, 21 January, CA.

⁹ *Drane v Evangelou* [1978] 2 All ER 437, CA (trespass); *Guppys (Bridport) Ltd v Brookling* [1984] 1 EGLR 29, CA (nuisance). The Housing Act 1988, s 28 entitles an unlawfully evicted tenant to a measure of damages which effectively consists of the profit which the landlord makes from the eviction.

¹⁰ *Ramzan v Brookwide Ltd* [2010] EWHC Ch 2453.

Personal injury

27.3 The rules which govern the assessment of damages for personal injury are complex; no more than an outline can be given here. One of the major problems is that the loss which flows from an injury falls into two very different categories. In the first place, the claimant may suffer monetary losses, such as medical expenses or loss of earnings; the guiding principle here is that the claimant is entitled, so far as is possible, to full restitution of what has been lost. Secondly, however, there is non-monetary loss, which includes such matters as pain and suffering and loss of amenity. It is obviously impossible to place a precise value upon such things, and the law's aim here is simply to ensure that compensation should be fair and reasonable. This involves attempting to devise a scale of injuries (so that, for example, a lost leg is treated as worth more than a lost eye) and also maintaining some degree of consistency between the amounts awarded in similar cases.[1] With these points, and especially these two categories, in mind, we may now consider the various heads of damage under which personal injury awards are usually itemised.

¹ See *Heil v Rankin* [2000] 3 All ER 138, CA.

Loss of amenity

27.4 The claimant is entitled to an award of damages in respect of the extent to which he or she is unable through injury to engage in previously enjoyed activities. Under this heading compensation may be awarded, for example, in respect of a lost limb or the impairment of senses or of sexual function. The seriousness of the deprivation, the claimant's degree of awareness of it, and the period for which it is likely to endure, are all factors which influence the size of the award. In *Daly v General Steam Navigation Co Ltd*,[1] a woman whose injuries made it difficult and painful to keep house for her family recovered under this heading for the period preceding the trial; as to the future, she was held entitled to the estimated costs of employing a housekeeper, whether or not she in fact intended to employ one.

Although this category appears to be based on a person's lost enjoyment of life, it was laid down by the House of Lords, in *H West & Son Ltd v Shephard*,[2] that it represents an objective loss. Consequently, even someone rendered immediately and permanently unaware of the loss may be entitled to a considerable sum. Of course, a claimant who is aware of the loss may be compensated for this under the heading of 'pain and suffering'.[3]

¹ [1980] 3 All ER 696, CA.
² [1963] 2 All ER 625, HL.
³ Para 27.5.

Pain and suffering

27.5 This head of damage includes not only the physical pain of the injury and subsequent surgical operations, but also mental anguish arising out of disability or disfigurement. It cannot by definition apply to claimants rendered permanently unconscious; nor, where a person is killed by a tort, can damages be awarded to the estate for that 'pain and suffering' which is really part of the death itself.[1]

As a general rule, the courts do not separate 'pain and suffering' from 'loss of amenity', but award a global sum to cover both categories. Where very severe injuries are involved, this can be a considerable amount.

[1] *Hicks v Chief Constable of the South Yorkshire Police* [1992] 2 All ER 65, HL.

Loss of expectation of life

27.6 A claimant whose life expectancy has been reduced is not entitled to damages for that fact.[1] However, this does not prevent a claim in respect of the suffering caused by awareness of the reduced lifespan,[2] nor for the money which could have been earned during the lost years.[3]

[1] Administration of Justice Act 1982, s 1(1).
[2] S 1(1)(b).
[3] S 1(2).

Medical and other expenses

27.7 The claimant is entitled to recover the cost, both past and future, of medical and nursing care including, where appropriate, the expense of living in a suitable institution or of adapting his (or her) own home. If the claimant has to live in an institution, a sum representing normal living expenses must be deducted from the damages awarded under this head, since these will no longer be incurred.[1] The claimant cannot recover damages for any expenses which ought reasonably to have been avoided, but it is not unreasonable to care for a severely injured person at home just because he (or she) could be catered for more cheaply than in an institution,[2] nor to seek private medical treatment rather than making use of the National Health Service facilities.[3]

Where necessary nursing services have been rendered to a seriously disabled claimant by a close relative, as where a mother has given up a job in order to look after her crippled child, it is established that the claimant can recover from the defendant a reasonable sum in respect of those services.[4]

[1] *Lim Poh Choo v Camden and Islington Area Health Authority* [1979] 2 All ER 910, HL.
[2] *Rialas v Mitchell* (1984) Times, 17 July, CA.
[3] Law Reform (Personal Injuries) Act 1948, s 2(4).
[4] *Donnelly v Joyce* [1973] 3 All ER 475, CA. However, this does not apply where it is the defendant who renders the services: *Hunt v Severs* [1994] 2 All ER 385, HL.

Loss of earnings

27.8 Earnings which the claimant has lost up to the date of the trial are relatively easy to measure, but loss of future earnings[1] must also be compensated, and here assessment is far less certain, especially where it appears that the claimant will never be able to work again. In such cases, the courts, having firmly refused to enter into detailed actuarial calculations,[2] simply multiply their prediction of the claimant's average annual income (net of income tax and national insurance contributions) by an appropriate multiplier. This is not simply the number of years' earnings which have been lost, but is discounted to reflect the chance of an earlier death and the benefit of having an immediate lump sum. It is not increased, however, to mitigate the effect which high rates of taxation will have upon the income produced by investing a large award of damages.[3] In *Wells v Wells*,[4] the House of Lords held that the multiplier should be calculated on the basis that the claimant would invest the damages in index-linked government securities and would thus be protected in inflation.

A person whose life expectancy is substantially reduced as a result of a tort is of course likely to be deprived of the opportunity to earn money during the lost years. Under the Administration of Justice Act 1982, s 1(2), a living claimant[5] can recover for prospective earnings during the lost years, although a deduction must be made in respect of what would have been spent on the claimant's support during that time. However, the courts will not make an award of this kind to a very young claimant, on the grounds that the loss is too speculative.[6]

Much of the uncertainty which surrounds this particular head of damage arises from the fact that, since damages are normally paid as a lump sum,[7] they must be assessed in advance. A limited exception to this is found in s 32A of the Senior Courts Act 1981; this provides that, in cases where there is a chance that the claimant's condition will deteriorate at some time in the future, the court may make an initial lump sum award on the basis that this will not happen, the claimant being at liberty to seek additional damages if it does.[8]

[1] Including loss or reduction of future pension rights: *Auty v National Coal Board* [1985] 1 All ER 930, CA.

[2] *Mitchell v Mulholland (No 2)* [1971] 2 All ER 1205, CA.

[3] *Hodgson v Trapp* [1988] 3 All ER 870, HL.

[4] [1998] 3 All ER 481, HL.

[5] The claim does not pass to the deceased's estate: see para 27.11.

[6] *Croke v Wiseman* [1981] 3 All ER 852, CA.

[7] The court has power to make an award of periodical payments, known as a structured settlement, provided it is satisfied that continuity of payment will be secure: Damages Act 1996, s 2, as amended by the Courts Act 2003, s 100.

[8] See *Willson v Ministry of Defence* [1991] 1 All ER 638.

Collateral benefits

27.9 A person who is injured in an accident may, as a result of this, receive sums of money from a wide variety of sources, such as insurance, sick pay or a pension from an employer, or social security benefits. To what extent, if at all, should this be regarded as relevant when the claimant comes to claim damages from the defendant in respect of his loss of earnings? Should the claimant be allowed to recover full damages and to keep the other benefit, and thereby be doubly compensated? Should damages be reduced, so that the defendant reaps the benefit of a payment designed to help the claimant? Or should the law seek to ensure that the money is in some way returned to the collateral fund?

To these questions, English law has no simple answers, largely because it has dealt with each type of collateral benefit as it has arisen, without attempting to lay down any general principles. Very broadly, the position now is that most state benefits received in the five years after the accident are deducted from the damages and then recovered from the defendant by the state.[1] Similarly, where a claimant has received treatment on the NHS for an injury, the defendant may be made to pay charges to the NHS for that treatment.[2]

Deducted from damages, but not recovered from the defendant, are wages, sick pay,[3] redundancy payments[4] and the like to which the claimant is actually entitled, together with any saving on living costs where the claimant is maintained at public expense in an institution.[5] The product of private insurance,[6] or a charitable payment, on the other hand, is non-deductible.[7] On the very borderline is a pension; in *Parry v Cleaver*,[8] this was held by a bare majority of the House of Lords to be non-deductible, on the ground that it is not intended to be an equivalent of wages lost and cannot therefore be said to reduce the loss which the claimant has suffered.

[1] Social Security Administration Act 1992, Part IV, as amended by the Social Security (Recovery of Benefits) Act 1997. After five years there is neither deduction nor recovery.

[2] Health and Social Care (Community Health and Standards) Act 2003, s 150.

[3] *Hussain v New Taplow Paper Mills Ltd* [1988] 1 All ER 541, HL.

[4] *Colledge v Bass Mitchells & Butlers* [1988] ICR 125, CA.

[5] Administration of Justice Act 1982, s 5.

[6] Even where paid for by the defendant employer: *McCamley v Cammell Laird Shipbuilders Ltd* [1990] 1 All ER 854, CA.

[7] *Bradburn v Great Western Rly Co* (1874) LR 10 Exch 1.

[8] [1969] 1 All ER 555, HL; followed unanimously by the House of Lords in *Smoker v London Fire and Civil Defence Authority; Wood v British Coal Corpn* [1991] 2 All ER 449, HL.

Death

27.10 The Law Reform (Miscellaneous Provisions) Act 1934 provides that most tort actions survive for and against the estates of the parties.[1] However, the Administration of Justice Act 1982, s 4 provides that a deceased person's estate may not be awarded damages for bereavement,[2] exemplary damages[3] or damages for loss of earnings during the lost years.[4] Apart from this, where an action is brought on behalf of a deceased person, the damages awarded are such as could have been recovered if the person had not died, which means that the headings considered above under 'personal injury' are again relevant, at least as regards the period between the tort and death.

[1] Actions for defamation do not survive.

[2] Para 27.11.

[3] Para 27.2.

[4] Para 27.8.

Fatal accidents

27.11 At common law, no tort action could be brought by A for loss caused by the death of B. However, a statutory right of action for the dependants of a person who is killed by a tort has long been in existence and is currently governed by the Fatal Accidents Act 1976, as amended by the Administration of Justice Act 1982, s 3. Dependants for this purpose bears a wide meaning, including spouses, all ascendants and descendants, brothers and sisters, uncles and aunts and their issue, provided, of course, that they truly were dependent upon the deceased. Moreover, since 1982, the Act has extended to a former spouse or cohabitee of the deceased, although the amount of damages payable must reflect the fact that he or she had no legal right to financial support by the deceased.

The cause of action given by the Fatal Accidents Act is quite separate from that which may have survived for the benefit of the estate itself. Normal practice is for the action to be brought by the personal representative of the deceased, on behalf of all the dependants; the court will then assess the total liability of the defendant before apportioning the damages between the various dependants. Since the action is an independent one, it has its own limitation period of three years from the date of death. Further, it seems that where the fault of one dependant (such as negligent driving) has contributed to the causing of death, the damages payable to that dependant, though not those payable to other dependants, may be reduced on the ground of contributory negligence.

Although the action is thus separate, it is still subject to the principle that it can only be brought where the deceased could have sued if he (or she) had been injured rather than killed. As a result, if the deceased had already sued to judgment or settled a claim against the defendant, or if legal action was barred by time or by an exemption clause, the dependants' rights are also defeated. So too, if the deceased was guilty of contributory negligence, damages awarded under the Fatal Accidents Act will suffer an appropriate reduction.

It is important to appreciate that the main purpose of this statutory cause of action is to compensate the dependants, not for their grief at losing a loved one, but for the loss of some benefit which has a monetary value (including, for example, services performed by a wife and mother[1] or unpaid help given by a son to his father's work[2]) and which would have come to the dependants because of their relationship with the deceased.[3] However, since 1982 there has been a limited exception to this principle, in that damages for bereavement (a fixed sum laid down by statutory instrument[4]) may be awarded to the widow(er) or, where the deceased is an unmarried minor at the date of death, to his (or her) parents.

In deciding how much to award for loss of dependency, the court must try to assess what the position would have been had the deceased lived and, in carrying out this task, the prospects of both the deceased and the dependants are of course relevant. However, the court is not to consider a widow's prospects of remarriage.

Section 4 of the 1976 Act provides that, in assessing damages, no account is to be taken of any benefits which accrue to the dependant in question as a result of the death, for example by way of inheritance or insurance policies.[5]

[1] *Mehmet v Perry* [1977] 2 All ER 529, DC.

[2] *Franklin v South Eastern Rly Co* (1858) 3 H & N 211.

[3] Funeral expenses incurred by the dependants are also recoverable: Fatal Accidents Act 1976, s 3(3).

[4] This is currently £10,000: Damages for Bereavement (Variation of Sum) (England and Wales) Order 2002.

[5] See *Pidduck v Eastern Scottish Omnibuses Ltd* [1990] 2 All ER 69, CA.

Damage to property

Measure of damages

27.12 A person whose property (whether land or goods) is destroyed or damaged as a result of a tort is in principle entitled to full restitution in money terms of what has been lost. Where property is totally destroyed (which will hardly ever apply to land), the usual measure of damages is at least the full value to the claimant of that property at the time and place of its destruction. This value, in the case of a profit-earning chattel such as a ship, should take into account its profitability at the time, in the light of its current engagements.[1] However, a claimant who receives this sum may yet be out of pocket, in that the acquisition of a suitable replacement may take time; in such a case, damages for loss of profit, or simply loss of use, may also be recovered.

Where the claimant's property is damaged by the defendant, the court has a choice of at least two possible measures[2] to award (which may or may not be the same): either the amount by which the value of the property has been reduced, or the cost of repairing it. In the case of goods, the courts have usually been prepared to award the cost of repair, unless this would be unreasonable. For example, the owner of a badly damaged car will not normally be allowed the cost of repair where this exceeds the write-off value of the vehicle.[3] A similar principle applies in respect of damage to land and buildings, so that the cost of reinstatement is usually appropriate, provided that the claimant's decision to repair is a reasonable one. Thus, in *Hollebone v Midhurst and Fernhurst Builders*,[4] where the claimant's house was damaged by fire, the judge held that the claimant was fully entitled to decide to rebuild what was in effect a unique property. That case also laid down that a claimant need not suffer any deduction from the damages awarded in respect of 'betterment', ie the amount by which the value of the restored property exceeds its pre-accident value.

Where the claimant has no intention of repairing the building (as in *C A Taylor (Wholesale) Ltd v Hepworths Ltd*,[5] where fire damaged a disused billiards hall on a site which the claimants had always intended to redevelop) damages should only reflect the diminution in value of the property. This is also true of cases where the cost of reinstatement would be out of all proportion to the loss suffered. In *Jones v Gooday*,[6] for example, where the defendant wrongfully removed soil from the claimant's field, the claimant was awarded only the amount by which the value of the field was reduced, and not the much greater cost of restoring it to its original condition. In *Heath v Keys*,[7] where the defendant wrongfully dumped spoil on a small area of woodland owned by the claimant, the award was something of a compromise; not the full cost of restoring the site to its original condition, but enough to pay the costs involved in removing most of the spoil and tidying the site, in addition to the diminution in value which would remain when this had been done.

Quite apart from the damages discussed above, a claimant is entitled to compensation for loss of profits or loss of use during the time taken to effect repairs, which may be assessed on the basis of the cost of hiring a reasonable substitute. What is reasonable is a question of fact, and may even include a prestige car.[8] It is important to note that the claimant is not required to show that the non-availability of the property has caused any actual loss. Consequently, in *The Mediana*,[9] where a damaged lightship was replaced for a time by a substitute which the claimants kept for just such an emergency, they were nevertheless awarded substantial damages for loss of use.

It is worth noting that, where a purchaser brings an action for negligence against a surveyor on whose advice he relied in deciding to purchase, the basic measure of damages will be not the cost of repairing defects which the surveyor ought to have discovered, but the difference between what the purchaser has been led to pay for the property and its actual value. This is because the surveyor has not actually damaged the property, but has merely led the purchaser to pay more than it is worth.[10]

[1] *Liesbosch Dredger v SS Edison* [1933] AC 449, HL.

[2] These are not the only possible measures; the court will select whatever is the most appropriate measure of compensation in all the circumstances. See *Dominion Mosaics and Tile Co Ltd v Trafalgar Trucking Co Ltd* [1990] 2 All ER 246, CA; *Farmer Giles Ltd v Wessex Water Authority* [1990] 1 EGLR 177, CA.

[3] *Darbishire v Warran* [1963] 3 All ER 310, CA.

[4] [1968] 1 Lloyd's Rep 38. Also see *Dominion Mosaics & Tile Co Ltd v Trafalgar Trucking Co Ltd* [1990] 2 All ER 246, CA.

[5] [1977] 2 All ER 784.

[6] (1841) 8 M & W 146.

[7] [1984] CLY 3568.

[8] *Daily Office Cleaning Contractors v Shefford* [1977] RTR 361, DC.

[9] [1900] AC 113, HL.

[10] *Watts v Morrow* [1991] 4 All ER 937, CA.

Date of assessment

27.13 Where damages fall to be based on the cost of repair, this is normally assessed as at the date on which the claimant ought reasonably to have repaired the property. In *Dodd Properties (Kent) Ltd v Canterbury City Council*,[1] where the claimants' garage was seriously damaged by building works carried on by the defendants on adjoining property, the claimants chose for sound financial reasons not to start repairs until they had recovered damages from the defendants. It was held by the Court of Appeal that the claimants were entitled to recover the full cost of repair at the date of trial, notwithstanding that this was much greater than the cost at the time the property was damaged.

¹ [1980] 1 All ER 928, CA.

Multiple tortfeasors

27.14 Where the claimant is harmed by the tortious conduct of more than one person, the first question to be asked is whether each tortfeasor has caused a separately identifiable part of the claimant's overall damage. If this is so, then each is liable only for the part which he or she has caused. More commonly, however, the damage to the claimant will be indivisible; if so, the claimant is entitled to recover damages in full from any or all of the tortfeasors, subject to the proviso that the total recovered cannot exceed what has been lost. Thus, for example, if the claimant is injured by the combined negligence of A and B in such circumstances that the court regards A as three-quarters and B as one-quarter to blame, the claimant may nevertheless choose to sue B alone and may recover full damages. The importance of this principle is seen in cases where A is insolvent and uninsured; the loss then falls upon B, who is after all guilty of some fault, rather than upon the claimant who is completely innocent.

In practice, it is desirable that the claimant should bring all the defendants into court in one action. To encourage this, s 4 of the Civil Liability (Contribution) Act 1978 provides that a claimant who brings successive actions against different tortfeasors will be unable to recover the legal costs incurred in all but the first action, unless the court finds that there were reasonable grounds for bringing the subsequent ones.

Contribution between tortfeasors

27.15 Section 1(1) of the Civil Liability (Contribution) Act 1978 provides that any person liable¹ in respect of any damage suffered by another person may recover contribution from any other person liable in respect of the same damage.² The recovery of contribution may be sought as part of the original action by the claimant (so long as both tortfeasors are parties to that action), or in a separate action between the tortfeasors.

The right of one tortfeasor (D1) to claim contribution from another (D2) is independent of the claimant's right of action. Thus, the fact that the claimant's claim against D2 would have been barred by lapse of time³ is irrelevant, provided that D1 brings an action for contribution within two years of the date on which the right to do so arises (this will normally be the date on which D1 pays compensation to the claimant).

In assessing the amount of contribution, the court is instructed to do what is just and equitable, and it seems that, in arriving at a fraction or percentage, it will rely on the same factors as in cases of contributory negligence.⁴ However, it should be noted that D2 cannot be ordered to pay more to D1 than he (or she) would have had to pay the claimant (eg where a contract with the claimant contained a clause which limited D2's liability): nor does the Civil Liability (Contribution) Act prevail against a right of indemnity which is contained in a contract between the tortfeasors.

¹ This includes liability in 'tort, breach of contract, breach of trust or otherwise'.
² The phrase 'the same damage' requires both persons to be liable to the same third party: *Birse Construction Ltd v Haiste Ltd* [1996] 2 All ER 1, CA.
³ Paras 27.20–27.24.
⁴ Para 19.9.

Damages: Key Points

- Damages in tort are almost always intended to compensate the claimant for injury, damage or loss.

- Damages for personal injury cover both monetary loss (medical expenses and loss of earnings) and non-monetary loss (pain and suffering and loss of amenity).

- Where a claimant receives some collateral benefit (such as an insurance payout or state benefits) in consequence of a tort, some (but not all) of these may have to be deducted from the damages payable by the defendant.

- Where a person is killed by a tort, that person's dependants may be entitled to recover damages for the financial loss which they suffer.

- Where property is damaged by a tort, the owner may be entitled to claim either the cost of repair or the amount by which the value of the property has been reduced.

- Where there is more than one defendant, each is potentially liable in full for the claimant's loss; a defendant who pays more than his (or her) fair share may then claim a contribution from the others.

Injunctions

27.16 An injunction is a specific decree of the court which orders the defendant to do or, more commonly, not to do something. Like all equitable remedies it is not available as of right, but lies in the discretion of the court. As a result, it is unlikely to be granted where damages would be an adequate remedy, where the harm suffered by the claimant is of a very trivial or temporary nature,[1] or where the claimant has actually or apparently acquiesced in the defendant's tort. For example, in *Armstrong v Sheppard and Short Ltd*,[2] the claimant assented in principle to the laying of a sewer by the defendants under certain land near his house, unaware that he in fact owned that land; upon discovering the truth, he sued the defendants in trespass. The Court of Appeal held that, since the defendants had been misled and the harm was trivial, the claimant was not entitled to an injunction but only to damages.

[1] *A-G v Sheffield Gas Consumers Co* (1853) 3 De Gm & G 304.
[2] [1959] 2 All ER 651, CA.

Kinds of injunction

27.17 A *prohibitory* injunction, the most common kind, is an order to the defendant to stop certain conduct which represents a continuing or repetitive infringement of the claimant's legal rights (eg by the commission of trespass or nuisance). In the absence of special circumstances, the grant of such an injunction is almost automatic, though its operation may on occasion be suspended for a period to enable the defendant to make alternative arrangements.

By contrast, a *mandatory* injunction, which orders the defendant to take positive steps to repair the wrong done, is reserved for those few cases in which the claimant will suffer very serious harm unless the injunction is granted. Further, unless the defendant has acted in flagrant disregard of the claimant's rights, the court must weigh up what it will cost the defendant to comply with the order. Thus, in *Redland Bricks Ltd v Morris*,[1] where the defendants' excavations on their own land had caused subsidence of part of the claimant's land and danger to the rest, the House of Lords refused to order the defendants to restore support, since the cost of doing this would be greater than the total value of the claimant's land.

In matters of urgency, where the preservation of the status quo is important to save the claimant from further loss, the court may grant an *interlocutory* injunction, a provisional order until a full trial takes place. Since the defendant may lose money because of this order, and then turn out to have been in the right all along, the claimant may be compelled to give an undertaking to pay compensation if this in fact is what happens. The principles on which a court should exercise its discretion in relation to interlocutory injunctions were laid down by the House of Lords in the case of *American Cyanamid Co v Ethicon Ltd*.[2] Briefly, these are that, if there is a serious question to be tried, the court must consider all the circumstances, particularly whether the preservation of the status quo is important, and whether the defendant will be adequately protected by the claimant's undertaking to pay damages.

In rare cases, where the claimant's cause of action depends on proof of damage, the court may issue an injunction *quia timet* ('because he is afraid') before such damage had actually occurred. In effect, this means that the defendant is held liable before a complete tort has been committed; not surprisingly, therefore such an order is only granted where damages is almost certain to occur and where it is imminent.

[1] [1969] 2 All ER 576, HL.
[2] [1975] 1 All ER 504, HL.

Damages in lieu of injunction

27.18 In any case where an injunction is claimed, the court has a discretion to refuse the injunction and award damages in substitution for it. In effect, such an order allows the defendant to purchase the right to commit a tort against the claimant, and the discretion is consequently to be used sparingly. It has been suggested that the court should only act in this way where it is shown that the injury to the claimant is small, capable of estimation in money terms and adequately compensated by damages, and that an injunction would cause great hardship to the defendant.[1]

In *Jaggard v Sawyer*,[2] the owners of a private road sought an injunction to prevent the occupiers of a new house from trespassing along the road. However, the Court of Appeal held that this was a case where damages should be awarded instead, since to award an injunction would in effect render the house uninhabitable. By contrast, in *Elliott v Islington London Borough Council*,[3] the Court of Appeal awarded an injunction compelling a local authority to cut down a tree which was encroaching onto the claimant's land, notwithstanding that the tree was an ancient horsechestnut which the local authority passionately wanted to preserve.

[1] *Shelfer v City of London Electric Lighting Co* [1895] 1 Ch 287 at 322, CA.
[2] [1995] 2 All ER 189, CA.
[3] [1991] 1 EGLR 167, CA.

INJUNCTIONS: KEY POINTS

- Injunctions are usually prohibitory but may, in limited circumstances, be mandatory—that is, the defendant may be ordered to do something positive.

- The award of an injunction is always at the court's discretion and, in certain cases, a court may refuse an injunction and award damages instead.

Other remedies

27.19 In the vast majority of tort cases which come to court, the claimant is seeking either damages or an injunction. However, in some circumstances other remedies may be of greater value, particularly an order for the specific restitution of goods or land.[1]

Although not popular with the courts, and therefore strictly controlled, a certain amount of self-help is tolerated, in the interest of avoiding unnecessary litigation. Examples of this principle, all of which we have considered at the appropriate place, are the ejection of a trespasser and re-entry on to land,[2] the abatement of a nuisance,[3] the detention of straying livestock[4] and the killing of a marauding dog.[5]

[1] Para 22.9.
[2] Para 22.10.
[3] Para 24.22.
[4] Para 25.10.
[5] Para 25.12.

Limitation of actions

27.20 Any civil action will be barred by lapse of time unless it is commenced within the prescribed limitation period. The rules which govern this matter are entirely statutory and are contained in the Limitation Act 1980. For present purposes, the main limitation periods are 12 years (recovery of land and contracts made by deed); six years (breach of simple contracts and tort); and three years (actions for both tort and breach of contract in respect of personal injuries). Special periods apply to certain types of claim, for example those arising under the Defective Premises Act 1972.[1]

[1] Para 21.29.

Commencement of limitation period

27.21 Whichever period is applicable, the basic rule is that it starts on the day when the claimant's cause of action accrues. In contract cases, this is almost invariably the date of the defendant's breach, and the same is true of those torts which are actionable per se, such as trespass. On the other hand, where proof of damage forms part of the tort itself, as in cases of negligence or nuisance, the cause of action does not arise until the damage occurs and, accordingly, time does not start to run until that date.

Clearly, it may sometimes be to a claimant's advantage to be able to sue in tort rather than in contract, and this is what gives such importance to those decisions which have held professional advisers liable to their clients in the tort of negligence as well as for breach of contract.[1] However, the advantage of a tort action is not always as marked as might be supposed. For example, where a solicitor gives negligent advice to a client, as a result of which the client executes an imprudent mortgage of property, it has been held that the damage is suffered as soon as the mortgage is executed, since the property is immediately rendered less valuable, rather than when the property is later seized by the mortgagee.[2] Similarly, where a surveyor negligently advises a client to purchase a badly constructed building, the client is regarded as having suffered loss at the date of exchanging contracts to purchase, rather than at the later date when the building itself suffers physical damage.[3] By contrast, where a mortgage lender sues the valuer on whose valuation the lender relied, the lender's loss is deemed to occur at the first moment when the amount of the outstanding mortgage debt (including any accrued interest) exceeds the value of the property.[4]

Continuing torts, such as certain kinds of trespass[5] or nuisance, give rise to a fresh right of action every day until they are abated. The consequence of this is that a claimant is entitled to sue for everything which has occurred during the past six years, even if the tort was first committed outside that period or, indeed, before the claimant acquired the property in question.[6]

[1] Para 16.16.
[2] *Forster v Outred & Co* [1982] 2 All ER 753, CA.
[3] *Byrne v Hall Pain & Foster* [1999] 1 EGLR 73, CA.
[4] *Nykredit Mortgage Bank plc v Edward Erdman Group Ltd (No 2)* [1998] 1 All ER 305, HL.
[5] Para 22.7.
[6] See *Masters v Brent London Borough Council* [1978] 2 All ER 664.

Personal injury

27.22 A particular problem may arise in cases where an injury, such as a progressive industrial disease, is not discovered (or, indeed, discoverable) by the claimant until some considerable time after it first occurs. To deal with this problem, s 11 of the Limitation Act 1980 provides that the limitation period in cases of personal injury based on 'negligence, nuisance or breach of duty'[1] shall be three years and shall not begin until the claimant has knowledge of a number of material facts, of which the most important are the significance of the injury (that is, that it is serious enough to justify taking legal action) and its attributability to an identified defendant. The claimant's 'knowledge' for this purpose includes knowledge which he (or she) might reasonably have been expected to acquire from personal observations or from such expert advice as ought reasonably to have been sought, taking account of the claimant's age, background, intelligence and disabilities.[2]

[1] This includes trespass to the person: *A v Hoare* [2008] UKHL 6, [2008] 2 All ER 1, HL.
[2] *Davis v City and Hackney Health Authority* [1989] 2 Med LR 366.

Latent damage

27.23 The problem of hidden damage is not confined to personal injury cases; negligence in building houses is another obvious example. As to this s 14A of the Limitation Act 1980, added by the Latent Damage Act 1986, effectively extends the limitation period for claims in tort for negligence,[1] other than in respect of personal injury.[2] It also permits an action for negligent damage to property[3] to be brought by a person who acquires that property after it has suffered damage but before the damage has become apparent.

The time limit on claims falling within s 14A is either:

- six years from when the cause of action accrued;[4] or

- three years from when the claimant (or his predecessor in title, if property has changed hands) had both the right to bring an action and knowledge of material facts.[5]

However, s 14B of the Act imposes an overriding time limit of 15 years from the defendant's breach of duty on which the action is based. After this, the action is barred whether or not the damage has become known or has even occurred.

[1] The Act does not apply to claims based on a contractual duty of care: *Société Commerciale de Réassurance v ERAS (International)* [1992] 2 All ER 82n, CA.
[2] Thus including both claims for both damage to property and pure financial loss.
[3] But not for other types of claim, eg for negligent professional advice.
[4] Ie when damage is suffered; see para 27.21.
[5] 'Knowledge' is defined in a similar way as for personal injury claims; see para 27.22. For the operation of the Act in respect of a negligent survey, see *Hamlin v Edwin Evans* [1996] 2 EGLR 106, CA.

Extension of time

27.24 It is provided by the Limitation Act 1980 that in certain circumstances the limitation period may either begin to run from a later date than normal or may simply be extended.

- Where there is fraud, concealment or mistake,[1] the limitation period does not begin to run until this has been or ought to have been discovered by the claimant. The question of concealment has arisen in a number of cases where defects in a building which are due to negligence by the builder have been covered up in the course of the construction work and have not come to light until many years later. It has been held that the mere fact that a builder continues with his work after something shoddy or inadequate has been done does not necessarily amount to concealment for this purpose.[2] The question is whether in all the circumstances it was unconscionable for the builder to proceed with the work so as to cover up the defect.[3]

- Where the claimant is a minor or is mentally ill, the limitation period does not begin to run until the removal of his disability or his death.[4] This provision has been held to apply where the claimant's unsoundness of mind is caused by the accident in respect of which he sues.[5]

- A sweeping change in the law governing limitation of actions was introduced by the Limitation Act 1980, s 33. This provision, which applies to all actions brought in respect of personal injuries, empowers the court simply to override the normal three-year period if it appears equitable to do so. In deciding how to exercise its discretion in this way, the court is instructed to have regard to all the circumstances of the case, and in particular to the extent to which each party would be prejudiced by an adverse decision, to the conduct of each party since the accident, and to the length and reasons for the delay.[6]

[1] Para 11.53. 'Concealment' for this purpose may take place either when the cause of action first accrues or at any time thereafter: *Sheldon v RHM Outhwaite (Underwriting Agencies) Ltd* [1995] 2 All ER 558, HL.
[2] *William Hill Organisation Ltd v Bernard Sunley & Sons Ltd* (1982) 22 BLR 8, CA.
[3] *Applegate v Moss* [1971] 1 All ER 747, CA.
[4] Limitation Act 1980, s 28.
[5] *Kirby v Leather* [1965] 2 All ER 441, CA.
[6] See *Thompson v Brown Construction (Ebbw Vale) Ltd* [1981] 2 All ER 296, HL; *Hartley v Birmingham City District Council* [1992] 2 All ER 213, CA.

Injunctions

27.25 Injunctions are equitable remedies and their award, therefore, is not subject to the provisions of the Limitation Act. However, equity has its own rules concerning delay, and these we discussed in para 11.55.

LIMITATION OF ACTIONS: KEY POINTS

- All actions in tort are subject to statutory time limits, and will fail if not commenced within the relevant period.

- The time limit for most torts is six years from the date on which damage is suffered.

- In certain cases (notably those involving personal injury and latent damage) there is an alternative time limit which does not commence until the claimant is aware of the material facts about his or her potential claim.

Questions

1. In what circumstances can a court award damages over and above what is required to compensate the claimant?

2. What are the main heads of damage which may be awarded in an action for personal injury?

3. To what extent can a person's death lead to a claim in tort?

4. Where a person's property is damaged as the result of a tort, how are the damages assessed?

5. If A is injured in a road accident caused equally by the negligence of B and C, who is liable and for how much?

6. In what circumstances will a court refuse to grant the claimant an injunction and substitute an award of damages?

7. What time limits are applicable to a claim for damage to property, in a case where the damage is not immediately discoverable?

PART IV

Land law

28

Land, its ownership and use

CHAPTER OVERVIEW

In this chapter we examine the following issues:

● the way in which the law defines 'land';

● the physical limits of land ownership;

● the classification of rights relating to land into proprietary and personal rights;

● the organisation of proprietary rights to land into estates and interests;

● how the law treats personal rights to use land.

28.1 The study of land law is the study of the law relating to the rights and interests (ie 'bundles of rights') which people may have in respect of land. It deals with the nature of these rights and interests and with how they are created, transferred to other people, and enforced against them. Theoretically, when speaking of land being bought, sold or valued, we are not referring to the physical entity itself, but rather to the abstract interests which people have in the property. However, although land law is, in principle, concerned with abstract rights and interests, its practical context of houses and flats, offices and shops, factories and farms should always be borne in mind when studying its rules.

28.2 Private[1] rights[2] to enter, use, occupy or own land can be infinitely variable in extent; they range from a short-lived permission for a child to come into a neighbour's garden to retrieve a ball, to a right to stay in a hotel for a week, to a right of way across neighbouring land, to a right to 'own' land either for a limited period or in perpetuity. Where all the elements of a contract are present[3], the law will enforce such rights as between the parties who created them. However, the doctrine of privity of contract[4] may confine enforcement to the contracting parties. This would be unsatisfactory in the context of land since the effective use and enjoyment of land often needs to be supported by rights which remain permanently enforceable. So, for example, if the only access to Whitelands is across part of Blacklands, it is essential that the right of access does not cease to be enforceable once the owner of Blacklands who first conferred the right of access either dies or ceases to own Blacklands.

For this reason, the law has long recognised that certain rights to land are 'proprietary' in nature, with the result that they are legally capable of being enjoyed by, and being enforced against, not simply those parties who first created the rights, but also future owners of the land to which they relate. It is with these proprietary rights that land law is largely concerned. However, we shall also briefly discuss non-proprietary, that is 'personal', rights to use land[5]. This not only helps to explain the distinction between proprietary and personal rights to land, it also demonstrates that personal rights to use land play an important practical role in the use and enjoyment of land.

[1] In this section we largely confine our discussion to private, as opposed to public, rights to enter land even though the latter (especially in the form of public rights of way) are of obvious importance in everyday life.

[2] We use the term 'rights' to distinguish a lawful presence on land as opposed to the illegal presence of a trespasser (as to which see ch 22 and para 28.41).

[3] See chs 4, 5 and 6.

[4] But note the effect of the Contract (Rights of Third Parties) Act 1999; see ch 14.

[5] See paras 28.41–28.45.

28.3 Proprietary interests in land may, broadly, be divided into two groups: those in respect of one's own land and those in respect of land belonging to another person. The former category we shall call 'ownership interests'; it may be further divided into that which in effect gives absolute ownership of the land, popularly referred to as the freehold interest, and those which give rise to a more limited ownership, of which the main modern example is the leasehold interest. The two main ownership interests are the freehold and the leasehold; although other forms of ownership can exist, there are rarely encountered today. These ownership interests may be enjoyed by a single owner or concurrently with other owners.[1]

As well as these ownership interests, a person may have interests in respect of land which is owned by another. These are usually referred to as 'third party' rights. Examples of such interests include a private right of way over neighbouring land (a species of easement[2]), a right to prevent a neighbour building on his land (an example of a restrictive covenant[3]), or a mortgage on land granted as security for a loan to its owner.[4]

[1] Chapter 31.

[2] Chapter 32.

[3] Chapter 33.

[4] Chapter 34.

28.4 What makes land law a subject of some complexity, and what makes buying and selling interests in land potentially more complicated than buying and selling a car is that it is usual for a number of interests to exist simultaneously in respect of one piece of land. For example, A may have a freehold interest in the property, and, at the same time, B may have a 21-year lease of the property. Meanwhile X, a neighbour, may have the benefit of a covenant restricting development on the property, Y may have a private right of way across it and Z may have a mortgage on A's freehold interest. The rules of land law are concerned with the extent of the rights enjoyed by each of these various people and with the protection of those rights, particularly in the event of the freehold of the land in question being sold.

What is land?

28.5 For a whole variety of reasons it may be crucial to know what exactly the law means by 'land'. For example, unlike most other contracts, contracts for the sale or disposition of an interest in 'land' must be in writing[1]. 'Land' is protected by the tort of trespass for which it is not necessary to prove damage[2]; while this strict protection has caused problems in the past over essential access to carry out repairs[3], it has also proved useful elsewhere, notably in the airspace cases considered at para 28.16 below. The meaning of 'land' is also important because items which are treated as part of land[4] will be included in a contract for the sale or lease of land and pass to the purchaser or tenant on a conveyance of land unless expressly excluded[5], and will form part of the security where land is mortgaged[6]. Furthermore, the question of whether or not an item is 'land' will dictate whether or not it can be the subject matter of a lease[7] and its treatment under the taxation regime.[8]

1 Law of Property (Miscellaneous Provisions) Act 1989; para 29.2.
2 See para 22.1.
3 See para 22.6.
4 See paras 28.8-28.14.
5 Law of Property (Miscellaneous Provisions) Act 1989 s 2, Law of Property Act 1925 (LPA 1925), s 62.
6 This was the issue in *TSB Bank plc v Botham* [1996] EGCS 149, CA: see para 28.11.
7 See *Chelsea Yacht & Boat Co Ltd v Pope* [2001] 2 All ER 409, CA and para 28.9.
8 See *Melluish (Inspector of Taxes) v BMI (No 3) Ltd* [1995] 4 All ER 453, HL.

General definition of land

28.6 Both common law[1] and statute[2] accept that the expression 'land' covers more than just the surface of the earth. Not only does 'land' include airspace and subsoil, it also includes physical things attached to it such as structures, buildings, fixtures and things growing naturally on the land (which we consider in the following paragraphs). Furthermore, in addition to these physical elements, 'land' also refers to intangible ('incorporeal') rights to use or restrict the use of the land such as easements; these we consider later.

1 *Mitchell v Mosley* [1914] 1 Ch 438, CA.
2 LPA 1925, s 205(1)(ix).

Physical extent

28.7 The notion that 'the grant of land includes the surface and all that is [above]— houses, trees and the like— ... and all that is [below], ie mines, earth, clay, etc'[1], is beyond doubt[2]. On this basis, in *Grigsby v Melville*,[3] where the conveyance to the claimant of his semi-detached house was of 'all that dwelling-house and premises situate on the west side of Church Hill', it was held that the claimant acquired ownership of the cellar beneath his house, even though it could not be reached from the house but only from the adjoining property. He became owner of all the land above and below the surface.

That said, this principle that ownership of land extends above and below its surface is, as we shall see, subject to important limitations[4]. Furthermore, it does not prevent an owner from expressly splitting up the land by means of horizontal boundaries[5], as may occur where the ownership of a building is divided, by floor, into separate office units or into individual flats. However, as we shall see, while English law has no problem with the theory of stratified ownership, it has until recently found it impossible to accommodate the many practical problems which flow from the horizontal division of land[6]. For this reason a stratified freehold title (often referred to as a 'flying freehold') has been virtually unknown and the ownership of horizontally divided land has invariably been conferred by way of a long lease. This is now set to change. The Commonhold and Leasehold Reform Act 2002 has introduced a new form of stratified freehold ownership known as commonhold; this is designed to replace the use of the long lease as a mechanism for the ownership of parts of buildings, especially but not exclusively in the context of residential properties.[7]

1 *Mitchell v Mosley* [1914] 1 Ch 438, CA.
2 *Bocardo SA v Star Energy UK Onshore Ltd* [2009] EWCA Civ 579.
3 [1973] 3 All ER 455, CA.
4 See paras 28.15–28.20.

⁵ Law of Property Act 1925, s 205(1)(ix). It may, of course, not always be easy to decide exactly where those horizontal boundaries are located; see *Davies v Yadegar* [1990] 1 EGLR 71, CA and para 28.23.

⁶ See para 33.4.

⁷ The commonhold aspects of Commonhold and Leasehold Reform Act 2002 came into force on 27 September 2004; see further para 28.35 and 34.5.

Artificial things brought onto land

28.8 *Classification* It has been held by the House of Lords[1] that items brought onto land fall into one of three categories. They either become part and parcel of the land, or they are fixtures (in which case they are treated as part of the land), or they remain as chattels (goods) and are, therefore, regarded as quite separate from the land[2].

¹ *Elitestone Ltd v Morris* [1997] 2 All ER 513, HL. In many instances there is no practical consequence of the distinction between an item that becomes part and parcel of the land and one that is a fixture. However, this is not always the case; for example, an item attached to property by a tenant which becomes part and parcel of the land cannot be removed. As we shall see in para 28.13, tenants, on leaving the property, are allowed to remove many of the fixtures which they have attached to the property during the course of the lease.

² While the ownership of chattels is, in principle, quite separate from that of the land on which they happen to be located, where the ownership of a chattel is unknown, there are circumstances in which the landowner may have first claim; see para 28.18.

28.9 *Items which are part and parcel of land* Whether or not something becomes part and parcel of the land is 'as much a matter of common sense as precise analysis'[1]. So, in *Elitestone Ltd v Morris*[2] the House of Lords decided that a wooden bungalow resting on, but not attached to, concrete pillars had become part of the land. As a dwelling house, which the evidence showed could not be removed and re-erected elsewhere without destroying it, it must, objectively, be regarded as having been intended to serve a permanent purpose. It did not matter that the bungalow was not physically attached to the land, nor was it relevant that the parties themselves believed that the bungalow was owned separately from the site on which it stood. By way of contrast, a building which is designed to be taken apart and re-assembled elsewhere will retain its character as a chattel[3]; equally, an item such as a houseboat which could readily be moved somewhere else, will not be regarded either as part and parcel of the land or as a fixture[4].

¹ Lord Lloyd in *Elitestone Ltd v Morris* [1997] 2 All ER 513, HL.

² [1997] 2 All ER 513, HL.

³ See *Potton Developments Ltd v Thompson* [1998] NPC 49 where it was held that portable units of bedroom accommodation erected at a public house had not become part of the land but remained chattels; the units had been put together off-site, transported by lorry and put in place by crane and could be removed in the same way.

⁴ See *Chelsea Yacht & Boat Co Ltd v Pope* [2001] 2 All ER 409, CA where it was held that a houseboat which, although attached to its mooring and having connected services, was not regarded as part and parcel of the land because it was designed to, and could readily be, moved.

28.10 *Fixtures* Whether or not an item brought onto land is a fixture is important. For example, an owner who has contracted to sell land cannot thereafter remove any fixture that has not been specifically excluded from the sale[1]. Similarly, if a property is subject to a mortgage, any fixtures added either before or after the date of the mortgage form part of the security.

Whether something on land is a fixture and thus treated as part of the land depends on all the circumstances. Two factors are particularly important: the degree of annexation and the purpose of annexation[2] (or, in other words, how securely the thing is attached to the land and the reasons behind its being attached). The law appears to be that if something is fixed to the land it is presumed to be land, and the more firmly it is fixed the stronger this presumption becomes. However, this presumption may be rebutted by evidence that it was not the intention behind fixing the thing to the land that it should become a permanent part of the land. For example, a poster pinned to the wall of a student's room would not be intended to become a permanent part of the land, and would not be a 'fixture'. If an item is resting on land by its own weight it is presumed to retain its own independent character and not to become part of the land, although this may be rebutted by evidence of intention. It is important to note that intention must be objectively assessed; the fact that parties may have agreed that an item is a chattel will be ignored by the courts in assessing whether or not it is a fixture.[3]

[1] This does not prevent the parties agreeing that an item which is a fixture may nevertheless be removed; see para 28.12 below.

[2] *Holland v Hodgson* (1872) LR 7 CP 328.

[3] See *Elitestone v Morris* [1997] 2 All ER 513, HL; *Melluish (Inspector of Taxes) v BMI (No 3) Ltd* [1995] 4 All ER 453, HL.

28.11 Illustrations of whether a chattel fixed to the land has retained its chattel nature or has become a fixture are provided by the following cases. *Leigh v Taylor*[1] concerned tapestries which were put on the walls of a house by being fixed to a framework of wood and canvas which was nailed to the walls, each tapestry then being surrounded by a moulding, itself attached to the wall. The House of Lords held that the tapestries did not become part of the land but remained chattels, since the reason they were fixed to the wall was so that they might be better enjoyed as chattels; this meant that they had not passed to the purchaser on the sale of the property. The case of *TSB Bank plc v Botham*[2] provided the court with a rare opportunity to consider whether a range of modern household items were fixtures or chattels. Here a lender was seeking to sell a re-possessed flat and needed to know what could be included in the sale as part of its security. The Court of Appeal ruled that fitted kitchen units and bathroom fittings (taps, showerheads, towel rails etc) were fixtures; all were necessarily attached to the property to enable those rooms to be used for their respective purposes. On the other hand, the following items were all considered to be chattels: fitted carpets, curtains, light fittings which were not part of the electrical installation, gas and electric fires, a 'slot-in' electric cooker, a plumbed-in washing machine and a refrigerator. Although all of these were in some way attached to the property, they could all be detached or disconnected without doing any damage to the fabric of the building. Furthermore, the purpose for which they were attached to the property was to enable the items themselves to function.

In contrast, in *Reynolds v Ashby & Son*,[3] the House of Lords held that machines which were let into concrete beds in the floor of a factory and fixed by nuts and bolts, but which could be removed without difficulty, became fixtures, since the purpose of annexation was to complete and use the building as a factory. Similarly, in *Aircool Installations v British Telecommunications*,[4] it had to be decided whether air-conditioning equipment had become a fixture. The internal units were bolted to the walls and were linked by pipework to external units which simply rested on their own weight; the system could have been removed and installed elsewhere. The court was nevertheless satisfied that the equipment had become a fixture. It was physically attached to the premises and the purpose of the annexation was manifestly for the better enjoyment of the building to which it was fixed.

It should also be noted that, on occasion, things not attached to land and resting purely by their own weight may, nevertheless, be treated as fixtures. Where items form part of a carefully integrated garden or interior design this may be treated as evidence of an overwhelming intention that they should form a permanent part of the land despite the absence of any physical attachment.[5]

¹ [1902] AC 157, HL.
² [1996] EGCS 149, CA.
³ [1904] AC 466, HL.
⁴ [1995] CLY 821.
⁵ See *D'Eyncourt v Gregory* (1866) LR 3 Eq 382 (statues forming part of a landscaping scheme); *Hamp v Bygrave* [1983] 1 EGLR 174 (a collection of co-ordinated garden ornaments).

28.12 While the legal principles governing the distinction between fixtures and chattels are relatively straightforward, their day to day application is notoriously difficult. The potential for disputes, especially on the sale of property, is well recognised. For this reason it has become usual, as part of the National Conveyancing Protocol[1], for the vendor and purchaser to agree, prior to the exchange of contracts, a list of which items are to be taken by the vendor and which are to be left for the purchaser. This is then incorporated into the contract and, in so far as any item is, objectively speaking, a fixture, there is an agreement that it can be removed by the vendor.

¹ The Law Society's definitive guide to best practice in domestic conveyancing.

28.13 *Fixtures added by a tenant* In principle it is immaterial who paid for or who previously owned items which have become fixtures. Accordingly, fixtures added by a tenant under a lease are treated as part of the land and are therefore regarded as belonging to the freeholder, who has absolute ownership of the land. However, in practice, the effect of this last rule is modified in many instances since it has long been recognised that it operates as a disincentive, particularly for tenants who use premises for commercial purposes. Accordingly, when leaving the premises at the end of a lease, a tenant is permitted[1] to remove any domestic or ornamental fixtures[2] that they have attached and which can be removed without substantial[3] damage to the fabric of the building, together with any fixtures[2] which they have attached for the purposes of their business.[4]

¹ Unless the lease clearly and unequivocally excludes the right to remove fixtures: see *Lambourn v McLellan* [1903] 2 Ch 268, CA.
² The right of removal attaches only to fixtures, not to items which have become part and parcel of the land: see para 28.9.
³ In *Young v Dalgety plc* [1987] 1 EGLR 116 it was held that light fittings could be removed by a tenant even though this would cause minor damage. Such minor damage as is caused must be made good so as to leave the premises in a reasonable condition: see *Mancetter Developments Ltd v Garmanson Ltd* [1986] 1 All ER 449, CA.
⁴ The common law did not allow farm tenants to remove agricultural (as opposed to trade) fixtures. The right of a tenant of an agricultural holding to remove agricultural fixtures is governed by the Agricultural Holdings Act 1986, s 10. The right of a tenant under a farm business tenancy to remove *any* fixture is governed by the Agricultural Tenancies Act 1995, s 8.

Things growing on the land

28.14 Things which grow naturally on the land such as grass, plants and trees which, though they may need attention when first planted, do not need attention each year to produce a crop, such as apple trees, are known as *fructus naturales* and are regarded as part of the land. On the other hand, cultivated crops, such as wheat and potatoes, which are known as *fructus industriales*, are not regarded as part of the land.

Limitations on the physical extent of a landowner's rights

28.15 We saw in para 28.7 that land includes not only the surface but also what is above and what is below the surface and that, on the face of it, the rights of a landowner extend over all the land as so defined. However, this must not be regarded as a rigid legal definition of land but rather as being a somewhat imprecise expression of the rights of a landowner[1]. While the principle at least makes it clear that the rights of a landowner normally extend above and below the surface, it is obviously fanciful to treat it as meaning that the landowner's rights literally extend upwards to the heavens and downwards to the centre of the earth, a notion which would lead to the absurdity of a trespass at common law being committed every time a satellite passes over a suburban garden.[2] On the other hand, the limits which may realistically be put on the height and depth to which the landowner's rights extend are not easy to determine. Those which can be identified will be dealt with briefly here.

¹ *Railways Comr v Valuer-General* [1974] AC 328, [1973] 3 All ER 268, PC.
² *Bernstein v Skyviews and General Ltd* [1977] 2 All ER 902 at 907.

Airspace

28.16 We have suggested in para 22.2, that, following *Bernstein v Skyviews and General Ltd*,[1] the rights of a landowner as regards the airspace above the surface of the land are restricted to such a height as is necessary for the ordinary use and enjoyment of the land and the structures on it. However, this begs the question of how high that is in any particular case. This means that whether or not a trespass to airspace has been committed in any particular instance depends on the facts of each case. However, it seems likely that, whenever the intrusion emanates from an over-hanging structure on adjoining land such as a building or tower crane, this will virtually always constitute a trespass[2]. However, intrusion into the airspace by a flying object, such as a hot air balloon, will not, of itself, amount to trespass[3]. Furthermore, statute ensures that the ordinary overflight of civil aircraft at a reasonable height is not a trespass[4]; however, this immunity will not apply to extraordinary activities such as unwarranted surveillance[5].

¹ [1977] 2 All ER 902.
² See, for example, *Anchor Brewhouse Developments Ltd v Berkley House (Docklands Developments) Ltd* [1987] 2 EGLR 173 in which it was held that a trespass occurred where the jib of a tower crane 'oversailed' neighbouring land.
³ *Pickering v Rudd* (1815) 4 Camp 219.
⁴ Civil Aviation Act 1982, s 76(1).
⁵ In *Bernstein v Skyviews and General Ltd* [1977] 2 All ER 902 it was held that the statutory immunity applied to a flight at a reasonable height involving ordinary commercial aerial photography.

Minerals

28.17 The conventional view is that the landowner's rights do indeed extend to the earth's core, and as mining techniques have improved this can be of practical importance. It certainly constitutes a trespass to tunnel into adjoining land to exploit minerals.[1] In *Bocardo SA v Star Energy UK Onshore Ltd*[2] it was made clear that, unlike the position with regard to airspace, a trespass to the substrata occurs irrespective of whether the landowner's use and enjoyment is affected. Although the general rule is that minerals are part of the soil and thus belong to the owner of the surface, there are exceptions, of which the following are examples. All gold and silver in gold and silver mines belong to the Crown; therefore such a mine cannot be worked by an individual even on their own land without a licence from the Crown.[3] Oil and natural gas in underground strata belong to the Crown.[4] Coal is vested in the Coal Authority[5]. It should also be borne in mind that, even where a landowner does own minerals, planning permission is required in order to be able to extract them[6].

¹ See *Bulli Coal Mining Co v Osborne* [1899] AC 351, PC.
² [2009] EWCA Civ 579.

[3] *A-G v Morgan* [1891] 1 Ch 432, CA.

[4] Petroleum Act 1998, ss 1(a), 2(1).

[5] Coal Industry Act 1994, ss 1(1), 7(3); a licence granted under this Act does not confer any right to drill under neighbouring land. Such a right can be compulsorily acquired under s 1 of the Mines (Working Facilities and Support) Act 1966 and it is against the background of the compensation provisions of this Act that any damages for trespass will be assessed, see *Bocardo SA v Star Energy UK Onshore Ltd* [2009] EWCA Civ 579.

[6] Town and Country Planning Act 1990, s 55(1); see para 39.2.

Things found on or under the land

28.18 In the absence of evidence as to their true owner, the law presumes that a land-owner in possession of the land, is entitled as against the finder to:

- things fixed or buried in the land[1];

- things on the land *where the landowner obviously intends to exercise control over the property and the things in it;*[2] and

- things on the land where the finder is a trespasser.[2]

However, finds of 'treasure'[3] belong to the Crown (or any franchisee of the Crown)[4] except where any rightful owner can be identified. Treasure may be returned to the landowner or finder;[5] this is likely to occur where the find is of little historical or archaeological significance. Where it is subsequently transferred by the Crown to a museum a reward may be payable to the finder, to the landowner on whose property the treasure was found, or may be shared between such persons.[6]

[1] *Waverley Borough Council v Fletcher* [1995] 4 All ER 756, CA is modern authority confirming the important distinction between items found *in* the land, and those found *on* the land. In the former case the landowner has the superior claim even in situations where he or she has no obvious intention to exercise control over the property and the things in it.

[2] *Parker v British Airways Board* [1982] QB 1004, [1982] 1 All ER 834, CA.

[3] 'Treasure' is widely defined in the Treasure Act 1996, s 1 with the aim of covering all finds of historical and archaeological importance; it is no longer confined to items of gold and silver, as was the case under the old law of treasure trove.

[4] Treasure Act 1996, s 4.

[5] Treasure Act 1996, s 6.

[6] Treasure Act 1996, s 10. The Code of Practice drawn up under s 11 of the Act clearly envisages that finders who were trespassing at the time of their find may receive either no reward at all, or a reduced reward.

Wild animals

28.19 Wild animals cannot, while alive, be owned but, once killed on the land, they become the property of the landowner,[1] whether killed by the landowner in the exercise of their common law right to kill and take wild animals found on their land[2], or by a trespasser such as a poacher.[3]

[1] *R v Townley* (1871) LR 1 CCR 315.

[2] Statute makes it an offence to kill certain wild animals: see, for example, Wildlife and Countryside Act 1981, s 9.

[3] *Blades v Higgs* (1865) 11 HL Cas 621.

Water

28.20 Water standing on the land in a pond or lake is part of the land and belongs to the landowner. Water percolating in undefined channels or flowing in defined channels through or past the land cannot be the subject of ownership but, although landowners do not own the water, they have certain rights in relation to it. The most important of these is the right of abstraction. The Water Resources Act 1991[1] s 24 lays down the general rule that the landowner may only abstract water from a 'source of supply' in pursuance of a licence obtained from the Environment Agency. Rivers, streams and water in underground strata all constitute 'sources of supply', as do those lakes, ponds or reservoirs which discharge into rivers or streams. However, a licence is not required for certain limited purposes.[2]

Where no Environment Agency licence is required, a landowner is quite at liberty to abstract water percolating in undefined channels through underground strata even if this prevents any reaching their neighbour's land.[3] There is no remedy for damage to neighbouring property caused by such abstraction.[4]

Where the owner of land contiguous with a river or stream (the riparian owner) needs no NRA licence for the proposed abstraction, common law still limits the amount that may be taken. The landowner is free to abstract what is needed for domestic purposes and for cattle without regard to the effect which this will have on landowners downstream,[5] but abstraction for other purposes (which must be connected with the land) is subject to the requirement that the water is put back in substantially the same volume and quality. The reason for this limitation is that at common law each riparian owner has the right to the flow of the river or stream unaltered in quantity and quality, and may enforce this right against owners upstream by an action in nuisance.[6] If water is abstracted in pursuance of an Environment Agency licence, the riparian owner has a defence to such an action.[7]

The riparian owner also has the right to fish in non-tidal waters, even where they are navigable rivers.[8]

[1] Which re-enacts the rules previously laid down in the Water Resources Act 1963, as amended by the Water Act 1989.

[2] Water Resources Act 1991, s 27.

[3] *Bradford Corpn v Pickles* [1895] AC 587, HL; para 15.11 above.

[4] *Langbrook Properties Ltd v Surrey County Council* [1969] 3 All ER 1424; *Stephens v Anglian Water Authority* [1987] 3 All ER 379, CA.

[5] *Miner v Gilmour* (1859) 12 Moo PCC 131.

[6] *John Young & Co v Bankier Distillery Co* [1893] AC 691, HL; *Tate and Lyle Industries Ltd v Greater London Council* [1983] 1 All ER 1159, HL.

[7] Water Resources Act 1991, s 48.

[8] *Cooper v Phibbs* (1867) LR 2 HL 149; *Pearce v Scotcher* (1882) 9 QBD 162, DC.

Demarcating the physical extent of land: boundaries

The general law

28.21 Clearly it is important for landowners to know the exact extent of their land, in order to know precisely what can be bought or sold, or to prevent neighbours encroaching, or to know how much space is available for building. As a matter of law a boundary is simply an imaginary line which marks the confines or line of division of two contiguous parcels of land; in practice, the location of a boundary is often marked by some physical object such as a wall, hedge or fence. Unfortunately, despite the obvious importance of ensuring that the line of the boundary is clearly delineated, this is often not achieved, with the result that the question remains to be settled after the property has been transferred, often as a result of a boundary dispute between neighbours.

28.22 When the title to land is first registered at the Land Registry[1], the land is generally described in the transfer deed merely as 'the land comprised in Title Number...', a form of words which thereby incorporates the verbal description of the land in the Property

Register of the register of title. This description normally gives only the postal address and refers to the title plan. Although this plan is an accurate Ordnance Survey plan, it has two drawbacks. First, it is small scale, usually on a scale of 1:1250 in urban areas and 1:2500 in rural areas[2]. Second, in law, it normally only fixes a 'general boundary' (in effect the land's location); it does not establish the exact line of the boundary[3]. Often, this causes no difficulty. The limits of the property are usually demarcated by a fence, wall or hedge which the adjoining owners never have cause to dispute. However, where the precise line of the boundary is for some reason crucial (eg where one of them needs to build right up to the edge of their land) the title plan may well not be sufficiently detailed, exact or authoritative.

In such cases the matter will have to be resolved either by agreement[4] or by litigation. In any legal proceedings the court will have regard to extrinsic evidence, such as the contract itself,[5] pre-registration deeds, auction particulars,[6] photographs and surveyors' oral evidence,[7] planning permission,[8] and any acts of ownership in relation to some boundary feature by one of the parties, such as the erection and maintenance of a boundary fence.

Occasionally, where there is no evidence as to the line of the boundary, the courts resort to certain rebuttable presumptions[9], which we consider in the following paragraphs.

[1] As to which see para 29.15.
[2] It should be noted that the Land Registry will always consider the use of a larger scale plan, notably where the topography of the land makes this desirable.
[3] Land Registration Act 2002, s 60.
[4] As to which, see para 28.27.
[5] *Spall v Owen* (1981) 44 P & CR 36.
[6] *Scarfe v Adams* [1981] 1 All ER 843, CA.
[7] *Mayer v Hurr* (1983) 49 P & CR 56, CA.
[8] *Stock v David Wilson Homes (Anglia)* [1993] NPC 83, CA.
[9] Ie rules which apply only in the absence of evidence to the contrary.

Presumptions

28.23 *Walls and floors* The outside of any external wall is presumed to be included in a sale or lease of the property[1]. Thus in one case[2] it was held to constitute trespass for a landlord to affix advertising hoardings to the outside wall of premises which he had let on the second floor of his property. As to where the legal boundary lies between two floors of a building, which have been separately let, it has been held that the ordinary expectation is that the lease entitles the tenant to occupy all the space between the floor of his flat and the underneath of the floor of the flat above.[3] Where a dispute concerns the upper boundary of a top floor flat, its resolution may require resort to general principles governing the ownership of airspace[4]. So, in *Davies v Yadegar*[5] it was held by the Court of Appeal that the tenant of a top floor flat was entitled to insert dormer windows into the roof above his flat. His lease, which had expressly included the roof and roof space, had not specified an upper boundary to his property and, consequently, he was a tenant not only of the flat but of the airspace above the flat, into which the proposed new windows could legitimately intrude.

[1] *Sturge v Hackett* [1962] 1 WLR 1257, CA.
[2] *Re Webb's Lease* [1951] Ch 808
[3] *Graystone Property Investments Ltd v Margulies* (1983) 47 P & CR 472, CA.
[4] See paras 28.7 and 28.16.
[5] [1990] 1 EGLR 71, CA. Note, however, that the circumstances may indicate that the airspace is not included even though the lease does include the roof, see *Rosebery Ltd v Rocklee Ltd* [2011] EWCA B1 (Ch).

28.24 *Hedges and ditches* Where parties are disputing the exact line of a boundary along which runs a hedge or bank together with a ditch, the presumption of the law is that the boundary runs along the edge of the ditch furthest from the hedge or bank. This presumption derives from the quaint notion that the ditch was originally dug by the landowner at the furthest edge of their land and then, to avoid trespass, the resulting earth was thrown back onto their own land thereby forming either a bank or ground in which a hedge was then planted.[1] This presumption only applies where there is a hedge (or bank) and a ditch together. It would appear to apply to registered land even though the title plan is based on the Ordnance Survey map on which boundaries are treated as running down the middle of any hedge.

[1] *Vowles v Miller* (1810) 3 Taunt 137. For more recent applications of the presumption see *Hall v Dorling* (1997) 74 P & CR 400, CA and *Alan Wibberley Building Ltd v Insley* [1999] 2 All ER 897, HL.

28.25 *Highways* It is presumed that, wherever land abuts a highway, the boundary line lies down the middle of the highway.[1] This presumption, which applies only where there is no other evidence as to the boundary, is easily rebutted, for example in the case of a building estate where the developer might intend to retain ownership of the roads for construction purposes and for dedication to the public. Where the highway has been adopted by the highway authority,[2] there vests in that authority the surface and so much above and below the surface as is necessary for the carrying out of their duties as highway authority; thus, in such cases the issue relates only to the ownership of the subsoil. In the case of registered land, it is not the practice of the Land Registry to show ownership of the subsoil where the highway is adopted.

[1] *Central London Rly Co v City of London Land Tax Comrs* [1911] 1 Ch 467 at 474.
[2] Ie under the Highways Act 1980.

28.26 *Rivers, etc* In the case of non-tidal rivers which form a boundary to land, it is presumed that the boundary runs down the middle of the river bed. The rights of fishing and abstraction, described in para 28.20, would therefore be divided midstream between opposite riparian owners. In the case of land bounded by a tidal river or by the seashore, the boundary lies at the medium high water mark, the foreshore being vested in the Crown. There appears to be no presumption to assist in determining the boundary where the land of several owners is bounded by a lake.

Alteration of boundaries

28.27 The line of a boundary may be altered by agreement of the parties. Since this will involve the transfer of land from one party to the other such an agreement should be by deed and completed by registration, so as to comply with the formalities required for the transfer of an interest in land[1]. Where, as is often the case, such formalities are not complied with, the courts may be able to give effect to the agreement by the operation of the doctrine of estoppel.[2] In recent times the Court of Appeal has, somewhat controversially, simply accepted that informal boundary agreements involving the transfer of small amounts of land are binding both on the parties who make them[3] and on subsequent owners[4] without any resort to the doctrine of proprietary estoppel.

The line of a boundary may also be changed by the alteration of the title register where the Land Registration Act applies,[5] or as a result of the rules relating to adverse possession (as where a landowner moves the boundary fence so as to incorporate some of the neighbouring land and remains in adverse possession for the requisite period).[6]

If a boundary dispute arises, it is possible that the parties may, informally, agree where the boundary between their properties lies. Such an agreement does not involve the transfer of any land and so it is not necessary for a deed to be used. However, it is likely that no consideration is provided with the result that the agreement has no contractual force.

Nevertheless, the courts will strive to give effect to the parties' intentions, either by resorting to the doctrine of estoppel,[7] or by treating the agreement as evidence of where the boundary lies. So, in *Davey v Harrow Corpn*,[8] where adjoining landowners had agreed to the erection of a post and wire fence along the boundary, the Court of Appeal ruled that this rebutted any presumption which might otherwise have been relevant in determining the boundary line between the two properties, which were separated by a hedge and a ditch but had been conveyed by reference to the Ordnance Survey map.

[1] See ch 29.
[2] As in *Hopgood v Brown* [1955] 1 All ER 550, CA. See further paras 30.11–30.15.
[3] *Joyce v Rigolli* [2004] EWCA Civ 79.
[4] *Haycocks v Neville* [2007] EWCA Civ 78.
[5] Paras 35.38–35.44.
[6] Paras 30.23–30.32.
[7] Paras 30.11–30.15.
[8] [1957] 2 All ER 305, CA.

Boundary structures

28.28 Obviously any boundary structure exclusively on one side of the boundary belongs to the owner of that side, even though the neighbour may have the right that it be maintained.[1] It may be that the owner of a boundary structure is unable to repair it (or other parts of his or her property) without going onto adjoining land. As we have seen, at common law, there is no automatic right of access for such purposes so that in the absence of an express right of access, or a temporary permission from the neighbour, the landowner would be committing a trespass which can be restrained by an injunction. This unsatisfactory state of affairs has been remedied by the Access to Neighbouring Land Act 1992.[2]

In practice many boundary structures straddle the line of the boundary. Irrespective of the nature of the structure it is known, in law, as a 'party wall'. In the ordinary case, party walls are regarded as being vertically severed, each side having the right to support from the other.[3]

The Party Wall etc Act 1996 provides a scheme under which works to existing party structures, the construction of new party structures, and excavations near to adjoining or neighbouring structures can be authorised and any disputes over such works resolved by a surveyor, without recourse to the courts.

[1] See para 32.12.
[2] Discussed at para 22.6.
[3] LPA 1925, s 38.

WHAT IS LAND?: KEY POINTS

- The law regards land as three dimensional; it therefore includes the surface, the airspace above and the subsoil below unless specifically subject to horizontal division (as occurs in a block of flats).

- Land also automatically includes certain items attached to, or located on, in or under it; the most important of these are buildings and permanent structures, fixtures, and things growing on land.

- Fixtures are items that are physically attached to the land or a building or structure on the land with the intention that they form a permanent part of it; the only fixtures that can be removed on the sale of the freehold are those that have been expressly excluded. Tenants' fixtures can be removed at the end of a lease.

- The physical extent of land is demarcated by a boundary the line of which may (or may not) be marked by a boundary feature such as a wall, fence or hedge.
- The exact line of a boundary is not necessarily that shown on the title plan; in boundary disputes the courts may have to look at other evidence or, as a last resort, apply legal presumptions.

Legal nature of proprietary rights to land

28.29 Having considered the legal nature of land and the physical extent of a landowner's rights, we now turn to a further discussion of those rights to occupy or use land which the law recognises as proprietary, rather than personal. These are rights that are legally capable of being enjoyed by, and being enforced against, not simply those parties who first created the rights, but also future owners of the land to which they relate. As we have mentioned[1] they can largely be categorised as either[2] 'ownership' interests, ie those which are enjoyed in respect of one's own land, or third party interests, ie those which are enjoyed in respect of land owned by another.

[1] See para 28.3.
[2] However a leasehold ownership interest is hybrid in nature. Although it confers on a tenant the right to exclusive possession of the land in question for the duration of the lease, the land to which a lease relates is also 'owned' by another, ie the landlord.

Ownership interests: estates and tenure

28.30 We start by addressing the nature of ownership interests in land. As a matter of legal theory, under English law, only the Crown can 'own' land[1]; individual subjects of the Crown merely 'hold' land from the Crown. This is the doctrine of tenure. While Crown land is held absolutely and in perpetuity, other land is held for a period of time. This 'holding' of land is categorised according to the length of time for which it will last, a notion which finds expression in the doctrine of *estates*. Thus, rather than speaking of owning land in perpetuity or for life, we speak of owning a particular 'estate'[2] in the land which will last for ever, or for the lifetime of its owner. We shall now briefly consider these two historical building blocks of English land law, the doctrine of *tenure* and the doctrine of *estates*.

[1] Land owned directly by the Crown is known as 'demesne' land.
[2] The term is here used in its technical land law sense, rather than as a synonym for 'land'.

Tenure

28.31 Feudalism, in which tenure (from the Latin, *tenere*, to hold) was the fundamental element, formed the basis of society after the Norman Conquest. The social structure was based on grants of land by the King (to whom all land was regarded as belonging as the spoils of victory) to his followers, not as theirs to own, but to 'hold of' him (or 'have possession of' from him) as their superior lord in return for their performing certain services, such as furnishing the King with armed horsemen or with provisions. These 'tenants-in-chief' in their turn granted some of this land to other 'tenants' to hold of them as superior lords in return for services, and so on. Each tenant,[1] then, held land in return for providing services to their lord. However, over time there was a decline in the practical significance of the system of tenure, with the benefits and obligations of tenure gradually disappearing, so that all that remains today is the legal theory that land is not owned outright but held of the Crown. That said, the theory remains alive; for example, there is a tenurial relationship between the landlord and tenant of a lease.

[1] We are here using the term 'tenant' in the feudal sense of someone who holds land by way of tenure, rather than in its modern connotation of someone who owns land by way of a lease.

Estates

28.32 Although we referred in the last paragraph to the tenant holding land, it is more accurate to speak of the tenant holding the land for a particular estate, ie having possession of the land for an interest of a particular duration. The two most important estates are popularly referred to as the freehold and the leasehold. Historically, the law recognised other estates, in particular the fee tail and the life estate; however, these are rarely encountered today and no further discussion of them is necessary[1].

[1] That said, readers may be more familiar with the fee tail (or entail) than they might suspect. The fee tail usually restricted the inheritance of land to the sons of the current owner. Viewers of the TV series *Downton Abbey* or readers of Jane Austen's *Pride and Prejudice* will be fully aware of the serious consequences, for the owner of entailed land, of producing only daughters!

28.33 *Freehold: the fee simple absolute in possession* The technical legal term for the freehold estate is the estate in fee simple absolute in possession[1]. The owner of a fee simple absolute in possession is equivalent to an absolute owner. He or she has the complete freedom to dispose of their rights to the land either during their lifetime or by will; in other words, the owner is completely free to transfer the land[2]. He or she can also carve lesser ownership interests out of the freehold, for example by granting a lease, and can grant rights over it (such as easements or mortgages) to others.

[1] LPA 1925, s 1.
[2] Subject to any statutory powers of compulsory acquisition.

28.34 *Freehold estate in commonhold land* The Commonhold and Leasehold Reform Act 2002[1] has introduced a new form of ownership—commonhold—which is designed to provide a form of landholding appropriate to those whose properties are necessarily interdependent. Classically it applies to the ownership of flats, but it should be appreciated that commonhold is not confined to residential properties. It is intended that commonhold will replace the use of the long lease as a method of dealing with the ownership of physically interdependent properties. Such leases have become increasingly unpopular and discredited, especially in the residential context. They are a wasting asset and thus, over time, become unmortgageable; furthermore, tenants often believe that landlords do not manage and maintain their buildings in an efficient and cost-effective way. Despite the alleged unpopularity of leasehold schemes, the take-up of commonhold has been disappointing; between 2004 and 11 June 2008 only 14 were registered[2].

It is possible to register a freehold[3] estate in land as being a freehold in commonhold land, provided that there is in place a memorandum of association of a commonhold association and a commonhold community statement ('CCS')[4]. Once the development is completed[5] and the first unit sold, the initial title is divided into what is effectively a community of freehold titles. The title to the common parts[6] is held by the commonhold association and the purchaser of each unit has a freehold title to that unit. Once the commonhold is active, only unit owners can be members of the commonhold association[7].

The CCS must define the units within the commonhold[8]; contain provisions governing the use, insurance, repair and maintenance of each unit[9]; and regulate the use of the common parts and oblige the commonhold association to insure, repair and maintain the common parts[10]. This new system is designed to ensure that unit holders have a freehold title (thus eliminating the problem of the wasting asset); that the use, repair and maintenance of both the units and the common parts are governed by provisions[11] contained in a single document (the CCS); and that the unit holders (as the only members of the commonhold association) are in charge of the management and maintenance of the common parts.

[1] The Commonhold and Leasehold Reform Act 2002 ('CLRA 2002') came into force on 27 September 2004.

[2] House of Lords Written Answers, 18 June 2008.

[3] Commonhold can exist only in relation to freehold land, CLRA 2002, s 1.

[4] CLRA 2002, s 1(1).

[5] It is possible to convert an existing leasehold scheme (of which there are very many) into a commonhold; however, the consent of all leaseholders holding a registered lease of more than 21 years, and all mortgagees is required, CLRA 2002 s 3(1). This is likely to block the conversion to commonhold of many existing large leasehold schemes. Hence it is likely that commonhold will tend to be confined to new developments and refurbishments and small leasehold schemes (where the required consents will be more readily obtainable).

[6] 'Common parts' are all parts of the commonhold which are not defined by the CCS as a commonhold unit, CLRA 2002, s 25(1).

[7] CLRA 2002, s 34, Sch 3.

[8] CLRA 2002, s 11(2). There must be at least two units.

[9] CLRA 2002, s 14.

[10] CLRA 2002, s 26.

[11] Which are likely to become standardised so that the provisions governing all commonholds will become very similar.

28.35 *Leasehold: the term of years absolute*[1] The leasehold interest is the second of the two estates recognised at law. The terminology used in the Law of Property Act 1925 (LPA 1925), s 1 for the leasehold interest is 'the term of years absolute'. This phrase need not detain us; it can be regarded as having no meaning other than to denote a leasehold interest. A person has a leasehold interest in land where another, the landlord or lessor, grants exclusive possession of property, as tenant or lessee, for a definite or certain period.[2]

The leasehold interest acquired by the tenant or lessee is known variously as a 'tenancy'—generally where it is of short duration, as in weekly, monthly or yearly tenancies—or as a 'lease', 'demise', 'term of years' or 'term certain'—generally where it is of longer, fixed, duration, perhaps of 21 or 99 years. Having granted a lease (or 'let', 'leased' or 'demised' the property) the landlord is said, somewhat inaccurately, to retain the 'reversion' on the lease, on the basis that physical possession of the land will revert on the ending of the lease. In the eyes of the law, of course, the landlord is still regarded as being in possession during the course of the lease because of the receipt of the rents and profits of the land.[3]

Since a leaseholder can usually[4] carve a further lease out of their own lease, there can be more than one lease in respect of the same piece of land. For example, A the freeholder may grant a 99-year lease of Whitelands to B and B then may grant a 10-year sub-lease to C. This means that, for the next 10 years C will actually occupy Whitelands and pay the rent fixed in the sub-lease to B; B will receive that rent from C and pay the rent agreed in the headlease to A. B's expectation will be that the rent he receives from C will exceed that which he has to pay to A. At the end of the 10 years B will become entitled to physical possession of Whitelands although he may, of course, choose either to renew the sub-lease to C or to grant an new sub-lease to D.

[1] Leaseholds interests are considered in more detail in chs 36 and 37.
[2] See paras 36.3–36.7.
[3] LPA 1925, s 205(1)(xix).
[4] The right to sublet may, however, be forbidden under the terms of a lease; see para 36.25.

Third party rights: interests in land

28.36 We have already mentioned[1] that the law recognises not only ownership rights in respect of land, but also rights which one person may have over land which belongs to another, such as private rights of way. Where such rights fall within certain legally defined categories[2] they are regarded as interests in land. Interests in land, which are usually referred to, somewhat confusingly, as 'third party' rights, are 'proprietary' in nature. This means that they are capable of binding future owners of the land to which they relate, in other words that future owners can be obliged to recognise such rights.[3]

[1] See para 28.3.
[2] The most important of which are dealt with in chs 32–34.
[3] The circumstances in which third party rights actually bind future owners are dealt with in ch 35.

Legal and equitable rights to land

28.37 The Law of Property Act 1925, s 1 distinguishes between legal estates and interests on the one hand, and equitable interests on the other. The freehold[1], or fee simple absolute in possession, and the leasehold, or term of years absolute, are now, by virtue of that section, the only estates that are able to exist at law. They are the two legal estates. Other forms of ownership, such as the life estate, which were formerly recognised by the law, today can only take effect as equitable interests (although they are rarely encountered today and are not further discussed).[2] The section also provides that only certain third party rights can exist at law[3]. The more important of these are easements[4] (rights of way, rights of support and the like) which have been granted for a period equivalent to a fee simple absolute in possession or term of years absolute, and charges by way of legal mortgage,[5] the most common device for mortgaging land. These are referred to as legal interests. Those third party rights which cannot take effect as legal interests now do so as equitable interests.

[1] Including its new variant, the freehold estate in commonhold land, see para 28.34.
[2] LPA 1925, s 1(3).
[3] LPA 1925, s 1(2), para 28.36.
[4] Chapter 32.
[5] Para 34.4.

What is an equitable interest?

28.38 An equitable interest is either (as explained in the previous paragraph) an interest which, after 1925,[1] can no longer exist at law, or it is one which is derived from the rules of equity (ie those principles of law which originated in the decisions of the former Court of Chancery[2]). As we shall see, apart from recognising rights for which the common law could find no place (such as restrictive covenants), equity was prepared to give effect to transactions which do not comply with the strict formalities demanded by the common law.[3] Whether a right is legal or equitable often makes little difference to its substance; however, the distinction can be crucial in determining its actual enforceability against future owners.[4]

[1] As a result of LPA 1925, s 1(3).
[2] Paras 1.5–1.8.

[3] Chapter 30.
[4] Chapter 35.

28.39 *The trust* One equitable concept which plays a particularly important part in the English law of property is that of the 'trust'. The idea which lies behind the trust is that of separating the management of property from the enjoyment of its benefits, such as possession of it and income from it. The device is said to have originated in the practice of those going on crusades of transferring their land to trusted friends to hold for the benefit of their wives and children while they were away, and in the practice of granting land to be held for the benefit of Franciscan friars who, by the rules of their Order, could not themselves hold land. In the eyes of the common law, only those to whom the land had been formally conveyed had rights in respect of it; those for whose benefit the land was supposed to have been held were viewed as having no rights. The Court of Chancery, however, took a very different approach, and recognised that the persons to whom the land was conveyed (who are today known as trustees) were in conscience bound to honour the trust placed in them. This court allowed those who were intended to benefit (who we now refer to as beneficiaries) to compel the trustees to permit them to use or take the income of the land. That the beneficiaries had these rights against the trustees effectively meant that the trustees had only the bare legal ownership of the land, whilst the beneficial ownership lay with the beneficiaries.

The trust has always been, and still is, used as a protective device under which the legal title and management responsibilities can be placed in the hands of an experienced and responsible trustee in order to guard the interests of a young and vulnerable (or, perhaps, not so young but irresponsible) beneficiary. However, it has always had other roles. From earliest times it was used as a pure conveyancing device. For example, it was possible to create a greater range of ownership rights in respect of the equitable interest in land than in the legal interest; further, it was possible to leave an equitable interest in land by will long before this was permitted at law. In more modern times, it became usual to create a trust of land where it was desired to give a number of different people ownership and other interests in the same piece of land, either in succession, or concurrently. In this way the legal title to the land, which would be held by a limited number of trustees, could be kept relatively straightforward; the complex equitable interests being kept 'behind' the trust. This latter use of the trust was greatly extended by the 1925 property legislation and is a topic to which we return in Chapter 31. Finally, equity has come to employ the trust as a means of compelling a common law owner of land, in appropriate circumstances, to hold 'his' or 'her' land for the benefit of another. So, for example, as we shall see,[1] where land is conveyed to A alone but B has contributed to the purchase price, equity may insist that A holds the land on trust for himself and B.

[1] See para 30.9.

THE LEGAL NATURE OF PROPRIETARY RIGHTS: KEY POINTS

- Proprietary rights to land are those that the law recognises as being enforceable not only by the parties who created them but also by and against future owners of the land to which they relate.

- Proprietary rights can be broadly categorised as either 'ownership' rights (which confer a right to the exclusive possession of the land) or 'third party' rights (which confer some sort of entitlement to land that is owned by another).

> - Modern ownership rights (ie 'estates') are either freehold (of which commonhold is a species) or leasehold; freehold effectively confers permanent ownership rights whilst a leasehold is time limited.
>
> - Proprietary rights can either be legal (ie recognised by the common law) or equitable (ie recognised only by equity); some interests, notably restrictive covenants, can only be equitable.
>
> - Whether or not a particular right is legal or equitable makes no difference to its substance; it does have a significant effect on its enforceability against future owners.

Personal rights to use land: licences

28.40 Owners of land are free to confer on others a right to use their land which does not amount to an interest in land. Such rights, although infinitely variable in content, are collectively known as 'licences'. The classic definition of a licence relating to land states that a licence passes no interest in the land but only makes lawful what would otherwise be unlawful.[1] It would appear, then, that a licence to enter on, or to occupy, property is a personal arrangement between the licensor and the licensee under which the licensee acquires no interest in the property. If a licence creates no property interest but is dependent on the permission of the licensor, why is the topic of licences included in the study of land law? First, because occupation of land by virtue of a licence has been common as a substitute for occupation by virtue of a tenancy, as a means of avoiding legislation which protects the rights of tenants[2], so that the courts have frequently been called upon to draw the fine line between a licence (which is not a property interest) and a lease (which is).[3] Second, because the courts may, in certain circumstances, recognise certain types of use and occupation of land which are, on the face of it, enjoyed merely by licence as having proprietary characteristics, in particular that of being enforceable against subsequent owners of the land.[4]

Most licences fall into one of the following two categories:

- gratuitous licences (sometimes referred to as 'bare' licences); or
- contractual licences.

The characteristics and nature of these types of licence will be discussed in the following paragraphs.

[1] *Thomas v Sorrell* (1673) Vaugh 330 at 351.
[2] Eg Housing Act 1988, Landlord and Tenant Act 1954.
[3] See paras 36.9 and 36.11.
[4] Paras 30.8–30.18.

Gratuitous licences

28.41 A gratuitous licence is, in essence, a permission to be on land for which no consideration[1] has been provided. The guest whom you invite to dinner has, when arriving, a gratuitous licence to be on your property. Your neighbour's young son, who with your permission enters your garden to retrieve his ball, is a gratuitous licensee. A householder who lives in a dwelling-house which has a path through the front garden to the street and does not keep the gate locked, is treated as giving an implied licence to any member of the public who has a lawful reason for doing so to proceed from the gate to the front door, and to inquire whether they may be admitted to conduct their lawful business.[2] Although most gratuitous licences are of the relatively trivial variety just mentioned, it should be remembered that this category is a residual one; consequently any licence not falling within one of the other categories is a gratuitous licence.[3]

In each of the above examples the right of the licensee to be on the land is dependent entirely on the permission, express or implied, of the landowner/licensor. Without that permission, the licensee would be a trespasser. Normally, the licensee has no right to prevent the revocation of the licence and the landowner may revoke the permission to be on the land at any time[2]. A withdrawal of permission does not mean that the licensee immediately becomes a trespasser. The law allows a reasonable time to leave the premises; what is reasonable will vary according to the circumstances of the case.[3]

Clearly a gratuitous licence, being entirely dependent on the permission of the landowner, is neither assignable by the licensee nor, in the absence of additional factors, enforceable against successors of the licensor.[4]

[1] See para 6.5.
[2] However, there are circumstances in which equity will prevent the revocation of a gratuitous licence; these are discussed at paras 30.8–30.18.
[3] *Robson v Hallett* [1967] 2 All ER 407 at 414.
[4] See, for example, *Horrocks v Forray* [1976] 1 All ER 737; but note para 28.45.

Contractual licences

Nature

28.42 A licence to enter land is a contractual licence if it is conferred by contract; hence, unless a deed is used, consideration must have been provided for the permission to be on the land. It is immaterial whether the right to enter the land is the primary purpose of the contract or is merely secondary.[1] An example of the former would be a contractual licence to hire a room for a function, or to occupy a room in a house as a lodger. (As we shall see,[2] in neither of these cases does the occupier have exclusive possession, hence there is no tenancy, merely a licence.) An example of a licence conferred as a secondary object of a contract is provided by *Hounslow London Borough Council v Twickenham Garden Developments Ltd*,[3] in which the primary object of the contract was that the defendants should build a housing estate for the claimants; it was held that this necessarily conferred on the defendants a licence to enter the site.

Not surprisingly, in order for a contractual licence to be valid, it must be shown that the essential requirements of a contract are present. In certain cases where there has been no express agreement between the parties, the courts have been able to discern the presence of the requirements of a contract and thereby imply the existence of a contractual licence between the parties. In *Chandler v Kerley*[4], the Court of Appeal was satisfied that an arrangement under which the defendant, a former co-owner of the property, agreed to sell it to the claimant for two-thirds of the asking price on the understanding that she and her children could continue to live there, amounted to a contractual licence. However, it is often impossible, particularly in a family context, to infer the necessary ingredients of a contract, notably any intention to create legal relations. So, in *Horrocks v Forray*,[5] the court was unable to treat an arrangement between a man and his mistress, whereby the former had for many years provided accommodation for the latter, as a contractual licence. In the absence of any additional factors[6] she was regarded as having only a gratuitous licence and could not resist his executors' claim for possession of the house in which she lived.

[1] *Hounslow London Borough Council v Twickenham Garden Developments Ltd* [1970] 3 All ER 326 at 343.

[2] Para 36.9.

[3] [1970] 3 All ER 326.

[4] [1978] 2 All ER 942, CA.

[5] [1976] 1 All ER 737, CA.

[6] Paras 30.8–30.18.

Revocability

28.43 A contractual licence is not an entity distinct from the contract which brings it into being, but merely a provision of that contract.[1] Thus the extent to which the licensor is free to revoke the licence depends on the terms, express or implied, of the contract. It is a question of construction of the particular contract whether a purported revocation by the licensor is or is not in breach of contract.[2] In the absence of express terms there is no general rule as to the revocability of a contractual licence,[3] although (where there is no other evidence of the parties' intentions) it appears that the courts will readily imply a term that the licence is revocable on reasonable notice being given;[4] what is 'reasonable' depends on the circumstances of the case.

Where a licensor purports to revoke the licence in breach of contract the licensee has a contractual right to remain on the property despite the wrongful revocation by the licensor. The licensee cannot be treated as a trespasser[5] and, if forcibly removed as a trespasser, may sue for damages for assault.[6] If it is practicable for the licensee to seek the assistance of the court, an injunction may be obtained to prevent any eviction or, in a case where the licensor refuses entry in the first place, an order of specific performance.[7] However, these orders are available only at the discretion of the court, and, for example, the court will not specifically enforce an agreement for two people to live peaceably under the same roof.[8] A licensee who cannot obtain a court order enforcing the contractual licence, either because in the circumstances it is not practicable for one to be sought,[9] or because the licence is not regarded as specifically enforceable, must, unless peaceable entry to the property can be achieved, accept the termination of the licence as a fait accompli and sue for damages for breach of contract.

[1] *Hounslow London Borough Council v Twickenham Garden Developments Ltd* [1970] 3 All ER 326 at 343.

[2] *Millennium Productions Ltd v Winter Garden Theatre (London) Ltd* [1946] 1 All ER 678, CA; rvsd sub nom *Winter Garden Theatre (London) Ltd v Millennium Productions Ltd* [1947] 2 All ER 331, HL.

[3] *Australian Blue Metal Ltd v Hughes* [1963] AC 74 at 99.

[4] *Winter Garden Theatre (London) Ltd v Millennium Productions Ltd* [1947] 2 All ER 331, HL; *Chandler v Kerley* [1978] 2 All ER 942, CA.

[5] *Winter Garden Theatre (London) Ltd v Millennium Productions Ltd* [1947] 2 All ER 331, HL.

[6] See *Hurst v Picture Theatres Ltd* [1915] 1 KB 1, CA.

[7] *Verrall v Great Yarmouth Borough Council* [1980] 1 All ER 839, CA.

[8] *Thompson v Park* [1944] 2 All ER 477 at 479.

[9] As where a customer is evicted from a theatre performance, or from a restaurant.

Enforceability against third parties

28.44 In principle, the modern view that a contractual licence has no existence independent of the contract which creates it[1] means that the licensee's contractual right to remain on land cannot be enforced against a successor of the licensor; the arrangement between licensor and licensee is a personal contractual arrangement giving the licensee no interest in the land capable of binding the third party.[2] Thus, for example, the occupier of a university hall of residence room under a contractual licence could not insist on remaining in the hall if it is sold by the university to a third party; the only remedy would lie in damages against the licensor.[3] It follows that, although a person may enjoy under the terms of a contractual licence rights which appear to be very similar to a lease or easement, the contractual licence does not possess that most important characteristic of an interest in land, that of being capable of binding third parties. This is confirmed by the decision of the Court of Appeal in *Ashburn Anstalt v Arnold*,[4] where it was held that a mere contractual licence to occupy land is not binding on a purchaser of the land even where the latter has notice of the licence. In reaching this decision, the Court of Appeal held that its earlier decision in *Errington v Errington and Woods*,[5] in which the contrary view was taken, could not stand with the decisions of the Court of Appeal in *Clore v Theatrical Properties Ltd*[6] and of the House of Lords in *King v David Allen & Sons Billposting Ltd*.[7]

However, there are instances in which the courts have been prepared to enforce the rights of both gratuitous and contractual licensees against a subsequent purchaser.[8] The devices used include the doctrine of proprietary estoppel and the constructive trust. These are discussed more fully at paras 30.8–30.18.

[1] Para 28.43.
[2] *Clore v Theatrical Properties Ltd* [1936] 3 All ER 483, CA.
[3] *King v David Allen & Sons Billposting Ltd* [1916] 2 AC 54, HL.
[4] [1988] 2 All ER 147, CA.
[5] [1952] 1 All ER 149, CA, 36.
[6] [1936] 3 All ER 483.
[7] [1916] 2 AC 54.
[8] See, for example, *Inwards v Baker* [1965] 1 All ER 446, CA.

PERSONAL RIGHTS TO USE LAND (LICENCES): KEY POINTS

- Personal rights to use land (known as licences) are either gratuitous or contractual and are normally only enforceable between the parties who created them.

- Gratuitous licences can be withdrawn at any time with the result that the licensee becomes a trespasser.

- A contractual licence can only be revoked in accordance with the terms of the contract and a court will, where appropriate, prevent a licensor from wrongly terminating it.

- Only in very exceptional circumstances will a court treat a future owner as being bound by a licence, usually under the principles of proprietary estoppel or constructive trust (as to which see later).

Questions

1. What is included in the legal definition of 'land'?

2. How is a landowner's property demarcated and how are disputes over its extent resolved?

3. How are rights to land classified?

4. What is the distinction between proprietary and personal rights to land?

5. What, in modern times, are the major forms of ownership?

6. What is a trust?

7. What are licences and to what extent can they be legally enforced?

29

The formal acquisition of rights to land

CHAPTER OVERVIEW

Statute requires that, when disposing of land, certain formalities must be complied with. In this chapter, we consider:

- the formalities applying to contracts for the sale or other disposition of land;
- the formalities with which the actual transfer or creation of legal or equitable rights to land must comply;
- the circumstances in which the transfer or creation of legal rights to land must be completed by registration at the Land Registry;
- the current proposals relating to the introduction of electronic conveyancing; and
- the typical process of negotiating and then transferring the ownership of freehold land from one person to another.

29.1 The context in which most people experience the operation of land law is that of the transfer or creation of rights to land. The most commonly encountered transactions relate to ownership rights such as the transfer of freehold ownership, the transfer (technically 'assignment') of the remainder of an existing lease, or the creation of a new lease. As part and parcel of any of these arrangements it will be usual for lesser *interests* in land such as easements or mortgages to be transferred or created, although such interests can, of course, be created quite independently of any transfer of ownership.

Many land transactions can, legally speaking, be broken down into three stages:

- a binding agreement to carry out the agreed deal (the contract);
- the actual creation or transfer of the interest in land (the conveyance or transfer); and
- registration at the Land Registry (where necessary).

As we shall see, the contract and the conveyance or transfer must *each* comply with *different* formal requirements; registration is applied for by the purchaser (or lessee or assignee where appropriate) and is effected by the Land Registry.

Not surprisingly, the common law always demanded that the *actual disposition* of interests in land should comply with strict formalities; however, these rules have long been enshrined in statutory provisions.[1] Furthermore, ever since the 17th century, legislation has dictated that *contracts* for the sale or other disposition of land should also satisfy formal requirements, albeit that these are different from those required for actual dispositions.[2] In practice, given the importance of such transactions to those involved, these formalities are normally observed, if only because it is usual for the parties to employ legal advisers. However, in those cases where these rules are not complied with, equity will sometimes intervene and give effect to the parties' intentions.[3] Furthermore, as we shall see, there are occasions where the law is prepared to acknowledge that, even in the absence of any documentary evidence, freehold ownership[4] or an easement[5] has arisen on the basis of long unchallenged possession or use.

The rules governing the creation and transfer of interests in land are further complicated by the process of registration of title. As we shall see,[6] most titles to land are already entered on a central Land Register. Any dealings with such land not only must comply with the general law, but must also be carried out in accordance with the specific rules laid down for registered land[7]. In cases where title is not yet registered, most transactions now trigger a requirement for the title to be registered so that compliance with registered land rules is also necessary[8]. Hence it is only in respect of transactions relating to unregistered land which do not trigger registration of title, or the creation of titles to registered land which do not require registration (eg short leases) that the Land Registry procedures can be ignored.

Major reforms to the process of creating and transferring interests in land are currently underway. The Government is committed to a move to electronic conveyancing and this project is making good progress. The Land Registration Act 2002 set out the necessary legal framework and, since 2003, the building blocks of the new system—notably the establishment of a secure intranet through which the process can be conducted—has been put into place. It is expected that the new system will be fully implemented by 2015.[9]

[1] Paras 29.11 and 29.12.
[2] Para 29.2.
[3] Paras 30.2–30.18.
[4] Paras 30.19–30.34.
[5] Para 30.19 and paras 32.40–32.51.
[6] Para 29.13.
[7] Para 29.18.
[8] Para 29.15.
[9] Para 29.20.

Formal requirements governing contracts for the sale of land

The statutory requirements

29.2 A contract for the sale or other disposition of land is a legally binding agreement under which an owner of a proprietary[1] interest in land becomes committed to transfer that interest, at some future date, to the purchaser.[2] It is *not* the actual transfer of the interest in question; this takes place at the second and third stages of the transaction.[3] Such[4] contracts must, of course, satisfy all the usual legal requirements relating to the formation of a contract.[5] In particular, any agreement for the sale of land will fail to meet the contractual prerequisite for certainty unless it identifies the parties, the price or other consideration, and the property which is being sold. However, contracts for the sale of land[6] must also comply with additional rules governing the form in which they must be made. Since the Law of Property (Miscellaneous Provisions) Act 1989 (LP(MP)A 1989),[7] such contracts must comply with the following requirements:

- the agreement must be in writing; and
- the document must be signed by or on behalf of each party; and
- all the terms expressly agreed by the parties must either:
  - be incorporated in one document; or
  - where contracts are exchanged, be set out in each of the identical documents; or
  - set out in a 'secondary' document which is expressly referred to in the signed 'master' document.

The 1989 Act specifically provides[8] that the following three types of land contract do not have to be in writing in order to be valid:

- contracts made in the course of a public auction;
- contracts to grant a lease not exceeding three years taking effect in possession at the best rent reasonably obtainable[9]; and
- contracts regulated under the Financial Services Act 1986.

Furthermore, the Act does not affect the creation of implied, resulting or constructive trusts.[10]

[1] Thus contracts for the use or occupation of land by way of a licence (see para 28.40) are not here being discussed.

[2] This also includes a contract between A and B under which A agrees to enter into a future contract to sell land to B (see *Sharif v Sadiq* [2004] EWHC 1931 (Ch)), or to C (see *Jelson Ltd v Derby City Council* [1999] 3 EGLR 91. A contract between A and B to sell to an as yet unidentified third party is not a contract for the sale of land, see *Nweze v Nwoko* [2004] 2 P & CR 33, CA and does not, therefore, need to be in writing.

[3] See para 29.11.

[4] Contracts that *relate to* land (but which do not dispose of an interest in land) are not covered. So, for example, a 'lock-out' agreement under which a vendor agrees not to negotiate with anyone else for a specified period (as to which see para 5.35) does not, therefore, have to be in writing: see *Pitt v PHH Asset Management Ltd* [1993] 4 All ER 961, CA. The same is true of an agreement that a landlord will pay the fit-out costs incurred by a new tenant when moving into a property, see *Tootal Clothing Ltd v Guinea Properties Management Ltd* (1992) 64 P & CR 452, CA.

[5] See chs 4, 5 and 6.

[6] LP(MP)A 1989, s 2(1).

[7] The same formal requirements also apply to the variation of an existing written contract: see *McCausland v Duncan Lawrie Ltd* [1996] 4 All ER 995, CA.

[8] LP(MP)A, s 2(5).

[9] For an example see *Looe Fuels Ltd v Looe Harbour* [2008] EWCA Civ 414.

[10] LP(MP)A 1989, s 2(5).

Amplification by the courts

29.3 In the vast majority of cases these statutory provisions give rise to no difficulties at all. Parties rarely embark on land transactions without professional advice and the procedures routinely followed[1] involve the signing and exchanging of standard form, written documents which almost invariably meet the requirements of s 2. That said, and although the 1989 Act was intended to eliminate the uncertainties which had come to surround the previous law, the legislation has spawned an unwelcome amount of litigation. This has clarified the following points.

[1] See paras 29.22–29.38.

Signatures

29.4 The signature of all parties[1] must appear on the same document. The only exception is where the standard conveyancing procedure of exchanging identical copies of the contract is followed, in which case the Act allows for each party to sign one copy. So, in *Commission for the New Towns v Cooper (Great Britain) Ltd*,[2] the Court of Appeal ruled that an exchange of (non-identical) letters each signed by one party did not amount to a contract. This decision appears to rule out the possibility of a contract arising as a result of the exchange of correspondence. The requirement for a signature is not met by the mere insertion of the name of a party; each party must write their name on the document in their own handwriting.[3]

---

[1] The decision in *Jelson Ltd v Derby City Council* [1999] 3 EGLR 91 that, where a contract between A and B gives B the right to require A to transfer property to C, then C must also be signatory seems to be incorrect, see *Nweze v Nwoko* [2004] 2 P & CR 33, CA.

[2] [1995] 2 All ER 929, CA.

[3] *Firstpost Homes Ltd v Johnson* [1995] 4 All ER 355.

More than one document

29.5 It is perfectly possible for a contract for the sale or disposition of land to comprise more than one document. Section 2 requires that, in such a case, there must be incorporation by reference. This means that there should be a 'master' document which has to be signed by both parties; this 'master' document must refer to the other document(s) (which themselves do not need to be signed[1]). The application of these rules is well illustrated by the case of *Firstpost Homes Ltd v Johnson*[2]. Here, a vendor agreed, in a letter addressed to the purchaser, to sell land which the letter identified by reference to an enclosed plan. The letter was signed by the vendor; the plan was signed by both parties. The court held that the letter and the plan must be treated as two separate documents. It therefore followed that, since the signed document (ie the plan) did not refer to the letter, there was no incorporation by reference and thus no contract had come into being.

---

[1] *Record v Bell* [1991] 4 All ER 471.

[2] [1995] 4 All ER 355.

Additional terms

29.6 Section 2 requires that all the terms that the parties have expressly agreed should be included in the contract documentation. However, where parties to a contract for the sale or lease of land have entered into additional agreements which do not appear in the written contract, one of them may, at a later date, seek to use this statutory requirement as a basis for arguing that no contract exists. Perhaps mindful that this can provide an unmeritorious escape route from an agreement that was originally regarded as binding, the courts have been generous in their approach. In many of the cases to date it has been held that these additional terms do not render the main contract invalid. The Court of Appeal has recently made it clear[1] that parties to a composite agreement are free to separate out[2] those terms that are genuinely distinct from the land contract without jeopardising the validity of the latter. However, where the land contract is conditional upon the performance of the other terms, their omission will be fatal and the land agreement will fail. The courts have also been able to save the contract by ruling the 'side' agreement to be a collateral contract.[3] It is also possible, in appropriate circumstances to order rectification[3] of the main contract so as to include the omitted terms[4].

---

[1] *North Eastern Properties Ltd v Coleman* [2010] EWCA Civ 277. Here the defendant sought to argue that he was not bound by a contract of sale because an agreement for a finder's fee had been omitted (at his request) from the contract. The court held that the land contract was not conditional upon payment of the fee and remained fully enforceable. See also *Tootal Clothing Ltd v Guinea Properties Management Ltd* (1992) 64 P & CR 452, [1992] 2 EGLR 80, CA (where a contract to grant a lease failed to include an agreed provision under which the landlord would pay for the tenant's fitting out costs but was, nevertheless held to be valid). By way of contrast, see *Dolphin Quays Developments Ltd v Mills* [2006] EWHC 931 where an agreement that the purchase price of a flat should be paid by way of set off against a debt owed to the purchaser by the vendor

was not included in the 'contract'. The court held that this term was an integral part of the sale and could not be described as a separate contract with the result that the requirements of s 2 had not been satisfied.

[2] The parties can help to reinforce this separateness by including in the contract an express term stating that the documentation 'contains the entire agreement between the parties', see *North Eastern Properties Ltd v Coleman* [2010] EWCA Civ 277.

[3] *Record v Bell* [1991] 4 All ER 471 (where a contract for the sale of residential property did not include an agreed condition that the vendor would supply office copies of Land Register).

[4] *Wright v Robert Leonard (Developments) Ltd* [1994] NPC 49, CA (where a contract for the sale of a show home did not contain the agreed schedule of furnishings to be included).

Options and rights of pre-emption

29.7 Two particular forms of land contract merit specific mention. An option to purchase a freehold or leasehold interest in land is traditionally viewed as a continuing offer to sell the land which the person to whom the option is granted has the right to convert into a contract for sale by notifying an acceptance of that offer.[1] While this analysis is not universally accepted,[2] it is clear that the initial grant of the option is itself a contract[3] to which s 2 of the 1989 Act applies. The difficulty is whether the exercise of an option gives rise to a second contract to which s 2 also applies. This question came before the court in *Spiro v Glencrown Properties Ltd*[4] where it was held that it is *only* the initial grant which needs to satisfy s 2; the actual exercise of the option, which usually takes the form of a unilateral notice signed only by the option holder, is not caught by the Act.

A right of pre-emption, or right of first refusal, is rather different. Here the grantee does not have a *right* to require the land to be transferred; all that is required is that the potential vendor will not sell the land without first giving the holder of the right of pre-emption the opportunity to buy on the agreed terms. Although it has been held that a right of preemption confers no immediate rights to the land,[5] in the same case it was indicated that such rights do arise as soon as the prospective vendor takes some steps indicating a desire to sell; at this point the right of pre-emption effectively converts into an option. Where this is the case, it would seem that, so long as the initial grant of the right of pre-emption satisfies s 2, its exercise can be by unilateral notice, as with an option. However, it has since been made clear that, where the initial grant does not set out the terms on which the right of pre-emption is to be exercised, there is no contract of sale unless the exercise of the right results in an agreement which satisfies s 2.[6]

[1] *Helby v Matthews* [1895] AC 471, HL. In order not to be void for uncertainty an option must be subject to an overall time limit and must either be at a fixed price or must contain a formula under which a price can be arrived at, eg open market value at the date of exercise.

[2] Alternative views are that an option is a conditional contract which the grantee is entitled to convert into a concluded contract, or that an option comprises two contracts, the first a unilateral contract and the second a concluded contract of sale.

[3] If the *initial grant* of the option is not supported by consideration as required under ordinary contractual principles it will need to take the form of a deed; see para 6.5 above. For the meaning of a deed, see para 29.11, below.

[4] [1991] 1 All ER 600.

[5] *Pritchard v Briggs* [1980] Ch 338, [1980] 1 All ER 294, CA. It should be noted that it is now provided that, in relation to registered land, rights of pre-emption are to be treated as giving rise to an interest in land at the date of its creation, Land Registration Act 2002, s 115.

[6] *Bircham & Co Nominees (No 2) Ltd v Worrell Holdings Ltd* [2001] EWCA Civ 775.

Compliance

29.8 Where the requirements of s 2 have been complied with and a valid contract to convey or create a legal estate or interest has been entered into, the purchaser has more than simple contractual rights. As we have seen,[1] the law regards every piece of land as unique, with the result that contracts for the sale or lease of land can normally be enforced by way of specific performance by either a purchaser or a vendor. For this reason the purchaser is regarded as having a right to the land from the moment the contract is entered into.[2] This equitable proprietary right is known as an estate contract. This means that if, for example, V contracts to sell to P[3] and then, in breach of that contract, conveys the land to X, P will usually[4] be able to compel X to convey the land to P rather than simply claim damages from V.

[1] Para 11.44.
[2] *Lysaght v Edwards* (1876) 2 Ch D 499.
[3] Or grants either an option or a right of pre-emption to P.
[4] For an explanation of the circumstances in which P's rights *will* bind X, see para 35.35.

Non-compliance

29.9 Where the requirements of s 2 are not satisfied there will, in most circumstances, be no contract[1]. However, an important issue arises where a person relies to their detriment on an agreement to sell land that does not comply with the statutory formalities. The courts have accepted that the principles of either proprietary estoppel[2] or constructive trust[3] can be used as a means of giving effect to such an agreement. In *Yaxley v Gotts*[4] the claimant had orally agreed with the defendant's father that, if the latter bought a house and the claimant carried out work on it to convert the property into flats, then Mr Yaxley would own the ground floor flats. Unknown to the claimant, the house was in fact transferred to the defendant and it was the son who, after Mr Yaxley had carried out the work and moved into the ground floor, was now trying to evict him. The Court of Appeal held that Mr Yaxley had an interest in the land—the court awarded him a 99-year lease free of any rent—on the basis of either a constructive trust or proprietary estoppel[5]. However, the House of Lords has, in *Yeoman's Row Management Ltd v Cobbe*,[5] expressed the view[6] that the principles of proprietary estoppel[7] cannot be used to side-step the requirements of s 2. Thus the role of proprietary estoppel in this context is now uncertain[8]. What is clear is that, where an oral agreement is expressed to be 'subject to contract'[9] or 'in principle', or where the claimant is a knowledgeable property professional,[10] it is unlikely that either proprietary estoppel or a constructive trust can be established since it will not be possible to prove that the informal agreement was relied upon.

[1] *United Bank of Kuwait v Sahib* [1997] Ch 107.
[2] See further paras 30.11–30.16.
[3] See further para 30.10.
[4] [2000] 1 All ER 711, CA . See also *Oates v Stimson* [2006] EWCA Civ 548 where the claimant was held to be entitled by way of constructive trust to enforce an oral agreement to acquire the defendant's share in a jointly owned property.
[5] [2008] EWHL1139.
[6] Although influential, this view is not binding because it was not necessary for the decision; on the facts of the case there was no concluded agreement that the appellant would sell its land to the respondent and so s 2 was, strictly, irrelevant.
[7] It appears that, where appropriate, a constructive trust can still be utilised where the statutory formalities have not been complied with since this is expressly excluded by s 2(5), see para 29.2. For a view that proprietary estoppel can still assist a claimant whose sale agreement does not comply with s 2, see *Herbert v Doyle* [2008] EWHC 1950 (decided after the House of Lords ruling in *Yeoman's Row*).
[9] See *James v Evans* [2000] 3 EGLR 1, CA.
[10] See *Yeoman's Row Management Ltd v Cobbe* [2008] EWHL 1139.

Reform: electronic documents

29.10 It is clear that, once it becomes compulsory for the second and third stage of the conveyancing process (ie the transfer and registration) to be electronic[1], the same will be true of the contract phase[2]. However, prior to the full implementation of e-conveyancing it will be necessary for s 2 of the 1989 Act to be amended so that electronic contracts are legally permissible. Accordingly, draft amendments to s 2 have already been drawn up[3]. While these have not been finalised and are not yet in force, they will extend the ambit of s 2 so that, in respect of contracts disposing of interests in registered land, its requirements will be satisfied by an agreement in electronic form[4].

[1] See para 29.20.

[2] Land Registration Act 2002, s 93 (which is not yet in force) will make it compulsory for dispositions of registered estates, charges or interests which are the subject of a notice in the register to be in electronic form; the section applies equally to contracts to make such dispositions.

[3] See the draft Land Registration (Electronic Communications) Order 2007, drawn up under the Electronic Communications Act 2000, s 8.

[4] See s 2 which will insert a new s 2A into the 1989 Act.

CONTRACTS FOR THE SALE OF LAND: KEY POINTS

- Contracts for the sale or disposition of land (as opposed to those that simply relate to land) must comply not only with the normal contractual rules but also with the statutory requirements as to their form.

- Section 2 of the LP(MP)A 1989 requires that all of the expressly agreed terms of such contracts must be set out in a written document that is signed by or on behalf of all of the parties.

- Section 2 makes it clear that the expressly agreed terms may be contained in other documents so long as these are referred to in a 'master' document that is signed by all parties.

- Section 2 also provides that where identical copies of a document setting out all the expressly agreed terms are to be exchanged (as is usual in residential sales) it is sufficient if each party signs one of those copies; they do not all have to sign every copy.

- In the case of options and rights of pre-emption it is usually sufficient that their initial grant satisfies the requirements of s 2; their exercise can be by a unilateral notice.

- An agreement that complies with s 2 creates not simply a valid contract but also an interest in land known as an estate contract; this is a proprietary right that can bind future owners.

- A failure to comply with s 2 means that there can be no legally enforceable agreement save in very exceptional circumstances.

Formal requirements governing the creation of legal and equitable interests

Legal estates and interests: the general law

29.11 In the preceding paragraphs we have dealt with the legal formalities governing the contract stage of a land transaction. We now turn to its second phase, that where the interest in question is created or transferred. The general rule governing the creation or transfer of legal estates and interests, which is laid down by the LPA 1925, s 52(1), is that they must be created and conveyed by means of a deed. Traditionally, a deed was a document which was 'signed, sealed and delivered'. Many features of this old definition of a deed had long been unsatisfactory and, in 1989, reforms were enacted by s 1 of the LP(MP)A 1989. A deed is now defined as an instrument which makes it clear on its face that it is intended to be a deed (eg 'signed as a deed') and which is validly executed as a deed. The requirements of valid execution vary according to whether the deed is being entered into by an individual or by a company. A deed is validly executed by an individual provided it is both signed (in the presence of a witness who attests the signature) and delivered as a deed[1]. The term 'delivery' is misleading since no physical handing over of the document is necessary. Any act or words by the maker of the document showing an intention to be bound constitutes 'delivery' even though the document remains in the possession of the grantor.[2] There is no longer any need for an individual to seal a deed.

In the case of a deed entered into by a company, execution can be effected by the affixing to the document of the company seal.[3] Equally, it is now perfectly valid for a company to execute a deed without the use of a seal; in this case the document must be expressed to be executed by the company and must either be signed by two authorised signatories or by a single director whose signature is attested by a witness.[4] Once a deed has been executed by a company, there is a presumption that it has been delivered unless a contrary intention is shown.[5]

It should be noted that s 91 of the Land Registration Act 2002 makes provision for 'electronic deeds' in connection with dispositions of registered land[6]. An electronic document that satisfies the conditions set out in s 91(3)[7] is deemed to satisfy the requirements of the 1989 Act[8]. The application of this section has been triggered so as to enable the operation of a pilot scheme of electronic mortgages[9]; it is expected that a pilot scheme for electronic transfers of registered estates will take place from early 2011.

[1] A solicitor or licensed conveyancer acting in the course of a conveyancing transaction is conclusively presumed to have the necessary authority to deliver a deed, LP(MP)A 1989, s 1(5).

[2] *Vincent v Premo Enterprises (Voucher Sales) Ltd* [1969] 2 All ER 941, CA.

[3] Companies Act 2006 (CA 2006), s 44(1)(a).

[4] CA 2006, s 44(2)(a)(b).

[5] CA 2006, s 44(5).

[6] See para 29.20.

[7] These are that the electronic document makes provision for the time and date from which it is to take effect and contains the certified electronic signature of every authenticating party.

[8] Land Registration Act 2002, s 91(4)(5).

[9] Land Registration (Electronic Conveyancing) Rules 2008.

Short lease exception

29.12 One important exception to the general rule that a deed must be used is that new leases taking effect in possession[1] for a term not exceeding three years (a definition which covers periodic leases such as yearly or weekly tenancies) may be created[2] orally or in writing so long as they are at the best rent reasonably obtainable[3] and not for a lump sum payment. This is provided for by the LPA 1925, s 54(2). Within this exception also falls the creation of a periodic tenancy by implication, arising from going into possession and paying rent which is accepted.[4]

[1] Ie the lease must come into effect immediately. If it is to come into operation at a future date it will not fall within the exception and must be created by deed: see *Long v London Borough of Tower Hamlets* [1996] 2 All ER 683.

[2] All transfers (assignments) of an existing lease must be by deed, irrespective of the length of the lease: see *Crago v Julian* [1992] 1 All ER 744, CA and para 36.28.

³ See *Fitzkriston v Panayi* [2008] EWCA Civ 283 where the court ruled that a written periodic tenancy had not been validly created because the agreed rent was below open market value. In *Hutchison v B & DF Ltd* [2008] EWHC 2286 a tenant was held to be bound by an oral three-year lease granted at a market rent.

⁴ Para 36.14.

Legal estates and interests: registration of title

29.13 Prior to 1925 compliance with the rules laid down in the preceding two paragraphs would have ensured that the purchaser or lessee immediately acquired the relevant legal estate or interest. This is no longer the case. In 1925 a system for registering the title[1] to land was introduced by the enactment of the Land Registration Act 1925. This Act used only to apply to certain parts of England and Wales, known as areas of compulsory registration; however, by 1990 it had come to apply to the whole country. The 1925 Act has been replaced by the Land Registration Act 2002 (hereafter 'LRA 2002')[2]. The main aims of the 2002 Act are to achieve universal registration[3] and to provide the framework for the introduction of electronic conveyancing. While the Act retains most of the underlying principles of the previous scheme, there have been some significant changes.

The system involves the registration of the title to the major legal interests in land, in the main the freehold and leases for terms in excess of 7 years. We explain the rules governing which titles must be registered at para 29.15. However, it should be appreciated from the outset that it is perfectly possible (and, indeed, commonplace) for one piece of land to be the subject of two or more registered titles; for example if A, the registered proprietor of the freehold title to Blacklands, grants a 25-year lease of it to B, then B will also have to be registered as proprietor of a leasehold title to Blacklands; if B then grants a 10-year sublease of the property to C, C will also have to register his title. If C then grants a five-year subunderlease to D, the latter will have a perfectly valid lease—so long as it is created by deed—but that subunderlease will not appear on the Land Register as it is for a term of seven years or less.

¹ The registered system of conveyancing is usually known as the 'registered land' scheme; this is, however, something of a misnomer, for what is registered is not the land itself, but the title to the land, ie the evidence of the owner's right to the land.

² The Land Registration Act 2002 (LRA 2002) came into force on 13 October 2003.

³ Although the current national scheme of registration has been in place since the beginning of 1926 many titles are not yet registered. This is because, until 1990 the system did not apply to all parts of England and Wales and the requirement to register a title was only triggered by a subsequent transaction on sale. Thus if the land was located in the 'wrong' area, or it is owned by a corporate body (which includes large landowning entities such as local authorities, the Church Commissioners and Oxford and Cambridge colleges) there may never have been any transaction (especially relating to the freehold) to provoke registration of title. In 2009 it was estimated that title to some 30% of land in England and Wales remains unregistered.

The Land Register

29.14 The Land Register comprises the computerised record of all registered titles. It operates through district registries which handle applications relating to land within their area. Any person may inspect and make copies of the register, together with any documents to which it refers, and any other document relating to an application which is held by the Registry.[1] The file of each title is divided into three parts: the Property Register, the Proprietorship Register and the Charges Register.

- *Property Register* This part of the register contains a description of the land, states whether it is freehold or leasehold, and refers to a title plan of the land. Where the land is leasehold, brief particulars of the lease are set out. The Property Register also contains notes of any rights which benefit the land, such as easements over neighbouring land.

- The title plan is prepared from the plans and description of the land in the title deeds and is based on the Ordnance Map. It denotes the land comprised in the title by red edging. Boundaries shown in the filed plan are general, not fixed, boundaries; this means that they do not show the exact line of the legal boundary.[2]

- *Proprietorship Register* This part states the class of title with which the land is registered, the name and address of the registered proprietor, the price paid or rent reserved, together with any restrictions[3] affecting the proprietor's right to deal with the land.

- *Charges Register* This part contains entries and notices of rights and interests which adversely affect the title, such as restrictive covenants, easements, mortgages and registered leases.

[1] LRA 2002, s 66. It is, however, possible to apply for an exemption in respect of commercially sensitive information (which does not include the price paid for the property).
[2] LRA 2002, s 62; para 29.22.
[3] Para 35.34.

Title not yet registered: first registration

29.15 *Compulsory registration of title* Although most titles to land are now registered there are many that are not and, by necessity, the grant of any new lease creates a title that cannot previously have been registered. LRA 2002, s 4 requires that the following specified transactions (which, where appropriate, can be on sale, by order of the court or by way of gift or bequest) now always trigger a first registration of title:

- the transfer of an unregistered freehold estate;
- the transfer (ie the assignment) of an unregistered lease having more than seven years to run;
- a grant of a new lease or sublease of more than seven years;
- the grant of a new lease or sublease of *any length* where the lease will not take effect in possession until more than three months after the date of grant;[1]
- the grant of a first legal mortgage over unregistered land;
- the appointment of a new trustee under a trust of unregistered land[2];
- the partitioning of unregistered land among the beneficiaries of a trust[2].

Neither the creation of a new lease not exceeding seven years, nor the transfer of an existing unregistered lease that has seven years or less to run, nor the creation of legal interests (apart from a first legal mortgage) relating to unregistered land, lead to a requirement to register title.

On the occurrence of a transaction within s 4, the legal estate will pass to the transferee or grantee on due execution of the deed[3]. However, the new owner or tenant is required to apply for first registration within two months of completion (or by such later date as is specified by the Registrar provided there is good reason for an extension of time)[4]. If no application for registration is made, the transaction becomes void as to the passing or creation of the legal estate[5]. In the case of a transfer of a freehold or of an existing lease, the legal estate reverts to the vendor who will hold it on trust for the purchaser[6]. Where the transaction comprises the grant of a new lease or a first mortgage, the grant takes effect as a contract to create the lease or mortgage[7]. In any event the purchaser/tenant/mortgagee has the right to require the legal estate to be transferred again and this time should ensure that title to it is properly registered; the purchaser will however be liable to the vendor/landlord/mortgagor for the additional costs[8].

[1] Such leases are a form of future ('reversionary') lease; see para 36.19.
[2] Added by Land Registration Act 2002 (Amendment) Order 2008, which came into force on 6 April 2009.
[3] See para 29.11.
[4] LRA 2002, s 6.
[5] LRA 2002, s 7(1).
[6] LRA 2002, s 7(2)(a).
[7] LRA 2002, s 7(2)(b).
[8] LRA 2002, s 8.

29.16 *Voluntary registration of title* It is not necessary to wait until one of the transactions specified in s 4 occurs before first registration. The owner of the following unregistered estates and interests may choose to apply at any time to have title registered[1]:

- a freehold estate;
- a lease with more than seven years left to run;
- a lease of any length where the term is discontinuous (eg a time share lease);
- a rentcharge (a sum of money charged on land);
- a franchise (eg a right granted by the Crown to hold a market or a fair);
- a profit a prendre in gross (such as a right to hunt game)[2].

[1] LRA, s 3. This process is further encouraged by a significant reduction in the fees charged for voluntary registration. It should, however, be appreciated that voluntary registration requires a landowner to incur the significant legal costs involved in proving title to the satisfaction of the Land Registry.
[2] See para 32.20.

29.17 *The effects of first registration* An application to the Registrar for first registration of title to land is made for one of three classes of title[1]: absolute, good leasehold, or possessory[2]. A fourth class, qualified title, may be given where the Registrar is unable to grant the class of title originally applied for.

In the vast majority of cases involving freehold land, and in an increasing number of those relating to leaseholds, absolute title can be granted[3]. Absolute title will be given where the applicant proves title to the satisfaction of the Registrar. It is not quite accurate to say that registration with absolute title affords an unqualified state guarantee of the registered proprietor's title, for there exists the possibility that the register may be altered, ie amended if it does not show what should be the true state of affairs[4]. However, subject to this possibility, registration with absolute title effectively guarantees that the registered proprietor is entitled to the legal estate, together with all the existing rights which benefit that estate (such as, for example, easements like rights of way)[5]. The only adverse interests to which the new registered proprietor will be subject[6] are:

- interests protected by an entry on the register;
- 'overriding interests' within Sch 1;
- interests acquired under the Limitation Act 1980 (ie squatter's rights) of which the proprietor has notice[7];

- where, the proprietor is a trustee, those rights of the beneficiaries of which he has notice; and
- in the case of leaseholds, the express and implied covenants in the lease[8].

In a few rare cases, the Registrar may decide that it is not possible to grant the title applied for because of some specific defect in the title. In such a case, the applicant for registration may be registered with a qualified title. The effect of registration with a qualified title is the same as the effect of registration with absolute title except that in addition to entries on the register and overriding interests, the registered interest is also subject to a specified qualification stated in the register, for example any rights arising before a specified date or under a specified document.[9]

[1] LRA 2002, ss 9 and 10.

[2] Possessory title is only appropriate where there are no documents of title. Occasionally this will be because title deeds have been lost or destroyed; more likely is the case where the claim to title is based on adverse possession (as to which see paras 30.19–30.36). Possessory title provides no guarantee of title at the date of registration but, after an appropriate period, an application can be made to upgrade the title to absolute.

[3] The proprietor of a lease can only be registered with an absolute title where the Registrar is satisfied both as to the title to the lease and as to the title to the freehold and any intermediate leasehold interests. This will only be the case where either the landlord's title and any intermediate titles are themselves registered, or where the applicant can produce proof of the landlord's unregistered title. Where an absolute title cannot be granted, a good leasehold title will be awarded: this offers the same guarantee as an absolute title save that the proprietor takes subject to any rights or interests affecting the landlord's title to grant the lease, LRA, s 12(6). Where, at a later date, the Registrar can be satisfied as to the landlord's title, a good leasehold title can be upgraded to absolute.

[4] LRA 2002, s 65 and Sch 4; see paras 38.35–38.43.

[5] LRA 2002, ss 11(3), 12(3).

[6] LRA 2002, ss 11(4),(5), 12(4) and (5), see further paras 35.16–35.37.

[7] Note that a squatter who is in actual occupation of the land may have an overriding interest under Sch 1: see para 35.29. In such a case the proprietor will be bound irrespective of whether he or she has notice.

[8] LRA 2002, s 12(4)(a).

[9] LRA 2002, ss 11(6), 12(6).

Title already registered

29.18 Once title to an estate in land has already been registered (as is usually the case) all[1] subsequent dealings with that title are thereafter governed by the LRA. A registered proprietor has the power to make any disposition permitted under the general law[2] and a purchaser is entitled to assume that the registered proprietor has the power to make a disposition, save where those powers are restricted by an entry on the register[3]. Most dispositions affecting a registered estate have to be completed by registration[4]. So,

1. Any subsequent transfer of the estate itself must be carried out by a registered disposition which must be completed by registration, ie by the Registrar entering the transferee of the land on the register as proprietor.[5]

2. Where the registered proprietor of the estate creates a new interest which is required to be registered with its own independent title[6] this again must be carried out by registered disposition. So, for example, where a lease of more[7] than seven years is created out of a registered estate, the lessee will be registered as proprietor of the leasehold interest which is accorded its own separate title. The grant of such a lease will also be noted on the landlord's title[8].

3. Where a registered proprietor of either a freehold or leasehold estate creates a legal *interest* affecting the land which does not itself have to be registered with its own

independent title[9], again it is not enough simply to use a deed; the disposition must be completed by registration if it is to be fully effective.[10] Here, 'completion by registration' means that the interest is noted on the titles of any properties to which it relates[11].

Unless and until such dispositions are completed by registration, no legal estate or interest is created or transferred[12]. The purchaser acquires only an equitable interest which is capable of being overridden if not protected under other provisions in the LRA.[13]

An important exception to the rule that the creation or transfer of legal estates and interests relating to registered land must be completed by registration arises where a registered proprietor grants a lease of seven years or less. Save for the exceptional case where such leases do have to be registered with their own independent title[14], a legal estate is created immediately on grant, provided that the general law on formalities has been complied with[15]. Where the lease is for a term of more than three years it can be (but does not have to be) protected by an entry against the landlord's title[16].

[1] It should be noted that, where the registered title is leasehold, this means that any assignment must be completed by registration even where the lease has seven years or less to run.

[2] LRA 2002, s 23.

[3] LRA 2002, s 26. As we shall see where, for example, a registered proprietor is a trustee with restricted powers to dispose of the land, a restriction to that effect can be entered in the register—see para 35.33.

[4] At the moment there is, inevitably, a gap between the making of the disposition (ie executing the deed) and its completion by registration. One of the important benefits of the introduction of electronic conveyancing (see para 29.20) is that the making of a disposition (which will then no longer be paper-based) and completion by registration will become simultaneous.

[5] LRA 2002, s 27(2)(a) and Sch 2, para 2.

[6] LRA 2002, s 27(2)(b) and Sch 2 para 3(2)(a).

[7] In some instances there is a requirement for a lease of seven years or less to be registered with its own title; this is where the lease will not take effect in possession until more than three months after it is granted (a form of future or reversionary lease—see para 36.19) and where the lease is for a discontinuous term (eg a time share lease).

[8] LRA 2002, Sch 2 para 3(2)(b).

[9] Notable examples are expressly created legal easements and legal charges.

[10] LRA 2002, s 27(1).

[11] LRA 2002 Sch 2, para 7(2).

[12] LRA 2002, s 27(1).

[13] See paras 35.20–35.37.

[14] See para 29.15.

[15] See paras 29.11 and 29.12.

[16] See para 35.35.

29.19 *The effect of a registered disposition* Where a disposition is duly completed by registration a purchaser for valuable consideration of a registered estate[1] is well protected and takes free from any interest affecting the land[2] except:

- a registered charge (mortgage)[3];
- any interest protected by way of a notice entered on the register[4];
- any 'overriding' interest within Sch 3[5];
- any interest excepted from the effect of registration[6];and
- where the estate being disposed of is leasehold, the obligations contained in the lease.

[1] Ie any estate that has been registered with its own title, LRA 2002, s 132.

[2] LRA 2002, s 29.

   [3] See ch 34.
   [4] See para 35.35.
   [5] As we shall see, these are the only interests affecting registered land that will routinely bind a purchaser even though there is no entry on the register; see para 35.20.
   [6] In the unusual case of a proprietor being registered with either a possessory or qualified title (see para 29.17) there is no protection against existing rights affecting the land.

Electronic conveyancing

29.20 The Land Register itself is already computerised and there is increasing on-screen access for both searches and the transmission of information. However, the Government is committed to the further step of introducing electronic conveyancing and the current projection is that this will be in place by 2015. The intention is that the whole transfer process from contract to registration will take place online, via a secure intranet. This will mean that those professional advisers who have access will be able to monitor not only their own transfer but also the progress of related transactions, notably those in the same chain of sales and purchases[1]. It is clear that the actual transfer and its completion by registration will become both electronic and simultaneous, so that there will no longer be any gap between transfer and registration and registered conveyancing will become a two-, rather than three-stage process. Furthermore, related matters such as the discharge of the vendor's mortgage, the completion of the purchaser's mortgage, and the payment of Stamp Duty will also be automatically and electronically effected at the same time.[2]

   [1] A six month pilot scheme—Chain Matrix—was trialled in 2007; see further para 29.23 below.
   [2] Steady progress has been made. A secure intranet is in place—the Land Registry portal was launched in 2008 and provides the basis for the Registry's web service. Since 2009 it has been possible to discharge mortgages electronically and to lodge certain applications electronically. Currently there is in place a pilot scheme under which charges are being created electronically and the intention is that a pilot scheme of electronic transfers will be introduced in late 2011.

Equitable interests

29.21 The LPA 1925, s 53 states the general rule that equitable interests, although not requiring the formality of a deed, must nevertheless be created or transferred by signed writing. Classically, s 53 applies to the express creation of trusts of land although, in practice, a deed is often employed. While s 53 must be complied with where equitable interests are deliberately created, as has already been indicated,[1] equity has traditionally given effect to some transactions which were intended to give rise to legal estates or interests but which failed to do so because the correct formalities[2] were not complied with. Here, as we shall see,[3] it is not necessary to comply with s 53. Equally there are other circumstances in which equitable interests can arise without the need to comply with s 53. The LPA 1925 specifically provides that the section does not affect the creation of resulting, implied or constructive trusts.[4] Furthermore, certain equitable interests may come into existence as a result of the operation of other equitable principles without any need for writing.[5]

   [1] See para 28.38.
   [2] See para 29.9.
   [3] See paras 30.2–30.6.
   [4] LPA 1925, s 53(2). See further paras 30.8–30.10.
   [5] See paras 30.11–30.18.

THE CREATION AND TRANSFER OF LEGAL AND EQUITABLE INTERESTS: KEY POINTS

- The creation or transfer of a legal estate or interest must be carried out by a deed (as opposed to a simple written document); the only exception is a short lease, ie a lease for three years or less and this can be created either orally or in writing.

- The creation or transfer of an equitable interest does not need to be by deed but can be achieved by signed writing; they are exceptions to this requirement where no formalities at all are necessary, notably in the case of implied, resulting and constructive trusts.

- In most cases the use of a deed alone is not now sufficient to create or transfer a legal estate or interest and the transaction must be completed by registration on the Land Register; this is always required where the title to the freehold or lease being transferred is already registered and a failure by the transferee to register as the new proprietor means that they will not become the legal owner.

- Where the vendor's title to a freehold is not already registered the purchaser will become the legal owner but will cease to be so unless a first registration is made within two months of the transfer.

- Where either a new lease for more than seven years is being granted, or an existing unregistered lease that has more than seven years to run is being assigned the new tenant must register as proprietor.

- The creation or transfer of a lease for seven years or less is an important exception to the requirement to register; such leases do not normally need to be registered with their own separate title although where they are for a term of more than three years they will usually be noted on the landlord's title.

- The Land Registry is making good progress with the introduction of electronic conveyancing; once in place this will ensure that the whole transfer process from contract to registration will take place online, via a secure intranet.

A typical sale of land

29.22 In order to place the legal rules governing the creation, transfer and registration of estates and interests into their practical context, we now outline the steps involved in a typical sale of a freehold interest in land. The sale of a leasehold interest follows essentially the same path.

Initial negotiation

29.23 The typical private sale[1] begins when the parties, often introduced by an estate agent, discuss and agree on a price for the property. Although it might appear that vendor and purchaser are now parties to a binding contract, this is not the case. As we have seen, even if it were their intention to be legally bound at this early stage, which is unlikely, a contract for the sale or lease of land must be in writing[2]. It is normal practice for this written contract to come into existence by exchange of contracts.[3]

The period between the initial agreement and the exchange of contracts is one during which either side can withdraw[4]. Such a withdrawal may be for perfectly legitimate reasons (eg an unsatisfactory survey, an unexpected lack of finance, or the loss of a purchaser for a party's existing property). However, one particularly irksome cause is where, in a rising market, a vendor backs out in order to achieve a higher price than that which has already been agreed with the present purchaser—a practice usually referred to as 'gazumping' (although it should be noted that the reverse can occur in a falling market, ie the purchaser can back out in order to force a lower price than that which has been agreed). Whatever the cause, a withdrawal after an agreement has been reached is not only distressing to the innocent party, it can also cause the loss of any expenditure already incurred in the expectation that the deal would go through (notably solicitor's and surveyor's fees).

Where the chances of a withdrawal are greater than usual, for example because the risk of gazumping is high because the market is volatile or where it is known that the period between initial agreement and exchange of contracts may become protracted, it is possible for the parties to enter into an option[5] or a 'lock-out' agreement.[6] The latter requires less formality[7] and is often the more realistic course since the vendor merely agrees not to negotiate with anyone else for a specified period. While a lock-out agreement cannot be used to compel the vendor to exchange contracts,[8] its breach will give rise to a claim in damages; this, at least, compensates the innocent party for wasted expenditure.

However, such safeguards are not usually regarded as appropriate in the case of a routine transaction and the previous government in 2007 introduced the Home Information Pack scheme in order to try to speed up the conveyancing process. The expectation was that the provision of much fuller information before the parties even started to negotiate an agreement would reduce the number of transactions which fall through once the full picture becomes known to the purchaser. It was also thought that HIPs would facilitate a more rapid exchange of contracts and that this would reduce the risk of gazumping. However, the timing of this—just as a property recession was taking hold—and the late decision to back-track on making the provision of a Home Condition Report a compulsory element meant that the HIPs quickly came to be regarded as an unnecessary inconvenience. The new Government had no hesitation in closing down the scheme[9].

Furthermore, it should be appreciated that the most usual stumbling block to a swift exchange of contracts is not the legal procedures but rather the financing practices underpinning the purchase of property, especially those in the domestic residential sector. As a result of the recent credit crunch, mortgages, especially for first time buyers, have become much more difficult to obtain; this can halt or delay a sale, and related transactions. In addition, purchasers who already own a house are rarely able to afford to purchase another until their existing property is sold. As a result, the sale of a residential property is seldom an isolated transaction but rather one in a chain of similar deals; if any one of these falls through, the chain breaks down so that the exchange of contracts on all the other dependent sales has to be delayed. However, the introduction of electronic conveyancing[10] will have a significant impact on this particular problem. The expectation is that, once in place, electronic conveyancing will also allow the details of the progress of each transaction in such chains can be viewed, online, by all involved in related sales; in this way problems can be spotted, and resolved, at an earlier stage.[11]

---

[1] Ie one concluded by negotiation rather than by auction.

[2] LP(MP)A 1989, s 2; para 29.2.

[3] Para 29.27.

[4] The Government estimates that nearly 30% of transaction fail after terms have been agreed.

[5] See para 29.7.

[6] See *Pitt v PHH Asset Management Ltd* [1993] 4 All ER 961, CA and para 5.35 above.

[7] Unlike an option, a lock-out agreement is not a contract for the sale of land and thus does not need to comply with the LP(MP)A 1989, s 2; see *Pitt v PHH Asset Management Ltd* [1993] 4 All ER 961, CA.

[8] *Tye v House* [1997] 2 EGLR 171.

[9] From 21 April 2010. Only one element of the HIP remains; it is still necessary to have commissioned an Energy Performance certificate before putting the property on the market.

[10] See para 29.20.

[11] A pilot project—Chain Matrix—was trialled by the Land Registry in 2007 and remains a key element of electronic conveyancing.

Inquiries and searches

29.24 The period between initial agreement and the exchange of contracts provides an opportunity for the purchaser to take further steps, some of which ought to be satisfactorily completed before it is sensible to become legally committed to the transaction. At this stage the wise purchaser will usually put matters in the hands of professional advisers: a surveyor to report to the purchaser on the structural state of the property and solicitors to carry out the transaction. Where, as is usually the case, the purchaser wishes to finance the purchase by means of a mortgage, this will need to be arranged. Apart from assessing the purchaser's personal creditworthiness, the lender will require a valuation of the property to be carried out, at the purchaser's expense. The purchaser will also now[1] institute the local searches described in the following paragraph. A set of standard inquiries about the property, dealing with such matters as boundaries, the fixtures and fittings included in the sale, and asking whether the vendor is aware of any adverse interests affecting the property will be sent to the vendor. Where the property is domestic, under the Law Society's National Conveyancing Protocol, the vendor now provides the purchaser with a completed Property Information Form and the Fittings and Contents Form which specifies what items are to be included in the sale.[2]

[1] Unless, as is often the case, these have been voluntarily provided prior to exchange of contracts

[2] This is intended to obviate the need to resort to the arcane rules under which items are identified as fixtures, see para 28.12.

Local land charges and supplementary inquiries

29.25 The results of a search of the local land charges register (not to be confused with the Land Register), maintained by the district council (or London borough council) under the provisions of the Local Land Charges Act 1975 will reveal such matters as revocations of planning permission, orders requiring the discontinuance of an existing use, building preservation notices, listings of buildings of special architectural or historical interest, and (charges of a private rather than a public character) light obstruction notices under the Rights of Light Act 1959.[1] Registrations of these matters are made against the land in question. A search may be personal or official (ie carried out by officials of the registry). By virtue of the Local Land Charges Act 1975, s 10, charges of a public character which are not registered nevertheless remain enforceable. However, if a personal search fails to turn up the existence of a charge because it was not registered, or an official search fails to reveal an existing charge, the purchaser will be entitled to compensation for any losses he has thereby suffered.[2]

At the same time as any official search of the local land charges register is sought, a list of optional inquiries is also usually submitted to the district council.[3] While these supplementary inquiries form an essential adjunct to a search of the local land charges register, the procedure has no statutory basis. The district councils merely voluntarily answer the inquiries; nevertheless they may be liable to be sued for negligence in answering them. These inquiries cover such matters as whether the roadways abutting on the property are maintained at the public expense, whether it is proposed to construct any road or flyover close to the property, whether the property is drained to a sewer, whether the property is in a slum clearance area and other matters within the knowledge of the district council.

   [1] Para 32.55.
   [2] Local Land Charges Act 1975, s 10.
   [3] Or London borough council.

Draft contract

29.26 Meanwhile, the vendor's solicitor will be preparing a draft contract of sale, usually based on the Standard Conditions of Sale. At this stage of the transaction it has become normal, where title is already registered,[1] for the vendor to send to the purchaser, along with the draft contract, official copies of the register of title (ie those provided and authenticated by the Land Registry), title plan and any documents referred to on the register which are filed at the Registry. Thus, the vendor, in practice, takes the first step in fulfilling his or her contractual obligation to prove title[2] before the contract is formally entered into.

   [1] See para 29.18.
   [2] Explained further in para 29.37.

Contract

Exchange

29.27 Once both sides are ready to be legally committed to the transaction they will enter into a formal contract. As we have seen, since 1989 most contracts for the sale or disposition of an interest in land must be made in writing.[1]

It is almost invariable conveyancing practice in the case of residential property for the contract to come into being by 'exchange of contracts', more accurately the exchange of identical copies of the contract signed by each party. In the past 'exchange' was effected in person but today it is usual practice to exchange by post or, increasingly, by telephone. Where exchange takes place through the post, it would seem that the contract is formed not when each party receives the other's copy of the contract, but when the second (vendor's) copy is posted.[2] In the case of sales of houses there is often a chain of transactions in which each purchaser needs to sell before the vendor's property can be bought, and each vendor needs to sell in order to buy another property. Here it is often vital that there be as near as possible simultaneous exchanges of contract in respect of each of these transactions. One method of achieving this object, sanctioned by the Court of Appeal[3] and regulated by the Law Society is the 'telephonic exchange'. In this case, either each solicitor holds the client's signed part of the contract or one solicitor holds both parts, and they then, by telephone, deem the contracts to be exchanged, the date of exchange then being entered on each part. Actual physical exchange by post follows.

   [1] LP(MP)A 1989, s 2, see para 29.2.
   [2] Para 5.21. The Standard Conditions of Sale explicitly provide that this shall be the case.
   [3] *Domb v Isoz* [1980] 1 All ER 942, CA.

Deposit

29.28 At exchange of contracts it is usual for the purchaser to pay a deposit. The purpose of this is that, in effect, it gives the vendor a remedy, which is available without bringing a court action, in the event of the purchaser failing to complete. This is because the vendor is normally entitled to keep the deposit where such a failure to complete amounts to a breach of contract. The court does, however, have an unqualified discretion to order the repayment of the whole deposit under the LPA 1925, s 49(2).[1] However, the court should start from the assumption that the deposit should not be repaid[2], although account must be taken of all the circumstances including the effects on the vendor of the failure to complete.[3] It is usual for the contract to fix the amount of the deposit at 10% of the purchase price although, increasingly, the amount of the deposit is negotiable.

The deposit is normally paid to the vendor's solicitor. The general rule is that the solicitor holds it as agent for the vendor[4] unless the contract provides that it should be held by the solicitor as stakeholder. In practice, except where the vendor is to be allowed to use the whole or part of the deposit towards the deposit on a property being purchased in a related transaction, it is usual for the contract to require it to be held by the vendor's solicitor as stakeholder.

---

[1] *Universal Corpn v Five Ways Properties Ltd* [1979] 1 All ER 552, CA. Where, for no particular reason, an unusually large deposit has been paid this may be regarded as a penalty, in which case the court may order the repayment of the whole sum; see *Workers Trust and Merchant Bank Ltd v Dojap Investments Ltd* [1993] 2 All ER 370, PC. On penalties generally see para 11.33.

[2] *Omar v El Wakil* [2001] EWCA Civ 1090.

[3] *Aribisala v St James Homes (Grosvenor Docks) Ltd (No 2)* [2008] EWHC 456

[4] *Ellis v Goulton* [1893] 1 QB 350, CA; *Tudor v Hamid* [1988] 1 EGLR 251, CA.

Terms

29.29 As we have said, the terms of the contract are largely based on those contained in the Standard Conditions of Sale, modified by any special conditions agreed to by the parties. So, for example, it is usual to specify a date for completion; any failure to meet that deadline would then be a breach of contract entitling the innocent party to damages.[1] There would only be an entitlement to terminate for breach where time is made of the essence;[2] it is normally provided that, while time is not automatically of the essence, either party can render it so by serving a notice to complete on the other side.

---

[1] *Raineri v Miles* [1980] 2 All ER 145, HL.

[2] Para 8.31.

Vendor's liability for defects

29.30 It is said that an underlying rule in contracts for the sale of land is *caveat emptor*, let the buyer beware; in other words, it is for the buyer to discover defects in the property that is being bought, and not for the seller to warn of them. However, this rule is subject to a number of important exceptions:

- The vendor may be liable for misrepresentation, which we discussed at paras 12.1 to 12.50 above.

- The vendor may be liable for breach of contract where the property is misdescribed; for example, if the contract describes the size of the property as being greater than it is.

- The vendor is under an implied contractual duty to disclose all latent defects in *title* to the property, ie defects which the purchaser could not discover on a reasonable inspection of the property. Thus, for example, the vendor is obliged to disclose that title is dependent on adverse possession, or that the property is subject to restrictive covenants.

The vendor's liability under each of these three heads is likely to be modified by the terms of the contract. Under the Standard Conditions of Sale, for example, the vendor is to disclose to the purchaser all known adverse interests and the purchaser is to accept the property in the physical state it is in when the contract is made. Furthermore, albeit that property information will have been provided by the vendor, the contract provides that the onus remains on the purchaser to make all the searches, inquiries and inspections which a prudent buyer would make and that the property is bought subject to such defects as they would reveal. As to liability for misrepresentation, the Misrepresentation Act 1967, s 3[1] should be borne in mind when drafting any clause restricting or excluding liability.

It will be appreciated from this that the vendor is not normally liable to the purchaser for *physical* defects in the property.[2] To guard against these the purchaser needs to have a structural survey carried out before entering into the contract.

[1] Paras 12.45–12.50.
[2] However, as we have seen, a vendor/builder may, in appropriate circumstances, be liable to his purchaser under the provisions of the Defective Premises Act 1972; see para 20.28.

Remedies

29.31 The contractual remedies of particular relevance to sales of land are of course applicable to contracts in general and little need be said here additional to our earlier discussion of these remedies.

29.32 *Rescission* It is open to a purchaser to rescind the contract in the face of misrepresentation by the vendor,[1] although it should be remembered that this may not be possible after completion has taken place in a case where the property is purchased with the aid of a mortgage, for the mortgagee will be a purchaser of an interest in the property for value.[2]

[1] Para 12.17.
[2] Para 12.19.

29.33 *Termination of the contract for repudiatory breach*[1] The injured party may not only accept the repudiatory breach of the defaulting party as terminating the contract but may also sue for damages for loss of the bargain or wasted expenditure and any other loss which is not too remote.[2]

[1] Para 8.10.
[2] Paras 11.2–11.24.

29.34 *Damages* As in the general case, a breach of the contract for the sale of the land gives the innocent party the option to sue for damages for loss of the bargain or for wasted expenditure and any other loss which is not too remote. The date at which damages for loss of bargain are assessed is normally the date of breach though some other date may be chosen where otherwise injustice might be caused.[1]

A vendor who cannot show good title may have represented otherwise in answer to inquiries. Where there has been any misrepresentation by the vendor, the purchaser may choose to sue for damages for misrepresentation, rather than for breach of contract, a matter which we discussed in paras 12.21 to 12.38 above.

[1] Para 11.12.

29.35 *Specific performance* It will be remembered that the law regards every plot of land as unique, with the result that contracts for the sale or lease of land are always on the face of it specifically enforceable by both a purchaser and a vendor.[1] This does not mean that the remedy will always be granted, since it is discretionary. Where the court refuses to grant specific performance to either party, it has a discretion to order the repayment of the deposit,[2] although this discretion should be exercised with caution.[3] Further, the court has a discretion to award damages in addition to, or in substitution for, specific performance. Where the innocent party obtains specific performance, but the order is not complied with by the party in breach, the innocent party, having elected to affirm the contract, cannot then unilaterally terminate for breach. An application to the court, under whose supervision the performance of the contract now is, must be made in order to seek enforcement of the order or dissolution of the order and termination of the contract.[4]

[1] Paras 11.44 and 29.8.
[2] LPA 1925, s 49(2).
[3] See para 29.28.
[4] *GKN Distributors Ltd v Tyne Tees Fabrication Ltd* (1985) 50 P & CR 403.

Sale by auction

29.36 Where a sale is conducted by public auction there is a legally binding contract as soon as the property is knocked down[1] to the highest bidder, despite the absence of writing.[2] A person wishing to bid for a property may make pre-contract inquiries and searches before the auction but it is more usual either for the vendor to produce the relevant evidence at the auction, or for the contract to provide for the searches to be made after the auction, giving the purchaser the right to rescind if the searches produce adverse results. In *Rignall Developments Ltd v Halil*,[3] where the contract deemed the purchaser to have made the relevant searches and to have knowledge of what would thereby be disclosed, it was held that the vendor, who was aware of the defect in the title which the searches would disclose, could nonetheless not require the purchaser to complete the transaction since he had not made full and frank disclosure of the known defect.

[1] See para 5.7.
[2] Sales at public auction are excluded from the requirement for writing, LP(MP)A 1989, s 2(5); para 29.2.
[3] [1987] 3 All ER 170.

Transfer stage

Registered land

29.37 *Proving title* During the period between contract and transfer it is for the vendor to carry out the contractual obligation to prove title, ie to prove the ability to sell what has been contracted. It is now usual that the first stage of this process will already have taken place in that the vendor will have furnished the purchaser with official copies of the register of title, etc prior to the exchange of contracts[1] These official copies can be relied on to the same extent as the originals[2] and do not need to be verified against them.

The vendor should also provide the purchaser with any available documentary evidence relating to any interests which do not appear on the register.[3] The purchaser's solicitor will inspect the official copies and any documents required to be furnished to ensure all is well. Requisitions on title will also be raised; these are inquiries of the vendor for further particulars, for example as to adverse entries on the register, or, more likely, simply point them out and require their removal.[4] A failure by the vendor to answer a proper requisition on title may lead to the purchaser terminating the contract for breach or may lead to an application to the court to require an answer under the summary procedure provided by the LPA 1925, s 49(1).

At this stage, also, the purchaser's solicitor should draft the transfer of title, using the prescribed form.[5]

The next stage of the procedure is for the purchaser to request an official search of the register. This search is, in effect, to check for any further entries which may have been made since the date of the official copies already provided by the vendor.[6] The official certificate of search which results ensures that, provided the transaction is completed and the purchaser applies to be registered as proprietor within 30 working days, the purchaser will not take subject to entries made in the register during that time.[7]

A person who suffers loss as a result of an error in an official search is entitled to an indemnity.[8] However any entry which the search fails to reveal is still binding.[9]

[1] Para 29.24.
[2] LRA, s 67.
[3] Such as interests that override; see para 35.20.
[4] See *Re Stone and Saville's Contract* [1963] 1 All ER 353, CA.
[5] LRA, s 25.
[6] If any such entries are discovered, it may be necessary to raise further requisitions, for example requiring their removal.
[7] See further para 35.36.
[8] LRA, s 103, Sch 8, para 1(1)(c); para 35.44.
[9] *Parkash v Irani Finances Ltd* [1969] 1 All ER 930.

29.38 *Completion and registration* Completion now takes place. The transfer is executed and the purchase price paid. The transfer is in simple form but it must, of course, be validly executed as a deed.[1] As we have seen, the deed of transfer itself does not pass the legal estate in registered land to the purchaser. Only registration of the purchaser as proprietor passes the legal estate.[2] The purchaser should therefore apply to the Registry for registration as proprietor.

Where the vendor's title was not registered, the sale to the purchaser will invariably trigger first registration. In this case the legal estate will pass to the purchaser on completion but an application to be registered as proprietor must be made, within two months, apply to the Land Registry within two months.[3]

[1] Para 29.11.
[2] Para 29.19.
[3] Para 29.15.

A TYPICAL SALE OF LAND: KEY POINTS

- In a typical sale of residential property the period between the initial agreement and the exchange of contracts is one during which either side can withdraw.

- While this does permit the unattractive practice of gazumping (whereby the vendor backs out in order to achieve a higher price from another party) it does allow the purchaser time to ensure that the property is physically sound (by carrying out a structural survey) and by allowing any prospective lender to be satisfied that the property is good security for any loan that is necessary to finance the purchase. These are steps that must be taken before any purchaser can commit to the transaction.

- The parties become legally committed once contracts are exchanged; it is usual at this stage for a deposit to be paid.

- Between exchange and completion the vendor must prove title to the satisfaction of the purchaser and the latter will carry out an official search of the land register to ensure that no intervening rights to the land have been created.

- At completion the transfer is executed, the purchase price is paid and the purchaser becomes entitled to take possession; however, the latter will not normally become the full legal owner until he or she is registered as the proprietor in the weeks following completion.

- Once electronic conveyancing is fully implemented both the contract and the transfer will take place electronically and online and, at completion, the transfer and registration of the new owner will take place simultaneously.

Questions

1. What is the function of a contract to sell a freehold and how does this differ from the transfer of a freehold?

2. With what formalities must a contract for the sale of land comply?

3. With what formalities must the creation or transfer of a legal estate or interest comply?

4. How does a deed differ from a written document?

5. In what circumstances must title to land be first registered?

6. What is the most important exception to the requirement that a new title must be registered?

7. What are the key stages in a typical sale of land?

8. Lord Vincent is the freehold owner of a large country estate; his title is unregistered. He agrees to sell a two hectare plot to Peter; this agreement takes the form of a document signed by both himself and Peter. He orally agrees to sell a 100 hectare plot to ABC Developments Ltd; he negotiated this deal with Harry (ABC's managing director) and Harry has written a letter confirming all the terms of their agreement and enclosing a plan of the land to be sold. He agrees to lease a house on the estate to Terry for a term of five years; his solicitor has drawn up a deed to this effect, which has been duly signed and executed.
   Advise Lord Vincent on:
   - whether or not his agreement with Peter is legally binding and, if so, the steps that must now be taken before legal title passes to Peter.
   - whether or not his agreement with ABC Ltd is legally binding. He has recently been offered a higher price by XYZ Ltd and would like to accept that offer.
   - Whether or not the lease to Terry is fully effective.

30

The informal acquisition of rights to land

CHAPTER OVERVIEW

In the vast majority of cases proprietary rights to land are created or transferred in accordance with the rules outlined in the previous chapter. However, where this does not happen there are situations in which some legal effect can be given to dealings in respect of which no formal documentation exists. In this chapter we deal with:

- the effect of transactions which ought to have been made by deed;
- the circumstances in which effect will be given to informal arrangements relating to land; and
- the operation of the statutory rules under which title to land can be acquired as a result of its use over a long period of time.

30.1 In the previous chapter we considered the formal rules which govern the creation and transfer of legal and equitable interests in land. As we have said, in practice virtually all transactions satisfy those requirements. However, situations do arise, often in family or domestic situations, where parties fail to act in accordance with strict legal niceties. Furthermore, landowners may exercise rights over their neighbour's land, or people use land as if it were their own, for very many years but without any proper documentary evidence of their legal right to do so. In such circumstances, the lack of paperwork and the absence of entries on the Land Register make it difficult for solicitors to spot the possibility that rights to land may nevertheless be in existence. This makes it vital that those professionals who do regularly carry out physical inspections of land, notably surveyors, are aware that those who actually occupy or use land may have acquired proprietary rights despite the lack of any paperwork.

Informal transactions

30.2 Where parties make a positive attempt to create an estate or interest in land which fails in the eyes of the law because the formality of a deed is not gone through, their efforts may nonetheless give rise to an interest in the eyes of equity. The same principles apply whatever the type of estate or interest was intended to be created or transferred; hence, the same approach is taken to attempts to transfer a freehold, or to create a lease, an easement,

or a mortgage. However, in order to demonstrate the application of the relevant principles, we will use the example of an informal lease, ie a lease which has not been created in
accordance with the formality required by law.

An example: informal leases

30.3 Suppose that L grants to T a seven year lease which is simply in writing (ie a document which does not comply with the legal requirements of a deed).[1] Such a lease is not
within the exception to the general rule for legal estates under the LPA, s 54(2),[2] and
should therefore have been made by deed.[1] The result, at common law, is that this document does not create a seven year lease. However, suppose further that, because the parties were not aware that they have failed to comply with the proper formalities, T goes into
possession and pays rent which L accepts. At common law, this gives rise to a periodic
tenancy by implication.[3] Accordingly, the operation of the common law rules leaves T
with a markedly inferior interest, a periodic tenancy (which can be terminated at any time
by the landlord serving an appropriate notice to quit[4]), rather than the seven year lease
which the parties had meant to create.

Equity, however, regards the matter differently; it will, where possible, treat the purported lease as if it were a contract to create a lease.[5] So, if court proceedings are actually
brought, equity will usually grant specific performance of the contract. This has the effect
of remedying the initial failure to comply with the formal rules, since the court order
compels the landlord to draw up (or the tenant to accept) a proper deed granting a seven
year legal lease.

However, what is T's position if, as is more likely, neither party goes to court to seek any
remedy? (The parties' failure to use a deed may well have arisen from the fact that they did
not appreciate that one was necessary, in which case they will have no cause to realise that
they need a remedy because both will have acted as though a legal lease had been created.)
In such circumstances equity applies one of its basic principles; ie it 'looks on that as done
which ought to be done'. Since, in equity's view, the informal lease is treated as a contract
to grant a lease, what ought to be done is that this contract should be performed. Equity
therefore regards the situation *as if* the agreement had been complied with and a seven
year lease granted. Accordingly, in the eyes of equity, an informal lease is regarded from
the outset as a lease.[6] But this lease is only recognised by equity; thus T has an *equitable*
seven year lease, which, as we shall see, falls short of a legal lease in some respects.

[1] Para 29.11.
[2] Para 29.12.
[3] Para 36.14.
[4] See para 36.95. It may be that L's right to serve a notice to quit is restricted by statute (see ch 38), in which
case the implied periodic tenancy may be less of a disadvantage to T.
[5] Since this contract is one which creates an interest in land, it must be in writing sufficient to satisfy the
requirements of the Law of Property (Miscellaneous Provisions) Act 1989, s 2 (see para 29.2). Accordingly,
equity cannot be of assistance to T where the informal lease is oral since an oral agreement to create an interest in land cannot, since 1989, amount to a contract.
[6] As we have seen, equity treats a formal contract to grant a lease in the same way; see para 29.8.

30.4 This means that where T has gone into possession and paid rent there are, in effect,
two parallel leases—the implied periodic tenancy recognised by the common law and the
seven year equitable lease. The potential conflict between these two leases was addressed
by the courts in the case of *Walsh v Lonsdale*.[1] Here, the parties entered into an agreement
that Lonsdale would grant Walsh a seven year lease of a mill. The agreement provided that
Walsh was to pay rent annually in advance. No deed was ever drawn up, but Walsh went

into possession, paying rent quarterly in arrears. On the basis of the principles explained in the previous paragraph Walsh held two 'parallel' leases; at common law the absence of a deed meant that he was a periodic tenant, in equity he held a seven year lease. The essential dispute in this case was whether Lonsdale was entitled to demand the payment of rent annually in advance (in accordance with the terms of the equitable lease) or whether Walsh could continue to pay rent in arrears (as was his right under the legal periodic tenancy). It was held that Lonsdale could demand the rent in advance since, where the rules of equity and law conflict, those of equity must prevail.[2] Accordingly, *as between the parties themselves*,[3] the terms of their equitable lease prevailed over the common law periodic tenancy. The principle of this decision, although adverse to the tenant on the facts, could have been of benefit to him (and to any tenant in his position) in other circumstances. If, for example, Lonsdale had been seeking to turn him out by notice appropriate to ending the periodic tenancy, this would not have been allowed. His seven year equitable lease, which could not be terminated during its fixed term, would have prevailed over the periodic tenancy.

[1] (1882) 21 Ch D 9.
[2] Supreme Court of Judicature Act 1873, s 25(11); now re-enacted in the Senior Courts Act 1981, s 49(1).
[3] As we shall see in para 30.5 and in ch 35, the equitable lease does not always bind a purchaser.

30.5 It has been said that, as a result of the decision in *Walsh v Lonsdale*,[1] a written agreement for a lease is as good as a lease. There are, however, some important differences between a legal lease and an equitable lease. First, equity will only treat the parties to an informal lease or an agreement for a lease as having a lease where it considers that specific performance ought to be granted. Specific performance is a discretionary remedy.[2] So, for example, should the tenant go into possession under the agreement and immediately break one of its terms, equity would refuse to order specific performance of the agreement.[3] The tenant would not then have a lease in the eyes of equity, although wherever rent has been paid and accepted there would still be a legal periodic tenancy.

Second, an informal lease is only an equitable interest. Thus, unlike a legal lease, it is not necessarily binding on subsequent purchasers of the landlord's estate.[3] In particular, as we shall see, in some circumstances (notably where the tenant does *not* occupy the premises) the tenant may need to protect the lease by an entry on the Land Register.[4] Since the parties to an informal lease were probably unaware of the legal requirement for creating a legal lease, the tenant is unlikely to know that an equitable lease should be protected in this way. Thus, where a tenant should have secured an entry on the Land Register and has failed to do so, and the landlord subsequently sells the freehold to a third party, the purchaser will not be bound by the tenant's equitable lease. The new landlord will be bound by any legal periodic tenancy which has arisen by implication, as this does not require to be entered on the Register; however, except where prevented by landlord and tenant legislation, this periodic tenancy can be terminated by notice.[5]

Further, legal and equitable leases differ in that certain easements which may, by virtue of the LPA, s 62, be implied on the grant of a formal lease may not be implied where there is only an informal lease.[6]

[1] (1882) 21 Ch D 9, CA.
[2] Para 11.45.
[3] See generally ch 35.
[4] Under the Land Registration Act 2002; see para 35.35. This cannot be done where the lease is for three years or less, LRA 2002, s 33.
[5] This discussion is subject to the caveat that where tenants are in actual occupation under the lease, their rights under the equitable lease will bind the purchaser as an overriding interest, see para 35.23.
[6] Para 32.38.

The overall principle

30.6 In summary, where parties try to create a legal estate or interest without using a deed, equity will often[1] be able treat them as having created the equitable equivalent. As we have seen in the preceding paragraphs, an attempt to create a lease for more than three years which does not employ a deed, results in an equitable lease. Similarly, any attempt to create a legal mortgage or a legal easement without using a deed will often result in an equitable mortgage or an equitable easement.

[1] Provided that, as explained at para 30.3, note 5, the attempt takes the form of a written document which satisfies the requirements of the Law of Property (Miscellaneous Provisions) Act 1989, s 2.

INFORMAL TRANSACTIONS: KEY POINTS

- Where parties try to create a legal estate or interest without using a deed, provided that attempt takes the form of a written document satisfying the requirements of s 2 of the Law of Property (Miscellaneous Provisions) Act 1989, equity will usually take the view that the equitable equivalent has been created.

- This will often (but not always) leave the parties in as good a position as if they had used a deed in the first place.

Informal arrangements

30.7 In the foregoing paragraphs we have been explaining how equity may give effect to *positive* attempts to create interests in land, ie those which have, at the least, got to the stage of being formulated in a written document which satisfies the requirements of the Law of Property (Miscellaneous Provisions) Act 1989, s 2. We now turn to those situations where matters have never reached this point; the parties may merely have a spoken or unspoken understanding that one has, or will have, some right to property owned by the other, or the words or actions of the landowner may have given rise to an expectation that another has, or is to have, a right to the land. In such circumstances, equity may sometimes either:

- accept that the parties intended a trust[1], or
- impose a trust, or
- order that either a legal, equitable or some personal interest in land be conferred.

In many of these cases the connecting thread is that the actions of the owner of the legal estate in land are such that, in fairness, they should either be regarded as holding the land (either wholly or partially) in trust for another, or be compelled formally to grant an estate or interest in the land to that other.

[1] See para 28.39 for an outline of the concept of a trust.

Implied, resulting and constructive trusts

30.8 As we have seen,[1] s 53 of the LPA 1925 requires that equitable interests, including trusts, be created by a written and signed document. However, the section expressly provides that this rule does not apply to the creation or operation of resulting, implied or constructive trusts.[2] Furthermore, implied trusts are excluded from the ambit of s 2 of the Law of Property (Miscellaneous Provisions) Act 1989.[3] Accordingly, the courts have been able to use the implied trust (of which the resulting and constructive trust are now usually regarded as the two constituent species) as a mechanism for conferring an equitable interest in land even in the absence of any written evidence at all.

[1]   Para 29.21.
[2]   LPA, s 53(2).
[3]   s 2(5), see paras 29.2 and 29.9.

Resulting trusts

30.9 Traditionally, a resulting trust arises where land is conveyed to A alone but where B has contributed either all or part of the purchase price. In such a situation it is presumed[1] that it was the intention that A should hold the land on trust for B to the extent of the latter's contribution.[2] Thus B will be regarded as either the sole or part owner in equity. So, in *Sekhon v Alissa*[3] a mother gave her daughter £22,500 (a sum representing most of the mother's savings) towards the purchase of a house which was conveyed into the daughter's name. Later, when the daughter wished to sell the property she claimed that the property was solely hers and that the mother's contribution had been a gift. It was held that, in the absence of any evidence that a gift had been intended, a resulting trust would be presumed; accordingly, the parties were entitled to share the proceeds of sale in proportion to their initial contributions.

Not surprisingly, the possibility of a resulting trust arises most commonly in the domestic situation where spouses, civil partners or co-habitees make financial contributions to the purchase of a home which is registered in the sole name of their partner. It is usual that, following the application of resulting trust principles, the parties are regarded as co-owners in equity; accordingly, this is a topic to which we shall return when dealing with co-ownership in Chapter 31.[4]

[1]   Unless a contrary intention is proved. It may, for example, be shown that B was making a gift or a loan; see *Re Sharpe (a bankrupt)* [1980] 1 All ER 198.
[2]   *Dyer v Dyer* (1788) 2 Cox Eq Cas 92. This presumption applies even where the property was put into A's name in order to achieve an illegal purpose (eg to enable B to make a fraudulent benefit claim), see *Tinsley v Milligan* [1994] AC 330.
[3]   [1989] 2 FLR 94.
[4]   At paras 31.12–31.15.

Constructive trusts

30.10 Under the doctrine of constructive trusts, the courts may in certain circumstances preclude a landowner from enjoying all or part of the beneficial interest in the land by constructively treating them as trustee for another person. Although modern courts sometimes use the terms 'resulting' and 'constructive' trust indiscriminately, it would appear that, in order to establish a constructive trust the following elements must be present:

- an agreement, arrangement, understanding or common intention that a property right has been or will be created; and

- detrimental reliance on that agreement, arrangement, understanding or intention.[1]

The constructive trust is often used to confer equitable co-ownership in domestic cases where a spouse, civil partner or co-habitee, who is not named as a legal owner of the family home, has not made direct financial contributions to the purchase price. Although unable to establish a true resulting trust, the claimant may be able to satisfy the requirements of a constructive trust. Again, we deal with this specific application of the constructive trust later.[2]

However, the constructive trust has also been employed in a very much wider context. Thus, in *Bannister v Bannister*,[3] the defendant had conveyed the freehold of two cottages to the claimant, her brother-in-law, at an under-value on the understanding that she would be allowed to live in one of the cottages, rent free, for the rest of her life. When he sought to evict her, the Court of Appeal held that he was unable to do so; he was a constructive trustee with his sister-in-law having an equitable life interest in the property. In *Lyus v Prowsa Developments Ltd*[4] it was held that a purchaser, by expressly agreeing with the vendor to honour the claimant's existing contract to purchase part of the land,[5] thereby became a constructive trustee and was obliged to complete that contract. More controversially, it has been suggested that a purchaser of land might be bound by a contractual licence by virtue of the imposition of a constructive trust. In *Ashburn Anstalt v Arnold*[6] the Court of Appeal opined that, where a purchaser expressly agrees to be bound by[7] an existing contractual licence, this stipulation may independently give rise to a constructive trust under which the purchaser must give continued effect to the rights of the licensee.[8]

[1] See, in particular, *Lloyds Bank plc v Rosset* [1991] 1 AC 107, [1990] 1 All ER 1111, HL.
[2] At paras 31.12–31.15.
[3] [1948] 2 All ER 133.
[4] [1982] 1 WLR 1044.
[5] Which was not otherwise binding on the purchaser because it had not been registered, see para 34.35.
[6] [1989] Ch 1.
[7] The court made it clear that merely taking with notice of a contractual licence is insufficient to give rise to a constructive trust; it must be shown that the purchaser was agreeing to be bound by the licensee's rights.
[8] It is worth noting that, today, claimants may, in such circumstances, be able to utilise the Contracts (Rights of Third Parties) Act 1999; see ch 13.

Proprietary estoppel

30.11 An early statement of the equitable doctrine of proprietary estoppel is to be found in the judgment of Lord Kingsdown in *Ramsden v Dyson*:[1] 'If a man...under an expectation, created or encouraged by the land[owner], that he shall have a certain interest, takes possession of such land, with the consent of the land[owner], and upon the faith of such... expectation, with the knowledge of the land[owner], and without objection by him, lays out money upon the land, a court of equity will compel the land[owner] to give effect to such...expectation'. Whilst the development of this doctrine was greatly restricted for over a century by the very much stricter rules laid down in *Wilmott v Barber*,[2] it re-emerged following the decision in *Taylor's Fashions Ltd v Liverpool Victoria Trustees Co Ltd*.[3] There, Oliver J identified as the primary question for the court 'whether, in particular individual circumstances, it would be unconscionable for a party to be permitted to deny that which, knowingly or unknowingly, he has allowed or encouraged another to assume to his detriment'.[4] Having returned to its more broadly based roots the doctrine has, as we shall see, come to be used more widely.

However flexible the court's approach may have become, certain elements must be present if the doctrine is to be established in any given case. These we consider in the following paragraphs.

[1] (1866) LR 1 HL 129 at 170.
[2] (1880) 15 Ch D 96.
[3] [1982] QB 133n.
[4] See also *Habib Bank Ltd v Habib Bank AG Zurich* [1981] 2 All ER 650, CA. This approach has been endorsed by the Privy Council in *Lim Teng Huan v Ang Swee Chuan* [1992] 1 WLR 113 and by the Court of Appeal in *Gillett v Holt* [2000] 2 All ER 289.

Expectation

30.12 First, the landowner must have given an assurance, made a representation or created an expectation that the claimant has, or is to have, rights over the land in question[1]. Where a positive statement is made it must be 'clear enough' and intended to be taken seriously'; whether or not this test is satisfied depends hugely on the particular circumstances and the court is more likely to be generous in a domestic context[2]. However, where the parties were in a professional or business relationship it is unlikely that undertakings that are understood to be non-binding, such as a 'subject to contract' or an 'in principle' agreement, will be treated as giving rise to a claim to rights by way of proprietary estoppel[3]. While it is usually necessary to prove that a positive statement has been made, the courts may infer the necessary assurance where the landowner has remained silent and allowed the claimant to incur expenditure or otherwise act to his or her detriment in the mistaken belief that they have rights to the land in question.

[1] The land in question must be identified with reasonable precision, see *Thorner v Major* [2009] UKHL 18.
[2] *Thorner v Major* [2009] UKHL 18.
[3] See *James v Evans* [2000] 3 EGLR 1, CA and *Yeoman's Row Management Ltd v Cobbe* [2008] UKHL and para 29.9.

Acts in reliance

30.13 Second, it must be shown that the claimant has acted in reliance on that representation. In most cases this is not difficult to prove; it is obvious that the claimant has taken some positive step as a direct result of the assurance. However, in some instances the evidence shows that the claimant's actions were only partly induced by the landowner's representation; a personal relationship between the two was also a compelling reason. The courts have made it clear that this can be sufficient. Once the representation has been made, it is for the landowner to disprove reliance[1]; this cannot be done simply by showing that the claimant had mixed motives.[2] A further difficulty can arise where, following the representation, the claimant's conduct does not change; in such circumstances the claimant must be able to show that he or she would not have continued to behave in that way had the representation been withdrawn. In *Wayling v Jones*[3] a young man had worked for many years in his homosexual partner's hotel for little or no pay. When seeking more money he was told that he would inherit all of the latter's property. After the defendant's death, his will to this effect turned out to be invalid. It was held that the claimant could establish an entitlement to the estate by way of estoppel. Although he had admitted that he would have continued to work in the hotel had no promise ever been made, the evidence also showed that, had it been withdrawn, he would then have left.

Acts in reliance often, in practice, comprise expenditure on, or improvements to, the land in question. So, in *Pascoe v Turner*,[4] the claimant, on leaving the defendant for another woman, represented to the defendant that the house in which they had been living as man and wife was hers. On the faith of this, the defendant spent money on repairs and decoration. When the claimant subsequently sought to determine what he alleged was a mere licence to occupy, the Court of Appeal held that he could not do so because the doctrine of proprietary estoppel gave rise to an 'equity' in favour of the defendant. In *Inwards v Baker*,[5] a father allowed his son to build a bungalow for himself on the father's land, which the son did, by his own labour, and sharing the expense with his father. The father had, by an old unrevoked will, left the land to someone else, and on his death his executors claimed possession of the land from the son. This the Court of Appeal refused, holding that the son, having spent money on the land in the expectation of being allowed to stay there, was entitled to remain on the property.

However, it is equally clear that other acts of reliance will suffice, for example, expenditure on one's own land in the mistaken belief of having a right over another's land. This is shown by the application of the doctrine in *ER Ives Investments Ltd v High*,[6] where the defendant had spent money constructing a garage on his own land in a position where it could be reached only across the yard of the neighbouring property. The neighbouring owners at that time (predecessors of the claimant) had stood by and, indeed, encouraged the defendant to do this, knowing that he believed, as a result of prior transactions, that he had a right of way across the yard. The decision in *Crabb v Arun District Council*[7] demonstrates that the doctrine also extends to the situation where a claimant merely acts to their detriment in reliance on the expectation encouraged by the landowner. Here, the claimant, believing himself entitled, as a result of negotiations with the defendant, to a right of way across the defendant's adjoining land, sold part of his land, leaving the remainder accessible only via this disputed right of way. The Court of Appeal held that the actions of the defendant, in encouraging the claimant's belief, raised an 'equity' in favour of the claimant.

[1] *Greasley v Cooke* [1980] 3 All ER 710.
[2] *Wayling v Jones* (1983) 69 P & CR 170; *Campbell v Griffin* [2001] EWCA Civ 990.
[3] (1983) 69 P & CR 170
[4] [1979] 2 All ER 945, CA.
[5] [1965] 1 All ER 446, CA.
[6] [1967] 1 All ER 504, CA.
[7] [1975] 3 All ER 865, CA.

Detriment

30.14 Finally, it is clear that, in order to found a claim based on proprietary estoppel, it must be shown that the claimant will suffer a detriment unless the court intervenes to offer protection. This detriment lies not simply in the expenditure that has been incurred, or the acts that the claimant has carried out, but rather in the disadvantage that would be suffered if the landowner were allowed to insist upon their strict legal position and, thereby, to deny the expected rights. This means that the claimant must satisfy the court that 'the defendant is acting in a way which is unconscionable, inequitable or unjust'.[1]

[1] *Crabb v Arun District Council* [1975] 3 All ER 865, CA.

Effect of the doctrine

30.15 The doctrine of proprietary estoppel operates to prevent what the court regards as the true arrangement envisaged by the parties being frustrated by their being left to their rights and duties at law.[1] Its effect is to give rise to what is often referred to as an 'equity' in favour of the claimant, which the court satisfies by making an appropriate order. It is clear that the court has a wide discretion in deciding on a suitable remedy, but there is considerable debate as to the exact basis of this discretion. In most cases it appears that the remedy is designed to give effect to the claimant's expectations. However, there may be circumstances, especially where the value of the claimant's reliance is far less than that of their expectation or, where it is difficult to measure the extent of the expectation, the remedy may be modified and may be more closely linked to the claimant's reliance, expenditure, or detriment[2]. The nature of the remedy may also be dictated by practicalities; it may, for example, be inappropriate to order the defendant to share property with the claimant where the two could not live happily under one roof[3]. Furthermore, it is possible that, by the time the matter comes to court, the circumstances may be such that it is no longer equitable for the court to intervene, so that the owner is entitled to recover possession of the land free from any further claim.[4]

Where the court decides to confer rights to the property itself, it is now more usual for these to take the form of a recognised proprietary right. It is relatively rare for the court to order the outright transfer of the freehold, but it can happen. Thus, in *Pascoe v Turner*[5] the court decided that, in the circumstances, the equity could be satisfied only by declaring that the freehold of the property was vested in the defendant.[6] More likely is a declaration that the claimant is entitled to some lesser proprietary right such as a share in the ownership of the property,[7] or a right akin to an easement.[8] A common course of action in the past was for the courts to give the claimant an irrevocable licence for life.[9] While this had the attraction of representing fairly accurately the true arrangement envisaged by the parties, it did give rise to uncertainties as to the legal effect of the rights conferred. For this reason, the court will now usually try to devise some alternative solution.[10]

However, the court may decide not to confer any rights to the property. For example, in *Dodsworth v Dodsworth*[11] the court merely protected the defendants' occupation until such time as they had been compensated by the claimant for their improvements to the property. In *Wayling v Jones*[12] the specific property which had been promised to the claimant had been sold and he was given a money award instead.

[1] *Chandler v Kerley* [1978] 2 All ER 942 at 946.
[2] In *Jennings v Rice* [2003] 1 P & CR 8 the Court of Appeal stressed the need for the remedy to be proportionate.
[3] *Dodsworth v Dodsworth* (1973) 228 Estates Gazette 1115, CA.
[4] *Sledmore v Dalby* (1996) 72 P & CR 196, CA. Here, by the time of the hearing, the defendant had already occupied the property rent free for 18 years and the claimant's need for the property was now very much greater than his. The court therefore decided that it was no longer equitable to fulfil the defendant's expectation that he would be allowed to remain in the property for the rest of his life, and the claimant was permitted to regain possession.
[5] [1979] 2 All ER 945, CA, para 30.13.
[6] See also *Dillwyn v Llewelyn* (1862) 4 De GF & J 517; *Voyce v Voyce* (1991) 62 P & CR 290, CA.
[7] *Lim Teng Huan v Ang Swee Chuan* [1992] 1 WLR 113.
[8] *Crabb v Arun District Council* [1975] 3 All ER 865, CA; *ER Ives Investment Ltd v High* [1967] 1 All ER 504, CA.
[9] Eg *Inwards v Baker* [1965] 1 All ER 446, CA; *Greasley v Cooke* [1980] 3 All ER 710, CA.
[10] In *Griffiths v Williams* (1977) 248 Estates Gazette 947, CA the court suggested that the parties should agree to the grant of a long lease, terminable on the death of the claimant, and subject to an absolute covenant against assignment.
[11] (1973) 228 Estates Gazette 1115, CA. See also *Baker v Baker* (1993) 25 HLR 408, CA.
[12] (1993) 69 P & CR 170.

Conveyancing problems

30.16 The doctrine of proprietary estoppel gives rise to potential conveyancing problems. A major difficulty is whether, prior to any determination of the matter by a court, the claimant has a proprietary right at all. His (or her) equity arises from the estoppel and is not created by the court.[1] It thus dates from the moment when the landowner unconscionably sets up their own rights against the legitimate expectations of the claimant.[2] It remains uncertain whether a claimant can, at this stage (ie prior to any ruling by a court) transfer the benefit of their estoppel rights to someone else. In some instances, it may be clear that the rights are personal and non-assignable[3], in other cases the suggestion is that the benefit is transferable[4]. The position as to the other side of the coin, ie whether estoppel rights can bind a purchaser of the affected land, is rather clearer. This equity was assumed to be capable of binding purchasers in *Ives v High*[5] and *Inwards v Baker*[6], and it has now been confirmed that this is indeed the case in relation to registered land.[7] Thus, a purchaser may[8] be bound to give effect to a right, which may be difficult to detect and the full extent of which will not be known until the court decides on the appropriate remedy.

Once a court has determined how the 'equity' arising from proprietary estoppel should be satisfied further conveyancing problems should not arise. In the past, the court sometimes decided to satisfy the equity negatively, by holding merely that the claimant had an irrevocable licence to occupy for life. This did cause difficulties. However, where a right to the property is awarded, the courts are now more likely to ensure that a recognised proprietary right is granted.

¹ *Re Sharpe (a bankrupt)* [1980] 1 All ER 198.
² *Lim Teng Huan v Ang Swee Chuan* [1992] 1 WLR 113 at 117.
³ *Maharaj v Chand* [1986] 3 All ER 107, PC.
⁴ *Brikom Investments Ltd v Carr* [1979] 2 All ER 753, CA.
⁵ [1967] 1 All ER 504, CA.
⁶ [1965] 1 All ER 446, CA.
⁷ LRA 2002, s 116.
⁸ We discuss the exact circumstances in which the equity *will* bind a purchaser in ch 35.

Proprietary estoppel and constructive trusts

30.17 It will be apparent from the foregoing paragraphs that there are strong similarities between the doctrine of proprietary estoppel and the constructive trust. Although the former doctrine has a quite distinct legal pedigree from the constructive trust and the two principles have developed separately without cross-fertilisation between them, it is clear that the two have come to bear a close resemblance, particularly when applied in the context of co-ownership.¹ That said, there remain important differences. Particularly in its more modern formulations,² the constructive trust appears to be based firmly on an express or implied *agreement* between the parties. Proprietary estoppel is more firmly directed towards fulfilling *expectations* created by the landowner. It is also possible that, under the doctrine of proprietary estoppel, the courts may accept a wider range of acts in reliance³ than is acceptable as a basis for imposing a constructive trust.⁴ Finally, there is little doubt that the doctrine of proprietary estoppel affords the court a far wider range of remedies. As we have seen,⁵ the court can confer a range of rights from a temporary licence through to full legal ownership. Where a constructive trust is imposed the almost invariable result is that the claimant has an equitable interest in the property which amounts either to sole or, more likely, a share in the beneficial ownership of the property.

In those cases where the facts do lend themselves to alternative claims based on either constructive trusts or proprietary estoppel (usually those involving claims to shared ownership), there are circumstances in which the claimant might prefer to rely on proprietary estoppel. This is because estoppel rights can be more effectively enforced against a purchaser or mortgagee than those arising under constructive trusts⁶. Where this issue has come before the courts, the claimant has not been allowed to resort to proprietary estoppel simply as a way of avoiding the consequences of the trust⁷.

¹ As to which see para 31.12.
² Notably in *Lloyds Bank plc v Rosset* [1990] 1 All ER 1111.
³ See, for example, *Greasley v Cooke* [1980] 3 All ER 710, CA and *Re Basham* [1986] 1 WLR 1498 in both of which the continued contribution of domestic labour and services were held to be sufficient.
⁴ It remains highly unlikely that the courts will regard the performance of 'ordinary' domestic duties as sufficient; see further para 31.14.
⁵ Para 30.15.
⁶ As we shall see in paras 31.26, 31.36, 35.13 and 35.27, beneficial interests under a trust can be overreached, in which case they are transferred from the land to the purchase money and do not bind a purchaser. Hence the claimant's rights become ones to money rather than the property itself. This is not the case with proprietary estoppel.
⁷ See *Birmingham Midshires Mortgage Services Ltd v Sabherwal* (1999) 80 P & CR 256.

The doctrine of benefit and burden

30.18 The doctrine of benefit and burden,[1] originally limited to those taking the benefit of a deed, may also be employed so as to protect rights arising from informal arrangements. This is well illustrated by the case of *ER Ives Investment Ltd v High*[2]. High's original neighbour W built a block of flats on his land, the foundations of which encroached on High's land by about one foot. High and W agreed that the foundations could remain where they were and that in return High could have a right of way across the yard of W's flats to gain access to a side road. W subsequently sold his property to X. While X owned the flats, High, to X's knowledge, built a garage in such a way that it could only be reached across the yard, and also contributed to the cost of resurfacing the yard. Later X sold the flats to Ives Ltd, expressly subject to High's right to cross the yard. Ives Ltd brought this action to restrain High from crossing the yard. The Court of Appeal, in addition to upholding High's right on the basis of proprietary estoppel,[3] held that, on the principle that 'he who takes the benefit must accept the burden', so long as the owners of the blocks of flats had the benefit of having their foundations in High's land, they had to allow High and his successors to have access over their yard. The converse equally applies: so long as High took the benefit of access across the yard, he had to permit the foundations to remain. This would suggest then that should High, for example, decide to abandon using the access across the yard, he could demand that the foundations be removed from his land, no doubt necessitating the demolition of the flats. Thus, where the doctrine of benefit and burden does apply, it operates to render a licence irrevocable for so long as the corresponding benefit is enjoyed.

It has been made clear by the House of Lords in *Rhone v Stephens*[4] that the doctrine does not mean that any party deriving *any* benefit from a conveyance has to accept *any* burden imposed by that conveyance; the exercise of the right must be conditional on or reciprocal to the burden. Accordingly, in that case, the defendant could not be required to repair a roof which overhung the adjoining cottage simply because she had the benefit of a right of support from that property. It is also clear that the person on whom the burden is said to be imposed must have had the opportunity to reject the benefit[5].

[1] See also para 33.10; and see *Tito v Waddell (No 2)* [1977] 3 All ER 129.
[2] [1967] 1 All ER 504, CA.
[3] Para 30.13.
[4] [1994] 2 All ER 65, HL.
[5] *Davies v Jones* [2009] EWCA Civ 1164.

INFORMAL ARRANGEMENTS: KEY POINTS

- The law is sometimes able to give effect to spoken or unspoken arrangements under which it is agreed or intended that one party has, or shall have, rights to the land of the other. A similar approach can be taken where one party has acted in a way which leaves another to believe that they have, or will have rights over that party's land.

- The principles used to achieve this effect are primarily the resulting or constructive trust or the doctrine of proprietary estoppel.

- The resulting trust can only be used where the claimant has made a direct financial contribution to the acquisition of the property.

- The constructive trust is more appropriate where it can be shown that the parties had an agreement, arrangement, understanding or common intention that the claimant has, or will have, an interest in the property and that the latter has relied on this to their detriment.

- Proprietary estoppel applies where a landowner has given an assurance or created an expectation that the claimant has, or is to have, an interest in the land and the latter has relied on that to their detriment.

- The constructive trust and proprietary estoppel have strong similarities. However, the former is more strongly founded on the agreement or common intention of the parties, while the latter needs only the giving of an assurance or the creation of an expectation by the landowner. Where a constructive trust is established it is more usual for the claimant to be accorded a share in the ownership of the property. In cases of proprietary estoppel the courts can utilise a wider range of remedies.

- The doctrine of benefit and burden is a common law principle under which a party who takes the benefit of an arrangement may be required to accept a corresponding and related burden.

Adverse possession

30.19 Finally, we turn to the circumstances in which legal estates and interests may be acquired despite the absence of any formal grant, agreement or even an understanding between the parties. Here we are considering those situations in which, due to possession or user enjoyed by the claimant over a long period of time, the law is prepared to validate the claim to the estate or interest in question. The only legal rights to land which can be acquired in this way are ownership rights (both freehold and leasehold) and an easement (such as a right of way). Ownership may be established by long use (or, more accurately, adverse possession). A claim to an easement is made under the rules relating to prescription. In this section we shall deal only with the acquisition of ownership by way of adverse possession; prescription is more conveniently dealt with in Chapter 32. It should be noted that the LRA 2002 introduces radical changes to the law governing the acquisition of title by adverse possession where land is registered. The following paragraphs deal almost exclusively[1] with these new rules.

[1] A brief summary of the law governing unregistered land is provided at para 30.21.

Introduction

30.20 A landowner whose possession is interrupted is entitled to take steps against the trespasser.[1] However, a person who takes possession, rather than simply intruding on a temporary basis, is often referred to as a 'squatter' rather than just a trespasser; here the landowner will need to recover possession of the land rather than simply suing in trespass.[2] Traditionally the law has placed a limit on the time within which an action to recover possession must be taken; it is the policy of the law, first, to protect undisturbed possession and, second, that lawful claims should be pursued with diligence. This is the principle of 'limitation of actions'.[3]

The effect of the limitation principle was that a person who had the right to possess land could lose that right if someone else took possession of the land and remained in possession for the statutory 'limitation period', which was, generally, 12 years.[4] In such a case, not only was the original owner's right to take action to recover possession terminated, but also his or her title to the land was extinguished.[5]

It should be appreciated that, while this principle sometimes operates to deprive land-owners of title to the whole, or large portions, of their land, its more usual application is far less dramatic (and rather more acceptable). Suppose, for example, that a boundary structure between A and B's properties was inadvertently erected in the wrong place so that A's garden included a strip of B's land. If this situation remains undisturbed for a period of 12 years, B's title to that strip is extinguished. In this way, minor boundary discrepancies can often be resolved in a relatively straightforward manner.[6]

This area of the law has been the subject of careful scrutiny in recent years, especially in its operation in respect of registered land. It has become increasingly unacceptable that, where the ownership of land can be readily ascertained by reference to the Land Register, a squatter can acquire title. Although it was eventually decided that the old rules relating to registered land did not breach human rights law[7], by then significant changes had been brought into effect by the LRA 2002[8]. These have addressed most of the criticisms and the law is now regarded as being in a very much more satisfactory state[9].

[1] Para 22.4.

[2] A landowner who chooses self-help rather than seeking a court order for possession should take care to avoid transgressing the criminal law; see para 22.10.

[3] Currently embodied in the Limitation Act 1980, as amended. As we shall see, this Act no longer applies where the title to the estate being claimed by the squatter is registered, LRA 2002, s 96. The 1980 Act still applies where title to the estate being claimed is not registered, see para 30.21.

[4] Limitation Act 1980, s 15(1).

[5] LA 1980, s 17.

[6] See para 28.27. Although, generally speaking, the changes introduced by the LRA 2002 make it more difficult for a squatter to acquire title, the role of adverse possession as a mechanism for resolving such minor boundary discrepancies is retained, see para 30.31.

[7] *Pye (Oxford) Ltd v United Kingdom* (2007) (Application No 44302/02), a decision of the Grand Chamber of the European Court of Human Rights that overturned the ruling by the Chamber of the Court that there had been a breach of human rights.

[8] See para 30.22.

[9] Although the law relating to unregistered land remains unchanged this has always been regarded as more acceptable; title to unregistered land is firmly rooted in possession and the principle of limitation adds significantly to its reliability.

30.21 *The law governing unregistered land* The Limitation Act 1980 still applies to unregistered land. It provides[1] that no action may be brought to recover land after the expiry of 12 years from the date on which the right of action accrued. The right of action is deemed to accrue on the date on which the person in possession was dispossessed or discontinued possession and continues only so long as another person is in adverse possession of the land.[2] Hence, in order for time to start running it must be established that:

- the 'paper' owner has either been dispossessed or has discontinued possession; and
- that the squatter has gone into adverse possession.

The adverse possession must continue, unbroken, for the full 12-year period. However, it is not essential that the same person is the squatter for the whole of that period.[3] So, if A (the 'paper' owner) is dispossessed by B for five years and then B is dispossessed by C, A's title will be extinguished once C has been in adverse possession for seven years. However, C will remain vulnerable to an action for possession brought by B for a further five years; only at that point does C's title become secure. Equally, B could have voluntarily transferred his or her rights to the land to C; in that case C's title would become unimpeachable after seven years.

In the case of unregistered land, the title of the person entitled to bring an action for possession is extinguished on the expiry of the limitation period.[4] The effect of the Limitation Act 1980 is not to convey from one to another but to extinguish;[2] hence, the squatter does not acquire the title or estate of the former owner,[5] but acquires a new freehold title. However, it is important to remember that the only rights extinguished for the benefit of the squatter are those of persons who might, during the statutory period, have brought, but did not in fact bring, an action to recover possession of the land.[6] Thus the squatter has no answer to the claim of a third party seeking to enforce, for example, an easement or a restrictive covenant over the land;[7] these rights continue to bind the land in accordance with normal principles.

[1] Limitation Act 1980, s 15(1).
[2] LA 1980, Sch 1, paras 1 and 8. As we shall see in paras 30.23–30.27, 'adverse' possession is very much more than simple trespass.
[3] *Mount Carmel Investments Ltd v Peter Thurlow Ltd* [1988] 3 All ER 129, [1988] 1 WLR 1078, CA.
[4] Limitation Act 1980, s 17.
[5] *Tichborne v Weir* (1892) 67 LT 735.
[6] *Fairweather v St Marylebone Property Co Ltd* [1962] 2 All ER 288, HL.
[7] *Re Nisbet and Potts' Contract* [1906] 1 Ch 386 at 409.

Land Registration Act 2002: claims to registered land

Introduction

30.22 The LRA 2002 has made radical changes to the law in this area. The Limitation Act 1980 no longer applies where a squatter is claiming title, by way of adverse possession, to a registered estate[1]. Such claims are now governed by LRA 2002, s 97 and Sch 6. In summary, these provide that a squatter who can establish adverse possession[2] for the immediately preceding 10-year period[3], is able to apply to be registered as proprietor[4]. This will prompt the Registrar to notify the registered proprietor of the squatter's application[5]. If, as is likely, the registered proprietor objects within 65 business days then, save in exceptional circumstances, the squatter's application will be rejected[6]. If there is no objection within that time limit, the squatter will be registered as the new proprietor[7]. Thus, by changing the procedure rather than the substantive law, the LRA 2002 has now made it very much more difficult to acquire title by adverse possession where title to land is registered.

[1] LRA 2002, s 96. However, where a squatter has already completed a period of 12 years adverse possession by 13 October 2003 (ie the date on which LRA 2002 comes into force), the old rules will still apply, LRA 2002 Sch 12, para 18. The squatter's right to apply for registration remained fully enforceable until 13 October 2006; since that date, such right will only be enforceable against a purchaser from the registered proprietor where the squatter is in obvious occupation of the land, see LRA 2002, LRA Sch 3, para 2(c).
[2] For the meaning of 'adverse possession' see paras 30.23–30.29.
[3] See para 30.28.
[4] LRA 2002, Sch 6, para 1(1), see para 30.30.
[5] LRA 2002, Sch 6, para 2, see para 30.30.
[6] LRA 2002, Sch 6, para 3(1), see para 30.31.
[7] LRA 2002, Sch 6, para 4.

Adverse possession

30.23 A squatter can only apply for registration by establishing adverse possession for the requisite period[1]. LRA 2002 expressly provides that the meaning of 'adverse possession' is to be the same as under s 15 of the Limitation Act 1980[2]; thus, those statutory provisions and the pre-existing case law remain relevant to the new law. These establish that a period of adverse possession only commences when:

- the 'paper' owner has either been dispossessed or has discontinued possession; and

- the squatter has gone into 'adverse possession'; this requires proof that the squatter has taken factual possession (as opposed to a temporary incursion or occupation) and has the requisite intention to possess.

The House of Lords has made it clear that although the term 'adverse possession' is used by statute, it should not be regarded as meaning anything different from ordinary possession.[3] It is, however, to be contrasted with a temporary incursion onto, or intermittent use of, land. It should also be appreciated that a squatter's initial use of land may not amount to adverse possession but can, over time, so develop. So, for example, in *Powell v McFarlane*[4] the court concluded that, although for a number of years the claimant had done some clearing of the defendant's land and had grazed animals on it, these acts had not amounted to adverse possession. Only later, when his activities on the property had become more extensive and his intention to possess more formulated, could it be said that he was in adverse possession and it was only from this later date that the requisite period could be said to run.

[1] As to the requisite period, see para 30.28.
[2] LRA 2002, Sch 6, para 11(1).
[3] *JA Pye (Oxford) Ltd v Graham* [2002] UKHL 30, [2002] 3 All ER 865. See also *Ofulue v Bossert* [2009] UKHL 16.
[4] (1977) 38 P & CR 452.

30.24 *Discontinuance or dispossession* The requisite period cannot start to run until the paper owner has either been dispossessed or has discontinued possession. Dispossession refers to a person coming in and putting another out of possession, while discontinuance refers to the case where the person in possession abandons possession and another takes it.[1] Abandonment of possession can be difficult to establish. The smallest act by the paper owner will be sufficient to show that there was no discontinuance[2] since the owner with the right to possession will be readily assumed to have the requisite intention to possess.[3] Thus, the acts of the paper owner, in *Leigh v Jack*[4] in repairing a fence on the land, and, in *Williams Bros Direct Supply Ltd v Raftery*[5] in measuring the land for development and depositing rubbish on it, were sufficient to show no discontinuance. However if, for example, the paper owner erects a fence which prevents *their own* access to the disputed land, this will be strong evidence of abandonment, particularly in the case of urban property.[6]

The fact that there is no discontinuance or abandonment of possession by the paper owner means only that the squatter's case must be based on the dispossession of the paper owner. As has now been made clear by the House of Lords, this term carries no suggestion that the paper owner has been ousted or ejected. It simply means that it has to be shown that it is now the squatter who is in possession of the land rather than the paper owner; 'if the squatter is in possession the paper owner cannot be'[7].

[1] *Powell v McFarlane* (1977) 38 P & CR 452.
[2] *Leigh v Jack* (1879) 5 Ex D 264, CA.
[3] *Powell v McFarlane* (1977) 38 P & CR 452.
[4] (1879) 5 Ex D 264, CA.
[5] [1957] 3 All ER 593, CA.
[6] *Hounslow London Borough v Minchinton* (1997) 74 P & CR 221, CA.
[7] *JA Pye (Oxford) Ltd v Graham* [2002] UKHL 30, [2002] 3 All ER 865, 875 per Lord Browne-Wilkinson.

30.25 *Factual possession* Whether a person has factual possession depends on the circumstances, particularly the nature of the land and the way in which land of that nature is commonly used or enjoyed. Basically, however, what is required is that the squatter's use of the land should amount to more than persistent trespass. They must have been exercising sufficient physical control over the land to amount to exclusive possession and must have dealt with the land in the same way as any occupying owner might have done. Clearly building on land, occupying and using a building,[1] or fencing[2] and then incorporating land into land already owned by the claimant[3] will amount to factual possession. Equally, acts falling short of such obvious control for example, rough shooting,[4] grazing and storage,[5] weeding, tending and putting a compost heap on land,[6] have all been regarded as sufficient to show factual possession, in the light of the nature of the land in question.

Contrary to the view taken in a number of earlier authorities,[7] it is not the case that a squatter can only be said to take possession against a paper owner who is not currently using the land but who plans to use the land for a particular purpose in the future (eg redevelopment), where the squatter's acts are inconsistent with those future plans.[8] It is possible that, in such circumstances, the acts of a would-be squatter are too trivial to amount to factual possession[9] or that, particularly if the squatter is aware of the owner's plans, the requisite intention has not been demonstrated.[10] However, it is clear that, as *Buckinghamshire County Council v Moran* shows, a squatter's claim can succeed, despite the fact that their possession does not interfere with the paper owner's future plans for the land.

[1] *Mount Carmel Investments Ltd v Peter Thurlow Ltd* [1988] 3 All ER 129.

[2] A claimant who fences the disputed land will almost always have done enough to demonstrate factual possession since this is viewed as 'the strongest possible evidence' (*Seddon v Smith* (1877) 36 LT 168). However, in some circumstances fencing will not provide proof of factual possession eg in *Boosey v Davis* (1987) 55 P & CR 83 (incomplete fence) and *Marsden v Miller* (1992) 64 P & CR 239 (fence in place for only 24 hours).

[3] *Buckinghamshire County Council v Moran* [1989] 2 All ER 225.

[4] *Red House Farms (Thorndon) Ltd v Catchpole* (1977) 244 Estates Gazette 295.

[5] *Treloar v Nute* [1976] 1 WLR 1295.

[6] *Hounslow London Borough v Minchinton* (1997) 74 P & CR 221, CA.

[7] Commencing with a dictum of Bramwell LJ in *Leigh v Jack* (1879) 5 Ex D 264 at 273; see also, in particular, *Williams Bros Direct Supply Ltd v Raftery* [1957] 3 All ER 593, CA.

[8] *Buckinghamshire County Council v Moran* [1989] 2 All ER 225, CA, a view that has been emphatically endorsed by the House of Lords in in *JA Pye (Oxford) Ltd v Graham* [2002] UKHL 30, [2002] 3 All ER 865 and by the Privy Council in *Wills v Wills* [2004] 1 P & CR 37.

[9] See, for example, *Boosey v Davis* (1987) 55 P & CR 83, CA.

[10] See, for example, *Pulleyn v Hall Aggregates (Thames Valley)* (1992) 65 P & CR 276, CA, where there was held to be no adverse possession since the squatter's acts were consistent with the paper owner's present plans for the land. However, it should be noted that in *JA Pye (Oxford) Ltd v Graham* [2002] UKHL 30, [2002] 3 All ER 865 it was made clear that this would rarely be the correct inference where the paper owner has been physically excluded from the land. For a further discussion of the role of the squatter's intention, see para 30.26.

30.26 *Intention* However, factual possession alone is not enough; the squatter must prove the requisite intention. At one stage it was thought that the squatter must establish an intention to exclude the world at large, including the owner with the paper title. This approach has been modified in more recent times. What is now required, according to *Buckinghamshire County Council v Moran*, is not that the squatter must intend to own or even to acquire ownership of the land but rather that they must intend to possess it for the time being[1]. Thus the fact that Mr Moran's intention was to use land belonging to the council (which he had incorporated into his garden and access to which he had barred by a padlocked gate) only unless and until a proposed bypass was built on it did not preclude his having the requisite intention. Equally, the fact that it can be shown that the squatter would be willing, if asked, to pay for the use of the land is not inconsistent with his being in possession in the meantime[2].

Evidence of the squatter's intention is likely to be derived from their actions. As in *Buckinghamshire County Council v Moran*, enclosure of the land by the squatter, for example by putting up a fence, is strong evidence not only of factual possession but also of the requisite intention. However, even fencing may be equivocal. It may, for example, be that, as in *Littledale v Liverpool College*,[3] it is done to protect a right of way enjoyed over the paper owner's land from interference by the world at large, rather than to establish possession of the land by the squatter[4]. That said, the House of Lords has expressed the view that where a squatter has occupied and made full use of the land in the way that an owner would, there is no need to prove any intention to possession; positive proof of intention is only necessary where their acts are equivocal[5].

[1] These views were affirmed by the House of Lords in *JA Pye (Oxford) Ltd v Graham* [2002] UKHL 30, [2002] 3 All ER 865. It is not fatal that a squatter erroneously believes the land to be their own (or is being leased to them) since the intention required is to *possess* rather than to *dispossess*; see *Hughes v Cork* [1994] EGCS 25, CA, and *Ofulue v Bossert* [2009] UKHL 16.

[2] *JA Pye (Oxford) Ltd v Graham* [2002] UKHL 30, [2002] 3 All ER 865.

[3] [1900] 1 Ch 19, CA.

[4] See also *Fruin v Fruin* [1983] CA Transcript, where a claimant who had erected a fence to prevent an elderly member of the family wandering off was held not to have been in adverse possession and *Inglewood Investment Co Ltd v Baker* [2003] 1 P & CR 23 where the fencing was to keep the squatter's sheep from straying.

[5] *J A Pye (Oxford) Ltd v Graham* [2002] UKHL 30, [2002] 3 All ER 865, at p 887 per Lord Hutton.

30.27 *Occupation as a licensee* Occupation cannot amount to adverse possession if it has a lawful basis. If therefore a person's use of land is with the express or implied[1] permission of the paper owner, it cannot found a claim to title. However, there must be a genuine factual basis for any finding by the court that there is such a licence from the paper owner. In *BP Properties Ltd v Buckler*[2] the paper owner wrote to the squatter unilaterally permitting her to remain in the property; although the squatter ignored this letter, incorrectly believing she was entitled to remain as of right, it was held that her continued occupation was attributable to the licence and could not therefore amount to adverse possession. This case suggests that the unilateral grant[3] to the squatter of a short-term licence to remain in the property could be a speedy, cheap and effective way of stopping time running in the squatter's favour.[4] By way of contrast, sending a letter which merely asserts the paper owner's right to possession, without more, is ineffective to prevent the squatter acquiring title.[5]

[1] In order for an implied licence to arise there must be some 'overt act' by the landowner or 'demonstrable circumstance' from which permission can be inferred, see *Batsford Estates (1983) Co Ltd v Taylor* [2005] EWCA Civ 489.

[2] [1987] 2 EGLR 168, CA.

[3] There must he an outright *grant* of permission; merely inviting the squatter to agree to a licence will not, where the squatter fails to respond, stop time running; see *Pavledes v Ryesbridge Properties* (1989) 58 P & CR 459.

[4] Although it should be noted that the *BP Properties* case has been criticised and might not be followed in the future.

[5] *Mount Carmel Investments Ltd v Peter Thurlow Ltd* [1988] 3 All ER 129, CA.

30.28 *Adverse possession for the requisite period* The LRA 2002 requires that the squatter must establish continuous adverse possession for a period of 10 years ending on the date of the application for registration[1]. It is not necessary for the applicant to have been in adverse possession throughout this period since any period during which the land has been in the adverse possession of a predecessor in title can be added provided that there has been continuity[2]. However if, during the 10-year period, there has been any action which stops the squatter's occupation from amounting to possession (such as the granting of a licence[3]) time will stop running; if the squatter's possession later re-commences a fresh period of 10 years must be completed.

[1] LRA 2002, Sch 6, para 1(1). A squatter who has completed a period of 10 years adverse possession and is then evicted without a court order by the registered proprietor can still apply for registration provided that this is done within six months of the eviction.

[2] LRA 2002, Sch 6, para 11. This will not be the case where the applicant has *dispossessed* (as opposed to have taken title from) a previous squatter.

[3] See para 30.27.

30.29 *The position prior to completing the requisite period of adverse possession* A squatter who has commenced adverse possession[1] is regarded at common law as having a freehold interest in the land, albeit one that can be defeated by the paper owner taking steps to recover possession. Given that the paper owner's title continues to be registered, this means that there are two competing freehold estates. The squatter's rights are, of course, proprietary and are capable of binding anyone to whom the paper owner sells[2]. So if, for example, the paper owner transfers their title to the land to a purchaser when the squatter has been in adverse possession for five years, that purchaser has only five years in which to regain possession. If this is not done, the squatter will have the right to apply for registration. As we shall see[3], the new rules mean that only rarely will a squatter be registered as proprietor; however, where this does happen, the squatter becomes the proprietor of the paper owner's estate and the 'parallel' freehold interest is extinguished[4].

[1] Note that a squatter's initial use of the land may not always amount to adverse possession, see para 30.23.

[2] A squatter who is in occupation of the land will have an 'overriding' interest which will normally bind any purchaser, see para 35.23.

[3] See para 30.30.

[4] LRA 2002, Sch 6, para 9(1).

The effect of completing the requisite period of adverse possession

30.30 Completion of the requisite period of adverse possession confers no additional rights to the land; it merely entitles the squatter to apply to be registered as proprietor[1]. On receiving such an application the Registrar must notify the existing registered proprietor and certain parties with interests in the land, such as the proprietor of any registered charge over the land[2]. If, within 65 business days[3], there is no objection from those notified, the squatter is entitled to be registered as the new proprietor of the paper owner's estate[4], subject to all existing third party rights such as easements or covenants[5]. In practice, those notified are highly likely to object in which case the squatter's application for registration will normally be refused[6], unless one of the exceptional cases dealt with in the following paragraph can be established.

[1] LRA 2002, Sch 6, para 1(1).

[2] LRA 2002, Sch 6, para 2.

[3] Land Registration Rules 2003, r 189.

[4] LRA 2002, Sch 6, para 4. However, if it is later shown that the squatter had not been in adverse possession, the paper owner can be restored as the registered proprietor, see *Baxter v Mannion* [2011] EWCA Civ 120.

[5] LRA 2002, Sch 6, para 9(2).

[6] LRA 2002, Sch 6, para 5. Note that, following such a refusal, the applicant is entitled, in some circumstances, to make a further application, LRA 2002, Sch 6, para 6 and para 30.32.

30.31 *Exceptional cases* Where objection is made to the squatter's application, registration will normally be refused. However, there are three instances where the squatter will be registered as the new proprietor even in the face of objections:

- where it would be unconscionable because of an equity by estoppel for the applicant to be dispossessed;
- where the applicant is for some other reason entitled to be registered as proprietor; and
- where the land in question is adjacent to land owned by the applicant, the line of the boundary between the two pieces of land has not been determined, and during the ten years of adverse possession the applicant has reasonably believed that the land belongs to them[1].

In the first two of these exceptional cases, it is clear that the applicant also has a quite independent claim to the land which could be pursued through the courts. It appears to have been envisaged[2] that an application under Sch 6 might afford such applicants an easier and cheaper way of achieving a remedy. However, it is arguable that anyone who occupies land by virtue of either proprietary estoppel or some other right cannot be in adverse possession[3] and is not therefore entitled to make an application under Sch 6.

It is the third exception that is the most important. This effectively preserves at least some aspects of one of the most useful and uncontroversial benefits of the law of adverse possession, namely that of giving effect to the mis-placed boundary feature[4]. It is not uncommon for fences to be erected which do not accord with the legal boundary; where these remain unchallenged for over 10 years, this exception will often allow the existing state of affairs to be preserved.

[1] LRA 2002, Sch 6, para 5(2).
[2] By the Law Commission, see Law Com No 271, para 14.36.
[3] Because they occupy with the consent of the paper owner, see para 30.27.
[4] See paras 28.27 and 30.20.

30.32 *Further application for registration* As has already been pointed out[1], where objections are raised to a squatter's application for registration, it will normally be refused save in the exceptional cases discussed in the previous paragraph. However, the policy underlying the new provisions requires that a paper owner (or other objector) does more than simply object; they are expected to take steps to recover possession. If this is not done, and the squatter remains in undisturbed adverse possession for a further two years, the latter is entitled to make a fresh application for registration[2]. In such a case the paper owner will not be notified, no objection can be made and the squatter has an automatic right to be registered as the new proprietor[3].

[1] See para 30.30.
[2] LRA 2002, Sch 6, para 6. Such an application cannot be made if the applicant is the defendant in current legal proceedings being taken to regain possession of the land, or if judgment for possession of the land has been obtained in the last two years or if he has been evicted from the land under a judgment for possession.
[3] LRA 2002, Sch 6, para 7.

Adverse possession and leases

Adverse possession against a tenant of an unregistered lease

30.33 Where a person occupies land adversely to a tenant holding under an unregistered lease for the 12-year statutory limitation period, the tenant's title is extinguished.[1] There is no transfer of the tenant's lease to the adverse possessor since the title acquired by the latter is to a freehold estate[2]. It follows that the squatter is not directly bound by covenants in the original lease[3] but, where (as is usual) there is a provision in the lease allowing the landlord to terminate in the event of any breach of covenant (known as a right of re-entry), this right is binding on the squatter.[4] Thus, unless the squatter complies with the covenants, the landlord will be able to re-enter the land and regain possession.[5]

[1] Limitation Act 1980, s 17.
[2] See para 30.29.
[3] *Tichborne v Weir* (1892) 67 LT 735.
[4] A right of re-entry in a lease is a legal interest binding on allcomers.
[5] Paras 36.63–36.66 and 36.70.

The position of the landlord of an unregistered lease

30.34 Although adverse possession by a squatter will extinguish the tenant's title, time only begins to run against the landlord when the lease expires.[1] So, for example, where T, the tenant under a 20-year lease[2] is dispossessed by S in the fifth year of the lease, T's title will be extinguished 12 years later (ie in the seventeenth year of the lease). Just over three years later, when the lease would have expired, the landlord becomes entitled to regain possession against S; only then does time start to run against the landlord. Accordingly, S is not secure against the landlord until he has been in adverse possession for a further 12 years.

Furthermore, it has been held, by the House of Lords in *Fairweather v St Marylebone Property Co Ltd*,[3] that where a tenant's title is extinguished as a result of 12 years' adverse possession, that title is only extinguished as against the squatter. As between the landlord and the tenant the lease remains on foot. Accordingly, in that case it was held that the tenant whose title had been extinguished could, nevertheless, surrender the lease to the landlord before the expiration of the term. This brought the lease to an end and enabled the landlord to take immediate action to recover the land from the squatter, since time then immediately began to run against the landlord.

[1] Limitation Act 1980, Sch 1, para 4.
[2] It should be noted that it has only become compulsory to register leases of more than seven years under LRA 2002, see para 29.15. Prior to the commencement of this Act leases of 21 years and less were not registered.
[3] [1962] 2 All ER 288, HL.

Adverse possession against tenants of registered leases

30.35 Where a squatter takes adverse possession of land held by way of a registered lease the LRA 2002 rules apply in much the same way as for freeholds[1]. On completion of the 10-year period the squatter can apply for registration; the registered proprietor of the lease (ie the dispossessed tenant) and the landlord will be notified and will normally make objections which, save in exceptional circumstances, will prevent the squatter from being registered. If no objections are made, or any of the exceptional circumstances apply, or the squatter is able to make a further application, the squatter will be registered as proprietor of the existing lease[2]. Because the squatter effectively takes a transfer of the lease, unlike the position with unregistered leases, they will be directly bound by the covenants in the lease. However, during the period of adverse possession (ie prior to any registration as proprietor), the squatter's rights are to a freehold[3] and they will not be directly bound by the covenants in the lease; as with unregistered leases, the landlord may be able to enforce the covenants indirectly[4]. Furthermore, as with unregistered leases, it would appear that, unless and until the squatter is registered as proprietor of the lease, the dispossessed tenant can surrender the lease to the landlord who will then be entitled to take immediate steps to regain possession[5].

[1] See paras 30.30–30.32.2.
[2] See para 30.30. It is clear that there is, in effect a transfer of the existing lease, see LRA 2002, Sch 6, paras 4, 5(1) and 7.
[3] See para 30.29. If and when the squatter is registered as proprietor of the lease their freehold estate is extinguished, LRA 2002, Sch 6, para 9(1).
[4] See para 30.33.
[5] See para 30.34.

Adverse possession by tenants

30.36 A tenant cannot be in adverse possession of the property held under the lease until the lease has come to an end[1] since their possession throughout the term is necessarily by consent. Thereafter if the tenant remains in possession without the landlord's consent and without paying rent, the normal rules will apply.[2]

A tenant who goes into adverse possession of land owned by a third party is presumed to have done so on behalf of their landlord; this means that title is acquired by the landlord and not by the tenant[3]. This presumption can be displaced and the further away the land is from the land being leased the more likely it is that a tenant will be regarded as acquiring title in their own right.[4] The same presumption applies where a tenant adversely possesses other land owned by their landlord. This means that, unless the presumption is rebutted, the tenant holds that land on the same terms as their leased land.[5]

[1] As to when leases end, see paras 36.90–36.99.
[2] It should be noted that, unless the nature of the former tenant's occupation changes dramatically, their possession will necessarily be regarded as adverse possession, see *Williams v Jones* [2002] EWCA Civ 1097.
[3] *Smirk v Lyndale Developments Ltd* [1975] Ch 317.
[4] *London Borough of Tower Hamlets v Barrett* [2005] EWCA Civ 923.
[5] *J F Perrott & Co Ltd v Cohen* [1951] 1 KB 705.

Adverse Possession: Key Points

- As part of the general law on limitation of actions the law recognises that a landowner who has been dispossessed of the land by a squatter can lose title if he or she does not recover possession within a specified period.

- The law will only recognise the claim of a squatter where the latter can prove 'adverse possession' of the land for the requisite period.

- 'Adverse' possession is in principle no different from ordinary possession; the squatter must be in exclusive possession of the land and exercise the same level of control over it that an ordinary landowner would. However, the courts will not readily regard a squatter as being in possession where:
  – the true owner carries out any actions on the land, or
  – where the squatter is no more than a persistent trespasser.

- Where a squatter (or series of squatters) has been in continuous adverse possession of unregistered land for a period of 12 years the true owner's title is extinguished and the squatter acquires a new freehold title; the existing rights of any third parties over the land remain effective.

- Where a squatter (or series of squatters) has been in continuous adverse possession of registered land for a period of 10 years the squatter becomes entitled to apply to be registered as proprietor. However, the existing registered proprietor will be notified and can (and invariably will) successfully object. Only if the registered proprietor does not then take steps to regain possession within the next two years can the squatter re-apply to be registered (in which case no further objection can be made).

- A squatter who is registered as proprietor takes a transfer of the previous owner's title.

- The same rules apply where the true owner of the property is a tenant although a successful squatter will not thereby acquire title as against the landlord; this will only be achieved by a further period of adverse possession after the end of the lease.

- A tenant who adversely possesses adjoining or nearby land can normally only acquire title on behalf of their landlord; they therefore hold the land acquired on the same terms as their lease.

Questions

1. Larry 'grants' Tony a five year lease; this takes the form of a written document which both of them have signed. Does this give Terry a legal lease and, if not, what is its effect?

2. Angela provides £30,000 towards the cost of a house which is then transferred into her daughter, Belinda's, name. Does this mean that she has a share in the ownership of the property and, if so, on what basis does this happen?

3. Steve and Jenny, an unmarried couple, have recently moved into a new house together. The house is registered in Jenny's name; she pays the mortgage and Steve pays all other household expenses. Does Steve have any rights to the house and, if so, on what basis?

4. What is 'adverse possession'?

5. For how long must a squatter be in adverse possession of unregistered land in order to claim title? Does it make any difference if the land in question is registered?

6. How can a registered proprietor prevent a squatter from obtaining title?

31

Concurrent ownership

CHAPTER OVERVIEW

It is commonplace for the ownership of land to be shared between two or more persons. In this chapter we consider the following topics:

- the forms of concurrent ownership;

- the circumstances in which such ownership exists;

- the potential problems posed where the ownership of land is shared and the ways in which these are addressed by the law; and

- the legal machinery for giving effect to co-ownership.

31.1 So far, we have tended to speak of 'an' owner of land or an interest in land. This over-simplistic view of land ownership must now be examined more closely since the ownership of a piece of land can be enjoyed by more than one person. It is possible to carve up the ownership of land so that limited 'slices' of it are enjoyed successively, ie by one person after another. While the practice of successive ownership (known as 'settlements') was very common in the past, it is extremely rare today and we devote no space to this area of the law. Far more prevalent is the concurrent ownership of land, ie where it is enjoyed by two or more persons at the same time. Concurrent or co-ownership poses particular problems; notably how to balance the sometimes competing interests of the various owners, and how to facilitate the sale and management of land in which a number of ownership interests co-exist.

The forms of concurrent ownership

Introduction

31.2 The law has long recognised both successive and concurrent ownership of land. Successive ownership, usually in the form of settlements, was widely employed until the middle of the 19th century since it provided a mechanism by which the major form of wealth and route to political power (ie land) could be tied to a particular family for very lengthy periods of time. However, as the economy changed and diversified, social and political attitudes changed, and taxation bit, this type of ownership became increasingly unattractive. In sharp contrast, modern social, political and economic conditions provide an environment in which the concurrent ownership of land thrives. It is now[1] common for domestic property to be co-owned; whilst this is usually in the context of a home occupied by a couple, residential property may, of course, be co-owned by family members or by friends. Concurrent ownership is also found in the commercial sphere; where a business is run as a partnership, its property will often be co-owned by the partners.

[1] Whereas the 'family' home always used to be owned solely by the husband, the picture has changed dramatically in the last 40 or so years. The vast majority of properties bought as a matrimonial home are now in the names of both husband and wife. Whilst this is increasingly the case where homes are bought by those in other forms of relationship, it is thought that only 30% of more than 2 million (2002 census) cohabitees live in properties that are in their joint names. Even where this is not so it is likely that, where any financial contribution is made to the purchase of property which is owned by another, the contributor will be accorded a share in its ownership; see para 31.12.

31.3 In the past there were various forms of concurrent ownership. Today, there are only two: joint tenancy and tenancy in common. ('Tenancy' in this context effectively means 'ownership'.) Both forms of co-ownership may exist in relation to freehold or leasehold interests.

We leave our discussion of the structural mechanisms under which co-ownership exists until later in this chapter.[1] However, it is helpful to realise from the outset that statute requires that co-ownership always takes the form of a trust. The trustees must hold the legal title as joint tenants.[2] The beneficiaries may hold their beneficial interests as either joint tenants or tenants in common (also known as 'undivided shares').[3] Hence when, in the following paragraphs we consider whether co-ownership is a joint tenancy or a tenancy in common, we are necessarily referring to the *beneficial* (ie equitable) interest, since the legal title (held by the trustees) can only be a joint tenancy.

[1] See paras 31.28–31.42.
[2] See para 31.29.
[3] See paras 31.30–31.31.

Joint tenancy

31.4 The essential characteristics of joint tenancy are:

- the right of survivorship; and
- the 'four unities'.

The right of survivorship

31.5 Where co-ownership takes the form of joint tenancy, a joint tenant's interest in the land passes automatically on death to the surviving joint tenants (and so on, until there is one survivor who is then the sole owner of the land). This is the right of survivorship; the ultimate survivor takes all. Should a joint tenant try to leave their interest in the land by will, this disposition has no effect. Nor do the rules of intestacy, which apply where a person dies without leaving an effective will, take precedence over the right of survivorship.

Although the right of survivorship might be thought to render the joint tenancy something of a lottery and therefore an unattractive form of co-ownership, this is not necessarily the case. It is very appropriate for those whose ownership allows them no financial stake in the land, notably trustees. Furthermore, for co-owners who wish their fellow co-owner(s) to succeed to the property on their death, the joint tenancy is simple and convenient; for this reason it is often used by married couples or by those in a stable relationship.

The four unities

31.6 The 'four unities' are the unities of possession, interest, title and time; if any of them is missing there cannot be a joint tenancy. Joint tenants share possession of the land, together having one interest in the land, deriving the one title to the property at the same time.

- *Unity of possession* Joint tenants enjoy unity of possession; each has the right to possession of all of the co-owned land. No one joint tenant can exclude the others from any part of the land. A co-owner cannot, by the very nature of co-ownership, point to one part of the land and say 'that is mine and no one else's'.

- *Unity of interest* Where there is joint tenancy, each co-owner is entitled jointly with the other joint tenants to the entire interest in the property. Each tenant's interest must, therefore, be the same and, necessarily, equal. There is one interest, freehold or leasehold, to which they are all entitled. This means that the joint tenancy is not appropriate where co-owners are to have unequal shares in the land.

- *Unity of title* Joint tenants must derive title to the property under the same document (or by simultaneously taking possession and acquiring it by adverse possession).[1]

- *Unity of time* For a joint tenancy to exist the co-owners must not have interests commencing at different times.

[1] This requirement also means that joint tenants must act jointly in respect of the legal title. Thus, where a lease is held by joint tenants they must all agree when ending a fixed term lease by surrender or by the service of a break notice. However, where the tenancy is a periodic one, it has been held that the service of a notice to quit by only one of joint tenants is effective to end the tenancy, see further para 36.95.

Tenancy in common

No right of survivorship

31.7 If co-ownership takes the form of tenancy in common, the interest of each co-owner does not automatically pass to the surviving co-owners. The reason is that each tenant in common has a fixed share in the land which may or may not be equal. On death this may be passed on by will, or under the rules of intestacy. Thus, unlike the joint tenancy, the tenancy in common is appropriate for those who do not necessarily wish their fellow co-owners to become entitled to their share on their death. Accordingly, the tenancy in common is likely to be used where friends are buying property together or by business partners. It must also be used where the shares of each co-owner are to be unequal. Although each tenant in common has a fixed share, the land is not, of course, physically divided to give effect to those shares; land subject to tenancy in common is referred to in the LPA 1925 as being held 'in undivided shares'.

Four unities not essential

31.8 Unity of possession is an essential characteristic of co-ownership, whatever form it takes, for there is clearly no co-ownership where a person possesses land to the exclusion of all others. However, the other unities are not essential to tenancy in common, although they are often present.

THE FORMS OF CONCURRENT OWNERSHIP: KEY POINTS

- There are two forms of concurrent ownership—the joint tenancy and the tenancy in common.

- By statute, concurrent ownership must exist in the form of a trust with the trustees always holding on a joint tenancy.

- For a joint tenancy to exist the four unities must be present and the right of survivorship applies on the death of a joint tenant.

- For a tenancy in common to exist the four unities may, but do not have to be, present and there is no right of survivorship—each tenant in common can leave their share by will or it will pass under the rules of intestacy.

How concurrent ownership arises

Express creation

31.9 In most instances concurrent ownership is expressly created. Prospective purchasers or tenants who wish to co-own the property ensure that the property is explicitly transferred, or leased, in the name of both (or all) of them. Where a testator leaves property by will to two or more beneficiaries, the executor will ensure that there is an express transfer to all. Where a donor gives land to more than one person, again, the documentation will be explicitly so drafted. As we have mentioned, whenever land is transferred to two or more persons as co-owners, statute requires that a trust be created[1]. This means that the legal title is always held on a joint tenancy and that the following discussion of whether a particular co-ownership is a joint tenancy or a tenancy in common relates only to the beneficial interest.

[1] Para 31.3 and para 31.29.

How to decide whether the beneficial interest is held on a joint tenancy or a tenancy in common

31.10 *Express declaration* In most instances where concurrent ownership is expressly created the relevant documentation (ie the transfer or will) will specify which form of co-ownership of the beneficial interest is intended, by declaring that the co-owners are to hold as 'joint tenants' or as 'tenants in common'; in the case of tenancies in common, the size of the shares of the parties may also be stated.[1] This declaration is conclusive, in the absence of fraud or collusion[2] as to the state of affairs at the date of the acquisition of the property.[3] The standard transfer forms used by the Land Registry make provision for such declarations to be made but unfortunately do not make them compulsory[4].

It may be, however, that when making any declaration wording other than 'joint tenancy' or 'tenancy in common' (or 'undivided share') is used[5]; in such cases the courts will have to decide on their meaning and effect. Any words which demonstrate that each co-owner is to take a particular share to the property, such as 'to A and B in equal shares' or 'to be divided among A and B' are known as 'words of severance'[6] and give rise to a tenancy in common. In *Re North, North v Cusden*[7] land was left in a will to two sons on condition that they paid to their mother the sum of ten shillings weekly 'in equal shares'. It was held that the sons should likewise hold the property 'in equal shares', ie as tenants in common. In addition, of course, words which confer unequal shares (eg 'two-thirds to A, one-third to B') create a tenancy in common.

¹ For a further discussion as to quantification of shares, see para 31.16.

² *Goodman v Gallant* [1986] 1 All ER 311, CA.

³ This can change as a result of subsequent events but any such change must either be documented in writing or satisfy the rules for implying a trust (see para 31.16).

⁴ Any declaration of trust contained in the transfer form is not entered on the Register; a copy of the form should, therefore, be retained as evidence of the declaration, should this ever prove necessary.

⁵ Non-technical language is more likely to be encountered in a home-made will than in documents such as transfers which are usually drafted by lawyers.

⁶ Since they destroy the essential unity which characterises a joint tenancy.

⁷ [1952] 1 All ER 609.

31.11 *No declaration* Where the documentation merely makes clear that the parties are to be co-owners (classically by a transfer of the legal title into joint names), but gives *no indication* as to the *form* of co-ownership, common law would always assume a joint tenancy.[1] In certain cases, however, equity infers the existence of a tenancy in common despite the presence of the four unities and the absence of words of severance. The rationale is that the right of survivorship, which benefits the co-owner who lives longest, might operate particularly unfairly in the following instances:

- where the purchase price for the land was provided by the co-owners in *unequal*[2] shares. However, the House of Lords[3] has now made it clear that this is not the position where the property being purchased is a home for those with a family or emotional relationship; here there is a strong[4] presumption that the beneficial interest is held on a joint tenancy and that the shares of the co-owners are therefore equal. Nevertheless it does appear that this new approach will not be taken in the commercial sphere, or where those with a personal relationship purchase property as an investment.[5] In these circumstances it seems that the old presumption that unequal contributions produce an equitable tenancy in common in shares proportionate to their input will be applied;

- where the land was acquired by business partners as part of the assets of the partnership;

- where money is lent by co-mortgagees. As between themselves, co-mortgagees are regarded as being tenants in common in relation to their interest in the land; the loan is repaid however into a joint account and the survivor can thus give a complete discharge for all money due;[6]

- where the co-owners hold the land for their separate individual business purposes.[7]

In each of these cases, equity presumes that each co-owner will wish to have the fullest ability to realise their investment. However, there is only a presumption of tenancy in common, and this can be rebutted by evidence to the contrary.

¹ *Morley v Bird* (1798) 3 Ves 628. This will be so even where the co-owners have contributed to the purchase price in unequal shares,

² Note that there was never an equitable presumption of a tenancy in common where the contributions are *equal*.

³ See *Stack v Dowden* [2007] 2 AC 432.

⁴ *Fowler v Barron* [2008] EWCA Civ 377 shows that the presumption of a joint tenancy in equity (and thus equal shares) can only be displaced by strong evidence of a common intention that the shares were to be unequal.

⁵ See *Laskar v Laskar* [2008] EWCA Civ 347 where a mother and daughter bought a property as an investment and were held to be tenants in common.

[7] *Malayan Credit Ltd v Jack Chia-MPH Ltd* [1986] 1 All ER 711, PC.

Co-ownership by implication

31.12 Co-ownership usually arises expressly; the co-owners opt to have property transferred to them both, or a testator or donor chooses to bequeath or give land to more than one person to share. However, this is not the only situation in which co-ownership arises. As we have seen,[1] in certain circumstances, where land is conveyed to one person alone, the courts may nevertheless imply that another has ownership rights. Much of the case law in this area has arisen in the context of a matrimonial home or one shared by a couple living together in a stable relationship where the property was transferred into the name of one partner only but the other claims a share. There is no principle in English law of community of property or family assets whereby property belonging to either of a couple is regarded as family property. Consequently, the claim to a share must, in general, be based on a claim to an interest arising under an implied trust.[2]

We have already discussed the basic principles governing resulting and constructive trusts.[1] Here we shall simply demonstrate how these principles are likely to be applied in the particular context of implied co-ownership cases. It should be appreciated that the case law in this area is not easy to rationalise, largely because the courts have not consistently discriminated between the resulting and the constructive trust. Accordingly, what follows is a very broad overview rather than a detailed analysis.

[1] Paras 30.8–30.10.
[2] Occasionally such interests have arisen on the basis of proprietary estoppel; see para 30.11.

Direct financial contributions

31.13 Where there have been *direct* financial contributions to the initial purchase price the principles of resulting trust will allocate to the contributing party a share commensurate to that contribution unless it can be shown that no share in the property was intended.[1] Originally the courts took a strict approach to what was a direct financial contribution. However, more recently the courts have taken a wider view. The following have now been accepted as falling into this category: contributions to mortgage repayments[2], council house discounts[3], improvements[4], unpaid work[5], and contributions to household expenses[6].

[1] See para 30.9.
[2] *Gissing v Gissing* [1971] AC 886; *Lloyds Bank plc v Rosset* [1991] 1 ACC 107; *Stack v Dowden* [2007] 2 AC 432.
[3] Ie where the only contribution made by a tenant purchasing a property under the right to buy scheme (as to which see para 37.18) is their entitlement to a discount on the price, see *Laskar v Laskar* [2008] EWCA Civ 347.
[4] For married couples and those in a civil partnership, this is made explicit by the Matrimonial Proceedings and Property Act 1970, s 37. It is thought that significant improvements made by other parties will also be taken into account, see *Stack v Dowden* [2007] 2 AC 432.
[5] Classically where a property registered in the name of A and occupied by A and B is paid for by the profits of A's business in which B works on an unpaid basis, see for example, *Nixon v Nixon* [1969] 1 WLR 1676.
[6] At least where these are necessary to enable the other party to meet the mortgage repayments, see *Gissing v Gissing* [1971] AC 886; *Le Foe v Le Foe* [2001] 2 FLR 970.

No direct financial contributions

31.14 Where there have been no direct financial contributions to the acquisition of the property, or where a share greater than that gained under ordinary resulting trust principles is being sought, resort must normally be had to the constructive trust. The circumstances in which a constructive trust will be imposed have been considered by the House of Lords on a number of occasions. The ruling in *Lloyds Bank plc v Rosset*[1] is generally regarded as setting out the relevant framework. It establishes that a constructive trust will arise in one of two situations. First, where, at some time prior to the acquisition of the property (or exceptionally, at some later date), there is *evidence* of some agreement, or arrangement or understanding between the parties that the property is to be shared beneficially. Once a finding to this effect is made, the partner asserting a claim to land registered in the name of the other partner must show that they have acted to their detriment or significantly altered their position in reliance on the agreement.[2] The House pointed out that, in considering the claims of a partner to have acted to their detriment, the court must distinguish between reliance on an expectation of sharing the practical benefits of occupying the home whoever owns it, and an expectation of sharing the ownership of the property asset which the home represents. Only in the latter case will a trust arise.

The second situation[3] in which a constructive trust will arise is where is *no evidence* to support a finding of an actual agreement or arrangement to share. Here, the court may be able to rely on the behaviour of the parties both as the basis on which to infer a common intention to share the property beneficially and as the conduct relied on to give rise to a trust. Their lordships were of the view that only direct contributions to the purchase price by the partner who is not the legal owner, whether initially or by payment of mortgage instalments would justify the inference of a common intention to share the property. However, subsequent case law[4] suggests that this is too narrow an approach and that contributions of the kind outlined in para 31.13 will be sufficient. Nevertheless, it seems clear that the contribution must be in money or money's worth and must relate to the acquisition of the property; 'merely' keeping house and raising a family will not suffice to give a non-owner a share in the home.[5]

In the *Rosset* case itself, Mrs Rosset alleged a constructive trust in her favour based on an express agreement with her sole proprietor husband that the property was to be jointly owned and detrimental reliance in the form of work that she had undertaken in the course of renovation of the property. The court found no evidence of such an agreement and felt that any work of renovation was trifling. As Mrs Rosset had made no financial contribution to the acquisition of the property, there was no basis on which the court could infer a common intention to share the property. Accordingly she was not a beneficial co-owner of the house.

[1] [1990] 1 All ER 1111.
[2] See, for example, *Eves v Eves* [1975] 3 All ER 768, CA and *Grant v Edwards* [1986] 2 All ER 426, CA.
[3] This second situation looks very similar to the resulting trust outlined in 31.13.
[4] See *Stack v Dowden* [2007] 2 AC 432; *Abbott v Abbott* [2007] UKPC 53.
[5] *Gissing v Gissing* [1970] 2 All ER 780, HL; *Burns v Burns* [1984] 1 All ER 244, CA.

Reform

31.15 It will be very apparent from the previous three paragraphs that this area of the law is full of uncertainty. Attempts by the Law Commission even to propose a new scheme foundered due to the complexity of finding ways to deal with all types of home sharers.[1] However, the Government later asked the Commission to examine afresh the position of unmarried cohabitees who are in an intimate relationship. A report was published in 2007.[2] This proposes that legislation be introduced under which a cohabitant whose relationship[3] has broken down could, in certain circumstances, apply to the court. Where appropriate, the court would have the discretion to order financial payments, property transfers and the sharing of pensions rights. No steps have yet been taken to implement these proposals.

How Concurrent Ownership Arises: Key Points

- Whenever concurrent ownership arises there is a trust and the trustees hold the legal estate as joint tenants.

- Where concurrent ownership is created expressly the parties usually declare whether the beneficial interest is to be held on a joint tenancy or tenancy in common—this declaration is normally conclusive.

- In some cases the courts may have to interpret the language used by the parties in order to decide whether they intend to create a joint tenancy or, by using words of severance, they intend a tenancy in common.

- In cases where concurrent ownership is expressly created, but without any declaration of what type that should be, the law will assume that the beneficial interest is to be held on a joint tenancy except where equity presumes a tenancy in common.

- There are circumstances in which concurrent ownership will be implied; this usually means that a sole owner will be treated as holding the property on trust for themself and another, but can mean that existing co-owners must hold the property on trust not just for themselves but also for an additional co-owner.

- Where a direct financial contribution has been or is being made to the acquisition of the property co-ownership will be implied on the basis of a resulting trust.

- Where no direct financial contribution has been made a constructive trust may arise where it can be shown that the parties had an agreement, arrangement, understanding or common intention that the property is to be shared beneficially and the claimant has relied upon that to their detriment.

Quantification of shares

31.16 Once it is settled that beneficial co-ownership exists (either as a result of an express declaration or following the rules for implied co-ownership) there can still be an issue as to the size of the shares enjoyed by each co-owner. Where property is expressly transferred into joint names (necessarily a joint tenancy) but without any express declaration as to how the beneficial interest is held, there is a very strong presumption that, where the co-owners are in a family or emotional relationship, the beneficial interest is also held on a joint tenancy.[1] This means that each 'share'[2] must necessarily be equal.

Where the co-owners have an equitable tenancy in common[3] their stake may be equal or unequal. They are, of course, free to declare in writing[4] when acquiring the property what their shares are to be; this declaration will be conclusive as to the position at that time.[5] Where no formal declaration is made, or where it is sought to argue that any declaration has subsequently been altered (otherwise than in writing) it is necessary for the courts to resort to the principles of implied trusts in order to decide upon the shares. At one stage, the courts would use resulting trust principles and allocate shares on the basis of financial contributions. However, more recently, a broader, less arithmetic approach has been adopted. Initially, it was held that shares should be decided on the basis of what is fair in the light of the couple's whole course of dealing in relation to the property.[6] This approach has since been rejected. The House of Lords has held[7] that the courts must seek to assess the intentions of the co-owners by taking account of all[8] of their conduct over the course of their relationship; an objective view of fairness cannot override the parties' intentions.

It is possible that, over time, the parties' initial intentions as to their respective shares can change. Provided that there is clear evidence of such an altered intention, the courts will make an appropriate adjustment to the previously agreed shares.[9]

[1] See para 31.11 and *Stack v Dowden* [2007] 2 AC 432. It should be noted that the House of Lords decided that, on the unusual facts of that case (unequal contributions to the purchase and a rigid separation of the couple's finances), the presumption of an equitable joint tenancy was displaced with the result that the parties' shares in the property were unequal.

[2] In strict law there are no 'shares' in a joint tenancy (see para 31.6); the term is however convenient for indicating how any proceeds of sale would be divided.

[3] Either as a result of an express declaration to that effect, or because of an equitable presumption, see para 31.11.

[4] Ie so as to comply with LPA 1925, s 53.

[5] *Goodman v Gallant* [1986] 1 All ER 311, CA. See para 31.10.

[6] *Oxley v Hiscock* [2005] Fam 211.

[7] *Stack v Dowden* [2007] 2 AC 432.

[8] And not just that in relation to the property.

[9] See *Holman v Howes* [2007] EWCA Civ 877 (where no such intention was proved). The basis for establishing an altered intention is not yet settled. In *Kernott v Jones* [2010] EWCA Civ 578, a majority in the Court of Appeal overturned the trial judge's decision that an intention to adjust shares by 50:50 to 90:10 had been shown; the case is now on appeal to the Supreme Court.

QUANTIFICATION OF SHARES: KEY POINTS

- Where the beneficial interest is held on a joint tenancy the co-owners' shares are necessarily equal.

- Where the beneficial interest is held on a tenancy in common the shares can be equal or unequal.

- Where the parties have made a written declaration as to their original shares (or as to any subsequent alteration in their shares) this is normally conclusive.

- In the absence of any declaration as to their shares the courts use the principles of implied trust as a basis for any decision.

- This means that the courts will seek to identify the parties' intentions judged over the course of their relationship.

The conversion of a joint tenancy into a tenancy in common: severance

31.17 Severance is a process by which joint tenants can convert their joint tenancy into a tenancy in common *during their lifetime*; a joint tenancy cannot be severed *by will* since a will only comes into effect after death, by which time the joint tenant's rights have already passed to the other joint tenant(s) under the right of survivorship[1].

As we shall see, co-ownership can now only exist in the form of a trust under which the trustees always hold the legal estate as joint tenants.[2] This legal joint tenancy can never be severed; the severance of a legal joint tenancy would create a *legal* tenancy in common, which cannot now exist.[3] Accordingly, severance affects only an *equitable* joint tenancy, converting it into an *equitable* tenancy in common.

The most important practical effect of severance is to defeat the right of survivorship since, once the joint tenant has become a tenant in common, their interest will, on death, pass either under any will or under the rules of intestacy. Severance would also be used where the main intention is to adjust the shares of the joint tenants from equal to unequal ones.

There are five methods[4] of severing an equitable joint tenancy. In the first two methods, severance is effected by destroying one of the four unities.[5]

[1] Para 31.5.

[2] Para 31.29.

[3] LPA 1925, s 1(6); para 31.30.

[4] The common law rule of forfeiture prevents a joint tenant who kills another joint tenant from taking the latter's 'share' under the rule of survivorship; the joint tenancy is in effect severed. The Forfeiture Act 1982 gives the court a discretion to modify this rule in respect of unlawful killings other than murder. It seems inappropriate to describe this as a 'method' of severing a joint tenancy.

[5] Para 31.6.

Acquiring a greater interest in the land

31.18 All the joint tenants have one identical interest in the land; if one acquires another interest, the unity of interest is destroyed. This is rarely encountered in practice.

By disposition of the equitable interest

31.19 A joint tenant who disposes of their equitable interest during their lifetime brings about a severance by destroying the unity of title, since the assignee derives title under a different document from the original co-owners. Thus, if A, a joint tenant with B and C, assigns his equitable interest in the land to X, X takes as tenant in common.[1] As between themselves, B and C remain joint tenants, for between them the four unities remain. X becomes a tenant in common, having a one-third share, with B and C who are joint tenants of a two-thirds share. The disposition in question need not be an outright transfer; severance may result, for example, where a joint tenant mortgages their interest.[2]

[1] The same will be true of involuntary dispositions of the equitable interest; the most obvious example is where a joint tenant becomes bankrupt; their equitable joint tenancy becomes a tenancy in common and their share vests in the trustee in bankruptcy.

[2] *First National Securities Ltd v Hegerty* [1985] QB 850.

By mutual agreement to sever

31.20 Equitable joint tenants may by mutual agreement sever that joint tenancy. The agreement may be one to sever, or one to deal with the property in a way which involves severance, for example where joint tenants agree that one will sell their share to the other. The agreement itself converts the joint tenancy into a tenancy in common. It would appear that the agreement itself need not be in writing, nor be specifically enforceable since it is not necessary for it to *bind* the parties; it needs merely to demonstrate a mutual intention to sever.[1]

[1] *Burgess v Rawnsley* [1975] 3 All ER 142, CA; see also *Hunter v Babbage* (1994) 69 P & CR 548.

By notice in writing

31.21 An equitable joint tenant may sever the joint tenancy by giving a notice in writing to that effect to the other joint tenant(s).[1] In practice this is by far the simplest method of severance; it does not require the agreement of the other joint tenant(s) but they are, by definition, informed of the position, which removes the possibility of subsequent disputes. Such a notice should always be served by legal advisers where the relationship between joint tenants has broken down; in such circumstances the right of survivorship becomes inappropriate. Even where a 'formal' notice has not been served it is sometimes possible that paperwork, which has been drawn up for other purposes, can also constitute a notice of severance[2]. All that is necessary is that the document demonstrates an unequivocal intention to sever.[3]

[1] LPA 1925, s 36(2).
[2] *Re Draper's Conveyance, Nihan v Porter* [1967] 3 All ER 853.
[3] *Harris v Goddard* [1983] 1 WLR 1203.

Course of dealings

31.22 In *Burgess v Rawnsley*[1] Lord Denning took the view that the negotiations which had taken place between the parties were a sufficient 'course of dealing' to bring about severance. The other members of the Court of Appeal thought, despite the unsatisfactory evidence, that there had been a mutual agreement to sever.[2] In that case, all were agreed that an uncommunicated declaration of an intention to sever, and realise one's share, is insufficient to bring about severance, but that a course of dealings between the parties sufficient to indicate a *shared* intention to sever will bring about severance.

[1] [1975] 3 All ER 142, CA.
[2] Para 31.20.

SEVERANCE: KEY POINTS

- Severance is the process by which, during the lifetime of a joint tenant, a joint tenancy can be converted into a tenancy in common; the usual objective is to prevent the application of the right of survivorship.

- Severance is achieved in any of five ways:
  – where one joint tenant acquires a greater interest than the other(s);
  – by a joint tenant disposing of the beneficial interest;
  – by a mutual agreement to sever;
  – by a unilateral written notice from one joint tenant to the other joint tenant(s);
  – by a course of dealings indicating a shared intention to sever.

Ending co-ownership

31.23 In practice, where concurrent owners no longer wish to co-own a particular property, they usually agree to sell it; their co-ownership of it will then cease[1]. However, co-ownership may also be ended by physical partition of the land or by union of the concurrent interests in a single co-owner.

Partition of the land destroys the unity of possession without which there can be no co-ownership. The parties agree physically to divide the land between them, the trustees transferring a part to each.[2] Sale may be ordered under the Trusts of Land and Appointment of Trustees Act 1996, s 14[3] as a substitute for partition and this will be particularly appropriate if partition is impractical, as where the property consists of a single house.

Union of the interests in the land in a sole tenant may occur by survivorship or by one tenant acquiring the interests of the others.

[1] We consider the sale of co-owned land in more detail at paras 31.36 and 31.37.

[2] LPA 1925, s 28. Such a transfer, in respect of unregistered land, now triggers first registration, see para 29.15.

[3] Para 31.41.

The potential problems arising from concurrent ownership

Some of the problems

31.24 Where more than one person has ownership rights in the same property the potential for difficulties exists. Suppose, for example, that A, B and C concurrently own the freehold of Blacklands and that X wishes to buy the property. In theory X may have to investigate three different titles to Blacklands; furthermore, A, B and C may not all agree that Blacklands should be sold. These difficulties will rapidly multiply if A, B and C are tenants in common and A dies, leaving his share to his four children P, Q, R and S; there are now six titles to investigate and six people to agree to any sale.

The old solutions

31.25 *The trust for sale* The problems faced by co-owners were not tackled until 1925 (largely because co-ownership was not, before that date, very often encountered as a way of owning land on a long-term basis). It was then decided that a particular form of trust, the trust for sale, should be the mechanism for co-ownership. The Law of Property Act 1925 required all concurrent ownership to exist in the form of a trust for sale. If land was conveyed[1] to co-owners without the express use of a trust for sale, one was imposed by statute. Thus, to revert to the example used in the previous paragraph, A, B and C were required to hold the legal estate, on a joint tenancy, as trustees on trust for sale for themselves as beneficiaries. As trustees, A, B and C were under an obligation to sell the property immediately, but could all agree to postpone any sale indefinitely. In this way the Act ensured that the legal title to the land was a single indivisible[2] one which could easily be investigated by any purchaser. As a result of the principle of overreaching[3], the purchaser had no need to (and was not entitled to) investigate the interests of the beneficiaries. In this way any sale of co-owned property was rendered much more straightforward.

[1] We have seen (at para 31.12) that co-ownership can arise by implication as a result of the operation of the doctrines of resulting or constructive trusts; where this occurred a trust for sale would also be imposed.

[2] It will be remembered that a joint tenancy must have unity of title (see para 31.6), that the right of survivorship (see para 31.5) means that the number of joint tenants can only diminish, and that there can be no severance of a joint tenancy of the legal estate (see para 31.17).

[3] See para 31.26.

31.26 *Overreaching* A fundamental feature of the trust for sale (and just as important to the new trust of land) is the concept of overreaching. Overreaching was an existing principle which applied where trustees of land exercised a power to sell that land. The LPA 1925 merely extended and regulated its operation. Where the trustees under a trust for sale actually sold the land then, provided the purchase money was paid to at least two trustees,[1] the interests of the beneficiaries ceased to relate to the land and attached henceforth to the proceeds of sale. In this way any purchaser who dealt with at least two trustees was certain to acquire the land free from the claims of the beneficial co-owners (ie A, B, and C in the example used above). The usefulness of this concept in freeing the title to land of equitable ownership interests is very clear and has been carried over into the new trust of land[2].

[1] LPA 1925, s 2(2).
[2] See further para 31.36.

31.27 *Disadvantages of the trust for sale* However, the imposition of a trust for sale in the co-ownership context came to pose its own difficulties. Even after 1925 concurrent ownership was not widespread, especially in circumstances where the co-owned land was to be retained; at that time co-ownership was either a means by which the income from property (as opposed to its occupation) could be shared, or a temporary state of affairs pending its sale (eg where property was given, or bequeathed to children). In the early 20th century many family homes would have been leased rather than held in freehold owner-ship; in either event, it would have been owned by the husband alone. Co-ownership by husband and wife only started to become commonplace well after the Second World War and has only become standard practice in the last 40 or so years. It was only then that the drawbacks of the trust for sale became really apparent. The imposition of a duty to sell (albeit theoretical) in the case of property which had been purchased for the purpose of occupation was not only confusing to purchasers who were buying a property in which to live, it also gave rise to technical legal difficulties. The courts had to adopt some deft footwork in order to provide workable rules on rights to occupy co-owned property and on its sale where the co-owners were in dispute as to whether it should be kept or disposed of. Reform of the mechanism for concurrent ownership had long been necessary.

THE PROBLEMS OF CONCURRENT OWNERSHIP: KEY POINTS

- Prior to 1925, when any number of co-owners could share the legal ownership of land, the conveyance of that land could be very difficult because:
  – the agreement of each and every co-owner would have to be obtained;
  – the purchaser would have to investigate the title of each and every co-owner.
- Between 1925 and 1996 these problems were resolved by the statutory imposition of a trust for sale but this form of trust came to pose its own problems particularly as concur-rent ownership became, over the years, the prevalent form of ownership for domestic residential property.

The modern mechanism for owning land concurrently: trusts of land

31.28 Although the trust *for sale* had proved an increasingly unsatisfactory mechanism for the co-ownership of land, the basic idea of requiring concurrent ownership to take the form of a trust was retained by the Trusts of Land and Appointment of Trustees Act 1996 (TLA 1996). This Act implemented proposals for reform made by the Law Commission in 1989 and came into effect on 1 January 1997. Broadly, the Act:

- leaves existing settlements[1] untouched;
- converts existing trusts for sale into 'trusts of land';

- ensures that concurrent ownership (and any other trust of land[2]) arising on or after 1 January 1997 takes the form of 'trusts of land' within the TLA 1996;[3] and

- allows for the express creation of a trust for sale but subjects such trusts to the same regime as the 'trust of land'.[4]

We now examine in a little more detail the machinery for creating concurrent ownership.

[1] See para 31.2.
[2] Such as a an implied, resulting or constructive trust: see TLA 1996, s 1(2)(a).
[3] TLA 1996, ss 1,2 and 5 and Sch 2.
[4] TLA 1996, s 4. Hence, there is little point, in practice, in creating an express trust for sale.

The imposition of a trust of land

31.29 In cases of concurrent ownership a trust of land is imposed by the Law of Property Act 1925; the relevant provisions have been amended by the TLA 1996 so that what previously were references to a trust for sale are now references to a trust of land.[1] The amended LPA 1925 requires that, in all cases of co-ownership, a trust of land must be used under which the trustees *must* hold the legal estate as joint tenants. Where co-ownership arises expressly it is normal practice to create an express trust. Where this is not done (and also where co-ownership arises by implication) the LPA 1925 automatically imposes a trust.[2] In the following paragraphs we explain the operation of the trust of land in the context of concurrent ownership.

[1] TLA 1996, s 5 and Sch 2, paras 3 and 4.
[2] LPA 1925, ss 34 and 36 (as amended by the TLA 1996).

Tenancy in common

31.30 A tenancy in common cannot exist in relation to a legal estate;[1] consequently, it takes effect only in equity. If legal title is inadvertently conveyed to a number of people as tenants in common, the LPA 1925 provides that the conveyance takes effect as if it were a conveyance of the legal estate to the co-owners (or, if there are more than four, to the first four named in the conveyance) *as joint tenants on trust* to give effect to the rights of the co-owners *as tenants in common in equity*.[2] Thus a tenancy in common can only exist behind a trust; it takes effect in relation to the beneficial, equitable interest in the land, but not the legal estate. The key to an understanding of the machinery of co-ownership is to consider separately the position of the co-owners in relation to the legal estate in the land (be it freehold or leasehold) and their position in relation to the equitable interests existing behind the curtain of the trust.

Thus, if land is granted to A, B and C in equal shares they will hold the legal estate as joint tenants and as trustees; the wording used[3] gives rise to a tenancy in common which will take effect in equity.

Should C die, his individual share under the tenancy in common may pass under his will or on intestacy (say to X); but the right of survivorship operates in respect of the joint tenancy of the legal estate:

$$\frac{\text{A, B – legal JT}}{\text{A, B, X – equitable TiC}}$$

[1] LPA 1925, s 1(6).
[2] LPA 1925, ss 34 and 35.
[3] Being words of severance; see para 31.10.

Joint tenancy

31.31 As in the case of tenancy in common there is a splitting of the legal and equitable ownership whenever a joint tenancy is created. The co-owners (or the first four of them) hold the legal estate as joint trustees for themselves as joint tenants in equity:[1]

$$\frac{\text{A, B, C – legal JT}}{\text{A, B, C – equitable JT}}$$

Should C die, the right of survivorship operates in respect of the joint tenancy both at law and in equity:

$$\frac{\text{A, B – legal JT}}{\text{A, B – equitable JT}}$$

[1] LPA 1925, s 36.

Why a trust?

31.32 It might reasonably be asked why there is any need to impose a trust where both the identity of the co-owners (in our examples, A, B and C), and the nature of their interests are the same. This is because the position may change at any time during the course of the co-ownership. We saw in para 31.30 that C might die and leave his share in the equitable tenancy in common to X; in the example given in para 31.31, following C's death, A might have severed her equitable joint tenancy and given her share in what is now an equitable tenancy in common to Y. However, because of the existence of the trust and the principle of overreaching, none of this is of any concern to a purchaser; they can safely pay the purchase price to at least two trustees and be sure that no beneficiary can make any claim to the land.[1]

[1] See further, para 31.36.

The position of the trustees

Powers and duties

31.33 There will normally be between two and four trustees of a trust of land[1]. In relation to the land, they have all the powers of an absolute owner of land.[2] This means that they can sell,[3] lease or mortgage the land. In doing so they must, under the general law of trusts, act in the best interests of the trust and have regard to the rights of the beneficiaries.[4] Where either the whole or part of the land is sold, or capital money is raised by the creation of other interests (eg the grant of an option or lease at a premium) the trustees must invest that money. They can do so by purchasing investments in accordance with the provisions of the Trustee Act 2000. Equally, they are empowered to purchase other land as an investment, for occupation by a beneficiary, or for any other purpose.[5] Where all of the beneficiaries are of full age and capacity, the trustees can compel the beneficiaries to take a conveyance of the land irrespective of whether the beneficiaries wish this to happen.[6]

When exercising any of their functions relating to land[7] the trustees are under an obligation, so far as is practicable, to consult all the beneficiaries who are entitled to a present interest in the land. They should, in so far as is consistent with the best interests of the trust, give effect to the wishes of the majority of the beneficiaries.[8]

The trustees can choose[9] to delegate all or any of their functions relating to the land[10] to any beneficiary(ies) of full age who are entitled to an interest in possession in the land, either for a limited time, or indefinitely. Such a delegation must be made by way of power of attorney (ie formally by deed) which must be given by all of the trustees jointly. This power of attorney may be revoked by any one of the trustees, and will automatically be revoked by the appointment of a new trustee. Any beneficiary to whom the functions of a trustee have been delegated has the same duties and liabilities as regards the exercise of those functions as a trustee.

[1] There need to be a minimum of two in order that overreaching can take place (see para 31.36; there can be no more than four trustees of land, Trustee Act 1925, s 34(1).

[2] TLA 1996, s 6(1).

[3] It should be noted that, in sharp contrast to the position of a trustee under the old trust for sale, there is merely a *power* to sell, not an obligation. Even if a trust of land contains an express provision *obliging* the trustees to sell, this can safely be ignored since the trustees always have a power to postpone sale for an indefinite period: TLA 1996, s 4.

[4] TLA 1996, s 6(5) and (6).

[5] TLA 1996, s 6(3) and (4), s 17(1).

[6] TLA 1996, s 6(2). Where all the beneficiaries are of full age and capacity it has always been possible for the *beneficiaries* to compel the trustees to convey the land to them: *Saunders v Vautier* (1841) 10 LJ Ch 354. The TLA now allows the trustees the same freedom. Provided the beneficiaries *consent*, the trustees can, instead, partition the land between them: TLA 1996, s 7.

[7] The trustees' functions relating to land do not extend to their powers and duties in respect of capital moneys, such as investment.

[8] TLA 1996, s 11.

[9] Delegation is a matter of discretion for the trustees and, in deciding whether or not to delegate, they must bear in mind that they will become liable for the consequences of any negligent delegation. Any beneficiary to whom they refuse to delegate could apply to the court under TLA 1996, s 14.

[10] Again (see note 7 above) the power to delegate does not extend to the trustees' powers and duties in respect of capital moneys. So, for example, any capital moneys received as a result of the sale of the trust property must be paid to the trustees.

Restrictions on powers

31.34 In the case of an express trust of land (as opposed to one which is *imposed* by statute[1] or the courts[2]) certain of the trustees' power can either be expressly excluded,[3] or their exercise made subject to the consent of some person(s)[4] by the terms of the instrument creating the trust. The powers which can be restricted in this way are only those conferred by the TLA 1996, ss 6 and 7. So, the all-important power to dispose of the land can be restricted, as can the power to require adult beneficiaries to take a conveyance of the land or the power to invest in other land. However, neither the other powers of investment, nor the power to delegate, can be excluded.

[1] Such as is imposed by the LPA 1925, ss 34 and 36 wherever co-ownership is created without the use of an express trust of land; see para 31.29.

[2] Such as a resulting or constructive trust in the case of implied co-ownership.

[3] TLA 1996, s 8.

[4] TLA 1996, s 10.

The position of the beneficiaries

31.35 There can be any number of beneficiaries of a trust of land and, naturally, the interest of each one will be equitable. Any co-owner has the right to occupy the trust land provided that:

- the purposes of the trust include the provision of land for the occupation of the beneficiary(ies); and

- the property is not unavailable or unsuitable for occupation.[1]

Where more than one beneficiary is entitled to occupation they can, of course, occupy the property together. Where joint occupation is not feasible, the trustees (and, if necessary, the courts) can resolve disputes over which of them should occupy.[2]

As we have seen,[3] any beneficiary of full age and capacity with a present interest in the land is entitled to be consulted when the trustees exercise any of their functions relating to the land. Where there is an express provision requiring their consent,[4] a beneficiary may be able to prevent the trustees exercising any of their functions relating to the land. Where delegation has taken place,[5] a beneficiary will be able to exercise all those functions which have been delegated, although in doing so he (or she) must act in the best interests of the trust.

The beneficiaries under a trust of land are not entitled to receive capital moneys directly from a purchaser even where there has been full delegation of the trustees' functions.[6] Furthermore, they have no right to control[7] the trustees in the exercise of their functions relating to the investment of capital moneys.

[1] TLA 1996, s 12.
[2] TLA 1996, ss 13 and 14. See para 31.42.
[3] See para 31.33.
[4] See para 31.34.
[5] See para 31.33.
[6] See para 31.33. It should be remembered that a purchaser would not wish to pay capital moneys to anyone other than the trustees since this would prevent the overreaching of the beneficial interests under the trust: see paras 31.26 and para 31.36.
[7] Either by way of consultation, consent or delegation since all of these relate only to the trustees' functions in so far as they relate to the land.

The sale of trust land

The basic principles

31.36 One of the major purposes of using the trust to give effect to concurrent ownership is to avoid complexity in conveyancing. The ready marketability of land would be seriously inhibited if purchasers (and, in law[1], 'purchasers' include mortgagees[2] and lessees) could not be sure that the interest which they are acquiring (or obtaining as security) is free from the claims of others (save where those claims are readily detectable and then either reflected in the price paid or otherwise dealt with to the satisfaction of the purchaser). We have seen[3] that, without the device of the trust, a purchaser of land which is owned concurrently would have a multiplicity of titles to investigate, and would take subject to the rights of any owner who would not co-operate in the sale or other transaction. The trust avoids these difficulties.

Trustees always hold an unfragmented legal estate, be it freehold or leasehold. They hold that estate as joint tenants; this means that there is unity of title, so that there is only one register of title for the purchaser to investigate.

Furthermore, a purchaser of land held on trust need not be concerned with the equitable ownership[4] interests behind the 'curtain' of the trust, no matter how many.[5] They are not part of the legal title to the property; they are 'off the title' and neither the existence of the trust nor its details are recorded in the Land Register.[6] A purchaser need only ensure that any purchase money (or loan or other capital moneys) is paid to the trustees, who must be at least two in number (or a trust corporation)[7]; this ensures that the beneficial interests under the trust are overreached by the conveyance.[8] This does not mean that those beneficial interests are destroyed; it means that they cease to relate to the land and are transmuted into equivalent rights to the proceeds of sale. We can illustrate this fundamental principle with two examples.

EXAMPLE 1

Suppose Blacklands is conveyed to H and W as joint tenants. This takes effect in the following way:

$$\frac{\text{H, W – legal JT}}{\text{H, W – equitable JT}}$$

On a sale of Blacklands the purchaser P only needs to investigate the single legal register of title of H and W. He would not be concerned with their beneficial interests; he does not have to check whether W has, for example, severed the equitable joint tenancy and disposed of her interest to X, or whether Y has acquired a beneficial interest by way of financial contribution to the mortgage on Blacklands. By paying the purchase price to H and W *as trustees* any potential complexity in relation to the beneficial ownership of the land need not concern him, for the conveyance overreaches the beneficial interests. H's beneficial rights (and any rights which X and Y may have) are now rights to a share in the moneys paid by the purchaser.

EXAMPLE 2

Suppose Whitelands is conveyed to A, B, C, D and E as tenants in common. This takes effect as follows:

$$\frac{\text{A, B, C, D – legal JT}}{\text{A, B, C, D, E – equitable TiC}}$$

Suppose A dies, leaving his interest in Whitelands to Z. The position now is:

$$\frac{\text{B, C, D – legal JT}}{\text{Z, B, C, D, E – equitable TiC}}$$

On a sale of Whitelands, a purchaser would only need to investigate the single title of B, C and D and would not be concerned with the beneficial interests in general or with what has happened to A's interest in the land, in particular. So long as the purchaser deals with and pays the purchase price to the trustees (B, C and D) the complexity in relation to the beneficial ownership of Whitelands is not a problem because the conveyance overreaches the beneficial interests. The rights of Z, B, C, D and E are now rights to a share of the proceeds of sale.

However, it should be appreciated that, while the principle of overreaching is highly convenient for those purchasing, or lending on the security of land, it can operate unfairly to deprive beneficiaries of their right to occupy trust property. In cases where the trustees and beneficiaries are different persons, the trustees might sell or mortgage the property without the knowledge or consent of the beneficiaries; their interests are automatically overreached and while, in certain circumstances, the beneficiaries may be able to sue the trustees for breach of trust[9], they will certainly not regain their rights to the land. This is well illustrated by the decision in *City of London Building Society v Flegg*.[10] Here the defendants had contributed to the purchase of a property in which they, and their daughter and son-in-law were to live. This was transferred into the names of the younger couple[11], with the result that they were trustees under a trust of land; they and the parents (by way of resulting trust[12]) were the beneficiaries. Some time later and unknown to the Fleggs, the young couple granted a mortgage on which they subsequently defaulted. When the claimant mortgagee sought possession, the Fleggs claimed that their rights as equitable co-owners were binding. The House of Lords held that this was not so; the Fleggs' rights had been overreached because the mortgage had been granted by the trustees. In 1989, the Law Commission proposed that the rights of adult beneficiaries who are occupying the property should not be overreached by transactions conducted without their consent,[13] but this suggestion has long been abandoned.

[1] LPA 1925, s 205(1)(xxi).

[2] A mortgagee of land is a person who makes a loan on the security of land; he or she is a person *to whom* a mortgage is granted by the landowner/mortgagor.

[3] See para 31.24.

[4] A purchaser does, of course, need to be concerned about equitable interests which are *not* ownership interests, eg restrictive covenants, since these may can continue to affect the land (see generally ch 35).

[5] LPA 1925, s 27(1).

[6] Any purchaser's lawyer checking title will, of course, realise that there is always a trust wherever there is more than one owner of the legal estate; however, the details of the trust is of no concern.

[7] Overreaching also occurs where capital moneys are not paid to the trustees at the time of the conveyance but later. In *State Bank of India v Sood* [1997] 1 All ER 169, CA the trustees executed a charge over trust property in favour of the bank, as security for present and future indebtedness on certain bank accounts. No loan was advanced at the time of the charge but the accounts became further overdrawn. When the bank wished to exercise its power of sale (as to which see para 34.29 below) it was held that it could do so free from the claims of the beneficiaries; their interests had been overreached at the time of the charge.

[8] LPA 1925, ss 2(1)(i) and 27(2).

[9] Eg because the trustees have failed to consult the beneficiaries as required by TLA 1996, s 11, see para 31.33.

[10] [1987] 3 All ER 435, HL.

[11] The parents declined legal advice to be joint registered proprietors; they could also have protected their position by insisting that their consent be required for any subsequent disposition (which would have included a further mortgage), see para 31.34.

[12] See para 31.13.

[13] In Law Com No 188 (1989), the sentiments of which were echoed by Peter Gibson LJ in *State Bank of India v Sood* [1997] 1 All ER 169, CA.

31.37 It may, of course, happen that a sale cannot proceed in the straightforward manner suggested by the examples given in the previous paragraph. The trustees may not agree that the land should be sold, or the beneficiaries may disagree with the trustees' decision to sell. In the typical co-ownership situation outlined in Example 1, it may be that H and W disagree as to whether a sale should take place, a state of affairs which completely rules out the possibility of overreaching since the purchaser would be unable to pay the money to at least two trustees. We discuss how these difficulties may be resolved in para 31.39 and 31.41.

Furthermore, in the examples so far employed, the existence of the trust has been apparent on the title because each property was expressly conveyed to more than one person. What is the position where there is no indication on the title of the existence of any trust? This situation will arise when land has been conveyed in the name of one person only but where that person is regarded by equity as holding it on trust either wholly, or partly for another. The most commonly encountered example of this is where equity implies co-ownership.[1] As we have seen, there is no doubting the existence of a trust of land in such circumstances,[2] the problem is that a purchaser (or mortgagee) may unwittingly hand over purchase money or otherwise deal with someone who is in reality a *sole* trustee. This means that the purchaser is deprived of the protection of overreaching which only applies to dealings with *two* trustees. As we shall see,[3] in such circumstances the purchaser or mortgagee may be bound by the interests of the implied (co) owner (who is a 'hidden'[4] beneficiary under the trust) unless careful investigations are carried out.

[1] See para 31.12.
[2] See para 31.29.
[3] See para 34.24 and 35.27.
[4] By 'hidden' we mean undetectable on the paper title; such beneficiaries are often, in practice, detectable since they are usually in occupation of the trust land. As we shall see in paras 34.24 and 35.27, the purchaser's (and mortgagee's) best protection is the careful inspection of the property and the investigation of the property rights of anyone who is occupying the property either with, or instead of, the vendor/mortgagor.

Disputes over trusts of land

31.38 Inevitably, there will be times when there are disputes over the operation of a trust of land. The trustees may disagree with each other over whether or not the land should be sold or retained, on whether (or which of) the beneficiaries should occupy the property, or on how it should be managed. The beneficiaries may be at odds with the trustees, or with each other.

These difficulties produce a total stalemate in the very common situation where the trustees and the beneficiaries are one and the same and where there are only two of them. Classically, this will occur where property is co-owned by a married couple, civil partners, or by co-habitees whose relationship has broken down. In practice, the legal title to their home will be vested in the two of them as trustees, and they will also be the only beneficiaries, holding either as joint tenants or tenants in common in equal shares (see Example 1 in para 31.36). Obviously, they may be able to agree on what should happen to the property; for example that it should be sold and the proceeds divided between them, or that one should buy the other out. Often, however, they will be unable to reach agreement, if only because their respective interests will have become diametrically opposed. One may wish to remain in the house with any children; the other will need to realise their share in the property in order to fund the purchase of another home.

'Matrimonial' property

31.39 Where the dispute concerns 'matrimonial'[1] property (eg where those, in the scenario described in the previous paragraph, are a married couple or in a civil partnership), it will be resolved by the courts under the Matrimonial Causes Act 1973[2] or Civil Partnership Act 2004,[3] as part of any divorce or separation proceedings. Those statutes give the court wide powers to make orders relating to what was 'matrimonial' property; it can order that the property be sold, or retained (especially where there are young children still living at home) and it can adjust the parties' rights to the property. So, it can order that one party transfer their share to the other.

[1] This includes property held by same sex couples who have entered into a civil partnership.

² Matrimonial Causes Act 1973, ss 23–25.
³ Civil Partnership Act 2004, s 72, Sch 5.

Other trust property

31.40 Where disputes concern trust land which is not co-owned by a married couple or those in a civil partnership, they must be resolved by the application of ordinary property principles. The TLA 1996 has sought to rationalise and improve the approach to differences arising in the context of trusts of land.[1] The courts have been given a wide jurisdiction to entertain applications from trustees or those with an interest in a trust of land.[2] They may make any order 'relating to the exercise by the trustees of any of their functions, including an order relieving them of any obligation to obtain the consent of, or to consult, any person in connection with the exercise of their functions'.[3] They may also make an order 'declaring the nature or extent of a person's interest' in the trust land.[4]

The Act sets out matters which the court should take into account when making *any* order;[5] there are also specific provisions dealing with a dispute as to which beneficiary(ies) should occupy the trust property.[6] Many of these principles are derived from the case law which was developed by the courts prior to 1997 so that, as we shall see, some pre-1997 cases provide an indication of how the courts are likely to apply these new statutory provisions.

In practice, most of the disputes concerning trust land concern one (or both) of two issues; whether the land should be sold or, which of the beneficiaries should occupy the trust property. We shall, therefore, address each of these in the following paragraphs.

¹ It should be remembered that the provisions of the Act which we are about to deal with apply to *all* trusts of land. In practice, however, most of the disputes arise in connection with *co-owned* land.
² TLA 1996, s 14(1).
³ TLA 1996, s 14(2)(a).
⁴ TLA 1996, s 14(2)(b). It should be noted that, in sharp contrast to the position regarding *matrimonial property* (see para 31.39 above), the court has no power to *vary* the interests of the beneficiaries.
⁵ TLA 1996, s 15.
⁶ TLA 1996, ss 13 and 15(2).

31.41 *Sale.* Where there is an application to court under the TLA 1996, s 14 because there is a dispute as to whether or not the trust land should be sold, it is clear that the court can:

- order a sale; or
- order a sale but suspend the order for the time being; or
- refuse a sale; or
- refuse a sale and make an order as to the occupation of the property.

When making its decision the court is required to take into account:[1]

- the intentions of the person(s) creating the trust;
- the purposes for which the trust property is held;
- the welfare of any child who occupies or might reasonably be expected to occupy the trust property as his home;
- the interests of any secured creditor of any beneficiary; and
- the wishes (of the majority by value) of any beneficiaries of full age and capacity.

Where an application under TLA 1996, s14 is made by a trustee in bankruptcy, the above principles do not apply. So where, for example, one of the co-owners becomes bankrupt[2] and their trustee in bankruptcy applies for an order of sale, it is the insolvency regime which applies.[3] Broadly, where the property is the home of the bankrupt or the bankrupt's spouse or former spouse, one year's grace following the bankruptcy is given; thereafter, on any application for sale by the trustee in bankruptcy the interests of the creditors are paramount so that, in practice, an order of sale will virtually always be made.[4]

[1] TLA 1996, s 15. The section makes it clear that what follows is not an exhaustive list, so that the court is free to take account of other matters as well.

[2] With the result that their beneficial interest will vest in their trustee in bankruptcy, see para 31.19.

[3] TLA 1996, s 15(4). This is now only the case where the trustee in bankruptcy applies for the sale of the property within 3 years of the bankruptcy, Insolvency Act 1986, s 283A (inserted by the Enterprise Act 2002, s 261).

[4] Insolvency Act 1986, s 335A; although a sale can be refused in exceptional circumstances the courts have generally been extremely reluctant to do so.

31.42 *Occupation* As we have seen,[1] beneficiaries often have the right to occupy the trust property and, in the case of concurrent ownership where the property was purchased for joint occupation, this will invariably be the case. Where two or more beneficiaries are entitled to occupy at the same time, but do not wish to occupy the property together and cannot agree a solution, the trustees are given the power to decide which of them can occupy and on what terms.[2] If a beneficiary is dissatisfied with the trustees' decision, an application to court under the TLA 1996, s 14 can, of course, be made. However, the more likely circumstance of an application to court will be where the trust arises as a result of co-ownership. Here, the trustees are usually the very same beneficiaries who no longer wish to share occupation and who cannot agree as to which of them should stay. Here, a court's intervention will be necessary. As can be seen from the cases considered in the previous paragraph, it may well be the case that the court considers the question of sale and occupation together.

The TLA 1996, s 13 sets out the powers of the trustees and the circumstances which they must take into account when arriving at a decision about the occupation of trust property. The section provides that the trustees may exclude or restrict the right to occupy where it is reasonable to do so. Where this is done, the occupying beneficiary can be required to make payments to the excluded beneficiary. Equally, the trustees can subject a beneficiary's occupation to reasonable conditions (such as, in particular, the payment of compensation to other beneficiaries and responsibility for any outgoings or expenses in respect of the land). In reaching any decision the trustees should have regard to the intentions of the person who created the trust, the purposes for which the land is held and the circumstances and wishes of the beneficiaries who are entitled to occupy.

If the matter goes to court it is now clear that the court must[3] take into account the factors set out in section 15[4] and it should be noted that these are wider than those applicable to the trustees. Commonly, the court is dealing with both the sale and occupation of co-owned land, Here, it is likely[5] that, where a sale is refused with the result that one of the co-owners is to remain in occupation, the occupier will be required to pay an occupation rent to the other (with credit being given for any mortgage payments being made by the occupier).

[1] See para 31.35.

[2] TLA 1996, s 13.

[3] See *Stack v Dowden* [2007] 2 AC 432.

[4] These are the same as those applicable where an order for the sale of the land is being sought and are set out in para 31.41.

[5] See *Murphy v Gooch* [2007] EWCA Civ 608.

Trusts of Land: Key Points

- Since 1997 all co-ownership exists in the form of a trust of land governed by the TLA 1996.

- The imposition of a trust means that the legal title is held on a joint tenancy by trustees who can be no more than four in number; this ensures that a purchaser only has to investigate a single unfragmented title.

- The beneficial interest can be held by any number of co-owners who can hold on either a joint tenancy or tenancy in common; these are of no concern to a purchaser of the land who complies with the requirements of overreaching.

- Provided a purchaser pays the purchase price to at least two trustees the interests of all beneficiaries are overreached; this means that those interests cease to relate to the land and become attached to the proceeds of sale and the purchaser takes the land free from any claims by the beneficiaries.

- The TLA 1996 gives the trustees all the powers of an absolute owner although they must consult all adult beneficiaries; they may delegate these powers to an adult beneficiary and the trust instrument may require the trustees to obtain the consent of a person (who may well be one of the beneficiaries).

- Provided the purposes of the trust include the provision of land for occupation, the beneficiaries have a *right* to occupy the land; the extent of their other powers depends on whether or not the trustees have delegated all or any of their functions and on whether or not the trust instrument has required the consent of a beneficiary to any particular action by the trustees.

- Whether or not trust land is sold is a decision for the trustees; this may well cause problems in many cases where the co-ownership is shared by two people (classically cohabitees) who are together the only trustees and the only beneficiaries and, because of a relationship breakdown, cannot agree on a sale.

- All disputes over the sale or occupation of trust land that cannot be resolved by the trustees will be dealt with by the courts.

Questions

1. What are the two forms of concurrent ownership and what are the differences between them?

2. What are 'words of severance'?

3. In what circumstances, and on what basis, may the courts treat a person as a co-owner of land that is registered in the name of another?

4. How are the shares in co-owned land quantified where the parties have made no express provision?

5. What is severance and how can it be achieved?

6. How does the imposition of a trust overcome the problems posed by the co-ownership of land?

7. Where the trustees of co-owned land sell it the interests of the beneficiaries can be 'overreached'; what does this mean and how is it achieved?

8. Fiona and George are an unmarried couple who bought a house together 10 years ago. The title to the property was registered in both their names; they made no declaration as to the ownership of the beneficial interest. They now have two children and their relationship has just come to an end. George wants the house to be sold so that he can realise his share; he needs the money in order to buy a new home for himself. Fiona needs the property as a home for herself and the children. Explain their legal situation as regards the house. Consider what legal procedures will be followed, and what principles will be applied, in order to resolve this impasse.

32

Easements

CHAPTER OVERVIEW

We now turn our attention to the more important of the third party rights, ie those proprietary rights that are enjoyed over land belonging to another. In this chapter we deal with easements and consider:

• the essential legal characteristics of an easement;

• the methods by which easements can be created or acquired; and

• certain specific easements.

32.1 Some third party rights, notably easements and restrictive covenants, can only exist between neighbouring properties, so that they are a benefit to one and a burden on the other. These rights are particularly important in dictating the way in which each piece of land can be used and enjoyed. Other third party rights, such as mortgages, options and rights of pre-emption, can be enjoyed by those who do not themselves have any rights to other land; these are therefore simply a burden on the land to which they relate, their benefit attaches to a person (who can, of course, usually transfer their rights to another) rather than to other land.

32.2 We start by considering one of the most important of the third party rights to land, the easement.[1] As we shall see, there are a number of different types of easement (such as rights of way, rights of support, rights of drainage, rights of light) but they all share the same basic characteristics. Easements are irrevocable rights which one landowner enjoys in respect of a neighbour's land and, as such, they provide what is often an essential basis for the full enjoyment of land ownership. Many pieces of land or buildings or parts of buildings cannot be properly utilised without the existence of rights over adjoining property: for example, the tenant of a first floor flat will need a right of way over the ground floor of the premises; the owner of a semi-detached house needs support from the adjoining 'semi'.

---

[1] The importance of easements is recognised in the Law Commission's Consultation Paper No 186 *Easements Covenants and Profits a Prendre* (2008). It proposes a number of important changes to this area of the law.

The nature of easement

32.3 An easement is a right which one landowner enjoys in respect of a neighbour's land; it may be legal or equitable.[1] Some idea of the nature of easements may be gathered from the following statement by Lord Denning:[2] 'There are two kinds of easements known to the law: positive easements, such as a right of way, which give the owner of land *a right himself to do something* on or to his neighbour's land: and negative easements, such as a right of light, which give him *a right to stop his neighbour doing something* on his (the neighbour's) own land.'

The nature of an easement is best explained by reference to four essential characteristics approved by the Court of Appeal in *Re Ellenborough Park, Re Davies, Powell v Maddison*.[3] In this case, the Court held that the right to use a park or garden adjacent to a group of houses was an easement attaching to those houses. The Court reached its decision by considering whether the following four requirements were satisfied:

- there must be a dominant and a servient piece of land;
- the easement must 'accommodate' the dominant land;
- the dominant and servient owners must be different persons; and
- the right must be capable of forming the subject matter of a grant.

Each of these will now be considered.

[1] Para 32.24.
[2] *Phipps v Pears* [1964] 2 All ER 35 at 33.
[3] [1955] 3 All ER 667, CA.

The essential characteristics of an easement

There must be a dominant and servient piece of land

32.4 There must be land which enjoys the right (the dominant land) and land which is subject to the right (the servient land). An easement takes effect for the benefit of *land*; it is annexed to that land and passes automatically on its transfer. An easement cannot exist independently of the ownership of land; it amplifies an owner's enjoyment of some estate or interest in a piece of land.[1] Thus there can be no grant of an easement at a time when the dominant land has not yet been identified; this means that it is not possible to create easements in favour of land which is to be acquired in the future.[2] Furthermore, where an easement exists for the benefit of one piece of land, it cannot later be used for the benefit of another, subsequently acquired, piece of land[3], save where the use of the easement for the extra land is genuinely ancillary[4].

[1] *Alfred F Beckett Ltd v Lyons* [1967] 1 All ER 833, CA.
[2] *London and Blenheim Estates Ltd v Ladbroke Retail Parks Ltd* [1993] 4 All ER 157, CA. See also *Voice v Bell* (1993) 68 P & CR 441, CA.
[3] *Jobson v Record* (1997) 75 P & CR 375, CA; *Peacock v Custins* [2001] 2 All ER 827, CA; *Das v Linden Mews Ltd* [2002] EWCA Civ 590.
[4] *Massey v Boulden* [2002] EWCA Civ 1634 and see para 32.53.

The easement must 'accommodate' the dominant land

32.5 An easement must be of benefit to the dominant land. There must be a clear connection between the enjoyment of the right and the enjoyment of the dominant land. In *Re Ellenborough Park*,[1] the court held that the park became a communal garden for the benefit and enjoyment of those whose houses adjoined it or were in its close proximity; it was the collective garden of the neighbouring houses. The necessary connection between the right and the land was thus shown. In contrast, a right given to the purchaser of a house to attend Lord's cricket ground without payment would not constitute an easement, for, although it would confer an advantage on the purchaser and doubtless would increase the value of the property, it would be wholly extraneous to, and independent of, the use of the house as a house.[2]

This does not mean that a right which primarily benefits a business cannot be held to accommodate the land from which that business is operated. Thus, in *Moody v Steggles*,[3] it was held that the right to affix an inn sign on adjoining property accommodated the claimant's public house. The question would seem to depend on whether the court is prepared to find a close connection between the right and the business conducted from the dominant land.[4]

However, where the right in question actually constitutes the business, there can be no easement. So, in *Hill v Tupper*,[5] the tenant of premises on the bank of the Basingstoke Canal was given the 'sole and exclusive right' by the owners to put pleasure boats on the canal. He subsequently brought an action against the defendant, who had also started to hire out pleasure boats on the canal, alleging that the latter was interfering with his easement. This claim failed; the court held that the claimant's right to put boats on the canal was merely a contractual licence, giving him rights against the licensors (the owners of the canal) but not against the defendant. The claimant was trying to set up, under the guise of an easement, a monopoly which had no normal connection with the ordinary use of his land but which was merely an independent business enterprise. Far from the right claimed accommodating the land, the land was but a convenient incident to the exercise of the right.

[1] [1955] 3 All ER 667, CA.
[2] [1955] 3 All ER 667 at 680.
[3] (1879) 12 Ch D 261. See also *William Hill (Southern) Ltd v Cabras Ltd* [1987] 1 EGLR 37, CA where the right to erect the name of a business on adjoining property was held to be an easement.
[4] In *Clapman v Edwards* [1938] 2 All ER 507 a *general* right to advertise on adjoining premises was held not to be an easement since there was no connection with the dominant land.
[5] (1863) 2 H & C 121.

32.6 It may not be possible to demonstrate the necessary connection between enjoyment of the right and the dominant land where the dominant and servient properties are at some distance from each other: 'a right of way over land in Northumberland cannot accommodate land in Kent'.[1] On the other hand, it is not necessary that the properties be adjoining. In *Re Ellenborough Park*,[2] a few of the houses having the benefit of the use of the park were some 100 yards from it: nonetheless, the court held that the necessary connection between dominant and servient tenement existed. Again, in *Pugh v Savage*,[3] the owner of field C was held entitled to an easement of way across field A to reach the nearby highway despite the existence of field B, which he had a licence to cross, between the two properties.

[1] *Bailey v Stephens* (1862) 12 CBNS 91.
[2] [1955] 3 All ER 667, CA.
[3] [1970] 2 All ER 353, CA.

The dominant and servient owners must be different persons

32.7 Clearly, since an easement is a right over another's land, one cannot have an easement over one's own land. However, the freehold owner of two plots may grant an easement over one plot to the tenant of the other, and a tenant may expressly or impliedly grant an easement to another tenant of the same landlord. Where an owner of two plots of land uses a way across one plot to reach the other, they are clearly doing so as owner rather than by virtue of an easement; nevertheless, it is said that in these circumstances there is a 'quasi-easement'. There are circumstances in which quasi-easements can become full easements; we deal with this in para 32.31.

The right must be capable of forming the subject matter of a grant, ie be capable of being granted

32.8 This requirement comprises a number of elements some of which are 'technical' and others of which are more policy based. It ensures that the right claimed must be one which can be formulated in a deed of grant by a capable grantor to a capable grantee. For example, a tenant cannot grant an easement in fee simple, nor can an easement be granted to a fluctuating group of persons.

However, this requirement also, and perhaps more importantly, acts as a filter for the recognition of new types of easement, a question that raises policy issues. Although there is no fixed list of easements, the courts do control the rights which will be recognised as easements. Easements are powerful rights which last for as long as the interest to which they are attached. So, an easement for the benefit of a freehold estate is, in reality, indefinite; an easement attached to a leasehold estate will continue for as long as the lease. Furthermore, as we shall see, easements do not always originate in an express agreement between neighbouring landowners; they can arise by implication or as a result of prescription (long use). For these reasons a court, when deciding whether a type of right *which has never previously been accepted as an easement*,[1] should be so recognised, will consider a variety of matters. However, it will often take into account four particular factors which are accepted as delimiting the nature of an easement.

[1] Once a type of right has been accepted by the courts as *capable* of being an easement, these policy issues will not normally be re-visited should the same type of right be litigated in future cases.

32.9 *Sufficiently definite* The first factor is whether the right claimed is one which is of too wide and vague a character,[1] rendering it difficult to define in a deed of grant. Thus a right to a view over neighbouring land cannot be an easement[2]. Similarly, the courts have also refused to allow as an easement a claim to a general right of light for one's land;[3] such rights can only exist as an easement in respect of a defined aperture.[4] Similarly, the right to the general passage of air over one's land cannot exist as an easement,[5] but a right to air to a defined aperture can.[6] The extent of the right claimed can in the latter case be expressed with some precision.

[1] *Re Ellenborough Park* [1955] 3 All ER 667, CA.
[2] *William Aldred's Case* (1610) 9 Co Rep 57b. A right to a view can only be protected indirectly by, for example, imposing restrictive covenants (as to which see ch 33) that prevent neighbours from building in a way which obstructs the view, see *Davies v Dennis* [2009] EWCA Civ 1081.
[3] See *Roberts v Macord* (1832) 1 Mood & R 230.
[4] Para 32.54.
[5] *Webb v Bird* (1861) 10 CBNS 268.
[6] *Bryant v Lefever* (1879) 4 CPD 172.

32.10 *No new negative easements* The second matter that will affect a court's consideration of whether to recognise a new right as an easement will be the question of whether the right is negative or positive. Although negative easements (ie those which operate to restrict what a servient owner can do on their own land[1]) do exist, notably easements of light and easements of support for buildings, those that do have been recognised for hundreds of years. Today, the law is reluctant to recognise new ones, largely because it is felt that rights which prevent a servient owner using their land in some way are better dealt with by way of expressly agreed restrictive covenants[2]. So, in *Phipps v Pears*,[3] the Court of Appeal had to decide whether the right to have one's property protected from the weather could exist as an easement. One of two houses, which were very close together but which did not actually support each other, was demolished, thereby exposing to the elements the wall of the other house, which had never been rendered or plastered. Reflecting the policy considerations which must always be present when a claim to a new type of easement is decided, the court rejected the claim to an easement on the basis that this was a claim to a *negative* easement, new examples of which the law should be wary of creating since they restrict servient owners in the enjoyment of their own land and hamper legitimate development[4]. Similarly, in *Hunter v Canary Wharf Ltd*[5], it was held that the right to receive an uninterrupted television signal could not exist as an easement.

[1] See para 32.3.
[2] See ch 33.
[3] [1964] 2 All ER 35, CA.
[4] It should be noted that, today, the claimant may well have been able to base a claim in tort, in either negligence or nuisance, see *Rees v Skerrett* [2001] EWCA Civ 760, [2001] 1 WLR 1541.
[5] [1997] 2 All ER 426, HL.

32.11 *No joint possession* Until recently it was thought that a claim to an easement must not amount to a claim to use and enjoy the servient land either exclusively, or jointly with the servient owner. An easement is a right which is compatible with the servient owner's right to exclusive possession of the land. In *Copeland v Greenhalf*,[1] the defendant claimed that he was entitled to an easement to store vehicles awaiting and undergoing repair on a strip of land opposite his premises. Upjohn J rejected the claim as being virtually a claim to possession of the servient land, since it involved the defendant and his employees being able to carry out repair work on the land and involved the defendant leaving as many vehicles on the land as he wished, thereby effectively treating the land as his own.[2] Similarly, in *Grigsby v Melville*[3] it was held that an unlimited right to store items in an adjoining cellar could not amount to an easement as it involved too extensive a use.

It did not follow, however, that an easement to store articles on another's land could not exist. The possibility was recognised in *A-G of Southern Nigeria v John Holt & Co (Liverpool) Ltd*,[4] and in *Wright v Macadam*[5] it was held, without argument on the point, that the right to store coal in a coal shed was clearly an easement. In *Miller v Emcer Products Ltd*,[6] a case demonstrating that the categories of easements are not closed, the Court of Appeal held that a right to use a neighbour's lavatory could exist as an easement. The court pointed out that, although at the times when the dominant owner exercised their right the owner of the servient tenement would be excluded, this was a common feature to a greater or lesser extent of many easements, such as a right of way, and in any case this did not amount to so complete an ouster of the servient owner's rights as was held to be incompatible with an easement in *Copeland v Greenhalf*.

This view of the law has been thrown into doubt by recent case law concerning the right to park vehicles on neighbouring land. Originally, the courts appeared to be holding to the traditional line. In *London and Blenheim Estates Ltd v Ladbroke Retail Parks Ltd*[7] the view was expressed that a right to park a car anywhere within a defined area can be an easement whereas a right to park in a particular slot, to the exclusion of the servient owner, would not be. In *Hair v Gillman*[8] it was held that a right to park one car anywhere within an area in which four cars could be parked was an easement; by way of contrast, in *Batchelor v Marlow*[9] an exclusive right to park six cars on a strip of land during working hours was held to be too extensive to be an easement. However, in *Moncrieff v Jamieson*[10], the House of Lords has disapproved of this approach. In confirming that a right to park can exist as an easement, their Lordships expressed the view that the effective exclusion of the servient owner from the land does not prevent a right being an easement. Specifically, this ruling seems to mean that a right to park in an allocated space or a garage can now be an easement. More generally, the case may create problems. It will now be more difficult to decide whether 'storage' rights are easements (ie limited rights over the land of another) or ownership rights (ie rights conferring exclusive possession) such as a lease. Where claims to such rights are based on long use the difference between adverse possession[11] and prescription[12] may be harder to distinguish.[13]

[1] [1952] 1 All ER 809.
[2] Such facts might provide a basis for a claim to the *ownership* of the land under the principles of adverse possession: see paras 30.19–30.36 above.

[3] [1973] 1 All ER 385.

[4] [1915] AC 599, PC.

[5] [1949] 2 All ER 565, CA.

[6] [1956] 1 All ER 237, CA.

[7] [1993] 1 All ER 307, affirmed by the Court of Appeal on another point.

[8] (2000) 80 P & CR 108.

[9] [2001] EWCA Civ 1051.

[10] [2007] 1 WLR 2620. Technically, this was an appeal dealing with the law in Scotland. The Court of Appeal has accepted that the ruling also represents the law in England and Wales, see *Waterman v Boyle* [2009] EWCA Civ 115.

[11] See paras 30.19–30.36.

[12] See paras 32.40–32.51.

[13] Given the increasing difficulty in succeeding in a claim based on adverse possession (see para 30.22) claimants may now try to characterise their possession as an easement in order to be able to proceed by way of prescription.

32.12 *No expense for servient owner* A fourth factor to be considered is that the easement claimed must not automatically involve the servient owner in expenditure. An easement is either a right to do something or a right to prevent something. A right *to have something done* is not an easement, nor is it an incident of an easement.[1] Thus an agreement by a landlord to supply hot water and heating to the tenants of a block does not give rise to an easement;[2] rights such as these can only exist as express contracts or covenants. However, both a right to a supply of water[3], and a supply of electricity,[4] through meters located on the servient land and for payment of which the servient owner was responsible, have been analysed as easements for the passage of water and electricity respectively. In both instances the dominant owner would, by implication, be liable to reimburse the servient owner for the costs of the supply to the dominant tenement.

An exception to the rule that the right claimed must not involve the servient owner in expenditure is provided by the long recognised easement of fencing. 'The right to have your neighbour keep up the fences is a right in the nature of an easement which is capable of being granted by law'.[5] The cases suggest that such easements are restricted to fencing against straying livestock. If this is so, an obligation to maintain a fence between two neighbouring houses does not amount to an easement; it will therefore bind only the contracting parties and cannot affect a new owner of the 'servient' property[6].

There is long-standing authority that the owner of the servient tenement is not bound, in the absence of an express or implied contractual obligation,[7] to carry out any repairs necessary to ensure the enjoyment of the easement by the dominant owner. It seems, however, that a servient owner may be liable in negligence or nuisance if they fail to take reasonable steps to repair defects of which they are aware or ought to have been aware which threaten to interfere with the dominant owner's easement.[8] It should be noted that the grant of an easement does, ordinarily, confer on the *dominant* owner the right to enter the servient property to effect essential repairs[9] and, where this is necessary to the enjoyment of the right, to make improvements (eg to a right of way).[10]

[1] *Jones v Price* [1965] 2 All ER 625 at 628, CA.

[2] *Regis Property Co Ltd v Redman* [1956] 2 All ER 335, CA.

[3] *Rance v Elvin* (1985) 50 P & CR 9, CA.

[4] *Duffy v Lamb* [1997] NPC 52, CA.

[5] *Crow v Wood* [1970] 3 All ER 425 at 429, CA.

[6] See *Jones v Price* [1965] 2 All ER 625, CA.

[7] See *Liverpool City Council v Irwin* [1976] 2 All ER 39, HL and *King v South Northamptonshire District Council* (1991) 64 P & CR 35, CA, two cases in which the courts were prepared to imply a contractual obligation on the part of a landlord to repair and maintain an essential means of access to the demised property; see para 36.46.

[8] *Bradburn v Lindsay* [1983] 2 All ER 408; see also para 23.16 and para 32.57.

[9] *Jones v Pritchard* [1908] 1 Ch 30.

[10] The dominant owner may not, however, carry out works which amount to an improvement which increases the burden on the servient land where the right has been acquired by prescription (for which see paras 32.40–32.51). See *Mills v Silver* [1991] 1 All ER 449, CA where it was held that the dominant owner was not entitled to improve the surface of a right of way.

Rights similar to easements

32.13 Under this heading we further explain the nature of easements by considering rights which are similar to easements and, in each case, what it is which differentiates them from easements.

Natural rights

32.14 Every landowner enjoys certain natural rights against neighbouring landowners. Unlike easements, these rights flow automatically from the ownership of land; they do not depend on any form of creation. Every landowner has the right to receive support for their land from that of their neighbour.[1] Further, as we have seen,[2] all landowners have certain limited right to water.

[1] See further para 32.57.

[2] Para 28.20.

Restrictive covenants[1]

32.15 A similarity between easements and restrictive covenants can be seen in that both require dominant and servient land.[2] Indeed, restrictive covenants were described by Sir George Jessel MR[3] as an equitable development of the concept of negative easements. However, there are important differences. Restrictive covenants must be expressly created; as we shall see, easements may be implied, and can be acquired as a result of long use (ie by prescription).[4] Again, as we shall see, restrictive covenants are equitable only, whereas easements may be legal or equitable. Furthermore, it may be that the content of a restrictive covenant is not limited in the same way as that of easements. So, for example, while the right to a view is too vague to exist as an easement,[5] the same objective may be achieved by the imposition of a restrictive covenant preventing development which obstructs the view.[6] Certainly, save for the requirement that a restrictive covenant be negative,[7] the courts do not exercise control over the type of rights which can exist by way of restrictive covenant; as we have seen,[8] policy considerations do dictate the nature of rights which will be accepted as easements. Finally, as we shall see,[9] there are recognised circumstances in which both the common law and, more particularly, statute specifically allows for restrictive covenants to be modified or discharged. There is no such general provision for the removal of easements; indeed, once created, the law is most reluctant to extinguish an easement.[10]

[1] See ch 33.

[2] See para 33.13.

[3] *London and South Western Rly Co v Gomm* (1882) 20 Ch D 562.

[4] See paras 32.40–32.57.

[5] *Aldred's Case* (1610) 9 Co Rep 57b.

[6] *Wakeham v Wood* (1981) 43 P & CR 40, CA, para 33.30; and see *Gilbert v Spoor* [1982] 2 All ER 576, CA, para 33.42 below.

[7] See para 33.12.

[8] Para 32.8.

[9] See paras 33.31–33.44.

[10] See para 32.52.

Public rights

32.16 An easement is a private right which one landowner can exercise against the land of another. Some rights to land can be exercised by any member of the public and one of the most commonly encountered is a public right of way. Those entitled to exercise such rights do so in their capacity as members of the public, they do not have to own dominant land. Public rights of way can be created expressly by statute, or at common law by dedication and acceptance[1]. The right of the public to have access over privately owned land was greatly extended by the Countryside and Rights of Way Act 2000.[2]

[1] Highways Act 1980, s 31(1).
[2] Part I of the Act confers a public right to roam over certain designated land (largely open country and registered common land) while Part II contains provisions governing the classification and recording of public rights of way.

Licences[1]

32.17 The right to walk across another's field, for example, may exist either as an easement, a public right of way, or a licence. A licence differs from an easement in that it can, in general, be revoked. Moreover, a licence is a personal right not a proprietary right; it requires no dominant land and, unless supported by some equity, can only be enforced against the licensor, and not against any subsequent owner of the licensor's land.[2]

[1] Paras 28.40–28.44.
[2] See para 28.44.

Non-derogation from grant[1]

32.18 A person who conveys or leases part of their land *for a specific purpose*, is under an obligation not to use the retained land in such a way as to render the land conveyed or leased unfit, or materially less fit, for the particular purpose for which the conveyance or lease was made.[2] *Aldin v Latimer Clark, Muirhead & Co*[3] illustrates how this principle may confer greater rights than may be conferred as an easement. Land was let to the claimant to enable him to carry on the business of a timber merchant. It was held that the landlord could not build on his retained land so as to interrupt the free passage of air to the claimant's timber-drying sheds. A general right to air such as this could not have existed as an easement; the easement to the free passage of air is limited to one through a defined aperture.[4]

[1] See, in the specific context of leases, para 36.35.
[2] *Browne v Flower* [1911] 1 Ch 219 at 226.
[3] [1894] 2 Ch 437.
[4] Para 32.9.

Profits à prendre

32.19 A profit à prendre is a right to take from another's land the natural produce of the land, minerals, or wild animals on the land. The most important modern day examples of profits are: the profit of pasture (ie a grazing right), whereby grass (a natural product of the land) is taken from the land by being eaten by the profit-owner's animals; the rights to take gravel and minerals from the land; the rights to catch fish and shoot game.

32.20 A profit may be legal or equitable.[1] In the case of registered land a profit which is not entered on the register is an overriding interest whether it is legal or equitable.[2]

A profit may be several or in common. A 'several' profit is owned by one person to the exclusion of others. A profit in common (or simply 'common') is owned in common with others. A common pasture is perhaps the most important type of profit in common. This is often encountered in hill-farming areas whereby a number of farms may enjoy the right to graze stock on the adjoining hills and mountains.

A profit may be appurtenant or in gross. If appurtenant, it is, like an easement, annexed to a dominant tenement. If so, the profit is limited to the needs of the dominant land. For example, an appurtenant profit of pasture will be limited to the number of cattle or sheep which the dominant land is capable of supporting. A several profit in gross is owned independently of land and is unconnected with any dominant tenement. Nevertheless, it is still a right in land and, indeed, the owner of such a right may now register title to it[3].

Profits are acquired in much the same way as easements, with some variations as to detail. In particular, a profit in gross cannot be acquired by prescription.

[1] The rules outlined in para 32.24 apply also to profits.
[2] Para 35.30.
[3] LRA 2002, s 3(1)(d); see para 29.16.

32.21 Under the Commons Registration Act 1965, any common right or common land (ie land subject to common rights) or town or village green existing before 2 January 1970 must have been registered in the appropriate county council's register of commons before 31 July 1970, otherwise it ceased to be recognised. Where new common land or a town or village green comes into existence registration is required[1]. The 1965 Act is in the course of being replaced by the Commons Act 2006. This is designed to improve the registration system and the management of common land. A registered common, or town or village green cannot be built on. Local inhabitants are increasingly realising that registration under the Commons Act[2] is a very effective way of preventing what they regard as undesirable development of land to which they have previously enjoyed access.

[1] Such registration is now under the 2006 Act.
[2] Broadly, registration as a town or village green can be made on proof of user as of right by a significant number of local inhabitants for lawful sports and pastimes for 20 years up to the date of the application.

Customary rights

32.22 Customary rights are not public rights, available to the general public at large, but are confined to the inhabitants of a particular locality. They differ from easements in that there is no necessity for dominant land and in that they are not capable of forming the subject matter of a grant, since a fluctuating body of inhabitants is not a capable grantee. A customary right must be ancient, continuous, certain and reasonable.[1] Examples include the right of fishermen of a particular parish to dry their nets on private land[2] and the right of the inhabitants of a village to hold a fair on private land.[3]

[1] Para 3.46.
[2] *Mercer v Denne* [1905] 2 Ch 538, CA.
[3] *Wyld v Silver* [1962] 3 All ER 309, CA.

THE NATURE OF EASEMENTS: KEY POINTS

- The right to use the land of another can only amount to the proprietary right known as an easement where it displays certain characteristics:
  - it must exist between two pieces of land, one of which benefits from the right (the dominant land) and the other of which is burdened by it (the servient land);
  - it must benefit the dominant land rather than simply the owner of the dominant land;
  - the owners of the dominant and servient land must be different persons; and

> – the right must be capable of forming the subject matter of a grant. This means that it must be of a type that the courts will recognise as an easement; this usually requires that the right is sufficiently definite, it is positive rather than negative, and that it does not directly involve the servient owner in expense. Traditionally, rights that allow a person to occupy the servient land have not been accepted as easements, but this approach is now being questioned, notably in cases involving the right to park cars.
>
> • Easements need to be distinguished from other rights that share some but not all of their features; these include natural rights, restrictive covenants, public rights, licences, profits à prendre, and customary rights.

Acquisition of easements

32.23 It is not sufficient for an easement to exist that a right exhibit the characteristics outlined above. It must also be created or acquired in a manner recognised by the law. In practice, most easements are created expressly by deed in the context of a sale or lease of part of the vendor's or lessor's land. However, it is important to note that easements can also be created by implication and as a result of prescription (ie long use).

We will first consider the difference between legal and equitable easements and then deal, in turn, with the various methods by which an easement can be created.

Legal and equitable easements

32.24 An easement is legal if it is created in fee simple or for a term of years absolute,[1] and is made by deed.[2] Easements created by implication, or by prescription are also legal easements. This is because, in such cases, it is either implied or presumed that a deed has been used.

An easement is necessarily equitable if it is created for a lesser interest than a fee simple or term of years, eg for life. Furthermore, an easement in fee simple or for a term of years will, if not created by deed, be equitable if created by means of an agreement which satisfies the requirements of the Law of Property (Miscellaneous Provisions) Act 1989, s 2.[3]

Where a proprietor of registered land expressly grants an easement, the disposition must be completed by registration in order for the easement to exist as a legal interest[4]. This means that the right will be entered in the property register of the dominant land and a notice will be entered in the charges register of the servient land.[5] Any legal easement affecting the title at the time of first registration will similarly be entered on the register of the servient land.[6] Certain legal easements are not required to be entered on the register; in practice, these are easements arising by implication, or by virtue of s 62 of the Law of Property Act 1925, or as a result of prescription.[7] These take effect as 'overriding' interests.[8]

All equitable easements must be protected by the entry of a notice on the title of the servient land; if this is not done, the equitable easement will not bind a purchaser of the servient land.[9]

---

[1] LPA 1925, s 1(2).
[2] LPA 1925, s 52.
[3] Para 30.6.
[4] LRA 2002, s 27(2)(d).
[5] LRA 2002, s 27, Sch 2, para 7. If this is not done the easement will only be equitable.
[6] LRA 1925, ss 37, 71.

Expressly created easements

32.25 An easement is usually created expressly on the transfer or lease by a landowner of part of their land. It can, however, be created, independently of the transfer of land, by two neighbouring landowners. It was made clear by the Court of Appeal in *IDC Group Ltd v Clark*[1] that, even where a right displaying all the features of an easement has been expressly created, there will be no easement unless the parties *intended* to create an easement. Accordingly, in that case, a right to use a fire escape route through a neighbouring building which the two neighbouring owners had created by deed, was held not to be an easement because it had been clearly described as a licence. This meant that the right was not intended to be proprietary and did not bind a purchaser of the 'servient' land.

[1] (1992) 65 P & CR 179, CA.

Grants and reservations

32.26 An easement is said to be *granted* where the vendor or lessor confers an easement over the land being retained in favour of the land that is being sold or leased. An easement is *reserved* where the vendor or lessor of land reserves a right over the land sold or leased in favour of the retained land. Any ambiguity in the terms of a grant will be resolved in favour of the purchaser/lessee and against the vendor/lessor; any ambiguity in the terms of a reservation is to be resolved in favour of the vendor/lessor.[1]

[1] *St Edmundsbury and Ipswich Diocesan Board of Finance v Clark (No 2)* [1975] 1 All ER 772, CA.

Implied easements[1]

32.27 There are circumstances in which, despite the fact that a transfer or lease does not expressly create an easement, the law will do so by implication[2]. This method of creation is applicable only where a landowner is selling or leasing a part of their land and is retaining the remainder (or disposing of the whole in parcels), because only in such a case is there a transaction into which the grant or reservation of an easement can be implied.

[1] The Law Commission is proposing that this area of the law should be simplified, see Consultation Paper No 186 *Easements Covenants and Profits à Prendre* (2008).

[2] Where an easement is implied into a deed, the easement will be legal rather than equitable.

Implied grants

32.28 The common law will fairly readily imply the grant of easements in favour of a purchaser or tenant. The underlying approach is that a purchaser or tenant is entitled to the benefit of such easements over the vendor's or landlord's retained land as they might reasonably have expected to receive. However, this broad policy is applied through the medium of three[1], sometimes overlapping, mechanisms:

- easements of necessity;
- intended easements; and
- easements within the rule in *Wheeldon v Burrows*.

We consider each of these in turn.

[1] Purchasers and tenants can also acquire easements that have not been expressly mentioned in their transfer of lease by virtue of LPA 1925, s 62; see paras 32.35–32.39.

32.29 *Easements of necessity* Where a vendor sells land which, as a result, is left without any legally enforceable means of access, ie which is 'landlocked', the law will imply from those circumstances that the parties intended a right of way of necessity to be granted.[1] It is for the vendor to select the route but it must, however, provide a convenient access. Such a right of way is limited to what was necessary in the circumstances of the original transaction. Thus, in *London Corpn v Riggs*,[2] following a sale, the defendant's agricultural land was left without access; since there was no mention of any easements of way in the conveyance this meant that he was entitled to a right of way of necessity. However, the defendant later sought to build refreshment rooms open to the public on his land. The claimant was held to be entitled to prevent him using the right of way for any purposes other than those connected with the agricultural use of the land.

[1] *Nickerson v Barraclough* [1981] 2 All ER 369, CA. Such an intention cannot be implied where there is any alternative access, even solely by water; see *Manjang v Drammeh* (1990) 61 P & CR 194, PC.
[2] (1880) 13 Ch D 798.

32.30 *Intended easements* The law will imply the grant of easements in order to give effect to the common intention of the parties as to the purposes for which the land granted is to be used. However, it is essential that the parties intend that the land sold should be used in some definite and particular manner;[1] it is, however, sufficient to establish the intended use on the balance of probabilities.[2]

It is arguable that the categories of easements of necessity and intended easements overlap. For example, reciprocal easements of support will be implied on the sale by their owner of one of two attached properties. This may be regarded as an easement of necessity, although some regard it as an intended easement.[3] Conversely, the case of *Wong v Beaumont Property Trust Ltd*[4] was held to concern an implied easement of necessity, although it could equally well have been treated as an intended easement. Here, cellar premises were let to a tenant who covenanted that he would carry on business as a restaurateur, would not cause any nuisance, and would control and eliminate all smells and odours in conformity with the health regulations. The tenant subsequently assigned to Wong. In order to comply with the health regulations, Wong sought the landlord's permission to affix a ventilation duct to the outside wall of the landlord's premises. The landlord refused but Wong obtained a declaration that he was entitled to attach the duct. The Court of Appeal held that, where a lease is granted which imposes a particular use on the tenant and it is impossible for the tenant so to use the premises legally unless an easement is granted, the law does imply such an easement as of necessity.

[1] *Pwllbach Colliery Co Ltd v Woodman* [1915] AC 634, HL. This is often easier to prove in the case of a lease of land (which often contains specific user covenants) as opposed to a freehold sale.
[2] *Stafford v Lee* (1992) 65 P & CR 172, CA. Note that the test for implied reservations is stricter, see para 32.33.
[3] *Jones v Pritchard* [1908] 1 Ch 630.
[4] [1964] 2 All ER 119, CA.

32.31 *Easements within the rule in Wheeldon v Burrows* In addition to the two bases of implication just discussed, there has evolved an extension of the doctrine of non-derogation from grant[1] known as the rule in *Wheeldon v Burrows*.[2] The rule states that where a landowner sells or leases part of their land, the *grant* (but *not* the reservation) of certain quasi-easements[3] will be implied into the conveyance (or into any contract to convey[4]). The quasi-easements which will pass to the purchaser or tenant as full easements are those which are 'continuous and apparent', necessary to the reasonable enjoyment of the property granted, and which have been and are at the time of the grant used by the owners of the entirety for the benefit of the part granted.[5] Thus, where, prior to the sale or lease, the owner has exercised some right over the part being retained which is necessary to the reasonable enjoyment of the part being sold, that right will pass to the purchaser or lessee as an easement, provided it is continuous and apparent.

It is said that, strictly, a 'continuous' easement is one that is enjoyed passively, without the need for action on the part of the dominant owner, such as the right of light. Something is 'apparent' if it is discoverable on a careful inspection by a person ordinarily conversant with the subject.[6] Thus the presence of a window on the dominant tenement receiving light from the adjoining land suggests a continuous and apparent easement of light. However, the courts have extended the concept of what is 'continuous and apparent' beyond these narrow confines; the phrase is regarded as being 'directed to there being on the servient tenement a feature which would be seen on inspection and which is neither transitory nor intermittent'.[7] Thus, it is well established that a right of way over a made-up road or worn track can pass as an easement under the rule in *Wheeldon v Burrows*, provided it is necessary to the reasonable enjoyment of the property.[8] Similarly, a right to use drains running through the vendor's retained land may also be created as an easement under this rule.[9]

It is clear that the requirement that the easement be necessary to the reasonable enjoyment of the property granted is less strict than that for easements of necessity.[10] In *Millman v Ellis*[11] it was held that the claimant, who had expressly been granted a right of way over part of a layby on the defendant's retained land which provided access to the road, was also entitled to an implied right of way over the remainder of the layby. The more extended right was reasonably necessary to the enjoyment of the claimant's property since, without it, access to the highway was dangerous. This can be compared with the decision in *Wheeler v JJ Saunders Ltd*[12] that a right of way over the defendant vendor's retained land would not be implied; given that there was a perfectly adequate alternative access, this second access was not necessary to the reasonable enjoyment of the claimant's land.

[1] Para 32.18 and para 36.35.
[2] (1879) 12 Ch D 31.
[3] Para 32.7.
[4] *Borman v Griffith* [1930] 1 Ch 493; *Sovmots Investments Ltd v Secretary of State for the Environment* [1976] 1 All ER 178.
[5] (1879) 12 Ch D 31 at 49.
[6] *Pyer v Carter* (1857) 1 H & N 916 at 922.
[7] *Ward v Kirkland* [1966] 1 All ER 609 at 616.
[8] *Borman v Griffith* [1930] 1 Ch 493.
[9] *Ward v Kirkland* [1966] 1 All ER 609.
[10] Para 32.29.
[11] (1995) 71 P & CR 158, CA.
[12] [1995] 2 All ER 697, CA.

Implied reservations

32.32 Easements in favour of a vendor or landlord can also be implied. However, the courts are far more reluctant to imply reservations than they are to imply grants (ie easements in favour of the purchaser or tenant). The reason for this is that, where a vendor or landlord sells or leases part of their land and wishes to reserve rights over the part sold or leased, in favour of the land being kept, this should be made clear. Reservations ought therefore to be express. To imply reservations imposes an unexpressed (and possibly unexpected) burden on the purchaser or lessee. However, in very limited circumstances, the courts will imply reservations, namely:

- easements of necessity; and
- intended easements.

It should be emphasised that neither the rule in *Wheeldon v Burrows*[1], nor LPA 1925, s 62[2] applies to reservations.

[1] See para 32.31.
[2] See paras 32.34–32.39.

32.33 *Easements of necessity and intended easements* The rules governing implied easements of necessity are the same for reservations as they are for grants[1]. However, where a landlord or vendor is seeking to show the *reservation* of an intended easement the test is stricter than it is for grants[2], since it must be shown that the facts are not reasonably consistent with anything but a common intention. In *Re Webb's Lease, Sandom v Webb*,[3] where a landlord sought to show that he had the right to use the outside wall of demised premises for displaying advertisements, the court held that the mere fact that the tenant knew of the presence of the advertisements at the time of the lease was insufficient to show an intention common to both parties that the landlord was to have a reserved right to maintain the advertisements. However, in *Peckham v Ellison*[4] the facts were strong enough for the Court of Appeal to imply the reservation of a right of way; the right had been exercised for many years and had been believed by all concerned to be legally valid.

[1] See para 32.29.
[2] See para 32.30.
[3] [1951] Ch 808, [1951] 2 All ER 131, CA.
[4] (1998) 31 HLR 1030, CA.

Creation of easements by the operation of the LPA 1925, s 62

32.34 The creation of easements under the LPA 1925, s 62 does not come about by implication in the conveyance; rather the words creating the easement are deemed by virtue of the section to have been expressed in the conveyance from the outset. However, it is convenient to treat s 62 here, because of the interrelation of the section and the rule in *Wheeldon v Burrows*.

The ambit of s 62

32.35 The section provides that a conveyance or transfer of land shall be deemed to include and shall by virtue of the Act operate to convey, with the land, all liberties, privileges, easements, rights and advantages, whatsoever, appertaining or reputed to appertain to the land or any part thereof, or, at the time of the conveyance, enjoyed with the land or any part thereof. Section 62 makes it clear that *existing* easements enjoyed with the land pass on a conveyance of the land. However, the section has a further most important effect, namely that it operates to convert mere privileges and advantages into *new* legal easements. In effect, s 62 states that a conveyance of a piece of land operates to convey with that land all advantages appertaining to, or, at the time of the conveyance, enjoyed with the land, so as to convert such advantages into legally enforceable rights.[1] These rights and privileges must actually be enjoyed at the time of the grant with the land granted or a part of it.[2] Where the rights are continuous and apparent it matters not that the dominant and servient land were both owned and occupied by the same person prior to the conveyance.[3] Where the rights are not continuous and apparent the section can only operate where, although the two pieces of land are in *common ownership*, they are separately occupied at the date of grant.[4]

It should be noted that the section does not operate to create easements out of rights not capable of existing as such; thus the right to protection from the weather,[5] or to the provision of hot water and heating,[6] cannot pass under s 62.

> [1] *Nickerson v Barraclough* [1981] 2 All ER 369 at 381–382.
> [2] *Payne v Inwood* (1996) 74 P & CR 42, CA. However, actual user must be judged not by reference simply to the moment of the conveyance, but rather in relation to a reasonable period leading up to that conveyance; see *Green v Ashco Horticulturist Ltd* [1966] 1 WLR 889. Furthermore, the operation of s 62 is *not* prevented where the use of the right has been *temporarily* interrupted at the date of the conveyance; see *Pretoria Warehousing Co Ltd v Shelton* [1993] NPC 98, CA.
> [3] *Broomfield v Williams* [1897] 1 Ch 602; *P & S Platt Ltd v Crouch* [2004] 1 P & CR 242.
> [4] *Sovmots Investments Ltd v Secretary of State for the Environment* [1977] 2 All ER 385, HL; *Long v Gowlett* [1923] 2 Ch 177.
> [5] *Phipps v Pears* [1964] 2 All ER 35, CA.
> [6] *Regis Property Co Ltd v Redman* [1956] 2 All ER 335, CA.

The operation of s 62

32.36 The operation of s 62 is illustrated by *International Tea Stores Co v Hobbs*.[1] A tenant, with the landlord's permission, made use of a roadway on the landlord's property. Subsequently, the tenant purchased the freehold and it was held that the right to use the roadway passed to him as an easement under s 62. Similarly, in *Wright v Macadam*,[2] a tenant was given permission by the landlord to use a coal shed belonging to the landlord. The Court of Appeal held that on the renewal of the lease the right to use the coal shed passed as an easement, although previously depending on permission. These cases constitute a warning to landlords to revoke all licences granted to a tenant prior to renewing the lease or selling the reversion, or, preferably, positively to exclude the operation of s 62.[3]

> [1] [1903] 2 Ch 165. see also *Hair v Gillman* (2000) 80 P & CR 108.
> [2] [1949] 2 All ER 565, CA.
> [3] Para 32.39.

32.37 Another warning as to the possible effect of the section appears from *Goldberg v Edwards*.[1] Edwards leased an annexe at the rear of her house to Goldberg. This annexe could be reached by an outside passage at the side of the house. Goldberg was allowed into possession before the lease was executed and was given permission to use a passage through the landlord's house to reach the annexe. The lease was executed some time later. Edwards subsequently let her house to Miller, the second defendant, who barred the door to Goldberg. Goldberg claimed he was entitled to a right of way either under the rule in *Wheeldon v Burrows*[2] or under s 62.

The Court of Appeal held that the claimed right of way had not passed under *Wheeldon v Burrows* since it was not necessary for the reasonable enjoyment of the annexe, which could conveniently be reached via the outside passage. However, the right did pass as an easement under s 62 since, at the time of the conveyance (ie when the lease was finally executed), the privilege of going through the house was being enjoyed with the annexe and thus passed as an easement when the lease was executed.

[1]   [1950] Ch 247, CA.
[2]   Para 32.31.

32.38 Section 62 operates only in respect of a 'conveyance', ie the transfer or creation of a *legal* estate; accordingly it will not operate to pass easements in an equitable lease.[1] Just as *Goldberg v Edwards* illustrates how an easement may pass by virtue of s 62 where *Wheeldon v Burrows* is inapplicable, so *Borman v Griffith*[1] shows how easements within the rule in *Wheeldon v Burrows* may pass where s 62 does not apply. Borman occupied a house in the grounds of Wood Green Park under an agreement for a seven-year lease. He made use of the main drive of the park which ran past the front of his house although the agreement contained no reference to a right of way and despite the fact that his house could be reached by an unmade track at the rear. Borman claimed a right of way along the main drive in this action against the tenant of the remainder of the park who had prevented Borman's use of the drive. The court rejected the claim based on s 62 as Borman had only an equitable lease. However, the court in effect held that, just as easements within the rule in *Wheeldon v Burrows* will be implied in the grant of a legal estate, so continuous and apparent easements necessary for the reasonable enjoyment of the property will be implied in an agreement for such a grant,[2] and, since the drive was plainly visible and was necessary for the reasonable enjoyment of the property, a right of way over it passed to Borman.

[1]   *Borman v Griffith* [1930] 1 Ch 493. In this case the claimant occupied on the basis of a contract for a seven-year lease; as we have seen in Note 6, para 30.3 above, this gives rise not to a legal lease but to an equitable one.
[2]   *Sovmots Investments Ltd v Secretary of State for the Environment* [1976] 1 All ER 178, HL.

Exclusion of s 62 and the rule in *Wheeldon v Burrows*

32.39 Neither the rule in *Wheeldon v Burrows* nor s 62 will apply in the face of a contrary intention and it is common for their operation to be expressly excluded by making it clear that rights which might otherwise pass are not intended to be conveyed.[1] Where there is no explicit exclusion, the courts may decide that other provisions in the conveyance necessarily exclude the implication of any easements. So, for example, it is possible that, where a purchaser covenants to erect a fence, this will prevent the implication of any access through that fence.[2] However, this will depend on the particular facts; in some circumstances it will be proper to treat the covenant to fence as permitting the inclusion of a gate, so that a right of access can still be implied.[3]

[1]   *Squarey v Harris-Smith* (1981) 42 P & CR 118, CA.
[2]   *Wheeler v JJ Saunders Ltd* [1995] 2 All ER 697, CA.
[3]   *Hillman v Rogers* [1997] NPC 183, CA.

Prescription

32.40 Prescription is the method whereby the law confers legality on the long enjoyment of a right, by presuming a lawful grant. An easement acquired by prescription is, therefore, a legal easement. The law of prescription has been described as unnecessarily complex and unsatisfactory[1] particularly because there exist side by side three methods by which a claim to have acquired an easement by prescription may be made: at common law, under the doctrine of lost modern grant, and under the Prescription Act 1832.

Whichever method is being relied on as the basis of a claim (and it may be advisable to rely on more than one method) it must be shown that there has been:

- continuous enjoyment of the alleged right,
- in fee simple,
- as of right.

[1] See Consultation Paper No 186 *Easements Covenants and Profits à Prendre* Law Commission (2008). This proposes that a new single form of prescription should be introduced.

Continuous enjoyment

32.41 This requirement does not mean that the right claimed must have been used ceaselessly day and night throughout the prescriptive period. What is continuous depends on the nature of the right being claimed and the circumstances of the case. In *Diment v NH Foot Ltd*,[1] the use of a path between six and ten times a year was considered sufficient in regularity and extent to constitute continuous enjoyment. The claim to a right of way by prescription was, however, unsuccessful for other reasons.

[1] [1974] 2 All ER 785.

In fee simple

32.42 An easement (other than one of light[1]) may only be acquired by prescription by one freehold owner against another freehold owner.[2] Hence prescription cannot be established during any period when the freeholds of the dominant and servient lands are in common ownership.

This requirement also means that, where the *servient* land is held by a tenant under a lease throughout the period of enjoyment on which the dominant owner's claim to have acquired an easement is based, the claim will usually be unsuccessful.

Furthermore, long enjoyment of a right by a tenant of the *dominant* land is treated as being on behalf of the freeholder; the easement is thus acquired by the freeholder and not by the tenant. This, coupled with the fact that a person cannot have an easement over their own land, means that a tenant cannot acquire a prescriptive right against their own landlord, nor can a tenant acquire an easement by prescription against another tenant of the same landlord.[3]

Note, however, that the position is different in the case of claims to a right to light under the Prescription Act 1832.[4]

[1] Para 32.55.
[2] *Wheaton v Maple & Co* [1893] 3 Ch 48, CA.
[3] *Kilgour v Gaddes* [1904] 1 KB 457, CA.
[4] See para 32.55.

As of right

32.43 A person claiming to have acquired an easement by prescription must show that their enjoyment of the right has been on the basis of an entitlement to do so on a permanent basis. This is achieved by showing that the use was neither by force, nor secretly, nor by permission. Furthermore, the user on which a prescriptive claim is based must not be illegal.[1] This latter rule gave rise to considerable difficulties to those whose rights of access to their properties (often, but not exclusively, over common land) have never been formally granted. Access by motor vehicle across the land of another without the consent of that person has long been a criminal offence[2] and it seemed that even long enjoyed rights of *vehicular* access could not, therefore, be legitimised by prescription.[3] The situation was rectified by statute and those who, but for the illegality, would otherwise have been entitled to their right of vehicular access by prescription, can now compel the servient owner to grant such rights at a statutorily fixed price[4]. Subsequently, the House of Lords has ruled in *Bakewell Management Ltd v Brandwood*[5] that the illegality rule is not an absolute one. Where consent by the servient owner would have negated the criminal offence and thus removed the illegality, prescription is possible. In such cases there is no need to resort to the statutory scheme and the payment of statutory compensation can be avoided.

¹ *Bakewell Management Ltd v Brandwood* [2004] 2 AC 519.
² Currently by virtue of LPA 1925, s 193(4) and the Road Traffic Act 1988, s 34.
³ *Hanning v Top Deck Travel Group Ltd* (1993) 68 P & CR 14, CA (later overruled by *Bakewell Management Ltd v Brandwood* [2004] 2 AC 519).
⁴ Countryside and Rights of Way Act 2000, s 68.
⁵ [2004] 2 AC 519.

32.44 *Without force* There can be no claim to an easement by prescription where the alleged right has been exercised by force or in the face of open and continuous opposition from the servient owner.

32.45 *Without secrecy* Where a servient owner does not know, or cannot discover, that a right over their land is being used,[1] they cannot be said to have acquiesced in that enjoyment; the use cannot therefore be as of right. So, it was not possible to claim by prescription an easement in respect of the support of a dry dock where none of the supporting rods was visible on the alleged servient land.[2] Similarly, the intermittent discharge of borax at night into a sewer could not, even over a long period, ripen into an easement; the servient owner clearly could not discover such a use.[3]

¹ *Dalton v Angus* (1881) 6 App Cas 740 at 801, HL.
² *Union Lighterage Co v London Graving Dock Co* [1902] 2 Ch 557 at 571, CA.
³ *Liverpool Corpn v H Coghill & Son* [1918] 1 Ch 307.

32.46 *Without permission* To succeed in a claim to have acquired an easement by prescription, it must be shown that the servient owner acquiesced in the dominant owner's enjoyment as if it were an established right, ie that the former knew, or had the means of knowing, that the right was being exercised and stood by and allowed the use to continue.[1] However, if a claimant's use is with the positive permission of the servient owner, or is subject to the control of the servient owner, this makes it clear that the latter did not regard the enjoyment as an established and irrevocable right, but merely as a licence which could be terminated at any time by the withdrawal of the permission.[2]

¹ *Mills v Silver* [1991] 1 All ER 449, CA.
² The need for the permission to be unequivocal and overt was stressed in *R (Beresford) v Sunderland City Council* [2003] UKHL 60. A user that has continued after the expiry of an express licence will be sufficient to found a claim to a prescriptive right, see *London Tara Hotel Ltd v Kensington Close Hotel Ltd* [2010] EWHC 2749.

The three methods of prescription

32.47 *Common law* Thus far we have said that a claim to have acquired an easement by prescription depends on showing long enjoyment as of right. Strictly, at common law, it is necessary to show enjoyment as of right since 'time immemorial' which, for historical reasons, is conveniently fixed at 1189. Obviously, a requirement positively to prove continuous enjoyment since before 1189 would in most cases be impossible to satisfy. Accordingly, where it is proved that a right has been enjoyed during living memory (usually treated as about 20 years) the courts will *presume* that enjoyment has been since time immemorial. However, this presumption can easily be rebutted, and the claim will fail, if it is shown that at some time since 1189 the right either did not exist or could not have existed. So, for example, in the case of a claim to an easement of support, or an easement of light, there can be no prescription at common law if there was no building on the land in 1189. Equally, there can be no prescription at common law where it can be shown that the dominant and servient lands have been in common ownership at any time since 1189.

Because common law prescription is often impossible to establish, the doctrine of lost modern grant was developed.

32.48 *Lost modern grant* Here prescription is based on the complete fiction that there was a comparatively recent deed granting the easement which has since been lost. In this way a lawful basis for long enjoyment is presumed without the need to show user since 1189. A lost modern grant will be presumed on evidence of 20 years' continuous use in fee simple[1] as of right, even where this period of user took place at some time in the past.[2] So, in *Tehidy Minerals Ltd v Norman*,[3] the fact that, during part of the 20-year period preceding the court action, the right could not be used because the servient land had been requisitioned by the Government was not fatal to a claim based on lost modern grant[4]. More than 20 user, prior to the date of requisition could be shown, and this was sufficient.

Lost modern grant is a strong presumption which cannot readily be rebutted. It cannot be defeated by evidence that no deed was ever drawn up[5] but only by evidence showing that a grant could not possibly have been made, eg where the grant was prohibited by statute.[6]

[1] Thus a tenant cannot acquire an easement under the doctrine of lost modern grant, nor can an easement be acquired on this basis by one tenant against a tenant of the same landlord: *Simmons v Dobson* (1991) 62 P & CR 485, CA; see para 32.42 above.

[2] An important advantage over the Prescription Act 1832, see paras 32.49–32.51. For a recent example of claim which would have failed under the 1932 Act but which succeeded under lost modern grant, see *London Tara Hotel Ltd v Kensington Close Hotel Ltd* [2010] EWHC 2749.

[3] [1971] 2 All ER 475, CA.

[4] This would, however, prevent a claim under the Prescription Act 1832, see para 32.50.

[5] *Dalton v Angus* (1881) 6 App Cas 740.

[6] *Neaverson v Peterborough Rural District Council* [1902] 1 Ch 557.

32.49 *Prescription Act 1832* 'The Prescription Act 1832 has no friends. It has long been criticised as one of the worst drafted Acts on the Statute Book'.[1] The Act was apparently drafted with the aim of avoiding the pitfalls involved in a claim at common law. In view of its complexity, the Act provides few advantages over the other two methods with which it co-exists. Nonetheless, it may, in fact, be of some utility to those claiming an easement by prescription.

The Act provides for a claim to an easement other than light to be based either on 20 years' enjoyment as of right without interruption, or on 40 years' such enjoyment. It deals separately with claims to easements of light and these provisions are dealt with in a later paragraph.[2]

[1] Law Reform Committee, 14th Report, Cmnd 3100 (1966), a view accepted by the law Commission in its Consultation Paper No 186 *Easements Covenants and Profits à Prendre* (2008).

[2] Para 32.55.

32.50 Where a claim under the Act to an easement other than light is based on 20 years' enjoyment as of right without interruption, it cannot be defeated by evidence that enjoyment began later than 1189, although it may be defeated in any other way in which a claim at common law may be defeated.[1] Thus it is still necessary to show that enjoyment was continuous, in fee simple, and as of right.

There must be some court action to confirm the embryonic right as an easement. This can take the form either of an action by a dominant owner for a declaration that they are entitled to an easement, or an action by the servient owner to prevent continued enjoyment, in which the dominant owner relies on the Act as a defence. The Act requires that the period of enjoyment must have *immediately preceded* the court action relating to the claim.[2] If there has been no enjoyment for some time prior to the court action, then even if there has been an earlier period of 20 years' enjoyment, a claim under the Act cannot, subject to the question of an interruption, succeed.[3]

Although the Act requires the enjoyment to be 'without interruption', it does define an interruption as an act which has been acquiesced in for one year.[4] So, if a landowner has enjoyed a right of way over neighbouring land for 15 years and the neighbour then physically bars the way, this will only constitute an interruption after the elapse of one year. If the use of the way recommences in *less than* twelve months and the 20-year period is then completed, a claim will succeed. However, if the exercise of the right is interrupted for a full year, a fresh period of 20 years user will then have to be established before an easement can be acquired. It also follows that, if that landowner had *already* enjoyed the right of way for 20 years before it was barred, an easement could still be claimed under the Act provided an action to claim the right is brought within one year of the commencement of the obstruction.

[1] Prescription Act 1832, s 2.
[2] Prescription Act 1832, s 4.
[3] Such a claim may succeed under the doctrine of lost modern grant, see para 32.48.
[4] Prescription Act 1832, s 7.

32.51 A claim to an easement under the Act based on 40 years' enjoyment as of right without interruption is deemed to be absolute and indefeasible unless it is shown that the enjoyment depended on written consent.[1] Again, the 40-year period must immediately precede some court action. 'Interruption' has the same meaning as in relation to the 20-year period.

Although a claim based on 40 years' enjoyment will only be defeated by proof of written permission, the enjoyment must nevertheless be 'as of right'. Therefore, enjoyment which depends on regular permission (written or oral)—as in *Gardner v Hodgson's Kingston Brewery Co*[2] where an annual payment of 15 shillings had to be made for the use of a right of way—will not ripen into an easement even if the permission is oral and the enjoyment has continued for 40 years, because the enjoyment is permissive and not as of right.[3] Oral permission given at the outset and not renewed will not defeat a claim based on the 40-year period, though it will defeat a claim based on 20 years' enjoyment.

[1] Prescription Act 1832, s 2.
[2] [1903] AC 229, HL.
[3] See also *Jones v Price and Morgan* (1992) 64 P & CR 404, CA.

THE ACQUISITION OF EASEMENTS: KEY POINTS

- Rights that demonstrate the characteristics of an easement will only be easements if they have been created in a way recognised by the law.

- While easements are usually created expressly they can also be created by implication, by virtue of s 62 of the Law of Property Act 1925, and as a result of long use (prescription).

- Expressly created easements relating to registered land must be completed by registration in order to be legal; this means that they are noted on the title of both the servient and dominant land.

- All equitable easements must be protected by the entry of a notice against the title to the burdened land.

- Easements created by implication, under s 62, or by prescription are legal although, by definition, they will not be referred to in any documentation and will not appear as entries on the Land Register; such easements normally bind a purchaser of the servient land as interests that override.

- Express easements are usually created where a landowner sells off part of his or her land. Where the easement is for the benefit of the land sold and is exercisable over the land retained it is said to be a 'grant'; where it for the benefit of the retained land and exercisable over the part sold it is called a 'reservation'.

- The creation of an easement may be implied despite the fact that it is not mentioned in a transfer or lease; the courts will more readily imply the grant of an easement to a purchaser or tenant than it will imply a reservation in favour of a vendor or landlord.

- Courts may imply the grant of an easement on the basis of necessity, intention or the rule in *Wheeldon v Burrows*.

- Reservations will only be implied on proof of necessity or intention.

- The grant of an easement can also occur on the transfer or lease of land by virtue of s 62 of the LPA 1925.

- Rights that have the characteristics of an easement can become full legal easements as a result of unbroken use for at least 20 years; this use must be as of right, by or on behalf of a freehold owner, and must satisfy one of the three types of prescription – common law, lost modern grant, or the Prescription Act 1832. The 1832 Act contains special rules governing the acquisition of a right to light; these are significantly easier to satisfy than those for other easements.

Extinguishment of easements

32.52 At common law easements may only be extinguished by being released, expressly or impliedly, by the dominant owner, or by ownership and possession of the dominant and servient properties falling into the same hands. In practice, implied release is extremely difficult to establish. It is not enough to show that the dominant owner is not using the right and has not used it over a long period,[1] or to prove that the obstruction of some aspects of the right has been acquiesced in.[2] It must be shown that the dominant owner intends to abandon the right, and abandonment of an easement can only be treated as having taken place where the person entitled to it has demonstrated a fixed intention never at any time thereafter to assert the right or to attempt to transmit it to anyone else.[3]

An easement can, effectively, be lost where the character of the dominant land is radically changed with the result that the burden imposed on the servient land is substantially increased. So, in *McAdams Homes Ltd v Robinson*[4], land used as a bakery had a right of drainage over adjoining land. The bakery was demolished and replaced by two dwellings, resulting in a significant increase in the use of the drains. The Court of Appeal held that the very nature of the dominant land had changed and that the servient owner was entitled to prevent the use of the drains. This result will not follow where the *existing* use of the dominant land increases significantly putting concomitant pressure on the use of the easement, nor where there is a change in the use of the dominant land but where this does not increase the use of the easement. In these instances there can be no complaint from the servient owner.

Unlike the case of restrictive covenants, there is no statutory scheme for the modification or discharge of easements.[5] Easements may, however, be expressly extinguished by specific statutes (as happened under the old Inclosure Acts). They can also be effectively suspended by a number of Acts under which land can be compulsorily acquired[6]; in such cases the owner of the dominant tenement can claim compensation.

[1] See *Benn v Hardinge* (1992) 66 P & CR 246, CA where it was held that there was no abandonment of an easement simply because no one had occasion to use the right during the previous 175 years.

[2] See *Snell & Prideaux Ltd v Dutton Mirrors Ltd* [1995] 1 EGLR 259, CA, where it was held that a right to use a passageway *both* as a right of way *and* for loading and unloading had not been abandoned simply because its use as a right of way had long been obstructed by the erection of a brick pillar.

[3] *Tehidy Minerals Ltd v Norman* [1971] 2 All ER 475 at 492, CA.

[4] [2004] EWCA 214.

[5] Paras 33.38–33.43. The Law Commission is suggesting that a new statutory scheme should be introduced that also applies to easements, see Consultation Paper No 186 *Easements Covenants and Profits à Prendre* (2008).

[6] See *R v City of London Corpn, ex p Mystery of the Barbers of London* (1997) 73 P & CR 59 where easements were suspended when the servient land was acquired for planning purposes under the Town and Country Planning Act 1947.

Particular easements

Rights of way

32.53 A right of way may be limited in extent, for example, as to the times it may be used or as to the purposes for which it may be used (eg agricultural purposes only) or as to the modes of enjoyment (eg on foot only), or it may be unlimited.

Disputes can often arise as to whether a dominant owner is making excessive use of their right of way. In resolving these, the method of creation of the easement is highly relevant. Where the easement was expressly granted or reserved, the question turns on the construction of the relevant deed in the light of the circumstances surrounding its making, in particular the nature of the road or track over which the right was granted.[1] However, in the absence of any special factors, the dominant owner is not confined to using the right of way for the purposes which existed at the date of grant but is entitled to use it for any lawful purposes to which the dominant tenement is later put.[2] Where the wording of the deed is unclear, ambiguities are resolved in favour of the person having the benefit of the easement.[3] In the case of easements of way arising by implication, enjoyment is limited by the situation prevailing at the time of the grant.[4]

The extent of enjoyment permitted in the case of an easement of way acquired by prescription is determined by the nature of the enjoyment during the prescriptive period;[5] however an increase in the frequency of use is unobjectionable unless it produces a change in the nature of the enjoyment.[6] For example, where a right of way had been acquired by prescription to a site used by a small number of caravans, the servient owner could not object to a considerable increase in the number of caravans using the site.[6]

Enlargement of the dominant tenement by the acquisition of additional land will not affect entitlement to a right of way to the original dominant tenement. However, the use of that right of way for the additional land will not be permitted save where that use is genuinely ancillary to that in respect of the dominant land.[7]

Whether or not an express right of way impliedly includes any right to park or a right to turn vehicles[8] can be an important issue. A right to park can be implied where, in the circumstances at the date of the grant, it is reasonably necessary.[9] It is not enough that a right to park is desirable.[10] Furthermore, where the transfer deals expressly with rights to park, a court is most unlikely to imply additional parking rights.[11]

Where a dominant owner is using a right of way in a manner or to an extent which exceeds that to which they are entitled, a nuisance is committed and the servient owner may seek an injunction to limit the use to the permitted level.[12] However, where the express terms of a right of way permit a level of use which, in other circumstances, might amount to a nuisance the servient owner has no remedy.[13]

[1] *Cannon v Villars* (1878) 8 Ch D 415; see also *Jelbert v Davis* [1968] 1 All ER 1182, CA; *National Trust for Places of Historic Interest or National Beauty v White* [1987] 1 WLR 907.

[2] *Alvis v Harrison* (1991) 62 P & CR 10, HL.

[3] *St Edmundsbury and Ipswich Diocesan Board of Finance v Clark (No 2)* [1975] 1 All ER 772, CA.

[4] *London Corpn v Riggs* (1880) 13 Ch D 798.

[5] *Mills v Silver* [1991] 1 All ER 449, CA.

[6] *British Railways Board v Glass* [1964] 3 All ER 418, CA.

[7] *Harris v Flower* (1904) 74 LJ Ch 127, CA; *Peacock v Custins* [2001] 2 All ER 827, CA; *Das v Linden Mews Ltd* [2002] EWCA Civ 590, [2002] 2 EGLR 76; *Massey v Boulden* [2002] EWCA Civ 1634, [2003] 2 All ER 87, CA.

[8] See *Property Point Ltd v Kirri* [2009] EWHC 2958.

[9] *Moncrieff v Jamieson* [2007] UKHL 42; *Bulstrode v Lambert* [1953] 1 WLR 1064 (where a right of way to business premises was held to include a right to stop for loading and unloading).

[10] *London & Suburban Land & Building Co (Holdings) Ltd v Carey* (1991) 62 P & CR 480.

[11] *Waterman v Boyle* [2009] EWCA Civ 115.

[12] *Rosling v Pinnegar* (1986) 54 P & CR 124, CA.

[13] *Hamble Parish Council v Haggard* [1992] 4 All ER 147.

Rights of light

32.54 There is no natural right to light. The right of light can exist only as an easement and then only in respect of a defined aperture, usually a window.[1]

[1] See *Levet v Gas Light and Coke Co Ltd* [1919] 1 Ch 24.

Acquisition by prescription

32.55 Although a right to light can be created expressly or by implication, it is more usually acquired by prescription and is then sometimes referred to as 'ancient lights'. Ancient lights can be acquired by all three methods of prescription, though acquisition at common law is highly unlikely since it is usually easy to prove that there was no building with windows on the site in 1189.[1]

Where reliance is placed on the Prescription Act 1832, special rules apply. Under the Act, a claim to an easement of light based on 20 years' enjoyment immediately preceding a court action, without interruption, gives rise to an absolute and indefeasible right, unless the light was enjoyed by written consent.[2] There is no requirement that enjoyment be as of right, so the fact that the light was enjoyed by virtue of regular oral permission is no bar to a claim to have acquired a prescriptive right. Furthermore, since it is not necessary to show enjoyment in fee simple, a tenant may acquire an easement of light against his own landlord or against another tenant of the landlord.[3]

The existence of a right to light can severely restrict a servient owner's ability to build on their land so it is particularly important for owners of undeveloped land to be able to prevent their neighbours from acquiring rights to light. Enjoyment of the light could, of course, be interrupted[4] by the erection of a structure blocking the light to the particular window, and traditionally this was done by the erection of a hoarding. However, this method would now fall foul of the planning laws, and so, as an alternative, the servient owner may apply under the Rights of Light Act 1959 for registration in the local land charges registry[5] of a notice, which is treated as being equivalent to an actual obstruction of the light. The application for registration must state the size and position of the opaque structure which the notice is intended to represent.[6] Before such a notice can be registered, the Lands Tribunal must certify that all those likely to be affected by the registration have been notified.[7] Registration is effective for one year, which is sufficient to constitute an interruption; this means that, in order to acquire an easement of light, a further 20 years' enjoyment must be established which can, where necessary, be interrupted by a further registration of a right to light notice.

[1] Para 32.47.
[2] Prescription Act 1832, s 3. Written consent is often given, and rights to light thereby excluded, by the inclusion in a sale or lease of part of land of a reservation allowing the vendor or lessor complete freedom to redevelop the retained land, see *RHJ Ltd v FT Patten (Holdings) Ltd* [2008] EWCA Civ 151.
[3] *Morgan v Fear* [1907] AC 425, HL.
[4] An act does not constitute an interruption for the purpose of the Act unless submitted to or acquiesced in for one year; Prescription Act 1832, s 4; see para 32.50 above.
[5] Para 29.25.
[6] Rights of Light Act 1959, s 3.
[7] Rights of Light Act 1959, s 2.

Extent of right

32.56 An owner of a right to light is not necessarily entitled to maintain the level of light which is currently being enjoyed; generally speaking, the entitlement is to sufficient light 'according to the ordinary notions of mankind' for the comfortable use and enjoyment of the property as a dwelling-house, if it is a dwelling-house, or for the beneficial use and occupation of the building if it is a warehouse, a shop, or other place of business.[1] Where there is a right of light, a dominant owner may only bring an action in respect of a reduction in the amount of light received where the reduction constitutes a nuisance; this will only be the case if the light[2] received is reduced below what is sufficient according to the ordinary notions of mankind. In determining this question, the court may take into account the nature of the locality and may have regard to the fact that higher standards may be expected as time goes by.[3] A right of light exists in respect of a defined aperture in a building; the internal arrangement of the rooms in the building is not necessarily relevant to ascertaining the extent of the right.[4]

It is sometimes possible to have a right to a higher than usual level of light. In *Allen v Greenwood*,[5] the claimants, who for at least 20 years had had a greenhouse in their garden, close to the boundary with the neighbouring property, sought an injunction restraining their neighbours from obstructing the light to the greenhouse. The obstruction was caused by a fence which the neighbours had erected and by the neighbours' caravan which was parked close to the greenhouse. Although the greenhouse still received enough light to read by, the Court of Appeal held that this was insufficient for the ordinary purposes of mankind for the use and enjoyment of a greenhouse as a greenhouse (which is regarded as a building with apertures). The question of the amount of light necessary for ordinary purposes is determined by the nature and use of the building, and thus a high degree of light may be necessary in a particular case. The court also held that it is possible to acquire a prescriptive right to a greater than ordinary amount of light. Just as the extent of enjoyment during the prescriptive period governs the extent of a prescriptive right of way,[6] so it also determines the extent of a right of light acquired by prescription. The greenhouse having enjoyed an extraordinary amount of light for 20 years, to the knowledge of the servient owner, a prescriptive right to that amount of light had been acquired.

A claimant whose right to light will be, or has been, infringed is normally entitled to obtain an injunction[7]. This will readily be granted where the infringement has not yet taken place; in this situation the defendant will either be prevented from erecting the offending structure, or will have to modify its design in order to accommodate the claimant's right. Where the infringement has already taken place, a claimant can still obtain an injunction unless the breach is trivial and can be compensated by an award of damages[8]. Thus a defendant can be ordered to demolish a newly constructed building or extension where they have failed to negotiate a settlement with a neighbour whose right to light has been infringed[9].

[1] *Colls v Home and Colonial Stores Ltd* [1904] AC 179 at 208, HL.
[2] It should be noted that the right is to natural light; the fact that a modern office building is artificially lit throughout the day is irrelevant, see *Midtown Ltd v City of London Real Property Co Ltd* [2005] EWHC 33 (Ch).
[3] *Ough v King* [1967] 3 All ER 859, CA.
[4] *Carr-Saunders v Dick McNeil Associates Ltd* [1986] 2 All ER 888.
[5] [1979] 1 All ER 819, CA.
[6] See para 32.53.
[7] See para 11.46.
[8] See para 33.30.
[9] See *HKRUK II (CHC) Ltd v Heaney* [2010] EWHC 2245 (Ch) where a demolition costing somewhere between £1m and £2m was ordered.

Rights of support

32.57 All landowners automatically have a natural right of support[1] which means that they may bring an action in nuisance should the support to their *land* be removed. For example, in *Redland Bricks Ltd v Morris*,[2] the claimant successfully sought damages when part of his market garden slipped into the defendants' land as a result of their digging for clay for their brickworks,[3] and, in *Lotus Ltd v British Soda Co Ltd*,[4] the claimant was held to be entitled to damages when the pumping of brine from boreholes on adjacent land resulted in withdrawal of support from and consequent subsidence of the claimant's land, with resultant damage to the buildings on it. In addition, in certain circumstances at least, landowners can expect their neighbours to take reasonable steps to prevent the potential removal of support to their land.[5]

There is no natural right of support in respect of *buildings*. Such a right of support must be acquired as an easement. However, as *Lotus v British Soda* shows, damages may be claimed in respect of damage to buildings which results from infringement of the natural right of support to the land on which they stand.

An easement of support for buildings may be acquired expressly, by implication or by prescription. A servient owner who by a positive act interferes with a right of support does so at their peril;[6] if support is removed an equivalent must be provided. There is, however, established authority that a landowner is under no strict obligation to repair that part of their building which provides support for a neighbour; it can be allowed to fall into decay. However, it is becoming clear that a servient owner may be liable in the tort of either negligence or nuisance where steps to prevent interference with a neighbour's right of support should reasonably have been taken. It should be noted that the owner of the *dominant* land may always enter the servient land in order to carry out repairs so as to ensure the support continues.[7]

[1] See para 32.14.

[2] [1969] 2 All ER 576, HL.

[3] He also sought, and failed to obtain, a mandatory injunction: para 27.18 above. Where the withdrawal of support causes no immediate collapse but merely the certainty of subsidence in the future, no action can be taken: *Midland Bank Ltd v Bardgrove Property Services Ltd* (1992) 65 P & CR 153, CA.

[4] [1971] 1 All ER 265.

[5] *Holbeck Hall Hotel Ltd v Scarborough Borough Council* [1997] 2 EGLR 213.

[6] *Brace v South East Regional Housing Association Ltd* (1984) 270 Estates Gazette 1286, CA.

[7] *Bradburn v Lindsay* [1983] 2 All ER 408; *Rees v Skerrett* [2001] EWCA Civ 760, [2001] 1 WLR 1541.

PARTICULAR EASEMENTS: KEY POINTS

- The more complex of the commonly encountered easements are: rights of way, rights to light, and rights of support.

- In each case it is important to know the exact extent of the right since any use in excess of the terms of the grant amounts to a breach.

- Rights of way are often created expressly and their extent will depend on the precise wording of the grant; where they are created by prescription their extent will depend on the nature of the use during the prescriptive period.

- Rights to light are not infringed simply because the amount of light received by the dominant land is reduced; what matters is that there is sufficient light left, taking into account the nature of the property and its location. Where the right to light has been acquired by prescription (as is often the case) it is possible to acquire the right to a higher than usual amount of light.

- All property owners enjoy a natural right to support for their land; in order to have a right of support for any buildings on the land, an easement of support must exist. While this prevents the owner of the servient land from positively removing support, it does not necessarily prevent the loss of support as a result of the physical deterioration of the supporting structure.

Questions

1. What are the characteristics that must be established if a right over the land of another is to be capable of being an easement?

2. Can a right to park exist as an easement? What legal difficulties do such rights pose?

3. What are the legal rules governing the express creation of an easement?

4. What is the difference between a grant and a reservation?

5. In what circumstances will the grant of an easement be implied?

6. In what circumstances will the reservation of an easement be implied?

7. Compare and contrast the operation of the rule in *Wheeldon v Burrows* and s 62 of the LPA 1925.

8. What are the basic principles that must be satisfied before any of the different forms of prescription can apply? How do the special rules, contained in the Prescription Act 1832, governing rights to light differ?

9. How do the courts decide whether or not a right of way is being used to excess?

10. Two years ago Valerie, the owner of The Manor, sold a field to Penny on which she has since built a house. Prior to the sale Valerie used a track across The Manor as a means of accessing the main road from that field. Penny's property has a direct access onto a side road but she has been claiming the right to use the track to the main road despite the fact that there is no mention of such a right in the transfer. Has she the right to do so?

33

Restrictive covenants

CHAPTER OVERVIEW

In the property context a covenant is a contractual agreement, usually occurring in a transfer or a lease, in which one party, the covenantor, agrees to do or not to do something for the benefit of another, the covenantee. We deal with leasehold covenants in Chapter 36. In this chapter, we shall be considering the circumstances in which:

- covenants arise where there is no relationship of landlord and tenant;
- the burden of such covenants will pass to a successor in title of the covenantor;
- the benefit of such covenants will pass to a successor in title of the covenantee;
- restrictive covenants will be discharged or modified.

33.1 Typical covenants which might be entered into between the parties to a transfer include covenants preventing building on the land transferred, or preventing the building of more than one house, or requiring the building of a boundary wall. The parties to a lease may enter covenants requiring the payment of rent and the carrying out of repairs, or preventing sub-letting. All these covenants, being contractual agreements, are enforceable between the original parties according to the ordinary law of contract. However, a covenant may also be a right in land, which is enforceable not only between the original parties to it, but also by and against their successors in title to the property concerned. These are of obvious importance to those who take a transfer or assignment from a freeholder or leaseholder.

Covenants where there is no relationship of landlord and tenant[1]

33.2 We leave until a later chapter our consideration of the circumstances in which covenants imposed between landlord and tenant will bind parties to whom the lease or reversion is transferred.[2] Here, we consider the question of the extent to which the *benefit* of a covenant 'runs' (ie passes) with the land of the covenantee, and the extent to which the *burden* of it runs with the land of the covenantor where there is no relationship of landlord and tenant. Suppose that P purchases 100 hectares of farmland from V and covenants with V that he will use the land for agricultural purposes only. If V then sells the remainder of her land to R, R will wish to know whether he can enforce the covenant entered into by V and P, ie whether the benefit of the covenant has run, with the land, to him. Were P subsequently to sell his land to A, A would wish to know if he was bound by P's covenant, ie whether the burden of the covenant has run with the land to him.

We are here dealing with the enforcement of covenants between persons who are not, either as original parties or as assignees, in the relationship of landlord and tenant. In other words, we are mainly concerned with the enforcement of covenants between free-holders, although it should be noted that these same rules apply should a landlord wish to enforce covenants against a sub-tenant since there is no direct relationship of landlord and tenant between such parties.[3]

In this area, common law and equity have separate rules. Both permit the benefit of a covenant to run with the land. Common law, however, does not allow the burden of a covenant to run, while equity allows the burden of negative covenants, which restrict the use of the land, to run. This means that the burden of positive covenants, which require the covenantor to do something in connection with the land, will not run with freehold land.

[1] It should be noted that the Law Commission is in the process of reviewing this area of the law, see Consultation Paper No 186 *Easements Covenants and Profits à Prendre* (2008) and para 33.45.

[2] Paras 36.71–36.86.

[3] Para 36.89.

33.3 Clearly, covenants entered into between freeholders, usually on the sale of part of land by one to another, are mutually enforceable between the original parties on the basis of the contract between them. Furthermore, like other contractual rights, the benefit of a covenant may be assigned to a third party who may then enforce the benefit in their own right.[1] In certain exceptional cases the LPA 1925, s 56 allows a person to enforce a covenant relating to property *as if they were* a party to it, even though they are not named as a party to the covenant; this is only allowed in respect of persons in existence at the time of the covenant, identified by it, and where the covenant purports to be made *with* that person.[2] Such a person is then assumed to be a covenantee. Furthermore only those who, *at the time the covenant was made*, were owners of adjoining land are deemed to be covenantees by virtue of s 56. In the case of covenants entered into after May 2000, it is possible that a wider range of persons might more readily be regarded as having the ben-efit of a covenant as a result of the Contracts (Rights of Third Parties) Act 1999. As we have seen[3], under this Act a party may sue on a covenant either where it is expressly provided that they can, or where the covenant purports to confer a benefit on that party. However, the 1999 Act can be expressly excluded and, in the property context, this practice is wide-spread with the result that it is not having a significant impact.

[1] See para 13.9.

[2] *White v Bijou Mansions Ltd* [1937] 3 All ER 269.

[3] See ch 13.

The running of the burden

Positive covenants

33.4 Where the parties are not in the relationship of landlord and tenant, the burden of a covenant does not run with the land at common law.[1] Since, as we shall see, equity allows the burden of restrictive (negative) covenants to run with the land of the covenan-tor, the practical effect of the common law rule is that the burden of positive covenants will not run with freehold land. This rule, 'the greatest and clearest deficiency' in the law of covenants,[2] is of considerable significance since it means that covenants which impose positive obligations, such as to keep premises in repair, to erect boundary walls, and to contribute to the maintenance of roads, cannot be enforced against successors of the original covenantor. Despite the criticisms of the rule, the House of Lords has declined to overrule it in *Rhone v Stephens*,[3] expressing the view that such a significant departure from long-established principles should be implemented by legislation rather than by judicial decision.[4]

An inability to ensure compliance with positive obligations to repair or to contribute to the cost of maintenance and other services is a grave disadvantage in the case of certain types of property such as a block of flats, an estate with common facilities or a commercial building in multiple occupation. Indeed, the rule has cast a blight on developments of freehold flats which for this reason (among others) are not considered to be a particularly good security for a mortgage. It has therefore become the usual practice for units within buildings in multiple occupation (such as blocks of flats) and estates with shared facilities to be sold on long leases, thus ensuring that positive covenants are enforceable[5]. However, over the years, long leasehold ownership has become very unpopular and after lengthy political pressure, things were supposed to change.

[1] *Austerberry v Oldham Corpn* (1885) 29 Ch D 750, CA, approved *Rhone v Stephens* [1994] 2 All ER 65, HL. Section 33 of the Local Government (Miscellaneous Provisions) Act 1982 provides that local authorities may enforce positive covenants made by deed against successors of the covenantor.

[2] Law Commission Report on the Law of Positive and Restrictive Covenants; Law Com No 127; a view endorsed in the most recent review, see Law Commission Consultation Paper No 186 *Easements Covenants and Profits à Prendre* (2008).

[3] [1994] 2 All ER 65, HL.

[4] For a discussion of proposals for reform see para 33.45.

[5] On the principles expounded in paras 36.71–36.86.

Commonhold

33.5 It is the difficulties over the enforcement of positive covenants which have helped to provoke the eventual implementation of a new type of land holding—commonhold—designed to facilitate the freehold ownership of flats in particular. The commonhold provisions of the Commonhold and Leasehold Reform Act 2002[1] came into force on 27 September 2004. In reality, the Act only applies to new developments. Although it is possible for existing leasehold schemes to convert to commonhold, the consent of all long leaseholders is required[2]; this is only likely to be practicable where the number of units is very low and those involved regard the expense of setting up the commonhold as acceptable. It is now possible to register a scheme as a 'commonhold'. Individual units therein (eg flats) are owned freehold, but the common parts are owned by the commonhold association (which is made up of the unit owners). That association is responsible for the maintenance of the common parts and for major expenditure; the positive obligation to contribute to the cost of such work is enforceable against the original unit holders and anyone to whom they sell their unit. In this way, albeit without any general reform of the law on positive covenants[3], it is possible for positive obligations to bind future owners of units within a commonhold. To date the take up of the new scheme has been disappointingly low[4] and it remains to be seen how quickly the landscape of flat ownership will be changed.

[1] Contained in Part I of the Act; see para 28.34.

[2] Commonhold and Leasehold Reform Act 2002, s 3(1)(b).

[3] As to which see para 33.45.

[4] See para 28.34.

Devices to achieve the enforcement of positive covenants

33.6 Not surprisingly, legal ingenuity has sought to devise methods of achieving the enforcement of positive obligations against successive freehold owners without transgressing the rule preventing the enforcement of positive covenants against successors of the covenantor. However, as the Law Commission has pointed out,[1] none of the devices used to achieve enforcement of positive obligations can be said to provide an effective general solution to the problem. However, since they are to some extent encountered in practice, we give a brief summary of them in the following paragraphs. It should be appreciated that, while some of these could be useful in enabling a developer or management company to enforce positive obligations against successive residents of a housing estate or block of flats, they do not enable the individual residents to enforce such obligations against each other.

[1] Consultation Paper No 186 *Easements Covenants and Profits à Prendre* (2008).

33.7 *Chain of indemnity covenants* By virtue of the LPA 1925, s 79, unless a contrary intention is expressed, a covenantor covenants that both he or she *and* subsequent owners will abide by the covenant. Should a subsequent owner fail to do so, the covenantee may sue the original covenantor for breach of contract. The covenantor (and each successive owner) should therefore ensure that purchasers provide an indemnity in the event of their being sued for non-performance of an obligation by any such purchaser. Such a chain of indemnity provides an indirect method of enforcing covenants, but like all chains it is only as strong as its weakest link.

33.8 *Rights of entry* A right of entry may be used to secure compliance with positive covenants even though the covenants themselves are not enforceable as such.[1] A person having a right of entry has the right to enter property should certain conditions occur and take possession of it, thereby ending the interest of the person holding the land. For example, a vendor of property might insert in the conveyance a covenant requiring the purchaser and any successors to keep the property in repair and reserve a right of entry should the property fall into disrepair. The threat of re-entry will ensure that the purchaser and any successors comply with a positive covenant to repair. However, such a right of entry suffers two disadvantages: first, it is equitable, and must, therefore, be positively protected by the entry of a notice in the Land Register.[2] Second, it is subject to the rule against perpetuities; that is, there is a limit to how far in the future the right may be exercised. To overcome these two disadvantages, it should be annexed to, ie incorporated with, an estate rentcharge, which we discuss in the next paragraph.

[1] *Shiloh Spinners Ltd v Harding* [1973] 1 All ER 90, HL.
[2] See para 35.35.

33.9 *Estate rentcharges* A rentcharge is any annual or other periodic sum charged on or issuing out of land, except rent reserved by a lease or tenancy or any sum payable by way of interest.[1] If it is perpetual or for a term of years it is a legal interest.[2] The Rentcharges Act 1977 prohibits the creation of rentcharges for the future, subject to the important exception of the estate rentcharge.

An estate rentcharge may be of two kinds. The first is one created for the purpose of making positive covenants enforceable by the person to whom the rentcharge is paid (the rent owner) against the owner for the time being of the land. Such a rentcharge must not be of more than a nominal amount.[3] This kind of estate rentcharge achieves its object of making positive covenants enforceable against successive landowners by having a right of entry annexed to it. A right of entry annexed to a rentcharge is a legal interest and is not subject to the rule against perpetuities.[4] Essentially, annexing a right of entry to this kind of estate rentcharge cures it of the defects which it suffers when not so annexed. Nonetheless, the remedy remains 'clumsy and draconian' and although the device of the estate rentcharge comes closest to providing a solution to the unenforceability of positive covenants, it is undoubtedly artificial and technical in the extreme.[5]

The Rentcharges Act 1977 also provides for a second kind of estate rentcharge, defined as one created for the purpose of meeting, or contributing towards, the cost of the performance by the rent owner of covenants for the provision of services, or for the carrying out of maintenance or repairs, or for the effecting of insurance or the making of any payment by him for the benefit of the land affected by the rentcharge. Such a rentcharge must be reasonable in relation to the cost to the rent owner of performing the covenant.[6] Examples of this kind of rentcharge are where the developer of a housing estate reserves a rentcharge from each purchaser to provide a fund to maintain the estate roads until adoption by the local authority; or where the management company of a block of flats reserves a rentcharge in respect of each flat to provide a fund for the maintenance of the common parts.

[1] Rentcharges Act 1977, s 1. A legal rentcharge created out of registered land is noted together with the right of entry in the Charges Register of the landowner's register of title, and the rent owner may be substantively registered as the proprietor of a rentcharge LRA 2002 27(2)(e), Sch 2, para 7.
[2] LPA 1925, s 1(2).
[3] Rentcharges Act 1977, s 2.
[4] LPA 1925, ss 1(2) and 4(3).
[5] Law Commission Consultation Paper No 186 *Easements Covenants and Profits à Prendre* (2008).
[6] Rentcharges Act 1977, s 2.

33.10 *Doctrine of benefit and burden* Another possible method of securing the enforcement of positive obligations against successive landowners is the doctrine of benefit and burden elaborated in the case of *Halsall v Brizell*.[1] Here, the developers of a private housing estate imposed a covenant on each purchaser, under which the latter covenanted to contribute towards the cost of maintaining the roads and footpaths of the estate, which were retained by the developer. Upjohn J held that as this covenant was positive it could not be enforced against successors of the original purchasers. However, by applying the doctrine that a person who takes the benefit of a deed is bound by any conditions in it, he held that if successors of the original purchasers wished to take advantage of the benefit of the roads and footpaths, which, of course, they had to do, they must also accept the burden of paying for their maintenance. It has recently been made clear that this doctrine does not mean that *any* condition can be rendered enforceable by attaching it to a right; the condition must be relevant to the right.[2] Furthermore, it is clear that the subsequent purchasers must have a real option to decline to take the benefit and thereby escape the burden[3]. This doctrine is, therefore, only of utility where the obligation is linked to a corresponding benefit of which the successors wish to take advantage.

[1] [1957] 1 All ER 371; para 30.18.
[2] *Rhone v Stephens* [1994] 2 All ER 65, HL.
[3] *Thamesmead Town Ltd v Allotey* [1998] 3 EGLR 97, CA; *Davies v Jones* [2009] EWCA Civ 1164.

Restrictive covenants

33.11 The particular contribution of equity, originating in the case of *Tulk v Moxhay*,[1] is to allow the burden of restrictive covenants, those which restrict the uses to which the land may be put, to run with the land. Consequently, although a vendor is not able to ensure that successors of a purchaser act positively in relation to the land, it is possible to make certain that they refrain from acting in particular ways: a vendor may, for example, restrict building on the land or the carrying on of any trade. Equity will allow the burden of a covenant to run with the land of the covenantor if:

- it is essentially negative;
- the covenantee retains land capable of being benefited by the covenant;
- the parties intend that the covenant should run with the land; and
- the requirements of registration or of the doctrine of notice are complied with.

Each of these will now be considered in turn.

[1] (1848) 18 LJ Ch 83.

The covenant must be essentially negative

33.12 The essence of the covenant, whether positively or negatively worded, must be negative or restrictive. The case of *Tulk v Moxhay*[1] provides an example. Tulk owned Leicester Square. He sold off the gardens in the centre and retained the surrounding land. The purchaser of the gardens covenanted that 'his heirs and assigns … would … at all times … keep and maintain the said piece of ground … in an open state'. This covenant was held to be binding on a successor of the purchaser. Although the covenant was phrased in terms of a positive obligation, 'keep and maintain in an open state', it was essentially negative, prohibiting building on the land. Conversely, a covenant 'not to let the premises fall into disrepair' is a positive covenant since the covenantor must take positive steps to carry out repairs.

Why did equity confine its intervention to negative covenants? As we have seen,[2] equity does not override a common law rule, thus it could not compel positive compliance with a contractual obligation entered into by the current owner's predecessor. However, the court of equity could take the view that, where land is sold subject to a *restriction*, this means that the purchaser, and anyone who subsequently purchases the land with notice of that restriction, simply never acquires that right to use the land which would otherwise have been enjoyed.[3] Any attempt to act in a way which contravenes the restriction will be restrained by the issue of an injunction, an equitable remedy which is particularly suitable for the enforcement of negative obligations.

[1] (1848) 18 LJ Ch 83.
[2] Para 1.7.
[3] See *Rhone v Stephens* [1994] 2 All ER 65 at p 68.

The covenantee must retain land capable of being benefited

33.13 The requirement that the covenant must have been imposed for the benefit of land retained by the covenantee is effectively the same as that in the law relating to easements, for there to be dominant land which is benefited by the easement.[1] It means that restrictive covenants are only enforceable as between neighbouring landowners. This rule was established in *LCC v Allen*,[2] where a developer covenanted with the London County Council (LCC) not to build on a plot which lay across the end of a proposed street. It was held that the LCC could not enforce this covenant against a successor of the developer since at no time did the council have any interest in any land capable of being benefited by the covenant.

The reversion on a lease gives the landlord a sufficient retained interest in the land to permit the enforcement against a sub-tenant of a restrictive covenant made by the tenant and contained in the headlease.[3] Such a covenant may be enforced by the landlord against a sub-tenant having notice of it, despite the absence of a contract or privity of estate between a landlord and sub-tenant. A mortgagee's (lender's) interest has also been held sufficient to allow the enforcement of restrictive covenants against successors of the mortgagor/covenantor.[4]

The courts will readily assume that the retained land is capable of being benefited by the covenant unless the defendant can show that the restriction cannot reasonably be said to be of value to the land.[5] Furthermore, the courts have been prepared to hold that a covenant restraining a purchaser from carrying on a business which competes with that carried on by the vendor on the retained land benefits the vendor's land. Both these points are illustrated in *Newton Abbot Co-operative Society Ltd v Williamson and Treadgold Ltd*[6] where a covenant imposed by the vendor prohibiting dealing in articles of ironmongery in the property sold was held to benefit the vendor's retained ironmonger's shop. Upjohn J stressed the enhanced price the vendor would realise on selling together the land and the business, as a result of the covenant.

There are some circumstances in which the requirement that the covenantee must retain land which is benefited by the covenant is manifestly inconvenient for public bodies. For this reason statute expressly permits local authorities, local planning authorities, the National Trust and the Nature Conservancy Council to enforce restrictive covenants despite the absence of any retained land.[7]

[1] Paras 32.5.

[2] [1914] 3 KB 642, CA.

[3] *Hall v Ewin* (1887) 37 Ch D 74.

[4] See *Regent Oil Co Ltd v J A Gregory (Hatch End) Ltd* [1965] 3 All ER 673, CA.

[5] *Wrotham Park Estate Co v Parkside Homes Ltd* [1974] 2 All ER 321. Contrast *Re Ballard's Conveyance* [1937] 2 All ER 691.

[6] [1952] 1 All ER 279.

[7] See Housing Act 1985, s 609, Town and Country Planning Act 1990, s 106(3), National Trust Act 1937, s 8 and Countryside Act 1968, s 15(4).

The parties must intend that the covenant should run

33.14 By the LPA 1925, s 79, which applies unless a contrary intention is expressed,[1] the parties are assumed to intend that the covenant should run with the land, rather than being merely personal to the parties.

[1] See *Re Royal Victoria Pavilion, Ramsgate* [1961] 3 All ER 83.

Registration and notice

33.15 In the case of registered land, the covenant must be protected by the entry of a notice in the Charges Register of the burdened land in order to bind the land of the covenantor.[1] The details of the covenant are set out in full on the register of the burdened land.[2] It should be noted that a restrictive covenant entered into between landlord and tenant cannot be registered[3]. Consequently, enforcement of such a covenant by the landlord against a *sub-tenant* depends on whether or not the title of the headlease is registered. If it is, the covenant is automatically binding[4]. Where it is only title to the sub-lease which is registered, the doctrine of notice would appear to dictate whether or not restrictive covenants in the (unregistered) headlease bind the sub-tenant.[5]

[1] LRA 2002, s 29(2); para 35.35.

[2] Inconveniently, the existence of the covenant is not noted on the title of the benefited land; this can make it difficult for those entitled to the benefit to be aware of their rights.

[3] LRA 2002, s 33(c).

[4] LRA 2002, s 29(2)(b).

[5] In such circumstances the sub-lessee could only have been accorded a good leasehold title which does not guarantee that the landlord had the right to grant the lease free from incumbrances; see para 29.17, note 3 and LRA 2002, s 12(6).

THE RUNNING OF THE BURDEN: KEY POINTS

- The burden of positive covenants does not pass to a new owner of freehold land; commonhold—aimed largely at new flat developments—is designed to overcome this problem but has not yet become widely used. Other devices to make positive covenants run remain largely untested.
- The burden of restrictive covenants does pass to a new owner of freehold land provided:
  - the covenantee retains land capable of being benefited by the covenant;
  - the parties intend that the covenant should run with the land; and
  - the requirements of registration or of the doctrine of notice are complied with.

The running of the benefit

33.16 As with the running of the burden, there are certain divergences between the rules of common law and of equity on this topic. To the extent that equitable rules differ from common law rules, they apply only to restrictive covenants. For our purposes therefore it is appropriate to retain the division of the subject matter into positive and restrictive covenants.

Positive covenants

33.17 At common law the benefit of a covenant will run with the land to a successor of the original covenantee if it is annexed to the land. This means that is incorporated with it so that on a transfer of the land the benefit automatically passes without the need for any mention being made of it. A covenant will be annexed and the benefit will run where the conditions set out in the following paragraphs are met.

The covenant must touch and concern the land of the covenantee

33.18 The covenant must either affect the way in which the land is occupied or it must be such that in itself, and not merely as a result of collateral circumstances, it affects the value of the land.[1]

In *Smith and Snipes Hall Farm Ltd v River Douglas Catchment Board*,[2] the Catchment Board covenanted with the owner of the land adjoining a brook that the Board would maintain the banks of the brook. The court held that the covenant touched and concerned the adjoining land, in that it affected the value of the land by converting it from flooded meadows to land suitable for agriculture.

A difficulty can arise where the benefited land is large, with the result that it may successfully be argued that the whole of that land cannot be benefited from the imposition of a covenant relating to land which adjoins only part.[3] While it is possible to prove that the whole of a very large property does in fact benefit from the covenant,[4] the problem can be avoided altogether by the inclusion of an express provision that the covenant is imposed for the benefit of 'all or any part of' the covenantee's land.[5]

---

[1] *Rogers v Hosegood* [1900] 2 Ch 388 at 395; see also *P & A Swift Investments v Combined English Stores Group plc* [1988] 2 All ER 885, HL.

[2] [1949] 2 All ER 179, CA.

[3] As in *Re Ballard's Conveyance* [1937] Ch 473.

[4] *Marten v Flight Refuelling Ltd* [1962] Ch 115.

[5] *Marquess of Zetland v Driver* [1938] 2 All ER 158, CA.

It was intended that the benefit should run

33.19 In the *River Douglas Catchment Board* case, the Court of Appeal held that it was plain from the language of the covenant, under which the Board undertook to maintain the banks of the brook 'for all time', that it was intended to take effect for the benefit of successive owners of the land. While in this case evidence of intention was sought and found in the language of the document creating the covenant, we shall explain in para 33.26 below that this may no longer be necessary.

The land to be benefited should be identifiable

33.20 In the *River Douglas Catchment Board* case, the document creating the covenant referred only to 'certain land situate between the Leeds and Liverpool Canal and the River Douglas and adjoining the Eller Brook'. This was, however, regarded as sufficient; extrinsic evidence was admissible to prove the precise extent and situation of the relevant land.

The successor must acquire a legal estate

33.21 The common law used to require that the person seeking to enforce the covenant should have the same legal estate as the original covenantee. However, in *Smith and Snipes Hall Farm Ltd v River Douglas Catchment Board*, the Court of Appeal held that the covenant could be enforced against the Board not only by Smith who purchased the freehold from the original covenantee, but also by Snipes Hall Farm Ltd to whom Smith had leased the land. The Court held that the LPA 1925, s 78 permits the benefit of a covenant to run to lessees and sub-lessees as well as to successors of the covenantee's legal estate. A further, more radical effect, of s 78 is considered in para 33.26, below.

It should be noted that it is not necessary that the covenant should have any connection with the land of the covenantor.

Restrictive covenants

33.22 As with the common law rules, the first requirement of the equitable rules, which apply to restrictive covenants, is that the covenant should touch and concern the land of the covenantee; this has already been discussed.[1] A successor in title of the original covenantee must then go on to show that the benefit has passed either:

- by annexation, or
- by assignment, or
- under a scheme of development.

[1] See para 33.18.

Annexation

33.23 We have already considered the common law rules on annexation. In practice these are rarely encountered for the very good reason that they apply only where the burdened land has not yet changed hands. Once that has occurred, the assistance of equity must be sought for both the running of the burden and the running of the benefit. In truth, the equitable rules as to annexation are almost certainly a more fully developed version of the common law rules.

33.24 *Annexation by express words* Where a positive obligation is imposed, it is often clear from the circumstances that it is intended to benefit particular identifiable land. This is not always the case with obligations imposed by restrictive covenants. The original approach was, therefore, that in order to annex the benefit of a restrictive covenant in equity express wording must be used which clearly identifies the land and indicates the parties' intention that the covenant is for the benefit of that land; that is, words which demonstrate either that the covenant has been entered into for the benefit of identifiable land or that it was made with the covenantee in his capacity as owner of that land[1]. As we shall see in the following paragraphs, it is now clear that it is not essential to use express words of annexation. Nevertheless, it is good conveyancing practice to put the matter beyond argument by formulating a restrictive covenant in a way which does itself achieve annexation[2].

It is also desirable for the wording to make clear that the covenant is intended to benefit *each and every part* of the covenantee's property. This serves two purposes. First, as we have seen, it ensures that, where the land to be benefited is unusually large, there will be no argument over the question of whether the land is in fact benefited.[3] Second, it also means that, as well as the benefit of the covenant passing by annexation to subsequent owners of the *entire* benefited land, it will, if the benefited land is divided up rather than remaining as an entity, pass also to the purchasers of *those parts*. However, where the wording of the covenant is unclear, the courts will now presume that annexation is to each and every part; hence if it is intended that the benefit of the covenant should pass only to successors to the whole of the benefited land this needs to be made explicit[4].

[1] *Renals v Cowlishaw* (1878) 9 Ch D 125; *Reid v Bickerstaff* [1909] 2 Ch 305.
[2] *Rogers v Hosegood* [1900] 2 Ch 388, CA.
[3] See *Marquess of Zetland v Driver* [1938] 2 All ER 158, CA and para 33.18.
[4] *Federated Homes Ltd v Mill Lodge Properties Ltd* [1980] 1 All ER 371, CA.

33.25 *Annexation by implication* However desirable, it is clear that the use of express words is not essential to bring about the annexation of the benefit of a covenant. It is a question of construction of the particular covenant. There is authority that annexation can be implied where, from the document creating the covenant, the land intended to be benefited and an intention to benefit the land can be clearly established.[1] As we have explained, these two matters, together with evidence that the covenant touches and concerns the land, themselves establish annexation.

[1] *Marten v Flight Refuelling* Ltd [1962] Ch 115; *Shropshire County Council v Edwards* (1982) 46 P & CR 270; *J Sainsbury plc v London Borough of Enfield* [1989] 2 All ER 817.

33.26 *Annexation under LPA 1925, s 78* A more important erosion of any requirement for express wording is the ruling by the Court of Appeal in *Federated Homes Ltd v Mill Lodge Properties Ltd*[1] that the LPA 1925, s 78 can cause the benefit of a covenant to be annexed, and hence to run with the land.

Section 78 provides that a covenant relating to any land of the covenantee shall be deemed to be made with the covenantee and any successors in title, including the owners and occupiers for the time being of the land of the covenantee intended to be benefited, and the persons deriving title under them, and shall have effect as if such successors and other persons were expressed.

Prior to the *Federated Homes* case, s 78 was regarded, like its mirror provision s 79, as merely a word saving provision with no substantive effect.[2] However, this view was rejected by the Court of Appeal which held that s 78 operates to annex the benefit of any post-1925 covenant which touches and concerns (ie 'relates to') the land of the covenantee. It is not necessary for the covenant to express any positive intention that the benefit should run[3] but it is now clear that the covenant itself, or the document in which it is contained, must identify the benefited land.[4] It is also settled that, where the covenant makes it clear that there is no intention for the covenant to run (for example by providing that it should not take effect for the benefit of successors unless the benefit is expressly assigned to them) s 78 does not cause the benefit to be annexed.[5]

Although the decision in *Federated Homes* was heavily criticised at the time, it has now remained unchallenged for 30 years. It radically simplifies the law relating to annexation which is of considerable assistance both to students learning the law and to those claiming the benefit of covenants. However, this simplification has its disadvantages; it is now much more difficult than hitherto for those ostensibly subject to the burden of covenants to escape liability on the grounds that there was no adequate annexation and thus no one entitled to enforce the covenant.

[1] [1980] 1 All ER 371, CA.
[2] A view which still prevails in relation to s 79; see *Tophams Ltd v Sefton* [1967] 1 AC 50, HL; *Rhone v Stephens* [1994] 2 All ER 65, HL.
[3] *Mohammad Zadeh v Joseph* [2006] EWHC 1040.
[4] *Crest Nicholson Residential (South) Ltd v McAllister* [2004] EWCA Civ 410.
[5] *Roake v Chadha* [1983] 3 All ER 503; see also *Sugarman v Porter* [2006] EWHC 331 (Ch).

Assignment

33.27 The traditional view of the law was that if the benefit of a covenant was not originally annexed to the land by the use of appropriate wording, it was necessary for a successor of the covenantee to show that the benefit of it had been separately expressly assigned to him or her at the same time as the land was transferred However, as we explained in the preceding paragraphs, it now appears to be the law that annexation may either be implied or be brought about by the LPA 1925, s 78. Thus the circumstances in which it will be necessary to resort to the law of assignment are limited. However, where there is no express or implied annexation of a pre-1926 covenant, assignment must be considered,[1] likewise where, as in *Roake v Chadha*,[2] annexation is expressly excluded.

Briefly, the rules as to the assignment of the benefit of a covenant are as follows. The assignment of the benefit of the covenant must be contemporaneous with the assignment of the land; a covenantee who has transferred the land can no longer enforce the covenant[3] and thus has no enforceable covenant to assign.[4] To be capable of assignment, a covenant must have been taken for the benefit of ascertainable land which is capable of being benefited by it. The existence and situation of the land to be benefited need not—and, since assignment is being resorted to in the absence of annexation, usually will not—be indicated in the terms of the covenant itself. However, it is sufficient that, on a broad and reasonable view, it can otherwise be identified with reasonable certainty.[5] The benefit of an assignable covenant may be assigned separately and at different times with parts of the benefited land.[6]

[1] *J Sainsbury plc v London Borough of Enfield* [1989] 2 All ER 817.
[2] [1983] 3 All ER 503; para 33.26 above.
[3] *Chambers v Randall* [1923] 1 Ch 149.
[4] *Re Union of London and Smith's Bank Ltd's Conveyance, Miles v Easter* [1933] Ch 611, CA.
[5] *Marten v Flight Refuelling Ltd* [1961] 2 All ER 696.
[6] *Chambers v Randall* [1923] 1 Ch 149.

Scheme of development

33.28 Where a developer wishes to impose a set of mutually enforceable restrictions on a number of plots of land, the rules of annexation and assignment cannot achieve the desired result. This can be illustrated by the following example:

Plot 1	Plot 2	Plot 3	Plot 4
A	B	C	D

Elm Avenue

Plot 5	Plot 6	Plot 7	Plot 8

When the developer sells Plot 1 to A, subject to a number of restrictive covenants, the benefit of those covenants can be annexed to, or assigned with, the developer's retained land (ie Plots 2, 3 and 4); when Plot 2 is sold to B, subject to the same restrictions, these can only be annexed to, or assigned with, the developer's retained land (ie Plots 3 and 4); the benefit of restrictions imposed on Plot 3 (sold to C) can only be for the benefit of Plot 4 and, by the time Plot 4 is sold to D, there is no longer any retained land to benefit. Hence it can be see that annexation and assignment do not allow the land of earlier purchasers to benefit from covenants imposed on land purchased later. So, in our example the restrictions imposed on A's land can be enforced by B, C and D, those imposed on B's land by C and D but not A, those on C's land by D but not A and B, and so on. This pattern would be extended by the sale of plots 5 to 8.

For this reason the rules relating to schemes of development were devised. A scheme of development exists where a landowner has disposed of their land in parcels, imposing, on each transfer of a parcel of land, restrictive covenants intended not simply for their advantage as owner of the land but for the advantage of each parcel purchased. Such schemes may be imposed to maintain the character of an area such as a housing estate. The scheme of covenants gives rise to what is in effect a local 'planning' law for the area of land disposed of, which is based on *reciprocal* rights and obligations.[1] However, the use of a scheme of development secures only the passing of the benefit of the covenants; in order to achieve the necessary reciprocity, it is essential that the restrictive covenants be properly registered[2] in order to ensure that they are mutually *binding*. If this is not done the whole scheme may collapse. As soon as the original vendor sells the first parcel of land, the scheme crystallises, and all the land within the area of the scheme (there must be a clearly defined area[3]) is bound, becoming subject to the 'local law'.[4]

Species of scheme of development which may be encountered include the building scheme, designed to provide for and regulate building development, and the letting scheme, under which a common set of restrictions is imposed on leasehold interests whether in relation to flats in a particular block, or houses on an estate, or a group of commercial premises[5].

[1] *Reid v Bickerstaff* [1909] 2 Ch 305 at 319, CA.
[2] See Preston and Newsom *Restrictive Covenants Affecting Freehold Land* (7th edn, 1992). See para 33.15.
[3] *Reid v Bickerstaff* [1909] 2 Ch 305, CA. The defined area of the scheme must be clear to both vendor and all the purchasers, see *Emile Elias & Co Ltd v Pine Groves Ltd* [1993] 1 WLR 305, PC.
[4] *Brunner v Greenslade* [1970] 3 All ER 833.
[5] In *Williams v Kiley* [2002] EWCA Civ 1645, [2003] 1 P & CR D 38 the principles of a letting scheme were, apparently for the first time, applied to a small arcade of shops. In this way the tenant of one shop was able to prevent the tenant of another breaching the user covenants in the lease in a way which competed with the claimant's business.

33.29 In the case of *Elliston v Reacher*,[1] Parker J laid down four requirements of a scheme of development:

- both claimant and defendant in the action to enforce the particular covenant must derive title from the same vendor;

- this vendor must have laid out the estate, or a defined part of it, for sale in lots, subject to restrictions which were intended to be imposed on all the lots, and which are consistent only with some general scheme of development;
- these restrictions must have been intended to be, and be, for the benefit of all the lots; and
- the lots must have been purchased from the common vendor on the basis that the restrictions to which they were subject were to take effect for the benefit of all the other lots. This is an important requirement.

More recent cases have shown that this list does not constitute an inflexible definition. For example, in *Baxter v Four Oaks Properties Ltd*,[2] the estate was not laid out in lots by the original vendor, rather he sold the land in parcels of whatever size the particular purchasers required. Nonetheless the area was held to be the subject of a scheme. In *Re Dolphin's Conveyance, Birmingham Corpn v Boden*,[3] the original owners of an estate, having sold off part in lots, gave the rest to their nephew who continued the process of selling the estate off in lots, imposing the same restrictions. Again, there was held to be a scheme of development, despite the absence of a common vendor. In these cases the intention to impose a scheme was evident in the conveyancing documents. Where such an intention is not evident, it is more necessary to consider whether Parker J's four requirements are complied with. Thus in *Emile Elias & Co Ltd v Pine Groves Ltd*,[4] where there was no evidence of a common intention to produce mutually enforceable covenants, the absence of a clearly defined area to which the alleged scheme applied and the lack of uniformity between the restrictions imposed on different plots, proved fatal to the existence of a scheme of development.

It must be remembered that a scheme of development is a scheme for the reciprocal enforcement of restrictive covenants and that for the burden to be enforceable restrictive covenants require protection by registration. Thus, every time a parcel is sold, the common vendor must have the covenants noted on the charges register of the purchaser's register of title,[5] as appropriate. Furthermore, since the vendor is impliedly bound by the restrictions (even in the absence of any express covenant), each purchaser should register the restrictions against the common vendor. Only if this is done can each purchaser enforce the restrictions against subsequent purchasers.

[1] [1908] 2 Ch 374.
[2] [1965] 1 All ER 906.
[3] [1970] 2 All ER 664.
[4] [1993] 1 WLR 305, PC.
[5] Para 33.15 and 35.35.

THE RUNNING OF THE BENEFIT: KEY POINTS

- The benefit of positive covenants passes to a purchaser of the original covenantee's land provided that:
  - the covenant relates to that land;
  - the benefited land is clearly identifiable;
  - it was intended that the benefit should pass;
  - the purchaser acquires the legal estate.
- The benefit of restrictive covenants that relate to the covenantee's land passes to a purchaser of the original covenantee's land by way of either:
  - annexation (usually automatically under s 78 of the LPA 1925 in the case of post-1925 covenants); or

- assignment; or
- a scheme of development; this allows all those who own land within the scheme to enforce restrictive covenants against each other.

Remedies

33.30 The equitable remedy of an injunction is particularly suitable for enforcing negative obligations such as restrictive covenants. Such a remedy achieves exactly what the claimant normally desires, namely the cessation of the activity which breaches the covenant, as opposed to mere compensation. Indeed, equitable remedies are, in principle, the only remedies available for the enforcement of restrictive covenants against a successor of the original covenantor. However, in such cases, the court has a discretion to award damages, as an alternative to granting an injunction.[1] A 'good working rule' for deciding whether to grant damages instead of an injunction was put forward in *Shelfer v City of London Electric Lighting Co.*[2] According to this an injunction will be granted unless:

- the injury to the claimant's legal rights is small;
- it is capable of being estimated in terms of money;
- it can adequately be compensated for by a small payment; and
- it would be oppressive to the defendant to grant an injunction.

It should be noted that this is only a good working rule and the court always retains its discretion to refuse an injunction.[3] In practice such a refusal is increasingly likely where a claimant fails to take immediate legal steps to protect their rights, eg by seeking an interlocutory injunction to stop any building in breach of covenant.[4] Where damages are awarded on a discretionary basis, as an alternative to an injunction, they can be based on the profit which has accrued to the defendant as a result of the breach of covenant.[5]

Nonetheless, in the majority of cases an injunction is the remedy which is sought and that which is granted. In appropriate cases, a mandatory injunction will be granted; for example requiring the demolition of a building, as in *Wakeham v Wood*,[6] where the defendant erected a house blocking the claimant's sea view in flagrant disregard of a covenant prohibiting him so doing.

In the event of a breach by an original covenantor, damages at common law will be available as of right; unlike damages awarded as an alternative to an injunction, these cannot be based on the profit which has been gained as a result of the breach; accordingly, in the absence of actual loss by the claimant, damages will only be nominal.[7] Where the breach is of a positive covenant damages will normally be the appropriate remedy, though specific performance may be granted in certain circumstances.[8] Where the breach is of a restrictive covenant the claimant will normally seek, and be granted, an injunction.

[1] Senior Courts Act 1981, s 50.
[2] [1891–4] All ER Rep 838.
[3] See, for example, *Wrotham Park Estate Co v Parkside Homes Ltd* [1974] 2 All ER 321.
[4] Although this will not be fatal where the defendant has been clearly warned of impending legal proceedings, see *Mortimer v Bailey* [2004] EWCA Civ 1514.
[5] *Wrotham Park Estate Co v Parkside Homes Ltd* [1974] 2 All ER 321; *Surrey County Council v Bredero Homes Ltd* [1993] 3 All ER 705, CA; *Jaggard v Sawyer* [1995] 2 All ER 189, CA.
[6] (1981) 43 P & CR 40, CA.
[7] *Surrey County Council v Bredero Homes Ltd* [1993] 3 All ER 705, CA.
[8] See, for example, *Jeune v Queens Cross Properties Ltd* [1973] 3 All ER 97.

Discharge of restrictive covenants

Development, planning law and restrictive covenants

33.31 Planning law and restrictive covenants exist side by side as a means of controlling development.[1] 'From the individual's point of view, control by private covenant has obvious advantages over planning control, in that it can cover matters of important detail with which a planning authority would not be concerned and the procedure of enforcement is available to a person who is entitled to the benefit of a covenant and is aggrieved by a breach, instead of depending on the planning authority's decision to act'.[2] In the words of a leading textbook on the subject, 'one thing that is abundantly plain is that there is no prospect whatever that restrictive covenants will become unnecessary and that their place will be taken by the planning laws. For planning standards are still too often below the standards imposed by restrictive covenants'.[3] Another point is that, as the Law Commission says,[4] certain changes of use and certain building operations to which a neighbour might reasonably object do not require planning permission. It is important to realise that the fact that an individual has planning permission for a particular project in no way permits or excuses the breach of a restrictive covenant burdening his land, though the grant of planning permission may be relevant, but far from decisive, in relation to an application to the Upper Tribunal (Lands Chamber)—the successor to the Lands Tribunal—for the modification or discharge of the covenant.[5] However, as we shall see,[6] where land is acquired for planning or other statutory purposes, a restrictive covenant will not be allowed to impede those purposes.

[1] For an outline of the law of development control and its enforcement, see ch 39 below.
[2] Law Commission, Report on Restrictive Covenants No 11, para 8.
[3] Preston and Newsom *Restrictive Covenants Affecting Freehold Land* (7th edn, 1992).
[4] Consultation Paper No 186 *Easements Covenants and Profits à Prendre* (2008).
[5] *Re Martin's Application* [1989] 1 EGLR 193, CA; para 33.42.
[6] See para 33.37.

33.32 A purchaser or would-be purchaser of land, discovering that the land is apparently subject to some long-standing restriction preventing intended development, may make an application to the Chancery Division for a declaration as to whether or not the land is, or would in any given event be, affected by the restriction; or as to the nature and extent of the restriction and whether it is enforceable and if so by whom.[1] Such a declaration, which will only be made after due publicity of the proceedings has been circulated to all nearby owners who might have the benefit of the covenant,[2] is conclusive; anyone not named in the declaration will lose the benefit of the covenant. It should be noted also that it is possible to take out a relatively inexpensive insurance policy against one's plans being thwarted by the enforcement of a restrictive covenant.

[1] LPA 1925, s 84(2).
[2] *Re Sunnyfield* [1932] 1 Ch 79; *Re Elm Avenue* [1984] 3 All ER 632.

33.33 There are various circumstances in which a person claiming the benefit of a restrictive covenant may be prevented from enforcing the covenant. At common law, there are four main possibilities:

- a change in the character of the neighbourhood;
- release of the covenant;
- unity of ownership; and
- acquisition for planning or statutory purposes.

Under statute, we consider applications to the upper Tribunal (Lands Chamber) to discharge or modify the covenant, and (briefly) applications under the Housing Act 1985.

Discharge at common law

Change in character of neighbourhood

33.34 In *Chatsworth Estates Co v Fewell*,[1] Fewell had opened a guest house contrary to a covenant that his house should be used as a private dwelling only. The estate company having the benefit of the covenant sought an injunction against him. Fewell claimed that the covenant was not enforceable on the ground that the character of the neighbourhood had completely changed since the covenant was made because some houses in the area were now used as guest houses, and some as schools. Farwell J rejected this argument holding that to succeed on this basis a defendant would have to show so complete a change in the character of the neighbourhood that there was no longer any value left in the covenant at all. This was clearly not so in this case.

[1] [1931] 1 Ch 224.

Release of the covenant

33.35 Release may be express or implied. In *Chatsworth Estates Co v Fewell*, the defendant also argued that the estate company, by allowing others to open guest houses, etc had impliedly released the benefit of the covenants. This, said Farwell J, was a matter of degree, to be decided in this case by reference to the question, 'have the claimants by their acts and omissions represented to the defendant that the covenants are no longer enforceable and that he is therefore entitled to use his house as a guest house?' Again, this was not so in this case.

Unity of ownership

33.36 If the burdened and benefited land come into the same ownership, any restrictive covenants are extinguished.[1] This follows from the fact that a person cannot have a third party right over their own land. Land subject to a scheme of development, however, forms an exception to this rule. Plots within the area of a scheme, which have fallen into common ownership, remain subject to the scheme and continue to do so if they are later sold off separately.[2] Thus, if the common vendor sells, subject to the scheme, a number of lots to a builder, who subsequently sells the lots to separate purchasers, the restrictions are enforceable between those purchasers even though their land had for a period been in common ownership.

[1] *Re Tiltwood, Sussex, Barrett v Bond* [1978] 2 All ER 1091.
[2] *Texaco Antilles Ltd v Kernochan* [1973] 2 All ER 118, PC; *Brunner v Greenslade* [1970] 3 All ER 833.

Acquisition for planning or statutory purposes

33.37 Where land is acquired by a local authority for planning purposes, restrictive covenants will not be allowed to impede the carrying out of works in accordance with planning permission,[1] whether these works are carried out by the local authority or by someone to whom the local authority has later transferred the land.[2] Equally, restrictive covenants will not be allowed to prevent the use of land acquired by other bodies for statutory purposes.[3] It matters not whether the acquisition was made under compulsory powers, or by agreement.[3] It is usual for the person entitled to the benefit of the restriction to be entitled to the payment of compensation.[4]

Technically, the covenant remains in existence; it is merely the right to enforce which is taken away. However, the covenant will still be enforced where it does not directly prevent the statutorily authorised use. So, where a covenant prevented the carrying out of building works to a hospital without prior approval, it was held that such approval must be sought. Only if that approval was actually refused would the statutory powers (to operate a hospital) be impeded and the right to further enforce the covenant be denied.[5]

[1] Town and Country Planning Act 1990, s 233.
[2] *R v City of London Corpn, ex p Masters, Governors and Commonlity of the Mystery of the Barbers of London* [1996] 2 EGLR 128.
[3] *Kirby v School Board of Harrogate* [1896] 1 Ch 436.
[4] Usually under the Compulsory Purchase Act 1965, s 10.
[5] *Cadogan v Royal Brompton Hospital National Health Trust* [1996] 2 EGLR 115.

Application to the Upper Tribunal (Lands Chamber)

33.38 Under the LPA 1925, s 84(1) the Upper Tribunal (Lands Chamber)—the successor to the Lands Tribunal[1] has jurisdiction on certain grounds to discharge, wholly or partly, or to modify, restrictive covenants affecting freehold or leasehold land. In the case of leasehold land, the power is limited to where the term is of more than 40 years of which at least 25 years have expired.[2] The majority of applications made to the Tribunal under this section are to modify a covenant; for example, to enable the owner of the land affected to build at a higher density than that permitted in the covenant, or to carry out such projects as the conversion of a house into flats,[3] the building of a house in the garden of an existing house, or the erection of a public house. The fact that an applicant has planning permission for the intended development is in no way decisive of an application under s 84, although the Tribunal must take into account the development plan for the area and the pattern of grants and refusals of planning permission in the area.[4]

Provision is made for those having the benefit of the relevant covenant to lodge an objection to the application. If the applicant considers that any objector is not entitled to the benefit of the covenant the Tribunal may make a preliminary determination of the matter,[5] the onus being on the objector to prove his entitlement.[6]

There is no rule preventing the original covenantor making an application under s 84, nor preventing modification of a covenant which has only recently been imposed.[7] These are merely factors to be taken into account in the exercise of the Tribunal's discretion.

The Tribunal may, in modifying a covenant, add other reasonable restrictions which are acceptable to the applicant.[8]

The Tribunal may exercise its jurisdiction to discharge or modify a covenant on one or more of the grounds outlined in the following paragraphs.

[1] Para 2.24.
[2] LPA 1925, s 84(12).
[3] See also para 33.44.
[4] LPA 1925, s 84(1B).
[5] LPA 1925, s 84(3A).
[6] *Re Edis's Application* (1972) 23 P & CR 421.
[7] *Ridley v Taylor* [1965] 2 All ER 51, CA; *Cresswell v Proctor* [1968] 2 All ER 682, CA; *Jones v Rhys-Jones* (1974) 30 P & CR 451, CA.
[8] LPA 1925, s 84(1C).

Obsolescence

33.39 A restrictive covenant may be modified or discharged on the basis that it ought to be deemed obsolete by reason of changes in the character of the property or the neighbourhood, or other material circumstances.[1]

In *Re Truman, Hanbury, Buxton & Co Ltd's Application*[2] the applicant brewers applied on this ground to have a covenant modified to permit the erection of a public-house. The covenant was imposed under a scheme to preserve the character of an estate as a residential area. On appeal from the Lands Tribunal, the Court of Appeal held that only when the original purpose of a covenant can no longer be achieved can it be said to be obsolete. In this case it would be necessary to show that what was intended to be a residential area had become a commercial area, which was not the case. Furthermore, it was clear that the object of the covenant was still capable of fulfilment since the Lands Tribunal had expressly found that the proposed development would injure the objectors.

[1] LPA 1925, s 84(1)(a).
[2] [1955] 3 All ER 559, CA.

Agreement

33.40 The second ground for modification or discharge is that the persons entitled to the benefit of the restriction have agreed either expressly or by implication, by their acts or omissions, to the discharge or modification.[1]

This ground is rarely relied on by an applicant at the outset for, if there is evidence of agreement to the discharge or modification, an application to the Tribunal is probably not worthwhile. However, an individual may amend an application to include this ground once it has become clear that those who are entitled to the benefit of the covenant have failed to object to the application or have withdrawn their objection. The application will then be granted, since the persons entitled to the benefit have shown by their acts or omissions that they agree to the proposals.[2]

[1] LPA 1925, s 84(1)(b).
[2] *Re Dare's and Beck's Application* (1974) 28 P & CR 354.

No injury

33.41 A restrictive covenant can be discharged or modified where this will not injure the persons entitled to the benefit of the restriction.[1] This ground has been described as a long-stop against frivolous or vexatious objections,[2] and is limited to cases where there is no merit in the objections.

[1] LPA 1925, s 84(1)(c).
[2] *Ridley v Taylor* [1965] 2 All ER 51 at 58.

Impedes reasonable use

33.42 The final and most widely used ground is where the restriction impedes some reasonable use of the land, and either:

- does not secure to persons entitled to the benefit of it any practical benefits of substantial value or advantage to them; or
- is contrary to the public interest;

provided that:

- money will be an adequate compensation for the loss or disadvantage (if any) which any such person will suffer from the discharge or modification.[1]

  The majority of successful applications are made on this ground. The leading case is *Re Bass Ltd's Application*.[2] The company wished to use a site, which was subject to a restriction limiting its use to dwelling-houses, as a loading area for articulated trucks. The site was zoned in the development plan for industrial use and planning permission had been granted. A large number of those having the benefit of the covenant, imposed under a scheme of development, objected. The Tribunal rejected the company's application, giving its decision in the form of answers to questions formulated by counsel. These have come to provide the usual approach to applications on this ground.

- *Is the proposed use which is impeded by the restriction reasonable?* This question is to be answered leaving aside for the moment the restrictions. Where planning permission has been granted it will be difficult to find the proposed use unreasonable.

- *Does impeding the proposed use secure practical benefits to the objectors?* The expression 'practical benefits' is very wide: the Tribunal is to consider the adverse effects of the applicant's proposal on a broad basis. Thus, in *Gilbert v Spoor*,[3] the preservation of a pleasant rural view enjoyed not from the benefited land but from a point a short distance away was held to be a practical benefit. The Tribunal in the *Bass* case answered this second question affirmatively, in view of the fact that the proposed development would give rise to increased noise, fumes, vibration, dirt and risk of accidents.

- *If yes, are the benefits of substantial value or advantage?* The Tribunal has stressed that the benefits are not to be assessed in terms only of financial value. In the *Bass* case the benefits were held to be of substantial advantage, as have been, in other cases, peace and quiet, an unobstructed view[4] and the advantage of not being overlooked.

- *Is impeding the proposed use contrary to the public interest?* Again, planning permission is relevant, but it must be remembered that planning permission does not necessarily imply that the proposed development is positively in the public interest. In the *Bass* case in view of the noise and amenity problem the development would cause, the economic interest of Bass Ltd could not be equated with the public interest. It is worth noting that the Tribunal has normally interpreted the requirement of public interest strictly and has rejected claims that impeding particular development is contrary to the public interest because, for example, housing land is in short supply or government policy favours high density development.

- *If the restriction does not secure benefits of substantial value and/or the proposed use is not contrary to the public interest, would money be an adequate compensation?* This question was not relevant to the *Bass* case and so was not dealt with. It is clear that a restriction can be discharged or modified without the payment of any compensation where no loss or disadvantage is suffered.[5] By definition, even where a loss or disadvantage is suffered, the levels of compensation are likely to be modest since a restriction which secures substantial benefits will not be modified or discharged in the first place. Equally, there are cases where money is not adequate compensation, for example where the application is being opposed by a local authority acting in the interest of the local community.[6]

---

[1] LPA 1925, s 84(1)(aa), (1A).
[2] (1973) 26 P & CR 156.
[3] [1982] 2 All ER 576, CA.

⁴ [1982] 2 All ER 576, CA.
⁵ See LPA 1925, s 84(1) and para 33.40.
⁶ *Re Martin's Application* [1989] 1 EGLR 193, but note *Re Willis' Application* [1997] 28 EG 137.

33.43 The Tribunal may order that the applicant pay to the objectors a sum by way of compensation intended either:

- to make up for any loss or disadvantage suffered in consequence of the discharge or modification of the restriction; or

- in an appropriate case to make up for any effect the restriction had, at the time when it was imposed, in reducing the price then received by the objector for the land affected by it. [1]

It was made clear in *Winter v Traditional & Contemporary Contracts Ltd*[2] that compensation must be assessed on the basis of the loss to the objectors and not on the gain to the applicant. Here the Court of Appeal declined to assess compensation by reference to any share in the development value.

¹ LPA 1925, s 84(1).
² [2007] EWCA Civ 1088.

Housing Act 1985, s 610

33.44 Application may be made under this section to a county court to vary a restrictive covenant to enable a house to be converted into two or more dwellings. The applicant must either have planning permission for the proposed conversion or prove to the court that (owing to changes in the character of the neighbourhood) the house cannot readily be let as a single dwelling but could if converted. The court must give interested parties an opportunity of being heard, and may vary the covenant (subject to such conditions and on such terms as it thinks just).[1]

¹ In *Lawntown Ltd v Camenzuli* [2007] EWCA Civ 949 the Court of Appeal expressed its surprise that more use is not made of this provision.

Proposals for reform

33.45 In 1984 the Law Commission produced a report and draft legislation[1] aimed at comprehensive reform of the law of covenants. The mainspring of their report was the need to deal with the unsatisfactory state of the law concerning positive covenants,[2] but they were equally unhappy with the complex and uncertain law relating to restrictive covenants. However, in 1998 it was announced that the report would not be implemented.

The Law Commission is currently engaged in a fresh examination of both easements and covenants. It has issued a Consultation Paper[3] and is expecting to produce a final report, together with draft legislation in June 2011. Its current view is that a new property interest—a Land Obligation—should be introduced. This would replace both positive and restrictive covenants. They are also suggesting that the statutory mechanism for modifying and discharging covenants should be modernised.

¹ The Law of Positive and Restrictive Covenants (1984) Law Com No 127.
² Para 33.4.
³ Consultation Paper No 186 *Easements Covenants and Profits à Prendre* (2008).

DISCHARGE OF RESTRICTIVE COVENANTS: KEY POINTS

- Restrictive covenants are not discharged where the owner of the burdened land obtains planning permission to carry out the activity prevented by the covenant.

- A restrictive covenant can very occasionally be discharged at common law where there is a complete change in the character of the neighbourhood, by an agreed release, or where benefited and burdened land come into common ownership.

- A restrictive covenant will be statutorily discharged where it would hinder the use of land that has been acquired by a local authority for planning purposes, or by other bodies for statutory purposes, or to enable a house to be converted into two or more dwellings.

- A restrictive covenant can be discharged or modified by the Upper Tribunal (Lands Chamber) under the jurisdiction conferred by s 84 of the LPA 1925; the most usual basis on which this occurs is where a covenant impedes some reasonable use of the land and does not secure to those benefiting practical benefits of any substantial value and for which money is an adequate compensation.

Questions

1. What is the difference between a positive and negative covenant relating to land?

2. In what circumstances, if any, will the burden of a positive covenant pass to the new owner of the freehold?

3. In what circumstances will the burden of a restrictive covenant pass to the new owner of the freehold?

4. In what circumstances will the benefit of a restrictive covenant pass to the new owner of the freehold?

5. What remedies are available for the breach of a restrictive covenant and what consequences can these have for the party in breach?

6. What is the legal position where the owner of land burdened by a restrictive covenant obtains planning permission to carry out some development that the covenant prevents?

7. What is the most usual basis on which the Upper Tribunal (Lands Chamber) will order the discharge or modification of a restrictive covenant?

8. Victor sells part of his very large garden to Bob's Builders Ltd. The transfer contains a covenant preventing the construction of more than one dwelling on the plot and one that requires the erection of a stone wall on the boundary between the two properties. Bob's Builders built a house on the site and sold it to Caroline. Victor has since sold his house to Darren. No stone wall has ever been put up and Caroline has just obtained planning permission to build a further house on her garden. Can Darren require Caroline to construct a stone wall and can he prevent her from building another house?

34

Mortgages

CHAPTER OVERVIEW

A mortgage of land is a transfer of an interest in the land as security for a debt. It enables the creditor, in the event of the debtor being unable or unwilling to pay off the debt, to enforce the debt against the land, usually by selling the land and recouping what is owed. In this chapter we consider:

- the ways in which mortgages of registered land can be created;
- the rights of the mortgagor;
- the mortgagee's remedies; and
- the order in which mortgages will be paid off where the security proves to be insufficient.

34.1 Mortgages are created most commonly where a building society or other institutional lender lends money towards the acquisition of either residential or commercial property. A mortgage may, however, be granted by a landowner to secure (ie as security for) a bank loan, or a loan from a finance company, or to secure a current account, as well as, in the commercial sphere, to secure a loan to finance the development of property or the expansion of a business. The creditor, the lender of the money to whom the mortgage is granted, is called the mortgagee, the debtor or borrower is called the mortgagor.

34.2 The law of mortgages is still heavily influenced by its historical development. This means that, in many respects, its provisions can appear artificial and outdated. That said, the actual operation of the law, especially in respect to registered land (on which this chapter concentrates) works reasonably well; this is in no small part due to the intervention of equity which has done much to ensure that, despite appearances, mortgages retain their essential character as security for a loan.

Creation of mortgages

Historical background

34.3 For several hundred years prior to the 1925 property legislation mortgages were created by the mortgagor (the borrower) transferring the ownership of the land to the mortgagee (the lender). Provided that the loan was repaid by the due date, the land would be re-transferred to the borrower; if not, the land would remain in the ownership of the lender subject, as we shall see, to the increasingly important equitable right to redeem[1]. Thus the form of the mortgage was not that of a mere security, but rather of a change of ownership.

In 1925 the creation of mortgages was modified by the LPA 1925. Mortgages by outright transfer could no longer be created. Henceforth they were to be created either by the grant of a 3,000-year lease (which would automatically come to an end when the loan was repaid) or by means of a charge by way of legal mortgage. While the grant of a long lease might have been preferable to an outright transfer of ownership, it still conferred on the mortgagee very considerable ownership rights which distorted the nature of a mortgage as a security.

[1] See para 34.8.

Modern mortgages

Legal mortgages

34.4 Today, mortgages of unregistered land are invariably created by way of a charge by way of legal mortgage. While this gives the mortgagee 'the same protection, powers and remedies' as if the mortgage had been created by long lease[1], it at least gives a more accurate impression of the mortgage as a security since the freehold remains vested in the mortgagor. Mortgages of registered land must now be created by legal charge[2]; in order to be legal the charge must be completed by registration[3] which means that the mortgagee is entered in the register as proprietor of the charge[4]. A registered charge takes effect as a charge by way of legal mortgage[5]; this means that the mortgagee has the benefit of the legal remedies afforded to mortgagees by the LPA 1925[6]. In law, any number of mortgages can be created in respect of one property; in practice, the number of mortgages that can be created will be limited by the value of the property[7].

[1] LPA 1925, s 87(1).
[2] LRA, ss 23(1)(a), 27(2)(f).
[3] It should be noted that it will soon be possible to create registered charges electronically, see para 29.20.
[4] LRA 1925, s 27, Sch 2 para 8.
[5] LRA 1925, s 51.
[6] Notably the statutory power of sale and the right to appoint a receiver; see paras 34.29 and 34.35.
[7] For the order in which a series of mortgages are paid off, see paras 34.41 and 34.42.

Informal mortgages

34.5 It is possible to create informal mortgages of registered land by way of an agreement to create a mortgage. Such an agreement falls within the Law of Property (Miscellaneous Provisions) Act 1989, s 2 and must therefore be made in writing and be signed by all parties[1]. Such a mortgage will not bind future purchasers of the land (including subsequent mortgagees) unless it is protected by the entry of a notice in the Land Register[2].

[1] See para 29.2.
[2] LRA 2002, s 29(2); see para 35.35.

CREATION OF MORTGAGES: KEY POINTS

- A legal mortgage in respect of unregistered land is created by a charge by way of legal mortgage.
- A legal mortgage of registered land is created by a registered charge.
- An informal mortgage can be created by a written agreement to create a mortgage that satisfies the requirements as to form imposed by s 2 of the Law of Property (Miscellaneous Provisions) Act 1989.
- Any number of mortgages can be created in respect of the same property.

Mortgagor's right to redeem (repay)

Commercial arrangements for repayment

34.6 Provisions in mortgages for the repayment of the debt, ie the principal sum borrowed plus interest and costs, vary considerably. In the traditional 'standing' mortgage, in relation to which the law of mortgages originally developed, the principal is repaid in a lump sum, although provision will normally be made for regular payments of interest in the interim[1]. An endowment mortgage is a variety of this type of mortgage. Under this scheme, the mortgagor makes regular monthly payments of interest to the mortgagee while at the same time paying premiums on an endowment assurance policy[2] which, on maturity (often in 20–25 years), will provide a lump sum for the repayment of the principal. Today, the most common form of mortgage in the domestic market is the true instalment mortgage (sometimes somewhat misleadingly described as a 'repayment' mortgage) under which both the principal and interest is repayable in monthly instalments spread over a lengthy period—again, often 20–25 years. Where a mortgage is created in order to secure an overdraft on a current account it is often made payable on demand.

Traditionally, mortgage interest rates have been variable, with the result that mortgagees have been able to change their rate of interest during the course of the mortgage in order to keep pace with general interest rates. Thus, if interest rates rise, a mortgagor's liability can increase in an often unpredictable and dramatic fashion. In recent years there has been a move towards mortgage loans at fixed rates for a specific period; this provides mortgagors with a greater degree of certainty as to their liabilities.

[1] When this form of mortgage is granted in respect of residential property it is often referred to as an 'interest only' mortgage.

[2] It is the poor stock market performance of such 'with profits' endowment policies that has led to the declining popularity of this type of mortgage.

The differing approaches of the common law and equity to repayment

Legal date of redemption

34.7 As we pointed out in para 34.3, prior to 1926 a legal mortgage of land was effected by an outright transfer of the mortgagor's estate to the mortgagee, subject to a provision for re-transfer on payment of the moneys due. The mortgage would provide that redemption (repayment) should take place on a fixed date. At common law, if the moneys due under the mortgage were not repaid on that date, there could be no re-transfer. Further, the mortgagor, despite having lost the right to have the land re-transferred, remained liable to repay the money owed.

The equity of redemption and the equitable right to redeem

34.8 This harsh common law rule was radically limited by equity. In equity, despite an apparent transfer of ownership to the mortgagee, the essence of a mortgage was always seen to be simply the provision of security for a debt; if that was repaid the mortgagee's rights to the land should cease. Equity recognised that, despite having transferred the legal estate to the mortgagee, the mortgagor still had an interest in the land. This interest, known as the 'equity of redemption', is best described as the sum of the mortgagor's interest in the property.[1] It can be represented in purely financial terms as the value of the mortgaged property minus the amount owing to the mortgagee. (So, if a house is worth £300,000 and there is an outstanding mortgage of £250,000, the mortgagor's equity of redemption is £50,000.) One of the vital rights attaching to the equity of redemption is the continuing right of the mortgagor to redeem the mortgage. Accordingly, even though the contractual (or legal) date for redemption had passed, the mortgagee would be compelled to re-transfer the land on payment of what was owed, ie the principal plus interest (and costs).

Once it was established that redemption was possible after the contractual date for repayment, that contractual date came to be fixed at a token date, conventionally six months from the date of the mortgage. This clearly did not affect the mortgagor's equitable right to redeem thereafter, but merely allowed for redemption at that early date if required. The reason why the contractual provision for redemption was retained was because, once the legal date fixed for repayment has passed, the mortgage money is regarded as due and a mortgagee is thereafter in a position to exercise their remedies for non-payment[2].

This remains the situation, despite the fact that, today, a mortgage cannot be created by an outright transfer.[3] Although a mortgagor now retains the legal estate, they are nevertheless still regarded as also having an equity of redemption in respect of the land, giving the right to redeem the mortgage despite the passing of the contractual date for redemption. In a standing mortgage and in certain instalment mortgages, an early date for redemption is still fixed, commonly at six months from the date of the mortgage. Neither party intends that the mortgage should be repaid at that date, the provision is inserted simply to bring into play the mortgagee's remedies, as the mortgage money is then due. In those instalment mortgages which do not provide for an early contractual date, it is usual for the parties to provide that the entire mortgage moneys become due should the mortgagor default in respect of one or two instalments.

Where the contractual date for redemption has passed, the mortgagor is entitled, subject to any express provision in the mortgage providing otherwise,[4] to redeem the mortgage by paying the principal plus interest on giving the mortgagee six months' notice or six months' interest in lieu of notice.[5]

---

[1] The equity of redemption will change in value during the course of the mortgage. It will increase as any capital debt is repaid and in line with increases in the market value of the property. Equally, in a falling market it can decrease sometimes to the extent that the borrower's equity becomes negative, meaning that the property is worth less than the outstanding loan.

[2] Para 34.29.

[3] Paras 34.3 and 34.4.

[4] But see paras 34.10 and 34.12.

[5] *Browne v Lockhart* (1840) 10 Sim 420; *Cromwell Property Investment Co Ltd v Western and Toovey* [1934] Ch 322.

Impediments to full redemption

34.9 Equity is careful to preserve the essential nature of a mortgage as a transaction involving the giving of security for a loan by protecting the mortgagor's equity of redemption. In particular, it requires that there should be 'no clogs or fetters on the equity of redemption', that is, that the mortgage should not contain terms which impede the ability of the mortgagor to redeem the property free of the conditions of the mortgage. We shall see that the case law in the following paragraphs establishes that the court will declare void any provision in a mortgage which either is inconsistent with the mortgagor's right to redeem the property unfettered by any term of the mortgage, or is unfair and unconscionable.[1]

It should also be noted that, like any other contract, a mortgage transaction may be set aside on the basis of misrepresentation or undue influence. Many of the modern cases on this subject have involved mortgages, notably where a mortgagor has persuaded their spouse or co-habitee to participate in a mortgage; as we have seen, this may mean that the victim can have the mortgage set aside.[2]

[1] It should be noted that equity's traditional role of protecting mortgagors is increasingly being over-taken by statutory regulation aimed at protecting consumers. In the mortgage sector this tends to mean those who have granted mortgages over residential property, see further paras 34.15–34.17.

[2] Paras 12.61–12.66.

Provisions excluding redemption

34.10 It follows from what we said in the preceding paragraph that a provision excluding redemption in a mortgage granted by an individual[1] is of no effect.[2] Thus where the mortgage deed confers on the mortgagee an option to purchase[3] the mortgaged property, that provision is void[4] because, of course, at the option of the mortgagee, the mortgagor may be forced to sell his or her property and thus lose the opportunity to redeem. However, there is nothing to prevent the parties, by a separate transaction genuinely independent of the mortgage, agreeing that the mortgagee should have an option to purchase the property[5]. A subsequent variation of a mortgage under which the mortgagee is given an option to purchase will be viewed not as a separate arrangement but as part of the original transaction and the option will, therefore, be void.[6]

A provision will be regarded as excluding the right to redeem where this is its real effect. Thus, in *Fairclough v Swan Brewery Co Ltd*,[7] the claimant mortgaged his 17½-year lease to the brewery, the mortgage containing a clause prohibiting redemption until six weeks before the expiry of the lease. This clause was held to be void since, for all practical purposes, it rendered the mortgage irredeemable.

[1] Under the provisions of the Companies Act 2006, s 739, a company may create an irredeemable mortgage.

[2] *Re Wells, Swinburne-Hanham v Howard* [1933] Ch 29 at 53.

[3] Para 29.7.

[4] *Samuel v Jarrah Timber and Wood Paving Corpn Ltd* [1904] AC 323, HL; *Lewis v Frank Love Ltd* [1961] 1 All ER 446.

[5] *Reeve v Lisle* [1902] AC 461, HL.

[6] *Jones v Morgan* [2001] EWCA Civ 995, [2002] 1 EGLR 125.

[7] [1912] AC 565, PC.

Oppressive or unconscionable terms

34.11 Equity[1] has long regarded itself as having a broad jurisdiction to strike down any provision in a mortgage which impedes full redemption of the mortgaged property unfettered by the terms of the mortgage or which is unfair, oppressive or unconscionable. This is well illustrated by *Cityland and Property (Holdings) Ltd v Dabrah*[2] where the mortgage provided for the repayment by instalments over six years of a sum representing the capital sum advanced together with a premium of 57%. On the mortgagor's default, the court refused to permit the mortgagee to enforce payment of the stated sum, allowing him only the principal plus interest, which (in 1967) was fixed at what, in 1967, was a moderate 7%. In the circumstances, the provision for the payment of a premium was unconscionable, particularly as this was not a bargain between trading concerns but a case of house purchase by a mortgagor of limited means.

However, the limits of this general jurisdiction were explained in *Multiservice Bookbinding Ltd v Marden*.[3] Here the mortgage provided for the repayment by instalments of the capital sum plus interest at 2% above the bank rate payable on the whole sum throughout the term of the loan. Further, each instalment was subject to index-linking in the form of a 'Swiss franc uplift'; that is, the amount payable was then to be increased (or, theoretically, decreased) in proportion to the variation in the rate of exchange between the pound and the

Swiss franc after September 1966. (Furthermore, the loan could not be called in, nor was the mortgage redeemable, for 10 years.) Browne Wilkinson J held that although the mortgage might be unreasonable this is not the relevant test; the question is whether any of the terms of the bargain are unfair and unconscionable which requires that the terms have been imposed in a morally reprehensible manner. In this case the parties were businessmen, who entered the agreement with their eyes open, with the benefit of independent legal advice and without any compelling necessity on the part of the company to accept the loan on these terms. The company was therefore bound to comply with the mortgage[4].

It is possible that a provision in a mortgage allowing the mortgagee to vary the rate of interest could be challenged as being unfair or unconscionable. However, it would appear that this would only succeed if it were shown that the lender had acted in a way that no reasonable lender would.[5] Any actions in respect of unfair variations might be better taken under consumer protection legislation.[6]

The general power to strike out unconscionable terms has been resorted to in two particular types of case which we consider in the following paragraphs.

[1] We have seen that statute, in the form of the Unfair Terms in Consumer Contracts Regulations 1999, controls unfair terms in consumer contracts; see paras 12.58–12.63. These Regulations may impact on terms in residential mortgages but it should be noted that they do not allow a challenge to price (which includes interest).

[2] [1967] 2 All ER 635.

[3] [1978] 2 All ER 489.

[4] A similar approach was adopted in *Jones v Morgan* [2001] EWCA Civ 995, [2002] 1 EGLR 125 where the court held that a mortgagor who had taken advice from his own solicitor could not escape 'unwise and improvident' mortgage terms by arguing that they were unconscionable.

[5] See *Nash v Paragon Finance plc* [2001] EWCA Civ 1466.

[6] See paras 34.15–34.17, although it should be noted that the borrowers were unsuccessful when proceeding in this way in *Nash v Paragon Finance plc* [2001] EWCA Civ 1466.

34.12 *Provisions postponing redemption* We have seen that provisions which render a mortgage irredeemable will be struck out.[1] Terms which merely *postpone* the right to redeem are not automatically void; their validity depends on whether or not they are unfair or unconscionable. In *Knightsbridge Estates Trust Ltd v Byrne*,[2] the claimant company, wishing to pay off an existing debt, sought a loan of £310,000 from the friendly society of which the defendants were trustees, at 5% interest repayable over 40 years. This was agreed and a mortgage was executed providing for repayment in half-yearly instalments over 40 years.

Five-and-a-half years later the claimant brought an action claiming to be entitled to redeem the mortgage, on the basis that the postponement of redemption for 40 years was a clog on the right to redeem. The Court of Appeal rejected its claim, holding that equity is concerned to see only two things—one that the essential requirements of a mortgage transaction are observed and the other that oppressive or unconscionable terms are not enforced. Equity does not interfere with mortgage transactions merely because they are unreasonable, which, in any event, this transaction was not.

Most instalment mortgages, although providing for repayment over a lengthy period, do not prevent early redemption; however, they often insist upon a period of notice or the payment of interest instead. Fixed rate interest mortgages do tend to prevent repayment of the mortgage within, say, two to five years; these provisions are designed to stop mortgagors moving to new providers should a better deal be offered. They have not as yet been tested in the courts and when they are, this may be under the new provisions for statutory regulation.[3]

[1] Para 34.10.

[2] [1938] 4 All ER 618, CA; affd on other grounds [1940] 2 All ER 401, HL.

[3] See paras 34.15–34.17.

34.13 *Provisions conferring collateral advantages* The parties may by their agreement confer on the mortgagee some advantage additional to repayment of the principal plus interest plus costs. Where such an additional advantage, such as an option to purchase, renders the mortgage irredeemable, it is clearly void, unless contained in some separate and independent transaction.[1] More complex are those cases in which mortgages impose some type of commercial tie such as that the mortgagor should only buy, and sell on the premises, beer or petrol supplied by the mortgagee. Originally the courts took the view that such provisions would be valid if limited to the period of the mortgage;[2] if designed to continue beyond redemption they would be invalid because they would then fetter the right to full redemption. Thus, in *Noakes & Co Ltd v Rice*,[3] a provision in a mortgage tying the mortgaged leasehold property to the mortgagee brewery not only for the duration of the mortgage but for the duration of the entire lease, was held void, for its effect would have been to permit the mortgagor, who mortgaged a free house, to redeem only a tied house thus fettering his right to redeem.

However, it is clear that the courts have become uncomfortable at the prospect of interfering with the terms of a bargain entered into by business people, often with the assistance of professional advice. Accordingly, various devices have been used to retreat from the position where the enforceability of a collateral advantage hinges entirely on the technicality of whether or not they last beyond redemption. As with provisions excluding the right to redeem, in some cases the court may be able to construe a provision contained in a mortgage deed which confers some additional advantage on the mortgagee as in fact being a separate transaction even though it is contained in the same deed.[4] In this way the advantage will not be struck down as being inconsistent with, or a clog on, the right to redeem. Thus, in *Kreglinger v New Patagonia Meat and Cold Storage Co Ltd*,[5] the mortgage between the claimant woolbroker and the defendant meat packers provided that for a period of five years, whether or not the loan was paid off earlier, the defendants would give the claimant the right to buy all sheepskins. The mortgage was redeemed after two years and the defendants disputed the claimant's right thereafter to the sheepskins. The House of Lords held that the claimant remained entitled to the skins. The grant of the right to purchase sheepskins was in substance independent of the mortgage.

However, certain of the judgments in the *Kreglinger* case went rather further, suggesting that, in any event, an advantage collateral to the security will not be held void unless it is:

- unfair or unconscionable; or

- in the nature of a penalty clogging the equity of redemption; or

- inconsistent with or repugnant to the contractual and equitable right to redeem. [6]

If this wider approach is accepted, the validity of a collateral advantage may now quite simply depend on whether or not it is unfair, oppressive or unconscionable, rather than on the period for which it is imposed.[7]

---

[1] Para 34.10.

[2] *Biggs v Hoddinott* [1898] 2 Ch 307, CA.

[3] [1902] AC 24, HL.

[4] *Kreglinger v New Patagonia Meat and Cold Storage Co Ltd* [1914] AC 25, HL; *Re Petrol Filling Station, Vauxhall Bridge Road, London, Rosemex Service Station Ltd v Shell Mex and BP Ltd* (1968) 20 P & CR 1.

[5] [1914] AC 25, HL.

[6] [1914] AC 25 at 61.

[7] Subject to what is said in the following paragraph concerning the doctrine of unreasonable restraint of trade.

Restraint of trade

34.14 In *Esso Petroleum Co Ltd v Harper's Garage (Stourport) Ltd*[1] the House of Lords held that the restraint of trade doctrine applies to provisions in a mortgage. Thus collateral advantages contained in a mortgage, perhaps providing for a commercial tie, may not only be invalidated as preventing full redemption or as being unfair and unconscionable, but also as being in unreasonable restraint of trade.

[1] [1967] 1 All ER 699, HL.

Statutory regulation

34.15 In the case of mortgages over residential property it is increasingly the case that statutory regulation is taking over equity's protective role. This was first introduced by the Consumer Credit Act 1974 which has since been amended and strengthened by the Consumer Credit Act 2006.[1] In the meantime the Financial Services and Markets Act 2000 has empowered the Financial Services Authority (the 'FSA') to implement a regulatory regime for those offering loans by way of mortgage.[2]

[1] See para 34.17.
[2] See para 34.16.

34.16 *Financial Services and Markets Act 2000* (FSMA 2000) This Act, which came into force in 2004, applies to a 'regulated mortgage contract'. This is a loan to an individual secured by way of a first legal mortgage on land of which at least 40% must be used or be intended to be used by the borrower as, or in connection with, a dwelling.[1] Accordingly the Act does not apply to second or equitable mortgages, or to loans to a company, or to mortgages in respect of property used solely for non-residential purposes. Mortgage lenders cannot enter into a regulated mortgage contract unless they are authorised by the FSA[2]; a breach of this requirement usually means that the mortgage is unenforceable against the mortgagor[3] (who can claim compensation[4]) and that the mortgagee is guilty of a criminal offence.[5] The regulatory regime has been implemented by means of the *Financial Services Authority Handbook, Mortgages: Conduct of Business*.[6] One of its overall objective is to ensure an appropriate degree of protection for consumers. It imposes standards on mortgage lenders in respect of mortgage advice and lending practices and requires transparency in the disclosure of all charges. The duties under the Act cannot be varied and sanctions for breach include compulsory reference to the Financial Services Ombudsman and, ultimately, an action for damages.[7]

[1] FSMA 2000 (Regulated Activities) Order 2001, art 61.
[2] FSMA 2000, s 22.
[3] FSMA 2000, s 26(1).
[4] FSMA 2000, ss 26(2), 28(2).
[5] FSMA 2000, s 23(1).
[6] The most recent edition of which came into force on 6 April 2007.
[7] FSMA 2000, s 150(1).

34.17 *Consumer Credit Acts 1974 and 2006* (CCA 1974 and 2006) The Consumer Credit Act 1974 (CCA 1974), as amended by the 2006 Act, does not apply to a regulated mortgage contract within the meaning of the Financial Services and Markets Act 2000[1], to 'buy to let' mortgages[2], nor to any mortgage granted to exempt bodies such as banks, building societies, local authorities and certain bodies (including insurance companies and friendly societies).[3] However, it applies to virtually all[4] other mortgages granted by individuals, typically second and subsequent mortgages to finance and credit companies.

It is these borrowers who are most at risk of exploitation since they are often higher risk and unable to secure loans from institutional lenders.

In its original form the 1974 Act gave the courts a power to 're-open extortionate credit bargains' and to 'do justice between the parties'. This test has been replaced by the new concept of an 'unfair relationship'; this applies to both new and existing credit agreements. A court may decide that a mortgage creates a relationship that is unfair to the mortgagor on account of its terms, or the way in which the lender has exercised or enforced its rights, or for any other act or omission by the lender whether before or after the mortgage is created.[5] Where an unfair relationship is found to exist the court has a wide range of powers. It can alter the terms of the mortgage, reduce the amount payable by the borrower, or require the lender to repay money to the borrower.[6] It remains to be seen whether or not the wide powers given to the court prove to be more effective than those under the old regime.

The Act contains further regulations which provide for the prospective mortgagor to be given an opportunity to withdraw from the transaction[7], which prescribe the form and content of the agreement[8], which prevent a higher rate of interest being charged on default[9], and which (and to be borne in mind in relation to the mortgagee's remedies) ensure that a mortgage regulated by the Act may only be enforced by order of the court.[10]

[1] See para 34.16.

[2] Legislative Reform (Consumer Credit) Order 2008.

[3] CCA 1974, s 16.

[4] The Act does not apply to loans exceeding £25,000 where the loan is predominantly for business purposes; where such a loan is made to 'high net worth' individuals, ie those with a net income exceeding £150,000 or net assets exceeding £500,000, the debtor can opt out of regulation.

[5] CCA 1974, s 140A.

[6] CCA 1974, s 140B.

[7] CCA 1974, s 58.

[8] CCA 1974, s 60.

[9] CCA 1974, s 93.

[10] CCA 1974, s 126.

MORTGAGOR'S RIGHT TO REDEEM: KEY POINTS

- The commercial terms governing the repayment of a modern mortgage differ from case to case; a 'repayment' mortgage requires the regular payments of both capital and interest, while under an 'interest only' mortgage the regular payments are of interest only with the capital being repaid at the end of the agreed period. Interest is either variable or the rate is fixed for a set period.

- A mortgagee always has an equitable right to repay the mortgage after the contractual date for repayment has passed.

- Equity has always fiercely protected the mortgagee's interest in the property (known as the equity of redemption); the contractual terms of the mortgage cannot exclude the right to redeem and cannot contain provisions that are oppressive, unconscionable, or in restraint of trade.

- The role of equity in protecting the mortgagee has now largely been replaced by statutory regulation; this applies, for the most part, to mortgages of residential property granted by private individuals.

Mortgagee's remedies

Possession of the mortgaged property

34.18 Strictly speaking, the right to take possession of the mortgaged property is not a *remedy* of the mortgagee. This is because, as a matter of legal theory, which has little relation to practical reality, the mortgagee rather than the mortgagor, has the legal *right* to possession right from the outset of the mortgage. In the absence of agreement to the contrary, the mortgagee may go into possession before the ink is dry on the mortgage. This is because the mortgagee has, in effect, a long lease of the property.[1] Thus the right of the mortgagee to possession has nothing to do with default on the part of the mortgagor and is not, therefore, properly described as a remedy. The rigour of this apparently harsh rule, that the mortgagee may have possession of the property at any time, is in fact mitigated in a number of respects; as a result, in practice, possession is almost invariably resorted to only as a remedy in the event of default and, even then, only as a preliminary step to an exercise of the power of sale, so that the sale may be made with vacant possession.

A legal mortgagee may take physical possession by peaceably entering on the property.[2] It is usual, in the case of a dwelling-house, to seek a possession order from a county court, requiring the delivery of vacant possession within a specified time.[3] However, it is now clear that a mortgagee does not have to take court proceedings in order to obtain possession of a dwelling-house[4]. The government is currently considering whether or not to change this position[5].

[1] *Four-Maids Ltd v Dudley Marshall (Properties) Ltd* [1957] 2 All ER 35 at 36. See para 34.3 and 34.4.
[2] This does not seem to be the case for mortgages that are regulated credit agreements under the Consumer Credit Act 1974, see para 34.15. Anyone taking possession of premises, needs to beware of falling foul of the Criminal Law Act 1977, s 6(1); this provides that an entry onto property that uses, or threatens the use of, violence is a criminal offence.
[3] A new Pre-Action Protocol applies where a mortgagee is seeking possession; this is designed to ensure that possession proceedings are used as a last resort.
[4] *Ropaigealach v Barclays Bank plc* [2000] QB 263, CA, *Horsham Properties Group Ltd v Clark* [2008] EWHC 2327; see further para 34.25.
[5] *Mortgages: Power of Sale and Residential Property* Ministry of Justice Consultation Paper, 2009.

Restrictions on the mortgagee's right to possession

34.19 The mortgagee's right to possession may be restricted in a number of ways. It may be limited:

- by an express provision in the mortgage;
- by an implied provision in the mortgage;
- (indirectly) by the obligation to account strictly while in possession;
- as a result of someone else's prior claim to possession; and
- (in the case of a dwelling) by the court.

Each of these will be examined in the following paragraphs.

Express restriction

34.20 The terms of the mortgage may expressly provide that the mortgagee may only go into possession in the event of default. This is increasingly the case in building society and similar mortgages.

Implied restriction

34.21 Although the legal mortgagee's right to possession should not be lightly treated as restricted,[1] the court may find that the mortgagee has by implication contracted out of the right to possession. In particular, the court will be ready to find an implied term that the mortgagor may remain in possession until default in an instalment mortgage. However, there must be something on which to hang such a conclusion other than the mere fact that it is an instalment mortgage;[2] this will be the case where, for example, the mortgage speaks of the mortgagee having the power to eject the mortgagor in the event of default.[3]

> [1] *Western Bank Ltd v Schindler* [1976] 2 All ER 393 at 396.
> [2] *Esso Petroleum Co Ltd v Alstonbridge Properties Ltd* [1975] 3 All ER 358.
> [3] *Birmingham Citizens Permanent Building Society v Caunt* [1962] 1 All ER 163.

Duty to account strictly

34.22 A mortgagee who goes into possession is liable to account *strictly* to the mortgagor. This goes well beyond a natural requirement that an account must be given for any income which has actually been received since taking possession; the duty to account *strictly* means that a mortgagee is also liable to the mortgagor for money which *ought* to have been received. Thus, where a mortgagee in possession (a brewery) leased[1] the mortgaged premises (a public-house) on the basis that it was tied to the brewery, the mortgagee was held liable to account to the mortgagor not only for the rent actually received but also for the (higher) rent which would have been received had the property been let as a free rather than a tied house.[2] While this duty to account strictly does not directly restrict a mortgagee's right to possession, any mortgagee who would have taken possession in order to receive the income of the mortgaged property so as to cover unpaid instalments is very much better advised not to do so and instead to appoint a receiver, a remedy which we consider at para 34.35.

> [1] For powers of leasing, see para 34.39.
> [2] *White v City of London Brewery Co* (1889) 42 Ch D 237, CA.

The existence of a prior claim to possession

34.23 *Existing leases* Where the mortgaged property is subject to a lease that was in existence prior[1] to the creation of the mortgage, this lease will normally bind the mortgagee[2] with the result that the latter will not be able to obtain physical possession of the property. The tenant cannot waive any statutory rights such as any protection under either the Rent Act 1977 or the Housing Act 1988[3]. The mortgagee can merely take legal possession by requiring the tenant of the mortgagor to pay rent directly[4].

> [1] For the position with regard to lease granted *after* the mortgage, see para 39.39.
> [2] An existing lease of registered land will bind a mortagee either because it will itself be registered with its own independent title and thus noted on the freehold title (leases of more than 7 years) or will usually rank as an 'overriding' interest under LRA, Sch 3, para 1 or para 2 (leases of 7 years or less); see para 35.22.
> [3] *Woolwich Building Society v Dickman* [1996] 3 All ER 204.
> [4] See *Davies v Law Mutual Building Society* (1971) 219 Estates Gazette 309, DC.

34.24 *The claims of implied co-owners*[1] One of the most serious impediments to the mortgagee's right to possession can occur where, unknown to the mortgagee, there is someone occupying the property—usually a spouse or cohabitee—whom equity regards as a co-owner of the property with the mortgagor. The rights of that implied co-owner can bind the mortagee. So, for example, in *Williams & Glyn's Bank Ltd v Boland*[2] a matrimonial home was in the sole name of the defendant; however his wife had contributed to the purchase and was therefore an implied co-owner in equity. He mortgaged the house to the claimant and then defaulted on the repayments. When the bank sought possession, the House of Lords held that the wife's equitable interest in the property was binding[3] on the bank and that it could not obtain possession against her.

Subsequent case law[4] has established that the courts will not normally regard the rights of an implied co-owner as having priority over a mortgagee where that co-owner knew that the mortgage was being obtained to *acquire* the property to which the co-owner has a claim. The mortgagee is also secure where the mortgage is granted by at least two legal co-owners of the property. The claims of any additional, implied, co-owners are not regarded as binding on the mortgagee because they are said to be 'overreached'[5].

Hence the mortgagee is only at risk in the case where a mortgage (often a second mortgage or a re-mortgage[6]) is created *after* the acquisition of the property. Here, it is vital that, prior to taking the mortgage, the mortgagee makes inquiries of any adult occupying the property in order to be satisfied that such persons are not implied co-owners. If they are, the mortgagee will require them to agree that their rights will not take priority over the mortgage[7].

[1] For implied co-ownership see para 31.12.

[2] [1980] 2 All ER 408, HL.

[3] As an 'overriding' interest; see para 35.28.

[4] *Bristol and West Building Society v Henning* [1985] 2 All ER 606, CA; *Abbey National Building Society v Cann* [1990] 1 All ER 1085, HL. See para 35.24.

[5] See *City of London Building Society v Flegg* [1987] 3 All ER 435, HL; see para 35.27.

[6] A re-mortgage occurs where the mortgagor grants a replacement mortgage, the proceeds of which are used to repay and discharge the existing loan.

[7] See para 35.26.

Restrictions on claims to possession of dwellings

34.25 The fact that a mortgagee's claim to possession is strictly a *right* rather than a *remedy* made it difficult for the courts to control the circumstances in which it was exercised. This was particularly important in the context of residential property where the consequence of a mortgagee taking possession is that a mortgagor loses their home. For this reason, in the 1970s, legislation was passed which gave the courts powers to ensure that mortgagees could not take possession where there was any chance that the mortgagor could repay the loan. The Administration of Justice Act 1970 applies where the mortgagee of a dwelling-house is seeking possession. Section 36 provides that the court can adjourn the proceedings, or make an order but suspend its operation, or make an order postponing the date for possession, if it appears to the court that the mortgagor is likely within a reasonable period to pay any sums due under the mortgage or to remedy any other default under the mortgage. It has recently become clear that the Act does not *require* the mortgagee to go to court in order to obtain possession,[1] and that s 36 is only engaged where there are court proceedings.[2] This means that a court is powerless where the mortgagee simply sells the property without seeking possession; a purchaser can then obtain possession without restriction.[3]

[1] Where a mortgage is a regulated credit agreement under the CCA 1974 it can only be enforced by a court order, see s 126 and para 34.17.

[2] *Ropaigealach v Barclays Bank plc* [2000] QB 263, CA.

[3] *Horsham Properties Group Ltd v Clark* [2008] EWHC 2327 where it was held that this is not breach of the mortgagor's human rights. The practice of selling property without first seeking a court order for possession has, to date, largely been used in respect of 'buy to let' mortgages rather than those taken out by owner occupiers and the Council of Mortgage Lenders has stated (2008) that its members will not use such tactics where a mortgagor uses the property as their home. Furthermore, the previous government indicated its intention to amend the law so that a lender cannot sell a dwelling-house without taking court proceedings, see *Mortgages: Power of Sale and Residential Property* Ministry of Justice Consultation Paper, 2009.

34.26 *The problem of instalment mortgages* A problem which rapidly emerged out of the original drafting of s 36 concerned the usual provision in instalment mortgages that, in the event of default, the *entire sums* due under the mortgage become immediately payable. It was obviously not Parliament's intention to give the court the power to delay possession only where the mortgagor could pay off the *whole* mortgage debt within a reasonable period, but this was all the original section achieved.[1] The Administration of Justice Act 1973, s 8 seeks to alleviate the problem. This provides that in the case of instalment mortgages, or other mortgages providing for deferred payment of the principal, which contain such a default clause, the sums due under the mortgage are to be regarded, for the purposes of s 36, as being the arrears of instalments or deferred payments. In such cases the court may exercise its power to delay possession where it appears likely that within a reasonable period the mortgagor will pay the *instalments* owing and keep up with the *instalments*.

Unfortunately, the wording of s 8 is far from ideal and litigation has been necessary to establish exactly what types of deferred payment mortgages fall within its ambit. It is now settled that the section applies to endowment mortgages,[2] but not to mortgages which secure an overdraft repayable 'on demand'.[3]

[1] *Halifax Building Society v Clark* [1973] 2 All ER 33.
[2] *Bank of Scotland v Grimes* [1985] 2 All ER 254, CA.
[3] *Habib Bank Ltd v Tailor* [1982] 3 All ER 561, CA.

34.27 *The court's discretion* Clearly the court will delay possession where there is a reasonable prospect of paying off the arrears within a reasonably short period.[1] In practice, however, by the time proceedings are actually brought the mortgagor is often in substantial default. The decisions of the courts have been notoriously inconsistent and it is difficult to discern a principled approach. However, it is clear that the court cannot postpone possession for an indefinite period[2]. Furthermore, in *First National Bank plc v Syed* [3] the Court of Appeal ruled that, in order to justify a postponement, the mortgagor must have a realistic ability to make payments which will cover current instalments and make some inroads into the arrears. In this case the mortgagor was only able to afford payments which fell below the interest charges and a postponement was refused.

A crucial issue is often the period over which the repayment of the arrears can be made; in other words, what is the reasonable period within which payment of the sums owing must take place? Initially, the courts seemed to take the view that this would be no more than two to four years (and, often very much shorter).[4] However, the position was reviewed by the Court of Appeal in *Cheltenham and Gloucester Building Society v Norgan*.[5] Here, most importantly, the court took the view that, in principle, the outstanding period of the loan should be regarded as a reasonable period within which any arrears should be paid off, at least in a case where the property is still adequate security for the loan. Accordingly, it would now seem that, where the mortgagor can make payments which will cover current instalments and pay off the arrears by the end of the loan period (which can be anything up to 25 years), possession will be postponed.

The court may also delay possession in order to give a mortgagor an opportunity to sell the property themself (in order to produce the funds to pay off the debt), since such a sale will normally result in a better price than one achieved by the mortgagee;[6] the court will not adopt this approach unless there is a realistic prospect of a speedy sale.[7] Furthermore, where the proceeds of sale will not discharge the debt, and where the mortgagee would prefer to conduct the sale, possession will not normally be postponed since the objective of the mortgagor in such a situation is not usually to obtain a better price but to hold up the eventual sale of the property.[8]

Sale

34.28 While it is possible for a mortgage to provide expressly for a power of sale, it is usual to rely on the statutory power conferred by the LPA 1925, or that power as modified by the terms of the mortgage. The major attraction of the statutory power is that there is no requirement for the mortgagee to obtain court approval for its exercise although, as we have just seen, where the mortgaged property is a dwelling-house, the mortgagee will, in practice, need to obtain a court order for possession[1] in order to be able to sell with vacant possession. However, it is now clear that a mortgagee can sell to a third party and that third party can readily obtain possession against the mortgagor whose rights to the property are terminated by the sale. In this way the court's powers to delay an order for possession are bypassed.[2]

[1] Paras 34.25–34.27.

[2] See *Ropaigealach v Barclays Bank plc* [2000] QB 263, CA, *Horsham Properties Group Ltd v Clark* [2008] EWHC 2327, see para 34.25.

The power of sale

34.29 Where the mortgage is made by deed and contains no expressed contrary intention, the LPA 1925, s 101 confers on the mortgagee the power to sell the mortgaged property when the mortgage money has become due. The mortgage money becomes due when the contractual date for redemption has passed, if such a date is fixed or, in the case of mortgages providing for repayment in instalments of principal and interest, when an instalment is due and unpaid. The contractual date of six months or earlier usually fixed in standing mortgages is incorporated therefore, not with the object that the mortgage should be redeemed at that time, but in order that the remedy of sale and other remedies for enforcing the security should become available at an early opportunity. As to mortgages providing for repayment by instalments of principal and interest, a mortgagee may only exercise the power of sale to enforce their security in respect of instalments in arrear,[1] unless, as is normal, it is provided that failure to pay one or more instalments causes the entire sum to become due. In endowment mortgages it is likewise usual for a default clause to provide that failure to pay instalments of interest makes the entire sum, principal and interest, due[2].

Although the mortgagee's power to sell *arises* when the mortgage money has become due, by virtue of the LPA 1925, s 103, it cannot be *exercised* unless and until:

- notice (in writing) requiring payment of the mortgage money has been served on the mortgagor, and payment has not, within three months thereafter, been made; or

- some interest under the mortgage is in arrear and unpaid for two months after becoming due; or

- there has been a breach of some provision contained in the mortgage deed or in the LPA 1925 other than the covenant for repayment.

The provisions of the mortgage deed itself may, and commonly do, vary or extend the statutory provisions,[3] for example by providing that the power of sale should be exercisable as soon as it arises.

  [1] *Payne v Cardiff RDC* [1932] 1 KB 241.
  [2] See para 34.8.
  [3] LPA 1925, s 101(3).

Exercise of the power

34.30 The power of sale is exercised, and the mortgagor's right to redeem thus barred, as soon as the mortgagee enters into a binding contract to sell.[1] A mortgagee may not purport to sell the land to themselves.[2] There is, however, no hard and fast rule that a mortgagee may not sell to a company in which they are interested. Where this is done, the mortgagee and the company seeking to uphold the transaction must show that the sale was in good faith and that the mortgagee took reasonable precautions to obtain the best price reasonably obtainable at the time.[3]

Although a mortgagee has only a term of years or equivalent charge in respect of the land, they have full power to convey the mortgaged freehold or leasehold together with fixtures attached to the land.[4]

The purchaser takes the estate subject to rights having priority to the mortgage, but freed from subsequent rights. The Act provides that the purchaser's title may not be challenged on the ground that the mortgagee's power was not, in fact, exercisable, or due notice was not given, or the power was otherwise improperly or irregularly exercised. The Act further provides that the purchaser is not concerned to inquire as to these matters.[5] It would thus appear that, unless the power of sale has not even arisen (in which case the purported sale takes effect as a transfer of the mortgage) the purchaser takes a valid legal title to the mortgaged land. However, it has been suggested that, if the purchaser becomes aware of any facts showing that the power is not exercisable, or that there is some impropriety in the sale, then a good title is not obtained.[6] In any event a person affected by an improper or irregular exercise of the power of sale has a remedy in damages against the mortgagee.[5]

  [1] *Property and Bloodstock Ltd v Emerton* [1967] 3 All ER 321, CA.
  [2] *Farrar v Farrars Ltd* (1888) 40 Ch D 395 at 409; *Williams v Wellingborough Borough Council* [1975] 3 All ER 462, CA.
  [3] *Tse Kwong Lam v Wong Chit Sen* [1983] 3 All ER 54, PC.
  [4] LPA, ss 88 and 89, and see LRA 2002, s 23(2).
  [5] LPA 1925, s 104.
  [6] *Lord Waring v London and Manchester Assurance Co Ltd* [1935] Ch 310 at 318.

34.31 *Price* It was established in *Cuckmere Brick Co Ltd v Mutual Finance Ltd*[1] that all mortgagees are under a duty to the mortgagor to obtain the best price reasonably achievable. In that case the duty was framed as one in the tort of negligence; however, it has since been made clear that the duty is one imposed by equity on the mortgagee alone.[2] A mortgagee does not discharge this duty by appointing a reputable professional to conduct the sale, and remains liable to the mortgagor for any deficiencies in the sale process.[3] A mortgagee's professional adviser owes no direct duty to the mortgagor[4] who must pursue any legal action against the mortgagee. The duty is owed not only to the mortgagor but also to anyone interested in the equity of redemption[5]; this has been held to include a guarantor[6] and a subsequent mortgagee[7]. Case law indicates that sale by auction does not necessarily show that reasonable care has been taken to obtain the proper price.[8] A mortgagee proposing to sell should consult professional advisers such as estate agents as to the method of sale and the measures which should be taken in order to secure the best price; this does not extend to any duty to improve the value of the property by, for example, obtaining planning permission.[9] However, this does not mean that the mortgagee must exercise the power of sale as a trustee would. On the contrary, the property can be sold for the mortgagee's purposes and at any time. It matters not that the moment may be unpropitious and that, by waiting, a higher price could have been obtained.[10] However, the property must be properly exposed to the market; a mortgagee can be liable for any shortfall where the property is sold in a 'crash sale'[11]. Furthermore, a mortgagee who, in advertising the property for sale, negligently fails to mention that it has the benefit of planning permission, will be liable to account to the mortgagor for the difference between the price obtained and 'a proper price' or 'the true market value'.[12] A purchaser in such a case would appear to be protected by the LPA 1925, s 104,[13] unless, perhaps, he or she was aware of the irregularity.

[1] [1971] 2 All ER 633, CA; see also *Predeth v Castle Phillips Finance Co Ltd* [1986] 2 EGLR 144, CA.
[2] *Downsview Nominees Ltd v First City Corporation Ltd* [1993] AC 295.
[3] *Cuckmere Brick Co Ltd v Mutual Finance Ltd* [1971] 2 All ER 633, CA.
[4] *Raja v Austin Gray* [2002] EWCA Civ 1965.
[5] *Silven Properties Ltd v Royal Bank of Scotland plc* [2004] EWCA 1409.
[6] *Standard Chartered Bank Ltd v Walker* [1982] 3 All ER 938, CA.
[7] *Downsview Nominees Ltd v First City Corporation Ltd* [1993] AC 295.
[8] *Tse Kwong Lam v Wong Chit Sen* [1983] 3 All ER 54, PC.
[9] *Silven Properties Ltd v Royal Bank of Scotland plc* [2004] EWCA 1409.
[10] *China & South Sea Bank Ltd v Tan* [1989] 3 All ER 839, PC; *Bank of Cyprus (London) Ltd v Gill* [1980] 2 Lloyds Rep 51.
[11] *Predeth v Castle Phillips Finance Co Ltd* [1986] 2 EGLR 144.
[12] *Cuckmere Brick Co Ltd v Mutual Finance Ltd* [1971] 2 All ER 633, CA.
[13] Para 34.30.

34.32 *Proceeds* The LPA 1925, s 105 provides that, first, any prior mortgages to which the sale was not made subject must be discharged. Then the proceeds are held by the selling mortgagee in trust:

- to pay the costs and expenses of the sale;
- to pay off the principal plus interest and costs due under the mortgage;
- to pay the surplus to any subsequent mortgagee of whom the mortgagee has notice (the Land Register or Land Charges Register as appropriate should therefore be searched), or, if there is no subsequent mortgagee, to the mortgagor.

Court's power to order sale

34.33 It will be appreciated from the foregoing paragraphs that the mortgagee's statutory *power* to sell is almost invariably more than adequate to allow the realisation of the security once the mortgagor is in default. However, there may be situations in which the mortgagee does not have a statutory power to sell because the mortgage is not by deed; in such a situation, a mortgagee wishing to sell will need to seek a court *order* of sale.[1] Further, as we shall see, where a mortgagee is seeking to foreclose,[2] the court may well choose to order a sale instead.[3]

In addition, there have been recent illustrations of applicants asking the court to exercise its jurisdiction to order a sale, despite the existence of a statutory power to sell. In *Arab Bank plc v Mercantile Holdings Ltd*[4] the mortgagee had already negotiated a sale which was the best that could be hoped for in the light of the fall in the property market. It asked the court to order a sale rather than rely on its statutory power because of strong evidence that the mortgagor would try, unjustifiably, to prevent the transaction going ahead. The court agreed to do so, especially given that the sale might well fall through unless the purchasers were confident that it could not be challenged.

Palk v Mortgage Services Funding plc[5] was a case in which, most unusually, it was the *mortgagor* asking the court to order a sale. Here, again, the value of the mortgaged property had fallen dramatically. The mortgagors wished to sell, albeit at a price well below their outstanding debt, in order to reduce the amount of capital owed and so to stem the ever-increasing interest charges. The mortgagee was refusing to co-operate,[6] taking the view that it would be better to let the property (even though the rent would not meet the interest payments) and wait for the market to improve. In these exceptional circumstances the Court of Appeal was prepared to order a sale. However, it has recently been made clear that the court will not allow the mortgagor to conduct a sale where it is clear that the mortgagee does wish to exercise its statutory power of sale (which was not the case in *Palk*); in such a situation, the mortgagor's motive is normally to delay the sale for as long as possible.[7]

¹ Under LPA 1925, s 91(2).
² See paras 34.33–34.36.
³ See para 34.36.
⁴ [1994] 2 All ER 74.
⁵ [1993] 2 All ER 481, CA.
⁶ A sale by the mortgagor could not, in practice, go ahead without the mortgagee undertaking to discharge the mortgage.
⁷ *Cheltenham and Gloucester plc v Krausz* [1997] 1 All ER 21, CA and para 34.25.

Action on the personal covenant

34.34 It should not be forgotten that a mortgage is a loan under which the mortgagor covenants to repay. Hence, in the event of any default, the mortgagee can sue on this personal covenant. In practice, a defaulting mortgagor will not usually have the funds to pay off the debt and the mortgagee will normally choose to rely on the security by taking possession and selling the property. However, there are occasions where the right to sue can be valuable. First, it can be utilised in addition to the mortgagee's other rights; thus, where the sale of the property fails to raise enough money to pay off the debt, the mortgagor can be sued for the balance. Since such an action can be brought up to 12 years after the initial default,[1] this means that the mortgagee can wait to see if the mortgagor's financial position improves.[2] The other circumstance in which the right to sue can be useful is where the mortgagee is unable to sell the property because possession cannot be obtained due to another (eg an implied co-owner) having priority.[3] Although the mortgagor in such a situation would be most unlikely to be able to pay, the mortgagee can then have them declared bankrupt. The trustee in bankruptcy will then usually, after a year, be able to obtain an order for the sale of the property[4] and the mortgagee will recover more of its money[5] than might otherwise be the case.

The date on which the right to sue arises depends on the form of the covenant to pay. Where the mortgage provides for repayment on a fixed contractual date, the mortgagee's right to sue arises in the event of failure to pay on that date. Where the mortgage provides for repayment in instalments, the mortgagee may sue for unpaid instalments. However, as we have seen,[6] it is usual to include a default clause providing that the whole sum becomes due in the event of failure to pay, perhaps, two instalments. Where the mortgage makes the whole sum payable on demand, the right of action accrues at the start of the mortgage unless, as is common, there is provision for notice to be given.[7] However, where a default clause in an instalment mortgage provides for default to result in the mortgage money becoming payable on demand, the demand must first be made before the right to sue accrues.[8]

[1] Limitation Act 1980, s 20. The limitation period for claims to interest is six years.
[2] In *Bristol & West plc v Bartlett* [2002] EWCA Civ 1181, [2002] 4 All ER 544 the mortgagee had, some eight years previously, sold three properties at prices which did not clear their mortgage debt. It was held to be entitled to sue the three mortgagors, each of whom still owed in the region of £60,000.
[3] See para 34.24.
[4] Insolvency Act 1986, s 335A. See para 31.4.
[5] Any prior claim must be paid before the mortgagee can take its share of the proceeds.
[6] See para 34.8.
[7] *Re Brown's Estate, Brown v Brown* [1893] 2 Ch 300.
[8] *Esso Petroleum Co Ltd v Alstonbridge Properties Ltd* [1975] 3 All ER 358.

Appointment of a receiver

34.35 In the case of commercial or tenanted properties, the mortgagee may wish to secure payment of any overdue instalment without necessarily taking action to sell. This can be achieved by appointing a receiver to manage the property and receive its income or rents; such a receiver can also sell the property where this turns out to be the appropriate way of securing payment of what is owed. In exercising their powers a receiver is under the same duties as the mortgagee.[1] The statutory power to appoint a receiver arises and is exercisable on the same conditions as the power of sale,[2] again subject to any extension or variation in the mortgage deed. The appointment and removal of the receiver must be in writing. A receiver appointed under the statutory power is deemed to be the agent of the mortgagor;[3] this does not mean that a receiver is under any greater duty to the mortgagor than is the mortgagee.[4] The mortgagee is liable to account to the mortgagor only for what is received from the receiver, and not for what, without wilful default, might have been received.[5] The receiver has power to demand and recover rents due but may not grant leases unless the mortgagee's power of leasing has been delegated or the sanction of the court has been obtained[6]. The receiver applies money received in the following order:

- in discharge of all outgoings affecting the mortgaged property;
- in making payments under prior mortgages;
- in payment of his or her own commission, of insurance premiums payable under the mortgage, and of the cost of carrying out repairs required by the mortgagee;
- in payment of interest due under the mortgage;
- in or towards paying off the principal if required by the mortgagee; and
- in paying the residue to the mortgagor.[7]

[1] *Medforth v Blake* [1999] 3 ALL ER 97; *Silven Properties Ltd v Royal Bank of Scotland plc* [2004] EWCA 1409, see para 34.31.
[2] LPA 1925, ss 101 and 109; paras 34.29 and 34.30.
[3] LPA 1925, s 109.
[4] *Silven Properties Ltd v Royal Bank of Scotland plc* [2004] EWCA 1409; as to the mortgagee's duties see para 34.31.

⁵ Which would be the position if the mortgagee took possession, see para 34.20.

⁶ *Re Cripps* [1946] Ch 265, CA.

⁷ LPA 1925, s 109.

Foreclosure

34.36 As soon as the mortgage money is due, or in the event of a condition of the mortgage being broken,[1] the mortgagee may apply to the court for foreclosure. When foreclosure is granted to the mortgagee it has the effect of putting an end to the mortgagor's right to redeem and vests the mortgaged property in the mortgagee, subject to any prior mortgages but freed from any subsequent ones[2]. On the face of it, this is, from the point of view of the mortgagor and any subsequent mortgagees, a harsh remedy; their rights in the property are extinguished, in theory, even where the value of the property exceeds the value of the debt owed to the foreclosing mortgagee[3]. For this reason both the mortgagor and any subsequent mortgagees must be made parties to the foreclosure action.

Because of the severity of the remedy it is in fact made subject to a number of restrictions which have had the effect that foreclosure is rarely sought; mortgagees usually prefer to enforce their security by seeking vacant possession of, and subsequently selling, the mortgaged property.

[1] Eg a covenant to pay instalments of interest, *Twentieth Century Banking Corpn Ltd v Wilkinson* [1976] 3 All ER 361.

[2] LPA 1925, s 88(2).

[3] But see para 34.38.

34.37 On an application for foreclosure, the court will first grant an order nisi. This requires accounts to be taken of what is due to the mortgagee in respect of principal, interest and costs, and orders the mortgagor, within (usually) six months thereafter, to pay the sums due or be foreclosed in default. In the event of non-payment an order absolute for foreclosure may be made. Where there are subsequent mortgagees, they too have the opportunity to redeem in order to avoid foreclosure.

The court has a discretion to extend the period given for repayment of the sums due or even to 'open the foreclosure' after an order absolute has been made. Furthermore, in cases of instalment (or other deferred payment) mortgages of dwelling-houses, power is conferred on the court by the Administration of Justice Act 1973, s 8 to adjourn the proceedings or suspend its order, where it appears likely that the mortgagor will pay the instalments owing and keep up with future instalments.[1]

[1] Paras 34.25–34.27.

34.38 Perhaps more influential than the foregoing in reducing the importance of foreclosure as a remedy is the fact that, under the LPA 1925, s 91(2), the court has power on the application of any interested party to order sale of the property instead of foreclosure.[1] Clearly, the court will be particularly willing to exercise this power where it is shown that the value of the property exceeds the amount due under the mortgage since, otherwise, the mortgagee reaps a windfall profit. Sale may be ordered on such terms as the court thinks fit; for example, it may even require that the mortgagor pay into court a sum sufficient to protect the mortgagee against loss. While it may order immediate sale, it may equally provide time for redemption of the mortgage. Conduct of the sale will usually be given to the mortgagor since he or she will be most concerned to realise the highest price for the property. A reserve price will be fixed, and the purchase money must be paid into court.

Given that sale of the mortgaged property is highly likely as a result of an application for foreclosure, it will be preferable for a mortgagee to exercise their statutory power of sale to realise the security. However, that power must have arisen and must be exercisable.[2]

In *Twentieth Century Banking Corpn Ltd v Wilkinson*,[3] the mortgage provided that, for the purposes of the LPA 1925, the mortgage money was not due until the end of the mortgage term. The mortgagor defaulted on his obligation in the meantime to pay instalments of interest and the mortgagee sought an order for sale or foreclosure. The court held that the mortgagee's statutory power of sale would not arise until the mortgage money became due, but that the mortgagee was entitled to seek foreclosure because the mortgagor was in breach of a condition of the mortgage. Since the mortgagee was entitled to foreclosure the court had a discretion to order sale instead, which it did.

[1] Para 34.33.
[2] Paras 34.29 and 34.30.
[3] [1976] 3 All ER 361.

Mortgagee's Remedies: Key Points

- Unless the terms of the mortgage provide to the contrary, a mortgagee always has the basic right to take possession of the property irrespective of whether the mortgagor is in default.

- In practice a mortgagee does not wish to take possession unless the mortgagor is in default and the sale of the property is required; where court proceedings are taken, and the property is residential, the court has a power to delay granting possession if the mortgagor is likely within a reasonable period to pay any sums due under the mortgage.

- The most important of any mortgagee's remedies is the statutory power to sell the property without the need for any court order as soon as the mortgagor is in default. When selling, the mortgagee is under a legal duty to obtain the best price reasonably achievable. Following a sale, the purchaser takes free from the rights of the mortgagor and of any mortgagee subsequent to the one who is selling. The proceeds of sale must be used to pay off the seller's loan and any subsequent mortgage in order of priority; any balance will be paid to the mortgagor.

- A mortgagee can sue on the mortgagor's personal covenant to repay for up to 12 years after default; this right can be exercised even after a sale where this has failed to satisfy the outstanding debt.

- Where a commercial mortgagor is in default it is common for the mortgagee to appoint a receiver.

- The remedy of foreclosure—which extinguishes the mortgagor's equity of redemption and results in the property belonging outright to the mortgagee—is rarely used.

Leasing

34.39 Both the mortgagor, while in possession, and the mortgagee, if possession has been taken or a receiver appointed,[1] are empowered by the LPA 1925, s 99[2] to grant leases in accordance with that section. The leases authorised by the section are agricultural or occupation leases for a term not exceeding 50 years, and building leases for a term not exceeding 999 years. Such leases must take effect in possession not later than 12 months from their date, must reserve the best rent reasonably obtainable, and must contain a covenant for payment of rent and a condition of re-entry in the event of breach.[3] The lessee must execute a counterpart of the lease. If in good faith a lease is granted which does not comply with these requirements, it takes effect in equity as a contract to grant an equivalent lease in accordance with the statutory power.[4]

Save in relation to mortgages of agricultural land[5] and the grant of new tenancies of business premises under the Landlord and Tenant Act 1954, Part II,[6] the statutory power applies only to the extent that it is not excluded by the parties. In fact it is normal practice to exclude the mortgagor's statutory power of leasing altogether. In this way the mortgagor is prevented from creating (without the positive consent of the mortgagee), for example, an assured shorthold tenancy within the Housing Act 1988,[7] which would devalue the mortgagee's security. Where the mortgage terms exclude the power to create any tenancy, any breach is commonly expressed to give rise to the mortgage money becoming due, and hence to the mortgagee's remedies becoming available. Where the mortgagor's power of leasing is excluded then any purported tenancy granted by the mortgagor is binding on the parties to it by estoppel[8] but does not bind the mortgagee[9]. It is not unusual, in practice, for such tenancies to be granted and for the tenants thereunder to be unaware of their vulnerable position until the mortgagee obtains a possession order against which they have no defence. Their situation has now been addressed by the Mortgage Repossessions (Protection of Tenants etc) Act 2010.[10] Such unauthorised tenants (along with authorised tenants and other occupiers) already have the right to be notified by the mortgagee of any possession proceedings.[11] They now have the right to appear at the hearing and to apply for the date of possession to be delayed by up to two months[12]. The mortgagee must also serve 14 days' notice on all occupiers that they are going to execute an order for possession.[13] If an unauthorised tenant has not previously applied for a two month delay, he (or she) can ask the mortgagee to grant such a delay and, if this is refused, can apply to court at this stage.[14]

[1] To whom the power of leasing may be delegated.
[2] See also LRA 1925, s 23(2).
[3] Further conditions are imposed in respect of building leases.
[4] LPA 1925, s 152(1).
[5] Agricultural Holdings Act 1986, Sch 14, para 12.
[6] See paras 37.25–37.29.
[7] Para 37.4.
[8] Para 36.18.
[9] *Iron Trades Employers Insurance Association v Union of House and Land Investors Ltd* [1937] 1 All ER 481; *Dudley and District Benefit Building Society v Emerson* [1949] 2 All ER 252, CA; *Britannia Building Society v Earl* [1990] 2 All ER 469, CA; and see *Quennell v Maltby* [1979] 1 All ER 568, CA.
[10] This came into force on 1 October 2010.
[11] Under the Civil Procedure Rules.
[12] Mortgage Repossessions (Protection of Tenants etc) Act 2010 (MR(PT)A 2010), s 1(2).
[13] MR(PT)A s 2.
[14] MR(PT)A, s 1(4).

Insurance

34.40 The mortgagee is empowered by the LPA 1925, s 101 to insure the mortgaged property against loss or damage by fire up to the amount specified in the deed or up to two thirds of the amount which would be required to reinstate the property in the event of total destruction.[1] The premiums become part of the mortgage debt. It is common expressly to provide that the mortgagor shall insure the property for a specified sum or the full value of the property or, particularly in building society mortgages, that the society will effect the insurance for a specified sum but the premiums will be payable by the mortgagor.

The mortgagee may require that all moneys received under an insurance of the mortgaged property effected under the terms of the Act or the mortgage deed be applied by the mortgagor in making good the loss or damage or be applied in or towards the discharge of the mortgage money.[1] Should the mortgagor independently of any obligation in the mortgage choose to insure the property, the mortgagee is not entitled to any money received, but where the money is payable in the event of fire it can be required to be used towards reinstatement,[2] and in any event it is common to exclude the mortgagor's power independently to insure the property.

[1] LPA 1925, s 108.
[2] Fires Prevention (Metropolis) Act 1774, s 83.

Priorities

34.41 The issue of priorities between competing mortgagees arises where the value of the mortgaged property is insufficient to provide security for all the mortgages to which the property is subject. The incidence of this problem is rare in times of rapidly increasing property values, so long as mortgagees act with care. However, as property recessions have shown, should the value of property decline, the difficulty does arise. In such a case, if the property is sold to realise the security, the various mortgagees do not share in the proceeds equally or rateably in proportion to the size of their mortgage; the mortgagee having priority is paid in full before any money is passed to the second in priority, and so on. We shall only consider the rules governing the priority of mortgages of registered land.

Priority

34.42 Registered charges[1] rank for priority as between themselves in order of registration.[2] A charge which has not yet been registered takes effect in equity only; it will be overridden by a subsequent registered charge but, being the first in time, it will take priority over any other unregistered charge[3].

[1] Para 34.4.
[2] LRA 2002, s 48.
[3] LRA 2002, s 30.

Tacking of further advances

34.43 Where a mortgagee makes a further loan, or advance, to the mortgagor, there are circumstances in which it may be 'tacked on' to the original mortgage so as to enjoy the priority of that mortgage. Tacking of further advances is particularly important where a person mortgages property to a bank to secure an overdrawn current account. The overdraft at the time of the mortgage represents the original debt for which the mortgage is security: each subsequently honoured cheque represents a further advance. The bank will, of course, wish to ensure that it does not lose priority in respect of these further advances to any intervening mortgage of the property created by the debtor.

The circumstances in which tacking will be permitted are:

- if there is an arrangement to that effect with the subsequent mortgagee;[1]

- if the mortgagee has received no notice from a subsequent mortgagee of the creation of the subsequent charge;[2]

- where the mortgagee is obliged to make further advances and that fact is noted on the register at the time the subsequent mortgage is created;[3]

- where the parties to the first mortgage have agreed a maximum amount for which the charge is security and that fact is noted on the register and the further advance is within that limit.[4]

[1] LRA 2002, s 49(6).
[2] LRA 2002, s 49(1). In practice a subsequent chargee will always give notice to a prior mortgagee.
[3] LRA 2002, s 49(3).
[4] LRA 2002, s 49(4).

Questions

1. How are legal mortgages created?

2. How does equity protect the position of a mortgagor?

3. What role does statutory regulation now have in the protection of mortgagors?

4. When does the mortgagee have the right to take possession of the property? In what circumstances is this right restricted?

5. When can a mortgagee sell the property and what are his or her duties in respect of the sale?

6. Where a mortgagee sells the property, how must the proceeds of sale be distributed?

7. Where a mortgagor has granted an unauthorised tenancy what are that tenant's rights where the mortgagee is seeking possession?

8. Fred and Geraldine purchased a house with the aid of a loan from Henry; this is secured by a registered charge over the property. At the beginning of last year Fred lost his job and the couple have not made any monthly repayments for the past six months. Henry has issued proceedings for possession and Fred and Geraldine have heard that he has agreed to sell their house to an old friend of his at a price that they believe is well below its market value.

   Advise Fred and Geraldine on their legal position.

35

Enforceability of interests in land

CHAPTER OVERVIEW

The essence of a proprietary right is that it is capable of binding future owners of the land to which it relates. However, whether or not a proprietary right actually binds a future owner—a matter of supreme importance to a purchaser of land—depends on rules which, with the increasing prevalence of registration, have become more straightforward. In this chapter we consider:

- the background to the current rules relating to the enforceability of proprietary rights affecting land; and

- the rules governing the enforceability of proprietary rights relating to registered land.

35.1 We have already seen[1] that one of the essential features of any proprietary right to use and enjoy land is that it must be *capable* of binding, not just the landowner who created the right, but also subsequent purchasers of the land to which the right relates. Rights, such as licences, which cannot in themselves[2] bind a purchaser are, by definition, purely personal. However, the fact that a right is proprietary does not mean that it will automatically bind a purchaser of the land. Now that we have discussed many of the most important proprietary rights to land, we turn to the final piece in the jigsaw and examine the circumstances in which such rights *will actually bind* a future owner. This is an issue that is of prime importance. The value, and indeed the very marketability, of land depends on a purchaser or lender[3] being able to discover exactly what rights relating to the land will continue to operate after the sale or mortgage since this can profoundly affect the decision to purchase or to lend (or the price to be paid or the amount of any loan). Equally, those who have the benefit of rights over land which belongs to another, wish to ensure that any transfer of that land will not result in the loss of their rights.

---

[1] Paras 28.2 and 28.9.

[2] Additional factors may persuade a court to invoke the constructive trust or the doctrine of proprietary estoppel as a means of protecting a licensee against a subsequent purchaser; see paras 28.44 and 30.10–30.16.

[3] A 'purchaser' includes 'a lessee, mortgagee or other person who for valuable consideration acquires an interest in property...', LPA 1925, s 205(1)(xxi).

The background

The pre-1926 rules

35.2 The pre-1926 rules governing the enforceability of proprietary rights depended simply on whether the right in question was *legal* or *equitable*.

Legal rights

35.3 It was always a basic principle of English land law that legal rights to land 'bind the whole world'. Thus a legal right always bound a purchaser irrespective of whether the purchaser knew of the right in question. So, for example, if A (a freeholder) granted a legal lease to B and then sold his freehold reversion to C, C was always bound by the lease. The same would be true if, instead of selling the freehold, A had granted a legal mortgage to D; D would also be bound by B's lease.

This rule rarely caused unfairness because it was easy for a purchaser to discover the existence of legal rights to land. As we have seen, common law usually required rights to land to be created by deed[1] with the result that there was documentary evidence of such rights which formed part of the title to the land. In those instances where the common law recognises rights despite the absence of a deed,[2] the owner of those rights was either in occupation of the land, or the rights were being openly exercising; accordingly they would be revealed by the physical inspection of the land which every prudent purchaser is assumed by the law to make.

[1] Para 29.11.
[2] Eg leases not exceeding three years (para 29.12), freehold ownership based on adverse possession (paras 30.19–30.36) and easements acquired by prescription (para 30.19 and paras 32.40–32.51).

Equitable interests

35.4 We have seen that equity's first foray into English land law was when the Court of Chancery started enforcing the trust by requiring the trustees, the legal owners of the land, to abide by the terms of the trust, thus recognising that it was the beneficiary who was entitled to the benefits of the land.[1] However, the beneficiary's rights against the trustees would be of little use if these benefits would be lost should the trustees transfer their ownership of the land to someone else. Gradually, the Chancellor came to hold that there were others besides the original trustees who were in conscience bound to give effect to the rights of the beneficiary. Thus, these rights came to be enforceable against a trustee's heir, against someone to whom a trustee left the land by will, against someone to whom the trustees gave the land, and against someone who bought the land knowing that the beneficiary was entitled to the benefit of it. As the class of persons against whom a beneficiary could enforce their rights was extended the effect was that their equitable interest became almost as good as the legal estate which was held by the trustees. However, the Court of Chancery stopped short of enforcing the beneficiary's rights against the whole world; their rights came to be enforceable against the whole world *except* a 'bona fide purchaser of a legal estate for value without notice of the equitable interest'.

In addition to beneficial interests under a trust, equity, over the years, came to recognise a number of rights in respect of land which were not recognised by the common law; for example the restrictive covenant.[2] Furthermore, as we have seen,[3] equity will sometimes give effect to rights despite the fact that they were created in ways which failed to comply with the formalities demanded by the common law and statute. The decision in *Pilcher v Rawlins*,[4] in 1872, made it clear that the rule that equitable rights were not enforceable against a bona fide purchaser of a legal estate without notice of their existence applied to all equitable interests, not just beneficial interests under a trust.

[1] Para 28.39.
[2] Chapter 33.
[3] See paras 30.2–30.6.
[4] (1872) 7 Ch App 259.

The bona fide purchaser of a legal estate for value

35.5 In order to appreciate the differences between the rules governing the enforceability of legal and equitable rights to land, we need briefly to examine the notion of the bona fide purchaser of a legal estate for value without notice. To fall within the exception and thus take free from prior equitable interests in the land, a purchaser must have acted bona fide, 'in good faith'; they must have acted honestly, and genuinely be without notice. As we have seen, the term 'purchaser' bears an extended meaning in law encompassing all those who acquire an interest in land[1] and includes a lessee and a mortgagee. However, the purchaser must have acquired the legal estate 'for value', ie for valuable consideration[2] or in consideration of marriage. Thus, where a person acquired the legal estate as a gift or under a will or on an intestacy[3] they would be bound by any equitable interests, even if they had no notice of them.

[1] Para 35.1.
[2] See ch 6.
[3] Ie where a person dies leaving no effective will.

35.6 *The doctrine of notice* We now turn to the concept of notice itself, of which three varieties came to be recognised: actual notice, constructive notice and imputed notice. A purchaser has actual notice of rights of which they know.

If actual notice were the only type of notice, a purchaser could have avoided knowledge of an equitable interest, and thus take the land free from it, by refraining from inspecting the land they were buying or by failing to investigate the title to it. To avoid this, equity also recognised that a purchaser has constructive notice of an equitable interest if its existence would have come to their knowledge if reasonable inquiries and inspections had been made. The onus was thus on the purchaser to make such reasonable inquiries and inspections as would be made by any prudent purchaser. A further aspect of constructive notice was the doctrine of *Hunt v Luck*,[1] whereby a person's occupation of property constituted constructive notice to others of his or her rights in respect of the property. Thus, a purchaser, on inspecting the property, needed to make inquiries of any person in occupation in order to establish whether that person had any rights in the property. Failure to do so would give constructive notice of those rights.

Finally, we should mention imputed notice. For fairly obvious reasons, equity also took the view that any notice, actual or constructive, which was acquired by a solicitor or other agent acting for the purchaser in the transaction was imputed to the purchaser.

[1] [1901] 1 Ch 45; affd [1902] 1 Ch 428, CA.

35.7 *The problems caused by the doctrine of notice* The application of the fully developed doctrine of notice undoubtedly came to cause problems for both a purchaser of land and an owner of any equitable interest. A purchaser was at risk of being bound by an undiscovered equitable interest because they could be deemed to have notice unless 'proper' pre-purchase inquiries had been made. Furthermore, and conversely, an equitable interest in land could be lost if the legal estate was acquired for valuable consideration by someone without notice of its existence. If these difficulties were not seriously to hinder dealings in land (which were, of course, by the end of the 19th century starting to increase quite dramatically) changes in the law were necessary, and it is to these which we now turn.

The solutions adopted in 1925

35.8 Two solutions were adopted in 1925 to ease these problems. In the case of some equitable interests which might loosely be described as 'commercial',[1] the concept of registration was introduced. Henceforth such interests could be protected by being registered in which case they would bind a purchaser; if they were not registered, they would not bind. A purchaser thus knows that, prior to a purchase, the relevant register must be searched to discover the existence of those interests which will be binding; equally, the owner of the interest knows that, by registering his or her interest, they will always be enforceable against all purchasers.

The second solution relates to those equitable interests of a 'family' nature, such as interests arising under a settlement or as a result of co-ownership.[2] We have already seen that, after 1925, all such interests are necessarily equitable and can now only exist behind a trust.[3] In the case of these trust interests it was felt unnecessary that they should bind a purchaser at all, and undesirable that the legal estate should permanently be encumbered with a string of beneficial interests. Consequently, the existing notion of 'overreaching' was extended. As we have seen,[4] this is the process whereby, on the sale of the trust land, the beneficial interests cease to bind the land, and are satisfied thenceforth out of the proceeds of sale instead.

[1] Eg estate contracts (para 29.8), restrictive covenants (ch 33) and mortgages (ch 34).
[2] Chapter 31.
[3] Para 31.29.
[4] Paras 31.26 and 31.36.

Two systems of registration

35.9 The detailed implementation of the policy of registering 'commercial' type proprietary rights was further complicated by the simultaneous introduction of the system of registration of *title*. While the introduction of a radically different system for the protection and enforcement of interests in land was a vital aspect of registration of title, the LRA 1925 had a much wider remit. As we have seen,[1] the 1925 Act put in place a scheme for the central registration of title to land which resulted in quite different procedures for the transfer and creation of rights to land once registration has taken place. For practical reasons which we have already explained, this had to be implemented on a gradual basis which, even now, is not yet complete.

Accordingly, in 1925 the legislators had to decide whether to leave unregistered land subject to the existing, unsatisfactory, rules on notice, or whether to introduce essentially temporary reforms, designed to apply until such time as the title to any particular piece of land was actually registered. In the event, the latter course was adopted with the result that there are two *quite separate and mutually exclusive* systems of registration. The first and far more limited scheme, is that which applies *only* to unregistered land and is contained in what is now the Land Charges Act 1972 (hereafter LCA 1972). The second is that which is now governed by the LRA 2002. We have already dealt with the conveyancing aspects of the LRA;[2] in this chapter we concentrate on its rules governing the protection and enforceability of third party rights to registered land.

Before providing a very brief summary of the Land Charges Act scheme of registration, we first consider the impact of registration on the traditional division of proprietary rights to land as either legal or equitable.

[1] Paras 29.13–29.20.
[2] Paras 29.13–29.20.

35.10 It will become very clear that the introduction of systems of registration has diminished the importance of a proprietary right being legal or equitable. As we shall see, the LCA and the LRA each classify proprietary rights in their own distinct way and it is that classification which then dictates the enforceability of those rights against future owners. However, it remains fair to say that whether a right is legal or equitable will often determine the category into which a right falls under each Act.

Unregistered land

35.11 Before concentrating on the position of registered land, we first summarise the rules relating to the protection of interests in land where the LRA does not apply because the title to land has not yet been registered. As we have just indicated, the key to understanding the rules governing the enforceability of rights in unregistered land lies in grasping the way in which such rights are now classified. The rights of third parties fall into one of two categories; they are either registrable under the LCA or they are not registrable. This second category can itself be further divided into two groups; those rights which are legal and those which are equitable. Again this second group, ie equitable rights which are not registrable under the LCA, can be further divided into those which are overreachable and those which are not. A different rule on enforceability applies to each category and we shall deal with each in turn.

35.12 *Rights made registrable by the Land Charges Act 1972* The policy of reducing the impact of the doctrine of notice, both to enable a purchaser more readily to discover interests affecting the land and to allow those entitled to those interests to fix the purchaser with notice of their existence, was given effect by the Land Charges Act 1925, now repealed and consolidated by the Land Charges Act 1972. The fundamental objective of this Act is to mechanise the doctrine of notice by requiring rights governed by the Act to be registered.[1] Such registration constitutes actual notice,[2] while a failure to register renders the right void against most purchasers; a failure to register does not however render the right void against a donee, a devisee (ie a beneficiary under a will) or a squatter.[3] If a right is void against a purchaser for non-registration then it is irrelevant that the purchaser actually knew about it.[4]

The rights made registrable by the LCA are mostly equitable and include estate contracts (ie contracts for the sale of land, options and rights of pre-emption), post 1925 restrictive covenants and some equitable easements.

---

[1] The LCA obliges the Land Registry, in addition to operating the system of registration of title under the LRA, also to maintain a Land Charges department operating the Land Charges Act 1972. This department keeps the Land Charges Register on computer at Plymouth.

[2] LPA 1925, s 198(1).

[3] LCA 1972, s 4(5) and (6).

[4] LPA 1925, s 199.

35.13 *Interests outside the Land Charges Act* As explained at the outset, the LCA system of registration was never intended to apply to all third party rights affecting unregistered land. In particular, it was always anticipated that virtually all *legal* interests, and those equitable interests to which the *overreaching* provisions apply, should not be registrable.

1. On the whole *legal* third party rights are not registrable under the LCA. For such rights the pre-1926 rules apply; namely that, as legal rights, they bind the whole world. Thus a purchaser is bound by such rights irrespective of whether they know about them or not; as we have already explained, in practice, it is generally quite easy for a purchaser to discover the existence of legal rights.[1]

2. We have already seen that certain *equitable interests arising under trusts* are overreachable. This means that, on a sale of unregistered land, the rights of beneficiaries do not bind a purchaser even where the purchaser is fully aware of them.

In the event of a sale or mortgage the rights of the beneficiaries are transferred from the land to the purchase or loan money. It must be remembered that, in order for overreaching to take effect, the purchaser or lender must pay the money to trustees who must be at least two in number (or a trust corporation).[2] If this is not done,[3] no overreaching occurs; in such a situation whether or not the purchaser takes free from the rights of the beneficiaries depends on the old doctrine of notice.

3. The LCA itself envisages that some other *equitable* interests are not registrable, eg pre-1926 restrictive covenants. Case law has made clear that certain other equitable interests, such as those arising by way of proprietary estoppel, are also not registrable[5]. In these cases also the doctrine of notice[6] governs whether the rights are enforceable against a purchaser.

---

[1] Para 35.3.

[2] Paras 31.26, 31.36 and 35.8.

[3] As already explained, this is most likely to occur in cases of implied co-ownership, where the title deeds often give the purchaser the impression that the property is solely owned so that he does not realise that any question of overreaching arises; see para 31.37.

[4] *Caunce v Caunce* [1969] 1 All ER 722.

[5] *E R Ives Investments Ltd v High* [1967] 1 All ER 504, CA.

[6] See para 35.6.

THE BACKGROUND: KEY POINTS

- Prior to 1926, whether or not a proprietary right was binding on a purchaser hinged on whether the right in question was legal or equitable; a legal right would always bind a purchaser, while an equitable right would only bind a bona fide purchaser for value without notice of the right.

- The 1925 property legislation tackled the increasing problem of the enforceability of proprietary rights in two ways:
  - It introduced a system of *registration of title* into which was incorporated an entirely new regime governing enforceability.
  - It amended the existing rules so as to improve the situation in relation to *unregistered land*; this system would gradually disappear as unregistered land moved onto the Land Register.

- Where title to land is *not yet registered*, the enforceability of third party rights depends on whether or not those rights are registrable under the Land Charges Act 1972 (which is quite different from the Land Registration Act):
  - Registrable rights are listed in the 1972 Act and will only bind a purchaser if they are actually registered in the land charges register (not to be confused with the Land Register).
  - Rights that are not registrable are either legal or equitable:
    - many of the unregistrable rights are legal and these will always bind a purchaser;
    - unregistrable equitable rights are either:
      - beneficial interests under a trust of land – these will be overreached on a sale by at least two trustees and will not then bind a purchaser, or
      - non-overreachable interests – whether or not these interests bind turns on the old doctrine of notice.

Registered land

Introduction

35.14 As we have said[1] the introduction of a new system of registration of title by the LRA 1925 offered an opportunity to adopt a fresh approach to the question of the enforceability and protection of third party rights and this process has now been refined and taken further by the LRA 2002. In order to be covered by the 2002 Act at all a third party right must relate to or be parasitic on an interest to which title has been registered.[2] So, for example, a restrictive covenant, a short lease or a mortgage, will only fall within the ambit of the LRA if the title to the freehold or lease to which it relates has been registered. First registration of title[3] provides a chance for the Land Registry to check all the existing evidence of rights affecting that title, to classify those rights and to record their existence by way of an entry in the register. By definition this initial investigation by the Land Registry will reveal, and result in the registration of, a far wider range of rights than are covered by the much more limited system of registration set up by the LCA. Since virtually all dealings with the land thereafter should be completed by registration[4] the register can be kept up to date by the addition, where necessary, of fresh entries.

[1] Para 35.9.

[2] We have discussed the circumstances in which title either must or can be registered at paras 29.15 and 29.16.

[3] Para 29.15.

[4] Para 29.18. Note that the grant of leases for seven years or less is an important exception to this requirement, see para 29.18 and note 1, para 35.17.

The classification of rights to registered land

35.15 The classification of rights to land by the LRA is its own. As we have seen,[1] title can only be registered to certain interests, largely but not exclusively, either freehold or leasehold estates; these are registrable interests. Rights affecting any interest to which the title has been registered fall into one of three categories: they are either registered charges; interests which will override first registration or a registered disposition; or minor interests which should be protected by an entry on the register. The enforceability against subsequent purchasers of rights affecting registered interests to which the title has been registered flows from the LRA classification and system of protection and not from whether the rights are legal or equitable.[2]

[1] Para 29.15 and 29.16.

[2] Although their LRA classification may hinge on whether they are legal or equitable.

The effect of registration of title

35.16 *First registration* Although the effects of registration of title have already been dealt with[1], it might be helpful to remind ourselves of these. When a title is registered (with absolute title[2]) for the *first* time that first registered proprietor is entitled to the legal estate, together with all the existing rights which benefit that estate (such as easements and restrictive covenants). More importantly for present purposes, the only adverse interests to which that first registered proprietor will be subject are:

- interests protected by an entry on the register;
- 'overriding' interests within Sch 1 to the LRA;
- interests already acquired under the Limitation Act 1980 (ie squatter's rights) of which the proprietor has notice;

- where the proprietor is a trustee, those rights of the beneficiaries of which the proprietor has notice; and

- in the case of leaseholds, the express and implied covenants in the lease.

[1] See paras 29.17 and 29.18.
[2] As is usually the case, see para 29.17.

35.17 *Subsequent dealings* Once a title has been registered for the first time, any *subsequent* dealing with that registered title must normally be carried out by way of a disposition which must be completed by registration[1]. A purchaser[2] for valuable consideration under a registered disposition of an interest with absolute title will take the registered estate together with the rights by which it is benefited. However, as compared to a *first* registered proprietor, a purchaser of an *already registered estate* takes subject to a *narrower* range of adverse interests, namely:

- a registered charge;

- interests protected by an entry on the register;

- 'overriding' interests within Sch 3[3] of the LRA;

- in the case of leaseholds, the covenants in the lease.

[1] Note that where a registered proprietor grants a lease for seven years or less the process does not normally have to be completed by registration (see para 29.18). This means that such leases do not normally appear on the register (although leases of more than three years *may* be protected by the entry of a notice—see para 35.35). Where a lease is not entered on the register it will normally be an interest that overrides—see para 35.22.
[2] Note that a purchaser includes a mortgagee; see note 3 para 35.1.
[3] As we shall see, the overriding interests within Sch 3 are a narrower group than those within Sch 1 which bind a *first* registered proprietor, see para 35.21.

35.18 We now consider in more detail the circumstances in which registered charges, 'overriding' interests, and those interests that can be protected by an entry on the register will bind either a first registered proprietor or a purchaser for valuable consideration of an already registered estate.

Registered charges

35.19 As we have seen, a mortgage of registered land must now be created by way of a legal charge[1]. It constitutes a 'registered disposition'[2] and must be completed by registration, ie the lender is registered as proprietor of the charge.[3] By definition, a registered charge cannot be in existence at the time of a first registration of title; they can only be created where title is already registered. A purchaser of an already registered title and a subsequent mortgagee will always be bound by an existing registered charge.[4] In practice, particularly in the case of residential property, existing registered charges are usually paid off by the vendor immediately prior to a sale so that a purchaser will not then be bound by the vendor's mortgage. It is likely, of course, that the purchaser will immediately create his or her own registered charge in order to finance the purchase.

[1] See para 34.4.
[2] LRA 2002, s 27(2)(f).
[3] LRA 2002, s 27, Sch 2, para 8.
[4] LRA 2002, s 29(2)(a)(i).

'Overriding' interests

Introduction

35.20 The land registration system has always accepted that there are some interests that must bind a purchaser or lender despite not being entered on the register. The LRA 1925 referred to such rights as 'overriding interests'. While the LRA 2002 discards this label (and makes some radical changes to this area of the law) the term remains a useful description and we retain the expression. At first sight, the existence of a category of rights, which bind the purchaser despite not being entered on the register, may appear surprising; it clearly invalidates any idea that the registered land scheme ensures that all interests affecting the land should be discoverable from an inspection of the Land Register. However, we have seen a number of situations where the law recognises that rights to land can be created outside the context of a formal transaction and without the use of documents.[1] In such instances the owner of the right is highly unlikely to be aware of any need to register their right if this were required. Accordingly, a registration system either has to decide that such rights effectively disappear in the event of a sale or mortgage—a stance that would inevitably reproduce the very unfairness that the informal conferment of rights was designed to eliminate—or it is accepted that, in certain circumstances at least, unregistered rights can bind a purchaser or mortgagee. It is the latter course that was followed by the LRA 1925. This approach has been accepted by the LRA 2002 although that Act has cut down the number of interests that can override and drawn a new distinction between unregistered rights that can bind a *first* registered proprietor, and those that can bind purchasers and mortgagees of an *already registered estate*. The aim is to strike a balance between fairness to the owner of what are often informally created or longstanding rights and the imposition of an unreasonable requirement to expect purchasers to discover the existence of unregistered rights.

[1] For example, the conferment of interests in land by the use of resulting or constructive trusts (see paras 30.9–30.10) or under the doctrine of proprietary estoppel (see paras 30.11–30.16). We have also seen that easements can be created by implication (see paras 32.27–32.33) or by prescription (see paras 32.40–32.51) and that squatters can acquire rights by way of adverse possession (see paras 30.19–30.36); in none of these situations will documents have been used.

35.21 *The distinction between first registration and subsequent dealings* The LRA 2002 has, for the first time, drawn a distinction between those overriding interests that bind a first registered proprietor and those that bind on any subsequent dealings with the registered estate. While the overriding interests themselves are broadly the same, those that bind on a first registration are more widely defined and are listed in Sch 1 to the Act[1]. Those that bind on subsequent dealings are more narrowly defined and are listed in Sch 3. The reason for the distinction is that first registration can take place voluntarily without the need for any transaction. Thus, there is not necessarily any purchaser or mortgagee to be burdened by the need to discover the existence of overriding interests; they are therefore more widely defined. In the case of subsequent dealings, the needs of a purchaser are given greater consideration with the result that overriding interests are, in this case, drawn more narrowly; in particular, account is often taken of how readily the rights can be discovered by a purchaser.

In practice, the vast majority of transactions are not first registrations but dealings with already registered estates. In the following paragraphs we will, therefore, deal primarily with those overriding interests that will bind a purchaser or mortgagee of such estates, ie those listed in Sch 3. However, where appropriate, we will draw attention to the way in which the Sch 1 equivalent differs.

[1] It should be noted that an applicant for first registration is obliged to inform the Land Registry of any known interests to which their estate is subject, LRA 1925, s 71. Where such interests fall within Sch 1 and are not excluded by s 33 (as to which see para 35.35) the Registrar is obliged to protect them by the entry of a notice. In this event, the interests take their protection from the entry of the notice and are not then overriding.

Short legal leases

35.22 Most legal leases not exceeding seven years are overriding interests under Sch 3, para 1.[1] The only exceptions are those few leases for seven years or less that are required to be registered with their own independent title;[2] of these, the most important are reversionary leases of any length that are to start at least three months after the date of grant.[3] The reasons why it is felt unnecessary to require short leases either to be registered with their own title, or protected by notice[4] are various. Such leases are often not transferred or mortgaged; there are very many of them (so that registration would have considerable resource implications); many (ie those for a term of three years or less) are entered into without formality and often without legal advice,[5] and tenants are usually in occupation so that the existence of the lease is readily discoverable.

[1] Leases exceeding seven years must be registered with their own title, see para 29.15.
[2] LRA 2002, s 4; see para 29.15.
[3] LRA 2002, s 4; see para 29.15.
[4] See para 35.35.
[5] Good examples are the short-term residential leases entered into by many students.

Rights of persons in actual occupation

35.23 Schedule 3, para 2 provides that 'interests belonging at the time of the disposition to a person in actual occupation of the land' will bind a purchaser of a registered estate. This replaces s 70(1)(g) of the LRA 1925, one of the most heavily litigated provisions in that Act. While there are important differences between s 70(1)(g) and para 2, some at least of the existing case law on the former provision remains relevant.

This is the most controversial and extensive category of overriding interest. Any proprietary right affecting registered land can fall within para 2 provided only that its owner is in actual occupation of the land to which it relates.[1] (It should be stressed that it is the *right* that is the overriding interest, not the occupation; occupation by someone without a proprietary right to the land can never give rise to an overriding interest.) While the LRA seeks to eliminate the doctrine of notice, para 2 may be regarded as affording very similar protection under the registered land system to that conferred by the doctrine in *Hunt v Luck*.[2] Indeed, para 2 may be regarded as even more extensive; while constructive notice cannot save an interest in unregistered land which should have been registered under the LCA,[3] para 2 can operate to protect a right which could have been entered on the Land Register; it makes no difference that the right protected by occupation might also have been protected by the entry of a notice on the register.[4]

[1] Thus, the right must relate to the land that is occupied; this means that the occupation of part of land cannot render overriding an interest over a larger whole. This overturns previous case law.
[2] [1902] 1 Ch 428, CA. Ie whereby a purchaser has constructive notice of the rights of any person in occupation of land; para 35.6.
[3] Land Charges Act 1972, s 4(5) and (6); see para 35.12.
[4] *Williams and Glyn's Bank Ltd v Boland* [1980] 2 All ER 408, HL; see para 35.28.

35.24 *Rights with reference to land* The only rights which can be protected by actual occupation under para 2 are 'rights with reference to land which have the quality of being capable of enduring through different ownerships of the land according to normal conceptions of title to real property', in other words, recognised proprietary interests.[1] Examples include unregistered estate contracts such as contracts for the sale of land and options,[2] rights of pre-emption[3], interests under any trust of land,[4] rights in the course of being acquired by a squatter[5], and interests arising by way of proprietary estoppel[6].

However, the courts have held that proprietary rights which are not intended to take priority over the purchaser cannot be overriding. So, where an implied co-owner knows that a mortgage is necessary in order to acquire the very property to which he or she will have rights, those rights cannot override the rights of the mortgagee, even though the implied co-owner is in actual occupation[7]. Rights to land that are not proprietary, such as contractual licences[8], cannot be overriding interests. It is expressly provided that certain interests are not covered by para 2; these are beneficial interests under an old strict settlement,[9] a spouse's rights of occupation under what is now the Family Law Act 1996,[10] reversionary leases that are not to commence for at least three months and have not yet taken effect[11], and overriding leases under the Landlord and Tenant (Covenants) Act 1995[12]. These must be protected by other means; either by registration in their own right (reversionary leases) or by the entry of a notice[13] or restriction[14].

[1] *National Provincial Bank Ltd v Ainsworth* [1965] AC 1175 at 1226.

[2] *Bridges v Mees* [1957] 2 All ER 577 (contract of sale); *Webb v Pollmount* [1966] 1 All ER 481 (option to purchase).

[3] Specifically dealt with by LRA 1925, s 115.

[4] *Williams and Glyn's Bank Ltd v Boland* [1980] 2 All ER 408, HL.

[5] Ie where a squatter has been in adverse possession of registered land for, say, five years and the land is then sold by the registered proprietor, the new registered proprietor will usually be bound by the five years of adverse possession. Time does not begin afresh for the squatter; he or she can apply for registration after a further five years adverse possession. See para 30.29.

[6] Specifically dealt with by LRA 1925, s 116; this resolves the previous controversy as to whether or not interests arising by way of proprietary estoppel could be regarded as overriding.

[7] *Bristol and West Building Society v Henning* [1985] 2 All ER 606: *Paddington Building Society v Mendelsohn* (1985) 50 P & CR 244; see para 34.24.

[8] See para 28.40.

[9] LRA 2002, Sch 3, para 2(a).

[10] Family Law Act 1996, s 31(10)(b).

[11] LRA 2002, Sch 3, para 2(d).

[12] Landlord and Tenant (Covenants) Act 1995, s 20(6). For the confusingly named overriding lease, see para 36.86.

[13] See para 35.35.

[14] See para 35.34.

35.25 *Actual occupation* It is expressly provided that, for the purposes of Sch 3, the occupation (*not* the right) must, except where the purchaser has actual knowledge, be 'obvious on a reasonably careful inspection of the land at the time of the disposition'. This is a new requirement which settles a long standing debate on whether, under the previous law, actual occupation was purely a question of fact or whether it should be readily discoverable by a purchaser. Under the new law it is clear that discoverability is now a key question.

This does not mean that there will not still be difficult questions to answer. There are bound to be issues over what amounts to a 'reasonably careful inspection'. It will also be necessary to clarify whether the occupation must be obvious to *a* purchaser, or to *the* purchaser. Equally there will continue to be issues over what constitutes actual occupation. Clearly, where the adult[1] owner of the right is in permanent occupation of the property, eg a wife or cohabitee living in the home to which she has implied rights of co-ownership, she will be in actual occupation[2]. The position would be the same were a permanent occupier be away on holiday or in hospital for a short time[3]. What of a more intermittent presence in the home[4]? What of a long holiday away from home, or leaving the property empty save for furniture[5]? Can actual occupation take place through an agent or employee[6]?

Under the previous law, there was for a long time uncertainty as to whether the actual occupation had to exist at the date of the disposition, ie completion of the purchase or mortgage, or at the date when the purchaser or mortgagee is registered[7]. Paragraph 2 makes it explicit that actual occupation must exist at the date of completion. This means that anyone going into occupation after completion but before registration (classically, a cohabitee who, unknown to a mortgagee financing the purchase, goes into occupation with the registered proprietor immediately after the mortgage is created but before it can be registered) cannot claim priority over that mortgagee.

[1] It has been held that minor children cannot be in actual occupation, see *Hypo-Mortgage Services Ltd v Robinson* [1997] 2 FLR 71.

[2] *Williams and Glyn's Bank Ltd v Boland* [1980] 2 All ER 408.

[3] *Chhokar v Chhokar* [1984] FLR 313.

[4] In *Link Lending Ltd v Bustard* [2010] EWCA 424, the Court of Appeal upheld a decision that the defendant, who spent lengthy periods in a psychiatric hospital, was in actual occupation; she had left her home involuntarily, made regular visits there and had a declared intention to return there.

[5] The decision in *Strand Securities v Caswell* [1965] 1 All ER 820 held that leaving furniture would not be sufficient.

[6] Possibly. Compare *Strand Securities v Caswell* [1965] 1 All ER 820, where occupation by a step-daughter was held not to be on behalf of her step-father with *Lloyds Bank plc v Rosset* [1989] Ch 350 where the Court of Appeal held that actual occupation by builders employed by the wife was sufficient for her to be so. (Note that this issue was not discussed by the House of Lords' ruling in that case.)

[7] Finally resolved in favour of the date of completion by the House of Lords in *Abbey National Building Society v Cann* [1990] 1 All ER 1085 at 1101.

35.26 *Inquiry* A purchaser or mortgagee of registered land should inquire of all those who are or appear to be in actual occupation of the property as to whether they have any rights in the land; the vendor's word should not be accepted.[1] Where such an inquiry is made of an occupier and that person does not disclose the right when he or she could reasonably have been expected to do so, that right will not then be an overriding interest.[2]

Particular care needs to be taken where a spouse or co-habitee whose name is not on the register is in occupation; a prospective purchaser or lender should ensure that a reasonable inspection of the property is undertaken[3] and where this reveals the presence of such an occupier, inquiries should be made of him or her. If, as in *Williams and Glyn's Bank Ltd v Boland*,[4] the occupier has rights (in that case as a beneficial co-owner of the property) and the purchaser or lender fails to make inquiry, the purchaser or lender takes subject to them. Where potential lenders become aware that persons other than the registered proprietor are in occupation of the property being offered as security, it is now standard practice for them to require those occupiers to sign a declaration under which any rights that they may have are postponed to the rights of the mortgagee.

[1] *Hodgson v Marks* [1971] Ch 892 at 931.

[2] LRA 2002, Sch 3, para 2(b).

[3] See para 35.25.

[4] [1980] 2 All ER 408, HL.

35.27 *Overreaching* Many of the cases concerning the LRA 1925, s 70(1)(g) involved the claims of implied co-owners and this is likely to continue under the new Sch 3. As we have seen[1] co-ownership gives rise to a trust of land with the result that, in many instances of implied co-ownership, the person who appears to be a sole registered proprietor is in law a trustee holding the property on trust for themselves and the implied co-owner. We have also seen that, where a purchaser deals with a sole trustee, the overreaching machinery is not triggered[2] so that the implied co-owner's rights may bind the purchaser. In unregistered land this will only be the case where the purchaser has *notice* of the rights of the co-owner.[3] In registered land those rights can, but are unlikely to be, protected by an entry in the register[4] or, where the implied co-owner is in actual occupation, they can bind a purchaser as an overriding interest under Sch 3. However, it has been made clear by the House of Lords in *City of London Building Society v Flegg*[5] that, where a purchaser (in that case a mortgagee) deals not with a sole trustee but with the trustees who are at least two in number, the rights of any other implied co-owners will be overreached even where the latter are in actual occupation.[6]

[1] Para 31.29.
[2] Para 31.37.
[3] Para 35.13.
[4] Para 35.35.
[5] [1987] 3 All ER 435, HL. For the facts of this case, see para 31.36.
[6] See also *State Bank of India v Sood* [1997] 1 All ER 169, CA.

35.28 *The operation of Schedule 3* There has, to date, been no significant case law on the operation of Sch 3. However, some flavour of how the provision is likely to work can be gained from looking at three cases under the old s 70(1)(g) since, if the facts of these were to be repeated today, the outcome would be the same. In *Hodgson v Marks*[1], Mrs Hodgson, the freehold owner of a house, transferred it, for nothing, to her lodger, Evans. This was not intended to be an outright gift, for the parties agreed that although Evans was to become the registered proprietor, the beneficial (equitable) ownership was to remain in Mrs Hodgson; in other words, Evans was to hold the land on (resulting) trust for Mrs Hodgson. The parties continued to live in the house as if nothing had changed: Mrs Hodgson as if owner and Evans as if lodger. Evans then sold the house to Marks who became registered proprietor. Marks was aware of Mrs Hodgson's presence in the house but not of any rights she might have in respect of it. Mrs Hodgson's interest under the trust could only bind Marks if either it was protected by an entry on the register, which it was not, or if it was an overriding interest by virtue of her occupation of the property. The Court of Appeal held that she was in actual occupation of the property and her rights under the trust constituted an overriding interest. The court held that simply because the vendor is, or appears to be, in occupation of the property does not mean that no one else can be in actual occupation.

In *Strand Securities Ltd v Caswell*[2], the defendant was the tenant under a sublease which, as the law then stood, was not required to have its title registered. He later allowed his stepdaughter and her family to live in the flat rent free. When his landlord's registered lease was later transferred to the claimants the latter claimed to take free from the defendant's sublease. The Court of Appeal held that the defendant could not have an overriding interest under s 70(1)(g)[3] since, although he owned a right having reference to land (ie the sublease), he was not in actual occupation of the flat. He did not live there and neither the presence of his furniture nor the occupation of his stepdaughter ranked as his actual occupation. Equally his stepdaughter did not have an overriding interest; although she was in actual occupation, she did not have a right with reference to land since she was only a licensee.[4]

In *Williams and Glyn's Bank Ltd v Boland*[5], Mrs Boland was, by virtue of her substantial contribution to its purchase price, an equitable tenant in common of the house which had been transferred into the sole name of her husband.[6] In order to raise money for his business, he later mortgaged the house to the bank which made no inquiries of Mrs Boland. On the husband defaulting, the bank started possession proceedings. It was held, however, that the wife had an interest with reference to land and was in actual occupation; she therefore had an overriding interest which had priority over the bank's mortgage and it could not therefore obtain possession against her.

1 [1971] 2 All ER 684, CA.
2 [1965] 1 All ER 820, CA.
3 The sublease did not meet the requirements of LRA 1925 s 70(1)(k).
4 The court went on to hold that, for other reasons, the defendant's sublease bound the claimants.
5 [1980] 2 All ER 408, HL.
6 Para 31.13.

35.29 *Rights of persons in actual occupation under Schedule 1* Because a first registration can take place voluntarily without the occurrence of any transaction, the definition in Sch 1 of the rights of persons in actual occupation is slightly different from that in Sch 3. Such rights will bind the first registered proprietor, even though the occupation is not obvious and even though inquiries may have been made of the occupier and the rights have not been disclosed[1]. This seems fair enough in the case of a voluntary registration, where there will normally have been no disposition and the new registered proprietor will be the existing owner. It seems less justifiable where there is a transaction and the first registered proprietor is a new owner; in such circumstances there seems no good reason for the new registered proprietor not being given the same protection as under Sch 3.

1 LRA 2002, Sch 1, para 2.

Easements and profits à prendre

35.30 *Schedule 3* Paragraph 3 of Sch 3 makes certain legal easements[1] and profits[2] overriding interests. It will be remembered[3] that expressly created easements and profits are dispositions that must be completed by registration[4]; this means that such rights will be noted on the register[5] and will not therefore be overriding interests. Accordingly, the only legal easements and profits that can be overriding interests under Sch 3 are those created under LPA 1925, s 62[6], those created by implication[7], and those acquired by prescription[8]. Even then, unless the dominant owner proves that the easement or profit has been exercised during the year preceding the disposition[9], it will not be overriding unless it was known to the purchaser and obvious on a reasonable inspection of the servient land[10]. However, these limitations do not apply to those easements and profits within Sch 3 that were created after the commencement of LRA 2002 (ie 13 October 2003) and during the following three years (ie prior to 13 October 2006)[11], with the result that all[12] legal easements and profits arising during that period are overriding. It should be noted that, unlike LRA 1925, the 2002 Act makes it clear that equitable easements and profits cannot be overriding interests; these will only bind a purchaser for valuable consideration where they are protected by the entry of a notice[13].

1 See Ch 32.
2 See paras 32.19–32.21.
3 See para 29.18.
4 LRA 2002, s 27(1).
5 LRA 2002, Sch 2, para 7(2).
6 See paras 32.34–32.38. LRA 2002, s 27(7) specifically provides that in such circumstances there is no requirement for there to be a disposition completed by registration; hence such easements can fall within para 3.
7 See paras 32.27–32.33.
8 See paras 32.40-32.51.
9 LRA 2002, Sch 3, para 3(2).
10 LRA 2002, Sch 3, para 3(1).

[12] Except for those that are *expressly* created; these must be created by registered disposition, LRA 2002, s 27.
[13] See para 35.35.

35.31 *Schedule 1* In the case of a first registration any existing legal easement or profit, whether created expressly or impliedly or acquired under LRA 1925 s 62 or by prescription, will bind a first registered proprietor of the servient land[1]. As with Sch 3, it is now clear that equitable easements cannot bind a first registered proprietor unless it was already registered under the LCA.[3]

[1] LRA 2002, Sch 1 para 3.
[2] See para 35.12.

Miscellaneous overriding interests

35.32 Both Schs 1 and 3 make a range of other rights overriding[1]; these include customary rights[2], public rights[3] and local land charges[4]. A further series of somewhat archaic rights (eg manorial rights and rights to payment in lieu of a tithe) are retained as overriding interests until 2013; after that period they will cease to have effect[6].

[1] LRA 2002, Sch 1, paras 4–9; Sch 3, paras 4–9.
[2] See para 32.22.
[3] See para 32.16.
[4] See para 29.25.
[5] LRA 2002, Sch 1, paras 10–14; Sch 3, paras 10–14.
[6] LRA 2002, s 117(1).

Interests that require protection by an entry on the register

35.33 Virtually all interests affecting a registered estate *can* be protected by an entry on the register, including those that, in the absence of such an entry, will be overriding interests. As we have seen[1], most of the rights that can be overriding interests are, in practice, unlikely to be protected by way of an entry on the register and the owners of such rights will usually need to depend for their protection on the overriding status of their rights. However, it should be appreciated that such rights *are capable* of being protected by an entry on the register.

For most practical purposes we are here dealing with third party rights affecting a registered estate which cannot be overriding interests. Such interests must be protected by entry on the register; however, the function of such an entry is not always to render the right binding on a purchaser. In some instances, notably entries in relation to the rights of beneficiaries under a trust of land, the purpose of the entry is to make any purchaser aware that the registered proprietors are trustees and that the overreaching machinery (ie payment of the purchase money to at least two trustees) needs to be complied with if the purchaser is to take free from the rights. In the other cases the function of the entry is indeed to inform the purchaser of rights which will be binding. There are now two methods of protecting interests by entry on the register.

[1] Para 35.20.

Methods of protection

35.34 *Restriction* A restriction can be entered in the Proprietorship Register of the register of title by, or with the consent of, the registered proprietor[1]. They can also be entered by the Registrar[2], by order of the court[3], or on the application of any person with a sufficient interest in the making of an entry[4]. A restriction does not operate to make interests binding on a purchaser. Rather, its object is to prevent dealings with the land unless a specified requirement has been complied with[5], such as the payment of the purchase money to trustees who must be at least two in number, or the obtaining of the consent of a particular person. It is also used to stop the registered proprietor dealing with the land, eg where the registered proprietor has been declared bankrupt. It can be used to protect any type of interest but one of its main uses is to protect beneficial (equitable) interests under a trust of land by ensuring that the overreaching provisions are complied with.[6]

[1] LRA 2002, s 43(1)(a) and (b).
[2] LRA 2002, ss 42 and 44.
[3] LRA 2002, s 46.
[4] LRA 2002, s 43(1)(c).
[5] LRA 2002, s 40.
[6] See para 31.36.

35.35 *Notice* A notice is an entry in the register in respect of the burden of an interest affecting a registered estate.[1] It can be used to protect any right except certain excluded rights[2]. The most important of the excluded rights are: beneficial interests under a trust (which as we have seen[3] are more appropriately protected by a restriction); any lease for a term of three years or less that is not required to be registered with its own title[4]; restrictive covenants between landlord and tenant. All other interests such as estate contracts, restrictive covenants between freeholders and adverse easements can be protected by notice. There are two alternative types of notice that can be entered; and agreed notice or a unilateral notice.

1. An agreed notice will be entered where either the registered proprietor makes the application (or consents to the application) or where the Registrar is satisfied as to the validity of the interest[5]. Its normal use is, therefore, where the registered proprietor accepts the validity of the interest (which is usually the case).

2. However, there are times when the registered proprietor disputes the validity of the interest being claimed and will not agree to the entry of a notice. In this event the owner of the interest can apply for the entry of a unilateral notice[6]. Where a unilateral notice is entered the registered proprietor must be informed and can apply for the entry to be cancelled[7]; where this happens, the owner of the interest will have to prove the validity of his or her claim in order to prevent the removal of the entry. Since the entry of a unilateral notice can damage the registered proprietor (it may, for example, prevent a sale of the property going ahead) the entry of such a notice without reasonable cause gives rise to a liability in damages[8].

The effect of the entry of a notice is to render the right binding on a subsequent purchaser for valuable consideration since a disposition by a registered proprietor takes effect subject to all rights protected by a notice;[9] however, it does not confer priority over an earlier, unregistered minor interest since, in such a situation, priority is governed by the order in which the interests are created.[10] The entry of a notice does not confer validity on an otherwise invalid interest.[11]

[1] LRA 2002, s 32(1).
[2] LRA 2002, s 33.
[3] See para 35.33.
[4] This means, in effect, that leases for a term exceeding three years but not more than seven years *can* be protected by an entry on the register. This is, of course, not necessary since such leases are overriding interests and will therefore bind a purchaser in any event. Leases of three years or less cannot be protected by the entry of a notice and will thus depend for their protection on their overriding status, save in those cases where such leases have to be registered with their own independent title (for which see para 29.15).

[5] LRA 2002, s 34(3).
[6] LRA 2002, s 34(2).
[7] LRA 2002, s 35.
[8] LRA 2002, s 77.
[9] LRA 2002, s 29(2).
[10] LRA 2002, s 28.
[11] LRA 2002, s 32(3).

The search procedure

35.36 As we have seen,[1] an intending purchaser (which, as always, includes a mortgagee) can request an official search of the register in order to discover the existence of interests protected by an entry on the register.[2] Once in receipt of an official certificate of search the purchaser has the benefit of a 30-day priority period in which to complete the transaction and apply for registration; provided this is done, the purchaser will not be bound by any adverse entries made on the register during that period.

[1] Para 29.37.
[2] LRA 2002, s 70.

Failure to register

35.37 The scheme of the LRA is designed to ensure that, in the case of interests that can be protected by an entry on the register, the state of the register should be paramount and that the doctrine of notice has no application. All a purchaser has to do is consult the register; they will take free from any interest not entered on the register. To this, as we have seen[1], there is one exception. Where the owner of an unregistered interest that could have been protected by an entry but has not been, is in actual occupation of the land to which the right relates, that interest will be regarded as an overriding interest within Sch 3. As such it will bind any purchaser.

The intention that the enforceability of interests affecting a registered estate should hinge solely on either an entry in the register or their overriding status, is made clear by LRA 2002, s 29. This provides that the purchaser of registered land for valuable consideration is bound only by entries on the register and overriding interests. However, there are always difficult issues where a purchaser either knows or ought to have known of an interest which ought to have been entered on the register but which has not been. Under the LRA 1925, there were situations in which the courts held that a purchaser was bound by an interest which was neither overriding nor entered on the register. These included cases of fraud[2], bad faith[3], and circumstances in which a constructive trust was imposed on the purchaser[4]. The LRA 2002 does not deal with this question explicitly; however, the Law Commission, in the Report containing the draft of the LRA 2002, has made it clear that neither actual notice nor bad faith will affect the statutory protection of the purchaser[5]. While it seems unlikely that a fraudulent purchaser will retain the protection of s 29, the clear intention is that, in all other cases, the owner of the unprotected interest will be left to any personal claims that they might have against the purchaser. These could include contractual rights, tortious liability for interference with contractual rights, or equitable liability for knowing receipt of trust moneys. The ambit of these liabilities in this context are at present unknown and it remains to be seen how ready the courts are to intervene. Too enthusiastic an approach would undermine the protection of purchasers and the whole system of registration of title.

[1] Para 35.23.
[2] *Jones v Lipman* [1962] 1 WLR 832. It should be appreciated that a purchaser will not be regarded as fraudulent simply because he knows of the unregistered minor interest; see *De Lusignan v Johnson* (1973) 230 Estates Gazette 499.

[3] *Peffer v Rigg* [1978] 3 All ER 745.
[4] *Lyus v Prowsa Developments Ltd* [1982] 2 All ER 953. See para 30.10.
[5] Law Com 271 (2001).

Alteration, rectification and indemnity

Alteration

35.38 It was pointed out earlier[1] that registration with absolute title does not, despite the name, absolutely guarantee the title, for there remains the possibility that the register of title may be altered (either by court order[2] or by the Registrar[3]). It is inevitable that errors can be made and that there should be the power to put these right. In some circumstances, where a person suffers loss as a result of a change in the register (or a refusal to change the register) there is an entitlement to an indemnity from state funds[4]. Broadly speaking, although the structure and terminology of the provisions governing alterations has been changed by LRA 2002, the substance of the law remains much as it was under LRA 1925. Thus previous case law will remain relevant.

LRA 2002 introduces the term 'alteration'; this applies to any change to the register. Some alterations, ie ones that involve correcting a mistake and which prejudicially affect the title of a registered proprietor, are known as 'rectification'. Thus rectification is narrower than alteration and, as we shall see, it is usually only rectification that gives rise to a right to an indemnity[4]. Under LRA 2002, s 65 and Sch 4 either the court or the Registrar can order the alteration of the register in three circumstances:

- to correct a mistake;
- to bring the register up to date; and
- to give effect to any interest excepted from the effects of registration.

In addition, the Registrar has the power to remove superfluous entries. Where a case falls within any of these heads the register must be altered, unless the circumstances are exceptional[5].

[1] Para 29.17.
[2] LRA 2002, Sch 4, para 2.
[3] LRA 2002, Sch 4, para 5.
[4] See para 35.44.
[5] LRA 2002, Sch 4, paras 3(3) and 5(3).

35.39 *Mistake* One of the most obvious mistakes that can be made is where someone who is not entitled to the land (or not to all of it) is wrongly registered as its proprietor[1]. Similarly, a fraud practised on the registry, as where a conveyance or mortgage is forged,[2] will also be regarded as a mistake. In these instances the register will be rectified (and an indemnity may well be payable[3]). However, where a *transferor* (as opposed to the registry) is defrauded, it will not be regarded as a mistake and the register will not be *rectified*[4] (although the register will be *altered* under·the jurisdiction to bring the register up to date.[5]) In such a case, no indemnity will be payable.

[1] *Re 139 High Street, Deptford* [1951] Ch 884.
[2] *First National Securities v Hegerty* [1984] 1 All ER 139.
[3] See para 35.44.
[4] *Norwich and Peterborough Building Society v Steed* [1993] 1 All ER 330, CA.
[5] See para 35.40.

35.40 *Bringing the register up to date* This covers the entry on the register of rights that arise after registration, such as easements acquired by prescription. As indicated in the previous paragraph, it will also cover cases where it was the transferor who was defrauded rather than the registry.

35.41 *Exceptions from registration* We have seen that, where a person is registered with a title less than absolute (eg he or she is registered with a possessory or qualified title), they do not take free from any existing rights[1]. If such rights become known to the registry they will be entered on the register.

> [1] See para 29.17.

35.42 *Removal of superfluous entries* The Registrar has jurisdiction to remove entries that cease to have effect. For example, a restriction[1] on all dealings with the land may have been imposed due to specific circumstances. If these come to an end, the restriction can be removed.

> [1] See para 35.34.

35.43 *Limits on the right to alter* Although the circumstances in which the register can be altered or rectified appear to be very wide, as under the LRA 1925, the 2002 Act limits the right to alter the register against a registered proprietor who is in physical possession[1]. (A registered proprietor who is a landlord, mortgagor, licensor or trustee is to be treated as being in possession where the land is occupied by a tenant, mortgagee, licensee or beneficiary respectively[2].) In these circumstances the register cannot be altered without his or her consent unless either the registered proprietor has by fraud or lack of proper care caused or substantially contributed to the mistake, or where it would be unjust not to rectify[3].

> [1] LRA 2002, s 131(1).
> [2] LRA 2002, s 131(2).
> [3] LRA 2002, Sch 4, paras 3(2) and 6(2).

Indemnity

35.44 Schedule 8 governs the payment of an indemnity. It is now tied to rectification, ie the correction of a mistake that adversely affects the title of the registered proprietor (and to a refusal to rectify that causes loss)[1]. A close consideration of the other alterations that can be made to the register show that these do not, in fact, cause loss to the registered proprietor. This is because they give effect to rights that would in any event have been binding; the alteration is being made in order to ensure that the register truly reflects the existing position. An indemnity is also available if loss is caused where the registry has made certain specified errors, notably if a mistake in making an official search[2] is made by the registry.

The indemnity payable where the applicant has caused or substantially contributed to the loss by fraud or lack of proper care may be reduced to such extent as is just and equitable.[3]

> [1] LRA 2002, Sch 8, para 1(1)(a).
> [2] LRA 2002, Sch 8, para 1(1)(b)–(g).
> [3] LRA 2002, Sch 8, para 5.

REGISTERED LAND: KEY POINTS

- Once title to land is registered the rules governing the enforceability of third party rights are those contained in the LRA 2002.

- A purchaser from a registered proprietor is bound only by registered charges, interests that are listed in Sch 3 as 'overriding', and interests that are protected by an entry on the register.

- A purchaser who becomes the registered proprietor following a first registration is bound by a slightly wider range of rights.

- A registered charge is a legal mortgage; it will be entered on the Land Register.

- Interests that are override rights that are not entered on the register and will always bind a purchaser; they are listed in Sch 3. The most important of these are:
  - legal leases for seven years or less;
  - proprietary rights of persons in obvious occupation of the property;
  - legal easements and profits à prendre that have not been expressly created; thus the only legal easements that are overriding are those that are created under s 62 LPA 1925, by implication, or by prescription.

- Interests protected by an entry on the register are, on the whole, those third party rights that cannot be overriding. Entry on the register is either by way of 'notice' or 'restriction':
  - a notice can be agreed or unilateral and can be used in respect of most third party rights apart from beneficial interests under a trust; the effect of a notice is to render the right in question binding on any purchaser;
  - a restriction does not make the right in question binding on a purchaser but is designed to ensure that correct procedures are followed. Classically it is used where there is a trust of land and will guarantee that a purchaser knows that it is essential to deal with at least two trustees so that overreaching takes place.

- Registration with absolute title is not a complete guarantee that the title is as entered on the register since the register can be altered or rectified; however, the circumstances in which this can be done are extremely limited and where it does occur an indemnity may well be paid.

Questions

1. For the purposes of enforceability, how are rights to unregistered land classified?

2. How are rights to registered land classified?

3. If an interest is one that 'overrides', what does this mean for a purchaser?

4. What legal requirements must be satisfied for the right of a person in occupation of registered land to bind a purchaser?

5. What is a 'notice' under the registered land system and what forms can it take?

6. What is a 'restriction' and what is its effect?

7. Does a registered proprietor with absolute title have a complete guarantee that the title is as reflected by the register?

8. Whiteacres—a large country estate—was recently sold by Philip (its registered proprietor) to Primrose who has been registered as the new proprietor. Primrose, who was abroad at the time of the sale has only just moved in. She discovers that one of the cottages on the estate is being occupied by Daphne, Philip's ex-wife; Daphne claims that he told her that she could live there for the rest of her life. Gerald, the owner of Blackacres—the neighbouring estate, tells her that next week his gamekeeper and a large party of his guests will be using one of the roads across Whiteacres to get to a stretch of river on Blackacres; he explains that this has been going on for years. There is no mention of Daphne or Gerald's alleged rights on the land register. Advise Primrose on her legal position.

PART V

The law of landlord and tenant

36

Landlord and tenant: the general law

CHAPTER OVERVIEW

Leasehold ownership is widespread across all the main property sectors—residential, commercial, industrial and agricultural. In this chapter we deal with:

- the essential features of leasehold ownership;
- the most commonly encountered of the obligations (ie covenants) imposed in a lease;
- the remedies available to both landlord and tenant in the event of a breach of covenant;
- the circumstances in which lease covenants are enforceable against those to whom either the lease or the landlord's interest (the reversion) may be transferred; and
- the termination of leases at common law.

36.1 We have, so far, given only passing consideration to leasehold ownership when dealing with the doctrine of estates[1] and the formal[2] and informal[3] creation of interests in land. This may have given a misleading impression for such ownership is widespread in England and Wales. The lease obviously provides an important medium through which essentially short-term occupation of both residential and commercial property can be enjoyed without the need for a capital contribution to its purchase. However, the long-term lease (eg for 99 years or even 999 years) for which a capital sum (known as a 'premium') is normally paid is commonplace. Such leases became, in the 20th century, a popular device for financing the development of land and for investing in land. In addition, they are still the usual mechanism for the occupation of a unit within a building (notably flats); this is because, as we have seen, obligations imposed under a lease are more readily enforceable against future owners of that lease than they would be if imposed on a freeholder.[4] However, as we have also seen[5], the Commonhold and Leasehold Reform Act 2002 introduces a new form of ownership—the commonhold—which is specifically (but not exclusively) aimed at facilitating the freehold ownership of flats. This came into force in 2004 and, given its disappointing take up[6], it will take many years before long leases of flats disappear.

[1] Para 28.35.
[2] Paras 29.11 and 29.12.
[3] Paras 30.3–30.5.
[4] Para 33.4 and para 36.72, note 1.
[5] Para 28.34.
[6] Para 28.34.

Characteristics of leasehold interests

36.2 In order for a lease to arise, exclusive possession of a defined area of land for a certain or ascertainable period of time must be conferred. Any occupation of land which fails to display these characteristics cannot be a lease and the occupier is a mere licensee.[1] While it is usual for rent to be paid this is not legally essential.[2] As will become apparent, the distinction between a lease and a licence has been fraught with difficulties because landowners have sought to devise agreements to occupy which do *not* amount to leases in order to avoid the statutory protection which is conferred on many tenants (but not on licensees).[3]

If a lease is to confer a legal estate it must comply with the required formalities; as we have seen, for leases in excess of three years a deed must be used, while those for three years or less may be created orally or in writing, provided that they take effect in possession[4] and are at the best rent reasonably obtainable.[5] A lease for a term in excess of seven years must always be registered with its own independent title[6]. Leases which fail to comply with these formal requirements may nevertheless take effect in equity.[7]

   [1] Paras 36.3–36.11.
   [2] *Ashburn Anstalt v Arnold* [1988] 2 All ER 147, CA.
   [3] The problem has diminished since the implementation of the Housing Act 1988; this Act has significantly reduced the protection given to residential tenants with the result that, since 1989, landowners have been happy to grant short-term tenancies of residential property. See paras 37.4–37.11.
   [4] A lease not exceeding three years which is to take effect on a future date must be created by deed; see *Long v London Borough of Tower Hamlets* [1996] 2 All ER 683 and para 29.9, note 1. Furthermore if it is to commence more than three months after the date on which it is created, it must also be registered with its own title, see para 29.15.
   [5] Paras 29.11 and 29.12.
   [6] LRA 2002, s 4 and para 29.15.
   [7] Paras 30.3–30.5.

Certainty of term

36.3 The requirement that a lease must be of certain duration means that, at the outset, it must have a certain commencement date[1] and a certain or ascertainable maximum duration (often referred to as 'certainty of term'). These days most leases are for a fixed term, eg for five years, and no problems of certainty of term arise. However, from time to time cases arise where leases have been granted for a period measured by reference to an uncertain event. Periodic tenancies have also given rise to difficulties on the question of certainty. In addition, the LPA 1925 deals specifically with some unusual types of lease which might otherwise be regarded as uncertain, in order to bring them within the framework of modern leasehold ownership.

   [1] *Harvey v Pratt* [1965] 1 WLR 1025.

Fixed-term leases

36.4 A fixed-term lease is one which is granted for a predetermined period of time. It is not necessary for the term to be continuous; thus there is a valid lease where a holiday home is let on a 'time-share' basis for one week per year for 80 years.[1] A fixed-term lease cannot be certain if it is expressed to last until an event which either may or may not happen, or which will happen but at an unpredictable date. So for example, a lease which was expressed to last for the duration of the war was declared to be void by the Court of Appeal in *Lace v Chantler*.[2] This rule was affirmed by the House of Lords in *Prudential Assurance Co v London Residuary Body*.[3] Here a lease granted until the land was required for road widening was held to be void for uncertainty.[4] Their Lordships emphatically rejected any suggestion[5] that a term can be certain where the event which is to bring about the termination of the lease is within the control of one of the parties.

Where a fixed-term lease is held to be void for uncertainty of term, the agreed 'lease' is of no effect but, provided the tenant has taken up occupation and paid rent, an implied periodic tenancy will arise.[6] This tenancy can be terminated by the service of an appropriate notice to quit. The courts will *not* imply that such a notice can only be served in the circumstances which would have brought about the end of the intended fixed term, since this would render the periodic tenancy uncertain. So, in the *Prudential* case, the tenants were held to be yearly tenants; the defendant landlords were entitled immediately to serve six months' notice to quit and were not obliged to wait until the land was required for road widening before serving such a notice.

---

[1] *Cottage Holiday Associates Ltd v Customs and Excise Comrs* [1983] QB 735. Note that such discontinuous leases *may* now be registered with their own title, see para 29.16.

[2] [1944] 1 All ER 305, CA.

[3] [1992] 3 All ER 504, HL.

[4] It is worth noting that the desired object can be achieved in such cases without offending the rule on certainty of term by including a 'break' provision (as to which see para 36.95); for example, in *Prudential*, the parties could have expressed the lease to be for, say, 99 years subject to a landlord's right to break when the land was required for road widening.

[5] See *Ashburn Anstalt v Arnold* [1988] 2 All ER 147, CA.

[6] See para 36.14.

Periodic tenancies

36.5 Periodic tenancies[1]—for example, weekly, monthly or yearly tenancies—do not determine (end) automatically at the end of the period, be it week or month or year, but continue from week to week, month to month, year to year, until ended by appropriate notice.[2] Thus, in one sense, at the outset of the tenancy its maximum duration is unknown and it has been said that the simple statement that the maximum duration of a term must be certainly known in advance of its taking effect does not directly apply to periodic tenancies.[3] However, this view has now been rejected by the House of Lords in the *Prudential* case.[4] Here it was held that periodic tenancies are subject to the same rule on certainty as fixed terms. A periodic tenancy is normally sufficiently certain because each party has the right to terminate it at the end of any period of the tenancy. Equally, such a tenancy will be valid where, at the beginning of the tenancy, it is agreed that one side cannot serve a notice to quit until after a *certain* time limit has elapsed (eg that the landlord will not serve a notice to quit for at least one year).[5] However, any agreement preventing one side determining the tenancy for an *uncertain* period (eg that the landlord will only serve a notice to quit if the property is required for the landlord's personal use) is not permitted.[6] Equally, a term under which the landlord can only serve a notice to quit provided the tenant is in breach of covenant, is also invalid[7]. A provision purporting to prohibit absolutely the giving of notice by one party is repugnant to the nature of the tenancy and therefore invalid.[8]

---

[1] As to periodic tenancies generally, see para 36.14.

[2] Para 36.95 below, and note, in particular, ch 37 as to the statutory regulation of the termination of tenancies.

[3] *Re Midland Rly Co's Agreement* [1971] 1 All ER 1007; see also *Ashburn Anstalt v Arnold* [1988] 2 All ER 147, CA.

[4] *Prudential Assurance Co v London Residuary Body* [1992] 3 All ER 504, HL, overruling *Midland Rly Co's Agreement* [1971] 1 All ER 1007 and *Ashburn Anstalt v Arnold* [1988] 2 All ER 147, CA on this point.

[5] *Prudential Assurance Co v London Residuary Body* [1992] 3 All ER 504, HL.

[6] *Prudential Assurance Co v London Residuary Body* [1992] 3 All ER 504, HL.

[7] *Berrisford v Mexfield Housing Co-operative Ltd* [2010] EWCA Civ 811.

[8] *Centaploy Ltd v Matlodge Ltd* [1973] 2 All ER 720.

Leases for life

36.6 Prior to 1926, it was possible to create a lease for life, despite the fact that such a term is far from certain. As a result of the LPA 1925, s 149(6), an attempt to create such a lease, at a rent or for a premium, now results in the grant of a 90-year term which may be ended after the death of the tenant by one month's notice in writing given on one of the usual quarter days (25 March, 24 June, 29 September, and 25 December).[1] This same rule applies to leases determinable on the marriage of the tenant.

[1] For a modern application of this provision see *Skipton Building Society v Clayton* (1993) 25 HLR 596, CA; here it was held that an arrangement whereby, in return for the grant of an option to purchase at one-third market value, a couple were to be given a right to occupy a property for their joint lives fell within s 149(6).

Perpetually renewable leases

36.7 Again, prior to 1926, it was permissible to grant a lease conferring on the tenant the right to have the lease renewed on the expiry of the existing term over and over again. Such leases were, by the Law of Property Act 1922, s 145 and Sch 15 converted into terms of 2,000 years commencing with the beginning of the then existing term. Any perpetually renewable lease granted since 1926 is likewise to take effect as a 2,000-year term. The term created by the statute is subject to the provision that the tenant may terminate the lease on 10 days' notice ending on a date on which it would have expired had it not been converted. It is, of course, highly unlikely that a landlord would deliberately create a perpetually renewable lease and the court leans against finding that a lease contains a perpetual right of renewal.[1] However, this may be the only possible conclusion, as is demonstrated by *Re Hopkin's Lease, Caerphilly Concrete Products Ltd v Owen*,[2] where a landlord granted a lease, for a term of five years at a rent of £10 per annum, containing a covenant to renew the lease at the same rent and subject to the same covenants, including the covenant to renew, with the result that the lease was perpetually renewable; the landlord had inadvertently created a 2,000-year term at a rent of £10 per annum.

[1] *Marjorie Burnett v Barclay* (1980) 258 Estates Gazette 642.
[2] [1972] 1 All ER 248 CA.

Exclusive possession

36.8 For a person to be regarded as having a leasehold interest in property, it is essential that they should have exclusive possession of a defined area of land.[1] There can be no lease where a landowner has the right to move the occupier to alternative accommodation.[2] Exclusive possession means that the tenant must have the right to exclude all others from the property, including the landlord. It is a fundamental principle that the landlord may only enter the property either with the permission of the tenant or under a right of entry[3] conferred by the lease. Without exclusive possession there can be no lease, only a licence. The latter confers only a personal permission to occupy property but does not give the occupier a stake in the property.[4]

[1] See *Clear Channel UK Ltd v Manchester City Council* [2006] 04 EG 168 where an agreement for the placement of advertising stations was held not to be a lease since there was no precise location for each of the stations.
[2] *Westminster City Council v Clarke* [1992] 1 All ER 695, HL.
[3] Such a right is of a limited nature and allows entry only for specified purposes, eg to inspect for repairs.
[4] *Marchant v Charters* [1977] 3 All ER 918, CA; para 28.41.

The distinction between a lease and a licence

36.9 The issue we are concerned with here is not simply an academic question of the difference between a personal right and a proprietary right, but also the practical question of whether in a given case a person is in occupation of property as a licensee or as a tenant. In some cases, particularly of shared occupation of residential premises, the grant of a licence to each occupier is more appropriate than the grant of a tenancy. However, the question has more often arisen where a landowner has deliberately sought to 'dress up' a lease as a licence in order to prevent the occupier qualifying for the statutory protection which is conferred on many tenants. This used to be a particular problem in the residential sector because of the extremely beneficial nature of the protection conferred by the Rent Act 1977 and its precursors;[1] this legislation has now been supplanted[2] by the Housing Act 1988[3] and landlords are not now seeking to use residential licences to the same extent. However, landlords of commercial property will sometimes seek to avoid the provisions of Pt II of the Landlord and Tenant Act 1954 by granting purported licences; furthermore, the application of other statutory regimes often distinguish between leases and licences[4]. In addition, licensees do not have the benefit of covenants that are statutorily implied into some tenancies, notably those requiring the landlord to keep the premises in repair[5].

In considering whether a transaction constitutes a licence or a tenancy, the court is to have regard not to the label ('lease' or 'licence') which the parties give to the document but to the substance of the transaction.[6] As Lord Templeman pointed out in a now famous dictum in *Street v Mountford*,[7] 'The manufacture of a five-pronged implement for manual digging results in a fork even if the manufacturer ... insists that he intended to make and has made a spade.'[8] In other words, if the parties' agreement has the hallmarks of a tenancy, it is a tenancy, even if the parties by their agreement 'intend' to enter into a licence.

The hallmarks of a tenancy are, according to the House of Lords, exclusive possession, for a fixed or periodic term, at a rent.[9] Since Mrs Mountford's agreement with Mr Street was admitted to give her exclusive possession of rooms owned by Mr Street at a rent for a term, she was a tenant even though she had signed an agreement under which she expressly accepted that it was only a licence which gave her no protection as a Rent Act tenant. Accordingly, subject to limited exceptions,[10] since *Street v Mountford*, the courts need only inquire whether or not an agreement to occupy confers exclusive possession (for a fixed or periodic term).

However, once it was made clear that the absence of exclusive possession precluded the grant of a tenancy, it became common for landlords wishing to avoid the provisions of protective legislation to make use of agreements which either stated that exclusive possession was not conferred, or which contained provisions which were designed to have the effect of taking away exclusive possession. So, for example, there might be included a term under which the owner was given the right to share the property with the occupier, or one which prevented the occupier from using the property during, say, the hours of 12 noon and 2 pm. Where a court is satisfied that terms of this kind do not truly represent the intentions of the parties (ie that they are 'sham' terms), they will be ignored and the occupier will be a tenant.[11] However, where, for example, the landlord provides attendance or services[12] which require the landlord or his employees to exercise unrestricted access to and use of the premises, or where access is genuinely needed in the particular circumstances,[13] the occupier will not have exclusive possession and will be a mere licensee.

[1] See para 37.3.
[2] The RA 1977 continues to apply to tenancies granted prior to 15 January 1989; accordingly the lease/licence distinction remains vital in such cases.

[3] See paras 37.4–37.11.

[4] See ch 37.

[5] See paras 36.45 and 36.46.

[6] *Shell-Mex and BP Ltd v Manchester Garages Ltd* [1971] 1 All ER 841 and 845.

[7] [1985] 2 All ER 289, HL.

[8] [1985] 2 All ER 289 at 299.

[9] [1985] 2 All ER 289 at 306. That is not to say that the payment of rent is an essential prerequisite of a tenancy, but rather that if the three hallmarks are present there is a tenancy: *Ashburn Anstalt v Arnold* [1988] 2 All ER 147, CA. 'Rent' does not include a mere contribution to the household expenses (eg to gas and electricity bills) of the property owner: *Bostock v Bryant* (1990) 22 HLR 449, CA.

[10] In *Street v Mountford* [1985] 2 All ER 289 it was acknowledged that there may be occasions when an occupier has exclusive possession yet is merely a licensee. Two situations referred to in that case were that of a service occupier (ie an employee who occupies employer's premises in order better to perform their duties as an employee) and where occupation has been conferred as an act of friendship or generosity (which negatives any intention to enter into legal relations and hence negatives the existence of a tenancy).

[11] See, for example, *Aslan v Murphy (Nos 1 and 2)* [1989] 3 All ER 130, CA.

[12] Such as cleaning the room and changing the linen: *Marchant v Charters* [1977] 3 All ER 918, CA.

[13] *Westminster City Council v Clarke* [1992] 1 All ER 695, HL.

36.10 *Sharers* In one particular situation the courts faced further difficulties in determining whether or not an occupier enjoyed exclusive possession. Where the use of accommodation was to be shared, landowners commonly required each sharer to sign a separate (but often identical) agreement conferring a right to occupy the whole of the premises, subject to the rights of the other occupiers. In this way it could be argued that none of the sharers had exclusive possession; each destroyed the others' exclusive possession. Not surprisingly, this matter came before the House of Lords in 1988 when appeals in two cases, *AG Securities v Vaughan* and *Antoniades v Villiers* were heard together.[1] Here it was decided that, in such instances, the approach should be two-stage. First, it should be decided whether or not the signing of *separate* agreements was genuine. If so, each sharer would have an individual, but not exclusive, right to use the property and could only be a licensee. However, if the signing of separate agreements was itself a pretence, then the sharers should be regarded as having together signed a single agreement; if this agreement genuinely conferred exclusive possession the sharers would be joint tenants.

In *AG Securities* four individuals sharing a four-bedroomed flat in a London mansion block, signed separate licence agreements at different times on different terms. They had not known each other prior to moving in to the flat. In these circumstances there was no artificiality about the separate agreements; it was clear that the purpose and intention of both parties to each agreement was that it should confer an individual right on the licensee named. Each was individually liable for the amount of rent to which he had agreed which, in that case, differed from the amounts paid by the others. There had been no grant of exclusive possession of any identifiable part of the flat to any individual and so each was a licensee.[2]

By way of contrast, in the *Antoniades* case, the defendant and a woman friend each signed a separate agreement for the occupation of a small one-bedroomed flat. Each agreement provided that the licensee was to have the use of the flat 'in common with the licensor and such other licensees or invitees as the licensor may permit from time to time to use the rooms'. The House of Lords found that there was an air of total unreality about these 'separate' documents, given the fact that the appellants were together seeking a flat as a quasi-matrimonial home. The documents were a pretence designed to disguise the true character of the agreement which, their Lordships held, should be regarded as a single contract. As the parties' subsequent conduct indicated, there was never any intention on the part of the landlord to share possession (either by himself or by introducing others) with the couple, who together had exclusive possession and were, therefore, joint tenants.

¹ [1988] 3 All ER 1058, HL.
² See also *Stribling v Wickham* (1989) 21 HLR 381, CA.

36.11 *Business premises* There is no suggestion that the approach to deciding whether the occupation of business premises is by way of lease or licence is any different in principle from that adopted in respect of residential property. In practice the issue is usually whether the landowner has retained such control over the premises as to preclude the grant of exclusive possession.¹ It can also happen that the occupation and use of commercial premises is dressed up to look like a licence when, in reality, the arrangement is a lease.²

¹ See *Shell-Mex and BP Ltd v Manchester Garages Ltd* [1971] 1 WLR 612 where the claimant retained extensive control over the management and layout of a petrol station and was held to have granted only a licence to the defendant. See also *National Car Parks Ltd v Trinity Development Co* [2001] 2 EGLR 43.
² See *Dellneed Ltd v Chin* [1987] 1 EGLR 75 where a so called 'management agreement' was held to be a sham; in the court's view the claimant was setting up its own independent business and was in truth a tenant.

CHARACTERISTICS OF LEASEHOLD INTERESTS: KEY POINTS

- A person who occupies land belonging to another will only be regarded as holding a legal lease where the following requirements are met:
  - The occupation is to be for a certain or ascertainable period.
  - The occupier is to enjoy exclusive possession.
- Where these requirements are not met the occupier has only a licence; a licensee does not have the benefit of most of the implied or statutory rights conferred on tenants and, in particular, does not enjoy any statutory security of tenure when the licence comes to an end.
- Where these requirements are met but the correct formalities have not been complied with, the occupier will often have an equitable lease.
- In cases where a landowner may be trying to dress up occupation as a licence rather than a lease the courts will be astute to detect and then disregard sham terms.

Particular types of tenancy

36.12 The great majority of leases are created expressly and tend, these days, to be for a fixed term. That said, periodic tenancies remain common, particularly in the residential sector. While many of these are expressly created, they also often come into being by way of implication. In this section we also consider a number of anomalous forms of tenancy and, finally, we explain forms of lease under which the tenant does not necessarily take an immediate entitlement to physical occupation.

Fixed-term leases

36.13 This is the simplest and most common form of lease. It arises where the tenancy is granted for a pre-determined period, eg for six months, for five years or for 99 years. The law sets no minimum or maximum period for such leases; all that is required is that the period of time for which the lease is to last is certain or ascertainable at the outset.[1] When the term for which the lease has been granted expires, the lease comes to an end automatically without the need for notice.[2] A fixed term lease must, in principle, run its course; it can only be brought to an end before the end of the term:

- by the agreement of the parties (ie a surrender[3]);

- where the tenant is in breach, by the exercise by the landlord of a right of re-entry (ie forfeiture[4]); or

- by the exercise, where present, of an option to terminate (usually known as a 'break clause')[5].

[1] See para 36.4.
[2] See para 36.95 below, but note that statutory protection may mean that the tenant does not have to leave the premises, see ch 37.
[3] See para 36.92.
[4] See paras 36.63–36.67 and 36.70.
[5] Para 36.95.

Periodic tenancies

36.14 A periodic tenancy is one which continues automatically from period to period until terminated by either side serving an appropriate notice to quit.[1] It is not a series of renewed tenancies but one continuous term which will run until brought to an end.[2] The most commonly encountered periodic tenancies are weekly, monthly and yearly tenancies. Such tenancies must, by definition, have a minimum duration of the initial period; as we have seen,[3] its maximum duration remains unknown until a notice to quit is actually served.[4]

Periodic tenancies are usually created expressly but may arise by implication.[5] A person allowed into occupation of property as a tenant, without any express agreement as to the duration of the tenancy, will be treated initially as a tenant at will.[6] If rent is then paid and accepted, an implied periodic tenancy, based on the periods by reference to which that rent is calculated, may then arise. Thus if the rent is fixed at £1,000 per annum, a yearly tenancy arises even if the rent is paid at more frequent intervals; if rent is fixed at £20 per week, a weekly tenancy arises.[7] As the case of *Manfield & Sons Ltd v Botchin*[8] shows, there is no room for the implication of a periodic tenancy where the parties expressly provide that the tenancy should remain at will. Furthermore, modern cases stress that whether or not a periodic tenancy arises as a result of the payment of rent depends on the intention of the parties.[9] Such an intention is particularly difficult to establish where a prospective tenant is allowed into occupation while in the course of negotiating a lease of the premises.[10] Furthermore, where a tenant is entitled by virtue of statutory protection to remain in occupation following the determination of a previous tenancy, it is now unusual for the court to imply a periodic tenancy.[11]

[1] For notices to quit see para 36.95.
[2] *Hammersmith and Fulham London Borough Council v Monk* [1992] 1 All ER 1, HL.
[3] Para 36.5.
[4] However, the fact that either side can ascertain the maximum term by serving a notice to quit is sufficient to render periodic tenancies sufficiently certain; see para 36.5
[5] Periodic tenancies are almost invariably legal. Provided the period on which the tenancy is based does not itself exceed three years (which would be very unusual) no formalities are required; LPA 1925 s 54(2), para 29.12.
[6] See para 36.15.
[7] See *Ladies' Hosiery and Underwear Ltd v Parker* [1930] 1 Ch 304.
[8] [1970] 3 All ER 143.
[9] *Javad v Aqil* [1991] 1 All ER 243, CA.

[10]   *Javad v Aqil* [1991] 1 All ER 243, CA and see para 36.14.

[11]   *Harvey v Stagg* (1977) 247 Estates Gazette 463, CA; *Longrigg, Burrough and Trounson v Smith* (1979) 251 Estates Gazette 847, CA.

Tenancy at will

36.15   A tenancy at will occurs where a person is let into, or allowed to remain in, possession of property as a tenant by the landlord on the basis that either side may terminate the arrangement whenever they wish. It may arise where a purchaser of the freehold is permitted to occupy the property prior to completion of the transaction or where a prospective tenant is allowed into occupation while the parties continue negotiating the detailed terms of the lease,[1] or where a fixed-term tenant is permitted to remain in occupation after the expiry of the term.[2] Consequently, it has been suggested by Scarman LJ in *Heslop v Burns*,[3] that it may be that the tenancy at will can now serve only one legal purpose, and that is to provide for occupation of property during a period of transition. It was certainly made clear in *Javad v Aqil*[4] that, in such a transitional situation, the court may conclude that the parties only intended a tenancy at will even though rent has been paid and accepted.[5] Although a tenancy at will often arises by implication, such a tenancy may be expressly granted, as in *Manfield & Sons Ltd v Botchin*[6] where such a tenancy was granted pending the landlord's application for planning permission to develop the site. An express tenancy at will may provide for the payment of rent by the tenant, in which case there will be no implication of a periodic tenancy.[7] If no provision is made for rent to be paid, the landlord is entitled to compensation for the use and occupation of the property.

[1]   *Javad v Aqil* [1991] 1 All ER 243.

[2]   Unless the tenant is staying in occupation by virtue of statutory protection; see ch 37.

[3]   [1974] 3 All ER 406 at 416.

[4]   [1991] 1 All ER 243, CA.

[5]   As opposed to a periodic tenancy; see para 36.14.

[6]   [1970] 3 All ER 143.

[7]   Para 36.14.

Tenancy at sufferance

36.16   A tenant at sufferance is, at common law, someone who wrongfully remains in possession ('holds over') without the landlord's consent after the tenancy has come to an end. Such a person is in effect a trespasser. The landlord may at any time claim possession of the property. The tenant at sufferance is essentially in the position of a 'squatter',[1] though liable under statute[2] to pay either a payment calculated at double the rental value of the property or, in certain circumstances, double the rent payable under the lease, for holding over in the face of a notice to quit. In practice, many tenants who hold over after the end of their tenancies do so by virtue of statutory protection[3] and are not, therefore, tenants at sufferance.

[1]   Para 30.36.

[2]   Landlord and Tenant Act 1730; Distress for Rent Act 1733.

[3]   Chapter 37.

Tenancy by estoppel

36.17   Where a person who has no power to do so purports to grant a lease or tenancy, they and the 'tenant' are estopped (ie prevented by the rules of evidence) from denying the validity of the 'lease'. Thus, as between the parties, a tenancy by estoppel has all the features of a valid tenancy; it will similarly bind assigns of the parties but will not bind third parties. A tenancy by estoppel could arise where a purchaser of land is allowed into possession prior to completion of the transaction and then purports to grant a lease, or where a mortgagor (borrower) purports to grant a lease where the power to do so has been excluded.[1] In the former case, the subsequent acquisition of the freehold estate by the purchaser is said to 'feed the estoppel' and confers on the tenant a valid tenancy.

 [1] Para 34.39.

Concurrent leases

36.18 A concurrent lease (sometimes called a 'side-by-side' lease, or a lease of the reversion) arises where a lease is granted which is to commence before the expiry of an existing lease of the same premises granted to another person. Accordingly the concurrent lessee becomes the landlord of the existing tenant. A concurrent lessee is entitled to receive the rent and to enforce the tenant's covenants and is obliged to honour the landlord's obligations under the existing lease. If the existing lease expires before the concurrent lease then the concurrent lessee becomes entitled, at that time, to physical possession of the property. If not, the concurrent lessee is only ever entitled to receive the income produced by the existing lease. The concurrent lease is thus a device by which income under an existing lease can be assigned for a fixed period of time, with or without any right to future physical occupation.

Reversionary leases

36.19 A reversionary lease is one which is granted now but which is to take effect at a future date, eg a lease for five years granted on 1 June 2011, to commence on 1 September 2011. A person may not create, or make a contract to create, a lease which is to take effect in possession more than 21 years after the date of the lease.[1] In order to create a legal estate, a reversionary lease must always be made by deed[2]. Where the lease is not to commence for at least three months, it must always[3] be registered with its own title.[4]

 [1] LPA 1925, s 149(3).
 [2] The 'short lease' exception, whereby leases of three years or less can be created orally or in writing applies only to leases taking *immediate* effect; see *Long v London Borough of Tower Hamlets* [1996] 2 All ER 683 and para 29.12, note 1.
 [3] Even if for a term of seven years or less, see para 29.15.
 [4] LRA 1925, s 4.

PARTICULAR TYPES OF TENANCY: KEY POINTS

- In modern times most leases are for a fixed term although periodic tenancies are still common.

- A fixed term tenancy is for a pre-determined period of time. It must normally run its course and will, at common law, end automatically on its contractual term date. A fixed term lease can normally only be brought to an end early by an agreed surrender, by the exercise of a contractual right to break, or by the landlord forfeiting the lease on account of the tenant's breach of covenant.

- A periodic tenancy is one that is granted for a period which automatically renews itself until terminated by either side serving a notice to quit.

- Other forms of lease are tenancies at will, tenancies at sufferance, tenancies by estoppel and concurrent and reversionary leases.

Rights and obligations under a lease: an introduction

36.20 In practice a lease does much more than simply confer ownership for a limited period; it imposes a range of rights and obligations on the parties. These will vary according to the length of the lease and the nature of the property. Where a lease is of very short duration the landlord will wish to impose strict controls on the tenant, but will invariably have to accept responsibility for the upkeep of the property. Where it is relatively long and at a market rent, a landlord of prime property will wish to impose such restrictions as are necessary to protect the value of their investment while, where possible, imposing substantial obligations on the tenant for the repair and maintenance of the premises. A landlord of secondary or tertiary property may well have to compromise on these aspirations. Where a lease is granted at a premium for a very long term (and thus very similar in economic terms to a freehold), the restrictions on the tenant will tend to be minimal; however they will be expected to carry all the responsibility for the upkeep of the property.

The primary source of the rights and obligations of the landlord and the tenant is, of course, the lease itself. The terms of a lease are usually referred to as 'covenants', whether or not the lease was made by deed, even though, strictly speaking, that word is reserved for contractual terms contained in a deed. It is possible, but increasingly unlikely, that nothing will be expressly agreed by the parties to the lease, other than its duration and the rent. In such a case, as we shall see, only the most minimal terms will be implied by the law. It is therefore preferable that the parties should agree terms for themselves even where the tenancy is only to be of very short duration.

Lease negotiations

Introduction

36.21 It should be borne in mind that, when negotiating the terms of a lease, both legal and commercial factors will affect the outcome, as will the state of the market. An occupier will become a tenant of premises in one of two ways, either by taking a new lease of premises from the owner thereof, or by taking an assignment of an existing lease from a tenant who no longer wishes to occupy the property. The approach to negotiating a new lease differs markedly from that of an assignment. The freedom to negotiate the terms of a lease also differs according to whether the premises are commercial or residential.

New leases

36.22 Where a prospective tenant is looking to take a new lease of premises negotiations will be direct with the landlord or their agent. In principle everything is negotiable—the parties start with a blank page. In reality the position may well be very different. Many landlords expect a tenant to accept their standard lease, but this may be more or less negotiable depending on the state of the market and the attractiveness of the prospective tenant. However, where the premises are only part of a building, complex, or shopping centre the landlord will not wish a lease of part to differ in any significant way from the leases of other parts. Furthermore, where the landlord is a tenant, the new lease being negotiated is a sublease. The terms that can be offered in a sublease are often constrained by the terms of the landlord's own headlease.

Existing leases

36.23 An occupier seeking premises may, as an alternative to taking a new lease from a landlord, take over an existing lease from the current tenant; this is known as an assignment. Where the premises are commercial, this may involve the quite separate matter of taking over that tenant's business. More usually the incomer simply wants the premises for their own purposes. This situation is very different from a negotiation of a new lease with a landlord. Here the bargaining is in essence with the current tenant although there are likely to be some dealings with the landlord. The lease in question is an existing package; although there may be scope for the re-negotiation of some terms (which must necessarily have the agreement of the landlord) this is likely to be limited. Where the existing lease contains unattractive terms that the landlord will not amend (classically a rent that is now above current open market levels) the prospective tenant must either walk away from the deal or persuade the existing tenant to make a financial payment to sweeten the pill (usually referred to as a reverse premium).

Commercial premises

36.24 It is in the commercial sector that the parties are most free to decide for themselves what the terms of their lease should be. There is no standard form of business lease[1], although many landlords have their own favoured form of lease and, in any event, solicitors never draft leases completely from scratch—they have their own lease precedents (ie templates) which are amended to suit the particular circumstances.

Despite the absence of any legal constraint on the terms of business leases, the Government has, in recent years, sought to encourage the negotiation of more flexible terms. This started in the face of mounting complaints that the lease terms offered by many landlords were hindering tenants in the operation of their businesses. The process adopted has been the agreement of a series of voluntary codes, the most recent of which is the Code for Leasing Business Premises in England and Wales 2007. This is designed to encourage landlords to offer tenants more choice on lease terms and to make tenants (particularly those operating small businesses) more aware of property issues. This edition, which annexes a set of model heads of terms and an occupier's guide, is more strongly worded than its predecessors and contains a range of firm recommendations. These will be alluded to, where appropriate in the following paragraphs.

---

[1] Various organisations, including the Law Society and the British Property Federation, have produced a standard form of lease for short business lettings. There is no evidence that these are widely used.

Residential property

36.25 The freedom to negotiate the terms of residential leases has long been constrained by statutory intervention (notably in the area of repairs[1] and service charges[2]). Where a residential tenancy is offered on a non-negotiable basis (more usual in short-term lettings) the Unfair Terms in Consumer Contracts Regulations 1999[3] apply. This means that the terms must be drafted in plain and intelligible language and can be reviewed for fairness by the courts. The Office of Fair Trading issues regular guidance on the type of terms that might be regarded as unfair.

---

[1] See para 36.45.
[2] See para 36.60.
[3] See paras 9.22–9.30.

Flexibility through form: absolute, qualified and fully qualified covenants

36.26 Flexibility in lease terms can be achieved not simply by the content of the lease covenants but also by their form. Inevitably a landlord will require that some of the restrictions imposed on the tenant are absolute, ie the tenant is totally prevented from carrying out the activity. However, in many instances, it is perfectly acceptable that a restriction can be removed or modified with the landlord's agreement; in such cases it is preferable, from a tenant's point of view, that the landlord's consent cannot unreasonably be withheld. This protects the tenant from arbitrary or unreasonable decisions. So, for example, a lease may state that a tenant cannot erect signs on the outside of the demised premises; this is known as an 'absolute' covenant. If the covenant states that the signs cannot be erected without the landlord's consent, it is known as a 'qualified' covenant. If it provides that the signs cannot be put up without the landlord's consent which cannot unreasonably be withheld, the covenant is known as a 'fully qualified' covenant. As we shall see in the following paragraphs, a tenant is significantly more restricted by a covenant that is in the absolute form than by one that is fully qualified.

LEASE NEGOTIATIONS: KEY POINTS

- The approach to the negotiation of lease terms varies according to the type of property, the state of the market and a range of individual factors.

- The negotiation of a new lease is very different from the bargaining that can take place on the assignment of an existing lease.

- Landlords of commercial premises are being encouraged to be more flexible when granting a new lease; the 2007 Lease Code contains a range of recommendations as to the terms that should be offered.

- Statute constrains the terms of certain residential leases.

- Flexibility for the tenant can be achieved not just by the content of lease provisions but also by their form; an absolute covenant is much stricter than one that is fully qualified.

The principal lease covenants

36.27 As we have noted, it is usual these days for a lease expressly to set out the obligations of the parties. Only rarely will express terms be supplanted or modified by statute.[1] Equally, in those infrequent cases where the parties do not expressly agree what their obligations are to be, those implied by the law are minimal. Covenants commonly found in leases include:

- a covenant restricting assignment, sub-letting or parting with possession;
- covenants dealing with the use and enjoyment of the premises;
- covenants relating to the repair and alteration of the property;
- covenants governing outgoings such as rent (including rent review), service charges and insurance.

We shall briefly consider these, and certain implied covenants, in the ensuing paragraphs; for a more detailed treatment, readers are advised to consult a specialist textbook on the law of landlord and tenant.[2]

[1] Importantly statute does supplant or modify express repairing obligations in respect of short-term residential tenancies (see para 36.45) and service charges in residential leases (see para 36.60).

[2] See, for example, P F Smith *The Law of Landlord and Tenant* (6th edn) 2002.

Disposition

Assignment, sub-letting, or parting with possession

36.28 *The form of covenant* At common law a tenant is completely free to deal with the lease; this would include an assignment[1] (ie an outright transfer of the remainder of the lease), a subletting (the carving of shorter lease[2] out of their own lease), a parting with possession, or using the lease as security. In practice it is usual for the lease to restrict the tenant's rights of disposition. An absolute[3] covenant against any assignment or sub-letting, etc is usually only found in short tenancies. Longer[4] leases often absolutely prohibit assignments or subletting of *part* of the property, but it is usual to allow the assignment or sub-letting of the *whole* provided that the tenant first obtains the landlord's consent which is not to be unreasonably withheld.[5] Should the landlord unreasonably refuse consent the tenant may go ahead with the proposed assignment or sub-lease, or may apply to court for a declaration that the refusal is unreasonable and, as we shall see, claim damages for any losses suffered.

An assignment or sub-letting in breach of covenant does not affect the validity of the assignment or sub-lease, but may expose the assignee or sub-lessee to the risk of forfeiture.[6]

[1] Note that any assignment must be by deed (LPA 1925, s 52(1)) even where the lease itself was not required to be created by deed (LPA 1925, s 54(2)); see *Crago v Julian* [1992] 1 All ER 744, CA. As to the liability of the assignee on the covenants in the lease, see paras 36.74, 36.75, 36.77, 36.79 and 36.80.

[2] A purported sub-lease for a term equal to or exceeding that of the tenant, takes effect as an assignment; see *Milmo v Carreras* [1946] 1 All ER 288, CA.

[3] See para 36.26.

[4] In very long leases, ie those for which a premium was paid and only a ground rent reserved, the lease will often do no more than require the tenant to inform the landlord of any assignment.

[5] Where a covenant requires the landlord's prior consent to any disposition, but does *not* expressly provide that this consent is not to be unreasonably withheld, the Landlord and Tenant Act 1927, s 19(1) operates to achieve this effect.

[6] *Old Grovebury Manor Farm Ltd v W Seymour Plant Sales & Hire Ltd (No 2)* [1979] 3 All ER 504, [1979] 1 WLR 1397, CA; and see paras 36.63–36.66.

36.29 *The procedure for obtaining consent* In the past landlords could often frustrate tenants who wished to assign by the simple device of delaying any decision. This problem was addressed by the Landlord and Tenant Act 1988 which imposes certain statutory duties on a landlord whose consent to an assignment or sub-letting is required. The landlord must respond in writing, within a reasonable time, to the tenant's written application for consent, giving consent unless it is reasonable not to do so. Where the consent is conditional, the conditions (which must be reasonable) must be specified. Where consent is refused the reasons for that refusal (which must be reasonable) must be given. Breach of any of these duties gives rise to liability in tort for breach of statutory duty. This means that the tenant can obtain either damages[1] or a mandatory injunction against a dilatory or unreasonable landlord. It is also clear that a tenant who is confident that the landlord has either failed to respond within a reasonable time or unreasonably refused consent can go ahead with the transaction[2].

What is a reasonable time will depend on the facts of every case. In *Dong Bang Minerva v Davina Ltd*[3] it was held that 28 days was sufficient and this has become an approximate rule of thumb. The Court of Appeal has emphasised that, in unusual or complex cases, a reasonable time may sometimes have to be measured in weeks rather than days, but should always be measured in weeks rather than months.[4] The time limit does not start until the landlord has received any information from the tenant that is reasonably required, but the landlord cannot use this as a delaying tactic and must promptly request the further details.[5]

---

[1] Damages will normally be compensatory but, where the landlord is shown to have acted deliberately to prevent the assignment punitive or exemplary damages may be awarded, see *Design Progression Ltd v Thurloe Properties Ltd* [2004] EWHC 324 (Ch).

[2] *Norwich Union Life Insurance Society v Shopmoor Ltd* [1999] 1 WLR 531.

[3] [1995] 1 EGLR 41.

[4] See *Go West Ltd v Spigarolo* [2003] EWCA Civ 17, [2003] 2 All ER 141.

[5] *Norwich Union Life Insurance Society v Shopmoor Ltd* [1999] 1 WLR 531.

36.30 *The reasonableness test*[1] In any case where the reasonableness of a landlord's refusal is in issue it is now[2] for the landlord to show that consent was reasonably withheld. In considering this question it is assumed that the purpose of such a covenant is to protect the landlord from having their premises used or occupied in an undesirable way or by an undesirable tenant or assignee. The court will take account of the purpose of the covenant and all the circumstances, including the statutory background, at the time when the consent is sought. A landlord is entitled to give priority to their own interests although, where the consequences of a refusal for the tenant are particularly serious, this may not be the case[3]. Whether or not the landlord is acting unreasonably is a question of fact in every case; previous case law should, therefore, be regarded as laying down guidelines rather than binding precedents.[4] That said, a landlord's refusal of consent will usually be regarded as reasonable where there are genuine doubts about the proposed assignee's ability to pay the rent[5], or to remedy serious breaches of covenant committed by the current tenant[6]. A refusal will normally be justified if the assignee intends to use the premises in breach of the user covenant[7]. However, the landlord will be regarded as unreasonable where the refusal is designed to achieve 'collateral' objectives outside those secured by the terms of the lease[8]. So, a refusal was held to be unreasonable where a landlord was seeking to force the tenant to give up possession[9], as was one where the proposed assignee was occupying other premises owned by the same landlord which would be difficult to re-let[10]. However, landlords who have refused consent to an assignment which would breach their tenant mix policy have been held to be reasonable.[11]

---

[1] This test can be modified in respect of assignments of post-1995 business leases; see para 36.31.

[2] Landlord and Tenant Act 1988, ss 1(6) and 3(5).

[3] *International Drilling Fluids Ltd v Louisville Investments (Uxbridge) Ltd* [1986] 1 All ER 321, CA.

[4] *Ashworth Frazer Ltd v Gloucester City Council* [2001] UKHL 59, [2002] 1 All ER 377.

[5] *British Bakeries (Midlands) Ltd v Michael Testler & Co Ltd* [1986] 1 EGLR 64. See also *Royal Bank of Scotland v Victoria Street (No 3) Ltd* [2008] EWHC 3052 where it was held that a landlord is entitled to leave out of account any continuing liability of the outgoing tenant (as to which see paras 36.74 and 36.81).

[6] *Orlando Investments Ltd v Grosvenor Estate Belgravia* [1989] 2 EGLR 74, CA.

[7] *Ashworth Frazer Ltd v Gloucester City Council* [2001] UKHL 59, [2002] 1 All ER 377.

[8] *Bromley Park Garden Estates Ltd v Moss* [1982] 2 All ER 890. CA.

[9] *Bates v Donaldson* [1896] 2 QB 241, CA.

[10] *Re Gibbs and Houlder Bros' Lease* [1925] Ch 575, CA.

[11] See *Crown Estate Commissioners v Signet Group plc* [1996] 2 EGLR 200; *Moss Bros Group plc v CSC Properties Ltd* [1999] EGCS 47.

36.31 *The reasonableness test: post 1995 business leases* The reasonableness test outlined in the previous paragraph is usually modified in the case of leases of commercial and industrial[1] premises entered into on or after 1 January 1996. Here the landlord is permitted to specify in the lease any objectively verifiable circumstances[2] in which consent to an *assignment*[3] will be withheld. Where consent is later withheld, or subjected to conditions, in those specified circumstances the landlord's refusal (or any condition subject to which a consent has been given) is deemed to be reasonable.[4] A refusal of consent on a ground which has not been pre-specified in the lease can still be challenged as unreasonable under the principles outlined in the previous paragraph. It is clear that landlords have been making full use of this ability to control assignments more tightly; it has been standard practice to include in commercial and industrial leases a list of circumstances in which consent to an assignment can be refused, and conditions to which any consent may be subject.[5] In particular, leases invariably require that the outgoing tenant will always[6] enter into an authorised guarantee agreement.[7]

[1] The new law does not apply to residential or agricultural leases, Landlord and Tenant Act 1927, s 19(1A), added by the Landlord and Tenant (Covenants) Act 1995, s 22.

[2] Ie circumstances which are essentially factual and which do not involve any value judgment, eg 'consent to an assignment to a company will not be given unless that company is a plc'.

[3] The new law applies only to consent to *assignments*; it does not apply to sub-lettings and other types of disposition.

[4] Landlord and Tenant Act 1927, s 19(1A), added by the Landlord and Tenant (Covenants) Act 1995, s 22.

[5] It remains to be seen whether these practices will change. The Code for Leasing Business Premises in England and Wales 2007 recommends that pre-specified conditions should not normally be used.

[6] The 2007 Code states that business leases should no longer provide that authorised guarantee agreements are automatically required.

[7] For authorised guarantee agreements, see para 36.81.

36.32 *Covenants restricting subletting* It is usual for leases to restrict a tenant's right to create a sublease; in particular it is common to find that subleases of *part* of the premises are absolutely prohibited in leases to occupational tenants. Generally such covenants are subject to the statutory rules outlined in the previous paragraphs.[1] It should be noted that the modifications introduced for leases of commercial and industrial premises[2] do not apply to covenants restricting subletting. In an effort to gain more control over subletting than the ordinary reasonableness test permits, landlords of such premises have[3] often resorted to the imposition of pre-conditions. These effectively provide that the tenant has no right to sublet at all unless certain conditions are met[4]. Only then will the tenant have the right to sublet, subject to the landlord's consent which will not unreasonably be withheld. This device is legally effective[5], and is difficult for a tenant to get round.[6] It can seriously affect a tenant's ability to off load unwanted premises in difficult market conditions.[7]

[1] In particular, the Landlord and Tenant Act 1927, s 19(1) and the Landlord and Tenant Act 1988.

[2] See para 36.31.

[3] The use of pre-conditions was common prior to 2007. The Code for Leasing Business Premises in England and Wales 2007 recommends that they should not be used and a significant number of the members of the British Property Federation have declared that they will restrict their use of pre-conditions. It remains to be seen how effective these voluntary measures will be in limiting the practice.

[4] Typically, on conditions that any sublease is on the same terms as the lease and at the higher of either the passing rent under the lease or open market rent.

[5] *Allied Dunbar Assurance plc v Homebase Ltd* [2002] 2 EGLR 23, CA.

[6] In *Allied Dunbar Assurance plc v Homebase Ltd* [2002] 2 EGLR 23, CA the sublease reserved the same rent as under the lease but a side letter between the tenant and the subtenant agreed that a lower rent would

in fact be payable; this was held to be ineffective to side-step the pre-condition as to rent. In *NCR Ltd v Riverland Portfolio No 1 Ltd* [2004] EWHC 921 the tenant paid a reverse premium to the subtenant to compensate it for the above open market rent that it was to pay under the sublease; it was held that this did not breach a similar pre-condition.

⁷ If the current open market rental value of the premises has fallen below the passing rent the tenant will not be able to assign as an incoming tenant will not want to take over that rent. A subletting at open market rent would at least allow the tenant to offset its losses but is usually precluded by a pre-condition.

DISPOSITION COVENANTS: KEY POINTS

- It is usual for a lease to contain terms that limit the tenant's ability freely to deal with their lease.

- Disposition covenants can vary greatly depending on the length and nature of the particular lease.

- Although some covenants may be partly absolute, it is usual for the restriction to be largely fully qualified with the result that the tenant can assign etc with the landlord's prior consent, which cannot unreasonably be withheld. A disposition covenant that is drafted in the qualified form is converted by statute into a fully qualified one.

- When a tenant seeks permission to assign, sublet or part with possession the landlord is subject to certain statutory duties imposed by the LTA 1988. These require a landlord to respond within a reasonable time and to give consent where it is reasonable to do so. A breach of these duties will entitle a tenant to go ahead with the proposed transaction; if the transaction has fallen through the tenant will be able to claim damages.

- The general rule is that it is for the courts to decide whether or not a landlord is acting reasonably when refusing consent; the landlord of a post-1995 lease of business premises is allowed to spell out in the lease grounds on which consent to an assignment may be refused; a refusal on such a ground cannot be unreasonable.

- Landlords can provide that a tenant's right to sublet is subject to pre-conditions; these are not subject to the reasonableness test.

Use and enjoyment

36.33 A lease will impose a variety of obligations on both the landlord and the tenant that affect the use and enjoyment of the demised premises. Even in the absence of any express terms a landlord will be subject to an implied covenant for quiet enjoyment[1] and to an obligation not to derogate.[2] Similarly, all tenants are automatically bound to use the premises in a tenant-like manner.[3] In practice these implied obligations are supplemented or supplanted by express obligations as to the use of the property. These we consider in the following paragraphs.

[1] See para 36.34.
[2] See para 36.35.
[3] See para 36.42.

Landlord covenants

36.34 *Covenant for quiet enjoyment* This obligation on the part of the landlord is often expressly included; if not, it will be implied into all leases as being essential to the relationship of landlord and tenant. Its primary purpose is to ensure that the tenant enjoys the use of the leased property free from disturbance by adverse claimants to the property and free from substantial physical interference by the landlord.[1] The implied covenant for quiet enjoyment extends only to the acts of the landlord and those claiming under the landlord (such as other tenants of the same landlord). It does not apply to protect the tenant from any adverse rights arising from a title superior to the landlord's or granted by the landlord's predecessor in title[2]; an express covenant for quiet enjoyment is usually similarly limited but may be worded so as to give the tenant protection against the acts of a superior landlord.[3]

The covenant will be breached if it emerges that the landlord had no right to grant the lease, or is unable to give vacant possession to the tenant at the outset of the lease[4], or if the landlord interferes with the tenant's access to the premises during the course of the lease[5]. It is also clear that the landlord must have regard to the covenant for quiet enjoyment when carrying out any other obligations under the lease; so, for example, when carrying out repairs to the premises a landlord must take reasonable precautions to ensure that the tenant's use of the premises is not unduly disrupted[6]. The covenant may also be broken where the landlord (or their agents) carry out excessively prolonged and intrusive works in the vicinity of the demised premises.[7] Furthermore, it is apparent that, at least where the landlord undertakes a management role in respect of a community of tenants, they may be held responsible—under the covenant for quiet enjoyment—for failing to take steps against tenants whose activities are causing excessive disturbance to other tenants. So, for example, a landlord has been held liable where the way in which one of its tenants was operating her business seriously disrupted that of another tenant[8]. In another case, a landlord was required to compensate one of its tenants where it failed to enforce lease covenants restricting parking against the other neighbouring tenants[9].

However, there are limits to a landlord's liability. In particular, the covenant for quiet enjoyment does not protect a tenant from disturbance by other tenants arising from the state of the premises as they existed at the start of the lease. So, a landlord will not be liable to upgrade sound-proofing in a block of flats in order to prevent one tenant from being disturbed by a neighbouring tenant's normal use of his flat[10]. Furthermore, the covenant only protects a tenant's possession of the property;; it does not guard the tenant from interference with privacy or amenities[11].

A particular use of this covenant is as a means of gaining compensation for unlawful eviction and harassment. Thus, the landlord was held liable in damages for breach of this covenant in *Perera v Vandiyar*[12] where, with the object of driving the tenant out, he cut off the electricity and gas supplies to the premises. It should be noted that a landlord of a residential occupier who indulges in such harassment will often be guilty also of a criminal offence under the Protection from Eviction Act 1977, s 1,[13] as will a landlord who unlawfully evicts a tenant. Furthermore, acts of harassment often also amount to a tort such as trespass or nuisance, in which case there may, in appropriate circumstances, be an award of exemplary damages.[14] However, such claims have become unusual; a residential occupier who is driven to give up occupation as a result of harassment or eviction, now has a statutory right to damages under the Housing Act 1988, s 27, based on the difference in value of the landlord's interest with and without the occupier being in occupation. This section is being widely used and the cases indicate that it is producing awards of damages which far outstrip those gained for breach of the covenant of quiet enjoyment or in the tort of trespass or nuisance.[15]

---

[1] *Hudson v Cripps* [1896] 1 Ch 265.

[2] *Jones v Lavington* [1903] 1 KB 253, CA; *Celsteel Ltd v Alton House Holdings Ltd (No 2)* [1987] 2 All ER 240, CA.

[3] As in *Queensway Marketing Ltd v Associated Restaurants Ltd* (1984) 271 EG 1106 where a subtenant was able to establish that its immediate landlord had breached its covenant for quiet enjoyment as a result of scaffolding erected by the head landlord.

⁴ *Miller v Emcer Products Ltd* [1956] 1 All ER 237.

⁵ *Hilton v James Smith & Sons (Norwood) Ltd* [1979] 2 EGLR 44, CA.

⁶ *Goldmile Properties Ltd v Lechouritis* [2003] EWCA Civ 49, [2003] 2 P & CR 1.

⁷ See *Mira v Aylmer Square Investments Ltd* [1990] 1 EGLR 45, CA.

⁸ *Chartered Trust plc v Davies* [1997] 2 EGLR 83, CA.

⁹ *Nynehead Developments Ltd v RH Fibreboard Containers Ltd* [1999] 1 EGLR 7.

¹⁰ *Southwark London Borough Council v Mills* [1999] 4 All ER 449, HL.

¹¹ See *Browne v Flower* [1911] 1 Ch 219 (landlord not in breach of this covenant where another tenant, with landlord's consent, erected an iron staircase outside the plaintiff tenant's window seriously affecting the plaintiff's privacy); contrast *Owen v Gadd* [1956] 2 QB 99, [1956] 2 All ER 28 (landlord in breach of this covenant where he erected scaffolding outside the entrance to tenant's shop).

¹² [1953] 1 All ER 1109, CA.

¹³ As amended by the Housing Act 1988. This does not, in itself give the tenant the right to any financial compensation.

¹⁴ See para 27.2.

¹⁵ See, for example, *Tagro v Cafane* [1991] 2 All ER 235, [1991] 1 WLR 378, CA where a monthly tenant was awarded damages of £31,000 under s 27, and the para 37.23.

36.35 *Non-derogation from grant* It is a principle of general application that a grantor may not take away with one hand what has been given with the other.[1] Accordingly, a covenant is implied into all leases that the landlord will not derogate from his or her grant. Thus, a landlord who leases part of their land to be used in a particular way, must not so act in relation to land retained as to make the demised premises materially less fit for their intended use.[2] It has been accepted that there is often an overlap between this obligation and a landlord's liability under the covenant for quiet enjoyment[3].

Examples of liability under non-derogation from grant include where a landlord, who leased to the tenant two floors of a block of flats for residential purposes, then leased the remainder to another tenant for business purposes.[4] It has also been held that a landlord who let retail premises was liable to the tenant under the principle of non-derogation where a neighbouring tenant of the same landlord used his premises in a way which amounted to a nuisance[5]. Similarly, a landlord who closed off an access, thereby restricting the flow of people going past a sales kiosk let to its tenant, was held to have breached this obligation[6]. The conversion of part of a mall in a retail centre into an additional unit could also incur liability to the other tenants in the centre.[7] However, letting adjacent or nearby property for a competing use will not normally amount to a breach[8], nor will moderate changes to the tenant-mix in a shopping centre found liability[9].

¹ *Birmingham, Dudley and District Banking Co v Ross* (1888) 38 Ch D 295 at 313.

² *Aldin v Latimer Clark, Muirhead & Co* [1894] 2 Ch 437; *Browne v Flower* [1911] 1 Ch 219.

³ *Southwark London Borough Council v Mills* [1999] 4 All ER 449, HL.

⁴ *Newman v Real Estate Debenture Corpn Ltd and Flower Decorations Ltd* [1940] 1 All ER 131. See also *Aldin v Latimer Clark, Muirhead & Co* [1894] 2 Ch 437, para 32.18 above.

⁵ *Chartered Trust plc v Davies* [1997] 2 EGLR 83, CA. It was of some significance that the landlord retained control of the common parts of the arcade in which both shops were located since this was why the court concluded that the landlord had a duty to act against the tenant whose activities were causing the problem. See also *Nynehead Developments Ltd v RH Fibreboard Containers Ltd* [1999] 1 EGLR 7.

⁶ *Platt v London Underground Ltd* [2001] 2 EGLR 121.

⁷ *Petra Investements Ltd v Jeffrey Rogers plc* [2000] 3 EGLR 120.

⁸ *Port v Griffith* [1938] 1 All ER 295; *Romulus Trading v Comet Properties* [1996] 2 EGLR 70.

⁹ *Petra Investements Ltd v Jeffrey Rogers plc* [2000] 3 EGLR 120.

36.36 *User covenant* A landlord will not normally enter into a covenant that restricts the use of any property that has been retained. However such covenants are encountered in one rather specialised situation. A landlord of a shopping centre, retail park or parade of shops may wish to maintain tight control of the use to which individual units are put in order to ensure an attractive mixture of tenants. As we shall see[1], where very restrictive user clauses are imposed on tenants, the rental value of the premises can be seriously depressed. However, this effect can be offset by the landlord covenanting that other units will not be used in a way that competes with the tenant's business[2]; by giving the tenant what is effectively a monopoly use within the centre the landlord can achieve control over tenant mix without sacrificing rental value.

[1] See paras 36.37, note 1 and 36.58, note 3.
[2] See for example *Walker v Arkay Caterers Ltd* [1997] EGCS 107.

Tenant covenants

36.37 Virtually all leases include provisions that restrict the way in which the tenant may use the premises. Such covenants vary enormously and their complexity will depend upon the nature of the premises in question. So, a lease of residential premises may simply restrict use to that of a single dwelling, whereas that of a retail unit in a shopping arcade or centre may strictly limit the use of the property to a narrow range, while forbidding certain specified uses[1]. Even where positively worded, user covenants are usually interpreted as imposing only a negative obligation restricting the tenant to the permitted use but without positively requiring the tenant to use the premises in that way[2]. However, in some retail centres tenants may be required positively to 'keep open' for their particular trade[3].

The words of a user covenants must be interpreted according to the meaning that they carried when the lease was first drafted; so a covenant in a lease drafted in the 1950s to use premises only for the purposes of selling 'groceries' may prevent the current tenant from using the property as a modern supermarket selling a significant proportion of non-food items[4].

User covenants can be framed as absolute, qualified or fully qualified obligations[5]. Where the covenant is absolute the landlord is free to refuse any request for a change of use or can charge the tenant, either by way of a premium or an increase in rent for any change to which he chooses to agree. Where the covenant is qualified or fully qualified, statute does provide that where the change of use does not involve any structural alteration the landlord is not permitted to charge for any consent[6]. The payment of a reasonable sum to compensate for any diminution in value of the demised premises or of the landlord's neighbouring premises can be required.

Where the covenant is merely qualified (ie subject to the landlord's consent) there is no statutory requirement that the landlord can only refuse consent where this is reasonable. Such a requirement must be expressly set out in the lease[7]. Where the landlord is specifically required to act reasonably, the approach to the test of reasonableness is much the same as for disposition covenants[8]. However, it should be noted that the Landlord and Tenant Act 1988 does *not* apply to applications for consent to a change of use. Accordingly, it is for the *tenant* to prove that the landlord is acting unreasonably in refusing consent and the landlord is not under the obligations imposed by that Act; the landlord is not, therefore required to respond to a tenant's application within a reasonable time and cannot be liable in damages for any losses caused by an unreasonable refusal.

[1] It should be noted that a very restrictive user clause may have a serious impact on rent at rent review, see *Plinth Property Investments Ltd v Mott, Hay and Anderson* (1978) 38 P & CR 361, CA (36% reduction due to a very tight user clause) and para 36.37.
[2] *Montross Associated Investments SA v Moussaieff* [1990] 2 EGLR 61, CA.

[3] Where such covenants are broken, eg by a retailer closing down its operation, the courts will not enforce the covenant by way of a mandatory injunction: In appropriate circumstances, notably where an 'anchor' tenant in a shopping centre closes, the landlord may obtain substantial damages, see para 36.39.

[4] *St Marylebone Property Co Ltd v Tesco Stores Ltd* [1988] 27 EG 72.See also *Joint London Holdings Ltd v Mount Cook Land Ltd* [2005] EWCA Civ 1171 where a prohibition against use for the business of a "victualler" was held to prevent premises being used as a sandwich shop.

[5] See para 36.26.

[6] Landlord and Tenant Act 1927, s 19(3). Where the covenant is qualified rather than fully qualified this does not prevent the landlord simply refusing consent outright and then, say, offering to grant the tenant a new lease at a higher rent.

[7] *Guardian Assurance Co Ltd v Gants Hill Holdings Ltd* [1983] 2 EGLR 36.

[8] See para 36.30.

Other restrictions on use

36.38 A tenant may find that their use of the demised premises is restricted by legal requirements other than those contained in the lease. A tenant, like any other occupier, must comply with any restrictions on use imposed under planning law.[1] Furthermore, a subtenant will be bound by any restrictive covenants affecting the freehold or contained in their landlord's head lease.[2]

[1] See ch 39.
[2] See ch 33 and para 36.89.

Enforcement of user covenants

36.39 User covenants in leases can be enforced by the parties in the same way as any other contractual obligation. Where loss can be proved a claim in damages can be brought. However, where a breach occurs, the other party may well wish to prevent its continuance; this can be achieved by obtaining an injunction. Where, as is usual, the user covenant is negative an injunction will, subject to the normal caveats, be granted.[1] However, where the covenant is positive—typically a 'keep open' for trade covenant—it is now settled that an injunction will not be forthcoming,[2] although a damages claim can succeed.[3]

It is not unusual for other tenants of the same landlord to have a very real interest in the enforcement of user covenants. Tenants in a block of flats may wish to ensure that one of their number does not breach a covenant preventing business use, or tenants in a shopping centre will want others to abide by their user covenants. Often, in such situations there is no difficulty because the landlord will take steps to remedy the breach. However, where this is not the case one tenant may wish to take action against another tenant and faces the problem that they have no direct contractual relationship. In principle, reliance may be placed on the Contracts (Rights of Third Parties) Act 1999[4], but this is often excluded from leases. There is also the possibility that an action can be brought under s 3 of the Landlord and Tenant (Covenants) Act 1995 but this is largely untested. In certain circumstances restrictive user clauses imposed on neighbouring tenants can be treated as a 'letting scheme';[5] this will make them mutually enforceable.[6]

[1] See paras 11.46–11.51.
[2] See *Cooperative Insurance Society Ltd v Argyll Stores (Holdings) Ltd* [1997] 3 All ER 297, HL.
[3] See *Costain Property Developments Ltd v Finlay & Co Ltd* [1989] 1 EGLR 237; *Transworld Land Co Ltd v J Sainsbury plc* [1990] 2 EGLR 255.
[4] See paras 13.3–13.9.
[5] A form of building scheme, see para 33.29.
[6] *Williams v Kiley* [2002] EWCA Civ 1645.

COVENANTS GOVERNING THE USE AND ENJOYMENT OF THE PROPERTY: KEY POINTS

- A landlord is always obliged to give the tenant undisturbed possession of the property under the covenant for quiet enjoyment; where the landlord lets part of their property there is always an obligation not to derogate from the grant.

- A tenant will invariably covenant to restrict the use of the premises. A tenant's user covenant may be absolute, qualified or fully qualified.

- Where the landlord is expressly required to act reasonably when refusing consent, the courts will apply the same reasonableness test as is generally used in relation to disposition covenants. However, the duties imposed by the LTA 1988 do not apply, although the landlord cannot charge for any consent in certain circumstances.

- User covenants are interpreted according to the meaning that the words used would have had at the date the lease was drafted.

- Generally a user covenant can be enforced by injunction, or damages claimed for any breach; however the courts will not enforce a positive user covenant by way of injunction.

Physical state

36.40 It is usually[1] of obvious importance to both parties to a lease that the premises are maintained in a good condition. The landlord will wish to protect the capital value of their asset and the tenant will want to ensure that the premises are in a suitable state for use and occupation. Where the demised premises are part of a building or complex it will also be necessary to deal with the obligation to repair adjoining premises. In certain circumstances the tenant may need to make alterations to the property and will want to be certain that this can be done without undue interference from the landlord. It is usual[2] for leases to include express provisions dealing with these matters. The circumstances in which the law will imply obligations relating to the physical state of the premises are limited and are an unsatisfactory[3] way of dealing with such an important topic.

[1] Landlords and tenants of poor quality commercial property that is nearing the end of its useful life may be content to compromise on repairing obligations in order to achieve a short-term, low-cost occupation that suits both sides, see para.36.48.

[2] As we shall see (para 36.45) statute imposes repairing obligations on landlords of short-term residential leases; in such cases the lease may well not record these provisions.

[3] Except in the case of short-term residential leases, see para 36.45.

Implied repairing obligations: tenants

36.41 In the absence of express covenants, a tenant is subject to two implied obligations; a periodic tenant is obliged to use the premises in a tenant-like manner and no tenant is allowed to commit waste.

36.42 *To use the premises in a tenant-like manner* This covenant is implied in all periodic tenancies.[1] According to Denning LJ, as he then was, in *Warren v Keen*, 'The tenant must take proper care of the place ... he must do the little jobs about the place which a reasonable tenant would do. In addition, he must, of course, not damage the house, wilfully or negligently, and he must see that his family and guests do not damage it, and if they do, he must repair it.'[2] The limited nature of this obligation should be appreciated. For example, the covenant does not necessarily oblige the tenant to lag water pipes; this depends on the circumstances, including the severity of the cold and the length of any contemplated absences from home.[3]

> [1] *Marsden v Edward Heyes Ltd* [1927] 2 KB 1; *Warren v Keen* [1954] 1 QB 15, [1953] 2 All ER 1118, CA.
> [2] [1954] 1 QB 15 at 20.
> [3] See *Wycombe Health Authority v Barnett* (1982) 47 P & CR 394.

36.43 *Waste* 'Waste' has been defined as 'any act which alters the nature of the land, whether for the better or for the worse'.[1] It is an ancient, tortious liability imposed on owners of limited interest in land in order to protect the interests of those with rights to the subsequent occupation of the property such as tenants under leases. It is rarely encountered in modern times because leases tend to contain express provisions which obviate the need to rely on the doctrine.[2]

Common law recognised two forms of waste, voluntary and permissive. Voluntary waste would be constituted by carrying out substantial alterations to the property, for example by pulling down a building, or, as in *Marsden v Edward Heyes Ltd*,[3] by gutting the ground floor of a building to convert the entire area into a shop. Permissive waste is damage caused by omission or neglect, as by letting the premises go to ruin. All tenants are liable for voluntary waste. A tenant holding under a periodic tenancy is not liable for permissive waste but is under the obligation to use in a tenant-like manner which covers much the same ground.[4]

> [1] Megarry and Wade *The Law of Real Property* (6th edn) p 80.
> [2] That said, for various technical reasons, the doctrine was resorted to in *Mancetter Developments Ltd v Garmanson Ltd* [1986] 1 All ER 449, CA.
> [3] [1927] 2 KB 1.
> [4] See para 36.42.

Implied repairing obligations: landlords

36.44 *Fitness for habitation* Common law does not imply, as a legal incident of the relationship of landlord and tenant, any covenant on the part of the landlord that the premises are or will remain fit for use.[1] There is one exception: where residential premises are let furnished, a condition is implied that they are fit for human habitation at the commencement[2] of the tenancy.[3] Further, in one other situation, of little practical relevance because of ridiculously low rental limits and restrictive interpretation by the courts, an obligation to maintain the dwelling in state that is fit for human habitation is imposed by statute.[4] However, the Housing Act 2004 has introduced a significant change in the governmental approach to the improvement of housing conditions by moving away from the concepts of unfitness for habitation and repair. While this Act does not directly affect the legal liabilities as between landlord and tenant, it does provide a basis on which local authorities can intervene more effectively where premises are in poor condition. Housing authorities now have obligations[5] to inspect residential properties in their area using the Housing Health and Safety Rating System. This is designed to identify hazards that could put occupiers at risk of harm. Where a serious ('Category 1') hazard is found to exist, the authority must take enforcement action[6] against the owner[7]; in less serious cases action is a matter of discretion.[8] In this way landlords can be encouraged and, where necessary, compelled to keep their properties in good condition.

> [1] *Hart v Windsor* (1844) 12 M & W 68.
> [2] But not throughout the tenancy.
> [3] *Wilson v Finch Hatton* (1877) 2 Ex D 336.
> [4] Under the Landlord and Tenant Act 1985, s 8, there is an implied condition in any letting of a dwelling-house at a rent not exceeding, in Greater London, £80 per annum, or elsewhere, £52, that the house is fit

for human habitation both at the commencement of, and during, the tenancy. In *Quick v Taff-Ely Borough Council* [1986] QB 809, [1985] 3 All ER 321, the Court of Appeal remarked that this section must have remarkably little application.

[5] Housing Act 2004, s 4. The housing authority must inspect premises where it becomes aware that a hazard may exist (eg on the complaint of a tenant).

[6] The method of enforcement depends on the seriousness and nature of the hazard(s). The authority is most likely to issue either an improvement notice requiring specified work to be carried out; or a prohibition notice that effectively closes all or part of the property; or a hazard awareness notice informing the owner of the hazard and recommending the steps that should be taken.

[7] Housing Act 2004, s 5(1).

[8] Housing Act 2004, s 7(1).

36.45 *Repairs*[1] There is no generally implied covenant that the landlord is obliged to repair. A statutory exception is contained in the Landlord and Tenant Act 1985, ss 11 to 14, which provide that where a dwelling-house is let for less than seven years, the landlord is obliged[2]:

- to keep the structure and exterior in repair; and
- to keep in repair and proper working order the installations in the house for the supply of water, gas and electricity, for sanitation, and for space- and water-heating.

A landlord is only liable for defects of which they have notice.[3] The landlord has the right, on giving 24 hours' written notice, to enter and view the premises at all reasonable times. The landlord's obligations under these provisions may, in the case of leases entered into on or after 15 January 1989, extend beyond the structure and exterior of the particular dwelling-house or the installations in it. Where the dwelling-house is a part only of a building, for example a flat, then, in the case of breaches affecting the tenant's enjoyment of the flat or the common parts, the landlord's obligation to keep in repair the structure and exterior extends to any part of the structure and exterior of the building in which the landlord has an estate or interest[4], eg the common parts of a block of flats. Likewise, the obligation to keep in repair and proper working order the utility installations applies also to all those installations serving the flat or dwelling-house which the landlord owns or controls or which are in a part of the building in which the landlord has an estate or interest.[5]

[1] For the meaning of 'repair' see para 36.49.

[2] Although this obligation is often described as an 'implied' obligation it should be appreciated that it applies not only where a lease is silent as to any repairing obligations but also in the face of any provisions to the contrary. Thus a landlord cannot shift these obligations onto the tenant (nor make the tenant contribute to their cost) and they could more accurately be referred to as 'imposed' obligations.

[3] *O'Brien v Robinson* [1973] 1 All ER 583, HL. Whilst this notice usually comes from the tenant, it can come from any reliable source, see *Dinefwr Borough Council v Jones* [1987] 2 EGLR 58 where a local authority landlord had been told of the disrepair by its environmental health officer.

[4] Where the tenant of a flat sublets it on a lease to which these extended obligations apply the subtenant will have no remedy in respect of disrepair to the common parts since the landlord (ie the tenant of the flat) has no estate or interest in the common parts, see *Niazi Services Ltd v van der Loo* [2004] EWCA Civ 53.

[5] Landlord and Tenant Act 1985, s 11(1A),(1B), added by the Housing Act 1988. For leases entered into prior to 15 January 1989, the landlord's obligation is limited to the structure and exterior of the particular flat and the installations therein: *Campden Hill Towers Ltd v Gardner* [1977] 1 All ER 739, CA, and see *Douglas-Scott v Scorgie* [1984] 1 All ER 1086, CA.

36.46 *Other implied obligations* There are other specific situations in which a landlord may be held responsible to the tenant for the physical state of the premises. It was held in *Liverpool City Council v Irwin*[1] that where parts of a building (in this case, a high-rise block of flats) have been let to different tenants and the essential means of access, such as stairs and lifts, are retained by the landlord, a term may be implied that the landlord will take reasonable care to keep those parts reasonably safe and reasonably fit for use. It has also been held that, where a tenant was expressly obliged to keep the interior of a dwelling in repair, a term could be implied[2], that the landlord must keep the exterior in repair[3]. In *Rimmer v Liverpool City Council*[4] it was held that a landlord who designed and built the demised premises owed a duty in the tort of negligence to the tenant (among others) to take reasonable care to ensure he would not suffer personal injury as a result of dangerous defects in the design and construction of the premises.[5] It should also be noted that a landlord has obligations under the Defective Premises Act 1972, s 4; these are discussed at para 21.30. Finally, it has been accepted[6] that public authority landlords are obliged[7] to ensure that the condition of any dwelling house does not infringe the tenant's rights under Article 8.1[8] of the European Convention on Human Rights; however, it is clear that the condition of the property must be particularly severe for a breach to occur.[9]

[1] [1977] AC 239, [1976] 2 All ER 39. See also *King v South Northamptonshire District Council* [1992] 1 EGLR 53, CA.

[2] See para 7.31.

[3] See *Barrett v Lounova (1982) Ltd* [1989] 1 All ER 351, CA, although it now appears that this decision may be confined to its own particular facts: *Adami v Lincoln Grange Management Ltd* [1998] 17 EG 148, CA.

[4] [1984] 1 All ER 930, CA.

[5] In *Targett v Torfaen Borough Council* [1992] 1 EGLR 275, CA it was expressly held that this liability has survived despite the House of Lords' decision in *Murphy v Brentwood District Council* [1990] 2 All ER 908.

[6] *Lee v Leeds City Council* [2002] 1 WLR 1488, CA.

[7] As a result of the Human Rights Act 1998, s 6(1) which obliges public authorities not to act in a way that is incompatible with a convention right.

[8] This confers on everyone a right to respect for their private and family life, home, and correspondence.

[9] In *Lee v Leeds City Council* [2002] 1 WLR 1488, CA it was held that condensation in the tenant's house had not produced conditions that were sufficiently severe to trigger liability.

Express repairing obligations

36.47 A variety of covenants providing for the liability of the landlord or the tenant to repair either the demised premises, the common parts of a building or complex, or the landlord's adjoining premises may be encountered. In the case of longer leases of whole buildings, it is often provided that the full legal and financial responsibility for repairing the demised premises is placed on the tenant. Equally, the repairing obligations may be split between landlord and tenant, with the landlord being liable for repairs to the structure and exterior of the property and the tenant being obliged to repair the interior.[1] In such cases great care must be taken to ensure that the parts of the building for which each party is responsible is very carefully defined.

Also common, where premises are occupied by a number of tenants, are so-called 'clear leases'. These are leases in which the landlord covenants to carry out all works of repair and maintenance to the common parts of the building or complex, including the structure and exterior, and to provide all services; however the tenants bear all the costs of these works (by way of a service charge[2]). The tenants are each responsible for the repair of the interior of their respective parts. As a result the rent reaches the landlord clear of all expenses and overheads.

In the case of short residential tenancies, as we have seen[3], the landlord is always liable under the Landlord and Tenant Act 1985, to keep in repair the structure and exterior of the dwelling and to keep service installations in working order; whether or not the tenant is obliged to repair the interior depends on the express terms of the agreement.

[1] This is more likely in the case of shorter leases of whole buildings.
[2] Para 36.60.
[3] Para 36.45.

36.48 *To repair or to keep in repair* Where the obligation imposed is either 'to repair' or to 'keep' in repair (which it usually is) this means that, where necessary, any *existing* disrepair must be remedied.[1] It is thus vital, where such a repairing obligation is being imposed on a tenant, that the property is structurally surveyed before the lease is entered into in order to identify the extent of any disrepair. It will then be a matter for negotiation whether the landlord puts the premises into repair (or pays the incoming tenant to do so), whether the tenant accepts the responsibility of carrying out the repairs, or whether the repairing obligation is modified so that the tenant is only required to maintain the premises in their existing state. In this latter case, it is essential that the existing state of the premises is properly recorded—usually by way of a schedule of condition—so as to avoid future disputes.

In any case where the landlord is under an obligation to keep in repair the demised premise, the liability to the tenant does not arise until the landlord has notice of the defect;[2] however, where a landlord is obliged to keep either their own adjoining premises, or common parts, in repair, this liability arises as soon as the disrepair occurs[3]. This is also the case where it is the tenant who is covenanting to keep in repair.

[1] *Proudfoot v Hart* (1890) 25 QBD 42, CA.
[2] *McCarrick v Liverpool Corpn* [1946] 2 All ER 646, HL.
[3] *British Telecommunications plc v Sun Life Assurance Society plc* [1995] 4 All ER 44, CA.

36.49 *The meaning of repair* Where the obligation imposed is one to 'repair' or keep in 'repair' it can often be a highly technical issue as to whether or not the work required to be done is, legally speaking, 'repair'. There can be no obligation to repair unless the premises are in 'disrepair'. This will only be the case where a part of the building to which the covenant relates has physically deteriorated since the date of its construction.[1] Thus the rectification of a defect arising in the course of construction (an 'inherent defect') will only fall within the ambit of a repairing covenant if it has given rise to some physical deterioration in the part of the building to which the covenant applies[2]. An inherent defect that gives rise to a loss of amenity (however severe) is not disrepair[3].

'Repair' connotes the idea of making good damage so as to leave the subject so far as possible as though it had not been damaged.[4] A covenant to repair may require renewal of subsidiary parts, but not renewal of the whole.[5] Repair will, inevitably, involve some element of improvement, but it must not result in premises which are wholly different in character from those which were demised.[6] Within these limits, a covenant to repair will cover works necessitated by inherent defects in the premises (so long as they have caused disrepair).[7] It is always a question of fact and degree whether the work in question can properly be described as repair; in coming to any conclusion the court will take account of many factors including the age of the building, its expected lifespan, the extent of the works required and their cost compared to that of replacing the building.[8]

[1] *Quick v Taff-Ely Borough Council* [1985] 3 All ER 321, CA. See also *Post Office v Aquarius Properties Ltd* [1987] 1 All ER 1055, CA. Note that the deterioration must have occurred since the date of *construction*; the date of the *lease* is irrelevant for this purpose.
[2] *Stent v Monmouth District Council* [1987] 1 EGLR 59, CA.
[3] *Quick v Taff-Ely Borough Council* [1985] 3 All ER 321, CA, where condensation damage caused by the defective design of window lintels was held not to amount to disrepair as neither the lintels nor the windows had deteriorated. See also *Lee v Leeds City Council* [2002] EWCA Civ 06, [2002] 1 WLR 1488.

⁴ *Anstruther-Gough-Calthorpe v McOscar* [1924] 1 KB 716, CA. It should be noted that where positive damage to premises is caused, eg destruction by fire, an obligation to repair requires the damage to be put right even if this involves complete re-building. It is, therefore important that such disasters are covered by insurance, in which case the obligation to repair will be stated to exclude insured risks.

⁵ *Lurcott v Wakely and Wheeler* [1911] 1 KB 905, CA.

⁶ *Pembery v Lamdin* [1940] 2 All ER 434

⁷ *Ravenseft Properties Ltd v Davstone (Holdings) Ltd* [1979] 1 All ER 929.

⁸ See, for example, *Brew Bros v Snax (Ross) Ltd* [1970] 1 QB 612 and *Ravenseft Properties Ltd v Davstone (Holdings) Ltd* [1979] 1 All ER 929.

36.50 *Obligations to do more than repair* It is perfectly possible for a lease to be so worded as to impose an obligation to do work that goes beyond 'repair' as explained in the previous paragraph. Clear language is required to achieve this effect. Thus a covenant to 'repair, amend, renew…' has been held to be insufficient to impose a requirement to rebuild[1]; however, one to 'keep the demised premises in good and substantial repair… and where necessary to rebuild reconstruct or replace the same' was held to do so[2]. It is also clear that a covenant can be drafted so as to impose more than one obligation and that, together, these may require works going beyond the normal concept of repair. For example, a covenant to 'repair and otherwise keep in good condition' has been held to have this effect[3].

¹ *Collins v Flynn* [1963] 2 All ER 1068.

² *Norwich Union Life Insurance Society v British Railways Board* [1987] 2 EGLR 137.

³ *Credit Suisse v Beegas Nominees* [1994] 4 ALL ER 803.

36.51 *Standard of repair* Where the covenant is simply 'to repair' the obligation is satisfied by keeping the premises in substantial repair[1]; there is no requirement to keep them in a pristine condition[2]. However, it is more usual for the covenant to be amplified by an epithet such as 'good' or 'tenantable'. 'Good tenantable repair' has been defined as being 'such repair as, having regard to the age, character and locality of the [property] would make it reasonably fit for the occupation of a reasonably minded tenant'.[3] In practice, much will depend on the individual facts and a good rule of thumb is that if the condition of the premises has deteriorated the covenantor will have to put that right.

¹ *Harris v Jones* [1832] 1 Moo & R 173.

² *Commercial Union Life Assurance Co Ltd v Label Ink* [2001] L & TR 29

³ *Proudfoot v Hart* [1890] 25 QBD 42.

36.52 *Method of repair* It will often be possible to repair in a variety of ways; in particular there can be the option of carrying out 'patch and mend' work rather than undertaking more permanent repairs. Generally speaking it is for the party under the obligation to choose which particular method to adopt[1], although the courts will not allow the covenantor to 'patch and mend' where the only sensible course is to 'do a proper job'.[2] Equally, a tenant cannot insist that a landlord 'do a proper job' without proving that continuing to patch and mend is inappropriate[3], and nor can a landlord insist that a tenant repair by way of replacement where an existing system is working satisfactorily.[4] However, in the case of a landlord's covenant to repair where it is the tenants who will meet the cost of those repairs[5], there is a requirement that a decision to carry out more expensive works than is strictly necessary must be one which a reasonably prudent owner who is paying for the work would carry out.[6]

¹ *Plough Investments v Manchester City Council* [1989] 1 EGLR 244, *Carmel Southend v Strachan & Henshaw* [2007] 3 EGLR 15.

² *Elmcroft Developments Ltd v Tankersley-Sawyer* (1984) 270 EG 140.

[3] *Murray v Birmingham City Council* [1987] 2 EGLR 53 where the tenant had not provided any evidence to support his contention that the landlord should replace his roof rather than simply patch it with new tiles.

[4] *Land Securities v Westminster City Council (No 2)* [1995] 1 EGLR 245, where a landlord could not force the tenant to replace an air conditioning system which, although near the end of its useful life, was still functioning adequately with only the occasional repair.

[5] Ie through a service charge, see paras 36.47 above and 36.60 below.

[6] *Plough Investments v Manchester City Council* [1989] 1 EGLR 244, *Fluor Daniels Properties v Shortlands Investments* [[2001] 2 EGLR 103.36.

Covenants against alterations

36.53 It is usual for a lease to restrict the tenant's ability to make alterations to the premises. The lease may distinguish between different types of work. So, for example, structural alterations may be absolutely prohibited, while those to the internal layout may be permitted with the landlord's consent. All depends on the terms of the particular lease. A tenant may be able to carry out works despite the fact that they are absolutely prohibited by the lease. A tenant of business premises who wishes to carry out improvements[1] can go ahead where the requirements of Part I of the Landlord and Tenant Act 1927 (LTA 1927) are complied with and where either the landlord fails to object or the court certifies the improvements as 'proper'[2]. Furthermore, alterations required by Part III of the Disability Discrimination Act 1995[3] can be undertaken by the tenant, irrespective of any provisions in the lease.

Where a lease provides that alterations cannot be undertaken without the consent of the landlord, statute ensures that consent cannot unreasonably be withheld where the alteration amounts to an improvement[4]. The landlord can, however, require as a condition of consent that the tenant pays reasonable compensation for any damage or diminution in value to either the demised premises or the landlord's neighbouring property.[5] Where the improvement does not add to the letting value the landlord can also, where it is reasonable to do so, require the tenant at the end of the lease to reinstate the premises to their former condition.[6] Given these provisions, it is often difficult for a landlord to establish reasonable grounds for refusing consent to a tenant's alterations; however, a landlord has been held to have reasonably refused consent where he was concerned as to the structural integrity of the proposed works[7], and where the tenant was proposing to use the altered premises to compete with the landlord's business on neighbouring property.[8]

[1] LTA 1927, ss 1, 3. The improvements must add to the letting value of the premises, be suitable in character and must not be carried out under an obligation to the landlord.

[2] LTA 1927, s 3.

[3] This came into effect on 1 October 2004 and requires the removal or alteration of any physical feature which makes it impossible or reasonably difficult for a disabled person to gain access to business premises offering goods facilities or services.

[4] LTA 1927, s 19(2). The Act does not define an improvement but, given the landlord's entitlement to claim compensation for any diminution in value, the courts have held that whether or not work amounts to an improvement must be looked at from the tenant's point of view and does not depend on whether the work adds to the letting value; see *FW Woolworth & Co v Lambert* [1937] Ch 37. In practice this makes it very difficult for a landlord to argue that alterations are not an improvement.

[5] LTA 1927, s 19(2).

[6] LTA 1927, s 19(2).

[7] *Iqbal v Thakrar* [[2004] 3 EGLR 21, CA.

[8] *Sargeant v Macepark (Whittlebury)* [2004] 4 All ER 662.

36.54 *Right to fixtures* For the tenant's right to remove fixtures at the end of the lease, see para 28.13 above.

COVENANTS RELATING TO THE PHYSICAL STATE OF THE PREMISES: KEY POINTS

- Where the physical state of leasehold premises requires attention it does not follow that it is the obligation of either the landlord or tenant to put things right. This depends on whether or not the work required is a 'repair' in the legal sense and on whether the part of the premises affected is covered by the covenant as drafted. Remedial works can be outside the legal obligations of both parties.

- In the case of non-residential leases there are no implied covenants to repair; the obligations of the parties will depend on the express terms of the lease.

- In the case of residential leases the only implied covenants of any importance are those imposed by ss 11–14 of the LTA 1985. These provisions apply to leases for less than 7 years and operate despite any provisions to the contrary. They require the landlord to keep in repair the structure and exterior of the premises and to keep the main service installations in working order.

- All other leases will invariably contain express provisions regarding repair. These vary greatly:
  - They may impose the obligation to repair the whole of the premises at their own expense on one or other of the parties (usually the tenant).
  - They may split the obligations between landlord and tenant.
  - Where a building or complex is in multiple occupation it is usual for the landlord to covenant to repair the structure and exterior of the building/complex and for the tenants to pay the cost of this via a service charge.

- A covenant to 'repair' to 'keep in repair' requires the rectification of existing disrepair; a prospective tenant of a second-hand building must consider whether or not this is acceptable.

- Where a covenant is one to 'repair', the covenantor is not obliged to do works that amount to a renewal of the whole or to improve the property; inherent defects can fall within the covenant so long as their rectification is a 'repair'.

- It is a question of fact and degree whether or not any particular work is a repair.

- Covenants may impose an obligation that is greater than one simply to repair although the courts require clear words to achieve this effect.

- A covenantor is not required to keep the premises in a pristine condition, but any significant deterioration will normally have to be put right.

- A lease will normally restrict the tenant's right to carry out alterations and will often absolutely prohibit those affecting the structure.

- Any qualified covenant restricting alterations is converted into a fully qualified one where the proposed works are improvements. Since an improvement is judged from the tenant's perspective this can make it very difficult for consent to be reasonably refused, although a landlord can require both compensation and re-instatement in certain circumstances.

Outgoings

Rent

36.55 The payment of rent, although a normal feature of leases, is not an essential legal requirement.[1] The rent payable by a tenant will generally take the form either of a market rent or a ground rent. A market rent is sometimes described as a 'rack' rent. Rent for commercial premises is normally paid quarterly and, often, on the 'usual' quarter days.[2] A ground rent, commonly paid in the case of long leases, is paid where the land has been leased partly in consideration of a lump sum payment (ie a premium) at the commencement of the lease, or in consideration of the tenant building on the land, this being reflected in the rent which is, in essence, a rent for the land only and not the buildings thereon. It is normally expressly provided that rent is payable in advance; if this is not done, rent is payable in arrears.

[1] *Ashburn Anstalt v Arnold* [1988] 2 All ER 147, CA. It is in the erroneous belief that rent is a legal requirement that some leases are granted at a 'peppercorn' rent, ie a nominal rent that is not expected to be paid.

[2] These are: Christmas Day (25 December); Lady Day (25 March); Midsummer (24 June); Michaelmas (29 September).

Rent reviews

36.56 It is usual in the case of longer[1] commercial leases to provide for the level of rent to be revised at prescribed intervals, for example every five years. The object of a rent review clause is to give the landlord the benefit of increases in property values and to provide protection from the effects of falls in the value of money by increasing the rent payable in line with the market. It has become the widespread practice for rent review to take the upward-only form[2]. Under such a provision, the rent at each review can only either stay the same or move up in line with market rents. Such clauses play a vital role in preserving for the landlord the value of the income stream produced by commercial property and do much to enhance the attraction of property as an investment. They can, however, cause substantial hardship to tenants during a recession. When market rents fall significantly and for a lengthy period tenants can find themselves locked into leases which cause their premises to be over-rented.

A well-drafted rent review clause should contain both a formula for determining the revised rent and machinery for agreeing the rent and resolving disputes between the parties (generally by way of reference to a chartered surveyor acting as expert or arbitrator[3]). Rent review clauses vary in their details with the result that each clause is, in principle, unique. What follows is, therefore, merely a brief indication of features that are commonly encountered in rent reviews. It should be noted that, in longer leases, a review being conducted today may well be under a form a rent review clause that would not be found in a lease as currently drafted; thus some awareness of older styles of rent review clause is always necessary.

[1] In recent years the length of commercial leases has been reducing. There are now many more leases of five years or less; such leases often do not contain any rent review at all or, where they do, the rent review may take the form of simple index-linking.

[2] Despite Government efforts to discourage such forms of review and the continuing recommendations of successive codes of practice for commercial leases that encourage landlords to offer alternative forms of review.

[3] See para 2.26 and para 36.59.

36.57 *The machinery of review* Many modern rent review clauses impose no formal procedure for the implementation of a rent review; they simply entitle the landlord to review the rent. Others (including older forms of clause) require the rent review process to be initiated by the serving of a landlord's notice (a 'trigger' notice). Sometimes (but rarely in modern forms of rent review clause) the tenant must respond with a counter-notice. The function of such counter-notices varies; some require a counter-proposal as to the rent, others provide a mechanism under which the tenant can elect to have the rent fixed by a third party where the parties are unable to agree.

In order to be valid, any notice under a rent review clause must be intended to have legal effect[1] and should convey its meaning in a manner that is clear to the other side[2]. In older forms of lease, it is usual to find that rent review notices are required to be served within specified time limits. It is now settled that time is not normally 'of the essence' (ie these time limits are not strict)[3] except where the parties have expressly or impliedly provided that this is to be the case[4]. The parties may include the phrase 'time to be of the essence' or employ other wording that has this effect. In addition, the use of a series of strictly timetabled requirements, coupled with provisions that deal with the consequences of a failure to comply with the time limits will usually make time of the essence.[5] It is also likely that where provisions for which time is always of the essence, notably tenants' break clauses[6], are linked to a rent review, this will also make time of the essence for the review.[7] Furthermore, where a provision within a rent review clause is either subject to a time limit that is not strict or is subject to no time limit at all, it is always possible for the other side to serve notice imposing a strict time limit.[8] Making time of the essence will not *compel* the landlord to carry out the review[9] but it will ensure that a tenant knows whether or not the review is to take place.[10] A tenant is only likely positively to want a review carried out where the clause is an upward/downward one and the market has fallen. In such cases the courts will only require the landlord to review the rent where the clause is worded in such a way as to impose a review[11]; if it merely, in effect, gives the landlord an option to review or provides for what is to happen in the absence of a review, then the tenant cannot insist on the rent being revised.[12]

[1] So that a 'subject to contract' notice will usually be invalid, see *Shirlcar v Heinitz* (1983) 268 Estates Gazette 362 and on 'subject to contract' generally, see para 5.34.

[2] *Amalgamated Estates v Joystretch Manufacturing* (1980) 257 Estates Gazette 489. CA. So, for example, where a counter-notice is required to operate as an election to have the rent decided by a third party, a notice must clearly do this; a letter that merely objects to the landlord's proposed rent will not be a valid notice, see *Fox & Widley v Guram* [1998] 1 EGLR 91.

[3] *United Scientific Holdings v Burnley Borough Council* [1978] AC 904, HL; see further paras 8.28–8.31.

[4] *United Scientific Holdings v Burnley Borough Council* [1978] AC 904, HL.

[5] *Starmark Enterprises Ltd v CPL Distribution Ltd* [2001] EWCA Civ 1252, [2002] Ch 306.

[6] See para 36.95.

[7] *Central Estates Ltd v Secretary of State for the Environment* [1997] 1 EGLR 239, CA.

[8] *United Scientific Holdings v Burnley Borough Council* [1978] AC 904, HL; *Barclays Bank plc v Savile Estates* Ltd [2002] 24 EG 142, CA.

[9] The landlord can simply ignore the notice and thereby lose the right to review.

[10] In practice tenants with upward only rent reviews will normally do nothing; although the new rent will always be back-dated to the review date, having the use of the money in the meantime is usually preferable.

[11] *Royal Bank of Scotland plc v Jennings* [1997] 19 EG 152.

[12] *Harben Style Ltd v Rhodes Trust* [1995] 1 EGLR 118.

36.58 *The valuation basis* The essence of a rent review is that, as at each review date[1], a current open market rental value for the premises is assessed and, where that exceeds the rent currently payable (ie the passing rent), the new figure is substituted as the new rent for the next review period. This process inevitably requires the hypothesis that the premises are vacant and available to let when, in reality, the property is being occupied by the current tenant. This means that, in order to ease the task of the valuer, the clause normally contains a variety of assumptions (eg as to the length and terms of this hypothetical letting and the state of the property) and 'disregards', ie matters which should be ignored (eg any improvements carried out and paid for by a tenant). So, for example, a very basic[2] rent review clause would usually provide that the reviewed rent is to be the rent that would be agreed, in the open market between a willing landlord and a willing tenant, for the demised premises with vacant possession, on a lease equal in length to the unexpired residue of, and on the same terms as, the actual lease[3]. It will be assumed that the premises are fitted out and ready for occupation[4] and that the tenant's covenants have been complied with[5]; any improvements carried out by someone who was at the time[6] a tenant of the property will be disregarded. It should be appreciated that, while assumptions and disregards are usually designed to do no more than create a fair basis for the rent review valuation, they can be used to manipulate a rental advantage (usually, but not exclusively, for the landlord). The courts will strive to avoid interpreting these in a way that departs from the underlying purpose of a review clause, namely to align rents with current market levels[7].

[1] Note that although rent reviews are usually not settled until after the review date, it is that date which is invariably the valuation date for fixing the new rent. It is also the date from which the new rent will be payable.

[2] It must be stressed that we here highlight only the main valuation elements of a rent review clause; in practice, all rent reviews will be more detailed and wide ranging.

[3] Thus, at rent review, the valuer must assess the rental impact of the actual lease terms so that, for example, if a tenant is subject to an unusually onerous repairing obligation, or a very narrow user clause, the reviewed rent will be discounted: see *Norwich Union Insurance Society v British Railways Board* [1987] 2 EGLR 137 (25% reduction in the reviewed rent due to an onerous repairing covenant), *Plinth Property Investments Ltd v Mott, Hay and Anderson* (1978) 38 P & CR 361, CA (36% reduction due to a very tight and absolute user clause).

[4] This is to ensure that a tenant cannot argue at review, for a discount to reflect the benefit of a rent free period for fitting out which is normally given to new tenants at the beginning of their lease: see *London and Leeds Estates Ltd v Paribas Ltd* [1993] 2 EGLR 149, CA.

[5] The most important of which is any tenant's covenant to repair; this means that, if the tenant has not complied with the repairing obligations, the rent will not be reduced to reflect the disrepair. Even in the absence of any express provision to this effect, the courts will imply a requirement that the premises be valued as if in repair: see *Harmsworth Pension Fund Trustees Ltd v Charringtons Industrial Holdings Ltd* [1985] 1 EGLR 97. Note that where it is the *landlord's* repairing obligations that have not been complied with, the premises will be valued in their existing state, see *Fawke v Viscount Chelsea* (1979) 250 Estates Gazette 855. These assumptions arise in order to avoid a wrongdoer from benefiting from their own default.

[6] It is not usually necessary for the improvements to have been carried out by the *current* tenant; thus where a tenant carries out improvements and then assigns the lease, the assignee will have the benefit of the disregard at the next rent review.

[7] So, in a series of conjoined appeals—*Co-operative Wholesale Society Ltd v National Westminster Bank plc* [1995] 1 EGLR 97, CA—the Court of Appeal strove to avoid holding that provisions in a rent review clause entitled the landlords to claim the headline, as opposed to the effective, rent for the properties.

36.59 *Resolving rent review disputes* Where the parties are unable to agree a rent review it is usual for the rent review clause to provide that the matter will be referred to a third party, usually a chartered surveyor (or sometimes a lawyer), acting as either an arbitrator or expert[1]. The capacity in which the third party is to act can have a significant impact on both the procedure and outcome of a rent review dispute.

Arbitrators act in a quasi-judicial capacity; their function is to resolve a dispute[2]. They must act impartially and give a fair hearing to both sides[3]; although they are now empowered to make their own investigations[4], they should normally base their decisions on the evidence put to them by the parties (although this does not necessarily have to comply with the strict rules of evidence[5]). They must normally give reasons for their decisions[6]. They are entitled to use their expertise to evaluate the arguments put by the parties, but not to substitute their own views (unless these are put to the parties and their comments are invited)[7], or to make rulings on points not raised in argument[8]. An arbitrator's decision ('award') is open to limited challenge in the courts. With the leave of the court, it can be set aside, varied or remitted where the arbitrator has made an error of law that is either obviously wrong or, where the issue is of general public importance, open to serious doubt[9]. An award can also be set aside or remitted where there has been a serious irregularity in the conduct of the arbitration, but only where this would give rise to a substantial injustice[10]. An arbitrator has a wide range of powers conferred by the Arbitration Act 1996, notably that to order disclosure of documents[11] and to award costs[12].

Experts are not governed by the Arbitration Act and have none of the statutory powers accorded to arbitrators; they cannot therefore order disclosure or, save where the lease gives the power to do so, make an award of costs. Experts do not act in a quasi-judicial capacity but merely as professional persons appointed to carry out a specific task—to fix the rent. They are not required to hear submissions from the parties (unless the rent review clause requires this). In practice, experts will usually invite the parties to put their case, but they are not obliged to base their decision on this evidence. Although experts may be required to give reasons for their decision, they will normally opt to give only a non-speaking valuation (ie one without reasons). They can be held liable in negligence should they act without due care[13] (although, to date, no expert has been found to have been negligent when determining a rent at rent review). A court will not readily disturb a determination made by an expert who has been given the exclusive jurisdiction to deal with the matter by the lease[14]. Exactly what aspects of the rent determination process are within the exclusive remit of the expert will depend on the precise wording of the rent review clause. It will usually be the case that the courts will always regard the valuation approach as a matter for the expert alone. However, it may be that the legal interpretation of the clause and what it properly requires the expert to take into account in the valuation is an area that the court will not necessarily regard as their exclusive territory[15]. Where this is the case, the court may set aside a determination where an expert has misinterpreted the rent review clause[16]. It will be easier, in practice, to challenge an expert's decision where it is a speaking (ie reasoned) award rather than a non-speaking one.[17]

[1] The rent review clause will almost invariably be specific as to the capacity of the third party; if it is not, the courts tend, in rent review cases, to assume that the appointment is as an expert: see *Safeway Food Stores Ltd v Banderway Ltd* (1983) 267 EG 850.

[2] This means that they are immune from any action in negligence, see para 16.25 and the Arbitration Act 1996, s 29.

[3] Arbitration Act 1996, s 33.

[4] AA 1996, s 34(1)(g).

[5] AA 1996, s 34(2)(f).

[6] AA 1996, s 52(4).

[7] *Fox v PG Wellfair Ltd* [1981] 2 Lloyd's Rep 514, CA. In *Checkpoint Ltd v Strathclyde Pension Fund* [2003] EWCA Civ 84, [2003] 14 EG 124, CA, the Court of Appeal made it clear that an arbitrator may have more leeway to use his own experience where the rent review clause specifically requires him to have expertise of a particular type.

[8] See *Guardcliffe Properties Ltd v City and St James* [2003] EWHC 215 (Ch), 147 Sol Jo LB 693.

[9] Arbitration Act 1996, s 69.

[10] AA 1996, s 68 and see *Checkpoint Ltd v Strathclyde Pension Fund* [2003] 14 EG 124, CA.

[11] AA 1996, s 34(2)(d).

[12] AA 1996, s 59–65.

[13] *Palacath v Flanagan* (1985) 274 Estates Gazette 143.

[14] *Jones v Sherwood Computer Services plc* [1992] 2 All ER 170, CA.

[15] *Mercury Communications Ltd v Director General of Telecommunications* [1996] 1 All ER 575, HL; *British Shipbuilders v VSEL Consortium plc* [1997] 1 Lloyd's Rep 106; *National Grid plc v M 25 Group Ltd* [1999] 1 EGLR 65, CA.

[16] *National Grid plc v M 25 Group Ltd* [1999] 1 EGLR 65, CA, where the Court of Appeal held that it could either rule on the meaning of the rent review clause before the expert had made his (non-speaking) determination (as was the case there) or, where an expert had made an error as to the meaning of the clause, set aside the determination after it had been made. See also *Level Properties Ltd v Ball Brothers Ltd* [2007] EWHC 744 (Ch) where what appears to have been a reasoned award was set aside and *Homepace Ltd v Sita South East Ltd* [2008] EWCA Civ 1 where a reasoned decision was set aside.

[17] In *Morgan Sindall plc v Sawston Farms (Cambs) Ltd* [1999] 1 EGLR 90, the Court of Appeal held that, in the case of a non-speaking determination, a court should not set aside an expert's determination after the event by speculating as to the expert's reasons. However, in *Homepace Ltd v Sita South East Ltd* [2008] EWCA Civ 1 the Court of Appeal suggested that there is no difference in principle between a challenge to a speaking and non-speaking award; it did however accept that misinterpretations can be difficult to identify where the valuation is non-speaking.

Service charges

36.60 Where buildings or complexes such as blocks of flats or offices, or shopping centres are in multiple occupation, it is usual for the landlord to undertake responsibility for the repair and maintenance[1] of the structure and exterior and other common parts, to insure, and to provide the services since this is the only practicable way of dealing with such matters. The tenants then covenant to pay the landlord's costs of carrying out these obligations. Service charges are a fertile source of disputes between landlords and tenants since the latter are always concerned that they may be being over-charged, or charged for works carried out to too high a standard. A service charge will define the items that fall within the service charge[2] and provide a mechanism for allocating payments between the various tenants (eg based on a percentage, relative floor space or rateable value); ideally it should also prescribe the information to be provided to tenants and lay down a procedure for resolving disputes. The courts will strictly construe service charge provisions and will not allow recovery for items unless they are clearly covered by the terms of the lease[3]. Where a lease allowed for the recovery of sums 'properly expended' by the landlord, the court took the view that although works of repair were an item within the service charge, they could not be charged to one of the tenants; its short lease was approaching its expiry date and the repairs had not been carried out for its benefit[4].

Service charges relating to residential property are the subject of strict statutory control. Briefly, service charge moneys must be held on trust in a separate account[5] and cannot normally be recovered unless demanded within 18 months of the cost being incurred[6]. Service charges[7] cannot be recovered unless they have been reasonably incurred and the work or services provided to a reasonable standard[8]. Either the landlord or the tenant can ask the leasehold valuation tribunal to make a determination on reasonableness[9]. Where works costing over a prescribed amount, or to be carried out under a contract for over 12 months, are planned, the landlord must consult the tenants and provide them with at least two estimates of the likely cost[10]. Tenants are also entitled to a regular statement of account and have wide rights to inspect estimates and accounts[11]. It is further provided that any administration charges (eg for approvals or the provision of documents) made by the landlord must be reasonable[12].

Service charges relating to commercial property are not subject to any statutory controls[13]. It was thought that there would always be an implied term that such service charges must be reasonable[14]. However, there is now some doubt as to whether or not this is the case[15].

[1] See paras 36.40–36.52.
[2] A landlord cannot, by way of a service charge, recover the cost of works falling within the statutory repairing obligations imposed by the Housing Act 1985, s11 (as to which see para 36.45), Housing Act 1985, s 11(4).
[3] See, for example, *Mullaney v Maybourne Grange (Croydon) Management Co* [1986] 1 EGLR 70; *Jollybird Ltd v Fairzone Ltd* [1990] 1 EGLR 253; *Morgan v Stainer* [1993] 2 EGLR 73.
[4] *Scottish Mutual Assurance plc v Jardine Public Relations Ltd* [1999] EGCS 43.
[5] Landlord and Tenant Act 1987 (LTA 1987), ss 42, 42A and 42B.
[6] LTA 1985, s 20B(1).
[7] As defined by the Landlord and Tenant Act 1985, s 18, as amended by the Commonhold and Leasehold Reform Act 2002 ('CLRA 2002').
[8] LTA 1985, s 19.

⁹ LTA 1985, s 19(2A) and (2B).

¹⁰ LTA 1985, s 20,20ZA (as substituted and added by the CLRA 2002).

¹¹ LTA 1985, ss 21, 21A (as substituted and added by the CLRA 2002).

¹² CLRA 2002), s 158 and Sch 11.

¹³ There is a voluntary code of practice in place and the Code for Leasing Business Premises in England and Wales 2007 recommends that this should always be adhered to *Service Charges in Commercial Property: A Guide to Good Practice* (2nd edn, 2000). The RICS has also issued a code of practice : *Service Charges in Commercial Property* 2006 with which its members are expected to comply.

¹⁴ *Finchbourne v Rodrigues* [1976] 3 All ER 581, CA.

¹⁵ *Havenridge Ltd v Boston Dyers Ltd* [1994] 49 EG 111, CA; *Berrycroft Management Co Ltd v Sinclair Gardens Investments (Kensington) Ltd* [1997] 1 EGLR 47, CA.

Insurance

36.61 Either the landlord will covenant to insure the property on the basis that the tenant will pay the premiums, or the tenant will be required to insure the property, often with a named company[1], to its full value. Failure to keep the property insured constitutes a breach.[2]

¹ Where the premises are a house, the tenant is entitled, provide certain conditions are met, to insure with any company, Commonhold and Leasehold Reform Act 2002, s 164.

² *Penniall v Harborne* (1848) 11 QB 368.

COVENANTS RELATING TO OUTGOINGS: KEY POINTS

- A lease invariably reserves a rent but rent is not a legal requirement.

- Without a provision to the contrary the rent would remain the same for the whole period of the lease; it is now normal for leases of any length to include a rent review. In commercial leases rent reviews are usually upward only.

- A rent review clause may set out the procedure for instigating a review; it will set out the valuation basis for arriving at the new rent and a process for resolving any dispute, either by reference to an arbitrator or an expert.

- Where a rent review clause does set out a procedure for review, time provisions are presumed not to be strict, ie time is not of the essence.

- The basis for the reviewed rent is normally the current open market rental value for a lease on the same terms, subject to a series of assumptions and disregards (which can have a significant impact on the new rent).

- Where a lease is of part of a building or complex it is usual for it to contain service charge provisions which oblige the tenant to contribute to the landlord's cost of repairs, maintenance and the provision of services.

- In the case of residential leases, service charges are subject to strict statutory controls. Service charges in non-residential leases depend entirely on the terms of the lease.

Remedies for breach of covenant

For breach of covenants other than for payment of rent

36.62 *Contractual remedies* For breach of covenants other than for payment of rent the injured party may pursue the normal contractual remedies, ie damages can be sought[1] or an injunction obtained in order to restrain the breach. These have already been discussed[2].

Peculiar to leases is the landlord's remedy of forfeiture of the lease. It should be noted that, where the breach is of the covenant to repair important variations to the basic rules sometimes apply.[3]

[1] It should be appreciated that a landlord may bring such an action not only against the current tenant, but also against a former tenant who remains liable either under the terms of the lease or as a result of entering into an authorised guarantee agreement, or any other guarantor; see paras 36.71–36.88.

[2] See paras 11.1–11.34 and 11.46–11.51.

[3] See para 36.67.

Forfeiture [1]

36.63 *The right to forfeit* The landlord normally has a right to claim forfeiture of the lease because a proviso for re-entry in the event of a breach of covenant is invariably expressly included in the lease.[2] Such a right of re-entry is a proprietary right and as such is enforceable not only against the tenant but also against assignees and sub-tenants (including mortgagees). In claiming forfeiture and exercising a right of re-entry the landlord is choosing to put an end to the tenant's interest in the property because of the breach. It is a remedy that needs to be exercised with some thought, especially in a depressed market, where the lease is at a market as opposed to a ground rent. In such circumstances, the tenant may regard the termination of the lease as a blessing and the landlord may be left with a property that cannot readily be re-let[3].

[1] It should be noted that the Law Commission published yet another report incorporating a draft bill, which proposes sweeping changes to the law on forfeiture; see Termination of Tenancies for Tenant Default 2006 Law Com No 303. There is no indication of when, if ever, this Report will be adopted by the Government.

[2] In those rare cases where the lease does not contain an express right of re-entry for breach, the landlord can only forfeit for breaches of those covenants which are framed as conditions (eg by the use of wording such as 'on condition that').

[3] See, for example, *GS Fashions Ltd v B & Q plc* [1995] 4 All ER 899.

36.64 *Waiver* The landlord may lose any right to forfeit for a breach of covenant where the right to do so has expressly or impliedly been waived. Implied waiver can only occur where the landlord (or agent), knowing of the breach, does some unequivocal act which, considered objectively without regard to the landlord's motive or intention, is consistent only with the continued existence of the lease.[1] The onus is on the tenant to show that waiver has occurred. The act most commonly relied on as constituting waiver is the acceptance of future rent. The very fact of acceptance of rent,[2] even as a result of a clerical error, amounts, as a matter of law, to waiver of the right to forfeit.[3] Whether or not other acts amount to waiver is a question of fact.[4] If the breach is of a continuing nature, for example a failure to insure or to repair, continued breach after the waiver revives the right of re-entry. Waiver only deprives the landlord of the right to forfeit; other remedies for the breach can still be pursued.

[1] *Matthews v Smallwood* [1910] 1 Ch 777 at 786; *Central Estates (Belgravia) Ltd v Woolgar (No 2)* [1972] 3 All ER 610, CA; *Expert Clothing Service and Sales Ltd v Hillgate House Ltd* [1985] 2 All ER 998, CA.

[2] A demand for future rent is similarly treated as waiver as a matter of law; see *David Blackstone Ltd v Burnetts (West End) Ltd* [1973] 3 All ER 782.

[3] *Central Estates (Belgravia) Ltd v Woolgar (No 2)* [1972] 3 All ER 610, CA.

[4] *Expert Clothing Service and Sales Ltd v Hillgate House Ltd* [1985] 2 All ER 998, CA.

36.65 *Procedure* The LPA 1925, s 146 provides that a right of re-entry or forfeiture for breach of a covenant or condition *other than one for payment of rent* may not be enforced unless and until the landlord serves on the tenant a notice which is designed to give the tenant reasonable information about what, if anything, has to be done in order to avoid forfeiture. In the case of a long lease (ie one for more than 21 years) of a dwelling, a landlord cannot issue a s 146 notice until at least 14 days after either the tenant has admitted the breach, or a leasehold valuation tribunal has determined that a breach has occurred[1]

A s 146 notice must:

- specify the particular breach complained of;
- require the lessee to remedy it (if the breach is capable of remedy[2]); and
- if desired, require the lessee to make compensation in money for the breach (if required).

Having served a s 146 notice, the landlord is compelled then to allow the tenant sufficient time to remedy the breach and to make reasonable compensation (where that was required) before he can take any further steps. Even where the breach is not capable of remedy, the tenant must still be given a short time in which to consider their position before the landlord proceeds to forfeiture.[3]

The landlord should normally forfeit by bringing a court action for possession. Although, there is the alternative of forfeiting by peaceably re-entering on the land, this is not to be recommended, for the following reasons. First, in the case of residential lettings, forfeiture must be effected by court proceedings while any person is lawfully residing in the premises.[4] Second, the landlord runs the risk of contravening the Criminal Law Act 1977, s 6 (which prohibits the use or threat of violence to secure entry) or some other provision of the criminal law. Third, forfeiting by way of peaceable re-entry does not, as was once thought, give the landlord an unchallengeable right to possession since a tenant, sub-tenant or mortgagee may still be able to claim relief.[5]

It should also be noted that a landlord of residential premises is not entitled to re-enter for non-payment of a service charge unless its amount has been admitted, agreed, or determined.[6] This is designed to prevent landlords threatening tenants (or their mortgagees) with the termination of their lease for non-payment of what might well be disputed service charge payments.

---

[1] Commonhold and Leasehold Reform Act 2002, s 168. Where the lease does not exceed 21 years, the landlord can serve a s 146 notice provided that this informs the tenant that the landlord cannot take the matter further (ie by actually re-entering) until the service charge amount is admitted, agreed or determined, Housing Act 1996, s 82.

[2] Certain breaches are, legally speaking, regarded as incapable of remedy. These include the breach of a covenant against immoral user (see *Rugby School (Governors) v Tannahill* [1935] 1 KB 87, CA) and that of a covenant against assignment or sub-letting (see *Scala House and District Property Co Ltd v Forbes* [1973] 3 All ER 308, CA). See generally *Expert Clothing Service and Sales Ltd v Hillgate House Ltd* [1985] 2 All ER 998, CA and *Savva v Hussein* [1996] 47 EG 138, CA. Where a breach is incapable of remedy the landlord may proceed to forfeit more rapidly (see note 3 below); furthermore, the tenant is less likely to be given relief, see para 36.66.

[3] *Horsey Estate Ltd v Steiger* [1899] 2 Qb 79, CA. Fourteen days' notice has been held sufficient in such cases: *Civil Service Co-operative Society Ltd v McGrigor's Trustee* [1923] 2 Ch 347.

[4] Protection from Eviction Act 1977, s 2, see further para 37.23. Section 2 applies where only part of the premises is used for residential purposes, *Pirbakaran v Patel* [2006] EWCA Civ 685 (where the premises were a shop with a flat above).

[5] *Billson v Residential Apartments Ltd* [1992] 1 AC 494, [1992] 1 All ER 141, HL; see para 36.66.

[6] Housing Act 1996, s 81.

36.66 *Relief* At any time from the service of the s 146 notice until the landlord has recovered possession of the property under an unassailable court order,[1] the tenant may apply to the court for relief from forfeiture.[2] The court has a complete discretion as to whether or not to grant relief and on what terms, if any, it thinks fit,[3] although the tenant will, invariably, be required to remedy the breach.

Where a lease is terminated by forfeiture this necessarily destroys any sub-leases and mortgages granted by the lessee. This, of course, would involve considerable hardship to an innocent sub-lessee or mortgagee and so, under the LPA 1925, s 146(4), they are entitled to apply to court for relief. This will normally only be given where the sub-tenant (or mortgagee) is prepared to remedy the tenant's breach. Where relief is given, a new lease, held direct of the landlord, will be vested in the applicant.

[1] *Billson v Residential Apartments Ltd* [1992] 1 AC 494, [1992] 1 All ER 141, HL. This means that, should a landlord forfeit by way of peaceable re-entry, a tenant (and, presumably a sub-tenant or mortgagee) can still apply to court for relief. It is this which makes it unwise for a landlord to re-enter peaceably.

[2] Under LPA 1925, s 146(2).

[3] LPA 1925, s 146(2).

For breach of repairing covenants

36.67 We have already mentioned that certain special rules apply in cases where the covenant which has been breached is that to repair. Where it is the *landlord* who is seeking a remedy the following restrictions apply.

First, an *injunction* or *specific performance* in order to enforce a tenant's obligation to repair cannot normally be obtained since damages will usually be an adequate remedy.[1]

Second, where a landlord is seeking *damages*, two special rules apply. In certain cases[2] an action for damages cannot be commenced without first serving a s 146 notice and, where the tenant so requires[3], without obtaining the leave of the court. Even where the landlord does obtain damages, the measure of those damages is limited by statute; they can, in no event, exceed the amount by which the value of the reversion is diminished and, where the landlord is planning to demolish or redevelop the premises at the end of the lease, damages cannot be recovered at all.[4]

Third, where a landlord is seeking to *forfeit* for breach of a repairing covenant a number of special rules apply. In certain instances[5] the s 146 notice must inform the tenant that the benefit of the Leasehold Property (Repairs) Act 1938 can be claimed by serving a counter-notice within 28 days. The landlord must prove that the tenant actually knows that the s 146 notice has been served.[6] Where the tenant does claim the benefit of the LP(R)A 1938 the landlord cannot proceed to forfeit without the leave of the court. This will not be given unless it is shown that the tenant is in breach and that the case is covered by one of the 1938 Act grounds.[7]

Finally, where the s 146 notice relates to internal decorative repairs, the tenant may apply to court for relief from all liability for such repairs, which the court may grant if in all the circumstances it considers the notice unreasonable.[8]

These restrictions on landlords' remedies can largely be avoided by the inclusion in the lease of a contractual provision under which the landlord can, where the tenant is in breach of repairing obligations, re-enter the premises, carry out the repairs and recover the cost of the work from the tenant[9]. It is now commonplace for such provisions to be included in leases of commercial premises.

Where it is the *tenant* who is seeking a remedy for the landlord's breach of the repairing obligations, not surprisingly, there are no special restrictions but, rather, additional rights. In the case of residential tenancies, there is no bar to the tenant being awarded specific performance,[10] and in any case the court has a general jurisdiction, which should be carefully exercised, to order a landlord to do some specific work pursuant to the covenant to repair.[11] It may also be noted at this point that the court has the power, at the suit of a tenant, to appoint a receiver to receive the rent and exercise the duties of the landlord,[12] a power which has been used where a landlord is in breach of a repairing covenant and has persistently failed to remedy the breach.[13] In the case of tenancies of flats, this general jurisdiction has been superseded by the right, given by Pt II of the Landlord and Tenant Act 1987, to apply to the leasehold valuation tribunal for the appointment of a manager where the landlord is in breach of an obligation, such as a repairing covenant, which is likely to continue[14]. Where this remedy does not solve the problem the tenants can apply for the compulsory acquisition of the landlord's interest under Pt III of the 1987 Act.

[1] There has been one reported case in which an order for the specific performance of a repairing covenant has been made against a tenant: *Rainbow Estates Ltd v Tokenhold Ltd* [1998] 2 All ER 860. Unusually, the lease contained neither a forfeiture provision, nor any right for the landlord to enter and carry out the repairs; in these circumstances it was clear that damages would not be an adequate remedy.

[2] Ie all leases (except those of agricultural holdings) granted for a term of seven years or more, of which at least three years remain unexpired; Leasehold Property (Repairs) Act 1938, s 1(2).

[3] Where the tenant serves a counternotice within 28 days of receiving the s 146 notice the landlord must then obtain the leave of the court; LP(R)A 1938, s 1(3).

[4] LTA 1927, s 18.

[5] Ie where the lease is covered by the Leasehold Property (Repairs) Act 1938; see note 2 above.

[6] LTA 1927, s 18(2).

[7] Leasehold Property (Repairs) Act 1938, s 1(5); see *Associated British Ports v CH Bailey plc* [1990] 1 All ER 929, HL.

[8] LPA 1925, s 147.

[9] After years of uncertainty the efficacy of such provisions was confirmed by the Court of Appeal in *Jervis v Harris* [1996] 1 ALL ER 303.

[10] Landlord and Tenant Act 1985, s 17.

[11] *Jeune v Queens Cross Properties Ltd* [1974] Ch 97, [1973] 3 All ER 97.

[12] Senior Courts Act 1981, s 37.

[13] See, for example, *Hart v Emelkirk* [1983] 1 WLR 1289; *Daiches v Bluelake Investments Ltd* [1985] 2 EGLR 67.

[14] Landlord and Tenant Act 1987, s 24.

For non-payment of rent

36.68 In the event of non-payment of rent, the additional[1] remedies available to the landlord are distress, an action to recover the rent[2], and forfeiture.

[1] Ie those over and above the contractual right to sue for the agreed sum (as to which see paras 11.35–11.40).

[2] It should be appreciated that such an action may be brought not only against the current tenant, but also against a former tenant who remains liable either under the terms of the lease or as a result of entering into an authorised guarantee agreement, or any other guarantor; see paras 36.71–36.88.

Distress [1]

36.69 This is an ancient remedy which the Law Commission has recommended should be abolished.[2] Its attraction to landlords is that it is available without recourse to the courts[3] and without prior notice to the tenant, thus making it extremely effective in practice. For this reason government has acceded to pressure that it should be retained for commercial property. Currently, the right of distress entitles the landlord, or rather his or her certificated bailiff, to enter the demised premises and impound goods found there[5] to provide security for the outstanding rent. Provided that notice is given to the tenant these goods may be sold after five days. Part 3 of the Tribunals, Courts and Enforcement Act 2007[6] abolishes distress and sets out a new procedure for what will be known as Commercial Rent Arrears Recovery ('CRAR'). This requires advance notice to be given to the tenant and will regulate the process to be followed for the seizure and sale of the tenant's goods. However, the implementation of Part 3 has already been postponed on several occasions; it is currently scheduled to be brought into force in April 2012.

¹ Distress for Rent Acts 1689 and 1733.
² Landlord and Tenant: Distress for Rent (1991) Law Com No 194.
³ Save in relation to tenancies of dwelling-houses falling within the Rent Act 1977 or Housing Act 1988, where leave of the county court is required; Rent Act 1977, s 147, Housing Act 1988, s 19.
⁴ Distress for Rent Consultation Paper, 2001.
⁵ Subject to certain limited exceptions.
⁶ Section 72, Sch 12.

Forfeiture

36.70 The landlord may claim forfeiture of the lease for non-payment of rent where the lease contains an express proviso for re-entry.[1] However, in the case of long leases (ie those of more than 21 years) of dwellings, a landlord cannot forfeit for non-payment of small amounts[2] of rent, service charges, or administrative charges[3] unless these have not been paid within a prescribed period[4]. At common law, the landlord cannot claim forfeiture without having first made a formal demand for the exact sum due, on the demised premises, between sunrise and sunset. The technicality of a formal demand is invariably dispensed with by an express provision in the lease.[5] A s 146 notice is not required in the case of forfeiture for non-payment of rent. (Thus, in theory at least, a landlord is usually able to forfeit for non-payment of rent without giving any prior warning to the tenant; in practice the tenant is likely to have been chased for payment for some time.) The law as to waiver and as to the exercise of the right of re-entry explained in paras 36.64 and 36.65 applies equally in cases of non-payment of rent.

Most applications for relief from forfeiture for non-payment of rent are heard in the county court[6]. If the tenant pays off all the arrears and the landlord's costs at least five days before the hearing date, the proceedings are automatically terminated[7]. Where this is not done and an order for possession is granted, this must be suspended for at least four weeks (or, at the court's discretion, for longer). If the arrears are paid off within this period (or within any extension granted by the court) then relief will be granted[8]. If this is not done then the order for possession will be enforced[9]. Even then the tenant has one further chance to obtain relief by applying to court within six months of the date on which possession was recovered by the landlord[10]. Mortgagees and sub-tenants may apply for relief either under LPA 1925, s 146(4) or under the County Courts Act. In the latter instance relief must be applied for within six months[11].

¹ Where this is not the case, the landlord will still be able to forfeit if the covenant to pay rent is framed as a condition of the lease.
² Currently set at £350 or less.
³ Commonhold and Leasehold Reform Act 2002, s 167.
⁴ Currently set at three years.
⁵ In any event, in cases where half a year's rent is in arrear and insufficient distrainable goods are available on the premises, there is no need for a formal demand: Common Law Procedure Act 1852, s 210. See also County Courts Act 1984, s 139(1), for actions brought in the county court.
⁶ It should be noted that, where an application for relief is made to the High Court, the rules are slightly different; we do not deal with these.
⁷ County Courts Act 1984 (CCA 1984), s 138(2).
⁸ CCA 1984, s 138(3).
⁹ CCA 1984, s 138(7).
¹⁰ CCA 1984, s 138(9A).
¹¹ *United Dominions Trust Ltd v Shellpoint Trustees Ltd* [1993] 4 All ER 310, CA.

REMEDIES FOR BREACH OF COVENANT: KEY POINTS

- Where a party to a lease is in breach of covenant the other side has all the usual contractual remedies; however they have certain additional remedies.
- Where a tenant is in breach of covenant a landlord has the right to forfeit the lease (ie terminate by re-entry) unless the landlord has lost this right by waiver.
  - Where the breach is of a covenant other than that to pay rent the landlord must serve a s 146 notice (and where the breach is of a repairing covenant there are additional requirements). No such notice is required in the case of non-payment of rent.
  - Peaceable re-entry is only possible in the case of non-residential leases. Re-entry by court proceedings is always preferable.
  - The tenant always has a right to apply for relief; this is automatic in some cases of non-payment of rent where the tenant has paid off the arrears. In other cases it is at the discretion of the court provided that the tenant remedies the breach.
- Where a tenant has failed to pay rent the landlord may be able to levy distress, ie enter the premises without notice and seize goods to the value of the rent owed and sell these if payment is not made.

Enforceability of covenants by and against assignees

36.71 We have indicated that, subject to any controls imposed by the lease,[1] a tenant may assign the lease to another, ie transfer the whole of the remainder of the term[2]. The longer the lease the more likely this is to happen and, in practice, assignments are commonplace. Equally, during the continuance of a lease, a landlord is completely free to transfer their interest in the land. We now need to consider the effect which such transfers will have on the enforceability of the covenants contained in the lease. To what extent will a new landlord be able to enforce the lease covenants against either the original tenant, or an assignee of the lease? Can a new tenant insist that the original landlord, or an assignee of the reversion, perform the obligations imposed by the lease terms?

The law in this area was radically overhauled by the Landlord and Tenant (Covenants) Act 1995 ('LT(C)A 1995'). This introduced a new regime on the enforceability of leasehold covenants, but only for leases entered into on or after 1 January 1996 ('new' leases); the previous rules, with limited modifications, continue to apply to leases granted before that date ('old' leases). Since 'old' leases will remain in existence for very many years to come, those dealing with property need to be equally familiar with both regimes. We turn first to the enforceability of covenants contained in 'old' leases.

[1] Para 36.28.
[2] This should not be confused with the situation where a tenant sublets, ie carves a shorter lease out of his own interest. For subleases, see para 36.89.

Leases entered into before 1 January 1996

36.72 The rules relating to the enforceability of covenants in 'old' leases are essentially two-fold. First, and obviously, all covenants, whether imposing positive or negative obligations, are mutually enforceable between the original parties to the lease as a matter of basic contract law. Second, as we shall see, where there has been an assignment of the lease or the reversion, or both, all covenants (whether positive or negative[1]) which 'touch and concern' the land which is the subject of the lease are mutually enforceable between the persons who are now in the relationship of landlord and tenant. This relationship is known as 'privity of estate' and is the very basis on which such covenants remain enforceable.

¹ Thus, where property is held by way of a lease, positive obligations will pass on to an assignee. This is in sharp contrast to covenants affecting freehold land where, as we have seen at para 33.4, only negative covenants can bind transferees.

Touching and concerning

36.73 Before examining the operation of these two rules, we must first consider what is meant by the phrase 'touch and concern'. It means that the covenant should relate to either the demised land, or to the reversion; it must be reasonably incidental to the relationship of landlord and tenant rather than merely of personal advantage to the particular covenantee and must affect the nature, quality, mode of enjoyment or value of the land¹.

Examples of covenants which have been held to touch and concern the property are a covenant to pay rent, a covenant to repair the property, a covenant not to assign, the landlord's covenant for quiet enjoyment, a covenant by a surety guaranteeing the rent and a covenant giving the tenant an option to renew the lease. Covenants which have been held not to touch and concern the land include a covenant not to open a public house within half a mile of the demised public house, a covenant to pay the tenant £500 unless the lease is renewed, a covenant to pay rates on other land, and a covenant giving the tenant an option to purchase the reversion.

¹ *P & A Swift Investments v Combined English Stores Group plc* [1988] 2 All ER 885, HL.

Assignment of the lease

36.74 *A single assignment* We now turn to consider the operation of the two basic rules relating to the enforceability of covenants in 'old' leases.

We first consider the case where the tenant has assigned the entire leasehold interest:

Here, T has assigned the lease to A. L and A are now in the relationship of landlord and tenant; they have 'privity of estate'. Therefore covenants in the lease which touch and concern the land are enforceable by L against A, and by A against L.¹ Thus, for example, A will be bound by a covenant to pay rent and L will be liable to A on the covenant for quiet enjoyment.

If A is in breach of a covenant touching and concerning the land, such as the covenant to pay rent, L could, and normally would, take action against A to remedy the breach.² However, it must be remembered that there is still a contract between L and T; under this contract T remains liable on the covenants for the rest of the lease³. This means that, should a successor of the tenant fail to perform a covenant, the original tenant is in breach of their *contractual* obligation. So, instead of, or as well as,⁴ suing A, L may also sue T in respect of A's breach of covenant. This continuing liability of T is often referred to as 'original tenant liability'.

It is to be noted that T will not be liable for the breach of any *new or changed* covenant inserted into the lease by L and A after the assignment from T to A.⁵ However T is liable in respect of any changes which occur after the assignment but which are the result of the operation of the terms of the lease as they existed at the date of the assignment; this means that, in particular, T is liable for rent which has been increased after the assignment in accordance with a rent review clause which was already in the lease.⁶

If L does sue T, T may then sue A in an attempt to recover money paid to L. This will be on the basis of a term implied by statute[7] that A will perform the covenants in the lease and, if not, will then indemnify T for any losses that T suffers as a result of A's breach of the lease covenants. In reality, A is unlikely to be able to pay T.

In practice, L is only likely to sue T where A has failed to pay rent and is without funds. However, during the recession of the early 1990s, it became commonplace for landlords to utilise their rights against original tenants and it was the latters' complaints which eventually persuaded the government to implement a reform of this area of the law.

In the event, most of the provisions of the LT(C)A 1995 apply only to leases entered into after 1 January 1996, leaving tenants under existing leases to the rigours of the old law. However, two of the new measures introduced by the 1995 Act do apply to 'old' leases. First, in order to be able to recover a 'fixed charge'[8] from a former tenant, the landlord must serve a default notice within six months of those sums becoming due.[9] This notice must specify the sums due. Second, a former tenant who pays all the sums specified in a default notice is then entitled to require the landlord to grant an overriding lease.[10] Broadly, this lease sits between the current tenant, A, and L; thus T becomes A's landlord and is able to take steps to enforce the covenants which A is breaking, and in particular, to forfeit A's lease[11]. This at least means that T then has the right either to occupy the premises, or to re-assign to a more reliable assignee than A has proved to be.

[1] *Spencer's Case* (1583) 5 Co Rep 16a.
[2] Paras 36.68–36.70.
[3] LPA 1925, s 79.
[4] The landlord may not, of course, recover twice in respect of the same loss.
[5] *Friends' Provident Life Office v British Railways Board* [1995] 48 EG 106, CA, LT(C)A 1995, s 18.
[6] LT(C)A 1995, s 18.
[7] LPA 1925, s 77(1)(c) and Sch 2.
[8] Broadly, rent and service charge payments; LT(C)A 1995, s 17(6).
[9] LT(C)A 1995, s 17(2), para 36.85.
[10] LT(C)A 1995, s 19(1), para 36.86.
[11] See paras 36.63 and 36.70.

36.75 *A further assignment*

Here T has assigned the lease to A (as in the previous example) but A has then later assigned the lease to B. This allows us to demonstrate the fundamental difference between T's liability, which is based on privity of contract, and that of A, which is based on privity of estate. Once A assigns the lease A ceases to be in a relationship of landlord and tenant with L (this now exists only between L and B); since there is no longer any privity of estate between them, A cannot be made liable for any subsequent breaches committed by B.[1] However, T's liability remains unaltered; T is still bound by the original contract and can be sued in respect of breaches committed by B (or any subsequent assignee).

However, it should be noted that, particularly in the case of commercial leases, it became the widespread practice for the basic rule concerning the liability of assignees to be varied by express agreement. It was usual for an assignee to be required to enter into a direct contract with the landlord under which the assignee agrees to be bound by the covenants contained in the lease for the remainder of the term; in this way the assignee accepts a contractual liability which is identical to that of an original tenant.[2] Thus, in our example, both A and B may have entered into a direct contract with L; if, and only if, this is the case, L can sue A in respect of breaches committed by B. If B assigns on, L can sue B in respect of subsequent breaches.

An assignee who remains liable to the landlord following a further assignment because of the imposition of a direct covenant is entitled to the limited benefits introduced by the LT(C)A 1995. Accordingly, an assignee must be served with a default notice where the sums specified in that notice are paid, an overriding lease can be called for. [3]

[1] *Onslow v Corrie* (1817) 2 Madd 330. For the same reason A is not liable for breaches which occurred before becoming the tenant, *Grescot v Green* (1700) 1 Salk 199.
[2] *J Lyons & Co Ltd v Knowles* [1943] 1 All ER 477.
[3] See para 36.74 and paras 36.85 and 36.86.

Assignment of the reversion
36.76

In this case, the landlord has assigned the reversion to R. R and T are now in the relationship of landlord and tenant. Covenants which touch and concern the subject matter of the lease are mutually enforceable between R and T.[1] Indeed *only* R can sue T; L is unable to enforce the lease covenants once the reversion has been assigned[2].

As with an original tenant, L remains contractually liable to T even after an assignment of the reversion (even though L can no longer enforce covenants *against* T).[3] However, since landlords do not, generally speaking, undertake obligations which are as onerous as those imposed on tenants, the continuing liability of landlords has not given rise to the same pressure for reform.[4]

[1] LPA 1925, s 141 provides that the *benefit* of such covenants passes to an assignee of the reversion; s 142 passes the *burden*.
[2] LPA 1925, s 141, *Re King, Robinson v Gray* [1963] 1 All ER 781, CA; *London and County (A & D) Ltd v Wilfred Sportsman Ltd* [1970] 2 All ER 600, CA.
[3] *Stuart v Joy* [1904] 1 KB 362, CA.
[4] Although, as we shall see in para 36.83, landlords under new leases can apply to be released from their obligations following an assignment of the reversion.

Assignment of both the lease and the reversion
36.77

Here both landlord and tenant have assigned their interest in the property. All covenants which touch and concern the land are mutually enforceable between R and A, the new landlord and tenant. In addition, where A is in default, R can also sue T whose contractual liability for the remainder of the lease[1] is owed to R just as much as it was to L.

It should be noted that it is provided by s 3 of the Landlord and Tenant Act 1985 that in the case of leases of dwellings, on assignment of the reversion, L remains liable to the current tenant (T or, as the case may be, A) in respect of any breach of covenant until either L or R gives written notice of the assignment and of R's name and address to the current tenant.

[1] See para 36.74.

Leases entered into on or after 1 January 1996

The broad effect of the LT(C)A 1995

36.78 The broad effect of the LT(C)A 1995, which applies to all[1] leases entered into on or after 1 January 1996[2] is as follows:

- the requirement that covenants should 'touch and concern' the land is abolished;[3]

- all tenants, whether original tenants or assignees, are automatically released from future liability on an assignment of their lease;[4]

- however, a landlord can often require an assigning tenant to enter into an agreement guaranteeing that the assignee will perform the obligations imposed by the lease;[5]

- while landlords are not *automatically* released from future liability when transferring their reversion, they can seek release from the tenant or from the court;[6]

- where landlords are able to hold a former tenant liable for breaches committed by the current tenant, they must serve a default notice within six months of any sums becoming due and, where these sums are paid, must if required to do so by that former tenant, grant an overriding lease;[7] and

- landlords are given greater control over the assignment of leases. This aspect of the 1995 Act has already been dealt with. [8]

We now deal, in outline, with each of these changes.

[1] The provisions of the Act cannot be avoided; any attempt to 'exclude, modify or otherwise frustrate the operation of any provision of this Act' is void; LT(C)A 1995, s 25(1).
[2] The major exception to this is where a lease is granted after 1 January 1996 as a result of the exercise of an option granted prior to that date; such leases are subject to the old rules.
[3] See para 36.78.
[4] See para 36.80.
[5] See para 36.81.
[6] See para 36.83.
[7] See paras 36.85 and 36.86. As we have seen in paras 36.55 and 36.56, these provisions also apply to 'old' leases.
[8] See para 36.31.

The transmission of covenants on assignment of the lease or the reversion

36.79 When either a lease or a reversion is assigned the benefit and burden of all landlord and tenant covenants passes to the assignee.[1] There is no longer any requirement that the covenants should 'touch and concern' the land, but covenants which are expressed to be personal will not pass.[2] A landlord or tenant covenant includes any term, condition or obligation, whether contained in the lease or in any collateral agreement entered into before or after the lease, which has to be complied with by either the landlord or tenant respectively.[3]

[1] LT(C)A 1995, s 3(1); the benefit of a landlord's right of re-entry also passes to the assignee of the reversion; LT(C)A 1995, s 4.
[2] LT(C)A 1995, s 3(6)(a).

³ LT(C)A 1995, s 28(1). Covenants which require third parties to discharge any function in respect of the demised premises (eg where a management company is required to carry out repairs, maintenance, etc) are treated as landlord or tenant covenants, as appropriate, and can, therefore, be enforced by assignees; LT(C) A 1995, s 12.

Release of tenant on assignment of the lease

36.80 A tenant who assigns a lease is released from the tenant covenants from the date of the assignment.[1] The only circumstances in which this release does not occur is where the assignment is 'excluded'; an assignment is excluded if it is made in breach of covenant (eg without consent where consent is required) or by operation of law (eg where a lease transfers automatically, on bankruptcy, to the tenant's trustee in bankruptcy).[2] As we shall see in the following paragraph, the practical benefits of this release are reduced where the landlord can, and does, require the assigning tenant to guarantee the obligations of the assignee.

¹ LT(C)A 1995, s 5 (2).
² LT(C)A 1995, s 11.

Authorised guarantee agreements

36.81 Although a tenant is released from the *tenant covenants* on assigning the lease, the Act expressly permits the landlord to require the creation of an agreement under which the outgoing tenant guarantees that the assignee will perform the tenant covenants.[1] This means that, if the latter is in breach of those covenants, the former tenant can then be sued under the *guarantee*. Such agreements are known as 'authorised guarantee agreements' ('AGAs'). A crucial restriction on AGAs is that they cannot impose liability on a former tenant once his or her immediate assignee has been released by a further, non-excluded, assignment.[2]

A landlord is entitled to require an assigning tenant to enter into an AGA in the following circumstances:[3]

- where the lease contains an absolute covenant against assignment (but the landlord is prepared to allow the assignment);

- where the landlord's consent is required in a lease of *commercial or industrial* premises and the lease contains an express requirement that, on assignment the tenant must enter into an AGA;[4] and

- in the case of any lease where the landlord's consent is required and a condition that the tenant enter into an AGA is *reasonable*.

In the period since the 1995 Act came into force, it has become clear that landlords of commercial and industrial premises are, as a matter of standard practice, including in their leases provisions which require their tenants to enter into an AGA as a condition of consent to any assignment; the *automatically* imposed AGA has therefore become a fact of life for such tenants.[5] Accordingly, the normal pattern of liability following the assignment of a business lease is that the outgoing tenant is released from the tenant covenants but will remain liable (under the AGA) for any breaches committed by an immediate assignee; only when that assignee further assigns will the original tenant be entirely free from any further obligation.

¹ LT(C)A 1995, s 16(1).
² LT(C)A 1995, s 16(4)(b).
³ LT(C)A 1995, s 16(2) and (3).
⁴ As we have seen in para 36.31, the LT(C)A 1995, s 22 has inserted a new s 19(1A) into the Landlord and Tenant Act 1927; as a result it is now possible for landlords of commercial and industrial premises to specify

in advance the conditions to which any consent to an assignment will be subject. Where this is done, any condition is deemed to be reasonable.

[5] This is despite the fact that the Code for Leasing Business Premises in England and Wales 2007 specifically recommends that AGAs should only be required where the assignee is, at the date of the assignment, of lower financial standing than the outgoing tenant, or is resident overseas.

Illustrations

36.82 It may be helpful to illustrate the principles outlined in the previous two paragraphs by three examples.

EXAMPLE 1

$$T \longrightarrow A_1$$

Provided T's assignment to A_1 is not excluded, T is released from the tenant covenants. However, where an AGA has been entered into, T will be liable on that agreement if A_1 breaches any tenant covenant.

EXAMPLE 2

$$T \longrightarrow A_1 \longrightarrow A_2$$

Provided both assignments are not excluded, T is now free from any further liability. Any AGA which T entered into when assigning to A_1 cannot have any further effect after A_1's assignment to A_2. A_1 will be released from the tenant covenants on assigning to A_2 but, where an AGA has been entered into A_1 will be responsible, under that AGA, for any breaches committed by A_2; A_1 will only be free from all liability when A_2 lawfully assigns.

EXAMPLE 3

$$T \longrightarrow A_1 \longrightarrow A_2$$

Here let us assume that T's assignment to A_1 is excluded because it was without consent. This means that T is *not* released from the tenant covenants; should A_1 breach those covenants, T is *directly* liable to the landlord. If A_1 lawfully assigns to A_2, T is then released from the tenant covenants (as is A_1). However, T may be required to enter into an AGA guaranteeing A_2's performance of the tenant covenants (as may A_1); in such a case T is not free from all liabilities until A_2 lawfully assigns.

Release of landlord on assignment of the reversion

36.83 A landlord is not automatically released from the landlord covenants when the reversion is assigned. Thus each successive landlord is, in principle, liable on the landlord covenants for the remainder of the lease.[1] It should be remembered that the continuing liability of a landlord is nothing like as onerous as that of a tenant; indeed, there has, as yet, been no reported decision in which a former landlord has been sued in respect of breaches committed by the current landlord.

That said, the 1995 Act does permit[1] a landlord who assigns the reversion to apply, in the first instance to the tenant, for release from the landlord covenants[2] within four weeks of any assignment. Where the tenant objects to such a release, the landlord can apply to court.[3] Where a landlord fails to apply for a release, or fails to achieve a release, a fresh application can be made should the assignee further assign.[4]

This procedure is cumbersome and may, in itself provoke tenants into objecting to any release. It is clear that the parties are free simply to agree a release following an assignment by the landlord[5]. It has also been held by the House of Lords[6] that it is permissible to draft a lease so that the landlord's liability is expressed to come to an end as soon as the reversion is transferred; the statutory release scheme applies only to liabilities that would otherwise continue.

[1] LT(C)A 1995, s 6(2). This differs from the position under an 'old' lease where only the original landlord continues to be liable following the assignment of the reversion; see para 36.76.

[2] This will not include covenants that are stated to be personal; see *BHP Petroleum Great Britain Ltd v Chesterfield Properties Ltd* [2001] EWCA Civ 1797, [2002] 1 All ER 821 where it was held that a landlord could not obtain release from a personal warranty against defects in the new building leased to the tenant.

[3] LT(C)A 1995, s 8.

[4] LT(C)A 1995, s 7.

[5] LT(C)A 1995, s 26(1)(a).

[6] *Avonridge Property Co Ltd v Mashru* [2005] UKHL 70.

Default notices and overriding leases

36.84 Despite the radical changes introduced by the 1995 Act, it is clear that the device of the AGA permits a former tenant to be liable for breaches committed by an immediate assignee; indeed, as we have seen, emerging practice suggests that in the case of commercial and industrial leases, this liability is turning out to be automatic.[1] However, the Act does contain provisions designed to alleviate the position of a former tenant who is being, or has been pursued, by the landlord. Landlords must now serve default notices wherever they wish to pursue a former tenant; furthermore, a former tenant who pays all the sums due under a default notice, is entitled to require the grant of an overriding lease. As we have seen, these provisions apply not only to 'new' leases but also to 'old' leases to which the Act does not otherwise apply.[2]

[1] See para 36.81.

[2] See para 36.74.

36.85 *Default notices* No former tenant can be held liable for a 'fixed charge' unless, within six months of that charge becoming due the landlord serves a prescribed form of notice which informs the recipient that the sum is now due, and the amount which is due, together with any interest thereon.[1] A 'fixed charge' is defined so as to cover rent, service charge payments and any other fixed sum payable in the event of a breach of covenant.[2] This prevents landlords allowing arrears to build up (on which a penal rate of interest is normally payable) without informing the former tenant. Where arrears continue to accrue the landlord must, of course, serve further default notices every six months in order to be able to pursue the former tenant.[3]

[1] LT(C)A 1995, s 17(2). Where parts of the fixed charge are yet to be ascertained – classically where a rent review has yet to be settled – the landlord must serve an additional default notice within six months of the final sum being fixed, *Scottish & Newcastle plc v Raguz* [2008] UKHL 65.

[2] LT(C)A 1995, s 17(6).

[3] The service of regular default notices is a matter which will normally be left to a landlord's managing agent.

36.86 *Overriding leases* A major defect in the law as it stood prior to 1995 was that a former tenant had no rights in respect of the demised premises. All original tenants, and any assignee who had signed a direct covenant,[1] could be held liable for all the obligations under the lease for the remainder of the lease, yet the current tenant could remain in occupation of the property.[2] The former tenants could sue the current tenant under their indemnity covenant (which would be worthless if the current tenant has no money) but could not regain the property. This has now been changed for all leases, 'old' and 'new'.

A former tenant who has paid all sums due under a default notice,[3] is entitled to require the landlord to grant an overriding lease.[4] This overriding lease is, in effect, a concurrent lease (or lease of the reversion)[5], which sits between the landlord's reversion and the current tenant's lease; thus the former tenant becomes a direct tenant of the landlord and the landlord of the current tenant. This means that the former tenant can now take steps, as landlord, against the current tenant. In particular, the former tenant can forfeit the current tenant's lease and then either occupy the premises on the basis of the overriding lease, or assign the overriding lease to a reliable assignee who will thus take over its obligations.

[1] See para 36.75.
[2] Obviously the *landlord* can always forfeit the lease, but may choose not to do so where there is a former tenant who is liable and able to meet all its obligations. This will particularly be the case where the premises are let on terms which are better than those which could now be achieved.
[3] See para 36.85.
[4] LT(C)A 1995, s 19(1).
[5] See para 36.18.

Sureties and sub-tenants

36.87 To conclude this section on the transmission of covenants we briefly consider the position of sureties and sub-tenants.

Sureties

36.88 For many years it has been the widespread practice of landlords to require a lease to be executed not just by the tenant but also by a surety (or guarantor). This does not make the surety a tenant, rather it commits the surety to the obligations imposed by the covenant of guarantee which is then included within the lease. The broad effect of such a covenant is to render the surety liable to the landlord in virtually[1] the same circumstances as the tenant would be liable; in other words the liability of the surety 'mirrors' that of the tenant being guaranteed. In particular this means that, where the tenant remains liable following the assignment of the lease, so does the surety. So, the surety of an original tenant under an 'old' lease will remain liable for the whole of the lease term, even after that tenant has assigned. So far as 'new' leases are concerned, the 1995 Act has been drafted so as to ensure that sureties incur no greater liability than the tenant whom they are guaranteeing, and enjoy the same benefits. So, where a tenant is released from the tenant covenants, so is the surety;[2] where a former tenant is entitled to a default notice or an overriding lease, so is the surety.[3]

[1] There are circumstances where a surety is released from liability where the principal is not, notably where, without the surety's consent, the terms of the lease are varied in a material way.
[2] LT(C)A 1995, s 24(2). It should be noted that to date, the courts have made it clear that a tenant's surety cannot be required to guarantee an assignee from that tenant either directly (by entering into the tenant's AGA) or indirectly by guaranteeing the tenant's AGA, *Good Harvest Partnership LLP v Centaur Services Ltd* [2010] EWHC 330, *K/S Victoria Street v House of Fraser (Stores Management) Ltd* [2010] EWHC 3006 (Ch). This is a controversial issue and the matter may well be taken to appeal.
[3] LT(C)A 1995, s 17(3), s 19(1). Note that these rights are accorded to sureties under 'old' leases as well.

Sub-tenants

36.89 The position where a tenant sub-lets is quite different from that where a tenant assigns:

L

T

S

Here a sub-lease has been created out of T's own lease. In this case while there is a contract (and a relationship of landlord and tenant) between L and T and a contract (and a relationship of landlord and tenant) between T and S, there is no contract between L and S, nor are L and S in a relationship of landlord and tenant. Therefore enforcement between L and S of covenants contained in the headlease between L and T depends not on the foregoing rules but on the rules described in Chapter 33. It should be noted that any covenant in a post-1995 head lease that restricts the use of the demised premises can be enforced against a subtenant even though there is no express mention of this in the sublease[1].

¹ LT(C)A 1995, s 3(5), *Oceanic Village Ltd v United Attractions Ltd* [2000] 1 All ER 975.

ENFORCEABILITY OF LEASEHOLD COVENANTS: KEY POINTS

- Once either a lease is assigned or the landlord's reversion is transferred it becomes vital to know the extent to which the covenants in the lease remain enforceable.

- The law in this area has been changed by the Landlord and Tenant (Covenants) Act 1995. The legal rules now depend on whether the lease was entered into before 1 January 1996 or on or after that date; many pre-1996 leases remain in force and so both sets of rules need to be understood.

- Pre-1996 leases:
  - Even after an assignment or transfer the original parties remain bound by all the covenants in the lease until the lease ends on the basis of privity of contract; this is particularly important for original tenants who can be sued by the current landlord in respect of breaches by any subsequent tenant.
  - The assignee of a lease or transferee of a reversion is bound by those lease terms that touch and concern or relate to the land; under the general law they are liable only for breaches of these covenants while they are the tenant or landlord. This is on the basis of privity of estate. It became a widespread practice for assignees of commercial leases to enter into a direct covenant; this makes the assignee contractually liable for breaches of all covenants for the remainder of the lease in the same way as is an original tenant.
  - A tenant who has been sued for a breach committed by their immediate assignee has a statutory right of indemnity.

- Post-1995 leases:
  - On the transfer of a reversion or assignment of the lease the benefit and burden of all 'landlord' and 'tenant' pass.
  - On a non-excluded assignment of a lease the tenant is released from all tenant covenants although the landlord may (and usually does) require the tenant to enter into an AGA. An AGA renders the outgoing tenant liable for breaches committed by the

immediate assignee. The tenant is released from the AGA if and when the lease is further assigned.
- A landlord who transfers the reversion is not automatically released from the landlord covenants but may apply to the tenant for such a release.
• The 1995 Act contains provisions that apply to all leases whenever granted. These govern:
- *Default notices*. A landlord cannot recover a 'fixed charge' (usually arrears of rent or service charge) from a former tenant or their guarantor without serving a default notice within six months of the charge first becoming due.
- *Overriding leases*. A former tenant who has paid the sums due under a default notice can require the landlord to grant an overriding lease. In this way the former tenant becomes landlord to the current tenant and thereby has direct remedies against the latter.

Bringing leases to an end: the common law

36.90 At common law a lease may come to an end in a number of different ways. Those which we have not already dealt with, we outline in the following paragraphs. We consider how the common law concerning termination of leases has been altered by statute in Chapter 37.

Forfeiture

36.91 So long as there is an express provision within the lease (known as a right of re-entry) a landlord can terminate a lease where the tenant is in breach of covenant. We have already considered forfeiture in paras 36.63 to 36.67 and 36.70.

Surrender

36.92 A lease comes to an end where it is 'swallowed up' by the immediate landlord's reversion and is thus extinguished. Surrender of a fixed term lease[1] may be effected by an express agreement[2] that the tenant is giving up the lease; this agreement should be in the form of a deed.[3] Surrender can also take place by operation of law. This will occur where the tenant gives up possession and the landlord unequivocally accepts[2] this as surrender, or where the tenant takes a new lease from the landlord during the currency of the existing tenancy—this existing lease disappears.

[1] In practice, surrender is only applicable to fixed-term leases that would otherwise continue until their contractual term date (see para 36.94 below). Where either party wishes to terminate a periodic tenancy they can (subject to statute) simply serve a notice to quit (see para 36.95 below).
[2] It must be stressed that a surrender is *not* a unilateral act; a tenant cannot simply 'decide' to give back the lease. The landlord must agree that the lease is at an end and will not readily do so where the premises cannot be readily re-let.
[3] LPA 1925, s 52(1), see para 29.11.

Merger

36.93 This occurs where either the landlord's and the tenant's interests are acquired by a third party in the same capacity, or where the tenant acquires the landlord's reversion. Provided that the parties so intend, the lease merges with the reversion and disappears.

Expiry

36.94 At common law a lease for a fixed term of years comes to an end when that term expires without the need for notice from either party. The common law position is, however, much affected by statute.[1]

[1] See ch 37.

Notice

36.95 A lease for a fixed term may not be determined by notice unless there is an express provision to that effect. Such options to terminate are known as break options or rights to break. Depending on the terms of the lease, they may be operated by either the landlord or the tenant. Tenants' rights to break are now commonplace as they mitigate the effect of a long lease by providing the tenant with an opportunity for earlier termination. It is usual for rights to break to be operable by the giving of a specified period of notice at a given point; so, a 10-year lease may contain a tenant's right to break on the giving of six months' notice expiring at the end of the fifth year of the term. It should be noted that any time provisions relating to break options must be strictly adhered to, ie time is always of the essence[1]. Any preconditions to the right to break, eg that the rent is fully paid up, or that the tenant is not in material breach of covenant, must also be completely complied with. Strict preconditions can make a right to break almost impossible to operate and should be avoided.

As we have seen,[2] periodic tenancies continue automatically until terminated by a notice to quit served by either party.[3] In the absence of any agreement to the contrary, a yearly tenancy may be determined by the service of no less than six months' notice expiring at the end of a period of the tenancy. In the case of other periodic tenancies, again in the absence of any agreement to the contrary, the minimum notice required at common law is equal to one full period of the tenancy; once again the notice must expire at the end of a period of the tenancy. So, a monthly tenancy can be terminated by the service of one month's notice expiring at the end of a month. These rules are subject to the overriding statutory requirement that, in the case of tenancies of residential premises, a notice to quit must be in writing[4] and must be for a minimum of four weeks.[5] Furthermore, the termination of leases by notice is also considerably affected in other respects by various statutes.[6]

[1] For a discussion of time of the essence generally, see paras 8.28–8.31. That concept is also referred to in the context of rent reviews at para 36.57.
[2] See para 36.14.
[3] Where there are joint tenants or joint landlords, a notice to quit served by one only, without the knowledge or consent of the other(s), is effective to terminate the tenancy: *Hammersmith and Fulham London Borough Council v Monk* [1992] 1 AC 478, HL. It should be noted that this rule only applies where the notice is a valid notice to quit of the required length expiring at the end of a period of the tenancy. Any other notice will, in law, operate as a break notice; this requires the co-operation of all joint owners, *Hounslow London Borough Council v Pilling* (1993) 25 HLR 305, CA.
[4] Protection from Eviction Act 1977, s 5(1)(a).
[5] PEA 1977, s 5(1)(b). It should be noted that, as a result of an amendment introduced by the Housing Act 1988, s 5 no longer applies to tenancies where the tenant shares the home of the landlord or the landlord's immediate family.
[6] See ch 37.

Enlargement

36.96 The LPA 1925, s 153 provides that where a lease has been granted for a term of not less than 300 years, of which not less than 200 years are left unexpired, and either no rent or no rent having any money value is payable, the term of years may be enlarged into a fee simple (freehold) by the tenant executing a deed to that effect. Such a combination of circumstances is no doubt unlikely.

Frustration

36.97 A lease can occasionally be terminated as a result of the operation of the contractual doctrine of frustration; this, together with its application to leases is discussed in ch 10.

Repudiation

36.98 We have seen that there are circumstances in which the breach of a contract by one of the parties can entitle the other party to repudiate, ie terminate, the contract[1]. Although a lease is a contract, it also creates an estate in land and, for this reason, it used to be thought that a lease could not be repudiated. However, it does now appear to be accepted that the principle can apply to leases[2]. Since a landlord can normally achieve the same effect by forfeiture[3], this development is of greatest interest to tenants who otherwise have no right to terminate in the face of substantial breaches of covenant by their landlords. However, it is clear that the only circumstances in which repudiation by a tenant will be allowed is where the landlord's breach effectively deprives the tenant of the benefit of the whole of the remainder of the lease. Breaches that do not have this effect should be remedied by an award of damages[4].

[1] See paras 8.9–8.15.
[2] See *Hussein v Mehlman* [1992] 2 EGLR 87 where a landlord's very serious breach of its repairing covenants was held to entitle the tenants to repudiate the lease. See also *Chartered Trust plc v Davies* [1997] 2 EGLR 83, CA where a landlord's breach of its obligation not to derogate from its grant was similarly treated, see para 36.35.
[3] See paras 36.63–36.67.
[4] See *Nynehead Developments Ltd v RH Fibreboard Containers Ltd* [1999] 1 EGLR 7.

Disclaimer

36.99 Where a tenant becomes insolvent the tenant's trustee in bankruptcy or, in the case of a company tenant, liquidator (to whom the lease passes by operation of law) may disclaim it where the lease is not readily saleable.[1] This terminates the lease as against the insolvent tenant; however, the lease remains on foot for other purposes so that others, such as former tenants, or sureties will remain liable to the landlord.[2]

[1] Insolvency Act 1986, ss 178, 315.
[2] *Hindcastle Ltd v Barbara Attenborough Associates Ltd* [1996] 1 All ER 737, HL. In *Shaw v Doleman* [2009] EWCA Civ 279, the Court of Appeal held that, where a former tenant's liability is based on an AGA, (as to which see para 36.81) only the very clearest wording will give rise to a release following the disclaimer of the lease.

Questions

1. Larry grants Tony a lease of part of an office building 'until Larry requires it back for his own business'. How does this arrangement take effect in law?

2. Leonora grants Teresa a three-month licence of a self-contained flat. At the end of the three months Teresa refuses to leave; she claims to have a tenancy and says that she has been told that as an assured shorthold tenant she must have at least six months' security of tenure. Advise Leonora.

3. What is a fixed term tenancy and how does it differ from a periodic tenancy?

4. What is the difference between an absolute, qualified and fully qualified covenant?

5. How do the courts decide whether or not a landlord is acting reasonably when refusing consent to an assignment and how does this differ for post-1995 lease of business premises?

6. Two months ago Theo wrote to Larry, his landlord, asking for consent to assign, as required by his lease. He has had no response. What is the legal position?

7. Trudi holds a lease of a shop; it is one of five located in a small suburban mall. Her lease requires her to use the shop as a 'grocer's store'. Her business in fact operates as a min-market selling both food and a wide range of non-food goods. Her success is adversely affecting the trade of the other shops whose tenants want to stop her selling non-food goods. Can they, or the landlord, do this?

8. Last month Tim took a lease of a rather run down small industrial unit. He carried out his own negotiations with the landlord and accepted a covenant 'to keep the premises in good repair'. The landlord is now trying to make him carry out a long list of repairs to the unit. Can he do this?

9. What is the legal meaning of 'repair'?

10. What matters are covered in a standard rent review clause?

11. To what extent are service charges subject to regulation?

12. What procedure must be followed by a landlord in order to forfeit a lease for the breach of a covenant other than that to pay rent? How does this process differ where the breach is:
    a. of a repairing covenant; or
    b. of the covenant to pay rent?

13. Following the assignment of a pre-1996 lease, for which and whose breaches of covenant is the original tenant liable? How does the position of an assignee differ?

14. What are the liabilities of a tenant under a post-1995 lease following its assignment?

15. What is an 'authorised guarantee agreement' and when can it be imposed?

16. What is a 'default notice' and when must one be served?

37

Landlord and tenant: statutory protection

CHAPTER OVERVIEW

A knowledge of the impact of the statutory regulation of the landlord and tenant relationship is an important part of the study of real estate management. Although, in a book of this nature, we cannot deal with this in great detail, in this chapter we will give an outline of:

- the statutory regulation of residential tenancies;
- the statutory protection of business tenants; and
- the statutory schemes applying to agricultural tenancies.

37.1 Our exposition of the law of landlord and tenant in the previous chapter deals with only half the story, for today the law relating to leases is much modified and qualified by statute. This statutory regulation is divided broadly into three areas: residential tenancies, business tenancies and agricultural tenancies. The hallmark of much of the legislation in all three sectors for a large part of the 20th century was the imposition of security of tenure, ie the right of the tenant to remain in occupation after the termination of their contractual lease, and, in the private residential sector, rent control. This approach is changing. Fearful that security of tenure (and, in the private residential sector, rent control) was discouraging landowners from letting their property, legislation in the late 1980s and 1990s heralded a much greater emphasis on freedom of contract in both private residential and agricultural tenancies, a move on which there appears to be political consensus. It is perhaps ironic that, on its face, it is the regime affecting tenants of business premises which now appears to confer the greatest security of tenure. However, as we shall see, it is possible for the parties to commercial leases to opt out of the scheme of protection.

It should also be appreciated that, during the last century, Parliament had to tackle the problem posed by long leases of residential property. Ever since the 19th century, the grant of such leases has been commonplace. This was partly because the long lease provided an effective mechanism for the large landowners to control the development of our cities. However, as we have seen, leasehold ownership was also the only practical basis for the ownership of flats. By the 1960s a significant number of these long leases had diminished to a length that was having a serious economic impact, notably that they were now too short to offer sufficient security for mortgage lending. This stirred the political conscience and it was then that the first steps down the thorny path of conferring on tenants a statutory right to enfranchisement (ie to acquire the freehold or a new long lease) were first taken. While this now horribly complex legislation will eventually be displaced if commonhold takes root, it will take many years before existing long leases are phased out.

Residential tenancies

Introduction

37.2 Although, inevitably, residential tenancies come in all shapes and sizes, for the purposes of statutory regulation one key practical distinction is usually that between long leases, ie those for more than 21 years, and those of a shorter duration. Most (but not all) leases of more than 21 years are granted at a premium, with the result that the rent is a low ground rent. Where the rent is low, neither the Rent Act 1977 nor the Housing Act 1988, can apply. This is no great disadvantage to the tenants under such leases since neither security of tenure nor rent levels are an immediate problem. The relationship between the landlord and the tenant at the outset of such leases is much more akin, at least in economic terms, to that between a vendor and purchaser of a freehold. However, there are problems for the tenants and these stem from the nature of their ownership, ie they hold a wasting asset and, where the property is a flat, it is usually the landlord who maintains the whole property and who provides services often, from a tenant's perspective, in an unsatisfactory way. These difficulties are addressed not by a regulatory scheme designed to protect tenants during and at the end of short leases, but by the prospect of enfranchisement (acquisition of the freehold or a lease extension) and self-management. Accordingly, there has come to be a complex statutory framework allowing for the enfranchisement of long leases of both houses and flats. The management problem has also been tackled by a variety of measures. These include the control of service charges affecting residential property[1] and the right of tenants to take over the management of the property[2]. Tenants of flats can apply for the appointment of a manager and, in extreme cases, can compulsorily acquire the landlord's interest[3].

The regimes governing tenancies where the rent is not low (and where lease lengths are usually, but not necessarily, short) are very different. Originally, the aim was to confer both security of tenure and rent control and this was the remit of a series of Rent Acts spanning the period 1915–1977. The change came in the late 1980s. The Housing Act 1988 in its original form abandoned rent control for new tenants but did still confer significant security of tenure. However, that Act made provision for a form of tenancy—the assured shorthold tenancy—under which tenants enjoyed little security. Subsequent amendments to the HA 1988 have ensured that the assured shorthold tenancy has become the dominant form in the private sector. Thus the traditional twin pillars of residential tenant protection—rent control and security of tenure—have all but disappeared.

Another key factor in the statutory framework is the divide between private and public sector provision. However, this is not, in terms of numbers, as significant as it used to be. As we shall see[4], much of the former public sector housing function has been handed over to housing associations and tenancies granted by these bodies are governed by the legislation relating to tenancies granted by private landlords.

Another important area of statutory provision in residential tenancies relates to harassment and unlawful eviction and the provision of information to tenants.

In this section we will deal with:

- private sector regulation—the Rent Act 1977 and the Housing Act 1988;
- public sector regulation—the Housing Act 1985;

- leasehold enfranchisement;
- miscellaneous statutory provision—harassment, unlawful eviction, the tenants' deposit scheme and information to tenants;
- the statutory protection of business tenants; and
- the statutory schemes applying to agricultural land.

[1] See para 36.60.
[2] See para 37.16.
[3] Para 36.67.
[4] Para 37.17.

Rent Act tenancies

37.3 The Rent Act 1977 applies to certain lettings[1] of dwelling-houses, granted *before 15 January 1989*. Excluded from its application are, for example, houses with an annual rent above £25,000 or of £1,000 or less in Greater London (or £250 or less elsewhere),[2] tenancies where the rent includes an element for board or attendance, lettings to students by universities and colleges, holiday lettings and tenancies where the landlord resides in another part of the same building (so long as this is not a purpose-built block of flats).

Rent Act tenancies terminate in accordance with the common law rules explained in Chapter 36; however, on the termination of a protected contractual tenancy, provided the tenant is occupying the premises as their residence, there immediately arises a statutory tenancy,[3] on the same terms. This confers on the tenant, not an estate in the land, but a 'status of irremovability'.[4] The landlord under either a protected or statutory tenancy (known collectively as 'regulated tenancies') may not recover possession save by order of a county court which will only be granted in accordance with the provisions of the Rent Act 1977, s 98 and Sch 15. Possession will only be granted where the court considers it reasonable to do so and either there is suitable alternative accommodation available to the tenant or the landlord makes out one of the discretionary cases for possession set out in the Act. The Act also provides for mandatory grounds for possession,[5] which, if made out, entitle the landlord as of right to regain possession.

On the death of a Rent Act tenant, the tenancy will not necessarily come to an end since a successor may be entitled to take over the tenancy[6]. On the death of an original tenant, a surviving spouse[7] can succeed to the tenancy and will continue to pay a fair rent[8]. If there is no surviving spouse, any member of the family[9] who was living with the deceased tenant for the previous two years can succeed but, in this case, the successor takes an assured tenancy[10] and must pay a market rent. It is these rights of succession which mean that it will still be some time before Rent Act tenancies disappear[11].

The Rent Act also imposes rent control. The landlord or tenant may apply to the rent officer for the area for the determination and registration of a fair rent,[12] which must not thereafter be exceeded and which takes effect for two years. Either party can, after two years (or earlier if the premises have been improved), apply for a re-registration of the rent; this is, in effect, the only means by which a landlord can achieve an increase in the rent. While it is now clear that fair rents must usually be fixed by reference to market rents in the locality[13], the Act requires that any element of scarcity must be ignored[14]. It is this disregard of scarcity which means that, although fair rents are now more closely linked to the market than used to be the case, they are still nearly always noticeably lower than market rents. Even so, the link to market rents has meant that fair rents have risen sharply; accordingly, a cap on increases to fair rents[15] has been introduced in order to protect the remaining Rent Act tenants who tend to be elderly and on low incomes.

[1] There must be a lease and not a licence; it is this requirement that provoked much of the litigation on the distinction between a lease and a licence referred to at para 36.9.

[2] Tenants under long tenancies (ie those in excess of 21 years) at a low rent qualify for the rights conferred by the Leasehold Reform Act 1967 and the Leasehold Reform, Housing and Urban Development Act 1993, paras 37.14 and 37.15.

[3] Rent Act 1977, s 2.

[4] *Keeves v Dean* [1924] 1 KB 685 at 686.

[5] These mandatory grounds usually only apply where the landlord has served notice to this effect on the tenant at the commencement of the tenancy.

[6] Rent Act 1977, s 2(1), Sch 1.

[7] This now includes a civil partner, Civil Partnership Act 2004, s 81, Sch 8, para 13. RA1977, Sch 1, para 2 defines surviving spouse so as to include any person living with the tenant as his or her wife or husband or civil partner.

[8] On the death of a surviving spouse or civil partner who has succeeded to a statutory tenancy there can be one further succession to a member of both the original tenant's and the successor's family who was living with the survivor for two years before his or her death. Any second successor takes an assured tenancy and must pay a market rent.

[9] While this will include blood relatives and adopted family, it will not normally extend to those who are not related to the tenant, see *Carega Properties SA v Sharratt* [1979] 2 All ER 1084, HL.

[10] Ie a tenancy governed by the Housing Act 1988, see paras 37.8–37.10.

[11] Although no new Rent Act tenancies have been created since 1989, it was estimated in 2007/8 that there were then about 120,000 such tenancies still remaining (some 4% of the private rented sector): Housing in England 2009 DCLG.

[12] The basis on which a 'fair rent' is to be ascertained is defined in the Rent Act, 1977, s 70.

[13] *Spath Holme Ltd v Chairman of Greater Manchester and Lancashire Rent Assessment Panel* (1995) 28 HLR 107, CA; *Curtis v London Rent Assessment Committee* [1997] 4 All ER 842, CA.

[14] Rent Act 1977, s 70(2).

[15] Rent Acts (Maximum Fair Rent) Order 1999. This limits increases to the increases in the RPI plus a further percentage.

Housing Act tenancies

Introduction

37.4 Where a tenancy of a separate dwelling-house is granted *on or after 15 January 1989* it will be governed by the Housing Act 1988, so long as the tenant is an individual who occupies the property as his or her only or principal home.[1] As with the Rent Act, certain tenancies are excluded, such as those of dwelling-houses let at a rent above or below prescribed limits[2] or let by educational institutions to students; also excluded are holiday lettings and tenancies granted by a resident landlord (the definition of which is much the same as under the Rent Act).[3] Housing Act tenancies are either assured shorthold tenancies[4] or assured tenancies[5]. Neither type of tenancy can be brought to an end by the landlord except in accordance with the Act[6]. Landlords are not restricted as to the rent they can charge, although a tenant under an assured shorthold tenancy can, in limited circumstances, ask a rent assessment committee to ensure that the initially agreed rent is no more than a market rent[7]. The Act provides a mechanism under which rent can periodically be increased in line with market rents[8], but the parties are not required to use the statutory scheme and can make their own provision for rent reviews. In the event of the death of a tenant holding under either an assured shorthold, or an assured, periodic tenancy there is a single right of succession to any spouse[9] of the deceased tenant who, at the date of the death was occupying the premises as his or her only or principal home[10].

[1] Housing Act 1988, s 1. In the case of joint tenants, each must be an individual, though only one need occupy the premises as their home. There has been considerable litigation, both under the Rent Acts and the Housing Act, as to the meaning of a separate dwelling-house. Suffice to say that the thrust of this is that

the premises should be capable of providing all the necessary attributes of a home; it has, however, been acknowledged that, in modern times, accommodation can be a home even though it is a single room (with ensuite facilities) that has no cooking amenities, see *Uratemp Ventures Ltd v Collins* [2001] UKHL 43, [2002] 1 All ER 46.

   [2] The rent limit for both assured and assured shorthold tenancies has been lifted from £25,000 pa to £100,000 pa, The Assured Tenancies (Amendment) (England) Order 2010. This came into effect on 1 October 2010 and applies both to tenancies created on or after that date and to those in existence at that date. The previous rent limit had never been altered since 1989 and the change will bring into the Housing Act scheme a large number of existing tenancies and greatly extends its application for the future. Tenancies at a rent of £1,000 pa or less (in Greater London) or £250 or less elsewhere are excluded.

   [3] HA 1988, s 1 and Sch 1.

   [4] See paras 37.5–37.7.

   [5] See paras 37.8–37.11.

   [6] HA 1988, ss 5, 7.

   [7] HA 1988, s 22, see para 37.7.

   [8] HA 1988, ss 13, 14, see para 37.11.

   [9] A 'spouse' includes a civil partner (Civil Partnership Act 2004, s 81, Sch 8, para 41) is defined so as to include a person who was living with the tenant as his or her wife or husband or civil partner, HA 1988, s 17(4).

   [10] HA 1988, s 17.

Assured shorthold tenancies

37.5 *The creation of an assured shorthold tenancy* Right from the outset the HA 1988 envisaged a form of assured tenancy under which tenants would enjoy minimal security of tenure and which landlords could terminate simply by serving notice—the assured shorthold tenancy. However, initially, the Act required that such tenancies could only arise where criteria additional to that for assured tenancies were satisfied. So, for tenancies created *on or after 15 January 1989 and before 28 February 1997* it was essential, in order for there to be an assured shorthold, that the tenancy was for a term of not less than six months (and did not contain any provision—other than a forfeiture provision— allowing the landlord to terminate the tenancy within six months) and that the landlord had served on all the tenants a statutorily prescribed form of prior notice stating that the tenancy was to be an assured shorthold tenancy. These preconditions caused problems. Many landlords found that, either through ignorance or incompetence, these requirements had not been met; as a result, the tenancy would be a fully assured one under which it was very difficult to regain possession[1].

The HA 1988 was therefore amended in 1997[2] and, for Housing Act tenancies created *on or after 28 February 1997*, the position is very different. All tenancies that satisfy the basic criteria of the Act[3], whether fixed term or periodic, are now assured shorthold tenancies unless the landlord gives notice that they are to be assured tenancies[4]. Accordingly the assured shorthold has now become the norm.

   [1] See para 37.10.

   [2] By the Housing Act 1996.

   [3] See para 37.4.

   [4] HA 1988, s 19A, Sch 2A as inserted by the Housing Act 1996, s 96. In practice it is most unlikely that a private landlord would ever give such a notice; registered providers of social housing are more likely to grant fully assured tenancies.

37.6 *Termination of assured shorthold tenancies* An assured shorthold tenancy can now[1] be either fixed term or periodic. Neither can be brought to an end by the landlord except in accordance with the Act[2]. The tenant is free to terminate the tenancy in accordance with the common law, subject to any express provisions in the agreement; accordingly he or she can, as appropriate, treat a fixed term tenancy as at an end on its contractual term date, or serve a notice to quit a periodic tenancy.

A landlord cannot regard a fixed-term assured shorthold tenancy as expiring on its contractual term date[3]. Unless the tenant chooses to leave, the tenancy is automatically replaced by a statutory periodic tenancy[4] under which the tenant can remain in possession until the tenancy is terminated in accordance with the Act. Where the assured shorthold tenancy is periodic from the outset, the landlord cannot serve a notice to quit[5]. The landlord will therefore normally terminate an assured shorthold tenancy by serving notice under the Act[6]. The tenancy can also be ended by obtaining a court order based on one of the statutory grounds for possession but this method will rarely be adopted given the simple alternative of serving notice[7].

The great attraction of the assured shorthold for landlords is the ability to regain possession[8] following the simple service of a statutory notice, without the need to prove any statutory ground. In order to terminate the tenancy in this way the landlord must serve at least two months' notice in writing[9]. While this can be served during the currency of any fixed-term tenancy, no order for possession can be obtained until such fixed term has expired[10]. A landlord's notice to terminate a periodic tenancy can, subject to any express provisions in the agreement, be served at any time; it must expire at the end of a period of the tenancy[11]. However, no order for possession will be granted until six months after the assured shorthold tenancy (whether fixed term or periodic) was first granted[12]; this is designed to ensure that all assured shorthold tenants have, if they choose, a minimum of six months' security of tenure.

[1] Ie for tenancies granted on or after 28 February 1997, see para 37.5.
[2] Housing Act 1988, ss 5, 7.
[3] HA 1988, s 5(1).
[4] HA 1988, s 5(2).
[5] HA 1988, s 5(1).
[6] HA 1988, s 21.
[7] HA 1988, ss 5, 7, 21. The notice method of termination can only be used at the expiry of a fixed-term tenancy. If a landlord wishes to terminate *during* a fixed term (eg where the tenant is in default) a statutory ground will have to be used, see para 37.10.
[8] It should be appreciated that, where a tenant refuses to leave following the service of a proper notice, the landlord will then need to obtain a court order for possession since it is a criminal offence simply re-enter residential premises: see Protection from Eviction Act 1977, s 3(1), para 37.23.
[9] HA 1988, s 21.
[10] HA 1988, s 21(1)(a).
[11] HA 1988, s 21(4)(a).
[12] HA 1988, s 21(5).

37.7 *Rent referral and rent review* The only theoretical drawback of an assured shorthold tenancy for landlords is that a tenant is entitled to refer the *initial* rent to a rent assessment committee during the first six months of the tenancy[1]; however, the committee's jurisdiction is limited and is designed only to ensure that the landlord does not charge a rent which is *in excess* of market rents and there is little evidence that such references are often made. The landlord of an assured shorthold tenancy is able to make use of the statutory provisions governing rent increases[2]. In practice, where a landlord does allow assured shorthold tenants to remain in occupation for a relatively lengthy period, it is usual either to include express rent review provisions in the original agreement[3], or to grant a series of short fixed term tenancies and to negotiate a new rent at the beginning of each.

[1] Housing Act 1988, s 22.
[2] HA 1988, ss 13, 14, see para 37.11.
[3] Which necessarily excludes the statutory machinery, HA 1988, s 13(1).

37.8 *Tenancy deposit schemes* It has become standard for landlords of short-term tenancies to require their tenants to pay a deposit as security for non-payment of rent, other breaches of covenant, and the rectification of damage to the property. In the light of evidence that the unfair withholding of such deposits was not uncommon, a mandatory statutory scheme for the protection of deposits has been put in place[1]. A landlord[2] who takes a deposit on the grant[3] of an assured shorthold tenancy must enter into either a custodial or an insurance backed scheme[4]. The Act requires the landlord to provide the tenant with details of the scheme being used and satisfy the initial requirements of the scheme within 14 days of receiving the deposit[5]. Under a custodial scheme the landlord pays the deposit to the administrator of the scheme who retains the money and pays it out at the end of the tenancy in accordance with any agreement between the parties[6]. Under an insurance scheme the landlord retains the deposit but gives an undertaking to the administrator to comply with any direction given regarding the deposit. In the event of a disagreement over the return of the deposit the landlord must then pay the disputed sum to the scheme where it will be held until the matter is resolved. The administrator must maintain insurance to cover the risk of the landlord failing to pay[7]. Any scheme must offer a dispute resolution service[8].

It was clearly intended that a landlord[9] who fails to comply with the statutory scheme should be subject to significant sanctions. Certainly no s 21 notice terminating the tenancy can be served at a time when a deposit is being held in a way that does not conform with the statutory scheme, or when the initial requirements of the scheme have not been complied with, or when the tenant has not been given the prescribed information about the scheme[10]. It is also provided that, on an application by the tenant[11], the court must order the landlord to pay to the tenant a sum equal to three times the amount of the deposit if the initial requirements of the scheme have not been complied with or where the landlord has failed to provide the required information[12]. However, the issue that has arisen is whether these penalties are irretrievably triggered once the landlord has failed to comply within the 14-day statutory time limit, or whether a landlord who complies, albeit belatedly, escapes sanction. A majority of the Court of Appeal has held[13] that breaches of the time limit are remediable and that a landlord who protects the deposit and provides the necessary information to the tenant by the date of the court hearing[14] is not subject to the statutory penalties.

---

[1] By the Housing Act 2004, ss 212–215 which came into effect on 6 April 2007.

[2] This includes any agent to whom the task of handling the deposit has been delegated, see *Draycott v Hannells Lettings Ltd* [2010] EWHC 217 (QB).

[3] It should be noted that from 1 October 2010 the rent limit for assured shorthold tenancies has been increased to £100,000 pa (see para 37.4, note 2). This applies to existing tenancies and brings them within the tenancy deposit scheme rules. Landlords under such tenancies must take steps to protect any deposits that they are holding. The ruling in *Vision Enterprises Ltd v Tiensia* [2010] EWCA Civ 1224 (see Note 13 below) does mean that intractable problems over the 14-day time limit will be avoided.

[4] HA 2004, s 213(1) and (2). It is for the landlord to choose which type of scheme to use.

[5] HA 2004, s 213 (3)–(6).

[6] HA 2004, Sch 10 paras 3 and 4.

[7] HA 2004, Sch 10, paras 5–8. This is paid for by the charges made to landlords using this scheme.

[8] HA 2004, Sch 10, para 10.

[9] Or any agent to whom the task of handling the deposit has been given, see *Draycott v Hannells Lettings Ltd* [2010] EWHC 217 (QB).

[10] HA 2004, s 215(1) and (2).

[11] Which may be by way of issuing proceedings or by counter-claiming in a landlord's action for possession.

[12] HA 2004, s 214(4). This is in addition to an order that the landlord must either repay the deposit to the tenant or pay it into a custodial scheme, ibid s 214(3).

[13] *Vision Enterprises Ltd v Tiensia* [2010] EWCA Civ 1224. This was a ruling by the majority; Sedley LJ, who dissented took the view that this decision emasculates the scheme.

[14] Even where, by the date of the hearing, the tenancy has come to an end, *Potts and Densley* [2011] EWHC 1144 (QB).

Assured tenancies

37.9 *Creation of assured tenancies* Where a tenancy complying with the basic criteria of the Act[1] is entered into on or after 28 February 1997, it will only be an assured tenancy (as opposed to an assured shorthold tenancy[2]) where a notice to that effect is served on the tenant.[3] Accordingly, Housing Act tenancies granted by private landlords will now invariably be assured shorthold rather than assured tenancies; however, those granted by registered social housing providers such as housing associations will often be fully assured since such bodies are encouraged to confer long-term security wherever possible[4].

[1] See para 37.4.

[2] See paras 37.5-37.7.

[3] Housing Act 1988, s 19A.

[4] In accordance with the tenancy standard issued by the Tenant Services Authority (which in 2010 took over the regulatory functions of the Housing Corporation). The TSA is itself now scheduled to disappear; if this does happen its functions will be transferred to the Homes and Communities Agency, see para 37.17.

37.10 *Termination of an assured tenancy* Where a fixed-term assured tenancy expires, a statutory periodic tenancy arises (the periods of which are those in respect of which rent was payable under the fixed term).[1] A periodic assured tenancy, including one arising on the ending of a fixed term, cannot be terminated by the landlord serving a notice to quit.[2] In contrast to an assured shorthold tenancy, a landlord cannot bring an assured tenancy to an end simply by serving notice; a court order based on a statutory ground for possession must be obtained[3]. To do this the landlord must first serve on the tenant a statutory notice in prescribed form specifying the ground(s) on which possession will be sought and stating that proceedings will commence within a specified period.[4] As with the Rent Act, the HA 1988 provides for discretionary and mandatory grounds for possession, though some of these grounds are new or differ in detail[5]. Most of the mandatory grounds are not available to the landlord until the expiry of any fixed-term tenancy[6] and also require the service of a prior notice on the tenant at or before the grant of the tenancy[7]. Most of the grounds that are available during the currency of any fixed term are based on tenant default (and thus effectively replace forfeiture as a method of termination); however, virtually all of these are discretionary grounds. A vitally important exception is Ground 8. This is a mandatory ground of possession based on at least two months' rent arrears. This is widely used in practice as it provides the only opportunity for a landlord, whose tenant is in default, to recover possession as of right during any fixed term assured or assured shorthold tenancy[8]. It should be noted that where the landlord of an assured tenancy is a registered provider of social housing, it can terminate that tenancy as against a tenant who has engaged in housing related anti-social behaviour or conduct involving the use of the premises for unlawful purposes by obtaining a demotion order[9]. Where it has obtained an order for possession based on anti-social behaviour or domestic violence, it can offer the tenant a family intervention tenancy[10].

[1] Housing Act 1988, s 5(2).

[2] HA 1988, s 5(1).

[3] HA 1988, s 5(1).

[4] HA 1988, s 8.

[5] HA 1988, s 7, Sch 2.

[6] HA 1988, s 7(6).

[7] HA 1988, Sch 2, Part 1.

[8] It should be noted that one of the most common reasons for the build up of rent arrears is a failure in the administration of housing benefit; this in itself is not a reason for the court to refuse an order for possession and nor can the court stay, suspend or postpone the order since it has no power to do so where a mandatory ground is made out, Housing Act 1988, s 9(6).

[9] Housing Act 1985, s 82A; this effectively deprives the tenant of any security of tenure for a period of 12 months, see para 37.18, note 12 and 37.21.

[10] HA 1985, s 12ZA; such a tenancy confers no security of tenure, see para 37.21.

37.11 *Rent review* The Housing Act 1988 does not in any sense impose rent control in the case of assured tenancies. The tenant has no right to refer the rent to a rent assessment committee[1]. The parties are free to include their own provisions for rent review, provided that these are genuine[2]. Wherever an assured periodic[3] tenancy does not contain its own provisions for rent review the Act provides a statutory mechanism under which a landlord can, by the service of a prescribed form of notice, seek to increase[4] the rent; such a notice can be served every year.[5] A tenant who objects to the landlord's proposed rent may refer the notice to a rent assessment committee, usually within one month of receiving the landlord's notice; where this is done the committee will determine the new rent by reference to open-market rental value.[6]

[1] Compare the position of an assured shorthold tenant: see para 37.7.

[2] If the tenancy agreement includes a rent review provision that is manifestly not intended to operate as a review but merely as a mechanism to force the tenant to quit, the provision will not be enforced. See *Bankway Properties Ltd v Pensfold-Dunsford* [2001] EWCA Civ 528, [2001] 2 EGLR 36 where there was a provision that, as from the last review date, the rent (of just over £4,500 pa) should automatically increase to £25,000 pa (ie above the then rent limit for assured tenancies).

[3] The statutory machinery does not apply during the currency of a fixed-term tenancy; it will, however, kick in once the fixed term expires and is replaced by a statutory periodic tenancy (see para 37.10), provided the tenancy agreement does not set out its own rent review provisions.

[4] Since only the landlord can serve the statutory notice it is inherently unlikely that there will ever be a proposal that the rent goes down.

[5] HA 1988, s 13.

[6] HA 1988, s 14.

SHORTER TERM PRIVATE SECTOR RESIDENTIAL TENANCIES: KEY POINTS

- Residential tenancies for a term of 21 years or less may, where granted by private landlords, enjoy protection under either the Rent Act 1977 or the Housing Act 1988. Generally, the Rent Act can only apply to tenancies granted before 15 January 1989; tenancies granted on or after that date will, where appropriate, be governed by the Housing Act 1989.

- Both Acts only apply where a house or part of a house is let as a separate dwelling; certain tenancies are excluded, notably those granted by resident landlords.

- The 1977 Act ensures that where the tenancy has ended the tenant can remain indefinitely so long as they continue to reside at the property; on death the tenant's statutory tenancy may pass to a surviving spouse or civil partner, or to a member of the tenant's family. The landlord can only regain possession on certain statutory grounds, many of which are discretionary. The Rent Act also ensures that the tenant pays no more than a 'fair' rent; this is normally below a market rent.

- Under the Housing Act 1988 all non-excluded tenancies granted on or after 28 February 1997 are assured shorthold tenancies unless the landlord serves notice that the tenancy is to be an assured tenancy (which normally only happens where the landlord is a provider of social housing). A landlord can terminate a fixed term AST by giving two months' written notice expiring at the end of the tenancy; if that is not done the tenant can remain as a statutory periodic tenant subject to termination by two months' notice. If the AST is periodic from the outset it can be ended by the landlord giving two months' written notice expiring at the end of a period. No order for possession will be granted until the tenant has been in possession for at least 6 months. There is no rent control under an AST. A landlord cannot regain possession before the end of the contractual term except on a statutory ground. An assured shorthold tenant has the benefit of the tenancy deposit scheme introduced in 2007.

- Assured tenancies under the 1988 Act are increasingly rare outside the social housing sector. An assured tenant can remain in occupation after the end of the tenancy and the landlord can only regain possession by serving notice and proving a statutory ground. The most important of these is the mandatory one based on two months' rent arrears. An assured tenancy is not subject to rent control and the rent can be increased either in accordance with the express rent review provision or under statutory provisions.

Long residential tenancies

Security of tenure

37.12 Tenants of residential premises let on leases in excess of 21 years at a low rent (ie an annual rent of £1,000 or less in Greater London, £250 or less elsewhere) are given security of tenure at the expiry of the term, by virtue of Schedule 10 to the Local Government and Housing Act 1989.[1] Their existing lease is automatically continued on the same terms, including as to rent. The continued tenancy may be terminated by the landlord giving to the tenant between six and twelve months' notice either offering an assured monthly tenancy, or stating that the landlord will seek a possession order from the court on grounds stated in the Act, which are essentially the same as the discretionary grounds provided for under the Housing Act 1988. This protection will now rarely be necessary since such tenants will often, in practice, exercise the rights to enfranchise or to extend their existing leases discussed in the following paragraphs.

[1] This replaces the previous scheme contained in Part I of the Landlord and Tenant Act 1954.

Enfranchisement

37.13 *Introduction* Tenants under long leases of both houses and flats now have extensive rights to enfranchise. Enfranchisement for tenants of houses was the first to be introduced – by the Leasehold Reform Act 1967 ('LRA 1967'). This scheme is necessarily more straightforward since the problems posed by the rules under which the burden of positive covenants cannot pass to a purchaser of freehold land[1] is not so acute in the case of houses.

It took nearly thirty years to devise rules under which tenants of flats—for whom the running of positive covenants is essential—could be given the right to enfranchise[2]. This was achieved by Part I of the Leasehold Reform, Housing and Urban Development Act 1993 ('LRHUDA 1993'). This complex piece of legislation was initially hampered by poor drafting and has been subjected to numerous amendments, most recently in 2002[3]. As we shall see[4], it conferred two alternative rights: either a significant majority of the tenants in the building could, collectively, acquire the freehold and thus effectively become their own landlord or, where such agreement could not be achieved, individual tenants could exercise a right to acquire a new extended lease.

It is now recognised by all political parties that the use of the lease as a mechanism for the long-term ownership of residential property is no longer acceptable. The introduction of commonhold[5] is seen as the correct approach for the future. However, although it is theoretically possible to convert the ownership of a building from long leasehold to a commonhold, this is very unlikely to occur to any great extent[6]. Accordingly, enfranchisement is the only realistic prospect for the owners of existing long leases.

[1] See para 33.4 and 36.72.

[2] Some tenants of flats had been given a right of first refusal by virtue of Part I of the Landlord and Tenant Act 1987.

[3] By the Commonhold and Leasehold Reform Act 2002.

[4] Para 37.15.

[5] Para 28.34 and 33.5.

[6] Largely because the conversion to commonhold requires the consent of 100% of those with any existing interest in the property, see Commonhold and Leasehold Reform Act 2002, s 3; thus the dissent of just one tenant will prevent any change.

37.14 *Leases of houses* The Leasehold Reform Act 1967, as amended, applies where a tenant has held[1], either for the last two years, or for periods amounting to at least two years during the last 10 years[2], a lease of a *house* which was originally granted for a fixed term of over 21 years[3].

A house[4] is any building designed or adapted for living in[5] and reasonably so called[6] whether or not it is structurally detached; where a building is divided horizontally, the flats or units into which it is divided are not 'houses' although the building as a whole may be, if reasonably so called[7]. Where a building is divided vertically (eg a semi-detached property or a terrace) it cannot, as a whole, be a 'house'[8] although the individual units may be.

In these circumstances[9] the tenant[10] can, by serving notice on the landlord, require that the freehold of the house and premises[11] be transferred to him or her, or alternatively that he or she be granted a new lease in substitution for the existing lease, for a term expiring 50 years from the end of the existing lease[12]. This latter alternative is rarely sought. The price or rent to be paid is to be determined in accordance with a formula laid down in the Act. The price to be paid on the acquisition of the freehold is calculated on one of two alternative bases, depending on the rateable value[13] of the property on the appropriate day[14]. For lower value properties the formula is very favourable to tenants; it is assumed that the vendor is selling subject to the tenancy as extended by 50 years and that any higher bid that might be expected from the sitting tenant (ie marriage value) is excluded[15]. For higher value property it is not assumed that the tenancy has been extended and the sitting tenant bid is not excluded (although the landlord's share of that is limited to 50%); the price is to be diminished by any increase in value attributable to improvements carried out and paid for by the present or previous tenants[16]. Furthermore the landlord has more extensive compensation rights, eg for diminution in value to other land, including loss of development value[17].

[1] There used to be a requirement that the tenant must have occupied the house as his or her residence. This has now been abolished, Commonhold and Leasehold Reform Act 2002, s 138; it means that a company or non-resident tenant can now enfranchise. This appears to have consequences that go beyond what Parliament might have intended; now that there is no longer any need for the tenant to be residing more difficult issues are arising as to whether or not the current use of the property will prevent it being regarded as a 'house', see Notes 5 and 6 below.

[2] This period used to be three years and has now been reduced to two: CLRA 2002, s 139.

[3] There used to be a requirement that the rent be 'low'; this has now gone, CLRA 2002, s 141. It should also be noted that, since 26 July 2002, business tenancies (as to which see paras 37.25–37.45) have been largely excluded from the scope of enfranchisement, LRA, s 1(1ZC), as inserted by the CLRA 2002. The only ones that may now qualify are those for terms in excess of 35 years; furthermore the tenant must also satisfy a residence requirement.

[4] As defined by LRA 1967, s 2.

[5] This involves considering the original design and purpose of the property and whether or not a subsequent adaptation has been for some other purpose than for living in; it does not matter that the premises

are now so dilapidated as to be unfit for immediate residential occupation, *Boss Holdings Ltd v Grosvenor West End Properties Ltd* [2008] UKHL 5. Furthermore, premises that were originally designed as a house and have been adapted into multiple residential units are a house for the purposes of the Act even though the current use is for the business of providing short-term tourist and business accommodation, *Hosebay Ltd v Day* [2010] EWCA Civ 748.

 [6] A building that was originally designed or has subsequently been adapted for living in will only be a house if it can reasonably be so called; this can include a property that is partly used for business purposes such as a purpose built shop with living accommodation, *Tandon v Trustees of Spurgeon's Homes* [1982] 1 All ER 1086, HL or even where premises are solely used for business purposes, see *Lexgorge Ltd v Howard de Walden Estates Ltd* [2010] EWCA Civ 748 (where no physical changes had been made to the original residential design). However, where the terms of the lease and a property's actual use limit the residential use to a very small proportion of the premises this can take the property outside the Act, *Prospect Estates Ltd v Grosvenor Estates Ltd* [2008] EWCA 1281. Severe dilapidation rendering a building unfit for occupation does not prevent it being a house reasonably so called, *Boss Holdings Ltd v Grosvenor West End Properties Ltd* [2008] UKHL 5.

 [7] Thus a purpose built block of flats will not be a 'house', whereas a house divided into two flats may well be, whether the flats are together occupied as a single residence (*Sharpe v Duke Street Securities* (1987) 55 P & CR 331, CA) or separately (*Malpas v St Ermine's Property Ltd* [1992] 1 EGLR 109).

 [8] LRA 1967, s 2(1)(b).

 [9] It should be noted the tenants of some types of landlord cannot enfranchise, eg the National Trust, local authorities and registered housing associations.

 [10] A surviving spouse or civil partner and certain other members of a deceased tenant's family who succeed to the tenancy can take the benefit of that tenant's accrued rights: LRA 1967, s 7.

 [11] The freehold can be acquired not only of the house but also of any garage, outhouse, yard, or garden which are let to the tenant with the house: LRA 1967, s 2(3).

 [12] LRA 1967, s 8.

 [13] For tenancies granted after 1 April 1990 (when domestic rates were abolished) rateable value limits have been replaced by a statutory formula based on the premium paid on the grant of the tenancy.

 [14] These vary according to the date on which the tenancy was first rated.

 [15] LRA 1967, s 9(1).

 [16] LRA 1967, s 9(1A), (1B), (1C).

 [17] LRA 1967, s 9A.

37.15 *Leases of flats* Tenants under long leases of *flats* now have, in certain circumstances, a right, together with other tenants in the same building, to acquire the freehold of that building. Alternatively, a tenant may exercise an individual right to acquire an extended lease; this takes the form of a new lease for 90 years plus the outstanding period of the old lease.

The right to collective enfranchisement applies only to residential flats within a self-contained building or part[1] of a building comprising at least two flats that are owned by 'qualifying tenants'[2]. At least two thirds of the total number of flats in the building must be occupied by tenants who qualify.[3] Buildings where more than 25% of the internal floor area is occupied for non-residential purposes are outside the Act, as are those comprising not more than four units where there is a resident landlord[4].

The right to collective enfranchisement can be exercised where at least half of the qualifying tenants wish to do so[5]. In order to 'qualify' the tenant must hold a lease for more than 21 years[6]; there is no longer a low rent requirement or any residence qualification[7]. A person who satisfies these requirements in respect of three or more flats in the same building cannot be the qualifying tenant of any of those flats[8]. The process is started by the service of a claim notice (the 'initial notice')[9]; this must specify the premises to be acquired, propose the price to be paid, provide the landlord with details of the qualifying tenants participating in the notice, and provide the name and details of the nominee purchaser[10]. Following the service of the initial notice it is the nominee purchaser (which may be an individual, a group of individuals or, more usually, a company formed by the participating tenants) which thereafter acts on behalf of the participating tenants and, ultimately acquires the freehold. The landlord must respond within a strict time limit[11] and can either: admit the right to enfranchise and state which of the proposals are accepted; challenge the right to enfranchise, giving reasons; or indicate that the landlord intends to redevelop so that there is then no right to enfranchise. Following this exchange of notices the parties may well be able to agree the terms of the acquisition. If not, any dispute will be resolved by the leasehold valuation tribunal[12]. The price to be paid is governed by a statutory formula[13]. This is based on the open market value, assuming that the freehold is encumbered by the existing leases. The landlord is entitled to a 50% share in any marriage value. Once the process is completed the freehold is vested in the nominee purchaser which becomes the landlord to all the tenants in the building.

It may be that there are tenants under long lease of flats who cannot participate in collective enfranchisement. This may be because the building does not qualify or because insufficient other qualifying tenants wish to acquire the freehold. Equally, there may be tenants who simply do not want to be involved in that process. Such tenants[14], provided they have held their existing lease for at least two years[15], are given an individual right to acquire a new long lease[16]. The procedure is similar to that for collective enfranchisement. The tenant must serve a claim notice, giving details of the flat, proposals as to the terms of the new lease, and the premium to be paid[17]. The landlord must respond to this in much the same way as for collective enfranchisement and any disputes as to the terms of the new lease, or the premium to be paid can be referred to the leasehold valuation tribunal[18]. The new lease will be for a term of 90 years from the expiry date of the existing lease at a peppercorn rent[19]. A premium, calculated by reference to a statutory formula, must be paid[20]. Again, this is based on market value and the landlord is entitled to a 50% share of any marriage value. The terms of the lease are to be the same as the existing lease save where this does not contain any provision for variable service charges; the new lease must provide for such service charges and their enforcement[21].

[1] Tenants of flats within a self-contained part of a building can enfranchise even though that part can itself be divided into self-contained parts, LRHUDA 1993, s 3(2), *41–60 Albert Place Mansions (Freehold) Ltd v Craftrule Ltd* [2010] EWHC 1230.

[2] LRHUDA 1993, s 3(1).

[3] LRHUDA 1993, s 3(1)(c).

[4] LRHUDA 1993, s 4(4).

[5] LRHUDA 1993, s 13(2)(b).

[6] LRHUDA 1993, s 5(1).

[7] Commonhold and Leasehold Reform Act 2002, ss 117 and 120. This means that a company, or a head tenant who holds a headlease of a whole building comprising several flats can now be a qualifying tenant, *Howard de Walden Estates Ltd v Aggio* [2008] UKHL 44.

[8] LRHUDA 1993, s 5(5).

[9] LRHUDA 1993, s 13.

[10] CLRA 2002, ss122-124 and Sch 8 contains provisions for the introduction of a requirement that the enfranchisement process be conducted by an RTE company rather than a nominee purchaser. These have not yet been implemented and, following a consultation process, it now appears that they have effectively been abandoned, *The right to enfranchise provisions (RTE)—consultation* 2010 DCLG.

[11] The date for the landlord's response must be set out in the claim notice; this must be not less than two months after the date on which the claim notice was served.

[12] LRHUDA 1993, s 24(1).

[13] LRHUDA 1993, s 32 and Sch 6.

[14] Who, where seeking an extension rather than collective enfranchisement (see text and note 8 above), can be the qualifying tenant of three or more flats. LRHUDA, s 39(3).

[15] Previously, qualifying tenants had to satisfy a residence test. This is no longer necessary, with the result that a head tenant of a whole building is now able to obtain lease extensions in respect of each individual unit, *Cadogan v 26 Cadogan Square Ltd* and *Howard de Walden Estates Ltd v Aggio* [2008] UKHL 44.

[16] LRHUDA 1993, s 39.

[17] LRHUDA 1993, s 42.

Right to manage

37.16 We have seen that where the landlord of a block of flats is guilty of failing to carry out repairing and insuring obligations, the tenants can apply for the appointment of a manager and, where this proves not to be an adequate remedy, they can compulsorily acquire the landlord's interest[1]. Part II of the Commonhold and Leasehold Reform Act 2002 introduces a new right for long leaseholders of flats to take over the management of their building despite the fact that their landlord is not in breach of these obligations. This right to manage arises in much the same circumstances as the right to collective enfranchisement[2]. It is exercisable by an RTM (right to manage) company which must be set up by the qualifying tenants[3]. Following the service of a notice of claim[4] and the elapse of the stated period of notice, the RTM company will take over the landlord's management functions, notably those with respect to services, repairs, maintenance, improvements, insurance and management[5].

1 See para 35.67.
2 See para 37.15.
3 Commonhold and Leasehold Reform Act 2002, s 74.
4 CLRA 2002, s 79.
5 CLRA 2002, ss 96, 97.

LONG RESIDENTIAL TENANCIES: KEY POINTS

- Residential tenants holding leases of more than 21 years have important rights to enfranchise or obtain an extended lease; tenants of flats also have a right to manage their building.

- Where the property is a house, the Leasehold Reform Act 1967 gives a long leaseholder who has held the lease for at least two years the right to acquire the freehold or to obtain an extended lease at a price in accordance with a statutory formula. The abolition of the residence test has opened up enfranchisement to company and other non-resident tenants and this is causing some unexpected difficulties where the current use of the premises is non-residential.

- Where the property is a flat within a self-contained building the requisite proportion of qualifying tenants who have held their leases for at least two years may collectively acquire the freehold and thus become the landlord, again at a price in accordance with a statutory formula. Individual tenants may have the right to an extended lease. The residence test has been abolished and, as with houses, this has opened up the process in unanticipated ways.

- Tenants of flats now have the right to manage; this can be exercised in much the same circumstances as collective enfranchisement.

Public sector tenancies

37.17 The Housing Act 1985, Pt IV, confers security of tenure on public sector tenants. It should be appreciated that the traditional role of local authorities in actually providing[1] housing is diminishing. Much social housing provision[2] is now undertaken by registered social housing providers such as housing associations; since 1989, new tenancies granted by such bodies are usually assured tenancies governed by the Housing Act 1988[3]. The secure tenancy regime is thus largely confined to the remaining tenants of local authorities and housing action trusts. Furthermore these bodies are now allowed to grant introductory tenancies under which the tenant has less security.

[1] Local authorities retain the vital function of allocating public sector accommodation, see Housing Act 1996 Part VI, ss 159–174 and the statutory guidance thereon, *Fair and flexible: statutory guidance on social housing allocations for local authorities in England*, 2009 DCLG.

[2] Following the implementation of the Housing and Urban Regeneration Act 2008 the Tenant Services Authority (the 'TSA') took over the operation of a single regulatory system for both public and private providers of social housing on 1 April 2010. As a result of the change of government this system is being reviewed; the TSA is to be abolished and its functions transferred to an independent committee within the Homes and Communities Agency and it is proposed that the level of regulation should be scaled back, see *Review of social housing regulation*, 2010 DCLG. This is only part of a radical review of social housing provision, see *Local decisions: a fairer future for social housing consultation*, 2010 DCLG.

[3] See paras 37.8–37.10.

Secure tenancies

37.18 Subject to certain exclusions[1], where a dwelling-house is let as a separate dwelling it will be a secure tenancy whenever both the landlord and the tenant condition are satisfied[2]. The landlord condition limits the type of landlord to a local authority, a new town corporation, an urban development corporation and certain housing co-operatives[3]. The tenant condition requires that the tenant is an individual who occupies the dwelling-house as their only or principal home[4]. The provisions as to security apply not only to tenancies but also to licences[5]; however, it is clear that the only licences covered by the HA 1985 are those that confer exclusive possession[6].

The landlord of a secure tenancy cannot recover possession without serving a notice on the tenant and then obtaining a court order based on one of the statutory grounds for possession[7]. Thus, any fixed-term tenancy does not end by expiry but is automatically replaced by a periodic tenancy[8], and the landlord cannot serve a notice to quit in respect of a periodic tenancy[9]. In order to terminate a tenancy the landlord must serve a notice on the tenant that specifies the grounds of possession on which the landlord will rely and which states a date after which proceedings will be commenced[10]. The grounds for possession are set out in Sch 2. Some, based largely on tenant default are discretionary[11], others are mandatory provided that suitable alternative accommodation is available to the tenant, and a third group is discretionary and also subject to the availability of suitable alternative accommodation. Where a statutory ground is made out the court may make a possession order[12]. Not surprisingly, given the role of public sector landlords, the courts are reluctant to order possession[13]. Even when granted, orders for possession are usually suspended especially where this will give the tenant a further opportunity to pay off arrears of rent. It used to be the case that the secure tenancy came to an end once an order for possession was granted (whether suspended or not). This caused very real problems where the landlord allowed the former tenant to remain in possession and the courts created the concept of the 'tolerated trespasser' as a means of resolving these difficulties. The law has now changed; a secure tenancy does not now come to an end until an order for possession is actually executed[14]. This means that no new tolerated trespassers can be created; existing tolerated trespassers have had their former tenancies restored[15].

Where a secure periodic tenant dies the tenancy will pass to any qualifying successor[16]. Priority is given to a surviving spouse or civil partner[17]; where there is no surviving spouse the tenancy can pass to any member of the deceased tenant's family who resided with him or her for the 12 months preceding the death[18]. The expression family is defined and includes a person living with the tenant as husband or wife or civil partner[19].

In addition to the rights conferred by the terms of their tenancy agreement, secure tenants currently have the benefit of the standards set by the TSA[20]. Most secure tenants also have a right to buy the freehold or acquire a long lease at a substantial discount. The details of this scheme are outside the ambit of this book. They are contained in the Housing Act 1985, Sch 1.

[1] The exceptions include, for example, land acquired for development and accommodation for homeless persons.

[2] Housing Act 1985, s 79(1) except, in the case of new tenants, where the landlord operates an introductory tenancy scheme, see para 37.20.

[3] HA 1985, s 80.

[4] HA 1985, s 81.

[5] HA 1985, s 79(3).

[6] See *Parkins v Westminster City Council* [1998] 1 EGLR 22, CA, *Westminster City Council v Clarke* [1992] 1 All ER 695, HL.

[7] In seeking possession the landlord must not discriminate against any disabled tenant, Disability Discrimination Act 1995, s 22(3)(c); see *London Borough of Lewisham v Malcolm* [2008] UKHL 43.

[8] HA 1985, s 86(1).

[9] HA 1985, s 82(1).

[10] HA 1985, s 83.

[11] This means that the court must be satisfied that it is reasonable to make an order for possession.

[12] However, where the tenant (or anyone living with them) has engaged in housing related anti-social behaviour or in conduct involving the use of the premises for unlawful purposes the landlord may apply for a demotion order, Housing Act 1985, s 82A, inserted by the Anti-Social Behaviour Act 2003. This will be granted by the court if it is reasonable to do so. A demotion order converts the secure tenancy into a demoted tenancy, see further para 37.21.

[13] All public sector landlords must comply with Article 8 of the European Convention on Human Rights; this requires that any order for possession is in accordance with the law and is, in the circumstances of the particular case, proportionate. It seems clear that the statutory requirement that an order for possession can only be made against a secure tenant where it is reasonable to do so automatically satisfies the proportionality test, see *Manchester City Council v Pinnock* [2010] UKSC 45.

[14] HA 1985, s 82(1A) as inserted by Housing and Regeneration Act 2008, s 299, Sch 11, Part 1.

[15] Housing and Regeneration Act 2008, s 299, Sch 11, part 2.

[16] HA 1985, s 89(1).

[17] HA 1985, s 89(2)(a).

[18] HA 1985, s 87(b).

[19] HA 1985, s 113(1)(a).

[20] This system of regulation is currently under review, see para 37.17, note 2.

Introductory, demoted and family intervention tenancies

37.19 *Introduction* Since 1996 various legislative initiatives have been taken to try to ensure that social landlords can more readily regain possession against tenants whose behaviour causes distress and disruption to their neighbours. The first of these was the introductory tenancy scheme which allowed local authorities to grant 'probationary' tenancies which would only blossom into fully secure tenancies after the tenants had proved themselves to be satisfactory. The success of this led to the introduction of a regime under which secure tenants who engage in anti-social behaviour can lose their security of tenure by having their tenancy reduced to a demoted tenancy. The most recent addition to this stable is the family intervention tenancy; this may be granted to a secure tenant whose tenancy has been terminated on the basis of anti-social behaviour or domestic violence. This type of tenancy must be accompanied by a behaviour support package designed to address the tenant's problems.

37.20 *Introductory tenancies* Since 1996 local authorities and housing action trusts have been permitted to choose, if they wish, to operate an introductory tenancy scheme.[1] This is designed to ensure that new[2] tenants are effectively 'on probation'[3] for a one-year period before becoming secure tenants. If they prove themselves to be poor tenants they can readily be evicted; if not, after the expiry of the one-year period, the tenancy will automatically convert into a secure tenancy. Once the scheme is adopted by a local authority or housing action trust, any periodic tenancy or licence which it then grants to a new tenant will be an introductory one rather than a secure tenancy[4]. This introductory tenancy will last for one year[5]; during this period the tenancy cannot be a secure one[6] but, after the expiry of the one-year period, it automatically becomes secure[7] unless the landlord has commenced possession proceedings[8]. During the introductory period the landlord can readily regain possession without having to prove a statutory ground[9]. Before seeking possession, the landlord must serve a preliminary notice[10]. This must set out the reasons[11] why the landlord has decided to retake possession, tell the tenant of the right to ask the landlord to review its decision and specify a date after which court proceedings for possession can be commenced. It used to be the case that, provided any review has been properly undertaken[12], the court had to order possession and had no power to review the landlord's decision. It is now clear that this does not satisfy the requirements of Article 8 of the European Convention on Human Rights[13], Accordingly, a court should not now grant an order for possession without considering whether or not this is proportionate in the particular tenant's circumstances[14]. However, it is necessary for the issue of proportionality to be raised by the occupier and the court should consider the matter summarily and dismiss it unless there is an arguable case. There will always be a strong case that the making of a possession order will be proportionate[15].

[1] Housing Act 1996, s 124.

[2] Existing secure tenants cannot be granted an introductory tenancy, HA 1996, s 124(2)(a).

[3] The scheme was always aimed at providing a means by which those whose anti-social behaviour manifested itself in the early stages of a tenancy could be easily removed (although it appears that, in practice, most of the evictions of introductory tenants are on account of rent arrears).

[4] HA 1996, s 124(2).

[5] HA 1996, s 125(1), (2). This period can be extended by 6 months where the landlord gives notice to that effect, ibid s 125A (inserted by the Housing Act 2004).

[6] HA 1985, Sch 1, para 1A inserted by HA 1996.

[7] Provided the conditions for a secure tenancy are then satisfied, see para 37.18 above.

[8] HA 1996, ss 127, 130.

[9] HA 1996, s 127(2).

[10] HA 1996, s 128(1).

[11] Which do not have to be based on anti-social behaviour or use of the premises for unlawful purposes.

[12] If it can be shown that this review has resulted in a decision that no reasonable person could have reached, the tenant can use the judicial review procedure to have that decision set aside, *Doherty v Birmingham City Council* [2008] UKHL 57. However, now that a possession order cannot be made without the court considering its proportionality (see text and notes 10 and 11) judicial review will become largely redundant.

[13] *Leeds City Council v Hall; Birmingham City Council v Frisby* [2011] UKSC 8.

[14] *Leeds City Council v Hall; Birmingham City Council v Frisby* [2011] UKSC 8.

[15] *Leeds City Council v Hall; Birmingham City Council v Frisby* [2011] UKSC 8.

37.21 *Demoted tenancies* Following the perceived success of introductory tenancies, it was decided to bring in a similar scheme to deal with anyone who already had a secure tenancy[1]. Where a court is satisfied that a secure tenant, a visitor or someone residing at the premises has engaged in housing related anti-social behaviour or conduct involving the use of the premises for unlawful purposes it may make a demotion order where it is reasonable to do so[2]. This has the effect of terminating the secure tenancy and replacing it with a demoted tenancy[3]. This tenancy lasts for 12 months, after which it will revert to being a secure tenancy unless the landlord commences proceedings for possession. In order to regain possession the landlord must follow the same procedure as applies to introductory tenancies[4]. It should be noted that the reasons for seeking possession are not limited to those for which the tenancy was originally demoted. It is now clear that, before making an order for possession, the court must satisfy itself that this is proportionate if this issue is raised by the occupier[5].

[1] The Anti-social Behaviour Act 2003 inserted new provisions into the Housing Act 1985 and the Housing Act 1996.
[2] Housing Act 1985, s 82A(4). The requirement that it must be reasonable to make the order is sufficient to ensure that it is proportionate for the purposes of Article 8 of the European Convention on Human Rights, see *Manchester City Council v Pinnock* [2010] UKSC 45.
[3] HA 1985, s 82A(3).
[4] HA 1996, ss 143E and 143F and see para 37.20.
[5] *Manchester City Council v Pinnock* [2010] UKSC 45; *Leeds City Council v Hall; Birmingham City Council v Frisby* [2011] UKSC 8 and see para 37.20.

37.22 *Family intervention tenancies ('FIT')* This form of tenancy was introduced in 2009[1]. A FIT may be offered to any secure tenant against whom a possession order based on either anti-social behaviour or domestic violence has been made, or could have been made[2]. The landlord's objective in granting such a tenancy must be to provide behaviour support services to the tenant or a person living with the tenant[2]. In order to create a FIT the landlord must serve a prior notice on the prospective tenant which provides prescribed information about the proposed tenancy and the support services[3]. The tenant enjoys no security of tenure and the landlord can regain possession by following a procedure similar to that for introductory and demoted tenancies[4]. In the light of the Supreme Court decision in *Manchester City Council v Pinnock*[5] and *Leeds City Council v Hall; Birmingham City Council v Frisby*[6] it seems likely that a court cannot make an order for possession without considering its proportionality.

[1] By the Housing and Regeneration Act 2008.
[2] HA 1985, s 4ZA(3) as inserted by the Housing Regeneration Act 2008.
[3] HA 1985 s 4ZA(4),(5), (7).
[4] Housing and Regeneration Act 2008, s 298; see para 37.20.
[5] [2010] UKSC 45, see paras 37.20 and 37.21.
[6] [2011] UKSC 8, paras 37.20 and 37.21.

PUBLIC SECTOR TENANCIES: KEY POINTS

- These days many tenancies of social housing are granted by landlords who are registered providers; most of these are therefore governed by the Housing Act 1988.

- Residential tenancies granted by local authorities are either secure tenancies or less protected forms of tenancy; in this latter group are introductory tenancies, demoted tenancies and family intervention tenancies.

- Where a property is let as a separate dwelling it will be a secure tenancy so long as the landlord is a local authority (or other designated public body) and the tenant is an individual residing in the property. The tenancy cannot be ended and the landlord cannot regain possession except by serving notice and proving one of the statutory grounds. Where the tenant dies a surviving spouse or civil partner, or members of the family, can succeed to the tenancy. Many secure tenants have a right to buy the freehold or acquire an extended lease at a discounted price.

- To address the problem of anti-social behaviour on local authority housing estates various types of tenancy have been introduced. These confer no security of tenure initially but can blossom into, or revert to, secure tenancies after 12 months satisfactory occupation. These tenancies are:

- *Introductory.* These are a form of probationary tenancy which convert to secure tenancies after a year. Within that year the landlord can regain possession without proving a statutory ground although, under human rights law, the court must be satisfied that the regaining of possession is proportionate.
- *Demoted.* Where a secure tenant has engaged in anti-social behaviour a court can make a demotion order. This terminates the secure tenancy and replaces it with a demoted tenancy. This operates in much the same way as an introductory tenancy.
- *Family intervention.* This arises in much the same circumstances as the demoted tenancy except that it can also be used where the tenant has been involved in domestic violence. It differs from a demoted tenancy in that the landlord's objective in granting the tenancy must be to offer behaviour support services.

Miscellaneous statutory provisions

Harassment and unlawful eviction

37.23 The Protection from Eviction Act 1977, as amended, confers basic protection against eviction and harassment on a wide range of residential occupiers[1]. It creates three criminal offences[2] and ensures that, in most circumstances, possession cannot be obtained without a court order while anyone is in residential occupation of the premises[3]. The Housing Act 1988 introduced a new statutory tort under which the victims of unlawful eviction can claim damages which are calculated at a penal rate[4].

The offence of unlawful eviction is committed where any person unlawfully deprives, or attempts to deprive, a residential occupier of occupation of the whole or any part of the premises, unless he or she proves a belief, and a reasonable cause to believe, that the occupier had ceased to reside on the premises[5]. The first offence of harassment is committed where any person does acts likely to interfere with the peace or comfort of the residential occupier or members of their household or persistently withdraws or withholds services reasonably required for the occupation of the premises as a residence, with the intent to cause the residential occupier of any premises to give up occupation, or to refrain from exercising any right or remedy in respect of the premises[6]. The intention required for this offence has made convictions difficult to secure. To overcome this, the Housing Act 1988 added a further offence of harassment which is designed to be easier to prove. This can be committed only where a landlord or their agent carries out any of the above acts; the intention required is merely a knowledge, or reasonable cause to believe, that this conduct is likely to cause the residential occupier to give up occupation or to refrain from exercising their rights or remedies[7]. There is, however, an absolute defence where the landlord or their agent can prove reasonable grounds for carrying out the conduct which would otherwise constitute the offence[8].

Conviction for a criminal offence does not in itself afford a remedy to the victim[9]. This is now provided by the Housing Act 1988 which creates a new statutory tort[10]. This imposes civil liability on a landlord who unlawfully evicts a residential tenant or where such a tenant leaves the premises because of the landlord's attempt at an unlawful eviction or as a result of the landlord's harassment[10]. It is not a pre-requisite of this civil liability that the landlord be convicted of the criminal offences of unlawful eviction or harassment. The measure of damages awarded is set out in the Act. Damages are to be assessed on the basis of the difference in value of the landlord's interest in the building in which the premises are situated subject to the occupier's right of occupation and the value of the landlord's interest free from that right[11]. Thus the more secure the occupier's rights, the greater the level of damages awarded; an unlawfully evicted assured tenant—against whom possession cannot readily be recovered—would obtain a much higher award of damages than an assured shorthold tenant.

[1] Covering both tenants and licensees, see Protection from Eviction Act 1977, s 1(1).
[2] PEA 1977, s 1(2), (3) and (3A).
[3] PEA 1977, ss 2 and 3. Tenants or licensees who share accommodation with their landlord, or a member of his family are excluded from this protection: PEA 1977, s 3A. Tenants who occupy premises for both residential and business purposes are protected, see *Pirbakaran v Patel* [2006] EWCA 685.
[4] HA 1988, ss 27, 28.
[5] Protection from Eviction Act 1977, s 1(2).
[6] PEA 1977, s 1(3).
[7] PEA 1977, s 1(3A).
[8] PEA 1977, s 1(3B).
[9] *McCall v Abelesz* [1976] 1 All ER 727, CA.
[10] HA 1988, s 27.
[11] HA 1988, s 28.

Information for tenants

37.24 Various statutory provisions require the landlord of residential premises to provide their tenants with certain information, either at the request of the tenant, or by way of inclusion in the tenancy agreement or on notices or demands. Landlords and managing agents need to be very aware of these since non-compliance may mean that payments under the lease are not, as a matter of law, due from the tenant and, as a result, remedies for non-payment cannot be pursued.

A residential tenant is entitled to request and be provided with the landlord's name and address. Failure to comply with such a request amounts to a criminal offence[1]. Where the reversion on a lease which includes residential premises has been assigned, the new landlord must, within two months, give the tenant notice of the assignment and of his name and address[2]. Failure to comply amounts to a criminal offence; furthermore until such notice is given the former landlord remains liable on the lease covenants[3].

The landlord of residential premises must, by notice[4], provide the tenant with an address in England or Wales at which notices may be served. Until this is done neither any rent or service charge is treated as legally due[6]. Any written *demand* for rent or other payments due under the lease must also contain the name and address[7] of the landlord; if it does not, any service charge will be treated as not due until this information is provided[8]. Any tenant or licensee of residential premises who is obliged to pay their rent on a weekly basis is entitled to be supplied with a rent book[9]. Where the tenancy is a Rent Act tenancy or an assured tenancy the rent book must contain prescribed information. A failure to comply with these requirements is a criminal offence. The tenant of an assured shorthold tenancy granted on or after 28 February 1997 can require the landlord to provide information on any of the terms of the tenancy that have not previously been evidenced in writing[10]. A failure to comply amounts to a criminal offence.

[1] Landlord and Tenant Act 1985, s 1.
[2] LTA 1985, s 3(1).
[3] LTA 1985, s 3(3A) and (3B).
[4] The inclusion of the landlord's name and address in the tenancy agreement is sufficient, see *Rogan v Woodfield Building Services Ltd* [1995] 1 EGLR 72, CA.
[5] LTA 1987, s 48(1).
[6] LTA 1987, s 48(2).

[7] Which must be in England or Wales: LTA 1987, s 47(1)(b).

[8] LTA 1987, s 47(1).

[9] LTA 1985, s 4(1).

[10] HA 1988, s 20A.

Business tenancies

Introduction

37.25 The general law of landlord and tenant governs the parties to a business lease during its contractual term[1]. However, their rights and obligations once the tenancy agreement is approaching its expiry have been regulated by statute ever since the 1950s[2]. Part II of the Landlord and Tenant Act 1954 ('LTA 1954') was first reviewed and then amended in 1969[3]. A second review was carried out by the Law Commission in 1992[4] and most[5] of the changes then proposed were implemented by the Regulatory Reform (Business Tenancies)(England and Wales) Order 2003 ('RRO 2003'). This came into force on 1 June 2004. Broadly speaking, Pt II of the Landlord and Tenant Act 1954 provides that a tenancy under which the tenant occupies premises for business or professional purposes[6] does not come to an end until terminated in accordance with the Act[7]. Until that happens the tenant is entitled to remain in the premises under a continuation tenancy on the same terms and at the same rent as under the contractual tenancy. Even when the current tenancy has been properly terminated the tenant is entitled to a new tenancy as of right (provided certain procedural steps are taken within the prescribed time limits)[8] unless the landlord can establish one or more of the statutory grounds of opposition[9]. The new tenancy will be on such terms as the parties agree; if they are unable to agree, both the terms and the rent will be fixed by the court (or, at the option of the parties, by an arbitrator or expert[10]) in accordance with the provisions of the Act[11].

[1] See ch 36.

[2] Ie by Part II of the Landlord and Tenant Act 1954.

[3] By the Law of Property Act 1969.

[4] *Landlord and Tenant: Business Tenancies: A Periodic Review of the Landlord and Tenant Act 1954 Part II* Law Com No 208 1992.

[5] Some relatively minor changes were made to the original proposals, see *Business Tenancies Legislation in England and Wales: The Government's Proposals for Reform* DETR 2001.

[6] Paras 37.26 and 37.27.

[7] Paras 37.30–37.32.

[8] Para 37.33.

[9] Paras 37.36–37.38.

[10] Ie under the voluntary PACT scheme set up by the Law Society and the RICS, see para 37.41 below. This was recently (2010) re-launched with new Guidance Notes that take account of the 2004 changes to the 1954 Act.

[11] Paras 37.42–37.45.

Tenancies within the Act

37.26 *The requirement for an occupying tenant* The LTA 1954 applies to any tenancy where the property comprised in the tenancy is or includes premises[1] which are occupied by the tenant and are so occupied for the purposes of a business carried on by the tenant or for those and other purposes[2]. It is essential that the occupation is by virtue of either a fixed term or periodic tenancy; occupation as a licensee or tenant at will is not sufficient[3]. It matters not whether the tenancy is a head lease or a sublease or even that it is a lease that has been granted in breach of covenant[4]. In principle, it is the tenant[5] who must be in occupation since it is the policy of the Act is to provide security of tenure for tenants who have established themselves in a business located at the premises in order that they can continue to carry on their business there. Thus a tenant who has parted with exclusive possession (usually by subletting)[6], or ceased trading[7] or vacated the premises[8] will not be protected. However, a tenant who has ceased trading or vacated for reasons beyond their control and who intends to resume business occupation as soon as possible retains protection[9]. A tenant will also be protected where, despite allowing another to occupy the premises, sufficient control is retained (usually by the provision of services which require the tenant's continued access to the demised premises) to be regarded as in occupation[10]. Furthermore, the Act makes specific provision for occupation in the case of leases held by trusts and by groups of companies[11].

[1] In practice business premises usually comprise buildings or other structures; however, where a business is carried out on open land, the Act will apply: see *Bracey v Read* [1962] 3 All ER 472 (race horse training gallops).

[2] LTA 1954, s 23.

[3] *Shell-Mex & BP Ltd v Manchester Garages Ltd* [1971] 1 All ER 841, CA (a licence held not to be within the Act); *Wheeler v Mercer* [1956] 3 All ER 631, HL (a tenancy at will held not to be within the Act). Where a prospective business tenant is allowed into occupation during the negotiations for a lease, the payment of rent will not normally be regarded as creating an implied periodic tenancy; the occupier will be treated as a tenant at will and so will not be statutorily protected, see *Javad v Aqil* [1990] EWCA Civ 1, see paras 36.14 and 36.15.

[4] *D'Silva v Lister House Development Ltd* [1970] 1 All ER 858; *Parc Battersea Ltd v Hutchinson* [1999] 2 EGLR 33.

[5] Acting either personally or through employees or agents. Occupation by a company in which the tenant holds a controlling interest is sufficient to confer protection on the tenant's lease, LTA 1954, s 23(1A) inserted by RRO 2003.

[6] *Graysim Holdings Ltd v P & O Property Holdings Ltd* [1995] 4 All ER 831, HL.

[7] *Aspinall Finance Ltd v Viscount Chelsea* [1989] 1 EGLR 103, CA. A tenant who has vacated, eg by subletting the whole, but who resumes business occupation even very shortly before contractual term date regains statutory protection, see *Pointon York Group plc v Poulton* [2006] EWCA Civ 1001.

[8] *Esselte AB v Pearl Assurance plc* [1997] 2 All ER 41, CA.

[9] See *Morrison Holdings Ltd v Manders Property (Wolverhampton) Ltd* [1976] 2 All ER 205 and *Flairline Properties Ltd v Hassan* [1999] 1 EGLR 137. In both of these cases the tenants had only vacated because their premises had been seriously damaged by fire and the court held that protection was retained because it was satisfied that the tenant intended to resume business occupation once the premises were reinstated.

[10] See *Lee-Verhulst (Investments) Ltd v Harwood Trust* [1972] 3 All ER 619, CA; *Linden v Department of Health and Social Security* [1986] 1 All ER 691; *Groveside Properties Ltd v Westminster Medical School* (1983) 47 P & CR 507, CA.

[11] LTA 1954, s 41(1) ensures that where a lease is held on trust, occupation by any of the beneficiaries qualifies the lease for protection; ibid s 42 provides that, where a lease is held by one group in a company, occupation by another company in the same group also suffices. S 42 has been amended by RRO 2003 so that it is no longer necessary for one company to be the subsidiary of the other; it suffices if both are under the control of the same company or person.

37.27 *The meaning of business* The term 'business' is very widely defined. Where the tenant is an individual the expression includes any trade, profession or employment[1]. It has been held that this means that where such a tenant carries on any undertaking of a non-commercial nature or something in the nature of a hobby, the lease will not be protected[2]. However, where the tenant is a body of persons, the statutory definition is widened so as to include any 'activity'. While this term has been held to carry some of the connotations of a business[3], it is clear that it covers non-profit making enterprises[4]. Where the terms of the tenancy prohibit all business use, the LTA 1954 cannot normally apply; where the tenancy permits a business use and, in breach of covenant, the tenant uses for another business use, the Act still applies[5]. The Act does not require the premises to be used only for business purposes, so that where premises are used for mixed business and residential use, the tenancy will be covered by the LTA 1954[6] rather than by any of the residential codes[7].

However, where the business use is incidental to any residential use, the LTA 1954 will not apply and the tenant will then be governed by the appropriate residential scheme[8].

[1] LTA 1954, s 23(2).

[2] See *Lewis v Weldcrest* [1978] 3 All ER 1226, CA (where a tenant who took in lodgers was, perhaps, surprisingly, held no to be conducting a trade; note that she did then qualify for protection under the Rent Act), *Abernethie v AH & J Kleiman Ltd* [1969] 2 All ER 790 (a tenant running a Sunday School for which no charge was made, was held to be engaging in a hobby and not a business).

[3] *Hillil Property and Investment Co Ltd v Naraine Pharmacy Ltd* (1979) 39 P & CR 67, CA.

[4] Such the running of a members' tennis club (*Addiscombe Garden Estate Ltd v Crabbe* [1957] 3 All ER 563, CA) a hospital (*Hills (Patents) Ltd v University College Hospital Board of Governors* [1955] 3 All ER 365, HL) and the provision of accommodation for students of a university medical school (*Groveside Properties Ltd v Westminster Medical School* (1983) 47 P & CR 507, CA).

[5] LTA 1954, s 23(4).

[6] *Cheryl Investments Ltd v Saldanha* [1979] 1 All ER 5, CA; *Broadway Investments Hackney Ltd v Grant* [2006] EWCA Civ 1709.

[7] Tenancies protected by the LTA 1954 are positively excluded by the Rent Act 1977, s 24(3), by the Housing Act 1985, s 79, Sch 1, para 11 and by the Housing Act 1988, s 1, Sch 1, para 4.

[8] *Gurton v Parrott* [1991] 1 EGLR 98, CA.

37.28 *Excluded tenancies* A variety of tenancies are expressly excluded from the protection of the LTA 1954[1]. These are: tenancies of an agricultural holding[2], farm business tenancies[3], mining leases, service tenancies[4], and tenancies granted for a fixed term not exceeding six months provided that the tenancy does not include any provision for renewal and that the tenant has not either been in occupation for a period exceeding 12 months, or has not succeeded to a business which has operated from the premises for such a period[5]. Leases of on-licensed premises used to be excluded from the Act; all such tenancies are now protected[6].

[1] LTA 1954, s 43.

[2] See para 37.47.

[3] See para 37.48.

[4] Ie any tenancy granted due to the fact that the tenant was an employee of the landlord.

[5] This means that the landlord cannot grant a series of short-term tenancies to the same tenant without the tenant automatically becoming protected once he or she has occupied for more than 12 months. A tenant who stays in possession after the expiry of a fixed-term tenancy cannot thereby claim to have a protected tenancy as a result of being in occupation for more than 12 months unless the facts establish the grant of a new periodic tenancy, see *Cricket Ltd v Shaftesbury plc* [1999] 2 EGLR 57.

[6] Landlord and Tenant (Licensed Premises) Act 1990.

37.29 *Contracted out tenancies* Originally, the LTA 1954 did not permit the parties to exclude ('contract out') its application to their tenancy. The Act was amended in 1969[1] so as to permit the parties to agree that the Act should not apply provided only that the approval of the court was obtained prior[2] to the grant of the tenancy. It appears that it was expected that this would only be done where a landlord wished to let on a very temporary basis[3]; however, no restrictions were imposed on the length of lease which could be contracted out and nor was the court given any power to refuse approval where the proper procedure had been followed and where both parties are properly advised[4]. Over the years, the practice of contracting out has certainly increased dramatically in numerical terms[5], although it is impossible to say whether or not there is any real increase in the proportion of contracted out tenancies relative to the number of new leases in the market place. Given the lack of any teeth to the court approval process this has now been replaced by a procedure under which prior notice must be given to the prospective tenant[6].

Where the parties to a fixed-term[7] tenancy wish to exclude it from the operation of the Act, the prospective landlord must serve on the prospective tenant a prescribed form of notice[8] that warns the recipient that the tenancy to be granted will not enjoy statutory protection and explains what this means. Provided that this notice is given at least 14 days in advance the tenant (or a person authorised by the tenant) may make a simple declaration and this will ensure that the lease is duly contracted out. The declaration must be made before entering into[9] the tenancy, and must state that 14 days' notice has been given and that the tenant has read and understood the consequences of excluding the Act. Where the prior notice is not given at least 14 days in advance[10], the tenant (or a person authorised by the tenant) must make a statutory[11] declaration before entering into the tenancy[12]; only then will the contracting out be effective. Due to concerns about the practical operation of the 14-day procedure, many solicitors are using the statutory declaration as a matter of routine. The previous government was in the process of considering amendments to address these problems; it remains to be seen whether these will be taken forward.

[1] LTA 1954, s 38(4) inserted by the Law of Property Act 1969. These provisions also applied to agreements to surrender.

[2] *Essexcrest Ltd v Evenlex Ltd* [1988] 1 EGLR 69, CA.

[3] Law Com No 17, 1969.

[4] *Hagee (London) Ltd v AB Erikson and Larson* [1975] 3 All ER 234, CA.

[5] Judicial statistics indicate that by 1989 the number of leases contracted out of the Act each year amounted to approximately 18,000; by 2000, this figure had increased to about 54,000.

[6] LTA 1954, s 38A as inserted by RRO 2003. These provisions apply equally to agreements to surrender.

[7] A fixed-term tenancy that includes a break clause can be contracted out, see *Metropolitan Police District Receiver v Palacegate Properties Ltd* [2000] EWCA Civ 33. However, the grant of a tenancy for a fixed term 'and thereafter from year to year' cannot be contracted out, see *Nicholls v Kinsey* [1994] 1 EGLR 131.

[8] The form of notice is prescribed by RRO 2003, Sch 1. A reference to the notice, to the agreement to contract out and to the appropriate declaration, must be contained in the tenancy agreement; this ensures that it is clear from the lease itself that it has been contracted out.

[9] Or becoming contractually obliged to take the tenancy.

[10] This alternative procedure was intended to be used only in emergencies where a tenant needed very quick access to new premises (eg following a fire or flood).

[11] Although the content of the statutory declaration is the same as the simple declaration, the former can only be made in the presence of an independent solicitor (ie not the solicitor of either the tenant or the landlord) who is authorised to administer oaths.

[12] Or becoming contractually obliged to take the tenancy.

Termination of tenancies governed by the LTA 1954

37.30 The LTA 1954 provides that a business tenancy does not come to an end by expiry or by a common law notice served by the landlord. Save where the tenant ceases business occupation by the end of the term,[1] it is statutorily continued[2] until terminated in accordance with the Act. The Act specifically recognises certain common law methods of termination. So, the parties can agree a surrender[3], the tenant can serve a notice to quit[4], and the landlord can forfeit the lease[5]. In all other circumstances, a statutory notice must be served in order to bring the tenancy to an end. It is important to appreciate that termination does not necessarily (and does not usually) mean that the tenant must leave the premises since, on the termination of the tenancy, the tenant is entitled to apply for a new tenancy[6]. Only if the landlord successfully opposes that application[7] will the tenant have to vacate. Accordingly, taking steps to terminate a tenancy is often simply the first stage of putting in place a new tenancy at a current open market rent[8].

[1] The cessation of business occupation means that the Act can no longer apply (see para 37.26 above), hence the tenancy will come to an end by effluxion: see *Esselte AB v Pearl Assurance plc* [1997] 1 EGLR 73, CA. This case (which has been confirmed by the insertion, by RRO 2003, of s 27(1A)) recognises the

important practical point that a fixed-term business tenant can walk away from the tenancy at the end of the lease without warning (see para 37.32).

[2] LTA 1954, s 24(1).

[3] LTA 1954, s 24(2). Note that while the parties can enter into a deed of surrender, a binding agreement to surrender at a future date is not effective without going through a prior notice procedure that mirrors that for contracting out (see para 37.29).

[4] A notice to quit is defined by LTA 1954 s 69 as including a contractual notice to terminate; this means that a tenant can terminate a periodic tenancy and also operate a break notice in a fixed-term tenancy.

[5] LTA 1954 s 24(1).

[6] See para 37.33.

[7] See paras 37.36–37.38.

[8] In most cases, by the time a business lease is at contractual term date the rent will last have been fixed by a rent review which took place five years previously. Thus, in a rising market, a landlord will normally be anxious to terminate the current tenancy and put a new lease in place simply in order to achieve a current open market rent.

37.31 *Termination by the landlord* The landlord[1] can only terminate the lease by serving on the tenant a section 25 notice in a prescribed form[2]. There are two alternative forms of section 25 notice depending on whether or not the landlord is opposing renewal[3]. Such a notice cannot be served if the tenant has already served a section 26 request.[4] A section 25 notice must state a date for termination which must be no earlier than the date on which the tenancy could be brought to an end at common law and give between six and twelve months' notice[5]. So, where the tenancy is for a fixed term, the earliest a section 25 notice can be served is 12 months prior to contractual term date. If the current tenancy is to end on contractual term date the latest date by which it can be served is six months before contractual term date. However, it must be stressed that there is no latest date for the service of a section 25 notice. Provided that a section 26 request has not been served and that no other termination method has been employed, a section 25 notice can be served at any time; the existing tenancy will simply continue until the date specified in that notice.

Where the landlord is not opposing renewal[7] the section 25 notice must set out proposals for the new tenancy[8]. It is not intended that these will be binding[9], but that the tenant should be given an early indication of what the landlord has in mind. Where the landlord wishes the tenant to leave, the section 25 notice must state that any application for a new tenancy will be opposed and set out the statutory grounds on which it is intended to rely[10]. A failure to do so means that the landlord will be unable to oppose a renewal.

[1] In order to be able to serve a section 25 notice, the landlord must be the 'competent' landlord: LTA 1954, s 44. Where the immediate landlord is the freeholder, he (or she) will always be the competent landlord. Where the immediate landlord is a leaseholder, he (or she) must hold a reversion which will last for a further 14 months; if this is not the case, the competent landlord is the next landlord up the chain whose reversion will continue for at least 14 months.

[2] LTA 1954, s 25.

[3] Prior to RRO 2003 there was one composite form to deal with both situations.

[4] LTA 1954, s 26(4): see para 37.32.

[5] LTA 1954, s 25(1), (2), (3), (4).

[7] See para 37.30.

[8] LTA, s 25(8), inserted by RRO 2003.

[9] This is clearly stated in the relevant prescribed form.

[10] LTA 1954, s 25(6), (7), see paras 37.36–37.38.

37.32 *Termination by the tenant* We have already seen[1] that a periodic tenant who wishes to leave the premises can serve a common law notice to quit; similarly, a fixed-term tenant who wishes to operate a break can serve an effective break notice. A fixed-term tenant who wishes to leave *at contractual term date* now has two options. He or she can either simply quit the premises by that date without any need to give notice[2], or a notice giving at least three months' notice expiring on contractual term date can be served[3]. However, where a fixed-term tenancy *has already been continued by the Act* (ie where the tenant has stayed on in business occupation beyond contractual term date) the tenant can only bring the tenancy to an end by serving a notice on the landlord giving three months' notice.[4]

A fixed-term tenant who wishes to remain in the premises does not normally need to take any positive steps. In the absence of any action by the landlord[5], the tenancy will be continued on the same terms and at the same rent[6] and, in a rising market, this will be to the tenant's obvious advantage. The position will be very different in a falling market, or where there are specific reasons to have a new tenancy in place. Here the tenant will need to take the initiative and can do so by serving a request for a new tenancy[7]. Such a request has the effect of terminating the existing tenancy[8]. The statutory requirements for a section 26 request largely mirror those for a section 25 notice[9]. The request (which cannot be served if the landlord has already served a section 25 notice[10]) must be in a prescribed form and must be served by the tenant[11] on the competent landlord. It must give between six and 12 months' notice and specify a date for the commencement of the new tenancy which must be no earlier than the contractual term date of the existing tenancy. It must set out the tenant's proposals as to the terms of the new tenancy[12]. The landlord can, within two months of being served with a section 26 request, serve a counter notice stating that the renewal will be opposed and setting out the grounds on which this will be done[13]. If the landlord does not serve such a counter notice the renewal cannot be opposed[14].

[1] Para 37.30.

[2] LTA 1954, s 27(1A) and see Note 1 para 37.30. It appears that this option is open to a tenant who has given the impression that it wishes to stay by applying for a new tenancy: see *Single Horse Properties Ltd v Surrey County Council* [2002] EWCA Civ 367, [2002] 2 EGLR 43.

[3] Landlord and Tenant Act 1954, s 27(1).

[4] LTA 1954, s 27(2).

[5] Such as the service of a section 25 notice.

[6] See para 37.30.

[7] LTA 1954, s 26.

[8] Immediately before the date specified in the request for the commencement of the new tenancy: LTA 1954, s 26(5).

[9] See para 37.31.

[10] LTA 1954, s 26(4).

[11] Certain tenants—those who hold under either a periodic tenancy or for a fixed term not exceeding one year—cannot serve a s 26 request: LTA 1954, s 26(1). This does not mean that such tenants cannot obtain a new tenancy, merely that they must wait for the landlord to initiate the process.

[12] LTA 1954, s 26(3).

[13] LTA 1954, s 26(6).

[14] Para 37.36.

The renewal process

37.33 *Application to court* It is in the area of the procedure for renewal that RRO 2003 has made the most significant changes. Previously, following the service of either a section 25 notice or a section 26 request, the tenant[1] had to make a court application for a new tenancy within a strict time limit[2]; this was invariably adjourned to allow the parties time to negotiate. In order to prevent these token applications, and to further encourage parties to negotiate for themselves without court intervention, the very strict time limits have been removed. Now, an application simply has to be made before the date specified for termination in either the section 25 notice or the section 26 request[3]. Furthermore, the parties are able to make a written agreement to extend this deadline[4]; further extensions can be agreed so long as they are entered into before a previous one expires. Only where no application to court has been made within any extended time limit will the tenant lose the right to apply for a new tenancy.

In order to give the landlord an opportunity to keep the process moving, he or she can now apply to court, either simply for a termination[5] of the current tenancy (which will only succeed if a ground of opposition is established) or for the grant of a new tenancy[6]. The tenant's right to apply for a new tenancy is, of course retained. In order to avoid multiple applications, only one application can be made[7].

In practice, the parties are usually able to reach agreement either that the landlord has made out a good ground of opposition, or that the tenant no longer wishes to take a new tenancy, or as to the terms of the new tenancy. The most usual reason for a court hearing is that the tenant challenges the landlord's ground(s) for opposing renewal[8].

[1] Under the old system only the tenant could apply to court.

[2] If this was not done the tenant would lose the right to a new; this set a 'time trap' into which less experienced tenants and their advisers often fell.

[3] LTA 1954, s 29A(2), as inserted by RRO 2003. If the renewal process has been commenced by way of a section 26 request, an application to court cannot be made until either at least two months after the making of the request or until after the landlord has served a counter notice opposing renewal.

[4] LTA 1954, s 29B as inserted by RRO 2003.

[5] LTA 1954, s 29(2) as substituted by RRO 2003.

[6] LTA 1954, s 24(1) as substituted by RRO 2003. The tenant can inform the court that he or she does not want a new tenancy and the landlord's application must then be dismissed, LTA 1954, s 29(5); if the court is satisfied that the landlord's application was properly made and that the tenant has used the proceedings as a means of prevaricating, the court can make the tenant pay the landlord's costs, *Lay v Drexler* [2007] EWCA Civ 464. The dismissal is automatic and dates from when the court receives the notification from the tenant; this means that, under LTA 1954 s 64 (see para 37.34), the current tenancy ends 3 months' later, *Windsor Life Assurance Co Ltd v Lloyds Bank plc* [2009] 47 EG 134.

[7] LTA 1954, s 29(3) as substituted by RRO 2003.

[8] See paras 37.36–37.38.

37.34 *Interim continuation* It is common for the tenant's position still to be unclear by the date specified for the termination of the existing tenancy in either the section 25 notice or section 26 request. This may be because the parties are still carrying out their own negotiations, they may have agreed an extension to the time limit for making a court application[1], or a court application may have been made and they are waiting for a court hearing or an appeal. The Act makes provision for this. By definition, by the date specified for termination, the parties must either have agreed an extension or an application to court must have been made. Where there is an agreed extension, the date originally specified for termination in the section 25 notice or section 26 request is effectively changed to the final date of that (or any further) extension[2]. Once an application to court has been made, the current tenancy will not terminate on the date specified in the notice or request or extension but will continue until three months after the date on which the application is either withdrawn or finally disposed of by the court[3]. This is known as 'interim continuation'.

[1] LTA 1954, s 29B, see para 37.33.

[2] LTA 1954, s 29B(4).

[3] LTA 1954, s 64.

37.35 *Interim rent* Under the original provisions of the Act, the tenant would continue to pay the existing rent throughout any period of interim continuation. The landlord would not get rent at a current open market level until the commencement of any new tenancy.

Not surprisingly, this encouraged tenants to drag their feet when negotiating new leases. This resulted in an amendment to the Act, which introduced the concept of interim rent[1]. The RRO 2003 has made further significant changes[2]. Either[3] the landlord or the tenant can apply[4] for interim rent. If the court so decides[5] (or the parties agree), this will be payable from the earliest date that could have been specified for termination in either the section 25 notice or the section 26 request[6]. This is designed to prevent the practice of seeking to preserve a rental advantage by serving a long section 25 notice or section 26 request. Interim rent is payable until the date when the current tenancy actually ends[7].

The level of interim rent is determined in accordance with the Act and RRO 2003 has introduced an alternative and more realistic basis which applies in the majority of instances. In all cases where the landlord has not opposed renewal, where the tenant was in occupation of the whole of the demised premises, and where the landlord actually grants a new tenancy of the whole of the property to the tenant, the interim rent will be equal to the rent payable under and at the commencement of the new tenancy[8]. In all other circumstances, interim rent is assessed according to the old rules. These provide that interim rent is to be the open market rent, as at the commencement of the interim period, but taking account of the existing rent and on the assumption of a yearly tenancy[9]. This can have the effect of cushioning the tenant from a substantial increase in the rent; however, this is now confined to cases where the tenant's future occupation of the premises is genuinely uncertain.

[1] LTA 1954, s 24A inserted by the Law of Property Act 1969.

[2] LTA 1954, s 24A has now been replaced by ss 24A –D, inserted by RRO 2003.

[3] Previously, a tenant could not apply for interim rent. It was not appreciated by those drafting LTA 1954, s 24A that, in a falling market, a tenant could wish to apply for interim rent; this has now been rectified.

[4] An application cannot be made more than six months after the termination of the tenancy, ibid, s 24A(3).

[5] The award of an interim rent is at the court's discretion, LTA 1954, s 24A(1).

[6] Thus an agreed extension (see para 37.33) does not affect the date from which interim rent is payable.

[7] In accordance with LTA 1954, s 64, see para 37.34.

[8] LTA 1954, s 24C. However, where there have been substantial changes in the market between the start date for interim rent and the commencement of the new tenancy, or where the terms of the new lease have a substantial impact on rent, the interim rent can be modified by the court, LTA 1954 s 24C(3).

[9] LTA 1954, s 24D. RRO 2003 has introduced one minor amendment; this is that account must be taken of the rent payable under any sub-tenancy of part of the premises, s 24D(1)(b).

Opposing renewal

37.36 A landlord can only oppose renewal where an intention to do so, on one or more specified statutory grounds has been stated, in either a section 25 notice, or in a counter notice to the tenant's section 26 request. The landlord[1] is limited to the grounds specified and cannot add to the stated grounds[2]. The statutory grounds are set out in s 30(1) (a)–(g). Those most widely used in practice are the ones based on tenant default (para (a)—breach of repairing covenant, para (b)—persistent delay in paying rent, and para (c)—breaches of other obligations), or para (f)—where the landlord intends to redevelop or para (g) where the landlord wishes to occupy the premises for his own business purposes. Grounds (e)—a more economic letting of the whole and ground (d)—the availability of suitable alternative accommodation—are rarely employed and have scarcely been litigated. The tenant default grounds are straightforward; they are, however, discretionary and the court tends to be generous towards tenants whenever there is any suggestion that they can retrieve the situation[3]. Paragraphs (f) and (g) are mandatory so that, where made out, the court must refuse to order a new tenancy. Where either is the sole basis on which the landlord has stated an intention to oppose renewal, compensation must be paid to the tenant if the latter quits the premises[4]. It is these two grounds that are the most frequently litigated.

[1] It should be noted that where, after serving a section 25 notice or counter notice to a section 26 request, the landlord's interest is transferred, the new landlord can rely on any grounds stated in that notice, *Morros Marks v British Waterways Board* [1963] 1 WLR 1008, CA.

[2] See *Smith v Draper* [1990] 2 EGLR 69, CA.

[3] See, for example, *Hurstfell Ltd v Leicester Square Property Co Ltd* [1988] 2 EGLR 105, CA. It is fair to say that, where a business tenant is in serious default, this may be an indication that the business is also in difficulties; in such cases the tenant may well choose not to take a new tenancy.

[4] See para 37.39.

37.37 *Redevelopment by the landlord* It is not the policy of the LTA 1954 to impede development. Accordingly, where the landlord intends to demolish or reconstruct the premises (or a substantial part of them) or to carry out substantial works of construction, the court must refuse to order a new tenancy[1]. The works to be taken into account must affect the structure of the premises[2]; this is usually easy to establish in the case of demolition, reconstruction, or where a new building or extension is being erected. It may be less easy to prove in cases of refurbishment where the core of an existing building is being left intact and where much of the work relates to the internal layout[3]. Demolition and reconstruction must affect the whole or a substantial part of the premises; works of reconstruction must themselves be substantial. Substantiality is, inevitably, a question of fact and degree to be decided by the trial judge; an appeal court will rarely intervene[4].

The landlord must establish the requisite intention by the date of any court hearing[5]. What must be proven is not simply a desire to carry out the works in question but rather a reasonable prospect of doing so[6]. Ideally, the landlord should have taken a formal decision to undertake the project[7], have put in place the necessary finance and building contracts, and obtained planning permission, where this is necessary. However, it is clear that a somewhat lesser state of readiness can suffice. So, for example, where a landlord has not yet been given planning permission, or has had an application refused, there can still be a successful opposition if it can be shown that there is a sufficient prospect of gaining planning permission that a reasonable landlord would persist with the proposal[8].

The project must be one for which the landlord requires possession of the premises; if the existing lease confers rights which allow the landlord access to do the work in question, a new tenancy will be ordered[9]. It must also be shown that it is the landlord who is going to carry out the redevelopment. Manifestly, this will be satisfied by the employment of a building contractor—the landlord does not have to do the work personally[10]. However, para (f) is not made out where the landlord is intending to sell the premises outright to a developer; it must be shown that the landlord retains control and this can be achieved by the grant to a developer of a building lease as opposed to selling the freehold[11] (unless, by the date of the hearing, the developer has become the competent landlord[12]).

Where a landlord has, in principle, satisfied all the requirements of paragraph (f) the tenant may turn to LTA 1954, s 31A. This allows the tenant to offer to take a new tenancy that gives the landlord rights of access to carry out the proposed works, or to take a letting of an economically severable part of the existing premises. However, the court will only allow this where the works will not interfere to a substantial extent, or for a substantial time, with the tenant's business at the premises[13]. What amounts to a substantial interference is a question of fact and degree; in one case[14] a new lease was ordered where the relevant works would take about two weeks to complete, in another[15] a new tenancy was refused where the works would take 12 weeks.

[1] LTA 1954, s 30(1)(f).

[2] See *Percy E Cadle & Co Ltd v Jacmarch Properties* [1957] 1 All ER 148, CA; *Joel v Swaddle* [1957] 1 WLR 1094, CA, *Romulus Trading Co v Trustees of Henry Smith's Charity* [1990] 2 EGLR 75, CA.

[3] See *Barth v Prichard* [1990] 1 EGLR 109, CA, *Global Grange Ltd v Marazzi* [2002] EWHC 3010.

[4] See *Global Grange Ltd v Marazzi* [2002] EWHC 3010.

[5] *Betty's Cafes Ltd v Phillips Furnishing Stores Ltd* [1957] 1 All ER 1, CA. If the tenant seeks to obtain summary judgment, the date of proving intention is that of the projected trial and not of the summary hearing, *Somerfield Stores Ltd v Spring (Sutton Coldfield) Ltd* [2010] EWHC 2084.

[6] *Cunliffe v Goodman* [1950] 1 All ER 720, CA—the landlord must have moved 'out of the zone of contemplation into the valley of decision'.

[7] Eg, where the landlord is a company, by making a formal board decision.

[8] See *Cadogan v McCarthy & Stone (Developments) Ltd* [2000] L & TR 249, CA; *Gatwick Parking Services Ltd v Sargent* [2000] 2 EGLR 45, CA, *Dogan v Semali Investments Ltd* [2005] EWCA Civ 1036. For a case where the court was satisfied that the landlord had no real prospect of obtaining planning permission: see *Coppin v Bruce-Smith* [1998] EGCS 55, CA.

[9] *Heath v Drown* [1972] 2 All ER 561, HL.

[10] *Gilmour Caterers Ltd v St Bartholomews Hospital Governors* [1956] 1 QB 387, CA.

[11] *PF Ahern & Sons Ltd v Hunt* [1988] 1 EGLR 74, CA.

[12] *Morris Marks v British Waterways Board* [1963] 1 WLR 1008, CA.

[13] It is irrelevant that the tenant can relocate his or her business for the period of the work; what matters is the period and extent of the disruption at the demised premises: *Redfern v Reeves* (1978) 37 P & CR 364, CA.

[14] *Cerex Jewels Ltd v Peachey Property Corpn* [1986] 2 EGLR 65, CA.

[15] *Blackburn v Hussain* [1988] 1 EGLR 77.

37.38 *Occupation by the landlord* A landlord may oppose the grant of a new tenancy on the basis of an intention to occupy the premises[1] for the purposes of his or her business[2] or residence[3]. As with para (f)[4], the landlord must demonstrate the requisite intention, namely a reasonable prospect of fulfilling his or her wishes[5]. So, it must be shown that the landlord has a fair chance of obtaining planning permission[6], where this is necessary, and has the necessary finance to set up the proposed business[7]. Provided that the court is satisfied that the landlord is intending to set up business at the premises, it matters not that there is a real risk that the business may not survive on a long-term basis; the landlord is entitled to try[8]. An important restriction on the right to rely on para (g) is the five-year rule. This prevents a landlord from using this ground where his or her interest in the property was acquired within five years preceding the date specified in the section 25 notice or section 26 request[9] and where throughout that period there has been a business tenancy of the premises[10]. This rule is designed to prevent landlords buying up reversions subject to business tenancies that are about to expire and then using para (g) to evict the tenant at the end of the lease.

The courts have made it clear[11] that the five-year rule is to be used as a guide on the operation of para (g) where a landlord's intention is to occupy for only a short period. If the landlord's intention is to make a gratuitous transfer within the five years following the regaining of possession, the requirements of para (g) are satisfied; however, if it is shown that the landlord intends to sell the premises within that period, renewal cannot be opposed[11]. Where a court is satisfied that, while no intention to sell within five years has been proved, such a sale is highly likely, it can legitimately conclude that no intention to occupy has been established[12].

[1] The test of occupation is the same as for tenants claiming the protection of the Act, see para 37.26. So, for example, where a landlord was intending to run a business which involved subletting the premises, it was held that para (g) was not satisfied because the landlord would not be in occupation: see *Jones v Jenkins* [1986] 1 EGLR 113, CA.

[2] The landlord must either solely own the business which is to operate from the premises, or be a partner in the business (in which case it is not essential to be intending to take an active part in it: see *Skeet*

v Powell-Sheddon [1988] 2 EGLR 112, CA); alternatively the business may be operated by a company in which the landlord has a controlling interest (LTA 1954, s 30(3)).

³ LTA 1954, s 30(1)(g).

⁴ See para 37.37.

⁵ Much of the case law on intention can be used interchangeably for either para (f) or (g).

⁶ *Gregson v Cyril Lord Ltd* [1962] 3 All ER 907, CA.

⁷ The failure to provide evidence of the availability of finance needed to set up a restaurant business was fatal to the landlord in *Zarvos v Pradhan* [2003] EWCA Civ 208.

⁸ *Cox v Binfield* [1989] 1 EGLR 97, CA; *Dolgellau Golf Club v Hett* [1998] L & TR 217, CA.

⁹ *Frederick Lawrence Ltd v Freeman, Hardy & Willis* [1959] 3 All ER 77.

¹⁰ LTA 1954, s 30(2).

¹¹ *Willis v Association of Universities of the British Commonwealth* [1965] 1 QB 140, CA.

¹² *Patel v Keles* [2009] EWCA Civ 1187.

37.39 *Compensation for disturbance* A landlord who opposes the grant of a new tenancy on the basis of paras (e)[1], (f) or (g) may become liable to pay compensation to the tenant[2]. Compensation is payable where the landlord has specified one or more of those grounds and no other and, as a result, the tenant either makes no application for a new tenancy, or withdraws that application, and then quits the premises[3]; it matters not that, by the time the tenant leaves, the landlord has abandoned his or her opposition[4]. Compensation may also be payable where the landlord specifies one of the compensatable grounds along with other grounds; however, in this instance the tenant must obtain a ruling from the court that the only ground on which a new tenancy was refused was a compensatable one[5]. It is possible to include in the tenancy agreement a clause contracting out of compensation. However, this ceases to have effect where the tenant has been in occupation of the premises for at least five years preceding the date on which the tenant is to quit the premises[6].

The amount of compensation is the product of a statutorily prescribed 'appropriate multiplier' (currently set at 1) and either the rateable value or twice the rateable value[7]. The higher rate of compensation is only payable where the tenant has been in occupation of the premises[8] for the whole[9] of the 14-year period preceding the date specified for termination by either the section 25 notice or section 26 request[10]. A tenant who makes the mistake of moving out of the premises prior to the date specified for termination in the landlord's section 25 notice will lose the right to the higher level of compensation[11].

¹ Which is very rarely used: see para 37.36.

² LTA 1954, s 37(1). This section has been reformulated by RRO 2003 but has largely the same effect as the old provision.

³ LTA 1954, s 37(1C).

⁴ As happened, for example, in *Bacchiocchi v Academic Agency Ltd* [1998] 2 All ER 241.

⁵ LTA 1954, s 37(1A) and (1B).

⁶ LTA 1954, s 38(2).

⁷ LTA 1954, s 37((2).

⁸ Or has taken over a business which has been operated at the premises by a business tenant for that period, LTA 1954, s 37(3)(b). A tenant who has occupied part of the premises for the 14-year period will only qualify for the higher rate of compensation in respect of that part, LTA 1954, s 37(3A) as added by RRO 2003.

⁹ The court will ignore short periods of non-occupation which have occurred for sensible operational reasons: see *Bacchiocchi v Academic Agency Ltd* [1998] 2 All ER 241.

¹⁰ LTA 1954, s 37(3)(a).

¹¹ *Sight and Sound Education Ltd v Books etc Ltd* [2000] L & TR 146.

37.40 *Compensation for misrepresentation* RRO 2003 has replaced the former provision[1] governing the award of compensation to a former tenant who had quit the premises on the basis of a misrepresentation or concealment by the landlord. Previously a tenant could only obtain compensation where an application for a new tenancy had actually gone to court and it was subsequently shown that the court had been induced to refuse a new tenancy on the basis of the landlord's misrepresentation or concealment of material facts. The new wording means that the tenant can also obtain redress where either a consent order is made, or where he (or she) quits the premises without making, or after withdrawing, an application for a new tenancy[2]. The Court of Appeal has held[3] that a landlord who not only served a section 25 notice based on s 30(1)(f) but who at the same time also informed the tenant of its present intention to redevelop[4], was liable to pay compensation when, prior to the tenant committing to new and more expensive premises, it decided not to go ahead with the development.

[1] LTA 1954, s 55 was regarded as ineffective and has been removed and replaced by a new s 37A.

[2] LTA 1954, s 37A(1) and (2).

[3] *Inclusive Technology Ltd v Williamson* [2009] EWCA Civ 718.

[4] The mere serving of a section 25 notice based on para (f) would not itself have been a representation of a present intention to redevelop since a landlord does not have to prove intention until the court hearing (see para 37.37). The critical factor was the landlord's accompanying statement of its intention to redevelop; it was this which amounted to a continuing representation of intention. When this later changed the landlord was obliged to inform the tenant; its failure to do so amounted to a misrepresentation for which compensation was payable.

The new tenancy

37.41 Unless the landlord succeeds in establishing a ground of opposition, the court must order the grant of a new tenancy[1]. The terms of the new tenancy (including the rent) are usually agreed by the parties. Where, or to the extent that, agreement is not possible, the court will settle them by applying ss 32-35 of the LTA 1954. Alternatively, the parties can opt to have the terms and the rent settled in accordance with the Act by a third party, appointed under the PACT scheme[2]. Accordingly, since the provisions of the Act will dictate the terms of the lease should the parties fail to agree, these must be borne in mind when seeking to negotiate out of court. Where the terms are settled by the court, or by a third party, the tenant has 14 days in which to decline the tenancy and to apply for the revocation of the order[3].

[1] Landlord and Tenant Act 1954, s 29(1).

[2] See para 37.25, note 10.

[3] LTA 1954, s 36(2).

37.42 *The premises* Unless the parties agree otherwise, the tenant is entitled to a new tenancy of the 'holding' ie those parts of the existing premises which he or she occupies at the date of the hearing[1]. So, if the tenant has sublet part of the premises there is no right to a new tenancy which includes the sublet part, although the landlord can require this to happen[2]. The tenant is entitled to have included in the new tenancy any rights such as easements which were previously formally enjoyed in connection with the holding[3].

[1] Landlord and Tenant Act 1954, ss 23(3), 32(1).

[2] LTA 1954, s 32(2).

[3] LTA 1954, s 32(3). The court will not order the inclusion of rights that were not contained in the old lease, see *The Picture Warehouse Ltd v Cornhill Ltd* [2008] EWHC 45.

37.43 *Duration of the new tenancy* The parties can agree any length of term they choose. Where they are unable to agree, the court can order a new tenancy of up to 15 years[1]. The court will take into account a whole range of factors when deciding on the appropriate duration (or on the insertion of a landlord's break option): the length of the current lease, the business requirements of both parties[2], the wish of the landlord to reoccupy[3] and the prospects of redevelopment[4] have all been regarded as relevant. A vexed question in today's market, where lease lengths are getting shorter, is whether tenants can insist on a lease that is shorter than their existing lease, simply as a matter of policy. This appears only to have been considered once, and then only in the county court[5]. The view was expressed that this will depend on the particular circumstances; the tenant in that case was given the shorter lease that it had requested[6]. It should always be remembered that, at the end of a renewed lease, the LTA 1954 will still, in principle, apply. Thus, the tenant will be entitled to a further statutory renewal unless the landlord can successfully establish a ground of opposition.

[1] LTA 1954, s 33. This upper limit was increased from 14 to 15 years by RRO 2003.

[2] Eg, where a tenant was due to retire on a particular date, he was given a lease which would last until then in order to avoid him having to re-locate for a short period: see *Becker v Hill Street Properties Ltd* [1990] 2 EGLR 78, CA.

[3] See *Upsons Ltd v E Robins Ltd* [1955] 3 All ER 348, CA where only a short new lease was granted because the landlord had only just failed to satisfy the five-year rule under para (g).

[4] See, eg, *Adams v Green* [1978] 2 EGLR 46, CA and *National Car Parks Ltd v Paternoster Consortium Ltd* [1990] 1 EGLR 99. In both cases landlord's break provisions were included so that the landlords could then seek to terminate should they be in a position to redevelop.

[5] See *Rumbelows Ltd v Tameside Metropolitan Borough Council* (1994) county court, noted at [1994] 15 EG 154.

[6] It should not be assumed that this will always happen since the outcome in *Rumbelows* turned on its particular facts.

37.44 *Lease terms other than rent* LTA 1945, s 35 gives the court a wide discretion to settle the terms of the lease other than rent. It does, however, require regard to be had to terms of the existing lease. It has been held that, where a party is proposing terms that are different from those in the current lease, it is for that party to justify the changes and to prove that they are fair and reasonable in all the circumstances; it was also suggested that a term is not necessarily fair and reasonable simply because it accords with current market practices in lease drafting[1]. This has produced a tendency for the terms of statutorily renewed leases to follow those of the existing lease, save where the parties are able to agree the change. So, a landlord may not be able to substitute a variable service charge for a fixed charge[2]; it has been held that a user clause could not be varied so as to exclude a use which was important to the tenant's business[3]; a 'keep open for trade' covenant was not excluded from the new tenancy because of the benefit it conferred on the landlord[4]; and a user covenant cannot be altered for the sole purpose of either enhancing[5] or diminishing[6] the rental value of the premises. It is specifically provided that the court can take into account the operation of the Landlord and Tenant (Covenants) Act 1995[7]; this means that the court can now approve the inclusion of a new style disposition covenant under which the landlord can stipulate specific requirements that do not have to be reasonable[8]. It has been held that this does not mean that the landlord can insist on the inclusion of a requirement that a tenant cannot assign without automatically entering into an authorised guarantee agreement; such a requirement must be subject to the reasonableness test[9]. It remains to be seen whether or not, when deciding the terms of a statutorily renewed lease, the courts will take account of the recommendations of the Code for Leasing Business Premises in England and Wales 2007[10].

[1] *O'May v City of London Real Property Co Ltd* [1982] 1 All ER 660, HL.

[2] It should however be noted that the renewal in *O'May* was for only a three-year term and the court considered that the risk of incurring the cost of expensive repairs was not reasonable for a short-term tenant.

[3] *Gold v Brighton Corpn* [1956] 3 All ER 442, CA.

[4] *Boots the Chemist v Pinkland Ltd* [1992] 2 EGLR 98.

⁵ *Charles Clement (London) Ltd v Rank City Wall Ltd* [1978] 1 EGLR 47, *Samuel Smith (Southern) Ltd v Howard de Walden Estates Ltd* [2007] 1 EGLR 107.

⁶ *Aldwych Club Ltd v Copthall Property Co Ltd* (1962) 185 Estates Gazette 219.

⁷ Landlord and Tenant Act 1954, s 35(2).

⁸ *Wallis Fashions Group plc v CGU Life Assurance Ltd* [2000] L & TR 520. See para 36.31 above.

⁹ *Wallis Fashions Group plc v CGU Life Assurance Ltd* [2000] L & TR 520.

¹⁰ See para 36.31.

37.45 *Rent* The rent can only be determined once all the other terms of the new lease have been settled[1]. This is required, by LTA 1954, s 34(1) to be that at which the premises might reasonably be expected to be let in the open market. It does not matter if this means that the rent is then set at a level that the tenant cannot afford to pay[2]. The appropriate valuation date is the commencement of the new lease[3]. The rent will usually be fixed by reference to appropriate comparable evidence; if this is not available account can be taken of general rent increases in the locality[4]. The rent will not be reduced to take account of disrepair where this is due to the tenant's default[5]; however, where it is due to the landlord's breach, the court can order that any increase in the rent cannot come into effect until repairs are carried out[6]. In those now rare cases where the existing lease does not contain any provisions for a rent review, the court may order the inclusion of a rent review clause in the new lease[7].

It is specifically provided that certain matters are to be disregarded when fixing the rent. These are: any effect on rent attributable to the tenant's occupation; any goodwill attaching to the premises by reason of the business carried on there by the tenant; in the case of licensed premises; any increase in value attributable to any tenant's licence; and any increase in value attributable to certain tenant's improvements[8]. The improvements to be disregarded are defined as those carried out by anyone who was at the time[9] the current tenant[10] provided that these were not carried out under an obligation to the landlord. All such improvements that were carried out under the *current* tenancy are disregarded[11]. Where such an improvement was made during a *previous* tenancy it will only be disregarded if it was completed not more than 21 years before the date of the application for the new tenancy; in addition, the premises must have at all times after the completion of the improvements have been the subject of a 1954 Act tenancy and, at the end of any such tenancy, no tenant must have quit the premises[12].

¹ *Cardshops v Davies* [1971] 2 All ER 721, CA, *Samuel Smith (Southern) Ltd v Howard de Walden Estates Ltd* [2007] 1 EGLR 107.

² *Giannoukakis Ltd v Saltfleet Ltd* [1988] 1 EGLR 73, CA.

³ *Lovely and Orchard Services Ltd v Daejan Investments (Grove Hall) Ltd* [1978] 1 EGLR 44. Since, technically, this is three months after the application is finally disposed of (see para 37.34) the valuation date is usually taken to be the hearing date.

⁴ *National Car Parks Ltd v Colebrook Estates Ltd* [1983] 1 EGLR 78.

⁵ *Family Management v Gray* [1980] 1 EGLR 46, CA.

⁶ *Fawke v Viscount Chelsea* [1979] 3 All ER 568, CA.

⁷ LTA 1954, s 34(3). In these very unusual cases, it now seems settled that the courts will insist on an upward and downward clause even though these are rarely encountered in practice, see *Fourbouys plc v Newport Borough Council* [1994] 1 EGLR 138.

⁸ LTA 1954, s 34(1).

⁹ Improvements carried out prior to the formal grant of the tenancy will not be disregarded, see *Euston Centre Properties v H & J Wilson* [1982] 1 EGLR 57.

¹⁰ Improvements carried out by a third party under a management agreement with tenant can be disregarded where these were under the control and effectively at the expense of the tenant, see *Durley House Ltd v Cadogan* [2001] 1 EGLR 60.

¹¹ LTA 1954, s 34(2).

¹² LTA 1954, s 34(2)(a), (b), (c).

Business Tenancies: Key Points

- Part II of the Landlord and Tenant Act 1954 applies to a tenancy under which the tenant occupies premises for business or professional purposes. The parties can agree to contract out of the Act by following a statutory notice procedure before the tenancy is granted.

- A protected tenancy does not come to an end until terminated in accordance with the Act; in the meantime there is a continuation tenancy on the same terms and at the same rent.

- The tenant is entitled to terminate the tenancy and quit by vacating at contractual term date (fixed term), serving a notice to quit (periodic tenancy), exercising a break provision, or by serving notice under section 27.

- Although the landlord is free to forfeit, they have no other unilateral right to end the tenancy except by serving a section 25 notice.

- A tenant who wishes to remain under a new tenancy can serve a section 26 request; this terminates the current tenancy.

- Where the current tenancy has been terminated by either a section 25 notice or a section 26 request the tenant is entitled to a new tenancy as of right provided certain procedural steps are taken within the prescribed time limits.

- The landlord can only prevent a renewal and obtain possession by establishing one or more of the statutory grounds of opposition.

- The new tenancy will be on such terms as the parties agree; if they are unable to agree, both the terms and the rent will be fixed by the court (or, at the option of the parties, by an arbitrator or expert) in accordance with the provisions of the Act.

Agricultural tenancies

37.46 Most agricultural tenancies are regulated by one of two statutory schemes of protection. Those granted prior to 1 September 1995 are, where appropriate, governed by the Agricultural Holdings Act 1986. Those granted on or after that date are given very much more limited protection under the Agricultural Tenancies Act 1995. Some of the detail of both of these schemes has been altered by the Regulatory Reform (Agricultural Tenancies) (England and Wales) Order 2006. These are designed to improve the viability of tenanted farms by encouraging diversification, allowing the re-structuring of holdings without the loss of rights, and improving flexibility while maintaining a balance between the interests of the landlord and the tenant[1].

[1] See *Guide to the Regulatory Reform (Agricultural Tenancies) (England and Wales) Order 2006*, DEFRA 2006.

Agricultural holdings

37.47 An agricultural holding is land (whether agricultural land or not), comprised in a contract for an agricultural tenancy. A contract for an agricultural tenancy is a contract of tenancy, other than one granted on or after 1 September 1995,[1] under which the whole of the land is let for use as agricultural land[2] for the purposes of a trade or business. 'A contract of tenancy' is defined so as to include a lease or agreement for a lease for a term of years or from year to year; furthermore, it is provided that any letting of land less than a tenancy from year to year, or any licence to occupy such land, is to take effect as if it were an agreement for a tenancy from year to year.

A tenancy for a fixed term of two years or more[3] continues, on expiry, as a tenancy from year to year unless and until either party serves a notice to quit; this provision is modified where the tenant dies before the term expires and may be contracted out of, with approval of the minister.[4] For tenancies originally granted before 12 July 1984 certain eligible close relatives are entitled to take over the tenancy on the death[5] or retirement[6] of the tenant. Although these rights have long been abolished for post-1984 tenancies of agricultural holdings, they will remain important for many years because they apply not only on the death or retirement of the original tenant but also on the death or retirement of a successor.

As a general rule, an agricultural tenancy may only be terminated by a notice to quit of at least 12 months. A landlord's notice to quit may take one of two forms. Where such a notice does not state any reasons, the tenant may serve a counter-notice, the effect of which is to prevent the notice to quit operating without the consent of the Agricultural Land Tribunal. Any consent must be based on one of six statutory grounds; these include where the landlord wishes to terminate the tenancy in the interest of good husbandry or the sound management of the estate[7]. However, even where one of these grounds is made out the Tribunal must still withhold its consent if satisfied that in all the circumstances a fair and reasonable landlord would not insist on possession. Where the notice to quit relies on one of eight statutory grounds[8], the tenant is precluded from serving a counter notice[9]. A tenant who wishes to contest the ground relied upon can in some instances serve a notice requiring the matter to be referred to arbitration[10]; in other cases the tenant must challenge the ground by way of defence in any proceedings.

The AHA 1986 confers some protection in respect of rent; either the landlord or the tenant may apply for the rent to be submitted to arbitration.[11] Such applications cannot be made more frequently than every three years.

Part V of the AHA 1986 provides for compensation to be paid by the landlord in respect of certain tenant's improvements where the tenant quits on the termination of a tenancy of an agricultural holding. This is fixed in accordance with various statutory formulae[12]. Quitting tenants may also qualify, where appropriate, for compensation in respect of any milk quota attached to the holding[13]; compensation for disturbance is also payable where the tenancy is terminated on grounds unconnected with tenant default[14]. The landlord can obtain compensation on the termination of the tenancy for deterioration to the holding[15].

[1] Agricultural Tenancies Act 1995, s 4(1). This section does provide for the Agricultural Holdings Act 1986 to apply in certain exceptional cases to tenancies granted on or after 1 September 1995.

[2] Defined as 'land used for agriculture' by AHA, s 1(4); 'agriculture' is defined by ibid, s 96. It is not necessary for the whole of the land to be used for agriculture but any other uses of part of the land must not substantially affect the character of the tenancy.

[3] It should be noted that, perhaps curiously, the scheme of the Act is such that a tenancy for a fixed term of at least 12 months but less than two years is a lease of an agricultural holding so that, for example, the other major statutory schemes of protection are excluded. However, it is *not* afforded any security of tenure under the AHA 1986 since it is not made to continue, after expiry, as a tenancy from year to year. See *Gladstone v Bower* [1960] 2 Qb 384, [1960] 3 All ER 353, CA. An attempt to challenge this decision was rejected in *EWP Ltd v Moore* [1992] Qb 460, [1992] 1 All ER 880, CA.

[4] AHA 1986, ss 1–5.
[5] AHA 1986, ss 36–48.
[6] AHA 1986, ss 50–58.
[7] AHA 1986, ss 25–27.
[8] AHA 1986, Sch 3.
[9] AHA 1986, s 26(2).

[10] The old rules governing agricultural land arbitrations have been abolished and such arbitrations are now governed by the Arbitration Act 1996.

[11] AHA 1986, ss 12, 84 and Sch 2.

[12] AHA 1986, Sch 9, para 2 ('old' improvements), s 66 ('new' improvements) and ss 64-69 (a special system of farming).

[13] AHA 1986, s 13 and Sch 1.

[14] AHA 1986, s 60.

[15] AHA 1986, ss 71, 72.

Farm business tenancies

37.48 The Agricultural Tenancies Act 1995 applies to farm business tenancies granted on or after 1 September 1995. A farm business tenancy is one[1] under which all or part of the land comprised in the tenancy is farmed for the purposes of a business and has been so farmed since the beginning of the tenancy.[2] It is essential that the character of the tenancy is, at all times, primarily or wholly agricultural,[3] with the result that the tenancy can move in and out of the ATA 1995. At any time when it is outside that Act, ie when the tenancy is not primarily or wholly agricultural, it could, provided that there is business use of part, move into the protection of Pt II of the Landlord and Tenant Act 1954.[4] This possibility can be avoided by each party giving notice to the other, at or before the beginning of the tenancy, that the tenancy is to be and to remain a farm business tenancy.[5]

A tenant under a farm business tenancy has only very limited statutory protection. Where the tenancy is a periodic tenancy other than a yearly tenancy, or where it is for a fixed term of two years or less, the tenancy comes to an end in accordance with the normal common law rules. Accordingly, it will either come to an end by expiry,[6] or by means of a normal notice to quit served by either party.[7] A tenancy for a fixed term of more than two years, can only be brought to an end by one of the parties serving a notice to terminate in writing of at least 12 months before it is due to take effect[8]. It used to be the case that such a notice had also to be for less than 24 months; the parties can now agree their own maximum period of notice[9]; in the meantime the tenancy continues as a tenancy from year to year[10]. Similarly, a yearly tenancy can only be brought to an end by the service of a notice to quit, in writing, given at least 12 months before the end of the tenancy.[11] In neither case is there a need for there to be any grounds for the termination of the tenancy.

Part II of the ATA 1995 sets out statutory provisions for rent review[12]. These apply in all cases unless there is an express provision in a written lease which provides otherwise[13]; the only[14] restriction on the parties' right to agree their own rent review formula is that this must not preclude a reduction in rent[15].

Part III of the ATA 1995 provides for compensation to be paid by the landlord in respect of certain tenant's improvements on the termination of a farm business tenancy. This is fixed in accordance with a statutory formula[16]. The parties are now able to agree an upper limit to the amount of compensation to be paid[17].

[1] Unlike the AHA 1986, the ATA 1995 does not apply to licences: see Agricultural Tenancies Act 1995, s 38(1).

[2] ATA 1995, s 1.

[3] ATA 1995, s 1(3).

[4] See paras 37.25-37.45.

[5] ATA 1995, s 1(4).

[6] See para 36.94.

[7] See para 36.95.

[8] ATA 1995, s 5(1).

[9] ATA 1995, s 5(1) as amended by Regulatory Reform (Agricultural Tenancies) (England and Wales) Order 2006, arts 13, 18 and Sch 2.

[10] ATA 1995 s 5(1).

[11] ATA 1995, s 6. Again, the maximum period for such a notice has been removed, see Note 9 above.

[12] ATA 1995, Part II.

[13] ATA 1995, s 9.

[14] The right of the parties to agree their own rent review provisions used to be more limited; these restrictions have been removed by Regulatory Reform (Agricultural Tenancies) (England and Wales) order 2006. The new regime applies to contractual provisions made on or after 19 October 2006.

[15] ATA 1995, s 9(c).

[16] ATA 1995, s 20.

[17] ATA 1995, s 20(4A) and (4B) as inserted by Regulatory Reform (Agricultural Tenancies) (England and Wales) order 2006.

AGRICULTURAL TENANCIES: KEY POINTS

- Tenancies of agricultural land are governed by one of two statutory schemes.

- Those granted before 1 September 1995 are normally covered by the Agricultural Holdings Act 1986; those granted on or after that date are usually farm business tenancies within the Agricultural Tenancies Act 1995.

- All tenancies within the 1986 Act (except one granted for a fixed term of at least 12 months but less than 2 years) is automatically continued and can only be terminated in accordance with the statutory procedures; these require the service of a notice to quit of at least 12 months which can only succeed where a statutory ground is made out. Where the tenancy was granted before 12 July 1984 certain eligible close relatives can take it over on the death or retirement of the tenant on two successive occasions. The Act gives some protection in respect of rent and makes provision for the payment of compensation when the tenant quits.

- The 1995 Act applies to all tenancies under which land is farmed for the purposes of a business. The character of the tenancy must at all times be primarily agricultural. In order to avoid the possibility that diversification will take the tenancy outside the Act, the parties can agree at the outset that the tenancy is to remain a farm business tenancy. The Act does not prevent the termination of the tenancy; in the case of yearly tenancies or those for a term of more than two years a notice to quit must be for a minimum of 12 months. The Act precludes any upward only rent review and makes provision for compensation for tenants' improvements.

Questions

1. Eleven months ago Leonard granted to Tina a one year lease of a flat. He wishes to regain possession at the end of the lease. Can he do so and, if not, how and when can he end the lease?

2. Explain the requirements of the tenancy deposit scheme.

3. What is leasehold enfranchisement? To what leases does it apply and why is the scheme relating to flats necessarily more complex than that governing houses?

4. When do secure tenancies arise?

5. What options are available to local authority landlords of housing estates that are plagued by families who engage in ant-social behaviour?

6. What basic requirements must be met if a tenant of business premises is to qualify for protection under Part II of the LTA 1954?

7. What procedure must be followed for the grant of a 'contracted out' tenancy?

8. How can a landlord unilaterally terminate a 1954 Act protected tenancy?

9. How can a tenant terminate a fixed term 1954 Act protected tenancy?

10. What procedural steps must be followed by a landlord who wants to prevent a 1954 Act tenant from renewing their lease?

11. On what basis are the terms for a statutorily renewed lease settled, and how do parties who are unable to agree resolve their differences?

12. What are the two schemes of statutory protection that apply to leases of agricultural land?

PART VI

Planning law

38

The operation of the planning system and its legal framework

CHAPTER OVERVIEW

In this chapter a short historical perspective on the planning system is given. We then consider:

- the legal framework of the planning system and key legislation;
- the operation and respective roles of central and local government;
- the development plan system and its significance; and
- the legal liabilities of local planning authorities.

Introduction

38.1 The creation of the planning system was intended to secure public control over the use and development of land. Public control is seen as essential to ensure that land use and development are reasonably systematic, or at least not determined solely by commercial or private interests. This enables the interests of the community at large or public interest to be taken into account.

The origins of the planning system

38.2 The origins of the planning system can be traced back to the turn of the 20th century. The first town planning legislation, the Housing and Town Planning Act, was passed in 1909. This largely stemmed from concerns over poor sanitation and public health and mainly addressed housing conditions. However, early attempts at preparing schemes (what we would now call plans) were thwarted by a lack of technical expertise and delay. Another particular issue which caused difficulty was how to deal with the consequent changes to land values which could decrease as a result of blight[1] as well as increase as a result of a grant of planning permission.

The modern planning system was created by the Town and Country Planning Act 1947 (TCPA 1947). The provisions of the TCPA 1947 contained four major elements which remain central to the planning system today:

- Local planning authorities were created by giving new functions to councils. Among their obligations was the production of development plans.[2]

- All land was made subject to planning control, whereby any person intending to carry out development[3] would require planning permission from the local planning authority. In making its decision, the planning authority would have regard to its development plan.

- Local planning authorities were given powers to enforce planning control.

- Local planning authorities were given additional powers to control land use outside the basic planning control system, including the preservation of buildings of historic or architectural interest[4], tree preservation, and the display of advertisements.

In addition to these elements, there is also statutory provision for the compulsory acquisition of property and compensation, but this is outside the scope of this book.

[1] Blight occurs when a planning proposal for say an airport or railway line adversely affects the sale of a property as uncertainty is created and the market value cannot be realised.

[2] These are statutory documents which set out a local authority's policies and proposals for the future development and use of land in their area (paras 38.21–38.28 below).

[3] Development is defined in the TCPA 1990, s 55(1) as 'the carrying out of building, engineering, mining or other operations in, on, over or under land', or 'the making of any material change in the use of any buildings or other land' (paras 39.2–39.17 below).

[4] Para 39.45 below.

The framework for planning control

Legislation

Principal Planning Acts

38.3 Since the Town and Country Planning Act 1947, planning legislation was consolidated by further Acts in 1968 and 1971. Major change did not then occur until the late 1980s and early 1990s. Four principal Acts replaced and restated the existing law taking the opportunity to correct technical anomalies. The four Acts are:

- Town and Country Planning Act 1990 (TCPA 1990);

- Planning (Listed Buildings and Conservation Areas) Act 1990 which deals with special controls in relation to buildings and areas of special historic interest.[1]

- Planning (Hazardous Substances) Act 1990;

- Planning (Consequential Provisions) Act 1990 largely to deal with issues of transition arrangements.

Another principal Act, the Planning and Compensation Act 1991 made important changes to a variety of things including development plans, appeals, enforcement powers and the definition of development.

The Planning and Compulsory Purchase Act 2004 (PCPA 2004) is the most significant post-1991 change. Some of the PCPA 2004's provisions are additional to those found in the TCPA 1990; other provisions repeal, amend or substitute provisions in the TCPA 1990. The PCPA 2004 introduced further changes to both the development plan system and to planning control. Amongst other things, it created a new statutory layer of plan at regional level known as regional spatial strategies[2] and replaced the old system of local plans with a local development framework.[3] Some of the more significant changes in relation to planning control were the removal of Crown immunity[4], the strengthening of enforcement powers[5], and the introduction of new processes for determining major infrastructure projects.

A further important change to the planning system occurred. Traditional planning considered the development or use of land. However, increasingly planners have to deal with a plethora of plans and initiatives. Traditional planning moved on to become spatial planning—'planning which goes beyond traditional land use planning to bring together and integrate policies for the use and development of land with other policies and programmes which influence the nature of places and how they function'.[6] This meant that regeneration, transport, health, economic and housing strategies could be considered alongside planning strategies. More than anything this involved a culture change within the planning sector. There was widespread recognition that spatial planning was about integrating development and its delivery. More emphasis was put on the implementation of plans and policies and a holistic approach to place making was taken. Coupled with this, s 39 of the PCPA 2004 provides that any person or body who exercises a function in relation to regional spatial strategies, local development frameworks or, in Wales, the Wales Spatial Plan must do so with the objective of contributing to the achievement of sustainable development.[7] Although the concept of sustainable development had been central to the planning system for many years, this was the first time it had been placed on a statutory footing.

The PCPA 2004 also required the new plans to be subject to a sustainability appraisal. In practice this is usually satisfied by meeting the requirements of strategic environmental assessment.[8]

The Planning Act 2008 (PA 2008) established a new system for dealing with nationally significant infrastructure projects such as water, waste, energy, and transport projects.[9] It established the Infrastructure Planning Commission to deal with such projects in line with national policy statements. Amongst other things, it also introduced the concept of the community infrastructure levy.[10]

Despite the extensive changes introduced by the PCPA 2004 and the PA 2008, the TCPA 1990 remains the principal planning Act. At the time of writing, major new legislation has been introduced in Parliament in the shape of the Localism Bill. A brief outline of the main provisions of the Localism Bill is included at the end of Chapter 39.[11]

[1] Paras 39.45–39.51.
[2] Para 38.22.
[3] Paras 38.23–38.25.
[4] For many years planning legislation did not bind the Crown.
[5] Para 39.52 below.
[6] So defined in PPS11 [note the PSS was cancelled in February 2010 but the definition remains useful]
[7] See para 38.27.
[8] Para 38.26.
[9] Defined in PA 2008, s 14.
[10] Owners and developers contribute in whole or in part to the cost of infrastructure required to support the development they are proposing.
[11] Para 39.68.

Human Rights legislation

38.4 The Human Rights Act 1998 has also had significant implications for planning. The Act is discussed in more detail elsewhere in Chapter 3.

Subordinate legislation

38.5 Beyond the principal Acts of Parliament, there is extensive subordinate legislation in the form of numerous rules, regulations, and orders which will be referred to where necessary. Its importance should not be underestimated. In planning law, subordinate legislation constitutes not so much small print as the sharp end of the system. In practical terms, it is in the rules, regulations, and orders, as well as in case law, that the answer is commonly to be found as to what may or may not be done.

Government policy: Planning Policy Guidance Notes, Planning Policy Statements and Circulars

38.6 Although it is not law, government policy is particularly important in the planning system. Government policy is a 'material consideration' for decision makers to take into account in deciding whether or not to grant planning permission. While policy, which is chiefly set out in Planning Policy Guidance Notes (PPGs) and their newer style replacements Planning Policy Statements (PPSs), is not binding on any decision maker, it is at least influential, and failure to pay due regard to it may lead to the decision being declared invalid in the courts[1].

There are over twenty PPGs and PPSs at the time of writing which set out Government policy on a range of planning issues including sustainable development[2], climate change, green belts, transport, and flood risk. The Secretary of State[3] also issues circulars which help to interpret the legislation.

In Wales a series of topic based technical advice notes and minerals technical advice notes are the equivalent of PPGs and PPSs in that they supplement two overarching policy frameworks, Planning Policy Wales and Minerals Planning Policy Wales. Procedural guidance is given in Welsh Office, National Assembly for Wales and Welsh Assembly Government circulars.

---

[1] For example, in *Fulford v Secretary of State* [1997] JPL 163, the court stated that relevant national policy (in that case PPG 15) was one of the necessary material considerations in deciding an application to demolish buildings in a conservation area.

[2] Para 38.27.

[3] Para 38.8.

FRAMEWORK FOR PLANNING CONTROL: KEY POINTS

- The planning system can trace its origins back to the turn of the 20th century and originally addressed concerns about health and poor housing conditions. One of the notable dates in the evolution of the planning system is the Town and Country Planning Act 1947. This introduced the need for local authorities to prepare development plans.

- Anyone wishing to develop land has to obtain planning permission from the local planning authority. The planning system operates in the public interest.

- The principal Planning Acts of relevance are the TCPA 1990 and the Planning and Compulsory Purchase Act 2004. This latter Act introduced regional spatial strategies and local development frameworks. In addition it strengthened enforcement powers, removed Crown immunity and introduced new processes for dealing with major infrastructure projects.

- As well as the principal Planning Acts, much of the day to day sharp end of practice in the planning system can be found in subordinate legislation which takes the form of numerous rules, regulations and orders.

- The Government produces planning policy guidance in the form of Planning Policy Guidance Notes and their replacements Planning Policy Statements. Matters of procedure are dealt with in Circulars.

The planning institutions—a mixture of central and local government

Central government

38.7 At the central government level, the key player in England is the Secretary of State (SoS) and the Department which he or she heads. Successive reorganisations of government have made this confusing. The names of planning law cases reported over the years refer to Ministers and Secretaries of State presiding over Housing and Local Government, Town and Country Planning, and Environment. Since May 2006 the Secretary of State responsible for planning has been the Secretary of State for Communities and Local Government.

In Wales, the National Assembly for Wales in some cases, and the Welsh Ministers in others, exercise the powers in respect of planning which are exercised in England by the Secretary of State. Hereafter references to the SoS must be read as referring to the National Assembly for Wales or the Welsh Ministers as the case may be.

The SoS has a wide range of powers and duties. These arise in respect of legislation (notably subordinate legislation), policy making and appeals.

The role of the Secretary of State

38.8 *Legislation* Despite the plethora and length of the various Acts many of them are simply statements of general principle. Much of the real 'teeth' of the planning system lie in regulations and orders. For example, the SoS has made three statutory instruments which affect the day to day practice of planning:

- Town and Country Planning (Use Classes) Order 1987 (UCO) which specifies numerous different types or 'classes' of development and is significant because it allows changes of use within each class and between certain classes to occur without the need to apply for a specific grant of permission.

- Town and Country Planning (General Permitted Development) Order 1995 (GPDO) which grants permission for certain categories of development such as some householder development without the need to apply for a specific grant of permission.

- Town and Country Planning (General Development Procedure) Order 1995 (GDPO) not to be confused with the similarly titled GPDO, this Order sets out the procedures to be followed.

This demonstrates the wide ranging powers the SoS has. By adding or removing a class to the UCO for example, it is possible to make the system more flexible and responsive to economic circumstances or by extending permitted development rights under the GPDO it may have the effect of removing several hundred applications from the system.

38.9 *Policy* The making of PPGs, PPSs, and other circular advice has already been mentioned.[1] Development plans, including the regional spatial strategies introduced by the PCPA 2004 and prepared by local planning authorities (LPA), must conform to Government policy. The SoS also has powers to direct a LPA to modify its development plan proposals and may also 'call in' development plans to ensure their compatibility with Government policy.

[1] Para 38.6.

38.10 *Appeals to the Secretary of State and 'call in' powers* The TCPA 1990 gives applicants for planning permission a right of appeal[1] against applications which have been
refused, against conditions imposed on a grant of permission which may be unacceptable
to the applicant, or against applications which are not determined within the statutory
timeframe.[2] There are other types of statutory appeal, such as those against enforcement
notices[3] which follow similar procedures. Whilst in practical terms appeals are usually
determined by an inspector appointed by the SoS, the SoS can 'call in' appeals of a controversial or significant nature for his (or her) own decision. This process, although provided
for by statute[4] is often regarded as controversial because it seems to permit intervention
on political grounds in an objective process. In *R v Secretary of State for Environment,
Transport and the Regions, ex p Alconbury Developments*[5], an attempt was made to
argue that the process of calling in an appeal by the SoS was contrary to the European
Convention on Human Rights[6], as being inconsistent with the right to a fair trial. The
House of Lords held that the call-in procedure was not incompatible with a fair hearing
even where, as here, the SoS was deciding an appeal concerning government land.

Some recent examples where the SoS has 'called in' applications include proposals for
the Stamford Bridge football stadium and terminal five at Heathrow Airport.

[1] TCPA 1990, s 78.
[2] Para 39.26.
[3] Para 39.62.
[4] TCPA 1990, Sch 6, para 3.
[5] [2001] UKHL 23, HL.
[6] Article 6(1). See also para 3.24 on human rights.

Local government: the local planning authority

The role of the LPA

38.11 The LPA has two main functions; the preparation of a development plan which
it must monitor and keep up to date and 'development management'. Historically, the
planning system dealt with the use of land. However, in the 2000s and as a result of the
PCPA 2004, the planning system was reformed and with it the functions of local authorities. Nowadays planning, or spatial planning as it is known, takes a much more holistic approach. Spatial planning delivers economic, social and environmental outcomes
in collaboration with the local community and other stakeholders. Spatial planning
begins with a vision for the area which identifies challenges and opportunities based on
evidence. Active collaboration with local people and businesses, and other groups and
organisations with a stake or interest in the area translates these objectives into priorities,
policies and programmes. This in turn means that investment and infrastructure can be
planned for, ensuring that the plan and its proposals are delivered. This means that LPAs
become 'place shapers'[1] and climate change and the achievement of sustainable development[2] are an integral part of the planning system's objectives.

'Development management' was coined as a phrase in the late 1990s. It is the way in
which the vision and plans prepared by the LPA are delivered. Described by the Planning
Advisory Service[3] as a 'single system that operates in the public interest through a combination of plan preparation and control over the development and use of land', development management should be seen as a proactive way for LPAs to help shape places,
manage investment opportunities and maximise benefits for their communities.

[1] See PPS12 (2008) for a further discussion on local spatial planning.
[2] Para 38.27.
[3] www.pas.gov.uk.

Identifying the LPA

38.12 At local government level, the main institution is the local planning authority (LPA). However, just as central government reorganisation of ministries and departments has made tracing the predecessors of the SoS problematic, so local government reform has made the identification of an LPA much less straightforward too.

Local government reorganisation in 1974 established a two-tier system of county or shire authorities and non-metropolitan districts across England. The exceptions to this were Greater London and six metropolitan counties. Reorganisation occurred again in the 1990s[1] and introduced single-tier administrations known as unitary authorities which have been established in some areas. It is not difficult to imagine that further changes will take place that will again alter this geography.

The PCPA 2004 introduced significant changes to the respective responsibilities of the authorities. Previously where the two-tier system existed in non-metropolitan areas, the County Council would have prepared a Structure Plan setting out the broad priorities for the area including new housing numbers. In addition the County Council would have dealt with minerals and waste. The District or Borough Council would have prepared a Local Plan which would be in general conformity with the Structure Plan and set out detailed policies and proposals. In those areas with a unitary authority, a unitary development plan would be prepared covering the same aspects as both the structure plan and local plan, but contained in one document. Under the PCPA 2004 this situation changed. The current system will be discussed in more detail later on in this chapter.

In the metropolitan areas of Greater Manchester, Merseyside, Tyne & Wear, West Midlands, South Yorkshire and West Yorkshire, the LPA is the relevant metropolitan borough council which, like the London boroughs, will also be a unitary authority.

The position of London is unique. The Mayor has responsibility for planning at a strategic level. The London boroughs are the local planning authorities for their area and the London Thames Gateway Development Corporation and the Olympic Delivery Authority are the LPAs for parts of east London. The boroughs must consult the Mayor[2] on planning applications of strategic importance[3] and the Mayor can 'call in' the application for decision. The boroughs consult the Mayor on their local development frameworks (which are discussed in more detail later on in this chapter)[4] and the Mayor must issue a statement as to whether the plan(s) are in general conformity with the spatial development strategy, currently the London Plan, which is the equivalent of a regional spatial strategy[5] elsewhere in England.

National Parks also have their own arrangements. National Park Authorities are the planning authorities for their area. The newest national parks are the New Forest (2006) and the South Downs (2011). It should also be noted that the Broads Authority is the LPA for the Broads.

There are 25 local planning authorities in Wales which consist of 22 county or county boroughs and are the equivalent of the unitary authorities in England, and the three national park authorities of Brecon Beacons, Snowdonia and the Pembrokeshire Coast. Each of the LPAs prepares a local development plan.

---

[1] Local Government Act 1992.
[2] Greater London Authority Acts 1999 and 2007.
[3] Defined and set out in the Town and Country Planning (Mayor of London) Order 2008.
[4] Paras 38.23–38.25.
[5] Para 38.22.

The operation of LPAs

38.13 We now turn to the operation of LPAs. Two groups of people play fundamental roles in the planning process:

- councillors;
- officers.

38.14 *Councillors* (who are also known as members) are elected[1] by the voters of the area. They represent sub-divisions of their city or district, which are often called wards. These in turn make up the council. The councillors often stand as candidates on behalf of one of the major political parties: Labour, Conservative or Liberal Democrat, or on behalf of a special interest group (such as a campaign against an airport development or to protect the Green Belt), or as independents. The councillors are the decision makers of the council. These posts are unpaid, although expenses are payable.

[1] Some areas have elections for the whole council every four years, while others have one third of the seats contested each year over a three year cycle.

38.15 *The Planning Committee* Councillors meet periodically as a Full Council, ie all together, but most of their business is transacted in committees. Most authorities have a separate *Planning or Development Committee*. This is a subdivision of the council as a whole, although attempts will have been made to ensure that the political parties are represented in approximately the same proportions as in the Full Council. If the Council has 50 members, of whom 20 are Labour, 20 are Conservative and 10 Liberal Democrat, the 10 members of the Planning Committee would be 4 Labour, 4 Conservative and 2 Liberal Democrat. Party politics is important in local government as it is in central government, because the members of a party group or bloc tend to vote together, so that support or opposition for a scheme by a party may well mean that all the party's councillors will support or oppose it. If the party has a majority, ie more than half the total councillors, it is in a position to ensure a particular outcome, assuming all councillors obey the party line.

Written reports prepared by officers, plans and other supporting documentation will also be available to the committee members. At the committee it is also usual for members to receive an oral report from the officers. Legal advice may also have been obtained from the council's legal department. Members of the public are able to attend the committee[1] and are also usually permitted to speak although in many councils the amount of time each person can speak or make a statement in support or against a proposal is limited to ensure that the business of the committee is completed in a timely manner. After discussion and sometimes a vote if the issue is finely balanced, members will usually make the decision in accordance with the recommendation from officers. Occasionally however members overturn the recommendations based on local knowledge or political grounds and so on. These cases are sometimes difficult for the council to defend when challenged on appeal or by judicial review particularly when the officers' professional recommendation was to approve a scheme, but members refused it.

[1] Local Government Act 1972, ss 100A and 100E.

38.16 *Officers of the council* The officers of the council are not elected. They are paid members of the council's workforce. The officers' task is to run the council; in this respect they are rather like managers or executives in a company, implementing the decisions of the councillors (who are somewhat like the board of directors) and handling day to day business. However, they are more than mere employees and may take on significant responsibilities.

A Chief Planning Officer or Head of Planning, for example, will be a well qualified and experienced professional planner, with a degree and membership of the Royal Town Planning Institute (MRTPI). Other officers will also be well qualified and experienced professionals.

38.17 Planning officers have a role in LPA decision making. In the past it was only councillors, as elected members, who could take decisions, which the officers would then put into practice. Today many planning applications are determined by officers under delegated powers[1]. The council will have established procedures known as 'standing orders' and these will provide for a scheme of delegation by which certain types or categories of application and decision making can be made by named officers such as the chief planner or other officers acting under their authority. In some authorities as many as 90% of the applications will be determined this way. However the planning committee will still tend to make the decision on any contentious proposals or ones where there may be political implications.

[1] Under Local Government Act 1972, s 101.

38.18 Planning officers have a role in committee work. Even when not acting under delegated powers, officers are still centrally involved in the council's planning functions. All committees, including the Planning Committee, are serviced by officers, who provide research, background preparation, technical knowledge and advice on the matters on the agenda items. For each planning application which goes before the committee a report usually containing details of the site's history and its characteristics, details of the proposal, the relevant national and local policies, consultation responses and so on together with a recommendation as to whether permission is granted or refused is prepared by officers.

38.19 Planning officers have a role in development plans. Officers have other significant planning functions besides their involvement in planning decisions. The task of preparing development plans once the overall strategy of the council has been set by members largely falls to the planning officer.

38.20 Planning officers have a role in enforcement. Another major planning task of officers is enforcement of planning control and this is dealt with in Chapter 39.[1]

[1] Para 39.52.

PLANNING INSTITUTIONS: KEY POINTS

- The Secretary of State in England and the Welsh Assembly Government and in some instances Welsh Ministers in Wales are responsible for planning.

- The role of the Secretary of State includes making legislation and preparing policy and guidance. The SoS also has 'call-in' powers.

- LPAs have two main functions; the preparation of a development plan and development management.

- Spatial planning is a proactive and positive system of place shaping. It takes a holistic approach to development bringing together a range of stakeholders and focuses on the delivery and implementation of plans and policies as well as a vision for an area.

- In England the LPA can be a district or borough council or a metropolitan borough, or a unitary authority. In Wales the county or county borough will be the LPA. In both England and Wales national park authorities are also the relevant LPA in their areas.

- Councillors or elected members together with officers of the council have different roles and responsibilities.

Development plans

Introduction

38.21 Development plans play a vitally important role in the planning system. We have in England and Wales what is often described as a 'plan-led' system. Decisions about the location, type and amount of new development and infrastructure, the determination of planning and other related applications, and enforcement action all spring from the development plan. Although the purpose of development plans has remained broadly the same since the TCPA 1947, there have been three major versions or iterations:

- The plans originally developed under the TCPA 1947.

- Plans initiated and prepared under the TCPA 1968 and continued by the provisions of the TCPA 1971 and the TCPA 1990. These plans comprised two basic elements, the structure plan prepared by the county council and a local plan prepared by the district council. The structure plan was a broad statement of strategic planning policies developed through studies and appraisals of the area and through consultation with the LPAs of the county and other stakeholders. The local plan set out detailed policies and specific proposals for the area and had to be in general conformity with the structure plan. It was to the local plan that developers and their professional advisers referred to for day to day guidance on planning decisions. Maps and diagrams in the local plan were especially useful for identifying specific sites. Structure plans were not intended to be site specific. After the local government reorganisation under the Local Government Act 1992 which enabled the creation of unitary authorities, unitary development plans were prepared in some areas. Unitary development plans combine the features of both structure plans and local plans. It should be noted that the phrase 'development plan' which is very important in the planning system, rarely refers to a single document. Under the 'old style' two-tier system described above, the development plan would have comprised both the structure plan and the local plan.

- The PCPA 2004 fundamentally changed the system of development planning and replaced the system of structure, local and unitary plans with a new single level plan called the local development framework. The PCPA 2004 also introduced a new layer of statutory plan at regional level called a regional spatial strategy.[1]

Transition period Most authorities are well advanced with the preparation of local development frameworks introduced by the PCPA 2004. However plans take a long time to prepare and at the time of writing (Spring 2011), some LPAs do not yet have local development frameworks in place. Therefore some 'old style' structure and local plans are still in force in some areas. During the transition period it is therefore quite possible for the development plan to comprise some old style local plans as well as new style local development frameworks.

It should also be noted that the PCPA 2004 allowed structure plans and local plans policies to be 'saved', ie remain in force for three years from the commencement of the Act. Gradually as LPAs progress work on the 'new style' local development frameworks, the 'old style' saved structure and local plan policies will be phased out and replaced by the plans and policies of the local development frameworks.

[1] Para 38.22.

Regional spatial strategies

38.22 Under the old style system, regional planning was done through regional planning guidance and had the status of a 'material consideration'[1]. Initially the existing regional guidance became the regional spatial strategy (RSS) for each region. A RSS contained broad policies for development over a 15–20 year period. It set out the scale and distribution of new housing and dealt with matters such as transport, environmental protection, and economic development. The RSS was revised by a regional planning board.

The PCPA 2004 gave more weight to regional planning by putting RSSs on a statutory footing[2]. This meant that the RSS formed part of the 'development plan'. Eight regions were defined, each covering a number of local authority or council areas. In London the Mayor's Spatial Development Strategy is the strategic planning document, the equivalent of the regional spatial strategy.

The Coalition Government indicated its intention to abolish RSSs in the Localism Bill published in December 2010. Until the RSSs are abolished, they remain part of the statutory development plan although the Coalition Government's intention to abolish them is a material consideration.

[1] Para 39.28.
[2] PCPA 2004, s 38(3).

Local Development Frameworks

38.23 The PCPA 2004 Part 2 sets out the detail in relation to local development. A LPA is required to review matters which will affect the proper planning of their area. Amongst these matters are demographic changes, physical, economic, environmental and social considerations, communications and transport systems, and the use of land.

The Local Development Framework (LDF) is not a single document, but can be regarded as a suite, or folder, or a portfolio, of different documents. The LDF consists of several different types of documents known as local development documents which is a generic term for all the documents in the LDF. There are two main types of document; development plan documents which are statutory and supplementary planning documents which are non-statutory and provide more detail or supplement the policies in a development plan document. The LDF will also include a local development scheme, a statement of community involvement and an annual monitoring report. Each is outlined below.

Local development scheme[1] This is a document which sets out the programme that the council will follow in producing documents: in other words it is a timetable or project plan for the LDF. Its purpose is to inform the public and other interested parties about what the LPA is proposing to do. It must also be kept under review.

Development plan documents These documents form part of the development plan for the area. They must be spatial in nature, ie not just cover land use, but also take economic, environmental and social considerations into account. There is also a formal scrutiny and appraisal process. Development plan documents comprise the following:

- A Core Strategy which sets out the long-term vision and key objectives. In other words it sets out the planning framework for the area. It is a key document because all other documents must conform to it and for this reason it must be kept up to date.

- Proposals Map. This shows the policies and proposals in the development plan documents which are capable of being shown on a map. Many councils now have interactive proposals maps on their websites.

- Site Specific Allocations. This document will specify an area and allocate land for new development such as new housing or mixed use.

- Area Action Plans. These plans are for specific locations or areas of change, opportunity, or conservation, ie they might cover an area in need of regeneration or an
  area of planned growth, or an area of historic importance which needs protection.
  These plans tend to focus on implementation making sure that development is of an
  appropriate mix, scale, density, and quality for a specific area.

Supplementary planning documents These are designed to provide further details and
support and supplement the implementation of policies and proposals in the LDF. They
often provide more practical guidance.

Statement of community involvement[2] This sets out how the council's proposals for
involving the local community and stakeholders in the preparation of its plans and policies. The minimum requirements for public engagement are set out in regulations, but
councils can do more if they wish.

Annual monitoring report[3] This is an assessment about the extent to which policies are
being achieved and monitors progress towards targets and milestones set out in the LDF.

[1] PCPA 2004 ss 15, 17. Also see PPS12 for further information.
[2] PCPA 2004, s 18.
[3] PCPA 2004, s 35.

Process

38.24 The process of preparing and adopting the various documents in the LDF is complex. A number of stages must be passed. At the outset it is usual for a number of studies
and surveys to be carried out on the economic, environmental and social characteristics of the area. This information will provide the evidence on which the plan making
can be based. It is important to recognise that this evidence or information gathering is
ongoing.

Early consultation then takes place with the community and other stakeholders on the
key issues which the plan needs to address and options are developed to deal with them.
Often this stage is called the 'issues and options' stage. After this has taken place further
refinement of those ideas and options occurs. More public and stakeholder engagement
is carried out. This stage is often referred to as the 'preferred options' stage. After further
consideration of this second stage of consultation, the document is finalised and submitted to the Government for independent examination. The Government then appoints
an inspector who holds an examination into the plan. This is held in public and involves
testing the plan to make sure it is sound.

The inspector then produces a report detailing whether the plan is sound and can be
formally adopted or whether further modifications need to be made. In deciding whether
the plan is sound, the inspector will apply twelve tests including whether the plan is justified, effective and consistent with national policy. In *Blythe Valley District Council v
Persimmon Homes (North East) Ltd*[1] the Court of Appeal quashed part of the plan because
it was inconsistent with national policy even though national policy had altered during
the preparation of the plan. The inspector's report is binding: this means that the inspector's modifications must be adhered to.[2] Once the LPA has incorporated the inspector's
modifcations into the plan, the council can then adopt the plan. Once the plan has been
adopted it becomes part of the development plan.

The SoS has powers to intervene in the preparation of plans. Before adoption, a direction modifying the plan can be issued if the SoS considers the plan to be unsatisfactory. In
addition the plan can be called in for the SoS's own approval. Finally the SoS can prepare
or modify a plan if it is considered that this function is not been carried out satisfactorily
by a council.

Legal challenges

38.25 Under the PCPA 2004¹ the validity of a plan can be challenged by an aggrieved person on one or other (or both) of two grounds:

- the document is not within the appropriate power; or

- a procedural matter has not been complied with.

¹ PCPA 2004, s 113.

Strategic environmental assessment

38.26 Development plans also need to comply with strategic environmental assessment.¹ This is an assessment of the environmental impacts of policies and proposals. The Directive on Strategic Environmental Assessment does not only apply to planning; it also applies to programmes in other fields such as transport, telecommunications and energy. Strategic environmental assessment is best regarded as a process or a generic tool.

The Directive brings a new emphasis to:

- 'collecting and presenting information on the environmental baseline and current problems, and their likely future evolution;

- predicting significant environmental effects of the plan or programme, including those of strategic alternatives;

- addressing adverse environmental effects through mitigation measures;

- consulting the public and authorities with environmental responsibilities as part of the assessment process;

- monitoring the environmental effects of the plan or programme during its implementation'.²

The rationale behind the strategic environmental assessment is that whilst individual major projects are assessed through environmental impact assessment³, it is also necessary to assess the broad range of plans and programmes before a plan is adopted. The aim of the Directive is to ensure that the environment is protected and that environmental considerations are taken into account with a view to promoting sustainable development.⁴ Therefore the Directive has a particular impact on regional spatial strategies, London's spatial development strategy and local development plans and documents.

The Directive does not prescribe who is to carry out the assessment, but usually it is carried out by, or on behalf of, the authority or body who prepares or adopts the plan.

¹ EU Directive 2001/42 EC.
² As stated in 'A Practical Guide to the Strategic Environmental Assessment Directive', 2005, ODPM.
³ Under Directive 85/337/EC.
⁴ Para 38.27.

Sustainable development

38.27 Sustainable development is primarily about ensuring that we do not deplete the Earth's natural resources, there is sustained economic growth and opportunity for all. In other words it is about our quality of life.

The PCPA 2004 requires persons or bodies responsible for exercising any function in relation to RSSs or LDFs to do so with the aim of contributing to the achievement of sustainable development[1]. This has been a key objective of the planning system for many years, but the PCPA 2004 put the objective on a statutory footing for the first time. Much has been written about sustainable development, but a widely used and helpful definition of sustainable development is 'development which meets the needs of the present without compromising the ability of future generations to meet their own needs'.[2] The planning system has an important role and contribution to make.

[1] PCPA 2004, s 39.
[2] Report of the World Commission on Environment and Development: *Our Common Future* (1987).

The significance of the 'development plan'

38.28 The planning system is plan-led. This is an important concept as the legal significance of the development plan is critical to the operation of the planning system and explains the importance of the forward planning function of LPAs. As already stated, the 'development plan' is a term which can encompass more than one document or plan. The PCPA 2004[1] provides that the development plan comprises the regional spatial strategy and the development plan documents that have been approved and adopted in relation to that area. In London the development plan comprises the spatial development strategy and development plan documents which have been approved or adopted. In Wales it is the local development plan approved or adopted in that area which constitutes the development plan.

Our starting off point in considering the significance of the development plan is the TCPA 1990 which states that in dealing with an application for planning permission, the LPA 'shall have regard to the provisions of the development plan, so far as material to the application, and to any other material considerations'.[2]

The meaning of this has been the subject of much case law. Cases like *Simpson v Edinburgh Corpn*[3] and *London Borough of Enfield v Secretary of State for Environment*[4] established that 'shall have regard to' did not mean that the LPA must 'slavishly adhere to' the development plan. Indeed if this had been the intention there would be little point in the Act referring to 'other material considerations'.

The Planning and Compensation Act 1991[5] then inserted a new provision into the TCPA 1990. Section 54A stated that 'where, in making any determination under the planning Acts, regard is to be had to the development, the determination shall be made in accordance with the plan unless material considerations indicate otherwise'.

This had the effect of giving the development plan primacy and reinforced the nature of the plan-led system as a framework in which future development can be encouraged as well as managed through planning control.

TCPA 1990, s 54A has now been repealed by the PCPA 2004. Section 38(6) of the PCPA 2004 now provides that 'if regard is to be had to the development plan for the purpose of any determination to be made under the planning Acts, the determination must be made in accordance with the plan unless material considerations indicate otherwise.' The change of wording from 'shall' to 'must' seems to further reinforce the importance of the development plan.

When considering how this presumption is to be applied, the courts have in the past consistently taken the view that account must be taken of the development plan and whether or not this has happened is a question of fact. However, the weight to be given to the development plan is a matter for the decision maker. It is therefore critical that they make it clear that they have considered the development plan. It is for this reason that most reports by officers and inspectors will at the very least indicate whether a proposal accords, or not, with the development plan. It is also very rare for there to be no development plan policies of relevance to a proposal. In fact it is much more likely that there will be a number of development plan policies which pull in different directions. For example, in *R v Rochdale MBC, ex p Milne*[6], the judge recognised that there were development plan policies which encouraged rural development for employment purposes and others which sought to protect the open countryside. In such cases it is for the decision maker to make a judgement by weighing up or balancing these often competing considerations.

In addition if there is a conflict between a policy in one development plan and a policy in another development plan, the conflict must be resolved in favour of the policy in the most recent plan to be adopted, approved or published.[7]

[1] PCPA, s 38.
[2] For an explanation of material considerations, see para 39.28.
[3] 1961 SLT 17.
[4] [1975] JPL 155.
[5] PCA 1991, s 26
[6] (2001) 81 P & CR 365.
[7] This is why it is important for LPAs to keep their local development documents up to date.

DEVELOPMENT PLANS: KEY POINTS

- We have a plan-led system.

- Regional spatial strategies and their equivalent in London, contain broad or strategic policies for the region for a 15–20 year period.

- A local development framework prepared by LPAs is a portfolio of different documents some of which are statutory and others are non-statutory.

- A regional spatial strategy and the statutory development plan documents in the local development framework taken together comprise the 'development plan'.

- All plans have to follow a prescribed process which includes community engagement, the involvement of a wide range of stakeholders and an examination by a planning inspector to see if the plan is 'sound'. Once a plan is found to be sound it can be adopted.

- The environmental impact of plans and policies is assessed using a process known as strategic environmental assessment.

- All plans must contribute to the achievement of sustainable development.

- The development plan is a significant term in planning. All decision makers determining planning applications must do so in accordance with the development plan unless material considerations indicate otherwise.

The legal liabilities of LPAs

38.29 The planning functions of the LPA bring it into a great deal of contact with the general public. Planning officers are required to communicate and negotiate with developers and their professional representatives and many other inquirers. The question therefore arises as to the position of the LPAs in terms of liability for their actions or statements.

The power of planning officers to bind the authority

38.30 In principle, the delegation of powers to planning officers should be capable of carrying with it the power to bind the council. The courts however, have not, with a few exceptions, viewed with much enthusiasm the proposition that a council should be deprived of its power to make a correct decision by an officer's indication that an incorrect one is appropriate.

The question has arisen whether a LPA can be protected by the doctrine of estoppel from exercising its powers as a result of a statement made by one of its planning officers. The doctrine of estoppel (not to be confused with the equitable doctrine of promissory estoppel referred to in Chapter 6) is a legal doctrine whereby, if a person misrepresents to another an existing fact and intends this misrepresentation to be acted on, and it is acted on by the other who suffers detriment in consequence, he cannot subsequently deny the truth of that fact.

In *R v East Sussex CC, ex p Reprotech (Pebsham) Ltd*,[1] Lord Hoffmann thought it unhelpful to introduce the doctrine of estoppel into planning law. Two subsequent cases, *Coghurst Wood Leisure Park Ltd v Secretary of State for Transport, Local Government and the Regions*,[2] and *Wandsworth LBC v Secretary of State for Transport, Local Government and the Regions and BT Cellnet*,[3] held that following the *Reprotech* case there cannot be any statutory jurisdiction to allow a planning appeal on the doctrine of estoppel. This means that if a binding decision is required as to whether a proposal requires planning permission then a formal application for a certificate of lawfulness must be made.

[1] [2002] UKHL 8, HL.
[2] [2002] EWHC 1091 (Admin).
[3] [2003] EWHC 622 (Admin).

Legitimate expectation

38.31 Legitimate expectation has caught the attention of the courts in relation to planning law. Legitimate expectation occurs when a public body unequivocally promises something. Where the principle of legitimate expectation applies, the public body which acts in breach of the legitimate expectation will be prevented from acting contrary to the expectation, ie the expectation will be enforced. A legitimate expectation will not be easily established. For example in *Coghurst Wood Leisure v Secretary of State*[1] it was accepted that some infrequent situations might occur in planning law where the principle could apply. In *Cox v First Secretary of State*[2], the High Court held that advice given by a planning officer which was misleading, but given in good faith, did not give rise to a legitimate expectation. Where the circumstances do not attract the principle of legitimate expectation, there may nevertheless be grounds for complaint to the Local Government Ombudsman.

[1] [2002] EWHC 1091 (Admin).
[2] [2003] EWHC 1290 (Admin).

Local Government Ombudsman

38.32 There is still the possibility of making a complaint to the Local Government Ombudsman although this remedy normally applies to areas of maladministration. In one case known to the author, a council erred in granting planning permission for a new house on land in a floodplain which was contrary to its own policies and those of the

Environment Agency. The applicants submitted a second application on the same site which was refused. The Ombudsman upheld a complaint and awarded compensation of £1,500: the council admitted its error in relation to the first application and accepted that compensation was justified as the second application had been futile.

LEGAL LIABILITIES OF LPAS: KEY POINTS

- The doctrine of estoppel is a legal doctrine whereby, if a person misrepresents to another an existing fact and intends the misrepresentation to be acted on, and it is acted on by the other who suffers detriment in consequence, he cannot subsequently deny the truth of that fact.

- Legitimate expectation occurs when a public body unequivocally promises something. Where the principle of legitimate expectation applies, the public body which acts in breach of the legitimate expectation will be prevented from acting contrary to the expectation, ie the expectation will be enforced. A legitimate expectation will not be easily established.

- Complaints in maladministration can be directed to the Local Government Ombudsman.

Questions

1. What is meant by spatial planning?

2. Describe the two main roles of the LPA.

3. What are the respective roles of a councillor and officer in determining planning applications?

4. Summarise the role and purpose of the different documents found in a LDF. Distinguish between statutory and non-statutory documents.

5. Explain the significance of the development plan if you are the decision maker determining a planning application.

6. Can an unadopted development plan document form part of the statutory development plan?

7. Your client, Animaland Ltd owns a large area of land attached to an agricultural holding. They want to sell off some land for new housing development. How would you advise your client in respect of the planning policy framework to ensure that their expectations were realistic?

39

The law of development management and enforcement

CHAPTER OVERVIEW

In this chapter we examine:

- what the different types of development are;
- the need for planning permission;
- the two important development orders which allow various operational development and changes of use to occur without the specific grant of permission;
- the planning application process from submission to decision;
- what material considerations are;
- the decision-making process;
- the appeal system and enforcement;
- the future of the planning system.

Introduction

39.1 Section 57(1) of the TCPA 1990 states that, subject to exceptions specified in s 57, 'planning permission is required for the carrying out of any development of land'. The exceptions specified by s 57 are:

- where planning permission to develop land has been granted for a limited period, planning permission is not required for the resumption, at the end of that period, of its use for the purpose for which it was normally used before the permission was granted (s 57(2));
- where by a development order planning permission to develop land has been granted subject to limitations, planning permission is not required for the use of that land which (apart from its use in accordance with that permission) is its normal use (s 57(3));
- where an enforcement notice has been issued in respect of any development of land, planning permission is not required for its use for the purpose for which (in accordance with the provisions of this Part of the Act) it could lawfully have been used if that development had not been carried out (s 57(4)).

In determining for the purposes of s 57(2) and (3) what is or was the normal use of land, no account may be taken of any use begun in contravention of present or previous planning control.

However, the basic requirement is that any development of land will require planning permission. This then begs the question 'what is development'?

The definition of development

39.2 Section 55 of the TCPA 1990 provides that 'development' may take one of two forms:

- *operational development*, meaning the carrying out of building, engineering, mining or other operations in, on, over or under land; and
- *material change of use,* meaning the making of any *material* change in the use of any buildings or other land.

Operational development

39.3 Whereas engineering and mining operations may be relatively straightforward to understand and the term 'other operations' has been considered in only a few judicial decisions, building operations has resulted in extensive case law.

39.4 *Building operations* The TCPA 1990, s 55 (1A) provides that this term includes:

- demolition of buildings;
- rebuilding;
- structural alterations of or additions to buildings;
- other operations normally undertaken by a person carrying on business as a builder.

In *Cheshire County Council v Woodward*[1] Lord Parker CJ had to consider a coal merchant's coal hopper, some six metres in height and mounted on wheels. Its installation was held not to be development. Lord Parker stated that, in defining a building as including '*any structure or erection, and any part of a building so defined*, but does not include plant or machinery comprised in a building', the definition refers to 'any structure which can be said to form part of the realty and to change the physical character of the land.... There is no one test; you look at the erection, equipment, plant, what it is, and ask: in all the circumstances is it to be treated as part of the realty?'

Normally, the change to the physical character of the land must have some degree of permanence. However, even this is not an infallible test, which emphasises Lord Parker's point about the need to look at all the circumstances. In *Barvis Ltd v Secretary of State for the Environment*[2] which involved the siting of a mobile crane at a depot, it was held that the approach taken to determining whether something is a building hinged on size, permanence, and physical attachment to the land. In this case it was found that the crane, which could be dismantled in a matter of days, was not a building. In *Skerritts of Nottingham Ltd v Secretary of State for Environment Transport and the Region (No 2)*[3] the Court of Appeal held that the erection of a large marquee for nine months each year in the grounds of a hotel constituted operational development. The Court took the view that to find otherwise would mean that anything which could be dismantled and removed for a short time period would fall outside the scope of planning control.

In determining such matters as appeals against enforcement notices and certificates of lawfulness, the Secretary of State (SOS) has also held that carports, portakabins, a plastic tree in the grounds of a public house, and play equipment fall within the definition of a 'building'. Although these determinations are not legally binding, LPAs and landowners are often reluctant to challenge the SoS's decision through the courts. More recently a series of decisions found that polytunnels placed and used during the growing season on farmland constituted a building operation[4].

[1] [1962] 2 QB 126.
[2] (1971) 22 P & CR 710.
[3] [2000] JPL 1025, CA.
[4] *R (on the application of Hall Hunter) v First Secretary of State* [2006] EWHC 3482 (Admin).

39.5 *Building operations which are not development* Operations required to maintain, improve or alter a building, or works which only affect the interior of the building, or which do not materially affect the external appearance of the building do not fall within the definition of a building operation. This essentially means that planning control does not extend to internal works except in the case of historic buildings.[1] However, the matter is not clear cut and questions arise as to what constitutes a 'material' change to the external appearance of a building. In *Burroughs Bay v Bristol City Council*[2] it was held that 'external appearance' should be taken to mean the way in which the exterior of the building would be seen by an observer outside the building. The degree of visibility would affect whether the change in appearance was material or not and would be judged by the impact on the whole building rather than a particular part of the building seen in isolation.

[1] Para 39.45.
[2] [1996] 1 PLR 78.

Material change of use

39.6 The other type of development is material change of use. Rather unhelpfully the term is not defined in the TCPA 1990, but the word 'material' should be noted. A change of use will only constitute development, if it is *material*. Although there has been case law which assists with the interpretation, the courts have largely left it to the LPAs to decide what is material or not. Often, therefore, it is largely a matter of fact and degree of the particular proposal itself and the interpretation of this may vary from LPA to LPA.

In extreme cases an apparently minor change of use can be material. A classic example of this was *Bendles Motors Ltd v Bristol Corpn*[1] where the installation of a free-standing vending machine selling eggs on the forecourt of a petrol station was held to involve a material change of use and thus to constitute development. This case demonstrates that not only may a material change of use be on the face of it relatively small, but also that a material change of use can occur when one use is joined by another. Thus a material change of use occurs not simply as a result of a switch from one use to another but also where an existing use is joined by an additional use. In the *Bendles* case there was a change of use from a garage and petrol filling station to a garage, petrol filling station and shop.

[1] [1963] 1 WLR 247.

What constitutes a material change of use?

39.7 The TCPA 1990 states[1] that, amongst other matters, the following *do* constitute a change of use:

- 'the use as two or more separate dwellinghouses of any building previously used as a single dwellinghouse'
- 'the deposit of refuse or waste materials on land…notwithstanding that the land is comprised in a site already used for that purpose, if

    (a) the superficial area of the deposit is extended or

    (b) the height of the deposit is extended and exceeds the level of the land adjoining the site'.

[1] TCPA 1990, s 55(3).

What does not constitute a material change of use?

39.8 The TCPA 1990 also states[1] that certain uses *do not* constitute development:

- 'the use of any buildings or other land within the curtilage of a dwellinghouse for any purpose incidental to the enjoyment of the dwellinghouse as such'. This is an area of much litigation. Various cases have indicated that 'curtilage' will not necessarily be the same as a garden area or land which is owned in common with the dwelling-house. Questions abound as to whether using a room in a house or separate outbuilding for business purposes constitutes a material change of use. The use of a kitchen to prepare sandwiches which were then delivered and sold to businesses and offices in the locality is considered to be development. This is generally because there may be deliveries to the dwelling, staff may be employed and vans will leave the dwelling to deliver the sandwiches. Other legislation such as food safety requirements will also have to be complied with due to the nature of the business. This can be contrasted with the use of a spare bedroom as an office where provided there are no visitors or deliveries, the use is usually low key and does not materially alter the primary use of the dwelling. The determination is a matter of fact and degree. Some of the more bizarre cases are found in this part of planning law. In *Croydon London Borough Council v Gladden*[2] the Court of Appeal refused to accept that keeping a lifesize model of a Spitfire (and other World War II memorabilia) in a garden was a use incidental to the normal enjoyment of a dwelling-house. The concept of 'normal' or 'reasonable' enjoyment within this provision was derived from *Wallington v Secretary of State for Wales*[3] where the Court of Appeal held that keeping 44 dogs in a house was not reasonably incidental to its enjoyment as a dwelling-house.

- 'the use of any land for the purposes of agriculture or forestry…and the use for any of those purposes of any building occupied together with land so used'. This provision has also been the subject of litigation as owners explore the boundaries of what they might do as part of an agricultural use in particular. The association of retailing and the serving of refreshments with agriculture/horticulture at farm shops and garden centres have provided material for dispute with planning authorities seeking to control commercial development in rural areas.

[1] TCPA 1990, s 55(2).
[2] [1994] JPL 723, CA.
[3] [1990] JPL 112, CA.

Other uses excluded from development

39.9 As well as uses incidental to the enjoyment of a dwelling-house and to agriculture or forestry, there is one other use which the TCPA 1990 expressly states does not involve the development of land. That is a change of use within the same use class (or between classes) as specified by the Town and Country Planning (Use Classes) Order 1987.

The Use Classes Order

39.10 The Use Classes Order classifies different uses which have a similar impact into groups. There are numerous different classes and a change of use *within* the same class will not constitute development and thus will not require the submission of a planning application. For example, a change under Class A2 Financial and Professional Services (see below) from a building society to a bank would not be a material change of use. The Use Classes Order also permits certain changes of use from one use class to another.

The Use Classes Order is divided into four parts:

A   shopping area uses;

B   business and industrial uses;

C   residential uses;

D   non-residential/institutional social and community uses.

The table offers a summary guide to the Use Classes Order and is the English version.

Class A1 (shops)	Class A2 (financial and professional services)	Class A3 (food and drink)	Class A4 (drinking establishments)	Class A5 (hot food takeaways)
retail sale of goods other than hot food; post office; ticket or travel agency; sale of cold food for consumption off the premises; hairdressing; direction of funerals; display of goods for sale; hire of domestic or personal goods; reception of goods for washing, cleaning or repair; internet café where the primary purpose is to access the internet	financial services; professional services (other than health or medical services); any other services (including betting) appropriate to a shopping area, provided principally to members of the public	use for the sale of food or drink for consumption on the premises	use as a public house, wine bar or other drinking establishment	sale of hot food for consumption off the premises

Continued

Class B1 (business)	Class B2 (general industrial)	Class B8 (storage/ distribution)		
office (other than financial or professional services); research and development of products or processes; any industrial process which can be carried out in a residential area without detriment to amenity	use for the carrying out an industrial process not falling within B1	use for storage or a distribution centre		

Class C1 (hotels)	Class C2 (residential institutions)	Class C2A (secure residential institution)	Class C3 (dwelling-houses)	Class C4 (houses in multiple occupation)
use as a hotel or boarding or guest house where no significant care element is provided	use for residential accommodation and care to people in need of care; hospital or nursing home; residential school, college, or training centre	prison; young offenders institution; detention centre; secure training centre; custody centre; secure hospital; military barracks	use as a dwelling-house occupied by a single person or family'; by not more than six residents living as a single household where care is provided for residents; or by not more than six residents living together as a single household where no care is provided (other than a use within Class C4)	use of a dwelling-house by not more than six residents as a house in multiple occupation

Class D1 (non-residential institutions)	Class D2 (assembly and leisure)			
for provision of medical or health services; as crèche, day nursery or day centre; for provision of education; for display of works of art; as a museum; as a public library or reading room; as a public hall or exhibition hall; for public worship or religious instruction	a cinema; a concert hall; a bingo hall or casino; a dance hall; swimming bath, skating rink, gymnasium, or for indoor or outdoor sports (not involving motor vehicles or fire-arms)			

39.11 *Classes E, F, G and H* Although little used, these classes are important. Class E's purpose is to encourage flexibility in the grant of planning permission. An example would be permission might be granted for a change of use from use 1 to use 2 *or* use 3. Classes F and G permit change of use from Class A1 or A2 to a mixed shop/flat use (ie shop with flat above it) or from such a mixed use to wholly Class A1 or A2 (eg to allow the flat above to be used for shop storage). Class H relates to the change of use from a casino to a Class D2 use.

39.12 *Sui generis uses* Not every use is allocated to a particular class and these are known as *sui generis*. A way to remember those uses which have not been classified is to think of the use as being 'in a class of its own'. Examples of *sui generis* uses are theatres, amusement arcades, launderettes, and scrapyards. Changes to a *sui generis* use always requires planning permission.

39.13 The principle of the Use Classes Order, then, is that change *within* classes will not require planning permission subject to various criteria because it is not a *material* change of use. However, change of use *between* classes usually does constitute a material change of use requiring the submission of a planning application. In *Rugby Football Union v Secretary of State for the Environment, Transport and the Regions*[1] the question arose whether Twickenham rugby stadium (whose use for sport fell within Class D2(e)) required planning permission if it was to be used for music concerts. The Court of Appeal[2] held that it did. It rejected the argument that planning permission was not necessary, because such use would fall within another category within Class D2 (Class D2(b) (concert hall), on the ground that an open air concert could not be classified as use as a concert hall given that a concert hall had to be enclosed by a roof and walls. The change of use was therefore not a change of use within Class D2.

[1] [2001] EWHC 927 (Admin).
[2] [2002] EWCA Civ 1169, CA.

39.14 *Abandonment* Before leaving change of use, the following additional points should be noted. Existing use rights can be lost by abandonment. If the use of a building or land is temporarily discontinued or interrupted, it would seem the resumption of that use is not development. However, if a use is permanently discontinued, the resumption of that use is development. Again this is an area of much litigation. Generally speaking it will depend on the circumstances; these include the time period of non-use, whether there has been any intervening use(s), and the intention of the owner.

39.15 *The planning unit* A significant factor in change of use can be the extent of the planning unit. Planning law is not concerned with the owners of land or buildings except on those rare occasions when a planning permission has been granted to a particular individual or family or business on a personal basis. Generally planning permission goes with the land or building. The exact physical or geographical extent of the land can be important in helping to determine whether the change of use is material or not. An example is that a large parcel of land can be subdivided and sold on to various owners and, provided the use does not change, it can be continued by all of the new owners. However, difficulties arise when land or a building is used for more than one purpose. Often there is a main use and an ancillary use. The general principle is that the use of land for a main or primary purpose also includes the right to use it for any purpose which is ancillary to the main use. However, if there are two or more physically separate and distinct uses in the same single unit, each area should be considered a separate planning unit. This often causes some uncertainty and difficulty. For example, an hotel with a restaurant could be a single unit with mixed C1/A3 use or it could be considered a C1 and an A3 unit respectively; this depends on the facts relating to both its physical and legal integration or separation. The issue becomes further complicated as any discussion of primary and ancillary uses must always relate to activities within the same planning unit.[1] It would be wise to ascertain the precise nature of the planning unit in physical and legal terms and the use(s) at an early stage when determining whether a material change of use would occur.

[1] *Westminster City Council v British Waterways Board* [1985] AC 676, HL and *Essex Water Co v Secretary of State for the Environment* [1989] JPL 914.

39.16 To further illustrate the relationship between primary and ancillary uses two cases are examined. In *Cocktails Ltd v Secretary of State for Communities and Local Government*[1] a change of use occurred from a motor vehicle dealership to a registered sex shop. The operators claimed that the motor dealership was retail use and therefore the use remained within Class A1. Although the sale of motor vehicles is a retail use, the site had various other uses including car repairs, offices and storage that were not demonstrated to be ancillary. The site therefore had a mixed use and a change from that mixed use was regarded as material.

In *Eagles v Minister for the Environment Sustainability and Housing and Welsh Assembly Government and another*[2] the conversion of a barn in the curtilage of an existing dwelling to living accommodation was regarded not to be ancillary; the barn was not only the size of a spacious dwelling, but its accommodation also exceeded the size of the original house. Beatson J's decision in this case left it open to the planning inspector to conclude that the conversion was not ancillary to the existing dwelling.

[1] [2008] EWCA Civ 1523, CA.
[2] [2009] EWHC 1028 (Admin).

The need for planning permission

39.17 We have seen that the TCPA 1990[1] provides that planning permission is required for the carrying out of any development of land. Planning permission can be granted in three ways: by development order, by the deemed grant of permission or as a result of an express grant of permission resulting from the submission of a planning application to the LPA. A development order is made by the SoS. One of the most important orders is the Town and Country (General Permitted Development) Order (GPDO) 1995.

[1] TCPA 1990, s 57(1). See para 39.1.

Permitted development

39.18 The Town and Country Planning (General Permitted Development) Order 1995 (the GPDO) specifies various categories of development which do not require the specific submission of a planning application. Development which falls within these classes is known colloquially as 'permitted development'.

As a generalisation the GPDO covers certain minor development proposals which would almost certainly be granted permission if an application were to be submitted. This reduces the burden placed on the planning and construction industry. As more technological advancements are made and become more commonplace (such as solar panels on dwelling-houses), more categories of development are likely to become 'permitted development'.

While it is not feasible to deal with each of the categories of permitted development here, a selection of the more frequently encountered categories is considered. It should be noted that all categories are subject to various restrictive criteria and this list is illustrative only.

Development within the curtilage of a dwelling-house Such development includes the:

- enlargement, improvement or alteration;
- addition or alteration to a roof;
- erection of a porch;
- provision (within the curtilage) of a building, enclosure or pool incidental to the enjoyment of dwelling-house;
- hard surface;
- installation of microwave antenna.

Minor operations Such operations include:

- gates, fences, walls or other enclosures;
- means of access to highways (other than trunk roads or classified roads);
- external painting.

Agricultural buildings and operations Certain erections and extensions of buildings are permitted on agricultural land where reasonably necessary for the agriculture on that unit, although this is subject to significant exceptions and conditions.

Local Development Orders

39.19 Local planning authorities also have the discretionary power to make Local Development Orders[1]. Such an order extends the permitted development rights given by the GPDO. The key difference is that the GPDO applies nationally, ie to England and Wales, whereas the local development order is determined locally and only applies in that local area. However, although this power has been available for some time, few LPAs have chosen to make local development orders, even though successive governments have encouraged them to do so.

[1] PCPA 2004, s 40.

Article 4 directions

39.20 Article 4 of the GPDO empowers the Secretary of State or the LPA to make a direction (referred to as an 'Article 4 Direction'), withdrawing certain classes of permitted development rights in a specified area. This would be done where the LPA wished to tighten control on particular types of development, either to protect the character or amenity of a particular neighbourhood or to deal with a perceived problem; it is often used in conservation areas which are areas of special architectural or historic interest.[1]

[1] Para 39.49.

Applications for planning permission

39.21 Having examined the meaning of 'development' and considered means by which, through the Use Classes Order and the GPDO, permission will not be required in some situations, it is now necessary to consider how planning permission is obtained via the planning application route.

Outline and full planning applications

39.22 There are two types of application for planning permission: outline and full.

Outline applications An outline application can only be made when permission is sought for the erection of a building(s). Such an application gives the developer the opportunity to find out at an early stage whether or not a proposal is likely to be acceptable. Often this method is used by developers seeking to establish the principle of, for example, residential development on a parcel of land before the land is purchased and before significant costs have been incurred. However, these days a great deal of information has to be submitted for an outline application. The outline application will almost always require the subsequent approval of what is known as 'reserved matters'. These are means of access, appearance, landscaping, layout and scale. No development may start until approval has been obtained for the reserved matters.

Full applications The full application will include full details of the proposal together with supporting information defined by national and local requirements. If full planning permission is granted it is usually granted subject to a number of conditions[1] and/or legal agreements known as planning obligations.[2]

[1] See para 39.31.
[2] See para 39.32.

Submitting an application

39.23 An application for planning permission to carry out development is made to the LPA in whose area the site is located. There is a standardised set of planning applications (known as 1APP) together with national information requirements, but many LPAs also set out additional local requirements. The forms and more information can be found on the individual LPA's website. Many applications are now submitted electronically through the Planning Portal website which also carries other useful information about the planning system. A range of information will accompany the form and might include site location plans, drawings or other documents. A fee[1] is also payable. At present the fees are set nationally, but at the time of writing (Spring 2011) the Government is currently consulting on proposals to allow LPAs to set their own level of fees. Most applications also require the submission of a *design and access statement*. This is a report which explains the design concept and principles behind the scheme and contains a statement about how issues relating to access to the development have been dealt with.[2] Applicants also need to complete a certificate[3] regarding land ownership and to declare whether the land in question is an agricultural holding.

The LPA is required to maintain a *planning register*[4] of all applications made to the authority and this must be available for public inspection. The register can be a very useful source of information as it usually includes application particulars, details of the decision including appeal decisions and so on. Other registers will hold details of enforcement action and other planning matters.

[1] TCPA 1990, s 303.

[2] TCPA 1990, s 62 (5) as substituted by PCPA 2004, s 42(1). The provision came into force on 10 August 2006.

[3] Article 7 of the Town and Country Planning (General Development Procedure) Order 1995.

[4] TCPA 1990, s 69.

What the LPA does on receipt of an application

39.24 Once the LPA has received a planning application, it will check that it is valid.[1] To be valid, the application must contain all the requisite information and drawings, correctly completed certificates, and the appropriate fee. The LPA will then acknowledge receipt. In certain circumstances, such as where the application is the same as another recently determined application, the LPA has the power to decline to determine an application.

Once the application has been validated it will be allocated to a planning officer, known as the case officer. Publicity and consultation will be carried out. Often the application will be publicised by sending notification to interested parties such as adjoining landowners. A site notice may also be posted at the site and an advertisement may go into a local newspaper. Council websites as well as the planning register will provide details of the applications received. Other bodies such as town or parish councils, the highways authority or other statutory consultees will also be notified. Special publicity must be given to certain types of development or development proposals which affect certain types of building or fall within particular areas such as conservation areas.

The case officer will examine all of the documentation and plans, make a site visit and write a report making a recommendation as to whether permission should be granted or refused so that the application can either be determined under delegated powers or by a planning committee. This process is described in more detail in Chapter 38.

[1] Paras 38.13–38.18.

The decision

39.25 Where an application is made to the LPA, the TCPA 1990[1] provides that planning permission may be:

- granted;
- granted subject to conditions as the LPA sees fit; or
- refused.

The LPA is required to give reasons for its decision. This is to ensure that the applicant and other interested parties understand the rationale behind the decision that has been taken.

[1] TCPA 1990, s 70(1).

39.26 *Determination time periods* Currently most applications have a statutory eight week period for determination and major applications a period of thirteen weeks. If an application is not determined within the respective time period, the applicant has a right to appeal against non-determination. In most cases however, it is sensible to wait for the LPA's decision and it is usually possible to agree a timeline with the LPA which is helpful to both parties.

39.27 As we have seen[1] the decision maker must determine the application in accordance with the development plan unless 'material considerations' indicate otherwise.[2] Chapter 38 contains a discussion of the purpose and types of development plans and their significance.[3] It must be remembered that the development plan is rarely a single document. At present the term 'development plan' comprises the regional spatial strategy[4] and any development plan documents which form part of the Local Development Framework[5]. Only an adopted or approved plan has the status of the development plan.

It is now important that we turn our attention to material considerations.

[1] Para 38.28.
[2] PCPA 2004, s 38 (6).
[3] Para 38.28.
[4] Para 38.22. It should be noted that the development plan system is likely to change with the abolition of regional spatial strategies.
[5] Para 38.23.

Material considerations

39.28 The term 'material considerations' referred to in the last paragraph covers a wide range of factors which may apply in any given situation. In *Stringer v Minister of Housing and Local Government*[1] Cooke J said '... it seems to me that any consideration which relates to the use and development of land is capable of being a planning consideration. Whether a particular consideration falling within that broad class is material in any given case will depend upon the circumstances.' From this it will be apparent that the courts have generally adopted a liberal approach. It is not practical to deal with every possibility here but some examples will be examined.

Many material considerations are straightforward in that they are what we might expect to be taken into account such as the number, scale, massing, design, height and location of buildings, means of access, landscaping, impact on neighbouring properties and so on. However, the courts have also held that a number of other considerations are material including:

- Government policy in the form of Planning Policy Guidance Notes, their replacements Planning Policy Statements, and Circulars;.

- previous appeal decisions ;

- the safeguarding of land for a road widening scheme;

- the risk of flooding to neighbouring landowners;

- the likelihood of the development being carried out;

- the availability of alternative sites;

- local economic need;

- risk of piecemeal development;

- fears of residents;

- protection of private interests;

- personal circumstances;

- precedent;

- health.

[1] [1070] 1 WLR 1281.

39.29 It will be seen from the above list that what constitutes a material consideration can be many and varied. A number of the more common misconceptions about material considerations will now be considered.

The planning system exists for the public benefit. However, the courts have held that the *protection of private interests* or *personal circumstances*, two factors which we might not expect to be taken into account, can be material considerations. It is clear that planning control is concerned with public interest, but where private rights are being interfered with the courts have seemed willing to intervene.

In *R v Vale of Glamorgan DC, ex p Adams*[1] a grant of permission to convert three barns to housing was quashed because planning committee members had not been aware that the personal circumstances of the occupier, who risked losing his tenure if permission were granted, could be considered. However, personal circumstances usually have to be compelling to overcome the public interest. In *Khan v Secretary of State for Environment*[2] the fact that a disabled child was to be accommodated in a residential extension was held not to be a material consideration capable of outweighing development plan policy guidelines on the dimensions of extensions.

Precedent in a non-legal sense of the term is a commonly misunderstood concept. In principle the LPA is able to refuse permission if to grant would lead to a spate of similar applications which would be then hard to resist. In fact it is very difficult to prove that applications are sufficiently similar as it will be very rare indeed to have two identical proposals and sites. LPAs also commonly argue that to allow one proposal would open the floodgates making it harder to resist proposals which might have a harmful cumulative impact. In *Anglia Building Society v Secretary of State for the Environment*[3] permission for a change of use from a retail unit to a building society was refused on the grounds that allowing the proposal would create a precedent which would undermine the LPA's policy of retaining retail uses in that area. Although one change of use in itself might not undermine the strategy, other proposals could come forward which would be difficult to resist and which together would reduce the retail character of the area.

The question as to what material considerations comprise was again raised in *R (on the application of Copeland) v Tower Hamlets LBC*[4]. In this case objectors to a planning application for a hot food takeaway close to a school had argued that the grant of permission would be wholly inconsistent with the school's healthy eating policy. The LPA refused to treat this as a material consideration. The court held that this was wrong; *health* is a material consideration and indeed this decision reflects others on telecommunications masts where it has been held that health concerns are material considerations.

[1] [2001] JPL 93.
[2] [1997] JPL B126.
[3] [1984] JPL 175.
[4] [2010] EWHC 1845 (Admin).

Making a decision

39.30 We have seen that making a decision on a planning application is a complex process. The decision maker be it a planning committee, a council officer under delegated powers or a planning inspector must first begin by taking into account the development plan and then go on to considering any material considerations, which in themselves can be many and varied.

Making the decision can be a finely balanced judgement. Often development plan policies will pull in different directions. It should be noted that a development plan which is not yet adopted or approved, but in the course of being prepared does not have the same status as an adopted plan. In *Nottinghamshire County Council and Broxtowe Borough Council v Secretary of State for the Environment, Transport and the Regions*[1], Sullivan J said '…there is a clear difference between a statutory obligation to determine an appeal in accordance with development plan policies unless material considerations indicate otherwise and an obligation to have regard to emerging policies as material considerations, even if the emerging policies are accorded considerable weight'.

Here the question of 'weight' is referred too. As the decision-making process is a matter of judgement, it follows that the decision maker must accord weight to each relevant issue. In cases where there is more than one issue, it is good practice to reach a conclusion on each particular issue and then reach a conclusion on the overall merits of the scheme. For example, in deciding whether permission should be granted for a large extension, there may be three issues: the effect on the character and appearance of the area, the effect on the living conditions of neighbouring occupiers in relation to loss of light or an overbearing impact, and the effect on a tree in the garden. The decision maker may find that in respect of the effect on neighbours and the tree the proposal is acceptable, but not in terms of the first issue. It will be necessary to balance those three issues and decide whether the harm caused outweighs the acceptability of the proposal in other respects.

[1] [1999] EGCS 35.

Grant of permission

Conditions

39.31 Almost all grants of permission are granted subject to conditions. Conditions are imposed not only to enhance the quality of a development, but also to reduce or ameliorate any of its harmful effects. In other words conditions permit applications to be granted that might not otherwise be given the go ahead. Although the statute[1] gives the LPA power to grant permission 'subject to such conditions as they think fit', case law has placed certain restrictions on this apparently very wide discretion. The leading case is *Newbury District Council v Secretary of State for the Environment*[2], where the House of Lords laid down three tests for validity:

- the condition must have a planning purpose;
- it must fairly and reasonably relate to the development in question;
- it must not be unreasonable within the general public law meaning of the word[3]: '*Wednesbury* unreasonableness'.

Beyond the *Newbury* tests, Circular 11/95 also sets out six 'tests' of a condition. As well as being necessary, relevant and reasonable, the conditions must also be precise and enforceable. These requirements are especially important as the applicant has the right of appeal against the imposition of conditions. It is important to look at conditions carefully to make sure that they meet these requirements and that the applicant can satisfy them. Often conditions take the form of requiring further action before a development is started or first occupied, but other conditions can relate to on-going requirements such as opening hours. If a condition is not complied with to the LPA's satisfaction, the LPA has the power to serve a Breach of Condition Notice.[4] There is no right of appeal against such a notice.

An example of the kind of condition which would offend against the *Newbury* tests can be seen in *R v London Borough of Hillingdon, ex p Royco Homes*[5], where a condition was imposed on the grant of permission to build houses that a number of the units must be offered for rent to people on the council's housing waiting list. This was held to be an invalid condition, since it was an attempt by the council to force the developer to take on part of its housing obligations. This was held to be *ultra vires*, ie beyond the council's powers.

Whether or not a condition 'serves a planning purpose' can be problematic. In *R v Bristol City Council, ex p Anderson*[6] permission was granted for student accommodation subject to a condition which required arrangements relating to welfare, support, and the supervision of students (including such items as car parking arrangements) to be approved by the LPA. Judge Collins decided that such a condition was 'too uncertain' and had little to do with fulfilling a proper planning purpose. However, the Court of Appeal allowed an appeal against this decision deciding that the amenities provided for students did have consequences as regards the development's impact on the locality.

Sometimes conditions restrict the use of a building to a particular type of occupier for example sheltered housing schemes or agricultural workers. This type of condition can be distinguished from a personal permission which is very rare as permission usually runs with the land rather than the applicant. Personal occupancy conditions need to be carefully worded though as illustrated by the cautionary tale (from the LPA's perspective) of *Knott v Secretary of State for the Environment*.[7] In *Knott* planning permission was granted for a dwelling subject to a condition that the permission 'shall enure solely for the benefit of Mr and Mrs Knott'. Clearly the intention was that only Mr and Mrs Knott could live in the property. However the court held that the condition was 'spent' as soon as the permission had been implemented and therefore if someone other than Mr and Mrs Knott lived in the dwelling subsequently this could not be controlled by this particular condition.

[1] TCPA 1990, s 70(1).
[2] [1981] AC 578, HL.
[3] *Associated Provincial Picture Houses v Wednesbury Corpn* [1948] 1 KB 223.
[4] See para 39.63.
[5] [1974] QB 720.
[6] [2000] PLCR 104, CA.
[7] [1997] JPL 713.

Planning obligations

39.32 Applications may also be granted subject to a legal agreement. It is a long standing principle that LPAs can enter into agreements with developers for regulating the use or development of land. Although planning agreements are a useful way of restricting land and have the advantage of binding future as well as current landowners, there was some evidence in the 1970s of agreements being used to secure benefits for the community which were unrelated to the proposal. This 'planning gain' led to accusations of 'chequebook' planning or 'buying and selling' permission. One of the many problems associated with the planning agreement was that the negotiation often took place behind closed doors and only the LPA and applicant were party to it. Accordingly the system has been tightened to prevent abuse and to increase transparency.

Planning obligations comprise both *section 106 agreements* (so called because of the section in the TCPA 1990 which gives the LPA the power to enter into such an agreement) and *unilateral undertakings*. A unilateral undertaking enables a developer to give a binding undertaking rather than having to reach agreement with the LPA.

Planning obligations are made in the form of deeds which are enforceable by LPAs. Guidance from the Planning Inspectorate[1] states:

'they are required to ensure new development does not put a strain on existing services and facilities, and cover the provision of, for example, open space, recreation and leisure facilities, roads, schools, libraries or other community services. They can also prescribe the nature of a development by, for example, requiring that a proportion of housing is affordable.'

To prevent further accusations of abuse of the system, the Government has published advice and guidance in the form of Circular 05/2005. This states that obligations must meet all of the following tests:

- be relevant to planning;
- be necessary to make the proposal acceptable in planning terms;
- be directly related to the proposal;
- be fairly and reasonably related in scale and in kind; and
- be reasonable in all other respects.

Examples of planning obligations include contributions to public transport, traffic calming measures, provision of public open space, public art, flood defence work, restriction on the age of occupiers, and affordable housing.

[1] Planning Inspectorate Good Practice Note 16, published 2010.

39.33 Further changes were made in the PCPA 2004[1] whereby developers can make planning contributions towards services and facilities relating to the proposed development . The Planning Act 2008[2] provides for a *community infrastructure levy*. The idea behind this is to capture the uplift in land values that a grant of permission gives and to fund the provision of infrastructure. LPAs are able to charge the levy on developers. Some LPAs have a 'menu' or price list of charges and the levy covers most forms of development. Broadly speaking the purpose of the community infrastructure levy is to ensure that development contributes to its impact on a locality and gives additional certainty to developers. It should be noted that the negotiated planning agreements between developers and the LPA are retained. Therefore section 106 agreements remain the way to secure contributions from developers in those local authority areas that choose not to implement the community infrastructure levy.

It is worth noting that this is an area of planning law which has been subject to significant change and it is likely that more will be made in the future.

[1] PCPA 2004, ss 46–48.
[2] PA 2008, s 205.

Development Management: Key Points

- Planning permission is required for the development of land. Development may take one of two forms; operational development and change of use. The most common types of operational development are known as building operations and this includes demolition, rebuilding, structural alterations, and other work usually carried out by a builder. Unlike operational development, material change of use is not defined in legislation. The courts have largely left it for LPAs to determine what constitutes a material change of use. Therefore it can take many forms, but is largely a matter of fact and degree.

- In order to reduce the burden on the construction industry, the Use Classes Order and General Permitted Development Order define certain types of development which do not require a specific or express grant of permission.

- Other types of development require the submission of a planning application. There are two types of planning application; outline and full. For each application a set of forms, drawings, supporting information, certificate of ownership and a fee are submitted to the LPA.

- The decision maker, be it a planning committee, council officer or planning inspector, must determine the application in accordance with the adopted development plan taking all material considerations into account. Often the decision is a finely balanced judgement.

- The LPA can grant permission, grant permission subject to conditions or refuse permission. Sometimes a planning obligation will also be entered into.

Appeals to the Secretary of State

39.34 There is a right of appeal to the Secretary of State,[1] from most decisions of local planning authorities. Whilst the majority of appeals are determined by a planning inspector and from the Secretary of State to the courts on a point of law, the SoS does have powers to recover the jurisdiction to decide an appeal from an inspector in any particular case and these are known as recovered cases. The most common appeals are against the refusal of planning permission or a grant of planning permission subject to conditions. Additionally there is the right to appeal if an application has not been determined by the LPA within the prescribed time period.[2]

Since April 2009[3] a new householder appeals service has been introduced. This service is for works or extensions to a dwelling or for development within the dwelling's boundary. It was introduced as an easier, quicker and more proportionate way of dealing with changes to an existing dwelling-house (with certain exceptions) and is much more streamlined than the general appeal route.

With the exception of householder appeals, a planning appeal must be lodged within six months of the decision or, in non-determination cases, after the expiration of the period the LPA would have had for dealing with the application. The time limit for householder appeals is twelve weeks.

Whilst there has been much speculation about the introduction of third party rights of appeal, presently only the applicant can lodge an appeal. However, once an appeal has been lodged by the applicant, third parties may be heard and participate in the appeal process either as objectors to, or in support of, the development.

[1] TCPA 1990, s 78.
[2] Para 39.26.
[3] TCPA 1990 as amended.

39.35 The Planning Inspectorate's Procedural Guidance on planning appeals and called-in planning applications[1] explains the procedure for handling appeals in England[2]. It should be noted that there are other appeal mechanisms for enforcement, certificates of lawfulness, listed building and conservation area, tree preservation order and advertisement cases.

Appeals are determined by planning inspectors appointed by the Secretary of State. Inspectors are civil servants from a range of professional backgrounds, usually with considerable experience of planning and usually accredited by the Royal Town Planning Institute or one of the other professional institutes. Appeals follow one of three procedures.

The Secretary of State has the power[3] to determine the procedure used and this is exercised on the SoS's behalf by the Planning Inspectorate based on which is the most appropriate and proportionate for each case. Each procedure has distinct characteristics. The three procedures are:

- written representations;
- informal hearings;
- public inquiries.

[1] PINS 01/2009.
[2] Under TCPA 1990, s 78 as amended.
[3] TCPA 1990, s 319A.

Written representations

39.36 This is the commonest and quickest way of determining appeals. Since the introduction of the Householder Appeal Service, over 85% of appeals are dealt with by 'written reps' (although the proportion varies from year to year). Written submissions and evidence are exchanged by the 'main parties' (the appellant and the LPA). Other third parties may also submit written evidence. The inspector reaches a decision on the basis of the written submissions and a site visit.

Informal hearing

39.37 This is an alternative to the written representation procedure and is more informal than a public inquiry. A hearing is usually suited to small-scale developments, where there are no complex legal or technical issues and where there is little or no third party interest. After the exchange of written evidence in advance of the hearing date, the inspector will lead a discussion between the parties and make a site visit. The hearing itself usually takes less than a day. Although a hearing is not as formal as a public inquiry, the need for rigorous examination of the issues is still essential. In *Dyason v Secretary of State for the Environment*[1], the 'dangers' of a more relaxed atmosphere were highlighted when Pill LJ said that the 'absence of an accusatorial procedure places an inquisitorial burden on the inspector'.

[1] [1998] JPL 778, CA.

Public inquiry

39.38 This is the most formal method of determining an appeal and is suitable for cases where there are complex issues or technical evidence which needs to be examined, usually through expert witnesses. An inquiry comprises a quasi-judicial process in which both appellant and LPA (and sometimes third parties) are normally represented by lawyers. The judicial nature of the process requires the proper consideration of all the evidence. In *West Lancashire District Council v Secretary of State for the Environment*[1], the absence, through illness, of an LPA expert witness on noise levels was fatal to an inspector's decision; the expert's evidence needed to be subjected to cross-examination and the absence of this meant that the inspector could not have weighed it properly.

A major inquiry, with legal representatives on both sides, and perhaps several expert witnesses each, may take several weeks rather than days and can prove enormously costly both in terms of fees and time. The most infamous inquiry is that relating to Terminal 5 at Heathrow Airport which lasted for 524 sitting days, the longest in history, and is said to have cost the participants in excess of £83 million.

[1] [1998] EGCS 33.

The inspector's decision

39.39 Whichever method of determining the appeal is used, the inspector's decision will be conveyed to the parties in the form of a written decision letter. The inspector's decision letter will be scrutinised carefully by the appellant and the LPA (and by third parties) and by their legal advisers. This is not only for the most obvious reason—to understand the outcome—but to assess whether there is any prospect of success in mounting a challenge in the courts to the appeal decision.[1]

[1] Under TCPA 1990, s 284.

39.40 *Correction of errors* There is a power[1] to correct simple errors in decision letters. Examples of such corrections would be typographical errors or other matters which would not change the substance of the decision or disadvantage either party.

[1] PCPA 2004, s 56–59.

Award of costs in appeals

39.41 It is a common misconception that costs will always be awarded to the successful party. However, the costs of an appeal are usually borne by each party regardless of the outcome of the appeal. Nevertheless it is possible for costs to be awarded against one party in favour of the other. The costs regime[1] exists to ensure that all parties behave in an appropriate way. An application for costs is likely to be successful if the party applying for costs does so in a timely way, the party against which costs are sought has acted unreasonably and the unreasonable behaviour has caused the applicant for costs to incur unnecessary costs or wasted expense in the appeal process. For example, appellants are at risk of an award of costs against them if the proposal is contrary to national policy on green belts, whereas a LPA may be at risk if conditions have not been imposed which could have reasonably overcome the objection. Both parties may risk an award of costs if they fail to adhere to the appeal timetable for submission of statements or do not provide relevant information.

Just as the inspectors must give reasons for reaching their decision on the planning merits of the appeal, clear reasons must also be given for a decision on costs.

[1] The criteria for the award of costs are set out in Circular 03/2009.

Challenging an inspector's decision

39.42 The TCPA 1990, s 288 provides a procedure, called 'statutory review', whereby a person aggrieved by an inspector's decision may question the validity of that decision by applying to the High Court. The application must be made within six weeks, and may only be made on the grounds that the inspector's decision is not within the powers of the TCPA 1990 or that a procedural requirement has not been satisfied. Thus, it is not enough simply that the person aggrieved disagrees with the inspector's decision.

The term 'person aggrieved' includes the applicant for planning permission and LPA. It *can* also include third parties. In *Eco-Energy (GB) Ltd v First Secretary of State*[1] it was held that someone who took a sufficiently active role in the planning process as a substantive objector (as opposed to somebody who objected and did no more) could fall within the definition. However, the courts are often strict in refusing standing to parties who are merely 'interested'. In *William Ashton v Secretary of State for Communities and Local Government and Local Government and Coin Street Community Builders Ltd*[2] both at first instance and in the Court of Appeal, the judges decided that Mr Ashton who was a local resident and had taken no part in the objections to a 43-storey building to the south-east of Waterloo Bridge, was not a person aggrieved.

A third party who is not a 'person aggrieved' may have a 'sufficient interest' to bring judicial review proceedings[3] because the threshold for a sufficient interest to bring such proceedings is lower than is required to be a person aggrieved in respect of statutory review proceedings.

[1] [2004] EWCA Civ 1566, CA.
[2] [2010] EWCA Civ 600, CA.
[3] Senior Courts Act 1981, s 31 and the Civil Procedure Rules, Pt 54.

APPEALS TO THE SECRETARY OF STATE: KEY POINTS

- An applicant for planning permission has a right of appeal against a refusal of planning permission or the non-determination of a planning application within the statutory time limits. There is also a right of appeal against any condition imposed on a grant of planning permission.

- There is no third party right of appeal.

- A householder appeals service for minor changes to dwellings or for development within the curtilage of a dwelling offers a streamlined appeals system for development of a more minor nature.

- There are three types of appeal procedure: written representations, informal hearings and public inquiries.

- Costs can be awarded to either of the main parties, ie the appellant or the LPA. Costs are only awarded when there has been unreasonable behaviour which has resulted in unnecessary costs or wasted expense in the appeal process.

- The High Court is the only authority that can reconsider a planning inspector's decision on the grounds that the order is not within the powers under the TCPA 1990 or that a procedural requirement has not been satisfied.

Environmental impact assessment

39.43 As a result of various European Union regulations and directives certain development requires the submission of an environmental impact assessment (EIA).[1] The requirement is made in domestic law through the Town and Country Planning (Environmental Impact Assessment) (England and Wales) Regulations 1999.

EIA is a process which allows the decision maker to decide whether a proposal should be granted permission after the consideration and assessment of a comprehensive set of information about the environmental impact of a project. It is a complex and specialist area of practice.

¹ Directives 85/337/EC, 97/11/EC.

39.44 The Regulations specify two sets of projects: Sch 1 development always requires an EIA and Sch 2 developments require an EIA in certain circumstances which include the size, nature and location of the proposed development. Examples of a Sch 1 development would be a crude oil refinery, nuclear power station, certain waste disposal installations and the construction of motorways or waterways.

Developers and their professional advisers must be alert as to whether their proposal is caught by the Regulations. It is possible to ask the LPA for a screening opinion to determine whether an EIA is required. The courts have taken an increasingly robust approach to the obligations imposed by EIA and it is another area of much litigation.

*R (on the application of Cooperative Group Ltd) v Northumberland County Council*¹ is illustrative of the issues concerning Sch 2 development. In this case, both the applicant and the LPA accepted that the development for a mixed retail, office, and residential scheme was within Sch 2. The applicants asked for a negative screening opinion which was issued by the LPA. This meant that an EIA was not required. The case centred on whether the LPA had had sufficient information to reach that decision as it is not permissible to adopt a negative screening opinion on the basis that more information about the environmental effects of a scheme will be provided at a later date. The information given to the LPA did not go into sufficient detail and relied on further details being provided in the future. Pelling J concluded that it would have been impossible (at the time the screening opinion was given) to reach a conclusion that there was no likelihood of significant environmental effects from the development. The LPA had not been supplied with sufficient information to make an informed judgement. Many of the issues that should have been subject to an EIA were put off for later consideration. Therefore the decision to grant planning permission was quashed. The application will be freshly considered on its merits. This shows how important it is to ensure that the statutory requirements are properly complied with.

¹ [2010] EWHC 373 (Admin).

ENVIRONMENTAL IMPACT ASSESSMENT: KEY POINTS

Certain types of development require the submission of an environmental impact assessment. The relevant regulations specify two sets of projects which require an EIA; Sch 1 development which always requires an EIA and Sch 2 development which requires an EIA in certain circumstances. Both types of development are specified in the regulations.

Listed buildings and conservation areas

Listed buildings

39.45 Listed building control is a special form of control intended to protect buildings of special architectural or historic interest from unrestricted demolition, alteration or extension. This is governed by the Planning (Listed Buildings and Conservation Areas) Act 1990 and the Planning (Listed Buildings and Conservation Areas) Regulations 1990. It is not intended to describe here in full detail the regime for the protection of buildings of special interest and conservation areas as this comprises an area of specialist practice. However, it should be noted that it is always worth seeking early, and specialist, advice in dealing with listed buildings.[1]

[1] Listed buildings can also include bridges, tunnels, lampposts and other structures.

39.46 The decision whether to list a building or group of buildings such as a terrace is the responsibility of the Secretary of State for Culture, Olympics, Media and Sport. In England, English Heritage makes recommendations to the SoS. In Wales Cadw, the historic environment service of the Welsh Assembly Government, compiles the list. Buildings are listed as:

- Grade I, buildings of exceptional interest;
- Grade II*, buildings of special interest and national importance; and
- Grade II, particularly important buildings of more than special interest.

The majority of listed buildings (over 90%) are Grade II listed. Whether or not a building is listed is recorded in the local land charges register which is maintained by the local authority.[1]

[1] Para 29.25.

39.47 As well as protecting the listed building itself, the legislation also ensures that the impact of nearby development on a listed building and its curtilage is carefully considered. Often it is thought that if a building is listed, very little can be done with it. However, the purpose of listing is not to preserve a building in aspic, but to ensure that any changes made are appropriate and will respect the special characteristics and integrity of the building.

39.48 Although there are moves afoot to streamline the consent regime, presently it is necessary to apply for *listed building consent* as well as planning permission. A grant of planning permission by itself does not give listed building consent and listed building consent does not give planning permission. Separate forms will be needed and separate decisions given by the LPA. If the requisite consents are not obtained, the special control over listed buildings is secured by criminal sanction.

Conservation areas

39.49 These are areas of special architectural or historic interest designated by LPAs. Such designations give the LPAs additional powers over development.

39.50 When determining applications in conservation areas, there is a special duty to ensure that the character or appearance of the area is preserved or enhanced[1]. As this is central to decision making on development in conservation areas, in addition to the usual material considerations, the meaning of this obligation has been subject to close scrutiny by the courts. In *Steinberg v Secretary of State for the Environment*[2], the High Court rejected the interpretation placed on it by a planning inspector in an appeal, that a vital question was 'whether the proposed development would *harm* the character of the conservation area'. The court regarded this as a negative duty, whereas the statute requires a positive one in the 'paying of special attention to the desirability of preserving or enhancing'. In *South Lakeland District Council v Secretary of State for the Environment*[3], the House of Lords decided that preserving the character or appearance of a conservation area can be achieved by a positive contribution to preservation or by development which was neutral in its effect in that its leaves the character or appearance of the conservation area unharmed.

¹ Planning (Listed Buildings and Conservation Areas) Act 1990, s 72.
² [1989] JPL 258.
³ [1992] 2 AC 141, HL.

39.51 Although an application for planning permission in a conservation area is made in the usual way, a further consent, known as a *conservation area consent* will be necessary if the proposal involves total or substantial demolition of an unlisted building in a conservation area.¹ LPAs may also have made Article 4 Directions² to remove or modify permitted development rights in conservation areas.

LPAs often have specialist officers and detailed guidance on their policies and approaches to development in conservation areas.

¹ *Schimizu (UK) Ltd v Westminster City Council* [1997] JPL 523.
² Para 39.20.

LISTED BUILDINGS AND CONSERVATION AREAS: KEY POINTS

- Buildings and structures of special architectural or historic interest are protected from demolition or harmful alterations and extensions through listed building control. Buildings are listed as Grade I, Grade II* or Grade II. Listed building consent is required for any alterations. This is in addition to any planning permission which will be needed.

- Listing does not mean that the building must be preserved as it is and that no alterations can take place, but it does mean that any alterations to the building and its surrounds must be appropriate and will respect the special characteristics and integrity of the building.

- LPAs are able to designate areas of special architectural or historic interest as conservation areas. This gives the LPA additional powers over development.

- There is a special duty when determining applications in conservation areas to ensure that the character or appearance of the area is preserved or enhanced.

Enforcement

39.52 Under the TCPA 1990, a breach of planning control occurs when development is carried out without the requisite planning permission or when any condition or limitation attached to a permission is not complied with. Surprisingly, perhaps, LPAs are not required to take enforcement action when a breach occurs: it is a discretionary activity and for this reason is often known as the 'Cinderella' of the planning system. Before taking any action, LPAs must be sure of the facts and there are numerous issues to be examined, including time limits¹ and established use rights.² Most breaches of planning control are brought to the LPA's attention via observation of its own officers or through complaints from neighbours or local residents or councillors.

A fundamental principle of the enforcement procedure is that, with the exception of removing surface soil from agricultural land, the development of land without planning permission does not constitute a criminal offence. However, LPAs have a range of powers³ to enable them to take action against unauthorised development, including the serving of an enforcement notice.⁴ This usually requires the removal of an unauthorised structure or building or the cessation of an unauthorised use. It should be noted that whilst the development of land without planning permission is not a criminal offence, non-compliance with an enforcement notice is.

Over the last few years enforcement powers have been strengthened, most notably by Part 1 of the Planning and Compensation Act 1991. These changes were brought in as a result of the Carnwath Report 'Enforcing Planning Control' published in 1989. This report highlighted weaknesses in dealing with breaches of development control and noted that these were leading to a loss of public confidence in the system.

One of the new procedures introduced by the 1991 Act is the planning contravention notice (PCN)[5] which makes it easier for LPAs to obtain the necessary information from property owners relating to suspected breaches of planning control. Difficulties with enforcing conditions on permissions were dealt with by the introduction of the breach of condition notice.[6] Despite these and numerous other changes designed to strengthen the enforcement system and to address lingering concerns over those who disregarded the planning system, further changes were made in the Planning and Compulsory Purchase Act 2004. This introduced a new temporary stop notice[7] procedure and removed Crown immunity from enforcement action.

Further changes are proposed in the Government's Localism Bill[8]. Under the Bill, LPAs would be able to decline to determine retrospective planning applications which are applications made after, rather than before, the development has taken place if an enforcement notice has been issued. They would also be allowed to take enforcement action against a breach of planning control despite the expiry of the relevant time limit for taking action if the breach has been concealed. It is widely thought that this last provision is a response to the few, but increasing number of cases, which have been deliberately concealed until after the relevant time limits.

[1] Paras 39.53–39.55.
[2] Paras 39.56–39.57.
[3] Paras 39.59–39.66.
[4] Para 39.61.
[5] Para 39.60.
[6] Para 39.63.
[7] Para 39.65.
[8] Published 13 December 2010.

Time limits

39.53 There are currently two time limits under TCPA 1990 for taking enforcement action[1]. The rationale behind the time limits is that within the time periods the LPA would have had adequate opportunity to take action if they thought it necessary to do so. These are discussed in more detail below.

[1] TCPA 1990, s 171B.

The four-year rule

39.54 Where the breach of development control consists of either:

- operational development; or
- change of use of a building to use as a dwelling-house,

the LPA must take enforcement action within four years of the date when the operational development was substantially complete or the change of use took place.

Unsurprisingly, there have been a number of cases relating to what constitutes substantially complete. In *Sage v Secretary of State for the Environment, Transport and the Regions and Maidstone BC*[1] the Court of Appeal held that a dwelling-house was not substantially complete if there was work still to be done in order for the building to be fit for habitation. However, the House of Lords disagreed taking the view that a holistic approach must be taken. In *First Secretary of State v Chelmsford BC*[2], the House of Lords' decision in *Sage* was applied and the High Court ruled that the bringing together of two static caravans onto land and bolting them together did not amount to substantial completion as cladding would have been subsequently added even though that in itself did not require planning permission.

[1] [2003] UKHL 22, HL.
[2] [2003] EWHC 2800 (Admin).

The 10-year rule

39.55 For all other material changes of use and for any breach of condition on a permission, the LPA must take enforcement action within 10 years of the date of the beginning of the breach.

Lawful use

39.56 If the LPA has not taken any action against the breach within the relevant time limits, the development in question becomes lawful. This does not mean that the development or breach gains permission, it means that enforcement action cannot be taken in respect of the breach and that it is therefore immune from action. This has important implications in property development and real estate management; it is a complex area of planning law. If a development or use is immune from action, it means that the development or use can continue. However, if changes are sought such as an extension or the intensification of the use, it is likely that this would be resisted by the LPA as this may compound any adverse impacts of the use. Additionally care should be taken in dealing with land or property with a lawful use as the value of land or property may be affected.

Certificates of lawfulness

39.57 An owner (or any other person such as a prospective purchaser) wishing to find out whether an existing use is lawful can apply to the LPA[1] for a certificate of lawfulness of existing use or development (a CLEUD). The onus is on the applicant to provide the relevant information and evidence, often in the form of sworn affidavits, to prove that the use or development has been in place for the relevant time period. If the LPA is satisfied that the use or development is lawful, it will issue a CLEUD and cannot therefore subsequently take enforcement action. If the LPA refuses the application, the applicant has a right of appeal to the Secretary of State.[2]

[1] Under TCPA 1990, s 191.
[2] TCPA 1990, s 195.

39.58 Sometimes it is necessary to find out whether a proposed use or development would be lawful. In these cases it is possible to apply for a certificate of lawfulness of proposed use or development (CLOPUD). This is a formal way of ascertaining whether a planning application is required to be submitted for a proposal. If a CLOPUD is not issued then a planning application would be required to be submitted in the usual way. In practice, unless there is a good prospect of the proposal being lawful, it is often quicker to apply for planning permission in the usual way (unless, of course, there is any risk that this will not be forthcoming).

Enforcement powers

39.59 If a breach of planning control occurs and subject to action not being barred by time limits or the issue of a CLEUD (or CLOPUD), the LPA may use one, or a combination, of its enforcement powers to remedy the breach.

39.60 *Planning contravention notice (PCN)*[1] The principal purpose of a PCN is to obtain information to help the LPA to decide whether or not to serve an enforcement notice and, of course, to enable the LPA to be sure of its facts. It may also have the ancillary benefit of alerting persons responsible for alleged contraventions to the need to comply with planning requirements. They might, for example, seek to regularise the position by coming forward with an application for planning permission or at least to discuss the matter with the LPA.

There is a degree of variation in practice between LPAs in their use of PCNs. Some are reluctant in using them, while others resort to them with relatively little encouragement. However, PCNs cannot be used without some basic justification. In *R v Teignbridge District Council, ex p Teignmouth Quay Co*[2] the court held that there must be *some* basic evidence of a possible breach before a PCN could be served; a merely uncooperative attitude by a landowner would not, of itself, be enough.

The PCN requires the owner or occupier of land upon whom it is served to state:

- whether the land is being used as alleged;
- when any use or operation began;
- the identity of any persons responsible;
- information about existing planning permission or why none is necessary; and
- the identity of persons having an interest in the land.

The PCN has two sanctions to encourage the occupier to reply within the 21 day time limit:

- it is a criminal offence to fail to reply or to reply misleadingly;
- the compensation which the occupier may claim if the LPA unjustifiably serves a stop notice[3] would be lost if it was discovered that the LPA was misled by receiving no response or partial information.

---

[1] TCPA 1990, ss 171C and 171D.
[2] [1995] JPL 828.
[3] Para 39.64.

39.61 *Enforcement notices* The standard method of taking action against breach of planning control is for the LPA to serve an enforcement notice[1]. As with a PCN, the LPA must have some justification for serving an enforcement notice and government guidance[2] makes clear that it is not for trivial breaches. Equally, an enforcement notice would be inappropriate if the unauthorised development would probably be granted planning permission. In other words it must be expedient to issue a notice having regard to the development plan and any other material considerations. The issue and service of an enforcement notice is a complex procedure with many opportunities for the process to go wrong. It is therefore important for all parties to ensure that the correct procedure has been followed and that the timetables for service and appeals are adhered to.

The enforcement notice is served on owners, occupiers and any other persons having an interest in the land (such as mortgagees).

The notice must state:

- the alleged breach;
- the steps required to remedy the breach (which could be less than the LPA is entitled to ask for: 'under-enforcement' is permitted);
- the date when the notice takes effect (at least 28 days from its service);
- the period for carrying out any remedial works;
- the reason for issuing the notice;
- the delineation of the site affected by the notice; and
- the existence of the right to appeal against the notice to the Secretary of State. This right of appeal, discussed in para 39.62, is significant because the effect of the enforcement notice is suspended during the appeal. Appeal is thus a favoured means of delaying the enforcement process, although a frivolous appeal could result in a costs order against the appellant.

Once the time limit has expired, the enforcement notice is confirmed and is registered against the property by the local authority. Breach of it, or continuing failure to comply with it, which amounts to the same thing, is an offence punishable by heavy fines, which can take account of the benefit to the owner of the breach.

A favourite tactic of defendants in enforcement proceedings was to reopen all the planning issues that had often been argued through the planning application and appeal processes to try to persuade the criminal court that the enforcement notice should never have been served. This defence was rejected by the House of Lords in *R v Wicks*[3], where it was held that the only thing to be decided was whether the enforcement notice had been breached. Its validity could only be challenged at the earlier stage of appeal to the Secretary of State. Similarly, in *Vale of White Horse District Council v Parker*[4], it was held that the defendants in a prosecution for breach of an enforcement notice would not be allowed to argue that the steps that it required were excessive. Again, this came too late in the day. The only valid defences to a prosecution would be for the owner to show that he had taken all reasonable steps to comply with the notice.

The proper means of responding to an enforcement notice is either to comply with it, to try to negotiate with the LPA a partial or complete withdrawal, or to appeal.

There is another important 'rule' with enforcement notices: that is 'once an enforcement notice always an enforcement notice'. Even if a notice is complied with, it continues to have effect. This means that should, for example, the use recommence the notice will bite again. This also applies to breach of condition notices.

[1] Under TCPA 1990, s 172 (1).
[2] PPG 18.
[3] [1997] JPL 1049.
[4] [1997] JPL 660.

39.62 *Appeals against enforcement notices* These are procedurally similar to appeals against refusal of planning permission. The principal differences are the time limit—an appeal against an enforcement notice must be lodged before the notice takes effect—and the grounds for appeal.

An appeal may be brought on any of the following grounds[1]:

- planning permission ought to be granted or the condition in question discharged;
- the matters alleged have not occurred or do not amount to a breach;
- the LPA has lost the right to enforcement (eg through time limits);
- the enforcement notice was not validly served;
- the steps required were excessive;
- the period for compliance was inadequate.

The Secretary of State can grant planning permission for any or all of the matters stated in the enforcement notice to constitute a breach of planning control or discharge a condition. So in effect success in an appeal against an enforcement notice is similar to that in an appeal against a refusal of planning permission; namely that permission is deemed to be granted for the development in question. For this reason, a fee is charged on appeal equivalent to the fee charged by LPAs with planning applications, so that appellants do not seek to avoid the application fees by this 'backdoor' route.

[1] TCPA 1990, s 174(2).

39.63 *Breach of condition notice (BCN)*[1] The purpose of a BCN is to take action against an alleged breach of a condition attached to a planning permission. The BCN will specify the alleged breach and the steps which the LPA consider ought to be taken (including cessation of activities in some cases) in order to secure compliance with the condition. The BCN must give a time limit for compliance which must not be less than 28 days from the service of the BCN.

Formidable features of the BCN are that failure to comply with it is an offence and that there is no appeal. This is a compelling reason why an applicant for planning permission should appeal to the Secretary of State promptly on receipt of permission if there are conditions which the applicant is unable or unwilling to accept.

[1] TCPA 1990, s 187A.

39.64 *Stop notices* Often the LPA can experience delay in the enforcement notice machinery. This can even be utilised as a tactic by the person in breach with legal challenges to the appeal decision further lengthening the process. In *R v Kuxhaus*[1], the Court of Appeal would not allow an enforcement notice to be confirmed until the last legal challenge had been exhausted, although the court has the power[2] to permit confirmation of the notice pending appeal if it appears to be justified. This delay can be overcome by the LPA's use of another of its powers: the issue of a stop notice[3]. A stop notice can only be issued in conjunction with an enforcement notice (and must refer to it) but unlike the latter, it has almost immediate effect (within three days or even less if the LPA can justify it). The LPA can, therefore, use this powerful weapon to procure an immediate cessation of the activity alleged to constitute the breach. Failure to comply with the stop notice is an offence.

Any appeal is against the enforcement notice and not the stop notice, but the difference, if the latter is used, is that the activity cannot continue pending the appeal. However, the LPA may have to pay a price for resorting to such an effective procedure. If the enforcement notice is subsequently withdrawn, or overturned on appeal to the Secretary of State, or declared invalid on appeal to the Secretary of State, or on judicial challenge, the LPA may be liable to pay compensation for the interruption to activity caused by the stop notice. The compensation may be considerable in some circumstances and this prospect can inhibit the use of stop notices by LPAs. In *Barnes and Co v Malvern Hills District Council*[4], it was held that compensation payable could include liquidated damages payable for delay under an interrupted building contract. Disputes as to compensation are settled by the Lands Chamber of the Upper Tribunal. No compensation is payable if the enforcement action was erroneously taken because of non-compliance with a PCN.

[1] [1988] 2 All ER 705, CA.
[2] TCPA 1990, s 289(4A).
[3] TCPA 1990, s 183.
[4] [1985] 274 Estates Gazette 830.

39.65 *Temporary stop notices* Introduced by PCPA 2004, s 52, these give LPAs power immediately to stop a breach of planning control for up to 28 days. This means that action can be swiftly taken without the need to wait for the service of an enforcement notice and can prevent the intensification of a use or development. They should not be confused with stop notices discussed above. The temporary stop notice has proved popular with LPAs as it is a useful procedure for stopping damage to historic buildings, trees and in cases of tipping. It should, though, be noted that a temporary stop notice cannot be used to halt the use of a building as a dwelling-house. In *R (on the application of Wilson) v Wychavon DC and anor*[1], the Court of Appeal held that the prohibition on the use of a temporary stop notice in the case of dwelling-houses, but not for caravans, discriminated against Gypsies; however, it concluded that the need to weigh up the risk of harm to caravan dwellers against the protection of the environment made it compatible with the European Convention on Human Rights, Article 14.

[1] [2007] EWCA Civ 52, CA.

39.66 *Injunctions* These are potentially the most powerful weapon available since a failure to comply with an injunction is potentially imprisonable. However, the high standards of proof required to obtain an injunction are perceived to be a deterrent and LPAs are reluctant to apply for them.

However, statute[1] and case law have sought to facilitate the use of injunctions by LPAs. In *London Borough of Croydon v Gladden*[2] the Court of Appeal upheld the use of an injunction under the TCPA 1990 with the encouragement that the standard of proof required to obtain it may not be as high as in the general law. In *Harborough District Council v Wheatcroft*[3] the court made clear that it was not necessary for every remedy (such as the enforcement notice and its appeal mechanism) to have been exhausted before resorting to an injunction. Indeed, an injunction could, in appropriate circumstances, be served at an early stage of enforcement proceedings or may be particularly useful if the perpetrator or persons with an interest in the site are unknown. In *South Cambridgeshire DC v Persons Unknown*[4], the Court of Appeal agreed that an injunction could be granted to restrain persons unknown from perpetuating identified breaches of planning control.

Despite this, few injunctions are applied for by LPAs; nevertheless, there is a high success rate when such an application is made.

[1] TCPA 1990, s 187B.
[2] [1994] JPL 723, CA.
[3] [1996] JPL B128.
[4] Times Law Reports, 11 November 2004, CA.

39.67 *Rights of entry* To underpin the specific enforcement powers set out above, the LPA has powers of entry to land for purposes of investigation[1]. A person duly authorised in writing by the LPA can enter any land without warrant at any reasonable hour, provided there is reasonable ground for doing so, to ascertain whether there has been a breach of planning control, whether enforcement action would be justified or whether any requirement arising from previous enforcement action is being complied with. Twenty-four hours' notice has to be given if the premises are residential. Further powers of entry are obtainable by warrant from a magistrate if the LPA can justify them[2].

[1] Under TCPA 1990, s 196A.
[2] Under TCPA 1990, ss 196B, 196C.

ENFORCEMENT: KEY POINTS

- A breach of planning control occurs when development is carried out without the requisite planning permission or when a condition attached to a grant of permission is not complied with.

- The LPA has various and discretionary enforcement powers when a breach of planning control occurs. The main remedy is to serve an enforcement notice which exists in perpetuity and can result in a criminal record if it is not complied with.

- Enforcement action must be taken within strict time limits; for operational development and changes of use of a building to a dwelling, the LPA must take action within four years. For other types of development, including other material changes in use, the time limit is ten years.

- There are two types of certificates of lawfulness. A certificate of lawfulness of proposed use or development determines whether a proposed use or development requires the submission of a planning application. The second type of certificate, known as a certificate of lawfulness of existing use or development, determines whether an existing use or development is lawful. If a use or development is lawful, it is immune from enforcement action. The onus is firmly on the applicant to prove that the use or development has been in existence for either the four or ten year period.

- If a breach occurs and is of a very serious nature, the LPA can issue a stop notice which has immediate effect or apply to the courts for an injunction.

- Temporary stop notices can be issued and give the LPA immediate power to stop a breach of planning control for up to 28 days.

The Localism Bill

39.68 In December 2010, the Coalition Government introduced the Localism Bill. The Bill devolves more power to councils and neighbourhoods giving local communities more control over decisions relating to housing and planning matters at a local level. This is in line with the Government's decentralisation programme. The Bill is not restricted to planning matters; it covers a wide range of provisions relating to local government including the possibility of directly elected mayors, the abolition of the standards regime and enables local people to hold referendums on any issue.

There are a number of proposals which herald further reform to the planning system. The first significant change is in relation to plan making. Regional spatial strategies are to be abolished. A new layer of plans at neighbourhood level will be introduced and it seems that the current local development framework will morph into a local plan. Parish and town councils and neighbourhood forums will be able to produce a neighbourhood plan if they so wish. This plan must comply with the local plan, but can propose more development locally so long as this has local support. This reflects the government's wider growth agenda.

Local planning authorities will be under a duty to cooperate or work together to ensure that the more strategic elements of plans which would have been considered at regional level are considered at the larger than local scale and to ensure that sustainable development is planned for. Minor revisions to some of the components of the LDF such as the annual monitoring report and local development scheme are also proposed.[1] In addition, the process of preparing and adopting plans is to be changed. The plans would still be subject to independent examination and checks for soundness, but the inspector's modifications would no longer be binding on the authority.[2] Additionally, neighbourhoods would have the option to prepare neighbourhood development orders, which would permit categories of development or development on a particular site. In effect this would mean that, subject to the usual checks and balances, a planning application might not be needed for certain types of development. Both the neighbourhood plan and neighbourhood development order would be subject to independent examination and a local referendum.

An important point to note is that where neighbourhood plans are adopted, they would become part of the development plan ie they would be statutory.

Communities would also be given a number of 'rights'. In relation to planning, the key one is the community right to build. This is a power given to groups of local people to deliver development such as new homes and community facilities in their area providing that local support can be demonstrated.

Other important changes are proposed in relation to the enforcement system, which is strengthened by giving the LPA power to decline a retrospective planning application if an enforcement notice has been issued in relation to any part of the development and by allowing enforcement action to be taken even if the time limits (the four and ten year rules) have been expired in cases where the breach has been concealed. Powers in relation to unauthorised advertisements are also changed.

If the Bill moves forward in its current format, it is expected to become law in the latter part of 2011 or 2012.

[1] Para 38.23.
[2] Para 38.24.

Questions

1. Outline the Use Classes Order and its purpose.

2. What is meant by the phrase 'permitted development'?

3. What is a local development order?

4. Describe the two types of planning application and when you might submit each type.

5. Explain what a material consideration is and give three examples of considerations.

6. Name the six tests of a planning condition.

7. What is the purpose of a planning obligation?

8. Describe the different types of planning appeal.

9. What is a breach of condition notice and when might an LPA wish to serve such a notice?

10. If Joel owns a florist shop and wants to sell it to Richard who wants to open a wine bar, what advice would you give to Joel and Richard to make sure that the requisite planning permissions were in place? If Richard wanted to extend the premises to make it bigger would this change your advice? If the building was listed would this change your advice?

Index

abandonment
material change of use 39.14
abatement
private nuisance 23.22
acceptance 5.9–23
by conduct 5.14
communication of 5.16–23
counter-offers
distinguished 5.11–13
dispensation from need for
communication of 5.19
general requirement of 5.2
Internet sales 5.18
postal acceptance 5.21–22
prescribed mode of 5.23
presumption of 5.20
requirements 5.9–10
rewards 5.10
tenders 5.15
access to neighbouring land 22.6
accord without
satisfaction 6.27
account of profits from
breach 11.38–40
accountants
professional liability 16.21
accumulation
strict liability 24.5
accuracy
ascertaining of
representation 7.20
acquisition for planning or
statutory purposes
restrictive covenants 33.37
act
tender by 8.5
act of God
strict liability 24.12
act of parties
termination of agency
by 14.22–23
act of stranger
strict liability 24.13
action of ejectment
trespass to land 22.9
active misrepresen-
tation 12.3–50
breach of contract 12.42–44
has become contractual
term 12.41–44
remedies for those which
have remained mere rep-
resentations 12.16–40

which have remained mere
representation 12.4–5
Acts of Parliament 1.4, 3.1,
3.3–4
commencement and
repeal 3.4
interpretation 3.10
literal construction 3.11–12
parts regarded as
intrinsic aids to
interpretation 3.20
purposive
construction 3.13–15
validity of 3.3
acts in reliance
proprietary estoppel 30.13
actual authority
agents 14.29
actual undue influence 12.60
administration of justice
historical perspective 1.6
adverse possession
against tenants 30.33–35
by tenants 30.36
exceptional cases 30.31
further application for
registration 30.32
leases 30.33–36
occupation as licensee 30.27
prescription and 32.11
requisite period 30.28–32
squatters 30.23–28
unregistered leases
30.33–36
advertisements
offer of invitation to treat 5.6
representation 12.12
advocates 16.26
affirmation
bar to rescission 12.19
termination of
contract 8.16–17
age
negligence 17.5
agency 14.1–47
agency of necessity 14.11
creation of 14.2
definition 14.1
effects of termination 14.27
termination 14.21–27
agency of necessity 14.11
agents
actual authority 14.29

appointment by express
agreement 14.4
appointment by implied
agreement 14.5
authority of 14.29–34
bribes 14.15
capacity 14.3
conflict of interest 14.15
contracts made by
deed 14.40
contractual liability 14.43
duties 14.12–16
fiduciary duties 14.15
indemnity 14.19
ostensible
authority 14.30–34
principal and 14.2–27
ratification 14.6–10
remuneration 14.17–18
quantum meruit 14.17
rights of 14.17–19
rights of third parties
against 14.44–46
role in contract 4.15
sale of goods through 7.25
secret profits 14.15
third parties and 14.39–46
tortious liability 14.46
trade usage 14.41
where principal in
reality 14.42
aggravated damages 27.2
agreements 5.1–38
agreement to agree 5.33
ascertaining 5.1
binding 6.1–28
conditions 6.6
as contract 6.1
essential element of
contract 4.1
made within course of
business 6.4
made within family 6.3
making binding 9.28
parties to 6.2
possibility of ignoring uncertainty in 5.32
rebuttal 6.4
restrictive covenants 33.40
'subject to contract' 5.34–35
uncertainty 5.30–32
written not whole
contract 7.5

agricultural holdings 37.47
agricultural tenancies 37.46–48
  statutory provisions 37.46
airspace
  landowner's rights 28.16
  trespass to land 22.2
alterations
  boundaries 28.27
  covenants against 36.53–54
  Land Register
    indemnity 35.44
    limits on right to 35.42
alternative dispute
    resolution 2.25–30
ambiguities
  exemption clauses 9.5
animals
  assumption of risk 25.7
  contributory negligence 25.7
  damage caused by 25.6
  dangerous animals 25.4
  dangerous species 25.5
  duty of care 25.3
  foreseeability 25.3
  liability 25.1–12
    defences 25.7
  negligence 25.3
  non-dangerous species 25.6
  public nuisance 25.2
  trespassers injured by 25.7
annexation
  express words 33.24
  implication 33.25
  restrictive
    covenants 33.23–26
  under Law of Property Act
    1925 33.26
anticipatory breach 8.26–27
  damages 11.27
  effects of 8.27
anxiety
  damages for 6.11
appeals 2.7
  High Court of Justice 2.13
  planning 38.10, 39.34–41
appellate civil jurisdiction
  Queen's Bench Division 2.11
appellate jurisdiction
  Chancery Division 2.9
application to court
  renewal of business
    tenancies 37.33
applications
  planning
    permission 39.21–24
appointment
  agent 14.4
apportionment 19.9
arbitration 2.26
  rent reviews 36.59

Area Action Plans
  development plan
    documents 38.23
Article 4 directions
  planning permission 39.20
articles of association 4.14
assignees
  enforceability of covenants
    by and against 36.71–89
    leases entered into on
      or after 1 January
      1996 36.78–86
    'old' leases 36.72–77
assignment 29.1
  consent 36.29
  contractual rights to third
    parties 13.9
  leases 36.28–31, 36.74–77
  reasonableness test
    36.30–31
  release of landlord on
    reversion 36.83
  release of tenant on 36.80
  restrictive covenants 33.27
  reversion 36.76, 36.79
assumption of
    responsibility 11.21–24,
    16.18–9
  inclusionary effect 11.24
  public authorities 16.24
assumption of risk
  animals 25.7
  defence to negligence 19.2–5
  occupiers' liability 21.17
  private nuisance 23.19
assured shorthold
    tenancies 37.5–8
  creation 37.5
  rent referral and review 37.7
  tenancy deposit schemes 37.8
  termination 37.6
assured tenancies 37.9–11
  creation 37.9
  rent review 37.11
  termination 37.10
auctioneers 14.47
auctions
  offer 5.7
  sale of goods 7.25
  sale of land 29.36
authorised acts
  course of employment 26.9
authorised guarantee agreements
    (AGAs) 36.81–82
authority
  breach 14.45

bailment 13.14
bankruptcy
  termination of agency by 14.26

battle of the forms 5.13
beneficiaries
  trusts of land 31.35
benefit
  award for 10.19–20
benefit and burden
  doctrine of 30.18, 33.10
bids
  offer 5.7
bilateral contracts 4.2
  consideration 6.8
bona fide purchaser of legal
    estate for value 35.5
borrowed employees
  vicarious liability 26.7
boundaries
  alteration 28.27
  general law
    governing 28.21–22
  land 28.21–8
  presumptions 28.23–26
  structures 28.28
breach of authority 14.45
breach of condition
  notice 39.63
breach of contract 8.6–27
  account of profits from
    breach 11.38–40
  active misrepresentation
    12.42–44
  avoidance of liability for 9.11
  contract of employment 11.6
  contract for sale of
    land 29.30
  contributory
    negligence 11.28–29
  damages for 8.8
  definition 8.6
  equitable relief 11.55
  injunctions 11.46–51
  injured parties 8.10–14
  lawful excuse for 8.7
  limitation periods 11.53–54
  liquidated damages
    11.20–22
  penalty clauses 11.32–33
  quantum meruit 11.41–42
  remedies 11.1–55
    damages 11.1–34
  repudiatory breach 8.8–25
  specific
    performance 11.43–45
breach of covenant
  contractual remedies 36.62
  forfeiture 36.63–66
  procedure 36.65
  relief 36.66
  remedies 36.62–70
  waiver 36.64
breach of duty 17.1–18

breach of repair
    covenants 36.67
breach of statutory duty 20.1–8
breach of trust
    tort and 15.6
breach of warranty 14.45
bribes
    agent 14.15
builders' liability 21.26–29
building contracts
    implied terms 7.31
building operations 39.4–5
building preservation
    notices 29.25
buildings
    listing 29.25
burden of proof
    damage 18.1
    negligence 17.15–18
business
    agreements made in
        course of 6.4
    definition 37.27
    sale of goods in course of 7.25
business premises
    exclusive possession 36.11
business tenancies 37.25–45
    background 37.25
    compensation for
        disturbance 37.39
    compensation for
        misrepresentation 37.40
    contracted out
        tenancies 37.29
    excluded tenancies 37.28
    opposing renewal 37.36–40
    renewal 37.33–35
        application to court 37.33
        interim continuation 37.34
        interim rent 37.35
        new tenancy 37.41–45
        requirement for occupying
            tenant 37.26
    statutory
        provisions 37.26–29
    termination under Landlord
        and Tenant Act
        1954 37.30–32
    types of 37.26–29
'business' test
    employee 26.6
'but for' test
    causation 18.3
byelaws 3.8

capacity
    agent 14.3
    contract 4.10–9
care
    agent's duty to exercise 14.14

causal connection
    damages 11.13
causation 19.8
    'but for' test 18.3
    damage 18.1–6
    'guilty' conduct 18.9
    'innocent' conduct 18.8
    intervening causes 18.6–13
    multiple causes 18.6
    policy considerations 18.20
    proof 18.4
    rescue cases 18.11
    statutory duty 20.7
caveat emptor doctrine 21.16
central government
    role in planning 38.7
certificate of lawfulness
    development 39.57–58
chain of indemnity covenants
    positive covenants 33.7
Chancery Division
    appellate jurisdiction 2.9
    High Court of Justice 2.9
    original jurisdiction 2.9
change of circumstances
    frustration 10.2–10
character of neighbourhood
    change in 33.34
Charges Register 29.14
chattels
    becoming fixtures 28.11
    fixed to land 28.11
    fixtures distinguished
        28.12
cheque
    conditional discharge by 8.3
children
    negligence 17.5
    occupiers' liability 21.13
circulars
    invitation to treat 5.6
civil courts
    structure of 2.1
civil law
    criminal law
        distinguished 1.1–3
civil liability 20.2
claimant
    conduct of 18.10
co-ownership *see* concurrent
    ownership
Code for Leasing Business
    Premises in England
    and Wales 36.24
collateral advantages
    redemption 34.13
collateral benefits
    damages 27.9
collateral contracts
    definition 7.6

express terms 7.6
    third parties 13.10
collateral negligence 26.24
collective
    enfranchisement 37.15
commencement
    Acts of Parliament 3.4
commercial property
    leases 36.24
Commercial Rent Arrears
    Recovery (CRAR)
    36.69
committee work
    planning officers 38.18
committees
    reports of as extrinsic aid to
        interpretation of Acts of
        Parliament 3.21
common law
    definition 1.4
    equity and 1.5–8
    equity prevails in conflict
        with 1.8
    legislation distinguished 1.4
    negligent misrepresen-
        tation 12.32–34
    position of occupier at 21.4
    positive covenants 33.17
    presumptions against
        alteration of 3.19
    restrictive covenants 33.33
        discharge 33.34–37
common law courts 1.5
commonhold 28.34
    introduction of concept 28.7
    introduction of 36.1
    positive covenants 33.5
commonhold community
    statement 28.34
commons 32.21
Commonwealth courts
    persuasive precedents 3.45
communication
    acceptance 5.16–23
community infrastructure levy
    planning permission 39.33
companies
    capacity to contract 4.11–15
    legal status 4.11
company incorporation 4.11
    UCTA not applicable to
        contracts relating
        to 9.14
company registration 4.14
compensation
    damages awarded for
        11.3–34
    disproportionate 9.28
    disturbance 37.39
    misrepresentation 37.40

completion
   contract for sale of
      land 29.38
   time 8.28–31
compliance
   contract for sale of land 29.8
compulsory registration
   title to land 29.15
conciliation 2.30
concurrent leases 36.18
concurrent ownership
      (co-ownership) 31.1–42
   assumption of joint
      tenancy 31.11
   background to 31.2
   by implication 31.12–15
   constructive trust 31.14
   ending 31.23
   express creation 31.9–11
   express declaration 31.10
   financial
      contribution 31.13–14
   forms of 31.2–7
   how arises 31.9–11
   joint tenancy 31.4–6
   modern approach
      to 31.28–42
   overreaching 31.26, 35.27
   potential problems of
      31.24–27
   problems of 31.1
   quantification of shares 31.16
   reform of law on 31.15
   statutory reform to 31.28
   tenancy in common 31.7–8
   trust for sale 31.25
   trusts of land 31.28–42
   types of 31.3
condition notice
   breach of 39.63
condition precedent 5.36
condition subsequent 5.37
conditional discharge
   cheque 8.3
conditions
   agreements 6.6
   ascertaining intention of
      parties 8.22
   breach of 8.21
   contract for sale of
      goods 8.23
   courts' approach to 8.22
   definition 8.21
   judicial classification 8.22
   operation of 5.36–37
   planning permission 39.31
   requirements for 8.22
conditions precedent 7.3
conduct
   misrepresentation by 12.5

value of 17.13
confidentiality
   fiduciary
      relationships 12.55–56
conflict of interest
   agent 14.15
conformity of goods 9.18
consent
   assignment 36.29
   defence to negligence 19.2–5
   express 19.4
   implied 19.5
   informed consent 19.3
   meaning of 19.3
consent of claimant
   strict liability 24.10
consequences
   seriousness of 17.12
consequential loss 16.13
   damages 11.11–12
   remoteness 11.11
conservation areas 39.49–51
consideration 6.5–24
   adequacy of 6.11
   contracts where there
      is no 4.5
   definition 6.7
   elements required for 6.5
   essential element of
      contract 4.1
   executed 6.8
   executory 6.8
   failure of 8.13, 10.16
   part payment of
      debts 6.18–20
   past consideration 6.9–10
   promise and 6.5
   promissory estoppel 6.21–24
   requirements for 6.5
   sufficiency of 6.12–17
constructive trusts
   concurrent ownership
      (co-ownership) 31.14
   interests in land 30.10
   proprietary estoppel 30.17
consumer
   dealing as 9.13
   definition 9.24
contemptuous damages 27.2
contributory negligence
   animals 25.7
continuity
   private nuisance 23.9
continuous enjoyment
   easements 32.41
contract
   actions in 2.3
   breach 8.6–27
   capacity to make 4.10–19
   discharge 6.25–27, 8.1–2

discharged by
      frustration 10.1–23
   e-mail 4.9
   enforcement by third
      parties 13.12
   essential elements 4.1–2
   evidenced in writing 4.8
   exclusion of liability by 21.2
   fiduciary
      relationships 12.55–56
   form 4.3–9
   illegality 4.20
   letter of intent 5.38
   limited liability
      partnerships 4.16–17
   made by deed 14.40
   must be in writing 4.7
   not necessarily extinguish by
      termination 8.15
   payment in anticipation of
      concluding 5.38
   relationship with tort 16.16
   rights of third parties against
      agents 14.44–46
   role of agents 4.15
   termination 8.10–17
   third party rights 13.1–16
   time of performance 8.28–31
   tort and 15.4
   trade usage 14.41
   ultra vires 4.14
   variation 6.28
   visitors under 21.11
   voiding for mistake 12.1
   written agreement not
      whole 7.5
contract of employment
   breach of 11.6
   implied terms 7.31
   injunctions 11.50
   reciprocal terms 7.31
   vicarious liability 26.3–7
contract for sale of land
   additional terms 29.6
   amplification by
      courts 29.3–8
   breach of contract 29.30
   completion 29.38
   compliance 29.8
   contract terms 29.29
   contractual duty 29.30
   damages 29.34
   deposit 29.28
   draft 29.26
   exchange 29.27
   misrepresentation 29.30
   more than one
      document 29.5
   non-compliance 29.9
   options 29.7

pre-emption rights 29.7
proving title 29.37
registration 29.38
remedies 29.31–35
repudiatory breach 29.33
rescission 29.32
signatures 29.4
specific performance 29.35
statutory requirements 29.2
termination for repudiatory
        breach 29.33
transfer 29.37–38
vendor's liability for
        defects 29.30
contract terms 7.1–34 *see also*
        express terms; implied
        terms
    active misrepresen-
        tation which has
        become 12.41–44
    contract for sale of land 29.6,
        29.29
    defences available to
        promisor 13.7–8
    determination of whether
        written term is term of
        contract 7.8–13
    exemption clauses 9.1–8
    express terms 7.1–21
    frequency of use 7.11
    implied terms 7.2
    interpretation of written 9.30
    irrevocably binding
        consumer to 9.28
    language written 9.25
    notice 7.10
    order forms 7.9
    reasonable notice 7.13
    representation
        distinguished 7.14–15
    residential leases 36.25
    right of third party to
        enforce 13.3
    tickets 7.9
    time penalty clauses 6.16
    to be regarded as not having
        been individually
        negotiated 9.27
    vague 5.31
contracted out tenancies
    business tenancies 37.29
contractors' liability
    defective property 21.28
contractual bailee
    duty of 26.23
contractual duty
    existing 6.15–16
    owed to third parties 6.17
contractual liability
    agents 14.43

contractual licences 28.42–44
    enforceability 28.44
    nature of 28.42
    revocability 28.43
contractual obligations
    contract for sale of
        land 29.30
    defaulting party 8.14
    imbalance in parties'
        rights 9.26–28
    injured parties discharged
        from 8.11
    lawful excuse for breach
        of 8.7
    renunciation of 8.26
    third parties 13.15–16
    transfer 9.28
contractual obligations
    third parties 13.14–16
contractual remedies
    breach of covenant 36.62
contractual rights
    assignment to third
        parties 13.9
    third parties 13.2–13
contribution between
        tortfeasors
    damages 27.15
contributory negligence 18.10,
        19.6–9, 20.8
    apportionment 19.9
    causation 19.8
    damages 11.28–29
    misrepresentation 12.30
    private nuisance 23.19
    standard of care 19.7
Convention rights 3.5, 3.24–31
    application of 3.31
    interpretation of legislation
        in context of 3.22
    judicial precedent and 3.43
    protecting 15.12
    restrictions on 3.30
conveyance 29.1
conveyancing
    proprietary estoppel 30.16
core strategy
    development plan
        documents 38.23
correction of errors
    planning appeals 39.40
costs
    planning appeals 39.41
councillors
    role in planning 28.14–15
counter-offers
    acceptance
        distinguished 5.11–13
county courts 2.2–7
    jurisdiction 2.3

position in court system
        hierarchy 3.41
course of dealings
    severance of joint tenancy
        in 31.22
course of employment 26.8–16
    authorised acts 26.9
    implied authority 26.10
    intentional
        wrongdoing 26.14
    ostensible authority 26.11
    prohibitions 26.12–13
Court of Appeal 2.14–16
    composition of 2.14
    jurisdiction 2.15
    position in court system
        hierarchy 3.38
Court of Chancery 1.5
    development of role of 1.7
Court of Justice of
        the European
        Union 2.19–20
    historical background 2.19
    jurisdiction 2.20
    position in court system
        hierarchy 3.36
    relationship with English
        courts 2.20
court system
    England 1.5
    hierarchy of 3.35–42
courts
    terms implied by 7.29–33
covenant for quiet
        enjoyment 6.11
covenants
    against alterations 36.53–54
    disposition 36.28–32
    enforceability by and against
        assignees 36.71–89
    form of 36.28
    leases 13.14, 36.27–32
    remedies for breach
        of 36.62–70
    restricting subletting 36.32
    sub-tenants 36.89
    sureties 36.88
creator
    private nuisance 23.14
crime
    tort and 15.3
criminal law
    civil law distinguished 1.1–3
Crown
    land 28.30
    presumptions against being
        bound 3.19
custom 3.46
    terms implied by 7.23–24
customary rights 32.22

damage
  animals 25.6–7
  burden of proof 18.1
  causation 18.1–6
  compensation for 15.8
  emergencies 18.12
  extent 18.18
  foreseeability 18.15–19
  intervening causes 18.7–13
  legal rights 18.13
  loss of chance 18.5
  manner of infliction 18.17
  multiple causes 18.6
  negligence 18.1–20
  policy considerations 18.20
  remoteness 18.14–19
  rescue cases 18.11
  statutory duty 20.5
  strict liability 24.9
  third parties 16.10–11
  type of 18.16
damage to property
  damages 27.12–13
    date of assessment 27.13
damages 27.1–15
  anticipatory breach 11.27
  anxiety 6.11
  assumption of
      responsibility 11.21–24
  breach of contract 8.8,
      11.1–34
  causal connection 11.13
  collateral benefits 27.9
  compensatory purpose of 11.2
  consequential loss 11.11–12
  contract for sale of
      land 29.34
  contributory
      negligence 11.28–29
  damage to property 27.12–13
    date of assessment 27.13
  death 27.10–11
  deceit 12.25–31
  disappointment 11.6
  discomfort 11.5
  distress 6.11, 11.6
  fatal accidents 27.11
  for what compensation can
      be awarded 11.3–34
  inconvenience 11.5
  in lieu of injunction 27.18
  in lieu of rescission 12.36–38
  limitation of action 11.52
    agreed sum in contract for
      sale of goods 11.36
  loss of amenity 27.4
  loss of earnings 27.8
  loss of expectation of
      life 27.6
  loss of expectations 11.3–10

medical expenses 27.7
misrepresentation 12.21–38
mitigation 11.25–27
multiple tortfeasors 27.14–15
  contribution between
      tortfeasors 27.15
negative terms 11.7
pain and suffering 27.5
personal injury 27.3–9
private nuisance 23.20
public nuisance 23.26
purpose of 11.1–2, 27.2
reasonable contemplation
      test 11.22–23
for recovery of agreed
      sum in repudiatory
      breach 11.37
reduced lifespan 27.6
reliance loss 11.8–9
trespass to land 22.7
types of 27.2
dangerous animals 25.4
dangerous premises
  liability 21.1–30
dangerous species 25.5
dangerous things
  liability 24.6
dealing as consumer 9.13
  qualification to
      definition 9.18
death
  damages 27.10–11
  excluding liability for 9.10
  frustration 10.6
  termination of
      agency 14.22–23
  termination of offer 4.29
deceit
  damages for 12.25–31
  statutory
      provisions 12.25–26
decentralization 39.68
decision
  EU law 3.48
  planning permission
      39.25–27, 39.30
decision making
  planning officers 38.17
deed
  contracts made by 4.4
  creation of interests in land
      by 29.11
  definition 4.6, 29.11
  execution 4.6
  short lease exception 29.12
deed of grant
  easements 32.8–12
default of claimant
  strict liability 24.11
default notices 36.84–85

defaulting parties
  contractual obligations 8.14
defective performance
  repudiatory breach 8.20–25
defective products
  economic loss 16.15
defective property 21.26–8
  caveat emptor doctrine 21.26
  common law
      developments 21.27–28
  landlord's liability 21.30
  statutory provisions 21.29
defects
  vendor's liability 29.30
defences
  animals
      liability 25.7
  negligence 19.1–9
      assumption of risk 19.2–5
      consent 19.2–5
  occupiers' liability 21.24
  private nuisance 23.18–19
  statutory duty 20.8
  straying livestock 25.9–10
  strict liability 24.10–7
  trespass to land 22.5
      easements 22.5
      preservation of life or
          property 22.5
      rights of way 22.5
defendant
  breach of statutory duty
      by 20.6
defendant's conduct
  private nuisance 23.10
defendant's state of mind
  private nuisance 23.12
delegated legislation 3.6–9
  ultra vires 3.9
delegation
  agent has duty not to 14.16
demised premises
  physical state 36.40
demoted tenancies 37.21
deposit
  contract for sale of
      land 29.28
description
  sale of goods corresponding
      to 7.25
designers
  defective property 21.28
destruction
  frustration 10.4
detention
  straying livestock 25.10
determination time periods
  planning permission 39.36
detriment
  proprietary estoppel 30.14

development
  Classes E, F, G and H 39.11
  conservation areas 39.49–51
  definition 39.2–8
  environmental impact
      assessment 39.43–44
  law relating to 39.1–68
  lawful use 39.56–58
  listed buildings 39.47
  material change of use
      39.6–8
  operational
      development 39.3–5
  planning
      permission 39.17–27
  statutory provisions 39.1
  sui generis uses 39.12
  uses excluded from 39.9–16
development plans 38.21–28
  documents 38.23
  planning officers 38.19
  role in planning
      system 38.21
  significance of 38.28
  transition period 38.21
devolution
  proposed under Localism
      Bill 39.68
dictionaries
  extrinsic aid to
      interpretation of Acts of
      Parliament 3.21
direct applicability
  EU law 3.49
direct effect
  EU law 3.49, 20.3
directives
  effect of untransposed 3.51
  EU law 3.48
  transposition 3.50
disappointment
  damages for 11.6
discharge
  by payment 8.3
  contract 6.25–27, 8.1–2
  mutual discharge 6.26
  restrictive
      covenants 33.31–37
  common law 33.34–37
  third parties 13.6
  unilateral discharge 6.27
disclaimer
  leases 36.99
disclosed principal 14.35
disclosure
  duty of 12.53
  insurance contracts 12.54
  latent defects 29.30
discomfort
  damages for 11.5

discontinuance
  existing use 29.25
  title to land 30.24
disposition of equitable interest
  joint tenancy 31.19
dispositions
  effect of registered 29.19
  power to make 29.18
dispossession
  title to land 30.24
dispute resolution
  rent reviews 36.59
  trusts of land 31.40
disrepair
  remedying 36.48
distress
  damages for 6.11, 11.6
  non-payment of rent
      36.69
disturbance
  compensation for 37.39
ditches
  boundaries 28.24
divisional courts
  position in court system
      hierarchy 3.39
dogs
  liability for 25.11
dominant land
  easement must
      accommodate 32.5–6
  easements 32.4
  owner must be different
      from owner of servient
      land 32.7
double liability
  protection from 13.13
drafting
  residential leases 36.25
drafting errors
  legislation 3.15
duress 12.57–9
  requirements for 12.59
  rescission 12.68
  types of 12.58
duty of care 16.1–28
  animals 25.3
  current position 16.6
  damage caused by third
      parties 16.10–11
  economic loss 16.12–5
  general principle 16.3–5
  lawful visitors 21.1–3
  occupiers' liability 12.12–17,
      21.22
  omissions 16.7–8
  protection 16.9
  purchasers 21.26–29
duty of disclosure 12.53–56
duty of fidelity 7.31

duty to act
  agent 14.12
duty to mitigate 11.26

e-mail
  contract 4.9
early neutral evaluation 2.27
earnings
  loss of 27.8
easements 22.5, 30.2, 30.5,
      32.1–57, 35.30
  acquisition of 32.23–51
  continuous enjoyment 32.41
  creation under
      statute 32.34–39
  deed of grant 2.9–12, 32.8
  dominant and servient piece
      of land 32.4
  essential characteristics
      of 32.4–12
  expressly created 32.25–26
  extinguishment 32.52–56
  fee simple 32.42
  grants and
      reservations 32.26
  implied 32.27–33
  implied reservations 32.32
  legal and equitable 32.24
  nature of 32.3
  of necessity 32.29, 32.33
  need to be sufficiently
      definite 32.9
  no joint possession 32.11
  no new negative 32.10
  prescription 32.40–51
      common law 32.47
      lost modern grant 32.48
      methods of 32.47–51
      statutory
          requirements 32.49–51
  as of right 32.43
  rights of light 32.54–56
  rights similar to 32.13–22
  rights of support 32.57
  rights of way 32.53
  servient owner must
      not be involved in
      expenditure 32.12
  types of 32.2, 53–56
  under Law of Property
      Act 1925 32.34–39
  within rule in *Wheeldon v
      Burrows* 32.31, 32.39
  without force 32.44
  without permission 32.46
  without secrecy 32.45
economic loss 16.12–15
  defective products 16.15
  'opening the floodgates' 16.12
  transferred loss 16.14

'egg-shell skull' principle 18.19
ejusdem generis rule 3.18
elderly
  negligence 17.5
election
  third parties 14.38
electronic
      conveyancing 29.10–11
  move towards 29.1
  progress towards 29.20
  statutory provisions 29.13
electronic mortgages 29.11
emergencies
  damage 18.12
employee
  'business' test 26.6
  control over 26.4
  definition 26.3
  function of 26.5
  relationship with
      employer 26.2
  vicarious liability 26.2–7, 15
employer
  relationship with
      employee 26.2
  vicarious liability 26.2–7
employer's rights 26.4
Employment Tribunals 2.22
enforceability
  covenants by and against
      assignees
  'old' leases 36.72–77
  interests in land 35.1–44
    background 35.2–8,
      35.10–3
    bona fide purchaser
      of legal estate for
      value 35.5
    doctrine of notice 35.6–7
    equitable interests 35.5
    legal rights 35.3
    pre-1926 rules 35.2–7
    solutions adopted in 1925
      35.8
    unregistered land 35.11–13
enforcement
  contracts by third
      parties 13.12
  covenants by and against
      assignees 36.71–89
    leases entered into on or
      after 1 January 1996
      36.78–86
  planning control 39.52–55
    four-year rule 39.54
    ten-year rule 39.55
    time limits 39.53
  planning officers 38.20
  positive covenants 33.6–10
  user covenants 36.39

enforcement notice 39.61
  appeals against 39.62
enfranchisement
  collective 37.15
  long residential
      tenancies 37.13–15
  tenants 37.1
English Heritage 39.46
enlargement
  leases 36.96
enquiries
  sale of land 29.24
entire agreement clauses
  effect of 7.7
  misrepresentation 12.47–48
entry as of right 21.9
Environment Agency
  licences from 28.20
environmental impact
      assessment
  development 39.43–44
equitable easements 30.6, 32.24
equitable interests 29.21
  definition 28.38
  disposition of 31.19
  interests in land
      enforceability 35.5
equitable lease 30.5
  legal lease distinguished 30.5
equitable relief 11.55
equity
  cannot be demanded as
      right 1.8
  common law and 1.5–8
  county court jurisdiction
      in 2.3
  development of rules of 1.7
  part payment of debts 6.20
  prevail in conflict between
      common law and 1.8
escape
  strict liability 24.7
estate agents 12.49, 14.47
  misrepresentation 12.46
  professional liability 16.21
estate in commonhold
      land 28.34
estate rentcharges
  positive covenants 33.9
estates 28.32–5
EU law 3.47–53
  direct effect 20.3
  environmental impact
      assessment 39.43–44
  interpretation 2.20, 3.54
  legislation 1.4
    interpretation in context
      of 3.22
  strategic environmental
      assessment 38.26

supremacy of 3.52
  validity of 3.53
European Court of Human
      Rights
  decisions of 3.45
European Court of Justice *see*
      Court of Justice of the
      European Union
exceptions
  Land Register 35.41
exchange
  contract for sale of
      land 29.27
excluded tenancies
  business tenancies 37.28
exclusion clauses *see* exemption
      clauses
exclusionary effect
  assumption of
      responsibility 11.22
exclusive possession
  business premises 36.11
  leasehold 36.8–11
  sharers 36.10
executed consideration 6.8
execution
  written contract 7.16
executory consideration 6.8
exemplary damages 27.2
exemption clauses 9.1–8
  ambiguities 9.5
  excepted agreements 9.14
  inconsistent
      undertakings 9.7
  interpretation 9.1–3
  liability can only be excluded
      by clear words 9.4
  limitation of liability for
      negligence 9.6
  limitations on application of
      9.7–8
  misrepresentation 9.7
  protection of third
      parties 13.4–5
  requirement of
      reasonableness 9.15
  restricting liability 11.32
  standard terms 9.2
  UCTA provisions 9.9–21
  varieties of 9.21
existing leases
  prior claim to
      possession 34.23
expectation
  damages for loss of 11.3–10
  proprietary estoppel 30.12
expectation of life
  loss of 27.6
experience of others
  reasonableness 17.6

expert determination 2.28
expiry
  leases 36.94
explanatory notes
  intrinsic aid to interpre-
    tation of Acts of
    Parliament 3.20
exposure for sale 5.5
express agreement
  appoint of agent by 14.4
express consent 19.4
express declaration
  concurrent ownership
    (co-ownership) 31.10
express obligations
  repairs 36.47–52
express restriction
  mortgagee's right to
    possession 34.20
express terms
  collateral contracts 7.6
  conditions precedent 7.3
  contract 7.1–21
  'entire agreement clauses' 7.7
  exceptions to notice 7.11
  future facts 7.19
  invalidating factors 7.4
  invitation to verify 7.18
  opinion 7.19
  parole evidence rule 7.1, 6
  statements of fact 7.19
  written agreement not whole
    contract 7.5
express words
  annexation by 33.24
extinguishment
  easements 32.52–56
extra-hazardous acts
  independent
    contractors 26.22
extrinsic aids
  interpretation 3.21

factual possession
  squatters 30.25
failure
  registration 35.37
fairness
  test for 9.25–27
family
  agreements made within 6.3
Family Division
  High Court of Justice 2.12
family intervention tenancies
    (FIT) 37.22
farm business tenancies
    37.48
fast track claims 2.5
fatal accidents
  damages 27.11

fault
  establishing 15.11
  private nuisance 23.12
fax
  acceptance by 5.17
fee simple
  absolute in possession 28.33
  easements 32.42
feudalism 28.31
fidelity
  duty of 7.31
fiduciary duties
  agent 14.15
fiduciary relationships
  contracts 12.55–56
financial contribution
  concurrent ownership
    (co-ownership) 31.13–14
fire
  statutory authority 24.15–16
  strict liability 24.15–17
first registration
  subsequent dealings
    distinguished 35.21
fitness for purpose 9.18
fixed charges 36.85
fixed-term leases 36.4, 36.13
fixtures 28.10
  added by tenant 28.13
  chattels becoming 28.11
  chattels distinguished 28.12
  right to 36.54
flagstone
  danger from 23.25
flats
  long residential
    tenancies 37.15
flexibility
  leases 36.26
floors
  boundaries 28.23
'follow the trail' 17.9
force
  easements without 32.44
foreclosure
  mortgages 34.36–38
foreseeability 12.34, 16.10–11
  animals 25.3
  damage 18.15–19
  frustration 10.13
  private nuisance 23.15
  psychiatric injury 16.28
foreseeability test
  remoteness 18.15
forfeiture
  breach of covenant 36.63–66
  breach of repair
    covenants 36.67
  leases 36.91
  non-payment of rent 36.70

form
  contract 4.3–9
four unities
  joint tenancy 31.6
  tenancy in common 31.8
four-year rule
  enforcement
    planning control 39.54
fraudulent misrepresentation
    12.19, 12.23, 12.31,
    12.50
  inducement 12.29
freehold
  acquiring 37.14–15
  estate in commonhold
    land 28.34
  fee simple absolute in
    possession 28.33
  restrictive covenants 33.3
  transfer 29.1, 30.2
frequency
  contract terms 7.11
frustration
  award for valuable benefit
    obtained 10.19–20
  change of
    circumstances 10.2–10
  contract discharged
    by 10.1–23
  death 10.6
  destruction 10.4
  effect 10.15
  express provision for 10.12
  fault of party 10.14
  foreseen and foreseeable
    events 10.13
  fundamental change of
    circumstances 10.5
  illegality 10.8
  leases 36.97
  limits 10.11
  money paid following 10.18
  money paid or payable
    before 10.16–17
  personal incapacity 10.7
  requirements for 10.1
  scope of doctrine 10.1–10
  statutory
    provisions 10.21–23
  unavailability 10.3
full planning applications
    39.22
fundamental change of
    circumstances
  frustration 10.5
further advances
  mortgages 34.43
further assignment 36.75
future facts
  express terms 7.19

good faith 9.28
grant
  planning
    permission 39.31–33
grants
  easements 32.26
gratuitous licences 28.41
ground rent 36.55
guard dogs 25.7
'guilty' conduct
  causation 18.9

habitation
  fitness for 7.28
harassment
  residential tenancies
    37.23
headings
  intrinsic aid to interpretation
    of Acts of Parliament
    3.20
hedges
  boundaries 28.23–24
Hedley Byrne doctrine
  16.18–20
hierarchy
  court system 3.35–42
High Court judges 3.40
High Court of Justice 2.8–13
  divisions of 2.8
highways
  boundaries 28.25
  independent
    contractors 26.21
  public nuisance 23.25
  statutory duty 23.25
hire
  sale of goods 7.26
hire purchase
  liability for breach of
    obligations arising
    from 9.17
  sale of goods 7.26
horizontal direct effect
  EU law 3.49
House of Lords
  position in court system
    hierarchy 3.37
  Supreme Court replaces 2.17
houses
  long residential
    tenancies 37.14
  Housing Act tenancies 37.4
human rights 15.12
  impact of Human Rights
    Act 3.25–26
  planning and 38.4
  statutory interpretation 3.27
human rights
  legislation 3.24–31

declaration of
  incompatibility 3.28
  unlawful actions 3.29
hypersensitivity
  strict liability 24.11

illegality
  contract 4.20
  frustration 10.8
immunity 16.27
  advocates 16.26
  judges and other decision-
    makers 16.25
implication
  annexation by 33.25
  concurrent ownership
    (co-ownership) by
    31.12–5
implied agreement
  appointment of agent by 14.5
implied authority
  course of employment 26.10
implied consent 19.5
implied easements 32.27–33
implied grants
  easements 32.28
implied obligations
  repairs 36.46
implied ownership
  prior claim to
    possession 34.24
implied periodic tenancy 30.4
implied reservations
  easements 32.32
implied restriction
  mortgagee's right to
    possession 34.21
implied terms 7.22–33
  building contracts 7.31
  by courts 7.29–33
  by custom or usage 7.23–24
  by statute 7.25–28
  contract 7.2
  contracts of
    employment 7.31
  giving effect to parties'
    imputed intentions 7.32
  leases 7.28, 7.31
  necessary incident of type of
    contract 7.30–31
  reasonable care and skill 7.27
  sale of goods 7.26
  supply of services 7.27
  tenancy agreements 7.31
  time 7.27
  transfer of property 7.26
implied trusts
  interests in land 30.8
inability to restore parties to
  original position

bar to rescission 12.19
incapacitation
  repudiatory breach 8.19
inclusionary effect
  assumption of
    responsibility 11.24
incompatibility
  human rights legislation 3.28
inconsistent undertakings
  exemption clauses 9.8
inconvenience
  damages for 11.5
indemnity
  agents 14.19
  alterations to Land
    Register 35.44
  cannot be awarded if
    rescission barred 12.40
  misrepresentation 12.39–40
indemnity covenants 33.7
independent contractors
  collateral negligence 26.24
  extra-hazardous acts 26.22
  general principle 26.16
  non-delegable duties 26.17
  occupiers' liability 21.16
  operations on highway 26.21
  statutory duties 26.18
  strict liability 26.20
  vicarious liability 26.16–24
  withdrawal of support 26.19
inducement
  misrepresentation 12.14–15,
    12.29
inequitable for promisor to
  resile
    requirement for promissory
    estoppel 6.22
inference
  negligence 17.18
informal acquisition
  rights to land 30.1–36
informal arrangements
  adverse possession 30.19–21
  doctrine of benefit and
    burden 30.18
  interest in land 30.7–18
informal hearings
  planning appeals 39.37
informal leases 30.3–5
informal mortgages 34.4
informed consent 19.3
injunction *quia timet* 27.17
injunctions 11.46–51
  breach of repair
    covenants 36.67
  contract of
    employment 11.50
  damages in lieu of 27.18
  definition 27.16

limitation period 27.15
planning control 39.66
private nuisance 23.21
restrictive covenants 33.30
specific performance
    contrasted 11.51
trespass to land 22.8
types granted in contract
    cases 11.45
types of 27.17
injured parties
    breach of contract 8.10–14
    discharged from contractual
        obligations 8.11
    entitled to refuse
        payment 8.12
    recovery of money by 8.13
injury
    likelihood of 17.11
    restrictive covenants 33.41
    statutory duty 20.5
'innocent' conduct
    causation 18.8
innocent
        misrepresentation 12.35
inquiry
    occupation 35.26
instalment mortgages
    problem of 34.26
instalments
    payment by 6.18
instantaneous communication
    acceptance 5.17
insurance 16.7
    leases 36.61
    mortgages 34.40
insurance contracts
    duty of disclosure 12.54
    UCTA not applicable 9.14
intended easements 32.30,
        32.33
intention
    essential element of
        contract 4.1
    implied terms giving effect to
        parties' imputed 7.32
    misrepresentation 12.13
    Parliament 20.2–3
    title to land 30.26
    to be legally bound 6.2–4
intentional wrongdoing
    course of employment 26.14
interest
    unity of 31.6
interests in land
    acquiring greater 31.18
    acquisition of 29.1–38
    constructive trusts 30.10
    creating 29.11–13, 30.2
    enforceability 35.1–44

background 35.2–13
bona fide purchaser
    of legal estate for
    value 35.5
doctrine of notice
    35.6–7
equitable interests 35.5
legal rights 35.3
pre-1926 rules 35.2–7
solutions adopted in 1925
    35.8
unregistered land 35.11–13
implied trusts 30.8
informal
        arrangements 30.7–18
    proprietary estoppel 30.11
    requiring protection by entry
        on register 35.33–37
    resulting trust 30.9
    third party rights 28.36
    UCTA not applicable 9.14
interference 23.3
    degree of 23.6
    sensitivity 23.7
    unlawfulness 23.5
    use and enjoyment 23.4
interim continuation
    business tenancies 37.34
interim rent
    business tenancies 37.35
interlocutory injunction 27.17
intermediate terms
    breach of 8.24–25
international conventions
    acts giving effect to 3.23
Internet sales
    acceptance 5.18
interpretation
    Acts of Parliament 3.10
    aids to 2.20–21
    EU law 3.54
    exemption clauses 9.1–3
intervening causes
    damage 18.6–13
intrinsic aids
    interpretation 3.20
introductory
        tenancies 37.19–20
intrusion
    trespass to land 22.3
invalidating factors
    express terms 7.4
invitation to treat
    advertisements 5.6
    circulars 5.6
    offer distinguished 5.4
    self-service shops 5.5
    tenders 5.8
    window displays
        distinguished 5.5

invitation to verify
    representation 7.18
Irish courts
    persuasive precedents 3.45

joint possession
    easements 32.11
joint tenancy 31.4–6
    acquiring greater interest in
        land 31.18
    assumption of 31.11
    conversion to tenancy in
        common 31.17–22
    disposition of equitable
        interest 31.19
    four unities 31.6
    mutual agreement to
        sever 31.20
    right of survivorship 31.5
    severance 31.17
    severance in course of
        dealings 31.22
    trusts of land 31.31
judges 16.25
    High Court 3.40
judicial classification
    condition 8.22
Judicial Committee of the Privy
        Council 3.45
judicial immunity 16.25
judicial precedent
    application 3.44–45
    Convention rights and 3.43
    as extrinsic aid to interpre-
        tation of Acts of
        Parliament 3.21
    as source of English
        law 3.32–45
judicial process 16.25–27
judicial review 2.11
    Queen's Bench Division 2.11

land
    actions for recovery of 2.3
    artificial things brought
        onto 28.8–10
    chattels fixed to 28.11
    Crown 28.30
    demarcating physical
        extent 28.21–28
    development 39.1–68
    dominant and servient
        piece of 32.4
    fixtures 28.10
    general definition 28.6
    legal definition 28.5
    legal and equitable rights
        to 28.37
    ownership and use
        28.1–44

land (*cont.*)
  personal rights to
    use 28.40–44
  physical extent of
    ownership 28.7
  private rights to enter, use,
    occupy or own 28.2
  proprietary interests 28.3
  proprietary rights 28.2
  rights with reference to 35.24
  scope of possession 22.2
  strict liability 24.4
  things growing on 28.14
Land Charges Act 1972
  pertaining to unregistered
    land 35.12–13
land law
  complexity 28.4
  scope 28.1
Land Register
  alterations 35.38–43
    indemnity 35.44
    limits on right to 35.42
  definition 29.14
  exceptions 35.41
  interests in land requiring
    protection by entry on
    35.33–37
  mistake 35.39
  notice entered in 35.35
  removal of superfluous
    entries 35.42
  search procedure 35.36
  updating 35.40
Land Registration Act 2002
  operation of Sched.3
    35.28–32
Land Registry 28.22, 29.1
landlord
  occupation by 37.38
  private nuisance 23.17
  redevelopment by 37.37
  release on assignment of
    reversion 36.83
  termination of business
    tenancy by 37.31
landlord covenants 36.34–36
landlord and tenant
  covenants where there is no
    relationship 33.2–3
  development of law on 37.1
  law relating to 36.1–99
  statutory protection 37.1–48
Landlord and Tenant Act 1954
  termination of business
    tenancies under
    37.30–32
landlord's liability
  defective property 21.30
  repairs 21.30

landlord's obligations
  repairs 36.44–46
landowner's rights 32.14–22
  airspace 28.16
  limitations on physical extent
    of 28.15
  minerals 28.17
  things found on or under
    land 28.18
  water 28.20
  wild animals 28.19
language
  contract terms 9.25
lapse of time
  bar to rescission 12.19
  termination of offer 5.28
latent damage
  limitation period 27.23
latent defects
  disclosure 29.30
law
  sources of 1.4
Law Commission
  proposals on concurrent
    ownership
    (co-ownership) 31.15
  reports of as extrinsic aid to
    interpretation of Acts of
    Parliament 3.21
Law of Property Act 1925
  annexation under 33.26
lawful use
  development 39.56–58
lawful visitors
  assumption of risk 21.17
  children 21.13
  duty of care 21.1–3
  entry as of right 21.9
  exclusion of liability by
    contract 21.2
  exclusion of liability by
    notice 21.3
  independent
    contractors 21.16
  limited permission 21.8
  occupiers' liability 21.1–11
  rights of way 21.10
  specialists 21.14
  trespasser distinguished 21.7
  visitors under contract 21.11
  warnings 21.15
leasehold 28.35, 36.1–99
  characteristics of 36.2–11
  exclusive possession 36.8–11
leases
  adverse possession 30.33–36
  assignment 36.28–31,
    36.74–77
  assignment of
    reversion 36.76–77

authorised guarantee
  agreements 36.81–82
breach of covenant 36.62–70
business tenancies
  new tenancy 37.44
certainty of term 36.3
concurrent leases 36.18
contract terms 36.25
covenants 13.14, 36.27–32
  disposition 36.28–32
creating 30.2
disclaimer 36.99
drafting language 36.25
ending 36.90–99
enforceability of covenants
  by and against assignees
  36.71–89
  leases entered into on or
    after 1 January 1996
    36.78–86
  'old' leases 36.72–77
enlargement 36.96
expiry 36.94
fixed-term leases 36.4, 36.13
flexibility 36.26
forfeiture 36.91
frustration 36.97
implied repairing
  obligations 36.41–43
implied terms 7.28, 7.31
informal 30.3–5
insurance 36.61
landlord covenants 36.34–36
landlord's
  obligations 36.44–46
licence distinguished 36.9
for life 36.6
long leases 37.1
merger 36.93
negotiations 36.21–26
  commercial
    premises 36.24
  existing leases 36.23
  new leases 36.22
  residential property 36.25
notice 36.95
outgoings 36.55–61
periodic tenancies 36.5,
  36.14
perpetually renewable 36.7
release of landlord on
  reversion 36.83
release of tenant on
  assignment 36.80
repudiation 36.98
reversionary leases 36.19
rights and obligations
  under 36.20–26
surrender 36.92
tenancy at sufferance 36.16

tenancy at will 36.15
tenancy by estoppel 36.17
tenant covenants 36.37
tenants' obligations 36.41–43
transfer of 29.1
use and enjoyment 36.33–37
user covenants 36.36–39
leasing
  mortgages 34.39
legal identity 4.12
legal lease
  equitable lease
    distinguished 30.5
legal mortgages 34.4
legal profession
  professional liability 16.21
legal relations
  intention to create 6.2–4
legal rights
  damage 18.13
  excluding or limiting 9.28
legal status
  companies 4.11
legislation 3.1–2
  common law
    distinguished 1.4
  definition 1.4
  drafting errors 3.15
  types of 3.1
legitimate expectations 30.16
  local planning
    authority 38.31
letter of intent
  contract 5.38
liability see also civil liability;
    contractors' liability;
    contractual liability;
    landlords' liability;
    occupiers'
liability; strict liability; tortious
    liability; vendor's
    liability; vicarious
    liability
  animals 25.1–12
  avoidance of arising from
    sale of goods 9.16–20
  avoidance of arising from
    supply of goods
    9.16–20
  avoidance for breach of
    contract 9.11
  avoidance for negligence 9.10
  breach of obligations arising
    from hire purchase 9.17
  can only be excluded by clear
    words 9.4
  civil 20.2
  dangerous premises
    21.1–30
  dogs 25.11

elements of 16.1, 20.4–8
  exclusion of occupiers'
    21.25
  limitation of for
    negligence 9.6
  limiting 9.28
  occupiers' liability 21.1–25
  private nuisance 23.14–17
  straying livestock 25.8–10
licence
  lease distinguished 36.9
licences
  contractual licences
    28.42–44
  Environment Agency 28.20
  gratuitous licences 28.41
  landowners 32.17
  personal rights to use
    land 28.40–44
light obstruction notices 29.5
limitation of actions 11.52,
    27.21–25, 27.29, 30.20
limitation period 27.20–25
  commencement 27.21
  extension of time 27.24
  injunctions 27.25
  latent damage 27.23
  personal injury 27.22
limitation periods
  breach of contract 11.53–54
  extending 11.54
limited liability partnerships
  capacity to contract 4.16–17
limited partnerships
  capacity to contract 4.18
limited permission
  lawful visitors 21.8
liquidated damages
  breach of contract 11.20–22
  parties' intention 11.34
listed buildings 39.45–48
  categories of listing 39.46
  listing 29.25, 39.46
  planning permission 39.48
literal construction
  Acts of Parliament 3.11–12
livestock
  dogs worrying 25.11–12
  liability for straying
    25.8–10
  protection of 25.12
  strict liability 25.3
local authorities
  defective property 21.27–28
  devolution of powers 39.68
  diminishing role in housing
    provision 37.17
Local Development
  Frameworks 38.23–25
  legal challenges 38.25

process of preparing and
    adopting 38.24
Local Development Orders
  planning permission 39.19
local development
    scheme 38.23
local government
  role in planning 38.11–20
Local Government
    Ombudsman
  planning 38.32
local land charges
  sale of land 29.25
local planning
    authorities 38.11–20
  identifying 38.12
  legal liabilities 38.29–32
  legitimate expectation
    38.31
  operation 38.13–20
  planning officers' power to
    bind 38.30
  role of 38.11
Localism Bill
  planning system 39.68
locality
  private nuisance 23.8
lock-out agreements 5.35
long residential
    tenancies 37.12–16
  enfranchisement 37.13–15
  flats 37.15
  houses 37.14
  right to manage 37.16
  security of tenure 37.12
long title
  intrinsic aid to
    interpretation of Acts of
    Parliament 3.20
Lord Chancellor
  development of role of 1.7
loss
  falling outside scope of law of
    tort 15.8
  reasonable contemplation
    of 11.15–20
  remoteness 11.14–20
loss of amenity
  damages 27.4
loss of chance 18.5
loss of earnings
  damages 27.8
loss of expectation of life
  damages 27.6
lost expectations 11.3–10
  difficulty of precise
    assessment 11.10
  time of assessment 11.12
lost modern grant
  easements 32.48

McGhee principle 18.4
maladministration
  planning 38.32
mandatory injunctions 11.46,
  27.17
manifest disadvantage 12.65
material change of use 39.6–8
  abandonment 39.14
  definition 39.7
  planning unit 39.15
  uses not constituting 39.8
material considerations
  factors constituting 39.28
  planning
    permission 39.28–29
'matrimonial' property
  trusts of land 31.39
measure of damages
  damage to property 27.12
measured duty of care 23.16
medical expenses
  damages 27.7
mental elements
  tort and 15.9
mental incapacity
  termination of agency by
    14.25
mere puffs
  misrepresentation of fact
    distinguished 12.7
mere representation 12.4–5
  remedies 12.16–40
merger
  leases 36.93
minerals
  landowner's rights 28.17
mischief rule 3.13
misrepresentation 12.1–56
  active misrepresentation
    12.3–50
  by word or conduct 12.5
  compensation for 37.40
  contract for sale of
    land 29.30
  contributory
    negligence 12.30
  damages for 12.21–38
  deceit 12.25–31
  duty of disclosure 12.53–56
  entire agreement
    clause 12.47–48
  estate agents 12.46, 49
  exemption clauses 9.7
  of fact 12.6–11
  indemnity 12.39–40
  inducement 12.14–15, 12.29
  intentional 12.13
  mistake 12.1
  non-disclosure 12.51–56
  requirements for 12.12

rescission 12.17–20
silence 12.11, 12.51–52
statutory
  provisions 12.43–50
types of 12.22
mistake
  conditions for voiding
    contract for 12.1
  Land Register 35.39
  misrepresentation 12.1
mitigation
  damages 11.25–27
mortgaged property
  possession 34.18
mortgagee
  power to sell 34.29–32
  restrictions on claims to
    possession 34.25–27
mortgagees
  court's power to order
    sale 34.33
  duty to account strictly to
    mortgagor 34.22
  express restriction on
    mortgagee's right to
    possession 34.20
  implied restriction on
    mortgagee's right to
    possession 34.21
  remedies 34.18–27
  restriction on right to
    possession 34.19–27
mortgages 30.2, 34.1–43
  appointment of
    receiver 34.35
  creation of 34.3–4
  foreclosure 34.36–38
  further advances 34.43
  historical background 34.3
  informal mortgages 34.5
  insurance 34.40
  law relating to 34.2
  leasing 34.39
  legal 34.4
  modern 34.4–5
  personal covenants 34.34
  priorities 34.41–42
  proceeds of sale 34.32
  provision for sale 34.29–32
  purpose of 34.1
  redemption
    commercial arrangements
      for 34.6
    legal date of 34.7
    oppressive terms 34.11–13
    restraint of trade 34.14
    statutory
      regulation 34.15–17
    unconscionable
      terms 34.11–13

mortgagors
  duty to obtain best
    price 34.31
  mortgagee's duty to account
    strictly to 34.22
  right to redeem 34.6–17
motive 15.10
multi-track claims 2.6
multiple causes
  damage 18.6
multiple occupation
  occupiers' liability 21.5
multiple tortfeasors
  damages 27.14–15
  contribution between
    tortfeasors 27.15
mutual agreement to sever
  joint tenancy 31.21
mutual discharge
  contract 6.26

National Parks
  planning 38.12
natural rights
  landowners 32.14
negative covenants 13.14
negative easements 32.10
negative obligations 36.72
negative stipulations 11.48–49
negative terms
  damages 11.7
negligence
  age 17.5
  animals 25.3
  avoidance of liability for 9.10
  breach of duty 17.1–18
  burden of proof 17.15–18
  children 17.5
  collateral negligence 26.24
  contributory 20.8
  contributory
    negligence 19.6–9
  damage 18.1–20
  defences 19.1–9
    assumption of risk 19.2–5
    consent 19.2–5
  definition 16.1
  duty of care 16.1–28
  elderly 17.5
  establishing 17.15
  inference 17.18
  limitation of liability for 9.6
  physical defects 17.4
  professional liability 16.21
  public authorities 16.22–24
  res ipsa loquitur 17.16–17
  surveyors 17.9
  tort and 15.9
  valuers 17.9
negligent advice 16.17

negligent misrepresentation
  common law 12.32–34
  statutory provisions 12.24
negligent statements
  16.17–21
negligent words 16.17
negotiation
  leases 36.21–26
    commercial
      premises 36.24
    existing leases 36.23
    new leases 36.22
    residential property 36.25
  sale of land 29.23
neighbourhoods
  devolution of powers 39.68
new tenancy
  business tenancies 37.41–45
    duration 37.43
    premises 37.42
    rent 37.45
    terms of lease 37.44
nominal damages 27.2
non-compliance
  contract for sale of land
    29.9
non-dangerous species 25.6
non-delegable duties
  independent
    contractors 26.17
non-derogation from
  grant 32.18, 36.35
non-disclosure
  misrepresentation 12.51–56
non-natural use
  strict liability 24.8
notice
  contract terms 7.10
  doctrine of 35.6–7
  entered in Land
    Register 35.35
  exceptions to 7.11
  exclusion of liability by 21.3
  leases 36.95
  must be contained in
    contractual document
    7.12
  reasonable 7.13
  restrictive covenants 33.15
nuisance 23.1–26 see also
    private nuisance; public
    nuisance
  scope 23.1
  types of 23.1

obey instructions
  agent's duty to 14.13
obiter dictum 3.34
objective standard
  reasonableness 17.3

obsolescence
  restrictive covenants 33.39
occupation
  actual 35.25
  by landlord 37.38
  inquiry 35.26
  rights of persons in
    actual 35.29
  trusts of land 31.42
occupation as licensee
  adverse possession 30.27
occupier
  common law position of 21.4
  private nuisance 23.15
occupiers' liability 21.1–25
  assumption of risk 21.17
  children 21.13
  conditions 21.21
  defences 21.24
  duty of care 21.12–7, 21.22
  entry as of right 21.9
  exclusion of liability 21.25
  independent
    contractors 21.16
  injury suffered on access
    land 21.23
  lawful visitors 21.1–11
  multiple occupation 21.5
  premises 21.6
  rights of way 21.10
  scope 21.20
  specialists 21.14
  statutory
    provisions 21.19–25
  trespassers 21.18–25
  visitors 21.7
  warnings 21.15
occupying tenant
  requirement for in business
    tenancies 37.26
offer
  advertisements 5.6
  auctions 5.7
  bids 5.7
  definition 5.3
  effect of counter-offer 5.11
  general requirement of 5.2
  invitation to treat
    distinguished 5.4
  termination 5.24–29
officers of the council
  role in planning 38.16
'old' leases
  enforceability of cov-
    enants by and against
    assignees 36.72–77
omissions
  duty of care 16.7–8
'opening the floodgates'
  economic loss 16.12

operational
  development 39.3–5
  building operations 39.4–5
opinion
  express terms 7.19
oppressive terms
  mortgages
    redemption 34.11–13
options
  contract for sale of land 29.7
oral acceptance 5.17
order of events
  private nuisance 23.11
order forms
  contract terms 7.9
Orders in Council 3.5–6
original civil jurisdiction
  Queen's Bench Division 2.11
original jurisdiction
  Chancery Division 2.9
ostensible authority
  agents 14.30–34
  course of employment 26.11
'out of pocket rule' 12.24, 26–28
outgoings
  leases 36.55–61
outline planning
  applications 39.22
over-flight
  trespass to land 22.2
overreaching
  concurrent ownership
    (co-ownership) 31.26
overriding interests 35.18,
    35.20–32
overriding leases 36.86
ownership 15.7
  land 28.3
  physical extent of land 28.7
  sale of goods 9.19
ownership interests in land
  nature of 28.30

pain and suffering
  damages 27.5
Parliament
  intention 20.2–3
parliamentary debates
  extrinsic aid to inter-
    pretation of Acts of
    Parliament 3.21
parole evidence rule 7.1, 7.6
part and parcel of land
  items becoming 28.9
part payment of debts
  consideration 6.18–20
  position in equity 6.20
partial performance 8.12
parties
  to agreements 6.2

parties' intention
  liquidated damages or
    penalty 11.34
parties' rights
  significant imbalance
    to 9.27–28
partnerships
  capacity to contract 4.18–19
  UCTA not applicable to
    contracts relating to 9.14
party structures 28.28
past consideration 6.9–10
payments
  after frustration 10.18
  in anticipation of concluding
    contract 5.38
  before frustration 10.16–17
  discharge of contract by 8.3
  injured parties entitled to
    refuse 8.12
  recovery 11.35
  retaining 9.28
  tender of 8.4
penalties
  liquidated damages 11.34
penalty clauses 11.32–33
performance 8.1–31
  discharge by 8.2
  duty imposed by law 6.13–14
  existing contractual
    duty owed to other
    party 6.15–16
  existing contractual
    duty owed to third
    parties 6.17
  time for 8.26–31
periodic tenancies 30.5, 36.5,
  36.14
  creation 29.12
  implied 30.4
  secure tenancy
    becomes 37.18
permission
  easements without 32.46
  limited 21.8
permissive waste 36.43
permitted development
  planning permission 39.18
perpetually renewable
  leases 36.7
personal covenants 34.34
personal incapacity
  frustration 10.7
personal injury
  damages 27.3–9
  excluding liability for 9.10
  limitation period 27.22
  suffered on access land 21.23
personal security
  protection of 15.7

persuasive precedents 3.45
physical damage 16.17–20
physical defects
  negligence 17.4
planning
  appeals to Secretary of
    State 38.10
  human rights and 38.4
  Local Development
    Frameworks 38.23–25
  Local Government
    Ombudsman 38.32
  local planning
    authority 38.11–20
  maladministration 38.32
  National Parks 38.12
  policy making 38.9
  procedural guidance 38.6
  public policy 38.6
  regional planning 38.22
  restrictive covenants 33.32
  role of councillors 28.14–15
  role of officers of the
    council 38.16
  secondary legislation 38.8
  statutory controls 38.8
  statutory instrument 38.8
  subordinate legislation 38.5
planning appeals 39.34–41
  award of costs 39.41
  challenging inspector's
    decision 39.42
  correction of errors 39.40
  determined by planning
    inspectors 39.35
  informal hearings 39.37
  inspector's decision 39.39–40
  public inquiry 39.38
  statutory review 39.42
  written representations 39.36
planning contravention
  notice 39.60
planning control
  breach of condition
    notice 39.63
  enforcement 39.52–55
    four-year rule 39.54
    ten-year rule 39.55
    time limits 39.53
  enforcement notice 39.61
    appeals against 39.62
  enforcement
    powers 39.59–67
  injunctions 39.66
  legislative framework 38.3–6
  planning contravention
    notice 39.60
  rights of entry 39.67
  stop notices 39.64
  temporary stop notices 39.65

planning inspectors
  planning appeals 39.35
planning institutions 38.7–20
planning law
  restrictive covenants 33.31
planning obligations
  planning permission 39.32
planning officers 38.17–20
  power to bind local planning
    authority 38.30
planning permission
  appeals to Secretary of State
    39.34–41
  applications 39.21–24
  Article 4 directions 39.20
  community infrastructure
    levy 39.33
  conditions 39.31
  conservation areas 39.49–51
  decisions 39.25–27, 39.30
  determination time
    periods 39.36
  grant of 39.31–33
  listed buildings 39.48
  Local Development
    Orders 39.19
  material
    considerations 39.28–29
  need for 39.17–27
  permitted development
    39.18
  planning obligations 39.32
  precedent 39.29
  revocations of 29.25
Planning Policy Guidance
  Notes (PPGs) 38.6
Planning Policy Statements
  (PPSs) 38.6
planning system 38.1–32
  Localism Bill 39.68
  origins 38.2
planning unit
  material change of use 39.15
policy making
  planning 38.9
positive covenants
  chain of indemnity
    covenants 33.7
  common law 33.17
  commonhold 33.5
  doctrine of benefit and
    burden 33.10
  enforcement 33.6–10
  estate rentcharges 33.9
  intention that benefit should
    run 33.19
  land to benefited should be
    identifiable 33.20
  must touch and concern land
    of covenantee 33.18

restrictive covenants 33.4–10
rights of entry 33.8
successor to acquire legal
    estate 33.21
positive obligations 36.72
possession
    court's discretion 34.27
    existence of prior claim
        to 34.23–24
    express restriction on
        mortgagee's right
        to 34.20
    implied restriction on
        mortgagee's right to
        34.21
    mortgaged property 34.18
    mortgagee's duty to
        account strictly to
        mortgagor 34.22
    non-payment of rent 36.70
    power of sale 34.29–32
    problem of instalment
        mortgages 34.26
    restriction on mortgagee's
        right to 34.19–27
    restrictions on claims
        to 34.25–27
    sale 34.28–33
    trespass to land 22.4
    unity of 31.6
possession of goods 15.7
possession of land 15.7
    recovering 30.20
    scope 22.2
postal acceptance 5.21–22
pre-contractual
        representation 7.16
pre-emption rights
    contract for sale of land 29.7
precautions
    cost of 17.14
precedent
    planning permission 39.29
premises
    business tenancies 37.42
    definition 21.6
prescription
    acquisition of rights of
        light 32.55
    adverse possession and 32.11
    easements 32.40–51
        common law 32.47
        lost modern grant 32.48
        methods of 32.47–51
        statutory
            requirements 32.49–51
preservation of life or
        property 22.5
presumed undue
        influence 12.62–65

types of 12.62–65
presumptions
    acceptance 5.20
    boundaries 28.23–26
    intentions of Parliament 3.19
price
    duty of mortgagor to obtain
        best possible 34.31
primary victims 16.28
principal
    agent and 14.2–27
    third parties and 14.28–38
    where agent is in
        reality 14.42
priorities
    mortgages 34.41–42
private nuisance 23.2–12
    abatement 23.22
    assumption of risk 23.19
    continuity 23.9
    contributory
        negligence 23.19
    created by trespasser 23.16
    creator 23.14
    damages 23.20
    defences 23.18–19
    defendant's state of
        mind 23.12
    fault 23.12
    foreseeability 23.15
    injunctions 23.21
    interference 23.3
    landlord 23.17
    liability 23.14–17
    locality 23.8
    naturally arising 23.16
    occupier 23.15
    order of events 23.11
    public nuisance
        contrasted 23.24
    remedies 23.20–22
    repairs 23.17
    scope 23.3
    statutory authority 23.18
    utility of defendant's
        conduct 23.10
    who is protected 23.13
privity of contract 13.9–10
privity of estate 36.72
Privy Council 3.45
procedural guidance
    planning 38.6
        appeals 39.35
proceeds
    sale of mortgaged
        property 34.32
professional liability 16.21
professional status
    reasonableness 17.7–9
profits à pendre 32.19–21, 35.30

prohibitions
    course of
        employment 26.12–13
prohibitory injunctions 11.46,
    27.17
promise
    consideration for 6.5
    performance of duty imposed
        by law 6.13–14
    performance of existing
        contractual duty owed
        to other party 6.15–16
promisor
    defences available to 13.7–8
promissory estoppel 6.21–24,
    6.27
    definition 6.21
    effect of 6.23
    requirements for 6.22
    shield not sword 6.24
proof see also burden of proof
    causation 18.4
Property Register 29.14
proposals map
    development plan
        documents 38.23
proprietary estoppel 30.11–18
    acts in reliance 30.13
    constructive trusts 30.17
    conveyancing 30.16
    detriment 30.14
    doctrine of 30.11
    effects of doctrine 30.15–16
    expectation 30.12
proprietary interests in
        land 28.3
proprietary rights
    interests in land 28.2,
        35.1–44
    legal nature of 28.29
Proprietorship Register 29.14
    restrictions entered in 35.34
protected class
    statutory duty 20.4
protection
    duty of 16.9
proving title
    contract for sale of
        land 29.37
proximity
    psychiatric injury 16.28
psychiatric injury 16.28
public authorities
    assumption of
        responsibility 16.24
    human rights and 15.12
    negligence 16.23–24
    statutory duties 16.22
    unlawful actions under human
        rights legislation 3.29

public inquiry
planning appeals 39.38
public interest
planning system 38.1
public liability insurance 16.7
public nuisance 23.23–6
animals 25.2
damages 23.26
highways 23.25
private nuisance
contrasted 23.24
scope 23.23
public policy
part payment of debts 6.19
planning 38.6
public rights
landowners 32.16
public sector
tenancies 37.17–22
demoted tenancies 37.21
family intervention
tenancies 37.22
introductory
tenancies 37.19–20
secure tenancies 37.18
security of tenure 37.17
punctuation
intrinsic aid to interpretation
of Acts of Parliament
3.20
punitive damages 27.2
purchasers
duty of care 21.26–9
'pure' economic loss 16.13
purposive construction
Acts of Parliament 3.13–15

quantum meruit 11.41–42, 14.17
quasi-easement 32.7
Queen's Bench Division
appellate civil
jurisdiction 2.11
High Court of
Justice 2.10–11
judicial review
jurisdiction 2.11
original civil
jurisdiction 2.11
quiet enjoyment 36.34

ratification
agents 14.6–10
doctrine of 14.6
effects of 14.7
how to ratify 14.10
what can be ratified 14.9
who can ratify 14.8
ratio decidendi 3.33
reasonable care and skill
implied terms 7.27

reasonable contemplation
loss 11.15–20
reasonable contemplation
test 11.22–23
'reasonable man' 17.2
reasonable use of land
restrictive
covenants 33.42–43
reasonableness 17.1–9
experience of others 17.6
professional status 17.7–9
requirement for 9.10, 9.15,
9.25
under UCTA 9.20
risk 17.10–14
test for 9.28
reasonableness test
assignment 36.30–31
rebuttal
agreements 6.4
receiver
mortgages 34.35
reciprocal terms
contracts of
employment 7.31
recklessness
tort and 15.9
recovery
money by injured parties
8.13
money paid before
frustration 10.16
payment 11.13
possession of land 30.20
recovery of land
actions for 2.3
redemption
equity of and equitable right
to redeem 34.8
impediments to full 34.9
mortgages
commercial arrangements
for 34.6
legal date of 34.7
restraint of trade 34.14
statutory
regulation 34.15–17
mortgagor's right to 34.6–17
oppressive or unconscionable
terms 34.11–13
provisions conferring
collateral advantages
34.13
provisions excluding 34.10
provisions postponing 34.12
redevelopment
by landlord 37.37
reduced lifespan
damages 27.6
regional planning 38.22

regional spatial strategies 38.22
registered charges 35.19
priority 34.42
registered disposition 35.19
registered land
claims to 30.22–29
classification of rights to
35.15
registration 35.14
registered leases
adverse possession against
tenants 30.35
Registrar of Companies 4.14
registration
contract for sale of
land 29.38
failure to 35.37
restrictive covenants 33.15
title 28.22, 29.13–19, 35.9–10
distinction between
first registration and
subsequent dealings
35.21
effects of first 29.17
effects of 35.16–8
first registration 35.16
overriding
interests 35.18–32
registered land 35.14
rights of persons in actual
occupation 35.23–29
short legal leases 35.33
subsequent dealings 35.17
regulation
EU law 3.48
release of covenant
restrictive covenants 33.35
reliance
damages for loss of 11.8–9
requirement for promissory
estoppel 6.22
relief
breach of covenant 36.66
breach of repair
covenants 36.67
remedies 1.7, 27.1–25
account of profits from
breach 11.38–40
active misrepresentation
which have remained
mere representa-
tions 12.16–40
breach of contract 11.1–55
breach of repair
covenants 36.67
contract for sale of
land 29.31–5
damages 27.1–15
breach of contract 11.1–34
equitable relief 11.55

injunctions 11.46–51, 27.16–18
limitation of
    actions 27.20–25
mortgagees 34.18–27
non-payment of
    rent 36.68–70
private nuisance 23.20–22
quantum meruit 11.41–42
restrictive covenants 33.30
specific
    performance 11.43–45
specific restitution 27.19
trespass to land 22.7–10
remoteness 12.34
    application of contractual
        rule of 11.18–20
    consequential loss 11.11
    damage 18.14–19
    foreseeability test 18.15
    loss 11.14–20
    policy considerations 18.20
    test for 11.17
remuneration
    agent 14.17–18
    quantum meruit 14.17
renewal
    business tenancies 37.33–35
        application to court 37.33
        interim continuation 37.34
        interim rent 37.35
        new tenancy 37.41–45
        opposing 37.36–40
rent 36.55–59
    business tenancies 37.45
    remedies for non-
        payment 36.68–70
Rent Act tenancies 37.3
rent control 37.1
    residential tenancies 37.3
rent referral
    assured shorthold
        tenancies 37.7
rent review
    assured shorthold
        tenancies 37.7
    assured tenancies 37.11
rent reviews 36.56–59
    dispute resolution 36.59
    procedure for 36.57
    valuation basis 36.58
renunciation
    repudiatory breach 8.18
repair covenants
    breach of 36.67
repairs 7.28
    definition 36.49
    express obligations 36.47–52
    going beyond 36.50
    implied obligations 36.46
    landlords' liability 21.30

landlord's
    obligations 36.44–46
    method 36.52
    private nuisance 23.17
    standard of 36.51
    statutory exception 36.45
    tenants' obligations 36.41–43
repeal
    Acts of Parliament 3.4
reports
    extrinsic aid to interpretation
        of Acts of Parliament
        3.21
representation
    advertisement 12.12
    ascertaining accuracy of 7.20
    contract terms
        distinguished 7.14–15
    importance of 7.17
    invitation to verify 7.18
    pre-contractual 7.16
    when contract term 7.15
repudiation
    leases 36.98
repudiatory breach 8.8–25
    contract for sale of
        land 29.33
    damages for recovery of
        agreed sum 11.37
    option to terminate or
        affirm 8.9–17
    termination 8.10–17
    types of 8.18–25
reputation
    protection of 15.7
requisite period
    adverse possession 30.28–32
res ipsa loquitur 17.16–17
rescission
    bars to 12.19
    basic object of 12.19
    contract for sale of
        land 29.32
    courts' power to refuse or
        recognise 12.20
    damages in lieu 12.36–38
    duress or undue
        influence 12.68
    effecting 12.18
    indemnity cannot be
        awarded if barred 12.40
    misrepresentation 12.17–20
    qualification to bars to
        12.19
    restitution not required
        for 12.19
rescue cases
    damage 18.11
reservations
    easements 32.26

residential property
    leases 36.25
residential tenancies 37.2–16
    assured shorthold
        tenancies 37.5–8
    background to 37.2
    Housing Act tenancies 37.4
    regulation 37.2
    Rent Act tenancies 37.3
    rent control 37.3
    status of irremovability 37.3
    surviving spouse 37.3
residential property
    problem of long leases on 37.1
residential tenancies
    assured tenancies 37.9–11
    harassment 37.23
    information for
        tenants 37.24
    long residential
        tenancies 37.12–6
    unlawful eviction 37.23
responsibility
    assumption of 16.18–9, 16.24
restitution
    not required for
        rescission 12.19
    tort and 15.5
restraint of trade
    redemption 34.14
restrictions
    entry in Proprietorship
        Register 35.34
restrictive covenants 13.14,
        29.30, 32.15, 33.1–45
    acquisition for planning or
        statutory purposes
        33.37
    agreement 33.40
    annexation 33.23–26
    application to the Upper
        Tribunal (Lands
        Chamber) 33.38
    assignment 33.27
    change in character of
        neighbourhood 33.34
    common law 33.33
    covenantee must retain
        land capable of being
        benefited 33.13
    discharge 33.31–37
        common law 33.34–37
    equitable rules of 33.22–29
    essentially negative 33.12
    freehold 33.3
    impedes reasonable use of
        land 33.42–43
    no injury to persons
        entitled to benefit of
        restriction 33.41

restrictive covenants (*cont.*)
  no relationship of landlord
    and tenant 33.2–3
  obsolescence 33.39
  parties must intend covenant
    should run 33.14
  planning 33.32
  planning law 33.31
  positive covenants 33.4–10
  proposals for reform 33.45
  registration and notice 33.15
  release of covenant 33.35
  remedies 33.30
  requirements for 33.11
  running of benefit 33.16–29
  running of the
    burden 33.4–15
  scheme of
    development 33.28–29
  statutory provisions 33.44
  typical 33.1
  unity of ownership 33.36
resulting trusts
  interests in land 30.9
retrospective effect
  legislation 3.19
reversion
  assignment 36.76, 36.79
  release of landlord on
    assignment 36.83
reversionary leases 36.19
rewards
  acceptance 5.10
right to manage
  long residential
    tenancies 37.16
right to sell 7.25
right to sue
  limitations on undisclosed
    principal 14.37
right to vote 15.7
rights 1.7
rights of entry
  planning control 39.68
  positive covenants 33.8
rights of light
  acquisition by
    prescription 32.55
  easements 32.54–56
  extent of 32.56
rights of support
  easements 32.57
rights to land
  acquisition of 29.1–38
  classification 35.15
  informal acquisition of 30.1–36
rights of way 21.10, 22.5
  easements 32.53
  trespass to land 22.3
riparian ownership 28.20

risk 17.10–14
  cost of precautions 17.14
  degree of 11.17
  knowledge of 19.3
  likelihood of injury 17.11
  seriousness of
    consequences 17.12
  value of conduct 17.13
risk management 17.13–14
rivers
  boundaries 28.26
rules 3.16–19
  rules of interpretation 3.16
running of benefit
  restrictive
    covenants 33.16–29
running of the burden
  restrictive covenants 33.4–15
Rylands v Fletcher
  strict liability 24.2–9

sale
  exercise of power 34.30–32
  possession 34.28–33
  straying livestock 25.10
sale of goods
  auction 7.25
  avoidance of liability arising
    from 9.16–20
  breach of condition 8.23
  by sample 7.25
  conformity of goods 9.28
  contracts of hire 7.26
  corresponding to
    description 7.25
  in course of business 7.25
  hire purchase 7.26
  implied terms 7.26
  limitation on action agreed
    sum 11.36
  ownership 9.19
  right to sell 7.25
  satisfactory quality 7.25
  statutory provisions 7.25–27
  through agent 7.25
sale of land 29.22–26
  auctions 29.36
  draft contract 29.26
  enquiries 29.24
  initial negotiation 29.23
  local land charges 29.25
  searches 29.24
  supplementary
    enquiries 29.25
  trust land 31.36–37
  trusts of land 31.41
sample 9.18
  sale of goods by 7.25
satisfactory quality
  sale of goods 7.25

schedules
  intrinsic aid to inter-
    pretation of Acts of
    Parliament 3.20
scheme of development
  restrictive
    covenants 33.28–29
Scottish courts
  persuasive precedents 3.45
searches
  Land Registry 35.36
  sale of land 29.24
secondary legislation
  planning 38.8
secondary victims 16.28
secrecy
  easements without 32.45
secret profits
  agent 14.15
Secretary of State for
    Communities and Local
    Government
  role in planning 38.8–10
secure tenancies
  public sector tenancies 37.18
securities
  UCTA not applicable to
    contracts relating to 9.14
security of tenure 37.1, 37.12
  public sector tenancies 37.17
self-redress
  trespass to land 22.10
self-service shops
  invitation to treat 5.5
seller
  definition 9.24
sensitivity
  interference 23.7
service charges 36.60
servient land
  easements 32.4
  owner must be different from
    owner of dominant
    land 32.7
servient owner
  must not be involved in
    expenditure relating to
    easement 32.12
severance
  joint tenancy 31.17
sharers
  exclusive possession 36.10
shield not sword
  promissory estoppel 6.24
short business lettings 36.24
short legal leases 35.33
short title
  intrinsic aid to inter-
    pretation of Acts of
    Parliament 3.20

signatures
   contract for sale of land 29.4
silence
   does not constitute misrep-
      resentation 12.51–52
   misrepresentation 12.11
single assignment 36.74
site specific
   development plan
      documents 38.23
skill
   agent's duty to exercise 14.14
   obligation to display 17.8
small claims track 2.4
social housing
   provision 37.17
specialist courts 2.21
specialists
   occupiers' liability 21.14
specific performance 11.43–45
   breach of repair
      covenants 36.67
   contract for sale of
      land 29.35
   injunctions contrasted 11.51
   when not granted 11.44
specific restitution 27.19
squatters 30.20–22
   adverse possession 30.23–28
   factual possession 30.25
   intention 30.26
standard of care 19.7
standard form of lease for short
      business lettings 36.24
standard terms of contract 7.11
   exclusion clauses 9.2
   written 9.12
statements of fact
   express terms 7.19
statements of law
   misrepresentation of fact
      distinguished 12.10
statements of opinion
   misrepresentation of fact
      distinguished 12.8
statements as to the future
   misrepresentation of fact
      distinguished 12.9
status of irremovability 37.3
statute
   terms implied by 7.25–28
statutory duty
   breach 20.1–8
   breach by defendant 20.6
   causation 20.7
   defences 20.8
   independent
      contractors 26.18
   protected class 20.4
   public authorities 16.22

type of injury 20.5
statutory instruments 1.4, 3.6–7
   planning 38.8
statutory interpretation
   as extrinsic aid to inter-
      pretation of Acts of
      Parliament 3.21
statutory liability
   strict liability 24.18
statutory review
   planning appeals 39.42
stop notices 39.64
   temporary 39.65
strategic environmental
      assessment 38.26
strict liability 24.1–18
   accumulation 24.5
   act of God 24.12
   act of stranger 24.13
   consent of claimant 24.10
   damage 24.9
   dangerous animals 25.4
   dangerous species 25.5
   dangerous things 24.6
   default of claimant 24.11
   defences 24.10–7
   escape 24.7
   fire 24.15–7
   hypersensitivity 24.11
   independent
      contractors 26.20
   land 24.4
   livestock 25.3
   non-dangerous species 25.6
   non-natural use 24.8
   Rylands v Fletcher 24.2–9
   statutory authority 24.14
   statutory liability 24.18
   tort and 15.9
sub-agents 14.16, 14.20
sub-bailments 13.16
sub-contractors
   defective property 21.28
sub-tenants
   covenants 36.89
'subject to contract'
   agreements 5.34–35
subjective duty of care 23.16
subletting
   covenants restricting
      36.32
subordinate legislation 1.4, 3.5
   planning 38.5
subsequent dealings
   first registration
      distinguished 35.21
successorship
   periodic tenancies 37.18
sui generis uses 39.12
superfluous entries

removal from Land
      Register 35.42
supplementary enquiries
   sale of land 29.25
supplier
   definition 9.24
supply of goods
   avoidance of liability arising
      from 9.16–20
supply of services
   implied terms 7.27
Supreme Court
   jurisdiction 2.18
   position in court system
      hierarchy 3.37
   replaces House of Lords 2.17
sureties
   covenants 36.88
surrender
   leases 36.92
surveyors
   negligence 17.9
surviving spouse
   residential tenancies 37.3
survivorship
   joint tenancy 31.5
   tenancy in common 31.7
sustainable development 38.27

Technology and Construction
      Court 2.21
telephone
   acceptance by 5.17
temporary stop notices 39.65
tenancies
   public sector 37.17–22
   residential 37.2–16
   types of 36.12–19
tenancy agreements
   implied terms 7.31
tenancy at sufferance 36.16
tenancy at will 36.15
tenancy by estoppel 36.17
tenancy in common 31.7–8
   conversion of joint tenancy
      to 31.17–21
   four unities 31.8
   no right of survivorship 31.7
   trusts of land 31.30
tenancy deposit schemes
   assured shorthold
      tenancies 37.8
tenant covenants 36.37
tenants
   adverse possession
      against 30.33–35
      registered leases 30.35
   adverse possession by 30.36
   fixtures added by 28.13
   information for 37.24

tenants (*cont.*)
  release on assignment of
    lease 36.80
  right to
    enfranchisement 37.1
  termination of business
    tenancy by 37.32
tenants' obligations
  repairs 36.41–43
tenders
  acceptance 5.15
  by act 8.5
  invitation to treat 5.8
  payment 8.4
tenure
  definition 28.31
term
  certainty of in
    leaseholds 36.3
termination
  agency 14.21–27
    effects of 14.27
  business tenancies under
    Landlord and Tenant
    Act 1954 37.30–32
  by affirmation 8.16–17
  communication of 5.26
  contract 8.10–17
  contract for sale of
    land 29.33
  death 4.29
  does not necessarily
    extinguish contract 8.15
  lapse of time 5.28
  offer 5.24–29
  position of defaulting party
    after 8.14
  time taking effect 5.26
  unilateral contracts 5.27
third parties
  action in tort 13.11
  agents and 14.39–46
  assignment of contractual
    rights to 13.9
  collateral contracts 13.10
  conduct of 18.8–9
  contractual duty owed to 6.17
  contractual
    obligations 13.14–16
  contractual rights 13.2–13
  damage caused by 16.10–11
  defences available to
    promisor 13.7–8
  discharge 13.6
  election 14.38
  enforcement of contract by
    13.12
  principal and 14.28–38
  protection in respect of
    exemption clauses 13.4–5

right to enforce contractual
    terms 13.3
  rights against
    agents 14.44–46
  statutory rights 13.2–9
  undisclosed principal 14.37
  undue influence by 12.66
  variation 13.6
third party rights 13.1–16
  easements 32.1–57
  interests in land 28.36
tickets
  contract terms 7.9
time
  implied terms 7.27
  performance 8.28–31
  termination of offer 5.26
  unity of 31.6
time of assessment
  lost expectation 11.12
time limits
  enforcement
    planning control 39.53
time penalty clauses 6.16
title
  registration 35.9–10
    distinction between first
      registration and
      subsequent dealings
      35.21
    effects of 35.16–18
    first registration 35.16
    overriding interests 35.18
    rights of persons in actual
      occupation 35.23–29
    short legal leases 35.33
    subsequent dealings 35.17
  unity of 31.6
title plan 29.14
title to land
  adverse possession 30.21–23
  discontinuance or
    dispossession 30.24
  dispositions 29.18–9
  effects of first
    registration 29.17
  factual possession 30.25
  first registration 29.15
  intention 30.26
  proving 29.37
  registration 28.22, 29.13–19
  statutory
    provisions 30.22–23
tort
  actions in 2.3
  aims and functions of law of
    15.1
  breach of trust and 15.6
  contract and 15.4
  crime and 15.3

definition 15.2
  law of 15.1–12
  mental elements 15.9
  negligence 15.9
  recklessness 15.9
  relationship with
    contract 16.16
  restitution and 15.5
  scope of law of 15.7–11
  strict liability 15.9
tortious liability
  agents 14.46
touching and
    concerning 36.72–73
trade usage 14.41
transfer
  contract for sale of
    land 29.37–38
transfer of property 7.26
transferred loss 16.14
transition period
  development plans 38.21
transposition
  EU law 3.50
trespass 15.8, 30.20
trespass to land 22.1–10
  access to neighbouring
    land 22.6
  common form 22.3
  defences 22.5
  intrusion 22.3
  possession 22.4
  remedies 22.7–10
  rights of way 22.3
  scope 22.2
trespassers 21.18–25
  injured by animals 25.7
  lawful visitor
    distinguished 21.7
  private nuisance 23.16
tribunals 2.22–24
  historical background 2.22
  jurisdiction 2.23
  position in court system
    hierarchy 3.41
trust
  concept of 28.39
  equitable interest in
    land 29.21
trust land
  sale of 31.36–37
trust for sale
  concurrent ownership
    (co-ownership) 31.25
  disadvantages of 31.27
trustees
  trusts of land 31.33–34
trustees' powers and duties
  trusts of land 31.33
    restrictions 31.34

trusts of land 31.28–42
  beneficiaries 31.35
  dispute resolution 31.40
  disputes over 31.38–42
  imposition of 31.29
  joint tenancy 31.31
  'matrimonial' property 31.39
  occupation 31.42
  position of trustees 31.33–34
  reasons for 31.32
  restriction on trustees'
      powers and duties 31.34
  sale of land 31.41
  tenancy in common 31.30
type 2A presumed undue
      influence 12.63
type 2B presumed undue
      influence 12.64

ultra vires
  contract 4.14
  delegated legislation 3.9
unavailability
  frustration 10.3
uncertainty
  agreements 5.30–32
  possibility of ignoring in
      agreements 5.32
unconscionable bargains 12.57,
      12.67
unconscionable terms
  mortgages
      redemption 34.11–13
underlying strata
  trespass to land 22.2
undisclosed principal 14.36
  limitations on right to
      sue 14.37
  third parties 14.37
undue influence 12.60–66
  actual undue influence
      12.60
  by third party 12.66
  presumed undue
      influence 12.62–65
  rescission 12.68
unequivocal promise
  requirement for promissory
      estoppel 6.22
unfair contract terms 7.34, 9.9–30
  consequences of
      including 9.29
  under UCTA 9.9–21
  under UTCCR 9.22–30
unilateral contracts 4.2
  consideration 6.8
  termination of offer 5.27
unilateral discharge
  contract 6.27
unincorporated associations

capacity to contract 4.12
  UCTA not applicable to
      contracts relating to 9.14
unity of ownership
  restrictive covenants 33.36
unlawful actions
  under human rights
      legislation 3.29
unlawful eviction
  residential tenancies 37.23
unlawfulness
  interference 23.5
unregistered land 35.11–13
  interest outside Land Charges
      Act 1972 35.13
  law governing 30.21
  rights made registrable by
      Land Charges Act 1972
      35.12
unregistered leases
  adverse possession 30.33–36
  position of landlord 30.34
updating
  Land Register 35.40
Upper Tribunal
  position in court system
      hierarchy 3.41
Upper Tribunal (Lands
      Chamber) 2.22, 2.24
  application to 33.38
US courts
  persuasive precedents 3.45
usage
  terms implied by 7.23–24
Use Classes Order 39.10–16
use and enjoyment 23.4
  leases 36.33–37
user covenants 36.36–39
  enforcement 36.39

validity EU law 3.53
valuation
  professional liability 16.21
valuation basis
  rent reviews 36.58
valuers
  negligence 17.9
variation
  contract 6.28
  third parties 13.6
  unilateral without valid
      reason 9.28
vendor's liability
  defects 29.30
vertical direct effect
  EU law 3.49
vicarious liability 26.1–24
  borrowed employees 26.7
  collateral negligence
      26.24

contract of
  employment 26.2–7
course of
  employment 26.8–16
  employee 26.15
  employer and
      employee 26.2–7
  independent
      contractors 26.16–24
  scope 26.1
visitors
  occupiers' liability 21.7
volenti non fit injuria 20.8
voluntary registration
  title to land 29.16
voluntary waste 36.43

waiver
  breach of covenant 36.64
walls
  boundaries 28.23
warnings
  occupiers' liability 21.15
warranty
  breach 14.45
waste
  common law
      definition 36.43
water
  landowner's rights 28.20
Welsh Assembly acts 1.4, 3.1
Wheeldon v Burrows
  easements within rule of
      32.31, 32.39
White Papers
  as extrinsic aid to inter-
      pretation of Acts of
      Parliament 3.21
wild animals
  landowner's rights 28.19
window displays
  invitation to treat
      distinguished 5.5
withdrawal of support
  independent
      contractors 26.19
words
  misrepresentation by 12.5
  must be understood in
      context 3.17
  negligent 16.17
writing
  contract evidenced in 4.8
  contract which must be
      in 4.7
written contract
  execution 7.16
written representations
  planning appeals
      39.36

Printed and bound by CPI Group (UK) Ltd, Croydon, CR0 4YY